Valuing a Business

Valuing a Business

The Analysis and Appraisal of Closely Held Companies

Fourth Edition

Shannon P. Pratt, DBA, CFA, FASA, MCBA
Managing Director
Willamette Management Associates

Robert F. Reilly, CPA, CFA, ASA, CBA
Managing Director
Willamette Management Associates

Robert P. Schweihs, ASA
Managing Director
Willamette Management Associates

McGraw-Hill
New York • San Francisco • Washington, D.C. • Auckland
Bogotá • Caracas • Lisbon • London • Madrid • Mexico City
Milan • Montreal • New Delhi • San Juan • Singapore
Sydney • Tokyo • Toronto

Library of Congress Cataloging-in-Publication Data

Pratt, Shannon P.
    Valuing a business: the analysis and appraisal of closely held companies / by Shannon
P. Pratt, Robert F. Reilly, Robert P. Schweis. —4th ed.
        p. cm.
    Includes bibliographical references (p.).
    ISBN 0-07-135615-0
    1. Corporations—Valuation. 2. Corporations—Valuation—Law and legislation—United
States I. Reilly, Robert F. II. Schweis, Robert P. III. Title.
    HG4028.V3P7   2000
    657'.73—dc21   00–029948
                                                                       CIP

McGraw-Hill

A Division of The McGraw·Hill Companies

    5 6 7 8 9 0   CCW/CCW   0 5 4 3

The sponsoring editor for this book was Kelli Christiansen and the production supervisor was Elizabeth Strange. It was set in 11/13 Times Roman by
Hendrickson Creative Communications.

Printed and bound by R.R. Donnelley & Sons Company.

This publication is designed to provide accurate and authoritative information in regard to the subject matter covered. It is sold with the understanding
that neither the author nor the publisher is engaged in rendering legal, accounting, or other professional service. If legal advice or other expert assistance is required, the services of a competent professional person should be sought.

        —From a Declaration of Principles jointly adopted
          by a Committee of the American Bar
          Association and a Committee of Publishers

McGraw-Hill books are available at special quantity discounts to use as premiums and sales promotions, or for use in corporate training programs. For
more information, please write to the Director of Special Sales, Professional Publishing, McGraw-Hill, Two Penn Plaza, New York, NY 10121-2298.
Or contact your local bookstore.

Information contained in this work has been obtained by The McGraw-Hill Companies, Inc. ("McGraw-Hill") from sources believed to be reliable.
However, neither McGraw-Hill nor its authors guarantee the accuracy or completeness of any information published herein and neither McGraw-Hill
nor its authors shall be responsible for any errors, omissions, or damages arising out of use of this information. This work is published with the understanding that McGraw-Hill and its authors are supplying information but are not attempting to render engineering or other professional services. If
such services are required, the assistance of an appropriate professional should be sought.

 This book is printed on recycled, acid-free paper containing a minimum of 50% recycled de-inked fiber.

To Millie

To Janet

To Mary Beth

Preface

The book is designed to serve three purposes:

1. A comprehensive and updated reference for currently active business appraisers.
2. An introductory text on business valuation for both academic courses and beginning practitioners.
3. A reference for nonappraisers who use and/or evaluate business appraisals.

The authors have endeavored to present the current state of the art, thinking, and practice of the business valuation profession, which has progressed significantly since the third edition in 1996. Where clear consensus on positions exist, such consensus is presented. Where there are differing opinions, we try to present the issues clearly and fairly, reflecting extensive outside review (see Acknowledgments). We also present considerable documentation of various courts' positions on controversial issues.

Emphasis on Valuations That Withstand Challenge

Virtually every business valuation is potentially subject to challenge from one party or another—one or more buying or selling parties, taxing authorities, ESOP beneficiaries, a spouse in a divorce, or any of a variety of interested parties. The section on valuations for specific purposes has been greatly expanded and enhanced by chapters and sections on court cases detailing which aspects of valuation in various contexts the courts have provided guidance on. These valuation contexts, with extensive discussion of legal challenges and the courts' positions include, especially:

- Gift and estate taxes.
- Income taxes.
- Employee stock ownership plans.
- Marital dissolutions.
- Dissenting stockholder and minority oppression actions.

It is very enlightening to see just what methods, procedures, and data have held up under challenge and what methods, procedures, and data (or omissions in any of these categories) have caused appraisers to be admonished or rebuked by the courts. These insights should help analysts to avoid pitfalls, and should help attorneys, clients, and other users of valuations to critically evaluate valuation work products in light of the legal contexts that may govern the acceptability of these valuations.

Other Changes Since the Third Edition

This edition reflects the substantial advances in the tools and sophistication in business valuation that have evolved during the last half of the 1990s. These advances fall broadly into two categories:

1. Major advances in the quantity, quality, and accessibility of empirical data available to support business valuation conclusions.
2. Growing consensus within the business valuation professional community on standards, methodology, and terminology.

With the publication by co-authors Robert Reilly and Robert Schweihs of the book, *Valuing Intangible Assets* (McGraw-Hill, 1999), which addresses in detail the important and growing business valuation–related discipline of the analysis and appraisal of intangible assets and intellectual properties, we were able to eliminate the three-chapter intangible asset section that had appeared in the third edition of this book. This has allowed space for additions and expansions in many other important areas:

•   Extensive court case analysis and citations, as noted in the previous section.
•   An added chapter on valuing stock options.
•   The new *International Glossary of Business Valuation Terms* (see Appendix A), jointly developed by the five North American professional business valuation organizations.
•   Greatly expanded data for the market approach.
•   For privately held company mergers and acquisitions, *Pratt's Stats* (entirely new since the third edition) and *Bizcomps, IBA Market Database,* and *Done Deals* (considerably expanded since the third edition).
•   For guideline publicly traded companies, EDGAR (the SEC Electronic Data Gathering and Retrieval System).
•   New chapters on control and acquisition premiums and other discounts.
•   A section on mediation added to the chapter on arbitration.
•   A revised chapter on reviewing a business valuation report, which has been adopted by the American Society of Appraisers for peer review of business valuation reports submitted for accreditation.
•   Hundreds of updated data sources and bibliographical references.

Business Valuation Continues to Be Dynamic

The momentum of business valuation developments of the last five years is sure to continue into the new millennium. Very importantly, the positions of various courts on many business valuation issues continue to evolve. We will reflect these developments in future editions. Please address your comments, observations, and suggestions to any of us at the addresses below.

In the meantime, Shannon Pratt will continue to provide timely updates through his two monthly newsletters: *Shannon Pratt's Business Valuation Update* and *Judges and Attorneys Business Valuation Update* and the *Business Valuation Online Library* (www.BVLibrary.com). Readers may receive complimentary current issues of these newsletters by contacting Shannon Pratt at the telephone number or e-mail address listed below or at (888) BUS-VALU.

Shannon P. Pratt
Willamette Management Associates
111 S.W. Fifth Avenue, Suite 2150
Portland, Oregon 97204
(503) 222-0577
(503) 222-7392 (fax)
shannonp@transport.com

Robert F. Reilly
Willamette Management Associates
8600 West Bryn Mawr Avenue, Suite 950
Chicago, Illinois 60631
(773) 399-4300
(773) 399-4310 (fax)
rfreilly@willamette.com

Robert P. Schweihs
Willamette Management Associates
8600 West Bryn Mawr Avenue, Suite 950
Chicago, Illinois 60631
(773) 399-4300
(773) 399-4310 (fax)
rpschweihs@willamette.com

Acknowledgments

As with previous editions, this fourth edition has benefited immeasurably from peer review by a dedicated group of professionals who provided valuable input and assistance. In addition to review by a diverse group of practitioners in the business valuation community, the tax, family law, and shareholder dispute chapters have benefited from review by leaders in the respective specialties in the legal community.

We wish to thank the following individuals who have reviewed the entire manuscript and provided commentary and suggestions for this edition. We believe this volume truly represents a consensus of a broad cross section of the practitioners from all facets of the business valuation community:

R. James Alerding
Clifton Gunderson LLC

Stephen J. Bravo
Apogee Business Valuations Inc.

M. Mark Lee
KPMG Peat Marwick

Gilbert E. Matthews
Sutter Securities Incorporated

Richard M. Wise
Wise, Blackman

Portions of the manuscript were also reviewed by the following individuals:

Mel H. Abraham
The Accounting Offices of
  Mel H. Abraham

Ronald D. Aucutt
McGuire Woods Battle & Boothe LLP

The Hon. William A Christian
Chief District Court Judge
State of North Carolina
11th District

James S. Rigby Jr.
The Financial Valuation Group

Bruce L. Silverstein
Young Conway Stargatt & Taylor, LLP

Gary R. Trugman
Trugman Valuation Associates Inc.

Several members of the staff of Willamette Management Associates provided assistance with this edition. The sample report (Chapter 21) was prepared by Brian M. Swift, an associate in our Chicago office. Chapter 6, Gathering Economic and Industry Data, was prepared by Victoria A. Platt, senior research associate in our Chicago office, and Charlene M. Blalock, research associate in our Portland office.

Matthew S. Maudlin, an associate in our Portland office, checked the accuracy of the mathematical formulas and calculations and prepared several exhibits. Charlene Blalock prepared the chapter bibliographies. Other members of the Willamette Management Associates staff reviewed or prepared portions of chapters. Thomas J. Millon, director of our McLean, Virginia, office reviewed portions of the manuscript. Chapter 32, Valuations for Employee Stock Ownership Plans, was prepared by Kim S. Abello, a senior associate in our Chicago office. Curtis R. Kimball, director of our Atlanta office, reviewed the estate tax chapters. We also would like to thank Portland office senior associate Terry G. Whitehead and Portland office associate Karen J. Damiano for their contributions.

The authors have reviewed and edited all of the chapters written and updated by others and take final responsibility for their content.

Mary McCallister was responsible for typing most of the manuscript. This was a monumental task that she performed well under very tight time schedules.

Charlene Blalock served as the project manager for this undertaking. This included acting as a liaison and coordinating with the authors, the publisher, and the outside reviewers. She was responsible for obtaining permission to use material reprinted in this book from other sources. Charlene also prepared the index and edited and proofread the manuscript. This book would simply not have been completed without Charlene's dedication and project management.

We wish to thank Kelli Christiansen, acquisitions editor at McGraw-Hill, for her assistance and patience with this project. We also wish to thank Laurie Hendrickson of Hendrickson Creative Communications who was responsible for the layout and typesetting of this book.

For permission to use material previously published, we especially wish to thank:

Applied Financial Information, LP
The Appraisal Foundation
Business Valuation Review
The Canadian Institute of Chartered Business Valuators
Ibbotson Associates
John Wiley & Sons
McGraw-Hill
Prentice-Hall
Standard & Poor's Corporation
Warren, Gorham Lamont

We express our gratitude to all of the people singled out above as well as to all those who have written letters and had discussions with us about many conceptual and technical points since the last edition. As always, final responsibility for all content and judgments rests with the authors.

Shannon Pratt   **Robert Reilly**   **Robert Schweihs**
Portland, Oregon   Chicago, Illinois   Chicago, Illinois

About the Authors

Dr. Shannon P. Pratt is a managing director and one of the founders of Willamette Management Associates. Founded in the 1960s, Willamette Management Associates is one of the oldest and largest independent valuation consulting, economic analysis, and financial advisory firms in the country. It has regional offices in Chicago; New York; Atlanta; San Francisco; McLean, Virginia; and Portland, Oregon. Willamette Management Associates is well known for its extensive research library, which has a constantly updated collection of books, articles, transactional data sources, and court cases involving valuation and economic analysis issues. This book draws heavily on that resource.

In addition to this book, Dr. Pratt is a co-author of *Valuing Small Businesses and Professional* Practices, 3rd ed. (McGraw-Hill, 1998) and a co-author of *Guide to Business Valuations*, 10th ed. (Practitioners Publishing Company, 2000). He is also the author of *Cost of Capital: Estimation and Applications* (John Wiley & Sons, 1998), *Business Valuation Body of Knowledge* (John Wiley & Sons, 1998), and *Judges and Lawyers Business Valuation Handbook* (American Bar Association, 2000). Dr. Pratt is editor-in-chief of *Shannon Pratt's Business Valuation Update* and *Judges & Lawyers Business Valuation Update*, monthly newsletters covering current developments in the field of business valuation; *Business Valuation Online Library*, an on-line source of court cases, articles, laws and regulations; and *Pratt's Stats*, a database of private company sale transaction details.

Dr. Pratt holds a doctorate in finance from Indiana University and a bachelor of arts in business administration from the University of Washington. He is a chartered financial analyst, an accredited senior appraiser (certified in business valuation) and fellow of the American Society of Appraisers (the highest designation awarded by that society), and a master certified business appraiser of the Institute of Business Appraisers. Dr. Pratt has held many offices of the various professional societies and has served on numerous committees. Currently, he is a life member emeritus of the Business Valuation Committee of the American Society of Appraisers, a life member emeritus of the Valuation Advisory Committee of The ESOP Association, and a life member of the Institute of Business Appraisers. He is a recipient of the *Magna Cum Laude* award of the National Association of Certified Valuation Analysts. He served for two three-year terms as a trustee of The Appraisal Foundation (the entity responsible for establishing, issuing, promoting, and improving the *Uniform Standards of Professional Appraisal Practice,* under the authorization of Congress). He is frequently called upon to testify in disputed business valuation matters.

Robert F. Reilly is a managing director of Willamette Management Associates. He is a certified public accountant, a certified management accountant, a chartered financial analyst, a certified business appraiser, and an accredited senior appraiser of the American Society of Appraisers (designated in business valuation). He is an accredited tax advisor and an enrolled agent. And, he is a certified real estate appraiser, a certified review appraiser, a state certified general appraiser, and a state certified affiliate of the Appraisal Institute. He also serves as an issues resource panel member of The Appraisal Foundation.

Mr. Reilly provides consulting services relating to business valuation, intangible asset appraisal, security analysis, and damages analysis. He has testified as an expert witness in federal, state, and international courts on numerous occasions, and he regularly provides clients with litigation support and dispute resolution services. Mr. Reilly has also served as a court-appointed arbitrator.

He is the co-editor of *The Handbook of Advanced Business Valuation* (McGraw-Hill, 2000) and a co-author of *Valuing Small Businesses and Professional Practices*, 3rd ed. (McGraw-Hill, 1998), *Valuing Intangible Assets* (McGraw-Hill, 1999), and *Valuing Accounting Practices* (John Wiley & Sons, 1997).

He has authored chapters in numerous books related to specialized topics, such as ad valorem property taxation, matrimonial law and marital dissolution, and employee owned corporations. He also has written over 300 articles on various valuation-related topics that have been published in various professional journals.

Mr. Reilly is often called upon to speak at seminars and conferences of various professional groups. He also has taught courses in business valuation both in the United States and abroad.

Prior to joining Willamette Management Associates, Mr. Reilly was a partner and national director of the Deloitte & Touche Valuation Group. Before that, he was vice president of Arthur D. Little Valuation, Inc., a national appraisal firm.

He received an MBA in finance from the Columbia University Graduate School of Business and a B.A. in economics from Columbia University.

Robert P. Schweihs is a managing director of Willamette Management Associates. He is an accredited senior appraiser of the American Society of Appraisers (designated in business valuation). He is also a member of The ESOP Association, the Institute of Property Taxation, and the Association for Corporate Growth. Mr. Schweihs also serves as a trustee of The Appraisal Foundation.

Mr. Schweihs provides consulting services relating to business valuation, intangible asset appraisal, security analysis, and damages analysis. He has testified as an expert witness in federal and state courts and regularly provides clients with transactional fairness opinions, solvency analyses, economic analyses, financial advisory services, and litigation support services.

He is the co-editor of *The Handbook of Advanced Business Valuation* (McGraw-Hill, 2000) and a co-author of *Valuing Small Businesses and Professional Practices*, 3rd ed. (McGraw-Hill, 1998), *Valuing Intangible Assets* (McGraw-Hill, 1999), and *Valuing Accounting Practices*. (John Wiley & Sons, 1997). He also has written numerous articles on valuation-related topics that have been published in various professional journals.

Mr. Schweihs is often called upon to speak at seminars and conferences of various professional groups. He has taught courses in business valuation both in the United States and abroad.

Prior to joining Willamette Management Associates, Mr. Schweihs was a partner and national director of Deloitte & Touche Valuation Group. Before that, he was a manager of Arthur D. Little Valuation, Inc., a national appraisal firm.

He received an MBA in economics and finance from the University of Chicago Graduate School of Business, and a B.S. in mechanical engineering from the University of Notre Dame.

Notation System Used in This Book

A source of confusion for those trying to understand financial theory and methods is the fact that financial writers have not adopted a standard system of notation. For this edition, we have studied dozens of financial texts and have developed a system of notation that reflects either the most commonly used conventions or ones that seem intuitively easy to understand. If other financial writers adopt this standardized system of notation, we believe it will go a long way toward removing ambiguity, clarifying communication, and making it easier for readers to absorb financial articles and texts.

Value at a Point in Time

PV = Present value

FV = Future value

MVIC = Market value of invested capital

Cost of Capital and Rate of Return Variables

k = Discount rate (generalized)

k_e = Discount rate for common equity capital (cost of common equity capital). Unless otherwise stated, it generally is assumed that this discount rate is applicable to net cash flow available to common equity.

k_p = Discount rate for preferred equity capital

k_d = Discount rate for debt (Note: For complex capital structures, there could be more than one class of capital in any of the above categories, requiring expanded subscripts.)

$k_{d(pt)}$ = Cost of debt prior to tax effect

k_{ni} = Discount rate for equity capital when net income rather than net cash flow is the measure of economic income being discounted

c = Capitalization rate

c_e = Capitalization rate for common equity capital (cost of common equity capital). Unless otherwise stated, it generally is assumed that this capitalization rate is applicable to net cash flow available to common equity.

c_{ni} = Capitalization rate for net income

c_p = Capitalization rate for preferred equity capital

c_d = Capitalization rate for debt (Note: For complex capital structures, there could be more than one class of capital in any of the above categories, requiring expanded subscripts.)

t = Tax rate (expressed as a percentage of pretax income)

R = Rate of return

R_f = Rate of return on a risk-free security

$E(R)$ = Expected rate of return

$E(R_m)$ = Expected rate of return on the "market" (usually used in the context of a market for equity securities, such as the NYSE or S&P 500)

$E(R_i)$ = Expected rate of return on security i

B = Beta (a coefficient, usually used to modify a rate of return variable)

B_L = Levered beta

B_U = Unlevered beta

RP = Risk premium

RP_m = Risk premium for the "market" (usually used in the context of a market for equity securities, such as the NYSE or S&P 500)

RP_s = Risk premium for "small" stocks (average size of lowest quartile of NYSE as measured by market value of common equity) over and above RP_m

RP_u = Risk premium for unsystematic risk attributable to the specific company

RP_i = Risk premium for the ith security

$K_1 \ldots K_n$ = Risk premium associated with risk factor 1 through n for the average asset in the market (used in conjunction with Arbitrage Pricing Theory)

WACC = Weighted average cost of capital

Income Variables

E = Expected economic income (in a generalized sense; i.e., could be dividends, any of several possible definitions of cash flows, net income, and so on)

NI = Net income (after entity-level taxes)

NCF_e = Net cash flow to equity

NCF_f = Net cash flow to the firm (to overall invested capital, or entire capital structure, including all equity and long-term debt)

PMT = Payment (interest and principal payment on debt security)

D = Dividends

GCF = Gross cash flow (usually net income plus noncash charges)

EBIT = Earnings before interest and taxes

EBITDA = Earnings before interest, and taxes, depreciation, and amortization

Periods or Variables in a Series

i = The ith period or the ith variable in a series (may be extended to the jth variable, the kth variable, and so on)

n = The number of periods or variables in the series, or the last number in the series

∞ = Infinity

$_o$ = Period$_o$, the base period, usually the latest year immediately preceding the valuation date

Weightings

W = Weight

W_e = Weight of common equity in capital structure

W_p = Weight of preferred equity in capital structure

W_d = Weight of debt in capital structure

NOTE: For purposes of computing a weighted average cost of capital (WACC), it is assumed that above weightings are at market value.

Growth

g = Rate of growth

Mathematical Functions

Σ = Sum of (add up all the variables that follow)

π = Product of (multiply together all the variables that follow)

$\times$ = Mean average (the sum of the values of the variables divided by the number of variables)

G = Geometric mean (the product of the values of the variables taken to the root of the number of variables)

Contents

Transactions Involving Company Insiders. Contingent Assets and Liabilities. Adjustments to Asset Valuations. *Marketable Securities. Other Assets.* Computation of Earnings Per Share. *Weighted Average Basis. Basic versus Diluted Earnings.* Computation of Book Value Per Share. An Example of the Effect of Alternative Accounting Methods. Adjusting the Balance Sheet to Current Values. Summary. Bibliography.

FMV Opinions, Inc., Study. Management Planning, Inc., Study. Summary of Empirical Studies on Restricted Stock Transactions through 1996. Studies of Private Transactions before Initial Public Offerings. *Robert W. Baird & Company Studies. Willamette Management Associates Studies. Criticisms of Willamette Management Associates Studies. Summary of Conclusions from Private Transaction Studies.* Other Analysis of Discounts for Lack of Marketability for Minority Ownership Interests. Discounts for Lack of Marketability for Controlling Ownership Interests. *Illiquidity Factors Affecting Controlling Ownership Interests. Benchmark for the Illiquidity Discount for Controlling Ownership Interests. Differences between Private and Public Company Acquisition Price/Earnings Multiples.* Factors That Affect the Discounts for Illiquidity and Lack of Marketability. *"Put" Rights. Dividend Payments. Potential Buyers. Size of Interest. Prospect of Public Offering or Sale of the Business. Information Access and Reliability. Restrictive Transfer Provisions.* Court Decisions on Discounts for Illiquidity and Lack of Marketability. *Mandelbaum v. Commissioner Reviews Lack of Marketability Factors. Estate of Barge v. Commissioner Considers Lack of Marketability Factors.* Summary. Bibliography.

Characteristics of Closely Held Preferred Stocks. *Dividend Rate. Liquidation Preference. Cumulative versus Noncumulative Dividends. Redeemable versus Nonredeemable. Put Option. Voting versus Nonvoting. Participating versus Nonparticipating. Convertible versus Nonconvertible.* Method of Valuation. *Assessing Dividend and Liquidation Payment Risk. Comparison with Publicly Traded Preferred Stocks. Capitalizing the Income Stream.* Marketability Aspects of Closely Held Preferred Stock. Revenue Ruling 83-120. Summary. Bibliography.

Process. The Property Tax Equalization Process. *Assessment Ratio Studies. Use of Assessment Ratio Studies in Administrative Appeals and Litigation.* The Property Tax Unitary Valuation Process. The Property Tax Appeal Process. *Steps in the Ad Valorem Taxation Valuation Process. The Assessing Authority's Objective. The Property Owner's Objective. The Independent Valuation Analyst's Objective.* Special Topics. *Identification and Quantification of Functional Obsolescence. Identification and Quantification of the Economic Component of External Obsolescence. Issues in Unit Valuation for Ad Valorem Purposes. Identification and Valuation of Intangible Assets in the Unit Method of Assessment.* Identification and Application of Appropriate Income Approach Methods for Ad Valorem Unitary Valuation. *Weaknesses of Using CAPM. Additional Difficulties. Alternatives to CAPM.* Problems with the Use of Stock Market Data in Property Tax Valuations. *Introduction. Income Approach Valuation Issues. Market Approach Valuation Issues. Differences in the Risk and Expected Return Investment Characteristics between Operating Property and Negotiable Securities.* Capitalization of Leased Equipment Rental Expense. *Introduction. Reasons Not to Capitalize Operating Lease Rental Expense.* Summary. Bibliography.

Passive Appreciation. *"Active" Appreciation a Marital Asset. "Active" Appreciation Must Be Proven.* Valuation Date. Goodwill. *The "Market Value of Goodwill" Paradox. Personal Goodwill Not a Marital Asset in Many States. Professional Goodwill Is a Marital Asset in Many States.* Valuation Methods in the Family Law Courts. *The Size Argument. The Liquidity Argument. The Risk Argument. The Cost of Flotation Argument.* Noncompete Covenants. Buy-Sell Agreements. *Cases Rejecting Buy-Sell Agreements. Cases Finding Buy-Sell Price Controlling. Buy-Sell Agreement May Be Considered.* Discounts for Lack of Control and Lack of Marketability. *Discount for Lack of Control. Discount for Lack of Marketability.* Adequacy of Evidence. Treatment of Tax Liabilities. Summary.

the Arbitrators' Discretion. Other Factors to Address. Selection of Arbitrators. *Criteria for Selection. Procedure for Selection. American Arbitration Association Procedure.* Engagement and Compensation of Arbitrators. The Arbitration Process. *Review of Arbitration Document. Initial Communication among Arbitrators. Field Visit. Hearings. The Valuation Meeting.* Reporting the Results of the Arbitration. Mediation. *How Mediation Differs from Arbitration and Litigation. Self-Determination Is the Fundamental Principle. Role of the Business Valuation Expert in Mediation. Mediation in Family Law. Mediation in Federal Tax Disputes.* Summary. Bibliography.

List of Exhibits

Part I

State of the Profession, the Engagement, and the Basic Theory

Chapter 1

Business Valuation Standards and Credentials

Growing Consensus on Business Valuation Standards

One of the most significant developments since the third edition of this book in 1996 is the growing consensus regarding business appraisal professional standards. This has been accompanied by a proliferation of business valuation professional education.

It is important that all those either providing or using business valuation services be aware of these standards. The days when there was virtually no generally accepted guidance and almost anything could pass as a business valuation are gone forever. Owners, investors, attorneys, government agencies, and the courts all demand that business valuation work live up to these higher standards.

This chapter provides the reader a roadmap to business valuation professional standards as they exist as of this writing. It also gives the reader the sources to get complete copies of current standards and to keep up to date as they evolve. The chapter also catalogs the current state of business valuation professional credentials.

Both the standards and the credentials are still evolving. Readers can keep up to date on the changes through two monthly newsletters: *Shannon Pratt's Business Valuation Update* and *Judges & Lawyers Business Valuation Update* (see bibliography at end of chapter).

The Appraisal Foundation

Background and Organization

The Appraisal Foundation was established in 1987 by nine appraisal organizations constituting the North American Council of Appraisal Organizations (NACAO) and six nonappraiser members including the American Bankers Association and the U.S. League of Savings Institutions. Eight of the nine appraisal organizations were composed entirely of real estate appraisers. One, the American Society of Appraisers, is multidisciplinary. The American Society of Appraisers awards certification in real estate appraisal, machinery and equipment appraisal, personal property appraisal, business valuation, and technical valuation.

The board of trustees of The Appraisal Foundation consists of representatives of the sponsor organizations plus trustees-at-large. The board of trustees appoints two independent boards:

1. The **Appraisal Standards Board** promulgates the *Uniform Standards of Professional Appraisal Practice* (see next page).
2. The **Appraisal Qualifications Board** promulgates appraiser qualifications. So far, it has done so only for real estate appraisers and personal property appraisers. As of this writing, the Appraisal Qualifications Board has left the issue of business appraiser qualifications to the various professional credentialling organizations, discussed in a subsequent section.

Uniform Standards of Professional Appraisal Practice (USPAP)

The Financial Institution Reform, Recovery, and Enforcement Act (FIRREA) makes compliance with USPAP mandatory for all federally related real estate transactions. Although not mandatory as of this writing for federally related transactions involving personal property and business appraisals, USPAP has been adopted by major appraisal organizations in North America and has become widely recognized as the generally accepted standards of appraisal practice.

The content of USPAP is summarized in Exhibit 1–1. Standards 9 and 10, covering business appraisal, were substantially modified effective January 1, 2000. A complete updated USPAP usually is published in November of each year to be effective the following January 1 (see bibliography at end of chapter for details).

Exhibit 1–1

Uniform Standards of Professional Appraisal Practice
Table of Contents

Preamble
Ethics Rule
Competency Rule
Departure Rule
Jurisdictional Exception Rule
Supplemental Standards Rule
Definitions

Standards and Standards Rules

Standard 1   Real Property Appraisal, Development
Standard 2   Real Property Appraisal, Reporting
Standard 3   Real Property Appraisal Review, Development, and Reporting
Standard 4   Real Property/Real Estate Consulting, Development
Standard 5   Real Property/Real Estate Consulting, Report
Standard 6   Mass Appraisal, Development and Reporting
Standard 7   Personal Property Appraisal, Development
Standard 8   Personal Property Appraisal, Reporting
Standard 9   Business Appraisal, Development
Standard 10   Business Appraisal, Reporting

Statements on Appraisal Standards

SMT-1   Standards Rule 3-1(g) (Appraisal Review)
SMT-2   Discounted Cash Flow Analysis
SMT-3   Retrospective Value Opinions
SMT-4   Prospective Value Opinions
SMT-5   Confidentiality Section of the Ethics Rule
SMT-6   Reasonable Exposure Time in Real Property and Personal Property Market Value Opinions
SMT-7   Permitted Departure from Specific Requirements for Real Property and Personal Property Appraisal Assignments
SMT-8   Electronic Transmission of Reports

SMT-9   Identification of the Client's Intended Use in Developing and Reporting Appraisal, Appraisal Review, or Consulting Assignment Opinions and Conclusions

Advisory Opinions

AO-1   Sales History
AO-2   Inspection of Subject Property Real Estate
AO-3   Update of an Appraisal
AO-4   Standards Rule 1-5(b)
AO-5   Assistance in the Preparation of an Appraisal
AO-6   The Appraisal Review Function
AO-7   Marketing Time Opinions
AO-8   Market Value vs. Fair Value in Real Property Appraisals
AO-9   Responsibility of Appraisers Concerning Toxic or Hazardous Substance Contamination
AO-10   The Appraiser-Client Relationship
AO-11   Content of the Appraisal Report Options of Standard Rules 2-2 and 8-2
AO-12   Use of the Appraisal Report Options of Standard Rules 2-2 and 8-2
AO-13   Performing Evaluations of Real Property Collateral to Conform with USPAP
AO-14   Appraisals for Subsidized Housing
AO-15   Using the DEPARTURE RULE in Developing a Limited Appraisal
AO-16   Fair Housing Laws and Appraisal Report Content
AO-17   Appraisals of Real Property with Proposed Improvements
AO-18   Use of an Automated Valuation Model (AVM)
AO-19   Unacceptable Assignment Conditions in Real Property Appraisal Assignments

Glossary
Index

SOURCE: *Uniform Standards of Professional Appraisal Practice* (Washington, DC: The Appraisal Foundation, 2000). Reprinted with permission.

Standards Published by Business Valuation Professional Organizations

Three U.S. professional associations that offer education and accreditation in the discipline of business valuation also publish business valuation standards. These are:

1. American Society of Appraisers (ASA).
2. Institute of Business Appraisers (IBA).
3. National Association of Certified Valuation Analysts (NACVA).

In all cases, the standards published by the above organizations are considerably more detailed than USPAP, but none of them is in direct conflict with USPAP.

Of the above, the standards developed by the Business Valuation Committee of the American Society of Appraisers are the most comprehensive.

The latest editions of the standards of all of the above organizations are available without charge from their respective headquarters. Contact information for each is shown in the bibliography for this chapter.

Other Organizations That Have Offered Guidance on Business Valuation Issues

Internal Revenue Service

Congress directs the U.S. Treasury Department to issue legislative and interpretive regulations to provide structure for the tax laws it passes. Interpretive regulations (e.g., revenue rulings) do not have the force of law, but present the position of the Internal Revenue Service (IRS) on various tax matters, including the valuation of businesses, business interests, and related intangible assets. Regulations are actually formulated by the IRS, but they are approved by the Secretary of the Treasury or his or her delegate. As an example, the regulations for Chapter 14 of the estate and gift tax laws require appraisers to use a special valuation methodology in certain circumstances with regard to family-owned businesses.

The IRS also issues pronouncements representing administrative (as opposed to legislative) tax authority. The pronouncements include: revenue rulings, revenue procedures, private letter rulings (PLRs), technical advice memorandums (TAMs), and general counsel memorandums. These pronouncements illustrate the treatment of certain issues not clearly addressed in the regulations. Over time, many of the positions espoused by the IRS through regulations and revenue rulings come up in court disputes. The resolution of these issues by the courts establishes case law precedent. Much, but by no means all, of the case law has been supportive of positions taken in the regulations and revenue rulings. The most important of the revenue rulings that relate to business valuation are:

59-60   Valuing closely held stock.
65-193   Deletes the final §4.02(f) of Revenue Ruling 59-60 dealing with the valuation of intangibles.

68-609　　Discusses "formula method" for determining fair market value of intangible assets of a business. Supersedes ARM 34. Theory in Revenue Ruling 59-60 applies to income and other taxes as well as to estate and gift taxes, and to business interests of any type, including partnerships and proprietorships, and to intangible assets for all tax purposes.

77-287　　Recognizes relevance of restricted stock studies (see Chapter 17) in determining discounts for lack of marketability.

83-120　　Discusses valuing preferred stock (see Chapter 24).

93-12　　Allows the application of minority interest discounts to partial interest transfers even when a family owns overall control of a closely held business. Supersedes and reverses Revenue Ruling 81-253, which disallowed such discounts, but was overturned by case law.

Representing less authority than revenue rulings, the private letter rulings, technical advice memorandums, and general counsel memorandums issued by the IRS are responses to specific inquiries from taxpayers (and/or from IRS field offices) and may not be cited as precedent. Nevertheless, these can be helpful in understanding the IRS's likely position on emerging issues for tax-related appraisals.

IRS internal publications and other official materials also provide useful insights. The February 1998 *IRS Valuation Training for Appeals Officers* is available through Commerce Clearing House or on-line (see bibliography).

Revenue rulings and other IRS pronouncements often are cited for valuation guidance for purposes other than taxes. This can be useful to the extent that the material contains general valuation guidance. However, as discussed extensively in this book, valuation methods may differ for different purposes, and all aspects of revenue rulings may not be appropriate for nontax purposes.

Department of Labor

Like the IRS revenue rulings, regulations issued by the Department of Labor (DOL) do not have the force of law. They represent the department's position with respect to interpretation of the law as it applies to certain issues.

In May of 1988, the DOL issued a proposed draft of a Regulation Relating to the Definition of Adequate Consideration (for ESOP stock). Hearings have been held and written comments have been received. The complete text of the 1988 proposed regulation was included as Exhibit 23–2 in Chapter 23 on ESOPs in the second edition of this book. On May 8, 1995, the DOL announced that it had withdrawn the proposed regulations, effective February 1, 1995.

Association for Investment Management and Research

The Association for Investment Management and Research (AIMR) publishes educational materials, conducts seminars, and confers the professional designation CFA, chartered financial analyst, which is discussed later in the chapter.

AIMR materials and the CFA exams are oriented primarily to the analysis of publicly traded securities and the management of investment portfolios. As the interaction between publicly traded and closely held companies (mergers, acquisitions, leveraged buyouts, spinoffs, and so on) has accelerated in recent years, the AIMR has given increasing attention to analysis and appraisal of closely held companies.

In 1990, the Institute of Chartered Financial Analysts (now the AIMR) published a monograph titled *Valuation of Closely Held Companies and Inactively Traded Securities* (see bibliography) based on a seminar by the same name.

The ESOP Association

The ESOP Association is an organization of companies that have employee stock ownership plans (ESOPs) and companies that provide professional advisory services to ESOP companies. One of the association's committees is the Advisory Committee on Valuation, composed of 25 professional practitioner members of leading companies regularly performing ESOP valuations.

The ESOP Association Advisory Committee on Valuation meets twice a year to discuss issues concerning the valuation of ESOP shares, primarily those in closely held companies. The ESOP Association neither certifies nor endorses business appraisers or any other specialists, nor does it issue standards as such. However, it publishes a very useful book, *Valuing ESOP Shares*, reflecting the deliberations and views of the Advisory Committee on Valuation on many issues affecting the valuation of ESOP shares. The address to obtain this book and other ESOP Association information is presented in the bibliography at the end of this chapter.

Recognition of Professional Standards by Courts

Most business valuations that are performed have the potential for a legal challenge. Courts like to have professionally accepted standards to rely on for guidance in deciding disputed issues. Courts may suspect poor appraisal work, but it helps them tremendously to be able to cite authority for rejection of work that fails to meet professional standards. The authors, and many other valuation analysts, have brought the authority of the standards and other professional guidance discussed in this chapter to bear very fruitfully in court on numerous occasions.

One result of previous editions of this book, and the development of the standards and other professional guidance discussed in this chapter, is an increased consensus and consistency in the resolution of business valuation issues, both in the courts and elsewhere. There have been numerous references to this book in reported decisions quoting testimony that ultimately assisted the court in reaching its decision. We believe this has contributed to the consistency of judicial decisions. The standards and other guidance discussed in this chapter continue to build consensus and consistency on business valuation issues. As these materials are more widely disseminated and recognized, undoubtedly they will significantly impact court decisions in the future.

International Acceptance of U.S. Standards and Practices

The United States is by far the world leader in both markets for and analysis of securities, companies, and business interests. This is true for both publicly traded securities and closely held businesses and business interests.

Two factors have combined to accelerate the spread of U.S. technology in financial appraisals and markets throughout the world:

1. Rapidly increasing international flow of capital.
2. Growing privatization of formerly socially owned businesses in almost every country of the world.

The standards and guidance in this chapter and throughout this book are becoming increasingly applicable to international as well as to domestic transactions as the world financial markets become more homogenous.

Parts or all of earlier editions of this book already have been translated into several foreign languages. Several governments have adopted USPAP and the ASA business valuation standards as mandatory criteria for business valuations for transactions involving privatization. The authors, and other ASA members, have taught material from this book, USPAP, and ASA business valuation standards in many countries throughout the world.[1] Such presentations have been made under the varied auspices of private business organizations, local professional appraisal societies, local governments, academic institutions, the United Nations, and the World Bank.

Most meetings of the professional organizations listed in this chapter are attended by representatives of many foreign countries. The worldwide appetite for translations and teachers of U.S. business appraisal standards and practices is challenging our professionals' ability to fill such demand. We believe this growing global homogeneity of business appraisal standards and practices will contribute positively to successful privatization, worldwide capital flows, and economic growth.

Professional Organizations Offering Accreditation in Business Valuation

Four organizations in the United States and one in Canada offer various professional accreditations in business valuation. These are:

- American Society of Appraisers
- Institute of Business Appraisers
- National Association of Certified Valuation Analysts
- American Institute of Certified Public Accountants
- The Canadian Institute of Chartered Business Valuators

A summary of the professional designations offered by each and the requirements for each designation are presented in Exhibit 1–2. Additional information about each of these organizations and their activities is shown in Exhibits 1–3 through 1–7.

The above organizations are undertaking certain cooperative efforts in an attempt to make business valuation practice more consistent. The five organizations have a joint Business Valuation Glossary Committee, which has prepared the first draft of a jointly approved glossary of business valuation terms. This glossary is presented in the appendix at the end of this book. Also, the four U.S. organizations have formed a Joint Business Valuation Task Force for the purpose of making recommendations to the Appraisal Standards Board of The Appraisal Foundation for revisions to USPAP.

---

[1] As of this writing, ASA business valuation courses have been taught in Brazil, Hong Kong, Kuwait, Mexico, Russia, Slovenia, Taiwan, and Yugoslavia.

Exhibit 1–2

Professional Accreditation Criteria

ORGANIZATION	CERTIFICATION	PREREQUISITES	COURSE/EXAM	REPORTS	EXPERIENCE / OTHER
American Institute of Certified Public Accountants (AICPA)	ABV – Accredited in Business Valuation.	AICPA member with current CPA license.	One-day exam.	None.	Substantial involvement in at least 10 business valuation engagements.
American Society of Appraisers (ASA)	AM – Accredited Member.	College degree or equivalent.	Completion of four courses of three days each, with successful completion of one half-day exam following each course, or successful completion of one all-day challenge exam. Successful completion of ethics exam and USPAP exam.	Submission of two actual reports to satisfaction of Board of Examiners.	Two years full-time or equivalent (e.g., 5 years of 400 hours business appraisal work per year equals one year full-time equivalent). One full year of requirement is granted to anyone who has a CPA, CFA, or CBI designation with five years of practice in that field.
	ASA – Accredited Senior Appraiser.	Met AM requirements, plus three years of full-time or equivalent experience.			
	FASA – Fellow of the American Society of Appraisers.	Met ASA requirements, plus voted into College of Fellows on the basis of technical leadership and contribution to the profession and the Society.			
Institute of Business Appraisers (IBA)	AIBA – Accredited by IBA.	Possess business appraisal designation from AICPA, ASA, or NACVA OR IBA-8001 workshop.	Four-hour exam.	Submit one report for peer review.	Provide references of character and fitness. Submit proof of continued professional development with 24 hours of advanced BV education every 24 months OR submit another report for peer review OR pass CBA exam and enter CBA review process OR demonstrate completion of ten business appraisal assignments in two years.
	CBA – Certified Business Appraiser.	Four years of college or equivalent.	Three and one-half hour exam.	Submission of 2 business appraisal reports showing professional competence.	Have done at least 2 assignments.
	MCBA – Master Certified Business Appraiser.	IBA member in good standing with CBA designation.			10 years' practice experience, OR credit for publication or lecturing. 4 work product references from certified business appraisers.
	FIBA – Fellow of the Institute of Business Appraisers.	Met all CBA requirements, plus voted into College of Fellows on basis of technical leadership and contribution to the profession and the Institute.			
	BVAL – Business Valuator Accredited for Litigation.	Business appraisal designation from IBA, AICPA, ASA, or NACVA.	Seven-day Litigation Support and Expert Testimony Workshop and four-hour exam.	None.	Letters of reference from attorneys OR complete 16 hours of education in the area of law the appraiser will testify in.
National Association of Certified Valuation Analysts (NACVA)	AVA – Accredited Valuation Analyst.	Business degree and/or MBA, and member in good standing of NACVA.	8-hour pre-qualification exam on accounting fundamentals, PLUS comprehensive exam including 30-50 hour take-home case study.	Case study for exam.	2 years' full time or equivalent business valuation or related experience OR 10 or more business valuations OR other evidence of substantial knowledge.
	CVA – Certified Valuation Analyst.	CPA.	Five-day course; take-home exam until 1999; half-day proctored exam starting 1999.	Sample case on exam.	Experience required for certification as CPA.
	GVA – Government Valuation Analyst.	College degree.	60-hour, take-home exam, which includes one case study and report writing requirement.	Sample case on exam.	Employed by government agency, GS-12 or higher, 2 years full-time business valuation experience.
The Canadian Institute of Chartered Business Valuators (CICBV)	CBV – Chartered Business Valuator.	College degree or equivalent.	Successful completion of six courses, including assignments and exams for each course plus the required experience, followed by the writing of the Membership Entrance Examination. Writing of exam can be challenged without successful completion of courses if applicant has at least five years full-time experience in business valuations.	None.	Two years full-time experience or the equivalent of part-time obtained over a 5-year period, attested to by a sponsoring CICBV member.
	FCBV – Fellow of the Canadian Institute of Chartered Business Valuators	Members who have rendered outstanding service to the business valuation profession, or whose achievements in their professional lives or in the community have earned them distinction and have brought honor to the profession.			

SOURCE: Updated from *Judges & Lawyers Business Valuation Update,* January 1999, p. 3. Reprinted with permission of Business Valuation Resources.

Exhibit 1–3

AMERICAN SOCIETY OF APPRAISERS (ASA)
P.O. Box 17265, Washington, D.C. 20041, (703) 478-2228, www.appraisers.org

Date formed:	1936	Ownership:	Owned by members

Description: Multidisciplinary professional organization offering courses and exams leading to designations in the appraisal of real estate, machinery and equipment, personal property, gems and jewelry, businesses and business interests (including intangible assets), and certain technical specialties.

Designations offered:

AM—Accredited Member:
Educational requirement: College degree or equivalent.

Courses/exams: Completion of four courses of three days each, with successful completion of one half-day exam following each of the three courses and a full-day exam following BV204, OR successful completion of one all-day challenge exam. In addition, successful completion of an ethics exam and a USPAP exam is required.

Reports: Submission of two actual appraisal reports to satisfaction of Board of Examiners.

Experience requirement: Two years full-time or full-time equivalent (e.g., five years of 400 hours business appraisal work per year equals one year full-time equivalent).

Related experience offset: One full year of the experience requirement is granted to anyone who has any of the following three designations with five years of practice in that respective field: Certified Public Accountant (CPA), Chartered Financial Analyst (CFA), or Certified Business Intermediary (CBI).

ASA—Accredited Senior Appraiser:
has met all requirements above plus an additional three years of full-time or full-time equivalent experience.

FASA—Fellow of the American Society of Appraisers:
has met all requirements above plus is voted into the College of Fellows on the basis of technical leadership and contribution to the profession and the society.

Courses: Each of the core courses (BV201–204) are three days; BV201 through 203 are followed by a half-day exam and BV204 is following by a full-day exam. BV205 and 206 are two days each.
BV201: Introduction to business valuation, part one
BV202: Introduction to business valuation, part two
BV203: Business valuation case study
BV204: Business valuation selected advanced topics
BV205: Appraisal of small businesses and professional practices
BV206: Employee stock ownership plans: valuing ESOP shares

Seminars and Conferences: Seminars on specialized topics lasting from two hours to two days and sponsored by various groups within the ASA.
Annual interdisciplinary meeting with two and a half days of technical presentations on each of the society's appraisal disciplines.
Annual Advanced Business Valuation Conference with two or two and a half days of advanced business valuation papers, presentations, and discussion.

Publications: *Business Valuation Review*, quarterly professional journal with articles accepted based on peer review. Published at P.O Box 24222, Denver, Colorado 80224, (303) 975-8895. The other valuation disciplines also have their professional journal, similar to *Business Valuation Review*.
Valuation, published on an irregular basis, contains articles on all of the disciplines of valuation within the ASA. Published at ASA headquarters (see title of exhibit for address).

Local chapters: Chapters with regular monthly meetings in 87 cities throughout the United States and Canada.

Exhibit 1–4

INSTITUTE OF BUSINESS APPRAISERS (IBA)
P.O. Box 17410, Plantation, Florida 33418, (954) 584-1144, www.instbusapp.org

Date formed:	1978	Ownership:	Florida not-for-profit corporation (privately owned)

Description: Offers programs of interest to members whose business valuation activities are less than full time and/or whose practice includes valuation of small to midsize businesses.

Certification offered:

AIBA—Accredited by IBA:

Educational requirement: Must have business appraisal designation from AICPA, ASA, or NACVA or have completed IBA 8001 workshop.

Courses/exams: Four-hour exam.

Reports: Submission of one report for peer review.

Experience requirement: Provide references; submit 24 hours CPE in business valuation every two years or another report for peer review every two years or demonstrate completion of 10 business appraisal assignments in two years or pass CBA exam and enter that process

CBA—Certified Business Appraiser:

Educational requirement: Four years of college or equivalent.

Courses/exams: Three-and-one-half hour exam.

Reports: Submission of two business appraisal reports demonstrating professional level of competence.

Experience requirement: Have performed at least two valuation assignments.

MCBA—Master Certified Business Appraiser:

has met all requirements above plus has 10 years' practice experience or has received credit for published writing or lecturing; needs four work product references from other CBAs.

FIBA—Fellow of the Institute of Business Appraisers:

has met all requirements above plus is voted into the College of Fellows on the basis of technical leadership and contribution to the profession and to the Institute.

BVAL—Business Valuator Accredited for Litigation:

has met all requirements above and completes a seven-day workshop and four-hour exam; must submit two letters of reference from attorneys or complete 16 hours of education in law.

Courses: Eight-day workshop, offered two to four times a year, in various locations
Two-day course on valuing small businesses using IBA market database
Seven-day workshop on litigation support and expert testimony

Seminars and Conferences: One-day seminars on business valuation held at various locations around the United States.
Annual conference held in different cities.

Publication: *Business Valuation Practice*, semiannual professional journal with peer-reviewed articles on practical aspects of business valuation and litigation support.

Local chapters: A few at present.

In addition to the above organizations, the Association for Investment Management and Research (AIMR) confers the professional designation of chartered financial analyst (CFA). Candidates must pass three rigorous all-day examinations, each a year apart. (The exams usually are given on the first Saturday of June each year.)

The emphasis in the CFA program is on analysis and portfolio management of publicly traded securities. However, the required readings and exams include material on valuing closely held companies (including portions of this book). The AIMR

Exhibit 1–5

NATIONAL ASSOCIATION OF CERTIFIED VALUATION ANALYSTS (NACVA)
1111 East Brickyard Road, Suite 200, Salt Lake City, Utah 84106, (801) 486-0600, www.nacva.com

Date formed:	1991 Ownership: Group of shareholders
Description:	NACVA is an association of CPAs, government valuers, and other professionals that perform valuation services. Its purpose is to promulgate the members' status, credentials, and esteem in the field of performing valuations of closely held businesses.

Certification offered:

AVA—Accredited Valuation Analyst:

Educational requirement:	Business degree and member in good standing of NACVA.
Courses/exams:	Eight-hour prequalification exam on accounting and comprehensive exam including 30–50-hour take-home case study.
Reports:	Only case study for exam.
Experience requirement:	Two years' full-time or equivalent business valuation or related experience or have performed 10 or more business valuations or demonstrate evidence of substantial knowledge.

CVA—Certified Valuation Analyst:

Educational requirement:	CPA
Courses/exams:	Five-day course and half-day proctored exam which includes one case study and report writing requirement (prior to 1999 there was a 60-hour, take-home exam).
Reports:	Only for sample case on exam.
Experience requirement:	Experience required for certification as CPA.

GVA—Government Valuation Analyst:

Educational requirement:	College degree
Courses/exams:	60-hour, take-home exam, which includes one case study and report writing requirement.
Reports:	Only for sample case on exam.
Experience requirement:	Employed by government agency, GS-12 or higher, two years full-time business valuation experience.

Courses: Five days of training consisting of the following:

Days 1–2:	Fundamentals, Techniques, and Theory
Day 3:	Case Analysis No. 1 and Report Writing
Day 4:	Using Valuation Master 4.0 Software
Day 5:	Working Effectively in the Litigation Environment

Seminars and Conferences:	Two conferences held annually. Semi-annual one-and-a-half day seminars on business valuation topics. Also one- and two-day seminars on key valuation topics, including symposiums.
Publications:	The Valuation Examiner, a bimonthly magazine.
Local chapters:	State chapters presently in 38 states and one in Mexico City.

Directory indicates that several hundred of the organization's 30,000+ members specialize in valuing closely held companies.

American Society of Appraisers

The American Society of Appraisers (ASA), formed in 1936, is a long-standing, multidisciplinary organization that offers education and professional accreditation in many appraisal disciplines, including real property, machinery and equipment, personal property, and a number of technical valuation specialties, as well as in business

Exhibit 1–6

AMERICAN INSTITUTE OF CERTIFIED PUBLIC ACCOUNTANTS (AICPA)
201 Plaza Three, Jersey City, New Jersey 07311-3881, (201) 938-3000, www.aicpa.org

Date formed:	1887	Ownership:	Organization-sponsored

Description: Recognizes business valuation as a CPA service niche and confers an accreditation credential reflecting this recognition for those in public practice, industry, government, and education.

Certification offered: *ABV—Accredited in Business Valuation:*

Prerequisite:	AICPA member with current CPA license.
Courses/exams:	One-day exam.
Reports:	None
Experience requirement:	Substantial involvement in at least 10 business valuation engagements.

Courses/Exams: Two three-day courses (FBVI and FBVII) and one two-day course (ABV-E). The exam for the designation of ABV is a one-day exam, offered once each year in November. In addition, AICPA offers a variety of one-day advanced courses in business valuation.

Seminars and Conferences: Annual National Business Valuation Conference

Publications: *CPA Expert*, a quarterly newsletter
The AICPA also publishes an extensive list of consulting service publications, generally referred to as "practice aids" or "special reports," including practice aids related to consulting with specific industry engagements.

valuation. From 1984 through 1999, the business valuation discipline was the ASA's fastest growing area of accreditation.

For details of professional designations and accreditation requirements, publication and other activities, see Exhibits 1–2 and 1–3.

Institute of Business Appraisers

The Institute of Business Appraisers (IBA), founded in 1978, offers seminars on business appraisal topics and several professional designations in the field of business appraisal. It also offers a variety of member support services.

Details of the IBA's professional designations, publications, and some of its activities are shown in Exhibits 1–2 and 1–4.

National Association of Certified Valuation Analysts

The National Association of Certified Valuation Analysts (NACVA) was formed in 1993 by a group of CPAs to provide certification and member support services specifically for certified public accountants and others performing business valuation services. Details of their certification criteria and activities are shown in Exhibits 1–2 and 1–5.

American Institute of Certified Public Accountants

The newest entrant in the field of business valuation accreditation is the American Institute of Certified Public Accountants (AICPA), which started a business valuation specialty accreditation in 1997.

Exhibit 1–7

THE CANADIAN INSTITUTE OF CHARTERED BUSINESS VALUATORS
277 Wellington St. West, Toronto, Ontario, Canada M5V 3H2, (416) 204-3396, www.businessvaluators.com

Date formed:	1971	Ownership: Non-profit federally incorporated corporation owned by members

Description: The CICBV is the largest professional valuation organization in Canada. It was established to promote high standards in business and securities valuations. Members are entitled to use the professional designation CBV (Chartered Business Valuator) following completion of rigorous study and practical experience requirements. The Institute's members and students provide a broad range of business valuation services to Canada's business, legal, investment, banking, and governmental communities.

Designation Offered: CBV (Chartered Business Valuator)
FCBV (Fellow of the CICBV—must be elected)

Educational Requirement: College degree or equivalent.

Courses/Examinations: Successful completion of a program of six courses including assignments and examinations for each course plus the required experience, followed by the writing of the Membership Entrance Examination. Writing of this examination can be challenged without successful completion of the six courses, provided the applicant has at least five years of full-time experience in the field of business valuations.

Experience Requirement: Two years of full-time experience or the equivalent of part-time obtained over a five-year period, attested to by a sponsoring CICBV member.

Courses: All courses are provided by correspondence, including mandatory assignments with proctored examinations. Courses are offered twice per year. The courses offered are: Introductory Business & Security Valuations; Law and Valuation; Intermediate Business & Security Valuations; Taxation in Business Valuation; Special Topics; and Litigation.

Subscription: Subscription service is available for a yearly fee, which entitles the subscriber to receive all publications issued by the institute and to be maintained on a mailing list to receive other mailings.

Seminars and Conferences: Seminars and workshops offered monthly in major cities across Canada
Biennial National Conferences (two full days)
Regional Conferences—one to one-and-one-half days

Publications: *The Valuation Law Review* is published twice yearly with three sections: Corporate Securities Law, Family Law, and Taxation.
Business Valuation Digest is published twice yearly and consists of articles on business valuations.
The Journal of Business Valuation contains the proceedings of the Institute's Biennial Conferences.
The Business Valuator is a quarterly publication dealing with the activities of the Institute.

Information on the CPA specialty accreditation in business valuation and other AICPA business valuation activities is shown in Exhibits 1–2 and 1–6.

The Canadian Institute of Chartered Business Valuators

The Canadian Institute of Chartered Business Valuators (CICBV), founded in 1971, provides educational meetings and the professional designation CBV, chartered business valuator.

The CICBV publishes the proceedings of its biennial professional meetings in *The Journal of Business Valuation*. It also publishes a code of ethics and CICBV Practice Standards. The CICBV accreditation requirements and other information are presented in Exhibits 1–2 and 1–7.

Summary

The first half of the 1990s marked the culmination of long-time efforts to develop business valuation standards on which the professional business valuation community could achieve general consensus. During the latter part of the decade, this consensus has spread. These standards are rapidly being disseminated and recognized, not only throughout the professional business appraisal community and the courts in the United States, but also worldwide.

We believe these developments have already had some positive impact on the average quality of business valuation work. Business valuation practitioners are becoming more knowledgeable and rigorous in their practices. The standards also provide attorneys, CPAs, business owners, courts, and others who rely on business appraisals some widely accepted criteria by which to judge the quality of a business valuation. Chapter 22 of this book, Reviewing a Business Valuation Report, will be helpful in evaluating a business valuation report against the background of these standards.

The standards will continue to undergo refinement, but a solid foundation is certainly in place.

The accreditations in business valuation are also achieving increased recognition, both by the courts in written opinions and by the legal community in selecting business appraisers.

Bibliography

American Institute of Certified Public Accountants, Harborside Financial Center, 201 Plaza III, Jersey City, New Jersey 07311-3881, (800) 862-4272, www.aicpa.org.

- *Business Valuation Videocourse*, moderated by Shannon P. Pratt (New York: American Society of Certified Public Accountants, 1993, workbook updated in 1996). The objective of this videocourse is to provide practitioners with an overview of the essentials of business valuation. Joining Dr. Pratt in the two-and-one-half hour video presentation are Robert F. Reilly, Robert P. Schweihs, and Jay E. Fishman. The videocourse and accompanying course handbook are available from the AICPA, P.O. Box 2209, Jersey City, New Jersey 07303-2209, (800) 862-4272. The course code number is 350115.
- *Conducting a Valuation of a Closely Held Business*, by Gary R. Trugman (Jersey City: AICPA, Management Consulting Services Division, 1993). A consulting service practice aid available from the AICPA.
- *The CPA Expert*, a quarterly journal.

American Society of Appraisers, P.O. Box 17265, Washington, D.C. 20041, (703) 478-2228, www.appraisers.org.

- Principles of Appraisal Practice and Code of Ethics—available free of charge from the ASA.
- Standards for Business Valuation—single copies available free of charge from the publisher of *Business Valuation Review*.

- *Business Valuation Review*, a quarterly publication of the Business Valuation Committee of the American Society of Appraisers. Subscriptions are available by calling or writing the publisher: P.O. Box 24222, Denver, Colorado 80224, (303) 975-8895. Back issues are also available.
- *Valuation*, published periodically by the ASA, is multidisciplinary.

The Appraisal Foundation, 1029 Vermont Avenue, N.W., Suite 900, Washington, D.C. 20005, (202) 347-7722, www.appraisalfoundation.org.

- *Uniform Standards of Professional Appraisal Practice*, published annually in November.
- Information Service. The Information Service is designed to provide summary-oriented information to appraisers, users of appraisal services, and others who have an interest in remaining current on the activities of The Appraisal Foundation, the Appraisal Standards Board (ASB), and the Appraiser Qualifications Board (AQB).
- Subscription Service. The Subscription Service is the complete source of information for appraisers, users of appraisal services, and others on the activities of The Appraisal Foundation, the Appraisal Standards Board (ASB), and the Appraiser Qualifications Board (AQB).

Association for Investment Management and Research, 5 Boar's Head Lane, P.O. Box 3668, Charlottesville, Virginia 22903, (804) 977-6600, www.aimr.org.

- *Financial Analysts Journal*, published bimonthly.
- *Valuation of Closely Held Companies and Inactively Traded Securities*, edited by E. Theodore Veit, 1990 (monograph).

Business Valuation Resources, 7412 S.W. Beaverton-Hillsdale Highway, Suite 106, Portland, Oregon 97225, (888) BUS-VALU (888-287-8258), www.BVLibrary.com.

- *Judges & Lawyers Business Valuation Update*, monthly newsletter on business valuation for the legal community; reports new developments on business valuation standards, regulations, and professional credentials of interest to the legal community.
- *Shannon Pratt's Business Valuation Update*, monthly newsletter for business appraisers, intermediaries, buyers, sellers, and financing sources; "Association News" and "Legal and Court Case" departments report changes in professional standards and credentials, regulations, and laws affecting business valuation.

The Canadian Institute of Chartered Business Valuators, 277 Wellington Street, W., 5th floor, Toronto, Ontario, Canada M5V 3H2, (416) 204-3396, www.businessvaluators.com

- CICBV Practice Standards.
- *Business Valuation Digest.*
- *The Journal of Business Valuation.*

The ESOP Association, 1100 17th Street, N.W., Suite 210, Washington, D.C. 20036, (202) 293-2971, www.the-esop-emplowner.org.

- *Valuing ESOP Shares*, 1994.
- *Report on Valuation Considerations for Leveraged ESOPs*, 1998.

Institute of Business Appraisers, P.O. Box 17410, Plantation, Florida 33418, (954) 584-1144, www.instbusapp.org.

- *Business Valuation Practice*, a semiannual journal oriented to practical applications in business valuation.

Internal Revenue Service, 1111 Constitution Avenue, N.W., Washington, D.C. 20224, (202) 566-5000, www.irs.gov.

- *IRS Valuation Training for Appeals Officers*, 1998. Available through Commerce Clearing House Publishers, (800) 248-3248. (This publication is also available through *Business Valuation Update Online*, www.BVLibrary.com.)

National Association of Certified Valuation Analysts, 1111 East Brickyard Road, Suite 200, Salt Lake City, Utah 84106 (801) 486-0600, www.nacva. com.

- *The Valuation Examiner*, bimonthly magazine with information on NACVA activities and business valuation articles.

Chapter 2

Defining the Assignment

*It is impossible to intelligently discuss methods of valuation without refer-
ence to some assumed definition of value . . .*[1]

Many people hold the mistaken notion that there can be only one "value." As
we will see in this chapter, there are many definitions of value, and the purpose of
the valuation usually determines the appropriate definition of value.

This chapter is designed to help the valuation analyst and the client (or the
client's legal and other advisers) to focus together on all the elements that need to
be specified in the valuation assignment, so that appropriate methodology will be
employed to accomplish the objective of the specific engagement.

Identifying and clearly defining the purpose and objective of the business valuation assignment go a long way toward eliminating many of the problems that
occur with the conclusions of business valuation projects. While it seems simple, and
should be simple to understand, failure to clearly define the elements of the valuation assignment *at the outset of the business valuation* is one of the greatest sources
of errors, delays, excess costs, and misunderstandings between client and appraiser in a business valuation.

Defining the valuation assignment is the logical beginning of the valuation
process, providing focus for all the valuation considerations and efforts to be undertaken. Inadequate specification of the valuation assignment often results in misdi-
rected efforts and invalid conclusions.

It may seem obvious that the first step is to define the task. However, when
asked to participate in finding a solution to a client's problem, the client often does
not know how to define the valuation assignment, and communication to agree on
and mutually understand the assignment is often the most critical step. In fact, valuation assignments that have turned out poorly are often due to a failure to carefully define the assignment at the outset.

The reason for this failure may be that the client lacks sufficient experience to
realize all the details that should be included in the valuation assignment or has not
thought through the implications of some aspects of the appraisal. People who do
not engage in business valuations on a regular basis are unlikely to consider all of
the key elements of a valuation assignment. The professional appraiser should help
the client (and/or the client's attorney) in these details. However, appraisers are not
lawyers and do not practice law. When legal issues are involved, it is the ultimate
responsibility of the attorney, not the appraiser, to frame those issues.

Regardless of why the shortcomings occur, time spent at the outset in being
thorough and explicit in defining the valuation assignment is time well spent.

Basic Elements of the Valuation Assignment

The basic elements of the valuation assignment are:

1. Name of the client and of the appraiser.
2. Definition of the legal interest or interests to be appraised.
3. Valuation date(s) (the date as of which the appraiser's opinion of value applies).
4. Purpose or purposes of the appraisal (the use to which the valuation exercise is
   expected to be put).

---

[1] James C. Bonbright, *Valuation of Property*, Vol. I (Charlottesville, VA: The Michie Company, 1965 [reprint of 1937 ed.]), p. 128.

5. Applicable standard (or definition) of value.
6. Going-concern versus liquidation premise of value.
7. Description of the specific ownership characteristics:
    a.   Size of interest relative to total.
    b.   Degree of marketability (e.g., public, private, and related matters).
8. Form and extent of written and/or oral report.
9. Special requirements, contingent or limiting conditions, or special instructions for the professional appraiser.

Often it is impossible to define at the outset all of the relevant details of the valuation assignment. In those cases, it may be helpful for the appraiser to list the elements that are understood and the elements remaining to be understood. The appraiser then can follow up to try to resolve such questions. Exhibit 2–1 presents a general checklist for defining the valuation assignment.

Writing valuation objectives and requirements forces those responsible for the valuation to think carefully through all of its essential elements. It also helps prevent misdirecting the valuation process and helps the various parties involved, such as the principals, brokers, attorneys, and professional appraisers, avoid misunderstandings that otherwise might arise.

As the appraisal assignment develops, the file containing information on it will grow. As the missing details from the original appraisal assignment are changed or filled in, the appraiser notes them by memorandums to the file as they are discovered.

Definition of Who Offered and Who Accepted the Assignment

The most obvious reason for clearly defining the client and the appraiser is to know who is responsible for providing the services and who is responsible for paying for the services.

Another reason is that the appraiser has a responsibility to release confidential information about the appraisal only to the client. Others receive confidential information about the appraisal only with the client's permission, or if required by law.

If the case involves pending or potential litigation, the attorney may prefer to have his or her law firm retain the appraiser, rather than have the client retain the appraiser directly. This relationship may protect the appraiser's work and files from subpoena by the opposing attorney, although the effectiveness of such protection varies greatly from one situation to another.

Even when a business transaction is likely to be the ultimate outcome, it is important to specify by whom the appraiser is engaged. The appraiser may be engaged by the board of directors of the buying or selling company, a special committee of the board, the employee stock ownership plan trustee, or one or more individual shareholders of the buying or selling company, for example. The appraiser's relationship to the parties involved should be clear.

When specifying who is to provide the valuation services, the important distinction is whether the client is retaining the appraisal firm itself or the individual appraiser employed by the firm. The common practice is to retain the firm rather than the individual appraiser even though expert witnesses testify based upon their individual expertise and opinions. This practice protects the client, since the firm is responsible for completing the assignment regardless of impairments to the individual's capability to perform the work. This practice also tends to provide continuity

Exhibit 2–1

Valuation Assignment Checklist

Name of entity: _____

Form of ownership:
    ❑ Regular corporation   ❑ Limited partnership
    ❑ S corporation   ❑ Sole proprietorship
    ❑ General partnership   ❑ Limited liability company (LLC)
    ❑ Limited liability partnership (LLP)   ❑ Other (please specify)_____

State in which incorporated or registered: _____

Valuation being performed on: ❑ stock basis, or   ❑ asset basis

(If asset basis, list assets and liabilities): _____

_____

Are there other classes of equity interests outstanding?   ❑ Yes   ❑ No

(If yes, please specify): _____

Proportion of total entity being valued: _____

Any restrictions on transfer? _____

Purpose or purposes of the valuation: _____

Applicable standard of value (If pursuant to a federal or state statute, corporate bylaw or other governing law or document, so indicate): _____

Valuation date: _____

Is covenant not to compete involved?   ❑ Yes   ❑ No

Is employment agreement(s) involved?   ❑ Yes   ❑ No

If independent appraiser is retained:

    Name of appraiser: _____

    Name of client: _____

    Form and extent of appraisal report: _____

    Expected completion date (specify due date of various phases): _____

    Special instructions: _____

    Fee arrangement: _____

SOURCE: Willamette Management Associates.

in retention of the working papers and related records, making them accessible if they are needed months—or even years—later, as they frequently are.

Description of the Legal Interest or Interests to Be Appraised

To determine the applicable valuation approaches and procedures to be performed, *exactly* what is to be appraised must be made clear. Much of the confusion and disagreement among appraisers and appraisal writings arises simply because it is not clear exactly what asset, property, or business interest is to be valued.

Description of the Business Entity

If the entity at issue is incorporated, both the official name and the state of incorporation are necessary to define the entity. The state of incorporation is necessary because two or more corporations that are incorporated in different states may have identical names. Furthermore, the laws of the state of incorporation may have a bearing on the value of a particular business interest.

If, on the other hand, the business is not a corporation but some other structure, the form as well as the name must be specified. Some of the most common forms of business organization are sole proprietorships, general and limited partnerships, and cooperatives. By the same token, if the entity's structure gives rise to special legal or tax considerations, that structure should be specified. Some of these forms include S corporations, limited liability corporations (LLCs), limited liability partnerships (LLPs), family limited partnerships (FLPs), professional corporations, real estate investment trusts (REITs), investment companies registered under the Investment Company Act of 1940, and personal holding companies. For FLPs and LLCs, the state is especially important, because each state's partnership or LLC laws may have different implications on the interest being valued.

Description of the Specific Business Interest

The definition of the specific business interest can be broken into two broad questions:

1. Is the valuation to be a valuation of assets or a valuation of securities?
2. In either case, exactly *what* assets or *what* securities are subject to valuation?

By *securities* in the above context, we mean ownership interests such as stock, debt, and partnership interests, as opposed to direct ownership of underlying assets of the subject business entity.

Assets versus Securities. An equity interest represents an indirect ownership interest in whatever bundle of assets and liabilities (actual and contingent) exists in the business. Stock or partnership ownership is quite different from direct ownership of assets and direct obligation for liabilities. If stock or a partnership interest is to be valued, it must be identified in the appraisal assignment. If assets are to be valued, those assets (and any liabilities to be assumed) must be specified. For example, the assignment might include language such as ". . . engaged to estimate the fair market value of the fixed assets, inventory, and goodwill, on a going-concern basis, of . . ." In the analysis of the stock or a partnership interest in a business as compared with the assets of a business, noteworthy tax, legal, and financial characteristics come into play. These may have a significant impact on the valuation.[2]

Partial Interests. If a partial interest in an entity is to be valued, the proportionate relationship of the partial interest to the whole is obviously important. If there is more than one class of stock, such as preferred and common, or voting and nonvoting common, the appraisal assignment should indicate which class of stock is being appraised. If the business to be appraised is only a portion of the entire entity, such as a division or branch, it is necessary to state explicitly which aspects are included in the project.

---

[2] See, for example, *Edwin A. Gallun v. Comm.*, 33 T.C.M. 284 (1974).

Equity or Invested Capital. The *value of the business* is an ambiguous term until it is clear exactly what elements of equity and debt are to be included in that value.

Equity means the ownership interest. In a corporation, equity is represented by stock. If there is more than one class of stock, the term *equity* by itself usually means the combined value of all classes of stock. If it is intended that the value represents only one class of stock in a multiclass capital structure, there should be a statement as to which class of equity the value purports to represent.

In a partnership, equity is represented by partners' capital. If it is a multiclass partnership (such as a limited partnership), there should be a statement as to which class or classes of partnership interests the value purports to represent.

In a sole proprietorship, equity is the owner's interest.

Invested capital is not always as clearly defined. Therefore, if the term is used, it should be supplemented by a definition of exactly what it means in the given valuation context.

Usually, invested capital means all equity and interest-bearing debt, whether short-term or long-term. Alternatively, some analysts understand *invested capital* to mean all equity and only long-term debt. Investment bankers often do not include the company's cash among the assets when assessing the value of "invested capital." There are so many variations that it is essential to pin down *exactly* what is and is not to be included on the left and right sides of the valuation balance sheet.

Enterprise Value. The term *enterprise value* unfortunately is used at best very ambiguously and at worst very carelessly. It means different things to different people, each of whom may believe that his or her definition is the right definition.

It is generally used to represent some sort of aggregate value of the company and is often used as a synonym for market value of invested capital (MVIC). However, enterprise value could mean aggregate value of minority stock, value of either all common equity or all equity on a control basis, value of all invested capital, value of some portion (or all) of the assets, or something else.

Both the *Uniform Standards of Professional Appraisal Practice* and the American Society of Appraisers define a *business enterprise* as "a commercial, industrial, or service organization pursuing an economic activity." However, neither USPAP nor ASA offers a definition of *enterprise value*. The ASA Business Valuation Standards Subcommittee has discussed this term since 1985, and thus far has failed to find a consensus as to its definition.

If one encounters the term *enterprise value*, it is best not to assume any definition, but to make an attempt to identify the definition intended in its use. If one uses the term, it is important to spell out the intended definition, or the reader might infer an unintended definition. Because of the ambiguity, we have generally avoided using the term in this book.

Interests Other than Direct Fee Simple Ownership

If the ownership is something other than direct fee simple ownership of the stock, partnership interest, or other interest, the ownership interest needs to be specified. For example, the interest being appraised could be a life or term estate or a reversionary or remainder estate.

Ownership is, in effect, a bundle of rights. If the bundle of rights is anything less than a direct, unencumbered, simple ownership, the exact specification of the bundle of rights being appraised may have a significant bearing on value.

Description of the Specific Ownership Interest Characteristics

The description of the specific ownership interest subject to appraisal—and the particular investment attributes with regard to that ownership interest—can have a material impact on the appropriate valuation methodology and ultimate conclusion.

The primary ownership interest characteristics that need to be addressed in almost every business valuation are the following:

1. Control or minority valuation basis (not necessarily a black-and-white issue—there may be elements of control without absolute control).
2. Degree of marketability.

As such, the descriptions of the specific ownership interest characteristics are often in the nature of modifiers (adjectives) to the standard of value, such as "fair market value on a nonmarketable, noncontrolling ownership interest basis."

Sometimes the characteristics of the specific ownership interest subject to appraisal can be imposed artificially in a particular legal context. To give an example, under California Corporations Code Section 2000 (the California corporate dissolution statute), the case law is generally interpreted to mean that a minority ownership interest is valued *as if* it were a proportional share of the value of 100 percent of the company taken as a whole.[3]

To the extent that ownership interest characteristics are legally mandated or have been agreed on between the parties, they should be specified in the valuation assignment, with documentation as to their source. In many cases, the appraiser must consult with counsel to determine which ownership interest characteristics are appropriate. Also, the ownership interest characteristics may not be totally black-or-white issues, but in some cases may be matters of degree. *The descriptions of ownership interests often are major issues in disputed business valuation cases.* Consultation with the attorney involved and careful consideration of the implications of the purpose of the valuation can help to clarify issues related to choosing the appropriate description of the ownership interest for the situation.

Control versus Minority

As discussed in considerable detail in Part IV, the rights of control usually add value to shares of stock, typically making them worth considerably more than noncontrolling shares.

The degree of control represented by the interest being valued often is not necessarily a clear-cut issue. The degree of control or lack of it may fall anywhere across a broad spectrum, depending on the percentage ownership, the distribution of other ownership interests, and state laws governing rights of various percentage ownership interests in circumstances pertinent to the valuation situation at hand.

In most valuation situations, the understanding as to the degree of control can be stated clearly and unequivocally at the outset. In some cases, however, the degree of

---

[3] See, for example, *Ronald v. 4-Cs Electronic Packaging*, 168 Cal. App. 3d 290 (1985) and *Brown v. Allied Corrugated Box Co.*, 91 Cal. App. 3d 477 (1979).

control represented in the interest being valued is a matter of controversy. The impact of the degree of minority or control ownership on value is discussed at length in Chapters 15 and 16.

Degree of Marketability

For the purpose of this book, we define *marketability* as the ability to convert the asset to cash very quickly, at minimal cost, and with a high degree of certainty of realizing the anticipated amount of proceeds.[4]

The benchmark usually used to represent full marketability is an actively traded stock of a public company, which the owner can sell at or very near the last reported transaction price, at an insignificant transaction cost, merely by a phone call to a broker or by trading on-line, receiving cash within three business days. The premise as to the extent to which the entity or business interest being valued is or is not marketable is usually considered in relation to this benchmark.

All other things being equal, investors prefer to own something that they can liquidate immediately without any depressing effect on value rather than something that is difficult, time-consuming, and/or costly to liquidate. As will be seen in Chapter 17 on this subject, the degree of marketability or lack of it has a much greater impact on value than most people realize. It is not uncommon for discounts to run as high as 50 percent and, in many instances, higher!

The impact of the issue of marketability may be legally mandated or may be agreed between or among the parties. More often than not, however, this issue is an important subject of the appraiser's analysis. To the extent that matters affecting marketability are known (e.g., rights or restrictions regarding transfer of the ownership interest), it generally is desirable to note them in the engagement letter.

Valuation Date

The date, or dates, at which the business is being valued is critically important because circumstances can cause values to vary materially from one date to another, and the valuation date directly influences data available for the valuation. Every day, observers of the public stock markets see sudden and substantial changes in the value of a particular company's stock. In many court cases, especially those involving tax litigation, significant changes in value over very short time spans have been justified because of changes in relevant circumstances.[5]

Many internal and external factors can cause changes in the value of an interest in a company. Obviously, a sudden change in a company's earnings, especially if unanticipated, can have a substantial effect on value. Also, the value of a business interest varies with the cost of capital, a factor over which individual businesses have little control. Major events, such as the signing or termination of a major customer contract, can also have a dramatic, immediate impact on value.

In most business valuations, the opinion of value will be based at least partly on other, similar transactions, such as the prices at which stocks in the same or a related

---

[4] Some writings make a fine distinction between *marketability* and *liquidity*, with marketability focusing on finding the appropriate market, preparing the property for sale, and executing the trade and liquidity focusing on realizing cash proceeds.

[5] See, for example, *Morris M. Messing*, 48 T.C. 502 (1967), *acq.* 1968-1 C.B. 2. Even though the company made a public offering at over $36 shortly after a gift of stock, the court upheld a value of $13 for gift tax purposes as of the date of the gift.

industry are trading in the public market relative to their earnings, assets, dividends, or other relevant variables, if such data are available. It is important to know the valuation date when using guideline companies in the valuation so that the guideline transaction data can be compiled as of the valuation date, or as near to it as is practically possible.

Sometimes there is more than one valuation date. For example, in a marital dissolution, the parties may be concerned with the change in value that occurred during the marriage. In estate tax cases, the trustee, executor, or personal representative will consider adopting the "alternative valuation date" (i.e., six months after the date of death) to determine which is more advantageous and thus would be interested in the value of the estate's property on two dates six months apart.

In some litigated cases, the valuation date itself is an issue to be resolved by the court. In such situations, the appraiser must be prepared to address the valuation as of several dates, sometimes without knowing until after the judgment is rendered which date the court determined to be relevant. Since the choice of valuation date in such cases will be a legal matter, the attorney for whom the expert appraiser will be testifying should take the responsibility, as part of defining the assignment, of considering all the potentially applicable valuation dates and instructing the appraiser to be prepared to address the value as of each date. Sometimes a court will give an advance ruling on the valuation date to avoid the expense of appraisers doing valuations as of dates that the court will not deem relevant.

Purpose of the Appraisal

No single valuation method is universally applicable to all appraisal purposes. The context in which the appraisal is to be used is a critical factor.

Different statutory, regulatory, and case precedent standards govern valuations of businesses and business interests under various jurisdictions for diverse purposes. *Many business appraisals fail to reach a number representing the appropriate definition of value because the appraiser failed to match the valuation methods to the purpose for which it was being performed. The result of a particular appraisal can also be inappropriate if the client attempts to use the valuation conclusion for some purpose other than the intended one.*

Valuation reports should contain a set of limiting conditions, and one of the typical limiting conditions is as follows:

> This valuation is valid only for the valuation date or dates specified herein and only for the valuation purpose or purposes specified herein. No other purpose is intended or should be inferred.

Litigation over business valuation is commonplace. Much of this litigation arises because the parties have failed to match the valuation methods to the appraisal's intended purpose.

The purpose of the valuation encompasses the use to which the valuation exercise is expected to be put. Subsequent chapters of this book explore how valuation methods are impacted by special and specific purposes to which the valuation analysis may be put (Part VII). Valuations for each of these different purposes are often affected by a mass of complex federal and state statutes and legal precedents.

A valuation conclusion prepared for one purpose may not be the appropriate valuation conclusion for another purpose. The purpose of the valuation often determines the applicable standard of value—that is, the definition of value being sought—and almost always influences it. Standards of value are discussed in the next section, and an exhibit following that section illustrates the matching of certain valuation purposes with applicable standards of value.

Standards of Value

The word *value* means different things to different people. Even to the same person, value means different things in different contexts, as we discussed in the previous section.

Without carefully defining the term *value*, the conclusions reached in the valuation report have no meaning.

Is the objective of the valuation to estimate fair market value, market value, fair value, true value, investment value, intrinsic value, fundamental value, insurance value, book value, use value, collateral value, ad valorem value, or some other value?

Clients rarely give it much thought. Many don't have enough technical background in business valuation to raise the right questions. One of the professional appraiser's most important tasks is to work carefully and thoroughly with the client and/or attorney to arrive at a definition of value that is appropriate to the specific purpose of the valuation engagement.

In this book, a *standard of value* is a definition of the type of value being sought. A *premise of value* is an assumption as to the set of actual or hypothetical transactional circumstances applicable to the subject valuation (e.g., going-concern or liquidation).

For many situations, the standard of value is legally mandated, whether by law or by binding legal documents or contracts. In other cases, it is a function of the wishes of the parties involved. The standard of value usually reflects an assumption as to who will be the buyer and who will be the seller in the hypothetical or actual sales transaction regarding the subject assets, properties, or business interests. It defines or specifies the parties to the actual or hypothetical transaction. In other words, the standard of value addresses the questions: "value to whom?" and "under what circumstances?" The standard of value, either directly by statute or (more often) as interpreted in case law, often addresses what valuation methods are appropriate and what factors should or should not be considered.

Fair Market Value

In the United States, the most widely recognized and accepted standard of value related to business valuations is *fair market value*. With regard to business valuations, it is the standard that applies to virtually all federal and state tax matters, such as estate taxes, gift taxes, inheritance taxes, income taxes, and ad valorem taxes. It is also the legal standard of value in many other—though not all—valuation situations.

Fair market value is defined by the ASA as "the amount at which property would change hands between a willing seller and a willing buyer when neither is acting under compulsion and when both have reasonable knowledge of the relevant facts."[6] This definition comports to that found in the Internal Revenue Code and Revenue Ruling 59-60.

---

[6] American Society of Appraisers, Business Valuation Standards—Definitions.

In most interpretations of fair market value, the willing buyer and willing seller are hypothetical persons dealing at arm's length, rather than any particular buyer or seller. In other words, a price would not be considered representative of fair market value if influenced by special motivations not characteristic of a typical buyer or seller.

There is also general agreement that the definition implies that the parties have the ability as well as the willingness to buy or to sell. The *market* in this definition can be thought of as all the potential buyers and sellers of like businesses or practices.

The concept of fair market value also assumes prevalent economic and market conditions at the date of the particular valuation. You have probably heard someone say, "I couldn't get anywhere near the value of my house if I put it on the market today," or, "The value of XYZ Company stock is really much more (or less) than the price it's selling for on the New York Stock Exchange today." The standard of value that those people have in mind is some standard *other than* fair market value, since the concept of fair market value means the price at which a transaction could be expected to take place under *conditions existing at the valuation date.*

The terms *market value* and *cash value* are frequently used interchangeably with the term *fair market value*. The use of these essentially synonymous standard of value terms is often influenced by the type of asset, property, or business interest subject to valuation.

In the United States, the most widely recognized and accepted standard of value related to real estate appraisals is *market value*. The Appraisal Foundation defines *market value* as follows:

> MARKET VALUE: Market value is the major focus of most real property appraisal assignments. Both economic and legal definitions of market value have been developed and refined. A current economic definition agreed upon by agencies that regulate federal financial institutions in the United States of America is:
>
> > The most probable price which a property should bring in a competitive and open market under all conditions requisite to a fair sale, the buyer and seller each acting prudently and knowledgeably, and assuming the price is not affected by undue stimulus. Implicit in this definition is the consummation of a sale as of a specified date and the passing of title from seller to buyer under conditions whereby:
> >
> > **1.** buyer and seller are typically motivated;
> > **2.** both parties are well informed or well advised, and acting in what they consider their best interests;
> > **3.** a reasonable time is allowed for exposure in the open market;
> > **4.** payment is made in terms of cash in United States dollars or in terms of financial arrangements comparable thereto; and
> > **5.** the price represents the normal consideration for the property sold unaffected by special or creative financing or sales concessions granted by anyone associated with the sale.
> >
> > Substitution of another currency for United States dollars in the fourth condition is appropriate in other countries or in reports addressed to clients from other countries.

Persons performing appraisal services that may be subject to litigation are cautioned to seek the exact legal definition of market value in the jurisdiction in which the services are being performed.[7]

The most salient change in the above definition of market value compared with definitions widely accepted a few years ago is the phrase "the most probable price" in substitution for "the highest price."

Investment Value

In real estate terminology, investment value is defined as "the specific value of an investment to a particular investor or class of investors based on individual investment requirements; distinguished from market value, which is impersonal and detached."[8] Fortunately, business appraisal terminology embraces the same distinction in most contexts.

One of the leading real estate appraisal texts makes the following comments regarding the distinction between market value and investment value:

> Market value can be called "the value of the marketplace." Investment value is the specific value of goods or services to a particular investor (or class of investors) based on individual investment requirements. Market value and investment value are different concepts; the values estimated for each may or may not be numerically equal depending on the circumstances. Moreover, market value estimates are commonly made without reference to investment value, but investment value estimates are frequently accompanied by a market value estimate to facilitate decision making.
>
> Market value estimates assume no specific buyer or seller. Rather, the appraiser considers a hypothetical transaction in which both the buyer and the seller have the understanding, perceptions, and motivations that are typical of the market for the property or interests being valued. Appraisers must distinguish between their own knowledge, perceptions, and attitudes and those of the market or markets for the property in question. The special requirements of a given client are irrelevant to a market value estimate.[9]

The distinctions noted in the above quote can be carried over to business appraisal. There can be many valid reasons for the *investment value* to one particular owner or prospective owner to differ from the fair market value. Among these reasons are:

1. Differences in estimates of future earning power.
2. Differences in perception of the degree of risk and the required rate of return.
3. Differences in financing costs and tax status.
4. Synergies with other operations owned or controlled.

The discounted economic income valuation method can easily be oriented toward developing an investment value. Whether or not the value thus developed also represents fair market value depends on whether the assumptions used would be accepted by a consensus of market participants.

---

[7] *Uniform Standards of Professional Appraisal Practice* (Washington, DC: The Appraisal Foundation, 1999).

[8] *The Dictionary of Real Estate Appraisal,* 3rd ed. (Chicago: Appraisal Institute, 1993), p. 190.

[9] *The Appraisal of Real Estate*, 11th ed. (Chicago: Appraisal Institute, 1996), p. 638.

If sound analysis leads to a valid conclusion that the investment value to the current owner exceeded market value at a given time, the rational economic decision for that owner would be to not sell until a particular buyer is found who is willing to pay the investment value that is higher than the consensus of value among a broader group of typical buyers.

Of course, the concept of investment value as described above is not completely divorced from the concept of fair market value, since it is the actions of many specific investors, acting in the manner just described, that eventually lead to a balancing of supply and demand through the establishment of an equilibrium market price that represents the consensus value of the collective investors.

Intrinsic or Fundamental Value

Intrinsic value (sometimes called *fundamental value*) differs from *investment value* in that it represents an analytical judgment of value based on the perceived characteristics inherent in the investment, not tempered by characteristics peculiar to any one investor, but rather tempered by how these perceived characteristics are interpreted by one analyst versus another.

In the analysis of stocks, *intrinsic value* is generally considered the appropriate price for a stock according to a security analyst who has completed a *fundamental analysis* of the company's assets, earning power, and other factors.

> *Intrinsic value.* The amount that an investor considers, on the basis of an evaluation of available facts, to be the "true" or "real" worth of an item, usually an *equity security*. The value that will become the market value when other investors reach the same conclusions. The various approaches to determining intrinsic value of the *finance* literature are based on expectations and discounted cash flows. See *expected value; fundamental analysis; discounted cash flow method.*[10]

> *Fundamental analysis.* An approach in security analysis which assumes that a security has an "intrinsic value" that can be determined through a rigorous evaluation of relevant variables. Expected earnings is usually the most important variable in this analysis, but many other variables, such as dividends, capital structure, management quality, and so on, may also be studied. An analyst estimates the "intrinsic value" of a security on the basis of those fundamental variables and compares this value with the current market price of this security to arrive at an investment decision.[11]

> The purpose of security analysis is to detect differences between the value of a security as determined by the market and a security's "intrinsic value"—that is, the value that the security *ought* to have and will have when other investors have the same insight and knowledge as the analyst.[12]

If the market value is below what the analyst concludes is the intrinsic value, the analyst considers the stock a "buy." If the market value is above the assumed intrinsic value, the analyst suggests selling the stock. (Some analysts also factor market expectations into their fundamental analysis.)

---

[10] W.W. Cooper and Yuri Ijiri, eds., *Kohler's Dictionary for Accountants*, 6th ed. (Englewood Cliffs, NJ: Prentice Hall, 1983), p. 285. Reprinted by permission of Prentice Hall, Inc., Englewood Cliffs, New Jersey.

[11] Ibid., p. 228.

[12] James H. Lorie and Mary T. Hamilton, *The Stock Market: Theories and Evidence* (Burr Ridge, IL: Irwin, 1973), p. 114.

It is important to note that the concept of intrinsic value cannot be entirely divorced from the concept of fair market value, since the actions of buyers and sellers based on their *specific* perceptions of intrinsic value eventually lead to the general consensus market value and to the constant and dynamic changes in market value over time.

Case law often refers to the term *intrinsic value*. However, almost universally such references do not define the term other than by reference to the language in the context in which it appears. Such references to *intrinsic value* can be found both in cases where there is no statutory standard of value and in cases where the statutory standard of value is specified as *fair value* or even *fair market value*. When references to *intrinsic value* appear in the relevant case law, the analyst should heed the notions ascribed to that term as discussed in this section.

Fair Value

To understand what the expression *fair value* means, you have to know the context of its use. For certain bookkeeping applications, fair value is defined in the relevant accounting literature. In business valuation, the term *fair value* is usually a legally created standard of value that applies to certain specific transactions.

In most states, fair value is the statutory standard of value applicable in cases of dissenting stockholders' appraisal rights. It is also commonly used in valuations in state minority oppression cases, which have been on the rise. In these states, if a corporation merges, sells out, or takes certain other major actions, and the owner of a minority interest believes that he or she is being forced to receive less than adequate consideration for his or her stock, he or she has the right to have his or her shares appraised and to receive fair value in cash. In states that have adopted the Uniform Business Corporation Act, the definition of fair value is as follows:

> "Fair value," with respect to a dissenter's shares, means the value of the shares immediately before the effectuation of the corporate action to which the dissenter objects, excluding any appreciation or depreciation in anticipation of the corporate action unless exclusion would be inequitable.[13]

Even in states that have adopted this definition, there is no clearly recognized consensus about the interpretation of fair value in this context, but published precedents established in various state courts have not equated it directly to fair market value. When a situation arises of actual or potential stockholder dissent or dissolution action, it is necessary to research carefully the legal precedents applicable to each case. The appraiser should solicit the view of counsel as to the interpretation of fair value and, in most cases, should not assume that there is a definition that is clear and concise.

The term *fair value* is also found in the dissolution statutes of those states in which minority stockholders can trigger a corporate dissolution under certain circumstances (e.g., California Code Section 2000). Even within the same state, however, a study of case law precedents does not necessarily lead one to the same definition of fair value under a dissolution statute as under that state's dissenting stockholder statute.

Several countries undergoing privatization have adopted the term *fair value* to apply to certain transactions, often involving specific classes of buyers, such as employees. Such statutes vary widely in their definitions of fair value.

---

[13] Oregon Revised Statutes, Section 60.551(4).

Exhibit 2–2 gives some examples of matching certain valuation purposes with applicable standards of value.

Going-Concern versus Liquidation Premise of Value

Virtually all businesses or interests in businesses may be appraised under each of these following four alternative premises of value:

1. *Value as a going concern*—Value in continued use, as a mass assemblage of income producing assets, and as a going-concern business enterprise.
2. *Value as an assemblage of assets*—Value in place, as part of a mass assemblage of assets, but not in current use in the production of income, and not as a going-concern business enterprise.
3. *Value as an orderly disposition*—Value in exchange, on a piecemeal basis (not part of a mass assemblage of assets), as part of an orderly disposition; this premise contemplates that all of the assets of the business enterprise will be sold individually, and that they will enjoy normal exposure to their appropriate secondary market.
4. *Value as a forced liquidation*—Value in exchange, on a piecemeal basis (not part of a mass assemblage of assets), as part of a forced liquidation; this premise contemplates that the assets of the business enterprise will be sold individually and that they will experience less than normal exposure to their appropriate secondary market.

While virtually any business enterprise may be appraised under each of these four alternative fundamental premises, the value conclusions reached under each premise, for the same business, may be dramatically different.

Each of these alternative premises of value may apply under the same standard, or definition, of value. For example, the fair market value standard calls for a "willing buyer" and a "willing seller." Yet, these willing buyers and sellers have to make an informed economic decision as to how they will transact with each other with regard to the subject business. In other words, is the subject business worth more to the buyer and the seller as a going concern that will continue to operate as such, or as a collection of individual assets to be put to separate uses? In either case, the buyer and seller are still "willing." And, in both cases, they have concluded a set of transactional circumstances that will maximize the value of the collective assets of the subject business enterprise.

The selection of the appropriate premise of value is an important step in defining the appraisal assignment. Typically, in a controlling interest valuation, the selection of the appropriate premise of value is a function of the highest and best use of the collective assets of the subject business enterprise. The decision regarding the appropriate premise of value is usually made by the appraiser, based upon experience, judgment, and analysis.

Sometimes, however, the decision regarding the appropriate premise of value is made "for" the appraiser. This occurs when the appraiser knows—or is told—that the subject business enterprise will, in fact, be continued as a going concern or will be sold in a certain set of transactional circumstances. For example, if the business assets are, in fact, going to be sold on a value in exchange basis, it is not relevant for the appraiser to consider the value in continued use—or going-concern—premise of

Exhibit 2–2

Examples of Matching the Purpose of the Valuation with the Standard of Value

Purpose of Valuation	Applicable Standard of Value
Gift, estate, and inheritance taxes and charitable contributions	Fair market value.
Purchase or sale	Generally fair market value, but in many instances investment value, reflecting unique circumstances or motivations of a particular buyer or seller.
Marital dissolution	No statutory standards of value. Courts have wide discretion to achieve equitable distribution. Requires careful study of relevant case law.
Buy-sell agreements	Parties can do anything they want. Very important that all parties to the agreement understand the valuation implications of the wording in the agreement.
Dissenting stockholder actions	Fair value in almost all states. Consider relevant statute and case law to determine how interpreted in the particular state.
Minority oppression action	Generally, fair value in those states that address it at all. Not always interpreted the same as fair value for dissenting stockholder actions.
Employee stock ownership plans (ESOPs)	Fair market value.
Ad valorem (property) taxes	Generally, fair market value with varied nuances of interpretation. In many states, intangible portion of value excluded by statute.
Going private	Fair value in most states; governed by state statutes.
Corporate or partnership dissolutions	Fair value minority oppression statutes.
Antitrust cases	Damages based on federal case law precedent; varies from circuit to circuit.
Other damage cases	Mostly governed by state statute and case law precedent; varies by type of case from state to state.

value. Of course, if valuing a minority ownership interest, one would normally adopt the premise of "business as usual" unless given reason to do otherwise.

In some circumstances, it may be relevant—and, in fact, critical—to appraise the subject business enterprise under several alternative premises of value. For example, it may be extremely important to conclude the value of the same business enterprise under several alternative premises of value in appraisals performed for bankruptcy and reorganization or for financing securitization and collateralization purposes.

Sources of Guidance as to Applicable Standards and Premises of Value

The experience and expertise of the professional appraiser include the skill to seek out and interpret guidance as to the standard and premises of value that are relevant to the assignment at hand. Some of the most important sources of guidance as to the applicable standard and premises of value for the given situation are the following:

- Statutory law (state and federal).
- Case law (cases decided under the controlling statutory or common law).

- Administrative rulings (e.g., IRS revenue rulings).[14]
- Company documents (e.g., articles of incorporation or partnership, bylaws, meeting minutes, agreements).
- Contracts between the parties (e.g., buy-sell agreements, arbitration agreements).
- Precedent established by prior transactions.
- Directives issued by the court (in some litigated cases where the standards or premises are not clear, the appraiser may take the initiative to seek direction from the court regarding the relevant definition of value).
- Discussions with an attorney involved in the valuation matter or experienced in similar matters.
- Legal case documents (e.g., complaint, response, and so forth).
- The appraiser's experience and judgment.

Form of the Work Product

In many cases, the purpose of the report will largely determine the form of the report. The appraiser's report to the client can be oral, written, or a combination.

An oral report can be anything from a quick phone call to lengthy meetings with the principals, attorneys, brokers, and/or other parties involved. The form and extent of a written report can range from a single-page letter report to a detailed, hundred-page-plus volume.

An oral report is common in estate planning engagements, especially when the purpose of the exercise is to help the client get an approximate idea of the business's value in order to decide what action to take. A preliminary oral report is often the first deliverable product when the business valuation is being conducted in a litigation context, since the client attorney is concerned with the expert's opinion before the legal strategy is finalized because, if put into in writing, it could be discovered and utilized by the opponents. Even oral reports, however, may be covered by USPAP. Although some departures from full reports are permitted, there must be a supportable basis for opinions expressed.

When the purpose of the assignment is to prepare a feasibility analysis for a potential employee stock ownership plan (ESOP), the client, or client's attorney, will usually require a brief opinion letter which can be utilized for further planning. Once the business's value is approximated, the rest of the ESOP team is engaged, the size of the ESOP can be determined, and the amount and cost of bank financing can be identified.

In most cases, especially those involving taxes or tax implications, such as gift or estate tax valuations, the appraiser will be required to prepare a formal written opinion report.

The valuation opinion report will typically include the following sections:

1. A valuation opinion letter summarizing the valuation procedures and conclusions.
2. Several sections summarizing the relevant valuation theory, methodology, procedures, analyses, and conclusions.

---

[14] Note that administrative rulings do not have the force of law, but represent the position of the agency administering the law as to their interpretation of the law and rules for applying it.

3. A valuation synthesis and conclusion.
4. An exhibit section presenting a summary of the quantitative and qualitative valuation analyses.
5. A listing of the data and documents relied upon by the appraiser.
6. A statement of valuation contingent and limiting conditions.
7. An appraisal certification.
8. The professional qualifications of the principal appraisers.

Whether or not the report needs to conform to USPAP is either a matter of law or agreement with the client. Starting in 1999, USPAP stated:

> Compliance with these standards is required when either the service or the appraiser is obligated by law or regulation, or by an agreement with the client or intended users, to comply.[15]

Scheduling

One of the most important tools for conducting a business valuation thoroughly and on a timely basis is a proper schedule. Most first-time, or infrequent, business valuation clients tend to underestimate the amount of lead-time necessary for the appraiser to prepare a thorough and professional opinion. Scheduling problems often arise because the client delays in committing to the project, hoping that the valuation problem will go away. When it doesn't, there is little time left for anything but a crash assignment. Another common source of scheduling conflicts is a major change in some aspect of the assignment midway through the project—another good reason for the client and the appraiser to carefully think through and agree on the details of the valuation assignment as thoroughly as possible at the outset.

The valuation assignment should describe when the work is expected to be completed. But it should also make clear that the appraiser's ability to meet the proposed schedule depends upon receipt of the necessary information on a timely basis, and that changes midway through the assignment will likely cause changes in the schedule. To expedite getting necessary data to the appraiser on a timely basis, we recommend that anyone engaging an appraiser refer to Exhibit 4–1, "Preliminary Documents and Information Checklist for Business Valuation of Typical Corporation" (the exhibit can be readily modified for noncorporate forms of organization), and make sure the information is readily available.

One tactic often used, especially during the month of December when clients make gifts of property or are conducting other estate planning activities, is to ask the appraiser to arrive at an oral opinion of value and later provide a formal, written, documented report.

Fee Arrangements

The valuation budget may be a fixed price, a range of estimated fees, or it may be based on an hourly or daily rate. The more clearly and thoroughly defined the scope

---

[15] *Uniform Standards of Professional Appraisal Practice* (Washington, DC: The Appraisal Foundation, 2000), p. 2.

of the assignment is, the more likely it is that the appraiser will be able to quote a total fixed fee or a narrow range.

If third-party independence of judgment is required of the appraiser—as in cases involving expert testimony in pending or potential litigation—the appraiser's fees must be fixed, hourly, or set in some manner totally independent of the outcome of any litigation, or the appraiser's independent third-party status will be jeopardized. For those appraisal assignments requiring independence, the independent professional appraiser is legally and ethically prohibited from entering into an arrangement making the appraiser's fee contingent on a certain settlement amount or the outcome of a court decision.

The fee arrangements should include the terms of payment as well as the basis for establishing the fee.

Summary

This chapter has provided guidance to both the appraiser and the client (or the client's attorney) as to matters that should be considered when entering into the valuation engagement. Most of these matters should be incorporated into the engagement letter; some will be resolved after execution of the engagement letter or left to the appraiser's judgment. Even for those matters discussed in this chapter that ultimately are left to the appraiser's judgment, it often is helpful for the appraiser and the client (or the client's attorney) to discuss them at the onset of the engagement.

The basic elements of the appraisal assignment are:

1. Name of the client and of the appraiser.
2. Definition of the legal interest or interests to be valued.
3. Effective valuation date(s) (the date as of which the appraiser's opinion of value applies).
4. Purpose or purposes of the appraisal (the use to which the valuation exercise is expected to be put).
5. Applicable standard and premise of value.
6. Form and extent of written and/or verbal report.
7. Schedule and fee arrangements.

At some point, whether in the engagement letter or some other transmittal, additional topics typically are addressed, such as contingent and limiting conditions, limited use of the appraisal (only for the purpose intended and the effective date of valuation), confidentiality, and compliance with USPAP and/or other recognized professional business valuation standards.

Exhibit 2–3 is a sample engagement letter that covers the elements discussed in this chapter, as well as a few other important points such as indemnification of the appraiser.

Exhibit 2–3

Sample Professional Services Agreement

Amanda Appraiser & Associates and Estate of Charles C. Client agree as follows:

1.   **Description of services.** We agree to perform certain professional services for you, described briefly as follows as to purpose and objective, with the understanding that any modification to the assignment as stated below will be by a letter agreement signed by both parties.

   Estimate the fair market value in continued use of a 35 percent interest in Charles Client Crane Company, a New York corporation, held by the estate of Charles C. Client, as of September 30, 1999, for estate tax purposes.

2.   **Date(s) services due.** We will begin performance upon receipt of all information requested of you, and will complete our assignment, unless delayed or prevented by matters beyond our control, according to the following schedule:

   Full, formal appraisal report due within 90 days of receipt of signed agreement and all requested documents.

3.   **Fees.** Our fees for such professional services will be calculated on standard hourly rates in effect at the time services are rendered for staff members assigned to this project, plus out-of-pocket expenses. The fee is estimated at a range of $_____ to $_____, exclusive of expenses such as travel, long-distance telephone, purchases of data, copying and printing costs, and clerical time. The fee will not exceed such estimate by more than 25% without prior notification to you.

4.   **Retainer.** $_____ is due as a retainer upon execution of this Agreement. Retainer paid by you will be applied to the final billings.

5.   **Payment terms.** You will receive regular twice-monthly invoices, including fees and expenses incurred, for which payments will be due at our offices within 15 days of dates of invoices. Balances which remain unpaid 30 days from dates of invoices will be assessed a finance charge of 1.5% monthly (18% annual percentage rate).

   If we are to provide expert witness testimony as part of our assignment, you agree that payment of all fees and expenses invoiced and/or incurred to date will be received at our offices before we provide expert witness testimony, or if travel for testimony is necessary, payment will be received before travel is incurred.

   You agree that the fees and expenses invoiced by us must be paid current per the terms of this Agreement before we provide any report or analysis conclusions.

6.   You understand that we will need prompt access to documents, materials, facilities, and/or company personnel in order to perform our services in a timely and professional manner, and you agree to fulfill all such requests in a timely manner and to cooperate fully with us. You further understand and agree that delays in providing data or information may result in a delay of the completion date of the project.

7.   We agree to perform our services in a professional and objective manner. You understand that we do not guarantee the results of any analysis which we may undertake, but only agree that any report or analysis shall represent our professional opinion based on the data given to us or compiled by us. We will attempt to obtain and compile our data from reliable sources, but we cannot guarantee its accuracy or completeness.

8.   You warrant that the information and data you supply to us will be complete and accurate in every respect to the best of your knowledge; that any reports, analysis, or other documents prepared by us will be used only in compliance with all applicable laws and regulations; and that you will hold us harmless for any breach of this warranty.

9.   You agree to indemnify and hold us harmless against any and all liability, claim, loss, cost, and expense, whatever kind or nature, which we may incur, or be subject to, as a party, expert witness, witness or participant in connection with any dispute or litigation involving you unless such liability, claim, loss, cost, and expense, whatever kind or nature, is due to our gross negligence and such gross negligence is not caused by, related to, or the result of information provided to us by you. This indemnity includes all out-of-pocket expenses (including travel costs and attorney fees) and payment for all our staff members' time at standard hourly rates in effect at the time rendered to the extent we attend, prepare for, or participate in meetings, hearings, depositions, trials, and all other proceedings, including travel time. If we must bring legal action to enforce this indemnity, you agree to pay all costs of such action, including any sum as the Court may fix as reasonable attorney fees.

10.   If this Agreement, or any moneys due under the terms hereof, is placed in the hands of an attorney for collection of the account, you promise and agree to pay our attorney fees and collection costs, plus interest at the then legal rate, whether or not any legal action is filed. If any suit or action is brought to enforce, interpret, or collect damages for the breach of this agreement, you agree to pay our reasonable attorney fees and costs of such suit or action, including any appeal as fixed by the applicable Court or Courts.

Dated this 20th day of December, 1999, at New York, New York.

Estate of Charles C. Client	**Amanda Appraiser & Associates**
By: _____	By: _____
Name: Charlotte Client, Executor	Name: Amanda Appraiser, CFA, ASA
Address: 11 North 25th Street, Yonkers, New York 11111	
Telephone: (914) 555-4455	
Fax: (914) 555-4456	

Chapter 3

Business Valuation Theory and Principles

One of the frequent sources of legal confusion between cost and value is the tendency of courts, in common with other persons, to think of value as something inherent in the thing valued, rather than as an attitude of persons toward that thing in view of its estimated capacity to perform a service. . . . Certainly, for the purpose of a monetary valuation, property has no value unless there is a prospect that it can be exploited by human beings.[1]

There continues to be much controversy about the appropriate criteria by which to measure the value of a business or business interest. The previous chapter reconciled the issues surrounding the choices that determine the standard of value and the premise of value. In many cases, criticism of business valuation conclusions is more properly criticism of the definition of the valuation assignment. Once the scope in which the value will be considered has been defined (i.e., value to whom and in which market), the basic principles of business valuation are considered. While there are controversies here too, they tend to be more related to matters of professional judgment.

Generally Accepted Theory

In the simplest sense, the theory surrounding the value of an interest in a business depends on the future benefits that will accrue to the owner of it. The value of the business interest, then, depends upon an estimate of the future benefits and the required rate of return at which those future benefits are discounted back to the valuation date.

Thus, the theoretically correct approach is to project some category or categories of the future benefits of ownership (usually some measure of economic income, such as cash flow, earnings, or dividends) and estimate the present value of those future benefits by discounting them based upon the time value of money and the risks associated with ownership. Direct implementation of this theoretically correct approach is discussed in Chapter 9, Income Approach: Discounted Future Economic Income Method. That chapter focuses heavily on net cash flow as a measure of economic income, both for conceptual reasons and also because it is the focus of most merger and acquisition income value analysis.

While there is general acceptance of a theoretical framework for business valuation, translating it into practice in an uncertain world poses one of the most complex challenges of economic and financial theory and practice. The reasonableness of the business valuation conclusions will usually depend upon whether the projections and assumptions used to estimate future economic income benefits are acceptable to the decision maker for whom the business valuation is being prepared (e.g., the buyer, the seller, the opponent, the IRS, the judge).

Getting two or more parties with different economic and business expectations to agree on projected future benefits and the risks associated with achieving those projections is, perhaps, the most difficult task for the business appraiser. Therefore, business valuation practitioners have developed various approaches that use historical rather than projected data to arrive at a valuation.

In general, approaches using current or historical data, if properly carried out, should yield a result that is reasonably reconcilable with what a well-implemented discounted economic income method would derive.

---

[1] James C. Bonbright, *The Valuation of Property*, Vol. I (Charlottesville, VA: The Michie Company, 1965 [reprint of 1937 ed.], p. 21.

Reliance on Projected versus Historical Benefits

In virtually any business valuation, there is more than one point of view. Business appraisers are rarely engaged to conduct an assignment unless the client anticipates that the conclusions of the assignment will be scrutinized and challenged by someone with an adverse interest. Very often, the challenges surround the predictability of future benefits as they compare with the historical record.

In court, the parties to an action and the judge rely on *evidence* to support a particular position. Historical facts are often considered more credible evidence in the eyes of the court than forward projections of what somebody thinks will happen. Therefore, when legal evidence is required, the focus tends to be on the historical record of financial performance; future benefits and their predictability as of the valuation date are more difficult to establish. The courts generally prefer provable historical results to unprovable expectations of future results. The extent to which a court will accept projections as evidence in a valuation case is probably a function of the degree of confidence the court has in the validity of those projections based upon information available as of the valuation date, as well as the credibility of the witness. While courts continue to apply judicial scrutiny to the reasonableness of specific projections, it is noteworthy that in recent years courts have become much more accepting of the application of the discounted cash flow method as a valuation methodology.

Businesspeople are trained to make and evaluate business and economic projections and to use them as a basis for daily decision-making. Businesspeople can (and should) use their knowledge and experience in allocating resources entrusted to them for the purpose of taking business risks, and accept calculated risks inherent in decision making based on predictions of an uncertain future. In some mergers and acquisitions, a discounted future economic income model is used to identify the price. In developing investment recommendations, analysts often make estimates of the future benefits of ownership, and, if the analyst is credible, investors will act on their projections.

When preparing a business valuation for reorganization proceedings under bankruptcy statutes, the parties will frequently rely on capitalization of anticipated future cash flow. This makes sense because, unless there is a reasonable expectation that the future will be more rewarding than the recent past, the reorganization would appear to be a fruitless exercise.

Other categories in which projections are usually necessary are antitrust; lost business opportunity; breach of contract; infringement of patents, copyrights, or trademarks; and certain other types of damage calculations that need to address the amount of value lost as a result of a wrongful act. Eminent domain, a legal taking of property often subject to compensation for lost value, may also give rise to projections of lost future economic income.

As a practical matter, because of the lack of a set of projections and assumptions acceptable to all parties, many business valuations end up relying on historical data, which are evaluated and often adjusted in order to reflect reasonable expectations about foreseeable future results.

In summary, this difference in focus between projections of the future and the historical record is dictated by what the respective decision makers are willing to rely on. There may be a big difference in this respect between an investment decision in the market, where future performance of the business interest is critical, and a judicial decision in a court, where evidence rules the day, and projections unmet would mistreat one party. To be practically useful, the business valuation method selected must conform to the criteria acceptable to those who ultimately decide what action to take as a result of the valuation process. There is some trend toward more court recognition of modern financial theory, which is based on discounting expected economic income at a discount rate that reflects the risk of achieving the expectations.

In the 1930s, Bonbright recognized the valuation controversy surrounding the reliance on historical earnings and projected earnings:

> **Realized Earnings versus Prophesied Earnings.** In the valuation of entire business enterprises or of shareholdings in these enterprises, one of the most sharply contested questions has concerned the relative weight to be given to the earnings actually realized, as shown by the companies' financial statements after proper auditing, and the future earnings as estimated by the witnesses for the two parties to the controversy. Sometimes, indeed, the controversy arises from a denial by one of the parties that prophesied earnings should even be admitted as competent evidence. It is alleged that these prophecies are necessarily too highly speculative to merit consideration; that they are based on guesses as to future business conditions and as to managerial efficiency, the validity of which cannot adequately be checked by cross-examination or by the countervailing testimony of opposing experts. Hence, it is argued, only the realized earnings, whose amount can be approximately established by a careful audit, should be brought to the attention of the tribunal for such weight as it sees fit to give this type of data. Lawyers who take this position generally concede that facts having a general bearing on the immediate prospects of the business may be brought to the attention of the court. They object, however, to the false appearance of precision which is given by any estimate, in monetary amounts, of future net earnings. Their objection is likely to be even more strenuous if the case is being tried by a jury or by any other unsophisticated tribunal. Such bodies are in danger of taking the prophecies at their face value, without applying those drastic discounts for risk of nonoccurrence which cautious appraisal experts would apply.

> These practical objections to the admission of prophesied gross and net earnings are well taken. Indeed, the courts have shown a wholesome tendency to belittle the significance of the prophecies, and even on occasion to refuse to let them get into the record. But the language by which they have justified their treatment of this type of evidence has not always been acceptable to appraisal theory and has sometimes been very confusing. At times the courts have come close to stating that, as a matter of principle, the present value of a business property depends on present earnings, and that future earnings are irrelevant because they will determine merely future value. More frequently they have stated that present value depends on both present and future earnings, but with the implication that the present earnings have the more direct bearing on the worth of the property as it exists today.

> In fact, neither of these two statements correctly expresses the relevance of realized earnings and of prospective earnings. *The truth is that, when earnings have once been "realized," so that they can be expressed with some approach to accuracy in the company's accounts, they are already water under the mill and have no direct bearing on what the property in question is now worth. Value, under any plausible theory of capitalized*

earning power, is necessarily forward looking. It is an expression of the advantage that an owner of the property may expect to secure from the ownership in the future. The past earnings are therefore beside the point, save as a possible index of future earnings.[2]

In a litigated appraisal, a more convincing argument for the capitalization of realized earnings, rather than of prophesied earnings, can be found in the possibility . . . of capitalizing the realized earnings at a rate objectively determined by rates established on the marketplace. Assume, for example, that the case at bar requires the valuation of a railroad enterprise, the net earnings of which have averaged $10 million per year. Assume also that the securities issued by this particular railroad have no established market value, since they are closely held. If the various securities of other, comparable railroad companies are quoted at prices which average twenty times current annual net earnings, a rate of 5 percent suggests itself as the appropriate rate at which the current earnings of the instant railroad company may fairly be capitalized. Of course, any such conclusion involves a number of highly shaky assumptions— assumptions, not only as to the comparability of the various railroad enterprises, but also as to the relevance of quoted security prices as bearing on the value of an entire enterprise. But the errors implicit in this method of arriving at a proper rate of capitalization are probably far less serious than are the errors implicit in any other method available to an inexpert tribunal.[3]

The above quotation, written more than 60 years ago, continues to offer wisdom regarding the same issues today.

Basic Variables Affecting Value

Whether using projections or relying on historical data as a proxy for reasonable future expectations, there are certain key variables on which the business valuation will focus. The relative importance of the relevant variables will vary in different types of situations. For generations, theorists will continue to argue about which variables deserve the most attention and should be given the most weight in various valuation situations.

There are internal valuation factors that are a function of the performance of the business and there are external valuation factors that are a function of the environment in which the business operates.

One way or another, the financial benefits of ownership of an interest in a business enterprise must come from the following sources:

1. Dividends, distributions, or other type of cash flow:
   a. from operations, or
   b. from investments (e.g., interest).
2. Liquidation or hypothecation of assets.
3. Sale of the interest.

Therefore, any valuation approach—at least from a financial point of view—must focus on quantifying the ability of the business interest to provide benefits to its owner from one or some combination of the above sources.

---

[2] James C. Bonbright, *Valuation of Property*, pp. 249–50 (emphasis supplied).
[3] Ibid, p. 263.

In many instances, value conclusions are tempered by other internal variables, often variables relative to the specific shareholding as opposed to the company as a whole, such as:

1. Size of the subject interest (reflecting not only magnitude but control issues).
2. The right to vote and to impact the direction of the business.
3. Restrictive provisions affecting ownership rights.
4. The marketability of the ownership position.
5. Special ownership or management perquisites.

There is no universal answer concerning which variable among the future benefit statistics deserves the greatest attention. Generally, earning power is the important internal variable affecting the going-concern value of the business. Earning power may be expressed in terms of the ability to realize cash flows, dividends, net income, or any of several other measures.

The external variables that affect a business's value are collectively referred to as "the market." The market determines the amount of expected return that is required to attract investment—the *cost of capital*. The cost of capital depends on the general level of interest rates and the amount of premium for risk (above the return available on a safe, fixed income investment) that the market demands, as well as the risks attributable to the subject business. Sometimes, a change in the value of a business interest is entirely attributable to external market conditions and the investors benefit more for being at the right place at the right time than for an improvement in the fundamental financial performance of the business.

Impact of Risk on Value

The analyst should consider the expected economic income in two dimensions: the magnitude of the expected economic income and the risk that this economic income will or will not be realized. For the purpose of discussion in this book, we will define *risk* as *the degree of uncertainty as to the realization of expected future economic income*. For a given level of expected future *economic income*, the market will pay more for a company's stock to the extent that a realization of that economic income is more certain or less to the extent that a realization is less certain. In other words, for a given level of expected future economic income (e.g., cash flow, dividends), the lower the risk, the higher the present value or, conversely, the higher the risk, the lower the present value.

Risk generally is reflected in the valuation through the discount or capitalization rates applied to the financial variables. The market determines a basic risk-free required rate of return and the amount of premium required for assuming various levels of risk. Of course, one thing the owners can do to lower their cost of capital— and thus increase the value of their enterprise—is to lower the degree of risk associated with it. All else being equal, the lower valuation analysts perceive the risk to be, the lower will be the cost of capital considered applicable in the valuation and, thus, the higher will be the resulting value.

Specific assessment and treatment of the all-important factor of risk is discussed in detail in the chapters on implementing the various valuation approaches.

Accepted Business Valuation Approaches and Methods

Background and Structure

Business valuation as it is practiced today reflects a blending of two streams of academic and professional background:

1. The securities profession, which deals with financial analysis of stocks, bonds, and other financial instruments, and with business acquisitions, divestitures, and mergers.
2. The real estate profession, which deals with the analysis of transactions in land and real property improvements.

The body of knowledge required to estimate the value of a business or business interest is more akin to that required by the securities profession than by the real estate profession. That fact is reflected by the material in this book and the typical academic and professional backgrounds of those practicing in the field of business valuation.

However, real estate appraisers dominate the generalized field of "appraisal" (defined by The Appraisal Foundation as "the act or process of estimating value"[4]). Among individual members of professional member organizations composing The Appraisal Foundation, real estate appraisers outnumber business appraisers more than 65 to 1. The field of real estate appraisal is far more familiar to both the public and the courts than is the field of business appraisal.

Consequently, the American Society of Appraisers Business Valuation Standards recognize an "income approach," a "market approach" (sales comparison approach), and an "asset-based approach" (somewhat similar to real estate's "cost" approach), thus following the three-pronged structure familiar to real estate appraisers. The term "method" is often used to refer to more specific ways to implement a business valuation within one of the three broad approaches. For example, *discounted cash flow* and *capitalization of earnings* may be considered methods within the broader category of the income approach, and the *guideline publicly traded company method* would fall within the market approach.

The presentation of business valuation methodology in this book parallels the real estate appraisers' traditional three-pronged structure, as well as the structure of the American Society of Appraisers Business Valuation Standards. Thus, the reader will find:

---

[4] *Uniform Standards of Professional Appraisal Practice* (Washington, DC: The Appraisal Foundation, 1999), p. 10.

Comparison with Real Estate Appraisal Approaches

Interrelationship of the Three Broad Approaches. It is important to note that, in both business and real estate appraisal, the three broad approaches are not independent of each other but are interrelated.[5] The income approach requires some kind of a rate of return at which to discount or capitalize the income. The forces of the market drive these rates. All comparative valuation approaches relate some market value observation to either some measure of a property's ability to produce income or to some measure of the condition of its assets. The cost (or asset-based) approach uses depreciation and obsolescence factors that are based, to a certain extent, on some measure of market values of assets. Thus, whether in business appraisal, or real estate appraisal, the three broad approaches discussed so often are not discrete from each other, but are interrelated.

Income Approach. Within the income approach, the real estate appraisal profession recognizes certain methods similar to economic income discounting and capitalizing used in business appraisal. For example, what real estate appraisers call *yield capitalization* uses procedures similar to what we refer to in Chapter 9 as the discounted future economic income method. What real estate appraisers call *direct capitalization* uses procedures similar to what we refer to in Chapter 10 as the capitalization of future economic income method. In business valuation, as in real estate appraisal, the two methods within the income approach require different rates at which to discount or capitalize the income stream. (See Chapters 9 and 10 for an explanation of the relationship between discount and capitalization rates in the context of business appraisal.)

While the valuation procedures are similar, in most cases, estimating the future benefits of owning an operating business is more difficult than estimating the future benefits of owning an apartment building, an office building, or a similar income-producing real estate property. Furthermore, the risks of owning an operating business are typically more complex to assess and quantify than are the risks of owning operating real estate, and the resulting cash flows tend to be more volatile. Hence, the selection of appropriate discount and capitalization rates is more difficult in the context of the business valuation. The business appraiser needs a broad understanding of relevant economic and industry factors, capital market conditions, business management, and accounting.

Pretax income streams from direct investment in real estate tend to be capitalized at lower required rates of return than comparably defined pretax income streams from investments in non–real estate oriented businesses. One reason for this is the lower perceived risk in the typical real estate investment. Another is that real estate investments often enjoy income tax deductions and credits that are not available to the comparable income stream earned by a business.

Real estate investors may accept a lower rate of return from their cash flow stream than they would accept from other assets because they expect extra return in the form of capital appreciation on the property. This is in sharp contrast to a business investment that includes machinery and equipment that will eventually lose value through wear and tear and/or obsolescence, or an investment that includes intangible assets that will become obsolete.

---

[5] For a discussion of this interrelationship with respect to real estate appraisal, see *The Appraisal of Real Estate*, 11th ed. (Chicago: Appraisal Institute, 1996), p. 449.

Market Approach. As for the market or sales comparison approach (covered in more detail in Chapters 11 and 12), the real estate appraiser will seek data on sales of comparable properties, and the business appraiser will seek data on transactions of comparable businesses. The business appraiser will interpret the transaction data for guidance in determining applicable valuation parameters—such as capitalization rates for earnings or cash flow—and ratios of the entity's market value to asset value measures, such as book value or adjusted book value.

There is a tendency for the market for businesses to change more rapidly than the market for real estate. After all, a business can be thought of as a collection of tangible and intangible assets, each with its own price volatility and risks of ownership. Effects of these risks can be observed in volatility of stock prices every day.

Asset-Based Approach. The business appraiser's asset-based approach (see Chapters 13 and 14) has some similarities to the real estate appraiser's cost approach. This is true whether the business appraiser uses the discrete asset accumulation method or the collective capitalized excess earnings method. The asset-based approach provides an indication of the value of the business enterprise by developing a fair market value balance sheet. All of the assets of the business are identified and listed on the balance sheet (note: this balance sheet is not the cost-based balance sheet that is prepared in accordance with generally accepted accounting principles), and all of the business's liabilities are brought to current value as of the valuation date.[6] The difference between the fair market value of the assets and the current value of the liabilities is an indication of the business enterprise equity value under the asset-based approach.

The use of the asset-based approach should not be confused with the selection of the appropriate premise of value for the subject business valuation. Some analysts mistakenly confuse the use of the asset-based approach with a liquidation premise of value (or with a liquidation valuation). Rather, the asset-based approach can be used with all premises of value—including (1) value in use as a going-concern business enterprise and (2) value in exchange as part of a forced or orderly liquidation. The asset-based approach focuses on the value of the enterprise's component assets, properties, and business units. The use of the asset-based approach does not dictate the premise of value that should be applied to the enterprise's component assets, properties, and business units.

Businesses Typically Owned through Securities. As discussed more fully elsewhere in the book, the fact that businesses typically are owned through corporate stock, partnership interests, or limited liability company membership units introduces an element of complexity not present in direct ownership of assets. These securities represent bundles of rights determined by articles of incorporation or partnership, limited liability company membership agreements, bylaws, and many contractual and legal rights and restrictions not relevant to direct ownership of physical assets. Valuation of stock, a partnership interest, or a membership interest requires an understanding of the bundle of rights and restrictions encompassed therein.

Also, the tax consequences of ownership and/or transfer of stock or partnership interests usually are quite different from those of ownership and/or transfer of direct investment in underlying assets. These tax implications often have a significant bearing on value.

---

[6] For example, if the company had a 6 percent bond outstanding due in 10 years, and the current market rate for a comparative bond was 8 percent, the bond would be revalued downward on the liability side of the balance sheet to a value equivalent of an 8 percent, yield to maturity bond, unless it was contemplated that the bond would be paid before maturity.

The U.S. Supreme Court firmly established the principle that ownership of stock was not tantamount to ownership of a company's assets clear back in 1925:

> The capital stock of a corporation, its net assets, and its shares of stock are entirely different things. . . . The value of one bears no fixed or necessary relation to the value of the other."[7]

As George Lasry explains it:

> A share of common stock does not represent a share in the ownership of the assets of a business.[8]
>   Only the corporation itself holds title to all its assets and liabilities. . . . A thirsty shareholder of a brewery cannot walk into "his" company and demand that a case of beer be charged to his equity account.[9]

Dozens of court cases have elaborated on the distinction between ownership of stock or partnership interests and direct ownership of assets.[10]

Fractional Interests. Stocks and partnership units are designed to be readily divisible into fractional interests in an enterprise, while fractional interests in direct investment in real estate or other assets are far less common and generally more cumbersome to transfer. To implement the market approach when valuing noncontrolling interests, market data on fractional interest transactions in direct investment in real estate are meager, at best, while noncontrolling interest public stock transactions abound.

Generally, noncontrolling holders of stocks and partnership units enjoy fewer rights if they are dissatisfied with management than do direct fractional interest holders in income-producing real estate. As a consequence, discounts from a pro rata portion of the control value of 100 percent of the business or property taken as a whole generally are greater for noncontrolling stocks and partnership interests than they are for direct fractional interests in income-producing real estate.

Impact of Controlling versus Noncontrolling Ownership Interest

The owner of a controlling interest in an enterprise enjoys some very valuable rights that the owner of a noncontrolling interest does not enjoy. Consequently, if ownership control is an issue in the valuation, the analyst should assess the extent to which the various elements of control do or do not exist in the particular situation and consider the impact of each element on the value of control. (The most important elements of control are discussed in Chapter 15, Control and Acquisition Premiums.) A noncontrolling ownership interest holder may still enjoy some of the elements of ownership control. For instance, a noncontrolling ownership interest holder may be in a position to cast a crucial swing vote and, to some degree, influence important business policies.

The distribution of ownership can affect the value of a particular business interest. If each of three stockholders or partners owns a one-third interest, no one has

---

[7] *Ray Consol. Copper Co. v. United States*, 45 S. Ct. 526 (1925).

[8] George Lasry, *Valuing Common Stock* (New York: AMACOM, 1979), p. 1.

[9] Ibid., p. 15.

[10] See, for example, *Charles S. Foltz, et al. v. U.S. News & World Report, et al.*, 865 F.2d 364 (D.C. Cir. 1989); *Sommers Drug Stores v. Corrigan Enterprises, Inc.*, 793 F.2d 1456 (5th Cir. 1986); and *Estate of Edwin A. Gallun*, 33 T.C.M. 1316 (1974).

complete control. However, no one is in a relatively inferior position unless only two of the three have close ties with each other. In this situation, the analyst could recognize that the discount from pro rata value for each equal interest normally will be lower than that for a minority interest that has no control whatsoever. In fact, it is possible that the owner of a one-third minority interest may extract a special-purpose price premium (such as a swing vote price premium) in a competitive bid from the other two one-third stockholders.

Many typical control rights may be denied to a company through relations with other stakeholders in the company, such as its banker. Indenture provisions in conjunction with debt obligations or senior classes of stock frequently prevent the company from taking such actions as dividend payments, increases in management compensation, liquidation of assets, acquisitions, or changes in the direction of the business, for example. Shareholder agreements also may contain several restrictions.

Government regulation of operations may preempt the usual prerogatives of control. Liquidating insurance companies and utilities can be a lengthy and sometimes impossible process, for example. Government regulations may prevent certain acquisitions and, similarly, prevent a company from selling out to certain other companies or investors.

State statutes can affect the respective rights of controlling and noncontrolling stockholders. In about half the states, a simple majority can approve major actions such as a merger, sale, liquidation, or recapitalization of the company. Other states require a two-thirds or greater majority to approve such actions, which means that a minority of just over one-third (or even less in some states) has the power to block such actions. Under California and some other states' statutes, minority stockholders enjoy certain rights under specific circumstances. The variations in state law concerning which rights are given to what proportion of ownership can have an important bearing on the valuation of certain percentage interests in some cases.

Voting rights constitute one of the most difficult variables to quantify in terms of impact on value. For extremely small minority ownership interests, the market accords very little value to voting rights. However, where swing votes or majority ownership interests are involved, the impact on value can be significant. In fact, a majority block of nonvoting stock may actually be worth less per share than a small block of voting stock, since there are fewer potential buyers for the large block without the right to vote on corporate matters.

In most cases, a noncontolling ownership interest is worth less than a pro rata proportion of the value of the entire business enterprise. The analysis and quantification of minority ownership values versus control ownership values are addressed in considerable detail in Chapters 15 and 16 on control and acquisition price premiums and lack of control discounts.

Impact of Marketability

Ready marketability adds value to a security. Conversely, lack of marketability detracts from the security's value as compared with a security that is identical in all respects but is otherwise marketable. In other words, the market pays a premium for liquidity, or exacts a discount for the lack of liquidity.

Since interests in closely held businesses do not, by definition, enjoy the ready market of a publicly traded stock, a share in a privately held company usually is worth less than an otherwise comparable share in a publicly traded one. Many factors affect the relative marketability of different business interests. Sometimes size of the interest is a factor; a smaller block may be easier to market than a larger block, and in other cases the reverse is true. In most cases, the lack of marketability factor harshly impacts minority interests. However, even controlling interests in closely held businesses obviously are not as readily marketable as shares of publicly traded stock.

The existence of shareholder agreements can severely affect the transferability of shares. Some buy-sell agreements require that the shareholders be employed by the company and be a resident of a certain state. Others determine the price at which, and the circumstances under which, the shares are to be voluntarily or involuntarily transferred, put and call provisions, and who may be entitled to a right of first refusal on transactions. The presence of practically any type of restrictive agreement tends to reduce the estimated market value of a closely held company's stock.[11]

Chapter 17, Discounts for Illiquidity and Lack of Marketability, presents extensive empirical evidence on the quantification of discounts for lack of marketability.

Distinction between Discount for Lack of Control and Discount for Lack of Marketability

Confusion can result when clients, analysts, and the audience for the analysis (e.g., the court) fail to distinguish between a discount for lack of ownership control and a discount for lack of marketability. These are two separate concepts, although they are somewhat interrelated. Sometimes people overlook the fact that discounts are meaningless until the bases from which they are to be taken have been defined.

The base from which the discount for lack of control is subtracted is its proportionate share of the value of the total equity (or at least the common equity), taken as a whole, including all rights of ownership control. The base from which the discount for lack of marketability is subtracted is the value of an entity or interest that is otherwise comparable but enjoys higher liquidity (that is, can more readily be sold and converted to cash).

If a noncontrolling ownership interest in a closely held business is valued by reference to the trading prices of publicly held stocks, noncontrolling ownership interests are being compared with other noncontrolling interests. The closely held stock should be discounted for its lack of marketability with respect to the public stock, but not for lack of control. If a noncontrolling ownership interest in a closely held business is being valued by capitalization of earnings, book value, adjusted book value, or some other statistic, but with such multiples based on controlling interest transactions, discounts may be appropriate in order to reflect both the lack of ownership control and the lack of marketability. Conversely, if a controlling ownership interest in a closely held business is being valued with reference to day-to-day trading prices of public stocks, which are noncontrolling interests, it may be appropriate to add a price premium for control to the price that otherwise would appear to be indicated.

When using a discounted future economic income method, such as the discounted cash flow method, it is common to develop the present value discount rate based on data from the publicly traded stock market—that is, transactions in publicly traded noncontrolling shares. This would imply that, when valuing a non-

---

[11] See, for example, W. Terrance Schreier and O. Maurice Joy, "Judicial Valuation of 'Close' Corporation Stock: *Alice in Wonderland* Revisited," *Oklahoma Law Review* 31 (1978), p. 865.

controlling ownership interest, it would be appropriate to adjust the results from the method for a discount for lack of marketability, but not for lack of control. This is a correct implication, providing that the cash flows being discounted are not adjusted for changes or factors that would benefit a controlling interest owner but would not inure to the benefit of a noncontrolling interest owner. This is discussed in some detail in Chapter 9, Income Approach: Discounted Future Economic Income Method, and in the subsequent chapters on valuation adjustments.

Even controlling ownership interests can suffer to some extent from a lack of marketability. Even 100 percent ownership interests in businesses are not liquid. And, majority but less than 100 percent control position may take longer to sell than a 100 percent ownership interest. Such an increased selling (or "market exposure") period reduces the present value of the proceeds from the sale of the majority ownership interest by the time value of money, for example. The relationship between the discount for lack of marketability and the discount for lack of control lies in the fact that—even after reducing the pro rata value of an ownership interest in a business in order to reflect its lack of complete control—it is usually much harder and more expensive to sell an ownership interest in a closely held company than a publicly traded one.

In some cases, the value of control just offsets the disadvantage of lack of marketability. However, this should only be the result after careful consideration of the specific circumstances surrounding those factors and not the result of only an uninformed assumption.

In many published court decisions, especially older ones involving valuations for gift and estate tax purposes, a single lump sum discount to reflect lack of control, lack of marketability, and sometimes other factors is taken. However, conceptual thinking in the valuation process, supported by the use of empirical data, usually can isolate and separately quantify the various valuation factors, especially the more important ones. In recent years, valuation practitioners and courts have been giving separate recognition to the impact of noncontrolling ownership interest and lack of marketability factors. A 1982 estate tax decision articulated the distinction between the lack of control and lack of marketability discounts very clearly:

> In their arguments, neither petitioner nor respondent clearly focuses on the fact that two conceptually distinct discounts are involved here, one for lack of marketability and the other for lack of control. The minority shareholder discount is designed to reflect the decreased value of shares that do not convey control of a closely held corporation. The lack of marketability discount, on the other hand, is designed to reflect the fact that there is no ready market for shares in a closely held corporation. Although there may be some overlap between these two discounts in that lack of control may reduce marketability, it should be borne in mind that even controlling shares in a nonpublic corporation suffer from lack of marketability because of the absence of a ready private placement market and the fact that flotation costs would have to be incurred if the corporation were to publicly offer its stock.[12]

Many subsequent court decisions have distinguished between the concepts of lack of control and lack of marketability. And, many subsequent court decisions have separately quantified their conclusions regarding the impact of the respective factors. Several of these decisions are cited in later chapters. In addition, some court decisions have failed to recognize the multiplicative (rather than the additive) impact of valuation adjustments.

---

[12] *Estate of Woodbury G. Andrews*, 79 T.C. 938 (1982).

Other Qualitative Factors Affecting Value

Qualitative factors bear on value. However, such qualitative factors often defy quantification on the basis of empirical data within the valuation factors discussed up to this point. In some cases, such factors may influence the analyst's judgment and be reflected in a specific adjustment in arriving at the value conclusion. The analyst may incorporate these factors into the analysis when choosing valuation pricing multiples or capitalization rates. In some cases, the qualitative factors may be important enough to warrant a separate, specific (and therefore quantified) adjustment to value.

An important qualitative factor in many closely held companies is reliance on one or a few key management personnel. Limited product diversity can restrict the categories of potential customers, the number of potential customers within a category, and increase the risks arising from shortages of critical supplies or competitive product information. Lack of vertical integration can leave a closely held business vulnerable to vagaries in sources of supply or to a particular customer relationship—an example being the original equipment component manufacturer who is vulnerable should the customer decide to manufacture in-house. These factors are discussed in Chapter 18, Other Valuation Adjustments.

Other factors to consider in various cases include the company's research and development efforts, industry position, quantity and quality of asset base relative to competitors, and the quality and relationship with its workforce.

Matching the Valuation Methodology with the Standard and Premises of Value

Perhaps the single most prevalent broad reason for many valuation work products to miss the mark is failure to use valuation approaches and methods that are consistent with the definition of value being sought.

In the previous chapter, we discussed standards and premises of value and ownership characteristics, and presented a chart giving examples of how the purpose of the valuation can affect the appropriate definition of value. In this chapter we have, at least broadly, introduced the topic of approaches to value and elaborated a bit further on two of the most important ownership characteristics to consider: controlling versus noncontrolling ownership interests and degree of marketability. *All these matters must be taken into consideration together in deciding exactly which valuation methods to use and what assumptions and data will go into the implementation of those methods.*

This art of matching the methodology to the valuation context will become clearer as the reader moves through Part III on Business Valuation Approaches and Methods and Part VII on Valuations for Specific Purposes. When either preparing or reviewing a business valuation report, always be alert to consider whether each step of the procedure is consistent with the standard and premises of value—and with the ownership characteristics—applicable to the specific valuation context.

Sum of Parts Not Necessarily Equal to Whole

Since partial interests in a business enterprise are impacted by discounts and premiums differently than are controlling ownership interests, the sum of the individual ownership positions may be less than the overall business enterprise value. In most cases, the sum of the values of the partial interests taken individually is less than what might be received if a single buyer purchased the entire entity. The company in its entirety has a different value because it conveys different rights and interests than the sum of all the interests taken on a minority ownership interest basis. This economic fact, of course, is a catalyst for both merger and acquisition activity and dissenting shareholder lawsuits.

It is also important for attorneys and other advisers to alert clients entering into buy-sell agreements at "fair market value" that this term usually means something less than a pro rata proportion of the total enterprise value, unless other provisions are specified.

Since estate tax planning is seriously impacted by the fact that the sum of the parts do not always equal the whole, Chapter 14, the special valuation provision of the Internal Revenue Code, was added by the Revenue Reconciliation Act of 1990. These provisions mandate certain departures from strict fair market value in valuations for certain family company recapitalizations. However, there still are many opportunities in estate planning to benefit from the market reality fact that the sum of the values of parts often is considerably less than the value of the whole. These issues and opportunities are discussed at some length in Chapter 27, Valuations for Estate and Gift Tax Purposes.

Summary of Business Valuation Principles

The specific methods and procedures for valuing a business or a business interest vary from one situation to another. However, several basic principles are fundamental to the business valuation discipline:

1. From a financial point of view, the value of a business or business interest is the sum of the expected future benefits to its owner, each discounted back to a present value at an appropriate discount rate.
2. The market for capital usually determines the appropriate discount rate. The discount rate is the expected rate of return that would be required to attract capital to the investment, which takes into account the rate of return available from other investments of comparable risk.
3. Projecting future benefits and determining an appropriate discount rate is difficult, especially when trying to bring two participants to either a transaction or a dispute to an agreement. There are accepted methods of estimating value by using current or historical—rather than projected—financial data. Even valuation methods that use current or historical financial data often require adjustments to the historical data to reflect the impact of future expectations. In addition, consideration should be given to expected growth rates, industry trends, and other microeconomic factors. Values estimated from such procedures should be reconcilable with estimates of value from a discounted future economic income method.

4. When relying on specific comparative market transactions for guidance in esti- mating the value of a subject business or interest, investors' specific expecta- tions regarding future returns and risk that are incorporated into capitalization rates, multipliers, and other valuation parameters are not known. This makes it imperative that financial variables utilized in the valuation be defined on a con- sistent basis between the guideline and subject companies and that measurements for estimating variables be taken as of the same point in time or over the same time period relative to the valuation date for the guideline companies and the subject company.

5. Shareholders have no direct claim on a corporation's assets because a corporate entity intervenes between the assets and the shareholder. Therefore, the value of a share of stock can be more than or less than a proportionate share of the underlying net asset value and sometimes bears little relationship to the under- lying net asset value.

6. Lack of control and lack of marketability are distinct concepts, although they are related. Both controlling and minority ownership interests may suffer some- what from lack of marketability, defined as the ability to convert the asset to cash very quickly, at minimal costs, with a high degree of certainty of realizing the anticipated amount of proceeds. The impact of both minority and marketabili- ty factors are influenced by both internal and external facts and circumstances as of the valuation date.

7. Noncontrolling shareholders lack control over various decisions affecting the business enterprise. Minority ownership interests may be worth considerably less than a pro rata portion of the business value if it were valued as a single, 100 percent ownership interest.

8. The market pays a premium for liquidity, or, conversely, demands a discount for lack of liquidity. Business interests that lack ready marketability generally are worth less than otherwise comparable business interests that are readily mar- ketable.

9. The sum of the values of individual fractional interests in a business is not nec- essarily, or even usually, equal to the value of a 100 percent ownership interest in the business.

Within the scope of these business valuation principles, different standards and premises of value and different ownership characteristics apply for different valua- tion purposes and within different legal contexts. These can affect both the valua- tion procedures to be utilized and the final determination of value. The appraiser should understand the applicable purpose and objective for the assignment and the implications of each.

These principles, though broad, provide a framework for consistency in the practice of the business valuation discipline. Many errors and unreasonable valua- tion conclusions can be avoided if these principles are understood and implement- ed. These principles provide the business valuation user with a basic perspective from which to review and evaluate a business valuation work product.

Bibliography

Booth, Laurence. "The Capital Asset Pricing Model: Equity Risk Premiums and the Privately-Held Business." *The Journal of Business Valuation* (Proceedings of the 4th Joint Business Valuation Conference of The Chartered Business Valuators and the American Society of Appraisers). Toronto: The Canadian Institute of Chartered Business Valuators, 1999, pp. 87–114.

"Bulls, Bears and Ivory Towers." *The Economist*, May 15, 1999, pp. 81–82.

Copeland, Tom, Tim Koller, and Jack Murrin. *Valuation: Measuring and Managing the Value of Companies*. New York: John Wiley & Sons, 1990.

Damodaran, Aswath. *Damodaran on Valuation: Security Analysis for Investment and Corporate Finance*. New York: John Wiley & Sons, 1994.

Hawkins, George B., and Michael A. Paschall. *CCH Business Valuation Guide*. Chicago: CCH Incorporated, 1999.

Mercer, Z. Christopher, and Terry S. Brown. "Fair Market Value vs. the Real World." *Valuation Strategies*, March/April 1999, pp. 6–15.

Miles, Raymond C. *Basic Business Appraisal*. New York: John Wiley & Sons, 1984.

Pratt, Shannon P. *Business Valuation Body of Knowledge: Exam Review and Professional Reference*. New York: John Wiley & Sons, 1998.

Pratt, Shannon P., Robert F. Reilly, and Robert P. Schweihs. *Valuing Small Businesses and Professional Practices*, 3rd ed. New York: McGraw-Hill, 1998.

Reilly, Robert F., and Robert P. Schweihs, eds. *The Handbook of Advanced Business Valuation*. New York: McGraw-Hill, 2000.

Trugman, Gary R. *Understanding Business Valuation: A Practical Guide to Valuing Small to Medium-Sized Businesses*. Jersey City, NJ: American Institute of Certified Public Accountants, 1998.

West, Thomas L., and Jeffrey D. Jones. *Handbook of Business Valuation*, 2nd ed. New York: John Wiley & Sons, 1999.

Part II

Gathering and Analyzing Data

Chapter 4

Gathering Company Data

Generalized Company Information Checklist
Financial Statements
    Relevant Time Period
    Levels of Financial Statement Preparation
    Impact of Enterprise Legal Structure
Federal Tax Returns
Interim Statements
Other Financial Schedules
    Current Assets and Liabilities
    Plant and Equipment
    Officers' and Directors' Compensation Schedule
    Distribution of Ownership
    Dividend or Partnership Withdrawal Schedule
    Schedule of Key Person Life Insurance
Off–Balance Sheet Assets or Liabilities
Related Party Transaction Information
Operating Information
    Company History
    Brochures, Catalogs, and Price Lists
    Key Personnel
    Customer and Supplier Base
    Contractual Agreements and Obligations
    Industry and Trade Association Information
List of Past Transactions in the Stock or Offers to Buy
Budgets and Forecasts
Capital Requirements
    Capital Expenditures
    Deferred Maintenance
    Working Capital Requirements
Company Documents Relating to the Rights of Owners
    Corporate or Partnership Records
    Buy-Sell and ESOP Agreements
    Employment and Noncompete Agreements
Summary

The first step in the valuation process, after carefully defining the assignment, is to gather the data necessary to conduct the assignment. These data can be categorized into three groups:

1. Company-specific data.
2. Data about the company's industry and economic environment.
3. Data about the subject property's market (market for ownership interests in the subject company).

The company-specific data are gathered from the subject company in written form and during site visits and interviews with people knowledgeable about the company. The gathering of this information is the subject of this and the next chapter.

Industry and economic data often can be provided by the subject company and can also be gathered from publicly available sources. This is the subject of Chapter 5. Data about the market for ownership interests in the subject company include information about changes in ownership of competitors, guideline company transactions, and premiums and discounts that might apply to the subject property. These two categories of information gathering are covered in subsequent chapters in Part III.

The manner and sequence in which the data are gathered are important only to the extent that the process is complete and efficiently carried out. For example, supporting analysts may be collecting industry, economic, rate of return, and guideline transaction information at the same time that the case manager is working directly with the management of the subject company. In any case, it is important to convey a sufficient overview of the company and of the assignment to all of the valuation team members at an early meeting so that all of the analysts will be in a position to recognize important data as they proceed on the project.

If time allows, information gathered should be reviewed before the visit to the company so as to focus the interviewing process on the most essential factors that affect the value of the company, thereby minimizing the inconvenience to the company that might be associated with the management interviews and also maximizing the productivity of the site visit.

Some of the information necessary to conduct the business valuation will need to be obtained through interviews with company management. Sometimes, however, the analyst merely inspects voluminous or highly sensitive documents and only gets copies of the information necessary for the performance of the assignment.

Generalized Company Information Checklist

Written company-specific information that is generally used in business valuations is presented in Exhibit 4–1. This list is generic. Not every item on the list will be required for every appraisal, and in many circumstances, documents not listed must be reviewed. Working with this list, nevertheless, will assist the analyst in developing a subject company–specific information request list. It will also be helpful to company officials and attorneys in the planning stages of a potential valuation engagement.

Financial Statements

According to the American Institute of Certified Public Accountants (AICPA), the term *financial statements* refers to a presentation of financial data, including accompany-

Exhibit 4–1

Preliminary Documents and Information Checklist
for Business Valuation of Typical Corporation

Financial Statements for Typical Corporation

Balance sheets, income statements, statements of changes in financial position, and statements of stockholders' equity for the last five fiscal years
Income tax returns for the same years
Latest interim statements and interim statements for comparable period(s) of previous year

Other Financial Data

Summary property, plant, and equipment list and depreciation schedule
Aged accounts receivable summary
Aged accounts payable summary
List of marketable securities and prepaid expenses
Inventory summary, with any necessary information on inventory accounting policies
Synopsis of leases for facilities or equipment
Any other existing contracts (employment agreements, covenants not to compete, supplier agreements, customer agreements, royalty agreements, equipment lease or rental contracts, loan agreements, labor contracts, employee benefit plans, and so on)
List of stockholders, with number of shares owned by each
Schedule of insurance in force (key person life, property and casualty, liability)
Budgets or projections, for a minimum of five years
List of subsidiaries and/or financial interests in other companies
Key personnel compensation schedule, including benefits and personal expenses

Company Documents

Articles of incorporation, bylaws, and any amendments to either
Any existing buy-sell agreements, options to purchase stock, or rights of first refusal
Franchise or operating agreements, if any

Other Information

Brief history, including how long in business and details of any changes in ownership and/or any bona fide offers recently received
Brief description of the business, including position relative to competition and any factors that make the business unique
Marketing literature (catalogs, brochures, advertisements, and so on)
List of locations where company operates, with size and recent appraisals
List of competitors, with location, relative size, and any relevant factors
Organization chart
Résumés of key personnel, with age, position, compensation, length of service, education, and prior experience
Personnel profile: number of employees by functional groupings, such as production, sales, engineering/R&D, personnel and accounting, customer service/field support, and so forth
Trade associations to which the company belongs or would be eligible for membership
Relevant trade or government publications (specially market forecasts)
Any existing indicators of asset values, including latest property tax assessments and any appraisals that have been performed
List of customer relationships, supplier relationships, contracts, patents, copyrights, trademarks, and other intangible assets
Any contingent or off–balance sheet liabilities (pending lawsuits, compliance requirements, warranty or other product liabilities, estimate of medical benefits for retirees, and so on)
Any filings or correspondence with regulatory agencies
Information on prior transactions in the stock or any related party transactions

ing notes, derived from accounting records and intended to communicate an entity's economic resources or obligations at a point in time, or the changes therein for a period of time, in accordance with a comprehensive basis of accounting.[1]

There are four traditional statements, along with the footnotes, which together comprise the financial statements of a business entity. These are:

---

[1] *AICPA Professional Standards*, Vol. A (Jersey City, NJ: American Institute of Certified Public Accountants, 1999).

1. Balance sheet (statement of financial position).
2. Income statement (statement of income, statement of operations, or statement of earnings).
3. Statement of cash flows (formerly, statement of changes in financial position).
4. Statement of stockholders' equity (or statement of partners' capital).

The amounts of a company's assets, liabilities, and equity, as determined by generally accepted accounting principles (not necessarily the fair market value of those accounts) as of a given point in time, is the statement of financial position, more commonly referred to as the company's balance sheet. In contrast, the statement of results of operations, or the income statement, presents a financial summary of a company's operating results for a certain period of time. The third statement, the statement of cash flows, is designed to provide information about the important changes in financial position that took place during the accounting period. This statement is useful if net cash flow is an important measure of economic income in the valuation (as it is in many cases) because the statement of cash flows is a source of information on capital expenditures and changes in working capital.

However, analysts should note that the statement of cash flows presents changes in balance sheet accounts as of two points in time. These changes may be unusual or temporary. In such cases, the statement of cash flows may not fully reflect the continuing cash flow generating capacity of the subject business.

Even within the scope of generally accepted accounting principles (GAAP), there are many decisions that management makes with respect to the accounting treatment of various company transactions. These include, for example, such things as choices of capitalizing or not capitalizing certain items, inventory accounting methods, and depreciation methods. The footnotes to financial statements and supporting schedules usually are helpful in understanding the company's treatment of such items.

The analyst's function is not to audit, but to express an opinion of value on the basis of available financial information. In some situations, nevertheless, the accountants' work papers and/or company books may provide additional insight that is relevant to the valuation, and the analyst may request to see such information.

Relevant Time Period

When asking for historical financial statements on the subject property, one should endeavor to study statements during a *relevant period*. The most commonly used period is five years. However, conceptually, the relevant period covers the most recent period of time immediately prior to the valuation date during which the statements represent the company's general operations.

If the company significantly changed its operations a few years before the valuation date, only the previous three or four years may represent the relevant period. On the other hand, if the business has a long history and some or all recent years were abnormal in some way (such as during a cyclical peak or trough in the company's industry), statements for the past seven, ten, or more years may constitute a relevant period for valuing it.

Levels of Financial Statement Preparation

In the United States, we sometimes take for granted the degree of standardization of the financial statement presentation to which we have become accustomed. One

only needs to work with financial statements from other countries to truly appreciate our financial reporting standards, as complicated and as curious as they are.

Valuation analysts prefer to work with audited financial statements because of
their completeness and reliability, but the large majority of closely held businesses
do not go to the trouble and expense of having their statements examined by an
independent auditor. There are various levels of scrutiny represented by audited,
reviewed, and compiled financial statements. The same company might have different
levels of scrutiny performed for different years.

Audited Statements. In *audited statements*, the independent auditor expresses an opinion, or if circumstances require, disclaims an opinion, regarding the fairness with which the financial statements present the financial position, the results of
operations, and the changes in financial position, in accordance with generally accepted accounting principles.

Reviewed Statements. The accountant expresses limited assurance in *reviewed
statements* that there are no material modifications that should be made to the statements in order for them to be in conformity with generally accepted accounting
principles. A review does not provide assurance that the accountant will become
aware of all significant matters that would be disclosed in an audit.

Compiled Statements. Finally, the *compiled statements* are management's representations presented in the form of financial statements, but the accountant has not
undertaken any efforts to express assurance on the statements.

Sometimes, statements are prepared internally by management without the services of an outside accountant.

As the level of outside review of the financial statements declines, the analysts
should make more extensive inquiries and use more judgment as to the quality of
the information available.

Impact of Enterprise Legal Structure

When the legal structure of the company is different from the traditional corporation, the analyst should be cognizant of the potential impact on the analysis. Several
of these legal organizations, and the valuation implications of the choice of legal structure, are discussed in later chapters.

It is important to point out that different legal status of the business can have an
impact on the valuation conclusions, especially when it comes to partnerships. For
example, in those cases where partners do not share the earnings (or losses) in the same
proportion as their partnership share is entitled to upon liquidation, the legal rights
and privileges of one equity owner could be substantially different from that of another owner. And, this could result in a substantially different value conclusion. The analyst valuing a partnership interest subject to any such complications will need to read
the partnership agreement to be sure that the partners' rights are understood.

Federal Tax Returns

There are common reasons for discrepancies between the amounts and items reported on financial statements and those reported on federal income tax returns. Many
of the differences are simply resulting from timing differences, such as different
methods of revenue recognition and cost recovery of capital expenditures.

For corporations filing Form 1120, U.S. Corporate Income Tax Return, a summary of differences between tax return reporting and financial statement reporting is found in Schedule M-1, Reconciliation of Income per Books with Income per Return.

If such differences exist, the analyst must use his or her professional judgment to determine which figures will provide the most appropriate basis for appraisal purposes. A general rule is that the analyst should select the statements that most closely conform to industry practices and would most fairly represent the company's financial position and earning power. Normally, financial data and ratios derived from tax return data of the subject company would not be comparable to the financial data and ratios derived from the audited financial statements of publicly traded guideline companies.

It is not unusual to find small companies without any formally prepared financial statements. In this case, the analyst has only the tax returns as a basis for financial statements. In this situation, the analyst may format financial statements in the conventional manner by recasting information from the tax returns.

There are many federal income tax forms that may contain relevant data for a particular valuation assignment. A discussion of the various forms and their use would be too detailed to fit within the scope of this book. *Package X* is a two-volume set of sample forms along with their instructions which is available from the Internal Revenue Service. The IRS website provides most forms along with information and instructions. The address is www.irs.gov.

Interim Statements

Interim statements are those prepared as of a date other than the last day of the fiscal year. Analysis of interim statements can give a more timely indication of the financial performance of the subject company and can provide a better understanding of businesses with highly seasonal operations whose trends the analyst may want to track on a monthly or quarterly basis.

Some privately held companies prepare interim statements monthly. It is important, however, that the analyst have an idea of these statements' usefulness before demanding the effort required to develop this information.

Several factors influence the usefulness of interim statements, particularly:

1. The proximity of the valuation date to the fiscal year-end.
2. The quality of the interim statements.
3. The importance of seasonality to the subject company.
4. The extent to which information in interim statements is likely to affect the conclusion.

Oftentimes, information regarding the latest 12 months (LTM) of operations can provide a worthwhile perspective about the company's condition. When LTM analysis is conducted, the interim statements for the subject period of time plus the interim statements for the corresponding period during the prior fiscal year are needed.

Interim statements usually do not contain certain adjustments for a variety of accrual items typically made when closing the books at year-end, such as a physical inventory inspection, prepaid expenses, and reserve for bad debt accounts.

Therefore, to interpret interim statements and to use them as if they were comparable to year-end statements, the analyst may need additional information with which to approximate such year-end adjustments.

Other Financial Schedules

The purposes of requesting financial information regarding equipment lists, aged receivables, aged payables, and prepaid expenses are (1) to give the analyst familiarity with the accounting policies of the company and (2) to alert the analyst to special situations that could affect the valuation. This information may assist the analyst in distinguishing excess assets from normal operating assets so that the excess assets can be separately valued. Also, when applying the asset accumulation approach to business valuation (see Chapter 14), the information from these schedules can assist in the underlying assets valuation process. Chapter 7, Analyzing Financial Statements, discusses when and how some of this information may be used.

Current Assets and Liabilities

Depending on the situation, any or all of the following schedules may be relevant:

- Aged receivables list.
- Aged payables list.
- Marketable securities list.
- Prepaid expense list.
- Inventory list.

Among other things, an understanding of a company's current assets and liabilities gives insight into the company's working capital needs.

Aged Receivables and Payables Lists. The *aged receivables list* can yield insight into the company's profitability, and even viability. However, many relatively small companies do not prepare them. Because the aged list gives the analyst a useful means for recognizing situations that could affect the company's value, the analyst should have either the client's accounting department or a member of his or her own staff prepare one, if appropriate.

The *aged payables list* may be particularly relevant if it appears that a company's working capital may be deficient.

Marketable Securities List. For companies that carry marketable securities, knowing what they are helps to understand how they should best be treated in the valuation process.

Prepaid Expense List. Adjustments to prepaid expenses may be appropriate in some cases, and a listing will help to make this determination as well as provide insight into working capital needs.

Inventory List. The amount of detail desired in the inventory list will vary from one appraisal to another. Depending upon the inventory's importance to the valuation conclusion and to the extent to which inventory accounting methods vary within the particular industry, the amount of inventory data to be gathered will vary. In any case, the total should be reconcilable with the inventory as shown on the financial statements, using whatever adjustments conform to the company's method of inventory valuation. The company's write-down policy may also call for a market value adjustment.

Plant and Equipment

Property Lists. Lists of property owned should include the acquisition date, a description adequate for identifying each piece or group, the original cost, the depreciation method and life used, and the net depreciated value. The totals of such schedules should reconcile with line items in the financial statements. For real estate, the schedule should show the size (acres of land and dimensions and square feet of floor space of buildings), with a brief description of the construction and any special features. It should also indicate the dates and costs of additions and remodeling.

Evidence of Real and Personal Property Values. Indicators of current real estate and equipment asset values can be helpful. An independent appraisal by a qualified practitioner, if available, usually is a more reliable guide to asset value than either a tax assessment or insurance appraisal. Tax assessments are usually readily available but may represent a standard of value that is different from the one required for the business valuation. Insurance appraisals have a tendency to use the replacement value standard instead of the market value standard and thereby overvalue used property. This different standard is often used for insurance appraisal purposes in an attempt to ensure that the insurance will be adequate to cover potential losses.

Officers' and Directors' Compensation Schedule

An officers' and directors' compensation and benefits schedule for the same number of years as the financial statements should be prepared, when appropriate. The income statement could conceivably be adjusted in order to identify the company's earning capacity (see Chapter 7). The benefits of ownership should be identified separately from compensation for performing a specific role for the company.

Employees related to the owners should be included on the list. The analyst should be mindful that the Internal Revenue Service sometimes attempts to depict compensation paid to C corporation owners as excessive, so as to reclassify a portion of the C corporation owner's compensation as a stockholder dividend. The analyst should be careful when describing any adjustments made to compensation in order to avoid unintentionally triggering unfavorable tax consequences for the client. These benefits of ownership may include:

- Base salary.
- Bonuses or commissions.
- Pension contributions.
- Profit sharing plans.
- Other employee benefit funds.
- Life insurance policies.
- Noncash contributions:
  - Stock options.
  - Related party transactions.
  - Company cars.

- Country club memberships.
- Other company property used (plane, boat, condominium, etc.).
- Expenses paid or reimbursed to the employee.

Distribution of Ownership

The list of equity owners should include each owner's name and number of shares or partnership units held as of the valuation date. The ownership list should describe and quantify individual and other entity ownership, especially if there is more than one class of equity. Family members and other relationships among the equity owners should be identified.

Dividend or Partnership Withdrawal Schedule

The *dividend schedule* normally should cover the same period of time as the financial statements. It should show the date of each dividend payment and the per share amount for each class of stock or per unit amount for each class of partnership unit.

Schedule of Key Person Life Insurance

In many companies, the loss of a single key employee can have a significant impact on the company's operations. It is always desirable to know how much of this risk is covered by life insurance. A schedule of *key person life insurance* will help identify how much key employee risk affects the value of the business.

Off–Balance Sheet Assets or Liabilities

There are many financial items that can significantly affect the business's value that do not appear as line items on the balance sheet, usually because they are of a contingent nature. Such items may or may not be referenced in footnotes.

One of the most common off–balance sheet assets or liabilities is a prospective award or payment arising from a lawsuit. The analyst should inquire about any pending or potential suits and note the details.

This category could also include the potential cost of compliance with environmental, OSHA, or other government requirements. The adequacy of reserves for claims or other product liability should also be explored. Overfunded pension plans are another potential hidden asset, or, conversely underfunded plans a hidden liability.

Information regarding intangible assets, both those shown on the balance sheet and off–balance sheet intangibles, such as patents, copyrights, and trademarks, should include a description of the property protected by this legal right and the expiration date of the right. The list of intangibles should include a brief description and enough information to understand these items. The importance to the business's value of these legal rights and degree of detail required varies from one situation to the next. The importance of intangible assets is covered elsewhere in this book along with some of the documentation necessary to reflect their impact on the business's value.

Related Party Transaction Information

When it comes to related party transactions, it is important that the analyst gather as much information as is available in order to determine the nature of the transactions and their propriety.

As the Financial Accounting Standards Board (FASB) states in its *Statement No. 57* regarding *related party transactions*:

> Related party[2] transactions may be controlled by one of the parties so that those transactions may be affected significantly by considerations other than those in arm's-length transactions with unrelated parties.[3]
>
> Without disclosure to the contrary, there is a general presumption that the transactions reflected in the financial statements have been consummated on an arm's-length basis between independent parties. . . . Because it is possible for related party transactions to be arranged to obtain certain results desired by the related parties, the resulting accounting measures may not represent what they usually would be expected to represent.[4]

Related party transactions may be controlled entirely by one of the parties so that those transactions may be affected significantly by considerations other than those in arm's-length transactions with unrelated parties.

In the absence of audited financial statements, which will include related party information in their accompanying notes, the analyst should have a list prepared that describes the terms of the transactions. These types of related party transactions could include loans to and from related parties, leases, or purchases from or sales to related parties, guarantees to—or for—related parties, and so on.

Operating Information

Company History

The history of the company should put the business in the proper context for the user of the valuation analysis. A relatively brief history will suffice in most cases. The history should indicate how long the company has been in business and some chronology of major changes, such as form of organization, controlling ownership, location of operations, and lines of business. Sometimes predecessor companies are a relevant part of the background. A detailed explanation of the history may be required in some instances, and sometimes certain transactions that fundamentally contributed to the company's composition, as of the valuation date, should be included.

Brochures, Catalogs, and Price Lists

The company should furnish the analyst with a set of its sales materials, such as brochures, catalogs, and price lists. These items will enable the analyst to become

---

[2] Defined in *Financial Accounting Standards Board (FASB) Statement No. 57*, Appendix B(f).

[3] *FASB No. 57*, Appendix A, para. 13 (1982).

[4] Ibid., para. 15.

familiar with the company's products, services, and pricing and to evaluate the written sales materials. As with many of the written items furnished, these will help the analyst get an overview of the company and prepare relevant questions for the visit to the company's facilities and inquiries of company personnel.

Key Personnel

Hiring, motivating, and retaining human resources is often the closely held business owner's biggest challenge. Key personnel include directors and officers, heads of departments or divisions, and anyone else who plays an important part in the company's operation. Data on key personnel should include the person's age, position, tenure with the company and in the industry, educational and professional credentials, and compensation. An organization chart may help the analyst identify key personnel.

Customer and Supplier Base

Customer Base. An analysis of the customer (or client) base is especially important for businesses that rely on only a few customers for a significant portion of their revenue and/or profit. Many businesses fall under the "80/20 Rule" where 80 percent of their revenue is attributable to 20 percent of their customers. The information to analyze the impact on value attributable to customer base includes a list, in order of size of revenue (or profit), of the largest customers. The list should include revenue by customer for the most recent fiscal period and the dollar amounts of revenue for several prior periods. The columns for the prior periods should also show customers that accounted for a significant proportion of the revenue in the prior period, even if they are not on the current period's largest customer list. Sometimes a budgeted figure for each customer for the forthcoming period is available.

Order Backlog. If the company's order backlog (customers orders yet to be filled) is a significant factor in the business, the analyst should compare the backlog on the valuation date with that on previous dates. Such comparison, especially with the backlog one year prior to the valuation date, is one indication of the company's future prospects.

Supplier Base. Like the customer base, the supplier base can be an important factor affecting the value of a business, especially if the future availability of supplies is uncertain enough to increase the company's risk. The supplier list could take the same format as the customer base.

Contractual Agreements and Obligations

There are a variety of other contractual commitments (e.g., leases, loans, franchise agreements, distributor agreements, customer contacts, etc.) that can have a significant impact on the value of a particular business interest. The list of potential contractual commitments is nearly infinite. The analyst should draw on personal experience to inquire about contracts that typically occur in certain lines of business and ask management whether any significant contracts exist. Some of the factors that should be analyzed are the time period of specific rights of ownership, restrictive covenants, transferability of commitments, favorable or unfavorable rates relative to rates available as of the valuation date, renewal options, personal guarantees, and the penalties that the company could suffer for lack of performance under these commitments.

Industry and Trade Association Information

Industry information can be provided by the subject company, in many cases, more readily than relying on independent research. A description of the industry, its trends, and competitive environment, is usually accessible from the company. It is also helpful if the company can furnish a list of trade associations to which it belongs, or is eligible to belong, along with the name and address of the executive director of each. The subject company can often readily supply copies of relevant publications from trade associations, governmental agencies, and other industry sources.

List of Past Transactions in the Stock or Offers to Buy

To the extent that past transactions in the stock were at arm's length, they provide objective evidence of value. Even if not accepted, a bona fide offer, particularly if submitted in writing, can at least corroborate the value. In such cases, it is important to verify if the bona fide written offer was a funded offer. If financing was not in place for the written offer, it may provide less evidence to the analyst than if it was a funded offer. In preparing the record of past transactions or offers, it is important to list any relationships among the parties in order to determine whether each transaction was at arm's length. The transaction record usually should go as far back as the number of years of financial statements used. On this basis, past transaction prices can be compared with prevailing book values, earnings, or other relevant variables.

If the company has made an acquisition, details of the acquisition may be an extremely relevant past transaction. This is an important category of past transactions that often is overlooked.

Budgets and Forecasts

Budgets or forecasts prepared by closely held companies vary widely from no written budget at all ("It's all in my head. It doesn't need to be written down.") to fairly detailed and accurate ones. Since the value of a business interest ultimately depends on what the business will accomplish in the future, reasonable estimates of future expectations should help in arriving at a value. A good way to test the quality of a company's budgeting process is to compare past budgets with actual results.

Budgets and forecasts are heavily relied upon in valuations for mergers and acquisitions. On the other hand, some courts are reluctant to accept budgets because the future is inherently unprovable and (in the case of divorce) because they may incorporate fruits of a spouse's future efforts. In most cases, however, a company that produces convincing budgets will command a higher value than one that does not.

Capital Requirements

The business's capital requirements play a part in the valuation because they are an integral part of estimating net cash flow and dividend-paying capacity. Capital requirements include items such as:

1. Capital expenditures.
2. Remedying deferred maintenance.
3. Increasing working capital.

The proper amount paid to the seller would be the total value of a properly financed business, less the amount of the required cash infusion. When cash infusions are known or reasonably expected to be required in the foreseeable future to support the expected earnings, they must be reflected as a cash outflow, the present value of which should represent a decrease in the value of the business as otherwise determined.

Capital Expenditures

Capital expenditures include replacements of worn-out or obsolete existing plant and equipment plus any additions to plant and equipment necessary to produce any revenues contemplated in the valuation. The latter category would include items needed to remain competitive and maintain the company's position, plus anything needed to support whatever level of growth is contemplated in the valuation methodology and parameters used.

Capital expenditures are a specific component in the discounted or capitalized net cash flow methods. When using a market comparison approach to valuation, capital expenditure requirements may influence valuation multiples chosen if the subject company's capital expenditure requirements are significantly different relative to guideline companies. Alternatively, abnormal capital expenditure conditions may be treated as a direct decrement or increment to value determined through income or market valuation methods.

Deferred Maintenance

Some businesses have not maintained plant and equipment to a competitive level of efficiency and productivity. While expenditures to remedy this may be expensed for accounting and tax purposes, they nevertheless require an outlay of funds which detracts from value. The treatment as to how they impact value can be handled essentially the same as capital expenditures.

Working Capital Requirements

A company's working capital requirements can be estimated based on analysis of its past operations, industry data, guideline company data, and discussions with management. It is common to find companies with either excessive or inadequate working capital. Excesses or inadequacies in the valuation data can be treated in the valuation much as other capital requirements can be treated.

If growth is anticipated, growth in working capital generally must also be anticipated. The analysis of changes in net working capital is a specific component in the discounted or capitalized net cash flow method. When using a market approach to valuation, working capital requirements that differ significantly from guideline companies may be reflected in valuation multiples.

Company Documents Relating to the Rights of Owners

Corporate or Partnership Records

The official documents of a corporation or partnership often hold facts that significantly affect the valuation of the entity or of certain specific interests in the entity. The articles of incorporation or the partnership agreement, along with any amendments, and documents specifying rights attaching to each class of outstanding equity, provide information that is particularly important for businesses with more than one class of equity. Other information in the articles or bylaws may be relevant to the value. Partnership agreements should describe the rights and privileges of each of the partners.

Board of directors' meeting and shareholders' meeting minutes may be important, especially regarding transactions with related parties.

Buy-Sell and ESOP Agreements

Buy-sell or repurchase agreements among stockholders or between stockholders and the company may contain provisions that can strongly affect the value of the shares to which they apply. These agreements often restrict the marketability of the subject shares and they can, correspondingly, affect the value of other classes of equity as well. Provisions in such agreements may address the question of value directly or may impose a restriction on transferability, which may bear on the value of the affected shares. On the other hand, in certain litigation scenarios, the restrictive provisions of a buy-sell agreement may not be applicable to the standard of value being sought, and, at the instruction of counsel, are to be ignored. Chapter 29 discusses buy-sell agreements and their impact on value.

If the company has an employee stock ownership plan (ESOP), the terms of the buy-back provisions can have a major bearing on the marketability of the shares involved and, thus, must be considered when valuing ESOP shares. In some cases, the existence of an ESOP may provide a limited market for non-ESOP shares. Chapters 32 and 33 discuss these issues in further detail.

Employment and Noncompete Agreements

Employment agreements with key personnel may affect the company's value, as may agreements not to compete. These agreements could have either a positive or negative effect on value depending on the relationship between the cost and the value to the company.

Summary

Gathering and analyzing the foregoing information will give the analyst the groundwork on which to base the company interview and pinpoint still-needed details that are relevant to the valuation assignment. The specific material needed will vary with the particular valuation assignment and is a matter of the analyst's judgment. Following the suggestions in this chapter will help the analyst to avoid the all too common pitfall of overlooking certain company data that may have a significant bearing on the value of the business or interest being valued. The chapter also should help company officers and/or their attorneys to be well prepared for an efficient and productive data gathering process.

Chapter 5

Site Visits

This chapter provides a guide for the valuation analyst to conduct an efficient site visit that will contribute in a meaningful way to the valuation process. It also should be a helpful tool for company officials and any attorney involved to know what to expect and to prepare for the visit in order to make it as productive as possible.

In many cases, the analyst's understanding and impressions of the business can be dramatically improved by seeing the operations firsthand and participating in face-to-face interviews. The historical financial statements and other written material and their implications can become more meaningful to the analyst as a result of the site visit. Current and potential changes that might cause the company's future to differ from that indicated by a mere extrapolation of the historical data can be identified. The field trip and interviews should focus on establishing the relationship between the data gathered and the existing and prospective company situation and economic environment.

The need for the valuation analyst to visit the company facilities and have personal contact with the company personnel and other related people varies greatly from one valuation to another. The extent of the necessary fieldwork depends on many things, including the purpose of the valuation, the nature of the operation, and the size and complexity of the case. Another determining factor is the degree to which the analyst was able to gather and interpret the written material described in the previous chapter.

The title of the person to be interviewed is not as important as the categories of topics to be probed. To cover the topics described in this chapter, the analyst may need to interview the company's president, chief operating officer, marketing or sales manager, and chief financial officer. In some companies, these job titles are all the responsibility of one person. In some companies, these responsibilities are carried out by people who are not even employees of the subject company. The analyst can work with the client to determine exactly who should be interviewed in order to gain an understanding of the important information that affects the value of the business.

This chapter presents a generalized discussion of interview topics. The actual topics and sequence of coverage will vary considerably from one situation to the next. The top-to-bottom comprehension of the business that the analyst is pursuing may not be provided in top-to-bottom order.

The limitless number of inquiries has such broad potential implications for the valuation and will vary from one company to another. Accordingly, only the most general discussion of these topics is possible within the scope of this chapter. The analyst should attempt to understand all of the major factors that affect the value of the subject company.

Gaining a broader perspective of the business and its operations is the primary objective of the site visit. In addition, details missing from an analysis of the written material can be filled in. Developing some level of comfort with people at the company is also an important objective of the fieldwork, so that if additional information is required after the fieldwork is complete, it can be more readily obtained.

Generally, it is advisable to prepare a thorough list of questions in advance of the site visit. By studying the financial statements and other basic information, the analyst can gain an overview of the company and prepare a list of specific questions that will make the fieldwork more meaningful and productive. Also, after seeing the operation and talking with management, the analyst will be able to read and analyze the written material with greater insight.

It is usually best to visit company facilities and interview management fairly early in the valuation process—after obtaining and reviewing enough preliminary information to get a general overview of the company. This way, other necessary steps can be planned or some previously planned steps can be dismissed as irrelevant. Other sources of information (e.g., trade associations, periodicals, governmental agencies, customers, suppliers, and competitors) can be identified.

History

An appropriate beginning of the fieldwork is often a discussion of the company's history. This will give the analyst a perspective on how the business evolved and can often put the valuation assignment in focus.

The history of the company should cover when the business, or any of its predecessors, was founded, any acquisitions or divestitures along the way, any changes in the basic form of organization, any major changes in lines of business, and any changes in the geographical areas served. It should cover major changes in ownership and how they came about.

Although the business's total history should be sketched briefly, the parts most relevant to the valuation analysis usually will be the most recent past. A chronology of major events will help the analyst decide how many years of the company's financial data are relevant to the current valuation assignment and identify any major changes in the business or special circumstances to consider in analyzing the financial statements.

Description of the Business

The analyst should try to gain an understanding of how the company perceives itself:

- What does the company do?
- Why does it need to be done?
- What makes this company particularly well qualified to do it?
- What is the company's perception of the economic niche into which it fits?
- How does it try to do the best job of fitting in its niche?
- What are the company's major strengths and weaknesses?
- What are the key factors that enable it to operate profitably?
- What is the company doing that will cause the future to differ from recent history?

The analyst should try to gain an understanding of how the company perceives the industry and the particular aspect within which it operates:

- What are the nature and rate of technological changes affecting the industry?
- What developments or trends are expected in the industry in the foreseeable future?
- What special industry factors have a bearing on this particular company?
- To what extent are its fortunes subject to outside forces over which it has no control?
- What is the progress and prognosis for new products or services, locations, channels of distribution, etc.?
- What other aspects of the operation and of the industry are in a developmental or transitional stage?
- How will all these forces impact the future compared with the recent history?

The analyst will want to know the company's program for corporate development, including further development of existing and/or new products and markets. The company's program for capital expenditures, acquisitions, divestitures, and research and development should be uncovered. These inquiries should cover capacity constraints, how much is being spent for what, and how much of it is being financed.

If future growth is to be financed by issuing additional stock, the analyst should assess the effect of the potential dilution. If the future growth is to be financed using debt, the analyst should consider both the direct expense and the risk of the additional financial leverage.

The present management's policies toward the future direction of the company are more important for the analyst to understand if a noncontrolling ownership interest—versus a controlling ownership interest—is the valuation subject. This is because a controlling stockholder can change management policies. Nevertheless, even in the case of a controlling ownership interest valuation, the perspective of the existing management team on the major opportunities and problems facing the company and how it plans to deal with them is an important area of inquiry.

The strength of the company's intangible assets, whether or not they are carried on the company's books, is an increasingly critical area of inquiry. Often, sometimes without necessarily realizing it, when responding to questions about what makes this company unique, management lists intangible assets. The analyst should be curious about the proprietary products and services, especially about the unique characteristics that generate a comparative advantage over their competition. Can management help quantify the benefit attributable to brand names, trademarks, copyrights, or patents? Does the company enjoy economic benefits from a favorable location, favorable supplier contracts, sustainable customer relationships?

Management and Management Compensation

Another critical factor is the assessment of management's competency, breadth, and depth. Many closely held companies are somewhat lacking when it comes to providing for management succession.

The analyst should inquire about management members' age, health, education and professional credentials, experience, background, and history with the company. Each key person's compensation package and level of compensation should be considered. This includes participation in all employee benefit plans, fringe benefits, expense allowances, and other perquisites. Part of the purpose of this inquiry is to help the analyst judge whether key people are being compensated well enough to discourage them from leaving the company, and part of the purpose is to judge whether there may be excess compensation that the company could reduce if it fell on hard times, by direct reductions or by replacement of certain personnel with others who could do a comparable job at a lower cost.

The time and effort devoted to the business by each key person should be discussed. Many closely held companies employ people—usually family members—at full salary even though they have only a figurehead role and work only occasionally. On the other hand, some senior people who devote only limited hours may make a significant contribution because of experience and acumen.

The matter of excess compensation should be considered after taking into account the manager's hours devoted to the company and the job responsibilities of the manager. Some managers in closely held companies are paid at what some consider to be excessive compensation levels.

In many cases, the management of the closely held business are also the owners. By taking income in the form of compensation for services rendered instead of in the form of dividends, owners of C corporations avoid a layer of income tax at the corporate level. A hypothetical buyer of the entire business would want to be able to separate the existing owner's take-home pay between the amount that the buyer would have to spend to pay a substitute employee to perform the same duties and the amount that is attributable to a return on the buyer's investment.

When the valuation subject is a controlling ownership interest in the company, the existing total compensation less a normal level of compensation may be considered excess compensation. Such excess compensation is adjusted out of the expense category and into income in order to better reflect the expected economic performance of the company on a go-forward basis. This is because new controlling owners are in a position to eliminate this excess compensation.

If the valuation subject is a noncontrolling interest where no control over compensation levels is part of the equity position being valued (such as in the case of a gift of a 10 percent interest in the equity of a business, for example), the excess compensation of the owner is generally not added back to the income statement. This is because ownership of the noncontrolling position does not possess the rights necessary to correct the imbalance.

In order to make the appropriate adjustments regarding executive compensation of the closely held business, the appraiser identifies the total compensation from all sources being paid to the existing executive and compares that to the total compensation required to attract an executive of similar skills. If public company executives are the appropriate basis for comparison, then total compensation from all sources paid to the public company executive (including stock options, bonus plans, pension plans, perquisites, etc.) should be evaluated along with the contribution to the company provided by the executive.

Operations

The objective when discussing operations of the company is to learn what operations the company carries out, how efficiently and effectively it does so, and the prospects for either improvement or deterioration.

Materials and Supplies

Supplies are vital to the operations of any business enterprise. To what extent does the company fabricate versus assemble, and how much flexibility does it have in this respect? How much is the make-or-buy decision within the company's control?

Access and pricing are the two key factors the analyst should pursue in questioning the company's supply situation. The extreme—which is less rare than one might think—is the existence of a single source for a critical supply that, if cut off, could shut down the company's operations. Most distributorships, for example, can be terminated on 30 days' notice. For many manufacturing companies, one or more raw materials with limited sources of supply are essential to the operation. For some companies, a reliable source for energy is a critical component of the subject company's prospects.

The analyst should identify key suppliers and alternates, including names of individuals with whom the company deals. It may be appropriate for the analyst to contact suppliers directly, whether for additional information about the present or potential supply situation or for references concerning the company's credit, reputation, or other attributes.

Labor and Government Relations

The availability and cost of labor can be another critical factor in the successful operation of the business. When on the facilities tour, the analyst should be alert to clues about labor morale and efficiency. What labor contracts exist? When do they expire, and what are the prospects for satisfactory renewal in terms of both acceptable costs and risk of work stoppage? How do company compensation policies compare with other companies in the industry and in this locale? What is the company's experience with personnel turnover, and how does this compare with industry norms?

Government relations may impinge on the company's operations. To what extent is the company subject to industry regulations, such as food quality standards or the rate of return limitations imposed on some utilities? Does the company face costs associated with environmental protection or with OSHA? Does the company have problems meeting these requirements? What is the impact of these regulations on the company's earning capacity, flexibility, and future prospects?

Plant and Equipment

When touring the company's facilities, the analyst should gain an understanding of the adequacy of the plant and equipment. The business valuation analyst can make a general evaluation and can get the assistance of appraisers specializing in real estate, machinery, or personal property when needed. It may be desirable to take a set of pictures, especially if the analyst will need to communicate some description of the facilities to someone not able to visit the facilities, such as a judge in a court case. It may be useful to note the size and the type of construction, too. Is the equipment well maintained, new, highly utilized? Is there unused capacity and room for expansion? In general, will the plant be a source of future cost savings or a source of increasing costs?

Inventory

Inventory consists of raw material, work in progress, and finished goods. The analyst is interested in getting some assistance in interpreting how much inventory is obsolete, damaged, excessive, or inadequate. The facilities tour is a good time to inquire about inventory turnover and quality. Since it can have a significant effect on reported earnings and net worth in some types of companies, the analyst should take into consideration near worthless inventory that is carried on the books at original cost or valuable inventory that has been written off.

Markets and Marketing

The objective of the marketing interview is for the analyst to identify and describe the company's markets and its program for reaching them. Who are its customers? Why do customers buy from this company instead of from the competition? Is its target market growing or shrinking? Overall, what are the company's prospects for the future?

What are the forces that determine the demand and changes in demand for the company's products or services? To what extent can the company rely on repeat business and customer continuity? Does the market have identifiable seasonal, cyclical, or secular characteristics?

Are there technological changes in progress or in prospect that will alter its share of the market? What is this business planning to do in order to remain competitive? What does the company do to anticipate and cope with market changes, and how effective are its efforts?

It is common for the marketing manager to understate the company's competition and overstate the defined market's potential. Asking questions on a similar topic from a slightly different perspective or at a different point in the interview will help the analyst verify the responses without challenging the respondent.

One of the most important aspects of the marketing interview is determining how the company competes. The analyst should endeavor to list the identified competitors for each product or service and in each target market segment. This leads to market share estimates and market share trends. What is the economic outlook for these markets, and what are the competitors' likely actions? Many companies, especially smaller ones, are blind-sided by competition that has not yet been identified.

The company's policies about pricing, warranty, providing quality services, on-time or in-stock delivery, and terms and conditions of sale are typical areas of inquiry.

The interview should also cover personnel. Does the company have its own direct sales force, or do they rely on dealers or distributors? What is the degree of turnover? How are new sales and marketing people identified, and where do terminated employees go? What are the structure and level of compensation for marketing people, and how do they compare with the competition?

With respect to the order backlog, how does this year's compare with last year's and next year's expectations? What is the customer turnover rate? To what extent is the company dependent on one or a few key customers? What are the customers' motivations in choosing to do business with this company or its competitors, and how is the company addressing those motivations?

What changes are anticipated for the marketing program? How does the company plan to capitalize on future opportunities? If competitive forces or other problems are building up, what is the company doing to protect itself?

At the conclusion of the marketing discussion, the analyst should have a good grasp of the future prospects of the company and potential constraints.

Finance

As an aid in financial analysis, the analyst may conduct interviews with the chief financial officer, controller, outside accountant, or attorney. Analyzing financial statements is covered in Chapter 7, and many of the most important lines of interrogation are discussed there.

Interviews can contribute a great deal toward genuine understanding of a company's financial position beyond simply what the financial statements show.

Current Assets

It may be important, given the scope of the assignment, to verify the cash and equivalents account and the company's cash management techniques. The accounts receivable account may be examined to understand the extent to which the figure represents an amount that is genuinely collectible and how long it will take to collect it. What is the prognosis for collection of any notes or other receivables? The company's policy for accounting for the inventory may be an important factor affecting value. The physical flow and the accounting flow are likely to be different in a manufacturing operation and may be treated differently between the subject company and its competitors. What is the write-off policy? To what extent does the inventory figure represent the value of the inventory in a going-concern context?

Fixed Assets

The subject company's real estate and equipment are presented on the balance sheet according to historical cost less depreciation, and may not represent the fair market value of those assets. The method for capitalizing assets and the depreciation method adopted by the subject company also may differ from the methods chosen by others in the industry and could affect the valuation conclusion. If a liquidation premise is to be considered, the analyst should discuss the probable time and cost of liquidating all or any part of the assets, as well as their potential net realizable value.

Intangible Assets

Management's perception of the factors that make the subject company different from its competitors usually introduces a discussion of the intangible assets of the company such as a trademark, patent, or copyright. It may be proprietary technology, a trained and assembled workforce, special know-how, customer relationships, supplier relationships, or other intangible assets that make the company a viable competitor and give it earning power. Some closely held business owners call these intangibles *blue sky* or *goodwill*. The accounting practices for these assets and the legal protection of these assets should be explored.[1]

Current Liabilities

The company's banking relationship may be an important factor to consider when considering the company's current liabilities. If the company has a line of credit, what are the costs and terms? Is it under pressure to pay down the line or is there unused

---

[1] For a detailed discussion of the valuation of intangible assets, see Robert F. Reilly and Robert P. Schweihs, *Valuing Intangible Assets* (New York: McGraw-Hill, 1999).

credit? How is the line used during the operating cycle? What are the relationships with suppliers, and what are the terms of payment? What are the terms, conditions, and expectations regarding other current liabilities items?

Capital Structure

If there is long-term debt maturing in the foreseeable future, what are the company's options and intentions about rolling it over? What is the company's debt capacity, and is it assumable by a hypothetical buyer? Are personal guarantees on the company loans necessary? Convertible notes, puts, calls, warrants, or options could mean the current shareholders will be facing dilution. What changes to the capital structure might be anticipated? In virtually every valuation case, the analyst will want to discuss who owns the shares currently outstanding and what the shareholders' relationships are with each other.

Off–Balance Sheet Items

Potential asset items and potential liability claims against the company should be investigated. If the company is involved in pending litigation, what is its substance, and are there any pending judgments that might be favorable or unfavorable? Are leases of real or personal property favorable or unfavorable? The pension liability may be underfunded or overfunded. Is there any potential tax liability or refund? Lack of compliance with environmental protection, OSHA, or other governmental regulations may mean that an unstated liability would be imposed on a hypothetical buyer of the company. Product liability claims or a generous warranty policy could represent a significant unstated liability.

The site visit may also be used to investigate off–balance sheet items that are physically present at the time of the field inspection. Such off–balance sheet items may include inventory, tools and equipment, and so forth.

Profitability

A review of past and current budgets can be a good starting point from which to gain greater insight into the company's profit history and potential. Budgeting is an important area of inquiry. How far into the future does the company budget its operations, and how often is the budget reviewed? In some industries, an evaluation of the company's sales outlook should include an analysis that distinguishes between changes in unit sales and price changes. The most profitable products or product lines, including the outlook for maintaining profitability, should also be considered. An analysis of fixed and variable expenses will help the analyst understand the extent to which increased or decreased volume will affect operating margins. What can be done to make the company more profitable and what are the associated costs?

Insurance

An uninsured catastrophe could wipe out a business. The questions about insurance should investigate the adequacy of the company's coverage for key person life insurance, product and other liability insurance, and casualty insurance, including fire, theft, and business interruption. If no insurance is carried, the analyst should assess adequacy of reserves.

Dividends

The analyst should try to obtain a complete record of past dividend payments. Beyond that, the analyst should assess both the company's dividend-paying capacity and intentions with regard to dividends if dividend-paying capacity exists.

Prior Arm's-Length Transactions or Offers

Verification of the completeness of the list of prior transactions or offers—and the circumstances surrounding them—is a good idea. Overlooking or overemphasizing prior transactions is a common area of controversy in business valuations. What price was paid for the stock? Was it really an arm's-length transaction? Was it a "clean" transaction for the stock or were various strings attached?

If there were one or more offers to buy stock but a transaction was not consummated, the offer may still provide an indication of value. If it was a bona fide, arm's-length offer, it may provide particularly good evidence of value. This is particularly true if the offer was funded (i.e., the financing was already in place to pay for the offer). The analyst should seek anything in writing about such an offer.

Prior transactions of significance may include acquisitions by the company as well as transactions in its own stock, so the analyst should inquire about acquisitions. If the company made a meaningful acquisition, it may be a useful comparative transaction to use in the valuation.

Catch-All Question

If the person performing the fieldwork for a valuation follows this chapter as an outline, the result should be a reasonably comprehensive facility visit and set of interviews. This will be especially true if the person is an experienced interviewer, because many interview subjects will call for more in-depth interrogation than shown here, and personal style and technique alone can uncover critical information. Depending on the analyst's assignment, the ramifications of certain topics may call for a different depth of questioning, beyond the scope of reasonable explanation in a single book, much less in one chapter.

Nevertheless, even the most experienced interviewer may fail to ask just the right questions to elicit responses on every aspect bearing on the valuation. Therefore, somewhere near the end of each interview, the analyst might ask each interviewee a catch-all question. This can be something like: "Is there any information that you know that hasn't been covered and that could have a bearing on the valuation of the company?" This helps protect the analyst against material omissions in the questioning process and places the burden on company management if they are deliberately withholding material information.

Interviews of Outsiders

It is usually a good idea to get the names of outsiders who are involved with the company because, although it may not be necessary to interview these people, an interview may be desirable. Sometimes interviews with the company's outsiders are helpful not only for specific technical information but for independent viewpoints on certain aspects of the company. However, for many valuation assignments, where the purpose of the assignment is confidential and sensitive, it is inappropriate to contact outsiders, especially without the client's permission and introduction.

Professionals Related to the Company

Attorney. There are times when the analyst may work very closely with the company's attorney. The wording of the legal documents when structuring a recapitalization, buy-sell agreement, or an ESOP, for example, may have a considerable bearing on the valuation. In these circumstances, the attorney may solicit the analyst's opinion about the impact on the valuation due to certain prospective provisions. On the other hand, the analyst may need a legal interpretation of a company document or contract or need an assessment of a pending lawsuit or potential litigation.

Independent Accountant. To get an explanation or interpretation of something on the financial statements, or to consult working papers for details that augment the financial statements, it may be necessary to interview the company's outside independent accountant. This is most often the case when the financial statements are not audited, not completely footnoted, or contain some kind of qualified opinion by the independent accountant.

Banker. If the company's banking relationship is important, or in jeopardy, it is a good idea to hear first-hand how the banker perceives it. The banker also may be a good source of general information about the company and the industry.

Other Possible Outside Interviews

Customers. The company's customers can be a good source of information about the subject company's products, strengths, and weaknesses. Customers can help provide an indication of the longer-term outlook of the subject company and help the analyst evaluate the continuing demand for products and services. Customers also may provide a viewpoint about the competition and the customer's perceptions of the differences in product design, quality, service, pricing, and the various intangible assets (e.g., trade name) among competitors. Under some circumstances, former customers could be contacted to find out why they no longer patronize the company.

Suppliers. Particularly if the subject company deals in a technological area, the suppliers may be able to explain technology changes in the industry and, in some cases, make some evaluation of the subject company's expertise.

Competitors. When it is appropriate to contact competitors, it is usually necessary to avoid violating confidentiality. The analyst may ask the competitor many of the same questions asked of the subject company regarding demand, supply, and pricing factors, technological changes in the industry, and relative merits of the products and services of the various companies in the industry, including, of course, the subject company.

Former Employees. Sometimes former employees may be useful as information sources—about why they left and other aspects of the company as seen in hindsight and from a different viewpoint.

Summary

A good analyst can gain a great deal of insight into a company through the field trip and management interview process. The preceding queries should provide the analyst with a perspective on the company being valued and yield a multitude of details relevant to the valuation assignment. What the analyst gets from the process will depend partly on the thoroughness of preparation and partly on the degree of cooperation provided by the subject company and those being interviewed.

It may be helpful for relevant company officials to review this chapter prior to the site visit in order to be prepared to make the visit as efficient and meaningful as possible. Also, it often is helpful for the attorney involved in the matter for which the valuation is being done to review the chapter prior to the visit.

Chapter 6

Researching Economic and Industry Information

It is difficult to overemphasize the importance of thorough and relevant economic and industry research for a well-prepared business valuation. First, Revenue Ruling 59-60 requires consideration of "the economic outlook in general and the condition and outlook of the specific industry in particular." Second, an understanding of the economic and industry outlook is fundamental to developing reasonable expectations about the subject company's prospects. This chapter introduces some of the most useful sources of economic and industry information that can bear on a company valuation.

This chapter is organized in a top-down fashion. Because the general economic outlook influences all industries and all companies, this chapter starts with a discussion of general economic research, highlighting useful sources for researching both the national and regional economies. The chapter then turns to the topic of industry research for both general industry information and composite company statistics. Since the potential sources are so numerous, the chapter concludes with references to several indexes of economic and industry data sources.

The economic and industry outlooks included in valuation reports should be clearly related to the company being valued. It is particularly important to point out how the outlooks will affect the subject company and to focus on those issues most relevant to a thorough understanding of the company's competitive position in its market. As a corollary to this issue, it is important to understand the subject company's relationship to the structure of the industry. Each segment of an industry or an economy may be affected differently by a particular trend or development. Therefore, it is important to focus on the logical impact of each relevant factor on the subject company, whether positive or negative. Applying economic and industry research to the valuation of the subject company is too often neglected.

National Economic Information

Generally, economic outlooks should include a discussion of each of the most important leading economic indicators. For example, it typically is appropriate for valuation reports to discuss such variables as economic growth—usually measured by gross domestic product (GDP) on a national level or real gross state product (GSP) on a state level—inflation, employment, consumer spending, business investment, construction, interest rates, and population trends. The following sections outline some of the most useful sources of economic information for both national and regional economic research.

In addition to the economic indicators discussed above, the economic outlook should include the most relevant national economic issues at the time of the valuation. In the economic environment of the late 1990s, for example, such issues would include inflation, electronic commerce, and the Asian economic crisis. Because of the huge variety of national economic data available, only a few of the most generally useful sources are mentioned. Beyond that, the reader is referred to the section at the end of this chapter on indexing services that can lead to the specific types of economic data sought.

The Federal Statistical System

The United States collects, analyzes, and disseminates more economic data than any other country. While most countries have central statistical offices, this has never been the case in the United States. The remarkable range and extent of the government's statistical efforts developed piecemeal, according to the dictates of legislation and in response to emerging needs. Thus evolved the far-flung, highly decentralized federal statistical system. Only about a half dozen federal agencies exist solely to create statistics, but over 100 other governmental units also participate in the statistical process.[1] Four of the most widely used publications are the *Federal Reserve Bulletin*, *Survey of Current Business*, *Statistical Abstract of the United States*, and the *Economic Report of the President*.

- *Federal Reserve Bulletin* (Washington, DC: Board of Governors of the Federal Reserve System). Published monthly, the *Federal Reserve Bulletin* includes such data as employment, industrial production, housing and construction, consumer and producer prices, GDP, personal income and savings, and key interest rates. Three years of annual historical data are usually presented for each set of statistics, and data for the current year are provided in monthly or quarterly units. It is usually available at public and university libraries and is partially available on-line at www.bog.frb.fed.us/pubs.
- *Survey of Current Business* (Washington, DC: U.S. Department of Commerce). This monthly publication has two sections. The first deals with basic business trends and starts with an article, "The Business Situation," that reviews business developments. The second section contains an extensive compilation of basic statistics on all phases of the economy. It is usually available at public and university libraries and is available on-line at www.bea.doc.gov/bea/pubs.htm.
- *Statistical Abstract of the United States* (Washington, DC: U.S. Department of Commerce). This annual publication contains statistics on all phases of U.S. life—economic, social, political, industrial—and some comparative international statistics. It is well-indexed and easy to use, and is available at most public libraries or at www.census.gov/statab.
- *Economic Report of the President* (Washington, DC: U.S. Council of Economic Advisers). This annual publication is another valuable source of summary data on the U.S. economy. Released each year in January or February, the document is essentially a report from the executive branch to Congress on the state of the economy. An important feature of the narrative section is a five-year outlook for the U.S. economy, including projections for GDP and other key indicators. Available at most public and university libraries and at www.access.gpo.gov/eop.

Banks

Bank letters are excellent sources for statistics, analysis, and projections of regional, national, and international economic and financial conditions. Several private and many government-owned banks, both in the United States and abroad, publish these periodicals and often distribute them free of charge.

The letters cover such areas as government policies, inflation rates, trade balances, employment, manufacturing, and investment for the reporting period (e.g., monthly or quarterly). Some bank letters end such summaries with predictions of trends in the economy, including changes in interest rates, wages and prices, and government monetary policies. A second part of these bank letters consists of a statistical summary of

[1] Michael R. Lavin, *Business Information: How to Find It, How to Use It*, 2d ed. (Phoenix, AZ: Oryx Press, 1992), pp. 326–27.

major economic indicators for the reporting period. Several banks will include a section of international economic statistics to compare their economic situations with other countries.

Most bank letters concentrate on their state, region, or country of origin. For example, several of the banks in the Federal Reserve System publish data only on the states within their districts (e.g., New England or the Southeast). Although bank letters may vary in size, three excellent bank letters are *Economic and Financial Perspectives* (Bank of America), *Economic Trends* (Federal Reserve Bank of Cleveland), and *U.S. Financial Data* (Federal Reserve Bank of St. Louis).

- *Economic and Financial Perspectives* (New York: Bank of America). Issues are published monthly and feature a particular aspect of the economy such as the U.S. economy long-term outlook; short-term outlook; and the global economy. Available from http://corp.bankofamerica.com/research/e_economic_analysis___research.html.
- *Economic Trends* (Cleveland: Federal Reserve Bank of Cleveland). This monthly publication is an excellent source of economic variables, ranging from GDP and its components to money supply aggregates. The figures for such indicators as consumer income, business fixed investment, housing starts, producer and consumer prices, and so on, are usually given quarterly and monthly. Most major libraries have *Economic Trends* on hand, along with publications of the other 11 Federal Reserve Bank Districts, which also contain economic information. Also available from www.clev.frb.org/pubs.htm.
- *U.S. Financial Data* (St. Louis: Federal Reserve Bank of St. Louis). This letter is published weekly and is an especially good compilation of statistics on the money supply, commercial paper and business loans, interest rates, and securities yields. Available at www.stls.frb.org/publications/index.html.

Business Periodicals and Statistical Services

Business periodicals, such as *Barron's, Business Week, Forbes, Fortune, The New York Times*, and *The Wall Street Journal*, are good sources of timely information on the national economy, as well as other types of information. In every issue, both *Business Week* and *Fortune* include forecasts for certain segments of the economy and articles on recent economic developments. They and other magazines also publish extensive economic forecasts in their January issues. *The New York Times* and *The Wall Street Journal* are particularly valuable sources for the most current national economic information, since they are published daily. In addition to frequent articles on the most recent economic developments, *The Wall Street Journal*, in particular, includes a great deal of information on the financial markets.

Standard & Poor's Statistical Service, which is updated monthly, is one of the best sources of summary economic data. It contains economic statistics with special emphasis on banking and finance, production and labor, commodities prices, and the levels of activity in such industries as building and building materials, metals, and chemicals.

The American Statistics Index is a comprehensive tool to locate statistical information in the United States. This annual publication is in two volumes with monthly updates. The first volume is an index that refers to one or more abstracts in the second volume, which also contains full citations to the source publication. It is published by the Congressional Information Service, Inc.

Regional Economic Information

In addition to data on the national economic outlook, it is often appropriate to gather data on the outlook for the region or regions in which the subject company operates. The regional economic outlook is more relevant in some valuation analyses than in others. More often than not, however, the outlook for a specific city, county, or group of counties, cities, or states is relevant to the valuation of a particular company. It is crucial to recognize the importance of properly defining the region to be researched for a particular valuation. Even within the same state, the economic outlook can differ dramatically in different locales.

The primary sources for regional economic data are bank economics departments, public utilities, chambers of commerce, and various state agencies, such as departments of economic development and bureaus of labor statistics. Much of this information can now be found on-line, although the quantity and quality of the data vary from state to state and from city to city.

Most major local banks publish statistical tabulations of economic indicators, although their availability is limited. The best way to obtain regional bank publications is to visit their web site or write or call the particular bank's economic department.

Some universities publish regional and local economic data that are sometimes focused on industries important to the region. Most states and multistate regions now have regular business magazines and newspapers that give economic statistics on business developments and offer economic analysis. The newspaper(s) for the major city in a particular state or region may also contain information on the state or local economy. Most newspapers have web sites, but the ability to search the archives by keyword varies greatly from one paper to another.

Additional sources of information on regional and local economies are listed below.

- *Regional Economies and Markets* (New York: The Conference Board, quarterly). This analysis looks at groups of states in terms of manufacturing production, employment, and income.
- *The Complete Economic and Demographic Data Source* (Washington, DC: Woods & Poole Economics, annual). Available in print or on CD-ROM, this is an excellent source for statistical profiles of metropolitan areas, counties, and states. Historical as well as projected data are included in this source. Other publications from Woods & Poole include *State Profiles* and *MSA Profiles*, which currently include statistical economic data and forecasts through the year 2020.
- *Survey of Buying Power* (New York: Bill Communications, annual). Published annually in *Sales & Marketing Management* magazine, this publication breaks down demographic and income data by state, metropolitan area, and county. Retail sales data are presented for store groups and merchandise lines. Also included are population and retail sales forecasts for local areas.

Industry Information

This section is divided into three parts. The first focuses on researching the industry outlook and briefly discusses some of the most useful sources for industry research.

The second covers the various sources of composite financial statistics that can be used for comparison with the subject company. The third overviews sources of information on management compensation.

After reviewing the standard industry sources and while gathering more detailed information on the industry, the researcher should begin developing an outline of the relevant factors and events influencing the industry outlook. It is also advisable to keep a thorough bibliography of all information gathered, including the full name of the source and the date of the publication or meeting. The researcher should also comb through sources for additional references. Many articles cite individuals or other sources that will provide more informative and authoritative data.

In addition, the researcher should analyze the information in order to evaluate how the subject company is—and will be—affected by the various industry trends. For example, how will it be affected by price increases for key commodities? How will it be affected by shifts in demand, changes in technology, or shifts in the competitiveness of the industry? The researcher should consider the possible answers to these questions in the analysis and valuation of the subject company. The industry section of the report should include the analyst's conclusion as to the impact of the industry outlook on the valuation of the subject company, particularly as to how the subject company may respond differently or to a different degree than the guideline companies. And, the industry section of the report should provide an overview of the industry outlook at the time of the valuation. These factors should be considered by the analyst in the selection of yield capitalization rates, direct capitalization rates, valuation pricing multiples, and other valuation variables.

General Industry Information

The first step in conducting industry research is to develop a general overview of the industry. This will allow the analyst to get a firm grasp on where the subject company fits into the industry and which industry factors or events are most relevant to the subject company. This general overview will also provide enough information about the overall industry to assist the researcher in finding additional information and analyzing the relevance of new information as it is gathered. Several standard industry sources provide this general overview for most industries.

Standard Industry Sources. Three standard sources that provide a very good overview of most industries are *U.S. Industry & Trade Outlook*, *Standard & Poor's Industry Surveys*, and *WEFA Industrial Monitor*.

U.S. Industry & Trade Outlook (formerly the *U.S. Industrial Outlook*) is produced annually by the U.S. Department of Commerce and published by McGraw-Hill. It provides information on the prospects for hundreds of industries, focusing on the structure of the industry and the most significant factors influencing it. The *Outlook* includes forecasts for industries' revenue growth for the coming year as well as over the long term. In addition, this publication provides a very useful list of additional references for each industry covered.

Standard & Poor's Industry Surveys is also a useful starting point in researching an industry. It is organized into 52 broad industry groups and indexed for reference into 500 subgroups. It gives each industry group a reasonably comprehensive background analysis approximately twice a year. *Industry Surveys* generally includes discussion of the industry's structure, trends and outlook, and a section with financial statistics on publicly traded companies in the industry.

WEFA Industrial Monitor, published annually by John Wiley & Sons, complements the Standard & Poor's service with analysis of over 130 industries. It provides reviews and forecasts covering sales, output, prices, and other key indicators.

Trade Associations and Trade Magazines. Perhaps the most valuable source of authoritative information on a particular industry is that industry's trade association(s). Trade associations often collect financial statements from their members and compile composite financial data. Trade associations also publish general industry information, and they may include annual industry reports or articles in their trade magazines. In the data gathering and site visit stages of the valuation, the analyst may inquire of company management as to what are the appropriate trade associations and trade magazines to research.

The *Encyclopedia of Associations*, published annually by Gale Research, and *National Trade and Professional Associations of the United States*, published annually by Columbia Books, are two good sources to identify the association or associations that represent a particular industry or business sector. Many of these associations have regular publications that provide a wealth of data on their respective industries. They often provide periodic reviews and forecasts as well as statistical data.

After identifying the appropriate periodicals, the researcher can usually obtain them directly from the publishers, from a local business library, or on the Internet. If the periodical is not available or indexed on the Internet, it is worthwhile to phone the publisher and ask if any articles on the industry were published over a time period relevant to the valuation date.

Government Agencies and Government Publications. Federal and state agencies compile astronomical amounts of data, most of which are indexed in some form or another. The *Statistical Abstract of the United States* (discussed in more detail above) can help direct the researcher to various federal agencies, state agencies, and other sources of industry information. Regulatory agencies are often good sources of data on industries that are—or used to be—regulated, such as communications, trucking, airlines, food, and drugs.

Business Press. A wide variety of business publications cover companies and industries on an intermittent basis. *The Wall Street Journal*, *Barron's*, *Business Week*, *Forbes*, and *Fortune* are but a few of the publications that frequently include industry articles. The best way to find these articles is (1) to perform an on-line search through an electronic database (e.g., ABI/INFORM, Business & Industry, Newsletter Database, Prompt, or Trade & Industry), or (2) to search web-based services such as Northern Lights, Powerize, or Dow Jones Interactive. Often, articles in the business press will provide valuable leads to authoritative sources or important industry observers.

Brokerage Houses. Brokerage houses provide current information in published report form on publicly traded companies. Such reports are an important source of information in order to gain insight into the functioning of an industry. In addition to providing information on publicly traded companies, brokerage houses often provide stock prices, financial data on companies, estimated earnings on those companies, information on interest rates, and historical graphs. Many brokerage houses publish weekly and monthly reports. Using analyst report services is an efficient method of obtaining reports (e.g., Investext, Multext, Northern Lights, and Profound's Brokerline) rather than directly from the brokerage house.

Composite Company Data

Business Source Books. The Business Source Books, prepared annually by the Statistics of Income Division, Internal Revenue Service, are by far the most comprehensive set of composite company statistics. However, they generally are about three to four years out of date. They include the *Corporation Source Book*, *Partnership Source Book*, and *Sole Proprietorship Source Book*.

Almanac of Business and Industrial Financial Ratios. The data used in the *Almanac* are compiled from corporate tax returns by the U.S. Treasury, Internal Revenue Service. They are disaggregated into 179 fields of business and industry.

Exhibit 6–1 is a typical data presentation from the *Almanac*, in this case for meat products. Each industry group is presented in two tables. One table includes corporations that reported a profit as well as those that did not; the second table includes only those that reported a profit.

Each group for which there are sufficient data is presented in 13 asset size categories, compared with six in the *RMA Annual Statement Studies* data. The *Almanac* gives more income statement line items than does *RMA*, while *RMA* gives more balance sheet line items and more ratios.

The various ratios used are defined in the front part of the *Almanac*. Computations of some of the ratios differ from computations used by *RMA*.

The biggest drawback to the *Almanac* is the degree to which the information is outdated. The 1999 edition covers tax returns for fiscal years ended July 1995 through June 1996, the most recent year for which authoritative figures derived from tax return data of the Internal Revenue Service are available. Nevertheless, operating figures for most industries have at least some degree of stability over time, and the *Almanac* offers some income statement items not found elsewhere.

RMA Annual Statement Studies. Probably the most popular source of composite company data, including privately owned company data, is the *RMA Annual Statement Studies*, which is a product of a national association of bank loan and credit officers. The 1998-1999 edition was based on more than 147,000 financial statements submitted by representatives of their member banks. One reason for the broad appeal of the *Annual Statement Studies* is the over 615 different industries it covers. *Annual Statement Studies* is also available in computerized form from several sources.

Exhibit 6–2 is a typical page from *RMA Annual Statement Studies*, in this case "Manufacturers—Poultry Slaughtering & Processing." Note that each industry group is presented in six size categories, based on total assets. Also, data are shown in the aggregate for five years, so that year-to-year comparisons can be made.

Each of the ratios presented is defined in a section several pages long at the beginning of each annual volume. Note that "all ratios computed by *RMA* are based on year-end statement data only." For example, the cost of sales/inventory (inventory turnover ratio) is computed by dividing the cost of goods sold for the year by the ending inventory. A truer picture of inventory would be derived by dividing cost of goods sold by average inventory, but the data on which the *RMA* ratios are based are not sufficient to make that computation.

Analysts should be aware that sometimes a very small number of respondents are reported in the *RMA* categories. For example, on Exhibit 6–2, there are only 12 respondents in the $100 million–$250 million asset size category. Accordingly, analysts should be aware that a small number of respondents may produce data that are not truly representative of industry conditions.

Exhibit 6–1

Sample Page from Almanac of Business and Industrial Financial Ratios

Table II												MANUFACTURING 2010
Corporations with Net Income												

MEAT PRODUCTS

MONEY AMOUNTS AND SIZE OF ASSETS IN THOUSANDS OF DOLLARS

Item Description for Accounting Period 7/96 Through 6/97	Total	Zero Assets	Under 100	100 to 250	251 to 500	501 to 1,000	1,001 to 5,000	5,001 to 10,000	10,001 to 25,000	25,001 to 50,000	50,001 to 100,000	100,001 to 250,000	250,001 and over
Number of Enterprises 1	1700	11	414	214	32	313	442	100	103	36	15	10	9
Revenues ($ in Thousands)													
Net Sales 2	63884613	133708	80378	238024	93266	931962	3254175	4497258	6821329	6312467	3430646	5240773	32850627
Portfolio Income 3	217152	3548	·	116	129	6824	6535	2706	9379	15401	5927	7239	159347
Other Revenues 4	526152	2184	·	·	25778	44001	59514	11059	42690	8360	24918	52571	255077
Total Revenues 5	64627917	139440	80378	238140	119173	982787	3320224	4511023	6873398	6336228	3461491	5300583	33265051
Average Total Revenues 6	38016	12676	194	1113	3724	3140	7512	45110	66732	176006	230766	530058	3696117
Operating Costs/Operating Income (%)													
Cost of Operations 7	86.0	81.6	49.4	71.1	86.6	77.0	72.3	84.1	84.2	88.8	82.9	87.0	88.0
Salaries and Wages 8	2.5	1.0	18.5	6.0	·	3.2	6.7	4.8	2.7	1.9	3.4	3.2	1.6
Taxes Paid 9	1.0	3.0	2.6	2.6	0.8	1.7	1.8	0.9	1.0	0.6	0.7	0.7	1.1
Interest Paid 10	0.8	0.1	·	·	0.3	0.6	0.8	0.6	0.7	0.5	0.7	0.5	0.9
Depreciation, Depletion, Amortization 11	1.2	0.5	1.1	3.1	1.2	0.8	1.5	1.0	1.3	1.0	1.7	1.8	1.1
Pensions and Other Benefits 12	0.7	0.4	·	1.7	·	0.3	1.2	0.6	1.0	0.6	0.8	0.7	0.7
Other 13	6.2	3.7	18.7	14.1	5.9	10.2	9.6	6.4	6.1	4.4	6.6	5.9	6.0
Officers Compensation 14	0.7	·	5.6	·	9.6	7.2	4.9	0.4	0.8	0.4	0.5	0.2	0.2
Operating Margin 15	1.0	9.7	4.0	1.5	·	·	1.3	1.3	2.4	2.1	2.8	·	0.4
Oper. Margin Before Officers Compensation 16	1.7	9.8	9.6	1.5	5.2	6.2	6.2	1.7	3.1	2.4	3.3	0.3	0.6
Selected Average Balance Sheet ($ in Thousands)													
Net Receivables 17	2080	·	1	34	·	120	514	2231	3974	10078	16989	24801	196153
Inventories 18	2145	·	5	15	226	76	544	1970	3305	5552	12940	24766	243511
Net Property, Plant and Equipment 19	4315	·	20	66	89	189	695	2062	5794	14672	30695	61706	503978
Total Assets 20	11920	·	33	160	315	650	2414	6892	15916	37802	73308	146328	1409306
Notes and Loans Payable 21	3610	·	17	·	·	76	903	2718	4418	11280	23054	44066	420875
All Other Liabilities 22	2554	·	7	50	21	56	500	1769	3533	9342	16429	32075	293821
Net Worth 23	5756	·	9	110	294	518	1011	2405	7965	17181	33825	70187	694610
Selected Financial Ratios (Times to 1)													
Current Ratio 24	1.8	·	1.5	1.9	10.6	2.8	2.0	1.5	1.8	1.7	1.6	1.5	1.9
Quick Ratio 25	1.0	·	1.0	1.6	0.0	2.2	1.0	0.8	1.0	1.1	0.9	0.8	0.9
Net Sales to Working Capital 26	16.6	·	45.9	24.8	14.2	12.7	11.4	29.9	16.7	22.7	17.2	26.3	14.6
Coverage Ratio 27	3.8	·	·	·	·	8.3	5.2	3.7	5.6	6.5	6.3	3.3	2.7
Total Asset Turnover 28	3.2	·	5.9	7.0	9.3	4.6	3.1	6.5	4.2	4.6	3.1	3.6	2.6
Inventory Turnover 29	·	·	·	·	·	·	9.2	·	·	·	·	·	·
Receivables Turnover 30	·	·	·	·	·	·	·	·	·	·	·	·	·
Total Liabilities to Net Worth 31	1.1	·	2.7	0.5	0.1	0.3	1.4	1.9	1.0	1.2	1.2	1.1	1.0
Selected Financial Factors (in Percentages)													
Debt Ratio 32	51.7	·	72.8	31.0	6.8	20.4	58.1	65.1	50.0	54.6	53.9	52.0	50.7
Return on Assets 33	9.1	·	24.0	10.8	·	23.0	12.6	14.2	15.7	13.7	13.5	6.1	6.6
Return on Equity 34	11.1	·	·	13.6	·	23.9	22.7	23.2	23.0	23.5	22.0	6.1	5.7
Return Before Interest on Equity 35	18.9	·	·	15.7	·	28.9	30.0	·	31.4	30.1	29.2	12.6	13.4
Profit Margin, Before Income Tax 36	2.1	14.0	4.0	1.6	23.4	4.4	3.3	1.6	3.1	2.5	3.6	1.2	1.6
Profit Margin, After Income Tax 37	1.7	12.0	4.0	1.4	23.4	4.2	3.1	1.3	2.8	2.3	3.3	0.8	1.1

Trends in Selected Ratios and Factors, 1991-2000										
	1991	1992	1993	1994	1995	1996	1997	1998	1999	2000
Cost of Operations (%) 38	86.5	88.1	88.3	88.0	88.0	86.6	86.3	85.0	84.7	86.0
Operating Margin (%) 39	1.0	1.2	0.9	0.8	1.4	1.6	1.5	2.3	1.6	1.0
Oper. Margin Before Officers Comp. (%) 40	1.6	1.8	1.4	1.2	1.9	2.2	2.0	2.9	2.2	1.7
Average Net Receivables ($) 41	1280	2009	2185	1714	1306	1970	1789	1671	4859	2080
Average Inventories ($) 42	876	1636	2077	1696	1281	1636	1864	1676	3376	2145
Average Net Worth ($) 43	2722	4484	4485	4369	3618	4484	4936	5023	9410	5756
Current Ratio (x1) 44	1.7	1.7	1.6	1.6	1.6	1.9	1.9	1.7	1.7	1.8
Quick Ratio (x1) 45	1.0	1.0	0.8	0.8	0.8	1.1	0.9	0.9	1.0	1.0
Coverage Ratio (x1) 46	4.5	4.9	3.3	3.8	4.4	5.2	4.7	5.3	4.4	3.8
Asset Turnover (x1) 47	4.2	4.0	3.4	3.5	3.9	3.5	3.4	3.3	2.4	3.2
Operating Leverage 48	0.8	1.2	0.7	0.9	1.9	1.1	0.9	1.5	0.7	0.6
Financial Leverage 49	1.1	1.1	0.9	1.1	1.1	1.0	1.0	1.0	1.0	1.0
Total Leverage 50	0.8	1.3	0.6	0.9	2.1	1.2	0.9	1.6	0.7	0.6

Exhibit 6–2

Sample Page from RMA Annual Statement Studies

198 MANUFACTURING—POULTRY SLAUGHTERING & PROCESSING SIC# 2015

| Current Data Sorted By Assets | | | | | | | Comparative Historical Data | |

0-500M	500M-2MM	2-10MM	10-50MM	50-100MM	100-250MM		4/1/94-3/31/95 ALL	4/1/95-3/31/96 ALL
						Type of Statement		
		3	9	6	7	Unqualified	36	40
		2	1			Reviewed	4	7
	1					Compiled	5	3
	1					Tax Returns	1	
1	1	2	8	1	5	Other	15	11
	23 (4/1-9/30/98)		25 (10/1/98-3/31/99)					
1	3	7	18	7	12	**NUMBER OF STATEMENTS**	61	61
%	%	%	%	%	%	**ASSETS**	%	%
			7.4		3.1	Cash & Equivalents	4.9	3.7
			16.1		12.2	Trade Receivables - (net)	20.2	21.4
			18.4		29.2	Inventory	22.4	23.7
			1.9		2.8	All Other Current	1.5	1.4
			43.7		47.3	Total Current	48.9	50.2
			51.4		42.5	Fixed Assets (net)	42.1	43.3
			.6		1.2	Intangibles (net)	1.7	1.7
			4.2		9.0	All Other Non-Current	7.2	4.8
			100.0		100.0	Total	100.0	100.0
						LIABILITIES		
			7.3		10.1	Notes Payable-Short Term	8.4	11.8
			3.9		2.6	Cur. Mat.-L/T/D	3.9	3.8
			10.2		7.9	Trade Payables	15.9	14.9
			.4		.3	Income Taxes Payable	.4	.2
			7.8		6.1	All Other Current	6.6	8.5
			29.6		27.0	Total Current	35.0	39.3
			24.4		21.5	Long Term Debt	20.9	18.4
			1.6		5.9	Deferred Taxes	3.5	3.5
			3.5		2.3	All Other Non-Current	3.4	3.7
			41.0		43.2	Net Worth	37.1	35.2
			100.0		100.0	Total Liabilities & Net Worth	100.0	100.0
						INCOME DATA		
			100.0		100.0	Net Sales	100.0	100.0
			15.3		13.8	Gross Profit	15.2	13.1
			11.6		11.1	Operating Expenses	12.0	9.6
			3.6		2.7	Operating Profit	3.2	3.5
			.7		.2	All Other Expenses (net)	1.2	1.0
			2.9		2.5	Profit Before Taxes	2.0	2.5
						RATIOS		
			2.2 / 1.5 / .8		2.3 / 1.9 / 1.5	Current	2.3 / 1.6 / 1.1	1.8 / 1.4 / 1.0
			1.4 / .7 / .4		1.0 / .7 / .4	Quick	1.3 / .7 / .4	1.0 / .6 / .4
		13 29.0 / 20 17.9 / 30 12.3			17 22.0 / 21 17.2 / 33 11.1	Sales/Receivables	18 20.7 / 22 16.6 / 27 13.3	16 23.3 / 21 17.3 / 26 13.8
		15 24.2 / 25 14.5 / 51 7.1			36 10.1 / 55 6.6 / 96 3.8	Cost of Sales/Inventory	17 21.5 / 34 10.7 / 61 6.0	20 18.6 / 31 11.9 / 51 7.2
		10 38.4 / 13 27.3 / 23 15.7			13 28.6 / 17 21.0 / 21 17.6	Cost of Sales/Payables	12 29.3 / 17 21.5 / 29 12.6	12 30.8 / 16 23.3 / 21 17.5
			8.9 / 14.8 / -48.9		5.3 / 9.0 / 12.3	Sales/Working Capital	9.4 / 16.7 / 92.1	11.3 / 24.8 / 211.9
			5.1 / 2.3 / 1.6		5.5 / 3.0 / .9	EBIT/Interest	9.8 / 3.3 / 1.2	6.6 / (60) 2.7 / 1.2
						Net Profit + Depr., Dep., Amort./Cur. Mat. L /T/D	(30) 11.0 / 3.4 / 1.0	(28) 8.5 / 3.1 / 1.7
			.6 / 1.4 / 2.7		.7 / 1.1 / 1.3	Fixed/Worth	.7 / 1.2 / 2.2	.9 / 1.2 / 2.4
			.8 / 1.9 / 2.7		.8 / 1.2 / 1.9	Debt/Worth	1.0 / 1.8 / 3.1	1.0 / 1.8 / 3.5
			39.1 / 14.9 / 3.6		21.3 / 10.1 / -.4	% Profit Before Taxes/Tangible Net Worth	(58) 37.1 / 16.0 / 3.6	(56) 46.6 / 22.4 / 5.4
			14.3 / 4.3 / 1.6		10.7 / 4.5 / -.2	% Profit Before Taxes/Total Assets	10.8 / 6.2 / .9	15.1 / 6.7 / .9
			10.5 / 5.6 / 2.8		6.3 / 4.8 / 3.3	Sales/Net Fixed Assets	12.6 / 5.9 / 4.0	10.8 / 7.6 / 4.5
			3.5 / 2.4 / 2.0		2.3 / 2.0 / 1.5	Sales/Total Assets	4.1 / 2.7 / 1.9	4.1 / 3.2 / 2.0
			(17) 1.2 / 1.7 / 3.1			% Depr., Dep., Amort./Sales	(49) 1.5 / 2.0 / 3.2	(54) 1.0 / 1.8 / 2.7
						% Officers', Directors', Owners' Comp/Sales		
755M	14453M	131805M	1155900M	1367187M	3605935M	Net Sales ($)	8281869M	7607633M
278M	3581M	36508M	444472M	478079M	1881063M	Total Assets ($)	3021489M	2888603M

© RMA 1999

M = $ thousand   MM = $ million
See Pages 11 through 20 for Explanation of Ratios and Data

SOURCE: *RMA Annual Statement Studies,* 1999–2000 (Philadelphia: Robert Morris Associates, 1999), p. 198.

Standard & Poor's Analyst's Handbook. One of the primary sources of composite financial information on the larger publicly traded companies is the *Standard & Poor's Analyst's Handbook*. The handbook is published annually, with income statement and balance sheet items and related ratios grouped by industry. Approximately 90 industry groups are included, with data going back 30 years.

Information on Management Compensation

As discussed later in this book, management compensation often must be adjusted when valuing a company on a control basis. Following is a brief overview of some of the sources of comparative information on management compensation.

RMA Annual Statement Studies, the *Corporation Source Book of Statistics of Income*, and the *Almanac of Business and Industrial Financial Ratios*, described earlier, provide information on management compensation as a percentage of revenues.

The *Officer Compensation Report*, published annually by Panel Publishers, a division of Aspen Publishing, is a valuable source of information on officer or management compensation. It is a comprehensive study of officer compensation at over 1,400 companies with annual revenues of under $60 million. Compensation data are presented by such categories as officer position, company size, profit performance, and general industry group (manufacturing, technology, general products manufacturing, or service). The survey reports the compensation in effect early in the year in which the report is published; therefore, the results are very timely.

Executive Compensation Survey Analysis, published annually by the National Institute of Business Management, provides compensation data for 57 industry categories. The tables provided give detailed information on base salary, extra compensation, and total compensation. The industries are further broken down by annual sales, so that one can use data from companies with similar annual sales as the subject company. The data provided are taken from the results of a survey of over 600 companies. Data are for the prior year.

The proxy statements of comparative publicly traded companies are another useful source, since they generally present detailed information on the compensation of companies' top executives. Trade associations are another frequent source of information on management compensation, depending on the industry. For particularly small businesses, *Financial Statement Studies of the Small Business*, published annually, is a useful source. Additional sources are listed in the bibliography at the end of this chapter.

On-Line Information

Sometimes information needs can best be met by a database search. On-line information retrieval is computer-assisted access to several hundred databases covering information that includes multifaceted aspects of business. Some databases provide references to magazines and newspaper articles; others cover conference papers, statistical data, and technical reports. The capability to access remote databases of business information provides the smallest information center with the same resources as a very large library.

The computer provides powerful flexibility and control for the researcher. A quick search can retrieve a specific bit of data, or a carefully composed strategy can be used to probe a complex problem or to assemble more comprehensive information. In addition to actual on-line searching, the Internet has made a major impact on the variety of on-line resources that are available to the general public. By registering for an individual or corporate account, one can search databases that have previously been available strictly to librarians.

The advantages of searching on-line for information include:

- Faster and more efficient information retrieval than is usually possible in printed sources.
- The timeliness of business news.
- The ability to combine different facets of a subject in a single search statement.
- The interactive search process that provides a means of adjusting search strategy until the desired information is found.
- The ease of searching several databases in sequence to produce a comprehensive survey of the available literature.
- The increased number of access points for standard reference sources.
- The growing amount of information accumulating in databases (which can be quickly scanned by the computer).
- The ability to retrieve data and store them on a disk for later editing and manipulation of figures.

Several thousand on-line services are presently marketed by dozens of database vendors. This number is increasing every day. Major vendors have concentrated on supplying full-text services for searchers who do not have large libraries at their disposal. One can choose from an extraordinary number of business-related databases.

Dow Jones Interactive runs the gamut from company directories, financial services, and statistical files, to news wires, periodical indexes, and full-text files of newspapers, journals, and newsletters.

LEXIS/NEXIS databases offer electronic editions of a growing number of publications including law reviews and medical journals. LEXIS/NEXIS business offerings include corporate annual reports, state corporation filings, Wall Street brokerage reports, and the complete text of newsletters, trade journals, and local business newspapers.

On-line systems remain the most heavily used electronic sources for business searching, but they are by no means the only medium at the researcher's disposal. Important business databases can be found with increasing frequency on the Internet. Because of the greatly reduced cost, database searching on the Internet has become an extremely popular alternative to on-line information retrieval in recent years. Many libraries subscribe to on-line services and Internet providers. Their patrons are allowed to search these services for themselves for a limited amount of time.

Information on how to contact database vendors is included in the bibliography at the end of this chapter.

Indexes to Economic and Industry Information

Several books and indexes are available to assist in finding additional sources of economic and industry data. Some indexes were already mentioned, such as the

American Statistics Index and *The Wall Street Journal/Barron's Index*. Other indexes, such as the *Business Periodical Index*, the *Public Affairs Information Service* (PAIS), which tend to have more economic information, and *Predicasts* generally are available in public libraries.

Information Access Company provides several business reference publications. Two of this company's publications, *Predicasts Basebook* and *Predicasts Forecasts*, provide summary information on economic indicators and refer the reader to the original source. The *Basebook* provides historical data on U.S. business and economic activities, while *Forecasts* cumulates both short- and long-range projections for products, markets, industries, and the economy. *Predicasts Forecasts* is published quarterly, with an annual cumulative volume. *Forecasts* is particularly valuable as a source of long-term inflation forecasts.

In addition to these indexes, several directories can provide additional sources of economic and industry information. Two particularly valuable resources are *Encyclopedia of Business Information Sources*,[2] and *Business Information: How to Find It, How to Use It*.[3]

Summary

This chapter has briefly described some of the sources of economic and industry data that appraisers and economists find particularly useful. Since the variety of potential sources is virtually boundless, the final section lists several of the most useful indexing services for locating sources relevant to a particular topic or industry. Locations of the sources' publishers and other information appear in the following bibliography.

To get maximum benefit from economic and industry research, the analyst must focus on the implications of the data for the value of the subject company. This focus must be maintained while conducting the research, using it in arriving at an opinion as to value, and including the research as an integral part of the ultimate appraisal report.

Bibliography

National Economic Information

Economic Report of the President. Washington, DC: Government Printing Office, annual.

Federal Reserve Bulletin. Washington, DC: Board of Governors of the Federal Reserve System, monthly, www.bog.frb.fed.us.

Monthly Labor Review. U.S. Bureau of Labor Statistics, Department of Labor. Washington, DC: Government Printing Office, monthly, www.bls.gov/opub/mlr/mlrhome.htm.

A compilation of economic and social statistics. Most are given as monthly figures for the current year and one prior year. Features articles on the labor force, wages, prices, productivity, economic growth, and occupational injuries and

---

[2] James Woy, ed., *Encyclopedia of Business Information Sources*, 13th ed. (Detroit: Gale Research, 1999).

[3] Michael R. Lavin, *Business Information: How to Find It, How to Use It*, 3d ed. (Phoneix, AZ: Oryx Press, 1999).

illnesses. Regular features include a review of developments in industrial relations, book reviews, and current labor statistics.

Standard & Poor's Statistical Service. New York: Standard & Poor's DRI, monthly, with cumulations, www.dri.mcgraw-hill.com.

Standard & Poor's Trends and Projections. New York: Standard & Poor's DRI, monthly, www.dri.mcgraw-hill.com.

This popular newsletter from Standard & Poor's is available as part of the looseleaf version of their *Industry Surveys* or as a separate subscription. The newsletter provides a two- to four-page narrative economic outlook, plus a table of key forecasts from S&P economists. The list of variables is extensive, including GDP and its major components, various measures of personal and corporate income, the personal savings rate, the CPI, several key interest rates, the Index of Industrial Production, housing starts, auto sales, and the unemployment rate. Projections are given for the coming two years (both quarterly and annually). Actual data for the latest current year are provided for comparative purposes.

Statistical Abstract of the United States. Washington, DC: Government Printing Office, annual, www.census.gov/statab.

Survey of Current Business. Washington, DC: Government Printing Office, monthly, www.bea.doc.gov/bea/pubs.htm.

U.S. Industry & Trade Outlook. New York: McGraw-Hill, annual, www.dri.mcgraw-hill.com.

U.S. Macroeconomic Report. Eddystone, PA: WEFA Group, monthly, www.wefa.com.

This on-line database is compiled by the WEFA Group, a respected econometric forecasting firm formed in 1987 through the merger of Wharton Econometric Forecasting Associates and Chase Econometrics. Although these databases cover a wide variety of economic time series, almost all historical data come from government sources. Data are not limited to broad economic indicators; many industry-specific series are also included. Among the latter are detailed price indexes from the CPI and PPI, industrial production indexes, employment by industry, and manufacturers' shipments and inventories.

Federal Reserve Bank Periodicals (a sampling)

Federal Reserve Bank of Atlanta. *Economic Review.*
Federal Reserve Bank of Atlanta. *Econ South.*
Federal Reserve Bank of Boston. *Regional Review.*
Federal Reserve Bank of Boston. *New England Economic Indicators.*
Federal Reserve Bank of Boston. *New England Economic Review.*
Federal Reserve Bank of Chicago. *Ag Letter.*
Federal Reserve Bank of Chicago. *Economic Perspectives.*
Federal Reserve Bank of Cleveland. *Economic Commentary.*
Federal Reserve Bank of Cleveland. *Economic Review.*
Federal Reserve Bank of Cleveland. *Economic Trends.*
Federal Reserve Bank of Dallas. *Economic & Financial Review.*
Federal Reserve Bank of Dallas. *Southwest Economy.*
Federal Reserve Bank of Kansas City. *Economic Review.*
Federal Reserve Bank of Minneapolis. *Fedgazette.*
Federal Reserve Bank of Minneapolis. *Quarterly Review.*
Federal Reserve Bank of New York. *Economic Policy Review.*
Federal Reserve Bank of Philadelphia. *Business Review.*

Federal Reserve Bank of Richmond. *Economic Quarterly*.
Federal Reserve Bank of Richmond. *Region Focus*.
Federal Reserve Bank of St. Louis. *International Economic Conditions*.
Federal Reserve Bank of St. Louis. *National Economic Trends*.
Federal Reserve Bank of St. Louis. *The Regional Economist*.
Federal Reserve Bank of St. Louis. *Review*.
Federal Reserve Bank of St. Louis. *U.S. Financial Data*.
Federal Reserve Bank of San Francisco. *Economic Review*.
Federal Reserve Bank of San Francisco. *Fed in Print* (index).
Federal Reserve Bank of San Francisco. *Economic Letter*.

Regional Economic Information

American Business Climate & Economic Profiles, 6th ed., Priscilla Cheng Geahigan, ed. Washington, DC: Gale Research, 1999.
This is a concise compilation of facts, rankings, incentives, and resource listings for all 319 metropolitan statistical areas (MSAs) and the 50 states.
City and County Databook and the *State Metropolitan Area Databook*. U.S. Bureau of the Census, Department of Commerce. Washington, DC: Government Printing Office www.census.gov/statab/www/ccdb.html.
Economic Census. U.S. Bureau of the Census, Department of Commerce. Washington, DC: Government Printing Office, www.census.gov.
The Economic Census is produced as 12 separate titles grouped according to type of business: accommodation and foodservices; administrative and support and waste management and remediation services; arts, entertainment, and recreation; construction; educational services; health care and social assistance; manufacturing; mining; professional, scientific, and technical services; real estate and rental and leasing; retail trade; and wholesale trade. Each title consists of three subseries: geographic data for each state, detailed industry data by SIC numbers, and a subject series for special topics, though for some titles the industry and subject series are combined. It profiles the U.S. economy every five years from the national to local levels.
Contains statistics on housing, population, construction activity, and many other economic indicators.
Survey of Buying Power. New York: Bill Communications, Inc., annual.
This survey, published annually by *Sales & Marketing Management* magazine, breaks down demographic and income data by state, metropolitan area, and county or parish. Retail sales data are presented for store groups and merchandise lines. Also included are population and retail sales forecasts for local areas.
The Complete Economic and Demographic Data Source. Washington, DC: Woods and Poole Economics, Inc., annual.
U.S. Bureau of Economic Analysis, Department of Commerce. Washington, DC, (202) 377-1986, www.bea.doc.gov.
This organization has a regional economics program that provides estimates, analyses, and projections by region, state, metropolitan statistical area, and county or parish. Regional reports are released approximately six times a year with summary estimates of state personal income.

Industry Information

Almanac of Business and Industrial Financial Ratios. Englewood Cliffs, NJ: Prentice Hall, annual.

Economic Census. Washington, DC: Government Printing Office, www.census.gov.

Corporation Source Book: Statistics of Income; *Partnership Source Book: Statistics of Income*; and *Sole Proprietorship Source Book: Statistics of Income.* Internal Revenue Service. Washington, DC: Government Printing Office, annual.

Encyclopedia of American Industries (2 volumes), 2nd ed., Kevin Hillstrom, ed. Detroit: Gale Research, 1998.

Provides information on many industries, broken down by SIC code. Information includes an industry "snapshot," organization and structure of the industry, current conditions, a discussion of industry leaders, information on the work force, foreign competition and trade information, and additional sources of information. This is a very useful book, although its infrequency of publication can make its information dated.

Industry Norms and Key Business Ratios. New York: Dun & Bradstreet, Inc., annual.

Balance sheet and profit and loss ratios based on a computerized financial statements file. The 14 key ratios are broken down into median figures, with upper and lower quartiles. Covers over 800 lines of business, broken down into three size ranges by net worth for each SIC.

Manufacturing USA, 6th ed. Detroit: Gale Research, 1998.

Profiles and top company rankings for about 460 manufacturing industries, organized by four-digit SIC code. Synthesizes relevant data from the *Census of Manufacturers*, the *Annual Survey of Manufacturers*, *County Business Patterns*, the *U.S. Industry & Trade Outlook*, and the *Industry-Occupation Matrix* produced by the U.S. Department of Labor. Profiles provide general industry statistics, indexes of change, selected ratios, product share, statistical analyses of states and regions, and more.

Market Share Reporter. Detroit: Gale Research, annual.

Presents comparative business statistics in a clear, straightforward manner. Arranged by four-digit SIC code, contains data from more than 2,000 entries. Each entry includes a descriptive title, data and market description, a list of producers/products along with their assigned market share, and more.

Moody's Industry Review. New York: Moody's Investors Service, biweekly.

Covers approximately 4,000 companies in nearly 150 industry groups. Every company is ranked within its industry by five financial characteristics (revenues, net income, total assets, cash and marketable securities, and long-term debt) and five ratios (profit margin, return on capital, return on assets, P/E, and dividend yield). Every industry report also provides additional data in an unranked display, including earnings per share, book value, and 12-year stock price summaries.

Predicasts Basebook. Foster City, CA: Information Access Company, annual.

This loose-leaf reference provides historical data on U.S. business and economic activities. Arranged by a modified, seven-digit SIC number, the industry statistics include production, consumption, plant and equipment expenditures, payroll, and exports/imports. The figures cover approximately 15 years. The sources of statistic and annual growth are also provided.

Predicasts Forecasts. Foster City, CA: Information Access Company, quarterly with annual cumulations.

Nearly 50,000 short- and long-range projections for products and industries, along with leading economic indicators for U.S. business are available in this reference. Arranged by modified seven-digit SIC code, each forecast gives the subject, quantities for a base year, short- and long-term projections, unit of measure, source of data, and projected annual rate.

Predicasts PROMT. Foster City, CA: Information Access Company, updated daily.
This multi-industry resource provides broad, international coverage of companies, products, markets, and applied technologies for all industries. Available through on-line services, *PTS PROMT* is comprised of abstracts and full-text records from more than 1,000 of the world's important business publications, including trade journals, local newspapers and regional business publications, national and international business newspapers, trade and business newsletters, research studies, S1 SEC registration statements, investment analysts' reports, corporate news releases, and corporate annual reports.

RMA Annual Statement Studies. Philadelphia: Robert Morris Associates, annual.

Service Industries USA: Industry Analyses, Statistics, and Leading Organizations, 4th ed., Arsen J. Darnay, ed. Detroit: Gale Research, 1998.
Organizes widely scattered and sometimes difficult-to-use federal economic information, as well as data from other sources, into a workable and easy-to-read format. Four indexes provide easy access to the material: SIC Index; services index containing keyword listings of services with references to SIC codes and page numbers; company institution; and occupation indexes.

Standard & Poor's Analyst's Handbook. New York: Standard & Poor's Corporation, Inc., annual.

Standard & Poor's Industry Surveys. New York: Standard & Poor's Corporation, Inc., biannual.

U.S. Industry & Trade Outlook. New York: McGraw-Hill, annual.

Industry Information Directories

Encyclopedia of Associations. Detroit: Gale Research, annual.
Available in print, electronic, and web based formats. This is the largest compilation of nonprofit associations and organizations available anywhere. Contains descriptions of professional associations, trade and business associations, labor unions, chambers of commerce, and groups of all types in virtually every field.

National Trade and Professional Associations of the United States. Washington, DC: Columbia Books, annual.
Excellent source book for trade and industry sources of industry information. Restricted to trade and professional associations and labor unions with national memberships.

Nelson's Directory of Wall Street Research. Rye, NY: W.R. Nelson & Company, annual.
The "Research Sources" section gives names, addresses, telephone numbers, and specialties of research personnel at over 600 firms.

Management Compensation Sources

Almanac of Business and Industrial Financial Ratios. Leo Troy, Ph.D., ed. Englewood Cliffs, NJ: Prentice Hall, annual.

Executive Compensation Assessor. Redmond, WA: Economic Research Institute, quarterly. www.erieri.com.
ERI's *Executive Compensation Assessor* reports salaries and bonuses for 311 top management positions within multiple industries. Data may be adjusted for geographic area, organization size, and compensation valuation date. This source provides analysis of data compiled from virtually all publicly available executive compensation surveys, along with direct analysis of SEC Edgar proxy data. Other compensation products are also available.

Executive Compensation: Survey Results. New York: National Association of Business Management, Inc., annual.

The Hay Report: Compensation & Benefits. Philadelphia: Center for Management Research, annual.

This study details the practices of thousands of companies and compensation activity by industry, job level, and function. Includes sections on prevailing compensation levels, team-based compensation, average monthly premium costs, and CEO reward practices.

Officer Compensation Report. New York: Panel Publishers, Inc., annual.

RMA Annual Statement Studies. Philadelphia: Robert Morris Associates, annual.

Source Book Statistics of Income. Washington, DC: Internal Revenue Service, annual.

Standard & Poor's Execucomp. New York: Standard & Poor's, quarterly, www.umi.compustat.com/cgi-mi-auth/mihome.cgi.

Available on-line or on CD-ROM, *Execucomp* is a comprehensive database that covers S&P 500, S&P mid-cap 400, and S&P small cap companies. The study includes over 80 different compensation, executive, director, and company items, including breakdowns of salary, bonuses, options, and director compensation information.

Watson Wyatt Data Services Compensation Survey Reports. Rochelle Park, NJ: Watson Wyatt Data Services, annual, www.watsonwyatt.com

Watson Wyatt publishes several different compensation surveys annually—some are industry specific (e.g., Survey of Hospital & Health Care Management Compensation) and some are position specific (e.g., Survey of Top Management Compensation). The companies surveyed rage from emerging growth businesses to *Fortune* 1000 companies. The surveys together encompass more than one million employees.

On-Line Information

You may contact these vendors directly for more information about their services:

CompuServe
5000 Arlington Center Boulevard
Columbus, Ohio 43220
800-524-3388
www.compuserve.com

The Dialog Corporation
11000 Regency Parkway, Suite 10
Cary, North Carolina 27512-8004
800-334-2564
www.dialog.com/homepage.shtml

Dow Jones Interactive
P.O. Box 300
Princeton, New Jersey 08543-0300
800-369-7466
www.djinteractive.com

LEXIS/NEXIS
Reed Elsevier Inc.
9393 Springboro Pike
P.O. Box 933
Dayton, Ohio 45401
800-346-9759
www.lexis-nexis.com

Wilsonline
The H.W. Wilson Company
950 University Avenue
Bronx, New York 10452
800-367-6770
www.hwwilson.com

Indexes and Guides to Business Information

American Statistics Index: A Comprehensive Guide and Index to the Statistical Publications of the U.S. Government. Washington, DC: Congressional Information Service, monthly, with annual cumulations.

Published by a reputable firm specializing in providing access to government publications, the *ASI* provides access to federal statistics. Each edition is two volumes, Index and Abstracts. Also included in the index volume are a title index, a guide to the Standard Industrial Classification code, the Standard Occupation Classification, and a list of standard metropolitan statistical areas (SMSAs).

The Basic Business Library: Core Resources, 3rd ed. Bernard S. Schlessinger. Phoenix, AZ: Oryx Press, 1995.

New electronic formats and new publications are covered in the annotated core list of nearly 200 prime information sources, including on-line and CD-ROM databases, periodicals, newsletters, and books. The bibliography, including over 300 abstracts covering the business reference literature, has been updated to 1994.

Business Information: How to Find It, How to Use It, 3rd ed. Michael R. Lavin. Phoenix, AZ: Oryx Press, 1999.

Combines in-depth descriptions of major business publications and databases with explanations of concepts essential for using them effectively. Readers will gain a greater appreciation of the enormous diversity of published information and the wide range of specific questions that can be answered.

Business Information Sources, 3rd ed. Lorna M. Daniells. Berkeley, CA: University of California Press, 1993.

Annotates sources arranged by subject, such as industry statistics. Indexed by title, author, and subject. An updated edition is forthcoming.

Business Periodicals Index (BPI). New York: H.W. Wilson, monthly, with quarterly and annual cumulations, www.hwwilson.com/Documentation/WilsonWeb/tecfaq7.html.

Subject index to approximately 350 periodicals in the business field. The periodicals indexed are English-based and come from trade and professional associations and government agencies. Articles indexed under specific business subject headings, including names of executives and corporations. Available in print, on CD-ROM disk, and on-line. Over 57,000 subject terms for immediate access—search by subjects, key words, company names, and SIC codes.

Business Valuation Data Directory. Portland, OR: Business Valuation Resources, annual. www.BVLibrary.com.

Published annually as a supplement to *Shannon Pratt's Business Valuation Update*, this resource lists hundreds of sources for compensation, industry, cost of capital, guideline company, and mergers and acquisitions data.

Directory of Business and Financial Services, 14th ed. Charles J. Popovich and M. Rita Costello. Washington, DC: Special Libraries Association, 1999.

A fine companion to the Daniells book, this source deals with services that provide regularly or irregularly updated information on some category of business activity.

Encyclopedia of Business Information Sources, 13th ed. James Woy, ed. Detroit: Gale Research, 1999.

A bibliographic guide to more than 24,000 citations covering over 1,100 subjects of interest to business personnel. Includes abstracting and indexing services, almanacs and yearbooks, bibliographies, biographical sources, directories, encyclopedias and dictionaries, financial ratios, handbooks and manuals, on-line databases, periodicals and newsletters, price sources, research centers and institutes, statistics sources, trade associations and professional societies, and other sources of information on each topic.

Government Information on the Internet, Greg R. Notess. Lanham, MD: Bernan Press, 1999.

This resource covers all of the changes in formats and accessibility of the new generation of government information sources, including the Internet, CD-ROM products, on-line databases, diskettes, electronic bulletin boards, and telephone hot line numbers, as well as print sources.

International Business Information: How to Find It, How to Use It, 3rd ed. Ruth A. Pagell. Phoenix, AZ: Oryx Press, 1998.

Covering both print and electronic sources, this reference includes all major business environments outside the United States, with special up-to-date examinations of the most recent sources on Eastern Europe, the former Soviet Union, and Asia.

Predicasts F&S Index United States. Foster City, CA: Information Access Company, weekly, with cumulations.

Provides comprehensive reference indexes of business and economic information. *PTS F&S Index* covers worldwide company, product, and industry information. One- and two-line article summaries offer access to information on international companies, business and financial activities, demographics, government regulations, and economics. Detailed coverage of more than 750 trade journals, newspapers (including *The Wall Street Journal*), government documents, and special studies.

PAIS Select Journals List. New York: Public Affairs Information Service, annual, www.pais.org/select/sellst.htm.

A selected subject list of the latest books, pamphlets, government publications, reports of public and private agencies, and periodical articles relating to economic and social conditions, public administration, and international relations.

Statistical Reference Index. Washington, DC: Congressional Information Service, monthly with annual cumulation, www.lexis-nexis.com/cispubs/Catalog/cis.

Since 1980, *Statistical Reference Index* has indexed and abstracted statistical reports from agencies other than the federal government. Nonprofit organizations, trade and professional associations, state government agencies, university research centers, and commercial publishers are just some of the sources of statistical information included. Since 1983, CIS also has published the *Index to International Statistics*, which includes statistical publications of over 50 international, intergovernmental agencies such as the United Nations and OECD.

Trade & Industry Index. Foster City, CA: Information Access Company, weekly.

Business journals relating to trade, industry, and commerce are indexed and selectively abstracted in *Trade & Industry Index*. This on-line database provides, in a single source, current and comprehensive coverage of major trade journals and industry-related periodicals representing all Standard Industrial Classifications. *Trade & Industry Index* provides indexing and selective abstracting of over 300 trade and industry journals, as well as comprehensive but selective coverage of business and trade information from nearly 1,200 additional publications

Articles Providing Research Information

Lang, Eva M. "Advanced Internet Research Techniques." Presentation to the annual Advanced Business Valuation Conference of the American Society of Appraisers, October 24, 1997. Available on www.BVLibrary.com.

_____. "Beating the Search Engines Odds." *CPA Expert*, Summer 1999, pp. 11–13.

_____. "Finding Private Company Benchmarking Data." *CPA Expert*, Special Issue 1999, pp. 11–13.

_____. "Finding the Trade Association Needle in the Internet Haystack." *CPA Litigation Service Counselor*, May 1998, pp. 9–10.

Tudor, Jan Davis. "Industry Information on the Internet: A Case Study." *CPA Expert*, Fall 1998, pp. 10–12.

_____. "The Internet as Librarian: Online General Info Sources." *CPA Litigation Service Counselor*, January 2000, pp. 5–6.

_____. "The U.S. Economy on a Roll: Check It Out on the Internet." *Business Valuation Review*, December 1997, pp. 183–186.

Tudor, Jan Davis, and Karin Zamba. "Sources of M&A Data for Business Valuations: Print or Electronic?" *Business & Finance Bulletin*, Fall 1997, pp. 19–24.

Chapter 7

Analyzing Financial Statements

Adequacy of Allowance and Reserve Accounts
  Allowance for Doubtful Accounts—Accounts Receivable
  Allowance for Doubtful Accounts—Notes Receivable
Inventory Accounting Methods
  FIFO, LIFO, and Other Methods
  Write-Down and Write-Off Policies
Depreciation Methods and Schedules
  Declining-Balance Method
  Sum-of-the-Years'-Digits Method
  ACRS and MACRS
  Analytical Implications
Depletion
Treatment of Intangibles
  Leasehold Interests
  Other Intangible Assets
Capitalization versus Expensing of Various Costs
Timing of Recognition of Revenues and Expenses
  Contract Work
  Installment Sales
  Sales Involving Actual or Contingent Liabilities
  Prior-Period Adjustments
  Accounting for Leases
Net Operating Loss Carryforwards
Treatment of Interests in Affiliates
Extraordinary or Nonrecurring Items
  Ordinary versus Extraordinary Items
  Other Nonrecurring Items
  Discontinued Operations
Operating versus Nonoperating Items
Management Compensation and Perquisites
Transactions Involving Company Insiders
Contingent Assets and Liabilities
Adjustments to Asset Valuations
  Marketable Securities
  Other Assets

The financial analyst knows that there is some latitude permitted in the preparation of financial statements. Even within the broad confines of generally accepted accounting principles (GAAP), rarely do any two companies follow exactly the same set of accounting practices in keeping their books and preparing their financial statements. When it comes to the typical closely held company, most are not audited and many prepare financial statements that deviate from GAAP, to put it kindly. Therefore, the analyst must evaluate each item and adjust for differences in accounting practices, where appropriate, in order to compare two or more companies or to measure a company against some industry or other standard.

When there is a choice among accounting practices, private companies tend toward a more conservative selection in order to minimize taxes, while public companies may account more aggressively in order to report more income so as to please shareholders. Also, some public companies have been accused of "managing" their earnings in order to minimize earnings peaks and valleys by making more conservative accounting decisions in good years and more aggressive accounting decisions in bad ones. Furthermore, the smaller the private company, the more pronounced the difference between public companies and private companies tends to be.

All discussions of financial statement analysis in this book are subject to the caveat that generally accepted accounting principles are constantly being reviewed and changed. Also, publicly traded companies are subject to certain disclosure requirements of the SEC, which continue to be challenged and interpreted by the courts.

There are complete books dedicated to the subject of financial statement analysis (see bibliography at the end of this chapter). The material presented in this chapter is only a refresher to those who are presented with the task of valuing a business or reviewing a business valuation made by others.

The purpose of analyzing income statements is to better understand and interpret the earning power of the subject company, since earning power is usually the most important element of the value of a business. Therefore, adjustments to the income statements, in order to better present the earning power of the business, generally fall into any or all of three categories:

1. Conventions the company has elected to account for its activities, as discussed earlier.
2. Nonrecurring events, discontinued operations, or other aspects of past operations that may not represent future earning power.
3. Certain discretionary items, such as generous management bonuses.

In different valuation situations, asset values may play a relatively important role and, therefore, adjustments to the balance sheet may be necessary for analytical purposes. Some variables adjusted for in the income statement analysis may or may not require that adjustments also be made in the balance sheet analysis. And, some adjustments to the balance sheet require that adjustments also be made to the income statement.

This chapter discusses the most common categories of adjustments to the income statement and balance sheet in the business valuation. It begins with adjustments for different ways of measuring asset and liability items. Then it examines a number of items arising from the treatment of revenue and expense items. Finally, it looks at a number of miscellaneous items. More complete discussions of financial statements and the appropriate adjustments of various financial statement accounts can be explored by the reader by referring to other sources, including those referenced in the bibliography at the end of this chapter.

Adequacy of Allowance and Reserve Accounts

It is common to find that a company is either under- or over-reserved for certain items. Some so-called reserve accounts should not be considered reserve accounts at all but merely portions of equity that management has chosen to earmark for some future expenditure or contingency. If under-reserved, the effect is an overstatement of earnings due to inadequate reserve charges to expenses, with an accompanying overstatement of net asset value. If over-reserved, the opposite occurs. The analyst may encounter a variety of reserve or allowance accounts from time to time and should question and analyze each on its own merits.

Allowance for Doubtful Accounts—Accounts Receivable

While examining accounts receivable, the analyst should check their creditworthiness and make any appropriate adjustments. Most companies carry accounts receivable and deduct some allowance for potentially uncollectible accounts. The typical policy is to increase the allowance for doubtful accounts at the end of each month by a percentage of that month's credit sales. This shows up as a deduction from accounts receivable on the balance sheet. Then, as individual uncollectible accounts are finally written off, they are credited against accounts receivable and debited against the allowance for doubtful accounts, with no direct effect on either earnings or net asset value at the time of the write-off.

Since the expense charge actually represents an estimate of future write-offs, the analyst may wish to make some judgment as to that estimate's accuracy, at least if the effect might be material. One way is to compare the historical percentage of bad debt losses from past credit sales with the percentage of current credit sales being charged to bad debt expense to see if too little or too much is currently being charged. Another approach is to compare the aged accounts receivable schedule allowance relative to the amount of overdue accounts. Some companies tend to carry receivables on their books indefinitely, with little or no doubtful account allowance, resulting in overstatement of earnings and net asset value. Other companies follow a very aggressive write-off policy, removing from their books many accounts that eventually are collected; this tends to understate earnings and net asset value.

Allowance for Doubtful Accounts—Notes Receivable

Notes receivable may be taken to improve the company's chance of collecting a delinquent trade receivable, but their collectibility may be in question. Notes receivable from stockholders may really be more in the nature of long-term loans, deferred compensation, or even undeclared dividends, even though they may be carried on the balance sheet in the current asset section. A review of balance sheets from prior periods to see how long some "current" items have been carried may lead to questions for management regarding the probability of collection during the company's normal operating cycle.

Inventory Accounting Methods

FIFO, LIFO, and Other Methods

The *FIFO*, or *first-in, first-out*, inventory accounting method, assumes, for accounting purposes, that the oldest unit of an inventory item purchased is the next unit sold. The *LIFO*, or *last-in, first-out*, method assumes that the most recently purchased unit of an inventory item purchased is the next unit sold. The difference between FIFO and LIFO accounting shows up in the ending inventory on the balance sheet, affecting both the cost of goods sold and earnings. To the extent that prices go up, LIFO produces lower figures for earnings and inventory than does FIFO. Since LIFO accounting is acceptable for federal income tax purposes, many companies have adopted LIFO over FIFO inventory accounting in response to inflation.

However, it should be noted that if inventory has been accounted for using LIFO, and if the level of inventory *declines* over the course of the year—that is, withdrawals from inventory exceed purchases—an accounting phenomenon known as *LIFO liquidation* occurs. This reduces inventories to a point at which cost layers from prior years are matched to current inflated prices. If prices from the "old" inventory are much lower than current prices, a distortion of income occurs. Audited and reviewed financial statements should disclose whether LIFO liquidation has occurred and the extent of its effects. If a decline in inventory that is being accounted for using LIFO occurs, and the financial statements lack proper disclosures, the analyst should conduct further examination and inquiry in order to eliminate the distorting effects of LIFO liquidation.

When comparing two or more companies for valuation purposes, all of the companies' earnings and asset values should have been derived based on the same inventory accounting method if the difference is substantial enough to affect the valuation. If they do not all use the same accounting method, the analyst can adjust the earnings and asset values to the same basis using information in the financial statements.

As a simple example, imagine a company that started its accounting period with 30 widgets, purchased for $10 each. Later in the period, it purchased 60 more widgets at $15 each, and before its next fiscal year-end it sold 50 widgets, ending the period with 40 widgets in inventory. The cost of goods sold would be computed under the FIFO and LIFO methods as shown in Exhibit 7–1. In other words, LIFO accounting assumes that the original units in the inventory are the ones that are still there. In the above case, if sales were $1,000, the gross margin would be $400 under FIFO accounting and $250 under LIFO accounting.

Exhibit 7–1

Cost of Goods Sold
FIFO and LIFO Methods

		FIFO		LIFO	
	Beginning inventory	30 Units @ $10 =	$300	30 Units @ $10 =	$300
Plus:	Purchases	60 Units @ $15 =	$900	60 Units @ $15 =	$900
Equals:	Goods available for sale		$1,200		$1,200
Less:	Ending inventory	40 Units @ $15 =	$600	30 Units @ $10 =	$300
				10 Units @ $15 =	$150
					$450
Equals:	Cost of goods sold		$600		$750

For most companies that report on FIFO, the information the analyst needs in order to adjust earnings and inventory to the LIFO basis is not readily available. If a company reporting on LIFO has audited statements, however, the footnotes will provide a figure for the LIFO in inventory reserve that the analyst can use to adjust earnings and inventory values from LIFO to FIFO. If the statements are not audited, the company's accountant should be able to provide the analyst with the necessary information for adjusting to a FIFO basis. Therefore, because of the availability of this information, if one or more companies' inventory accounting needs to be adjusted for comparative purposes, the analyst usually should adjust the LIFO-reporting companies to a FIFO basis rather than vice versa.

The analyst should keep in mind that (1) if earnings are adjusted from LIFO to FIFO and (2) if after-tax income or after-tax cash flow are used as the appropriate measure of economic income, then the adjustment should be net of the income tax effect (either additional taxes or benefit) associated with it. Choosing the correct income tax rate to use in making the adjustment may be more complicated than just using the effective or the marginal income tax rate. The analyst should carefully scrutinize the income tax characteristics of the company whose income is being adjusted to determine the most likely consequences of the additional income or losses, as adjusted, on income taxes.

Besides adjusting the income statement from a LIFO to a FIFO basis, it may be necessary to adjust the balance sheet, generally in three areas. First, the inventory level should be adjusted to the FIFO basis. Second, an income tax liability account should be adjusted to account for the additional income taxes that would have resulted from the adjustment to inventory. Third, retained earnings should be adjusted by the net difference between the inventory and income tax liability adjustments.

Continuing with our widget company example, let's assume that the company is using LIFO accounting and the appropriate tax rate for the adjustment is 30 percent. The company has a LIFO reserve of $150; therefore, to adjust the inventory to FIFO, the analyst adds $150 to the ending inventory level of $450 to reach an adjusted inventory level of $600. Then the analyst adds $45 ($150 × 30% tax rate) to an income tax liability account and $105 ($150 – $45) to retained earnings. Exhibit 7–2 illustrates the calculations.

In some lines of business, specific inventory items are clearly identifiable from the time of purchase through the time of sale and are accounted for and costed on this basis. Some companies also account for inventory on some type of *average cost*

Exhibit 7–2

Adjusting LIFO to FIFO

Continuing with Exhibit 7-1:

Assume:	
Tax rate	30%
LIFO reserve	$150
Adjust ending inventory to FIFO:	
LIFO inventory	$450
Add LIFO reserve	150
Adjusted ending inventory	$600
Compute accrued income tax liability, and add to income tax liability account:	
LIFO reserve	$150
Multiply by tax rate	0.30
Addition to accrued income tax liability	$ 45
Add net effect to retained earnings:	
LIFO reserve	$150
Less related accrued income tax	45
Addition to retained earnings	$105

---

basis.[1] In particular, in some industries it is possible to adjust inventory from LIFO only to average cost, not to FIFO. The adjustment is calculated in the same way as the adjustment to FIFO.

Write-Down and Write-Off Policies

Regardless of whether the company uses FIFO, LIFO, specific identification, or average cost inventory accounting, most companies adhere to the *lower-of-cost-or-market* principle, which says that the carrying value should be reduced if the market value is less than cost. *Market value* for this purpose is defined as "current replacement cost except that market shall not be higher than net realizable value nor should it be less than net realizable value reduced by the normal profit margin."[2] Implementation of the lower-of-cost-or-market principle varies tremendously—one company may have stockrooms full of obsolete inventory and another an aggressive program of automatic write-downs and write-offs of inventory based on the number of months it has been in stock. If the company goes to one extreme or the other in its implementation of this principle, the analyst may need to adjust earnings and asset values.

Depreciation Methods and Schedules

The five most common methods of computing depreciation charges—all acceptable to the IRS for income tax purposes—are the straight-line, declining-balance, sum-of-the years'-digits, accelerated cost recovery systems (ACRS), and modified accelerated cost recovery system (MACRS) introduced by the Tax Reform Act of 1986.

---

[1] For a discussion of the average cost method, see Leopold A. Bernstein and John J. Wild, *Analysis of Financial Statements: Theory, Application, and Interpretation*, 6th ed. (New York: McGraw-Hill, 1997), pp. 168–69.

[2] Ibid., p. 170.

The method that produces the largest, quickest depreciation deductions is the one most often selected by closely held businesses, since they are most eager to minimize reported taxable income.

For income tax reporting purposes, the Internal Revenue Code defines the period and the amount per period over which the cost of most depreciable assets can be recovered.

The *straight-line method* simply charges depreciation on the asset in even increments over the asset's useful life. The declining-balance, sum-of-the-years'-digits, ACRS, and MACRS methods are called *accelerated methods* because, unlike the straight-line method, they charge a higher proportion of the total depreciation in the early years of the asset's useful life than in later years.

Declining-Balance Method

The *declining-balance method* uses some multiple, such as two times or one and one-half times the straight-line depreciation rate. For example, if an asset had a useful life of 10 years, straight-line depreciation would be at the rate of 10 percent per year. Double-declining-balance depreciation would be at twice that rate, or 20 percent, but with the percentage always applied to the remaining book value. For example, in the first year, a $100,000 piece of equipment with a 10-year life would be depreciated at 20 percent of $100,000 or $20,000, leaving a depreciated balance of $80,000. In the second year, the asset would be depreciated at 20 percent of $80,000, or $16,000, leaving a depreciated balance of $64,000.

Sum-of-the-Years'-Digits Method

In the *sum-of-the-years'-digits method*, the depreciation charge is a fraction whose denominator is the sum of the years' digits of the asset's useful life and whose numerator is the number of years of remaining useful life. Thus, for a 10-year useful life, the denominator is 55 $(1 + 2 + 3 + 4 + 5 + 6 + 7 + 8 + 9 + 10 = 55)$, and the numerator the first year is 10. Therefore, the first year's depreciation charge is 10/55 of the asset's cost, in the second year 9/55, and so on.

For some assets, the company assumes a residual or salvage value at the end of the depreciable life. In these cases, the difference between the cost and salvage value is the depreciable amount. Salvage value may not be deducted from cost when applying the declining-balance method, however, because that method never results in the asset being depreciated to zero.

ACRS and MACRS[3]

The fourth widely used depreciation method is *ACRS*, (accelerated cost recovery system), which was enacted as part of the Economic Recovery Tax Act of 1981. It is used mainly for federal tax purposes. The Tax Reform Act of 1986 revised the use of ACRS for property placed in service after 1986, thus creating the MACRS (modified accelerated cost recovery system). One can consult a periodic tax guide for a presentation of the original and revised provisions of ACRS.

---

[3] The MACRS example is quite complex and beyond the scope of this book. The reader may wish to refer to the *U.S. Master Tax Guide*, 82nd ed. (Chicago: Commerce Clearing House, 1999), for a comprehensive discussion of MACRS.

Still another depreciation method sometimes used is *units of production*, (also referred to as *units of utilization*). For example, if a $100,000 asset is expected to provide 10,000 hours of useful service, it might be depreciated on the basis of $10 for each hour it is used.

Exhibit 7–3 illustrates the depreciation computations under the straight-line, declining-balance, sum-of-the-years' digits, and ACRS methods assuming an asset with a cost of $50,000, no salvage value, and an estimated useful life of five years.

Analytical Implications

The analyst should make some judgment of the appropriateness of the depreciation schedule, both as it stands alone and in relation to other companies, if such comparisons are to be made. For example, a company may use an eight-year useful life for equipment that it manufactures and leases to customers, but most other companies in the industry may use a six-year useful life for the same type of equipment, assuming that the machinery will be technologically obsolete in six years. In valuing the company using an eight-year depreciation schedule, the analyst might apply a downward adjustment to both the earnings base and the equipment's net remaining book value to reflect the relatively inadequate depreciation charges, if such an adjustment would be material. There can be a fairly wide range of normal practices within any industry, and the analyst must be prepared to do considerable research to reach an informed judgment of the reasonable depreciation life for some types of assets.

Let's say we are valuing a closely held company using a multiple of earnings method and that 10 times earnings is appropriate based on capital market multiples of publicly traded guideline companies. Suppose, however, that the publicly traded guideline companies are reporting straight-line depreciation for financial statement purposes while the subject company is reporting on an accelerated depreciation basis. If the difference is material, the analyst may want to adjust the closely held company's earnings to a straight-line basis (remembering to also adjust the related income taxes) before applying the publicly traded company multiple so that the earnings to be capitalized will be stated on a comparable basis. Usually a reasonable approximation suffices for this kind of adjustment.

Depletion

Depletion is the process of charging the cost of a natural resource to expense over the time during which it is extracted. It applies to such natural resources as metals and hydrocarbons in the ground and to timber stands. The basic concept of depletion accounting is simple: If a natural resource costs $1 million and 5 percent of it is removed in a year, the depletion expense charge is 5 percent × $1,000,000 = $50,000. A like amount is credited to the allowance for depletion account on the balance sheet, reducing the net carrying value of the natural resource asset. The IRS also accepts this method of calculating depletion and refers to it as *cost depletion*.

An unrelated method, *percentage depletion*, also appears in the Internal Revenue Code and is defined so as to allow an excess tax deduction in prescribed circumstances. Percentage depletion, as defined by the IRS, has no conceptual basis and is allowed

Exhibit 7–3

Alternative Depreciation Methods

Data used for the following examples:

Piece of equipment, purchased at beginning of Year 1
Original cost of equipment $50,000
Salvage value   0
Estimated useful life   5 years

Year	Computation			Annual Depreciation Charge	Balance Accumulated Depreciation	Book Value at Year-End
Straight-Line Method						
1	1/5 (20%)	×	$50,000	$10,000	$10,000	$40,000
2	20%	×	50,000	10,000	20,000	30,000
3	20%	×	50,000	10,000	30,000	20,000
4	20%	×	50,000	10,000	40,000	10,000
5	20%	×	50,000	10,000	50,000	0
200% Declining-Balance Method						
1	40%	×	$50,000 a	$20,000	$20,000	$30,000
2	40%	×	30,000	12,000	32,000	18,000
3	40%	×	18,000	7,200	39,200	10,800
4	40%	×	10,800	4,320	43,520	6,480
5	40%	×	6,480	2,592	46,112	3,888
Sum-of-the-Years'-Digits Method						
1	5/15	×	$50,000 b	$16,667	$16,667	$33,333
2	4/15	×	50,000	13,333	30,000	20,000
3	3/15	×	50,000	10,000	40,000	10,000
4	2/15	×	50,000	6,667	46,667	3,333
5	1/15	×	50,000	3,333	50,000	0
Modified Accelerated Cost Recovery System						
1	20.00%	×	$50,000 c	$10,000	$10,000	$40,000
2	32.00%	×	50,000	16,000	26,000	24,000
3	19.20%	×	50,000	9,600	35,600	14,400
4	11.52%	×	50,000	5,760	41,360	8,640
5	11.52%	×	50,000	5,760	47,120	2,880
6	5.76%	×	50,000	2,880	50,000	0

a.   Based on double the straight-line rate of 20 percent, multiplied by the undepreciated book value.

b.   Numerator is the remaining estimated useful life. Denominator is the sum of the years (5 + 4 + 3 + 2 + 1 = 15).

c.   Statutory percentages for MACRS five-year property used for federal income tax purposes.

Note: The above are examples of the more popular depreciation methods now in use. An introductory accounting text can be consulted for a thorough presentation of potential depreciation methods. The modified accelerated cost recovery system (MACRS) was enacted as part of the Economic Recovery Tax Act of 1986 and is used for federal tax purposes. One of the periodic tax guides can be consulted for a thorough presentation of the provisions of MACRS.

only for calculating a depletion deduction for tax purposes. The problems of applying depletion are basically ones of measurement. How much of the natural resource is there? What is included in the "cost" of a natural resource undergoing continuous development? If depletion is involved, the analyst should ask how it is measured and how thoroughly the company's depletion accounting practices conform to (or depart from) industry norms. Although depletion is relatively easy to define, it is very difficult to measure. Reasonable estimates can be subject to wide variations.

Treatment of Intangibles

It may be necessary to adjust the balance sheet and income statement for the diverse accounting treatments (or lack thereof) for intangible assets.

Leasehold Interests

If a company owns a leasehold at something other than fair market rent, the balance sheet may be adjusted by the analyst to show an asset or liability representing the present value of the difference between the leasehold (contract) rent and the current fair market rent. The formula for this calculation is as follows:

Formula 7–1

$$PV = \sum_{i=1}^{n} \frac{A}{(1+k)^i}$$

where:

PV	=	Present value
A	=	Amount of difference per period between leasehold rent and fair market rent
n	=	Number of periods remaining on the lease
k	=	Before-tax discount rate per period at which to capitalize the leasehold interest
i	=	ith period

For example, suppose a company has 25 months remaining on its lease at $5,000 per month and a new lease on comparable space today would cost $6,500 per month. (Alternatively, the company could sublet the space at $6,500 per month for the 25 months remaining on the lease.) The company's before tax cost of capital is 12 percent per annum. The present value of the company's leasehold interest is computed as follows:

Formula 7–2

$$PV = \sum_{i=1}^{25} \frac{\$6,500 - \$5,000}{\left(1+\dfrac{0.12}{12}\right)^i}$$

$$= \sum_{i=1}^{25} \frac{\$1,500}{(1+0.01)^i}$$

An upward adjustment of $33,035 could be made by the analyst to the asset side of the balance sheet to recognize the value of the leasehold interest.

Other Intangible Assets

Effective for acquisitions after August 10, 1993, all "Section 197 intangibles" must be amortized over 15 years. . . Much like MACRS, §197 forces the taxpayer to use the 15-year period even if the useful life is actually more or less than 15 years. Section 197 intangibles include a number of items such as goodwill, going-concern value, covenants not to compete, information bases such as customer or subscription lists, know-how, customer-based intangibles, governmental licenses and permits (e.g., liquor licenses, taxicab medallions, landing or takeoff rights, regulated airline routes, television or radio licenses), franchises, trademarks, and trade names.[4]

The following are some other examples of intangible assets:

1. Patents.
2. Copyrights.
3. Employment contracts.
4. "Intangible drilling costs" or similar natural resource development costs.
5. Natural resource exploration rights.

Financial accounting principles state that intangibles are to be carried on the books at cost and amortized over their useful economic lives. However, for federal income tax reporting purposes:

The costs of developing, maintaining, or restoring intangibles which are unidentifiable, have indeterminate lives, or are inherent in a continuing enterprise should be expensed as incurred. By contrast, such intangible assets which are purchased must be carried at cost and amortized over their useful lives and cannot be written down or written off at date of acquisition.[5]

Thus, a company may have spent a great amount of money internally developing valuable intangible assets without showing their value on the balance sheet, while another company may show comparable intangible assets on the balance sheet and be charging amortization expenses as deductions from earnings because it purchased the intangibles instead of developing them internally. If a company's intangible assets have true economic value, that value is likely to be reflected in increased earnings. In comparing companies with very different accounting practices, one way for an analyst to adjust for intangible items on the financial statements is to eliminate (1) all intangible assets from the balance sheets and (2) all amortization expense from the income statements.

Capitalization versus Expensing of Various Costs

Many cost items fall into a "gray" area, in which the decision to expense or to capitalize the expenditure is subjective. One such decision is the dividing line between maintenance expenditures, which are expenses, and capital improvements, which are capitalized. For example, many seasonal operations, such as resorts and food processing plants, employ skeletal crews year-round. Their compensation generally is

---

[4] James W. Pratt and William N. Kulsrud, eds., *Federal Taxation 1995* (New York: McGraw-Hill, 1994), pp. 9-35. Reprinted with permission.
[5] Ibid., p. 176.

expensed, even though they make improvements during the slow period that probably would be capitalized if outside contractors were hired for the same job. Companies that want to report higher earnings will capitalize items that fall into this gray area, and companies that want to minimize income taxes will elect to expense rather than capitalize whenever possible. In analyzing the quality of the company's earnings and balance sheets, the appraiser should watch for opportunities to choose between capitalization and expensing and should ask management about the company's practice of accounting for these items.

Timing of Recognition of Revenues and Expenses

Certain types of companies have considerable latitude in their choice of accounting practices in the timing of recognition of some of their revenues and expenses.

Contract Work

Contract work can be accounted for either on a completed-contract or percentage-of-completion basis. To better match revenue with expenses, the latter is conceptually preferable, but it can be implemented only under strict guidelines established by the AICPA.[6] Furthermore, the method is only as good as the estimates of the percentages completed. If the company being valued is in the contracting business, its accounting practices deserve careful scrutiny. This can be one of the most difficult areas for the outside analyst to evaluate critically. If it is a major issue in the valuation, it may necessitate considerable inquiry into the company's records as well as investigation of industry experience in comparable situations.

Installment Sales

When is a sale a sale? For years many companies booked huge profits by selling land on high-face-value contracts with 5 percent or 10 percent down and the balance over extended periods at a low floating interest rate. The down payments were not high enough to deter many buyers from defaulting, and even good contracts were worth nowhere near their face value because of the low cost of debt. In 1982, the FASB released *Statement of Financial Accounting Standards No. 66*[7] to help prevent such abuses, but there is still some latitude for differences in treatment from one company to another. If installment sales are a significant part of the company's business, the analyst should look into their accounting treatment.

Sales Involving Actual or Contingent Liabilities

Generally, sales involving actual future liabilities are those in which certain services are due to the customer in conjunction with the transaction. Such sales would include service contracts and subscriptions or products with future servicing warranted for some period. The unearned portion of the revenues is usually carried on the balance sheet

---

[6] *AICPA Statement of Position*, 81-1
[7] *FASB Statement of Financial Accounting Standards No. 66*, "Accounting for Sales of Real Estate."

as a liability item, commonly labeled deferred income, and then transferred to income as it is earned. Knowing when to recognize such income as revenues may require considerable judgment. Thus, the analyst should scrutinize the accounting treatment in companies that make sales involving future liabilities.

Sales involving contingent liabilities most commonly are those in which the customer has rebates, allowances, or certain rights to return products for a refund of revenue already recorded. If contingent liabilities exist, the analyst should assess the adequacy of their accounting treatment because they will affect the reported earnings and assets.

Prior-Period Adjustments

For a variety of reasons a company may find that its revenues or expenses, or both, were understated or overstated in certain prior accounting periods. The most common reasons are errors in accounting and underpayment or overpayment of income taxes. The company usually records such an adjustment in the accounting year in which it is discovered by charging the adjustment to the opening balance of retained earnings. Thus, the adjustment does not affect net income during the current period. In assessing the company's earnings history, the analyst should spread the effect of the adjustment back over the prior periods to which it applies. Sometimes the information needed for accurately allocating the adjustment to the appropriate prior periods is not available. Even if a rough estimate of the appropriate prior-period allocation is the best one can make, usually it is better, for analytical purposes, to spread the adjustment on the basis of such an estimate rather than leave it in the single period in which it was reported.

Accounting for Leases

The analyst may decide to make adjustments for analytical purposes to the company's accounting treatment for leases. According to the *Statement of Financial Accounting Standards No. 13* as amended and interpreted, leases that are of a financial nature (those that transfer essentially all of the benefits and risks incident to ownership of the property) must be capitalized as assets on the lessee's balance sheet. All other leases are accounted for as operating leases—that is, the lease payments are simply expensed as they are incurred. Since there is sometimes room for argument about which method of accounting is appropriate (and because unaudited closely held companies are less prone to strictly adhere to GAAP than are audited public companies), the analyst may want to examine leases.

Net Operating Loss Carryforwards

An item that frequently causes controversy in a business valuation is the value of a net operating loss carryforward. The amounts are presented in the footnotes to the financial statements rather than in the body of the balance sheet. This is because their value is contingent upon generating future profits against which to use them. The company's ability to generate such profits usually is questionable, since the company has generated net operating losses as part of its operating history.

As far as the income statement is concerned, net operating loss carryforwards properly are classed as extraordinary credits in the periods in which they are used. They should probably be adjusted out of the earnings base in those periods for analytical purposes. It may be reasonable to spread back the tax loss carryforward credits that actually were used to offset the losses in the periods in which the tax loss carryforwards were generated to normalize the taxes in the historical loss periods.

In terms of the valuation of net operating loss carryforwards, it is noteworthy that it may take years for the buyer of the subject business to take advantage of the use of the loss carryforwards. In this regard, the analyst should be aware that there are time limits to the period in which net operating losses may be carried forward. In addition, there are serious restrictions as to (1) the seller's ability to transfer net operating losses and (2) the buyer's ability to use transferred net operating losses subsequent to a corporate acquisition.

Treatment of Interests in Affiliates

If a company owns 50 percent to 100 percent of another company's stock, it generally prepares consolidated statements. However, in some situations the parent company properly accounts for the subsidiary by the equity method, defined below. If a company owns 20 percent to 50 percent of another company's stock, it may account for it by either the equity method or the cost method, depending on whether the parent exerts "significant influence"[8] over the company in which it holds the ownership interest. If a company owns less than 20 percent of another company's stock, it almost always accounts for it by the cost method, although accounting principles leave the door open for using the equity method if a significant degree of control can be demonstrated.

Consolidated statements treat the parent and subsidiaries as if they were all one company, with minority interests in subsidiaries, if any, shown as deductions on the financial statements. When accounting is done by the equity method, the parent's share of the subsidiary's earnings or losses (net of intercorporate eliminations, if any) is shown on its income statement, and the carrying value of the interest in the subsidiary is adjusted accordingly on its balance sheet. When subsidiaries are accounted for by the cost method, the parent shows only dividends received on its income statement and continues to carry the investment on its balance sheets at cost. This is true except if the subsidiary has a permanent impairment in its value, in which case accounting principles state that the investment should be written down. Frequently an analyst would consider an adjustment appropriate on the basis of the evaluation, even though the account would not necessarily recognize permanent impairment.

The greatest distortions in the reporting of a parent company's overall results, of course, arise under the cost method, which does not reflect earnings or losses of the subsidiary interest in the parent's financial statement. If a subsidiary's earnings and losses are significant, the analyst may wish to make appropriate adjustments. On the other hand, presenting consolidated statements or accounting using the equity method implies that a dollar of the subsidiary's earnings is worth a dollar to the parent, which is not necessarily true. There may be restrictions on distributions of the subsidiary's earnings due to loan agreements, regulatory authorities, or other reasons. Also, the analyst should ensure that the parent has allowed for any income taxes incident to potential transfer of funds from subsidiary to parent.

[8] *APB Opinion No. 18*, 1971.

Extraordinary or Nonrecurring Items

In analyzing a company's historical earnings as a guide to estimating the company's earnings base, the analyst should make every reasonable effort to distinguish between past earnings that represent ongoing earning power and those that do not. The analyst should adjust the income statements to eliminate the effects of past items that would tend to distort the company's current and future earning power. Implementation of this analysis and adjustments requires much judgment.

Ordinary versus Extraordinary Items

Accounting Principles Board Opinion No. 30, issued in 1973, is very restrictive as to what may be reported as an "extraordinary" gain or loss. *APB Opinion No. 30* states that an item must be *both* unusual in nature and infrequent in occurrence to be categorized as extraordinary. It defines these two requirements as follows:

> *Unusual nature*—the underlying event or transaction should possess a high degree of abnormality and be of a type clearly unrelated to, or only incidentally related to, the ordinary and typical activities of the entity, taking into account the environment in which the entity operates.
> *Infrequency of occurrence*—the underlying event or transaction should be of a type that would not reasonably be expected to recur in the foreseeable future, taking into account the environment in which the entity operates.[9]

If an item meets these definitions, it almost certainly cannot be considered representative of ongoing earning power. That does not necessarily mean it should be totally ignored, however, since an extraordinary item could indicate a risk that the company may face again in the future.

Other Nonrecurring Items

Since the use of the *extraordinary* designation is so restrictive, obviously many items do not meet the strict definition for accounting purposes but nevertheless should be regarded as nonrecurring for analytical purposes. Some examples of such items would be:

1. Gains or losses on the sale of assets, especially when the company clearly lacks a continuing supply of assets available for sale.
2. Gains or losses on disposition of a segment of the business.
3. Insurance proceeds from life insurance on a key person or from some type of property and casualty claim.
4. Proceeds from the settlement of lawsuits.
5. Effects of a strike or of an extended period in which critical raw materials are unavailable.
6. Effects of abnormal price fluctuations, especially those of a very short-term nature that are due to regulatory, industry, or other aberrations that are not likely to be repeated.
7. Write-offs and other expenses related to an acquisition.

---

[9] *APB Opinion No. 30*, 1973

It is possible, of course, for most of these unusual events to recur, resulting in a greater or smaller effect on the company's financial results. The analyst must carefully consider the likelihood of their recurrence and decide whether and how to adjust the financial statements to produce a best estimate of the company's continuing earning power.

Discontinued Operations

Apart from any one-time gain or loss associated with the disposal or discontinuation of an operating segment, the analyst must also determine how to treat the operating earnings or losses that were generated by that segment before its discontinuation. If the amounts can be distinguished from the results of the ongoing operations, the analyst may decide to adjust the earnings of the ongoing operations by removing the effect of the discontinued operations. The analyst must also consider the effect on the company's overall resources, however, because lost earnings from one source may be replaced by redeploying the resources in other efforts.

Operating versus Nonoperating Items

Depending on the method of valuation, it may be useful to distinguish between operating and nonoperating earnings even if the latter are recurring. The nonoperating item most commonly found on financial statements is income from investments. We suggest elsewhere in this book that it may be appropriate to value certain portions of a company, such as investments, with a market value approach and operating portions primarily on a capitalization of earnings approach. If the analyst values nonoperating assets separately, he or she should exclude any income generated or expenses incurred by the nonoperating assets from the earnings base capitalized in valuing the company's operations.

Management Compensation and Perquisites

In closely held companies, compensation and perquisites to owners and managers may be based on the owners' personal desires and the company's ability to pay rather than on the value of the services these individuals perform. How much to adjust the earnings base to reflect discrepancies between compensation paid and value of service performed depends on the valuation's purpose.

Owners of successful closely held businesses tend to take out what normally would be considered profits in the form of compensation and discretionary expenses. This practice may be an effort to avoid the double taxation that arises from paying a corporate income tax and then paying a personal income tax on what the closely held business pays to the owner in the form of dividends. It is not uncommon to find an owner/manager of a successful company with annual compensation greater than the amount an equivalent nonowner employee would earn as compensation.

If the above owner/manager wants to sell the business and retire, the difference between the compensation and the cost to replace the owner's services will become available as a part of pretax profits, and the company's earning power should be adjusted accordingly in establishing the business's selling price. If, on the other hand, the principal owner plans to continue working and maintain a similar compensation program for a long period after the valuation date, after establishing an ESOP for example, the analyst may not adjust the earnings base since the level of compensation can be expected to continue.

It is also common for management to be undercompensated because the company lacks the ability to pay. Usually the analyst should assume that the underpayment will be corrected when adequate resources are available and should make an appropriate upward adjustment to the management compensation expense in estimating the company's earnings base.

In general, adjustments for compensation, if appropriate, will be made when valuing controlling interests, because it will be within the power of the controlling interest's owner to change such compensation. Adjustments for compensation may or may not be appropriate when valuing noncontrolling interests, because the noncontrolling stockholder may receive no benefit from such compensation and lacks the power to change it.

Transactions Involving Company Insiders

The analyst should carefully scrutinize and evaluate material transactions involving owners or management. One of the most common situations is one in which the business leases premises from a person associated with the company. In such cases, the analyst usually should evaluate whether the lease amounts are equivalent to what the company would pay on an arm's-length basis. If not, the appropriate adjustment will depend on the situation, especially the length of time over which the present lease arrangement can be expected to continue, and the ability of the stockholder whose stock is being valued to change the arrangement.

Another common occurrence in closely held businesses is loans to or from stockholders or officers. Here the analyst should examine the borrower's ability and intent to repay. If there is little or no likelihood of collecting a receivable from an insider, it should be removed from the balance sheet for analytical purposes. If interest is being accrued and is unlikely to be collected, it should be adjusted out of the earnings used to evaluate the earning power. It is also common to find a demand note payable in the current liability section of the balance sheet, even though there is no intent to pay the note any time soon or even ever. Interest may or may not be paid on it. For analytical purposes, it may be more appropriate to treat such an item as if it were long-term debt or even subordinated capital of a nature more like equity than debt.

Contingent Assets and Liabilities

One of the most difficult categories of items to treat analytically for valuation purposes is contingencies. The very fact that an item is a contingency defies precise quantification. Nevertheless, the valuation analyst must try to discover contingent assets and liabilities, whether or not they are on the financial statements in some form, and deal with them within the scope of the available information.

The most common categories of contingent assets and liabilities are those that arise from existing or potential litigation. If the outcomes were known, there would be no need for litigation. These situations are so varied that it is virtually impossible to generalize about how to treat them for valuation purposes. The analyst should at least be alert to opportunities to investigate and evaluate contingencies. When necessary, the analyst should seek legal opinions with regard to the likely occurrence of certain contingencies.

Adjustments to Asset Valuations

Marketable Securities

It is generally agreed that marketable securities should be adjusted to fair market value for most asset valuation purposes. However, there is not necessarily total agreement that such an adjustment should be accompanied by a partially offsetting adjustment for the related income tax effects, implied by the unrealized gain or loss to which the adjustment gives rise. The argument that the tax consequence of recognizing the fair market value of marketable securities should be ignored for analytical purposes is generally based on whether a tax strategy is available that delays or avoids recognition of the capital gain or loss.

Other Assets

The appropriateness of adjusting various other categories of balance sheet assets for financial analysis purposes is controversial and depends on the purpose of the assignment. Revenue Ruling 59-60 states that for gift and estate tax purposes, values of assets of an investment nature (as opposed to operating assets) should be adjusted. The theory apparently is that such assets could be liquidated without impairing the company's operations. Sometimes, however, that will not be true, such as if the assets must be maintained as loan collateral or are necessary for maintaining certain financial ratios that lenders or regulatory agencies require. Other portions of this book, especially Chapter 14, Asset-Based Approach, discuss the appropriateness of adjusting different categories of asset values under various circumstances.

Computation of Earnings Per Share

Weighted Average Basis

Earnings per share should be computed on a weighted average basis, that is, the number of shares weighted by the length of time they have been outstanding. Let's say that a company had 100,000 shares outstanding at the beginning of the year and issued 30,000 more shares on May 1. The 100,000 shares would be outstanding for four months and the 130,000 shares for eight months, or two-thirds of the year. The weighted average number of shares outstanding for the year would be computed as follows:

$1/3 \times 100,000$	=	33,333
$2/3 \times 130,000$	=	86,667
Weighted average shares outstanding	=	120,000

If the earnings were $300,000, earnings per share would be $300,000 ÷ 120,000 = $2.50.

Basic versus Diluted Earnings

In general, basic earnings per share are computed by dividing the earnings available to common equity by the weighted average number of common shares outstanding, plus "dilutive common stock equivalents." The definition and computations can be very technical, and the reader who needs this detail should turn to a technical, accounting-oriented manual, such as Bernstein's.[10]

For analytical purposes, it seems that the earnings per share are best stated on a diluted basis, that is, showing the maximum potential dilution that could have resulted had all likely conversions and exercises of options and warrants been exercised. Naturally, the effect of any interest or dividends paid on the convertible issues would have to be added back to the earnings base. Any conversions that would be antidilutive in their effect should not be included.

Computation of Book Value Per Share

Book value per share is based on the number of shares outstanding at the end of the accounting period rather than the weighted average used in computing earnings per share. Also, book value normally is computed without considering possible dilutive effects of conversions, although the analyst may wish to make such a computation for analytical purposes. Thus, the computation of book value per share usually is a simple matter of dividing the total common equity by the number of shares outstanding. (Treasury stock—that is stock once issued and subsequently reacquired— is *not* included in the number of shares outstanding.) On most balance sheets, the common equity consists of the common stock account, any paid-in capital in excess of par or stated value, and the accumulated retained earnings or deficit. Of course, if there were any contingent payments on senior securities not shown on the balance sheet, such as preferred dividends in arrears, such amounts would have to be deducted from common equity in computing book value per share. Several investment services, including *S&P Corporation Records* (referenced elsewhere in this book), exclude intangibles in their computed book values per share.

An Example of the Effect of Alternative Accounting Methods

Exhibit 7–4 illustrates the impact on reported earnings of using different methods of accounting for a particular set of operations.

---

[10] Bernstein, *Financial Statement Analysis*, pp. 326–36.

Exhibit 7–4

Example of the Effect of the Variety of Accounting Principles on Reported Income

Rival Manufacturing Company
Consolidated Statement of Income
for Year Ended 19xx

| | Method A | Adjustments | | | Method B |
		Debit		Credit	
Net sales	$365,800,000				$365,800,000
Cost of goods sold	(276,976,200)		[1]	1,730,000	
			[2]	88,000	
			[3]	384,200	
			[4]	346,000	
			[5]	78,000	(274,350,000)
Gross profit	88,823,800				91,450,000
Selling, general, & administrative expenses	(51,926,000)		[6]	9,226,000	(42,700,000)
Operating profit	36,897,800				48,750,000
Other income (expense):					
Interest expenses	(3,085,000)	10,000			(3,095,000)
Net income—subsidiaries	1,538,000	78,000			1,460,000
Amortization of goodwill	(390,000)		[7]	220,000	(170,000)
Miscellaneous expenses	(269,000)			40,000	(229,000)
Total other income (expense)	(2,206,000)				(2,034,000)
Income before taxes	34,691,800				46,716,000
Taxes:					
Income taxes—deferred	(556,000)	294,000			(850,000)
Income taxes—current	(13,906,500)	4,733,000			(18,639,500)
Net income	$20,229,300				$27,226,500
Earnings per share	$6.98				$9.39

Explanations:

[1]	Inventories	Difference:	$1,730,000
	A uses last-in, first-out		
	B uses first-in, first-out		
[2]	Administrative costs	Difference:	$88,000
	A includes some administrative costs as period costs		
	B includes some administrative costs as inventory costs		
[3]	Depreciation	Difference:	$384,200
	A uses sum-of-the-years'-digits method		
	B uses straight-line method		
[4]	Useful lives of assets	Difference:	$346,000
	A uses conservative assumption—8 years (average)		
	B uses liberal assumption—14 years (average)		
[5]	Pension costs	Difference:	$78,000
	A uses realistic assumptions regarding rates of return on assets and future inflation		
	B uses less realistic assumptions regarding rates of return on assets and future inflation		
[6]	Executive compensation	Difference:	$840,000
	A compensates executives with cash bonuses		
	B compensates executives with stock options		
[7]	Goodwill from acquisition	Difference:	$220,000
	A amortizes over 10 years		
	B amortizes over 40 years		

SOURCE: Leopold A. Bernstein, *Financial Statement Analysis: Theory, Application and Interpretation,* 6th ed. (New York: McGraw-Hill, 1997), p. 309. Reprinted with permission.

Adjusting the Balance Sheet to Current Values

If it is appropriate to rely heavily on an asset approach in the valuation, the analyst may prepare a pro forma balance sheet with some or all of the line items adjusted to current values. Depending on the valuation criteria to be used, the adjustments may affect only nonoperating assets or may affect all assets (see Chapter 14, Asset-Based Approach). The treatment of the tax effect on impounded capital gains on the unrealized appreciation remains a matter of some controversy, as noted earlier. Consensus is building among financial analysts that the built-in capital gains tax should be recognized one way or another (at least with regard to the valuation of C corporations), either in the form of a balance sheet adjustment or some type of a discount.[11]

Summary

Adjustments to the financial statements require both analytical judgment and an understanding of accounting principles. This chapter has presented the categories of financial statement adjustments that are most frequently encountered in the course of the business valuation process. The chapter has presented both the accounting mechanics and also some discussion of the judgmental factors that the analyst should consider in analyzing the financial statements for appropriate adjustments. The analyst should be guided by common sense, experience, and an understanding of the company in determining what adjustments should be made to present the statements in the manner most appropriate for valuation purposes. In some cases, there may not be enough information to make certain adjustments, or the process may be too time-consuming relative to the results achieved. Which adjustments to make should be a matter of professional judgment as to their materiality in the context of the specific valuation objective.

Bibliography

Articles

Bergevin, Peter M., and Lisa K. Miller. "Financial Statement Analysis: The Research Process in a Business Library." *Journal of Business & Finance Librarianship,* (Volume 1, Number 4, 1993), pp. 49–59.

Brown, Terry S., "Assessing the Quality of Company Earnings." *CPA Litigation Service Counselor*, March 1999, pp. 8–9.

Clark, Lynne. "Demystifying Dilution." *CA Magazine,* May 1993, pp. 62–64.

Craig, Thomas, and Timothy Hoerr. "Recasting Income Statements in Valuations of Closely Held Businesses." *Business Valuation Review,* September 1993, pp. 134–39.

Davis, Harry Zvi, and Yoram C. Peles. "Measuring Equilibrating Forces of Financial Ratios." *Accounting Review,* October 1993, pp. 725–47.

---

[11] For example, see *Estate of Artemus D. Davis v. Commissioner*, 110 T.C. 35 (June 30, 1998).

Dennis, Michael C. "Understanding Cash Flow Statements." *Business Credit,* January 1994, pp. 40–42.

Evans, Frank C. "Analyzing a Financial Statement." *Management Review,* November 1993, pp. 52–53.

Fridson, Martin S. "Financial Statement Analysis for Perilous Times." *Corporate Cashflow,* October 1992, pp. 46–50.

Greenberg, Herb. "Ebitda: Never Trust Anything That You Can't Pronounce." *Fortune*, June 22, 1998, pp. 192, 194.

King. Alfred M. "GAAP Financial Statements: Turning Myth into Reality." *Business Credit,* November/December 1992, pp. 333–35.

Kristy, James E. "Conquering Financial Ratios: The Good, the Bad, and the Who Cares?" *Business Credit,* February 1994, pp. 14–19.

Lee, Cheng F., and Chunchi Wu. "Rational Expectations and Financial Ratio Smoothing." *Journal of Accounting, Auditing & Finance*, Spring 1994, pp. 283–306.

Miller, Barry E. "Mastering Cause-and-Effect Ratio Analysis." *Business Credit,* February 1993, pp. 24–27.

Posner, Bruce G. "Minding Your Ratios—Annual Statement Studies/Industry Norms & Key Business Ratios." *Inc.,* November 1993, p. 136.

Schuppe, Walter. "Cash Flow, Liquidity and Solvency—Getting behind the Numbers." *Secured Lender,* July/August 1993, pp. 42–45.

Speece, Fred H. "Assessing the Quality of Earnings and Management." In *Equity Research and Valuation Techniques.* Charlottesville, VA: Association of Investment Management & Research, 1998, pp. 16–19.

Taub, Maxwell J. "Valuing a Minority Interest: Whether to Adjust Elements of a Financial Statement over Which the Minority Shareholder Has No Control." *Business Valuation Review*, March 1998, pp. 7–9.

Turner, Mark A. "Accounting for Inventory in a Reorganization or Liquidation." *Management Accounting,* February 1993, pp. 29–32.

Reference Books

Bailey, Larry P. *1999 Miller GAAS Guide*. New York: Harcourt Brace Professional Publishing, 1998.

Bandler, James. *How to Use Financial Statements: A Guide to Understanding the Numbers.* New York: McGraw-Hill, 1994.

Bernstein, Leopold A. *Analysis of Financial Statements*, 5th ed. New York: McGraw-Hill, 1999.

_____. *Financial Statement Analysis: Theory, Application, and Interpretation*, 6th ed. New York: McGraw-Hill, 1997.

Fraser, Lyn M., and Aileen Ormiston. *Understanding Financial Statements*, 5th ed. Englewood Cliffs, NJ: Prentice-Hall, 1997.

Fridson, Martin S. *Financial Statement Analysis: A Practitioner's Guide*, 2nd ed. New York: John Wiley & Sons, 1996.

Stickney, Clyde P., and Paul R. Brown. *Financial Reporting and Statement Analysis: A Strategic Perspective*, 4th ed. New York: Dryden Press, 1998.

Szurovy, Geza, and S.B. Costales. *Guide to Understanding Financial Statements*, 2nd ed. New York: McGraw-Hill, 1993.

White, Gerald I., Ashwinpaul C. Sondi, and Dov Fried. *The Analysis and Use of Financial Statements*, 2nd ed. New York: John Wiley & Sons, 1997.

Williams, Jan R. *2000 Miller GAAP Guide*. New York: Harcourt Brace Professional Publishing, 1999.

Chapter 8

Financial Statement Ratio Analysis

Use and Interpretation of Ratio Analysis

When used properly, analysis of financial statement ratios can be a useful tool in a business valuation. In particular, it can help identify and quantify some of the company's strengths and weaknesses—both on an absolute basis and relative to other companies or industry norms. Accordingly, financial ratio analysis is an important process within the business valuation.

The implications gleaned from financial statement analysis may be considered in arriving at the value of the business or business interest in several ways. The point in the valuation process where the financial statements ratio analysis has the greatest impact is in the selection of various fundamental financial multiples (e.g., MVIC/EBIT multiple) to apply to the subject company. To the extent that the ratios indicate sustainable growth, the business should be worth a higher multiple than it would if they did not indicate growth. The higher the degree of risk factors the ratios reveal, the lower the business's worth should be relative to earnings, book value, and other fundamental financial variables.

One use of ratio analysis is to compare a company's own figures over time, a method sometimes called *trend analysis*. In this way, aspects of the business that demonstrate any trends of improvement or deterioration can be identified. It can also indicate levels of the different variables that have been normal within the period studied, as well as ranges that reveal high and low points for each variable over time.

Another way to use ratio analysis is to compare the subject company with other companies, either specific companies or industry averages. Patterns of strength in the subject company relative to guideline companies would tend to support a multiple in the high end of the industry range. Conversely, poor performance ratios relative to similar companies would suggest lower multiples for the subject company.

In comparing ratios from one period to another or from company to company, the analyst should understand the extent to which comparative ratios are based on comparable accounting policies. The previous chapter noted that different choices among accounting methods can result in wide variations in reported figures. When making a comparative analysis of a company's financial statements over time, the analyst should allow for any changes in accounting policies that occurred during the period. When comparing a company with others in its industry, the analyst should allow for any differences in accounting policies between the subject company and industry norms.

Another consideration is whether to calculate the ratios before or after any adjustments in the balance sheet or income statement, such as for nonrecurring items or for inventory, or pro forma adjustments. In many cases, these adjustments can significantly affect the magnitude of the company's ratios.

Two factors should guide the analyst in making this decision. First, if the ratios are to be compared with those of similar publicly traded companies, the analyst should make the same adjustments to the statements of both the subject company and the guideline companies. Second, if the computed ratios are to be compared with industry norms, the analyst should make only those adjustments that are likely to put the subject company on a basis comparable to other companies in the industry. In most cases, however, ratios calculated on adjusted statements will reveal a more accurate picture of the company's financial health.

The relative significance of the various ratios will differ in each valuation. Certain ratios have greater significance for value in particular industries. A ratio may be especially significant in some situations because it departs markedly from industry norms.

The analyst must apply judgment to each individual case in selecting and evaluating the significance of figures as they apply to the particular situation.

If the analyst does the ratio computations prior to making the field trip to interview company personnel, the ratio analysis will usually generate some questions about departures from industry norms. Of course, if the ratio work follows the field trip, the analyst can cover such questions in later telephone interviews.

This chapter discusses ratios that help evaluate the company's financial position. First, it looks at those that measure short-term liquidity, followed by the commonly used longer-term balance sheet leverage ratios. Then the chapter discusses a variety of operating ratios. Each ratio is illustrated with an example from our hypothetical company, Warm Chicken Company. A summary of Warm Chicken Company ratios appears in Exhibit 21–6 in Chapter 21, Sample Report. All exhibits referred to in this chapter may be found at the end of Chapter 21.

Common-Size Statements

A common first step in ratio analysis of financial statements is to prepare what are sometimes called *common-size statements*. On these statements, each line item is expressed as a percentage of the total. On the balance sheet, each line item is shown as a percentage of total assets. On the income statement, each item is expressed as a percentage of sales.

Exhibit 21–3 shows five years of balance sheets and Exhibit 21–4 shows five years of income statements for Warm Chicken Company presented on a common-size basis.

Short-Term Liquidity Measures

Generally, *liquidity ratios* demonstrate the company's ability to meet its current obligations. Liquidity ratios can help resolve one of the common controversies in business valuations: whether the company has any assets in excess of those required for its operating needs or, conversely, whether its assets fall short of its needs.

Current Ratio

The most commonly used short-term liquidity ratio is the *current ratio*, which is defined as current assets divided by current liabilities. Its greatest significance is as an indicator of the company's ability to pay its short-term liabilities on time. A single rule of thumb—that, for example, a satisfactory current ratio is 2.0:1—is not widely followed because of vastly different conditions typical in various industries, such as accounts receivable collection periods and inventory turnover periods. As with most ratios, the adequacy of the current ratio for a given company can be better gauged by comparison with industry norms than by comparison with any absolute standard.

Using figures from Exhibit 21–3, the current ratio for Warm Chicken Company for 1998 is calculated as follows:

Formula 8–1

$$\frac{\text{Current assets}}{\text{Current liabilities}} = \frac{\$149,692,000}{\$81,565,000} = 1.84\!:\!1$$

Quick (Acid-Test) Ratio

The next most commonly used ratio is the quick ratio, which some analysts refer to as the *acid-test ratio*. It is defined as the sum of cash and cash equivalents plus receivables (usually all current assets listed above inventory) divided by current liabilities. For most companies, the only other significant current asset is inventory—usually the slowest of the current assets to be converted to cash. One old rule of thumb is that a satisfactory quick ratio is 1.0:1; but, as with the current ratio, comparison with industry norms is more meaningful in most cases than comparison with an absolute standard.

Using figures from Exhibit 21–3, the quick or acid-test ratio for 1998 is calculated as follows:

Formula 8–2

$$\frac{\begin{matrix}\text{Cash} + \text{Cash equivalents}\\ + \text{Investments}\\ \text{(generally marketable securities)}\\ + \text{Receivables}\end{matrix}}{\text{Current liabilities}} = \frac{\begin{matrix}\$298,000 + \$14,000\\ + \$50,120,000\end{matrix}}{\$81,565,000} = 0.62\!:\!1$$

It is important to realize that both the current ratio and the quick ratio measure liquidity at a point in time and may not reflect a company's use of short-term credit to finance its short-term liquidity needs. To be most meaningful, the investments that qualify as current assets should be computed at market value.

Activity Ratios

Activity ratios generally measure how efficiently a company uses its assets.

Accounts Receivable Turnover

The *accounts receivable turnover* can be expressed either as the number of times per year the accounts turn over on average or as the average number of days required for collecting accounts. A slow accounts receivable turnover (long average collection period) not only puts a strain on a company's short-term liquidity, it can indicate excessive bad debt losses. On the other hand, a fast accounts receivable turnover (short average collection period) can indicate an overly stringent credit policy that may be limiting sales.

The accounts receivable turnover typically is computed by dividing net credit sales by average accounts receivable. If cash sales (as opposed to credit sales) are insignificant, or if the available figures do not distinguish between cash and credit sales, total sales may be used in the computation. Because of limitations on available data, average accounts receivable may have to be computed by averaging the receivables at the beginning and at the end of the period. The procedure of averaging receivables figures at the end of each quarter or each month gives a more accurate picture, especially if the business is subject to seasonal variations. In any case, if the ratio is for comparative purposes, the amount of data available for the guideline companies may limit the extent of fine-tuning that is possible in computing this ratio.

Using data from Exhibits 21–3 and 21–4, the accounts receivable turnover for Warm Chicken Company for 1998 is computed as follows:

Formula 8–3

$$\frac{\text{Fiscal 1998 Sales}}{\left(\begin{array}{c}\text{Accounts receivable FYE 1998 +} \\ \text{Accounts receivable FYE 1997}\end{array}\right) \div 2} = \frac{\$743,999,000}{\left(\begin{array}{c}\$50,120,000 \\ +\$46,910,000\end{array}\right) \div 2} = 15.34 \text{ times}$$

The accounts receivable turnover is divided into 365 days to express this variable in terms of average collection period. For Warm Chicken Company, we divide 365 days by the turnover of 15.34 times a year for an average collection period of 23.8 days. Incidentally, some analysts use 360 days instead of 365 days—one of many inconsistencies in valuation practice.

The sales-to-receivables ratio reported in *RMA Annual Statement Studies*[1] is net sales for the year divided by accounts and trade notes receivable *as of the end of the year*. Therefore, if the analyst wishes to compare the subject company with RMA statistics, the ratio for the subject company should be computed in the same manner as the RMA ratio. For Warm Chicken Company, this simplifies the computation to the following:

Formula 8–4

$$\frac{\text{Fiscal 1998 Sales}}{\text{Accounts receivable FYE 1998}} = \frac{743,999,000}{50,120,000} = 14.84 \text{ times}$$

This level of accounts receivable turnover is equivalent to $(365 \div 14.84) = 24.6$ average days collection period.

Inventory Turnover

The *inventory turnover ratio* typically is computed by dividing the cost of goods sold by the average inventory. As is true of accounts receivable turnover, a slow inventory turnover (long average holding period) not only puts a strain on the company's liquidity but can indicate obsolete or otherwise undesirable inventory. On the other hand, a fast inventory turnover may indicate that sales are being lost due to insufficient inventory on hand.

Also, as with accounts receivable turnover, the ratio is more meaningful if it can be computed using quarterly or monthly inventory data, especially for companies with seasonal aspects in their operation; however, data limitations more often than not make these computations impractical.

Using data from Exhibits 21–3 and 21–4, the inventory turnover for Warm Chicken Company for 1998 is computed as follows:

---

[1] *RMA Annual Statement Studie*s (Philadelphia: Robert Morris Associates, 1999), published annually.

Formula 8–5

$$\frac{\text{Fiscal 1998 Cost of goods sold}}{\left(\begin{array}{c}\text{Inventory FYE 1998}\\+\text{ Inventory FYE 1997}\end{array}\right)\div 2} = \frac{\$672,290,000}{\left(\begin{array}{c}\$92,805,000\\+\$111,437,000\end{array}\right)\div 2} = 6.58 \text{ times}$$

Like accounts receivable turnover, inventory turnover can be expressed as the average number of days in inventory. For Warm Chicken Company, average days in inventory is calculated by dividing 365 days by an inventory turnover of 6.58 times per year for an average of 55.5 days needed for selling inventory.

RMA Annual Statement Studies reports inventory turnover in the same manner as accounts receivable turnover—dividing cost of sales *by ending inventory*. For making comparisons with RMA data, this ratio should be computed by RMA's formula. For Warm Chicken Company, this ratio is computed as follows:

Formula 8–6

$$\frac{\text{Fiscal 1998 Cost of goods sold}}{\text{Inventory FYE 1998}} = \frac{\$672,290,000}{\$92,805,000} = 7.24 \text{ times}$$

From an inventory turnover of 7.24 times per year, we calculate an average of 50.4 days in inventory ($365 \div 7.24 = 50.4$).

Sales to Net Working Capital

Net working capital is defined as current assets minus current liabilities. If a company's current ratio, accounts receivable collection period, and inventory turnover remain constant as its sales go up, the working capital must rise, because the company will have to carry more receivables and inventory to support the increased sales level. A simple way to compute the sales-to-net-working-capital ratio is to divide sales for the fiscal year just ended by net working capital at the fiscal year-end. This ratio can be useful in comparing the company's own history with those of other companies in the industry.

Using the figures from Exhibits 21–3 and 21–4, the sales-to-net-working-capital ratio for Warm Chicken Company is calculated as follows:

Formula 8–7

$$\frac{\text{Sales}}{\begin{array}{c}\text{Current assets}\\-\text{ Current liabilities}\end{array}} = \frac{\$743,999,000}{\begin{array}{c}\$149,692,000\\-\$81,565,000\end{array}} = 10.9:1$$

A more reasonable way to compute the ratio would be to use average net working capital rather than ending net working capital as the denominator. Again, using the figures from Exhibits 21–3 and 21–4, sales to average net working capital is calculated as follows:

Formula 8–8

$$\frac{\text{Fiscal 1998 Sales}}{\left(\begin{array}{c}\text{Working capital FYE 1998}\\+\text{ Working capital FYE 1997}\end{array}\right)\div 2} = \frac{\$743,999,000}{\left[\begin{array}{c}\left(\$149,692,000 - \$81,565,000\right)\\+\$166,919,000 - \$93,398,000\end{array}\right]\div 2} = 10.5$$

A high ratio of sales to net working capital results from a favorable turnover of accounts receivable and inventory and indicates efficient use of current assets. However, a high sales-to-net-working-capital ratio also can indicate risk arising from possibly inadequate short-term liquidity. The economy and most industries are subject to some degree of cyclicality in economic activity and liquidity that do not necessarily run exactly in tandem. In order to assess the company's ability to meet peak needs, the analyst should consider the highest reasonable level of sales that might be anticipated, couple it with the largest accounts receivable and longest inventory turnover periods that might occur, and assess the adequacy of the working capital under that scenario.

Sales to Fixed Assets and Total Assets

Sales-to-fixed-assets and *sales-to-total-assets ratios*, sometimes called *asset utilization ratios*, measure how efficiently a company's assets are generating sales. They are calculated by dividing sales by either ending assets levels or by an average of the asset levels over the last two years. The results indicate the number of dollars of sales being generated by a dollar of assets. When observed over time, these ratios can indicate changing levels of asset productivity and reveal possible nonoperating assets relative to comparative companies.

Using the figures in Exhibits 21–3 and 21–4, the simplest way to calculate these ratios is as follows:

Formula 8–9

$$\frac{\text{Sales}}{\text{Fixed assets}} = \frac{\$743,999,000}{\$99,984,000} = 7.4{:}1$$

$$\frac{\text{Sales}}{\text{Total assets}} = \frac{\$743,999,000}{\$295,902,000} = 2.5{:}1$$

Another approach would be to use the average asset levels over the last two years. In this instance, monthly or quarterly figures are less important, since one would not expect to see seasonality in total assets or fixed assets levels in the same manner as current assets. Using the figures in Exhibits 21–3 and 23–4, the calculation of these ratios using this method is as follows:

Formula 8–10

$$\frac{\text{Fiscal 1998 Sales}}{\left(\begin{array}{l}\text{Fixed assets FYE 1998}\\ + \text{Fixed assets FYE 1997}\end{array}\right) \div 2} = \frac{\$743,999,000}{\left(\begin{array}{l}\$99,984,000\\ +\$109,016,000\end{array}\right) \div 2} = 7.1{:}1$$

$$\frac{\text{Fiscal 1998 Sales}}{\left(\begin{array}{l}\text{Total assets FYE 1998}\\ + \text{Total assets FYE 1997}\end{array}\right) \div 2} = \frac{\$743,999,000}{\left(\begin{array}{l}+\$295,902,000\\ +\$321,154,000\end{array}\right) \div 2} = 2.4{:}1$$

These ratios are subject to misinterpretation. The age and, thus, depreciated book value of the assets used in these calculations should be considered, particularly when comparing them to those of other, similar companies.

Risk Analysis

At this point it is appropriate to briefly investigate risk analysis, since it is closely related to the leverage ratios and coverage ratios discussed in the following sections. The purpose of risk analysis is to ascertain the uncertainty of the income flows to the company's various capital suppliers. Generally, there are two classes of capital suppliers—those that provide debt capital and receive a fixed return and those that provide equity capital and receive a variable return but can participate in the company's growth through increased future returns. The higher the risk to any category of capital suppliers to the company, the higher the cost of that class of capital.

The capital asset pricing model suggests using the factor called *beta* to measure risk. However, because of a lack of regularly quoted market prices for their stocks, betas for most closely held companies cannot be measured directly. One can make a good case for the fact that the nonsystematic portions of risk (those not reflected in beta) are more important for closely held companies than for publicly traded companies. Therefore, the risk analysis portion of financial statement analysis is a very important part of the valuation process.

It is possible to examine the uncertainty of income to the various suppliers of capital by investigating the uncertainty of income to the company. The greater the uncertainty of income to the company, the greater the uncertainty of income to the investor in the company. There are two general classes of risk of the company: business risk and financial risk.

Business Risk

Business risk is the uncertainty of income due largely to two factors: (1) fluctuation in sales and (2) the level of the company's fixed operating costs, which is a function of how the company operates. There are basically two ways to measure a company's business risk.

The first—and simpler—way is to measure the coefficient of variation of earnings, which is equal to the standard deviation of net income divided by the mean of net income:

Formula 8–11

$$\text{Business risk} = \frac{\text{Standard deviation of net income}}{\text{Mean of net income}}$$

For example, using the figures from Exhibit 21–4, the standard deviation of net income is $7,669,800 and the mean of net income is $5,178,600. (Note that all numbers are before effect of the accounting change.) Substituting into the above equation produces a measure of business risk:

Formula 8–12

$$\text{Business risk} = \frac{\$7,669,800}{\$5,178,600} = 1.48$$

For many companies, sales volatility is the most important determinant of the fluctuation of net income measured by the standard deviation. Although companies may have some control over annual sales volume, sales volatility is, to a considerable extent, a function of the economy's overall health and consumers' willingness to spend their disposable income.

The second method used to measure business risk is the calculation of the degree of operating leverage. *Operating leverage* reflects both the variability of sales and the level of the company's fixed operating costs. These fixed operating costs are a function of the manner in which the company produces its product. The operating earnings of companies with high variable operating costs fluctuate at about the same rate as sales do, whereas those of companies whose production processes entail high fixed operating costs fluctuate more widely than sales.

Operating leverage is measured by the percentage change in operating earnings relative to the percentage change in sales during any given period:

Formula 8–13

$$\text{Degree of operating leverage} = \frac{\text{Percentage change in operating earnings}}{\text{Percentage change in sales}}$$

Financial Risk

The second type of risk to investigate is financial risk. Whereas business risk, as measured by operating leverage, reflects the incidence of fixed operating costs and their effect on the income flows to capital suppliers, *financial risk* reflects the incidence of fixed financial costs, or interest, and their effect on the fluctuation of income flows to investors. A company's financial risk occurs in addition to business risk. If there were only business risk, the fluctuation of earnings available to stockholders would be the same as that of operating earnings. However, when fixed financial costs—that is, the interest associated with the use of financial leverage—are introduced, the fluctuation of earnings available to shareholders is greater than that of operating earnings. When the company uses debt to finance some of its activities, the payments to the holders of this debt come before any payments to shareholders. During good times, there is plenty left over for the shareholders. In bad times, however, the company's operating earnings are used to pay the interest on the debt and little may be left over for the shareholders, increasing the fluctuation in their earnings.

Financial risk is measured in two ways: (1) through calculating the degree of financial leverage and (2) through calculating various leverage ratios. The degree of financial leverage is similar to the degree of operating leverage in that both measure relative volatility. Financial leverage measures the fluctuation of earnings available to the common shareholders relative to the fluctuation of operating earnings (measured as earnings before interest and taxes (EBIT)):

Formula 8–14

$$\text{Degree of financial leverage} = \frac{\text{Percentage change in income to common stockholders}}{\text{Percentage change in EBIT}}$$

For example, using the figures from Exhibit 21–4, the degree of financial leverage for Warm Chicken Company for 1998 is:

Formula 8–15

$$\text{Degree of financial leverage } = \frac{\dfrac{(\$2,883,000 - \$1,864,000)}{\div \$1,864,000}}{\dfrac{(\$10,883,000 - \$11,073,000)}{\div \$11,073,000}} = -31.86$$

This result indicates that a 1.0 percent change in operating income is accompanied by approximately a negative 31.9 percent change in income available to common shareholders.

The higher the degree of financial leverage, the more risk exists for the company's equity investors, because there is a greater possibility that they will receive lower cash flows both today and in the future.

The balance sheet leverage ratios discussed in the next section are also used to measure financial leverage. They are used in conjunction with the degree of financial leverage to indicate the company's overall financial riskiness.

Balance Sheet Leverage Ratios

The general purpose of capital structure or *balance sheet leverage ratios* is to aid in making some quantifiable assessments of the long-term solvency of the business and its ability to deal with financial problems and opportunities as they arise. As with most ratios, such analysis generally is most meaningful when compared with other companies in the same industry. Comparisons within the same company over time also can be useful.

There are numerous variations of balance sheet leverage ratios, but the following are the ones most frequently used.

Total Debt to Total Assets

Of the various balance sheet ratios designed to measure the long-term adequacy of the company's capital structure, the *total-debt-to-total-assets ratio* probably is the most popular. It is defined as total debt divided by total assets and measures the total amount of the company's funding provided by all categories of creditors as a percentage of the company's total assets.

Using the figures from Exhibit 21–3, the total-debt-to-total-assets ratio for Warm Chicken Company at the fiscal year-end of 1998 is calculated as follows:

Formula 8–16

$$\frac{\text{Total liabilities}}{\text{Total assets}} = \frac{\$168,957,000}{\$295,902,000} = 0.57$$

Equity to Total Assets

The *equity-to-total-assets ratio*, or simply *equity ratio*, is computed by dividing the company's total equity by its total assets. It is equal to 1 minus the total-debt-to-

total-assets ratio. Since these two ratios are merely alternative ways of stating the same thing, most analysts would include one or the other, but not both, in the presentation.

Using figures from Exhibit 21–3, the equity-to-total-assets ratio for Warm Chicken Company at the fiscal year-end of 1998 is calculated as follows:

Formula 8–17

$$\frac{\text{Total equity}}{\text{Total assets}} = \frac{\$126,945,000}{\$295,902,000} = 0.43$$

Long-Term Debt to Total Capital

Unfortunately, there is considerable ambiguity in the terminology of financial statement analysis, especially in ratio definitions. By debt ratio, some analysts mean "debt divided by total assets," the ratio just discussed, but others mean "long-term debt divided by total capital." Therefore, to avoid misinterpretation, it seems best to avoid the term debt ratio entirely and use the more specific term *long-term-debt-to-total-capital ratio*. Total capital is sometimes defined as total assets minus current liabilities (with the current liabilities balance excluding the current portion of long-term debt). However, many analysts include all interest-bearing debt as part of total capital.

Using figures from Exhibit 21–3, and using the first definition above, the long-term-debt-to-total-capital ratio for Warm Chicken Company is computed as follows:

Formula 8–18

$$\frac{\text{Long - term debt}}{\begin{array}{c}\text{Total assets}\\ -\text{ Current liabilities}^*\end{array}} = \frac{\$61,231,000}{\$295,902,000 - \$78,812,000} = 0.28$$

* excluding the current portion of long-term debt

The analyst should check to ensure that any ratios used for comparisons actually are computed by the same definitions, or the comparisons may be misleading. For example, some analysts include deferred taxes in the denominator as part of long-term capital, and others do not.

Equity to Total Capital

The *equity-to-total-capital ratio* is simply 1 minus the long-term-debt-to-total-capital ratio, so there usually is no need to compute both.

Using the figures from Exhibit 21–3, the equity-to-total-capital ratio for Warm Chicken Company at the fiscal year-end of 1998 is calculated as follows:

Formula 8–19

$$\frac{\text{Total equity}}{\text{Long - term debt + equity}} = \frac{\$126,945,000}{\$61,231,000 + \$126,945,000} = 0.67$$

Fixed Assets to Equity

One can get another view of the company's leverage by looking at the proportion of the fixed assets that are financed by equity as opposed to long-term debt. A larger value for the *fixed-assets-to-equity ratio* indicates that much of the company's productive capacity is being financed by borrowed funds rather than owners' funds.

Using the figures from Exhibit 21–3, the fixed-assets-to-equity ratio for Warm Chicken Company in 1998 is calculated as follows:

Formula 8–20

$$\frac{\text{Net fixed assets}}{\text{Total equity}} = \frac{\$99,984,000}{\$126,945,000} = 0.79$$

Debt to Equity

Sometimes the company's debt is expressed as a ratio to equity rather than to total assets. Again, some analysts prefer to focus on total debt and others just on long-term debt. *RMA Annual Statement Studies* uses total debt and only *tangible equity*. In other words, the RMA *debt-to-equity ratio* is computed as follows:

Formula 8–21

$$\frac{\text{Total liabilities}}{\text{Total equity} - \text{Intangible assets}}$$

This ratio is also sometimes expressed in reverse, that is, equity to total debt or equity to long-term debt.

Income Statement Coverage Ratios

In general, *income statement coverage ratios* are designed to measure the margin by which certain of the company's obligations are being met.

Times Interest Earned

The most popular income statement coverage ratio is times interest earned (referred to as the *interest coverage ratio*). It is designed to measure the company's ability to meet interest payments. The *times-interest-earned ratio* is defined as earnings before interest and taxes (EBIT) divided by interest expense.

Using figures from Exhibit 21–4, the times-interest-earned ratio for Warm Chicken Company for 1998 is:

Formula 8–22

$$\frac{\text{Earnings before interest and taxes}}{\text{Interest expense}} = \frac{\$4,804,000 + \$6,079,000}{\$6,079,000} = 1.8 \text{ times}$$

Note that the Warm Chicken Company statements are presented in the conventional manner, showing interest expense as a separate deduction after operating income. Since some closely held companies do not present the statements in this way, the EBIT figure may have to be computed rather than taken directly from a line item on the income statement.

Another way to look at interest coverage is to calculate the ratio based on earnings before depreciation, interest, and taxes (EBDIT) rather than EBIT. EBDIT is basically pretax, pre-interest cash flow that is available to pay the interest expense.

Using figures from Exhibit 21–4, the EBDIT interest coverage ratio for Warm Chicken Company for 1998 is computed as follows:

Formula 8–23

$$\frac{\text{Earnings before depreciation, interest, and taxes}}{\text{Interest expense}} = \frac{\$4,804,000 + \$20,949,000 + \$6,079,000}{\$6,079,000} = 5.2 \text{ times}$$

Coverage of Fixed Charges

The *coverage of fixed charges* is a more inclusive ratio than the times-interest-earned ratio in that it includes coverage of items in addition to interest. It is defined as the sum of earnings before interest and taxes and fixed charges divided by fixed charges. This definition leaves open an almost unlimited spectrum of possibilities for determining which items of fixed charges to include. The most common items are lease payments and required installments of principal payments toward debt retirement.

In the Warm Chicken Company example, the information shown in Exhibits 21–3 and 21–4 is inadequate for computing this ratio. Typically, the analyst must request some schedules or ask questions beyond the normal statement presentations in order to acquire the information necessary for computing this ratio. Audited financial statements normally contain such information in the footnotes.

Let's assume that the current portion of long-term debt (in this example, notes and mortgage payable, as shown in the current liability section of the balance sheet in Exhibit 21–3) is an annual required reduction of debt principal and that the operating expenses shown in Exhibit 21–4 include $4,000,000 per year lease payments on the premises the company occupies. The coverage of fixed charges for Warm Chicken Company, then, can be computed as:

Formula 8–24

$$\frac{\text{Earnings before interest and taxes + Lease payments}}{\text{Interest + Current portion of long-term debt + Lease payments}}$$

or

$$\frac{\$4,804,000 + \$6,079,000 + \$4,000,000}{\$6,079,000 + \$2,753,000 + \$4,000,000} = 1.16 \text{ times}$$

Income Statement Profitability Ratios

The four most commonly used measures of operating performance are *gross profit from sales, operating profit from sales*, pretax income from sales, and *net profit from sales*. Since all are percentages of sales, they may be read directly from the common-size income statements shown in Exhibit 21–4.

Return on Investment Ratios

Analysts will argue until doomsday whether return on equity, return on investment, or return on assets is the most meaningful measure of investment return. Proponents of return on equity say that the return on stockholder investment is what counts, and most adhere to this argument. Return on investment recognizes both the shareholders and the debtholders and can be quite important if the company is contemplating a change in the capital structure. However, proponents of return on assets say that management should be measured by the return on total assets utilized, without regard for the company's capital structure, which can have a considerable bearing on return on equity if return on assets is held constant. Each measure is useful for its own purpose.

Return on Equity

Return on equity usually means return on common equity capital. If a company has preferred stock outstanding, the analyst might consider computing return on total equity and return on common equity, since both can be useful measures. If comparing one or more ratios of return on equity for other companies with preferred stock outstanding, the analyst should ensure that the ratios are being computed on the same basis for the subject company as for the guideline companies.

Unless otherwise specified, return on equity means *after* taxes. Once in a while, someone—perhaps a broker trying to sell a business—quotes return on equity computed on a pretax basis. This definition can be very misleading, since *income taxes are a very real cost*, and the investor's return is what remains after corporate taxes. In fact, if the computation is being made for an S corporation, a partnership, or a sole proprietorship, many analysts recommend that the taxes the company would pay if it were a regular corporation be deducted from the net income before making the calculations. Sometimes there are legitimate reasons for comparing companies' returns on equity on a pretax basis, but when doing so it should be clearly specified—and recognized by the parties using the data—that it is a departure from the conventional meaning and computation of return on equity. Perhaps the best way to specify this is to use the expression *pretax return on equity* when that is what in fact is being shown.

One other issue to be resolved in the return on equity analysis is whether the selected equity base is the one at the beginning of the period, the end of the period, or the average for the period. There is consensus among analysts that the average equity provides the basis for the most meaningful analysis. However, an emerging group believe that beginning equity is the most important measure, since that is the equity base on which the earnings are generated. Still, the most commonly used method is to divide the earnings for the year by the average of the beginning and ending equity. If adequate information is available, return on equity can be further fine-tuned by averaging quarterly or monthly equity figures.

Since return on equity is a percentage, the result should be the same whether the computations are made on a total-company basis or on a per-share basis, at least if there is no dilution. If a weighted average number of shares has been used in the per-share earnings computation, the calculation will work out if the average equity base is weighted in the same manner.

Using the data from Exhibits 21–3 and 21–4, the return on equity for Warm Chicken Company for 1998 is calculated as follows:

Formula 8–25

$$\frac{\text{Net income}}{\begin{array}{c}\text{Average common}\\\text{stockholders' equity}\end{array}} = \frac{\$2,883,000}{\left(\begin{array}{c}\$126,945,000\\+\$124,291,000\end{array}\right) \div 2} = 2.3\%$$

Using beginning equity in this case yields the same percentage, as follows:

Formula 8–26

$$\frac{\text{Net income for 1998}}{\text{Stockholders' equity for 1997}} = \frac{\$2,883,000}{\$124,291,000} = 2.3\%$$

On a per-share basis with 1,577,420 shares outstanding for Warm Chicken Company, the computation is as follows:

Formula 8–27

$$\frac{\text{Earnings per share}}{\text{Average book value per share}} = \frac{\$1.83}{(\$80.48 + \$78.79) \div 2} = 2.3\%$$

Another way to look at the above ratio (i.e., net income divided by equity)—and perhaps to understand and appreciate it more fully—is in terms of the components that make up return on equity. These components of return on equity are:

Formula 8–28

$$\text{ROE} = \text{Profitability} \times \text{Turnover} \times \text{Leverage}$$

Stated more completely:

$$\frac{\text{Net income}}{\text{Equity}} = \frac{\text{Net income}}{\text{Sales}} \times \frac{\text{Sales}}{\text{Assets}} \times \frac{\text{Assets}}{\text{Equity}}$$

The formula above is commonly referred to as the *DuPont formula*, since the DuPont Company was widely known to use that formula as an integral part of its financial planning and control.

Return on Investment

The computations for *return on investment*, sometimes called *return on total capital*, are similar to those for return on equity. One key difference is that interest should be added back to net income to reflect the return to *both* equity *and* debt. Whether interest should be adjusted for taxes depends on the information to be conveyed in the ratio presentation. The analyst should adjust interest for income taxes by multiplying interest by 1 minus the tax rate—a product that is the equivalent of computing the ratio on an invested capital basis, as if all of the investment was in the form of equity. If, on the other hand, there is no adjustment for income taxes, the ratio will reflect the return under the company's existing capital structure. Again, the issue of average investment versus beginning investment should be recognized. In addition, the debt portion of the investment figure in the denominator could be long-term debt plus interest-bearing short-term debt, since the interest expense in the numerator is *total* interest expense.

Looking at it all four ways and using figures from Exhibits 21–3 and 21–4, the computation of return on investment for Warm Chicken Company for 1998 is as follows:

Formula 8–29

$$\frac{\text{Net income} + \text{Interest} (1 - \text{Tax rate})}{\left[\left(\begin{array}{c}\text{Beginning stockholders' equity} \\ + \text{Long-term debt}\end{array}\right) + \left(\begin{array}{c}\text{Ending stockholders' equity} \\ + \text{Long-term debt}\end{array}\right)\right] \div 2}$$

$$\frac{\$2{,}883{,}000 + \$6{,}079{,}000(1 - 0.40)}{\left[(\$124{,}291{,}000 + \$75{,}797{,}000) + (\$126{,}945{,}000 + \$61{,}231{,}000) \div 2\right]} = 3.4\%$$

or

$$\frac{\text{Net income} + \text{Interest}}{\left[\left(\begin{array}{c}\text{Beginning stockholders' equity} \\ + \text{Long-term debt}\end{array}\right) + \left(\begin{array}{c}\text{Ending stockholders' equity} \\ + \text{Long-term debt}\end{array}\right)\right] \div 2}$$

$$\frac{\$2{,}883{,}000 + \$6{,}079{,}000}{\left[(\$124{,}291{,}000 + \$75{,}797{,}000) + (\$126{,}945{,}000 + \$61{,}231{,}000)\right] \div 2} = 4.6\%$$

Based on beginning investment, return on investment becomes:

Formula 8–30

$$\frac{\begin{array}{c}\text{Net income} \\ + \text{Interest} (1 - \text{Tax rate})\end{array}}{\begin{array}{c}\text{Beginning stockholders' equity} \\ + \text{Long-term debt}\end{array}} = \frac{\$2{,}883{,}000 + \$6{,}079{,}000(1 - 0.40)}{\$124{,}291{,}000 + \$75{,}797{,}000} = 3.3\%$$

or

$$\frac{\text{Net income} + \text{Interest}}{\begin{array}{c}\text{Beginning stockholders' equity} \\ + \text{Long-term debt}\end{array}} = \frac{\$2{,}883{,}000 + \$6{,}079{,}000}{\$124{,}291{,}000 + \$75{,}797{,}000} = 4.5\%$$

Conceptually, the amount of interest expense that should be added back is only the interest expense that relates to the company's long-term debt, since that is the figure in the denominator. However, in practice, while one may be able to get this information for the subject company, the data for the guideline companies will rarely be available. Another alternative is to use total interest expense in the numerator and total interest-bearing debt in the denominator. The problem with this, however, is that often the fiscal year-end amount of short-term interest-bearing debt does not relate to the amount of interest expense that was paid during the year on the average amount of short-term interest-bearing debt utilized. To correct for this, one would have to find out what the average amount of short-term interest-bearing debt was over the course of the year and that depth of analysis may not be justified.

Due to these complexities, for practical purposes it is acceptable to use the ratio as we have defined it. However, the analyst is well advised to research both the subject and guideline companies' use of short-term debt to determine whether to adjust this ratio to include all interest-bearing debt.

The analyst should be aware of two other potential problems with the above formula. First, the comparisons among rates of return may not be meaningful when comparing companies with dissimilar capital structures. Second, the rates of return can be misleading in the cases of many (especially smaller) companies that show on their balance sheet short-term liabilities that actually are being used as long-term financing.

Return on Total Assets

The computations for *return on total assets* are similar to those for return on investment, with the same issues of income tax adjustments and beginning or average assets. A realistic analysis of return on total assets should not be influenced by how the company chooses to use debt in its capital structure.

Again, using figures from Exhibits 21–3 and 21–4, the computation of return on assets for Warm Chicken Company for 1998 is as follows:

Formula 8–31

$$\frac{\text{Net income} + \text{Interest}\,(1 - \text{Tax rate})}{\left(\begin{array}{l}\text{Beginning total assets} \\ + \text{Ending total assets}\end{array}\right) \div 2} = \frac{\$2{,}883{,}000 + \$6{,}079{,}000(1 - 0.40)}{\left(\begin{array}{l}\$321{,}154{,}000 \\ + \$295{,}902{,}000\end{array}\right) \div 2} = 2.1\%$$

or

$$\frac{\text{Net income} + \text{Interest}}{\left(\begin{array}{l}\text{Beginning total assets} \\ + \text{Ending total assets}\end{array}\right) \div 2} = \frac{\$2{,}883{,}000 + \$6{,}079{,}000}{\left(\begin{array}{l}\$321{,}154{,}000 \\ + \$295{,}902{,}000\end{array}\right) \div 2} = 2.9\%$$

Based on beginning assets, the ratio becomes:

Formula 8–32

$$\frac{\text{Net income} + \text{Interest}\,(1 - \text{Tax rate})}{\text{Beginning total assets}} = \frac{\$2{,}883{,}000 + \$6{,}079{,}000(1 - 0.40)}{\$321{,}154{,}000} = 2.0\%$$

or

$$\frac{\text{Net income} + \text{Interest}}{\text{Beginning total assets}} = \frac{\$2{,}883{,}000 + \$6{,}079{,}000}{\$321{,}154{,}000} = 2.8\%$$

Use care when comparing these ratios to published ratios to determine whether the bases are an average or beginning or year-end figures. The return-on-investment ratios shown in Exhibit 21–6 are calculated using both average and ending equity and both average and ending total assets.

Asset Utilization Ratios

Asset utilization ratios indicate how efficiently the company is employing its assets in its operations. These are almost always based on average asset levels, unless a study used for industry comparative ratio analysis calculates them using year-ending asset figures. This series of ratios relates sales to each of several assets or asset groups. Ratios sometimes computed include sales to cash, to accounts receivable, to inventories, to working capital, to fixed assets, to other assets, and to total assets (discussed under the "Activity Ratios" section).

Summary

Comparative ratio analysis helps identify and quantify some of the company's strengths and weaknesses, both on an absolute basis and relative to guideline companies or industry norms.

The analyst should allow for changes in the subject company's accounting policies during the period under analysis and differences in accounting policies between the subject company and the guideline companies or industry norms. The analyst should also be aware of off–balance sheet financing that may not be reflected in the ratio analysis.

Analysis of the various ratios will help the analyst to evaluate the subject company's financial position and to understand the risks it may be facing. The relative significance of the various ratios will differ in each valuation.

A further discussion of the valuation implications of these comparative ratios is included in Chapter 21, Sample Report.

Part III

Business Valuation Approaches and Methods

Chapter 9

Income Approach: Discounted Future Economic Income Method

THEORY OF VALUATION

. . . the value of an asset is the present value of its expected returns. Specifically, you expect an asset to provide a stream of returns during the period of time that you own it. To convert this estimated stream of returns to a value for the security you must discount this stream at your required rate of return. This process of valuation requires estimates of (1) the stream of expected returns, and (2) the required rate of return on the investment.[1]

Value today always equals future cash flow discounted at the opportunity cost of capital.[2]

This chapter presents the most commonly accepted methods of discounting expected economic income. It is the very heart of valuation. The next chapter deals with capitalizing economic income. We present discounting first because, as we will show in the next chapter, capitalizing is merely a short-cut version of discounting. We believe that the reader needs a basic grounding in discounting in order to thoroughly understand the theory of capitalizing and to evaluate the reasonableness of any capitalization method that may be presented.

This chapter necessarily has many algebraic formulas and quantitative examples. We have tried to present each formula clearly and precisely, with each variable defined in understandable terms, and with examples. In doing so, we hope to make a somewhat technical topic clear and understandable not only to appraisers, but also

[1] Frank K. Reilly, *Investment Analysis and Portfolio Management*, 5th ed. (Fort Worth, TX: The Dryden Press, 1997), p. 434.
[2] Richard A. Brealey and Stewart C. Myers, *Principles of Corporate Finance*, 5th ed. (New York: McGraw-Hill, Inc., 1996), p. 73.

to accountants, attorneys, business owners, and other appraisal users who do not necessarily have a finance background.

Introduction: Theoretical and Practical Soundness of Approach

What is someone who buys a company or an interest in a company really buying? Management? Markets? Technological skills? Products? Although each of these factors may be involved in the investment decision, what is actually being bought is a stream of prospective economic income.

It may be worthwhile to define the term, *economic income*, as we will use it in this discussion of the income approach to valuation. As the term implies, we define income according to the economists' definition and not the accountants' definition. In the landmark text, *Economics*, Paul D. Samuelson and William D. Nordhaus define income as: "The flow of wages, interest, payments, dividends, and other receipts accruing to an individual or nation during a period of time (usually a year)."[3]

For purposes of this discussion of the income approach, we will use a similarly broad definition of economic income. We define economic income as any inflow into an economic unit in exchange for goods, services, or capital.

In this definition, the economic unit can be either a business entity (e.g., corporation, partnership, professional practice) or an individual (e.g., an individual investor). And, the inflow can be gross (before recognition of any outflows) or net (after recognition of certain outflows). So, from the perspective of a business entity, economic income could mean, among other things, gross revenues, gross profits, net operating profits, net income before tax, net income after tax, operating cash flow, net cash flow before tax, net cash flow after tax, or net cash flow available for distribution to owners (e.g., dividends). Any of these measures of economic income could be converted into a value indication, based upon a discount (or capitalization) rate appropriate to the measure of economic income. Of course, different discount (or capitalization) rates would be appropriate to each different measure of economic income.

In theory, the value of a business or an interest in a business depends on the future benefits that will accrue to it, with the value of the future economic benefits discounted back to a present value at some appropriate discount rate. In other words, the basic concept of the income approach is to project the future economic income associated with the investment and to discount the projected income stream to a present value at a discount rate appropriate for the expected risk of the prospective economic income stream.

The income approach is based upon the economic principle of anticipation (sometimes also called the principle of expectation). In this approach, the value of the subject investment (i.e., the subject business interest) is the present value of the economic income expected to be generated by the investment. As the name of this economic principle implies, the investor "anticipates" the "expected" economic income to be earned from the investment. This expectation of prospective economic income is converted to a present worth—that is, the indicated value of the subject business interest.

For valuation purposes, the measurement of economic income to be analyzed can be defined in several different ways, as discussed in various sections of the

---

[3] Paul A. Samuelson and William D. Nordhaus, *Economics*, 14th ed. (New York: McGraw-Hill, 1992), p. 738.

chapter. Different measurements of economic income that are commonly analyzed in this approach include:

1. Payouts (e.g., dividends, interest, security sale proceeds, partnership withdrawals).
2. Cash flow (often measured as net cash flow).
3. Some measure of accounting earnings (often net income or net operating income).

In any event, it is essential that the economic income stream that is projected be clearly defined and that a discount rate appropriate for that definition of economic income be used in the analysis.

The discounted economic income method of the income approach to valuation is often used in the context of merger and acquisition analysis. In these instances, this method is not always used to estimate a fair market value conclusion. This is because the projections and the discount rate used in a merger and acquisition analysis may be specific to the individual acquirer, as suggested by the first quote above. Accordingly, such an analysis would estimate investment value, use value, acquisition value, or some other buyer-specific standard of value.

However, the same discounted economic income analysis could be performed—but with market-derived projections of economic income and with a market-derived discount rate, as suggested by the second quote above—in order to estimate the fair market value of the subject business interest.

The discounted economic income method also may be used to value a wide range of valuation subjects. For example, this method may be used in the valuation of both controlling and noncontrolling ownership interests, provided that: (1) the prospective economic income stream is consistent with the business interest subject to valuation, and (2) the discount rate is appropriate for that measure of economic income and for that particular valuation subject.

Since the value of a business interest depends on its prospective economic income, the correct application of this approach requires a projection of the economic income that is relevant to the valuation subject, be that dividends, cash flow, accounting earnings, or some other measure of economic income. The discounted economic income method is practical only to the extent that the projections used are reasonable to the decision-maker for whom the valuation is being prepared. Without supportable projections, the discounted economic income method can convey an aura of precision that is not justified.

Such economic income projections may be difficult to make—and even more difficult to get two or more parties with different investment perspectives and transaction expectations to agree on. Therefore, valuation analysts have developed various other approaches to valuation, based on both historical and prospective economic data. These approaches are discussed in subsequent chapters.

However, the valuation analyst should keep in mind that the value of an investment is a function of what it will do for an owner in the future, not what it has done for an owner in the past. Therefore, regardless of what valuation approach is used, in order for it to make rational economic sense from a financial point of view, the results should be compatible with what would result if a well-supported discounted economic income analysis were carried out. Of course, the discounted economic income analysis should include both (1) projected income from the operations of investment for a discrete period of time and (2) projected proceeds from the sale of the investment at some reversionary (or terminal) period.

The Basic Discounted Economic Income Framework

The basic arithmetic of the present value calculation is presented in Exhibit 9–1.

The basic formula for valuation using the discounted economic income method is as follows:

Formula 9–1

$$PV = \sum_{i=1}^{n} \frac{E_i}{(1+k)^i}$$

LEARN Formula (handwritten)

where:

PV = Present value

Σ = Sum of

n = The last period for which economic income is expected; n may equal infinity (i.e., ∞) if the economic income is expected to continue in perpetuity

E_i = Expected economic income in the ith period in the future (paid at the end of the period)

k = Discount rate (the cost of capital, e.g., the expected rate of return available in the market for other investments of comparable risk and other investment characteristics)

i = The period (usually stated as a number of years) in the future in which the prospective economic income is expected to be received

This basic formula can be expanded very simply as follows:

Formula 9–2

$$PV = \frac{E_1}{(1+k)} = \frac{E_2}{(1+k)^2} + \frac{E_3}{(1+k)^3} + \ldots + \frac{E_n}{(1+k)^n}$$

where:

$E_{1,2,3,etc.}$ = Expected economic income in the 1st, 2nd, 3rd periods, and so on

E_n = Expected economic income in the nth or last period in which an element of income is expected. (An investment with an expected perpetual life can be assumed to terminate at some point, since income in the remotely distant future will have only negligible impact when discounted to present value.)

k = Discount rate

This basic valuation model, which is central to the income approach to valuation, has only two variables:

1. The amount of the expected prospective economic income in each period.
2. The required rate of return (or yield rate) by which each of the expected prospective economic income receipts should be discounted.

Before attempting to quantify the numbers to go into the above model, it is first necessary to more specifically define each of the variables.

Exhibit 9–1

Arithmetic of Discounting vs. Compounding

COMPOUNDING

The formula to estimate the future value of an amount invested at annually compounded interest for a certain number of years is as follows:

$$FV = PV(1+k)^i$$

where:

FV	=	Future value
PV	=	Present value
k	=	Rate of return
i	=	ith year (the number of years into the future that the principal plus the compound rate of return will be received)

Example

Assume that we invest $1,000 for 3 years at 10% interest. Substituting in the above formula gives us the following:

$$
\begin{aligned}
FV &= \$1,000(1 + .10)^3 \\
&= \$1,000(1.10 \times 1.10 \times 1.10) \\
&= \$1,000(1.331) \\
&= \$1,331
\end{aligned}
$$

DISCOUNTING

Start with the formula for compounding:

$$FV = PV(1+k)^i$$

As we learned in basic algebra, we can divide both sides of an equation by the same factor:

$$\frac{FV}{(1+k)^i} = \frac{PV(1+k)^i}{(1+k)^i}$$

Also, if the same factor appears in both the numerator and the denominator of an expression, we can cancel them out:

$$\frac{FV}{(1+k)^i} = \frac{PV(\cancel{1+k})^i}{(\cancel{1+k})^i}$$

We then have the formula for discounting from a future value to a present value! Since it is customary to put the dependent variable (the value we are solving for) on the left hand side, the basic formula for discounting is written as follows:

$$PV = \frac{FV}{(1+k)^i}$$

Example

If we can earn 10% annually compounded interest, how much do we have to invest today to get a lump sum payment of $1,331 exactly three years from now? Substituting in the above formula gives us the following:

$$
\begin{aligned}
PV &= \frac{\$1,331}{(1+10)^3} \\
&= \frac{\$1,331}{1.331} \\
&= \$1,000
\end{aligned}
$$

DISCOUNTING A SERIES OF FUTURE ECONOMIC INCOME FLOWS

Discounting a series of future economic income flows simply involves discounting each individual future flow, and adding up the present values of each flow to get a total present value for the series of flows. The formula for discounting a series of future economic income flows may be written as follows:

$$PV = \sum \frac{FV^1}{(1+k)^i}$$

continued

Exhibit 9–1

Arithmetic of Discounting vs. Compounding (continued)

The capital Greek letter Sigma (Σ) stands for "sum of." It means to add up each of the components that follow, in this case the present values of each of the expected future amounts.

Example

Let's assume that a bond pays $100 interest at the end of each year for three years, and pays $1,000 principal at the bond's maturity date at the end of three years. If the market requires a 10% total rate of return on bonds of this quality and maturity at this time, what is the present value of the bond? Substituting in the above formula gives us the following:

$$PV = \frac{\$100}{(1+.10)} + \frac{\$100}{(1+.10)^2} + \frac{\$100}{(1+.10)^3} + \frac{\$100}{(1+.10)^3}$$

$$= \frac{\$100}{1.10} + \frac{\$100}{(1.10 \times 1.10)} + \frac{\$100}{(1.10 \times 1.10 \times 1.10)} + \frac{\$1,000}{(1.10 \times 1.10 \times 1.10)}$$

$$= \$90.90 + \$82.64 + \$75.13 + \$751.31$$

$$= \$1,000$$

It can readily be seen from the above that if the discount rate (i.e., the rate of return required to attract capital to the investment) goes up, then the present value goes down, and vice versa.

Note: In all the examples in this book, unless otherwise indicated, for simplicity it is assumed that compounding is on an annual basis, and that all returns are received at the end of each year. With minor adjustments in the arithmetic, assumptions of semi-annual, quarterly, monthly, daily, or even continuous compounding can be accommodated. It can also be assumed that proceeds are received at some time other than the end of the year. For example, proceeds received at the middle of the year, or more or less evenly throughout the year, may be accommodated by the "mid-year discounting convention."

The Numerator: Expected Prospective Economic Income

NEED TO KNOW

Income Associated with What?   The answer to this question depends on the answer to one of the questions in Chapter 2, "What exactly are we valuing?" Usually the focus is on the amount of economic income available to one of the following categories of investments:

1.   One class of common equity.
2.   All classes of common equity.
3.   All classes of equity.
4.   All equity and all long-term debt.
5.   All equity and all interest-bearing debt.
6.   All equity and all debt (i.e., total business assets).

When debt is included in what is being valued, the result is often referred to either as "the value of the business entity," "the business enterprise value," "the total capital value," or "market value of invested capital" (MVIC). For more discussion of defining the capital structure when debt is included, see the subsequent section on defining the capital structure under the discussion of discounting returns to overall capital.

Of course, we are sometimes interested in projecting economic income associated with other types of investments, such as: asset/property investments (e.g., income-producing real estate), security investments (e.g., minority interests in shares of stocks or in bonds), or intangible asset investments (e.g., patents, trademarks, or copyrights).

Obviously, the economic income to be measured should be that level of income that is associated with—and available to—whatever business or investment interest is being valued.

Definition of Economic Income Measured. Depending partly on the answer to the question, "Income associated with what?", there can be many definitions of economic income to be estimated. Some of the most common measurements of economic income include the following:

1. Dividends (or other payouts to security holders, such as partnership withdrawals).
2. Net cash flow to equity (NCF_e in the notation used in this book):

    Net income (after taxes)
    + Noncash charges (e.g., depreciation, amortization, deferred taxes)
    − Capital expenditures (the net changes in fixed and other noncurrent assets)*
    − Changes in net working capital*
    + Net changes in long-term debt*
    = Net cash flow to equity**

    *   Assumes that the amounts are the levels necessary to support projected business operations.
    ** If there are preferred dividends, they would have to be subtracted, of course, if the objective is to estimate net cash flow available to common equity holders. If one wants to project net cash flow available to all equity and interest-bearing debt holders, then interest needs to be added to the income measurement, but changes in long-term debt need not be considered (see following point 3).

3. Net cash flow to overall invested capital (NCF_f in the notation used in this book):[4]

    Net income (after taxes) available to common shareholders
    + Noncash charges
    − Capital expenditures*
    − Changes in working capital*
    + Interest expense, net of the tax effect (interest expense × [1 − tax rate])
    + Preferred dividends, if any
    = Net cash flow to overall invested capital
    *   Assumes that the amounts are the levels necessary to support projected business operations.

4. Net income (after taxes)

It is noteworthy that the capital expenditures, net changes in working capital, and net changes in long-term debt components to net cash flow may be negative. In other words, if there are not reductions (sales) of capital assets, decreases in net working capital, or decreases in long-term debt, these components would represent negative numbers. And, the subtraction of a negative number (e.g., a decrease in net working capital) would represent an increment—instead of a decrement—to net cash flow.

It is also noteworthy that the measures of cash flow defined above (i.e., to equity and to overall invested capital) are a different measure of cash flow than that reported in a Statement of Cash Flows prepared in accordance with generally accepted accounting principles.

Of course, many other variables representing some relevant measurement of economic income may be estimated. These might include, for example, pretax

---

[4] An alternative formula for net cash flow to overall invested capital is the following:

    Earnings before interest and taxes
    − Taxes on EBIT at effective tax rate
    + Noncash charges
    − Capital expenditures
    − Changes in working capital
    = Net cash flow to overall invested capital

income, net operating income, or some other measure of accounting income. However, for many of these other economic income measures, it may be difficult, if not impossible, to develop an empirically supportable discount rate.

The Denominator: The Discount Rate

Definition of a Discount Rate. In economic terms, a present value discount rate is an "opportunity cost," that is, the expected rate of return (or yield) that an investor would have to give up by investing in the subject investment—instead of in available alternative investments that are comparable in terms of risk and other investment characteristics.

The discount rate is the cost of capital for that particular category of investment. The discount rate is determined by market conditions as of the valuation date as they apply to the specific characteristics of the subject contemplated investment.[5]

Matching the Discount Rate with the Definition of the Prospective Economic Income. The choice of the discount rate is driven by the definition of economic income used in the numerator. The discount rate used in the analysis must be appropriate for the definition of the economic income in the numerator and for the class of capital (or other type of investment) to which it applies.

As a practical matter, the choice of economic income used in the numerator may be constrained by the ability, or lack of it, to develop an empirically supportable discount rate. For this reason, we sometimes find definitions of economic income used in market approach methods, where a market-derived capitalization rate is available, that are not used in discounting methods. In the next chapter, we explain the relationship between discount rates and capitalization rates.

In any case, we cannot overemphasize how important it is that *the discount rate developed must be matched conceptually and empirically to the definition of economic income being discounted*. Also, the discount rate must reflect the degree of risk, discussed in some detail later.

Constant or Variable Discount Rate? A question that sometimes arises is whether the discount rate should remain constant over the projection period or whether it should vary with time. The argument for varying it is that the investment risk may be greater—or less—later in the projection period than it is at the beginning of the projection period. This is a highly judgmental (and usually quite subjective) matter. Most commonly, analysts use a constant discount rate—reflecting the average amount of investment risk—throughout the projection period.

Estimating the Discount Rate

As noted in Chapter 3 on business valuation theory and principles and earlier in this chapter, in a valuation estimating fair market value *the discount rate is a market-driven rate. It represents the expected yield rate—or rate of return—necessary to induce investors to commit available funds to the subject investment, given its level of risk.*

---

[5] To the extent that a particular buyer or seller chooses to use a discounted economic income analysis using a discount rate that would deviate from the market consensus rate as of the valuation date, the resulting indicated value would depart from the strict standard of *fair market value* and, likely, approximate *investment value*, as defined in Chapter 2.

Return and Rate of Return Defined

When we speak of *return* and *rate of return*, we are referring to the *total yield to the investor*, reflecting all dividends, interest, or other cash or cash equivalent received, plus or minus any realized or unrealized appreciation or depreciation in the investment's value. The yield rate, or rate of return, on an investment for a given time period is as follows:

Formula 9–3

$$R = \frac{\text{Ending price} - \text{Beginning price} + \text{Cash distributions}}{\text{Begining price}}$$

where:

$$R = \text{Rate of return (for the period)}$$

This formula simply says that the investment yield—or rate of return—is equal to the ending price of an investment, minus the beginning price, plus any cash flows received from holding that investment, divided by the initial price. For example, if Paola Pizza Parlours stock started the year at $10 per share, paid $0.50 in cash dividends during the year, and ended the year at $11.50 per share, then the total investment yield or rate of return for the year would be computed as follows:

Formula 9–4

$$R = \frac{\$11.50 - \$10.00 + \$0.50}{\$10.00} = 0.20$$

Given a series of prices for a particular investment and the economic income received by the owner of that investment, it is possible to calculate the rate of return over any time period—or over any number of subperiods.

The *discount rate* is the expected total yield rate—or rate of return—that investors require for the particular class of investment.

Components of the Discount Rate

Broken down into its simplest components, the discount rate, or the rate of return that investors require, incorporates the following elements:

1. A "risk-free rate" (the amount that an investor feels certain of realizing over the holding period). This includes:
   a. A "rental rate" for foregoing the use of funds over the holding period.
   b. The expected rate of inflation over the holding period.[6]
2. A premium for risk. This includes:
   a. Systematic risk (that risk that relates to movements in returns on the investment market in general).
   b. Unsystematic risk (that risk that is specific to the subject investment).

---

[6] This assumes that the forecasted returns are in nominal terms, that is, including expected inflation over the forecast period. In economies characterized by hyperinflation, the practical procedure is to perform the discounted income analysis in "real" terms—that is, removing inflation from both the income forecast and also the discount rate. In any case, the forecast income and the discount rate must "match" in this respect—that is, either both the forecast and the discount rate include inflation or neither of them do.

Other important characteristics of an investment that sometimes are incorporated into the discount rate are: (1) the degree of minority ownership versus control position represented by the investment and (2) the degree of ready marketability or lack of marketability.

It is noteworthy that *discount rates developed through traditional capital asset pricing model (CAPM) analysis are based on noncontrolling transactions in highly marketable publicly traded securities. Therefore, discount rates based on CAPM relate to marketable, minority ownership positions in the subject investment.* Any considerations of investment control and/or lack of marketability require separate consideration and are addressed elsewhere in the book. Although there are exceptions, valuation analysts often explicitly treat the important valuation issues of ownership control and lack of marketability separately rather than implicitly incorporating those issues in the estimation of the appropriate discount rate.[7]

The Risk-Free Rate

The "risk-free" rate generally used is that rate available on instruments considered to have virtually no possibility of default, such as U.S. Treasury obligations. As noted above, such instruments compensate the holders for renting out their money and for the expected loss of purchasing power (inflation) during the holding period.

The ultimate riskless security is considered to be the short-term U.S. Treasury bill. However, in estimating cost of capital for equity investments, the short-term Treasury bill has an important shortcoming: Its maturity does not match the anticipated investment horizon (or holding period) of most equity investors. The Treasury bill rate is much more volatile than longer-term Treasury rates, and the yield may not reflect longer-term inflation expectations. Therefore, most valuation analysts prefer to use a long-term Treasury bond yield—such as the 20-year U.S. Treasury bond—as the risk-free component for estimating the cost of equity capital.[8]

The Equity Risk Premium

Over and above a risk-free return, investors must expect some additional rate of return to induce them to invest in non-Treasury bonds, in equities, or in similar securities—to compensate them for the additional risk incurred in such an investment. In the context of cost of capital, we define *risk* as *the degree of uncertainty as to the realization of the expected future returns*.

For a given level of expected future returns, the market will pay more to the extent that realization of those returns is more certain and less to the extent that their realization is less certain. In other words, for a given level of expected prospective economic income (e.g., cash flow, dividends, accounting earnings, and the like), the lower the risk, the higher the present value, or conversely, the higher the risk, the lower the present value.

---

[7] One notable exception is in the field of venture capital, where buyers of interests often incorporate the lack of marketability characteristic into their required rate of return in their discounted economic income analysis.

[8] The reason for using 20-year rather than 30-year Treasury bonds is that Ibbotson Associates publishes equity risk premium data related to 20-year Treasury bond maturities, but no such equity risk premium data are available for 30-year maturities.

The mechanism by which the assessment of risk is translated into its effect on value normally is the discount rate.[9]

Since the cost of capital is one of the most important variables in the valuation of a business or a business interest, both academicians and practitioners have expended an enormous amount of theoretical and empirical research effort in the attempt to quantify the effect of risk on the cost of capital for equity investments. The state of the art at the end of the 20th century involves incorporating one or all of the following elements into the discount rate to reflect risk:

1. A basic equity risk premium over the risk-free rate selected as the base.
2. One or more coefficients modifying the basic equity risk premium based on industry or other characteristics expected to affect the degree of risk for the subject investment.
3. An element reflecting the size effect.
4. A final adjustment reflecting judgments about investment-specific risk for the subject investment not captured in the first three elements.

Extensive empirical research is available that attempts to quantify the effect on the discount rate of the first three of the elements above. Nonetheless, there are choices to be made based on informed analysis of the evidence at each step. The fourth element, the unsystematic risk specific to the subject business or business interest, still remains largely a matter of the analyst's judgment, without a commonly accepted set of empirical support evidence. The analyst will base this judgment on factors discussed in Part II of this book, such as financial statement and comparative ratio analysis and the qualitative matters to be considered during the site visit and management interviews. However, after carefully analyzing these elements of investment-specific risk, there is no specific model for quantifying the exact effect of these factors on the discount rate. The analyst must depend on experience and judgment in this final element of the discount rate development, but should explicitly describe the factors that impact this final element.

Exhibit 9–2 gives a schematic summary of the elements of a discount rate applicable when net cash flow is the measure of economic income being discounted. The basic equity risk premium, modifications to it, and the effect of company size on the equity risk premium are discussed in some detail in subsequent sections.

Later in the chapter, a procedure is presented to convert a discount rate applicable to net cash flow to a discount rate applicable to net income, providing that certain fairly stringent assumptions are met.

The Capital Asset Pricing Model

The capital asset pricing model (CAPM) is part of a larger body of economic theory known as *capital market theory*. Capital market theory also includes *security analysis* and *portfolio management theory*, a *normative theory* that describes how investors *should* behave in selecting common stocks for their portfolios, under a

---

[9] Bierman and Smidt, two Cornell professors, make a convincing argument that the theoretically most correct way to handle the element of risk is to adjust the future expectations stream to what they call a *certainty adjusted equivalent*. They adjust the expectations downward by some factor that reflects the probability that the expectations will be achieved. They then apply the same cost of capital to the valuation of all alternative investment choices. They do quite a good job, in our opinion, of explaining the rationale for this approach (Harold Bierman, Jr., and Seymour Smidt, *The Capital Budgeting Decision*, 8th ed. (Englewood, NJ: Prentice-Hall, 1992)). Notwithstanding Bierman and Smidt's fine presentation, the more commonly used approach to incorporating risk in the valuation of a business is to reflect it in the cost of capital.

Exhibit 9–2

Schematic Diagram and Example of Elements of a Discount Rate Applicable to Expected Net Cash Flow Available to Common Equity

Risk-free rate	In the United States, usually 20-year, 5-year, or 30-day U.S. Treasury obligation yield available as of the valuation date. (Empirical equity risk premium data are available to match each of these three Treasury instrument maturities.)	6.83	20-year U.S. Treasury bond yield as of December 31, 1999. Source: *The Wall Street Journal*.
Equity risk premium (reflecting systematic risk)	Data available from Ibbotson Associates based on S&P 500 stock returns over income yields on 20-year, 5-year, or 30-day U.S. Treasury instrument rates. May be modified by one or more coefficients, such as beta, based on the capital asset pricing model, and/or other coefficients based on the arbitrage pricing model theory.	$8.00 \times 1.30 = 10.40$	Long horizon expected equity risk premium times beta. Source for long horizon equity risk premium: *SBBI Valuation Edition: 1999 Yearbook*, p. 51. Source for beta: median of beta from Standard & Poor's *Compustat* for industry.
Impact of size effect on risk	Incremental addition to the discount rate to reflect research showing additional returns to stocks of companies smaller than S&P 500. In this case we add the Ibbotson estimate of return in excess of CAPM for the smallest 10 percent of companies on the NYSE.	4.35	Expected size premium. Source: *SBBI Valuation Edition 1999 Yearbook*, p. 104.
Investment-specific risk	Matter of analyst's judgment. May be based on ratio analysis of subject compared to industry averages or specific guideline companies and/or on qualitative factors such as depth and quality of management, competitive position, and so on. This element of the discount rate will be supported conceptually by the analysis done pursuant to part II of this book. However, there is no widely accepted model or set of formulas to convert the results of these analyses into an exact quantified effect on the discount rate.	3.00	Based on analyst's judgment regarding results for subject company compared with guideline companies used.
Total discount rate Total discount rate (rounded)		<u>24.58</u> <u>25</u>	Given the number of significant digits in the estimation of the investment-specific risk factor (and other cost of equity capital components), it is not uncommon to see the discount rate rounded to a full percentage point.

given set of assumptions. In contrast, the CAPM is a *positive* theory, meaning it describes the market relationships that *will* result *if* investors behave in the manner prescribed by portfolio theory.

The CAPM is a conceptual cornerstone of modern capital market theory. Its relevance to business valuations is that businesses and business interests are a subset of the investment opportunities available in the total capital market; thus, the determination of the prices of businesses theoretically should be subject to the same economic forces and relationships that determine the prices of other investment assets.

Systematic and Unsystematic Risk

In the previous section, we defined risk conceptually as *the degree of uncertainty as to the realization of expected future returns*. Capital market theory divides risk into two components: systematic risk and unsystematic risk. Stated in nontechnical terms, *systematic risk* is the uncertainty of future returns due to the sensitivity of the return on the subject investment to movements in the return for the investment market as a whole. *Unsystematic risk* is a function of characteristics of the industry, the individual company, and the type of investment interest. Company characteristics could include, for example, management's ability to weather economic conditions, relations between labor and management, the possibility of strikes, the success or failure of a particular marketing program, or any other factor specific to the company. Total risk, therefore, depends on both these systematic and unsystematic factors.

The fundamental assumption of the capital asset pricing model is that the risk premium portion of the expected return of a security is a function of that security's systematic risk. This is because capital market theory assumes that investors hold or have the ability to hold common stocks in large, well-diversified portfolios. Under that assumption, the unsystematic risk attaching to a particular company's stock is eliminated because of the portfolio's diversification. Therefore, the only risk pertinent to a study of capital asset pricing theory is systematic risk.

Beta: The Measure of Systematic Risk

Systematic risk is measured in the capital asset pricing model by a factor called *beta*. Beta is a function of the relationship between the return on an individual security and the return on the market as measured by a broad market index such as the Standard & Poor's 500 Stock Composite Index. It is sometimes measured as a function of the excess return on an individual security relative to the *excess* return on the market index. By the "excess return," we mean the return over and above the return available on a risk-free investment (e.g., U.S. Treasuries).

For the market index as a whole, the average beta, by definition, is 1.0. If a stock tends to have a positive excess return greater than the market when the market return is greater than the risk-free return, and a negative excess return greater than the market when the market return is less than the risk-free return, then the stock's beta is greater than 1.0. If the difference between the stock's return and the risk-free return tends to be less than the difference between the market return and the risk-free return, then the stock's beta is less than 1.0.

In other words, beta measures the volatility of the excess return on an individual security relative to that of the market. Securities that have betas greater than 1.0

are characterized as aggressive securities and are more risky than the market. Securities that have betas of less than 1.0 are characterized as defensive securities and have systematic risks lower than the market.

It is possible (although not very common) for securities to have a negative beta (i.e., a beta less than zero). Such a beta would indicate that the returns of these securities are counter-cyclical to the returns of the broad investment market index.

One common method for calculating beta is illustrated in Exhibit 9–3. (The computation may be performed by regressing the excess stock return compared with the excess market return.)

(Is there a variability measurement that can identify stocks that go up more than the market when the market goes up, and down less than the market when the market goes down? Unfortunately, the answer is no. This is because research shows that stocks that have demonstrated such a pattern in the past do not tend to continue to demonstrate the same pattern in the future.)

Exhibit 9–3

Illustrative Example of One Common Method for the Calculation of Beta

Month End, t [a]	Return on Security A [b]	Return on S&P Index [c]	Calculated Covariance [d]	Calculated Variance [e]
1/89	0.041	0.069	0.00211	0.00325
2/89	(0.007)	(0.029)	0.00045	0.00168
3/89	0.052	0.021	0.00043	0.00008
•				
•				
•				
10/98	0.113	0.077	0.00709	0.00423
11/98	0.033	0.057	0.00131	0.00203
12/98	(0.016)	0.055	(0.00086)	0.00185
Sum	0.500	1.488	0.21060	0.26240
Average	0.004	0.012	0.00176 [f]	0.00219 [g]

$$\text{Beta} = \frac{\text{Covariance (Security A, S \& P Index)}}{\text{Variance of S \& P Index}} = \frac{0.00176}{0.00219} = 0.80$$

a. 10 years or 120 months.
b. Returns based on end-of-month prices and dividend payments.
c. Returns based on end-of-month S&P Index.
d. Values in this column are calculated as:
   (Observed return on Security A – Average return on Security A) × (Observed return on S&P Index – Average return on S&P Index)
   0.00211 = [(0.041 – 0.004) × (0.069 – 0.012)]
e. Values in this column are calculated as:
   (Observed return on S&P Index – Average return on S&P Index)^2
   $0.00325 = (0.069 – 0.012)^2$
f. The average of this column is the covariance between Security A and the S&P Index.
g. The average of this column is the variance of return on the S&P Index.

Using Beta to Estimate Expected Rate of Return

The capital asset pricing model leads to the conclusion that the equity risk premium (the required excess rate of return for a security over and above the risk-free rate) is a linear function of the security's beta. This linear function is described in the following univariate linear regression formula:

Formula 9–5

$$E(R_i) = R_f + B(RP_m)$$

where:

$E(R_i)$ = Expected return on an individual security

R_f = Rate of return available on a risk-free security (as of the valuation date)

B = Beta

RP_m = Equity risk premium for the market as a whole (or, by definition, the equity risk premium for a security with beta of 1.0)

To illustrate using the above formula as part of the process of estimating a company's cost of equity capital, consider stocks of average size, publicly traded companies i, j, and k, with betas of 0.8, 1.0, and 1.2, respectively, a risk-free rate in the market at the valuation date of 7 percent (0.07), and the market equity risk premium of 8 percent (0.08). The expected investment rate of return on common equity for stocks of these companies would be computed as follows:

Formula 9–6

$$
\begin{aligned}
E(R_i) &= 0.07 + 0.8(0.08) \\
&= 0.07 + 0.64 \\
&= 0.134 \\
E(R_j) &= 0.07 + 1.0(0.08) \\
&= 0.07 + 0.08 \\
&= 0.15 \\
E(R_k) &= 0.07 + 1.2(0.08) \\
&= 0.07 + 0.096 \\
&= 0.166
\end{aligned}
$$

Exhibit 9–2 and later sections of this chapter discuss sources for the market risk-free rate, the equity risk premium, and betas.

The above linear relationship is presented schematically in Exhibit 9–4, which presents the security market line. According to capital asset pricing theory, if the combination of the expected rate of return on a given security and its risk, as measured by beta, places it below the security market line, such as security X in Exhibit 9–4, that security (e.g., common stock) is mispriced. It is mispriced in the sense that the return on that security is less than what it would be if the security were correctly priced, assuming fully efficient capital markets.

For the return on a security to be appropriate for that security's risk, the price of the security must decline, allowing the rate of return to increase until it is just sufficient to compensate the investor for bearing the security's risk. All common stocks in the market, in equilibrium, adjust in price until the rate of return on each is sufficient to compensate investors for holding them. In that situation, the systematic risk/expected rate of return characteristics of all those securities will place them on the security market line.

Exhibit 9–4

Security Market Line

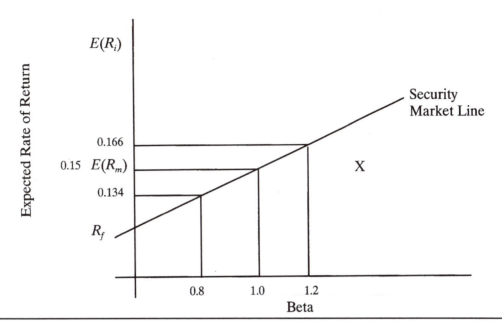

In the above diagram:

$E(R_i)$ = Expected return for the individual security

$E(R_m)$ = Expected return on the market

R_f = Risk-free rate available as of the valuation date

In a market in perfect equilibrium, all securities would fall on the security market line. The security X is mispriced, with a return less than it would be on the security market line.

Levered and Unlevered Betas

Published betas for publicly traded stocks reflect the actual capital structure of each respective company. As such, they can be referred to as *levered betas*, betas reflecting the actual financial leverage of the company's capital structure. If the leverage of the company subject to valuation differs significantly from the leverage of the guideline companies selected for analysis, it may be desirable to adjust the guideline betas for use in estimating the required rate of return on equity in the context of the CAPM.

This adjustment is performed by first computing *unlevered betas* for the guideline companies. An *unlevered beta* is the beta the company would have if it had no debt. The second step is to decide where the subject company's risk would fall on an unlevered basis relative to the guideline companies. The third and final step is to re-lever the beta for the subject company on the basis of one or more assumed capital structures. The result will be a market-derived beta that has been specifically adjusted for the degree of financial leverage of the subject company.[10]

---

[10] Robert S. Hamada, "Portfolio Analysis, Market Equilibrium and Corporation Finance," *Journal of Finance*, 24 (March 1969), pp. 19–30.

To summarize, the steps are as follows:

1. Compute an unlevered beta for each of the guideline companies.
2. Decide where the risk would fall for the subject company relative to the guideline companies assuming all had 100 percent equity capital structures.
3. Relever the beta for the subject company based on one or more assumed capital structures.

The formulas and an example for carrying out this process are presented in Exhibit 9–5. Of course, this financial leverage adjustment procedure takes as given all of the assumptions of the capital asset pricing model.

Keep in mind that capital structures for both the guideline and for the subject companies are assumed to be at market value in this process. If the relevered beta is used to estimate the *market value* of the company on a controlling ownership basis, and if it is anticipated that the actual capital structure will be adjusted to the proportions of debt and equity in the assumed capital structure, then only one assumed capital structure is necessary. However, if the amount of debt in the subject capital structure will *not* be adjusted, an iterative process may be required. The initial *assumed* capital structure for the subject will influence the cost of equity, which will, in turn, influence the relative proportions of debt and equity at market value. It may be necessary to try several assumed capital structures until one of them produces an estimate of equity value that actually results in the assumed capital structure.

This process of unlevering and relevering betas to an assumed capital structure is based upon the assumption that the business interest subject to valuation has the ability to change the capital structure of the subject company. In the case of the valuation of a noncontrolling ownership interest, for example, the valuation subject may not have that ability.

Assumptions Underlying the Capital Asset Pricing Model

The assumptions underlying the capital asset pricing model are as follows:

1. Investors are risk averse.
2. Rational investors seek to hold efficient portfolios—that is, portfolios that are fully diversified.
3. All investors have identical investment time horizons (i.e., expected holding periods).
4. All investors have identical expectations about such variables as expected rates of return and how capitalization rates are generated.
5. There are no transaction costs.
6. There are no investment-related taxes (i.e., there may be corporate income taxes).
7. The rate received from lending money is the same as the cost of borrowing money.
8. The market has perfect divisibility and liquidity (i.e., investors can readily buy or sell any desired fractional interest).

Obviously, the extent to which the above assumptions are or are not met in the real world will have a bearing on the application of the CAPM for the valuation of

Exhibit 9–5

Computing Unlevered and Relevered Betas

The following is the formula for computing an unlevered beta (a beta assuming 100% equity in the capital structure).

$$B_U = \frac{B_L}{1 + (1-t)(W_d \div W_e)}$$

where:

B_U	=	Beta unlevered
B_L	=	Beta levered
t	=	Tax rate for the company
W_d	=	Percent debt in the capital structure
W_e	=	Percent equity in the capital structure

Example:

Assume that for guideline company A:

Levered (published) beta: 1.2
Tax rate: 0.40
Capital structure: 30% debt, 70% equity

$$B_U = \frac{1.2}{1 + (1 - 0.40)(0.30 \div 0.70)}$$

$$= \frac{1.2}{1 + 0.60(0.429)}$$

$$= \frac{1.2}{1.257}$$

$$= 0.95$$

Assume that you made the above calculation for all the guideline companies, the average unlevered beta was 0.90, and you believe the riskiness of your subject company, on an unlevered basis, is about equal to the average for the guideline companies. The next step is to relever the beta for your subject company based on its tax rate and one or more assumed capital structures. The formula to adjust an unlevered beta to a levered beta is as follows:

$$B_L = B_U \left(1 + (1 - t)(W_d \div W_e) \right)$$

where the definitions of the variables are the same as in the formula for computing unlevered betas.

Example:

Assume for the subject company:

Unlevered beta: 0.90
Tax rate: 0.30
Capital structure: 60% debt, 40% equity

$$\begin{aligned} B_L \; &= \; 0.90\,(1 + (1-0.30)(0.60 \div 0.40)) \\ &= \; 0.90\,(1 + 0.70\,(1.5)) \\ &= \; 0.90\,(2.05) \\ &= \; 1.85 \end{aligned}$$

closely held businesses. While these assumptions appear unrealistic on their face, a "modified CAPM," which includes adjustments for size and specific company risks, is generally accepted.

The Size Premium

Several research studies demonstrate convincing evidence that, on average, smaller companies have higher rates of return than larger companies.[11] The *total* risk, or standard deviation of annual returns, also increases with decreasing company size.[12]

The SBBI 1999 Yearbook, Valuation Edition, states:

> The greater risk of small stocks does not, in the context of the capital asset pricing model, fully account for their higher returns over the long term. In the CAPM, only systematic or beta risk is rewarded; small company stocks have had returns in excess of those implied by their betas.[13]

The implication would seem to be that the market does not ignore unsystematic risk and, indeed, demands and achieves extra return for accepting it. The 1999 Ibbotson data showing higher returns to higher standard deviation stocks are consistent with Shannon Pratt's research as far back as 1966, which showed increasing returns to risk as measured by the standard deviation.[14]

We believe that the reflection of this unsystematic risk in the discount rate is especially important for the valuation of closely held stocks. Most owners of closely held businesses or interests in closely held businesses do not diversify their investment portfolios nearly to the extent to which investors diversify their holdings of publicly traded stocks. Thus, since the unsystematic portion of total risk is unlikely to be diversified away to the same extent as for a portfolio of publicly traded securities, it is worth considering reflecting at least some part of unsystematic risk—as well as systematic risk—in estimating an appropriate expected rate of return.

An explanation of the data quantifying the size premium is contained in a later section on sources of data.

A series of small stock premium studies have been developed by Roger Grabowski and David King of PricewaterhouseCoopers. In their first series of studies, they used eight different measures of size:

- Market value of equity.
- Book value of equity.
- Five-year average net income.
- Market value of invested capital.
- Book value of invested capital.
- Five-year average EBITDA.
- Sales.
- Number of employees.

---

[11] See, for example, Eugene Fama and Kenneth French, "The Cross Section of Expected Stock Returns," *Journal of Finance*, Vol. 47, 1992, pp. 427–65; Eugene Fama and Kenneth French, "Common Risk Factors in the Returns on Stocks and Bonds," University of Chicago Working Paper No. 360, November 1992; Eugene Fama and Kenneth French, "The Economic Fundamentals of Size and Book-to-Market Equity," University of Chicago Working Paper No. 361, September 1992; Christopher B. Barry and Stephen J. Brown, "Differential Information and the Small Firm Effect," *Journal of Financial Economics*, Vol. 13, 1984, pp. 283–94; and Rolf W. Banz, "The Relationship between Return and Market Value of Common Stocks," *Journal of Financial Economics*, Vol. 9, 1981, pp. 3–18. Also, see Chapter 4 of *Stocks, Bonds, Bills & Inflation: Valuation Edition 1999 Yearbook* (Chicago: Ibbotson Associates, 1999).

[12] *Stocks, Bonds, Bills & Inflation: Valuation Edition 1999 Yearbook* (Chicago: Ibbotson Associates, 1999), p. 100.

[13] Ibid., p. 102.

[14] Shannon P. Pratt, "Relationship between Variability of Past Returns and Levels of Future Returns for Common Stocks, 1926–1960" (abridged version, previously unpublished), in *Frontiers of Investment Analysis*, revised ed., E. Bruce Fredrikson, ed. (Scranton, NY: Intext Educational Publishers, 1971), pp. 338–53.

The first of their small stock studies covered the period from 1963–96. As shown in Exhibit 9–6, there was a positive equity risk premium associated with all eight of the size variables.

Grabowski and King conducted another series of risk premium studies using three measures of risk from companies' accounting data.[15] The three risk measures and their correlation coefficients with observed equity risk premiums are as follows:

- **Operating margin** (five-year mean of operating income net of depreciation divided by sales). The lower the operating margin, the higher the risk. This had the highest R squared at 76 percent.
- **Coefficient of variation in operating margin** (standard deviation of operating margin over the prior five years divided by the mean operating income for the same years). This had an R squared of 54 percent.
- **Coefficient of variation of return on book value of equity** (net income before extraordinary items minus preferred dividends divided by book value of common equity; the calculation then is the standard deviation of return on book value of equity for the prior five years divided by the mean return on book value of equity for the same years). This also had an R squared of 54 percent.

This study covered the period 1963–1998. This is because Standard & Poor's Compustat was established in 1963 and the study uses companies that are covered on both Compustat and the database of the Center for Research in Security Prices (CRSP) at the University of Chicago.

The results using the five-year average operating margin are summarized in Exhibit 9–7.

Exhibit 9–7 indicates that the operating margins are inversely correlated with company size. They make the point that these studies further support the validity of the small stock premium. However, the premiums could also be viewed as indications of specific company risk.

Analyses of size differentials relating to cost of capital on the *Pratt's Stats*, *Bizcomps* and *IBA Market Database* all show that the size effect continues to carry on down to smaller companies. For example, relative median valuation multiples for 12 industry groups from *Bizcomps* and *Pratt's Stats* are shown in Exhibit 9–8. It is very clear that the average transaction size is significantly lower and the valuation multiples similarly significantly lower for the *Bizcomps* companies compared with the *Pratt's Stats* companies.

The Discounted Cash Flow Method of Estimating the Cost of Capital

To use the discounted cash flow (DCF) method for estimating the cost of equity capital for a closely held company, one must select a group of publicly traded companies with risk characteristics similar to the subject. These usually are companies in the same industry, and may be the group of companies selected as guideline publicly traded companies in the market approach.

---

[15] This abstract is based on Roger Grabowski and David King, "New Evidence on Equity Returns and Company Risk," *Business Valuation Review*, September 1999, pp. 112–30, and on a presentation of the material at the American Society of Appraisers Advanced Business Valuation Conference in New Orleans, November 1999. Details of this and other PricewaterhouseCoopers studies can be found on the Ibbotson Cost of Capital Center web site: valuation.ibbotson.com.

Exhibit 9–6

Equity Risk Premium Study for Various Size Measures

Prior research has demonstrated a significant "size effect" in the sense that smaller companies have higher equity risk premiums than would be explained by their betas (in the context of the capital asset pricing model). The size used in these prior studies has been the aggregate market value of common equity.

    This study extends the prior research in several ways, most importantly by testing the comparative results using several different measures of size. As can be seen in the table below, the size effect is quite strong regardless of which size measure is used.

    Readers can approximate an equity required rate of return reflecting various size measures by adding the appropriate equity risk premium from the table below to the 20-year Treasury bond rate. Information to use the data along with a beta in the context of CAPM is contained in the full paper.

Size Rank	Market Value of Equity		Book Value of Equity		5-Year Avg. Net Income		Mkt. Value of Inv. Capital	
	Average Size	Arithmetic Equity Risk Premium	Average Size	Arithmetic Equity Risk Premium	Average Size	Arithmetic Equity Risk Premium	Average Size	Arithmetic Equity Premium
		%		%		%		%
1	40,860	5.21	10,255	5.43	1,572	5.62	52,246	5.02
2	12,776	3.94	4,664	5.01	575	5.81	17,601	3.49
3	7,619	3.53	2,866	5.80	367	5.19	10,828	4.48
4	5,069	6.16	2,104	5.24	238	5.15	6,883	4.54
5	4,280	4.20	1,575	6.52	188	5.78	5,608	5.37
6	3,288	6.26	1,335	7.50	141	8.57	4,532	8.36
7	2,502	6.74	1,087	6.82	110	6.74	3,733	7.12
8	2,156	7.52	893	6.31	95	7.61	2,958	6.21
9	1,957	6.16	752	6.02	76	7.05	2,483	6.44
10	1,610	7.94	652	7.62	67	6.44	2,124	7.47
11	1,368	8.01	577	9.39	55	9.72	1,896	6.47
12	1,181	8.55	472	9.50	46	8.12	1,676	8.37
13	1,017	7.53	415	7.61	37	9.14	1,438	8.81
14	864	8.79	363	8.68	33	7.90	1,188	8.73
15	710	8.60	314	9.00	28	9.46	996	9.64
16	586	9.25	281	9.89	24	9.21	832	9.53
17	496	8.07	237	8.83	20	10.99	673	8.91
18	408	10.56	208	8.48	16	10.44	572	7.57
19	344	9.21	174	9.52	14	9.22	494	10.20
20	285	9.21	146	10.70	11	10.72	396	11.14
21	225	11.32	125	10.00	9	11.45	316	10.34
22	170	10.34	100	11.62	7	12.13	237	11.71
23	130	12.10	84	10.72	5	11.52	186	10.43
24	85	12.45	60	11.52	3	12.11	126	12.25
25	30	15.83	24	14.17	1	13.67	46	15.55

Size Rank	Book Val. of Inv. Cap.		5-Year Average EBITDA		Sales		Number of Employees	
	Average Size	Arithmetic Equity Risk Premium	Average Size	Arithmetic Equity Risk Premium	Average Size	Arithmetic Equity Risk Premium	Average Size	Arithmetic Equity Premium
		%		%		%		%
1	22,397	4.64	4,860	5.92	33.180	6.43	181,966	5.98
2	9,282	4.43	1,856	5.29	11,821	5.37	59,133	6.66
3	5,790	5.10	1,213	5.84	8,159	7.14	40,819	7.17
4	4,173	6.28	788	5.61	5,673	7.58	31,672	7.93
5	2,978	6.58	603	6.76	4,174	8.69	24,425	8.52
6	2,323	7.72	472	8.31	3,344	7.85	17,962	8.43
7	1,896	6.81	361	7.76	2,776	7.74	15,419	7.42
8	1,646	5.56	318	6.42	2,332	7.06	12,828	7.68
9	1,383	6.16	264	6.47	2,007	6.77	10,385	8.98
10	1,241	7.40	226	7.48	1,596	7.94	8,437	9.04
11	1,018	7.70	189	8.68	1,345	8.87	6,863	9.01
12	815	8.13	157	9.55	1,128	11.00	6,260	8.95
13	741	8.07	141	10.46	1,003	11.77	5,417	9.31
14	630	10.54	112	8.52	892	7.84	4,655	8.61
15	526	8.87	92	8.27	753	9.00	3,938	9.98
16	469	8.78	84	10.49	678	8.37	3,520	9.60
17	407	9.55	69	10.01	583	10.45	2,928	8.63
18	342	10.91	59	10.21	521	8.99	2,438	8.63
19	285	10.39	50	10.55	420	9.46	2,173	7.92
20	243	10.14	40	8.84	336	9.85	1,787	11.21
21	198	8.86	33	10.52	279	9.21	1,446	9.91
22	152	10.27	27	11.68	235	9.75	1,101	10.75
23	121	11.03	20	12.80	177	13.09	875	10.98
24	88	12.24	13	12.82	123	11.38	595	10.65
25	36	14.03	5	13.09	47	13.55	223	13.55

SOURCE: Roger Grabowski and David King, "Size Effects and Equity Returns: An Update," *Business Valuation Review*, March 1997, pp. 22–26, and "New Evidence on Size Effects and Equity Returns," *Business Valuation Review*, September 1996, pp. 103–15. More recent data is available on the Ibbotson Associates cost of capital web site: valuation.ibbotson.com.

Exhibit 9–7

Companies Ranked by Five-Year Average Operating Margin

Historical Equity Risk Premium: Average Since 1963
Data through Year Ending December 31, 1998

Portfolio Rank by Risk	Median Operating Margin	Log of Median Op Margin	Number as of 1998	Beta Annual Since '63	Standard Deviation of Returns	Geometric Average Return	Arithmetic Average Return	Arithmetic Average Equity Risk Premium	Smoothed Average Equity Risk Premium	Average Debt/MVIC
1	35.6%	-0.45	85	0.89	17.82%	12.44%	13.76%	6.20%	5.76%	32.57%
2	28.6%	-0.54	71	0.85	15.40%	11.20%	12.24%	4.68%	6.41%	37.09%
3	25.0%	-0.60	64	0.93	16.29%	12.36%	13.53%	5.97%	6.80%	33.79%
4	21.9%	-0.66	75	1.00	17.65%	13.02%	14.42%	6.86%	7.18%	27.01%
5	19.2%	-0.72	72	1.00	17.29%	13.18%	14.59%	7.03%	7.55%	22.66%
6	17.2%	-0.77	78	1.07	19.21%	14.04%	15.63%	8.07%	7.89%	19.64%
7	15.5%	-0.81	83	1.09	19.86%	13.65%	15.35%	7.79%	8.19%	19.89%
8	14.1%	-0.85	84	1.11	20.54%	13.72%	15.56%	8.00%	8.47%	20.63%
9	13.0%	-0.89	87	1.12	20.67%	14.87%	16.69%	9.13%	8.70%	21.45%
10	12.1%	-0.92	68	1.15	20.63%	13.41%	15.30%	7.74%	8.92%	22.46%
11	11.3%	-0.95	74	1.29	24.10%	13.79%	16.26%	8.70%	9.11%	23.03%
12	10.6%	-0.98	69	1.25	24.28%	14.85%	17.34%	9.78%	9.30%	23.50%
13	9.9%	-1.00	107	1.20	23.28%	15.04%	17.44%	9.88%	9.49%	24.31%
14	9.3%	-1.03	96	1.21	22.53%	13.86%	16.11%	8.55%	9.68%	24.25%
15	8.8%	-1.06	74	1.27	24.39%	16.41%	18.95%	11.39%	9.85%	26.88%
16	8.2%	-1.08	105	1.23	24.47%	15.20%	17.90%	10.34%	10.04%	27.76%
17	7.7%	-1.11	78	1.28	25.66%	16.83%	19.56%	12.00%	10.24%	28.15%
18	7.2%	-1.14	101	1.30	27.08%	16.21%	19.22%	11.66%	10.44%	29.60%
19	6.6%	-1.18	126	1.24	24.89%	15.95%	18.60%	11.04%	10.67%	31.02%
20	6.1%	-1.22	105	1.28	26.31%	17.25%	20.17%	12.61%	10.91%	32.47%
21	5.5%	-1.26	98	1.37	27.75%	17.36%	20.52%	12.96%	11.22%	32.64%
22	4.8%	-1.32	97	1.28	26.51%	15.47%	18.50%	10.94%	11.60%	33.31%
23	4.0%	-1.39	142	1.27	27.41%	17.34%	20.44%	12.88%	12.11%	35.66%
24	3.1%	-1.51	129	1.38	31.16%	15.97%	19.91%	12.35%	12.87%	35.21%
25	1.6%	-1.79	194	1.22	27.38%	16.09%	19.16%	11.60%	14.74%	33.50%
High financial risk			538	1.63	40.69%	15.18%	21.14%	13.58%		54.33%
Large Stocks (Ibbotson SBBI data)						12.59%	13.72%	6.16%		
Small Stocks (Ibbotson SBBI data)						14.99%	17.77%	10.21%		
Long-Term Treasury Income (Ibbotson SBBI data)						7.53%	7.56%			

Equity Risk Premium Study: Data through December 31, 1998
Data Smoothing with Regression Analysis
Dependent Variable: Average Premium
Independent Variable: Log of Median Operating Margin

Regression Output:

Constant	2.753%
Std Err of Y Est	1.185%
R Squared	76%
No. of Observations	25
Degrees of Freedom	23
X Coefficient(s)	-6.716%
Std Err of Coef.	0.778%
t-Statistic	-8.64

Smoothed Premium = 2.753% - 6.716% * *Log(Operating Margin)*

Smoothed Premium vs. Unadjusted Average

SOURCE: Roger Grabowski and David King, "New Evidence on Equity Returns and Company Risk," *Business Valuation Review*, September 1999, p. 128.

Exhibit 9–8

Comparison of Median Valuation Multiples

	Bizcomps Data				Pratt's Stats Data			
	Medians of Sale Price/ Gross Sales	Medians of Sale Price/ SDCF	Median Sale Price (in $000s)	Median Gross Sales (in $000s)	Medians of Sale Price/ Gross Sales	Medians of Sale Price/ SDCF	Median Sale Price (in $000s)	Median Gross Sales (in $000s)
Publishing businesses	1.01	2.82	305	300	1.26	6.52	14,600	10,398
Printing businesses	0.55	2.34	148	238	0.55	5.96	9,125	19,213
Manufacturing: machine shops	0.67	2.12	315	479	0.66	6.58	7,200	9,439
Distributor: automotive	0.18	1.49	170	538	0.34	6.58	3,144	13,655
Distributor: industrial supplies	0.29	1.58	86	600	0.55	6.1	8,690	16,961
Distributor: food products	0.34	1.92	175	663	0.22	2.9	665	2,491
Retail: food markets	0.18	1.26	149	639	0.22	2.82	298	1,622
Bakeries: wholesale and retail	0.41	2.27	121	244	0.86	6.07	2,732	2,869
Restaurants: family	0.30	1.78	81	320	0.36	2.51	275	805
Delicatessans: retail	0.37	1.65	64	198	0.52	2.73	72	142
Retail: florists	0.29	1.64	68	245	0.62	2.69	325	525
Daycare centers	0.46	1.82	72	147	0.67	4.28	831	791

SDCF = Seller's discretionary cash flow.

SOURCE: *Bizcomps* 1998 Eastern Edition and *Pratt's Stats* year-end 1998.

The procedure is called the *DCF method* because it uses the DCF formula. Since the present value of the publicly traded company stock is known, the formula is merely rearranged to solve for the implied expected rate of return.

The expected dollar amounts of returns used as inputs to the formula usually are five years of analysts' earnings estimates from one of the estimates sources, such as Compustat's ACE (Analysts Consensus Estimates), or I/B/E/S, or First Call. The next five years' projections usually are an industry projection for years six through ten. Beyond the tenth year, it is usually assumed that earnings will increase at the projected rate of inflation. There are also simpler versions, but the "three-stage model" just described tends to produce the most reliable results.

Because the inputs are earnings estimates, the variable to which the implied cost of capital applies is net income rather than net cash flow, as discussed elsewhere in this chapter. Many valuation analysts feel that this long-run cost of capital estimate for net income is not significantly different than the long-run cost of capital applicable to net cash flow. The validity of this assumption depends on the extent to which net income and net cash flow tend to even out for the industry in question over the long run.

Cost of capital estimates by the DCF method are presented in Ibbotson's *Cost of Capital Quarterly* (see example in Exhibit 9–13).[16]

---

[16] An entire chapter is devoted to the DCF method of estimating the cost of equity capital, including examples, in Shannon P. Pratt, *Cost of Capital: Estimation and Applications* (New York: John Wiley & Sons, 1998).

Arbitrage Pricing Theory

The concept of the arbitrage pricing theory (APT) was introduced by academicians in 1976,[17] but it was not until 1988 that data in a commercially usable form became generally available to permit the application of the theory to the estimation of required rates of return in day-to-day practice.

As noted in the previous section, the CAPM is a univariate model—that is, it only recognizes one risk factor: systematic risk relative to a market measure. In a sense, APT is a multivariate extension of the CAPM, in that it recognizes a variety of risk factors that may bear on an investment's required rate of return, one of these being systematic or "market timing" risk. However, in another sense, it may be argued that the CAPM and APT are not mutually exclusive, nor are they of greater or lesser scope than one another. It can be argued that the CAPM beta implicitly reflects the information included separately in each of the APT "factors." Under APT, the required rate of return for an investment varies according to that investment's sensitivity to each risk factor. The APT model takes the following form:

Formula 9–7

$$E(R_i) = R_f + (B_{i1}K_1) + (B_{i2}K_2) + \ldots + (B_{in}K_n)$$

where:

$E(R_i)$	=	Expected rate of return on the subject security
R_f	=	Rate of return on a risk-free security
$K_1 \ldots K_n$	=	Risk premium associated with factor K for the average asset in the market
$B_{i1} \ldots B_{in}$	=	Sensitivity of security i to each risk factor relative to the market average sensitivity to that factor

The risk factors considered in current APT applications, in addition to market timing risk, include:

- Confidence risk.
- Time horizon risk.
- Inflation risk.
- Business cycle risk.

Each of these risk factors is discussed in Exhibit 9–9. Like the CAPM, APT ignores risk factors that are unique to a particular company, since investors theoretically could avoid such risks through diversification.

Ibbotson and Brinson make the following observations regarding APT:

In theory, a specific asset has some number of units of each risk; those units are each multiplied by the appropriate risk premium. Thus, APT shows that

---

[17] Stephen A. Ross, "The Arbitrage Theory of Capital Asset Pricing," *Journal of Economic Theory* (December 1976), pp. 341–60, and Stephen A. Ross, "Return, Risk, and Arbitrage," in *Risk and Return in Finance*, ed. Irwin I. Friend and J. Bisksler (Cambridge, MA: Ballinger, 1977), pp. 189–218. See also, Stephen A. Ross, Randolph W. Westerfield, and Jeffrey F. Jaffe, *Corporate Finance*, 3d ed. (New York: McGraw-Hill, 1993), Chapter 11, "An Alternative View of Risk and Return: The Arbitrage Pricing Theory," pp. 315–37.

Exhibit 9–9

Explanation of APT Risk Factors

Confidence Risk

Confidence Risk is the unanticipated changes in investors' willingness to undertake relatively risky investments. It is measured as the difference between the rate of return on relatively risky corporate bonds and the rate of return on government bonds, both with 20-year maturities, adjusted so that the mean of the difference is zero over a long historical sample period. In any month when the return on corporate bonds exceeds the return on government bonds by more than the long-run average, this measure of confidence risk is positive. The intuition is that a positive return difference reflects increased investor confidence because *the required yield on risky corporate bonds has fallen relative to safe government bonds*. Stocks that are positively exposed to this risk then will rise in price. (Most equities *do* have a positive exposure to confidence risk, and small stocks generally have greater exposure than large stocks.)

Time Horizon Risk

Time Horizon Risk is the unanticipated changes in investors' desired time to payouts. It is measured as the difference between the return on 20-year government bonds and 30-day Treasury bills, again adjusted to be mean zero over a long historical sample period. A positive realization of time horizon risk means that the price of long-term bonds has risen relative to the 30-day Treasury bill price. This is a signal that investors require a lower compensation for holding investments with relatively longer times to payouts. The price of stocks that are positively exposed to time horizon risk will rise to appropriately decrease their yields. (Growth stocks benefit more than income stocks when this occurs.)

Inflation Risk

Inflation Risk is a combination of the unexpected components of short- and long-run inflation rates. Expected future inflation rates are computed at the beginning of each period from available information: historical inflation rates, interest rates, and other economic variables that influence inflation. For any month, inflation risk is the unexpected surprise that is computed at the end of the month, i.e., it is the difference between the actual inflation for that month and what had been expected at the beginning of the month. Since most stocks have negative exposures to inflation risk, a positive inflation surprise causes a negative contribution to return, whereas a negative inflation surprise (a deflation shock) contributes positively toward return.

Industries whose products tend to be "luxuries" are most sensitive to inflation risk. Consumer demand for "luxuries" plummets when real income is eroded through inflation, thus depressing profits for industries such as retailers, services, eating places, hotels and motels, and toys. In contrast, industries least sensitive to inflation risk tend to sell "necessities," the demands for which are relatively insensitive to declines in real income. Examples include foods, cosmetics, tire and rubber goods, and shoes. Also companies that have large asset holdings such as real estate or oil reserves may benefit from increased inflation.

Business Cycle Risk

Business Cycle Risk represents unanticipated changes in the level of real business activity. The expected values of a business activity index are computed both at the beginning and end of the month, using only information available at those times. Then, business cycle risk is calculated as the difference between the end-of-month value and the beginning-of-month value. A positive realization of business cycle risk indicates that the expected growth rate of the economy, measured in constant dollars, has increased. Under such circumstances firms that are more positively exposed to business cycle risk—for example, firms such as retail stores that do well when business activity increases as the economy recovers from a recession—will outperform those such as utility companies that do not respond much to increased levels in business activity.

Market Timing Risk

Market Timing Risk is computed as that part of the S&P 500 total return that is not explained by the first four macroeconomic risks and an intercept term. Many people find it useful to think of the APT as a generalization of the CAPM, and by including this market timing factor, the CAPM becomes a special case: If the risk exposures to all of the first four macroeconomic factors were exactly zero, then market timing risk would be proportional to the S&P 500 total return. Under these extremely unlikely conditions, a stock's exposure to market timing risk would be equal to its CAPM beta. Almost all stocks have a positive exposure to market timing risk, and hence positive market timing surprises increase returns, and vice versa.

A natural question, then, is: "Do confidence risk, time horizon risk, inflation risk, and business cycle risk help to explain stock returns better than I could do with just the S&P 500?" This question has been answered using rigorous statistical tests, and the answer is very clearly that they do.

SOURCE: Presented in a talk based on a paper, "A Practitioner's Guide to Arbitrage Pricing Theory," by Edwin Burmeister, Richard Roll, and Stephen A. Ross, written for the Research Foundation of the Institute of Chartered Financial Analysts. The exhibit is drawn from Notes for "Controlling Risks Using Arbitrage Pricing Techniques" by Edwin Burmeister.

the equilibrium expected return is the risk-free rate plus the sum of a series of risk premiums.

APT is more realistic than CAPM because investors can consider other characteristics besides the beta of assets as they select their investment portfolios.[18]

Research suggests that, on average, the cost of equity as estimated using APT tends to be slightly higher than the cost of equity as estimated using CAPM. Early research also suggests that the multivariate APT model explains expected rates of return better than the univariate CAPM.[19]

A source of data for required rates of return using APT is included later in this chapter.

Sources of Data to Estimate the Cost of Equity Capital

Risk-Free Rate

The risk-free rate should be the yield available to investors as of the valuation date. In the United States, the yield most often used is for 20-year, 5-year, or 30-day U.S. Treasury obligations, because those are the maturities for which matching equity risk premium data are available.

The Ibbotson risk premium data are based on yields on U.S. government coupon bonds. Therefore, the coupon bond yield as of the valuation date is appropriate to use with the Ibbotson equity risk premium data.

Equity Risk Premium

Ibbotson Associates publishes its three equity risk premium series annually, as presented in Exhibit 9–10. These are based on arithmetic (as opposed to geometric) means of differences between stock market returns and riskless security returns, for reasons explained in Exhibit 9–11. This is the most widely (but not universally) accepted procedure for estimating the equity risk premium.[20]

Beta

Since privately held companies by definition have no market quotes and thus no market fluctuations, they have no observable betas. The most common procedure in using CAPM to develop a discount rate for a privately held company is to derive an estimate of betas from publicly traded guideline companies, most often guideline companies in the same industry as the subject company.

---

[18] Roger G. Ibbotson and Gary P. Brinson, *Investment Markets* (New York: McGraw-Hill, 1987), p. 52. For a more extensive discussion of APT, see Frank K. Reilly, *Investment Analysis and Portfolio Management*, 5th ed. (Fort Worth, TX: The Dryden Press, 1997), pp. 297–300.

[19] Tom Copeland, Tim Koller, and Jack Murrin, *Valuation: Measuring and Managing the Value of Companies*, 2nd ed. (New York: John Wiley & Sons, 1994), p. 267.

[20] For example, the Ibbotson view that the arithmetic mean is appropriate for estimating discount rates is supported in one of the leading corporate finance texts: Brealey and Myers, *Principles of Corporate Finance*, 5th ed., p. 147. However, for a contrary view (i.e., that the geometric mean differences more closely approximate the market's required return) see Tom Copeland, et al., *Valuation: Measuring and Managing the Value of Companies*, 2nd ed., pp. 261–63.

Exhibit 9–10

Key Variables in Estimating the Cost of Capital

	Value
Yields (Riskless Rates)*	
Long-term (20-year) U.S. Treasury Coupon Bond Yield	5.4%
Intermediate-term (5-year) U.S. Treasury Coupon Note Yield	4.7
Short-term (30-day) U.S. Treasury Bill Yield	4.5
Risk Premia**	
Long-horizon expected equity risk premium: large company stock total returns minus long-term government bond income returns	8.0
Intermediate-horizon expected equity risk premium: large company stock total returns minus intermediate-term government bond income returns	8.4
Short-horizon expected equity risk premium: large company stock total returns minus U.S. Treasury bill total returns[†]	9.4
Expected default premium: long-term corporate bond total returns minus long-term government bond total returns	0.4
Expected long-term horizon premium: long-term government bond income returns minus U.S. Treasury bill total returns[†]	1.4
Expected intermediate-term horizon premium: intermediate-term government bond income returns minus U.S. Treasury bill total returns[†]	1.0
Size Premia***	
Expected mid-capitalization equity size premium: capitalization between $918 and $4,200 million	0.5
Expected low-capitalization equity size premium: capitalization between $252 and $918 million	1.1
Expected micro-capitalization equity size premium: capitalization below $252 million	2.6

*   As of December 31, 1998. Maturities are approximate.

** Expected risk premia for equities are based on the differences of historical arithmetic mean returns from 1926–1998. Expected risk premia for fixed income are based on the differences of historical arithmetic mean returns from 1970–1998.

***See Chapter 7 for complete methodology.

[†] For U.S. Treasury bills, the income return and total return are the same.

Many different financial reporting services publish betas for publicly traded securities. These include *Value Line Investment Survey*, Wilshire Associates, and *Tradeline*. See the bibliography at the end of the chapter for details on locating these sources.

One will find significant differences among betas for the same stock published by different financial reporting services. This is because of differences in computation methods. See Exhibit 9–12 for a discussion of the controversy over different details of computing betas, which can sometimes lead to widely divergent results. One of the implications is that betas for guideline companies used in a valuation

Exhibit 9–11

Ibbotson Associates' Discussion of Arithmetic versus Geometric Mean for Calculating the Expected Equity Risk Premium for Estimating Cost of Capital (Discount Rate)

Arithmetic versus Geometric Differences

For use as the expected equity risk premium in the CAPM, the *arithmetic* or *simple difference* of the *arithmetic means* of the stock market returns and riskless rates is the relevant number. This is because the CAPM is an additive model where the cost of capital is the sum of its parts. Therefore, the CAPM expected equity risk premium must be derived by arithmetic, *not geometric*, subtraction.

Arithmetic Versus Geometric Means

The expected equity risk premium should always be calculated using the arithmetic mean. The arithmetic mean is the rate of return which, when compounded over multiple periods, gives the mean of the probability distribution of ending wealth values. (A simple example given below shows that this is true.) This makes the arithmetic mean return appropriate for computing the cost of capital. The discount rate that equates expected (mean) future values with the present value of an investment is that investment's cost of capital. The logic of using the discount rate as the cost of capital is reinforced by noting that investors will discount their expected (mean) ending wealth values from an investment back to the present using the arithmetic mean, for the reason given above. They will therefore require such an expected (mean) return prospectively (that is, in the present looking toward the future) to commit their capital to the investment.

For example, assume a stock has an expected return of +10 percent in each year and a standard deviation of 20 percent. Assume further that only two outcomes are possible each year—+30 percent and –10 percent (that is, the mean plus or minus one standard deviation) and that these outcomes are equally likely. (The arithmetic mean of these returns is 10 percent, and the geometric mean is 8.2 percent.) Then the growth of wealth over a two-year period occurs as shown below:

Note that the median (middle outcome) and mode (most common outcome) are given by the geometric mean, 8.2 percent, which compounds up to 17 percent over a 2-year period (hence a terminal wealth of $1.17). However, the *expected value*, or probability-weighted average of all possible outcomes, is equal to:

	(.25	×	1.69)	=	0.4225
+	(.50	×	1.17)	=	0.5850
+	(.25	×	0.81)	=	0.2025
TOTAL					1.2100

Now, the rate that must be compounded up to achieve a terminal wealth of $1.21 after 2 years is 10 percent; that is, the expected value of the terminal wealth is given by compounding up the *arithmetic*, not the geometric mean. Since the arithmetic mean equates the expected future value with the present value, it is the discount rate.

Stated another way, the arithmetic mean is correct because an investment with uncertain returns will have a higher expected ending wealth value than an investment that earns, with certainty, its compound or geometric rate of return every year. In the above example, compounding at the rate of 8.2 percent for two years yields a terminal wealth of $1.17, based $1.00 invested. But holding the uncertain investment, with a possibility of high returns (two +30 percent years in a row) as well as low returns (two –10 percent years in a row), yields a higher expected terminal wealth, $1.21. In other words, more money is gained by higher-than-expected returns than is lost by lower-than-expected returns. Therefore, in the investment markets, where returns are described by a probability distribution, the arithmetic mean is the measure that accounts for uncertainty, and is the appropriate one for estimating discount rates and the cost of capital.

Growth of $1.00

should all come from the same source. If all betas for guideline companies are not available from a single source, the best solution probably is to use the source providing betas for the most guideline companies, and to not use betas for the others. Otherwise an "apples-and-oranges" mixture will result.

Exhibit 9–12

Beta Measurement Problems

A major weakness of using CAPM for its original purpose of understanding the value of securities in a portfolio is the measurement of the various components of the CAPM equation. In particular, there is no single accepted source of data or method for measuring the beta coefficient component of the model.

First, different financial reporting services provide different estimates of beta—for the same industry, and even for the same individual security. And, there are at least a dozen reputable financial reporting services that analysts may refer to in order to obtain a beta for a particular security.

Second, different market indexes provide different estimates of the "market risk premium" component of CAPM. Some financial reporting services use the Standard & Poor's 500 as their benchmark market index; some use the Value Line index; some use the Russell 1000, 2000, or 3000; and so on.

Third, different time frames for beta estimates obviously can provide different estimates of the subject beta. In order to compare the subject security prices to the guideline market index, some financial reporting services use weekly observations, some use monthly observations, some make their observations on the last trading day of each, some make their observations on the last Friday of each month (or of each week), and so forth. These differences in data collection—particularly the differences between weekly observation and monthly observation—can have a material impact on the estimation of beta for the same security.

These first three beta measurement problems are illustrated by the data in the table below; this table presents the beta measurement characteristics of several commonly used financial reporting services.

Fourth, betas are typically measured infrequently; therefore, they can be "out of date" as of the particular valuation date. It is common that the most recent betas reported in reputable financial reporting services may have been estimated several months before the publication date of the financial service. And, most financial reporting services do not estimate individual betas on a real-time basis. Rather, they will estimate the beta for an individual security periodically—typically only a few times each year.

Fifth, betas are not available for many securities. For example, betas are not generally available for infrequently traded securities. And, there are literally thousands of publicly listed securities that are not followed by the financial reporting services. So, published betas are not readily available for those securities.

Therefore, with all of these beta measurement problems, the analyst is often uncertain as to:

1. What is the correct beta for the selected guideline companies used in the subject valuation analysis, and
2. What is the correct beta for the subject company (whether or not a "published" beta is estimated directly or a beta based upon guideline companies is estimated indirectly)?

Beta Measurement Characteristics of Common Financial Reporting Services

Financial Reporting Service	Market Index	Measurement Interval	Measurement Time Period
CompuServe	S&P 500	Weekly (Friday close)	5 years
Media General Financial Services	Media General Composite Index (6400+ common stocks)	Per market movement of 5% (up or down)	No set time span
Merrill Lynch	S&P 500	Monthly	5 years
S&P Compustat	S&P 500	Monthly (end of month)	5 years
Tradeline	S&P 500	Weekly (Friday close)	3 years
Value Line	NYSE Composite	Weekly	5 years
Wilshire Associates	S&P 500	Monthly	5 years

Size Premium

As noted earlier, a substantial body of published research indicates that the size of the company is important in that stocks of smaller companies are riskier than larger ones and that small-company stocks command a higher expected rate of return in the market. Ibbotson Associates quantifies this in the *SBBI Yearbook* in the chapter on "Firm Size and Return" as presented in Exhibit 9–10.

Starting with the *1995 Yearbook*, SBBI has expanded the size premium data to include three tiers based on data from the University of Chicago Center for Research on Security Prices (CRSP). What used to be called the *small stock premium* size tier is now called the *micro-capitalization equity size premium*. It still includes the smallest 20 percent of stocks on the New York Stock Exchange as measured by market value of common equity—in 1998 up to approximately $252 million.

The two size premium categories added in the *1995 Yearbook* are the "low-capitalization equity risk premium," which includes the sixth through eighth NYSE size deciles, encompassing market values of common equity from about $252 million to $918 million, and the "mid-capitalization equity risk premium," covering market value of common equity from $918 million to about $4.1 billion.[21]

It is noteworthy that the size premium is *in addition* to the basic equity risk premium already modified by the effect of the beta, and betas for smaller stocks tend to be greater than for larger stocks. The correct formula, reflecting *both* beta and the size premium, is the following:

Formula 9–8

$$E(R_i) = R_f + B(RP_m) + RP_s$$

where:

$E(R_i)$ = Expected return on an individual security

R_f = Rate of return available on a risk-free security (as of the valuation date); when using the Ibbotson size premium data, the risk-free rate should be 30-day, 5-year, or 20-year government bond yields, used in conjunction with the corresponding equity risk premium

B = Beta

(RP_m) = Equity risk premium for a security with a beta of 1.0

RP_s = Risk premium for size (size premium)

Investment-Specific Risk

The estimation of the effect of investment-specific (unsystematic) risk is often a matter for the analyst's professional judgment. The risk factors will be developed as part of the quantitative and qualitative analyses discussed in Part II of this book, and the significant positive and negative factors related to these analyses should be noted in the valuation report. These analyses will reveal many things that will affect the economic income projections, as well as the risk of achieving those projections. The analyst should be careful to distinguish between those factors that influence the *magnitude* of the projection (the numerator in the model) and those factors which affect the *degree of uncertainty* of achieving the mathematical expectation projection (that is, the *risk*, which determines the discount rate, the denominator in the model). The analyst must be especially careful to avoid undue double counting, such as reflecting a negative factor fully by a reduction in the same economic income projection, and then magnifying the effect by an increase in the discount rate—for the negative factor.

There is no specific model or formula for quantifying the exact effect of all the investment-specific risk factors on the discount rate. This ultimately is based on the analyst's experience and judgment. It is noteworthy that the analysis may lead to the conclusion that the subject company is *less risky* than industry or guideline company averages, in which case the investment-specific risk adjustment may *reduce* the discount rate.

---

[21] *SBBI: Valuation Edition 1999 Yearbook*, p. 99.

Arbitrage Pricing Theory Factors

Two major sources exist for arbitrage pricing theory data. The Alcar Group, Inc., markets a software package and database service called *APT!* that estimates bond ratings using standard financial ratios. Birr Portfolio Analysis, Inc., publishes *BIRR Risks and Returns Analyzer*, a PC-based software text. The contact information for these sources can be found in the bibliography at the end of this chapter.

Rate of Return Allowed to Regulated Companies

Additional cost of capital data are available when estimating the appropriate discount rate for a regulated company.

Public utility commissioners in all 50 states allow regulated utilities to charge rates to their customers that provide what supposedly is a fair rate of return on investment (often called the *rate base*). These allowed rates of return generally are based on the respective commissions' perceptions of the cost of debt capital and the cost of equity capital based on studies by their staffs. Utility commissions' allowed rate of return orders usually also specify an allowed overall rate of return on invested capital, based on their conclusions as to the appropriate capital structure. Megamillions of dollars are involved in these rate-setting decisions, based on hard-fought negotiations and hearings that sometimes culminate in lawsuits and rate base decisions rendered in court.

Regulated companies usually are regulated because they have a captive market and are in a monopoly position to supply a needed service; thus, their cost of capital should be considerably lower than that for an average company. Therefore, allowed rates of return for regulated companies can be viewed as a reasonable benchmark for a minimum boundary of the overall cost of capital.

Ibbotson Associates *Cost of Capital Quarterly*

Starting in 1995, Ibbotson Associates combined in one publication several of the above data items plus other information relevant to estimating the cost of equity, and also other information useful for valuation work. Exhibit 9–13 is an example of the information offered in *Cost of Capital Quarterly* for each of over 350 SIC code groups (see the bibliography at the end of this chapter).

This is a convenient and potentially powerful compilation of data for use in valuation work. We caution readers who use it, however, to carefully study the definitions of all data items before using them in a valuation analysis. Some definitions are not completely implied by the short titles describing the data points in the tables. Other definitions are not what we may ideally desire, usually because of limitations on the availability of data. The definitions *are* explained in detail. Used carefully, this can be a very useful reference source for the valuation analysis.

Discounting Economic Income Available to Overall Capital

Until now in this chapter, we have focused on discounting economic income available to the common equity holders. In some situations (which will be described elsewhere

Exhibit 9–13

Sample Page from Cost of Capital Quarterly

STATISTICS FOR SIC CODE 201

Meat Products

This Industry Comprises 13 Companies

Industry Description

Establishments primarily engaged in processing or manufacturing meat products including meat packing plants; sausages and other prepared meat products; poultry slaughtering and processing.

Sales (million$)

Total	31,323
Average	2,409.4

Three Largest Companies

IBP INC	12,848.6
TYSON FOODS INC -CL A	7,414.1
SMITHFIELD FOODS INC	3,867.4

Three Smallest Companies

DOUGHTIE'S FOODS INC	85.2
RYMER FOODS INC	33.9
SMITHFIELD COMPANIES INC	20.5

Total Capital (million$)

Total	15,241
Average	1,172.4

Three Largest Companies

TYSON FOODS INC -CL A	6,901.5
HORMEL FOODS CORP	2,827.0
IBP INC	2,438.9

Three Smallest Companies

DOUGHTIE'S FOODS INC	23.8
SMITHFIELD COMPANIES INC	18.1
RYMER FOODS INC	2.7

Annualized Statistics for Last 10 Years (%)

	Average Return	Standard Deviation
S&P 500	20.00	15.83
Ind. Composite	12.76	24.33
Lg. Composite	12.08	27.48
Sm. Composite	17.79	41.99

Distribution of Sales & Total Capital (million$)

	Sales Latest	Sales 5 Yr. Avg.	Total Capital Latest	Total Capital 5 Yr. Avg.
90th Percentile	6,704.8	5,564.3	2,749.4	2,454.5
75th Percentile	3,261.0	2,619.2	1,365.0	984.7
Median	521.4	795.1	272.6	270.9
25th Percentile	127.9	114.5	119.3	103.5
10th Percentile	44.2	83.4	19.3	17.3

Number of Companies & Total Capital (billion$)

	Large Cap	Mid Cap	Low Cap	Micro Cap	Total Cap
AAA, AA, A					
	1	1	0	0	2
	6.9	2.4	0.0	0.0	9.3
BBB					
	0	1	0	0	1
	0.0	1.4	0.0	0.0	1.4
BB, B, CCC, CC, D					
	0	0	1	0	1
	0.0	0.0	0.7	0.0	0.7
Not Rated					
	0	1	0	8	9
	0.0	2.8	0.0	1.0	3.9
Totals					
	1	3	1	8	13
	6.9	6.6	0.7	1.0	15.2

☐ S&P Debt Rating

Industry Sales, Income & Market Capitalization (billion$)

	Sales	Operating Income	Net Income	Equity Capital	Debt Capital
Current Yr.	31.3	1.8	0.5	11.0	4.2
Last Yr.	31.1	1.4	0.5	11.8	3.8
2 Yrs. Ago	28.7	1.2	0.3	10.1	3.5
3 Yrs. Ago	26.5	1.8	0.7	9.1	3.0
4 Yrs. Ago	25.2	1.5	0.4	8.6	2.4

Compound Annual Equity Return (%)

	5 Yrs.	10 Yrs.
75th Percentile	3.66	6.94
Median	1.38	3.59
25th Percentile	-8.00	-3.47
Ind. Composite	8.99	10.26
Lg. Composite	7.50	8.80
Sm. Composite	0.96	10.70

Growth Over Last 5 Years (%)

	Net Sales	Operating Income	Net Income
75th Percentile	8.93	12.86	15.49
Median	4.25	5.93	5.86
25th Percentile	1.94	-7.79	-10.77
Ind. Composite	5.90	8.38	2.59
Lg. Composite	4.11	8.27	0.59
Sm. Composite	2.95	-9.65	-6.44

Unlevered Betas

	Adj OLS	Adj Sum
75th Percentile	0.69	0.67
Median	0.54	0.52
25th Percentile	0.25	0.20
Ind. Composite	0.68	0.29
Lg. Composite	0.74	0.35
Sm. Composite	0.64	0.55

Levered Betas

	Raw OLS	Adj OLS	Adj Sum
75th Percentile	0.89	0.89	0.87
Median	0.64	0.77	0.78
25th Percentile	0.42	0.65	0.52
Ind. Composite	0.85	0.86	0.42
Lg. Composite	0.90	0.90	0.49
Sm. Composite	0.86	0.87	0.78

Capital Structure Ratios (%)

	Debt/Total Capital Latest	Debt/Total Capital 5 Yr. Avg.	Debt/MV Equity Latest	Debt/MV Equity 5 Yr. Avg.
75th Percentile	36.59	47.45	36.59	90.29
Median	30.18	35.59	30.18	55.26
25th Percentile	20.09	21.79	20.09	27.86
Ind. Composite	26.76	25.78	36.53	34.73
Lg. Composite	25.14	23.03	33.59	29.91
Sm. Composite	39.78	33.37	66.05	50.08

Margins (%)

	Operating Margin Latest	Operating Margin 5 Yr. Avg.	Net Margin Latest	Net Margin 5 Yr. Avg.	Asset Turnover Latest	Asset Turnover 5 Yr. Avg.	Return on Inv. Capital Latest	Return on Inv. Capital 5 Yr. Avg.	Return on Assets Latest	Return on Assets 5 Yr. Avg.	Return on Equity Latest	Return on Equity 5 Yr. Avg.
75th Percentile	8.69	7.64	3.76	2.14	372.07	326.65	7.82	8.26	7.01	6.60	7.28	8.21
Median	4.34	4.03	1.38	1.67	225.58	248.68	5.85	4.54	5.75	4.28	5.32	5.76
25th Percentile	2.38	3.07	0.34	0.30	190.61	214.23	0.23	1.75	0.52	1.46	0.53	3.08
Ind. Composite	5.71	5.42	1.50	1.67	258.57	281.59	4.95	6.16	3.87	4.69	4.09	4.88
Lg. Composite	5.96	5.69	1.57	1.88	253.15	280.48	5.10	7.00	3.97	5.27	4.05	5.07
Sm. Composite	2.45	3.53	1.03	1.92	262.82	310.55	3.50	7.30	2.72	5.95	5.66	9.44

Equity Valuation Ratios (Multiples)

Div. Yield (% of Price)

	Price/Earnings Latest	Price/Earnings 5 Yr. Avg.	Market/Book Latest	Market/Book 5 Yr. Avg.	Price/Sales Latest	Price/Sales 5 Yr. Avg.	Price/Cash Flow Latest	Price/Cash Flow 5 Yr. Avg.	Price/Operating Income Latest	Price/Operating Income 5 Yr. Avg.	Latest	5 Yr. Avg.
75th Percentile	190.14	32.46	2.42	2.12	0.64	0.54	NMF	NMF	8.54	6.21	1.42	2.18
Median	18.78	17.36	1.47	1.50	0.28	0.24	21.21	144.81	7.26	5.57	0.49	0.84
25th Percentile	13.74	12.18	1.17	1.24	0.13	0.13	15.88	21.34	4.96	4.11	0.00	0.52
Ind. Composite	2.99	3.31	2.22	2.24	0.37	0.34	65.65	49.53	6.41	6.29	0.78	0.93
Lg. Composite	3.32	3.73	2.18	2.35	0.39	0.37	69.28	37.92	6.50	6.50	0.87	0.98
Sm. Composite	1.61	2.11	1.05	1.26	0.18	0.20	17.64	115.02	7.46	5.75	0.84	1.47

Growth Rates (%)

	Analysts
75th Percentile	13.86
Median	10.38
25th Percentile	8.14
Ind. Composite	12.74
Lg. Composite	12.00
Sm. Composite	NMF

Cost of Equity Capital (%)

	CAPM Adj OLS	CAPM + Sm Prem	3-Factor Fama-French	Discounted Cash Flow Analysts	Discounted Cash Flow 3 Stage
75th Percentile	12.98	14.11	19.31	14.78	14.90
Median	11.02	11.97	14.80	13.91	11.50
25th Percentile	9.27	11.19	7.20	12.38	9.85
Ind. Composite	12.75	13.24	13.95	12.87	11.80
Lg. Composite	13.07	13.56	15.18	12.90	12.20
Sm. Composite	12.87	15.47	7.78	12.89	13.40

Weighted Average Cost of Capital (%)

	CAPM Adj OLS	CAPM + Sm Prem	3-Factor Fama-French	Discounted Cash Flow Analysts	Discounted Cash Flow 3 Stage
75th Percentile	11.37	12.25	13.27	13.61	13.36
Median	9.84	10.46	9.22	11.68	10.73
25th Percentile	9.05	9.39	7.62	8.64	9.00
Ind. Composite	10.91	11.28	11.80	11.00	10.20
Lg. Composite	11.22	11.59	12.82	11.09	10.56
Sm. Composite	11.20	13.02	7.63	11.21	11.57

Copyright © 1999
Ibbotson Associates

Cost of Capital Quarterly
1999 Yearbook

SOURCE: *Cost of Capital Quarterly 1999 Yearbook*™ (Chicago: Ibbotson Associates, 1999), pp. 2–3. Used with permission. All rights reserved.

in this book), it is desirable to value more than just the common equity—often all the equity and all the interest-bearing debt (sometimes referred to as the *entire capital structure* or *the value of the company* or *market value of invested capital (MVIC)*).

In these instances, the projected cash flow (or other economic income) must include that which is available to *all* the components of the capital structure being valued. The discount rate must be the weighted average of the cost of each of the components in the capital structure, *each weighted average based on the market value of that capital component.* This is called the *weighted average cost of capital* (WACC). In other words, the cost of a company's overall capital is the weighted average of the costs of all of its financing sources in its capital structure.

Defining the Capital Structure

When people refer to "the value of the company" (as opposed to just the value of equity), they usually mean the value of the company's capital structure. However, this still may leave ambiguity as to exactly what is included in the "capital structure."

Treatment of Interest-Bearing Debt. The most commonly used conceptual definition of *capital structure* is all equity and all long-term debt (including current maturities of long-term debt). However, to value the capital structure by this definition using the discounted economic income method, it is necessary to include the interest on the long-term debt in the income being discounted and treat other interest (such as on a bank operating line of credit) as an expense. If it is not practical to get the necessary information to separate the two elements of interest, then a commonly used solution to the problem is to define the capital structure to include all interest-bearing debt. Interest-bearing debt may be defined to include the permanent portion of interest-bearing current liabilities. This would be the case if, for example, 90-day notes payable (otherwise classified as a current liability) are used as a permanent source of capital for the subject company. Using all interest-bearing debt eliminates a judgment call by the analyst as to the appropriate levels of long-term versus short-term debt.

Treatment of Noninterest-Bearing Items. Another issue in some cases is whether or not to include certain noninterest-bearing long-term liabilities in the capital structure. This may include, for example, such items as deferred taxes and pension liabilities. If any such items were to be included, some portion of the capital structure would have zero cost of capital.

Conceptually, the most commonly accepted answer is that they should be included if it is expected that they will be paid and excluded if not. This, then, requires a judgment call. The analyst should also keep in mind that weightings of the components of the capital structure for the purpose of estimating a WACC are at *market value*. Therefore, if noninterest-bearing liabilities are to be included, an estimate of when they will be paid is required so the face value can be discounted to a present market value to determine their weight. As a practical matter, noninterest-bearing liabilities usually are not included in calculations of a WACC, but there are times that they are important enough to consider.

In any case, when discounting economic income available to the company, it is important to specify what is assumed to be included in the capital structure.

Weighted Average Cost of Capital (WACC) Formula

The basic formula for computing the after-tax WACC is as follows:

Formula 9–9

$$WACC = \left(k_e \times W_e\right) + \left(k_d[1-t] \times W_d\right)$$

where:

$WACC$	=	Weighted average cost of capital
k_e	=	Company's cost of common equity capital
k_d	=	Company's cost of debt capital
W_e	=	Percentage of equity capital in the capital structure
W_d	=	Percentage of debt capital in the capital structure
t	=	Company's effective income tax rate

Assume:

Cost of equity capital	0.25
Cost of debt capital	0.10
Proportion of equity in capital structure	0.70
Proportion of debt in capital structure	0.30
Income tax rate	0.40

The above data would be substituted into this formula as follows:

$$(0.25 \times 0.70) + (0.10[1 - 0.40] \times 0.30)$$
$$= 0.175 + (0.06 \times 0.30)$$
$$= 0.175 + 0.018$$
$$= \underline{\underline{0.193}}$$

So, the overall cost of capital in the above example is 19.3 percent.

In many cases, there is a more complex capital structure, perhaps with preferred stock and more than one class of debt. The above formula would simply be expanded to include a term for each class of capital.

Should an Actual or Hypothetical Capital Structure Be Used?

If the company is to be valued *as it is* (under the strict fair market value standard, assuming the capital structure will remain intact), then the amount of debt in the company's actual capital structure should be used. Certainly, if a minority ownership interest is to be valued by a procedure involving (first) valuing overall capital and (then) subtracting debt, the company's actual amount of debt in its capital structure would seem appropriate. This is because it would be beyond the power of a noncontrolling stockholder to change the capital structure.

The analyst should keep in mind that the weightings in the capital structure are at market value. Therefore, if there is a fixed amount of debt and the WACC is used to estimate market value of equity, computations may need to be iterated with different assumed capital structures until the estimated market value of equity results in the assumed market value capital structure weights.

If a controlling ownership interest is to be valued and the standard of value is fair market value, an argument can be made that an industry-average capital structure should be used. This is because a control buyer would have the power to change the capital structure and the industry average could represent the most likely result. However, it would be important to understand how the industry-average capital structure is derived and whether or not it is reasonable to expect the subject company to achieve it, given (1) the current conditions of the company itself and (2) the current financial market conditions. If a controlling ownership interest is to be valued under the standard of investment value, then the buyer's or owner's capital structure could be used.

Specific Projection Period Plus a Terminal Value

So far, we have presented the basic discounted economic income model, where specific projections of economic income are made over the life of the investment. However, as a practical matter, there are very few investments for which reliable projections can be made over the entire life of the investment. Variations of the model reflect this limitation.

The most common multistage variation of the discounted economic income model is a two-stage model that projects economic income for a finite number of periods, usually one business cycle of somewhere between 3 and 10 years, and then assumes a *terminal value* at the end of the discrete projection period.

This terminal value is sometimes also called the *residual value*, the *reversionary value*, or the *future value*. The formula for this model can be generalized as follows:

Formula 9–10

$$PV = \frac{E_1}{(1+k)} + \frac{E_2}{(1+k)^2} + \ldots + \frac{E_n}{(1+k)^n} + \frac{FV}{(1+k)^n}$$

where:

$E_1 \ldots E_n$ = Expected amounts of the economic income (often net cash flow) in each of periods E_1 through E_n

k = Discount rate

n = Number of periods in the discrete projection period

FV = Future value or terminal value (the prospective value as of the end of the discrete projection period)

The immediately obvious characteristic of the above formula is that it depends partly on a projection of the value of the subject several periods in the future to estimate the value of the subject today! It is not uncommon for the present value of the terminal value in this formulation to account for over half of the total present value. Therefore, the matter of how the terminal value is estimated is an important part of the estimate of present value.

If one assumes that the business will continue indefinitely as a viable going concern after the number of years for which discrete projections were made, two procedures are commonly used to estimate the terminal value:

1. Capitalization of ongoing economic income.
2. An estimated market multiple of the economic income projected for the last year of the discrete projection period.

The capitalization method is the procedure favored by most business appraisers. It is discussed in some detail in the next chapter.

Many investment bankers are prone to use the market multiple method. If one is discounting returns to equity, this method involves a multiple of some measure of income available to equity, most typically a price/earnings (P/E) multiple. If one is discounting returns available to overall capital, this method involves a multiple of some measure of income available to overall capital, most typically EBIT (earnings before interest and taxes) or EBITDA (earnings before interest, taxes, depreciation, and amortization).

The market multiple method introduces into the income approach the added dimension of projecting a market multiple as of the end of the projection period. As noted earlier, the terminal value often accounts for half or more of the value indicated by the DCF method. The market multiple brings a major element of the market approach into the income approach. Many valuation analysts prefer to keep the income approach and market approach as discrete from each other as possible. Many believe that using the Gordon growth model capitalization procedure described in the next chapter does a better job of keeping income approach and market approach indications of value as independent of each other as possible.[22]

Under certain circumstances, the terminal value may be based on the premise that the company will be liquidated at the end of the discrete projection period. This terminal value requires an estimate of liquidation value of the subject company assets as of that future date.

The "Midyear Discounting Convention"

In the formulas presented up to this point, we have implied (by using whole integer exponents) that the cash flows (or other economic income) are expected to be received at the *end* of each period. This is reasonable, since many closely held companies wait until the end of their fiscal year to see how things are and assess capital requirements and decide on shareholder distributions.

On the other hand, sometimes it seems more reasonable to assume that cash flows are received (or at least available) more or less evenly throughout the year. This projection can be reflected in the discounted economic income model by using the *midyear discounting convention*. This convention projects cash flows being received at the middle rather than the end of each year, thus more or less approximating the valuation effect of even cash flows throughout the year.

The modification to Formula 9–10 to accommodate the midyear discounting convention results in the following:

Formula 9–11

$$PV = \frac{E_1}{(1+k)^{0.5}} + \frac{E_2}{(1+k)^{1.5}} + \ldots + \frac{E_n}{(1+k)^{n-0.5}} + \frac{FV}{(1+k)^{n}}$$

where the variables are defined the same as in Formula 9–10.

The following chapter explains how the terminal value calculation can be modified for the midyear convention (see Formula 10–12).

----

[22] Whether using a market multiple or the Gordon growth model to estimate the terminal value, the resulting implied growth rate and market multiple, respectively, should be checked for reasonableness.

Of course, the failure to use the midyear discounting convention slightly decreases the indicated present value. This is because the midyear discounting convention assumes that the cash flows will be received earlier on the average than the year-end discounting model assumes.

The valuation model can be varied to accommodate any material assumptions about the timing of cash flows, such as monthly, quarterly, or irregularly. For example, a toy company may have predictably high seasonal cash flows in the fourth quarter, or an accounting firm may have a predictable bulge in cash flows during tax season. The calculations for any such variations can be done on any modern, inexpensive pocket financial calculator.

Example of Application of Discounted Economic Income Methods

In a series of exhibits, we present several of the basic discounted economic income methods applied to value 100 percent of the equity of Global Consulting, Inc., as of December 31, 1999. The basic information, including the December 31, 1999, balance sheet, three years of projected balance sheets, income statements, cash flows to equity, cash flows to invested capital, and other information are presented as Exhibit 9–14A.

The example projects stable growth for the entire projection period. This projection allows us to show how any of four methods can be used, all resulting in the same value:

1. Discounted net cash flow available to equity.
2. Perpetual growth model using net cash flow available to equity.
3. Discounted net cash flow available to all invested capital (market value of invested capital) less value of debt.
4. Perpetual growth model using net cash flow available to all invested capital (market value of invested capital) less value of debt.

Estimating an Equity Discount Rate

Exhibit 9–14B illustrates the estimation of the cost of equity capital for the subject company using the capital asset pricing model. The sources of all components are footnoted in the exhibit, so that one can seek out the sources and replicate the work.

Discounting Net Cash Flow to Equity

Exhibit 9–14C illustrates discounting the cash flow to equity using the projected net cash flows to equity from Exhibit 9–14A and the discount rate developed in Exhibit 9–14B. This example uses the perpetual growth model to estimate the terminal value.

With a very short specific projection period, the terminal value constitutes over half of the total value. The shorter the specific projection period and the lower the discount rate, the higher the proportion of the total value will be accounted for by the terminal value.

Exhibit 9–14A

Global Consulting, Inc.

Balance Sheets (in 000s)

End of Year	Actual 1999	Projected 2000	Projected 2001	Projected 2002
Current assets	$30,000	$31,500	$33,075	$34,728
Plant & equipment	90,000	101,000	112,550	124,677
Less: Accumulated depreciation	60,000	69,000	78,450	88,372
Net plant & equipment	30,000	32,000	34,100	36,305
Total assets	$60,000	$63,500	$67,175	$71,033
Current liabilities	$10,000	$10,500	$11,025	$11,576
Long-term debt	40,000	42,000	44,100	46,305
Equity	10,000	11,000	12,050	13,152
Total liabilities & equity	$60,000	$63,500	$67,175	$71,033

Income Statements (in 000s)

	2000	2001	2002
Sales	$200,000	$210,000	$220,500
Cost of sales	120,000	126,000	132,300
Gross margin	80,000	84,000	88,200
General operating expenses	52,000	54,600	57,330
Depreciation	9,000	9,450	9,922
Earnings before interest & taxes (EBIT)	19,000	19,950	20,948
Interest (10% of beginning LTD)	4,000	4,200	4,410
Taxable income (EBT)	15,000	15,750	16,538
Income taxes (40%)	6,000	6,300	6,615
Net income	$9,000	$9,450	$9,923

Other Information

Expected growth rate in perpetuity is 5% (applies to all income statement items, net working capital, capital expenditures, and long-term debt).

Capital expenditures year 2000: $11 million

Market value of long-term debt = Book value of long-term debt

All net cash flow to equity will be paid out in dividends.

Calculation of Net Cash Flow to Equity (in 000s)

		2000	2001	2002
	Net income	$9,000	$9,450	$9,922
+	Depreciation	9,000	9,450	9,922
−	Capital expenditures	11,000	11,550	12,127
−	Increase in net working capital	1,000	1,050	1,102
+	Increase in long-term debt	2,000	2,100	2,205
=	Net cash flow to equity	$8,000	$8,400	$8,820

Statements of Stockholders' Equity (in 000s)

		2000	2001	2002
	Balance at beginning of year	$10,000	$11,000	$12,050
+	Net income	9,000	9,450	9,922
−	Dividends paid	8,000	8,400	8,820
=	Balance at end of year	$11,000	$12,050	$13,152

Calculation of Net Cash Flow to Invested Capital (in 000s)

		2000	2001	2002
	Net income	$9,000	$9,450	$9,922
+	Depreciation	9,000	9,450	9,922
−	Capital expenditures	11,000	11,550	12,127
−	Increase in net working capital	1,000	1,050	1,102
+	Interest expense (net of 40% income taxes)	2,400	2,520	2,646
=	Net cash flow to invested capital	$8,400	$8,820	$9,261

Exhibit 9–14B

Illustrative Example of Discount Rate Applicable to Equity

	Risk-free rate (20-year U.S. Treasury bond) [a]		6.83%
+	Systematic risk:		
	Long-horizon expected equity risk premium [b]	8.00	
×	Beta [c]	1.30	
			10.40
+	Expected size premium [d]		4.35
+	Specific (unsystematic) risk [e]		3.00
=	Discount rate (indicated)		24.58
	Discount rate (rounded)		25.00

a.   Rate available as of December 31, 1999, per *The Wall Street Journal*.
b.   *Stocks, Bonds, Bills and Inflation: Valuation Edition 1999 Yearbook*, p. 51.
c.   Median beta of guideline companies from Standard & Poor's *Compustat*.
d.   *Stocks, Bonds, Bills and Inflation: Valuation Edition 1999 Yearbook*, p. 104.
e.   Analyst's estimate.

Exhibit 9–14C

Estimation of Value of Equity (Discounted Cash Flow Method)

	2000		2001		2002		Terminal Value
	$\dfrac{\$8,000,000}{(1+0.25)}$	+	$\dfrac{\$8,400,000}{(1+0.25)^2}$	+	$\dfrac{\$8,820,000}{(1+0.25)^3}$	+	$\dfrac{\$46,305,000}{(1+0.25)^3}$
		+		+		+	
=	$\dfrac{\$8,000,000}{(1.25)}$	+	$\dfrac{\$8,400,000}{(1.25)^2}$	+	$\dfrac{\$8,820,000}{(1.25)^3}$	+	$\dfrac{\$46,305,000}{(1.25)^3}$
=	$6,400,000	+	$5,376,000	+	$4,515,800	+	$23,708,200
=	$40,000,000 Indicated value of equity						

Estimating a Weighted Average Cost of Capital

Exhibit 9–14D illustrates the estimation of the weighted average cost of capital (WACC) using the information provided in Exhibit 9–14A and the equity discount rate developed in Exhibit 9–14B.

Discounting Net Cash Flow to Invested Capital

Exhibit 9–14E illustrates discounting the cash flow available to all invested capital using the projected cash flow to invested capital from Exhibit 9–14A and the WACC from Exhibit 9–14D.

In this example, with the short projection period and the WACC, which is much lower than the equity discount rate, the terminal value accounts for over three-quarters of the total market value of invested capital! Some market multiples that might be used as a check on the reasonableness of the terminal value are discussed in Chapter 12 on the guideline transaction method.

Exhibit 9–14D

Estimation of Weighted Average Cost of Capital

Capital Component	Amount	Percent of Capital		Cost of Capital		Weighted Average Cost
Market value of debt	$40,000,000	0.50	×	0.06*	=	0.030
Market value of equity	$40,000,000	0.50	×	0.25	=	0.125
Weighted average cost of capital						0.155

* Cost of debt × (1–income tax rate) = 0.10(1–0.40) = 0.06.

Exhibit 9–14E

Estimation of Market Value of Invested Capital (Discounted Cash Flow Method)

	2000		2001		2002		Terminal Value
	$\dfrac{\$8,400,000}{(1+0.155)}$	+	$\dfrac{\$8,820,000}{(1+0.155)^2}$	+	$\dfrac{\$9,261,000}{(1+0.155)^3}$	+	$\dfrac{\$92,610,000}{(1+0.155)^3}$
=	$\dfrac{\$8,400,000}{(1.155)}$	+	$\dfrac{\$8,820,000}{(1.155)^2}$	+	$\dfrac{\$9,261,000}{(1.155)^3}$	+	$\dfrac{\$92,610,000}{(1.155)^3}$
=	$7,272,700	+	$6,611,600	+	$6,010,500	+	$60,105,200
=	$80,000,000	Market value of invested capital					
Less	$40,000,000	Value of debt					
Equals	$40,000,000	Indicated value of equity					

The market value of debt, as of the valuation date, is then subtracted from the MVIC to arrive at the market value of equity.

Caveats in Using Discounted Economic Income Methods

The discounted economic income methods are extremely sensitive to changes in the input variables—that is, the projected cash flows and the discount rate. This is especially true of the market value of invested capital (MVIC) version, where one values the entire invested capital using a WACC discount rate and then subtracts the value of existing debt to get an estimate of the value of the equity. This issue is discussed further in the following chapter where estimates of terminal values using a capitalization method are explored in detail.

Because such large impacts may result from relatively small changes in input variables, it is often enlightening to perform some sensitivity analysis in conjunction with a discounted economic income method. This could take the form of a sensitivity table showing the impact of a range of discount rates, terminal value multiples, growth rates, and cash flow projections.

Converting a Discount Rate Applicable to Net Cash Flow to a Discount Rate Applicable to Net Income

If it can be assumed that the relationship (ratio) of net income to net cash flow is constant over time, then the formula to convert a discount rate applicable to net cash flow to a discount rate applicable to net income for use in the multiperiod discounted economic income model is as follows:[23]

Formula 9–12

$$k_{ni} = \left[\frac{NI}{NCF_e}(k_e - g) \right] + g$$

where:

k_{ni} = Discount rate applicable to net income

$\dfrac{NI}{NCF_e}$ = Assumed constant ratio of net income to net cash flow to equity

k_e = Discount rate applicable to net cash flow

g = Annual compound growth rate in perpetuity for both net income and net cash flow

Note carefully the *critical assumptions* inherent in the above formula:

1. Net income and net cash flow bear a constant relationship to each other over time.
2. Both grow at the same constant annual compound rate in perpetuity.

One way to assess whether these assumptions are realistic is to compute the ratio of net income to net cash flow for the subject company for several years in the past to see whether the ratio has been steady historically. One would still need to judge whether this stability would be expected to continue to hold true.

Another avenue is to research publicly traded companies in the industry to see the extent to which the ratio is reasonably consistent from company to company and over time. One would then have to analyze the extent to which the subject company could be expected to parallel the public companies in this respect.

If the subject company comes close enough to the above assumptions to realistically use this formula, then it is useful to know the following characteristics about how it works out:

1. The higher the cash flow discount rate, the higher the difference between the cash flow discount rate and the net income discount rate.
2. The higher the ratio between net income and net cash flow, the higher the difference between the net cash flow discount rate and the net income discount rate. For any given combination of discount rate and growth rate, this relationship moves proportionately with changes in the percentages by which net income exceeds net cash flow.
3. The higher the growth rate, the less the difference between the net cash flow discount rate and the net income discount rate.

Examples of the application of this formula are presented in Exhibit 9–15. As can be seen, the greatest differences between net cash flow discount rates and net

---

[23] For a proof of the derivation of this formula, see Z. Christopher Mercer, *Valuing Financial Institutions* (New York: McGraw-Hill, 1992), pp. 262–64.

Exhibit 9–15

Differences between Net Cash Flow Discount Rate and Net Income Discount Rate

Formula:

$$k_{ni} = \left[\frac{NI}{NCF_e}(k_e - g) \right] + g$$

	\multicolumn{6}{c}{**Constant Ratio of Net Income to Net Cash Flow**}
	150%	**140%**	**130%**	**120%**	**110%**	**100%**
$k_e = 30\%$ **Growth Rate**						
2%	14.0%	11.2%	8.4%	5.6%	2.8%	0.0%
4%	13.0%	10.4%	7.8%	5.2%	2.6%	0.0%
6%	12.0%	9.6%	7.2%	4.8%	2.4%	0.0%
8%	11.0%	8.8%	6.6%	4.4%	2.2%	0.0%
$k_e = 25\%$ **Growth Rate**						
2%	11.5%	9.2%	6.9%	4.6%	2.3%	0.0%
4%	10.5%	8.4%	6.3%	4.2%	2.1%	0.0%
6%	9.5%	7.6%	5.7%	3.8%	1.9%	0.0%
8%	8.5%	6.8%	5.1%	3.4%	1.7%	0.0%
$k_e = 20\%$ **Growth Rate**						
2%	9.0%	7.2%	5.4%	3.6%	1.8%	0.0%
4%	8.0%	6.4%	4.8%	3.2%	1.6%	0.0%
6%	7.0%	5.6%	4.2%	2.8%	1.4%	0.0%
8%	6.0%	4.8%	3.6%	2.4%	1.2%	0.0%

where:

k_{ni}	=	Discount rate applicable to net income
$\dfrac{NI}{NCF_e}$	=	Constant assumed ratio of net income to net cash flow to equity
k_e	=	Discount rate applicable to net cash flow to equity
g	=	Annually compounded growth rate in perpetuity for both net income and net cash flow

income discount rates are found in situations of high net cash flow discount rates, high ratios of net income to net cash flow, and low growth rates.

Net cash flow is generally lower than net income or any other economic income measures that the appraiser is likely to discount or capitalize. Therefore, the discount rate applicable to other measures is almost inevitably higher than the discount rate applicable to net cash flow.

CAUTION: The above critical assumptions for the conversion of a discount rate applicable to net cash flow to equity to a discount rate applicable to net income are rarely met in real world situations. Therefore, we strongly recommend the use of net cash flow as the measure of economic income to utilize in the discounted economic income method.

It is also noteworthy that the discount rate conversion procedures described above are appropriate for the multiperiod (or yield capitalization) discounted economic income model. They are not necessarily appropriate for the single-period (direct capialization) or capitalization or capitalization of economic income model.

Does the Discounted Economic Income Model Produce a Control or a Minority Value?

As noted earlier in the chapter, the discounted economic income model can produce either a control value or a minority value, depending on the model inputs regarding the valuation variables. Generally, if the inputs in the valuation model reflect changes that only a control owner would (or could) make (e.g., changed capital structure, reduced owner's compensation, and so on), then the model would be expected to produce a control value.

If the economic income projections merely reflect the continuation of present policies, then the model would be expected to produce a minority value. If every facet of the company is being so well optimized that a control owner could not improve on it, then there is little or no difference between a control value and a minority value. Further discussion of this notion will be found in Chapters 15 and 16 on control premiums and discounts for lack of control.

The argument is often made that, because discount rates typically are developed from minority trades in publicly traded stocks, the discount rate is a minority interest discount rate and the value indicated by a discounted economic income model must, therefore, be a minority value. There are at least two problems with this argument. First, *most, if not all, of the difference between a control value and a minority value in a discounted economic income model results from differences in the projected economic income (the numerator) and not from differences in the discount rate.* Second, while the costs of equity capital are estimated from trades of minority ownership interests, the capital structure (i.e., the percent of debt versus the percent of equity) of the subject company is clearly influenced by the controlling stockholder. And, the capital structure mix is at least as important as the cost of equity capital in the estimation of a company's overall WACC—that is, the discount rate associated with net cash flow. In other words, the cost of equity capital may be the same, or nearly the same, whether a control or a minority interest is being transacted. However, the controlling owner (and, generally, not the minority owner) influences the projection of economic income (the numerator in the model) and the capital structure component of the WACC (the denominator in the model).

What Standard of Value Does a Discounted Economic Income Model Produce?

As with the control/minority ownership issue, the answer to this question depends to some extent on the individual valuation variable inputs that go into the model.

If valuing a company on a stand-alone basis, the use of that company's own economic income projections and a market-derived cost of capital as the discount rate would be expected to estimate the *fair market value* of the subject business enterprise. If, on the other hand, a particular acquirer with a lower cost of capital would discount an economic income projection at that acquirer's lower cost of capital, then the result would be *investment value*, the value of the subject—but only to that individual acquirer. Similarly, if a potential acquirer were to include synergistic benefits or other enhancements in the economic income projections, then the result would be *investment value* rather than *fair market value*.

Common Errors

While simple in basic concept, the application of the discounted economic income method provides virtually limitless opportunities for errors. The following are a few of the common errors that are made:

Mismatching the Discount Rate with the Economic Income Measure

The most common error in application of the income approach is using a discount or capitalization rate that is not appropriate for the definition of economic income being discounted or capitalized. This general category of error has almost infinite variations. The following are only a few.

Using a "Safe" Rate to Discount or Capitalize a Risky Return. While not the most common error, this certainly is one of the most egregious. Some analysts have even erroneously discounted a highly risky series of projected economic income by the Treasury bill rate!

Applying a Discount Rate to an Income Variable Defined Differently Than That to Which the Discount Rate Is Applicable. This general error in itself has many variations. As discussed earlier, most of the methods and sources for developing discount rates used in the practical application of contemporary financial theory and discussed in this book produce a rate at which to discount net cash flow, as defined in an earlier section. The *SBBI: Valuation Edition 1999 Yearbook* makes the following point: "It is implicit that the market return data represents returns after corporate taxes but before personal taxes."[24]

Applying a Discount Rate in Real Terms to an Economic Income Projection in Nominal (Current) Terms. Some analysts erroneously subtract the anticipated inflation rate from the discount rate and then apply the adjusted discount rate to an economic income projection that includes inflation (and vice versa). It is noteworthy that all the Ibbotson data are in nominal terms—that is, including inflation.

Confusing Discount Rates with Capitalization Rates

The *discount rate* is the cost of capital, and applies to all prospective economic income. The *capitalization rate* (as discussed in the following chapter) is a divisor applied to some particular economic income (e.g., latest 12 months' earnings, cash flow, and so on). Only when the expected level of economic income is constant in perpetuity are these two rates equal, other than by sheer coincidence.

Nevertheless, some appraisers fall into the trap of using the discount rate (i.e., cost of capital) as a capitalization rate. We also see the opposite from time to time: using a capitalization rate to discount prospective cash flow or other expected economic

---

[24] *SBBI: Valuation Edition 1999 Yearbook*, p. 62.

income to a present value. The relationship between discount rates and capitalization rates is explained in the next chapter.

Projecting Growth Beyond What the Capital Being Valued Will Support

As businesses grow, they typically need additional working capital and capital expenditures to support the increased level of operations. One of the many advantages of using net cash flow as the prospective economic income measure is that it forces the analyst to explicitly consider these needs. Nevertheless, they are often underestimated but can be addressed if the projections include a balance sheet along with the income statement.

Projecting That Extrapolation of the Recent Past Represents the Best Estimate of Future Results

All economic, finance, and regulatory literature makes it clear that valuation is a function of expected prospective economic income. The past history is relevant only to the extent that it may, in some cases, provide useful guidance in projecting future economic income. Nevertheless, it is not as uncommon as one might think to see "projections" which are nothing more than a statistical extrapolation of past results, with no analysis as to the extent to which the future generating forces will or will not duplicate the recent past. Usually, they will not.

Discounting a Terminal Value for an Incorrect Number of Periods

Referring back to Formula 9–10, it can be seen that the terminal value usually is assumed to be the value at the *beginning* of the period immediately following the discrete projection period. Therefore, it usually should be discounted back to a present value by the same number of years as the last term in the discrete projection period (n in the formula). A common error is to discount the terminal value for $n + 1$ periods, which would be appropriate only if the terminal value represented the estimated value one year following the end of the discrete projection period.

Internally Inconsistent Capital Structure Projection

"Debt-free" methods and methods using betas adjusted for leverage require projections about the subject company's capital structure. These projected capital structures are on the basis of *market value*. Often appraisers assume a capital structure in the process of estimating a market value of equity, and the resulting estimated market value of equity makes the capital structure, at the estimated market value, different from that which was assumed.

   In such cases, the assumed capital structure needs to be adjusted and the process iterated until the estimated market value of equity results in a capital structure consistent with that which is projected in estimating the cost of capital.

Assumptions That Produce a Standard or Premise of Value Other Than That Called for in the Valuation Engagement

A common example of this type of error is making unsupported adjustments to projected economic income that only a control owner could cause to happen (e.g., lowering the control owner's salary) when valuing a minority ownership interest.

Another common error is projecting a capital structure other than the company's actual capital structure (thereby getting a weighted average cost of capital different from the company's actual WACC) when the standard of value is fair market value on a noncontrolling basis. If an acquirer were to use its own WACC, the implied result would be *investment value* to that acquirer instead of fair market value. Moreover, if the interest is a noncontrolling interest, the holder could not force a change in capital structure.

Summary

This chapter has presented the rationale of the discounted economic income method and step-by-step explanations of each important aspect of its implementation. The chapter has explained the conceptual elements of discount rates and sources of information to develop estimates of appropriate betas.

The discounted economic income method can be used in conjunction with almost any combination of standards of value and ownership characteristics, as long as the projections underlying the valuation variables used in the calculation are consistent with the definition of value being sought.

Bibliography

Articles

Abrams, Jay B. "Cash Flow: A Mathematical Derivation." *ASA Valuation*, March 1994, pp. 64–71.

Annin, Michael. "Fama-French and Small Company Cost of Equity Calculations." *Business Valuation Review*, March 1997, pp. 3–13.

_____. "Using Ibbotson Associates' Data to Develop Minority Discount Rates." *CPA Expert*, Winter 1997, pp. 1–4.

Annin, Michael E., and Dominic A. Falaschetti. "Equity Risk Premium Still Produces Debate." *Valuation Strategies*, January/February 1998, pp. 17–19, 44.

Becker, Brian, and Ian Gray. "Does a Small Firm Effect Exist When Using the CAPM? Not Since 1980 and Not When Using Geometric Means of Historical Returns." *Business Valuation Review*, September 1999, pp. 104–11.

Bendixen, Christian L. "Improved Estimation of Equity Risk Premiums." *Business Valuation Review*, March 1994, pp. 22–32.

Bielinski, Daniel W. "How to Sort Out the Premium Drivers of Post-Deal Value." *Mergers & Acquisitions*, July/August 1993, pp. 33–37.

_____. "Putting a Realistic Dollar Value on Acquisition Synergies." *Mergers & Acquisitions*, November/December 1992, pp. 9–12.

Black, Fischer. "Estimating Expected Return." *Financial Analysts Journal*, September–October 1993, pp. 36–38.

Booth, Lawrence. "The Capital Asset Pricing Model: Equity Risk Premiums and the Privately-Held Business," *The Journal of Business Valuation* (Proceedings of the 4th Joint Business Valuation Conference of The Canadian Institute of Chartered Business Valuators and the American Society of Appraisers). Toronto: The Canadian Institute of Chartered Business Valuators, 1999, pp. 87–114.

Burns, Richard M. "Business Valuations Using DCF Analysis." Presentation to the 1999 National Conference of the Institute of Business Appraisers. Available on www.BVLibrary.com.

Danielson, Morris G. "A Simple Valuation Model and Growth Expectations." *Financial Analysts Journal*, May/June 1998, pp. 50–57.

Dilbeck, Harold R. "A Constant-Dollar Discount Rate for Closely Held Businesses Based on Risk Premiums from Five-Year Holding Periods." *Business Valuation Review*, March 1994, pp. 11–18.

Dukes, William P., and Oswald D. Bowlin. "A Comparison of Valuation Techniques for Closely Held Firms." *Business Valuation Review*, June 1993, pp. 80–91.

Evans, Frank C. "Making Sense of Rates of Return and Multiples." *Business Valuation Review*, June 1999, pp. 51–57.

Fama, Eugene, and Kenneth French. "Common Risk Factors in the Returns on Stocks and Bonds." *University of Chicago Working Paper No. 360*, November 1992.

_____. "The Cross Section of Expected Stock Returns." *Journal of Finance*, Vol. 47 (1992), pp. 427–65.

Good, Walter R. "Yes, Virginia, There is a Risk Premium, But. . ." *Financial Analysts Journal*, January–February 1994, pp. 11–12.

Goodman, Barry R. "Analysis of Ibbotson's Small Cap Premium." Presentation to the 16th Annual Advanced Business Valuation Conference of the American Society of Appraisers (1997), available on www.BVLibrary.com

Grabowski, Roger, and David King. "New Evidence on Equity Returns and Company Risk." *Business Valuation Review*, September 1999, pp. 112–30.

_____. "New Evidence on Equity Returns and Company Risk: A Revision." *Business Valuation Review*, March 2000, pp 32–43.

_____. "New Evidence on Size Effects and Rates of Return." *Business Valuation Review*, September 1996, pp. 103–14.

Harper, Charles P., and Lawrence C. Rose. "Accuracy of Appraisers and Appraisal Methods of Closely Held Companies." *Entrepreneurship Theory & Practice*, Spring 1993, pp. 21–33.

Hickman, Kent, and Glenn H. Petry. "A Comparison of Stock Price Predictions Using Court Accepted Formulas, Dividend Discount, and P/E Models." *Financial Management*, Summer 1990, pp. 76–87.

Howitt, Idelle A. "Valuing Closely Held Stock." *CPA Journal*, September 1993, pp. 44–45+.

Jackson, Marcus. "The Gordon Growth Model and the Income Approach to Value." *Appraisal Journal*, January 1994, pp. 124–28.

Kenny, Thomas J. "Closely-Held Corporation Valuation: Determining a Proper Discount Rate." *Business Valuation Review*, March 1992, pp. 22–30.

King, David W. "The Equity Risk Premium for Cost of Capital Studies: Alternatives to Ibbotson." *Business Valuation Review*, September 1994, pp. 123–29.

King, David W. and Roger J. Grabowski. "Equity Risk Premiums" (Chapter 3). In *Handbook of Advanced Business Valuation*, Robert F. Reilly and Robert P. Schweihs, eds. New York: McGraw-Hill, 2000.

Knight, Ray A., and Lee G. Knight. "Three Key Methods for Valuing Profitable Closely Held Companies." *Journal of Corporate Accounting & Finance*, Autumn 1993, pp. 79–94.

LeClair, Mark S. "Valuing the Closely-Held Corporation: The Validity and Performance of Established Valuation Procedures." *Accounting Horizons*, September 1990, pp. 31–42.

Lippitt, Jeffrey W., and Nicholas J. Mastracchio, Jr. "Valuing Small Businesses: Discounted Cash Flow, Earnings Capitalization, and the Cost of Replacing Capital Assets." *Journal of Small Business Management*, July 1993, pp. 52–61.

Mard, Michael J., and James S. Rigby. "New Research to Estimate Cost of Capital." *CPA Expert*, Fall 1995, pp. 9–12.

Maxson, Mark J. "Will You Get Your Money's Worth?" *Financial Executive*, May/June 1993, pp. 54–58.

Miller, Warren D. "Assessing Unsystematic Risk." *CPA Expert,* Summer 1999, pp. 1–5.

Moyer, R. Charles, and Ajay Patel. "The Equity Market Risk Premium: A Critical Look at Alternative Ex Ante Estimates." Working paper (1997) available on www.BVLibrary.com.

Paschall, Michael A. "Do Smaller Companies Warrent a Higher Discount Rate for Risk?" *Business Valuation Alert*, December 1999, pp. 3, 10–12.

Peters, Jerry O. "Adjusting Price/Earnings Ratios for Differences in Company Size." *Business Valuation Review*, June 1999, pp. 71–85.

Pratt, Shannon P. "The Income Approach—Estimating the Cost of Capital" (Chapter 1). In *Handbook of Advanced Business Valuation*, Robert F. Reilly and Robert P. Schweihs, eds. New York: McGraw-Hill, 2000.

Pratt, Shannon P., and Ralph Arnold. "Misuse of the Discounted Future Returns Valuation Method." *Fair$hare*, March 1990, pp. 3–5.

Schilt, James H. "Still another Look at Betas." *Business Valuation Review*, March 2000, pp. 16–18.

Sharpe, William F. "Capital Asset Prices with and without Negative Holdings." Nobel Lecture, December 1990, The Nobel Foundation, Royal Swedish Academy of Sciences, Sweden.

Shiffrin, Daniel. "Tax Court Determines Weight of Asset-Based and Earnings-Based Valuation Approaches." *CPA Litigation Service Counselor*, February 2000, pp. 3, 12.

Sliwoski, Leonard. "Capitalization Rates, Discount Rates, and P/E Ratios: One More Time." *Business Valuation Review*, September 1992, pp. 122–34.

Stanton, Thomas C. "The Anatomy of Beta: Getting Down to Basics." *Business Appraisal Practice*, Fall 1999, pp. 34–38.

_____. "The Market Model: An Alternative to the CAPM." *Business Valuation Review*, March 1999, pp. 12–15.

Swad, Randy. "Discount and Capitalization Rates in Business Valuations." *CPA Journal*, October 1994, pp. 40–46.

"Update on IRS Position on Valuation Discounts and Small Stocks." *Journal of Taxation*, December 1999, pp. 379–81.

Vander Linden, Eric. "Cost of Capital Derived from Ibbotson Data Equals Minority Value." *Business Valuation Review*, December 1998, pp. 123–27.

Wiggins, C. Donald. "Matching Cash Flows and Discount Rates in Discounted Cash Flow Appraisals." *Business Valuation Review*, March 1999, pp. 26–35.

Reference Texts

Bierman, Harold, Jr., and Seymour Smidt. *The Capital Budgeting Decision: Economic Analysis of Investment Projects*, 8th ed. Englewood, NJ: Prentice-Hall, 1992.

Brealey, Richard A., and Stewart C. Myers. *Principles of Corporate Finance*, 5th ed. New York: McGraw-Hill, 1996.

Copeland, Tom, Tim Koller, and Jack Murrin. *Valuation: Measuring and Managing the Value of Companies*, 2nd ed. New York: John Wiley & Sons, 1994.

Damodaran, Aswath. *Damodaran on Valuation: Security Analysis for Investment and Corporate Finance*. New York: John Wiley & Sons, 1994.

Dewing, Arthur Stone. *The Financial Policy of Corporations*, 5th ed. New York: Ronald Press, 1953.

Ehrhardt, Michael C. *The Search for Value: Measuring the Company's Cost of Capital*. Boston: Harvard Business School Press, 1994.

Pratt, Shannon P. *Cost of Capital: Estimation and Applications*. New York: John Wiley & Sons, 1998.

Reilly, Frank K., and Keith C. Brown. *Investment Analysis and Portfolio Management*, 5th ed. Fort Worth, TX: Dryden Press, 1997.

Reilly, Robert F., and Robert P. Schweihs, eds. *Handbook of Advanced Business Valuation*. New York: McGraw-Hill, 2000.

Ross, Stephen A., Randolph W. Westerfield, and Jeffrey F. Jaffe. *Corporate Finance*, 4th ed. New York: McGraw-Hill, 1996.

Sharpe, John. *Texas Property Tax Manual for Discounting Oil and Gas Income*. Austin, TX: Texas Comptroller of Public Accounts, 1994.

Sharpe, William F., Gordon J. Alexander, and Jeffrey V. Bailey. *Investments*, 6th ed. Englewood Cliffs, NJ: Prentice-Hall, 1998.

Williams, John Burr. *The Theory of Investment Value*. Cambridge, MA: Harvard University Press, 1938.

Arbitrage Pricing Theory Data Sources

Birr Portfolio Analysis, Inc.
BIRR Risks and Returns Analyzer
Durham, North Carolina
(919) 687-7053
www.birr.com

The Alcar Group
APT!
Skokie, Illinois
(847) 967-4200
www.alcar.com

Sources of Beta

CompuServe
5000 Arlington Centre Boulevard
P.O. Box 20212
Columbus, Ohio 43220
(800) 848-8990
www.compuserve.com

Ibbotson Associates
The Beta Book
225 North Michigan Avenue,
 Suite 700
Chicago, Illinois 60601
(312) 616-1620
www.ibbotson.com

Merrill Lynch
Merrill Lynch Capital Markets
Global Securities Research &
  Economics Group
World Financial Center
North Tower, 19th Floor
New York, New York 10281-1320
(212) 449-1069
www.research.ml.com

Tradeline
IDD Information Services
100 Fifth Avenue
Waltham, Massachusetts 02154
(781) 890-7227
www.idd.net

Wilshire Associates Inc.
1299 Ocean Avenue, 7th Floor
Santa Monica, California 90401-1085
(310) 451-3051
www.wilshire.com

Other Cost of Capital Data
Ibbotson Associates
Cost of Capital Quarterly
PriceWaterhouseCoopers Risk Premia Study
Stocks, Bonds, Bills and Inflation
Stocks, Bonds, Bills and Inflation:
  Valuation Edition
225 North Michigan Avenue, Suite 700
Chicago, Illinois 60601
(312) 616-1620
www.ibbotson.com

Standard & Poor's Compustat and
Standard & Poor's Stock Reports
Standard & Poor's Corporation
25 Broadway
New York, New York 10004
(212) 208-8000
www.standardpoor.com
www.compustat.com

Value Line Investment Survey
220 East 42nd Street, 6th Floor
New York, New York 10017
(212) 907-1500
www.valueline.com

Chapter 10

Income Approach: Capitalized Future Economic Income Method[1]

---

[1] Much of this chapter is adapted from Chapter 15, The Capitalized Economic Income Method, in Shannon P. Pratt, Robert F. Reilly, and Robert P. Schweihs, *Valuing Small Businesses and Professional Practices*, 3rd ed. (New York: McGraw-Hill, 1998).

There are two variations of the capitalized future economic income method that are widely used in business valuation today:

1. The perpetual economic income stream model.
2. The constant growth model (with a variation commonly referred to as the *Gordon growth model*).[2]

This chapter transitions the reader from the discounted future economic income method of valuation to the capitalized future economic income method, and presents the mechanics, applications, and caveats in utilizing the various frequently used versions of the capitalized income method.

Essential Difference between the Discounting Model and the Capitalization Model

A *discount rate* converts *all* of the expected future return on investment (however defined) to an indicated present value.

In contrast to the more comprehensive method of discounting *all* of the expected returns, a *capitalization rate* converts *only a single return flow number* to an indicated present value.

Discount rate	A rate of return used to convert a monetary sum, payable or receivable in the future, into a present value.
Capitalization rate	Any divisor (usually expressed as a percentage) that is used to convert income into value.[3]
Capitalization	A method used to convert an estimate of a single year's income expectancy into an indication of value in one direct step, either by dividing the income estimate by an appropriate rate or by multiplying the income estimate by an appropriate factor.[4]

In property appraisal terminology, the above definition is called *direct capitalization*, the basic subject matter of this chapter. It is distinguished from what property appraisers call *yield capitalization*, which is comparable to the business appraiser's *discounted economic income*, the subject of the previous chapter.

The capitalized economic income method means the application of one divisor (or multiple) to one economic income measure. The result is an indication of value derived from that single division or multiplication.

For example, let's assume that the next year's net cash flow is expected to be $200,000,000 and the appropriate direct capitalization rate is 25 percent. In this case, the indicated value of the business is $800,000,000:

$$\frac{\$200,000,000}{0.25} = \$800,000,000$$

Note from the definition above that the method is based on *expectancies*. Like the discounted economic income method, it is a method to convert *anticipated* income to a present value.

---

[2] There can be other variations, such as capitalizing an income stream with a finite life. One who understands the details of the last chapter and this chapter should be able to construct capitalization rates for such variations.

[3] American Society of Appraisers, Business Valuation Standards, Definitions (Herndon, VA: American Society of Appraisers, 1994).

[4] *The Dictionary of Real Estate Appraisal*, 3rd ed. (Chicago: Appraisal Institute, 1993), p. 100.

The capitalized economic income method is used as frequently as the discounted economic income method, and probably even more frequently in the valuation of smaller businesses. So why does this text put the discounted economic income method first? Because, *the capitalized economic income method is simply an abridged version of the discounted economic income method.* The discounted economic income method is presented first because the valuation theory that is applied in the discounted economic income method is more comprehensive. And once the analyst has a grasp of the discounted economic income method, the valuation theory that is applied in the capitalized income method can be grasped more easily.

The Perpetual Economic Income Stream Model

Consider the case of a preferred stock that has no maturity and no call provision (i.e., no expected redemption), paying a fixed dividend in perpetuity. The basic discounted economic income formula would value this preferred stock as follows:

Formula 10–1

$$PV = \sum_{i=1}^{n} \frac{E_i}{\left(1 + k_p\right)^i}$$

where:

PV = Present value

$\sum$ = Sum of

n = The last period for which economic income is expected; n may equal infinity (i.e., ∞) if the economic income is expected to continue in perpetuity

E_i = The expected amount of economic income in each ith period in the future

k_p = Rate of return on preferred stock

i = The period (usually stated as a number of years) in the future in which the prospective economic income is expected to be received

It can be shown mathematically that where the expected economic income is a constant amount in perpetuity, the above formula can be simplified to:

Formula 10–2

$$PV = \frac{E}{k}$$

where:

E = An expected amount of economic income in every period ahead in perpetuity

k = Discount rate (cost of capital for that level of economic income)

In this unique case, the result is that the expected level amount of economic income can be capitalized by dividing it by the discount rate, and the capitalization rate equals the discount rate. Thus, in this case:

Formula 10–3

$$c = k$$

where:

  c = Capitalization rate
  k = Discount rate (cost of capital for that level of economic income)

In other words, *in the unique case where the expected economic income is a net level amount in perpetuity, the discount rate is equal to the capitalization rate.*

In any other case, where expected future amounts of economic income differ from the amount used in the capitalization formula, the difference between expected prospective amounts and the amount being capitalized is reflected in the difference between the appropriate discount rate (i.e., total yield or total required rate of return) and the capitalization rate (the divisor by which a single period return is converted to an estimate of value).

The simplest example of this is a noncallable preferred stock that pays a fixed dividend in perpetuity. Assume the following valuation variables:

  Annual dividend rate $5 per share
  Required rate of return 10%

In this case, the stock would be valued as follows:

$$\frac{\$5}{0.10} = \$50 \text{ per share}$$

Converting a Discount Rate to a Capitalization Rate—The Constant Growth Model

Discounting, for which a *discount rate* is used, is a process applied to one or a series of specific expected income amounts as of a specified time or times in the future, to convert those expected amounts to an estimate of present value. The discount rate is applied to all the expected future economic income. Therefore, any expected future growth in returns is captured in the numerator of the discounted economic income formula.

Capitalizing, for which a *capitalization rate* is used, is a process applied to an amount representing some measure of economic income for some single period, to convert that economic income amount to an estimate of present value. Capitalization procedures can be used with expected, current, historical, or "normalized" (or "stabilized") measures of economic income. If growth is expected from the base level of economic income being capitalized, then that expected growth is reflected in the capitalization rate.

This leads to the logical answer to the difference between the discount rate and the capitalization rate: *For an investment with perpetual life, the difference between the discount rate and the capitalization rate is the annually compounded percentage rate of growth or decline in perpetuity in the economic income variable being discounted or capitalized.*

If the level of economic income expected in the 12 months immediately following the valuation date is expected to increase after that time at a constant average annually compounded rate in perpetuity, then it can be demonstrated mathematically that the basic discounted economic income formula of:

Formula 10–4

$$PV = \sum_{i=1}^{n} \frac{E_i}{(1+k)^i}$$

can be simplified to:

Formula 10–5

$$PV = \frac{E_1}{k-g}$$

where:

PV = Present value

E_1 = Expected amount of economic income in the period immediately ahead

k = Discount rate (required total rate of return)

g = Expected growth rate of E, annually compounded in perpetuity

The above relationship can be expressed as an algebraic formula as follows:

Formula 10–6

$$c = k-g$$

where:

c = Capitalization rate (a rate to be used as a divisor to convert a return flow variable, such as net cash flow, to an indication of value)

k = Discount rate

g = Annually compounded rate of growth in the economic income variable being capitalized over the life of the investment (if there is an expected rate of decline, the g is negative, so the effect is that the rate of decline is *added* to the discount rate to conclude the capitalization rate)

This leads to the basic capitalization formula:

Formula 10–7

$$PV = \frac{E_1}{c}$$

where:

PV = Present value

E_1 = Expected economic income in the period immediately ahead

c = Capitalization rate

In this formula, it is noteworthy that the capitalization rate is the reciprocal of a valuation pricing multiple. For example, if next year's economic income is projected to be $1.00, and the stock is priced at $12.50, it is selling at 12.5 times next year's income. This equates to a capitalization rate of 8 percent—that is, $1 \div 12.5 = 0.08$.

A simple example of the perpetual growth model would be a stock for which we have an economic income estimate for the year immediately following the effective valuation date, and for which we expect a constant growth rate in that amount of income in the years to follow. Assume the following:

Next year's expected economic income (E_1) $10

Discount rate (k) (required total rate of return)   15%

Sustainable income growth rate (g)   5%

In this case, the share of stock would be valued as follows:

$$\frac{\$10}{0.15-0.05}=\frac{\$10}{0.10}=\$100$$

The Gordon Growth Model

As noted earlier, the direct capitalization model assumes that the base level of normalized economic income to be capitalized is the expected income in the period *immediately following* the effective valuation date (i.e., E_1 in our notation system).

If the normalized economic income for the period *immediately* preceding the effective valuation date is considered a reasonable base level from which to project sustainable growth, the *Gordon growth model* version of the capitalized economic income method is appropriate. Using net cash flow as the economic income measure, the formula for the Gordon growth model is as follows:

Formula 10–8

$$PV=\frac{E_o(1+g)}{k-g}$$

where:

PV = Present value
E_o = Amount of economic income in the period immediately past
k = Discount rate (required yield rate or total rate of return)
g = Growth rate of E, annually compounded in perpetuity

Formulas 10–5 and 10–8 are often referred to as the *Gordon growth model*, the *dividend growth model*, or the *constant growth model*.[5] They represent a technically correct simplification of the basic discounted economic income model, *provided that the critical assumption underlying this simplification is met—that is, the economic income variable is expected to have a constant average annually compounded rate of growth in perpetuity.*

Since this assumption is rarely met in the real world, this growth model is often used only as the final stage of a multistage discounted economic income model. For example, it is common to make specific income forecasts for some period (often five years or until the company is expected to reach a reasonably stable state), and then use the constant growth model to reflect income expectations from that point forward. An example of this will be shown later in the chapter.

In this case the investment would be valued as follows:

$$\frac{\$10(1+0.05)}{0.15-0.05}=\frac{\$10.50}{0.10}=\$105$$

Sensitivity to Growth Rate Assumptions

Changes in the growth rate projected, sometimes seemingly small, can result in striking changes. In the basic constant growth example, we had the following:

[5] For a mathematical proof of this formula, see, for example, Richard A. Brealey and Stewart C. Myers, *Principles of Corporate Finance*, 5th ed. (New York: McGraw-Hill, 1996), pp. 38–39.

$$\frac{E_1}{k-g} = \frac{\$10}{0.15-0.05} = \frac{\$10}{0.10} = \$100$$

Now let's just increase the assumed growth rate by 1 percent. Now we have:

$$\frac{E_1}{k-g} = \frac{\$10}{0.15-0.06} = \frac{\$10}{0.09} = \$111.11$$

One percentage point change in the growth rate produced more than an 11 percent change in the indicated value!

Taking the example a step further, let's assume a 10 percent weighted average cost of capital, with $100 debt and a 5 percent growth rate:

$$PV_f = \frac{NCF_f}{k-g} = \frac{\$10}{0.10-0.05} = \frac{\$10}{0.05} = \$200$$

less debt	100
value of equity	$100

Now let's increase the assumed growth rate by 1 percent. Now we have:

$$PV_f = \frac{NCF_f}{k-g} = \frac{\$10}{0.10-0.06} = \frac{\$10}{0.04} = \$250$$

less debt	100
value of equity	$150

In this leveraged investment a one percentage point change in the growth rate resulted in a 25 percent increase in the indicated value of invested capital and a 50 percent increase in the indicated value of equity!

Obviously, the closer the growth rate to the discount rate, the greater the sensitivity. When the projected growth rate reaches or exceeds the discount rate in the perpetual growth model, mathematically, the capitalization rate is zero or negative. This relationship leads to the generally unreasonable conclusion that the company is infinitely valuable.

Because such large impacts may result from relatively small changes in input variables, it is often enlightening to perform some sensitivity analysis in conjunction with a discounted or capitalized economic income method. This could take the form of a sensitivity table showing the impact of a range of discount rates, terminal value multiples, growth rates, and cash flow projections.

When to Use the Discounting versus the Capitalization Method

The obvious implication of all this, when one stops to think about it simplistically, is that *the difference between the discounting model and the capitalization model is how one treats anticipated changes in future income over time*:

1. In discounting, *changes over time in the expected economic income are treated specifically in the terms of the numerator of the present value equation.*
2. In capitalizing, *changes over time in the expected economic income are treated as a single average percentage change, and that annualized percentage is subtracted (assuming it is positive) from the cost of capital in the denominator.*

The important conceptual underpinning of the capitalized economic income valuation model is that there is either a constant annual income stream in perpetuity or a constant annualized rate of growth (or decline) in the economic income variable being capitalized in perpetuity. Obviously, this constant growth rate projection is rarely met in the real world.

Unlike the discounted economic income model, the capitalization model does not take into consideration the timing of future changes in expected economic income. The greater the differences in the anticipated changes over time, especially in the early years, the more the analyst is encouraged to apply the discounted economic income method rather than the capitalized income method.

This leads to some generalizations about the relative attractiveness of the two basic income approach valuation methods:

1. *Stable or evenly growing economic income flow.* If the economic income flow is either stable or growing (or declining) at a fairly even rate, the capitalized economic income method should conclude as accurate a value indication as the discounted economic income method.
2. *Predictable but uneven changes.* If there are reasons to believe that changes will be significant but predictable, even though uneven, the discounted economic income model should produce a more accurate valuation.
3. *Short- or intermediate-term supergrowth.* If growth is expected to be quite high in the immediate future, the discounted economic income model should produce a more accurate valuation. One of the most common mistakes in the application of this method is to use a 10 percent growth for the first few years (even though it may not be sustainable over the long term) and then subtract that 10 percent from the present value discount rate. This mistake will result in a low capitalization rate and in an overvaluation of the subject company.
4. *Changes that are erratic and unpredictable as to timing.* If the company's economic income is unstable and also more or less random as to timing, the company's risk increases, and thus the present value discount rate increases. However, the discounted economic income method may not be able to produce any more accurate a value indication than the direct capitalization method.

Equivalence of the Discounting and Capitalization Methods

Exhibit 10–1 shows that, with the same set of assumptions, the discounted economic income method and the capitalized economic income method will produce an identical valuation indication. Therefore, an analyst using the capitalized economic income method should understand its parent method (the discounted economic income method) and think through, as a form of mental verification of reasonableness, "If I carried out the full discounting procedure, would I get approximately the same answer?" If not, the valuation variables used in the capitalization method should be reexamined, or perhaps the capitalization method should only be used for a terminal value in conjunction with the discounting method.

Exhibit 10–1

Equivalence of Discounted Economic Income Method and Capitalized Economic Income Method under Constant Growth Rate Scenario

Projection scenario: $8,000,000 net cash flow to equity in Year 1, 5 percent perpetual annual growth rate from Year 1 forward, and a 25 percent present value discount rate.

Discounted Economic Income Method

Projection period:		Year 1		Year 2		Year 3		Terminal Value
Indicated value of business entity*	=	$\dfrac{\$8,000,000}{(1+0.25)}$	+	$\dfrac{\$8,400,000}{(1+0.25)^2}$	+	$\dfrac{\$8,820,000}{(1+0.25)^3}$	+	$\dfrac{\dfrac{\$8,820,000\,(1.05)}{0.25-0.05}}{(1+0.25)^3}$
	=	$\dfrac{\$8,000,000}{1.25}$	+	$\dfrac{\$8,400,000}{(1.25)^2}$	+	$\dfrac{\$8,820,000}{(1.25)^3}$	+	$\dfrac{\dfrac{\$8,820,000\,(1.05)}{0.20}}{(1.25)3}$
	=	$6,400,00	+	$5,376,000	+	$4,515,800	+	$\dfrac{\$46,305,000}{(1.25)^3}$
	=	$6,400,000	+	$5,376,000	+	$4,515,800	+	$23,708,200
Indicated value of business entity	=	$\underline{\$40,000,000}$						

Capitalized Economic Income Method

Projection period:	Year 1
Economic income to equity	$\underline{\$8,000,000}$
Present value discount rate minus expected long-term growth rate	0.25–0.05
Indicated value of business entity	$\underline{\$40,000,000}$

* using Formula 10–19

Implementing the Capitalized Economic Income Method

As we have seen, like the discounted economic income method, the essence of the capitalized income method is twofold:

1. *Projecting an anticipated economic income stream.* As opposed to projecting the amount and timing of each individual economic income flow the business is expected to produce for its owner, the direct capitalization method requires projecting a single, sustainable amount of future economic income (the *numerator* in the arithmetic formula).

2. *Capitalizing the expected economic income amount to produce a present value.* This second step involves dividing the expected economic income by a rate that reflects the risk (degree of certainty or uncertainty) of receiving that expected amount on a regular basis. In other words, the starting point is the *present value discount rate*, as discussed in the previous chapter. However, the numerator reflects only a *single period* of economic income, not any future changes. Therefore, if changes are expected, the present value discount rate should be modified by adding or subtracting the anticipated rate of growth (or decline) in the economic income flow to convert the present value discount rate into a direct capitalization rate (the *denominator* in the arithmetic formula).

Projecting the Basic Economic Income Level and the Growth Rate

The projections needed for the capitalized economic income method are twofold:

1. The normalized and sustainable expected base economic income.
2. The expected long-term growth rate.

These projections may be prepared by the company or by the valuation analyst, ideally with some involvement by both. The arithmetic of this valuation method could not be more simple. However, this fact implies the extreme importance of the realism of the expectations impounded in the base expected economic income estimate and the expected long-term growth rate.

Start with Sustainable Expected Economic Income

In order for the capitalized economic income method to produce a realistic value indication, the numerator should be a realistic sustainable base of expected economic income. The expected economic income should be either stable or expected to change at a somewhat constant average rate over a long period of time.

As with the discounted economic income method, this method requires carrying out the adjusted income statement procedures discussed in Chapter 7. Of course, if the operational economic income variable is net cash flow, the adjustments to reach that measure (as defined in the previous chapter) also should be made.

Again, the capitalized economic income method is a forward-looking analysis, just as the discounted economic income method is. The economic income measure capitalized should represent *expected* future economic income. A simple average—or a weighted average—of past operating results is not an adequate procedure in and of itself to develop this projection. The historical average should be used only if the analyst is able to justify the notion that this past average is indeed a reasonable proxy for future economic income expectations. Of course, the analyst may consider company budgets, plans, forecasts, and other forward-looking data in the estimation of the normalized (or sustainable) economic income measure.

The Projected Long-Term Growth Rate

Treating the Impact of Inflation. If the build-up procedure or the CAPM procedure is used to develop the present value discount rate from which the growth rate is to be subtracted in order to derive a direct capitalization rate, that discount rate should incorporate the expected rate of inflation as part of the required rate of return. The implication is that the selected long-term growth rate should also reflect the impact of expected inflation on the economic income variable being capitalized.

For example, if the projection of the financial performance for the company assumes no real growth, but it is expected that the economic income will grow enough to keep up with the general level of expected inflation, the consensus long-term inflation rate should be subtracted from the present value discount rate in order to arrive at the appropriate direct capitalization rate.

Sustainability. The economic income capitalization method has impounded in it the implied projection that the growth rate used to arrive at the direct capitalization rate is a long-term sustainable growth rate. In fact, technically, it is a growth rate expected *in perpetuity*.

As a practical matter, discount rates and capitalization rates for investments in small businesses and professional practices are relatively high compared with most other investments. Therefore, changes in the growth rate after 15 or 20 years would have almost no impact on the present value. However, misspecification of the projected growth rate during the first 10 years or so can have a major impact on the indicated value.

As suggested earlier, if significant changes in the growth rate are expected within the first 10 years, the discounted economic income model probably is preferable to the economic income capitalization model. The economic income capitalization model can be incorporated to estimate the terminal value in the discounted economic income calculations, as explained further in a subsequent section.

If some changes in the growth rate are expected but are either too minimal or too unpredictable as to timing to justify using the discounted economic income method, some subjective adjustment to the projected growth rate using the capitalized economic income method might be an acceptable compromise. To the extent that the higher growth is expected in the early years, the long-term average growth rate used might be raised slightly, and vice versa.

Defining the Components in the Capitalization Method

It is noteworthy that, as presented above, this is a *very generalized* formula. To actually use this valuation method, the analyst should be specific about the same points as in the discounted economic income method:

1. Is the analyst valuing *all invested capital* or just the *common equity* with these calculations?
2. What measure of economic income is being projected to be used as the numerator (e.g., net cash flow, net income, or some other economic income measure)?
3. The direct capitalization rate (c) represents the cost of what kind of capital (e.g., weighted average for net cash flow to invested capital, net cash flow available to equity, or something else)? In other words, the direct capitalization rate is a single figure representing the cost of a certain type of capital (the present value discount rate), modified by the projected annual percentage growth (or decline) in the economic income flow available to the capital structure being valued. *The direct capitalization rate must be appropriate for the definition of economic income being capitalized.*

Valuing Equity versus Invested Capital

The same fundamental principles apply with regard to the valuation of equity versus invested capital as those that apply in the discounting method.

Whichever measure of capital is selected as the valuation subject—owners' equity or invested capital—all of the economic income accruing to that class of capital should be included in the numerator.

It is noteworthy, however, that the direct capitalization model is much more sensitive to the projected rate of growth when it is applied to all invested capital than when it is applied only to owners' equity. This is because the present value discount rate is the *weighted average cost of capital* for invested capital (blended debt rate and equity rate). And, that rate is lower than the cost of equity capital alone. If the same percentage growth rate is projected on economic income available to invested capital as to owners' equity, the growth rate will have a greater impact on the resulting value of the invested capital.

Selecting the Appropriate Measure of Economic Income

As with the discounted economic income method, most valuation professionals today prefer to use *net cash flow* whether valuing equity or invested capital, for the same reasons as discussed in the previous chapter.

If you are considering using *net income*, the entire discussion in the previous chapter applies and should be read and applied in conjunction with this chapter.

We believe that capitalization of other income variables (e.g., gross revenue; owner's discretionary earnings; gross cash flow; and earnings before interest, taxes, depreciation and amortization) are better handled within the scope of the market approach. That is because capitalization rates for those economic income variables are better developed by direct observations of transactions in the market than by modifications to a built-up or CAPM present value discount rate.

Modification of the Capitalized Economic Income Method to Reflect the Midyear Discounting Convention

The basic capitalized economic income method, as presented so far, reflects the implicit assumption that the income becomes available to the owners of the subject business at the end of each period (usually assumed to be a year). This is a reasonable assumption for some businesses. This is because, at the end of the year, the owners assess the operating results and capital requirements, and distribute income in some form—such as dividends, partner withdrawals, or bonuses to owners.

If a more realistic scenario is that economic income will be available for distribution to the business owners more or less evenly throughout the year, a simple modification to the capitalized economic income formula can reflect this assumption:

Formula 10–9

$$PV = \frac{E_1(1+k)^{0.5}}{k-g}$$

where:

PV = Present value

E_1 = Expected economic income in the full period immediately following the effective valuation date

k = Present value discount rate (i.e., the cost of capital)

g = Expected long-term growth rate in E

Similarly, if the Gordon growth model version of the capitalized economic income method is used, the modified formula is as follows:

Formula 10–10

$$PV = \frac{E_0(1+g)(1+k)^{0.5}}{k-g}$$

where:

PV = Present value

E_0 = Expected economic income in the full period immediately preceding the effective valuation date

k = Present value discount rate (i.e., the cost of capital)

g = Expected long-term growth rate in E

This modified formula for the economic income capitalization method accomplishes the same result as the midyear discounting convention described in the previous chapter on the discounted economic income method.[6] Since this convention reflects earlier availability of economic income to the business owners, it slightly raises the indicated value of the business from what it would be using the end-of-the-year convention.

A simple example of the Gordon growth model would be a stock for which we know the economic income (or have estimated the normalized economic income) for the year immediately preceding the effective valuation date, and for which we expect a constant growth rate in that amount from last year's base amount. Assume the following:

Last year's economic income	$10
Discount rate (required total rate of return)	15%
Sustainable expected economic income growth rate	5%

For a simple example of the capitalized economic income model reflecting the midyear convention, use the stock in our previous example, but assume that the cash flows are received evenly over each year rather than at the end of each year. In this case, the investment would be valued as follows:

$$\frac{\$10(1+0.05)(1+0.15)^{0.5}}{0.15-0.05} = \frac{\$10.50(1.15)^{0.5}}{0.10} = \frac{\$10.50(1.0723)}{0.10} = \frac{\$11.26}{0.10} = \$112.60$$

This example demonstrates the principle that in the capitalization method, as in the discounting method, the midyear convention produces a higher indicated value because of the assumption that the cash flows will be received earlier.

Using the Capitalized Economic Income Method to Develop a Terminal Value for the Discounted Economic Income Method

Why the Capitalized Economic Income Method Is Preferable

As noted in the previous chapter, the discounted economic income method often involves projecting cash flows for some discrete time period, followed by a *terminal value* as of the end of the discrete projection period. It is not uncommon for the

---

[6] Proof of the accuracy of this method was presented in Todd A. Kaltman, "Capitalization Using a Mid-Year Convention," *Business Valuation Review*, December 1995, pp. 178–82.

present value of the terminal value to be 50 percent or more of the total value indicated by the discounted economic income method.

There are a variety of ways to develop a terminal value. The most common methods are (1) the capitalized economic income method or (2) a pricing multiple of some economic income variable, such as EBIT or EBITDA. Between these two methods, we recommend the capitalized economic income method.[7]

One reason for this recommendation is that multiples of EBIT, EBITDA, and other economic income variables used in estimating a terminal value should be market derived. That is, they should be dependent on pricing multiples observed in actual market transactions. (It should be noted that future pricing multiples may be lower than currently observed pricing multiples.) Terminal value multiples should not be estimated by modifying a discount rate or capitalization rate to be applicable to that economic income variable. Such pricing multiples are best developed through the use of the market approach, for which two chapters are included in this edition.

If the terminal value is estimated for the discounted economic income method using a market-derived pricing multiple of some economic income variable other than that used for the interim economic income flows, the analysis is not a pure income approach. Rather, the analysis is a mixture of a market approach and income approach. The greater the impact of the terminal value on the total present value, the more important this distinction becomes.

We have seen valuations where the present value of the interim cash flows was zero or even negative, and the terminal value was based on a market-derived multiple of EBIT or EBITDA. Such an analysis should in no way be classified as an income approach (as we've described it). Rather, such an analysis is driven entirely by what we have classified as a market approach.

A major problem with using a market-derived pricing multiple method to estimate the terminal value is estimating what that multiple will be 3 to10 years from now. Unlike the current pricing multiples used in the market approach, that future multiple can't be directly observed in the marketplace. Rather, it must be estimated. The procedure most commonly used is to naively assume that the future multiple will be the same as the current multiple. However, current pricing multiples impound investors' expectations about future changes, especially expectations regarding growth (including acquisitions). Companies in some industries often sell at high multiples reflecting high short-term growth expectations. If the expected future growth will be less following the terminal value date (due to, for example, maturity of the company and/or its industry), using the current pricing multiple will reflect too high a growth expectation following the terminal value date. This will have the effect of overstating the terminal value. We suspect that using a market-derived pricing multiple for estimating the terminal value, on balance, has a tendency to upwardly bias the valuation indication.

One of the primary objectives of using market price methods is to weight and check the results of each multiple against each other for reasonableness. When using a multiple of only a single variable, any possible benefit of comparing the indicated results from using multiples of several variables is lost. For the reasons discussed, we believe that this differentiation of methods is best accomplished by using the economic income capitalization method rather than a market multiple method to estimate the terminal value within the discounted economic income method.

---

[7] Whether using a market multiple or the Gordon growth model to estimate the terminal value, the resulting implied growth rate and market multiple, respectively, should be checked for reasonableness.

Implementation of the Capitalized Economic Income Method to Estimate the Terminal Value

The *terminal value* is the expected value of the entity *as of the end of the discrete projection period*.

Constant Income Scenario. If the economic income is expected to be constant following the discrete projection period, the formula for the terminal value is as follows:

Formula 10–11

$$PV = \frac{E_{(n+1)}}{c}$$

where:

PV	=	Present value
$E_{(n+1)}$	=	Expected economic income in the period immediately following the end of the discrete projections
c	=	Direct capitalization rate (which is equal to k, the present value discount rate, when the expected economic income is a constant amount in perpetuity)

Constant Growth Scenario. One of the most common ways to estimate the terminal value is to use the constant growth model presented earlier. This assumes that, after the discrete projection period, the economic income will grow at some constant compound rate in perpetuity. This version of the terminal value estimate merely continues the projection of prospective economic income with a simplifying assumption of a constant growth rate past the discrete projection period. Using the constant growth model to estimate the terminal value results in the following formula:

Formula 10–12

$$PV = \frac{E_1}{(1+k)} + \frac{E_2}{(1+k)^2} + \ldots + \frac{E_n}{(1+k)^n} + \frac{\frac{E_n(1+g)}{k-g}}{(1+k)^n}$$

where:

PV	=	Present value
$E_1 \ldots E_n$	=	Expected amounts of the economic income (often net cash flow) in each of periods E_1 through E_n
k	=	Discount rate
n	=	Number of periods in the discrete projection period
g	=	Annually compounded growth rate in perpetuity for the prospective economic income, beyond the discrete projection period

In Exhibit 9–14C in the previous chapter, we simply provided a terminal value without discussing how we arrived at it. Exhibit 10–2 presents that same DCF model, using the Gordon growth model to estimate the terminal value, assuming 5 percent annual growth beyond Year 3.

It is noteworthy that, with a very short discrete projection period, the terminal value often constitutes over half the total value. The shorter the discrete projection period and the lower the discount rate, the higher the proportion of the total value will be

Exhibit 10–2

Estimation of Value of Equity Using Gordon Growth Model to Estimate Terminal Value

	2000		2001		2002		Terminal Value
	$\dfrac{\$8,000,000}{(1+0.25)}$	+	$\dfrac{\$8,400,000}{(1+0.25)^2}$	+	$\dfrac{\$8,820,000}{(1+0.25)^3}$	+	$\dfrac{\dfrac{\$8,820,000(1.05)}{0.25-0.05}}{(1+0.25)^3}$
=	$\dfrac{\$8,000,000}{(1.25)}$	+	$\dfrac{\$8,400,000}{(1.25)^2}$	+	$\dfrac{\$8,820,000}{(1.25)^3}$	+	$\dfrac{\dfrac{\$9,261,000}{0.20}}{(1.25)^3}$
=	6,400,000	+	5,376,000	+	4,515,800	+	$\dfrac{\$46,305,000}{(1.25)3}$
=	$6,400,000	+	$5,376,000	+	$4,515,800	+	$23,708,200
=	$40,000,000 Indicated value of equity						

accounted for by the terminal value. When using the perpetual growth model to estimate the terminal value, it may be useful to check its reasonableness by computing implied pricing multiples and comparing the implied pricing multiples to pricing multiples currently observed in the market (see Chapters 11 and 12 on the market approach). This is not to suggest that market approach pricing multiples should be used to estimate the income approach terminal value. Rather, it suggests that the terminal value pricing multiples implied by the perpetual growth model can be checked for reasonableness by reference to observable market-derived pricing multiples.

Midyear Discounting Scenario. If the economic income for the discrete projection period was discounted using the midyear discounting convention, consistency would suggest using the direct capitalization formula modified to reflect the midyear convention. This procedure was presented in a prior section. Using the midyear convention for the terminal value makes the complete DCF formula as follows:

Formula 10–13

$$PV = \frac{E_1}{(1+k)^{0.5}} + \frac{E_2}{(1+k)^{1.5}} + \ldots + \frac{E_n}{(1+k)^{n-0.5}} + \frac{\dfrac{E_n(1+g)(1+k)^{0.5}}{k-g}}{(1+k)^n}$$

where:

PV = Present value
E_n = Expected economic income in the final (nth) increment of the discrete projection period
g = Long-term sustainable growth rate in E
k = Present value discount rate (i.e., the cost of capital)

Number of Periods by Which to Discount Terminal Value. In all of the above formulations, the terminal value is then discounted back to a present value at the present value discount rate (k) for n periods, the same number of periods for which the final increment of the discrete projection period was discounted. This is because the terminal value is the value *at the beginning* of the time immediately following the discrete projection period. This is exactly the same point in time as *the* *end* of the discrete projection period. (A common error is to discount the terminal value for $n + 1$ periods instead of n periods.)[8]

Does the Capitalized Economic Income Method Produce a Control Value or a Minority Value?

The answer to this question is the same as was presented for the discounted economic income method (the value indication can be either a control value or a minority value, depending primarily on the normalization adjustments made to the economic income flow being capitalized). If the adjustments include changes that only a control owner could make, such as normalization of compensation, then the value generally would represent a control ownership position. If such adjustments are not made, the value generally would represent a noncontrolling ownership position. If adjustments are not reasonably available for a control owner to make, it is possible that there may be little difference between a control value and a minority value—at least before consideration of marketability factors. (For example, the more the minority stockholder's access to the business's net cash flow is restricted, the greater the discount for lack of marketability. See Chapter 17 for more discussion of this topic.)

What Standard of Value Does the Capitalized Economic Income Model Produce?

The answer to this question is also essentially the same as was presented for the discounted economic income method.

If the economic income capitalized and the direct capitalization rate used reflect the condition of the company as it is on a stand-alone basis, the value indication should be *fair market value*. If synergies or circumstances peculiar to a particular investor are reflected in the economic income stream or in the direct capitalization rate, the value indication would reflect those elements of *investment value*.

Since the capitalized economic income method can be used to develop either fair market value or investment value, and most family law courts lean toward one or the other of those two standards of value, the capitalized economic income method is often used in valuations for purposes of marital dissolution.[9]

---

[8] If midyear discounting is used, a mathematical equivalent to using the modified (midyear) capitalization model is (1) to use the standard capitalization model (typically the Gordon growth version) and (2) to discount the indicated terminal value by $n - 0.5$ periods. While this procedure produces exactly the same answer, it seems that using the modified capitalization formula is a conceptually preferable presentation. This is because the modified formula, along with explanatory text, would make it easier for the valuation reader to understand the calculations.

[9] See, for example, *DeLucia v. DeLucia*, No. FA950249319s, 1997 WL 16832 (Conn. Super. Ct., Jan. 10, 1997), and *Backhaus v. Backhaus*, No. A-94-1083, 1996 WL 737590 (Neb. App., Dec. 17, 1996); *Giuliani v. Giuliani*, No. CA 9305268865 Conn. Super. Ct., 1996 WL 409324 (June 19, 1997); *Neuman v. Neuman*, 842 P.2d 575 (Wyo. 1992); *Bidwell v. Bidwell*, 504 N.Y.S.2d 327 (N.Y. App. Div. 1986); *Thomas v. Thomas*, 407 N.W.2d 124 (Minn. Ct. App. 1987); *Siegel v. Siegel*, 523 N.Y.S.2d 517, 521 (N.Y. App. Div. 1987).

Relationship between the Capitalized Economic Income Method and the Market Approach

In the capitalized economic income method, we divide an indication of income by a capitalization rate. We noted earlier in the chapter that the reciprocal of the capitalization rate is a multiplier. In the market approach, we use multipliers of income variables to derive indications of value. So what is the difference between the capitalized economic income method and the market approach using multiples of income variables?

There are two primary differences:

1. The way that capitalization rates are derived in the income approach versus the way that multiples are derived in the market approach.
2. The economic income variables typically capitalized in the income approach versus the economic income variables for which multiples are applied in the market approach.

Derivation of Income Approach Capitalization Rates versus Market Approach Multiples

As we have seen in this chapter, in the income approach, capitalization rates are derived from discount rates. To repeat, the capitalization rate is the discount rate minus the sustainable long-term growth rate.

In the market approach, multiples of income variables are derived from direct observation of the multiples in the market, as we will see in the next chapter.

Economic Income Variables Used in the Income Approach versus the Market Approach

In the income approach, the economic income variable generally preferred is net cash flow, either to equity or to overall invested capital, as defined in the previous chapter. This is partly because net cash flow is the discretionary amount that owners can take out of the business on an ongoing, sustainable basis without disrupting continuing operations, the variable on which many investors and corporate finance people will ultimately focus. It is also partly because net cash flow is the income variable that most analysts consider most appropriate to match with Ibbotson Associates equity risk premium data. The only other income variable widely used in the income approach is net income, as discussed in the previous chapter.

As will be seen in the next chapter, the market approach uses all kinds of economic income variables *except* expected net cash flow. Remember, in the income approach, the amounts of capital expenditures and changes in net working capital used to derive net cash flow are "amounts necessary to support projected business operations." In the market approach, it is difficult to determine for any given company whether or not amounts of capital expenditures and/or changes in net working capital meet that criterion. Therefore, while other cash flow–related measures of economic income (e.g., EDITDA) are used, net cash flow is not often used in the market approach.

By observing these differences, and by using the perpetual income or the Gordon growth model rather than a market multiple for the terminal value, the income and market approaches are quite discrete from each other and, if there are good data for both, can provide good checks against one another.

Summary

There are three principal variables in the direct capitalization of economic income method:

1. The projected base-level economic income flow.
2. The present value discount rate (i.e., the cost of capital).
3. The expected long-term growth rate by which the present value discount rate is to be modified to derive the direct capitalization rate.

The capitalized economic income method is essentially an abridged version of the discounted economic income method. The primary difference is in the treatment of future changes in the expected economic income. In the discounted economic income method, future changes in economic income are specifically reflected in the discrete income projections in the numerator of the arithmetic equation. In the capitalized economic income method, future changes in economic income are combined into a single growth rate. This single growth rate is subtracted from the present value discount rate in the denominator of the arithmetic equation.

The economic income flow to be capitalized can be either the amount available to equity or the amount available to all invested capital (usually defined to include owners' equity plus long-term interest-bearing debt, although other definitions are sometimes used).

The economic income flow that is projected is usually net cash flow (at least that is the preference of a consensus of valuation professionals), although other definitions of economic income are sometimes used.

Like the discounted economic income method, the capitalized economic income method is a forward-looking exercise. Using some average of actual past economic income is only appropriate if that average does, in fact, represent the expected level of sustainable economic income in the future.

The projected base-level sustainable economic income flow is divided by a direct capitalization rate, which is typically calculated as the present value discount rate less an expected long-term growth rate in the economic income being capitalized. This expected long-term growth rate is projected to be constant in perpetuity.

The development of the present value discount rate is the same as for the discounted economic income method, as discussed in Chapter 9. If either a build-up procedure or the CAPM procedure is used to develop the discount rate, that rate includes expected inflation. Therefore, the growth rate used should also reflect inflation—to the extent that it impacts the economic income variable being capitalized.

The results are extremely sensitive to changes in the growth rate factor, especially when valuing invested capital. This is because the analysis of invested capital starts with a lower present value discount rate than for equity only.

It is essential that the direct capitalization rate be developed so that it is appropriate for the definition of the economic income flow being capitalized. One of the most common errors in implementing the capitalized economic income method is using a direct capitalization rate that is not appropriate for the particular definition of economic income that is being capitalized.

The capitalized economic income method is also an excellent method for developing the terminal value in the discounted economic income method.

Bibliography

Agiato, Joseph A., and Thomas L. Johnston. "The Relationship between the Earnings Yield and the Cash Flow Yield." *CPA Expert*, Winter 1996, pp. 6–9.

Bakken, John E. "Capitalization of Earnings—an Income Approach." Chapter 17 in *Handbook of Business Valuation*, 2nd ed., Thomas L. West and Jeffrey D. Jones, eds. New York: John Wiley & Sons, 1999, pp. 192–200.

Evans, Frank C. "Recognizing the Key Factors in the Income Approach to Business Valuation." *Business Valuation Review*, June 1996, pp. 80–86.

Greer, Willis R. "The Growth Rate Term in the Capitalization Method." *Business Valuation Review*, June 1996, pp. 72–79.

Hawkins, George B. "Is the Capitalization Rate Reasonable?" *Fair$hare*, June 1997, pp. 2–7.

Kaltman, Todd A. "Capitalization Using a Mid-Year Convention." *Business Valuation Review*, December 1995, pp. 178–82.

Lippitt, Jeffrey W., and Nicholas J. Mastrachhio Jr. "Developing Capitalization Rates for Valuing a Business." *The CPA Journal*, November 1995, pp. 24–28.

Mercer, Z. Christopher. "Adjusting Capitalization Rates for the Differences between Net Income and Net Free Cash Flow." *Business Valuation Review*, December 1992, pp. 201–7.

Pratt, Shannon P. "Discounting versus Capitalizing." Chapter 4 in *Cost of Capital: Estimation and Applications*. New York: John Wiley & Sons, 1998.

_____. "NACVA Advisory Board Member Challenges Methods Taught." *Shannon Pratt's Business Valuation Update*, February 1996, pp. 9–11.

Reynolds, Kevin B. "Where Do Capitalization Rates Come From?" *CPA Litigation Service Counselor*, November 1999, pp. 9–11.

Rigby, James, and Michael J. Mattson. "Capitalization and Discount Rates: Mathematically Related, But Conceptually Different." *CPA Expert*, Fall 1996, pp. 1–3.

Schilt, James H. "Selection of Capitalization Rates—Revisited." *Business Valuation Review*, June 1991, pp. 51–52.

Sliwoski, Leonard. "Capitalization Rates Developed Using the Ibbotson Associates Data: Should They Be Applied to Pretax or After Tax Earnings?" *Business Valuation Review*, March 1994, pp. 8–10.

_____. "Capitalization Rates, Discount Rates, and P/E Ratios: One More Time." *Business Valuation Review*, September 1992, pp. 122–34.

Swad, Randy. "Discount and Capitalization Rates in Business Valuations." *CPA Journal*, October 1994, pp. 40–46.

Chapter 11

Market Approach: Guideline Publicly Traded Company Method

The use of comparable publicly held corporations as a guide to valuation, as a practical matter, may be the most important and appropriate technique for valuing a privately held operating business. Obviously finding a business exactly the same as the enterprise to be valued is an impossibility. The standard sought is usually one of reasonable and justifiable similarity. This degree of likeness is attainable in most cases.[1]

In the market determined price of a stock, thousands of investors act through Adam Smith's "invisible hand" to arrive at an equilibrium value.[2]

While the income approach discussed in the previous chapters is the core of valuation theory, actual market transaction data can provide compelling empirical evidence of value.

There is an enormous storehouse of reliable guideline transaction data from the day-to-day transactions in publicly traded companies, of which over 12,000 operating companies and another 4,000 holding companies are reasonably actively traded in the United States alone. We agree with the above quote that publicly traded corporation capital market data may provide relevant valuation guidance in many cases.

Exhibit 11–1 summarizes the several mechanisms available to effect a public offering. The size requirements for a public offering and public trading are far less than many people think. Many closely held companies that might be thought of as small actually are large enough to go public if they so desired. However, it is not necessary for a company to be eligible to go public in order to use valuation guidance from the public market. The capital markets provide general guidelines as to how securities in many industries are being priced.

The public capital markets in the United States (as well as in other countries) reprice thousands of stocks every day, mostly through transactions among financial buyers and sellers who are well-informed (because of stringent disclosure laws, at least in the United States) and have no special motivations or compulsions to buy or to sell. This constant repricing gives up-to-the-minute evidence of prices that

---

[1] Frank M. Burke, Jr., *Valuation and Valuation Planning for Closely Held Businesses* (Englewood Cliffs, NJ: Prentice-Hall, Inc., 1981), p. 49.

[2] Kent Hickman and Glenn H. Petry, "A Comparison of Stock Price Predictions Using Court Accepted Formulas, Dividend Discount, and P/E Models," *Financial Management*, Summer 1990, p. 84.

Exhibit 11–1

Mechanisms for Going Public in the United States

Registration statements are of two main types: offering registrations, filed under the Securities Act of 1933; and trading registrations, filed under the Securities Exchange Act of 1934.

Offering Registrations

Offering registrations are used to register securities with the SEC before they are offered to investors. Part I of the registration statement serves as a preliminary prospectus (sometimes called a "red herring") and contains information that will be included in the final prospectus. This includes:

- Description of securities to be registered
- Use of proceeds
- Risk factors
- Determination of offering price
- Potential dilution
- Selling security holders
- Plan of distribution
- Interests of named experts and counsel
- Information with respect to the registrant

Part II of the registration statement contains information not required in the prospectus. This includes:
- Expenses of issuance and distribution
- Indemnification of directors and officers
- Recent sales of unregistered securities, undertakings, exhibits, and financial statement schedules

Types of Offering Registrations

Offering registrations vary in purpose and content according to the type of organization issuing stock.

S-1   Companies reporting under the 1934 Act for less than one year. Permits no incorporation by reference and requires complete disclosure in the prospectus. The S-1 is used most often for Initial Public Offerings (IPOs).

S-2   Companies reporting under the 1934 Act for one year or more but not meeting the minimum voting stock requirement. Reference to 1934 Act reports permits incorporation and presentation of financial information in the prospectus or in an annual report to shareholders delivered with the prospectus.

S-3   Companies reporting under the 1934 Act for one year or more and having at least $150 million of voting stock held by non-affiliates, or as an alternative test, $100 million of voting stock coupled with an annual trading volume of 3 million shares. Allows minimal disclosure in the prospectus and maximum incorporation by reference of 1934 Act reports.

S-4   Registration used in certain business combinations or reorganizations.

S-6   Filed by unit investment trusts registered under the Investment Act of 1940 on Form N-8B-2.

S-8   Registration used to register securities to be offered to employees under stock option and various other employee benefit plans.

S-11   Filed by real estate companies, primarily limited partnerships and investment trusts.

F-1   Registration of securities by foreign private issuers eligible to use Form 20-F, for which no other form is prescribed.

F-2   Registration of securities by foreign private issuers meeting certain 1934 Act filing requirements.

F-3   Registration of securities by foreign private issuers offered pursuant to certain types of transactions, subject to the 1934 Act filing requirements for the preceding year.

F-4   Registration of securities issued in business combinations involving foreign private registrants.

F-6   Registration of depository shares evidenced by the American Depository Receipts (ADRs).

F-7   Registration of certain Canadian issues offered for cash upon the exercise of rights granted to existing security holders.

F-8   Registration of certain Canadian issues to be issued in exchange offers or a business combination.

F-9   Registration of certain investment-grade debt or investment-grade preferred securities of certain Canadian issues.

F-10   Registration of certain Canadian issues.

SB-1   Registration for small business offerings less than $10 million. Less information is required than in an S-1 registration.

SB-2   Registration for small businesses with revenues and public market float of less than $25 million. Less information is required than in an S-1 registration.

Rule 462(b)   Registration of up to an additional 20 percent of securities that were previously registered. Applicable to the following forms: S-1MEF, S-2MEF, S-3MEF, F-1MEF, F-2MEF, F-3MEF, S-11MEF, SB-1MEF and SB-2MEF.

SOURCE: *Guide to SEC Filings* (Bethesda, MD: Disclosure Incorporated, 1999). Available at www.primark.com/pfid.

---

buyers and sellers agree on for securities in all kinds of industries relative to the fundamental variables perceived to drive their values, such as dividends, cash flows, and earnings. Pricing multiples of these and other relevant financial variables are important investor valuation yardsticks.

Furthermore, companies already public are high on the list of potential acquirers for many private companies. And, valuation parameters of the potential acquirers' stock may influence the pricing of a potential acquiree. If the subject company *could* be a candidate to go public, this makes the comparison of the guideline publicly traded companies to the subject company more relevant.[3]

Overview of the Guideline Publicly Traded Company Method

The purpose of compiling guideline company statistics is to develop value measures based on prices at which stocks of similar companies are trading in a public market. The value measures thus developed will be applied to the subject company's fundamental data and correlated to reach an estimate of value for the subject company or its shares or other interests.

A "value measure" is usually a multiple computed by dividing the price of the guideline company's stock as of the valuation date by some relevant economic variable observed or calculated from the guideline company's financial statements. Some variables, such as projections of next year's earnings, may be estimated by security analysts. The reciprocal of the pricing multiple is the capitalization rate for that variable.

Income statement variables often used to develop pricing measures from guideline companies are the following:

- Net sales.
- Net income after taxes.
- Gross cash flow (net income plus noncash charges).
- Net cash flow (gross cash flow adjusted for capital expenditures, changes in working capital, and sometimes changes in debt).
- Net income before taxes.
- Gross cash flow before taxes (earnings before depreciation, other noncash charges, and taxes, sometimes called EBDT).
- Dividends or dividend-paying capacity.

In addition to business value measures using only the value of the common stock to develop the pricing multiple, some measures address the value of *all* the invested capital. In this case, the numerator for the value measure multiple is often called *market value of invested capital* (MVIC). This measure is also sometimes called *adjusted market value of capital structure, aggregate market value of capital structure,* or *enterprise value.* This measure includes the market value of all classes of stock and all interest-bearing debt. Many analysts deduct cash and marketable securities in situations where they are analyzing the performance of operating assets. The denominator used to compute the pricing multiples should include the returns available to all classes of capital reflected in the numerator—for example, preferred dividends and interest.

Income statement variables often used to develop business value measures for MVIC are:

- Net sales.
- Earnings before interest and taxes (EBIT).
- Earnings before interest, taxes, depreciation, and amortization, (or EBITDA).

---

[3] It should be noted that noncontrolling stockholders cannot initiate or consummate a public offering. This fact typically is recognized by a discount for lack of marketability for private company shares when valued by reference to guideline publicly traded company shares. This valuation adjustment is discussed in detail in Chapter 17, Discounts for Illiquidity and Lack of Marketability.

- Net cash flow available to invested capital.
- Revenues.

The above variables usually are computed on a operating basis, with nonoperating items treated separately. Any of the above income variables may be measured for any or all of a variety of time periods to create the denominator for a value measure. The typical time periods used are:

- Latest 12 months (LTM).
- Latest fiscal year (if LTM not available).
- Estimates for the forthcoming year.
- Simple average of some number of past years.
- Weighted average of some number of past years.

All of the above performance variables and time periods may have various other permutations, depending on availability and relevance of data.

In certain industries business value measures also may be developed based on balance sheet data. Such measures normally are developed by dividing the price as of the valuation date by the balance sheet variables as of a date as close as possible preceding the valuation date for which both guideline company and subject company data are available. Balance sheet variables typically used are:

- Book value.
- Tangible book value.
- Adjusted book value.
- Adjusted tangible book value.

As with value measures based on operating data, value measures based on asset values may also be performed on a value of total capital basis. In such cases, the market value of the senior equity and interest-bearing liabilities generally is added into both the numerator and the denominator in developing the business value measure.

Note that *unlike* operating variables, which are measured over one or more *periods* of time, asset value variables normally are measured only at the latest practical *point* in time.

The actual value measure applied to the subject company may be anywhere within (or sometimes even outside) the range of value measures developed from the market data. Where each value measure should fall will depend on the quantitative and qualitative analysis of the subject company relative to analysis of the companies that comprise the market transaction data.

When Is the Guideline Publicly Traded Company Method Most Useful?

The initial value derived from the guideline publicly traded company method, before adjustment for shareholder-level factors such as size of the block and degree of marketability or lack of it, is often called a *publicly traded equivalent value* or *as if freely traded value*—that is, the price at which the stock would be expected to trade if it were traded publicly. In other words, the value indication is appropriate for a marketable, minority ownership interest, using the premise of value in continued use, as a going-concern business.

The method can be used in conjunction with a valuation for any standard of value, certainly most importantly for fair market value. Use of the method in conjunction with each of the standards of value is discussed next. That discussion is followed by an explanation of the adjustments that are necessary when the method is used to value a nonmarketable minority stock and to value controlling ownership interests.

Finally, we discuss the impact of the quantity and quality of available data on the use of the method.

Standard of Value

Fair Market Value. While the guideline company method can be used in conjunction with any standard of value, it generally is most useful when the standard of value is fair market value. By definition, the method is based on making comparisons between the subject stock and transactions in guideline publicly traded stocks.

Fair market value is the standard of value in most income tax–related transactions. (Revenue Ruling 59-60 references the public markets no less than seven times.) It is also the standard of value for all ESOP valuations.

Fair Value. As noted in Chapter 2, fair value is a statutorily mandated standard of value. In the United States, it is applicable in almost all states to dissenting stockholder actions and, in the few states that have corporate and partnership dissolution statutes, to such dissolutions. It is interpreted by judicial precedent in each state. As a generality, in most states it is a broader standard that incorporates market value along with values indicated by income and asset approaches. Therefore, we would say that a guideline publicly traded company method usually would be a part of the analysis when fair value is the standard.

Investment Value. This is the standard of value that could depart the most from the value developed by a strict application of the guideline publicly traded company method. The guideline publicly traded company method would be expected to develop a value based on a *consensus* of market participants, as evidenced by their transactions. Investment value, by definition, is the value to a *particular* buyer or seller. Therefore, the income approach gives more opportunity for a specific party to project income flows and use discount and capitalization rates that are appropriate to his or her individual investment criteria.

Even a party primarily interested in investment value, however, generally would want to have some notion of what a consensus value would be. Furthermore, the analyst interested in investment value can always adjust the financial variables on a pro forma basis reflecting anticipated changes in the subject company and use the guideline publicly traded company method to test the sensitivity of market value to various possible changes in the financial variables.

Ownership Characteristics

Marketable versus Nonmarketable. The guideline company method would be most ideal, of course, when valuing marketable shares by direct comparison with marketable shares.

Marketability, or lack of it, like most shareholder-level attributes of securities, is often an issue that is not totally black or white. For example, private placements of stocks that already have a public market generally will be restricted for a time and then will enjoy full marketability. Most ESOP stock by law enjoys the right of a "put," which guarantees a market at the appraised price at the occurrence of specified triggering events. There are many data and precedents for adjusting for the limited marketability in such situations.

The use of the guideline publicly traded company method to value stocks of closely held companies that have no market has been significantly enhanced in the late 1980s and early 1990s by two important developments.

1. A vastly increased number of available actively traded public companies to choose from, especially smaller companies which may be more comparable in many respects to many closely held companies than those traded in public markets a decade ago.
2. Development of extensive new databases that provide empirical guidance not previously available to assist in quantifying the discount for lack of marketability between a publicly traded security equivalent value and an otherwise similar closely held security value. These data are described in detail in Chapter 17, Discounts for Illiquidity and Lack of Marketability.

Control versus Minority. Since guideline public company shares are, by definition, noncontrolling ownership interests, their trading prices are most directly relevant for valuation of other noncontrolling ownership interests.

In applying the guideline publicly traded company method, qualitative and quantitative differences between the guideline and subject companies are reflected in arriving at the publicly traded equivalent value of the subject stock, usually in the choice of multiples applied to the subject's fundamental data relative to the guideline companies' multiples. Adjustments also may be made for other factors such as relative excess assets or deficiencies in arriving at a publicly traded equivalent value. Thus, having arrived at a publicly traded equivalent value, the only remaining adjustment necessary for a minority interest value is the shareholder-level attribute of lack of marketability. As already noted, there are a plethora of empirical data on which to base this adjustment.

When valuing controlling interests, it may be preferable to apply the market approach by using only guideline controlling interest transactions, which is the subject of the next chapter. However, the practical reality is that there are far more reliable guideline public company noncontrolling interest transaction data available than guideline merged and acquired controlling interest transaction data. Therefore, it often is useful to use the guideline publicly traded company method even when valuing controlling interests. (This method requires consideration of a premium to reflect the prerogatives of control.) This premium may be offset in part or even fully by a discount for lack of marketability. This is a complicated issue, which is addressed briefly toward the end of this chapter in the section on typical adjustments to reach the value conclusion and in considerable detail in Chapters 15 through 17.

Going-Concern versus Liquidation Value

In almost all cases, the public market is pricing stocks on the assumption that they will continue as a going concern. Unless there is evidence to the contrary, the guideline publicly traded company method would be expected to produce a value on the premise that the subject is expected to continue as a going concern. In contrast, the various forms of liquidation value are addressed in Chapter 14 on the asset-based approach.

Quantity and Quality of Available Data

As with any valuation method, the quantity and quality of relevant data available to implement it will have an important bearing on the usefulness of the method. As noted earlier, there are more publicly traded companies, especially small ones, than most people realize, and it is important to search them out.

After discussing criteria for selection of companies, we address the question of how many guideline publicly traded companies would ideally be used in this method. The method needn't be rejected just because we were not satisfied with either the number or the degree of comparability of available guideline companies. In the final analysis, the quantity and quality of the guideline company data compared with the quantity and quality of data available for other methods will influence the weight accorded the method in correlating the results of various methods and reaching a value conclusion.

Criteria for Guideline Company Selection

One succinct quote summarizes the essence of the key characteristic that should be present in a guideline company: "Do the underlying economics driving this comparable company match those that drive our company?"[4] Of course, this quote does not suggest that the economics of the guideline companies be a perfect match to the economics of the subject company. Although this relationship is ideal, analysts rarely encounter it in the real world. Rather, this quote indicates that the microeconomic factors that drive the guideline companies should be sufficiently similar to the microeconomic factors that drive the subject company. Otherwise, the guideline companies will not provide meaningful pricing guidance to the analyst.

In Revenue Ruling 59-60, the IRS, one of the strongest proponents of the guideline publicly traded company method, makes the following observation:

> Although the only restrictive requirement as to comparable corporations specified in the statute is that their lines of business be the same or similar, yet it is obvious that consideration must be given to other relevant factors in order that the most valid comparison possible will be obtained.[5]

In analyzing (1) whether or not a particular publicly traded company should be considered an appropriate guideline or (2) which of the guideline publicly traded companies are most comparative to the subject company (and therefore deserve more weight in the valuation), the analyst should consider several important factors.

The comparability of guideline publicly traded companies used in a valuation frequently has become a central issue in litigated valuations, partly because of the difficulty of choosing truly comparative companies. In *Tallichet v. Commissioner*, the Tax Court emphasized that there are "guideposts in determining comparability."[6] According to the Court, the following factors are among those to consider in determining comparability:

1. Capital structure.

---

[4] Daniel W. Bielinski, "The Comparable-Company Approach: Measuring the True Value of Privately Held Firms," *Corporate Cashflow Magazine*, October 1990, pp. 64–66.

[5] Revenue Ruling 59-60 (1959-1 C.B. 237), Section 4(h).

[6] *Tallichet v. Commissioner*, 33 T.C.M. 1133 (1974).

2. Credit status.
3. Depth of management.
4. Personnel experience.
5. Nature of competition.
6. Maturity of the business.

In *Estate of Victor P. Clarke*, the Tax Court reemphasized that it is "imperative that the characteristics of the subject company and the purportedly comparable company relevant to the question of value be isolated and examined so that a significant comparison can be made."[7] In that case, the Court cited the following as relevant factors:

1. Products.
2. Markets.
3. Management.
4. Earnings.
5. Dividend-paying capacity.
6. Book value.
7. Position of company in industry.

Although these lists seem comprehensive, depending on the nature of the industry, the analyst may need to consider additional factors, such as number and size of retail outlets, sales volume, product mix, territory of operations, and customer mix. Clearly, even this additional list is not exhaustive, and we cannot overemphasize the necessity of tailoring the list of factors to be considered to fit each valuation. Much of this information can be gathered in a thorough review of each public company's Form 10-K, but it may also be necessary to consult additional sources such as industry and trade publications (discussed in Chapter 6, Researching Economic and Industry Information) or to call the company for additional information.

It is also useful to analyze the financial statements for both the subject company and the guideline companies to uncover similarities and differences to consider in the valuation. Bearing in mind the company being valued and the nature of the industry, we generally compare the performance of the subject company to the guideline companies by analyzing financial ratios that measure liquidity, leverage, activity, and profitability, as well as historical trends in revenues, expenses and profitability. This type of analysis is illustrated in Chapter 8, Comparative Ratios. In particular, if this analysis indicates that the guideline companies' capital structures differ significantly from that of the subject (one of the examples cited by the IRS in Revenue Ruling 59-60 regarding factors relevant to comparability), this difference can sometimes be factored out by using market value of invested capital procedures referred to earlier.

In many valuation situations, the subject company is so unique that it is difficult to find a set of good guideline companies. In these cases, the analyst may find a group of companies that can shed some light on the valuation question but may consider one or a few more directly comparable to the subject company than the rest. In such cases, the analyst may tabulate data for the whole group but elect to accord more weight to the data for those guideline companies considered most comparable.

Sometimes, though, the subject company seems so unique that even an exhaustive search produces no companies for use as guideline companies. The appraiser should keep in mind that there are over 30,000 small public companies out there that have sold stock through public offerings at one time or another and are still

---

[7] *Estate of Victor P. Clarke*, 35 T.C.M. 1482 (1976).

operating. Also, if the valuation is for federal gift and estate taxes, Revenue Ruling 59-60 states that the companies may be in the same "or similar" industries. This phrase gives the analyst latitude to exercise reasonable judgment in selecting companies from related industries if unable to find guideline companies in the subject company's industry group or companies with adequate trading volume.

In considering "the same or similar lines of business," the analyst should keep in mind the comparability of the driving underlying investment risk and expected rate of return characteristics of the guideline companies and the subject company. Important investment risk and expected rate of return factors include the market(s) into which the company sells, its brand acceptance, or lack of it, and, sometimes, the raw material supply conditions. Three quick examples will help to illustrate the point.

Example 1: Industrial Equipment Manufacturer
We were retained to value a company whose line of business was the manufacture of electronic control equipment for the forest products industry. We found plenty of manufacturers of electronic control equipment, but none for whom the forest products industry was a significant part of their market. Therefore, for guideline companies, we selected manufacturers of other types of industrial equipment and supplies that sold to the forest products and related cyclical industries. We decided that the markets served were more of an economic driving force than the physical nature of the products produced.

Example 2: The Gallo Wine Company
At the valuation date in the *Estate of Mark Gallo*,[8] there was only one publicly traded wine company stock, a tiny midget compared with the huge Gallo and, for other reasons as well, not a good guideline company. Experts for both the taxpayer and the IRS recognized this, and used as guideline companies distillers, brewers, soft drink bottlers, and food companies that enjoyed strong brand recognition and were subject to seasonal crop conditions and grower contracts.

Example 3: The Hallmark Greeting Card Co.
In the *Estate of Joyce Hall*,[9] there was only one good publicly traded greeting card guideline company as of the valuation date. The expert for the IRS used that company and also other companies that manufactured consumer consumable products and whose consumer brand names commanded the dominant market share for their respective products. The court commented very positively on this procedure.

However, the analyst who finds it difficult finding suitable guideline companies should also remember that in several cases, courts have decided that the comparability between the subject company and the guideline publicly traded companies was insufficient. In *Righter v. U.S.*, for example, the court decided companies that manufactured toys or toys and games were not sufficiently comparable to a company that produced two types of games, partly because their products appealed to and were used by different age groups.[10] In *Estate of Joseph E. Salsbury*, the Tax Court rejected several companies one of the experts had chosen as comparable because they

---

[8] *Estate of Mark S. Gallo*, 50 T.C.M. 470 (1985).
[9] *Estate of Joyce C. Hall*, 92 T.C. No. 19 (1989).
[10] *Righter v. U.S.*, 439 F.2d 1244 (1971).

"did not even have divisions engaged in the animal and poultry health industry" (which was the subject company's business). As a result, the Court concluded that the selection of these companies "fails to satisfy the 'same or similar line of business' requirement of the regulations."

A problem also arises if an appraiser establishes criteria that are too restrictive. By unnecessarily limiting the number of guideline companies considered, an appraiser may miss relevant market evidence that would have led to a different valuation. Several court cases have noted that experts were too selective, excluding companies that would have provided useful valuation guidance. In *Estate of Victor P. Clarke,* the Tax Court addressed this problem forcefully by stating that the definition of a guideline corporation cannot be "unduly restrictive, as it strips the inquiry into the valuation of closely held stock of the flexibility needed to make an informed judgment."[11] The U.S. Court of Claims stated its opinion on this issue quite succinctly in *Central Trust Company v. U.S.* In employing the guideline publicly traded company method, "every effort should be made to select as broad a base of comparative companies as is reasonably possible, as well as to give full consideration to every possible factor in order to make the comparison more meaningful."[12] In *Estate of Mark S. Gallo*, this point was again emphasized when the Tax Court commended one of the experts for making "careful and reasoned comparisons with each comparable instead of arbitrarily relying upon the outer limit of a range."[13] Clearly, the message of these cases is that the appraiser must choose guideline companies logically and be able to justify their selection.

How Many Guideline Companies?

The answer to this question depends on a number of factors:

1. Similarity to the subject—the more similar, the fewer needed.
2. Trading activity—again, the more actively traded, the fewer needed.
3. Dispersion of value measure data points—the wider the range of relevant value measure data points, the more companies it takes to identify a pattern relevant to the subject company.

In the *Gallo* and *Hall* cases cited earlier, where companies in other industries but with related characteristics were used, the guideline company lists encompassed 10 to 16 companies. In *Hall*, the court rejected the reliance by one appraiser on the only other company in the greeting card industry, even though it was an excellent comparable, stating "one company does not a market make."

We have used as few as two or three guideline companies. However, in those cases we would be reluctant to rely on the guideline publicly traded company method exclusively. Our confidence rises sharply when we can find four to seven good guideline publicly traded companies. In those rare cases where it seems that there are a dozen or more good guideline companies in terms of line of business, we often narrow down the criteria in terms of size, earning pattern, and other factors to utilize what our analysis indicates to be the best ones.

---

[11] *Estate of Victor P. Clarke*, p. 1501.
[12] *Central Trust Company v. U.S.*, 305 F.2d 393 (Ct. Cl., 1962).
[13] *Estate of Mark S. Gallo*, 50 T.C.M. 470 (1985).

Time Period to Consider

In the absence of a compelling reason to do otherwise, the time period most commonly used for analysis of operating data is five years. This conventional time period should not, however, be blindly and mechanistically adopted. The operative phrase is "relevant time period."

For a cyclical industry, a complete economic cycle for that industry is widely considered to be a good choice of time period from which to develop average operating results to be used as the basis for value measures. This has led us on occasion to use averages of operating data for as long as 10 years.

Sometimes the relevant time period is constrained by major changes that affected either the subject company or the industry as a whole. Such events may render comparative financial data before such changes irrelevant for valuation purposes. In these cases it may only be relevant to use one or a few years' comparative data.

Once in a while, the historical data include an aberration that is so clearly nonrecurring for either the subject company or the industry that the best thing to do is just to omit that year when computing the value measures. In such cases, however, the data normally are tabulated and presented and the reason for omitting that year from the value measure calculations is given.

Typically, the same time period that is used for gathering and presenting data also is used for both income statement and balance sheet data. Value measures based on income statement data typically are computed by dividing the valuation date price by the income variables or averages of variables for one or a number of prior periods, usually (but not necessarily) years. Value measures based on balance sheet variables (e.g., price/book value) typically are computed by dividing the valuation date price by the most recent balance sheet variable. The reason for collecting and presenting several years of balance sheet information is to identify and interpret comparative trends among the guideline and subject companies, although the earlier years' balance sheet data usually are not used directly in the computation of value measures.

Deciding Which Value Measures to Use

As we noted earlier in the chapter, there is a wide variety of financial variables for which capitalization rates for the guideline companies can be computed. For the income variables, there is also a wide choice of time periods and possible weighting schemes for each variable. The analyst's skill, experience, and judgment play an important role in making these choices and, ultimately, in deciding the appropriate weight to accord to each. This section discusses criteria to consider in order to make relevant choices in each case.

Influence of the Ownership Characteristics

Controlling Ownership Interest versus Noncontrolling Ownership Interest Value. When valuing a controlling ownership interest, emphasis is often placed heavily on measures of the market value of invested capital (MVIC) rather than of the equity only, because the controlling interest holder would be able to make the financial decision to change the capital structure if so desired. Conversely, when valuing a noncontrolling ownership interest, focus logically is on measures that directly value the subject equity interest. Sometimes, however, measures of the MVIC are used to value noncontrolling ownership interests, subtracting the debt to reach an indication of the value of equity. This procedure is most often used when the subject and guideline companies have wide variations in capital structure, to even out the effects of the differences in leverage.

Marketable versus Nonmarketable. Public companies tend to focus more on net income than do private companies, while private companies tend to focus more on cash flows than do public companies. Therefore, when valuing a private company, one may choose to focus a bit more on cash flow variables than net income variables. However, even though public company reports and press releases tend to focus on income variables, the market pricing for many public companies will be found to be more oriented to cash flows than to net income.

Going-Concern versus Liquidation Value

Going-concern value tends to be based largely—and sometimes entirely—on income and cash flow analyses. Liquidation value often involves an analysis of individual asset values, so the emphasis is on balance sheet items. As noted earlier, however, the guideline publicly traded company valuation method is often used in connection with a going-concern premise of value.

Type of Company

Operating versus Holding Companies. In the broadest general sense, valuation of operating companies tends to focus on earning power variables, while valuation of holding companies tends to focus on asset value variables. Therefore, for operating companies, focus tends to be on ratios of price to cash flows, earnings, and dividends. For holding companies, focus tends to be on ratios of price to book value or price to adjusted book value.

Stage of Company in Life Cycle. The more mature or stable the company, the more the focus may be on cash flow variables, whereas companies in a growth phase may focus more on net income. In fact, young companies in a very high growth phase may be expected to have negative net cash flow for years, so that net cash flow would be meaningful in a long-term discounted cash flow valuation method but meaningless for the same company in a capital market approach using current guideline publicly traded company data. This is not to imply diminished importance of ultimate ability to produce meaningful net cash flows, but only because multiples of negative current numbers are meaningless.

Line of Business. The more meaningful the assets are to the type of business, the more they should be considered in the value measures computed. Usually, assets that are more liquid and not "special purpose" are more important. Furthermore, they are easier to deal with in valuation if their GAAP values are close to their market values. For example, for financial institutions, the financial assets and liabilities are extremely important, and price-to-book-value ratios are much more important than for most other types of operating companies. For distribution companies (especially wholesalers, but also retailers), inventories (and in some cases receivables) are a major part of their asset mix, usually making price to book value a relevant measure to consider. For manufacturing companies, plant and equipment vary tremendously from one to another, both in age and condition and also in importance to their operations, so that price-to-asset-value measures are difficult to implement on a comparative basis and frequently are not very meaningful. For service companies, assets typically play a very minor role, if any, in value measures.

Availability of Data

We often face the frustrating obstacle of lack (or limited availability) of data for the value measures we would conceptually most prefer to use in the guideline publicly traded company method. The analyst should perform the most thorough possible search for the data he or she would *prefer* to use, and then should make the best possible use of whatever is available.

Gross Cash Flow versus Net Cash Flow. A good example of this problem is the choice between gross cash flow and net cash flow as an economic income variable in a guideline company value measure. In the discounted future economic income method, we generally prefer—and generally use—net cash flow, and most experienced analysts tend to prefer this measure in the guideline publicly traded company method as well. If one is willing to do the work, using the statement of cash flows along with the income statements and balance sheets, one can compute net cash flow for most public companies for each year. However, if data such as capital expenditures have been subject to wide variations, as they frequently are, these data generally are harder to adjust objectively for abnormal or nonrecurring items than most other data. Therefore, gross cash flow is more commonly used because it is straightforward, easier to compute, and simple to explain.

Multiples of Market Prices to Asset Values. When using multiples of market prices of stock or invested capital to underlying tangible asset values, it is more meaningful if the tangible asset values are adjusted to their respective fair market values. For example, publicly traded, closed-end investment companies are required to reprice their tangible assets at market value regularly, so the multiple of price to adjusted net tangible asset value is available for such companies.

Real estate investment trusts (REITs) and other real estate holding companies are not required to disclose market prices of their assets, but many choose to do so. Thus, if one is valuing a real estate holding company and has market values for the subject company tangible assets, one may limit guideline company selection to those that report market values of their holdings. Alternatively, one may use those that report market values for a price-to-adjusted-net-asset-value measure and a broader list for income-related value measures. (The availability of market prices of assets does not necessarily mean that assets are the primary value drivers. For example, at this writing, REIT prices are heavily driven by yields.)

Data on values of timber holdings for many forest products companies are available from Wall Street analysts. Therefore, when valuing a company with timber holdings, a value measure of price to net asset value adjusted for timber holdings can sometimes be developed.

For most other types of public companies, market values of asset holdings are not available. This leaves the analyst with no choice, if desiring to use a measure based on asset value in the guideline company method, but to use a simple price-to-book-value multiple. As noted earlier in the "Type of Company" section, the price-to-book-value multiple tends to have more relevance if assets are of such a nature that book values tend to be fairly close to market values.

Use of Only a Portion of the Guideline Companies for Some Value Measures. It is not necessary to use every guideline company selected for every value measure utilized. Not all public companies have earnings estimates, for example. Also, one of the guideline companies may have had deficit net income, so it can't be used for the price-to-earnings (P/E) pricing multiple. However, that guideline company may still have had meaningful gross cash flow so that it could be used in developing a price-to-gross-cash-flow pricing multiple. Sometimes an industry group includes a good guideline company that went public recently, say only three years ago. That guideline company would not be available for the calculation of the price-to-five-year-average-income pricing multiple, but it would be available for calculation of the price-to-latest-12-months'-income pricing multiple. Likewise, earnings projections may not be available for all of the guideline companies. The analyst should use caution and careful judgment, however, to be sure that the use of certain guideline companies for the calculation of some pricing multiples and not others does not introduce bias or distortion to the pricing multiple implications.

This section has touched on some of the more common general problems of availability of data to implement the guideline company method. Sometimes, we find that the guideline company data we have been able to develop are not as strongly and compellingly convincing of value as we would like. Generally, to the extent that they provide some general guidance with respect to value, we still would tend to present them rather than ignore them. And, the strength of the data leads to the judgment as to the weight ultimately accorded to them among the various value measures within the guideline publicly traded company method, and accorded to the guideline publicly traded company method among other valuation methods.

Compiling Guideline Company Tables

The purpose of gathering data on guideline publicly traded companies is to derive some benchmarks by which to value the subject privately held company. For example, public companies in the industry selling at price-to-earnings multiples higher than the overall market average indicate that the public market is optimistic about the industry's future relative to its recent earnings, and this optimism should also be reflected in the private companies' P/E multiples. Similarly, the public market can provide benchmarks concerning the relation of stock prices to such variables as book values, adjusted underlying net asset values, dividends, and gross revenues. Any or all of these parameters can be relevant to a specific valuation situation, as discussed throughout this book.

Compiling a comprehensive list of guideline publicly traded companies is not simple. No single source provides an exhaustive list. It is much easier to find good guideline companies in some industries than in others. A complete search requires creativity, ingenuity, and experience. This chapter presents the most comprehensive general sources available. If not satisfied with the list developed through these sources, the analyst can consult trade association membership lists and regional investment publications or ask the management of the subject company and of the companies discovered through the conventional search for additional prospects.

Of all the criteria by which different companies may be judged as comparable for valuation purposes, the one that typically receives the most attention is the industry in which the subject company operates. In fact, Revenue Ruling 59-60 specifically states that of the factors that "are fundamental and require careful analysis in each case" for gift and estate tax valuations, one is "the market price of stocks of corporations engaged in the same or a similar line of business having their stocks actively traded on a free and open market, either on an exchange or over-the-counter."[14]

Therefore, the starting point in compiling a list of guideline companies is to form a list of the companies that operate in the subject company's industry group. Still, the most widely accepted categorization of industry groups is the U.S. government's *Standard Industrial Classification Manual*, which publishes and defines Standard Industry Classification (SIC) codes. (The SIC code is the statistical classification standard underlying all establishment-based federal economic statistics classified by industry.) In 1997, the North American Industry Classification System (NAICS) replaced the 1987 U.S. SIC system and the classification systems of Canada and Mexico. NAICS is erected on a production-oriented conceptual framework. It is not a grouping of products but a grouping of producing units which allows for the collection of data on inputs and outputs on a comparable basis for production-oriented (not market-oriented) analysis. NAICS uses a six-digit coding system that resembles SIC codes. It is expected to eventually supersede the SIC system.

The search for guideline publicly traded companies should be as exhaustive as the scope of the particular valuation case permits. Frequently, the most obvious public companies in an industry are the largest ones and, for this and related reasons, may be less comparable to most closely held companies than some of the smaller, more obscure public companies. A comprehensive search for guideline companies also demonstrates that the analyst took into account all companies that might be considered reasonably comparable and selected for analysis the most comparative companies available. The analyst must establish and adhere to an objective set of selection criteria so that the final list will not tend to bias the valuation result either upward or downward.

Developing a List of Guideline Companies

The use of the SIC code as a means of identifying potential guideline publicly traded companies has already been discussed. The starting point in a search for developing similar guideline publicly traded enterprises is a search for the appropriate SIC code which applies to the subject company. Data concerning publicly traded companies by SIC group are found in a number of sources, including in printed material, on CD-ROMs, and in on-line databases.

Print Sources. *Moody's Manuals.* This service consists of annual hardback volumes updated by loose-leaf reports with detailed financial information and bond ratings in separate sets according to type of business or government entity. There is a

---

[14] Revenue Ruling 59-60 (1959-1 C.B. 327), Section 4.

master index to identify the industry volume in which each of the over 15,000 public companies is included.

SEC Directory. The *Directory of Companies Required to File Annual Reports with the Securities and Exchange Commission under the Securities Exchange Act of 1934* is published annually. It lists companies alphabetically and classified by industry group according to the *Standard Industrial Classification Manual.*

Standard & Poor's Corporation Records. In cases in which budget or time constraints do not permit an exhaustive search for guideline companies, a shortcut is to use the "Classified Index of Industrial Companies" published annually as part of the *Standard & Poor's Corporation Records.* The index, classified by SIC code, includes every public company that appears in the *S&P Corporation Records.* The two limitations are (1) that the *Corporation Records* excludes some smaller public companies included in the S&P Register and (2) there is no distinction for primary SIC code.

Standard & Poor's Register. The *S&P Register* is perhaps the most comprehensive directory of companies by SIC group, but it does not distinguish which companies are public and which are private. However, if a company is public and has been quoted in the *National Daily Quotation Service,* it will be listed in the *National Monthly Stock Summary.* Therefore, the *S&P Register* and the *National Monthly Stock Summary* can be used together to develop a list of publicly quoted companies in a particular SIC group.

CD-ROM. *Compact D/SEC.* This source contains lengthy extracts from major SEC documents for over 15,000 public companies. Its powerful capabilities and user-friendly approach have made it one of the best-selling CD-ROMs for business libraries. Produced by Disclosure Incorporated, Compact D/SEC provides extensive reports—a typical report is about 12 pages with over 200 variables, including a narrative description of the company, primary and secondary SIC codes, annual sales, and earnings information. The information is updated monthly.

Dialog on Disc. Produced by Knight-Ridder Incorporated, this CD-ROM product provides detailed descriptions of general operations, financial structure, sales, earnings, and corporate news for over 12,000 public companies. This information is also updated monthly.

Compustat. This is the most complete database of U.S. and Canadian public companies available. It includes information on over 10,000 companies with stock actively traded on U.S. exchanges and over 9,000 inactive public companies, as well as information on over 1,000 Canadian companies. Annual and quarterly financial data is provided along with pricing, dividend, earnings, and beta information. This product is provided on CD with on-line updates available on certain data items.

On-Line Databases. There are numerous on-line databases, and the list of available on-line services is rapidly increasing. The following paragraphs describe a representative sample of on-line services.

Company Intelligence. This is a combined directory and company news file published by Information Access Company. It contains current addresses, financial, and marketing information on approximately 150,000 private and public U.S. companies. Approximately 90,000 of these companies are listed in the three-volume set of *Ward's Business Directory.* A search for primary SIC code on public companies can be accomplished in powerful command-based language.

Media General Plus. This database provides timely and detailed financial and stock price information on approximately 5,100 public companies. It covers New York Stock Exchange and American Stock Exchange companies, plus all Nasdaq National Market System companies and selected over-the-counter companies.

Moody's Corporate Profiles. This database provides descriptive and financial information on important publicly traded U.S. companies. The file covers all companies on the New York and American Stock Exchanges, and approximately 1,300 of the most active, emerging companies traded over the counter. The data include concise narrative descriptions of the most essential company information and, for most companies, five-year financial histories and key statistics.

None of the databases can guarantee complete accuracy, and variables may be defined differently from one source to another. Therefore, if complete accuracy and consistency are essential, it often is necessary to go to the original source documents.

EDGAR. With the EDGAR system, analysts can access "as reported" financial data from companies required to file with the Securities and Exchange Commission (SEC). There is no charge for the data when accessed directly through the Internet. The EDGAR database, conceptualized by SEC Chairman John Shad in 1983 and started in 1984, is an effort to improve the speed and collection of financial documents required by the various U.S. securities laws and regulations. Since 1996, all public companies subject to the Securities Act or the Exchange Act have been required to file specific documents electronically. Although EDGAR does not hold every single type of disclosure document, it does contain the disclosure documents most valuable to analysts, such as Forms 10-K, 10-Q, and 8-K.

The EDGAR database is accessible from the Internet, as well as from a variety of commercial vendors. With an Internet connection, analysts can access disclosure documents free of charge from both the SEC and New York University (NYU) Stern School of Business Internet home pages, as well as other sources such as www.freeedgar.com. The formatting is not good, but there is freeware available to convert the documents to a more convenient format. Several companies provide EDGAR documents with value-added features, such as Boolean search capabilities or preformatted documents.

To take the value-added features a step further, commercial vendors such as Disclosure have added all sorts of bells and whistles to their traditional database products in order to maintain their market share in selling public company financial data. For example, Disclosure developed a product called *Global Access*, which indexes EDGAR documents so that analysts can perform sophisticated searches and obtain selected portions of documents in a short amount of time. In other words, when analysts access the EDGAR database from the SEC site or *LivEDGAR*, they cannot limit the printout to specific portions of a 10-K, such as company, name, ticker symbol, SIC Code, balance sheet, and statement of operations. With Disclosure's *Global Access*, researchers can essentially perform a guideline publicly traded company search and download only the portions of the source documents of the selected guideline companies that are needed. However, this value-added database comes with a price, and analysts need to consider the costs associated with using such a service.[15]

---

[15] This section was adapted from Shannon P. Pratt, Robert F. Reilly, and Robert P. Schweihs, *Valuing Small Businesses and Professional Practices*, 3rd ed. (New York: McGraw-Hill, 1998).

Financial Statement Adjustments to Guideline Companies

Generally, the same types of adjustments should be made to the financial statements of the guideline companies as are made to the financial statements of the subject company. Some main categories of adjustments are the following:

- Remove nonrecurring items (and any required tax effects) from income statements.
- Put guideline and subject companies on a comparable accounting basis (e.g., adjust any companies accounting for inventory on LIFO basis to FIFO basis, use consistent depreciation methods and lives).
- Adjust for nonoperating items.
- Adjust for discontinued operations.

Comparative Ratio Analysis

For purposes of comparative performance and other ratios between the subject company and the guideline companies, the comparisons will be more meaningful if the ratios are computed *after* the adjustments to the financial statements of the guideline companies as well as the subject company.

On the other hand, it is much faster and cheaper to use ratios for publicly traded companies from one of the many handy on-line or CD-ROM services, such as Dialog on Disk, Compustat, Compact D/SEC, or Media General Plus. Whether to use ratios computed by a service or to compute them oneself depends on the analyst's judgment as to the extent to which the difference in results is likely to justify the cost, which is a case-by-case decision.

An example of comparative ratio analysis based on guideline companies is included in Exhibit 21–8G and 21–8H in Chapter 21, Sample Report. This is a part of the analysis that helps guide the analyst's judgment as to where the various value measures for the subject company should fall relative to the range of the respective value measures for the guideline companies.

Typically, the comparative ratio analysis exercise is done only for the latest available comparative year, or the latest 12 months, even if value measures are based on several years' average results. If the comparative ratio analysis is used to help decide where the subject's value measures should be relative to the guideline companies' value measures, the analyst should be careful to recognize any distortions or abnormalities in the year for which the ratios were calculated that would cause the ratios to be misleading for use in pinpointing a relevant value measure. It may be helpful to calculate the ratios for past years, as well, to identify any possible distortions.

Obtaining the Guideline Companies' Market Value Data

If the value measures to be used are only those that relate to common equity, then all that is needed is the price for each guideline company's stock as of the valuation date.

If value measures based on the market value of invested capital (MVIC) are to be used, then the market value of all the components of the invested capital needs to be estimated. Some of the guideline companies' senior securities (e.g., debt and/or preferred stock) may not be publicly traded. In that case, book value often is used as a proxy for market value. If, however, the analyst suspects that the book value may be far enough apart from market value to create a significant distortion in the value measure computed, the senior securities should be revalued to market value. (Chapters 23 and 24 on Valuing Debt Securities and Valuing Preferred Stock, respectively, discuss how to do this.)

Presenting Guideline Company Tables

Guideline company tables may be presented on a direct equity basis or on an invested capital basis. They usually show the names of the guideline companies, the market in which they are traded (e.g., New York Stock Exchange, American Stock Exchange, Nasdaq, and so on), the per-share market price as of the valuation date, the financial fundamentals (e.g., EBIT, EBITDA, MVIC), and the resulting valuation multiple (the price divided by the financial fundamental). The table typically has a line at the bottom showing the comparable financial fundamental for the subject company.

For each valuation multiple presented, the table typically presents a low, high, mean average, and median. The sample report in Chapter 21 shows guideline publicly traded company tables for a variety of financial fundamentals.

A question often arises as to what extent value measures that were not ultimately used in reaching the value conclusion should be presented in the tables in the report. There is no clear-cut, right or wrong answer to this. We might suggest that there is not much point in presenting value measures that were never seriously considered to be used. If, however, a value measure was considered but discarded because of the nature of the data (perhaps a very wide dispersion of value multiples), it might be worth while to present it, so the reader can see the data that led to its being discarded in the final analysis.

Selecting and Weighting Multiples for the Subject Company Based on Guideline Companies

The result of the guideline company analysis is an array of pricing multiples for each of several value measures. At this point, it is necessary to again visit the question of which measures to use in reaching an indication of value and the relative weight to be accorded to each of those used.

For each value measure used, it is also necessary to decide what the pricing multiple for the subject company should be relative to the observed multiples for the guideline companies.

Impact of Guideline Company Data Evaluation

The same general thought processes and decision criteria apply to both deciding on whether or not to rely on any particular value measure at all and also to deciding on the relative weight to be accorded each value measure ultimately used in reaching the opinion of value.

The earlier discussion of the relative conceptual significance of different value measures as more or less applicable to different types of companies and with different ownership characteristics applies here, of course. However, a study of the data developed may lead to greater or lesser reliance on certain value measures than one might have expected before compiling the data.

Number of Data Points Available. If it turns out that very few data points are available for a particular value measure, that problem may lead one to abandon that measure or to put relatively little weight on it, even though it might be quite conceptually significant if there were more data. A common example is price to latest 12 months' earnings. If only two of seven guideline companies had meaningful positive earnings (and thus meaningful P/Es), the analyst has to decide whether the two convey enough information to be accorded weight in the final analysis. The analyst might, for example, decide instead to use a price-to-gross-cash-flow multiple or a price to some number of years average earnings. One must be careful, however, that this procedure does not give undue weight to companies with losses if the subject is a profitable company.

Comparability of Data Measurement. Another issue to consider is the extent to which the analyst is satisfied that the adjustments, if any, to the subject and guideline companies' financial fundamentals have resulted in stating the data on a comparable basis. The analyst's confidence regarding the comparability of fundamental data may influence his or her judgment regarding the use of, or weight accorded to, value measures based on that particular fundamental variable.

Comparability of Data Patterns. Another factor in assessing comparability is the extent to which the data for the subject company "track" with the data for the guideline companies. For example, if the subject and six of the seven guideline companies had a generally upward earnings trend, but one guideline company had a downward trend, the analyst may omit the aberrational company when deciding on appropriate pricing measures relative to earnings.

In the case of one annual valuation, the subject company's earnings always followed a pattern somewhat similar to a good group of guideline companies. Each year, we put considerable weight on the multiple of price to latest 12 months' earnings. Then, one year, the company had a banner year while the guideline group struggled. First we satisfied ourselves that this sudden divergence was an aberration. Then, in that year, we placed most of the weight on the price to five years' average earnings multiple instead of on the latest 12 months pricing multiple, which would have resulted in an inflated valuation.

Apparent Market Reliance. The extent to which the value measures are tightly clustered or widely dispersed tends to indicate the extent to which the market tends to focus on that particular measure in pricing stocks in the particular industry. For this reason, when analyzing the guideline companies, the analyst may want to calculate not only measures of central tendency (such as mean and median), but also measures of dispersion (such as standard deviation and coefficient of variation).

Generally, the lower the dispersion of the value measure, the greater the weight the analyst might consider according to that measure. In some cases, the guideline company table may lead the analyst to conclude that the value measures based on some particular financial fundamental are so widely dispersed that those measures have no usefulness as guidance to value.

Measures of Central Tendency and Dispersion

Measures of Central Tendency. The *median* (the number in the middle of the array) usually, but not always, provides a better measure of central tendency for ratios than the *mean* (the arithmetic average).[16] This is because one or a few outliers (extreme observations) may have more of a distorting effect on the mean than on the median.

Another problem with the arithmetic average is that when it is used to summarize ratios that have stock price or MVIC in the numerator (such as the P/E multiple), it weights each guideline company in proportion to that company's ratio. It does not give equal weight to each guideline company. For example, the arithmetic mean P/E multiple of two guideline companies' P/E multiples of 15 and 5 is 10. While it might appear that this mean is giving equal weight to each company, it actually gives three times as much weight to the first company because its P/E multiple is triple the second's. Assuming that we invest a total of $200 in both companies, the only way the resulting portfolio's P/E multiple is 10 is by investing $150 (for $10 of earnings) in the first company and $50 (for $10 of earnings) in the second.

The harmonic mean is used to give equal weight to each guideline company in summarizing ratios that have stock price or MVIC in the numerator. It is the reciprocal of the average of the reciprocals of the guideline company multiples. In the example above, the reciprocal of the P/E multiple of 15 is 0.0667, the reciprocal of the P/E multiple of 5 is 0.200, the average of the two reciprocals is 0.1334, and the reciprocal of the average is 7.5. This P/E multiple of 7.5 is the same as the P/E multiple of a $200 portfolio with $100 invested (for $6.67 of earnings at a P/E multiple of 15) in the first company and $100 invested (for $20 of earnings at a P/E multiple of 5) in the second company. With the $200 invested equally in each guideline company, the total earnings are $26.67, and the P/E multiple is 7.5.

Measures of Dispersion. A simple but important measure of dispersion is the range—that is, the spread between the highest and lowest observation. Generally, the tighter the range of the data points, the less room for judgmental error in deciding on the appropriate multiple for the subject company relative to the guideline companies.

Occasionally, differences between the subject and guideline companies lead the analyst to conclude that a multiple for the subject should be outside the range for the guideline companies. When this occurs, it is important that the analyst explain carefully the reason for choosing a multiple outside the guideline company range.

The most familiar measure of dispersion is the *standard deviation*.[17] When using the standard deviation, it is generally helpful to focus primarily on the *coefficient of variation*, which is the standard deviation divided by the mean. By using the coefficient of variation, the relative dispersion of data for different value measures with different mean or median values can be compared directly with each other.

Multiples of Earnings or Cash Flow

Multiples of economic income variables (price/earnings multiples, price/cash flow multiples, and so on) are the reciprocals of the capitalization rates applicable to those variables. For example, a pricing multiple of 8 is the inverse of a capitalization rate of 0.125 ($1 \div 8 = 0.125$). Therefore, valuation pricing multiples are influenced by the same forces that influence capitalization rates, the two most important of which are:

---

[16] A little knowledge of statistics is helpful here, but beyond the scope of this book. Relevant basic references would be, for example, Gerald I. White, Ashwinpaul C. Sondhi, and Dov Fried, *The Analysis & Use of Financial Statements*, 2nd ed. (New York: John Wiley and Sons, 1997), and Robert D. Mason and Douglas A. Lind, *Statistical Techniques in Business and Economics*, 9th ed. (New York: McGraw-Hill, 1996).

[17] For the mathematical formula for the standard deviation, see one of the statistics books referenced in the prior footnote. In any case, many pocket calculators are programmed to compute standard deviations.

1. Risk.
2. Expected growth in the operating variable being capitalized.

Therefore, in order for the analyst to make an intelligent estimate of what multiple is appropriate for the subject company relative to the multiples observed for the guideline companies, the analyst must make some judgments as to the relative risk and growth prospects of the subject compared with the guideline companies.

Relative Risk. Since a closely held stock does not have a regular price trading history from which to compute a *beta* (as described in Chapter 9), other means must be used to assess relative risk. One such means is a study of comparative financial ratios between the subject and guideline companies, as discussed in Chapter 8. Operating and financial leverage ratios are of the greatest importance in assessing relative risk. The analyst can then use judgment to adjust multiples up or down from those of the guideline companies to reflect relative risk as revealed by the comparative financial ratios.

Another way to assess relative risk is to compare historical earnings or cash flow volatility between the subject and the guideline companies. Any of several measures of dispersion, such as a standard deviation, may be used for this purpose. It then becomes a matter of analysts' judgment as to how much to adjust multiples from those observed for the guideline companies to reflect differences in risk evidenced by differences in earnings or cash flow volatility.

The size factor is also an important indicator of risk. We presented data in Chapter 9 that showed that companies of the size of the smallest decile of the New York Stock Exchange required a discount rate several points above the average for the New York Stock Exchange. This differential in the discount rate can translate directly into a difference in the capitalization rate.

Relative Growth. As discussed in Chapter 9, the expected growth rate in perpetuity for cash flow translates point for point into the capitalization rate for that variable. Therefore, if the subject company has very long-term growth prospects above or below those of the guideline companies, those growth rate differentials should be reflected in the capitalization rates chosen. Be careful, however, not to understate the proper capitalization rate by making a large adjustment for growth prospects that are only short or intermediate term.

An Example. We will continue with the example where the guideline company indicated price/cash flow ratio is 8, resulting in a capitalization rate for cash flow of 12.5. Let's assume that the comparative risk analysis leads us to conclude that the discount rate for the subject company would be five percentage points higher than for the guideline companies, which would bring the capitalization rate to 17.5 (12.5 + 5.0 = 17.5). On the other hand, let's assume that our smaller, riskier company had two percentage points higher infinitely sustainable long-term growth prospects than the guideline companies. This offsetting factor would bring the capitalization rate back down to 15.5 (17.5 − 2.0 = 15.5). This, then, equates to a valuation multiple of 6.5 (1 ÷ 15.5 = 6.5).

Capitalization of Dividends or Dividend-Paying Capacity

Dividends from operations ultimately are possible only as a result of earnings and adequate available cash flow. Therefore, capitalization of dividends or dividend-paying capacity may or may not be analyzed as a valuation method separate from capitalization of earnings and/or cash flow, depending on the circumstances and the valuation's purpose. Revenue Ruling 59-60 states that dividends or dividend-paying capacity should be one factor in the valuation of a business interest for federal estate or gift tax purposes. Most potential acquirers are not specifically interested in the acquiree's dividend-paying capacity, since the acquiree will not continue to operate as an independent entity.

If the valuation is of a controlling interest, dividend-paying capacity is more important than actual dividends paid, since the controlling stockholder has the discretion to pay or not pay dividends as long as the company has the capacity to do so. In valuing a noncontrolling interest, however, the actual dividends the company pays usually are more important than the dividend-paying capacity, since the noncontrolling stockholder generally cannot force the company to pay dividends even if it unquestionably has the capacity to do so.

When the capitalization of dividends method is used as an element in valuation, it usually is by reference to dividend yields on guideline publicly traded companies. For example, if guideline publicly traded companies were found to have an average dividend yield (annual dividends per share divided by market price per share) of 5 percent and the subject company paid dividends or was estimated to have a dividend-paying capacity of $1 per share, the capitalization of dividends method would be to simply divide the dividend-paying capacity per share by the appropriate capitalization rate or dividend yield—in this case, 0.05, which implies a $20 per share value by the capitalization of dividends method.

An estimate of dividend-paying capacity may be based in part on typical payout ratios of publicly traded companies in the subject company's industry. For example, if public companies in that industry typically pay out 30 percent of their earnings in dividends, 30 percent of earnings might be a good starting point from which to estimate the subject company's dividend-paying capacity. However, the typical closely held company is less well capitalized than its publicly traded counterpart and may have less dividend-paying capacity per dollar of earnings capacity than most of the publicly traded companies with which it might be compared. This factor must be considered in estimating the subject company's dividend-paying capacity.

Multiples of Revenue

Multiples of revenue tend to be most highly correlated with return on sales, but the strength of the correlation varies greatly from one industry to another. Therefore, when considering using a multiple of sales, it is useful to first see whether the guideline company multiples of revenue are well correlated with return on sales. This value measure tends to be more useful for industries where such a correlation is high than for those where it is not. In a way, capitalization of revenues can be considered a shortcut to capitalization or earnings, since generally there is an implicit assumption that a certain level of revenues should be able to generate a specific earnings level in a given type of business.

Capitalization of revenues is applied most frequently to start-up companies and to service businesses, such as advertising agencies, insurance agencies, mortuaries, professional practices, and some types of publishing operations.

One can find guidance in arriving at an appropriate multiple of revenues for a particular business in both public stock market data and merger and acquisition data. There are quite a few publicly traded companies in most service business categories, such as insurance agencies, advertising and public relations firms, and securities brokers. If the subject company's true return on sales is known, an estimate of a reasonable price/sales multiple can be derived by simple regression analysis using guideline companies' price/sales ratios and returns on sales.

Exhibit 11–2 illustrates the relationship between return on sales and price to revenue multiples for publicly traded insurance agency companies as of December 31, 1998. The exhibit also presents the computation of a suggested price to revenue multiple for a subject insurance agency company realizing a 6 percent return on revenue at that time.

Valuations by multiples of revenue are particularly susceptible to distortion because of differences in capital structure between subject and guideline companies. Therefore, this valuation pricing multiple should be calculated on a market value of invested capital basis, as discussed in a later section.

One step removed from a multiple of revenues is a multiple of some measure of unit volume or capacity. Examples would include nursing homes at so much per bed, forest products plants at so much per thousand board feet of production, service stations and fuel distributors at so much per gallon sold per month, wireless telephone and cable television companies at so much per subscriber, and so on. The implication of this method is that so much volume can be expected to translate into some anticipated amount of sales and economic income.

Exhibit 11–2

Correlation between Price/Revenues and Return on Revenues

Company	December 31, 1998	
	Return on Revenues	Price/Revenues
Marsh & McLennan Companies, Inc.	11.1%	2.09
Hilb, Rogal & Hamilton Co.	8.3%	1.33
E.W. Blanch Holdings, Inc.	14.9%	3.15
Arthur J. Gallagher & Co.	10.4%	1.44
Brown & Brown, Inc.	15.0%	3.07

$$r^2 = 0.948$$

The regression formula to be solved is $y = a + bx$. The price/revenues multiple = $a + b$ (return on revenues),
    where:
        a = price/revenues multiple (y) intercept
        b = slope of the line
Using a calculator capable of linear regression analysis, the analyst can calculate the y intercept a and
slope of the line b using return on revenues and price/revenues multiple data from the guideline companies.
Using the returns on revenues and price/revenues multiple data for 12/31/98, we calculate:
    $a = -1.1838$
    $b = 28.5149$
    $y = -1.1838 + 28.5149(x)$
Substituting in the subject company's return on revenues (0.10), we compute an indicated price/revenues
multiple:
    $y = -1.1838 + 28.5149(0.10)$
    $y = -1.1838 + 2.85$
    $y = 1.67$

Return on revenues = Net income divided by net sales
Price/Revenues = stock price divided by revenues per share

1998 Tax Rates	
Marsh & McLennan Companies, Inc.	39.0%
Hilb, Rogal & Hamilton Co.	41.1%
E.W. Blanch Holdings, Inc.	40.3%
Arthur J. Gallagher & Co.	32.9%
Brown & Brown, Inc.	38.5%

Multiple of Stock Value to Asset Value

When the analyst has determined that book value or some adjusted book value figure provides a useful representation of the company's underlying net asset values, the next step is to translate that figure into its implication for the value of the shares of stock or partnership interest being valued. This usually is accomplished by referring to the relationship of the prices of guideline companies' stocks to their respective underlying net asset values. The data for the guideline companies may be based on prices of stocks traded on the open market, prices paid in acquisitions, or both, depending on several factors, including the percentage ownership interest being valued.

As in any aspect of valuation based on comparisons with other companies, the analyst should use experience and expertise to ensure that the comparisons are as valid as possible within the limitations of data availability.

Price/Book Value Multiple. It may be possible to compute the multiple of market price to book value for a group of guideline companies that have stock trading in the public market and apply a multiple somewhere within the range of such multiples to the subject company's book value. If the book values of the subject and guideline companies were computed on comparable bases, and if the assets' composition is comparable, this procedure may provide a reasonably realistic figure for the value of the business interest.

If accounting methods for the subject and guideline companies differ significantly, the analyst should make appropriate adjustments before computing the market price/book value multiples and applying them to the valuation. There can be additional significant differences, such as in asset mix, that challenge the validity of using one company's price to book value multiple in valuing another's stock.

Often the value measure multiples are computed on only *tangible* book value. This may help to avoid distortions, since some companies may have created their own intangibles, and thus expensed them for accounting purposes, while others may have acquired their intangibles, and thus carry them on the balance sheet.

If the subject company's return on equity is high relative to the guideline companies', the appropriate price to asset value multiple probably should be in the upper end of the relevant range, and vice versa. As common sense would suggest, empirical tests indicate a significant degree of correlation between price/book value multiples and return on equity for both publicly traded stocks and acquisition prices in most industries. As a consequence, an analysis of the relationship between price/book value ratios and return on equity for the guideline companies often can provide objective guidance in deciding on an appropriate price/book value multiple for the subject company. If the correlation between the price/book value multiples and return on equity for the guideline companies is reasonably good, the analyst may use a simple linear regression to compute an indicated price/book value multiple for the subject company based on market data. The mechanics of this analysis are the same as for the price/revenues analysis presented in Exhibit 11–3.

Price/Adjusted Net Asset Value. For a limited number of industries, data on market values of underlying assets are available. Where this is the case, it is possible to compute pricing multiples of the public stock's price to its adjusted net asset value.

In particular, market values for some real estate companies are provided in *Realty Stock Review*. Also, estimates of timber values for many forest products companies are available from brokerage house analysts. When using multiples of price

Exhibit 11–3

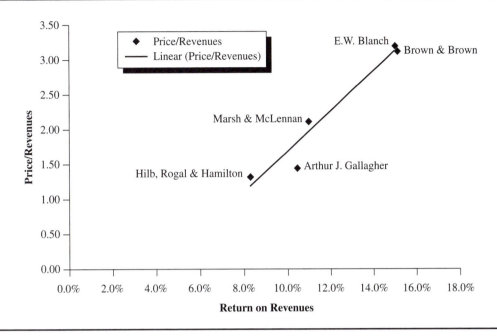

Price/Revenues Compared to Return on Revenues

to adjusted net asset value, it is important to make the same kinds of adjustments to the subject company as have been made to the asset values for the guideline companies. For example, some real estate company adjusted net asset values are reported net of impounded capital gains taxes and some are not.

The use of the various price/asset value pricing multiples are market approach valuation procedures. The use of these pricing multiples is independent of, and should not be confused with, the use of asset-based approach valuation methods (such as the asset accumulation method or the capitalized excess earnings method).

Treating Nonoperating Assets, Excess Assets, and Asset Deficiencies

If the subject company has significant nonoperating assets, excess assets, or asset deficiencies that distinguish it from the guideline companies, adjustments for those items may be appropriate. If some of the guideline companies also have such asset anomalies, it is important, of course, to make similar adjustments to them for consistency.

Nonoperating Assets

Many privately held companies own assets that are not part of their operations. Such assets may add some value to the closely held stock over and above the values indicated by the ratios of guideline company stock prices to their underlying financial fundamentals.

If nonoperating assets are to be given separate consideration, they should be separated from the operating company data (and from the guideline companies). Any income they generate (or expenses incurred on behalf of their maintenance) should be removed from earnings or cash flows capitalized. If a price/asset value multiple is used based on guideline companies, the nonoperating assets should be removed from the asset value. These financial statement adjustments should be made before the ratio analysis of the financial statements, if such analysis is to be used to help decide on multiples relative to guideline company multiples.

The question then becomes, "How much extra value do these assets contribute to the stock?"

The theory of valuing nonoperating assets separately from operating assets rests on the assumption that the nonoperating assets could be liquidated without impairing operations. Thus, if the market value of nonoperating assets is higher than their book value and the analyst is going to mark the nonoperating assets up to the market value to perform the valuation, the analyst should also consider offsetting factors. These factors might include the capital gains or ordinary income tax, as the case might be, that the company would have to pay if it liquidated the assets, any costs of liquidation, and any discounts that might be appropriate in reflecting the estimated time required to liquidate and the risk that the actual amounts realized might be less than the estimated market values as of the valuation date.

From there, it often makes a significant difference whether one is valuing a noncontrolling interest or a controlling interest. It also is important to know, if possible, the likelihood of sale of the assets. The market attributes very little weight to non–income producing, nonoperating assets, unless they are likely to be sold, because their existence provides little, if any, benefit to the noncontrolling stockholder. Even when valuing a controlling interest, they normally would be discounted from their net realizable value, because most control buyers would rather buy a pure operating company and not have to deal with disposing of nonoperating assets.

Marginal Operating Real Estate

An issue that often is a gray area in stock valuations is whether certain real estate should be valued separately when using the guideline company valuation method.

One factor is the degree of comparability. If the subject company owns its real estate and the guideline companies do not, then it often is appropriate to value the real estate separately. This is more true for controlling ownership interests than for noncontrolling ownership interests—for the same reasons discussed in connection with nonoperating assets. Of course, if the real estate is valued separately, then the company's income statement should be adjusted to reflect a market rent expense.

Real estate used in operations but used far below its highest and best use is often controversial. This becomes a matter of the analyst's judgment. Certainly, the imminence—or lack of it—of prospective development or sale of the real estate will play a role in the judgment.

Excess Assets or Asset Deficiencies

An often controversial area for possible adjustment may arise when the subject company has significantly greater amounts of some assets relative to its operations than do the guideline companies. The most common assets giving rise to such a potential adjustment are cash and marketable securities.

If it appears that some assets may be held in excessive amounts, the analyst should ask the company officials if there is a rationale for why such apparent excesses may be necessary for operations. If they are not necessary, then some adjustment may be appropriate. The same reasoning regarding noncontrol and control valuation premises discussed earlier also applies here.

It is also common to find the reverse situation—that is, one in which it might be appropriate to value the company by a capitalization of earnings method but then to subtract an amount reflecting the inadequacy of operating assets. This can easily be the case if net working capital is inadequate to support the level of business, if an adverse legal judgment is predictable, or if certain plant and equipment are in imminent need of replacement or major repair. Evaluating such inadequacies may require more subjective judgment than would assessing excess or nonoperating assets, but the potential problem of measurement does not render recognition of the concept of asset inadequacy any less important.

Multiline Companies

There are a variety of ways to handle multiline companies within the application of the guideline company method.

Procedures for Valuation

Separate Valuations. When a company has two or more separate and different operations, and if the financial information can be adequately segregated between them, the valuation of the combined operations might be handled as if it were two or more separate and independent valuations, using the valuation multiples most applicable for each.

Blended Valuation Multiples. More often, it is not possible to separate revenues and expenses so that values of different operating groups can be estimated separately. In this case, valuation multiples from the respective guideline company industry groups may be weighted in accordance with the subject company fundamental weights, such as sales or gross margin dollars.

Use of Conglomerates. One alternative for multiline companies is to use value measures from publicly traded conglomerates. We would recommend this procedure only if the industry lines of the subject company bear some reasonable resemblance to the industry lines of the guideline company conglomerates used.

"Portfolio Effect"

Multiline companies sometimes are valued at some discount from the sum of the indicated values of their various operations. This is because most buyers tend to seek a participation in a particular industry, and are less enthusiastic about a participation in somebody else's predetermined combination of some group of industries. This discount tends to apply whether valuing a noncontrolling or a controlling ownership interest. Guidance for quantifying this discount can sometimes be observed in the marketplace by comparing prices of conglomerate companies with the aggregate values of their parts, sometimes referred to as their breakup value.

Typical Adjustments to Reach a Value Conclusion

As discussed earlier, the guideline company method is based on minority interest, day-to-day transactions in publicly traded stocks. Therefore, if valuing a closely held noncontrolling ownership interest, it would not be appropriate to take a discount for lack of control, but it would be appropriate to take a discount for lack of marketability (discussed in Chapter 17, Discounts for Illiquidity and Lack of Marketability).

If a controlling interest is being valued, it may or may not be appropriate to apply a premium for control. This is discussed in Chapter 15, Control and Acquisition Premiums. Also, as discussed in Chapter 17, a control premium may be fully or partially offset by a discount for lack of marketability.

Value Measures Using Market Value of Invested Capital

Sometimes it is desirable to address the value of the entire invested capital. As noted in the section on defining the capital structure in Chapter 9, Income Approach: Discounted Future Economic Income Method, the most commonly used conceptual definition of *invested capital* is all equity and long-term debt (including current maturities of long-term debt).

Valuing the entire capital structure often is useful when valuing a controlling interest, since a control buyer is usually interested in the value of the entire company irrespective of its current capital structure, which a control buyer might change.

Valuing all of the invested capital based on guideline company values and then subtracting the value of the senior securities may also be useful for valuing noncontrolling interests where the capital structures differ significantly between the subject and guideline companies. This procedure can even out distorting effects of widely differing capital structures.

As a practical matter, when using the guideline company method, it generally is necessary to include *all* interest-bearing debt. Unless repayment at face is imminent, it usually should be valued at market. It often is difficult or even impossible to separate out how much of each of the guideline companies' interest expenses is attributable to long-term versus short-term debt.

Therefore, the numerator for market value of invested capital (MVIC) ratios in the guideline company method usually is the aggregate market value of all equity (including options and warrants) and all interest-bearing debt. Some practitioners subtract cash, which then would be added on at the end of the valuation procedures.

As noted earlier in the chapter, the denominators for MVIC measures typically are the following:

- Gross or net sales.
- Earnings before interest and taxes (EBIT).
- Earnings before interest, taxes, depreciation, and amortization, (EBITDA).
- Net free cash flow available to invested capital.

Exhibit 11–4 presents a simple illustration of a valuation exercise using MVIC for three guideline companies where the capital structures for the guideline companies differed significantly from the subject company. As can be seen in Exhibit 11–4, the range of indicated values for the subject company using MVIC for the guideline companies is tighter than the wide scatter using typical straight equity value measures. In particular, the straight equity measures distort the price/book value multiple on the high side and the price/revenues multiple on the low side.

The analysis suggests that a control buyer might be willing to pay $27 to $32 a share for the equity on the assumption that the buyer could leverage the purchase with debt similar to the industry average. On the other hand, a minority buyer could not take advantage of the leverage opportunity, and probably would not be willing to pay nearly as much.

Common Errors

The guideline publicly traded company method can be a powerful and useful tool in the valuation of closely held business interests. Proper application of it, however, requires some expertise in the analysis of publicly traded securities. This section discusses a few of the most common categories of errors frequently encountered in the use of the guideline publicly traded company method.

Failure to Conduct an Adequate Search for Guideline Company Data

As noted early in the chapter, there are thousands of publicly traded stocks. Some services report only a fraction of them, usually the largest ones. It is common to see reports that say something to the effect that, "We searched for publicly traded companies in the industry, but there were none," when, in fact, a more thorough search might unearth several. A related error is to use only companies in some service such as *Value Line Investment Survey*, which generally covers larger companies, when smaller companies not included in *Value Line* may be more comparative to the subject company.

Failure to Make Appropriate Financial Statement Adjustments to Guideline Companies

We frequently see a good job done on adjustments to the subject company statements, but little or no consideration given to possible appropriate adjustments to the guideline companies' financials. It is important that the analyst peruse the financial statements of the guideline companies to determine whether adjustments may be appropriate for one or more of the companies to put them on a basis as comparative as possible to the subject.

Along the same line, we generally like to use the guideline companies' original financial statements and SEC filings rather than secondary sources, especially if the guideline company method is to be the primary method relied on. Secondary sources often do not provide the detail of data needed for certain adjustments. Also, people sometimes are not careful to understand the definition a secondary source may use

Exhibit 11–4

Market Value of Invested Capital Valuation Using Guideline Publicly Traded Companies with Different Capital Structures than the Subject Company
$000s

	Guideline Company A	Guideline Company B	Guideline Company C	Subject Company
Comparative Balance Sheets				
Current assets	$25,000	$15,000	$12,000	$10,000
Net plant and equipment	45,000	35,000	18,000	15,000
Total assets	$70,000	$50,000	$30,000	$25,000
Current liabilities	$15,000	$10,000	$10,000	$5,000
Long-term debt	30,000	20,000	10,000	—
Stockholders' equity	25,000	20,000	10,000	20,000
Total liabilities and equity	$70,000	$50,000	$30,000	$25,000
Book value of invested capital (equity + interest-bearing debt)	$55,000	$40,000	$20,000	$20,000
Comparative Income Statements				
Sales	$90,000	$60,000	$40,000	$30,000
Cost of sales	55,000	35,000	25,000	18,000
Gross margin	35,000	25,000	15,000	12,000
General and administrative	16,000	12,000	7,000	5,500
Earnings before interest, taxes, depreciation, and amortization (EBITDA)	19,000	13,000	8,000	6,500
Depreciation	7,000	5,000	3,000	2,500
Earnings before interest and taxes (EBIT)	12,000	8,000	5,000	4,000
Interest	3,000	2,000	1,000	—
Net income before taxes	9,000	6,000	4,000	4,000
Taxes	4,000	2,500	1,500	1,500
Net income	$5,000	$3,500	$2,500	$2,500
Market value per share	$6.00	$5.00	$25.00	
Shares outstanding	10,000	6,000	1,000	1,000
Aggregate market value of equity	$60,000	$30,000	$25,000	
Add: Market value of debt [a]	30,000	20,000	10,000	—
Market value of invested capital	$90,000	$50,000	$35,000	
Debt/equity ratio (at market)	0.33	0.40	0.290	0.00

	Guideline Company A	Guideline Company B	Guideline Company C	Average	Implied Value of Subject [b] ($000)	Implied Value Per Share
Valuation Multiples						
Price/book value	2.4	1.5	2.5	2.1	42,000	$42.00
Price/sales	0.7	0.5	0.6	0.6	18,000	18.00
Price/earnings	12.0	8.6	10.0	10.2	25,500	25.50
Price/gross cash flow (net income + depreciation)	5.0	3.5	4.5	4.3	21,500	21.50
MVIC/BVIC	1.6	1.3	1.8	1.6	32,400	32.40
MVIC/Sales	1.0	0.8	0.9	0.9	27,000	27.00
MVIC/EBIT	7.5	6.3	7.0	6.9	27,600	27.60
MVIC/EBITDA	4.7	3.8	4.4	4.3	27,950	27.95

a. Assumes market value of debt = book value of debt

b. Using averages of guideline company multiples in all cases, since fundamentals are similar except for capital structure.

for certain data, and thus may get caught in a mismatch when using it to value the subject company.

Multiples that Mismatch Numerator and Denominator

There are many ways to mismatch the numerator in a value multiple (the multiple selected on the basis of guideline company market evidence) with the denominator (the fundamental data for the subject company to which the numerator is applied to get an indication of value). Two of the most common are mismatched time periods and mismatched definitions.

Mismatched Time Periods. It is not uncommon to find value multiples computed from guideline company data for some time period applied to subject company data for a different time period. This inconsistency can result in serious distortions, especially if industry conditions differed significantly between the time periods. At a market turning point for a cyclical industry, a single quarter's difference in the fundamental data used between the guideline companies and the subject company can result in seriously misleading value multiples.

In order to avoid such distortion, it is often necessary to work with interim (versus fiscal year-end) data for the guideline companies in order to match time periods as closely as possible with available subject company data closest to the effective date of the valuation. This usually requires more work on the part of the analyst but often is worth it to produce a more reliable result.

Mismatched Definitions of Variables. If a value multiple is computed based on guideline company data defined in a certain way, that multiple should be applied to fundamental data defined the same way for the subject company. Looking at the same point another way, if subject company data are defined in a certain way, the same definition should be used for guideline company data from which a value multiple is computed.

Elementary as this sounds, inexperienced analysts often make data mismatches. A few of the more common data mismatches are:

- Fully diluted data used for the guideline companies or the subject company, but not for both.
- Subject company—but not guideline company—data adjusted for nonrecurring items.
- After-tax pricing multiples for guideline companies applied to pretax data for subject company.
- Income data after officers' compensation for guideline companies applied to subject company income data before owner/officer compensation.

The above list provides a flavor of typical mismatches. Analysts should be on the lookout to avoid them.

Simple Reliance on Average of Guideline Company Multiples without Comparative Analysis

Unless the guideline and subject companies are extremely homogenous in their financial characteristics, the mean or median of the guideline company pricing multiples may not be the most appropriate pricing multiples for the subject company. Yet analysts often use the mean or median guideline company pricing multiple with no explanation to justify the implied notion that the subject company's characteristics indicate that it should be valued right at the average of the guideline companies.

A section of this chapter was devoted to selecting the pricing multiple for the subject company relative to guideline company pricing multiples. Such analysis is little more than common sense, yet it is surprising how often it is ignored!

Summary

This chapter has presented the procedures and sources for implementing the guideline company method of valuing the equity ownership of a business. It is widely used and accepted, but it must be implemented very carefully.

Exhibit 11–5 summarizes the steps in carrying out the guideline company method.

The guideline company method usually uses measures that indicate the value of the equity directly, such as price/earnings multiples. However, sometimes the market value of the total invested capital is estimated and the value of debt subtracted to reach an indicated value for the equity.

Because the guideline company method usually uses publicly traded minority interest stock transactions, the value reached usually is minority interest value on a

Exhibit 11–5

Steps in the Guideline Publicly Traded Company Method

1. Set criteria for selection of guideline publicly traded companies.

2. Search for and identify the companies that meet the criteria.

3. Decide on the relevant time period for comparative analysis of the subject company and the guideline companies.

4. Obtain the guideline companies' financial statements for the time period decided in Step 3.

5. Broaden or narrow the criteria, if necessary, to provide the best group of guideline companies, adding or deleting companies according to the revised criteria.

6. Analyze and adjust the subject and/or guideline company financial statements as appropriate (Chapter 7).

7. Compile comparative financial ratios for the subject and guideline companies (Chapter 8).

8. Decide which guideline company value measures to use.

9. Obtain the market price of each guideline company's stock as of the valuation date. (If market value of invested capital is used in any of the value measures, it is necessary to obtain the market value of all the guideline companies' securities that are included in their invested capital.)

10. Compile guideline company value measure tables for the value measures decided in Step 8.

11. Based on analysis of the value measure tables in conjunction with the comparative financial analysis of the subject and guideline companies, decide on the appropriate multiple for the subject company for each value measure to be used.

12. Multiply each value measure to be used by the relevant financial variable for the subject company to get indications of value according to each value measure.

13. Weight or otherwise correlate the indications of value from Step 11 to reach an estimate of "value as if publicly traded" (a marketable, minority ownership interest value).

14. Make adjustments to this value, if appropriate, for factors in the definition of value but not reflected in the value as if publicly traded, such as discount for lack of marketability and/or premium for control. Also, adjust any other elements of value, if appropriate, that were adjusted out of the guideline company analysis, such as nonoperating assets.

fully marketable basis. If the analyst is valuing a minority ownership interest in a private company, he or she should normally make an adjustment for lack of marketability. If the analyst is valuing a controlling ownership interest, a premium for control may or may not be appropriate, and such a premium may be fully or partially offset by a discount for the lack of liquidity of the privately held company controlling interest.

The chapter should be helpful both for those preparing a valuation utilizing the guideline company method, and also for those reviewing and evaluating a valuation report that uses the method.

Bibliography

Articles

Alford, Andrew W. "The Effect of the Set of Comparable Firms on the Accuracy of the Price-Earnings Valuation Method." *Journal of Accounting Research*, Spring 1992, pp. 94–108.

Bates, Mary Ellen. "Where's EDGAR Today? Finding SEC Filings Online." *Database*, June 1996, pp. 41–50.

Bielinski, Daniel W. "The Comparable-Company Approach: Measuring the True Value of Privately Held Firms." *Corporate Cashflow Magazine*, October 1990, pp. 64–68.

Bjorklund, Victoria B., and Susan A. Meisel. "Valuation: When Are Comparables Comparable Enough?" *Practical Tax Lawyer*, Spring 1991, pp. 45–47+.

Crow, Matthew R. "Developing Valuation Multiples Using Guideline Companies." *CPA Litigation Service Counselor*, September 1999, pp. 8–9.

"Enhanced EDGAR Site Has Email Capabilities and Integrates with Microsoft Excel 97." *Shannon Pratt's Business Valuation Update*, September 1997, p. 5.

Fowler, Bradley A. "How Do You Handle It?" *Business Valuation Review*, September 1996, pp. 136–37.

Goeldner, Richard W. "Adjusting Market Multiples of Guideline Companies." Presentation to the 18th Annual Advanced Business Valuation Conference of the American Society of Appraisers, October 29, 1999. Available on www.BVLibrary.com.

_____. "Bridging the Gap between Public and Private Market Multiples." *Business Valuation Review*, September 1998, pp. 97–101.

Graham, Michael D. "Selection of Market Multiples in Business Valuation." *Business Valuation Review*, March 1990, pp. 8–12.

Hickman, Kent, and Glenn H. Petry. "A Comparison of Stock Price Predictions Using Court Accepted Formulas, Dividend Discount, and P/E Models." *Financial Management*, Summer 1990, pp. 76–87.

McDonagh, Christopher S., and John M. McDonagh. "Valuing a Target's Ability to Compete in the Market." *Mergers & Acquisitions*, September/October 1995, pp. 22–25.

Nath, Eric W. "How Public Guideline Companies Represent "'Control' Value for a Private Company." *Business Valuation Review*, December 1997, pp. 167–71.

O'Leary, Mick. "The Many Faces of Disclosure." *Database*, October/November 1996, pp. 91–92.

Penhollow, John, and Gary Purnhagen. "EDGAR." In *Securities Filings* 1996, by Alan K. Austin. New York: Practicing Law Institute, 1996, pp. 33–131.

Peters, Jerry O. "Adjusting Price/Earnings Ratios for Differences in Company Size." *Business Valuation Review*, June 1999, pp. 71–85.

Randisi, Martin P. "Comparable Company Method of Valuing a Closely-Held Business." *Fair$hare*, January 1991, pp. 3–5.

Reilly, Robert F. "Problems in Using Capital Market Data to Value Operating Business Assets." *Valuation Strategies*, January/February 1999, pp. 17–19, 44, 46.

Slee, Robert T. "Is the Subject Company Similar?" *Valuation Strategies*, May/June 1998, pp. 4–7, 34.

Summers, S. Chris. "The Myth of Public Company Comparisons." *Business Valuation Review*, June 1992, pp. 59–62.

Wise, Richard M. "Multiple-of-Revenues as a Valuation Method." *Business Valuation Digest*, October 1996, pp. 1–4.

Sources of Guideline Publicly Traded Company Data

Compact D/SEC
Disclosure Incorporated
(a Primark company)
(800) 843-7747
www.primark.com/pfid

Compustat
Standard & Poor's Corporation
www.compustat.com
(800) 523-4534

Dialog on Disc
Knight-Ridder Information
www.dialog.com
(800) 334-2564

Directory of Companies Required to File Annual Reports with the Securities and Exchange Commission under the Securities Exchange Act of 1934
U.S. Government Printing Office
(202) 512-1800
www.gpo.gov

EDGAR Database
Securities and Exchange
   Commission
www.sec.gov/cgi-gin/srch-edgar

New York University
   Stern School of Business
www.edgar.stern.nyu.edu

EDGAR Conversion Software (freeware)
Available from the above two sources, as well as from Business Valuation Resources, www.BVLibrary.com

Moody's Manuals
Moody's Corporate Profiles
Moody's Investors Service
www.moodys.com
(800) 700-1709

Standard & Poor's Corporation Records
Standard & Poor's Register
Standard & Poor's Corporation
www.standardpoor.com
(800) 221-5277

Chapter 12

Market Approach: Guideline Merged and Acquired Company Method

*The most difficult decision an executive faces in negotiating an acquisition
is the price to be paid. The decision is difficult because there are so many
factors to consider—the process by which the target company is being sold,
the expected competition, the future profitability of the target, expected synergies, complex tax rules, alternate legal forms of effecting a transaction and
accounting considerations.*[1]

The essential difference between this chapter and the previous chapter on the
guideline publicly traded company method is the nature of the market data used as
a starting point. In the previous chapter, we started with noncontrolling ownership
interest transactions, mostly in the public stock market and thus fully marketable. In
this chapter, we start with data on transfers of controlling ownership interests, usually (but not entirely) 100 percent ownership interests.

The business interest transferred often includes the entire capital structure, not
necessarily just equity. The company being sold may have been either public or private before the transaction. The nature of the transaction and the nature and availability of data about it vary much more than public market guideline company transaction data.

The quote introducing this chapter helps explain why there may be different values under different valuation criteria and different circumstances. It also explains
why we should examine merger and acquisition transactions as carefully as possible
when using them as guidance in the market approach to valuing a company, and why
we need to be very careful in interpreting and applying the results of our analysis.

Overview of the Merged and Acquired Company Method

The previous chapter dealt with data on day-to-day trading prices of securities.
However, one also can derive indications of value from the prices at which entire companies or operating units of companies have been sold or the prices at which significant interests in companies have changed hands. Such data are harder to find
than daily stock trading data, since there is no centrally organized mechanism for collecting and making such price information available.

The general notion of merger and acquisition analysis is the same as guideline
public company analysis—one relates the price at which the transaction took place
to financial fundamentals that affect the value. As noted earlier, the financial variables used in the valuation of the entire company usually focus on the market value
of the entire invested capital rather than on the equity alone. This is because the
transaction often involves the entire capital structure, or if it does not, at least the
acquiring control owner usually has the power to change the capital structure.

Also, it is common to consider transactions over a fairly long time. This might
involve analyzing transactions in the subject company's industry or similar industries over several years. This is partly because there are fewer transactions and also
because acquisition pricing multiples seem to fluctuate somewhat less over time
than public stock market pricing multiples.

Generally, the criteria for selection of merged and acquired guideline company
transactions are similar to those for selecting publicly traded stock guideline com-

---

[1] Joseph H. Marren, *Mergers & Acquisitions: A Valuation Handbook* (New York: McGraw-Hill, 1993), p. v.

panies. However, in situations where limited transaction data are available, the criteria may have to be broadened somewhat.

When Is the Guideline Merged and Acquired Company Method Most Useful?

The initial value derived from the guideline merged and acquired company method, before adjustment for factors such as size of the subject block and degree of marketability, is an indication of transaction prices of major ownership interests, usually controlling ownership interests. The characteristics of each transaction need to be analyzed carefully to make judgments as to what adjustments may be necessary in order to use the transaction pricing multiples as guidance in a specific valuation assignment.

Standard of Value

Merger and acquisition transaction prices may be representative of *fair market value*, *investment value*, or somewhere in between. At one end of the spectrum, a sale to a pure financial buyer (one who is buying strictly for a return on investment from the company as a stand-alone entity) usually would be representative of fair market value, although even financial buyers may have some special motivations and advantages. At the other end of the spectrum, the more unique the synergies between the acquirer and the acquiree, the more the transaction is representative of investment value rather than fair market value, because the pricing may reflect the synergistic benefits to a *particular* buyer rather than the price a typical *hypothetical* buyer would pay (as required in the definition of fair market value).

William D. Rifkin explains how investment value characteristics often influence merger and acquisition prices:

> The same acquisition target will have different values to different buyers, due both to perception and reality. Potential buyers will have different views on: (1) the expected financial performance of the target; (2) what can be done to enhance performance; and (3) the risk of deviation from expected results. Certain potential buyers, regardless of their perception of the future, may have a true economic advantage over others. This could be due to tax factors (such as ability to utilize net operating loss carry forwards), potential economies of scale, or opportunities to achieve synergies. Economic benefits which may result from the combination of two going concerns would not, for instance, be available to a so-called financial buyer, such as a leveraged buyout firm. Unless a company is purchased for immediate resale, as in a "bust-up" acquisition, the potential acquiror's first step must be a determination of what the target is worth specifically to it, not others—and this requires a careful and honest assessment of what the acquiror can do with the combined company.[2]

---

[2] William D. Rifkin, "Valuing and Pricing Mergers and Acquisitions I: Concepts and Mechanisms," Chapter 3 in *Mergers, Acquisitions, and Leveraged Buyouts*, Robert Lawrence Kuhn, ed. (New York: McGraw-Hill, 1990), p. 39. Reprinted with permission.

The same distinction arises when using merger and acquisition data in the context of fair value. Most state statutes defining fair value specifically exclude the value of any benefits arising from the merger itself.

There is no formula to sort out the amount by which a price that was paid in a transaction reflected synergistic value over and above a strict, stand-alone fair market value price. This is a continuing source of contention when using merger and acquisition data to resolve disputed valuations and when challenging another analyst's judgment.

Ownership Characteristics

Marketable versus Nonmarketable. Whether to adjust for marketability or lack of it when estimating value on a control level is unresolved among business valuation professionals.

In many respects, this controversy is more semantic than real. Everyone recognizes that the sale of a controlling or major ownership interest in a company obviously is not as marketable as a publicly traded stock, which can be sold in seconds at or very near a recently established and known price, with cash delivered to the seller within three business days. Thus, if merger and acquisition data are used as guidance to estimate fair market value—a cash equivalent value as of a certain date—certain adjustments may be appropriate. This issue is discussed more fully in Chapters 15 through 18.

Control versus Lack of Control. Since mergers and acquisitions usually represent control transactions, they are most directly relevant for valuation of controlling ownership interests.

When valuing a noncontrolling ownership interest, it usually would be necessary to apply a discount for lack of control to a value indicated by merger and acquisition data. It also may be appropriate to apply a further discount for lack of marketability.

Going-Concern versus Liquidation Value

Sometimes, but not often, it is possible to analyze a transaction to estimate the extent to which a price represents a going-concern value or a liquidation value. Often, a transaction price reflects some combination of the two, where some assets acquired will be liquidated while others will be operated as part of a going-concern business. This is a matter that varies on a case-by-case basis.

Quantity and Quality of Data Available

Some industries are characterized by lots of acquisition activity while others are not. Even one good transaction generally is better than nothing, if it is a reasonably good guideline transaction and the data are complete and reliable. We generally would want to see at least a few transactions, however, if we were to weight the guideline transaction heavily in the final analysis.

If the acquiree(s) were public, generally adequate data are available. On the other hand, if the acquirees were private, good, verifiable data may be limited. If the private company is acquired by a public company in a transaction, that might be material to the public company, the buyer discloses the transaction by filing Form 8-K. Reported purchase prices may not reflect considerations such as covenants not to compete or employment contracts. It is often difficult to determine exactly what assets were included in the purchase price or what liabilities were assumed. It is often difficult to get any reliable data on profitability. All of these problems must be factored into the decision whether to use private company acquisition data and, if so, the weight to be accorded to it in the final analysis.

Control Transaction (Acquisition) Value Measures

When valuing a controlling ownership interest, the analyst often focuses on guidance from other controlling interest transactions (mergers and acquisitions). Control transaction valuation analysis typically focuses on market value of invested capital (MVIC, as defined in Chapter 11) or on *aggregate consideration*, defined as "*purchase price of equity plus total debt less cash*."[3] This is common sense, since the control owner has the power to change the capital structure, and control buyers very frequently do.

This, of course, means that all the returns available to both equity and debt should be included in the denominator when computing the pricing multiple. Control transaction value measures (often called *deal multiples or acquisition multiples*) often use the following measures of returns in the denominator:

*   Revenues.
*   Operating income available to invested capital (EBIT).
*   Operating cash flow available to invested capital (EBIT plus depreciation, and amortization).
*   Tangible book value.
*   Discretionary earnings (also called seller's discretionary cash flow, defined as EBIT plus *all* noncash charges plus all compensation and benefits for one owner operator, used primarily for smaller businesses with heavy owner/manager involvement).

The above assumes that nonoperating income, expenses, and the assets and/or liabilities that produce them are treated separately if they are significant. (As a practical matter, we believe that practitioners tend to separate out nonoperating items more carefully when calculating operating cash flow than when calculating operating income.)

Exhibit 12–1 presents a typical example of the use of the merger and acquisition method to develop an indicated value range for an acquisition candidate. Note that five value measures are computed, but only three of them are used in the valuation analysis applied to the subject company. The reason seems obvious: Three value measures fall into a fairly tight range while the other two are widely dispersed. Note that the preferred three involve aggregate consideration as the numerator (defined similarly to our definition of market value of invested capital, but not exactly the same). Had the tangible book value ratio also been computed on the basis of aggregate consideration instead of only price paid for equity securities, the range for that value measure may have been applied.

---

[3] Marren, *Mergers & Acquisitions: A Valuation Handbook*, p. 188.

Exhibit 12–1

Example Application of Merger and Acquisition Method
Analysis of Selected Transactions Involving Building Material Retailers
(Figures in millions except ratios)

Date Final	Target/Acquirer	AC PP	Sales AC/Sales	OCF AC/OCF	EBIT AC/EBIT	Net Income PP/Net Income	TBV PP/TBV
7/89	Scotty's/	$303.8	$574.4	$32.4	$19.4	$11.9	$174.6
	GB Inno BM SA	$243.9	0.53 ×	9.40 ×	15.70 ×	20.50 ×	1.40 ×
10/88	Payless Cashways/	$1,189.3	$1,844.9	$131.0	$93.0	$52.4	$397.5
	PCI Acquisition Corp.	$911.9	0.64 ×	9.10 ×	12.80 ×	17.40 ×	2.29 ×
3/88	Pay 'N Pak Stores/	$292.3	$398.1	$29.6	$19.3	$5.7	$100.1
	PNP Prime Corp.	$212.6	0.73 ×	9.90 ×	15.10 ×	37.30 ×	2.12 ×

Statistical Summary					
Low:	0.53	9.08	12.79	17.40	1.40
High:	0.73	9.87	15.66	37.30	2.29
Mean:	0.64	9.44	14.53	25.07	1.94
Median:	0.64	9.38	15.15	20.50	2.12
Sample:	3	3	3	3	3

PP = Purchase price for all equity securities including options and convertible debt.
AC = Aggregate consideration (PP plus total debt less cash).
EBIT = Earnings before interest and taxes.
OCF = Operating cash flow (EBIT plus depreciation and amortization).
TBV = Tangible book value (total book value less intangibles).

Comparable Transactions Valuation Analysis
(Figures in millions except ratios)

	Comparable Transaction Multiples		Target Company LTM [a] Results	Valuation Range	
	Mean	Median		Mean	Median
Aggregate consideration [b] sales	0.64	0.64	$1,050	$668	$677
Aggregate consideration [b] operating cash flow [c]	9.44	9.38	55	519	516
Aggregate consideration [b] EBIT	14.53	15.15	35	509	530
			Range	$509	$677

a. Aggregate consideration equals purchase price of equity plus total debt less cash.
b. Operating cash flow equals EBIT plus depreciation and amortization.
c. LTM means last 12 months.

SOURCE: Joseph H. Marren, *Mergers & Acquisitions: A Valuation Handbook* (New York: McGraw-Hill, 1993), pp. 188-189. Reprinted with permission.

Robert Kuhn recognizes that comparative transaction data are widely used in the merger market, but also cautions to carefully analyze differences between companies, time period differences, and market aberrations:

> In merger market valuation models, we compare prices among similar companies, much like comparison shopping for a consumer item among similar retail stores. Merger market value arrays reasonably similar transactions (i.e., similar industry, company size, financial structure, time frame, etc.) and uses these prices to judge the relative worth of the target company. Investment bankers favor this technique, generating long lists of comparable transactions to advise clients on both buy and sell sides.
>
> In theory, the M&A market is the true reflection of current interaction between willing sellers and willing buyers. In the real world, however, this is rarely the case. Corporations are not yellow pencils, quickly stacked and easily matched; it is difficult to make true comparisons of complex situations—in one way or another virtually every M&A sale can be considered special or extraordinary. Furthermore, the M&A market often evinces aberrations—companies selling too low when suffering distressed conditions and companies selling too high when faddish or foolish buyers are over-eager to acquire. The feeding frenzy of M&A in recent years—the search for synergy and hostile takeover battles—have bid up many M&A prices to unrealistic levels.[4]

Caveat: Check the Deal Structure

Deal Terms

For guideline valuation purposes, and certainly if the standard of value is fair market value, it is necessary that the deal price used to develop a value measure be a cash or cash equivalent price. In many acquisitions, the consideration paid is all or partly something other than cash, such as common or preferred stock (sometimes convertible), notes (also sometimes convertible), and so on. The cash value of such consideration often is less than its face value (rarely more). If using a guideline transaction in which the consideration paid was not all cash, the analyst should make the best possible effort to convert the consideration paid to a cash equivalent value.

Exactly What Was Transacted?

When using publicly traded guideline company stock transactions, we know that what was sold was stock. When entire companies are sold, however, the deal is often structured as an asset sale. In such instances, it is important to know exactly what assets were sold and what liabilities assumed. In addition to the fact that not everything on the seller's balance sheet (or off–balance sheet assets or liabilities) may have been included in the transaction, the income tax ramifications of an asset sale usually are considerably different than for a stock sale.

Differences in the structure between the guideline transaction and the contemplated subject transaction should be noted and adjusted or accounted for appropriately in

---

[4] Kuhn, *Mergers, Acquisitions, and Leveraged Buyouts*, p. 61.

developing value measures. This is of particular importance when the guideline transaction was an asset sale instead of a stock sale.

Noncompete and Employment or Consulting Agreements

Noncompete and employment or consulting agreements are often executed in conjunction with change of control transactions. If these are of significant importance, as for middle-market and smaller company transactions, they should be carefully analyzed for each comparative transaction used.

The noncompete or employment agreement usually (although not always) is the property of the individual rather than the selling corporation or partnership. In marital dissolution, dissenting shareholder, and bankruptcy cases, the ownership of noncompete and employment agreements often is an issue.[5]

If a noncompete or employment agreement is included in a transaction, the value allocated is included in the deal price in *Pratt's Stats*, *Bizcomps*, and the Institute of Business Appraisers database. If using multiples for comparative purposes, the multiples shown in the above sources often need to be adjusted if they are to be applied to a valuation where the agreements should not be considered a part of the entity value. This situation is especially a problem in valuations for marital dissolutions and is discussed more fully in Chapter 38 on that subject.

Sources of Merger and Acquisition Data

Sources for Large Company Transactions

Generally, sources of price and underlying financial data on control transactions are more expensive and less consistent in content and reliability than public market stock transaction data. Public stock financial data are subject to very consistent reporting requirements by the SEC and the accounting profession. Data on acquisitions of private companies are not subject to any such regulation, and data on mergers and acquisitions of public companies vary tremendously in scope and format.

The bibliography at the end of the chapter gives contact information for several merger and acquisition data sources.

Information about mergers is obtained from disclosure filings, the news media, and business intermediaries (business brokers and investment bankers). When publicly held companies are involved, the participants must submit disclosure documents such as SEC Form 8-K and others known collectively as William's Act reports. The major filings are Forms 14D-1, 13D, and 8-K. Companies attempting to purchase another company in the open market (called a tender offer) submit the Form 14D-1. Individuals purchasing 5 percent or more of a company's stock with the intent to obtain substantial voting control or otherwise influence the management of the company file form 13D. There are also many other relevant required reports, depending on the transactions, such as 14D-9s, proxy statements, and prospectuses. News stories, including press releases from the participants, are the primary source of information

---

[5] For a discussion of this issue with case references, see Shannon P. Pratt, "Ownership of Personal Intangibles: A Frequent Subject of Controversy," *Valuation Strategies*, May/June 1999, pp. 5–9.

on private transactions. The business media also can provide additional details on mergers involving public companies.

An amazing variety of reporting services, newsletters, and on-line databases utilize information from disclosure filings, company announcements, the media, and business intermediaries to provide extensive, organized analysis of merger transactions as they unfold. General business indexes and news databases can be useful in conducting merger research, but the following sources provide specific coverage of merger and acquisition activities. As with any secondary sources, errors and inconsistencies occur, so the original source documents are the only guarantees of absolute accuracy.

Mergerstat Review is published annually in book form by Applied Financial Information, LP. This source provides extensive analysis of the transaction data. In particular, it contains useful analysis of control premiums. Since 1997, they also have published a separate *Mergerstat Transaction Roster* on an annual basis (prior to 1997 the transaction roster was part of *Mergerstat Review*), which covers transactions announced during the year and either completed or still pending at year-end.

The *Merger & Acquisition Sourcebook* is published annually by NVST.com Inc. This reference tool contains detailed analysis of transactions in every industry. Of special interest is the section that presents the average purchase price ratios to seller's sales, earnings, and net worth for acquisitions in every industry. Typically, more than 3,000 transactions are included and organized by SIC code. Also published by NVST is a weekly newsletter, *Corporate Growth Report*, covering transactions announced or completed after the last *Sourcebook* was published.

The *Merger Yearbook* is published annually by Securities Data Publishing. All the data contained in the *Yearbook* are collected, analyzed, verified, and compiled by the staff of Securities Data Company, a leading provider of merger and acquisition and financial information worldwide. Drawing upon an extensive proprietary database of merger and acquisition information, The *Merger Yearbook* is very comprehensive.

Mergers & Acquisitions magazine is published bimonthly by Securities Data Publishing. Most issues contain articles about mergers and acquisitions and also a "Mergers & Acquisitions Roster." The rosters list every corporate acquisition over $1 million that the publisher can identify, including private transactions. Securities Data Publishing also publishes *Acquisitions Monthly*. This magazine covers the world marketplace.

Several newsletters cover the merger and acquisition scene. Among them are *Buyouts*, published every other week by Securities Data Publishing; *Mergers & Acquisitions Report*, published weekly by Securities Data Publishing; and *Mergerstat*, published monthly by Applied Financial Information, LP. The newsletters vary in price, but most tend to be expensive.

In addition to traditional print sources, on-line databases provide a variety of information sources for tracking merger and acquisition–related information.

SDC Platinum, produced by Securities Data Company, is the most extensive and thorough database available. *SDC Platinum* allows you to identify the information you need and create impressive reports and rankings. Preformatted standard reports range from brief and concise summaries to in-depth and comprehensive analyses. You may also customize your own reports or rankings using an extensive selection of data elements. Reports can also easily be downloaded to a spreadsheet file for additional formatting or analysis.

In addition to the previously mentioned print sources, *Mergerstat* provides several of their products electronically. Using various pricing plans and subscription services, the following sources include *Mergerstat* data: Bloomberg (www.bloomberg.com), FactSet (www.factset.com), Lexis-Nexis (www.lexis-nexis.com), and Data Downlink (www.mergerstat@xls.com).

Many of the sources mentioned above are available on-line through www.nvst.com for an additional charge.

Sources for Middle-Market and Smaller Company Transactions

Practical application of the guideline transaction method for companies valued under $100 million has been enhanced significantly since the last edition of this book by the development of databases covering "middle-market" and smaller company transactions. These databases are less expensive than those devoted to large company acquisitions.

There are at least four databases devoted to middle-market and small company controlling ownership interest transactions:

1. *Pratt's Stats.*
2. *Done Deals.*
3. *Bizcomps.*
4. *IBA Market Database.*

The bibliography at the end of the chapter gives contact information for each of these databases.

Pratt's Stats. *Pratt's Stats*, started in 1997, is the official database of the International Business Brokers Association. Information is collected from M&A intermediaries, business brokers, CPAs, and other sources. It is by far the most comprehensive of the private company databases in terms of detail (over 70 data points) per transaction. Exhibit 12–2 is a sample printout from *Pratt's Stats*. Exhibit 12–3 is a sample transaction input form.

Exhibit 12–4 presents the distribution of the *Pratt's Stats* transactions by deal size as of September 1999. The database is available either on-line or in print and diskette form. *Pratt's Stats* included a little over 3,000 transactions as of June 2000.

Exhibit 12–5 shows the results of our analysis on all eight valuation multiples for each of the restaurants and restaurant chains in the database with revenues from $1,000,000 to $75,000,000, along with the range, mean, median, and coefficient of variation for each valuation multiple.

Done Deals. *Done Deals* was started in 1996 by the World M&A Network and is now owned by NVST. Unlike the other three databases discussed in this chapter, all of the *Done Deals* data are collected from SEC filings. The database includes both public and private companies acquired by public companies.

Exhibit 12–6 presents a sample transaction from the *Done Deals* database. Exhibit 12–7 presents the distribution of the *Done Deals* transactions by deal size as of September 1999. The database is available either on-line or on diskette.

Bizcomps. The *Bizcomps* database is published in a series of four editions; each is issued once a year. There are three geographical editions: Western, Central, and Eastern, which cover mostly small transactions. In addition, there is a National Industrial Edition, which includes larger transactions drawn as a subset from the other

Exhibit 12–2

Sample Page from the Print Version of Pratt's Stats

Pratt's Stats™ Private Business Sale Transaction Record

Intermediary Name:	Papay, Gary	Firm Name:	CK Associates

SIC Code:	5172	0000	NAICS:	42272	City of Sale:	LaFargeville	State of Sale: NY	Date of Report: 2/25/99

Product/Service Description: Petroleum Distributor

Company Name: | | Years in Business: | | Number of Employees: |

Income Data	**Asset Data**	**Transaction Data**	
☑ Data is "Latest Full Year" Reported	☐ Data is "Latest Full Year" Reported	Income Statement Date:	12/31/97
☐ Data is Restated (See Notes field for any additional explanation)	☑ Data is "Purchase Price Allocation agreed upon by Buyer and Seller"	Balance Sheet Date:	12/31/97
		Date Sale Initiated:	8/1/96
Net Sales: $5,899,443.00	Cash and Equivalents:	Date of Sale:	12/4/98
COGS: $4,321,983.00	Trade Receivables: $200,000.00	Length of Time on Market: (Months)	27.6
Gross Profit: $1,577,460.00	Inventory: $100,000.00	Asking Price:	$4,000,000.00
Yearly Rent:	Other Current Assets:	Equity Price:	$2,600,000.00
Owner's Compensation: $50,000.00	Total Current Assets: $300,000.00	Amount of Down Payment:	$2,600,000.00
Other Operating Exp.: $1,145,964.00	Fixed Assets: $936,000.00	Deal Price:	$2,600,000.00
Noncash Charges: $168,137.00	Real Estate: $175,000.00	Stock or Asset Sale	Asset
Total Operating Exp.: $1,364,101.00	Intangibles: $1,189,000.00	Company Type: (C or S Corp., LLC, LLP, Sole Prop., etc.)	S Corporation
Operating Profit: $213,359.00	Other Noncurrent Assets:	Was there an Employment/Consulting Agrmnt?	
Interest Expense: $100,197.00	Total Assets: $2,600,000.00	☑ Yes ☐ No	
EBT: $113,162.00	Liabilities Assumed: $0.00	Was there an Assumed Lease in the sale?	
Taxes: $325.00	Emplymnt/ConsltAgrmnt: $50,000.00	☐ Yes ☑ No	
Net Income: $112,837.00	Noncompete Value: $250,000.00	Is there a Renewal Option with the Lease? ☐ Yes ☐ No	

Additional Transaction Information

Was there a Note in the consideration paid?   ☑ Yes ☐ No   Was there a personal guarantee on the Note?   ☐ Yes ☑ No

Financing, Terms of Loan Balance: (Length, Rate, Payment, Balloon Payment, etc.)

Considerations paid in cash.

Balance of Assumed Lease: (Months) | | Terms of Lease: |

Noncompete Length: (Months)   60   Noncompete Description: (Miles Radius, etc.)   75 mile radius of business location

Employment/Consulting Agreement Description: (Obligation, Length of Time, Services Required, etc.)

Owner to assist in transition period and manage the business for 6 months after closing. Compensation: $50,000.

Additional Notes:

Non-compete agreement paid as follows: $250,000 paid over 5 years at $50,000 per year.

Valuation Multiples

Equity Price/ Net Sales	EquityPrice/ Gross Cash Flow	Equity Price/ EBT	Equity Price/ Net Income	Deal Price/ Discretionary Earnings	Deal Price/ Net Sales	Deal Price/ EBITDA	Deal Price/ EBIT
0.44	9.25	22.98	23.04	6.03	0.44	6.82	12.19

Copyright Business Valuation Resources, LLC 2000   Page 1 of 1

SOURCE: *Pratt's Stats* (Portland, OR: Business Valuation Resources, 1999).

Exhibit 12–3

Pratt's Stats Submittal Form

Do you wish to have your name and firm associated with the reported information? Yes ☐ No ☐ Date of Report: [____]

Intermediary Name: [____]   Firm Name: [____]

Location of Firm, City: [____]   State: [__]   Phone: [____]

Product/Service Description of Company Sold: [____]

SIC Code: [__]   SIC Sub Code: [__]   NAICS: [__]   Company Name: [____]

Years in Business: [__]   Number of Employees: [__]   City of Sale: [____]   State of Sale: [__]

Income Data	Asset Data	Transaction Data
☐ Data is "Latest Full Year" Reported	☐ Data is "Latest Full Year" Reported	Income Statement Date: [____]
☐ Data is Restated (See Notes field for any additional explanation)	☐ Data is "Purchase Price Allocation agreed upon by Buyer and Seller"	Balance Sheet Date: [____]
		Date Sale Initiated: [____]
Net Sales: [__]	Cash and Equivalents: [__]	
COGS: [__]	Trade Receivables: [__]	Date of Sale: [____]
Gross Profit: [__]	Inventory: [__]	Asking Price: [____]
Yearly Rent: [__]	Other Current Assets: [__]	Selling Price: [____]
Owner's Compensation: [__]	Total Current Assets: [__]	Amount of Down Payment: [____]
Other Operating Exp.: [__]	Fixed Assets: [__]	Stock or Asset Sale [____]
Noncash Charges: [__]	Real Estate: [__]	Company Type: (C or S Corp., LLC, LLP, Sole Prop., etc.) [____]
Total Operating Exp.: [__]	Intangibles: [__]	
Operating Profit: [__]	Other Noncurrent Assets: [__]	Was there an Employment/Consulting Agrmnt?
Interest Expense: [__]	Total Assets: [__]	Yes ☐ No ☐
EBT: [__]	Liabilities Assumed: [__]	Was there an Assumed Lease in the sale?
Taxes: [__]	Emplymnt/ConsltAgrmnt: [__]	Yes ☐ No ☐
Net Income: [__]	Noncompete Value: [__]	Is there a Renewal Option with the Lease? Yes ☐ No ☐

Additional Transaction Information

Was there a Note in the consideration paid?   Yes ☐ No ☐   Was there a personal guarantee on the Note?   Yes ☐ No ☐

Terms of Loan Balance or Financing Information: (Length, Rate, Payment, Baloon Payment, etc.)

[____]

Balance of Assumed Lease: (Months) [__]   Terms of Lease: [____]

Noncompete Length: (Months) [__]   Noncompete Description: (Miles Radius, etc.) [____]

Employment/Consulting Agreement Description: (Obligation, Length of Time, Services Required, etc.)

[____]

Additional Notes:

[____]

Send to: **Business Valuation Resources, 7412 SW Beaverton-Hillsdale Hwy., Suite 106, Portland, OR 97225; Fax to (503) 291-7955**
If you have any questions, please call us toll free at (888) BUS-VALU
Copyright Business Valuation Resources, LLC 2000   Revised 1/99

SOURCE: *Pratt's Stats* (Portland, OR: Business Valuation Resources, 1999).

Exhibit 12–4

Distribution of Deal Value in Pratt's Stats

	Average Sell Price	Median Sell Price	% of Total Observations
$0–$500,000	$222,018.77	$195,000.00	14.3%
$500,001–$1,000,000	$721,412.12	$700,000.00	3.9%
$1,000,001–$5,000,000	$2,817,832.93	$2,700,000.00	21.4%
$5,000,001–$10,000,000	$7,277,053.14	$7,093,750.00	15.4%
$10,000,001–$20,000,000	$14,328,117.39	$14,000,000.00	16.7%
$20,000,001–$50,000,000	$31,694,996.88	$30,216,000.00	18.1%
$50,000,001–$100,000,000	$71,523,180.36	$70,000,000.00	9.5%
$100,000,001 +	$114,930,556.58	$111,000,000.00	0.6%

SOURCE: Distribution of deal value in *Pratt's Stats* database as of September 1999.

three editions. In 1999, *Bizcomps* also issued a special Restaurant Edition. The combined data are also available on disk, updated annually at the beginning of each year.

IBA Market Database. The Institute of Business Appraisers (IBA) maintains an empirical database of information on the actual sales of closely held businesses, primarily small businesses. Information for the *IBA Market Database* is obtained from IBA members and other sources having actual knowledge of the subject sales. The amount of information about each sale is limited by practical considerations such as (1) the amount of information that sources have about the sale of a closely held business and (2) the willingness of IBA members to take the time to record transactional data and to submit them to the IBA.

The IBA database contains a total of over 14,000 transactions that span a period over the last 20 years. It is available at no charge to IBA members, or on-line through www.BVLibrary.com, with subscription including IBA membership.

Exhibit 12–8 summarizes the four private company databases.

Adjusting for Time Period Differences

A major difference between merger and acquisition guideline transaction analysis and publicly traded guideline company analysis is the proximity of the guideline transaction date to the subject company's effective valuation date. In the publicly traded guideline company method, guideline transaction prices usually are as of the same date as the subject company effective valuation date. In the merger and acquisition method, guideline transaction dates are whenever they occurred.

This creates the additional problem of adjusting for differences in conditions between the guideline transaction dates and the subject company effective valuation date. If enough transactions are available, the analyst may wish to omit those that occurred when economic conditions were significantly different rather than try to make drastic adjustments to account for the differences.

The most common way to adjust for time differences is through either industry average stock price differences or industry average differences in valuation multiples, such as price/earnings multiples. Generally, we have found adjusting for industry valuation multiples more effective than adjusting for industry price indexes if the

Exhibit 12–5

Restaurants with Net Sales from $1,000,000 to $75,000,000

#	SIC	Net Sales	Equity Price	Deal Price	Equity Price/ Net Sales	Equity Price/ Gross Cash Flow	Equity Price/ EBT	Equity Price/ NI	Equity Price/ Discretionary Earnings	Deal Price/ Net Sales	Deal Price/ EBITDA	Deal Price/ EBIT
1	5812	$1,100,000	$290,000	$290,000	0.26	0.62	2.11	2.11	0.57	0.26	0.62	2.11
2	5812	$1,170,948	$350,000	$350,000	0.30	2.69	4.12	4.12	2.77	0.30	2.77	4.30
3	5812	$1,267,993	$500,000	$500,000	0.39	4.61	4.69	4.69	1.81	0.39	4.59	4.68
4	5812	$1,361,559	$300,000	$300,000	0.22	3.53	6.20	6.20	1.84	0.22	2.90	4.49
5	5812	$1,504,000	$350,000	$350,000	0.23	2.57	3.80	3.80	1.72	0.23	2.57	3.80
6	5812	$2,696,550	$3,100,000	$3,800,000	1.15					1.41		
7	5812	$3,138,726	$1,750,000	$1,800,000	0.56	18.26	NM	NM	10.56	0.57	10.86	24.96
8	5812	$3,537,215	$2,325,000	$2,325,000	0.66					0.66		
9	5812	$4,255,552	$4,750,000	$4,750,000	1.12	15.52	17.85	17.85	10.87	1.12	16.39	19.01
10	5812	$5,901,207	$3,700,000	$3,700,000	0.63	35.85	NM	NM	27.90	0.63	27.90	NM
11	5812	$8,456,540	$500,000	$500,000	0.06					0.06		
12	5812	$9,778,875	$12,000,000	$12,000,000	1.23	8.09	9.42	9.42	8.09	1.23	8.09	9.42
13	5812	$10,460,347	$450,000	$4,450,000	0.04				0.89	0.43	8.80	
14	5812	$11,969,000	$4,265,000	$4,265,000	0.36	9.56	5.73	9.56	3.35	0.36	5.33	5.33
15	5812	$13,875,572	$14,000,000	$14,000,000	1.01	4.85	5.45	5.45	4.85	1.01	4.85	5.45
16	5812	$26,674,248	$21,100,000	$21,100,000	0.79	8.12	13.95	13.95	7.39	0.79	7.39	11.92
17	5812	$29,710,001	$52,000,000	$52,000,000	1.75	16.21	25.45	19.91	15.60	1.75	15.60	19.00
18	5812	$32,167,408	$8,631,415	$10,150,188	0.27	6.20	15.43	15.43	6.20	0.32	7.29	18.14
19	5812	$42,330,000	$31,500,000	$58,000,000	0.74	13.09	29.01	29.01	7.28	1.37	13.41	19.29
20	5812	$60,119,261	$47,000,000	$47,000,000	0.78	13.20	17.78	18.43	8.04	0.78	8.04	9.72
21	5812	$61,283,000	$94,749,000	$94,749,000	1.55	10.06	8.40	13.09	7.04	1.55	7.04	8.40
22	5812	$65,680,000	$53,000,000	$68,000,000	0.81	20.83	19.81	32.48	9.68	1.04	12.42	14.90

			High		1.55	20.83	29.01	32.48	15.60	1.55	16.39	24.96
			Low		0.06	2.57	2.11	2.11	0.89	0.22	2.57	3.80
			Median		0.64	8.84	8.91	11.32	7.04	0.64	7.39	9.57
			Mean		0.66	9.84	11.82	12.84	6.35	0.73	8.14	11.43
			C. V.		0.62	0.59	0.70	0.70	0.63	0.59	0.53	0.60

Notes:
Transaction number 11 was a company in the process of complete liquidation under Chapter 11 (see transaction's notes field).
Deal price = equity price + liabilities assumed.
Equity price and deal price are equal where no liabilities are assumed.
C. V. = Coefficient of variation and equals the standard deviation/mean.
Only positive values of multiples were used.
90 percent of the data was used to calculate the summary statistics, 10 percent of the data was discarded.
NM = not meaningful.

SOURCE: Pratt's Stats On-line (www.PrattsStats.com), August 1999 (2113 transactions). (c) 1999, *Business Valuation Resources.*

subject and guideline companies are similar in terms of profitability and other operating characteristics. However, it should also be recognized (as discussed more fully in Chapters 15 and 16) that the relation between market multiples and acquisition multiples varies over time.

Past Subject Company Transactions

Past transactions involving the subject company may be fruitful subjects to analyze for guidance as to value.

Exhibit 12–6

Sample Done Deals Transaction

World M&A Network

Mid-Market M&A Deals Completed

Closing	Description					
7/ 1/96	*Buyer* AirSensors, Inc. 16804 Gridley Place Cerritos, CA 90703 Thomas M. Costales, CFO 810-860-6666	*Seller* Ateco Automotive Pty. Ltd. (Australia)		*Seller Description* A private company that distributed AirSensors, Inc.'s GASEOUS FUEL CARBURETION SYSTEMS and devices for use with internal combusion engines Type: Private	*Terms* $6.5MM cash ($4MM financed by Bank of Ameirca, $1.9MM by A/R)	*SIC* 5013

Price	*Assets*	*Stk. Equity*	*Revenue*	*Income*	*Cash Flow*	*P/A*	*P/SE*	*P/R*	*P/E*	*P/CF*
$6.5MM	$4.7MM 6/96	$2.6MM 6/96	$6.4MM in 12 mo. end 6/96	$0.361MM in 12 mo. end 6/96	$1.1MM in 12 mo. end 6/96	1.4	2.5	1.0	18.0	5.9

SOURCE: *Done Deals* (Bellevue, WA: NVST.com, 1999).

Exhibit 12–7

Distribution of Transaction Prices in Done Deals

Acquisition Transaction Price	Percent of Report Transactions
$0–$1,000,000	4.9%
$1,000,001–$10,000,000	38.0%
$10,000,001–$50,000,000	41.5%
$50,000,001–$100,000,000	11.1%
$100,000,001 +	4.5%

SOURCE: Distribution of transactions prices in *Done Deals* database as of September 1999.

Exhibit 12–8

Comparison of Private Company Sales Databases as of September 1999

	Pratt's Stats	Done Deals	Bizcomps	IBA Database
Type of transactions	Private companies	Private and public	Private companies	Private companies
Number of transactions	2,200	2,900 total (1,600 private)	3,500	14,000
Data points on each transaction	70	20	15	10
Range of sale prices	<$100,000 to $100,000,000	$1,000,000 to $100,000,000	$175,000 to $15,000,000	$100,000 to $10,000,000

Past Subject Company Changes of Control

If the subject company itself has changed control in the last few years, the transaction may be an excellent source of value measures. The value measures used would generally be the same as those discussed earlier. The value measures indicated by the prior transaction may need some adjustment to reflect internal changes in the company or changes in the industry or market conditions.

Bona Fide Offers

Documentable, arm's-length, bona fide offers to buy or sell may also be useful evidence of value. Funded bona fide offers (i.e., offers for which the financing for the offer is already in place) should be given more weight and more consideration than unfunded bona fide offers. It is usually difficult, however, to obtain adequate documentation or to verify the arm's-length relationship of the potential buyer/seller.

Past Acquisitions by the Subject Company

If the company has made one or more acquisitions in the last several years, such transactions may prove to be excellent sources of value measures. Again, adjustments may be necessary for changes between the dates of the acquisitions and the relevant valuation date.

It may be easy to overlook such acquisitions, because they may not come to light in any of the search procedures normally used to identify merger and acquisition transactions. The subject company may be the *only* source for such data, but typically is a very comprehensive and reliable source. Therefore, if considering using a merger and acquisition method, it often is a good idea to ask the company whether it has made any acquisitions.

Formulas or Rules of Thumb

Some industries have rules of thumb (sometimes given an aura of credibility by being referred to as industry valuation formulas) about how companies in their industry are valued for transfer of controlling ownership interests. On the one hand, if such rules of thumb are widely disseminated and referenced in the industry, they probably should not be ignored. On the other hand, there usually is no credible evidence of how such rules were developed nor how well they actually comport to actual transaction data.

Rules of thumb usually are quite simplistic. As such, they obscure much important detail. They fail to differentiate either operating characteristics or assets from one company to another. They also fail to differentiate changes in conditions for companies in various industries from one time period to another.

Furthermore, it is common for companies in many industries to sell on terms rather than for cash, so the "prices" generated by the rules of thumb often are not cash equivalent values. The terms may vary considerably from one transaction to another, but usually are worth less than cash equivalent value. Rules of thumb, therefore, may tend to overstate a cash equivalent value. Consequently, rules of thumb rarely, if ever, should be used without other, more reliable valuation methods.

In an article targeted primarily to valuations for divorce, and still widely quoted after 15 years, Jay Fishman offers the following summary:

> There are no "quick fixes" to the valuation of closely held entities. It is essential to remember that industry formulas or rules of thumb are commonly not market derived representations of actual transactions. Since most industry formulas or rules of thumb are derived from textbooks, trade publications, verbal representations, or other similar sources of information, they are poor substitutes for the Direct Market Comparison Approach.[6]

Under a heading "Cautions about Using Formulas" in his book *Handbook of Small Business Valuation Formulas and Rules of Thumb*, Glenn Desmond makes the following observations:

Formulas Are General in Nature

Formulas are general in nature. Adjustments must be made to account for variations in revenue and cash-flow trends; location; lease; condition of the plant, fixtures, and equipment; reputation with customers, suppliers, bankers, and others; special skills required; difficulty in starting the business; and so forth.

There Is No Single, All-Purpose Formula

There is no single formula that will work for every business. Formula multipliers offer ease of calculation, but they also obscure details. This can be misleading. Net revenue multipliers are particularly troublesome because they are blind to the business's expense and profit history. It is easy to see how two businesses in any given industry group might have the same annual net revenue (ANR), yet show very different cash flows. A proper valuation will go beyond formulas and include a full financial analysis whenever possible.[7]

Nonoperating Assets, Excess Assets, and Asset Deficiencies

If the subject company has significant nonoperating assets, excess assets, or asset deficiencies that distinguish it from the guideline companies, adjustments for those items may be appropriate. The same principles apply as were discussed in the previous chapter on the guideline publicly traded company method.

Selecting and Weighting Multiples for the Subject Company Based on Guideline Transactions

The result of the guideline transaction analysis is an array of pricing multiples for each of several value measures. At this point, it is necessary to again visit the questions of

---

[6] Jay E. Fishman, "The Problem with Rules of Thumb in the Valuation of Closely-Held Entities," *Fair$hare: The Matrimonial Law Monthly*, December 1984, p. 13.

[7] Glenn M. Desmond, ASA, MAI, *Handbook of Small Business Valuation Formulas and Rules of Thumb*, 3rd ed. (Camden, ME: Valuation Press, 1993), p. 12.

(1) which measures to use in reaching an indication of value and (2) the relative weight to be accorded to each of the measures used.

For each value measure used, it is also necessary to decide what the pricing multiple for the subject company should be relative to the observed multiples for the guideline transaction companies.

Impact of Guideline Transactional Data Evaluation

The same general thought processes and decision criteria apply to (1) both deciding on whether or not to rely on any particular value measure at all and (2) deciding on the relative weight to be accorded each value measure ultimately used in reaching the opinion of value. A study of the transactional data may lead to greater or lesser reliance on certain value measures than one might have expected prior to compiling the data.

Number of Data Points Available. If it turns out that very few data points are available for a particular value measure, that problem may lead one to abandon that measure or to put relatively little weight on it. This is true even though it might be quite conceptually significant if there were more data. A common example is the pricing multiple of price to the latest 12 months' earnings. If only two of seven comparative transaction companies had meaningful positive earnings (and thus meaningful price to earnings multiples), the analyst has to decide whether the two convey enough information to be accorded weight in the final analysis. The analyst may, for example, decide instead to use a price to cash flow pricing multiple or a price to some number of years average earnings pricing multiple.

Comparability of Data Measurement. Another issue to consider is the extent to which the analyst is satisfied that the adjustments, if any, to the subject company and to the guideline companies' financial fundamental data have resulted in presenting the data on a comparative basis. The analyst's confidence regarding the comparability of fundamental financial data may influence the analyst's judgment regarding the use of or weight accorded to value measures based on that particular financial variable.

Comparability of Data Patterns. Another factor in assessing comparability is the extent to which the data for the subject company "track" with the data for the guideline merged and acquired companies. For example, if the subject company and six of the seven guideline merged and acquired companies had a generally upward earnings trend but one guideline company had a downward trend, the analyst may omit the aberrational company when deciding on appropriate pricing multiples relative to earnings.

Apparent Market Reliance. The extent to which the value measures are tightly clustered or widely dispersed tends to indicate the extent to which the market focuses on that particular value measure in pricing companies in the particular industry.

Multiple of Stock Value to Asset Value

When the analyst has determined that either book value or some adjusted book value figure provides a useful representation of the subject company's underlying net asset values, the next step is to translate that figure into its implication for the value of the interest being valued. This translation usually is made by referring to the relationship of the transactional prices of the guideline companies to their respective underlying net asset values.

It may be possible to compute the multiple of market price to book value for a group of guideline transaction companies and to apply a multiple somewhere within the range of such multiples to the subject company book value. If (1) the book values of the subject company and guideline transaction companies were computed on comparable bases, and (2) the asset composition is comparable, this procedure may provide a reasonably realistic estimate for the value of the subject business interest.

If accounting methods for the subject company and for the guideline companies differ significantly, the analyst should make appropriate adjustments before (1) computing the market price to book value multiples and (2) applying them in the subject valuation. There can be additional significant differences, such as in asset mix, that challenge the validity of using one company's price to book value multiple in valuing another company's stock.

Reaching the Value Conclusion

Relative weighting of valuation multiples is similar to that used in the guideline publicly traded company method, except that assets may get a little more weight in a control valuation, since the control owner has discretion over their use or disposal. The same observations apply to nonoperating assets, excess assets, and asset deficiencies. (See Chapter 11, Market Approach: Guideline Publicly Traded Company Method, for a detailed discussion of these topics.)

One should recognize, of course, that an actual accomplished merger or acquisition observed in the market usually has been consummated at the highest possible value to the seller, not at some average of possible values. For every such transaction observed, many unsuccessful attempts at transactions were usually made. Furthermore, many transactions reflect some synergistic value, which would contain elements of investment value over and above pure fair market value. All these factors must be considered when deciding on what multiples to apply to the subject transaction, and the relative weight to be accorded to each.

Since merger and acquisition value analysis usually focuses on market value of invested capital, the value of the debt must be subtracted to reach the value of equity. This debt would be valued at market if it is expected to remain outstanding, but usually at face if it is expected to be retired in conjunction with the transaction.

If a noncontrolling interest is being valued, both lack of control and lack of marketability discounts should be considered. Even in the case of a controlling interest, it may be appropriate to make some adjustment for lack of marketability (or "lack of liquidity") relative to the values indicated from actual consummated transactions. This is discussed in Chapter 17.

Summary

The merger and acquisition method is similar in concept to the guideline publicly traded company method, seeking valuation guidance from actual sale transactions in the market. Since the transaction data used usually are controlling interests, it is most directly applicable for valuing other controlling ownership interests, although it can be used for noncontrolling interest valuations with proper adjustments.

Merger and acquisition data come from diverse sources and are less consistent (and sometimes less reliable) than data on day-to-day public stock market transactions. Sometimes, past transactions involving the subject company are a good source of value measures.

Since merger and acquisition transaction dates almost always differ from the subject company effective valuation date, adjustments often are needed to reflect differences in economic and industry conditions between the dates.

Merger and acquisition prices often, to some extent, reflect synergies and/or strategic advantages between acquirer and acquiree. To the extent that this is true, a transaction may be more reflective of *investment value* (value to that particular buyer) than *fair market value* (the value to a hypothetical, typically motivated buyer). For this reason, the circumstances of the merger and acquisition transactions must be carefully analyzed.

Bibliography

Desmond, Glenn M. *Handbook of Small Business Valuation Formulas and Rules of Thumb*, 3rd ed. Camden, ME: Valuation Press, 1993.

Fishman, Jay E. "The Problem with Rules of Thumb in the Valuation of Closely-Held Entities." *Fair$hare: The Matrimonial Law Monthly*, December 1984, p. 13.

Kuhn, Robert Lawrence, ed. *Mergers, Acquisitions, and Leveraged Buyouts*. New York: McGraw-Hill, 1990.

Marren, Joseph H. *Mergers & Acquisitions: A Valuation Handbook*. New York: McGraw-Hill, 1993.

Pratt, Shannon P. "Insights on Private Company Sale Pricing." *The Journal of Business Valuation* (Proceedings of the 4th Joint Business Valuation Conference of The Canadian Institute of Chartered Business Valuators and the American Society of Appraisers). Toronto: The Canadian Institute of Chartered Business Valuators, 1999, pp. 133–40. Also available on www.BVLibrary.com.

_____. "Ownership of Personal Intangibles a Frequent Subject of Controversy." *Valuation Strategies*, May/June 1999, pp. 5–9.

West, Thomas L., ed. *Business Reference Guide*, 9th ed. Concord, MA: Business Brokerage Press, 1999.

Sources of Transactions
Bizcomps
Jack R. Sanders
P.O. Box 711777
San Diego, California 92171
(619) 457-0366
www.bizcomps.com

> *BIZCOMPS National Industrial Edition (annual)*
> *BIZCOMPS Western, Central, and Eastern States Regional Studies (annual)*
> *BIZCOMPS Restaurant Edition (special edition 1999)*

Also available through various valuation software packages, through www.nvst.com, and through www.BVLibrary.com.

Business Valuation Resources
7412 S.W. Beaverton-Hillsdale Highway, Suite 106
Portland, Oregon 97225
(888) 287-8258
www.BVLibrary.com

Pratt's Stats

Institute of Business Appraisers
P.O. Box 1447
Boynton Beach, Florida 33425
(561) 732-3202
www.instbusapp.org

IBA Market Database

Also available through www.BVLibrary.com.

Applied Financial Information, LP
1933 Pontius Avenue
Los Angeles, California 90025
(310) 966-9492
www.mergerstat.com

Mergerstat Review (annual)
Mergerstat Transaction Roster (annual)
Mergerstat (monthly)

NVST.com,Inc.
777 108th Avenue N.E., Suite 1750
Bellevue, WA 98004
(425) 454-8098
www.nvst.com

Corporate Growth Report (weekly)
Mergers & Acquisitions Quarterly (quarterly)
The Merger & Acquisition Sourcebook (annual)
Done Deals Database

Securities Data Publishing Company
Thompson Financial Securities Data
40 West 57th Street, Suite 1000
New York, New York 10019
(212) 765-5311
www.securitiesdata.com

Some of the products listed below are also available on-line through
www.nvst.com.

BUYOUTS newsletter (biweekly)
Mergers & Acquisitions (bimonthly)
Acquisitions Monthly
Mergers & Acquisitions Report newsletter (weekly)
Mergers & Corporate Policy newsletter (weekly)
The Merger Yearbook (annual)

Chapter 13

The Capitalized Excess Earnings Method

As will be discussed in Chapter 14, the asset-based approach can be applied on either (1) a collective basis or (2) a discrete basis. When the asset-based approach is applied on a collective basis, all of the intangible value of the business—in excess of its tangible asset value—is estimated in the aggregate. When the asset-based approach is applied on a discrete basis, the individual intangible assets of the business are identified and quantified. The capitalized excess earnings method is a common method for estimating the collective intangible value in the nature of goodwill of the business. This chapter will describe the capitalized excess earnings method (or the collective basis application) of the asset-based valuation approach.

Some analysts consider the excess earnings method to be an income approach valuation method. In truth, the classification of any valuation method is purely a semantic matter. The classification of a particular valuation method in no way affects the applicability (or lack of applicability) of that method.

In this book, we classify the capitalized excess earnings method as an asset-based approach method. That is because the conclusion of the application of the capitalized excess earnings method is an indication of the value of an asset: the company's intangible value in the nature of goodwill. Of course, goodwill is an intangible asset of a business. And, the valuation of a business by reference to its component assets (both tangible and intangible)—whether the intangible assets are appraised on a collective basis or a discrete basis—is the very definition of an asset-based approach.

Some analysts disparage the capitalized excess earnings method. They allege that this method is obsolete and that it is formulaistic and mechanical.

First, the fact that a valuation method has stood the test of time does not make it invalid. For example, John Marshall first published a description of the three generally accepted valuation approaches (i.e., the cost approach, the market approach, and the income approach) in 1890 in his landmark text, *Economics*. The very fact that a valuation method is old means it has passed the test of time. It does not mean it is outdated and inapplicable.

Second, it is true that the capitalized excess earnings method is sometimes referred to as "the formula method." This does not mean that the method is formulaistic or mechanical. Rather, the application of the capitalized excess earnings method requires a great deal of analysis and judgment. In fact, one conclusion of this chapter is that the capitalized excess earnings method requires as much (or more) analysis and judgment on the part of the analyst as do other business valuation methods.

Some analysts assert that the capitalized excess earnings method—while often used—is often misused. It is sometimes applied by analysts who do not appreciate the subtle complexities of this method. That allegation may be true. The objective of this chapter is to educate readers about how to deal with these subtle complexities.

The History of the Capitalized Excess Earnings Method

The capitalized excess earnings method is sometimes called the *Treasury method*. This is because this valuation method originally appeared in a 1920 publication by the U.S. Treasury Department entitled Appeals and Review Memorandum Number 34 (ARM 34). It was adopted in order to estimate the intangible value of goodwill that breweries and distilleries lost because of the legal imposition of prohibition in the U.S. Treasury Department laws.

Since then, both taxpayers and the Internal Revenue Service have often used (and often misused) this valuation method in connection with business valuations for gift tax, estate tax, and other taxation purposes. Also, (1) perhaps partly because of its fairly wide dissemination and (2) partly because of its apparent simplistic nature, this valuation method is widely adopted in one form or another for other valuation purposes, such as marital dissolution, shareholder dispute, buy-sell agreement formula, and other transactional and controversial purposes.

In 1968, the Internal Revenue Service updated and restated the ARM 34 valuation method. This restatement was promulgated in Internal Revenue Service Revenue Ruling 68-609. This revenue ruling is reproduced as Exhibit 13–1. Revenue Ruling 68-609 is still in effect today.

The reader should keep in mind that the excess earnings method was originally created for the purpose of valuing the intangible value of a business, *not* for the purpose of valuing the company as a whole. Consequently, perhaps the most appropriate application of the excess earnings method is for the purpose of *allocating* total value between tangible and intangible assets. Examples of such purposes include:

- Marital dissolution cases, in jurisdictions where personal goodwill value is considered a personal rather than a marital asset and therefore needs to be separately valued from the rest of the business enterprise.
- Conversions from C corporation status to S corporation status.
- Eminent domain cases, where the tangible asset values and intangible asset values have to be recognized separately.
- Property tax cases, where a company's tangible assets are subject to property taxation but its intangible assets are not.
- Economic damage or deprivation cases, such as a breach of a contract or the infringement of a patent or trademark.

The capitalized excess earnings method is most often used to value small- and medium-sized businesses; however, it may be used to value larger businesses, especially for the purposes listed above.

The Capitalized Excess Earnings Valuation Method

Practical Application of This Method

There are several variations in the application of this valuation method. The most typical procedures in the capitalized excess earnings method are summarized as follows:

1. Estimate the net tangible asset value for the subject business. The tangible assets should be appraised at a standard of value and a premise of value consistent with the standard of value appropriate to the business enterprise value. The various standards of value and premises of value related to tangible assets are discussed in Chapter 14, with regard to the asset accumulation method.

   It is noteworthy that this estimate of value relates to the net tangible assets of the company only. As we will see, net tangible assets may or may not include such discrete intangible assets as leasehold interests, patents, trademarks, and copyrights.

2. Estimate a normalized level of economic earnings. There are many different definitions of economic earnings that may be used in this method. These various measures of economic earnings were discussed in Chapter 9 related to the income approach.

Exhibit 13–1

Revenue Ruling 68–609

The "formula" approach may be used in determining the fair market value of intangible assets of a business only if there is no better basis available for making the determination; A.R.M. 34, A.R.M 68, O.D. 937, and Revenue Ruling 65–192 superseded.

SECTION 1001.—DETERMINATION OF AMOUNT OF AND RECOGNITION OF GAIN OR LOSS

26 CFR 1.1001-1: Computation of gain or loss.   Rev. Rul. 68–609[1]
(Also section 167; 1.167(a)-3)

The purpose of this Revenue Ruling is to update and restate, under the current statute and regulations, the currently outstanding portions of A.R.M. 34, C.B. 2, 31 (1920), A.R.M. 68, C.B. 3, 43 (1920), and O.D. 937, C.B. 4, 43 (1921).

The question presented is whether the "formula" approach, the capitalization of earnings in excess of a fair rate of return on net tangible assets, may be used to determine the fair market value of the intangible assets of a business.

The "formula" approach may be stated as follows:

A percentage return on the average annual value of the tangible assets used in a business is determined, using a period of years (preferably not less than five) immediately prior to the valuation date. The amount of the percentage return on tangible assets, thus determined, is deducted from the average earnings of the business for such period and the remainder, if any, is considered to be the amount of the average annual earnings from the intangible assets of the business for the period. This amount (considered as the average annual earnings from intangibles), capitalized at a percentage of, say, 15 to 20 percent, is the value of the intangible assets of the business determined under the "formula" approach.

The percentage of return on the average annual value of the tangible assets used should be the percentage prevailing in the industry involved at the date of valuation, or (when the industry percentage is not available) a percentage of 8 to 10 percent may be used.

The 8 percent rate of return and the 15 percent rate of capitalization are applied to tangibles and intangibles, respectively, of businesses with a small risk factor and stable and regular earnings; the 10 percent rate of return and 20 percent rate of capitalization are applied to businesses in which the hazards of business are relatively high.

The above rates are used as examples and are not appropriate in all cases. In applying the "formula" approach, the average earnings period

and the capitalization rates are dependent upon the facts pertinent thereto in each case.

The past earnings to which the formula is applied should fairly reflect the probable future earnings. Ordinarily, the period should not be less than five years, and abnormal years, whether above or below the average, should be eliminated. If the business is a sole proprietorship or partnership, there should be deducted from the earnings of the business a reasonable amount for services performed by the owner or partners engaged in the business. See *Lloyd B. Sanderson Estate v. Commissioner*, 42 F. 2d 160 (1930). Further, only the tangible assets entering into net worth, including accounts and bills receivable in excess of accounts and bills payable, are used for determining earnings on the tangible assets. Factors that influence the capitalization rate include (1) the nature of the business, (2) the risk involved, and (3) the stability or irregularity of earnings.

The "formula" approach should not be used if there is better evidence available from which the value of intangibles can be determined. If the assets of a going business are sold upon the basis of a rate of capitalization that can be substantiated as being realistic, though it is not within the range of figures indicated here as the ones ordinarily to the adopted, the same rate of capitalization should be used in determining the value of intangibles.

Accordingly, the "formula" approach may be used for determining the fair market value of intangible assets of a business only if there is no better basis therefor available.

See also Revenue Ruling-59-60, C.B. 1959-1, 237, as modified by Revenue Ruling 65-193, C.B. 1965-2, 370, which sets forth the proper approach to use in the valuation of closely-held corporate stocks for estate and gift tax purposes. The general approach, methods, and factors, outlined in Revenue Ruling 59-60, as modified, are equally applicable to valuations of corporate stocks for income and other tax purposes as well as for estate and gift tax purposes. They apply   also to problems involving the determination of the fair market value of business interests of any type, including partnerships and proprietorships, and intangible assets for all tax purposes.

A.R.M. 34, A.R.M. 68, and O.D. 937 are superseded, since the positions set forth therein are restated to the extent applicable under current law in this Revenue Ruling. Revenue Ruling 65-192, C.B. 1965-2, 259, which contained restatements of A.R.M. 34 and A.R.M. 68, is also superseded.

---

[1] Prepared pursuant to Rev. Proc. 67-6, C.B. 1967-1, 576.

SOURCE: Rev. Rul. 68–609, 1968-2 C.B. 327.

---

3. Quantify the amount of excess earnings. First, estimate an appropriate fair rate of return on the estimated net tangible asset value of the subject business. Next, multiply the estimated net tangible asset value (from Step 1) by the estimated fair rate of return. This product estimates the amount of economic earnings that would be attributable to the company's net tangible assets. Next, subtract that fair return on net tangible assets amount from the normalized level of economic earnings estimated in Step 2. The result of this procedure is sometimes called the *excess earnings* or the *excess economic income*. This residual is the amount of economic earnings above a fair rate of return on the net tangible asset value of the subject company.

4. Estimate an appropriate direct capitalization rate to apply to the amount of excess economic earnings. These excess earnings are the economic earnings attributable to the intangible value in the nature of goodwill of the subject business (as opposed to being attributable to the net tangible assets of the subject business).

5. Capitalize the excess economic earnings at that estimated direct capitalization rate.
6. Add the values from Step 1 (i.e., the net tangible asset value) and Step 5 (i.e., the intangible value in the nature of goodwill). The sum of these two values indicates the value of the subject business.

The Seeming Simplicity of This Method

In a subsequent section, we will consider the many analytical decisions and judgments encountered in each of the above valuation procedures. The discussion will indicate that the application of this valuation method is anything but simple. First, let's consider an illustration of an application of the capitalized excess earnings method.

An Illustration

In this illustration, let's assume that Client Corporation has a net tangible asset value of $20,000,000 as of December 31, 2000. Let's also assume that Client Corporation is expected to earn a normalized level of economic earnings (that we will define as net income in this illustration) of $8,000,000 per year. For the purpose of this example, we have estimated a fair rate of return of 15 percent on the Client Corporation net tangible assets. Also, for purposes of this illustration only, we have estimated that the appropriate direct capitalization rate for excess earnings to Client Corporation is 20 percent. (The issue of the estimation of direct capitalization rates is discussed later in the chapter.)

In this simplified application of the capitalized excess earnings method, the business enterprise value of Client Corporation is estimated in Exhibit 13–2.

In this simple illustration, the Client Corporation business enterprise value is $45,000,000. This value is the sum of (1) a $20,000,000 value of net tangible assets and (2) a $25,000,000 intangible value in the nature of goodwill.

Analysis of the Capitalized Excess Earnings Method

Even though the capitalized excess earnings method has been criticized by some analysts, it is commonly used for many business valuation purposes. Therefore, this section will consider the future analytical strengths and weaknesses of this valuation method.

First, it is worth reiterating that the Treasury Department did not promulgate this valuation method to estimate the value of the total business enterprise. Rather, this valuation method was promulgated to value the goodwill, or the total intangible value (in excess of the net tangible asset value), of breweries and other companies affected by the Prohibition of the 1920s. Nonetheless, it is logical from an economics perspective that the intangible value identified by the capitalized excess earnings valuation method should be added to the net tangible asset value of a company in order to estimate the total business enterprise value.

Exhibit 13–2

Client Corporation
Business Enterprise Value Capitalized Excess Earnings Method
As of December 31, 2000

Net tangible asset value		$20,000,000
Normalized economic earnings	$8,000,000	
Less: Economic earnings attributable to net tangible assets		
($200,000,000 × 15%)	(3,000,000)	
"Excess" economic earnings	$5,000,000	
Indicated intangible value of capitalized excess economic earnings		
($5,000,000 ÷ 20%)		25,000,000
Indicated Client Corporation business enterprise value		$45,000,000

Unfortunately for analysts, Internal Revenue Service Revenue Ruling 68-609 contains many ambiguities, undefined variables, and unanswered questions. Various valuation analysts have adopted a wide variety of interpretations to these ambiguities and undefined variables.

In the following section, we will discuss these ambiguities and undefined variables. We will consider these ambiguities and variables in the same order as they were presented in the "Practical Application of This Method" section above.

Estimation of the "Net Tangible Asset Value"

The first procedure in the capitalized excess earnings method is the estimation of the net tangible asset value for the subject business. Unfortunately, Revenue Ruling 68-609 does not specifically define what it means by *net tangible asset value*. For example, the Revenue Ruling does not provide substantive guidance with respect to the important question "net of what?"

Definition of Net Tangible Asset Value. Revenue Ruling 68-609 offers little procedural guidance to analysts with respect to either (1) the appropriate standard of value or (2) the appropriate premise of value that should be used when estimating *net tangible asset value*. This lack of specificity may be appropriate, however. This is because the Revenue Ruling does not imply that there is a single answer as to the appropriate standard of value or premise of value. Rather, these determinations have to be made by the analyst based on the requirements of the subject valuation.

As with the application of other business valuation methods, the determination of standard of value and premise of value with respect to the capitalized excess earnings method should be concluded after the analyst's consideration of (1) the purpose and objective of the individual appraisal, (2) the quantity and quality of available data, and (3) the highest and best use of the subject business interest.

There is general agreement among analysts that the most common definition of *net tangible asset value* is the fair market value standard and the value in continued use premise. Typically, this standard of value and premise of value would be measured by one or more of the generally accepted asset appraisal approaches which will be discussed in Chapter 14 related to the asset accumulation method.

IRS Private Letter Ruling 79-05013 takes the position that the appropriate standard of value for the net tangible assets should be fair market value:

Rev. Rul. 68-609 addresses the determination of fair market value of intangible assets by the formula approach, and for this reason it is proper that all terms used in the formula be consistent. The formula uses value in terms of fair market value, so the term '. . . value of the tangible assets used in a business,' in the formula, should be in terms of fair market values, as defined in Rev. Rul. 59-60.[1]

As a practical matter, analysts do not always rely upon fair market value appraisals of all of the subject tangible assets in the capitalized excess earnings valuation of a large company. This is because it would be very time consuming and, often, prohibitively expensive to conduct real estate and personal property appraisals of all of the tangible assets of a substantial business.

Therefore, analysts often resort to using the book value of the subject tangible assets simply because it is too complicated and time consuming of a process to obtain appraisals of tangible asset fair market value. This use of book value for estimating the value of the subject net tangible assets is not preferred. However, tangible assets are often such a major component of the business value for large corporations that it would not be practical to use the capitalized excess earnings method if this simplifying assumption was not made.

Should Asset Value Adjustments Be Tax-Affected? Because the objective of the analysis is to estimate the value of subject net tangible assets on a continued use basis—on which a reasonable rate of return should be earned—the analyst normally does not make any adjustment to recognize the income tax effect of unrealized (built-in) gains or losses. This is because the business will not, in the normal course of business, sell its tangible assets at their appraised values. Therefore, in reality, no income tax liability will arise.

However, analysts should not just ignore income tax considerations. For example, there could be cases (e.g., a large inventory write-up where a tax payment on the sale of the inventory is imminent) where an income tax adjustment may be appropriate.

Are Intangible Assets Included or Excluded? Typically, as the phrase *net tangible asset value* implies, intangible asset values should be removed from the subject company balance sheet before performing the capitalized excess earnings analysis. However, some analysts leave on the balance sheet those intangible assets that are already capitalized on the subject company financial statements. Examples of intangible assets that may already be recognized on the company's financial statements would include purchased goodwill, purchased computer software, computer software internally developed in anticipation of resale, and so forth.

It is noteworthy that, so far, this discussion assumes the application of the capitalized excess earnings method to estimate the company's total intangible value in the nature of goodwill (i.e., the collective value of intangible assets). If the subject company's intangible assets are valued discretely (using, for example, the asset accumulation method), this conclusion would be different.

In that case, the capitalized excess earnings method is used to estimate the residual value of the company's goodwill—after all of its individual intangible assets have already been valued and included in the amount of net assets subject to the capitalized excess earnings analysis.

Treatment of Nonoperating Assets. There is general agreement among analysts that it is preferable to remove nonoperating and/or excess assets from the balance

---

[1] Priv. Ltr. Rul. 79-05013 (Oct. 24, 1979).

sheet (and the related economic income from the income statement) and to treat such items separately in the capitalized excess earnings method.

Treatment of Leased Real Estate. In some closely held corporations (including substantial corporations), the real estate is owned separately by the business owners and leased to the company. In these cases, it is important for the analyst to ensure that the real estate rent is adjusted to market rent. And, if the real estate lease is a long-term lease, it is not uncommon for analysts to capitalize the lease—that is, to treat the real estate as if it was owned instead of leased.

Estimation of Net Tangible Asset Value. There is no universally accepted conclusion as to what accounts should be "netted out" in the estimation of net tangible asset value. For example, various analysts have interpreted net tangible assets to mean any one of the following:

1. Gross assets net of accumulated depreciation (i.e., current market value of the tangible assets net of economic depreciation).
2. Net current value of the financial assets and the tangible assets less current liabilities only.
3. Net current value of the financial assets and the tangible assets minus all liabilities.

The most common interpretation of the term *net tangible asset value* is alternative 2—that is, net current value of the financial assets and the tangible assets less current liabilities only. However, if properly applied, alternative interpretations, such as the "average" of net tangible assets employed during the year, may be equally relevant.

In fact, the interpretation of what accounts are "netted out" in net tangible asset value is not particularly important to the application of the capitalized excess earnings method. That is, the final product of this method (the indicated value of the subject business enterprise value) should be unaffected by which definition of net tangible asset value is used.

This is because there should be a different fair rate of return and a different direct capitalization rate for each measure of net tangible asset value. The most important aspect of this method is not an academic debate over the conceptually correct definition of net tangible asset value. Rather, the most important aspect of this method is consistency. That is, the measure of net tangible asset value has to be consistent with (1) the measure of fair rate of return and (2) the measure of the direct capitalization rate. As long as all of the capitalized excess earnings method variables are applied consistently, this method will provide a valid estimate of business enterprise value.

Estimation of the Value of Debt. The conceptual answer to the question of the amount of debt to be deducted in this method is that it depends on when the debt is likely to be paid. If payment at face value is imminent (e.g., if a payment is triggered by the very transaction for which the valuation is being conducted), then it is appropriate to value the subject debt at face value. If the debt may remain outstanding for a period of time, many practitioners would value the subject debt at its fair market value.

Estimation of the "Normalized Level of Earnings"

Step 2 in the capitalized excess earnings method is the estimation of a normalized level of earnings. This is also called a normalized level of economic income. This more generic description is particularly appropriate because Revenue Ruling 68-

609 does not specifically define the term *earnings*. It does, however, make the key statement that the earnings *"should fairly reflect the probable future earnings"* (emphasis supplied).

When suggesting the use of past years' earnings as a basis for estimating future earnings, the Revenue Ruling notes that abnormal years should be eliminated from consideration. Analysts generally agree that nonrecurring income and/or expense items should be eliminated from any historical period that is used for the earnings base for projecting future normalized earnings.

Treatment of Nonoperating Income. Consistent with the removal of nonoperating assets from the net tangible asset base, related nonoperating income typically should be removed from the earnings base.

Treatment of Owners' Compensation. Revenue Ruling 68-609 states that "if the business is a sole proprietorship or partnership, there should be deducted from the earnings of the business a reasonable amount for services performed by the owner or partners engaged in the business." Analysts generally agree that owner/employee's abnormal compensation should be adjusted to a normal level of compensation in the valuation of a closely held business. This is true whether the owner/operator compensation is either above normal levels or below normal levels. The "normal level" of compensation is generally considered to be the expense of employing a nonowner/employee to perform the services currently performed by the owner/employee.

Treatment of Income Taxes. The measure of earnings—or economic income— to be capitalized should normally be net of federal and state income taxes paid by the subject business. Some closely held businesses operate as S corporations or other pass-through entities. It often is appropriate to tax-affect the economic income even where the subject business does not pay income taxes. The reason for this is, if the subject business were to be sold to a corporation that would have to pay income taxes on the subject's income, in estimating that buyer's investment value, the buyer almost surely would tax-affect the economic income. If that actual buyer were also the typical "willing buyer," the tax-affected earnings would also be the appropriate measure of economic income to use in estimating fair market value. Also, a significant (and not uncommon) problem arises when tax liability flows through to an owner but the earnings giving rise to the tax liability are not paid out. Tax-affecting the subject business earnings is one of several possible ways to treat this problem for purposes of valuation.

Again, with regard to the income tax issue, what is most important is consistency in application. That is, the measure of "earnings" or economic income that is selected—whether it is net income, net cash flow, or operating cash flow and whether it is before tax or after tax—should be consistent with (1) the measure of the fair rate of return and (2) the measure of the direct capitalization rate.

Definition of "Earnings." Revenue Ruling 68-609 does not provide a definition of the term *earnings*. Is it net income? Net cash flow? Or some other measure of economic income?

There is some agreement among analysts that the economic variable best suited to represent earnings in the context of the capitalized excess earnings method is cash flow. However, even within this general agreement, there is a difference in opinion about whether (1) net cash flow or (2) operating cash flow are the best measures of economic income. These different measures of economic income were discussed in Chapter 9, related to the income approach. The trend among analysts is to favor net cash flow. This is because that measure of income is the amount that the stakeholders can take out of the business without disrupting operations.

For many large businesses, the difference between net income and any measure of cash flow can be substantial. Again, there is some discretion in the analyst's selection of the appropriate measure of economic income to use in the excess earnings method. As long as the measure of economic income is used consistently, this method will provide a valid indication of value. That is, (1) the measure of economic income, (2) the fair rate of return, and (3) the direct capitalization rate should be consistently measured—on either a net cash flow basis or on an operating cash flow basis.

Appropriate Rate of Return on Tangible Assets

Several alternative procedures are used to quantify the appropriate rate of return on the subject company's net tangible assets. Most analysts agree that the required return is dependent largely on the asset mix. The riskier the assets, the higher the rate of return required to support them.

One common procedure is to use a weighted average of the company's cost of debt and cost of equity, with the weighting based on the proportions of the various asset classes that can be financed by debt. The following is an example of this appropriate rate of return procedure.

Asset Class	Percent Asset Value	Borrowing Financible	Capacity
Receivables	$10,000,000	80%	$8,000,000
Inventory	20,000,000	60%	12,000,000
Fixtures and equipment	20,000,000	50%	10,000,000
	$50,000,000		$30,000,000

If the company's borrowing cost is 10 percent and its cost of equity is 20 percent, then the weighted average would be calculated as follows:

Debt	@ 10% × 0.6 (i.e., $30,000,000 ÷ $50,000,000)	=	6%
Equity	@ 20% × 0.4 (i.e., $20,000,000 ÷ $50,000,000)	=	8%
Weighted average required rate of return on net tangible assets		=	14%

If the subject company is a C corporation that pays income taxes, the cost of debt would be tax-affected by multiplying the cost of debt by 1 minus the income tax rate. For example, if the company's income tax rate is 30 percent, the cost of debt would be $10\% \times (1 - 0.30) = 10\% \times 0.7 = 7\%$.

If the borrowing capacity of a closely held corporation is dependent on personal guarantees of the business owners, this is an additional debt cost factor. While no empirical support for the amount of this cost factor exists, it is reasonable to add to the cost of debt if personal guarantees are involved. Such guarantees carry risk to the guarantor and limit the guarantor's borrowing capacity for purposes unrelated to the subject closely held business.

Some analysts use historical industry average rates of return. The problem with this is that required rates of return, by definition, are based on the future expectations and alternative opportunity cost of the investor. The historical industry rate of return may not be representative of future expectations.

Appropriate Direct Capitalization Rate for Excess Earnings

Since the company's debt rate and the "safe part" of the company's equity rate are typically used in the estimation of the rate of return for net tangible assets, the direct capitalization rate applicable to excess earnings normally would have to be higher than the company's required equity rate.

Most analysts agree that one of the most important factors in the estimation of the direct capitalization rate for excess earnings is the perceived persistence of the excess earnings. The longer the time period and the greater the certainty of the expectation of the excess earnings, the lower the direct capitalization rate. Direct capitalization rates that are equal to the company's cost of equity capital assume a solid earnings base expected to continue well into the future. A low capitalization rate is usually applicable only for a very long and very predictable persistence of the excess earnings.

The selection of the excess earnings direct capitalization rate by these typical considerations is one of the more subjective judgments that are made within the various business valuation methods. However, ultimately, the weighted average of the capitalization rates for the net tangible assets and excess earnings (weighted by the amount of value ascribed to each of the two components) should be the same as the company's overall direct capitalization rate.

Commentary on the Estimation of Direct Capitalization Rates. Analyst David Bishop offers the following insights regarding the application of the excess earnings method (EEM):

> Before beginning our journey, let's review a few foundational thoughts with respect to the EEM.
>
> - The EEM is widely used regardless of the views of some practitioners.
> - The EEM is more frequently used on mid-size to smaller businesses.
> - Despite the intent of the EEM's birth documents (ARM-34 and RR 68-609) many practitioners mutate the EEM to indicate a value at the enterprise level.
> - The EEM is more appropriate when a business has a material investment in tangible assets. With respect to businesses with only a minor tangible investment, an overwhelming portion of the total earnings become excess earnings, with the result being the EEM becomes very similar to the single period capitalization method.[2]

Bishop offers the following useful advice with regard to the estimation of the appropriate direct capitalization rates (i.e., excess earnings capitalization rate, or EECR):

> Selecting the EECR is one of the most difficult decisions required of business appraisers. Rooted in theory is the view that the rate used to capitalize excess earnings will be at or above the high end of a range of reasonable rates because intangible assets are among the most perishable if not nurtured. In a worst-case scenario, amounts invested in intangible assets lack even a modicum of investment protection in the form of salvage value. There are

[2] David M. Bishop, "Excess Earnings Cap Rate—Six Market Influences," *Business Appraisal Practice*, Winter 1999, p. 4.

six primary *influences* to the selection of the EECR. They are listed below and then discussed more fully.

1. The rate used to capitalize or discount normalized benefits attributable to both tangible and intangible assets, e.g., in the single period capitalization method.
2. The rate used in the EEM as the rate of return applicable to tangible assets.
3. The persistence of the intangible assets.
4. The company's financial structure, and the stability and quality of its earnings.
5. The type of earnings or cash flow selected for use in the excess earnings method.
6. Whether or not a premium for illiquidity is built into the EECR.[3]

In addition, Bishop offers helpful commentary with regard to what procedures not to use in the estimation of the appropriate direct capitalization rates:

Automatic reliance on industry rates such as the return on total assets, tangible net worth or equity (e.g., RMA rates) can neither assure a reasonable rate of return on tangible assets nor provide support for the development of the EECR. The inappropriateness of the automatic use of such rates is explained as follows:

1. Industry return rates are calculated on book values and the appraisal process requires fair market values.
2. Industry return rates attribute all earnings to those book valued assets. The objective in the EEM is to segregate the return stream appropriate to the FMV of the tangibles and attribute the excess earnings, if any, to the intangible assets.
3. Industries with poor performance will have low rates of return and industries with excellent performance will have higher rates of return. When an appraiser (or valuation software program) automatically uses these rates, the higher rates of the more successful industries produce lower values; conversely, the lower rates of poor industries indicate higher values.

These differences invalidate the use of such rates despite their surface appeal. The objective is to determine the *expected market* rates not simply the *achieved book rates*. Automatic use of industry rates implicitly assumes *achieved* rates are equal to *expected* rates. While expected rates may be found to be equal to *achieved* rates, this relationship must be determined, not assumed.[4]

Comprehensive Example

Exhibits 13–3 through 13–8 present a comprehensive example of the application of the capitalized excess earnings method in the valuation of a substantial closely held corporation.

---

[3] Ibid., p. 7.
[4] Ibid., p. 6.

Exhibit 13–3

Substantial Close Corporation
Summary Balance Sheet
(Historical Cost Basis)
As of December 31, 2000

ASSETS		LIABILITIES AND OWNERS' EQUITY	
Current assets	$10,000,000	Current liabilities	$10,000,000
(cash, receivables, and inventory)		(payables and accruals)	
Tangible assets	20,000,000	Long-term debt	10,000,000
(real estate and equipment—		Owners' equity	10,000,000
net of accumulated depreciation)			
		TOTAL LIABILITIES AND	
TOTAL ASSETS	$30,000,000	OWNERS' EQUITY	$30,000,000

Substantial Close Corporation
Summary Income Statement
for the 12 Months Ended December 31, 2000

Net revenues	$50,000,000
Operating expenses	
Cash expenses	37,000,000
Depreciation expense	2,000,000
Interest expense	1,000,000
Total expenses	40,000,000
Profit before taxes	10,000,000
Income taxes	4,000,000
Profit after taxes	$6,000,000

Substantial Close Corporation
Summary Results of Operations
for the 12 Months Ended December 31, 2000

Net cash flow (invested capital basis):

	Profit after taxes	$6,000,000
Plus:	Tax-affected interest expense ($1,000,000	
	interest expense less $400,000 income tax expense)	600,000
Equals:	Profit after taxes—invested capital basis	$6,600,000
Plus:	Depreciation expense	2,000,000
Less:	Capital expenditures (during 2000)	2,000,000
Less:	Increase in net working capital (from 12/31/99 to 12/31/00)	1,000,000
Equals:	Net cash flow (invested capital basis)	$5,600,000

Operating cash flow (invested capital basis):

	Profit after taxes	$6,000,000
Plus:	Tax-affected interest expense	600,000
Equals:	Profit after taxes—invested capital basis	$6,600,000
Plus:	Depreciation expense	2,000,000
Equals:	Operating cash flow (invested capital basis)	$8,600,000

Exhibit 13–3 presents the historical financial statements for the illustrative company, Substantial Close Corporation (hereinafter "Substantial"). Exhibit 13–3 presents a balance sheet, income statement, and cash flow statement for Substantial.

The objective of this valuation is to estimate the fair market value of 100 percent of the owner's equity of Substantial, on a marketable, controlling ownership interest basis, as of December 31, 2000.

Exhibit 13–4 presents two alternative measures of (or definitions of) net tangible asset value for Substantial:

1. Accounting book value of Substantial net tangible assets.
2. Appraised fair market value of Substantial net tangible assets.

Exhibit 13–5 presents, with simplified assumptions, estimates of the direct capitalization rates applicable to the fair market value of net tangible assets and to the "excess earnings."

Readers should note that the estimation of the direct capitalization rate applicable to excess earnings is the most subjective procedure in the excess earnings method. It is a matter of the analyst's informed judgment. There is no generally accepted procedure to estimate the direct capitalization rate without first valuing the overall business enterprise. And, there is little or no market-derived empirical evidence with regard to the selection of the excess earnings direct capitalization rate.

Exhibit 13–6 applies these estimated direct capitalization rates to Substantial (based on the fair market value of net tangible assets) in order to arrive at an indicated value by the excess earnings method.

We know that the blended, or overall, direct capitalization rate for the entire capital structure should be equal to the company's weighted average cost of capital, less the estimated long-term growth rate in the economic income variable being capitalized. When valuing a controlling ownership interest, analysts typically value the overall capital structure of the subject business as opposed to just the equity of the subject business.

Exhibit 13–7 illustrates the estimate of the overall required rate of return (WACC) and overall direct capitalization rate for Substantial.

As a "reasonableness check" on the value indications from the excess earnings method in Exhibit 13–6, we can apply this direct capitalization rate to the Substantial net cash flow to invested capital, and then compare the results:

$$\frac{\$5,600,000}{0.15} = \$37,330,000$$

The value indication is reasonably close to the $37,400,000 indicated value of the Substantial invested capital as developed in Exhibit 13–6. If the results were not within a reasonable range of each other, it would be appropriate (1) to examine the assumptions of each method and (2) to make some revisions in order to make one or the other of the two methods more realistic.

The weights assigned to the capital structure components (generally debt and equity) usually should be the "target" weights for the subject company—that is, "the proportions of debt and equity that the firm targets for its capital structure over the long-term planning period."[5] This often is based on industry average capital structures.

Let's look back for a moment to other measures of net tangible asset value as presented in Exhibit 13–4. We should consider the implications of these other measures

[5] Alfred Rappaport, *Creating Shareholder Value*, rev. ed. (New York: The Free Press, 1998), p. 37.

Exhibit 13–4

Substantial Close Corporation
Application of Capitalized Excess Earnings Method
Alternative Measures of Net Tangible Asset Value

Measure #1
Accounting Book Value of Net Tangible Assets

		"Accounting Book Value" from 12/31/00 Balance Sheet
Current assets		$10,000,000
Minus:	Current liabilities	10,000,000
Equals:	Net working capital	–
Plus:	Tangible assets	20,000,000
Equals:	Book value of net tangible assets	$20,000,000

Measure #2
Appraised Fair Market Value of Net Tangible Assets

		Appraised Fair Market Value as of 12/31/00
	Current assets	$10,000,000
Minus:	Current liabilities	10,000,000
Equals:	Net working capital	–
Plus:	Tangible assets	25,000,000
	(based on contemporaneous market value appraisals of real estate and equipment)	
Equals:	Fair market value of net tangible assets	$25,000,000

for the estimates of capitalization rates for net tangible asset value and for excess earnings.

In the case of Measure #1, accounting book value, we know that accounting book value understates the fair market value of the net tangible assets. Consequently, it is reasonable to assume that a higher proportion of the net tangible assets as measured by accounting book value could be financed by debt, with the result that the required return on net tangible assets would be lower than if measured by fair market value. Similarly, this leaves a higher proportion of the net cash flow attributable to intangible assets, suggesting a higher direct capitalization rate for that component.

Exhibit 13–8 illustrates the value estimate for Substantial using accounting book value as the net tangible asset base, an 8 percent return on net tangible assets, and a 30 percent direct capitalization rate on excess earnings.

Not surprisingly, since accounting book values bear little relationship to appraised fair market values, the $33,333,330 from Exhibit 13–8 is not as close to the $37,333,330 as we concluded using appraised fair market values in Exhibit 13–6. However, most analysts probably would still consider this conclusion to be within a reasonable range of value.

The principal reason the alternative applications of this method appear to yield different value indications is that there are no precise methods for estimating the two direct capitalization rates, especially the direct capitalization rate for excess earnings.

In the comprehensive example, we did not illustrate the effect of the alternative growth rate projections on the excess economic income, on the direct capitalization

Exhibit 13–5

Substantial Close Corporation
Summary Balance Sheet
(Historical Cost Basis)
As of December 31, 2000

In this application of the capitalized excess earnings method, we use asset-specific required rates of return and asset-specific direct capitalization rates. That is, the required rate of return for each category of the Substantial net assets is specific to the investment risk associated with that class of asset investment. Also, the direct capitalization rate to be applied to the excess economic income is a rate that is specific to the risk of that measure of economic income—that is, the risk associated with the intangible goodwill of the subject company.

We could perform this asset-specific capitalized excess earnings analysis based upon any—and all—of the two measures of net tangible asset value illustrated in the previous exhibit. For simplicity, we only illustrate the asset-specific application of the capitalized excess earnings method using one measure of net tangible asset value: Measure #2, with net tangible asset value estimated at contemporaneously appraised fair market value, the most common formulation of the method.

From Exhibit 13–3, we recall that the net working capital balance for Substantial is zero (i.e., $10,000,000 current assets minus $10,000,000 current liabilities). This was a conscious simplifying assumption for illustrative purposes only. The asset-specific application of required rates of return and direct capitalization rates can work with any level of positive—or negative—net working capital.

While it will have no impact on our final business value estimate, let's estimate an asset-specific rate of return for the Substantial net working capital. Net working capital is usually considered a very low risk asset investment capital. Accordingly, a short-term, risk-free rate is often used as the asset-specific rate of return for net working capital. For purposes of this illustration, let's assume a short-term risk-free rate of 6% to be applied against this low risk asset investment category.

From Exhibit 13–4, we recall that the fair market value of the Substantial tangible assets (i.e., real estate and personal property) is $25,000,000. This value is based upon a current appraisal of the subject real estate and personal property.

Let's assume that the appropriate asset-specific rate of return on the Substantial tangible assets is 10%. This would be a rate of return specific to the risk and expected return of these tangible assets. For purposes of this illustration, let's assume that this 10% is the cost of financing for these tangible assets. In other words, let's assume that Substantial could borrow funds, using some equity, at a blended rate of 10% for the purposes of purchasing such tangible assets.

It is noteworthy that in the application of the asset-specific rate of return procedure, there could be several asset-specific rates of return: one for land, one for buildings, one for machinery and equipment, and so on.

At this point, we need to estimate an asset-specific direct capitalization rate for goodwill (based on the premise that we are subsuming all of the Substantial intangible value in the asset called "goodwill"). If we believe that a buyer would pay for four years of expected earnings from the company's goodwill (which assumes a reasonably reliable and persistent expected income stream from the goodwill), then the direct capitalization rate would be 25% ($1 \div 4 = 0.25$). The application of these asset-specific direct capitalization rates is presented in Exhibit 13–6.

---

rate, and (ultimately) on the estimation of goodwill. This omission was also due to space constraints. The effect of growth rate projections on the estimate of economic income and on the selected direct capitalization rate is discussed in detail in Chapter 10, related to the income approach.

The Treatment of Negative Goodwill

The capitalized excess earnings method is an asset-based valuation approach method. In a strict application of this method, all of the subject entity's assets—both tangible and intangible—are valued. However, the capitalization of excess economic income procedure itself only values one asset: the entity's intangible value in the nature of goodwill. This intangible value in the nature of goodwill is the value of the company's economic income (if any) over and above a reasonable rate of return on the company's net tangible assets. A significant conceptual and practical question is: What if the subject company's economic income is less than a reasonable rate of return on the net tangible assets?

Exhibit 13–6

Substantial Close Corporation
Application of Capitalized Excess Earnings Method
Capitalization of Asset-Specific Excess Earnings Using Fair Market Value of Assets
As of December 31, 2000

Net Tangible Asset Value Measure #2 (at Appraised Fair Market Value)

	Net cash flow (after-tax)		$5,600,000	(Exhibit 13-3)
	Fair market value of net tangible assets	$25,000,000		(Exhibit 13-4)
Times:	Asset-specific required rate of return on net tangible assets	× 10%		(Exhibit 13-5)
	Required level of economic income		2,500,000	
	Excess economic income (i.e., net cash flow less required level of economic income)		3,100,000	
Divided by:	Direct capitalization rate (based upon applying an asset-specific required rate of return on goodwill)		25%	(Exhibit 13-5)
Equals:	Estimate of intangible asset value in the nature of goodwill		12,400,000	
Add:	Fair market value of net tangible assets		25,000,000	
	Implied value of Substantial invested capital (including existing equity and debt)		37,400,000	
Less:	Existing debt		10,000,000	
Indicated value of Substantial equity			**$27,400,000**	

The result of this phenomenon (i.e., the amount of economic income is less than a fair return on net tangible assets) is often referred to as *negative goodwill*. Negative goodwill indicates that the collective going-concern value of the total subject entity is less than the sum of the individual values of the entity's total tangible assets.

In such a situation, the subject company's economic income is insufficient to justify buying the business on the basis of the collective value of its individual tangible and intangible assets. In such an instance, the collective value of the company's assets (including tangible assets and any discrete intangible assets) would be reduced to the level of economic value indicated by the conclusion of the capitalized excess earnings analysis. In other words, the negative economic value associated with the company's goodwill would partially offset the positive economic value of the company's tangible assets and discrete intangible assets.

Should the adjusted net asset value indicated by the application of the company's negative goodwill fall below the liquidation value of the company's net assets, an analyst may conclude that the business would be worth more on a liquidation basis than on a going-concern basis. That is, a liquidation of the subject business would be a rational economic choice.

Common Errors in Applying the Capitalized Excess Earnings Method

As mentioned previously, the capitalized excess earnings method is often misused in business valuation. This may be due to the apparent simplicity of this valuation

Exhibit 13–7

Substantial Close Corporation
Application of Capitalized Excess Earnings Method
Overall Required Rate of Return and
Overall Direct Capitalization Rate

After-Tax Weighted Average Cost of Capital

Assumptions: (a) Let's assume that the blended interest rate on the Substantial long-term debt is 10%. Let's also assume that the required risk-adjusted rate of return on the owners' equity of Substantial is 24%.

            (b) As indicated in Exhibit 13–3, the effective income tax rate for Substantial is 40%; the cost of debt capital (i.e., the interest rate) is affected by this income tax rate, where the cost of equity capital is already "paid" from after-tax dollars.

Type of Capital Component in Capital Structure	Before-Tax Cost of Capital Component	After-Tax Cost of Capital Component	Weighting in Capital Structure	Weighted Cost of Capital Component
Long-term debt	10%	6%	50%	3%
Owners' equity	24%	24%	<u>50%</u>	<u>12%</u>
Total	100%	15%		
After-tax weighted average cost of capital (rounded)				15%

Direct Capitalization Rate

As explained in Chapter 10 related to the income approach, the direct capitalization rate can be mathematically derived as follows:

$$c = k - g$$

where:

c = direct capitalization rate
k = present value discount rate
g = expected long-term growth rate

One procedure for estimating a company's present value discount rate is to calculate its weighted average cost of capital.

Since we have just calculated the Substantial weighted average cost of capital to be 15%, we use that indication as the appropriate present value discount rate. For purposes of simplicity, we assume a zero percent expected long-term growth rate. Therefore, we use 15% as the direct capitalization for the estimated net cash flow.

---

method. In any event, the most common errors in the application of this valuation method are discussed in the following sections.

Failure to Allow for Shareholder/Employee Salary

As noted in Revenue Ruling 68-609 (Exhibit 13–1), "If the business is a sole proprietorship or partnership, there should be deducted from the earnings of the business a reasonable amount for services performed by the owner or partners engaged in the business."

This guidance is equally valid with regard to the valuation of even the most substantial closely held corporations. And, this guidance is noteworthy whether the shareholder/employees are receiving compensation (and other perquisites) that are materially greater than or less than industry norms. For example, in established and financially successful corporations, shareholder/employees sometimes pay themselves executive compensation in amounts that are materially greater than non-shareholder/employees

Exhibit 13–8

Substantial Close Corporation
Application of Capitalized Excess Earnings Method
Capitalization of Asset-Specific Excess Earnings
Using Book Value of Assets

Net Tangible Asset Value Measure #1 (Accounting Book Value)

	Net cash flow (after-tax)		$5,600,000	(Exhibit 13-3)
Book value	Book value of net tangible assets	$20,000,000		(Exhibit 13-4)
Times:	Asset-specific required rate of return on net tangible assets	× 8%		(from text)
	Required level of economic income		1,600,000	
	Excess economic income (i.e., net cash flow less required level of economic income)		4,000,000	
Divided by:	Direct capitalization rate (based upon applying an asset-specific required rate of return on goodwill)		30%	(from text)
Equals:	Estimate of intangible asset value in the nature of goodwill		13,333,333	
Add:	Book value of net tangible assets		20,000,000	
	Implied value of Substantial invested capital (including existing equity and debt)		33,333,333	
Less:	Existing debt		10,000,000	
Indicated value of Substantial equity			**$23,333,333**	

would earn for the same services. Also, in development stage or unprofitable corporations, shareholder/employees sometimes pay themselves less than what they would pay to nonshareholder/employees for the same services. This is because the shareholder/employees would rather maximize the value of their business as opposed to maximizing their current (taxable) individual incomes.

Nonetheless, analysts often perform valuations using the capitalized excess earnings method without including a reasonable (or industry normal) allowance for executive compensation to the shareholder/employees for the services that they perform. This error results in (1) an understatement of the true economic income in the established company case mentioned above and (2) an overstatement of the true economic income in the development stage company case. Accordingly, this error in turn leads to (1) an understatement of the true economic value of the established company and (2) an overstatement of the true economic value of the development stage company.

Failure to Use Realistic Estimate of Future Normalized Earnings

To the extent that this valuation method is valid, it depends on a reasonable estimate of the subject business's normalized earnings. As noted in Revenue Ruling 68-609: "The past earnings to which the formula is applied should fairly reflect the probable future earnings."

However, this valuation method is sometimes applied naively either (1) to the latest year earnings of the subject business or (2) to some simple or weighted average of recent years' earnings of the subject business. This measure of normalized earnings is calculated without considering whether the earnings measure being used fairly reflects the probable future earnings.

Inconsiderate use of some historical earnings base usually results in either an undervaluation or an overvaluation of the subject business. As the guidance provided by Revenue Ruling 68-609 indicates, historical earnings should only be used in the application of this method to the extent that those historical earnings provide a reasonable indication of future normalized earnings.

Errors in Selection of the Appropriate Direct Capitalization Rates

The selection of the two direct capitalization rates is critical to the validity of the result of the capitalized excess earnings method. A conceptual approach to the selection of the appropriate direct capitalization rates was discussed in an earlier section of this chapter. However, one clearly erroneous procedure for the selection of the direct capitalization rates is to use the illustrative rates suggested in the ruling itself.

The revenue ruling, written in 1968, suggests capitalization rates of 8 percent to 10 percent on net tangible assets and capitalization rates of 15 percent to 20 percent to be applied to the excess earnings. However, the revenue ruling itself states that:

> The percentage of return . . . should be the percentage prevailing in the industry involved at the date of the valuation. . . . The above rates are used as examples and are not appropriate in all cases. . . . The capitalization rates are dependent upon the facts pertinent thereto in each case.[6]

Both the wording of the revenue ruling and common sense indicate that the specific capitalization rates mentioned in the ruling are illustrative only. The appropriate direct capitalization rates depend on the facts at the time of the valuation. These contemporaneous facts relate to (1) current economic indicators, (2) current capital market indicators, (3) current industry conditions, and (4) current company-specific conditions.

In spite of that, even in the year 2000, some analysts naively use the capitalization rates for the capitalized excess earnings method originally published in the ARM 34 example back in 1920, and repeated in Revenue Ruling 68-609 published in 1968.

Commentary on Capitalized Excess Earnings Method Problems

Because of the common errors that result from an inconsiderate application of the capitalized excess earnings method, some analysts disparage the use of this method. In an article in *Fair$hare*, Kalman Barson provides the following commentary with respect to the problems regarding the capitalized excess earnings method:

> Rev Ruling 68-609 requires the business investigator and valuator to make a number of subject determinations, many of which are also necessary for other approaches to valuation. For instance:

---

[6] Revenue Ruling 68-609, 1968-2 C.B. 327.

- Normalization adjustments. Were there out of the ordinary happenings in the business during the subject years; or perquisites taken which really had no business purpose?
- Reasonable compensation. The compensation taken by owners of a company isn't necessarily the appropriate compensation that would be taken by those same people for those same services had they been hired at an arm's length arrangement by the company as contrasted to owning it.
- Return on investment. Because 68-609 determines the intangible (or goodwill) value in a closely held company, it requires first that we subtract from the company's net income a return on investment, to reflect the return on the tangible assets of the business, before we go on to determining the value of the intangible assets. This raises certain issues such as what rate of return to use and how much should the tangible assets be adjusted in the context of this approach. (We also need to deal with the question of whether the rate of return should be based on pre or post tax income.)
- Capitalization rate. After all the income and operational adjustments have been made, we are left with a net income which then has to be capitalized to determine the goodwill value of that business. This involves another judgment—what is the appropriate capitalization rate, or multiple. Again, this type of judgment call is common to many other valuation approaches.
- Book value or net worth adjustments. Though not necessarily required in all cases, many situations call for adjusting fixed assets to reflect a more true economic depreciation, or making other adjustments to the book value balance sheet.

All in all, 68-609 calls for perhaps more judgment calls than most other approaches to valuation. As such, it provides more opportunities for errors, and for judgment versus factual basis.[7]

In the conclusion of his article, Barson reminds us that the capitalized excess earnings method may not be applicable in all valuation engagements. And, even when this method is applicable, it may not be the best method to use in the case of the instant valuation:

It is my belief that the time has come when other valuation approaches, valid (and sometimes more appropriate), should be used instead of relying on Revenue Ruling 68-609. It is important that the judicial and legal communities recognize that a valuation report is not necessarily deficient or suspect simply because it uses approaches to valuation other than 68-609, or it doesn't use 68-609 at all. Indeed, Revenue Ruling 68-609 says that, *"The 'formula' approach should not be used if there is better evidence available from which the value of intangibles can be determined.... Accordingly, the 'formula' approach may be used for determining the fair market value of intangible assets of a business only if there is no better basis therefor available."*[8]

---

[7] Kalman A. Barson, "Is it Time to Bury Revenue Ruling 68-609?" *Fair$hare: The Matrimonial Law Monthly*, January 1998, pp. 7–8.
[8] Ibid., p. 8.

Summary

The capitalized excess earnings method (also called the *formula method* or the *Treasury method*) dates back to the period of Prohibition. It was the U.S. Treasury Department method of determining the amount to compensate distilleries for the loss of their intangible value in the nature of goodwill as a result of the effects of Prohibition.

The Service's current position with regard to this business valuation method is embodied in Revenue Ruing 68-609 and in Private Letter Ruling 79-05013, both referenced in this chapter.

The capitalized excess earnings method is one of the most widely used (and sometimes misused) methods of business valuation—particularly with regard for valuations performed for taxation and litigation purposes. This is because analysts often carelessly apply the mechanics of this "formula method" without considering the sophisticated nuances of this conceptually elegant methodology.

In addition, analysts often ignore the professional guidance regarding the proper implementation of this method promulgated in the above Internal Revenue Service references. Therefore, the result of a naïve application of this method is a plethora of misapplications of a fundamentally sound (and potentially analytically rigorous) valuation method.

This chapter has developed the proper use of the capitalized excess earnings method. It has quoted the relevant guidance provided in each of the Internal Revenue Service references cited above. And, it has provided guidance on how to develop the four key variables in the capitalized excess earnings method:

1. Net tangible asset value.
2. Earnings base to be capitalized.
3. Reasonable rate of return on net tangible assets.
4. Direct capitalization rate to be applied to the "excess earnings."

The chapter has concluded with a discussion of several of the more common errors found in the inexperienced application of the capitalized excess earnings method. By following the guidance in this chapter, the analyst should be able (1) to properly apply the capitalized excess earnings method and (2) to identify common errors resulting from a naïve application of the capitalized excess earnings method.

Bibliography

Barson, Kalman A. "Is It Time to Bury Revenue Ruling 68-609?" *Fair$hare*, January 1998, pp. 7–8.

Bishop, David M. "Excess Earnings Cap Rate: Six Market Influences." *Business Appraisal Practice*, Winter 1999, pp. 4–9.

Fishman, Jay E., and William J. Morrison. "Capitalization of Excess Earnings for Talent-Based Personal Service Business." *Fair$hare*, February 1996, p. 13.

Lippitt, Jeffrey W., and Nicholas J. Mastriacchio. "Developing Capitalization Rates for Valuing a Business." *The CPA Journal*, November 1995, pp. 24–28.

Mastracchio, Nicholas J., and Jeffrey W. Lippitt. "A Comparison of the Earnings Capitalization and the Excess Earnings Models." *Journal of Small Business Management*, January 1996, pp. 1–12.

"Practitioners Disagree Strongly on Excess Earnings Methodology." *Shannon Pratt's Business Valuation Update*, April 1997, pp. 1–3.

Pratt, Shannon P. "The Excess Earnings Method: How to Get a Defensible Result." *Shannon Pratt's Business Valuation Update*, October 1996, p. 1, 20–21.

Shayne, Mark. "A Re-examination of Revenue Ruling 68-609." *Fair$hare*, July 1992, pp. 5–8.

Summers, S. Chris. "The Excess Earnings Method," Chapter 15. In Thomas L. West and Jeffrey D. Jones, eds. *Handbook of Business Valuation*. New York: John Wiley & Sons, 1992, pp. 167–76.

Chapter 14

Asset-Based Approach: Asset Accumulation Method

For the most part, business financial statements are prepared based on the *cost principle* of accounting. That is, assets are usually recorded at their historical purchase/acquisition cost. Generally, business assets are not restated from historical cost for financial accounting purposes, even if the current economic value of the assets has changed considerably in comparison with their historical cost. This is a fundamental financial statement presentation concept under generally accepted accounting principles (GAAP).

There are some exceptions to the application of the cost principle. Companies in certain industries may report their financial statements in compliance with a statutory basis of accounting other than GAAP. And under GAAP, assets that have been permanently impaired have to be written down from their historic cost to their market value. Also under GAAP, some companies report certain assets at the lower of their historical cost or market value. And, some companies in certain industries report their financial assets (such as investments in marketable securities) at their current market value. Accordingly, analysts who use any asset-based approach valuation method should be sure that they understand the accounting principles that were used to prepare the subject company financial statements.

Under GAAP, wasting assets, such as real estate (other than land) and tangible personal property, are depreciated over their expected useful lives. Therefore, at any point in time, the balance sheet presents the depreciated historical cost for these types of tangible assets. The depreciated historical cost of assets recorded on the balance sheet is often referred to as *book value*. The total depreciated historical cost of the recorded assets minus the total historical values of the recorded liabilities is often referred to as the *net book value* (or sometimes "book value") of the business owners' equity.

A fundamental *accounting* principle is: The book value of assets minus the book value of liabilities equals the book value of the business owners' equity. This formula is an accounting identity.

A fundamental business *valuation* principle is: The current value of assets minus the current value of liabilities equals the current value of the business owners' equity. This formula is an economics identity.

In a business valuation, the relevant standard of value for both the business and the component business assets is the standard that is defined by the purpose and objective of the valuation. Chapter 2 presented several alternative standards of value, including fair market value, fair value, intrinsic or fundamental value, and investment value. Any of these standards of value may be used in a business valuation performed using asset-based approach methods.

Based on the purpose and objective of the valuation, the analyst will apply the appropriate standard of value to the subject equity interest. If an asset-based approach is used, the analyst will apply a corresponding appropriate standard of value to all of the assets and liabilities of the subject company. It is noteworthy that the standard of value for the individual assets and liabilities may be different from the standard of value for the subject equity interest. For example, the analyst may apply the fair market value standard to the individual assets and liabilities even though a different standard of value is determined for the subject equity interest.

In the asset accumulation method, the analyst restates all of the assets and liabilities of the subject company from their historical cost basis to the appropriate standard of value. For the purpose of this discussion, let's assume that the appropriate standard of value is fair market value. After the revaluation of all asset and liability accounts from their historical cost basis to fair market value, the analyst can then apply the axiomatic "assets minus liabilities" formula to indicate the value of the subject business enterprise.

At this point, the asset accumulation method will typically indicate the value of 100 percent of the subject company equity, on a marketable, controlling ownership interest basis. If the ownership interest valuation subject is some other level of value, then appropriate valuation discounts and/or premiums may be applied.

In some cases, a discount for lack of marketability and/or other valuation discounts or premiums may be appropriate even when valuing an overall business enterprise. The application of such valuation discounts or premiums at the enterprise level may be appropriate depending upon which standard of value is being estimated.

Fundamentals of the Asset Accumulation Method

If properly applied, asset-based approach methods are some of the more complex and rigorous valuation analyses. The costs and benefits of using asset-based approach valuation methods are described below. Before we consider these costs and benefits, or the various asset-based approach valuation methods, several fundamentals should be reiterated.

First, in the asset accumulation method, historical cost–based financial statements are the starting point, not the ending point, in the analysis. Analysts use the company's cost-based balance sheet only as a point of departure from which to begin the valuation. The presentation format of the value-basis balance sheet may be similar to the formal historical cost–basis balance sheet (e.g., assets on the left side and liabilities on the right side). However, the content of the value-basis balance sheet is different from the content of the cost-basis balance sheet.

The value-basis balance sheet may be materially different from the cost-basis balance sheet in two ways: (1) the balances in the asset and liability accounts have been revalued and (2) several new asset and liability accounts may be added.

Second, all assets and liabilities should be restated to an appropriate standard of value. This standard of value should be consistent with (but not necessarily the same as) the standard of value selected for the business valuation. As described below, if certain asset and liability accounts are immaterial or if the revaluation change is immaterial, the analyst may decide to leave those account balances at their cost basis. Otherwise, the analyst will separately consider and analyze each asset and liability account, either item by item or by category.

Third, *all* of the company's assets and *all* of the company's liabilities should be considered for revaluation to the selected appropriate standard of value. In many cases, the analyst may need to rely on experts in real estate appraisal, in machinery and equipment appraisal, or in other asset appraisal disciplines.

Often, many of a company's most valuable assets may not be recorded on the company's cost-basis balance sheet. This includes the whole category of the company's intangible assets. These intangible assets are typically not included on a cost-basis balance sheet (unless the intangible assets were acquired as part of a business acquisition that was accounted for under the purchase method of accounting).

Also, many of a company's more significant liabilities may not be recorded on the company's cost-basis balance sheet. This includes the whole category of the company's contingent liabilities. Accordingly, as part of the asset accumulation method, new asset and, possibly, new liability accounts may be recorded on the value-basis balance sheet.

Asset-Based Approach versus Book Value

It is important to distinguish between the application of any asset-based approach valuation method and simple reliance on accounting "book value" to conclude a value estimate. Under any standard of value, the true economic value of a business enterprise equals the company's accounting book value only by coincidence. More likely than not, the true economic value of a company will be either higher or lower than its accounting book value. There is no theoretical support, conceptual reasoning, or empirical data to suggest that the value of a business enterprise (under any standard of value) will necessarily equal the company's accounting book value.

From a valuation perspective, the terms *book value* or *net book value* are merely accounting jargon. This is because book value is not related to economic value, or to the valuation process, at all. As an accounting convention, the book value of a company is the historical cost of all of the company's assets—less total accumulated depreciation. Net book value is the book value of the company's assets less the recorded liabilities. Net book value (often called book value, in the vernacular) is synonymous with the amount of owners' equity recorded on the company's cost-basis balance sheet. Therefore, net book value can also be calculated as the sum of the owners' equity investments in the company plus the cumulative amount of the company's retained earnings.

In any event, accounting book value is not a recommended business valuation method. In fact, accounting book value is not a business valuation method at all, although it is popular in buy-sell agreement formulas. The quantification of accounting book value is not an asset-based valuation method. It is generally inappropriate to estimate a business valuation based solely on accounting book value. The values presented on the cost-based balance sheet are usually not representative of a current economic value for business valuation purposes. Also, there may be one or more intangible asset accounts or contingent liability accounts that should be considered in a business valuation—but that are not presented on the cost-basis balance sheet at all.

Asset Accumulation Method and Capitalized Excess Earnings Method

In the valuation literature, there are several names for the asset-based approach method that is based on the discrete revaluation of all of the company's individual assets and liabilities. This individual asset revaluation analysis is sometimes referred to as the *net asset value method*, the *adjusted net asset value method*, the *adjusted book value method*, the *asset build-up method*, or the asset accumulation method. In fact, these are all different names for the same general method. As a convention, in this chapter (and in this book) we refer to this individual asset revaluation analysis as the *asset accumulation method*.

There are two general methods in the asset-based approach to business valuation:

1. The collective revaluation of all of the company's assets and liabilities. This analysis is usually conducted through the application of the capitalized excess earnings method, which was discussed previously in Chapter 13.
2. The individual revaluation of all of the company's assets and liabilities. We call this analysis the asset accumulation method. This method is the subject of the present chapter.

In order to illustrate the practical differences between these two asset-based approach methods, the following discussion will compare and contrast (1) the capitalized excess earnings method and (2) the asset accumulation method.

Capitalized Excess Earnings Method—Collective Revaluation

In the *capitalized excess earnings method*, the revaluation of all of the company's assets and liabilities is made—in the aggregate—and in one analysis. Depending on the particular analytical procedure used, this collective revaluation quantifies all of the incremental value over and above either (1) the book value or (2) the fair market value of the subject's net tangible assets. In the capitalized excess earnings method, the company's intangible value in the nature of goodwill is equal to the appreciation (or depreciation) in the total value of the company above and beyond the value of the company net tangible assets.

In this collective revaluation analysis, the value of the company equity is (1) the value of the net tangible assets plus (2) the value of the total intangible value, in the nature of goodwill. This total intangible value (or total appreciation in the value of the business over net tangible asset value) is usually quantified using the capitalized excess earnings method, which was presented in Chapter 13.

From the perspective of the asset-based approach, the capitalized excess earnings method is the collective application of the principle of revaluing all of the subject's assets and liabilities from their cost basis to the appropriate standard of value.

Asset Accumulation Method—Individual Revaluation

In the asset accumulation method, all of the subject's individual asset and liability account categories are analyzed and valued separately. This method involves a separate identification and individual revaluation of the company's:

1. Financial asset account categories (e.g., cash, accounts receivables, prepaid expenses, inventory).
2. Tangible personal property (e.g., machinery and equipment, furniture and fixtures, trucks and automobiles).
3. Real estate (e.g., land, land improvements, buildings, building improvements).
4. Intangible real property (e.g., leasehold interests, easements, mineral exploitation rights, air and water rights, development rights, and so on).
5. Intangible personal property (e.g., patents, trademarks, copyrights, computer software, trade secrets, customer relationships, going-concern value, goodwill, and so on).
6. Current liability account categories (e.g., accounts payable, taxes payable, salaries payable, accrued expenses, and so on).

7. Long-term liability account categories (e.g., bonds, notes, mortgages, and debentures payable, and so on).
8. Contingent liabilities (e.g., pending tax disputes, pending litigation, pending environmental concerns, and so on).
9. Special obligations (e.g., unfunded pensions, earned vacations or other leaves of absence, ESOP repurchase liabilities, and so on).

In the asset accumulation method, the value of the individual assets (both tangible and intangible) less the value of the liabilities (both recorded and contingent) represents the subject business value. Theoretically and practically, the business value concluded under the collective revaluation method (i.e., the capitalized excess earnings method) should equal the business value concluded under the individual revaluation method (i.e., the asset accumulation method).

The determination of which asset-based method to use in a given valuation engagement should be a function of:

1. The experience and judgment of the analyst.
2. The quantity and quality of available data.
3. The purpose and objective of the valuation.
4. The scope, budget, and timing of the valuation assignment.

As will be discussed below, there are both costs and benefits associated with the use of the asset accumulation method vis-à-vis the use of the capitalized excess earnings method.

Combining Elements of Asset Accumulation Method and Capitalized Excess Earnings Method

Sometimes it is only practical to revalue some of—but not all of—the company's individual assets and liabilities. In these instances, it is possible to combine elements of the asset accumulation method and the capitalized excess earnings method.

The asset accumulation method may be used to quantify a portion of the business value, based on the asset/liability accounts that it is practical to revalue. The capitalized excess earnings method may then be used to "finish the job." That is, the capitalized excess earnings method may be used to quantify the remaining portion of the business value, based on an analysis of the remaining intangible value that was not already identified by the asset accumulation method.

In this combination of asset-based methods, those assets and liabilities that can be individually revalued are individually revalued. The value-basis balance sheet at this point would then have some accounts stated at current value and some accounts still stated at historical cost.

The capitalized excess earnings method is then applied at this point. The result of this capitalized excess earnings analysis is an indication of the remaining business enterprise value that has not already been captured in the revaluation of the individual asset/liability accounts. When using elements of both the asset accumulation method and the capitalized excess earnings method in the same valuation, the analyst should pay particular attention to the selection of (1) the required rates of return and (2) the capitalization rates used in the excess earnings component of the valuation. When selecting the required rates of return and the capitalization rates to apply to the company "excess earnings," the analyst should consider the extent to which the excess earnings are (1) the result of revalued assets and (2) the result of assets still recorded on the value-basis balance sheet at their historical cost.

This combination of the two asset-based methods is sometimes used when the analyst has current appraisals of some asset categories available—but not of all asset categories. For example, the subject company may have current appraisals of its real estate—but not of its machinery and equipment. This combination of the two methods is sometimes used when it is possible for the analyst to value some of the subject company's discrete intangible assets (e.g., computer software) but not other of the company's intangibles (e.g., trademarks or contractual relationships).

If this combination of both asset-based approach methods is properly applied, it should conclude the same business value indication as would be concluded from either (1) the asset accumulation method or (2) the capitalized excess earnings method. Of course, the components of value will be different from those in the separate application of either method. For example, there may be a different attribution of value between tangible assets and intangible assets in the different methods. But, the final result of the analysis—that is, the estimate of business owners' equity value—should be essentially the same regardless of which asset-based method is used.

The collective capitalized excess earnings method of the asset-based approach was discussed in detail in Chapter 13. The remainder of this chapter will focus on the discrete revaluation method—or the asset accumulation method—of the asset-based approach.

Asset Accumulation Method Procedures

This section lists and briefly discusses the practical application of the asset accumulation method, as divided into the following six procedures:

1. Obtain or develop a cost-basis balance sheet.
2. Determine which assets and liabilities on the cost-basis balance sheet require a revaluation adjustment.
3. Identify off–balance sheet intangible assets or contingent assets that should be recognized and valued.
4. Identify off–balance sheet or contingent liabilities that should be recognized and valued.
5. Estimate the value of the various asset and liability accounts identified in steps 2 through 4.
6. Construct a value-basis balance sheet, based on the indicated values concluded during steps 1 through 5, and quantify the subject value.

Obtain or Develop a Cost-Basis Balance Sheet

First, the analyst starts with the subject business cost-basis balance sheet. Ideally, the cost-basis balance sheet will be prepared in accordance with GAAP. Also ideally, this balance sheet will be prepared as of the valuation date. If a cost-basis balance sheet is not available because the valuation is conducted as of an interim date, the analyst has three options:

1. The client (or an accountant retained by the client) may prepare a cost-basis balance sheet as of the valuation date and give it to the analyst.

2. The analyst may prepare a cost-basis balance sheet as of the valuation date from the company's trial balance or general ledger, assuming that the analyst has the requisite basic accounting expertise to prepare such a financial statement.

3. The analyst may rely on the most recent cost-basis balance sheet prepared at the fiscal period end prior to the valuation date. Typically, a recent fiscal period end balance sheet will require more revaluation adjustments than a valuation date balance sheet. However, using a recent fiscal period end balance sheet is usually better than not having a balance sheet to start with at all.

Identify Assets and Liabilities to Be Revalued

Second, the analyst will carefully analyze and understand each material asset account and liability account recorded on the subject company financial statements. The objective of this analysis is to determine which recorded assets and liabilities will need to be revalued—based on (1) materiality and (2) the selected standard of value appropriate for the subject business valuation.

As a convention throughout the remainder of this discussion, we will assume that fair market value is the appropriate standard of value for the subject business valuation. Accordingly, in this step, the analyst will decide which asset accounts and liability accounts on the company financial statements should be revalued in order to estimate fair market value.

Identify Off–Balance Sheet Assets

Third, the analyst will identify which unrecorded (sometimes called "off–balance sheet") assets need to be recognized on the value-basis balance sheet. For example, intangible assets are not normally recorded on financial statements prepared under GAAP. However, they often represent the largest component of overall business enterprise value in many industries.

The company's tangible and intangible assets represent the allocation of the elements of the overall business value into specific assets. They represent the identification of the specific factors (i.e., the specific asset accounts or asset categories) responsible for the company's earning capacity, cash flow–generating capacity, and dividend-paying capacity. Intangible assets created internally by a company normally do not appear on the balance sheet. Usually intangible assets are only recorded on the balance sheet if they are acquired in a purchase.

Some tangible assets may have been expensed rather than capitalized when they were acquired. Other tangible assets may be fully depreciated (and "written off") on the financial statements, even though they still have a remaining useful life and a considerable economic value (e.g., tools, dies, molds). For these reasons, the analyst should look for unrecorded tangible assets as well as for unrecorded intangible assets.

Identify Off–Balance Sheet and Contingent Liabilities

Fourth, the analyst will identify which unrecorded material contingent liabilities, if any, need to be recognized on the value-based balance sheet. If there are potential environmental liabilities, a specialized expert opinion may be needed.

Under GAAP accounting, contingent liabilities are typically not recorded on a cost-basis balance sheet. However, in audited and reviewed financial statements, material contingent liabilities are usually discussed in the explanatory footnotes to the financial statements.

Compared with the valuation of intangible assets, the identification and valuation of contingent liabilities is a relatively less common step in the asset accumulation method. This is only because not all businesses have material contingent liabilities. However, the analyst should consider this procedure in each application of the asset accumulation method.

Certainly, for those companies that have material pending litigation against them, income or property tax claims against them, environmental claims against them, and so forth, these contingent liabilities have a significant (and often quantifiable) effect on the risk of the business. Therefore, these material contingent liabilities may have a significant effect on the business enterprise value.

Value the Accounts Identified Above

Fifth, after (1) the analysis of recorded assets and liabilities and (2) the identification of unrecorded assets and liabilities, the analyst will begin the quantitative process of revaluing each of the asset accounts and, if necessary, each of the liability accounts.

Typically, the analyst will perform these valuation analyses by category of assets. The standard categories of assets for purposes of applying the asset accumulation method are: (1) financial assets, (2) tangible personal property, (3) real estate, (4) intangible real property, and (5) intangible personal property. For some of these asset categories, the analyst may need to rely on specialized asset appraisal experts.

The general valuation approaches, methods, and procedures for appraising these asset categories (and the individual tangible and intangible assets) will be summarized later in this chapter.

Construct a Value-Basis Balance Sheet

Sixth, after estimating the defined value for all of the individual tangible and intangible assets—the analyst will construct a value-basis balance sheet, as of the valuation date.

From this value-basis (as opposed to cost-basis) balance sheet, it is a simple procedure to subtract the value of the company's liabilities (recorded and contingent) from the value of the company's assets (tangible and intangible). The remainder of this subtraction procedure is the value of a 100 percent interest in the company owners' equity. This value indication is typically related to a marketable, controlling ownership level of value.

At this point, the asset accumulation method has indicated the value of the total owners' equity of the company. Of course, if the company has several classes of equity securities outstanding, additional valuation and value allocation procedures may be required.

In addition, if the subject valuation assignment relates to something less than the overall business value (e.g., to a particular class of securities or to nonmarketable or noncontrolling ownership interest levels of value), then additional valuation discount analyses may be required.

Premise of Value for Individual Assets

Before considering the various valuation methods with respect to the individual assets of a company, the analyst should first consider both (1) the appropriate standard of value and (2) the appropriate premise of value for each asset category. Usually (but not always), the appropriate standard of value selected for each asset category is the same as the standard of value selected for the overall business valuation.

Also, before the individual assets are valued, analysts should consider which premise of value to apply in the asset valuation process. Presumably, the analyst has already determined the appropriate premise of value with regard to the overall business valuation. This determination is made when the analyst considers the highest and best use of the business interest subject to valuation.

However, the highest and best use for the individual business assets may be different from the highest and best use of the overall business enterprise. Therefore, the most appropriate premise of value for the individual business assets may be different from the appropriate premise of value for the overall business enterprise. For individual asset valuation purposes, each of the premises of value may apply to each of the standards of value.

The standard of value answers the general question "value to whom?" The premise of value answers the general question "value under what set of hypothetical transactional conditions?" For example, under the same fair market value standard of value, the same asset category may be appraised under each of several alternative premises of value.

Under the fair market value standard, the question of "value to whom?" is answered by "a hypothetical willing buyer and a hypothetical willing seller." The selected premise of value answers the question "in what type of market transaction will these two willing parties interact?"

The alternative premises of value for individual asset valuation are (1) value in continued use, as part of a going concern; (2) value in place, as part of a mass assemblage of assets; (3) value in exchange, in an orderly disposition; and (4) value in exchange, in a forced liquidation.

Value in Continued Use, as Part of a Going Concern

Under this premise, it is assumed that the subject assets are sold as a mass assemblage and as part of an income-producing business enterprise.

This premise of value contemplates the mutually synergistic relationships (i.e., the value enhancement) (1) of the company's tangible assets to the intangible assets and (2) of the company's intangible assets to the tangible assets.

Value in Place, as Part of a Mass Assemblage of Assets

Under this premise, it is assumed that the subject assets are sold as a mass assemblage. And it is assumed that the mass assemblage is capable of being, but is not currently operating as, an income-producing business enterprise.

This premise of value contemplates some of the mutual contributory value (i.e., value enhancement) (1) of the tangible assets to the intangible assets and (2) of the intangible assets to the tangible assets. However, while there is a value in place component to the subject assets, this premise may exclude some of the contributory value of such common intangible assets as a trained and assembled workforce, going-concern value, and intangible value in the nature of goodwill.

Value in Exchange, in an Orderly Disposition

Under this premise, it is assumed that the subject assets are sold piecemeal, and not as part of a mass assemblage. It is assumed that the assets are given an adequate level of exposure in their normal secondary market.

However, due to the orderly disposition market transaction assumption, this premise does not contemplate any contributory value effect of the subject tangible assets on the intangible assets or of the subject intangible assets on the tangible assets.

Value in Exchange, in a Forced Liquidation

Under this premise, it is assumed that the subject assets are sold piecemeal, and not as part of a mass assemblage. It is also assumed that the assets are not allowed a normal level of exposure to their normal secondary market. Rather, the assets are permitted an abbreviated level of exposure to a market of the highest bidders present (who may or may not represent the collective demand-side marketplace for such assets), such as in an auction environment.

Due to the forced liquidation market transaction assumption, this premise assumes no contributory value (or other economic interrelationships) from the subject tangible assets to the subject intangible assets, or vice versa.

Selecting the Appropriate Premise of Value

Any of the four premises of value may be applied to the same asset (or asset category) under the same standard of value. For example, an analyst may apply the fair market value standard and then assume that a willing buyer and a willing seller will transact to exchange an asset (i.e., a value in exchange premise).

The selected premise of value describes the assumed market conditions under which this willing buyer and willing seller will meet and transact—that is, (1) during the sale of a going-concern business, (2) during the sale of a temporarily closed business, (3) during the brokered sale of individual assets, or (4) during the auction sale of individual assets.

The analyst will select the appropriate premise of value for the individual asset valuation (1) based on the purpose and objective of the business valuation, and (2) based on the most likely form of the ultimate sale of the subject business assets.

Two other factors influence the selection of the appropriate premise of value for the individual asset valuations:

1. *The actual condition and operation of the subject assets.* That is, the analyst should ascertain whether the subject assets are actually in use, in place, or held out for sale (either in an orderly disposition or in a forced liquidation environment).
2. *The highest and best use of the subject assets.* That is, the analyst should select the premise of value that will result in the greatest estimated value for the subject individual business assets.

Needless to say, the selection of the appropriate premise of value is an important decision in the application of the asset accumulation method. This is because, even under the same standard of value, the subject business can have materially different values—based on the premise selected for valuing the individual business.

Individual Asset Valuation Procedures

After the appropriate premise of value is selected, the next step in the asset accumulation method is to value each individual asset category.

The conceptual cornerstone of the asset accumulation method is the identification and valuation of all of the company's assets. This includes the financial assets, the tangible assets (real and personal), and the intangible assets (real and personal).

In Chapter 7, the procedures related to adjusting the balance sheet were discussed. Those adjustment procedures should be considered when analyzing the company's balance sheet in preparation for the application of *any* business valuation approach or method. The procedures discussed below are individual asset valuation procedures, as compared with common balance sheet adjustment procedures. Each of these asset valuation procedures should be considered when using the asset accumulation method.

Since this is not a text devoted to individual asset valuation, this discussion will be introductory in nature. Valuation analysts who desire a more detailed description of individual asset valuation procedures should consult the many specialized textbooks related to real estate appraisal, machinery and equipment appraisal, intangible asset appraisal, and so forth. A sampling of these books may be found in the bibliography at the end of this chapter.

Financial Assets

The most common assets included in this category include cash, accounts and notes receivable, and prepaid expenses.

With regard to cash, no revaluation procedures need to be performed, of course.

In the sale of a business, it is common for the seller to retain some or all of the cash balances on hand. This is true in a transaction involving the sale of stock as well as in a transaction involving the sale of assets. Accordingly, in a transactional valuation, the analyst should verify the amount of cash, if any, that will actually be transferred with the business enterprise.

With regard to accounts and notes receivable, the analyst may estimate the net realizable value of these receivables. The net realizable value is, essentially, the present value of the expected realization of (i.e., collection of) the receivables.

For businesses with audited or reviewed financial statements (or more sophisticated accounting systems), a reserve for uncollectible accounts is typically established as a contra-asset valuation account. Particularly if the valuation date is other than a fiscal period end, the analyst may assess the adequacy of this reserve for uncollectible accounts. For businesses that have not established reserves for uncollectible accounts, the analyst may assess the ultimate collectibility of the gross receivables. Based on this assessment of historical collection patterns, the analyst may revalue the gross accounts receivable in order to conclude an estimate of net cash collections. Finally, if the expected realization of the receivables is anticipated to occur over an extended period of time (i.e., longer than the normal collection cycle) the analyst also may apply a present value analysis to the longer-term receivables.

The net balance of the accounts and notes receivable, after the analysis for uncollectible accounts and the present value of extended period receivables (if applicable), represents the net realizable value of this asset category.

With regard to prepaid expenses, the analyst may estimate the net realizable value of this asset category. Prepaid expenses typically include deposits and prepaid rent, insurance, utilities expenses, and so forth.

Normally, the business will realize the economic benefit of these assets within the normal course of one business cycle. Therefore, normally, no revaluation adjustment is required with respect to recorded prepaid expenses. However, if the analyst determines that the company will not enjoy an economic benefit from a prepaid expense during a normal business cycle, then a revaluation adjustment may be appropriate. For example, if the company has recorded prepaid rent expense on a facility it is no longer using, that asset will likely have little economic value. The expected realization of the prepaid expenses represents the net realizable value of this asset category.

Real Estate

Real estate includes such assets as owned land, land improvements, buildings, and building improvements.

Technically, in the appraisal literature, real estate represents the tangible element of real property ownership. Real estate is distinguished from intangible real property. Intangible real property represents the bundle of legal rights associated with real estate. For example, a real property interest would be a limited legal interest (i.e., less than a fee simple ownership interest)—such as a leasehold estate—in real estate.

There is a prodigious body of literature with respect to the valuation of real estate. And, both the appraisal regulatory agencies and the various professional appraisal organizations have promulgated professional standards with respect to its valuation.

All real estate is valued by reference to three generally accepted appraisal approaches: (1) the cost approach, (2) the income capitalization approach, and (3) the sales comparison approach. Each of these three approaches represents a general category of several discrete appraisal methods. Each of these approaches is described briefly below.

Cost Approach. The cost approach is based on the economic principle of substitution. That is, no one would pay more for an asset than the price required to obtain (by purchase or by construction) a substitute asset of comparable utility. This assumes, of course, that the subject asset is fungible. In other words, the cost approach assumes that substitute properties of comparable utility may be obtained. If, in fact, the subject asset is unique in one or more respects, the cost approach may not be a viable valuation approach.

Using the cost approach, the value of land is valued separately from the value of all appurtenances to land. The subject land is valued as if vacant and unimproved. The subject land is also valued at its highest and best use. The value of vacant land is typically estimated by reference to the sale of comparable land parcels in the reasonably proximate marketplace.

The analyst collects and analyzes data with respect to recent sales of vacant land parcels. If necessary, quantitative adjustments are made for important factors such as size, access, services, frontage, topography, instance, time of sale, and special terms of sale. Based on an analysis of these adjusted comparable property sales data, the analyst estimates the value of the subject land.

The subject buildings and improvements are valued by reference to the current cost to recreate their functional utility. There are several commonly used cost approach methods. One of the common methods is the depreciated reproduction cost method. This method is described as follows:

	Reproduction cost new of buildings and improvements
Less:	Allowances for incurable functional obsolescence
Equals:	Replacement cost
Less:	Allowance for physical deterioration
Equals:	Depreciated replacement cost
Less:	Allowance for external obsolescence
Less:	Allowances for curable functional obsolescence
Indicates:	Market value of buildings and improvements

To complete the cost approach, the value of the land is added to the value of the buildings and improvements. The sum of these two values indicates the market value of the subject real estate.

Income Capitalization Approach. The income capitalization approach is based on the economic principles of (1) risk and expected return investment analysis and (2) anticipation. Using this approach, the value of the real estate is the present value of the expected economic income that could be earned through the ownership of the property.

There are two categories of valuation methods under the income capitalization approach: (1) the direct capitalization method and (2) the yield capitalization method. From an investment analysis perspective, these two methods are conceptually similar. Therefore, from a theoretical perspective, both methods should conclude essentially the same value for the same real estate parcel.

Using the direct capitalization method, the analyst first estimates the normalized level of economic income that would be earned from the rental (whether hypothetical or actual) of the subject real estate. Economic income may be defined many ways (i.e., before tax, after tax, before interest expense, after interest expense, and so on). However it is important to note that the level of income that is included in the direct capitalization analysis is the income related to the ownership of the real estate only—and not the income related to the operation of the business that occupies the real estate. In other words, the level of income that should be included in the analysis is a hypothetical real estate lessor's income—not the business operating income of the actual property owner/operator.

The most common definition of economic income used in the direct capitalization method of real estate valuation is (before-tax) net operating income. This estimate of economic income is normalized to represent an average or typical period's rental income (including normal repairs, maintenance, etc.).

The normalized economic income is capitalized, typically, as an annuity in perpetuity. The capitalization rate used in this procedure should be (1) commensurate with the risk of investment and (2) consistent with the measurement of economic income. For example, if projected economic income is measured on an after-tax basis, the capitalization rate should be derived on an after-tax basis. If economic income is measured before tax, the capitalization rate should be derived before tax, and so forth.

Consistent with the definition of economic income as before-tax net operating income, the most common derivation of the direct capitalization rate is a blended debt and equity rate (or a weighted average cost of capital). The capitalization rate should be the blended cost of capital related to the subject property, and not the blended cost of capital related to the business that is the owner/operator of the property. The appropriate real estate valuation capitalization rate considers the mortgage interest in the property, the replacement rate of return to a real estate investor, and the loan-to-value ratio appropriate to a mortgage on the subject property. The capitalization rate should not consider the cost of debt, the cost of equity, or the capital structure of the business that is the owner/operator of the property.

The equity component of this blended rate represents the typical real estate investor's current income yield expectation for similar rental properties. It excludes the investor's derived long-term capital appreciation expectation for the subject property. The debt component of this blended rate represents the typical mortgage debt rate for similar rental properties. It includes a yield component for the amortization of mortgage principal as well as the payment of mortgage interest.

The debt component and the equity component are blended, or weighted together, based on the typical loan-to-value ratio for new mortgages offered on comparable real estate properties. The result of this analysis is the direct capitalization rate.

Using the direct capitalization method, the value of the real estate is presented algebraically, as follows:

$$\text{Value} = \frac{\text{Normalized economic income}}{\text{Direct capitalization rate}}$$

Using the yield capitalization method, the value of the subject real estate is the present value of the projected economic income to be derived from the property over a discrete period of time. While there is no universally correct projection period, discrete projection periods of from 5 to 10 years are common. These projection periods usually correspond to the typical investment holding period for institutional real estate investors.

The analyst projects the economic income to be derived from the rental of the subject property for each year in the discrete projection period. Again, before-tax net operating income is the most common measurement of economic income.

The analyst next derives a present value discount rate to calculate the present value of the discrete projection of economic income. This present value discount rate is often called the *going-in capitalization rate*. The analyst then estimates the normalized economic income to be generated by the property after the conclusion of the discrete projection period. This is sometimes called an estimate of the residual value (or reversionary period) income. This is the average or typical level of income to be generated by the property after the end of the projection period.

The analyst next derives a capitalization rate consistent with the estimate of residual value (or reversionary period) income. This rate is often called the *residual (or reversionary) capitalization rate.* It is sometimes called the *coming-out capitalization rate*. The coming-out capitalization rate is often different from the going-in capitalization rate due to the changing relative remaining life of the property and the different risk positions of the two investment periods.

The estimate of residual normalized economic income is capitalized by the residual capitalization rate. The result is the estimated value of the property at the end of the discrete projection period. This residual value is brought back to its present value, using the discrete projection period present value discount rate.

Finally, under the income capitalization approach, the value of the real estate is the sum of discrete projection period present value plus the residual value present value.

Sales Comparison Approach. The sales comparison approach is based on the economic principles of (1) efficient markets and (2) supply and demand. That is, when there is a relatively efficient and unrestricted secondary market for comparable properties and when that market accurately depicts the activities of a representative number of willing buyers and willing sellers, the market is most determinative of the value of the subject property.

Using the sales comparison approach, the analyst first collects data with regard to relatively recent sales of comparable real estate properties. Next, the analyst analyzes each of these sale transactions to determine if any quantitative adjustments are necessary due to the lack of comparability of the subject property when compared with the comparable properties.

The analyst considers these factors, among others, when determining if quantitative adjustments to the sales comparison data are necessary:

1. Age of each transaction (i.e., elapsed time from the valuation date).
2. Land-to-building ratio of each property.
3. Absolute location and relative location of each property in relation to population centers, highways, and so forth.
4. Age of each property.
5. Physical condition of each property.
6. Municipal and other services available to each property.
7. Frontage and access of each property.
8. Topography of land and soil type of each comparable property.
9. Environmental aspects of each property.
10. Special financing or other terms regarding each sales transaction.

Accordingly, if necessary, the analyst adjusts the sales comparison data to make each transaction as comparable to the subject property as possible. Based on these adjusted sales comparison data, the analyst will conclude a market-derived pricing multiple. This pricing multiple is often expressed in terms of price per square foot of improved building space. Next, the analyst applies the market-derived pricing multiple to the size characteristics of the subject property. The resulting product is the estimate of value of the real estate according to the sales comparison approach.

Final Value Reconciliation. To reach a final valuation synthesis and conclusion regarding the real estate, the analyst will carefully consider the quantitative results of each of the valuation approaches used. In reaching the valuation conclusion, the analyst will consider the quantity and quality of available data used in each approach. The analyst will also assess the appropriate degree of confidence in the applicability and validity of each approach with respect to unique characteristics of the subject real estate. Based on these factors, the analyst will synthesize the results of each approach and conclude an overall value for the real estate.

Tangible Personal Property

The tangible personal property category of assets includes inventory, office furniture and fixtures, computer and office automation equipment, store racks and fixtures, manufacturing machinery and equipment, processing equipment, tools and dies, trucks and automobiles, and material handling and transportation equipment.

There is a considerable body of literature with regard to the appraisal of industrial and commercial tangible personal property. There is also authoritative literature regarding the appraisal of special-purpose and technical tangible personal property, such as scientific and laboratory equipment, medical and healthcare equipment, mining and extraction equipment, and so forth.

All of the various tangible personal property valuation methods and procedures can be grouped into three approaches: (1) the cost approach, (2) the income approach, and (3) the market approach.

Inventory. With regard to inventory, the analyst should distinguish between (1) the work-in-process inventory of a professional services firm (e.g., accounting firms, law firms, and so on) and (2) the merchandise inventory of a manufacturer/processor or of a wholesale/retail company.

The work-in-process inventory of a professional services firm is essentially the unbilled receivables of the firm. Therefore, the same net realizable value rules discussed with respect to accounts and notes receivable would apply to this asset as well. With regard to tangible merchandise inventory, there are three common valuation methods: (1) the cost of reproduction method, (2) the comparative sales method, and (3) the income method. These valuation methods apply equally to raw material, work-in-process, and finished goods inventory.

While these three inventory valuation methods are discussed elsewhere in the valuation literature, they are concisely summarized in Internal Revenue Service Revenue Procedure 77-12.[1]

Revenue Procedure 77-12 (presented in Exhibit 14–1) was originally issued with respect to the valuation of merchandise inventory for purchase price allocation purposes. Nonetheless, these valuation methods provide reasonable guidance for the appraisal of merchandise inventory as part of a business valuation, as well.

The cost of reproduction method generally provides a good indication of fair market value if the inventory is readily replaceable in the volume and in the mix equal to the subject quantity on hand. In valuing inventory under this method, however, other factors may be relevant. For example, a well-balanced inventory available to fill customers' orders in the ordinary course of business may have a fair market value in excess of its cost of reproduction. This is because such an inventory provides a continuity of business. However, an inventory containing obsolete merchandise unsuitable for customers may have a fair market value of less than the cost of reproduction.

The comparative sales method uses the actual or expected selling prices of finished goods to customers as a basis of determining the fair market value of that inventory. When the expected selling price is used as a basis for valuing inventory, consideration should be given to the time that would be required to dispose of this inventory, the expenses that would be expected to be incurred in such disposition, applicable discounts (including those for quantity), sales commissions, and freight and shipping charges, and a profit commensurate with the amount of investment and degree of risk.

---

[1] Rev. Proc. 77-12, 1977-1 C.B. 569.

Exhibit 14–1

Revenue Procedure 77-12

26 CFR 601.105: Examination of returns and claims for refund, credit or abatement; determination of correct tax liability. (Also Part I, Section 334; 1.334-1.)

Rev Proc. 77-12

SECTION 1. PURPOSE.

The purpose of this Revenue Procedure is to set forth guidelines for use by taxpayers and Service personnel in making fair market value determinations in situations where a corporation purchases the assets of a business containing inventory items for a lump sum or where a corporation acquires assets including inventory items by the liquidation of a subsidiary pursuant to the provisions of section 332 of the Internal Revenue Code of 1954 and the basis of the inventory received in liquidation is determined under section 334(b) (2). These guidelines are designed to assist taxpayers and Service personnel in assigning a fair market value to such assets.

SEC. 2. BACKGROUND.

If the asets of a business are purchased for a lump sum, or if the stock of a corporation is purchased and that corporation is liquidated under section 332 of the Code and the basis is determined under section 334(b) (2), the purchase price must be allocated among the assets acquired to determine the basis of each of such assets. In making such determinations, it is necessary to determine the fair market value of any inventory items involved. This Revenue Procedure describes methods that may be used to determine the fair market value of inventory items.

In determining the fair market value of inventory under the situations set forth in this Revenue Procedure, the amount of inventory generally would be different from the amounts usually purchased. In addition, the goods in process and finished goods on hand must be considered in light of what a willing purchaser would pay and a willing seller would accept for the inventory at the various stages of completion, when the former is not under any compulsion to buy and the latter is not under any compulsion to sell,

both parties having reasonable knowledge of relevant facts.

SEC. 3. PROCEDURES FOR DETERMINATION OF FAIR MARKET VALUE.

Three basic methods an appraiser may use to determine the fair market value of inventory are the cost of reproduction method, the comparative sales method, and the income method. All methods of valuation are based on one or a combination of these three methods.

.01 The cost of reproduction method generally provides a good indication of fair market value if inventory is readily replaceable in a wholesale or retail business, but generally should not be used in establishing the fair market value of the finished goods of a manufacturing concern. In valuing a particular inventory under this method, however, other factors may be relevant. For example, a well balanced inventory available to fill customers' orders in the ordinary course of business may have a fair market value in excess of its cost of reproduction because it provides a continuity of business, whereas an inventory containing obsolete merchandise unsuitable for customers might have a fair market value of less than the cost of reproduction.

.02 The comparative sales method utilizes the actual or expected selling prices of finished goods to customers as a basis of determining fair market values of those finished goods. When the expected selling price is used as a basis for valuing finished goods inventory, consideration should be given to the time that would be required to dispose of this inventory, the expenses that would be expected to be incurred in such disposition, for example, all costs of disposition, applicable discounts (including those for quantity), sales commissions, and freight and shipping charges, and a profit commensurate with the amount of investment and degree of risk. It should also be recognized that the inventory to be valued may represent a larger quantity than the normal trading volume and the expected selling price can be a valid starting point only if customers' orders are filled in the ordinary course of business.

.03 The income method, when applied to fair market value determinations for finished goods, recognizes that finished goods must generally be valued in a profit motivated business. Since the amount of inventory may be large in relation to normal trading volume the highest and best use of the inventory will be to provide for a continuity of the marketing operation of the going business. Additionally, the finished goods inventory will usually provide the only source of revenue of an acquired business during the period it is being used to fill customers' orders. The historical financial data of an acquired company can be used to determine the amount that could be attributed to finished goods in order to pay all costs of disposition and provide a return on the investment during the period of disposition.

.04 The fair market value of work in process should be based on the same factors used to determine the fair market value of finished goods reduced by the expected costs of completion, including a reasonable profit allowance for the completion and selling effort of the acquiring corporation. In determining the fair market value of raw materials, the current costs of replacing the inventory in the quantities to be valued generally provides the most reliable standard.

SEC.4 CONCLUSION.

Because valuing inventory is an inherently factual determination, no rigid formulas can be applied. Consequently, the methods outlined above can only serve as guidelines for determining the fair market value of inventories.

SOURCE: Rev. Proc. 77-12, 1977-1 C.B. 569.

Whether the quantity of inventory to be valued is a larger than normal trading volume should also be recognized. Also, the expected selling price can be a valid starting point only if customers' orders are filled in the ordinary course of business.

The income method, when applied to the fair market value estimation of inventory, recognizes that inventory should generally be valued in a profit-motivated business. Since the amount of inventory may be large in relation to the normal trading volume, the highest and best use of the inventory will be to provide for a continuity of the marketing operation of the going-concern business.

Additionally, the inventory will usually provide the only source of revenue of the subject business during the period it is being used to fill customers' orders. The historical financial data of the company can be used to estimate the amount that could be attributed to inventory in order to pay all costs of disposition and provide a return on the investment during the period of disposition.

The analyst will apply one or more of these inventory valuation methods (1) based on the quantity and quality of available data and (2) based on the most likely ultimate disposition of the subject inventory. The analyst will estimate the value of the subject inventory based on the results of these inventory valuation methods.

Other Tangible Personal Property. The conceptual underpinnings of the cost approach for tangible personal property are essentially identical to those for real estate. Again, the cost approach is based on the economic principle of substitution. Particularly with respect to tangible personal property, a willing buyer will pay no more to a willing seller than the cost associated with replacing the subject with an asset of comparable functional utility.

As with real estate, there are several common cost approach methods. These methods include the depreciated reproduction cost method, the depreciated replacement cost method, the creation cost method, and the recreation cost method.

For special-purpose tangible personal property (which may experience a considerable amount of incurable obsolescence), the depreciated reproduction cost method is a common valuation method. However, for most general-purpose tangible personal property, the depreciated replacement cost method is the more common valuation method.

The depreciated replacement cost method for tangible personal property is presented algebraically below:

	Replacement cost new
Less:	Allowance for physical deterioration
Equals:	Depreciated replacement cost
Less:	Allowance for external obsolescence
Less:	Allowance for curable functional and technological obsolescence
Indicates:	Fair market value

If the subject asset is no longer produced, the replacement cost of the most comparable available substitute asset is used as the starting point in the cost approach (and, specifically, in the depreciated replacement cost method).

Using the income approach, the value of the tangible personal property is often quantified as the present value of the rental income from the hypothetical rental of the subject property over its remaining useful life.

First the analyst estimates the remaining useful life of the subject asset. This is typically the shortest of the asset's remaining physical, functional, technological, or economic lives.

Second, the analyst estimates a fair rental rate for the subject asset. This gross rental income is reduced by insurance, maintenance, and other expenses that are the responsibility of the lessor. The result is a projection of the net rental income (real or hypothetical) to be derived from the subject asset over the asset's expected remaining life.

Next, the analyst derives an appropriate present value discount rate. This discount rate is intended to provide for a fair, risk-adjusted rate of return to the property lessor over the term of the lease. The present value of the projected rental income over the expected remaining life of the property represents the value of the subject asset, per the income approach. (Since tangible personal property has a finite life, analysts typically do not have to consider a residual value to tangible personal property—as would be appropriate with regard to real estate.)

Using the market approach, the value of the subject asset is the price that it would command in its appropriate secondary market. This approach is based on the economic principle of efficient markets. It assumes that an efficient secondary market exists with regard to the exchange of the subject asset. It also assumes that reliable information is available regarding this tangible personal property exchange market.

Using this approach, the analyst first obtains data regarding secondary transactions with respect to comparable assets. Next, the analyst analyzes these data with regard to a set of reasonable comparability criteria. The market transactional data are adjusted, if necessary, to enhance their comparability and applicability to the subject asset. Based on the adjusted transactional database, the analyst selects comparable sales most indicative of a hypothetical transaction involving the subject asset. These adjusted sales data are used to indicate the value of the subject asset.

Finally, the analyst concludes an overall value of the subject asset based on a synthesis of the results of the various appraisal approaches used. Based on the analyst's perceived reliability of, and confidence in, the various approaches, the analyst will reach a final value estimate for the subject tangible personal property.

Intangible Real Property

Intangible real property assets represent intangible legal claims on tangible real estate. The type of assets encompassed by this category of assets includes leasehold interests (and various other leasehold estates), possessory interests (associated with franchise ordinances or other permits), exploration rights, air rights, water rights, land rights, mineral exploitation rights, use rights, development rights, easements (including scenic easements), and other intangible rights and privileges related to the use or exploitation of real estate. As intangible claims on real estate, the value of these assets is generally a subset of, or a derivative of, the value of the associated real estate.

As with real estate, there are many individual methods and techniques to appraise intangible real property. All of these methods can be grouped into the same three approaches: (1) the cost approach, (2) the income capitalization approach, and (3) the sales comparison approach. Each of these approaches (and some associated methods) was discussed above with respect to the value of real estate. Those general discussions will not be repeated here.

It is noteworthy, however, that the cost approach is usually not relied on to value intangible real property. Intangible real property typically represents a legal claim on the use of, exploitation of, development of, or forbearance of real estate. Accordingly, the cost of the underlying real estate is generally irrelevant to the intangible property right holder.

The income approach is typically the most widely used approach with respect to the valuation of intangible real estate interests.

The sales comparison approach also is used to value certain intangible real estate interests. For example, there is a reasonable sales transaction secondary market for certain intangible real estate interests—such as the unexpired portion of assignable, below-market industrial and commercial leases (i.e., leasehold interests).

As with the appraisal of real estate, the appraisal of intangible real property interests is based on (1) a synthesis of all available valuation data and (2) the conclusions of whatever valuation approaches were used. The analyst considers and synthesizes the results of the various valuation approaches and estimates the value for the subject intangible real property interests.

Intangible Personal Property

This discussion of the identification, valuation, and remaining life analysis of intangible assets will be somewhat cursory. There are two reasons for this. First, the topic of this book is business valuation and not intangible asset valuation. From this perspective the valuation of intangible assets is one procedure within one method (the asset accumulation method) within one approach (the asset-based approach) to business valuation. Second, there is already a substantial body of literature available on the topic of intangible asset valuation. Analysts who want to research this topic in greater detail are referred to the book, *Valuing Intangible Assets* by Robert F. Reilly and Robert P. Schweihs.[2]

Analysts experienced with intangible asset valuation could create a list of a hundred intangibles commonly found in the industrial and commercial environment. For an intangible asset to exist from an economic valuation perspective, it should posses certain attributes such as:

- It should be subject to specific identification and recognizable description.
- It should be subject to legal existence and protection.
- It should be subject to the right of private ownership, and this private ownership must be legally transferable.
- There should be some tangible evidence or manifestation of the existence of the intangible asset (e.g., a contract, a license, a document, or a registration document).
- It should have been created or have come into existence at an identifiable time or as the result of an identifiable event.
- It should be subject to being destroyed or to a termination of existence at an identifiable time or as the result of an identifiable event.

There should be a specific bundle of legal rights (and/or other natural properties) associated with the existence of an intangible asset. For an intangible asset to have a quantifiable value, it should possess certain additional attributes such as:

- It should generate some measurable amount of economic income to its owner. This economic benefit could be in the form of an income increment or a cost decrement. This economic income may be measured in any of several ways, including present value of net income, net operating income, net cash flow, and so on.

---

[2] Robert F. Reilly and Robert P. Schweihs, *Valuing Intangible Assets* (New York: McGraw-Hill, 1999).

- It should enhance the value of other assets with which it is associated; the other assets may include tangible personal property, real estate, or other intangible assets.

Categorization of Intangible Assets

Individual intangible assets are often grouped into distinct categories. Intangible assets in each category are generally similar in nature and function. Intangible assets are grouped in the same category when similar valuation and economic analysis methods apply to that group of assets. A common categorization of intangible assets follows:

- *Technology-related* (e.g., engineering drawings and technical documentation).
- *Customer-related* (e.g., customer lists and customer relationships).
- *Contract-related* (e.g., favorable supplier or other product/service contracts).
- *Data processing–related* (e.g., computer software, automated databases).
- *Human capital–related* (e.g., employment agreements, a trained and assembled workforce).
- *Marketing-related* (e.g., trademarks and trade names).
- *Location-related* (e.g., leasehold interests, certificates of need).
- *Goodwill-related* (e.g., going-concern value).
- *Engineering-related* (e.g., patents, trade secrets).
- *Literary-related* (e.g., literary copyrights, musical composition copyrights).

There is a specialized classification of intangible assets called *intellectual properties*. Intellectual properties manifest all of the legal existence and economic value attributes of other intangibles. Because of their special status, intellectual properties enjoy special legal recognition and protection.

Unlike other intangibles, which are created in the normal course of business operations, intellectual properties are created by human intellectual and/or inspirational activity. Such activity (although not always planned) is specific and conscious. Such creativity can be attributed to the activity of identified, specific individuals. Because of this unique creation process, intellectual properties are generally registered under, and protected by, specific federal and state statutes.

Like other intangibles, intellectual properties may be grouped into like categories. The intellectual properties in each category are generally similar in nature, feature, method of creation, and legal protection. Similar valuation methods would apply to the intellectual properties in each category. A common categorization of intellectual properties follows:

- Creative (e.g., copyrights).
- Innovative (e.g., patents).

Valuation of Intangible Assets

The three previously discussed valuation approaches apply equally to tangible assets and to intangible assets. However, within each approach, different methods and procedures may be appropriate to value individual intangible assets.

Market Approach. The market approach provides a systematic framework for estimating the value of an intangible asset based on an analysis of actual sale and/or license transactions of intangibles that are comparable to the object. This approach requires comparing the subject intangible to intangibles that have been listed for sale/license or have been sold/licensed in their appropriate primary or secondary markets. Correlations between actual sale/license transaction prices are also examined. The following are some of the factors considered in the selection of comparative intangible asset sale/license transactions:

- The economic income–generating capacity of the comparative intangible asset.
- The markets served by the comparable intangible.
- The historical and expected return on investment earned by the comparative intangible.
- The historical age and the expected remaining useful life of the comparable intangible.
- The time of the sale/license transaction.
- The degree of—and the future risk of—obsolescence of the comparative intangible (including physical, functional, technological, and economic obsolescence).
- Special terms and conditions of the sale/license (such as special seller financing, an earn-out agreement, noncompete agreement provision, and so on).

These comparability selection factors are analyzed separately for each intangible asset transaction. Based on any differences in these factors between the subject intangible and the comparative intangible, the comparative sale/license transactional data may need to be adjusted as appropriate.

Generally, it is difficult for analysts to use the market approach to value intangible assets. This is true for several reasons. First, discrete intangible assets are not often sold separately from other business assets. In other words, they are often (but not always) sold as part of a going-concern business. In these cases, the analyst faces the problem of allocating a lump-sum transaction price among all of the assets transferred—including the subject intangible asset. Second, more than in the case of transactions involving the sale of real estate or tangible personal property, buyers and sellers of intangible assets tend to keep actual transactional data private. So analysts face difficulty in obtaining, verifying, and confirming transactional data on the actual terms of arm's-length sales/licenses of intangible assets.

The analyst also faces the challenge of data purification and cash equivalency analysis. That is, even if the comparative intangible was sold/licensed without any accompanying fixed assets, there are often short-term servicing agreements and long-term noncompete agreements that accompany the transfer of the comparative intangible. And, if there is an earn-out or other payment terms (as is often the case with the transfer of intangible assets), the analyst has to perform a cash equivalency analysis in order to estimate the actual transaction price to be used for further analysis.

It is true that when they can be used, market approach methods are often the best methods to estimate intangible asset value. It is equally true for intangible assets as for tangible assets that an actual and active secondary market provides the best indicator of value for any asset, property, or business interest. An active secondary transfer market exists for the sale/license of many intangible assets. In these cases, the analyst may obtain verifiable transaction pricing data regarding the actual asset/license transfers of comparative intangible assets.

Some intangibles do lend themselves to the market approach. These would include situations where there are often "naked sales" of intangibles within an industry. A naked sale occurs when the subject intangible asset is sold "naked"—or separately and independently from any other tangible assets or intangible assets. For example, in the financial institution industry, bank "core deposit" accounts, loan portfolios, credit card portfolios, mortgage servicing rights, and trust customer accounts are often—in negotiated arm's-length transactions—sold separately and independently from the rest of the financial institution.

In the real estate industry, leasehold interests, possessory interests, air rights, water rights, mineral rights, other development rights, easements, and other real estate–related intangible assets are often—in an active secondary marketplace—bought and sold separately from the actual underlying real estate (and separately from any other intangible assets).

In the aviation industry, airport landing rights (sometimes called "slots" at controlled airports), airline routes, airline reservation systems, FAA licenses, aircraft parking or "tiedown" rights, and airport gate positions are frequently—in negotiated arm's-length transactions—bought and sold independently from the rest of the assets of the going-concern airline business.

In fact, many licenses and permits are sold separately from other business assets. This may include Federal Communication Commission (FCC) licenses, liquor licenses, franchise agreements, territory development agreements, certificates of need, and so forth.

Income Approach. The income approach provides a systematic framework for estimating the value of an intangible asset based on economic income capitalization or on the present value of future "economic income" to be derived from the use, forbearance, license, or rental of that intangible.

Under the income approach, *economic income* can be defined in many ways, including:

- Net income before tax.
- Net income after tax.
- Net operating income.
- Gross or net rental income.
- Gross or net royalty or license income.
- Operating cash flow.
- Net cash flow.

The income capitalization procedure can also be accomplished in several ways, including:

- Capitalizing current year's economic income.
- Capitalizing an average of several years' economic income.
- Capitalizing a normalized or stabilized period's economic income.
- Projecting prospective economic income over a discrete time period and estimating a present value.

Quantifying the appropriate direct capitalization rate or present value discount rate is an essential element of the income approach. The appropriate direct capitalization rate or present value discount rate should reflect a fair return on the stakeholders' investment in the subject intangible. In selecting the rate, the analyst should consider the following:

- The opportunity cost of capital (i.e., expected return on alternative investments).
- The time value of money (including consideration of a real rate of return and the expected inflation rate over the investment time horizon).

- The term of the investment (including consideration of the expected remaining useful life of the subject intangible asset).
- The risk of the investment.

The most important factor with regard to estimating the appropriate direct capitalization rate or present value discount rate is that the selected rate must be consistent with the measurement of economic income used. For example, a before-tax capitalization rate should be applied to a before-tax measurement of economic income. An after-tax capitalization rate should be applied to an after-tax measurement of economic income. An economic income stream representing a return to stockholders only should be capitalized by a rate based on a cost of equity capital only. An economic income stream representing a return to all stakeholders (i.e., both debt holders and equity holders) should be capitalized by a rate based upon a blended—or weighted average—cost of debt and equity capital.

There are many ways to assign an economic income stream to a particular intangible. With regard to intangible assets, economic income can be derived from two categories of sources: (1) increments to revenue or (2) decrements to cost. From a valuation perspective, either source of economic income is a valid contributor to the value of the subject intangible.

With regard to incremental revenue, certain intangibles may allow the asset owner or licenser to sell more products (than otherwise), sell products at a higher average selling price, gain a larger market share, enjoy a monopolistic market position, ensure a relatively sure source of recurring customers, ensure a relatively sure source of future business, generate add-on or renewal business, develop new markets, introduce new products, and so on.

With regard to decremental costs, certain intangibles may allow the asset owner or licenser to incur lower labor costs, incur lower material costs, incur lower scrap (or other waste) costs, enjoy lower rent expense, enjoy lower utilities expense, enjoy lower advertising or promotional expenses, defer the costs to recruit and train employees, avoid start-up costs, avoid construction period interest, avoid interest in an otherwise greater level of receivables or inventory, avoid or defer design or development costs, supply a low-cost and dependable source of financing, avoid or defer software development or ongoing data processing costs, and so on.

Some intangibles lend themselves very well to the application of the income approach. Such contract-related or customer-related intangible assets as favorable leases, favorable supply contracts, favorable labor agreements, customer lists, and customer contracts are likely candidates for an application of the income approach. Other technology-related, engineering-related, and marketing-related intangible assets are also likely candidates for an application of the income approach. These intangible assets may include patents, proprietary technology or processes, trademarks and trade names, copyrights, and so forth.

When using an income approach method, the expected remaining useful life of the subject intangible is important. The economic income projection associated with the subject intangible should not extend beyond the term of the expected remaining useful life for that intangible.

Also, "double-counting" the economic income associated with the subject intangible is a common error. The analyst should ensure that the same stream of economic income (whether it represents a revenue increment or a cost decrement) is not assigned to more than one asset. For example, the same stream of excess earnings for a particular business should not be assigned both to the company's patent and to the company's trademark. Clearly, only one of these intangible assets deserves to be associated with that specific stream of economic income. The other intangible in this example, though it has legal existence, may have little or no incremental economic value.

Only that stream of economic income that associates with the subject intangible asset should be considered. A fair return on the tangible assets used or used up in the production of income related to the subject intangible should be assigned. This fair return on associated tangible assets should be subtracted from the economic income stream assigned to the subject intangible in order to avoid the "double-counting" of asset values.

Cost Approach. The cost approach provides a systematic framework for estimating the value of an intangible asset based on the economic principle of substitution. A prudent investor would pay no more for a fungible intangible than the cost that would be incurred to replace the subject with a substitute of comparable utility or functionality.

Replacement cost new typically establishes the maximum amount that a prudent investor would pay for a fungible intangible. To the extent that an intangible is less useful than an ideal replacement asset, the value of the subject should be adjusted accordingly. The subject's replacement cost new is adjusted for:

- Physical deterioration (which is unusual in the case of intangible assets).
- Functional obsolescence.
- Technological obsolescence (a specific form of functional obsolescence).
- External obsolescence (economic obsolescence is a specific form of external obsolescence).

Physical deterioration is the reduction in value due to physical wear and tear resulting from continued use. Physical deterioration is quite rare with respect to most intangibles.

Functional obsolescence is the reduction in value due to the intangible's inability to perform the function (or yield the periodic utility) for which it was originally designed.

Technological obsolescence is a decrease in value due to improvements in technology that make the intangible less than the ideal replacement for itself. Technological obsolescence occurs when, due to improvements in design or engineering technology, a new replacement produces a greater standardized measure of utility production than the subject intangible.

External obsolescence is a reduction in value due to the effects, events, or conditions that are external to—and not controlled by—the current use or condition of the intangible. The impact of external obsolescence is typically beyond the control of the asset's owner. Therefore, external obsolescence is typically considered incurable.

In estimating the amounts (if any) of functional obsolescence, technological obsolescence, and external obsolescence related to the subject intangible asset, the consideration of the asset's actual age—and its expected remaining useful life—is important.

A common cost approach formula for quantifying an intangible's value is as follows:

	Reproduction cost new
Less:	Incurable functional and technological obsolescence
Equals:	Replacement cost new
Less:	External obsolescence
Less:	Curable functional and technological obsolescence
Indicates:	Fair market value

An intangible's deficiencies are considered curable when the prospective economic benefit of enhancing or modifying it exceeds the current cost (in terms of material, labor, and time) to change it. An intangible's deficiencies are considered incurable when the current costs of enhancing or modifying it (in terms of material, labor, and time) exceed the expected future economic benefits of improving it.

Reproduction cost is the cost to construct, at current prices, an exact duplicate or replica of the subject. This duplicate would be created using the same materials, standards, design, layout, and quality of workmanship used to create the original intangible. An intangible's reproduction cost encompasses all of the deficiencies, "superadequacies," and obsolescence that exist in the subject intangible asset. Many of these conditions or characteristics are inherent in the subject and are, therefore, incurable.

The replacement cost of an intangible is the cost to create, at current prices, an asset having equal utility to the subject. However, the replacement asset would be created with modern methods and constructed according to current standards, state-of-the-art design and layout, and the same quality of workmanship.

The difference between reproduction cost and its replacement cost is typically the quantification of incurable functional and technological obsolescence. That is, in an ideal replacement intangible, all elements of incurable functional and technological obsolescence are removed or "reengineered" from the subject.

Intangible asset replacement cost is sometimes quantified using a *green-field* approach. That is, the replacement cost is the cost to redesign and reengineer an ideal replacement intangible on the drawing board from scratch—that is, on a green field.

With respect to both reproduction cost and replacement cost, four elements of cost should be considered in the analyses:

1. *Direct costs* (including material, labor, and overhead).
2. *Indirect costs* (including associated legal, registration, engineering, administrative, etc.).
3. *Developer's profit* (a fair return on the intangible asset creator's time and effort).
4. *Entrepreneurial incentive* (the economic benefit required to motivate the intangible asset development process).

Some intangibles lend themselves to the cost approach. Examples of this include computer software and automated databases, technical drawings and documentation, blueprints and engineering drawings, laboratory notebooks, technical libraries, chemical formulations, food and other product recipes, and so forth.

Remaining Useful Life Analysis of Intangible Assets

One factor that has been mentioned in all three approaches is the estimation of remaining useful life. This estimation (sometimes called *lifing* the intangible asset) is obviously important in the market approach. This is because the analyst should select comparative sale/license transactions where the sold/licensed intangible has a similar remaining useful life to the subject. This estimation is important in the income approach. The analyst should estimate the time period or duration over which to project (and capitalize) the economic income. This estimation is also important in the cost approach. The analyst should make an assessment of the remaining functionality or utility of the subject intangible in order to quantify elements of functional obsolescence, technological obsolescence, and external obsolescence.

Analysts should consider each of these measures when estimating the remaining useful life of intangible assets.

1. *Remaining legal (or legal protection) life* (e.g., remaining term of trademark protection).
2. *Remaining contractual life* (e.g., remaining term on a lease).
3. *Statutory or judicial life* (e.g., some courts have allowed a "standardized" life of five years for computer software).
4. *Remaining physical life* (e.g., some intangible assets just wear out from continued use, such as blueprints or technical libraries).
5. *Remaining functional life* (e.g., some intangible assets just become dysfunctional with the passage of time, like chemical formulations that need to be continuously updated).
6. *Remaining technological life* (e.g., period until the current technology becomes obsolete, for patents, proprietary processes, etc.).
7. *Remaining economic life* (e.g., period after which the intangible asset will no longer generate income, such as a legally valid copyright on a book that is out of print).
8. *Actuarial/analytical life* (e.g., estimating the remaining life of group intangible assets, such as customer accounts, by reference to the historical turnover—or mortality—of such accounts).

Typically, the shortest resulting measurement of remaining useful life will be appropriate for the valuation.

Example

To illustrate the application of the asset accumulation method, let's consider the hypothetical Seller Company, Inc. ("Seller"). Seller is a successful closely held manufacturing company. The owners of Seller are contemplating an ownership transaction by way of the sale of the business.

Therefore, the objective of the valuation is to estimate the fair market value of the entire business enterprise as of December 31, 2000. In other words, the appropriate level of value is a marketable, controlling ownership interest. The purpose of the valuation is to provide an independent opinion to the current owners as to the most likely transaction price regarding the sale of the company.

In order to identify the components of the Seller business value for potential buyers, we will use the asset accumulation method. We will estimate the fair market value of all of the tangible and intangible assets of Seller as of the valuation date after considering the successful operations of the company and the current owners' plans to sell the business as a going-concern business. We will use the premise of value in continued use for the individual assets.

Exhibit 14–2 presents the statement of financial position (i.e., balance sheet) of Seller as of the December 31, 2000, valuation date. This statement of financial

Exhibit 14–2

Seller Company, Inc.
Statement of Financial Position
as of December 31, 2000
(in 000s)

ASSETS		LIABILITIES AND OWNERS' EQUITY	
Current assets:		Current liabilities:	
Cash	$2,000	Accounts payable	$6,000
Accounts and notes receivable	6,000	Wages payable	1,000
Prepaid expenses	2,000	Taxes payable	1,000
Inventory	8,000	Accrued liabilities	2,000
Total current assets	18,000	Total current liabilities	10,000
Noncurrent assets:		Noncurrent liabilities:	
Land	2,000	Bonds payable	2,000
Buildings and improvements	12,000	Notes payable	4,000
Office furniture and fixtures	2,000	Mortgages payable	6,000
Machinery and equipment	8,000	Debentures payable	2,000
Tools and dies	3,000	Total noncurrent liabilities	14,000
Total plant, property, and equipment	27,000		
Less: Accumulated depreciation	12,000	Owners' equity:	
Net plant, property, and equipment	15,000	Capital stock	1,000
Other noncurrent assets:		Additional paid-in capital	4,000
Long-term notes receivable	2,000	Retained earnings	7,000
Note receivable from supplier	1,000	Total owners' equity	12,000
Total other noncurrent assets	3,000		
		TOTAL LIABILITIES AND	
TOTAL ASSETS	**$36,000**	**OWNERS' EQUITY**	**$36,000**

position is prepared in accordance with generally accepted accounting principles. In other words, Exhibit 14–2 is prepared on a historical-cost basis. This balance sheet will be the beginning point in the asset accumulation method analysis.

Exhibit 14–3 presents the final summary of the Seller asset accumulation method valuation. Exhibit 14–3 presents both the cost-basis values for all Seller recorded asset and liability accounts (slightly rearranged from the cost-basis balance sheet presentation) and the fair market values for all of the asset (both tangible and intangible) and liability accounts of the company.

Let's review each of the asset and liability fair market value conclusions in Exhibit 14–3. The following paragraphs describe an illustrative valuation analysis for each individual asset and liability account.

The cash balance remains at its historical cost value. The analyst confirmed that the cash balances would be transferred to the new owner when the business is sold.

The accounts and notes receivable assets remain at their historical cost value. This conclusion was reached based on the analyst's assessment of the timing and collectibility of the receivables.

Prepaid expenses remain at their historical cost value. This conclusion was reached based on the analyst's assessment of the economic value of the prepaid expenses to the going-concern business.

Inventory is revalued upward. This revaluation is based on the sales comparison method described in Internal Revenue Service Revenue Procedure 77-12.

Exhibit 14–3

Seller Company, Inc.
Business Enterprise Valuation
Asset-Based Approach
Asset Accumulation Method
as of December 31, 2000 (in 000s)

	At Historical Cost	At Fair Market Value
ASSETS		
Financial assets:		
Cash	$2,000	$2,000
Accounts and notes receivable	6,000	6,000
Prepaid expenses	2,000	2,000
Inventory	8,000	10,000
Long-term notes receivable	2,000	2,000
Note receivable from supplier	1,000	—
Total financial assets	21,000	22,000
Real estate:		
Land	2,000	4,000
Buildings and improvements	12,000	10,000
Less: Accumulated depreciation	6,000	—
Net real estate	8,000	14,000
Tangible personal property:		
Office furniture and fixtures	2,000	2,000
Machinery and equipment	8,000	6,000
Tools and dies	3,000	3,000
Less: Accumulated depreciation	6,000	—
Net tangible personal property	7,000	11,000
Intangible real property:		
Leasehold interests	—	2,000
Net intangible real property	—	2,000
Intangible personal property:		
Trademarks and trade names	—	2,000
Computer software	—	3,000
Patents and patent applications	—	2,000
Favorable supplier contracts	—	2,000
Goodwill	—	1,000
Net intangible personal property	—	10,000
TOTAL ASSETS	**$36,000**	**$51,000**
LIABILITIES AND OWNERS' EQUITY		
Current liabilities:		
Accounts payable	$6,000	$6,000
Wages payable	1,000	1,000
Taxes payable	1,000	1,000
Accrued liabilities	2,000	2,000
	10,000	10,000
Total current liabilities	20,000	20,000
Noncurrent liabilities:		
Bonds payable	2,000	2,000
Notes payable	4,000	4,000
Mortgages payable	6,000	5,000
Debentures payable	2,000	2,000
Total noncurrent liabilities	14,000	13,000
Contingent liabilities:		
Contingent claims	—	2,000
Total contingent liabilities	—	2,000
Total liabilities	24,000	25,000
TOTAL LIABILITIES AND OWNERS' EQUITY	**$36,000**	**$51,000**
TOTAL OWNERS' EQUITY	**$12,000**	**$26,000**

Long-term notes receivable are valued at their historical cost. This conclusion is based on (1) an analysis of the stated interest rate versus current interest rates for similar risk notes and (2) the historical and likely prospective payment pattern regarding the notes.

The note receivable from a supplier is revalued to zero. Some years ago, Seller extended a loan to one of its key suppliers. This decremental revaluation was based on the following facts: (1) the supplier has made no payments on the note for the last several years, (2) there is no security related to the note, (3) the documentation of the debt is not particularly good, so (4) it is unlikely that Seller could enforce collection of the note even if it attempted to do so.

Land is revalued upward. This incremental revaluation is based on a contemporaneously prepared market value appraisal of the land, as if vacant and unimproved, at its highest and best use, using the sales comparison approach.

Buildings and improvements are revalued incrementally, as market value exceeds the (depreciated) historical cost of these properties. This revaluation is also based on a contemporaneously prepared market value appraisal of the Seller facilities. This appraisal was based on the depreciated replacement cost of the subject facilities.

Office furniture and fixtures, machinery and equipment, and tools and dies are revalued incrementally. That is, the market value conclusions for each asset category exceed their (depreciated) historical cost. The depreciated replacement cost method would be a typical valuation method for the valuation of this category of assets.

A leasehold interest is identified and capitalized on the value-basis balance sheet. In this example, Seller enjoys a favorable rental advantage (i.e., below-market rental rates) on some warehouse space that it leases. The analyst used the income capitalization approach to project and capitalize this favorable (below-market) lease rate advantage and to conclude the market value of the leasehold interest. This leasehold interest intangible asset was not previously recorded on the Seller cost-basis balance sheet.

The entire category of intangible personal property typically would not be recorded on a cost-basis balance sheet. However, individual intangible assets will be identified and valued as part of this business enterprise valuation.

Trademarks and trade names are an important intangible asset for Seller. Company management spends a great deal of time and money promoting and protecting the company's name. They advertise, send promotional announcements, sponsor booths at trade shows, and so forth. They have actively defended the company name and market against any possible infringement. The analyst used the recreation cost method to quantify the value of this intangible asset. The analyst estimated the current cost required for the company to recreate its current level of customer awareness, brand recognition, and consumer loyalty. The estimated cost to recreate this level of name awareness is capitalized as the value of this intangible.

Computer software also is an important intangible asset for Seller. This computer software was internally developed and maintained by an in-house data processing department. The value of such computer software typically would not be recorded on a cost-basis balance sheet.

The systems analysts at Seller have developed and implemented an automated materials requirement planning (MRP) system. This system is extremely useful to the company with regard to material purchasing, labor scheduling, and production planning.

The analyst used the market approach to estimate the value of this intangible asset, as there is a relatively similar (in terms of functionality) MRP system available on the market from a commercial software vendor. After consideration of the market value of a comparable commercial system, and after including the costs of customization, installation, testing, and training, the analyst estimated the value in continued use of the Seller computer software.

Seller holds a number of patents and patent applications. The Seller products have certain unique and proprietary technological feature advancements compared with the products manufactured by Seller's competitors. And, other manufacturers cannot reverse-engineer and copy the Seller product advanced features because these products are protected by the company patents.

Because of the advanced features (protected by the several patents), Seller management estimates that (1) Seller sells more widgets than it otherwise would, (2) Seller has a greater market share than it otherwise would, and (3) Seller's average selling price per unit is higher than its competitors' prices. Accordingly, the analyst used the income approach to estimate the value of the Seller patents and patent applications.

Seller also has a favorable supply contract with a key supplier. The materials buyer for Seller is a skilled negotiator. Using these superior negotiating skills, the materials buyer convinced the key supplier to agree to supply an essential raw material to Seller at 20 percent below the prices that the supplier normally charges to its other, similar-sized customers. This long-term agreement is documented in a written five-year-term supply contract. The analyst used the income approach to estimate the economic value of the Seller favorable supply contract.

Goodwill is sometimes considered the accumulation of all the other elements of economic value of a business enterprise not specifically associated with (or allocated to) individual tangible and intangible assets. The analysis and quantification of goodwill (or the lack of goodwill) is an important component in the application of the asset accumulation method to a company like Seller.

With respect to the subject company, the analyst used the capitalized excess earnings method to value the Seller goodwill. First, the analyst identified and valued all of the other individual Seller assets—both tangible and intangible. Second, the analyst assigned a fair rate of return against each Seller asset category—both tangible and intangible. Third, the analyst compared the total calculated fair return on the total tangible and intangible assets with the total economic income actually earned by the company. Fourth, any excess economic income (above a fair return on all identified tangible and intangible assets) was capitalized as an annuity in perpetuity. The capitalized excess earnings method is described in Chapter 13.

The conclusion of the capitalized excess earnings analysis is the indicated value of the Seller intangible value in the nature of goodwill.

The current liabilities of Seller also were analyzed. Given the short-term nature of these monetary liabilities, the analyst estimated their fair market value at their historical cost carrying amounts.

The noncurrent liabilities also were analyzed. The analyst considered the terms and conditions of these liabilities and concluded that the stated interest rates approximated current market rates for comparative debt instruments. Accordingly, the analyst estimated the fair market value of the bonds, notes, and debentures at their historical cost carrying amounts.

The mortgage payable, however, has a substantial remaining term and a fixed interest rate which is considerably below current market rates. The analyst confirmed with the mortgage bank that they would allow Seller to pay off the mortgage at a discount compared to the principal balance. The analyst estimated this discount by reference to the difference in the imbedded interest rate and the market interest rate over the remaining term of the mortgage. The analyst reduced the liability by the present value of the imbedded interest rate advantage and then estimated the fair market value of the mortgage payable.

There is an outstanding lawsuit against Seller. The plaintiff, a former distributor, alleges that Seller violated the distributor's exclusive marketing territory agreement. Although there were extenuating circumstances, Seller management recognizes that it did violate the agreement and that it owes damages to the former distributor.

While the trial is not yet scheduled, and no one can predict the court's decision regarding either liability or damages, both Seller management and Seller legal counsel believe that an offer of $2,000,000 will be adequate to settle the case and to satisfy all future liability to the plaintiff.

The analyst reviewed this estimate and used it to recognize a contingent liability on the Seller value-basis balance sheet.

In the final step, the analyst summed the estimated fair market values for all of the Seller tangible and intangible assets, and summed the estimated fair market values for all of the Seller recorded and continent liabilities. The analyst subtracted the total liability value from the total asset value. The remainder is an indication of the fair market value of the Seller total owners' equity, as of December 31, 2000, as indicated by the asset accumulation method.

Advantages of the Asset Accumulation Method

As should be apparent from the discussion of the theoretical concepts and the practical applications of this method, there are a number of analytical advantages of the asset accumulation method.

First, the results of the asset accumulation method are presented in a traditional balance sheet format. This format should be familiar to anyone who has ever worked with basic financial statements. Therefore, business buyers and sellers, commercial and investment bankers, judges and lawyers, and individual and institutional investors should all be familiar with the basic balance sheet presentation of the results of this valuation method.

Second, this method componentizes all of the subject business value. In the example above, the valuation conclusion was slightly greater than two times accounting book value for Seller. Other business valuation methods would, presumably, reach the same valuation conclusion. But those methods would not explain why the subject company is worth more than two times accounting book value. The asset accumulation method identifies (1) exactly which assets (tangible and intangible) are contributing economic value to the company and (2) exactly how much economic value each asset is contributing.

Third, this method is useful when structuring the sale of a business. This method can quickly quantify the effects on business value of many common seller structural considerations, such as these:

1. What if the seller retains the company's cash on hand or accounts receivable?
2. What if the seller retains (or leases back to the company) the operating real estate facilities?
3. What if the seller personally retains title to the patents or to some other intangible asset owned by the company?

4. What if the seller personally retains any or all of the debt instruments (or other liabilities) of the company?

Fourth, this method is useful to the seller when negotiating the sale of the company. If the buyer offers a lower price than the asset accumulation method indicates, the seller can ask, "Since you're not willing to pay for all of the assets of the business, which of these assets don't you want to include as part of the transaction?"

Fifth, this method is useful to the buyer when negotiating the purchase of the company. If the seller wants a higher price than the value indicated by the asset accumulation method, the buyer can ask, "What other assets will be included in the transaction—in addition to the assets included on this value-based balance sheet—to justify the price you are asking?"

Sixth, after the sale transaction is consummated, this business valuation method allows for a ready and reasonable allocation of the lump-sum purchase price among the assets acquired. This purchase price allocation is often required for both financial accounting purposes and tax accounting purposes. This is important because the tangible assets are subject to depreciation cost recovery—and the intangible assets are subject to amortization cost recovery—for both financial accounting and federal income tax purposes.

Seventh, this method is useful with regard to financing the subject transaction. Typically, all categories of lenders (secured, unsecured, mezzanine, etc.) will want to know the value of all of the company's individual assets—both tangible and intangible—before they will commit to financing the business purchase deal. This valuation method generally provides the acquisition lenders with the information they need.

Eighth, this method is particularly useful in litigation and other controversial matters. Since it identifies the individual value components of the individual assets of the company, it allows for the easy measurement of the impact of certain alleged actions (or lack of actions) on the overall business enterprise value. Also, this method can be used to allocate assets (as well as—or instead of—stock) in a stockholder/partner dissolution dispute or in a marital dissolution dispute.

Ninth, this method can be used with any standard of value or with any premise of value. In other words, using the same comparative balance sheet format, analysts can value the same business enterprise under several alternative standards of value. Likewise, using the same comparative balance sheet format, analysts can value the same business enterprise under several alternative premises of value. Therefore, the impact of changing standards of value or premises of value can quickly be identified and quantified.

Tenth, this method requires the most rigorous analysis and thorough understanding of company operations on the part of the analyst. This method requires the analyst to understand the microeconomic dynamics of the subject business enterprise. For example, this method would require the analyst to consider the functional and technological status of the company's facilities and equipment, the degree of company dependence on employees versus customers versus suppliers, the extent to which the company has documented and protected its valuable intellectual property, and so on. Such rigorous analyses can only help enhance the quality of the valuation. Also, this method generally requires more active participation on the part of company management in the valuation process. This active participation can only help enhance the quality of the business valuation.

Disadvantages of the Asset Accumulation Method

The primary disadvantage of the asset accumulation method is that, if taken to an extreme, it can be very expensive and time consuming. It also may necessitate the involvement of appraisal specialists in several asset valuation disciplines. The costs and efforts of these appraisal specialists may be prohibitive with regard to the valuation of larger or complex businesses.

Also, as described in this chapter, this method requires the valuation of all of the company assets—the intangible assets as well as tangible assets. Many intangible asset values depend, in good measure, on the income valuation approach. Therefore, the value indication of the asset accumulation method may ultimately depend as much on the economic income capitalization variables as it does on the values of tangible assets. This is especially true for larger and more complex businesses. Of course, ultimately, the value of all assets, properties, or business interests depends on their economic income–generating capacity.

Summary

The asset accumulation method is a common asset-based approach method. The theoretical underpinning of this method is simple: The value of the business enterprise is the value of the business assets (both tangible and intangible) less the value of the business liabilities (both recorded and contingent). Basically, this method recognizes that all of the economic value of a business has to come from—and can be identified with—the productive assets of the business.

The asset accumulation method involves the separate identification and individual valuation of all business asset categories. In addition, this method involves the identification and valuation of all business liability categories. In these individual asset and liability valuations, it is important for the analyst to apply both (1) a standard of value and (2) a premise of value that are consistent with the purpose and objective of the business enterprise valuation.

It is conceptually incorrect to automatically conclude that the value of a business is based only on the value of its tangible assets. Likewise, it is also conceptually incorrect to conclude that the value of a business is equal to its accounting book value—without the use of generally accepted valuation procedures and rigorous fundamental analyses to support that conclusion.

The intangible assets of the company often contribute substantial economic value. In some cases, a company's intangible assets may even contribute negative economic value, which is recognized as external obsolescence. External obsolescence is recognized as a decrease in the value of the tangible assets of the company. Again, the application of the asset accumulation method requires a structured, rigorous, and comprehensive valuation analysis of all the company's assets.

There are numerous advantages to the asset accumulation method. These advantages include application to transaction pricing and structuring, deal negotiation, acquisition financing, purchase accounting, and dispute resolution.

However, there are costs associated with the application of the asset accumulation method. This method requires more time and effort on the part of the analyst than many other business valuation methods. It requires more access to company facilities and to company management than many other valuation methods. It requires more access to company data, particularly operational data, than many other valuation methods. And, it requires more time and effort on the part of company management and more involvement of company management in the valuation process.

Finally, the asset accumulation method requires that the analyst have expertise in the identification and valuation of both tangible assets and intangible assets. Certainly, this method is only recommended for analysts who have adequate experience and expertise in the valuation of individual business assets. The use of other experts with the requisite experience and qualifications may fill the void for a particular asset type for which the analyst lacks technical expertise.

Bibliography

Alico, John, ed. *Appraising Machinery and Equipment*. Herndon, VA: American Society of Appraisers, 1989.

Altman, Edward I. "Mark-to-Market and Present Value Disclosure: An Opportunity or a Costly Annoyance?" *Financial Analysts Journal*, March–April 1993, pp. 14–16.

The Appraisal of Real Estate, 11th ed. (Chicago: Appraisal Institute, 1996).

Baxter, William. "Asset and Liability Values (Complexities of Current Value Accounting)." *Accountancy*, April 1994, pp. 135–37.

Cheung, Joseph K., and Mandy Li. "Income Tax Effects on Asset Valuation and Managerial Analysis." *Abacus*, March 1992, pp. 98–106.

Churchill, Michael. "Asset Valuation." *Australian Accountant*, April 1992, pp. 35–39.

Crawford, Robert G., and Gary C. Cornia. "The Problem of Appraising Specialized Assets." *Appraisal Journal*, January 1994, pp. 75–85.

Dandekar, Manoj P., and Pamela Garland. "Tangible Personal Property Remaining Useful Life Estimation Analysis." *Willamette Management Associates Insights*, Winter 1996, pp. 13–20.

Dandekar, Manoj P., and Robert F. Reilly. "Tangible Personal Property Valuation Approaches, Methods, and Procedures." *Willamette Management Associates Insights*, Winter 1996, pp. 1–12.

DeThomas, Arthur R., and Robert R. Neyland. "Asset Valuation: A Practical Approach for Decision Making." *CPA Journal*, September 1991, pp. 82–83.

Fowler, Bradley A., and Edward C. Fowler. "Coordinating 'Business Valuation Overlay' with Asset Based Valuations." *Business Valuation Review*, December 1996, pp. 171–73.

Godfrey, Austin E. "The Valuation of Assets Subject to Lease Transaction." *Secured Lender*, September/October 1993, pp. 62–64+.

Jacoby, Henry D., and David G. Laughton. "Project Evaluation: A Practical Asset Pricing Method." *Energy Journal*, 1992, pp. 19–47.

Jones, P. C., W. J. Hopp, and J. L. Zydiak. "Capital Asset Valuation and Depreciation for Stochastically Deteriorating Equipment." *Engineering Economist*, Fall 1992, pp. 19–30.

Lynn, Daniel M., and Robert R. Neyland. "Asset Valuation: Softening the Bankruptcy Blow." *Bank Management*, April 1992, pp. 48–49.

McCrodan, Andrew. "Tackling Tax-Related Troubles." *CA Magazine*, April 1993, pp. 45–48.

Reilly, Robert F., and Robert P. Schweihs. *Valuing Intangible Assets*. New York: McGraw-Hill, 1999.

_____. "Valuation of Trademarks and Trade Names." *Valuation Strategies*, November/December 1999, pp. 7–13, 45–46.

Schmidt, Richard M. "Valuing the Assets of a Manufacturing Company." *The Appraisal Journal*, April 1997, pp. 120–23.

Shiffrin, Daniel. "Tax Court Determines Weight of Asset-Based and Earnings-Based Valuation Approaches." *CPA Litigation Counselor*, February 2000, pp. 3, 12.

Tole, Thomas M., Sammy O. McCord, and Charles P. Edmonds. "How Much Is the Business Worth?" *Real Estate Review*, Summer 1993, pp. 39–43.

Part IV

Discounts, Premiums, and the Value Conclusion

Chapter 15

Control and Acquisition Premiums

The most common valuation premiums and discounts relate to (1) degree of ownership control, or the lack of it (i.e., noncontrolling ownership interest status), and (2) the degree of the subject business interest marketability, or lack of it (i.e., nonmarketable ownership interest status). The issue of the value increment associated with ownership control of a business enterprise is the subject of this chapter. The analysis of the related issue of the discount for lack of control is the subject of the next chapter. The matter of the discount for lack of marketability is the subject of Chapter 17.

Critical to the discussion of valuation discounts or premiums is the notion that they have no meaning until the base of value to which they are applied has been clearly defined. Unfortunately, there have been many buy-sell agreements and business valuation opinions that refer to discounts or premiums—with no reference to the base of value from which those discounts or premiums are to be taken. This is a typical error committed. Throughout the discussions of premiums and discounts in the next several chapters, we will attempt to be very specific as to what premiums and/or discounts are properly applied to what base of value.

In Chapter 3, we discussed the fact that ownership control and marketability are, for practical purposes, separate and distinct valuation concepts. On the conceptual level, these two characteristics of ownership are somewhat interrelated. This is because the difficulty in liquidating a noncontrolling ownership interest in a closely held company generally is much greater than the difficulty in liquidating a controlling ownership interest. Two schematic presentations of the relationship—and the difference between the two ownership characteristics of control and marketability are presented as Exhibits 15–1 and 15–2.

The diagram presented in Exhibit 15–1 reflects the value influence of the ownership characteristics of control versus the noncontrolling stockholder's situation, as discussed in Chapter 16. This schematic usually would represent the *fair market value standard of value* on a *going-concern basis premise of value*. In some cases, there may be yet another layer of value, which may reflect synergies with certain third-party buyers (as examples of: (1) reducing combined overhead by the consolidation of operations or (2) raising prices by reducing competition). There is not yet a widely used term for this additional layer of price premium over fair market, going-concern value. However, this price premium—when combined with the ownership control premium—is sometimes called an *acquisition premium*. The standard of value reflecting these synergies usually would be considered *investment value*. This is because it reflects the *value to a particular buyer*, generally referred to as the *synergistic buyer*, rather than value to the hypothetical willing buyer. This "hypothetical" typical willing buyer acquires the subject company strictly because of its financial merits, and is generally referred to as a *financial buyer*.

It is noteworthy that the issue of ownership control (versus the lack of ownership control) covers a broad spectrum of factors that influence value. One category of factors is the degree of control elements that may or may not be present in any specific ownership interest. Another factor is the ability of a controlling shareholder to implement policies and practices that will enhance the value of the controlling shares—at the expense of the noncontrolling shares. This chapter discusses how a particular set of facts and circumstances may impact the value of a controlling ownership interest (vis-à-vis a noncontrolling ownership interest).

Exhibit 15–1

Levels of Value in Terms of Characteristics of Ownership

Notes:

a. Control shares in a privately held company may also be subject to some discount for lack of marketability, but usually not nearly as much as minority shares.

b. Minority and marketability discounts normally are multiplicative rather than additive. That is, they are taken in sequence:

$10.00	Control value
−3.00	Less minority interest discount ($0.30 \times \$10.00$)
$7.00	Marketable minority value
−2.80	Less: lack of marketability discount ($0.40 \times \$7.00$)
$4.20	Per share value of nonmarketable minority shares

c. Note that neither the minority/control nor the marketability issue are "all or nothing" matters. Each covers a spectrum of degrees.

SOURCE: Jay E. Fishman, Shannon P. Pratt, J. Clifford Griffith, and D. Keith Wilson, *Guide to Business Valuations*, 10th ed. (Fort Worth, TX: Practitioners Publishing Company, 2000). Reprinted with permission.

The Concept and Importance of Ownership Control

The following is a list of 20 of the more common prerogatives of ownership control of a business enterprise:

1. Appoint or change operational management.
2. Appoint or change members of the board of directors.
3. Determine management compensation and perquisites.
4. Set operational and strategic policy and change the course of the business.
5. Acquire, lease, or liquidate business assets, including plant, property, and equipment.
6. Select suppliers, vendors, and subcontractors with whom to do business and award contracts.
7. Negotiate and consummate mergers and acquisitions.
8. Liquidate, dissolve, sell out, or recapitalize the company.

Exhibit 15–2

Which Value Is Fair Market Value for 100%

SOURCE: Z. Christopher Mercer, "Understanding and Quantifying Control Premiums: The Value of Control vs. Synergies of Strategic Advantages, Part II," *The Journal of Business Valuation* (Proceedings of the Fourth Joint Business Valuation Conference of The Canadian Institute of Chartered Business Valuators and the American Society of Apprasiers, September 24 and 25, 1998) (Toronto: The Canadian Institute of Chartered Business Valuators, 1999), p. 51.

9. Sell or acquire treasury shares.
10. Register the company's equity securities for an initial or secondary public offering.
11. Register the company's debt securities for an initial or secondary public offering.
12. Declare and pay cash and/or stock dividends.
13. Change the articles of incorporation or bylaws.
14. Set one's own compensation (and perquisites) and the compensation (and perquisites) of related-party employees.
15. Select joint venturers and enter into joint venture and partnership agreements.
16. Decide what products and/or services to offer and how to price those products/services.
17. Decide what markets and locations to serve, to enter into, and to discontinue serving.
18. Decide which customer categories to market to and which not to market to.
19. Enter into inbound and outbound license or sharing agreements regarding intellectual properties.
20. Block any or all of the above actions.

From the above list, it is apparent that the owner of a controlling ownership interest in a business enterprise enjoys some very valuable rights that the owner of a noncontrolling ownership interest does not enjoy.

In its quarterly *Control Premium Study*, Mergerstat defines a control premium as "the additional consideration that an investor would pay over a marketable minority equity value (i.e., current, publicly traded stock prices) in order to own a controlling interest in the common stock of a company."[1]

A controlling interest is considered to have greater value than a minority interest because of the purchaser's ability to effect changes in the overall business structure and to influence business policies. Control premiums can vary greatly. Factors affecting the magnitude of a given control premium include:

- The nature and magnitude of nonoperating assets.
- The nature and magnitude of discretionary expenses.
- The perceived quality of existing management.
- The nature and magnitude of business opportunities which are not currently being exploited.
- The ability to integrate the acquiree into the acquiror's business or distribution channels.[2]

How the Applicable Standard of Value Affects Control Premiums

As discussed in Chapter 2, the applicable standard of value for most valuation situations typically falls into one of four categories: (1) fair market value, (2) investment value, (3) intrinsic value, or (4) fair value. The applicable standard of value is determined primarily by the purpose and objective of the valuation. In some situations, the applicable standard of value is mandated by law. In other situations, the selection of the appropriate standard of value may be determined by the analyst and/or the valuation client.

Fair Market Value

As discussed in Chapter 2, the *fair market value* standard implies a price at which an arm's-length transaction would be expected to occur between normally motivated investors under open market conditions, without considering any special benefits for any particular buyer or seller. Considering the economic unattractiveness of noncontrolling ownership interests in closely held companies to most investors, the lack of control discount from a proportionate share of enterprise value under the fair market value standard may be quite large. There are substantial amounts of transactional data (presented in Chapter 16) to assist the analyst in the quantification of the lack of control discount when the appropriate standard of value is fair market value. Later in this chapter, we will discuss the empirical data sources that are

---

[1] *Control Premium Study*, 4th quarter 1999 (Los Angeles: Applied Financial Information, LP, 1999), p. ii.
[2] Ibid.

frequently used to quantify the ownership control premium in valuations where the appropriate standard is fair market value.

Investment Value

In Chapter 2, we defined the *investment value* standard as the value to a particular investor considering that investor's cost of capital, perception of risk, and other unique characteristics. Because of the particular attributes of ownership that may have unique appeal to any specific investor, the investment value of a noncontrolling ownership interest in a certain business enterprise may be equal to, greater than, or less than fair market value. And, it also may be equal to, greater than, or less than a pro rata portion of the total business enterprise value.

Investment value, by definition, depends on the attributes of a particular buyer or seller. Therefore, there are not readily available market data to assist the analyst in quantifying premiums or discounts directly relative to that standard of value. This is because the price premiums or discounts would vary with each individual buyer or seller—rather than necessarily representing a market consensus as in the case of fair market value. Of course, market evidence would have a bearing on appropriate premiums or discounts under the investment value standard. However, the quantification of the discounts and premiums would be more judgmental, based on analysis of the individual facts and circumstances than under the fair market value standard.

This suggests that under the investment value standard, the analyst may be more inclined to select a valuation method that directly indicates the desired level of value—rather than to select a method that indicates a different level of value and then have to adjust the indicated value with either a lack of control discount or control premium.

A study in *Buyouts* distinguishes between price multiples of EBIT paid by strategic buyers versus price multiples paid by financial buyers. This study is presented in Exhibit 15–3.

Certainly, the excess of the pricing multiples paid by strategic buyers over those paid by financial buyers represents elements of investment value over fair market value. However, it also should be recognized that some elements of investment value are also often present in financial buyer transactions. For example, financial business buyers will not expect operational synergies (other than by replacing inefficient management). This is because they do not own other businesses that provide either horizontal or vertical integration opportunities. However, they may expect financial synergies. The financial buyer may pay a price premium for the ability to (1) change the target's capital structure or (2) finance the target with lower cost capital sources or with more capital to exploit expansion opportunities.

Exhibit 15–3

Average Acquisition to EBIT Multiples

	1989	1993	1995
Financial buyers	7.41	5.40	6.50
Strategic buyers	7.76	6.11	7.24

SOURCE: Jennifer Lea Reed, "Purchase Multiples Press to Rarefied Heights," *Buyouts*, February 20, 1995, p. 1.

While it is intuitively appealing to conclude that strategic buyers generally pay higher prices for acquisitions than financial buyers, that intuitive conclusion is not always supported by empirical data. Some analysts believe that strategic buyers do not always have greater prices—and greater control or acquisition price premiums—than financial buyers.

It has been asserted recently that control premiums have disappeared from the present equity markets, that only strategic mergers offer any significant control premiums today. After having examined a database of 1,446 transactions between 1992 and 1997, I have found no support for this theory. Control premiums have varied within a fairly narrow range for the last six years with no discernible trend and no distinction between the level of control premiums for strategic and non-strategic mergers although it does appear that strategic mergers as a percentage of all mergers have declined substantially in the last six years. The statistics also show no significant differences in control premiums for any of the specific years. There is also no significant difference between the median values for value or control premiums when the acquiring company and acquisition have different or the same primary SIC codes except that there may be a slight premium for circumstances in which the two companies are not in the exact same primary SIC codes but are very close to each other. Finally there are some significant distinctions between the valuation measures and control premiums by industry classification of the acquisition.[3]

Intrinsic Value

Intrinsic value (sometimes called *fundamental value*), as defined in Chapter 2, is the value inherent in the characteristics of the investment itself. It is less frequently used as a standard of value in and of itself. More commonly, the term is referred to, and some of the notions it implies are used, in the context of one of the other three standards of value.

As it is used by capital market security analysts, intrinsic value usually is a publicly traded, minority ownership value. If this is the case, then an ownership control premium could be applicable if the exercise of elements of ownership control could enhance the value elements reflected in the intrinsic value analysis.

Fair Value

As noted in Chapter 2, there is not a consistent definition of the *fair value* standard from one context to another. It most often arises as the statutory standard of value applicable to valuations performed under dissenting stockholders' appraisal rights or rights to dissolution. Such valuations, by their nature, typically involve noncontrolling ownership interests. The need to interpret the meaning of this standard of value from a study of the legal precedents in noncontrolling stockholder rights actions in each of the 50 states (and Canada) is a continuing challenge to the business valuation profession.

---

[3] George P. Roach, "Control Premiums and Strategic Mergers," *Business Valuation Review*, June 1998, p. 42.

Certain precedents—including those pursuant to California Corporation Code Section 2000—have suggested that fair value may be interpreted to mean fair market value without a noncontrolling ownership interest discount (i.e., a proportionate share of the overall business enterprise value).

Even when a proportionate share of the business enterprise value is an indicated interpretation of "fair value," precedent as to (1) which factors to consider and (2) the relative weights to accord to each factor varies considerably. Generally, but not always, unless the liquidation of the subject business is an imminent possibility, emphasis will be on factors that bear on the business enterprise going-concern value rather than on its liquidation value. Therefore, precedent may indicate not only what premiums and/or discounts may or may not be applicable, but also how such premiums or discounts are defined (and the value base to which they should be applied). It is necessary to research the specifically applicable legal precedent in each context to which the fair value standard is determined to apply.

Impact of State Statutes on the Value of Control

Statutes affecting noncontrolling stockholders' rights vary greatly from state to state. These statutes, and the judicial precedent developed pursuant to each, can have an extremely important bearing on the values of controlling ownership interests in many situations.

Requirements for Supermajority Votes

In some states, a simple majority can approve major actions such as a merger or sale of the company. Other states require a two-thirds—or even greater—majority to approve such actions. This means that a noncontrolling ownership interest of just over one-third has the power to block many corporate actions. This legal right gives large but noncontrolling ownership interests a form of blocking power.

Both the types of actions that require a supermajority vote and the size of the supermajority required for each action vary considerably from state to state. And, the statutes of many states are regularly undergoing review and change.

Dissenting Stockholder Appraisal Rights

Most states have statutes allowing noncontrolling stockholders to dissent if a company merges, sells essentially all its assets, or undergoes other fundamental change. In most cases, the dissenters' remedy is to have their shares valued and be paid that value in cash. In most (but not all) states, the standard of value for dissenting stockholder rights actions is "fair value," as discussed in Chapter 2. Standards of valuation under state dissenting stockholder rights laws vary considerably, and the analyst who practices in this area should become familiar with the relevant statutory authority and judicial precedent.

Most states require that if a noncontrolling stockholder dissents to a corporate action, the decision must be registered in writing at—or within a few days following—the stockholder meeting at which the action is approved by the majority of stockholders. This registration of the dissent often is referred to as *perfecting dissenters' appraisal rights*. The courts have been fairly consistent in prohibiting dissenters' appraisal rights unless they have been perfected within the time specified in the statute.

Rights to Dissolution or Sale of Stock

A few states have statutes enabling noncontrolling shares aggregating some specified percentage of the total outstanding to petition the courts to force the dissolution of the subject corporation under specified circumstances. Such statutes generally provide that controlling stockholders can prevent dissolution in such cases by paying the fair value of their shares to those who petition for dissolution. By far, the largest amount of litigation regarding the value of shares under such statutes has been pursuant to California Corporation Code Section 2000.

In states that have such dissolution statutes, the judicial precedent does not necessarily interpret fair value the same for dissolution statutes as it does for dissenting shareholder statutes. Usually, states that have such statutes provide noncontrolling stockholders with some of the elements of ownership control.

Market Evidence Regarding Control and Acquisition Price Premiums

The market evidence available to quantify ownership control premiums generally compares acquisition prices of publicly traded companies with preacquisition announcement prices of the same publicly traded stock.

The general idea of control premium studies is to measure the price premium over the noncontrolling ownership interest transaction prices at which a controlling ownership interest in the same company is transacted. Such studies compare capital market prices for publicly traded stock before (1) the announcement of a merger or acquisition to (2) the final merger or acquisition price. The percentage of the acquisition price that was finally paid over the pretransaction stock trading price is commonly called the control premium.

An important question is: Does this pre-deal versus deal stock price analysis capture only the price premium paid by the buyer for ownership control? Or, does this analysis capture additional price increments, in addition to the price premium related to control?

Clearly, all of the published studies that we will introduce quantify the entire transaction price premium. This entire transaction price premium includes some price increment for ownership control, more likely than not. However, the entire transaction price premium probably also includes other increments of value as well.

These other increments of value are sometimes called an acquisition premium, a synergy or synergistic premium, a consolidation premium, a post-merger expectations premium, a speculative premium, and so forth. And, while not all capital transactions pundits agree, most analysts concur that it is perfectly rational for acquirers to pay transaction prices that include (1) a noncontrolling ownership value plus (2) an ownership control premium plus (3) an additional acquisition price premium (above the control premium) related to the expected economic benefits of the merged companies.

The inclusion of acquisition price premiums in excess of stand-alone control premiums may taint the commonly used control premium data sources, but analysts should realize that these data sources are still the best empirical evidence generally available to quantify the control premium. The alternative—of customized transactional analyses of deals involving financial buyers only (that is, the exclusion of all strategic buyer deals)—is a rarely used and expensive option. However, this alternative is available to isolate the ownership control premium component of acquisition price premiums.

The problem is that valuation analysts often need to estimate the stand-alone value of the subject business—on a controlling ownership interest basis. This stand-alone value concept is consistent with the fair market value standard that is required for many taxation, regulatory, administrative, and legal purposes.

Nonetheless, none of the "control premium" data sources directly disaggregates the control premium only—that is, the ownership control value increment—from the total transaction price premium. Therefore, these data sources, which analysts frequently rely upon to estimate a "stand-alone business enterprise value" (on an ownership control basis), typically include both a "stand-alone business enterprise value" plus the "value of expected post-merger synergies." Or, in other words:

> If the buying company is going to create value for its shareholders the acquisition price must be no greater than the stand-alone value of the selling company plus the value created by acquisition synergies. These synergies increase the cash flows for the combined company over the expected level of cash flows for the two companies operating separately. At an economic breakeven, that is, when the acquiring company shareholders earn just their risk-adjusted rate of return, the following holds true:

> Acquisition price = Stand-alone value of seller + Value of synergies

> Note that the acquisition price minus the stand-alone value of the seller is the premium paid. Thus, the above break-even formula can be expressed more simply as:

> Premium paid = Value of synergies

> This formula captures the difficulty that buying companies have in creating value from mergers and acquisitions. To create value, the present value of synergies must be greater than the premium paid. Remember, the buyer pays the premium up front and buys an option on uncertain future synergies. In other words, the premium is an advance payment on a speculative synergy bet.[4]

Mergerstat Review Studies

Mergerstat Review describes its database as follows:

> Mergerstat® tracks formal transfers of ownership of at least 10% of a company's equity where the purchase price is at least $1,000,000 and where at least one of the parties is a U.S. entity. When a transaction involves less than 100% of an entity, the percentage bought is stated after the seller's name. When

---

[4] Alfred Rappaport, *Creating Shareholder Value: A Guide for Managers and Investors* (New York: The Free Press, 1998), pp. 145–46. Reprinted with the permission of The Free Press, a division of Simon & Schuster, Inc. Copyright © 1986, 1998 by Alfred Rappaport.

REM accompanies this percentage the buyer already owns a portion of the selling entity and this transaction will lead to 100% ownership. Data is collected for publicly traded, privately owned and foreign companies.[5]

Exhibit 15–4 presents average and medium acquisition price premiums offered over market price for transactions collected according to the above criteria. To convert the price premiums to discounts from the acquisition price, the formula is:

$$1 - \frac{1}{(1 + \text{Premium})}$$

For example, using the 1999 median premium, the discount would be:

$$1 - \frac{1}{(1 + 0.346)} \approx 0.26$$

Note that Exhibit 15-4 states that the noncontrolling interest trading price from which the acquisition price premium is computed is five business days before the initial transaction announcement. Published academic studies have indicated that stock prices have some tendency to increase somewhat earlier than the actual transaction announcement. This phenomenon is typically due to industry speculation of a possible takeover. Thus, the *Mergerstat Review* data may tend to understate the relevant acquisition price premium—at least with regard to a strictly "unaffected price."

The *Mergerstat Review* data indicate a strong inverse relationship between (1) the general level of the stock market (as measured by P/E multiples) and (2) the price premiums paid over the market average P/E multiple in acquisition transactions. When the general stock market is low, the P/E multiples offered relative to the general stock market P/E multiple are high, and vice versa. Exhibit 15–5 presents this relationship. Many times individual stocks, and even entire industries, may be overpriced. In those instances, it would not be prudent for acquirers to make takeover bids high enough in order to be successful. In such instances, a public market noncontrolling interest stock price may be equal to—or even greater than—a controlling interest stock price.

Mergerstat Acquisition Premium Studies

There is a similar set of acquisition premium data published on a quarterly basis, with an annual compilation. In an attempt to overcome the potential distortion caused by stock price increases in speculative anticipation of a possible deal, the *Control Premium Study* show, stock prices one day, one week, one month, and two months before the acquisition announcement date, as well as a "Mergerstat Unaffected Price." This "unaffected price" involves (1) an analysis of price and volume data and (2) the selection of a price just before observed changes in normal pricing activity.

The average and median *Mergerstat Control Premium Study* price premiums calculated tend to be somewhat greater than the price premiums calculated by *Mergerstat Review*, as shown in Exhibit 15–6. Note, however, as Exhibit 15–7 shows, at least for the fourth quarter of 1999, that the premiums over prices one month and two months before the announcement date were even higher than the Mergerstat control premium.

---

[5] *Mergerstat Review* 1999 (Los Angeles: Applied Financial Information, LP, 1999), p. ix. For further information, see www.mergerstat.com.

Exhibit 15–4

Premium Offered over Market Price

	DJIA High	DJIA Low	Premium Offered		Base
			Average	Median	
1990	2,999.75	2,365.10	42.0%	32.0%	175
1991	3,168.83	2,470.30	35.1%	29.4%	137
1992	3,413.21	3,136.58	41.0%	34.7%	142
1993	3,794.33	3,241.95	38.7%	33.0%	173
1994	3,978.36	3,593.35	41.9%	35.0%	260
1995	5,235.62	3,817.28	44.7%	29.2%	324
1996	6,560.91	5,032.94	36.6%	27.3%	381
1997	8,259.31	6,391.69	35.7%	27.5%	487
1998	9,374.27	7,539.07	40.7%	30.1%	512
1999	11,497.12	9,120.67	43.3%	34.6%	723

Note: Premium calculations are based on the seller's closing market price five business days before the initial announcement. These calculations exclude negative premiums.

SOURCE: *Mergerstat Review 2000* (Los Angeles: Applied Financial Information, LP, 2000), p. 24.

Exhibit 15–5

Price to Earnings Multiples*
Percent Offered over S&P 500
1990-1999

	S&P 500 P/E**	Average P/E Offered	Average P/E Offered Relative to S&P 500 P/E
1990	15.2	20.1	32.2%
1991	18.6	20.0	7.5%
1992	24.2	22.7	–6.2%
1993	23.4	24.4	4.3%
1994	19.9	24.5	23.1%
1995	16.6	23.8	43.4%
1996	19.2	26.2	36.5%
1997	22.4	27.4	22.3%
1998	26.9	25.1	–6.7%
1999	32.6	24.3	–25.5%

* Excludes negative P/E multiples and P/E multiples larger than 100.
** Based upon an average of weekly prices and quarterly earnings.

SOURCE: *Mergerstat Review 2000* (Los Angeles: Applied Financial Information, 2000, p. 21.

Exhibit 15–6

**Mergerstat Control Premium Study
Comparative Results
1996–1999**

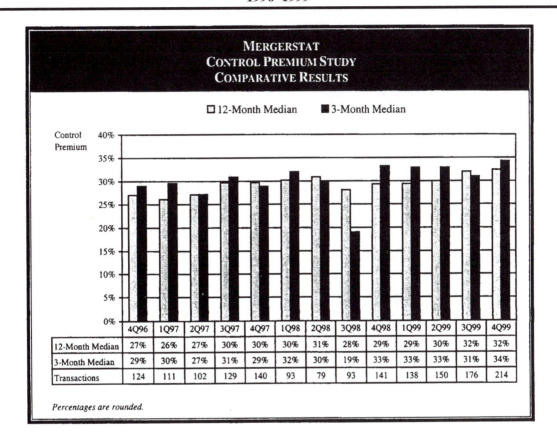

	4Q96	1Q97	2Q97	3Q97	4Q97	1Q98	2Q98	3Q98	4Q98	1Q99	2Q99	3Q99	4Q99
12-Month Median	27%	26%	27%	30%	30%	30%	31%	28%	29%	29%	30%	32%	32%
3-Month Median	29%	30%	27%	31%	29%	32%	30%	19%	33%	33%	33%	31%	34%
Transactions	124	111	102	129	140	93	79	93	141	138	150	176	214

Percentages are rounded.

SOURCE: *Mergerstat Control Premium Study*, 4th quarter 1999 (Los Angeles: Applied Financial Information, LP, 2000), p. 2.

Negative Control Premiums

From time to time, the acquisition price premium data presented in *Mergerstat Review* and the *Control Premium Study* report control event merger and acquisition transactions that have been consummated at a below-market price. This phenomenon usually occurs when the general stock market prices (and, therefore, the general stock market price/earnings multiples) are particularly high.

In a recent editorial, Shannon Pratt reported on this phenomenon:

Valuation analysts who use the guideline public-company valuation method and then automatically tack on a percentage "control premium" based on *Mergerstat Review* control premium averages, had better reconsider their methodology.

Exhibit 15–7

Mergerstat Control Premium Study
Price Premium Range

		Mergerstat Control Premium	Premium 1 Day	Premium 1 Week	Premium 1 Month	Premium 2 Months
Range	High	428.0%	222.2%	277.0%	236.4%	281.9%
	Low	2.2%	−58.4%	−56.0%	−57.2%	−58.6%
Median		31.7%	24.1%	30.5%	38.1%	40.7%
Average		45.4%	30.9%	38.0%	45.8%	52.8%

SOURCE: *Mergerstat Control Premium Study*, 4th quarter 1999 (Los Angeles: Applied Financial Information, LP, 2000), p. 52.

When stock market prices are as high as they have been in recent years, there often is no room for a control premium. In most cases, the company with the high-flying stock simply does not get any takeover offers. Once in a while, a company is taken over at a price less than the recent public market price.

Many discounts, some quite large

But during the third quarter of 1998, fully 20 of the 58 domestic transactions reported in the *HLHZ Control Premium Study* sold at discounts from their prior public trading prices. This is over a third of the transactions, not only without premiums but at discounts—many of them quite substantial! (See Exhibit 15–8.)[6]

Summary

When quantifying valuation discounts and/or premiums—such as the ownership control premium—it is important for the analyst to be very precise as to the level of value to which the discount or premium applies. This also means the valuation work product should be precise in its identification of the level of value that is being estimated. It is both practically and conceptually important that the level of valuation discounts and/or premiums be appropriately matched to the level of value estimated in the valuation.

This chapter discussed the concept of ownership control and the economic advantages of ownership control (compared with the fewer economic benefits available to a noncontrolling stockholder). There are numerous regulatory, legal, and contractual factors that affect the applicability and the quantification of the ownership control premiums. The degree of ownership dispersion or concentration and the degree to which the controlling shareholder can effectively (and legally) divert economic income or perquisites from the noncontrolling stockholder to the con-

---

[6] Shannon P. Pratt, "Control Premiums? Maybe, Maybe Not—34% of 3rd Quarter Buyouts at Discounts," *Shannon Pratt's Business Valuation Update*, January 1999, pp. 1–2.

Exhibit 15–8

Control Transactions at Discounts from Public Price
Third Quarter 1998

Target Name	Purchase Price Per Share	HLHZ Unaffected Price	HLHZ Control Premium	Price 1 Day Before	Premium 1 Day Before
Award Software International, Inc.	7.89	14.25	-44.6%	14.25	-44.6%
BankAmerica Corp.	62.87	76.44	-17.8%	76.44	-17.8%
Bristol Hotel Co.	23.08	27.63	-16.5%	27.63	-16.5%
Camco International Inc.	52.22	71.88	-27.4%	62.25	-16.1%
CBT Corp.	32.81	33.25	-1.3%	33.25	-1.3%
Dime Financial Corp.	31.84	33.00	-11.6%	36.00	-3.5%
Domain Energy Corp.	9.69	12.50	-22.5%	12.50	-22.5%
Dresser Industries Inc.	29.44	37.69	-21.9%	37.69	-21.9%
FTP Software, Inc.	0.91	2.00	-54.5%	2.00	-54.5%
Hyperion Software Corp.	30.40	38.13	-20.3%	38.13	-20.3%
IBS Financial Corp.	15.75	20.00	-21.3%	20.00	-21.3%
John Alden Financial Corp.	22.50	28.44	-20.9%	22.63	-0.6%
Oncormed Inc.	1.93	3.31	-41.8%	3.31	-41.8%
Retirement Care Associates Inc.	7.39	8.63	-14.4%	9.00	-17.9%
Saks Holdings Inc.	28.06	43.38	-35.3%	40.69	-31.0%
Teleport Communications Group	55.29	60.13	-8.0%	57.75	-4.3%
US Rentals Inc.	20.57	30.19	-31.9%	30.19	-31.9%
Western Atlas Inc.	64.48	79.75	-19.2%	79.95	-19.2%
Whitehall Corp.	18.67	22.00	-15.1%	22.00	-15.1%
Zero Corp.	28.48	28.88	-1.4%	28.88	-1.4%

SOURCE: Shannon P. Pratt, "Control Premiums? Maybe, Maybe Not—34% of 3rd Quarter Buyouts at Discounts," *Shannon Pratt's Business Valuation Update*, January 1999, p. 1.

trolling stockholder are important factors in the application of an ownership control premium.

As in many areas of business valuation, the empirical data available to quantify the ownership control premium are not perfect. The reason is that all generally available control premium studies actually report—and quantify—transactional acquisition price premiums, not just ownership control premiums. The reported data capture the value increment associated with ownership control. However, it is also likely that the reported data capture other value increments as well. These other value increments (or components of the acquisition price premium in addition to the stand-alone control premium) are sometimes called acquisition premiums, synergy premiums, merger benefit premiums, and so on.

The difference between total acquisition price premiums and the control premium element only deserves careful attention:

Each company that an analyst is valuing must be carefully analyzed to estimate the amount of an appropriate control premium, or even whether any premium is warranted at all. The actual answer may well be a discount from what we commonly call the "publicly traded equivalent value."

It is also important to recognize that what we historically have called the "control premiums" in the public market are actually "acquisition premiums."

In this sense, the premium paid typically reflects synergies between buyer and seller, not just what another owner may be able to do with the target company on a stand-alone basis.[7]

Nonetheless, these empirical data sources are the best data available to quantify ownership control premiums (absent expensive customized studies involving transactions consummated only by nonstrategic, financial buyers). Nonetheless, the analyst should be cognizant of these data limitations when selecting and applying the ownership control premium percentage.

A casual reading of the transactions roster in the 1997 [*Mergerstat Review*] book (or 1996 or 1995) will suggest that most of the acquisitions reported by far represent companies that have been acquired by companies in the same or similar business as the company acquired.[8]

Control premiums [in] typical appraisals may not be as large for private companies as many of us think. . . .[9]

Nonetheless, while there may be imperfections in the empirical control premium data, there is often a real economic value associated with ownership control of a business enterprise. And, depending on which valuation method is used to estimate the business value, it is a common valuation procedure to recognize this economic value increment by reference to the addition of an ownership control premium.

Bibliography

Annin, Michael. "Understanding and Quantifying Control Premiums: The Value of Control vs. Synergies or Strategic Advantages, Part I." *The Journal of Business Valuation* (Proceedings of the 4th Joint Business Valuation Conference of The Canadian Institute of Chartered Business Valuators and the American Society of Appraisers). Toronto: The Canadian Institute of Chartered Business Valuators, 1999, pp. 31–35.

Curtiss, Rand M. "A Practical Methodology for Determining Premiums and Discounts." *Business Valuation Review*, December 1997, pp. 172–79.

Fishman, Jay E., Shannon P. Pratt, J. Clifford Griffith, and D. Keith Wilson. "Premiums and Discounts in Business Valuations." Parts I and II. *Fair$hare*, May and June 1992, pp. 11–17, 14–16.

Garber, Steven D. "Control Premiums vs. Acquisition Premiums—Is There a Difference?" Presentation to the International Conference of the American Society of Appraisers, June 1998. Available on www.BVLibrary.com.

Hitchner, James R., and Gary Roland. "Marketability and Control Govern Value of Family Businesses." *Taxation for Accountants*, January 1994, pp. 24–28.

Julius, J. Michael. "Using Control Premium Statistics." *CPA Litigation Service Counselor*, July 1999, pp. 8–10.

Lease, Ronald C., John J. McConnell, and Wayne H. Mikkelson. "The Market Value of Control in Publicly-Traded Corporations. *Journal of Financial Economics 11* (1983), pp. 439–71.

---

[7] Ibid.

[8] Z. Christopher Mercer, "Understanding and Quantifying Control Premiums: The Value of Control vs. Synergies or Strategic Advantages, Part II," *The Journal of Business Valuation*, 1999, p. 50.

[9] Ibid., p. 52.

Mercer, Z. Christopher. "A Brief Review of Control Premiums and Minority Interest Discounts." *The Journal of Business Valuation* (Proceedings of the 12th Biennial Business Valuation Conference of The Canadian Institute of Chartered Business Valuators). Toronto: The Canadian Institute of Chartered Business Valuators, 1997, pp. 365–87.

_____. "Understanding and Quantifying Control Premiums: The Value of Control vs. Synergies or Strategic Advantages, Part II." *The Journal of Business Valuation* (Proceedings of the 4th Joint Business Valuation Conference of The Canadian Institute of Chartered Business Valuators and the American Society of Appraisers). Toronto: The Canadian Institute of Chartered Business Valuators, 1999, pp. 36–54. Also available at www.BVLibrary.com.

Nath, Eric W. "Control Premiums and Minority Interest Discounts in Private Companies." *Business Valuation Review*, June 1990, pp. 39–46.

_____. "Tale of Two Markets." *Business Valuation Review*, September 1994, pp. 107–12.

Pratt, Shannon P. "Control Premiums? Maybe, Maybe Not—34% of 3rd Quarter Buyouts at Discounts." *Shannon Pratt's Business Valuation Update*, January 1999, pp. 1–2.

Roach, George P. "Control Premiums and Strategic Mergers." *Business Valuation Review*, June 1998, pp. 42–49.

Schubert, Walt, and Les Barenbaum. "Control Premiums and the Value of the Closely-Held Firm." *Journal of Small Business Finance*, Vol. 1, No. 2 (1991), pp. 155–59.

Tiernan, Peter B. "How 50% Ownership Affects Estate Planning for Closely Held Stock." *Journal of Taxation*, October 1999, pp. 232–40.

Treynor, Jack L. "The Value of Control." *Financial Analysts Journal*, July–August 1993, pp. 6–9.

Chapter 16

Discount for Lack of Control

This chapter discusses the valuation of noncontrolling ownership interests in businesses. This type of ownership interest is often referred to in the valuation literature and in court cases as a *minority interest* or *minority ownership interest*. This type of ownership interest should be more properly referred to as a noncontrolling ownership interest.

This nomenclature is more consistent with the concepts of marketability and lack of marketability. A marketable ownership interest is one that is reasonably liquid. In other words, it can be sold and converted into cash quickly and at a low transaction cost. A business interest or security that does not enjoy this economic attribute is said to be nonmarketable. In the valuation process, that nonmarketable security may be valued by the application of a lack of marketability discount—or a "discount for lack of marketability."

Consistent with the standard industry jargon with regard to marketable ownership interests, an ownership interest that enjoys the economic "perquisites of control" is called a controlling ownership interest. The perquisites of control will be discussed later in this chapter. A business interest or security that does not enjoy the perquisites of control is said to be noncontrolling. In the valuation process, that noncontrolling security may be valued by the application of a lack of control discount—or a "discount for lack of control."

Therefore, in this chapter, we will use the phrase "noncontrolling ownership interests" to refer to so-called minority ownership interests. Readers should be aware that these two terms usually mean the same thing as what courts (and others) sometimes refer to as a *minority interest*.

This chapter discusses one aspect of the economic phenomenon that occurs when a particular ownership interest in a business is worth less than its pro rata percentage of the overall business enterprise value. That is, this chapter will explore why a 20 percent ownership interest in a business may be worth less (in some cases, materially less) than 20 percent of the overall enterprise value of that very business. The aspect that will be discussed in this chapter is the decremental effect on the value of an equity investment due to fact that its owner is not able to totally control the financial, operational, or legal aspects of the subject business.

This decremental effect on the pro rata value of an ownership interest is correctly called the lack of control discount. In this chapter, we will investigate how to identify and quantify the lack of control discount. Again, readers should be cognizant of the fact that this valuation adjustment is often referred to as the "minority interest discount," or simply the "minority discount," in many judicial decisions.

There is a conceptually important reason for this preferred nomenclature. This economic phenomenon—that is, a valuation adjustment—is caused by the fact that the subject equity investment is a noncontrolling ownership interest, not because it is a minority ownership interest. What is the difference? Let's consider two examples with regard to the valuation of substantial closely held corporations.

In the first example, one individual owns 40 percent of the common stock of the corporation. Sixty other individuals each own 1 percent of the common stock of the corporation. Technically, the 40 percent owner has a minority ownership interest. No one stockholder enjoys ownership control. However, the 40 percent stockholder probably enjoys management and operational control of the company. Unless almost all of the other shareholders vote unanimously in opposition, the 40 percent shareholder will receive the economic benefits of many of the elements of control.

In the second example, let's assume that Mister X owns 60 percent of XY Corporation and Mister Y owns 40 percent of XY Corporation. Clearly, Mister X enjoys voting control. However, he does not enjoy absolute control of XY Corporation. The various levels of control will be summarized in this chapter and were described in greater detail in Chapter 15, regarding control and acquisition price premiums. Depending on state statutes, Mister X can probably not squeeze out Mister Y. In fact, under state security statutes, Mister X may have a fiduciary duty of fair dealing to Mister Y.

And, Mister X may not have enough ownership control to effectuate either a merger or corporate dissolution. Depending on (1) state statutes and (2) the corporation's articles of incorporation, Mister Y may be able to block many of Mister X's desired corporate actions.

In the first example above, the stock of the 40 percent "minority" shareholder may be valued by consideration of some level of a control premium. In the second example above, the value of the stock of Mister X, the "control" stockholder, some level of discount may be considered—due to a lack of absolute control.

There are other scenarios when a lack of control valuation adjustment should be applied to something other than a minority ownership interest. We will introduce some of these scenarios later in this chapter.

As a final introductory comment, some analysts refer to minority ownership interests as *fractional ownership interests*. They define a fractional ownership interest as anything less than a 100 percent ownership interest. However, with regard to business valuation, this term is not commonly used in the literature, in the appraisal standards, or in the judicial precedent. The term *fractional ownership interest* is commonly used in the appraisal of less than a 100 percent ownership interest in real estate. In real estate appraisal jargon, a divided ownership interest in a real estate parcel is often called a fractional ownership interest.

Elements of Absolute Ownership Control

The following is a list of 20 of the more common prerogatives of absolute business ownership control:

1. Appoint or change operational management.
2. Appoint or change members of the board of directors.
3. Determine management compensation and perquisites.
4. Set operational and strategic policy and change the course of the business.
5. Acquire, lease, or liquidate business assets, including plant, property, and equipment.
6. Select suppliers, vendors, and subcontractors with whom to do business and award contracts.

7. Negotiate and consummate mergers and acquisitions.
8. Liquidate, dissolve, sell out, or recapitalize the company.
9. Sell or acquire treasury shares.
10. Register the company's equity securities for an initial or secondary public offering.
11. Register the company's debt securities for an initial or secondary public offering.
12. Declare and pay cash and/or stock dividends.
13. Change the articles of incorporation or bylaws.
14. Set one's own compensation (and perquisites) and the compensation (and perquisites) of related-party employees.
15. Select joint venturers and enter into joint venture and partnership agreements.
16. Decide what products and/or services to offer and how to price those products/services.
17. Decide what markets and locations to serve, to enter into, and to discontinue serving.
18. Decide which customer categories to market to and which not to market to.
19. Enter into inbound and outbound license or sharing agreements regarding intellectual properties.
20. Block any or all of the above actions.

As the equityholder enjoys fewer and fewer of these elements of ownership control, his or her position changes from absolute control to relative control to lack of control to absolute lack of control. Along this spectrum: (1) The control premium begins to decrease, (2) then becomes zero, and finally (3) changes to a lack of control discount.

The above list is also presented in Chapter 15. In that chapter, we discussed the economic value associated with the ability to exercise all of these elements of ownership control. In this chapter, we discuss the decrease in economic value associated with the inability to exercise all of these elements of ownership control. The business owner who can exercise all 20 elements of control enjoys absolute control. In such a case, a substantial ownership control premium is appropriate.

In instances when a business owner owns more than a 50 percent equity interest but cannot exercise many of these elements, then a much smaller ownership control premium may be appropriate. This situation may even be the case when the owner of 100 percent of a business operates in a highly regulated industry: In that case, the government—and not the business owner—may enjoy many of the elements of control.

In this chapter, we will explore the situation where the equityholder enjoys few—or none—of these elements of control. This dissipation of control could occur due to (1) contractual agreement (e.g., the equityholder forgoes these elements of control in a FLP or shareholder agreement), (2) government or other regulatory authority (e.g., supervision by a federal bankruptcy court), or (3) the equityholder owns less than 50 percent of the outstanding equity interests.

From the above list of control elements, it is apparent that the owner of an absolute controlling business ownership interest enjoys some very valuable rights not enjoyed by an owner not in such a controlling ownership position. While the controlling owner may not elect to exploit the economic benefits of the control position, what is important is that the control owner has the ability to exercise those economic benefits. Also, while the controlling owner may not exercise the perquisites of control to the economic disadvantage of the noncontrolling party (i.e., the control owner may not decide to disproportionately divert company resources), what is important is that the control owner has the ability to divert economic benefits from the noncontrolling owner.

From a valuation perspective, the concepts of the control premium and the lack of control discount depend on the control owner's ability to control events. The fact that the control owner has not exercised that ability historically may affect the magnitude of the premium or discount to apply—but it will not affect the conceptual applicability of the control premium or the lack of control discount.

Degree of Ownership Control

The matter of a controlling ownership position versus a noncontrolling ownership position is not an either/or proposition. Relevant state statutes, the subject company's articles of incorporation and bylaws, and the way the overall ownership of the subject company is distributed have an important bearing on the relative rights of the noncontrolling and of the controlling stockholders.

Effect of State Statutes

Statutes affecting the relative rights of controlling versus noncontrolling stockholders vary from state to state.

Supermajority Vote Requirements. In some states, a simple majority vote can approve major actions such as a merger, sale of all of the assets, or liquidation of the company. Other states require a two-thirds—or even greater—majority vote in order to approve such corporate actions. In these instances, a stockholder with just over a one-third ownership interest in the company (and in a few states, even less) has the power to block such actions. This is true even if there is a stockholder with a clear majority (i.e., over 50 percent) ownership position. In that case, the "majority" stockholder may enjoy relative control of the business—but not absolute control of the business.

State Dissolution Statutes. Under the statutes of a majority of the states, noncontrolling stockholders enjoy certain legal rights under some circumstances that noncontrolling stockholders in some other states generally do not enjoy. For example, under certain circumstances, noncontrolling stockholders can bring suit to dissolve the corporation. If the suit is successful and if the controlling stockholders wish to avoid dissolution, the remedy is to pay the noncontrolling stockholders the "fair value" for their stock. For this reason, the variations in state law concerning legal rights attributable to various equity ownership percentage interests have an important bearing on the valuation of a noncontrolling ownership interest.

Effect of Articles of Incorporation and Bylaws

As with state statutes, a company's articles of incorporation or bylaws may require supermajorities for certain actions. Also, the company's articles of incorporation or bylaws may confer special rights to noncontrolling stockholders under certain conditions. The possibilities are almost without limit. In performing the valuation of a noncontrolling ownership interest, the analyst should develop an understanding of the articles of incorporation and the bylaws (and all amendments thereto) in order to understand any factors affecting the noncontrolling stockholders' (1) degree of ownership control and (2) ability to restrict the absolute level of control of the controlling stockholder.

Effect of Distribution of Equity Ownership

If one person owns 49 percent of the stock and another person owns 51 percent, the 49 percent holder typically has little or no control of the company. However, if two stockholders each own 49 percent and a third stockholder owns 2 percent, the 49 percent stockholders may be on a par with each other—depending on who owns the other 2 percent. The 2 percent stockholder may be able to command a considerable price premium over the pro rata value for that particular block of stock because of its "swing vote" power.

If each of three stockholders (or partners) owns a one-third ownership interest, no one may have absolute control. On the other hand, no one owner may be in a relatively inferior position to the other two. This is true unless two of the three owners have close ties with each other (that are not shared by the third).

This three-stockholder example provides an excellent illustration for why the analyst should develop an understanding of the company's articles of incorporation and bylaws. Let's say that the three stockholders are Alpha, Beta, and Gamma. Each owns exactly one-third of the outstanding shares, but Alpha is the company president. The company articles of incorporation provide that the president can exercise all of the perquisites of control described previously. And, the removal of the president requires a vote of more than 50 percent of the outstanding stock. Under this set of circumstances, unless Beta and Gamma came together to vote the removal of Alpha, Alpha's one-third "minority" ownership interest is in a substantially superior position to the one-third interests owned by Beta and Gamma. As this example illustrates, the analyst should consider all of the specific circumstances related to each unique fact set when analyzing the applicability of lack of control discounts.

Normally, equal individual ownership interests are each worth less than a pro rata proportion of what the total business enterprise is worth. What this means is the sum of the values of the individual ownership interests normally is less than the amount that the total business enterprise could be sold for to a single "absolute control" buyer. However, the percentage valuation adjustment from pro rata value for each of such equal ownership interests would not normally be as great as for an ownership interest that had no control whatsoever. On the contrary, if one shareholder in the three equal shareholder example were to auction his or her shares to the other two, the price could conceivably exceed pro rata value.

Each situation has to be analyzed individually with respect to (1) the degree of control, or lack of it, and (2) the implications for the value of the subject noncontrolling ownership interest.

Distinction between Discount for Lack of Control and Discount for Lack of Marketability

Some inexperienced analysts do not understand the important differences between (1) a discount for lack of ownership control (also called a minority interest discount) and (2) a discount for lack of marketability. These are two separate concepts, although there is some subtle interrelationship between them.

Some judges also do not distinguish between the lack of control discount and the lack of marketability discount—either in their published opinions or in their quantitative decisions. Unfortunately, it is not that uncommon for a judicial decision to conclude a "combined" lack of control and lack of marketability discount of, say, 50 percent or 60 percent. Such a combined conclusion does not educate either the lay reader of the case or the legal scholar as to the judge's thinking with regard to the two separate components of the total combined discount. It is understandable when judges (who are usually not trained as valuation analysts) combine or confuse these two separate valuation discounts. However, it is not acceptable for a valuation analyst with even rudimentary training to confuse these two separate valuation discounts.

Many judges, of course, do understand the difference between the lack of control discount and the lack of marketability discount. And, some judges fault valuation expert witnesses for failing to distinguish between these two discounts.

In a recent tax case, the court was dissatisfied with the taxpayer's valuation because that valuation did not disaggregate these two discounts.

> As for discounts, the Court agreed with the taxpayer's expert that a discount should be applied for both lack of control and lack of marketability: "A minority discount reflects the minority shareholder's inability to compel liquidation and thereby realize a pro rata share of the corporation's net asset value. A discount for lack of marketability reflects the fact that there is no ready market for the stock of a closely held corporation."
>
> The Court also faulted the taxpayer's expert for failing to explain why he selected a 35 percent discount for minority interest and lack of marketability while the IRS's expert indicated a 10 percent minority interest. The taxpayer's expert "did not specify how much of the 35 percent combined discount that he applied was attributable to the fact that decedent did not own a controlling stock interest in B & W Longview on the valuation date. On brief, petitioner, who has the burden of proof, does not insist that a minority discount in excess of 10 percent be applied in this case."[1]

The concept of *noncontrolling ownership interest* deals with the relationship between the ownership interest being valued and the total business enterprise. This relationship is based on the factors discussed earlier in this chapter. The primary factor bearing on the value of the subject noncontrolling ownership interest in relation to the value of the total entity is how much ownership or operational control the noncontrolling ownership interest does—or does not—have over the particular entity.

The concept of *marketability* deals with the liquidity of the subject ownership interest—that is, how quickly and certainly it can be converted to cash at the owner's discretion. This topic is discussed in the next chapter.

Analysts sometimes overlook the fact that valuation adjustments (in this case, discounts) are meaningless until the base from which the adjustment is to be taken has been clearly defined. Since a noncontrolling ownership interest discount reflects a lack of control, the base from which the discount should be subtracted is its proportionate share in the total enterprise value (including all of the rights of ownership control). Since a discount for lack of marketability reflects a lack of liquidity, the base

---

[1] James R. Hitchner, "50% + 50% ≠ 100%," *CPA Expert*, Winter 1998, pp. 14–15 (review of *Estate of Thomas A. Fleming, et al. v. Commissioner*, T.C. Memo 1997-484 (October 27, 1997)).

from which the discount should be subtracted is the value of an enterprise or ownership interest that is otherwise comparable but that enjoys higher liquidity.

Even controlling ownership interests suffer to some extent from a lack of marketability. For example, it may take several months (or longer)—and a significant amount of expense and effort on the part of a single owner—to sell a 100 percent ownership interest in a company.

The relationship between the discount for lack of marketability and the discount for lack of control lies in the fact that, even after discounting a noncontrolling ownership interest for its lack of control, it still is usually much harder to sell a noncontrolling ownership interest than to sell a controlling ownership interest in the same business.

> The controlling interest value is generally considered to represent the value of an entire business. This value encompasses the rights, risks and rewards of having controlling power in a business. . . .
>
> We should note that controlling interests can be considered to be "marketable" in that they can generally be sold. However, controlling interests in companies are not "marketable" in the sense of publicly traded minority interests, where cash is available in three days upon entering a sale order with a broker. . . .[2]

For this reason, it is often useful to distinguish between (1) the lack of marketability of a noncontrolling ownership interest and (2) the lack of marketability of a controlling ownership interest. Unless the subject company has been "prepared" for sale and exposed to the market for some period of time, even a 100 percent ownership interest in a closely held business enterprise may suffer from some lack of marketability. As will be discussed in the next chapter related to lack of marketability, a company is prepared for sale after the owner has incurred the time and expense to, for example, prepare audited financial statements, have all company legal documents and board resolutions and minutes in order, have all leases and contracts prepared for transfer, have all elements of intangible asset ownership documented, have all contingent liabilities documented, retain a business broker or investment banker, and so forth.

In order to distinguish between these two different levels and applications of the lack of marketability discount, some analysts have suggested the following nomenclature:

1. *Lack of marketability discount* applies to noncontrolling ownership interest valuations.
2. *Illiquidity discount* applies to controlling ownership interest and business enterprise valuations.

Both of these terms, lack of marketability discount and illiquidity discount, effectively describe the same type of value decrement economic phenomenon. The reason to distinguish the two terms is that the order of magnitude of the phenomenon is (typically) so much greater for noncontrolling ownership interests than for controlling ownership interests.

When valuing a noncontrolling ownership interest in a closely held company by comparing it with values of publicly held securities, the analyst should apply a dis-

[2] Z. Christopher Mercer, "A Brief Review of Control Premiums and Minority Interest Discounts," *1997 Journal of Business Valuation* (Proceedings of the 12th Biennial Business Valuation Conference of The Canadian Institute of Chartered Business Valuators, 1996), pp. 366–67.

count only for lack of marketability. This is because a noncontrolling ownership interest discount is already implicit in the public stock's trading price.

Exhibit 16–1 illustrates the relationship between controlling ownership interest value, noncontrolling ownership interest value if readily marketable, and noncontrolling ownership interest value if not readily marketable.

How the Business Valuation Approach Affects the Lack of Control Discount

Each business valuation approach, depending on the specific methodology applied, indicates a value with certain assumed ownership characteristics (e.g., control/noncontrol, marketable/nonmarketable). The level of value (including assumed ownership characteristics) each approach may indicate was discussed in the chapters on the respective approaches. The ownership characteristics of the value indicated by the approach affect, to a large degree, the premiums and/or discount(s) appropriate for (1) the standard and (2) the premise of value being estimated. This section discusses how the selection and application of the business valuation approach(es) impact the discount for lack of control.

The Income Approach

The various methods within the income approach all have two basic elements in common:

1. A numerator consisting of an amount or amounts of expected economic income.
2. A denominator consisting of a rate of return at which the economic income is either discounted or capitalized.

Of these two analytical components, the more significant influence on the control versus noncontrol ownership level in the income approach is found in the numerator—the expected economic income—rather than in the denominator—the discount or capitalization rate.

For example, let's assume that a public company acquires a controlling ownership interest in another company, whether public or private. The acquirer generally will not be willing to accept a lower rate of return than its cost of capital (i.e., based on its own publicly traded minority stock) just because it is acquiring control. This is because a lower expected rate of return would be dilutive and detrimental to the acquirer's existing stockholders. Typically, acquiring control reduces risk compared with acquiring a noncontrolling ownership interest. And, that reduced level of risk should be reflected in a lower discount rate. This risk reduction phenomenon may well be a major factor in certain instances. For example, the reduced risk associated with ownership control may affect the selection of a discount rate (or hurdle rate) in the acquisition pricing decisions of individual investors or closely held corporate acquirers. However, surveys show that in instances of public company acquirers, the control versus noncontrol issue has relatively little impact on the discount rate used in the acquisition pricing decision.

More importantly, many analysts believe that the appropriate discount rate to use in the valuation should be the target's cost of capital, not the acquirer's cost

Exhibit 16–1

Example of Relationships between Levels of Ownership Interest and Applicability of Valuation Discounts

Level of Ownership Interest	Example of Ownership Interest Type	Type of Applicable Valuation Adjustment	Illustrative Impact of Value Decrement	Illustrative Percentage Discount[a]
Marketable, controlling ownership interest	100% ownership of a business that is offered for sale.	No discount applicable.	$10.00 per share	N/A
Nonmarketable, controlling ownership interest	Less than 100% (but controlling) ownership of a business.	Discount for illiquidity at the business enterprise level.	$9.00 per share	10%
Marketable, noncontrolling ownership interest[b]	Shares of registered stock in a publicly traded corporation.	Discount for lack of control (also called minority interest discount).	$6.30 per share	30%
Nonmarketable, noncontrolling ownership interest	Shares of stock in a closely held or family owned business.	Discount for lack of marketability at the share level.	$3.78 per share[c]	40%

a.   The magnitude of the valuation discounts are selected for illustrative purposes only and not to indicate recommended levels (or even orders of magnitude) of specific valuation adjustments.
b.   This level of ownership interest is often called the "as if freely traded value" or "publicly traded equivalent value" because it indicates what the subject security would sell for if it was freely traded on an organized stock exchange.
c.   The cumulative impact of a 10 percent, a 30 percent, and a 40 percent discount is a total 62.2 percent discount (and not an 80 percent discount). This is because the application of valuation discounts is multiplicative and not additive. Also, the order of the application of the valuation discounts will not affect the cumulative amount of the valuation adjustment.

of capital. That certainly is true if the selected standard of value is fair market value. Even if the selected standard of value is investment value, the greater risk of the target may increase the acquirer's overall cost of capital. This would imply that the risk of the subject controlling ownership interest may affect the acquirer's selection of a discount rate (or hurdle rate) for acquisition pricing purposes.

With regard to the effect of the discount rate on the level of value estimated by the income approach, there are two conceptual components to the discount rate selection process:

1.   Estimation of the appropriate cost of capital components (i.e., the cost of debt, the cost of equity).
2.   Estimation of the appropriate ratio of capital components in the subject capital structure (i.e., the "mix" of the debt to equity components).

We indicated above that, typically, the level of value will not materially affect the cost of the capital components. However, the level of value may materially affect the ratio of the capital components. In this regard, the selection of a "control" discount rate versus a "noncontrol" discount rate would have a material effect on the value indication.

For example, let's assume that the valuation subject is a noncontrolling ownership interest in a closely held business. The business is currently financed 100 percent with equity. And, the current market-derived cost of equity capital for such a business is 20 percent. For the valuation of the noncontrolling ownership interest, the analyst uses a discount rate around 20 percent.

Now, let's assume that the valuation subject is a controlling ownership interest in the same closely held business. Based on market-derived evidence, the analyst has concluded that the typical willing buyer would capitalize the company with 50 percent debt and 50 percent equity. And, the current market-derived (after-tax) cost of debt capital for such a business is 10 percent. For the valuation of the controlling ownership interest, the analyst uses a discount rate around 15 percent.

Obviously, the difference between a 20 percent discount rate (applicable to a noncontrolling ownership interest) and a 15 percent discount rate (applicable to a controlling ownership interest) will have a material effect on the value estimates.

Nonetheless, the more significant difference between control and noncontrol ownership in the income approach is generally found in the economic income projections. To the extent that the economic income projections reflect the ability of a controlling shareholder to realize more for the controlling interest than a noncontrolling shareholder could realize under the status quo, the income approach reflects the impact of control. And, the indicated value would represent an ownership level encompassing those elements of control. If a controlling stockholder could enhance value to controlling shares, but the impact of such potential actions is not reflected in the economic income projections, then the indication of value would be on a noncontrolling ownership basis. And, a premium for ownership control over the indicated value could be warranted if the valuation subject is a controlling ownership interest.

The most common example of economic income projections that would lead to either noncontrol or a control value is whether or not owners' compensation is adjusted to reflect the true economic value of the services rendered. Such an adjustment would move the income approach value indication toward a control ownership level of value rather than a noncontrol ownership level of value.

The implication of this discussion is that (1) the justification for and (2) the amount of any lack of control discount—or any control premium—over the value indications of the income approach largely depend on the ability of a control owner to increase the economic income paid to the control shares—over and above the amounts of economic income already accounted for in the income approach. The amounts of the (1) economic income adjustments and (2) discount rate adjustments to make in order to convert the income approach value indication from a noncontrol level to a control level (or vice versa) should be assessed based on the facts and circumstances in each particular case.

Market Approach—Guideline Publicly Traded Company Method

By definition, since the guideline publicly traded company method derives a value based on publicly traded shares, this method typically indicates a marketable, noncontrolling ownership level of value. If conditions in the market for companies in the industry at the valuation date are such that controlling ownership interests can be sold for more than the aggregate value of the publicly traded minority shares, then the application of a control premium is probably appropriate if the subject is a controlling ownership interest. (Such a control premium may be partially or fully offset by a discount for lack of marketability, as discussed in the next chapter.)

Market Approach—Guideline Merged and Acquired Company Method

Most (but not all) merger and acquisition transactions involve controlling ownership interests. Therefore, if an indication of value is developed based on empirical merger and acquisition transactional data, an additional control premium generally would not be appropriate. If valuing a noncontrolling ownership interest, a lack of control discount usually would be appropriate.

This is because the values indicated by this method generally are control values. So, premium for ownership control is already implicit in (1) the market-derived pricing evidence and (2) the indicated values. The application of an additional control premium is not necessary in order to reach the controlling ownership interest level of value. However, the application of a discount for lack of control is usually necessary in order to reach the noncontrolling ownership interest level of value.

Asset-Based Approach—Asset Accumulation Method

The asset accumulation method—also called the adjusted net asset value method—generally indicates a controlling ownership interest level of value. This is because only a controlling stockholder could decide (1) to replace or liquidate the subject assets or (2) to put the subject assets to their highest and best use in a going-concern context. If the economic value of all of the subject company intangible assets is captured in the asset-based approach valuation, then noncontrolling shares typically would sell at a lack of control discount from the indicated value. In other words, if the application of the asset accumulation method encompasses both (1) the value of all the tangible assets (and their highest and best use) and (2) the economic value of all the intangible assets, then the indicated lack of control discount would normally need to be applied in order to indicate a noncontrolling ownership interest level of value.

We would like to think that if the income approach, the market approach, and the asset-based approach were all properly applied for a controlling ownership interest level of value, we would reach the same indicated value by all three approaches. And, the amount of the lack of control discount to move from a control to a noncontrol level of value would be the same. However, rarely do the data allow us to make such a simple adjustment. In the typical situation (and especially when using the guideline publicly traded company method), one set of market-derived data provide guidance for a lack of control discount to move from a marketable control to a marketable noncontrol level of value. And then, another set of market-derived data provide guidance for a lack of marketability discount to move from a marketable, noncontrol to a nonmarketable, noncontrol level of value.

When using the asset-based approach, analysts may have to use this two-step discounting process in order to indicate a nonmarketable, noncontrolling interest level of value. The data for the lack of control discount portion of this process are better for some industries than for others. When using adjusted net asset value as a base, however, some empirical data unfortunately aggregate the lack of control and lack of marketability phenomena so that they cannot be separately quantified. This is especially true for limited partnership interests, as will be seen in a later section. If an analyst is starting from adjusted net asset value as an indicator of a controlling ownership interest, and the objective is to value a nonmarketable, noncontrolling interest, the analyst can either (1) discount first for lack of control and then take a separate lack of marketability discount or (2) aggregate the two separate factors into a single combined discount. Which of these two procedures is preferable in each valuation depends on the type of company and the quality of the empirical data available for quantification of the particular discounts.

Asset-Based Approach—Capitalized Excess Earnings Method

The excess earnings method can be viewed as a specialized application of the asset accumulation method by (1) adjusting tangible assets to fair market value and (2) aggregating all the intangible asset value into a single calculation—based on a capitalization of excess earnings. The amount of earnings included in this analysis typically is adjusted to reflect the prerogatives of ownership control. If the measure of earnings subject to capitalization corresponds to the earnings available to a control owner, then the capitalized excess earnings method would indicate a control level of value.

If the measure of earnings does not, however, reflect the prerogatives of ownership control, and the tangible assets are not adjusted to market value, then the capitalized excess earnings method would typically indicate a noncontrolling ownership level of value. Therefore, when considering whether a control premium or discount should be applied to a value derived from the capitalized excess earnings method, the analyst should consider whether or not the prerogatives of ownership control have been reflected in the economic income used in the calculation.

How the Applicable Standard of Value Affects Minority Ownership Interests

As discussed in Chapter 2, the applicable standard of value for most business valuations falls into one of four categories: (1) fair market value, (2) investment value, (3) intrinsic value, or (4) fair value. The applicable standard of value is determined primarily by the purpose and objective of the appraisal. In some situations, the applicable standard of value is mandated by law. In other situations, the choice of the standard of value lies within the discretion of the parties involved.

Fair Market Value

The fair market value standard implies the most likely price at which an arm's-length transaction would be expected to take place between normally motivated investors under open market conditions, without considering any special benefits that may be related to the transaction for any particular buyer or seller. Considering the relative unattractiveness of noncontrolling ownership interests in closely held companies to investors in general, under the fair market value standard, the valuation discount from a proportionate share of the business enterprise value would normally be quite large.

Investment Value

In Chapter 2, *investment value* was defined to include the value to a *particular* buyer or seller. We noted that consideration could be given to (for example) the investor's particular cost of capital, specific perception of risk, and other characteristics unique to that investor.

When valuing noncontrolling ownership interests, one characteristic unique to a particular investor that may be important is the investor's relationship with the other owners of the subject business. Such a relationship may give the particular noncontrolling owner some elements of control—or economic benefits—that would otherwise only be available to a controlling owner. It is noteworthy that some family law courts give recognition to such relationships, while the U.S. Tax Court (adhering to the standard of fair market value) does not.

Intrinsic Value

Intrinsic value, as noted in Chapter 2, arises from analysis of the characteristics of the investment, such as value of the company's assets, likely future earnings, likely future dividends, and likely future dividend rates.

The relative importance of these factors, however, may be different for noncontrolling ownership valuations than for control ownership valuations. Dividends may take on increased importance for a noncontrolling equity investor. This is because dividends may be the only periodic cash flow that the noncontrolling equity investor enjoys. Asset values, on the other hand, may have little or no importance to a noncontrolling equity investor, unless the noncontrolling equity investor perceives that the assets will somehow translate into a real economic benefit. The same thing can be said of the expected future earnings and growth of the subject company.

Fair Value

The fair value standard suffers from a lack of consistent definition from one context to another. It arises most often as the statutory standard of value applicable to valuations prepared under dissenting stockholders' rights. Such valuations, by their nature, are analyses of noncontrolling ownership interests. The need to interpret the meaning of this standard of value from a study of the legal precedents in dissenting stockholder actions in each of the 50 states and Canada poses a continuing challenge to the business valuation profession.

Certain state-specific precedents have suggested that fair value be interpreted to mean fair market value without a noncontrolling ownership interest discount (i.e., a proportionate share of the overall enterprise value). However, it should be reiterated that research as to the applicable legal precedent is important in each context to which the fair value standard applies.

Approaches to the Valuation of Noncontrolling Ownership Interests

There are three basic ways of approaching the valuation of noncontrolling ownership interests:

1. The discount approach—based on a proportionate share of the overall business enterprise value, less a specific valuation lack of control discount applied to the enterprise value.
2. The direct comparison approach—based on a direct comparison of the subject ownership interest with the values of other noncontrolling ownership interests.
3. The bottom-up approach—based on the estimation of the economic benefits that the noncontrolling ownership interest holder expects to realize over the expected holding period of the subject investment.

Conceptually, there is some analogy of the above-mentioned approaches to the three generally accepted approaches to individual asset appraisal: the cost approach, the market approach, and the income approach. The discount approach considers the "cost" of lack of control to the security holder in terms of a specific value decrement. The direct comparison approach relies on market-derived data regarding the sales of guideline or comparable noncontrolling securities (e.g., sales of other blocks of noncontrolling stock in the same closely held corporation). And, the bottom-up approach values the subject noncontrolling security by reference to the present value of all components of economic income that will be derived from the ownership of that noncontrolling security.

The Discount Approach

A common way to approach the valuation of a noncontrolling ownership interest is to apply the following four-step process:

1. Estimate the overall value of the subject business enterprise.
2. Calculate the noncontrolling owner's pro rata allocation of the business enterprise value.
3. Estimate the amount of the valuation adjustment—that is, the lack of control discount applicable to the pro rata allocation of the overall business enterprise value in order to properly reflect economic disadvantage of the noncontrolling owner vis-à-vis the controlling owner.
4. Subtract the lack of control discount from the controlling owner pro rata allocation of the overall business enterprise value. (In most cases, one would then also subtract a lack of marketability discount.)

The value of the overall business enterprise should be estimated on a controlling ownership level of value as discussed previously in this book. The proportionate value is normally a straightforward calculation. However, occasionally there may be complications due to special rights of different classes of partners or stockholders.

The amount of the valuation adjustment—or discount—to reflect the noncontrolling ownership interest should be a matter of rigorous analysis. The degree of ownership control, or the lack of it, has a bearing on the magnitude of the applicable valuation discount. However, there is no single formula to quantify this valuation adjustment.

Also, the valuation discount is generally lower for stocks that pay cash dividends or partnerships that distribute considerable cash flow, than for those that do not. However, there is no simple formula to quantify that factor either. Some guidance with regard to typical discounts—and to typical ranges of discounts—related to noncontrolling ownership interests is presented in later sections of this chapter.

The Direct Comparison Approach

If data are available on actual sales of comparative noncontrolling ownership interests, the analyst may be able to reach a conclusion of value by direct comparison to such transactions. This analysis can be performed without ever going through the step of estimating a value for the total business enterprise. The analyst can value the subject noncontrolling ownership interest using market valuation approach procedures similar to those used for valuing a total company. Such procedures include, for example, the capitalization of earnings, the capitalization of cash flow, the capitalization of dividends (or partnership withdrawals), the application of a market-derived multiple of price to book value, the application of a market-derived price to adjusted net asset value, and so on.

Guidance with regard to the quantification of the market-derived pricing multiples comes from an analysis of comparative noncontrolling ownership interest transactional data.

Sources of Comparative Data. One obvious source of comparative data would be prior arm's-length transactions involving noncontrolling ownership interests in the subject company.

There is no generally available source of data on any broad group of noncontrolling ownership interest transactions in closely held companies. There is, of course, a readily available database on daily transactions in minority equity interests in literally thousands of publicly traded companies. Subject to several limitations discussed earlier in the book, guidance with respect to market-derived pricing multiples for the valuation of noncontrolling ownership interests may be drawn from the prices of comparative publicly traded stocks.

Adjustments for Risk and for Lack of Marketability. As discussed earlier in the book, if the comparison with public stock prices procedure is performed, adjustments need to be made for differences in (1) risk, (2) liquidity, and (3) other factors. The most important of these factors is the lack of marketability of the noncontrolling ownership interest in the closely held company, compared with the virtually instant marketability of publicly traded stock.

This difference in marketability is a more important factor with respect to valuation than many people realize. The fair market values of noncontrolling ownership interests in closely held companies typically cluster between 35 percent to 50 percent less than prices of comparative noncontrolling equity interests in liquid, publicly traded companies, all other things being equal. This topic is discussed in great detail in the following chapter on discounts for lack of marketability.

The Bottom-Up Approach

In the two above-described approaches, the noncontrolling ownership interest valuation started with an estimated value. In the discount approach, the methodology applied a valuation discount (or two) in order to estimate the value of the noncontrolling ownership interest. In the direct comparison approach, the analysis started with the known values of comparable security sale transactions. In the bottom-up approach, the methodology starts with a *tabula rasa* (empty slate) and estimates what the noncontrolling equity interest owner may realize on the basis of a fundamental economic analysis.

In most cases, the economic benefits that the noncontrolling ownership interest holder may realize fall into two categories:

1. Dividends or partnership withdrawals (i.e., current economic income).
2. Proceeds from the ultimate sale of the ownership interest or liquidation of the subject business (i.e., including any long-term appreciation in the value of the security interest itself).

This approach is really analogous to an application of the discounted economic income method of the income approach to business valuation. The income approach is discussed in Chapter 9. The general procedures in the bottom-up approach to noncontrolling ownership interest valuation are as follows:

1. Project the expected income distributions (i.e., dividends, property distributions, or partnership withdrawals).
2. Project an investment holding period and a price at which the subject ownership interest can be expected to be sold. The projected holding period is often the amount of time before a "control event" (such as an IPO, sale of the company, liquidation of the company, etc.) is expected to occur.
3. Estimate an appropriate present value discount rate, using the methods and information discussed in Chapter 9.
4. Discount the projected periodic income distributions and the projected ultimate security sale price to a present value, using the present value formula presented in Chapter 9.

Analytical Caveat

We have previously suggested that, when developing the company's earnings capacity as part of the business enterprise valuation process, the analyst may remove from expenses such discretionary items as the controlling shareholder's excess compensation and the cost of the controlling shareholder's discretionary expenditures. That previous discussion was relevant to the valuation of the entire company. These discretionary expense adjustments assume that it is within the controlling owner's discretion to remove such expenses with no significant impairment to company revenues. The noncontrolling stockholder, however, has no such power to eliminate these discretionary expenses. Therefore, these adjustments may not be relevant in estimating an earnings base for the valuation of noncontrolling ownership interests. This is true unless there is reason to believe that the discretionary expense changes are actually going to be made.

The same general concept applies to adjustments to the balance sheet to reflect the values of excess or nonoperating assets. Unless the controlling business owner is expected to take some immediate action to liquidate these assets, their values to the noncontrolling stockholders are remote.

Discounts from Net Asset Value

As noted several times in this book, net asset value (or adjusted net asset value) is not equal to the true economic value of a company's stock unless a complete asset revaluation analysis—recognizing all intangible assets and all forms of obsolescence—has been conducted. Thus, the discount from some measure of the underlying net asset value at which a transaction occurs does not necessarily represent a pure lack of control discount. Nevertheless, there are many instances in which valuation guidance can be found in the relationship between transaction prices and some measure of net asset value. This section describes some of those categories of data.

Holding Companies

Adjusted net asset values are available for most publicly traded closed-end investment companies (including both REITs and operating real estate companies), for some real estate holding companies, and for some companies with significant timber holdings. If one were to assume the company could be liquidated for its adjusted net asset value (and, therefore, that value represented a control level of value) then the price at which minority shares traded may be an indication of a lack of control discount. There could also be other factors affecting this adjusted net asset value to price difference, however. For example, the amount of income taxes on the built-in gains related to unrealized appreciation of asset values could affect these security prices.

One published study indicated significantly greater discounts from net asset value for real estate operating companies than for REITs. The author of the study opined that:

> The primary reason for the different median discounts is that, by law, shareholders in REITs receive almost all of the cash flow generated. Because the cash flow is paid directly to shareholders, they control how that cash is used.[3]

The same study identified four factors that affect the size of the discount:

1. Revenues.
2. Earnings.
3. Dividend payout ratio.
4. Unrealized capital gains.

Exhibit 16–2 shows the effects of these factors graphically.

Limited Partnerships

Most market transactions in limited partnership interests in recent years have been at substantial price discounts from underlying net asset values. Unlike stocks, most limited partnerships sold in public offerings never develop a secondary public trading market. Hence, without liquid public markets, most of the transactions are individually negotiated. Therefore, unlike most stocks, where one body of empirical data helps to quantify lack of control discounts and another discount for lack of marketability, the discounts from net asset value for limited partnership transactions encompass aspects of both (1) the lack of control discount and (2) the lack of marketability discount.

One study tabulated discounts from net asset value for 146 syndicated limited partnerships that traded in the secondary market in April and May 1993. The study

---

[3] Lance S. Hall, "Valuation of Fractional Interests: A Business Appraiser's Perspective," *The Appraisal Journal*, April 1989, p. 175.

Exhibit 16–2

Minority Ownership Interest Discounts for Publicly Traded Real Estate Companies

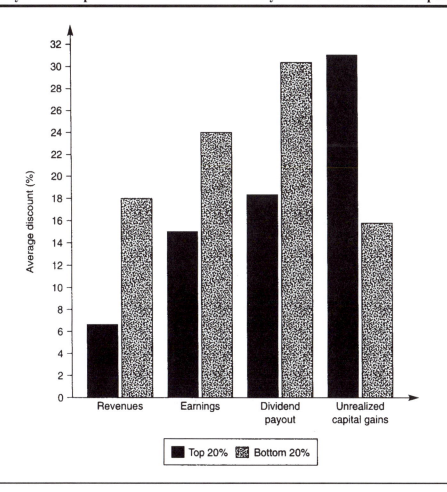

SOURCE: Lance S. Hall, "Valuation of Fractional Interests: A Business Appraiser's Perspective," *The Appraisal Journal*, April 1989, p. 175.

found an average price discount of 38 percent.[4] The study also found that those with no cash distributions sold at significantly greater price discounts than those with cash distributions.

An article in *Trusts & Estates* cites such empirical evidence of lack of control discounts for real estate limited partnerships, apparently influenced to some extent by less than optimum marketability:

> A comparison of net asset values and secondary market prices for 85 real estate-based partnerships reported that actual transactions occurred at an average discount of 44 percent from liquidation values. For 21 of the 85 partnerships, the trading discount was 60 percent or more. Partnerships not

---

[4] Steven Kam, Hans Schroeder, and Curt Smith, "Pricing Non-Publicly Traded Limited Partnerships," *Houlihan Valuation Advisors Valuation Report*, Spring 1994, p. 5.

currently distributing cash to investors tended to have larger discounts. This survey focused on partnerships whose units were traded relatively more frequently and in better organized markets. For other partnerships and related entities, the market imperfections would be larger and the discounts greater.[5]

Trust and Estate Sales Study

H. Calvin Coolidge, a bank trust officer responsible for administering trusts and estates that owned all or portions of closely held businesses, performed two studies several years ago in which he compiled data on actual sales prices of closely held businesses. As an introduction, Coolidge offers the following generalities:

> A number of years of experience has demonstrated that it is extremely difficult to find any market for minority interests . . . , despite efforts to do so. . . . On the relatively rare occasions when an offer is made to buy a minority interest, it is almost always for an amount far less than the fiduciary and the beneficiary expect to get.[6]

In his first study, Coolidge compiled data on 30 actual sales of noncontrolling ownership interests. He found that the average transaction price was 36 percent below book value, and he concluded with the following observations:

> Only 20 percent of the sales were made at discounts less than 20 percent. A little more than half the sales (53⅓ percent) were made at discounts that ranged from 22 percent to 48 percent, and 23⅓ percent of the sales were made at discounts of from 54.4 percent to 78 percent.
>
> It would be dangerous to draw too many generalizations from the survey, but those sales where the discounts were below 20 percent involved, with one exception, purchases from close relatives where friendly relations existed. The exception was the sale by a holder of swing shares who used his leverage well, but still took a 4.3 percent discount. At the other end of the spectrum was the settlement of a three-year bitter dispute between two families; the majority family raised its token offer only after threat of a lawsuit, but the price the minority interest took nonetheless represented a 78 percent discount.[7]

It is noteworthy that the discounts in the foregoing surveys were from accounting book value and not from the market value of the subject business enterprise. Accounting book value, of course, recognizes no appreciation in asset values above their depreciated original cost. Although, in a very few cases in the above survey, the price discounts were computed from an adjusted book value, reflecting appreciation in real estate values. One would expect that the subject business enterprise value would be above the book value in most cases. If that expectation is correct, then the discounts from the owners' proportionate shares of the total enterprise value would be even greater than the discounts as presented in the survey (which were from accounting book value).

---

[5] Mark S. Thompson and Eric S. Spunt, "The Widespread Overvaluation of Fractional Ownership Positions," *Trusts & Estates*, June 1993, p. 63, citing Partnership Profiles, Inc., "LP Secondary Market Discounts How Much?" *The Perspective*, May/June 1992, pp. 1-2.

[6] H. Calvin Coolidge, "Fixing Value of Minority Interest in Business: Actual Sales Suggest Discount as High as 70%," reprinted with permission from *Estate Planning*,© Spring 1975, p. 141, Warren, Gorham & Lamont, 31 St. James Avenue, Boston, MA 02116, (800) 950-1216.

[7] Ibid., p. 141.

An update published in 1983 indicated a trend toward even higher discounts when disposing of noncontrolling ownership interests in closely held corporations. That study concluded a much higher concentration of discounts from accounting book value at the high end of the range, and the average discount for the two studies combined was approximately 40 percent. The updated study concludes as follows:

> Each of the sales used in the survey involved a combination of factors that made it somewhat unique. To use any of the data, or any classification of the data, as definitive proof of the discount to be applied in a prospective valuation would be dangerous. This should not, however, obscure the true significance of the data, which is that in the actual marketplace, the typical discount is not of token size, but of substantial magnitude.[8]

Discounts for Direct Undivided Ownership Interests in Real Estate

Empirical market data on sales of fractional ownership interests in real estate are scarce. However, the available data do support the concept that fractional ownership interests in real estate, when they are sold, generally are priced at less than a pro rata portion of the market value of the total real estate parcel.

One study covered 54 undivided interests, with the undivided ownership interest price discounts ranging from zero to 82 percent, with a median price discount of 35 percent.[9] Another study covered 21 undivided ownership interests, with the undivided ownership interest price discounts ranging from 5 percent to 94 percent, with a median price discount of 30 percent.[10]

Real estate undivided ownership interest discounts tend to be considerably smaller than lack of control discounts for stocks or partnership interests. This probably is explained in large part by differences in the respective rights of the ownership interests. An owner of an individual ownership interest in real estate may sue for partition—that is, to have the property divided and to give each owner his or her pro rata share. If the court finds that the property is not divisible, then it may order the property to be sold. Owners of noncontrolling stock and partnership ownership interests have no such rights.

It is interesting to note that the U.S. Tax Court has distinguished between (1) lack of control (i.e., minority interest) and (2) lack of marketability discounts for an undivided interest in real estate. The court stated:

> "A minority interest discount for an interest in real property may be allowed on account of the lack of control which accompanies co-ownership." The minority interest discount should consider "the cost, uncertainty, and delays attendant upon partition proceedings. . . The marketability discount, by contrast, measures the diminution in value attributable to the lack of a ready market for the property." This two-step process is similar to prior Tax Court decisions regarding corporate and partnership interests.[11]

---

[8] H. Calvin Coolidge, "Survey Shows Trend Toward Larger Minority Discounts," *Estate Planning*, September 1983, p. 282.

[9] Peter J. Patchin, "Market Discounts for Undivided Minority Interests in Real Estate," *Real Estate Issues,* Fall/Winter 1988, pp. 14-16.

[10] Don L. Harris, Philip A. McCormick, and W.D. Davis Sr., "The Valuation of Partial Interests in Real Estate," *ASA Valuation,* December 1983, pp. 62-73.

[11] *Samuel J. LeFrak v. Commissioner*, 66 T.C.M. 1297 (1993).

Other Factors That Influence the Lack of Control Discount

Articles of Incorporation and Bylaws

A myriad of possible provisions in companies' articles of incorporation and bylaws can impact the relative degree of control or lack of it for any particular block of stock or partnership interest. For example, even in a state that requires only a simple majority for any corporate action, many companies write requirements for super-majorities for certain actions into their articles of incorporation.

The analyst should understand any provisions in company documents (or other shareholder agreements) that may impact the degree of control when quantifying a lack of control discount (or a control premium) for a specific ownership interest.

Potential Dilution

Another factor that can affect the degree of control—or lack of control—is a change in the relative distribution of ownership as a result of either issuance of shares or redemption of outstanding shares. Many companies have stock options outstanding, the exercise of which could affect the balance of control. An ESOP could have control at a point in time, but lose that control position as a result of retiring participants exercising options to "put" their stock to the company. Even if an ESOP has a right of first refusal, it may not always have the resources available to exercise the right.

Preemptive Rights

Some companies give their stockholders *preemptive rights*. The *Encyclopedia of Banking & Finance* defines this right as follows:

> **PREEMPTIVE RIGHT** Stockholders' privilege to subscribe to new issues of voting stock, usually the common stock or securities convertible into voting stock, before such offerings are made to nonstockholders. A preemptive right is often referred to as a privileged subscription right. The preemptive right has been eroded in recent years.[12]

Such rights are designed to protect stockholders from dilution. However, they can make it awkward for a company to issue new shares, first having to offer stock to existing stockholders in accordance with the preemptive right provisions. For this reason, the trend in recent years has been toward elimination of preemptive rights.

Even if preemptive rights exist on paper, they may not be of equal efficacy to each respective holder of such rights because one owner may have adequate resources to exercise such rights while another owner may not.

---

[12] Charles J. Woelfel, *Encyclopedia of Banking & Finance,* 10th ed. (Burr Ridge, IL: Probus Publishing Company, 1994), p. 912. Reprinted with permission.

Cumulative versus Noncumulative Voting

Either state statutes or a company's articles of incorporation may allow for cumulative voting. Under noncumulative voting, a simple majority of the stock can elect *all* the directors. Under cumulative voting, votes may be "cumulated" for a single director. For example, if five directors are to be elected, the owner of a share of stock could cast five votes for a single director, thus enabling minority shareholders with a sufficient number of shares to elect one or more directors.

The *Encyclopedia of Banking & Finance* offers the following formula for determining how many shares are required to elect one or more directors with cumulative voting:

$$\frac{\text{Total number of shares voting} \times \text{Number of directors desired}}{\text{Total number of directors} + 1} + 1$$

To illustrate: If there are five directors to be elected and 500 shares are outstanding and voting for the election of directors, the minimum number of shares necessary to elect one director would be 84 shares. Proof: 84 shares times five directors to be elected equals 420 votes, all cast for one director. Assuming the rest of the stock (416 shares) votes en bloc as the majority, such total of 2,080 votes distributed among five directors would be 416 votes each. Therefore, the individual representing the minority and receiving its 420 votes is sure to get one of the places on the board, the majority getting the other four places. The minority in this example must be sure to vote all of its 420 votes for one director; if it distributed the 420 votes among two, it obviously would not win any places on the board.

Cumulative voting, therefore, does *not* automatically assure the minority of representation on the board; the minority must have the minimum shares necessary for election of the directors desired and, second, must concentrate its cumulative votes properly. A good general rule to remember is Dr. Harry G. Guthmann's generalization: The minority for election of at least one director fraction of the total board must own the next lower fraction plus one share; e.g., on a board of five directors, the minority must have one-sixth of the stock plus one share; six directors, one-seventh of the stock plus one share, etc. Cumulative voting, moreover, requires a majority of the stock to be able to elect a majority of the board; in the above example, to elect three of the five directors, 251 shares are necessary, or a majority of the 500 shares total.[13]

Contractual Restrictions

Many ownership control rights may be denied to a company (or to the controlling owner) due to contractual restrictions. For example, indenture provisions in conjunction with debt obligations frequently prevent dividend payments, increased management compensation, liquidation of assets, acquisitions, or changes in the direction of the business.

---

[13] Ibid., p. 276.

Financial Condition of Business

Many of the rights associated with ownership control are rendered economically empty—or of little economic value—simply because of the company's financial condition. These could include the right to decide on management compensation, dividends, stock or asset purchases, or acquisition of other companies. Alternatively, companies that are generating a superior rate of return may not deserve a substantial control premium if most advantages of control are already being enjoyed by the shareholders.

Highly Regulated Industries

With respect to companies in highly regulated industries, a lack of control discount may apply even if the subject is a 100 percent equity ownership interest. This is because the controlling stockholders of a highly regulated business do not have all of the perquisites of control that owners of less regulated businesses have. In some industries, governmental authority is needed to buy, sell, or merge a company. In some industries, government authority is needed to liquidate or otherwise shut down a company (or a part of a company)—even when company operations have turned unprofitable. And in some industries, government authority is needed to open a new branch (or sell a new product or provide a new service).

For these highly regulated companies, a lack of control discount may be applicable to the overall business value. This is because the government—not the 100 percent stockholder—enjoys many of the prerogatives of ownership control. In such instances, there may be a greater discount for lack of control applicable to a non-controlling block of stock than to a controlling block of stock. But the difference in the two levels of lack of control discounts would not be as great as in a less regulated industry. This is because in a highly regulated industry, neither the noncontrolling stockholder nor the controlling stockholder enjoys absolute control.

Buy-Sell and Other Shareholder Agreements

In some companies, all shareholders have entered into buy-sell agreements or into other shareholder agreements. The provisions of such agreements usually dictate the valuation of the company stock for purposes of transactions (1) between the company and shareholders and (2) among shareholders.

If the language of the relevant agreements indicates that minority blocks of stock will be valued on a controlling ownership interest level of value, a full lack of control discount will not apply to the transactions to which the provision is applicable. For example, the agreement may say that the subject shares will be valued "on an enterprise basis" or as "a per share portion of the overall company value." In such instances, the company stockholders have agreed to deal with each other on a controlling ownership interest basis—according to the terms of the agreements.

Fiduciary Duties

Sometimes, controlling stockholders cannot or do not exercise all of the prerogatives of ownership control. This may occur when the controlling stockholder has a fiduciary or other special duty to the noncontrolling stockholders. In such cases, controlling stockholders and noncontrolling stockholders could be treated equally with regard to economic benefits of equity ownership.

In such instances, the lack of control discount may not be so great as it otherwise would be. This is because the base to which the discount would apply—that is, the overall business enterprise value—may not be inflated due to the influences of ownership control. And this is because all stockholders—noncontrolling and controlling—would expect to share equally in the economic fruit of the company's commercial success. However, there are very few situations in which a fiduciary obligation would require treating a noncontrolling stockholder on a basis equivalent to a controlling stockholder. Under most state laws, a controlling stockholder can even sell the control stock without requiring that any offer be made to purchase noncontrolling stock.

Private Company with Public Securities

Some privately owned companies have publicly traded securities that are subject to the Securities and Exchange Commission (SEC) registration process. This situation generally occurs when all of the company's common stock is closely held but some of the company's bonds are publicly traded. In this circumstance, the company is generally subject to all of the periodic disclosure requirements of other public companies.

In such instances, the discount for lack of control may be less than it would otherwise be. Due to the SEC public reporting requirements, the controlling stockholder would have to disclose information not normally available to noncontrolling stockholders, such as detailed financial statements, officers' compensation, transactions between the company and shareholders, and so forth. Therefore, some of the benefits of ownership control are lost due to these public disclosure requirements. Also, the controlling stockholder would always be aware of the applicable regulatory authority of the SEC. Accordingly, the controlling stockholder may not always act like a controlling stockholder would in a company not subject to SEC scrutiny.

Private Company That Operates Like a Public Company

Even if they don't have public debt outstanding, some closely held companies operate very much like publicly owned companies. They follow the business, accounting, and legal formalities of public companies. They have independent directors on their boards of directors. And, they believe in full disclosure to all stockholders.

In such an instance, the lack of control discount is usually less than it would otherwise be. One reason is that in such a case the controlling stockholder is (presumably on a voluntary basis) not exercising all of the prerogatives of control.

Control Has Already Been Dissipated

Earlier, we mentioned the case of three equal shareholders. Let's consider slightly more extreme cases. What happens if there are 10 or 20 equal (or relatively equal) stockholders? Such a scenario may not be uncommon at all in family-owned businesses or in professional practices. For example, consider a consultancy corporation with 20 shareholder/consultants. In such instances, ownership control may have already been dissipated.

In such circumstances, the lack of control discount is often less than it would otherwise be. That is because when all owners are sharing (relatively) equally in the wealth of the business, the overall business enterprise value may not be affected by the actions of a controlling owner. Consequently, the base to which the lack of control discount is applied is lower than it would otherwise be. And with all owners sharing (relatively) equally in the wealth of the business, there is no significant disparity between the economic benefits available to noncontrolling owners and to majority owners.

Summary

The types and amounts of appropriate discounts and/or premiums are often major matters of dispute in the resolution of business valuation controversies. The primary discounts are for lack of control and lack of marketability. Empirical market evidence indicates that these discounts may be quite substantial, generally greater than most people realize until they have become acquainted with the actual market-derived data.

When dealing with discounts and/or premiums, it is essential to be very precise as to the base of value to which the discount or premium applies. (This also means the basic valuation work product should be precise in its identification of the level of value it has estimated.) It is essential that the level of discounts and/or premiums be appropriately matched to the level of value estimated.

Many of the same indicators of market value (price/earnings multiples, capitalization of dividends, discounted economic income, price/book value multiples, and so on) used in valuing controlling ownership interests can also be used to value noncontrolling ownership interests. However, in valuing noncontrolling ownership interests, the focus of value normally is on the business as a going concern—rather than in either total or partial liquidation. And, relatively more emphasis is directed to the analysis of operating variables, such as earnings and dividends, and relatively less emphasis is directed to the analysis of asset values—than when valuing a controlling interest. Also, the assumptions underlying the noncontrolling ownership interest ownership valuation usually reflect business as usual rather than any changes that an outside control buyer would introduce.

If existing or potential litigation is involved, it is important to understand if there are any required standards of value and premises of value that should be estimated. The range of court case outcomes in disputes regarding valuations of noncontrolling ownership interest is extremely wide, even under comparable statutory law. Therefore, in controversy situations, an understanding of the facts and circumstances of the particular interest is essential, along with strong supporting data and careful reasoning that lead to an objective conclusion that is consistent with applicable statutes and legal precedent.

This chapter discussed the concepts, factors influencing, and empirical data sources to help quantify the lack of control discount. The next chapter presents and analyzes empirical data regarding the discount for lack of marketability.

Bibliography

Berkery, Peter M., Jr. "IRS Approves Minority Discounts." *Accounting Today*, March 1, 1993, p. 6.

Bolotsky, Michael J. "Adjustments for Differences in Ownership Rights, Liquidity, Information Access, and Information Reliability: An Assessment of 'Prevailing Wisdom' Versus the 'Nath Hypotheses.'" *Business Valuation Review*, September 1991, pp. 94–110.

Burkert, Rodney P. "Valuing the Minority Interest: To Adjust or Not to Adjust?" *Business Valuation Alert*, December 1999, pp. 4, 13–14.

Coolidge, H. Calvin. "Fixing Value of Minority Interest in Business: Actual Sales Suggest Discounts as High as 70%." *Estate Planning*, Spring 1975, pp. 138–41.

Curtis, Andrew M. "Discounting Minority Stock Interests in Closely Held Corporations: When and How Much?" *Journal of Taxation of Estates and Trusts*, Spring 1991, pp. 26–30.

Curtiss, Rand M. "A Practical Methodology for Determining Premiums and Discounts." *Business Valuation Review*, December 1997, pp. 172–79.

DenHollander, Darlene. "Minority Interest Discounts and the Effect of the Section 2704 Regulations." *Tax Lawyer*, Spring 1992, pp. 877–87.

Fishman, Jay E., Shannon P. Pratt, J. Clifford Griffith, and D. Keith Wilson. "Premiums and Discounts in Business Valuations." Parts I and II. *Fair$hare*, May and June 1992, pp. 11–17, 14–16.

Hall, Lance S. "Minority Interests in Closely Held Real Estate: Lessons from Estate of Berg." *Journal of Real Estate Taxation*, Winter 1993, pp. 170–77.

Hall, Lance S., and Timothy G. Polacek. "Strategies for Obtaining the Largest Valuation Discounts." *Estate Planning*, January–February 1994, pp. 38–44.

Herber, William C., Patrick K. Schmidt, and Robert J. Strachota. "Fairness in Minority Interest Valuation." *Business Valuation Review*, September 1992, pp. 140–46.

Hitchner, James R. "50% + 50% ≠ 100%." *CPA Expert*, Winter 1998, pp. 13–15.

Hitchner, James R., and Kevin J. Rudd. "The Use of Discounts in Estate and Gift Tax Valuations." *Trusts & Estates*, August 1992, pp. 49–52, 60.

Hopson, James F., and William J. Sheehy. "Valuation of Minority Discounts in Closely-Held Companies." *National Public Accountant*, December 1993, pp. 30–33.

Janiga, John M., and Louis S. Harrison. "Valuation of Closely Held Stock for Transfer Tax Purposes: The Current Status of Minority Discounts for Intrafamily Transfers in Family-Controlled Corporations." *Taxes*, May 1991, pp. 309–17.

Jankowske, Wayne C. "Valuing Minority Interests in Relation to Guideline Firms." *Business Valuation Review*, December 1991, pp. 139–43.

Lauer, Eliot, and Bernard V. Preziosi, Jr. "A Fair Share for Minority Shareholders." *New York Law Journal*, June 1, 1992, p. 7.

Lerch, Mary Ann. "Quantitative Measures of Minority Interest Discounts." *Business Valuation Review*, March 1991, pp. 14–20.

Maher, J. Michael. "An Objective Measure for a Discount for a Minority Interest and Premium for a Controlling Interest." *Taxes*, July 1979, pp. 449–54.

Mercer, Z. Christopher. "A Brief Review of Control Premiums and Minority Interest Discounts." *Journal of Business Valuation* (Proceedings of the 12th Biennial Business Valuation Conference of The Canadian Institute of Chartered Business Valuators). Toronto: The Canadian Institute of Chartered Business Valuators, 1997, pp. 365–87.

_____. "Understanding and Quantifying Control Premiums: The Value of Control vs. Synergies or Strategic Advantages, Part II." *Journal of Business Valuation* (Proceedings of the 4th Joint Business Valuation Conference of The Canadian Institute of Chartered Business Valuators and the American Society of Appraisers). Toronto: The Canadian Institute of Chartered Business Valuators, 1999, pp. 36–54.

Moroney, Robert E. "No Minority Discount for Interest in Trust." *Estate Planning*, May/June 1986, p. 167.

Murdock, Charles W. "The Evolution of Effective Remedies for Minority Shareholders and its Impact upon Valuation of Minority Shares." *Notre Dame Law Review*, Vol. 65 (1990), pp. 425–89.

Nath, Eric W. "Control Premiums and Minority Interest Discounts in Private Companies." *Business Valuation Review*, June 1990, pp. 39–46.

_____. "Tale of Two Markets." *Business Valuation Review*, September 1994, pp. 107–12.

Polacek, Timothy C., and Richard A. Lehn. "Tax Court Allows Sizable Fractional Interest Discounts." *Trusts & Estates*, September 1994, pp. 29–40.

Reynolds, Bruce M. "IRS Modifies Position and Allows Discounts on Intra-Family Stock Transfers." *Taxes*, June 1993, pp. 381–87.

Rothschild, Gideon. "IRS Turns around on Discounts for Intra-Family Gifts of Businesses." *Practical Accountant*, April 1993, pp. 59–60.

Shenkman, Martin M., and Cal R. Feingold. "Minority, Marketability Discounts Affect Valuation of Partnership Interest." *Real Estate Finance Journal*, Summer 1993, pp. 18–25.

Shishido, Zenichi. "The Fair Value of Minority Stock in Closely Held Corporations." *Fordham Law Review*, October 1993, pp. 65–110.

Simpson, David W. "Minority Interest and Marketability Discounts: A Perspective, Part I." *Business Valuation Review*, March 1991, pp. 7–13.

Sirmans, C.F., John C. Doiron, and Krisandra A. Guidry. "A Survey of Appraisers Regarding Factors in Discounting Partial Interests." *Appraisal Journal*, October 1993, pp. 600–07.

Tiernan, Peter B. "How 50% Ownership Affects Estate Planning for Closely Held Stock." *Journal of Taxation*, October 1999, pp. 232–40.

Warnken, Wayne L., and Pamela R. Champine. "Securing the Minority Discount for Family Business Transfers." *Trusts & Estates*, April 1993, pp. 49–50+.

Wise, Richard M. "Valuing Minority Shareholdings." *Canadian Tax Highlights*, March 16, 1993, pp. 20–21.

Chapter 17

Discounts for Illiquidity and Lack of Marketability

All other things being equal, an ownership interest in a business is worth more if it is readily marketable. An ownership interest in a business is worth less if it is not readily marketable. This is because business owners—and all investors—prefer liquidity to illiquidity. Ownership interests in closely held businesses—even substantial closely held businesses—are illiquid relative to many other types of investments. This phenomenon may be further compounded by restrictions on the transfer of ownership interests often found in close corporation buy-sell agreements or shareholder agreements. Therefore, analysts have to identify and quantify the valuation adjustment associated with (1) the illiquidity of the subject business enterprise and (2) the lack of marketability in the subject business ownership interest.

For purposes of this chapter, we will use the term *illiquidity* to mean the inability of the owner of an entire business enterprise to convert his or her investment into cash quickly and at a reasonably low and predictable cost. We will use the term *lack of marketability* to mean the inability of the owner of a noncontrolling equity interest to convert his or her investment into cash quickly and at a reasonably low and predictable cost.

These two concepts of illiquidity and lack of marketability are related but distinctly different. As with all valuation adjustments, it is important to identify the base of comparison to which the adjustment relates.

The measurement base for the discount for illiquidity relates to "control event" transfers (i.e., asset sales, stock sales, or mergers) of controlling ownership interests or entire business enterprises. This discount quantifies the inherent liquidity differences between the subject business enterprise and the selection of guideline merged and acquired companies that are used as a benchmark for estimating the subject business enterprise value.

The measurement base for the discount for lack of marketability relates to noncontrol event transfers (i.e., sales of small blocks of securities on organized stock exchanges). This discount quantifies the inherent liquidity differences between the subject noncontrolling equity interest and the selection of guideline publicly traded company securities that are used as a benchmark for estimating the value of the subject securities.

First, this chapter will discuss the theoretical concepts of illiquidity and lack of marketability. Second, this chapter will present the most recent empirical studies that are frequently used by analysts to quantify these valuation adjustments.

Concept and Importance of Marketability

The concept of *marketability* deals with the liquidation of the subject business ownership interest. That is, how quickly can the business ownership interest be converted to cash at the investor's discretion?

In this text, we will define *marketability* as the ability to convert the business ownership interest (at whatever ownership level) to cash quickly, with minimum transaction and administrative costs in so doing and with a high degree of certainty of realizing the expected amount of net proceeds.

Our definition is consistent with the definition offered by the *Encyclopedia of Banking & Finance*, which focuses on securities for which *some* public market already exists:

> **Marketability.** The relative ease and promptness with which a security or commodity may be sold when desired, at a representative current price, without material concession in price merely because of the necessity of sale. Marketability connotes the existence of current buying interest as well as selling interest and is usually indicated by the volume of current transactions and the spread between the bid and asked price for a security—the closer the spread, the closer are the buying and selling interests to agreement on price resulting in actual transactions. To look at it from the standpoint of a dealer maintaining the MARKET, the closer his [or her] bid to current transactions and the smaller his [or her] markup is to asking prices, the larger the volume will be. By contrast, inactive securities that rarely trade or for which buyers have to be located or sales negotiated are characterized by large spreads between the bid and asked prices.[1]

With respect to the ownership characteristics of operating assets (such as operating real estate and tangible personal property), the terms *marketability* and *liquidity* are sometimes interchangeable. The *Encyclopedia of Banking & Finance* offers the following:

> **Liquidity.** The amount of time required to convert an asset into cash or pay a liability. For noncurrent assets, liquidity generally refers to marketability. . . .
>
> In economics, liquidity is the desire to hold assets in the form of cash. Common elements often included in the concept of liquidity include marketability, realizability, reversibility (as to the difference between buying and selling prices), divisibility of the asset, predictability or capital certainty, and plasticity (ease of maneuvering into and out of various yields after the asset has been acquired). Firms and individuals often prefer to hold money for the sake of holding money. Liquidity may be desired for the following reasons: (1) the transactions motive, (2) the precautionary motive, and (3) the speculative motive. Money is desired to carry out future monetary transactions, to save for a rainy day, or to take advantage of movements in the price level.[2]

Barron's Dictionary of Business Terms defines marketability and liquidity as follows:

> **Marketability.** Speed and ease with which a particular product or investment may be bought and sold. In common use, *marketability* is interchangeable with *liquidity*, but *liquidity* implies the preservation of value when a security is bought or sold.[3]

---

[1] Charles J. Woelfel, *Encyclopedia of Banking & Finance*, 10th ed. (Burr Ridge, IL: Probus Publishing Company, 1994), p. 729. Reprinted with permission.

[2] Ibid., p. 703.

[3] Jack P. Friedman, ed., *Barron's Dictionary of Business Terms*, 2nd ed. (Hauppauge, NY: Barron's, 1994), p. 363.

The market for securities in the United States is generally considered to be the most liquid market for any kind of property anywhere in the world. This is one of the reasons that companies are able to raise investment capital from both institutional and individual investors: the ability to liquidate the investment immediately, at little cost, and with virtual certainty as to realization of the widely publicized market price. Empirical evidence suggests that investors are willing to pay a price premium for this level of liquidity. Conversely, investors extract a price discount relative to actively traded securities for stocks or other investment interests that lack this high degree of liquidity.

Adjustment for Lack of Marketability for Noncontrolling Ownership Interests

For a valuation "adjustment" to have a precise meaning, there should be a precise definition of the level of value from which the adjustment is made. When noncontrolling business ownership interests are valued by reference to the prices paid for guideline actively traded securities, the benchmark for the lack of marketability of the noncontrolling ownership interests is the active public securities markets. This publicly traded counterpart value is often called the *publicly traded equivalent value* or the *freely traded value*.

In the U.S. capital markets, a security holder is able to sell a security over the telephone or the Internet in seconds, usually at or within a small fraction of a percent of the last price at which the security traded, with a relatively small commission cost, and to receive the cash proceeds within three working days.

By contrast, the universe of potential buyers for most noncontrolling business ownership interests is an infinitesimal fraction of the universe of potential buyers for publicly traded securities.

Besides the problem of actually trying to sell the subject ownership interest, the liquidity of noncontrolling business ownership interests is further impaired by the relative unwillingness of banks and other lending institutions to accept them as loan collateral the same way they would accept public stock.

Because of these extreme contrasts between the ability to sell or hypothecate noncontrolling business ownership interests as compared with publicly traded stock, empirical evidence suggests that significant valuation discounts for lack of marketability are appropriate. These lack of marketability discounts for noncontrolling business ownership interests tend to cluster in the range of 35 percent to 50 percent from their publicly traded counterparts. Naturally, each valuation should be analyzed on the basis of the individual facts and circumstances. Accordingly, each individual noncontrolling equity interest valuation may justify a discount for lack of marketability above or below this typical range.

Evidence for the Quantification of Discount for Lack of Marketability

There are two general types of empirical studies designed to quantify the valuation adjustments associated with the lack of marketability of noncontrolling ownership interests in closely held businesses:

1. Discounts on the sale of restricted shares of publicly traded companies.
2. Discounts on the sale of closely held company shares—compared with prices of subsequent initial public offerings of the same company's shares.

As noted earlier, the above empirical studies indicate that the base from which to take the indicated lack of marketability discount is the actual (or estimated) price at which the shares would sell if registered and freely tradable in a public stock market.

The immediately following sections of this chapter summarize the findings of these two extensive lines of empirical evidence. The second line of empirical studies is more recent. More importantly, the transactions are more similar to noncontrolling privately held business ownership interest transactions. This is because that is what they are, even though the subject company may have contemplated a public offering at the time of the transaction. Therefore, this second category of empirical studies may be more relevant in the estimation of the discount for lack of marketability for most noncontrolling privately held business ownership interests.

The data presented in this chapter relate to the quantification of the discount for lack of marketability only. As mentioned previously, the discount for lack of marketability is separate and distinct from the discount for lack of control. The discount for lack of control is discussed in the previous chapter.

The body of empirical evidence from which to quantify illiquidity discounts for controlling business ownership interests is much less extensive and of a different nature. This subject will be covered later in the chapter.

Marketability Discounts Extracted from Prices of Restricted Stocks

One body of empirical evidence specifically isolates the pricing implications of marketability from all other valuation-related factors: the body of data on transactions in letter stocks. A *letter stock* is identical in all respects to the freely traded stock of a public company except for the fact that it is restricted from trading on the open stock market for a certain period. The duration of the restrictions may vary from one security to another. Since marketability is the only difference between the letter stock and its freely tradable counterpart, the analyst may quantify differences in the price at which letter stock transactions take place compared with open market transactions in the same stock on the same date. This difference will provide some evidence of the price spread between (1) a readily marketable security and (2) one that is otherwise identical but subject to certain restrictions on its marketability.

Publicly traded corporations frequently issue letter stock when making acquisitions or when raising private capital. This is because the time and cost of registering the new stock with the SEC would make registration at the time of the transaction impractical. Also, company founders or other insiders may own portions of a publicly traded company stock that has never been registered for public trading. Even though such stock cannot be sold to the public on the stock market, it may be sold in private transactions under certain circumstances. Such transactions usually must be reported to the SEC. Therefore, these private transactions become a matter of public record. Accordingly, empirical data on the prices of private transactions in restricted securities—or letter stocks—can be used for comparison with prices of the same but unrestricted securities eligible for trading on the open market.

Since these data represent hundreds of actual arm's-length transactions, anyone who is considering a deal involving such securities (for example, receiving letter stock in connection with selling out to a public company) would be well advised to become familiar with the information. Furthermore, courts have often referenced the data on letter stock price discounts when estimating the discount for lack of marketability appropriate to noncontrolling ownership interests in closely held companies.

It is particularly noteworthy that the restrictions on the transfer of letter stock eventually lapse, usually within 24 months up to 1997 and generally within a year since that time. At that point, the holder can sell the shares into the existing market, subject to whatever volume and other restrictions may be imposed. Consequently, all other things being equal, shares of closely held stock—which may never have the benefit of a public market—would be expected to require a higher discount for lack of marketability than that applicable to stock that would trade on an organized exchange but is restricted from doing so. In fact, the market does impose a higher discount on closely held noncontrolling ownership interests than on restricted stock of a public company, as we will see in a later section.

SEC Institutional Investor Study

In a major SEC study of institutional investor actions, one topic was the amount of discount at which transactions in restricted stock (or letter stock) occurred compared with the prices of identical but unrestricted stock on the open market.[4] The most pertinent summary tables from that study are reproduced in Exhibits 17–1 and 17–2.

Exhibit 17–1 presents the price discount from stock market prices on letter stock transactions disaggregated by the market in which the unrestricted stock trades. The four categories are the New York Stock Exchange, American Stock Exchange, over-the-counter (OTC) reporting companies, and over-the-counter nonreporting companies. A *reporting company* is a publicly traded company that must file Forms 10-K, 10-Q, and other information with the SEC. A *nonreporting company* is one whose stock is publicly traded OTC but is not subject to the same reporting requirements. A company whose stock is traded OTC can avoid becoming a SEC reporting company either by maintaining its total assets under $1 million or by keeping its number of stockholders under 500.

Because most closely held businesses (even substantial close corporations) are much smaller than typical well-known public companies, the smaller nonreporting public companies may have characteristics that are more comparable with the subject closely held business. However, since these nonreporting public companies need not report to the SEC, the analyst may have trouble obtaining annual and interim reports for them.

Exhibit 17–1 indicates that, compared with their free-trading counterparts, the price discounts on the letter stocks were the least for NYSE-listed stocks and increased, in order, for AMEX-listed stocks, OTC reporting companies, and OTC nonreporting companies. For OTC nonreporting companies, the largest number of observations fell in the 30 percent to 40 percent price discount range. Slightly over 56 percent of the OTC nonreporting companies had price discounts greater than 30 percent on the

[4] "Discounts Involved in Purchases of Common Stock," in U.S. 92nd Congress, 1st Session, House, *Institutional Investor Study Report of the Securities and Exchange Commission* (Washington, DC: Government Printing Office, March 10, 1971, 5:2444B2456, Document No. 92-64, Part 5).

Exhibit 17–1

Table XIV–45 of SEC Institutional Investor Study: Discount by Trading Market

Trading Market	−15.0% to 0.0% No. of Trans-actions	−15.0% to 0.0% Value of Purchases	0.1% to 10.0% No. of Trans-actions	0.1% to 10.0% Value of Purchases	10.1% to 20.0% No. of Trans-actions	10.1% to 20.0% Value of Purchases	20.1% to 30.0% No. of Trans-actions	20.1% to 30.0% Value of Purchases	30.1% to 40.0% No. of Trans-actions	30.1% to 40.0% Value of Purchases	40.1% to 50.0% No. of Trans-actions	40.1% to 50.0% Value of Purchases	50.1% to 80.0% No. of Trans-actions	50.1% to 80.0% Value of Purchases	Total No. of Trans-actions	Total Value of Purchases
Unknown	1	$1,500,000	2	$2,496,583	1	$205,000	0	$0	2	$3,332,000	0	$0	1	$1,259,995	7	$8,793,578
New York Stock Exchange	7	3,760,663	13	15,111,798	13	24,503,988	10	17,954,085	3	11,102,501	1	1,400,000	4	5,005,068	51	78,838,103
American Stock Exchange	2	7,263,060	4	15,850,000	11	14,548,750	20	46,200,677	7	21,074,298	1	44,250	4	4,802,404	49	109,783,439
Over-the-Counter (reporting companies)	11	13,828,757	39	13,613,676	35	38,585,259	30	35,479,946	30	58,689,328	13	9,284,047	21	8,996,406	179	178,477,419
Over-the-Counter (nonreporting companies)	5	8,329,369	9	5,265,925	18	25,122,024	17	11,229,155	25	29,423,584	20	11,377,431	18	13,505,545	112	104,253,033
Total	26	$34,681,849	67	$52,337,982	78	$102,965,021	77	$110,863,863	67	$123,621,711	35	$22,105,728	48	$33,569,418	398	$480,145,572

Exhibit 17–2

Table XIV–47 of SEC Institutional Investor Study: Discount by Size of Transaction and Sales of Issuer

Sales of Issuer (Thousands of Dollars)	0.1% to 10.0% No. of Trans-actions	0.1% to 10.0% Size of Trans actions	10.1% to 20.0% No. of Trans-actions	10.1% to 20.0% Size of Trans-actions	20.1% to 30.0% No. of Trans-actions	20.1% to 30.0% Size of Trans-actions	30.1% to 40.0% No. of Trans-actions	30.1% to 40.0% Size of Trans-actions	40.1% to 50.0% No. of Trans-actions	40.1% to 50.0% Size of Trans-actions	50.1% or More No. of Trans-actions	50.1% or More Size of Trans-actions	Total No. of Trans-actions	Total Size of Trans actions
Less than 100	9	$12,566,000	6	$12,267,292	16	$12,197,394	17	$19,642,364	7	$2,554,000	11	$2,894,999	66	$62,122,049
100-999	2	3,877,500	1	1,018,500	1	500,000	0	0	2	1,221,000	7	474,040	13	7,091,040
1,000-4,999	3	2,295,200	10	9,351,738	15	9,865,951	12	10,675,150	13	8,170,747	8	4,605,505	61	44,964,291
5,000-19,999	47	12,750,481	24	21,441,347	25	27,238,210	13	25,986,008	4	1,147,305	6	1,620,015	119	90,183,366
20,000-99,999	17	36,481,954	18	22,231,737	8	11,817,954	6	11,499,250	3	4,372,676	3	605,689	55	87,009,260
100,000 or More	7	10,832,925	10	24,959,483	3	7,903,586	2	2,049,998	0	0	2	1,805,068	24	47,551,060
Total	85	$78,804,060	69	$91,270,097	68	$69,523,095	50	$69,852,770	29	$17,465,728	37	$12,005,316	338	$338,921,066

SOURCE: *Institutional Investor Study Report of the Securities and Exchange Commission*, Chapter XIV, Section F.8., "Discounts Involved in Purchases of Common Stock," H.R. Doc. No. 64, Part 5, 92d Cong., 1st Sess. (1971), pp. 2444-56.

sale of their restricted stock—compared with the stock market price of their free-trading stock. A little over 30 percent of the OTC reporting companies were discounted over 30 percent, and over 2 percent had price discounts over 20 percent.

Using midpoints of the price discount range groups from Exhibit 17–1—and even including those that sold at price premiums for one reason or another—the overall mean average price discount was 25.8 percent and the median price discount was about the same. The study also noted, "Average discounts rose over the period January 1, 1966, through June 30, 1969," and average discounts were "27.9 percent in the first half of 1969."[5] For nonreporting OTC companies (which are more comparative with smaller businesses), the average price discount was 32.6 percent, and the median price discount again was about the same.

Since the time of the SEC study, the efficiency of the OTC market has improved considerably. This has been aided by the development of inexpensive and virtually instantaneous electronic communications and the advent of the Nasdaq system. Since the market in which restricted OTC shares will eventually trade once the restrictions expire (or are removed) is now somewhat more efficient, one would expect the differential in price discounts for restricted listed versus OTC stocks to be less pronounced. This generally has been the case.

Exhibit 17–2 presents the discounts from open market prices on letter stock transactions, disaggregated by the subject companies' annual sales volume into six groups. Companies with the largest sales volumes tend to receive the smallest discounts, and companies with the smallest sales volumes tend to receive the largest discounts. Well over half the companies with sales under $5 million (i.e., the three smallest of the six size categories used) had price discounts of over 30 percent. However, this may not be a size effect but just further evidence of the influence of the trading market. This is because most of the largest companies were listed on the NYSE, by far the most liquid market at that time.

Gelman Study

In 1972, Milton Gelman published the results of his study of prices paid for restricted securities by four closed-end investment companies specializing in restricted securities investments.[6] From 89 transactions between 1968 and 1970, Gelman found that (1) both the arithmetic average and median price discounts were 33 percent and that (2) almost 60 percent of the purchases were at price discounts of 30 percent and higher. The distribution of price discounts found in the Gelman study is presented in Exhibit 17–3.

Trout Study

In a study of letter stocks purchased by mutual funds from 1968 to 1972, Robert Trout attempted to construct a financial model that would provide an estimate of the price discount appropriate for a private company's stock.[7] His multiple regression model involved 60 purchases and found an average price discount of 33.45 percent for restricted stock from freely traded stock. As the SEC study previously indicated,

[5] Ibid., p. 2452.

[6] Milton Gelman, "An Economist-Financial Analyst's Approach to Valuing Stock of a Closely Held Company," *Journal of Taxation*, June 1972, pp. 353–54. Copyright © 1972 by Warren Gorham & Lamont, 31 St. James Avenue, Boston, MA 02116, (800) 950-1216.

[7] Robert R. Trout, "Estimation of the Discount Associated with the Transfer of Restricted Securities," *Taxes*, June 1977, pp. 381–85.

Exhibit 17–3

Gelman Study
Distribution of Price Discounts

Size of Discount	No. of Common Stocks	% of Total
Less than 15.0%	5	6
15.0–19.9	9	10
20.0–24.9	13	15
25.0–29.9	9	10
30.0–34.9	12	13
35.0–39.9	9	10
40.0 and Over	32	36
Total	89	100

SOURCE: Milton Gelman, "An Economist-Financial Analyst's Approach to Valuing Stock of a Closely Held Company," *Journal of Taxation*, June 1972, p. 354.

Trout also found that companies with stock listed on national exchanges had lower discounts on their restricted stock transactions than did companies with stock traded over-the-counter.

Moroney Study

In an article published in the March 1973 issue of *Taxes*, Robert E. Moroney presented the results of a study of the prices paid for restricted securities by 10 registered investment companies.[8] The study reflected 146 purchases. The average price discount for the 146 transactions was 35.6 percent, and the median price discount was 33.0 percent.

Moroney points out:

> It goes without saying that each cash purchase of a block of restricted equity securities fully satisfied the requirements that the purchase price be one, "at which the property would change hands between a willing buyer and a willing seller, neither being under any compulsion to buy or to sell and both having reasonable knowledge of relevant facts." Reg. Sec. 20.2031-1(b)[9]

Moroney contrasts the evidence of the actual cash deals with the lower average price discounts for lack of marketability adjudicated in most prior court decisions on gift and estate tax cases. He points out, however, that the empirical evidence on the prices of restricted stocks was not available as a benchmark for quantifying lack of marketability discounts at the time of the prior cases. And, he suggests that higher price discounts for lack of marketability be allowed subsequently based on relevant data available.

---

[8] Robert E. Moroney, "Most Courts Overvalue Closely Held Stocks," *Taxes*, March 1973, pp. 144–54.
[9] Ibid., p. 151.

Maher Study

Another well-documented study on lack of marketability discounts for closely held business ownership interests was performed by J. Michael Maher and published in *Taxes*.[10] Maher's analytical method was similar to Moroney's in that it compared prices paid for restricted stocks with the market prices of their unrestricted counterparts. Maher found that mutual funds were not purchasing restricted securities during 1974 and 1975, which were very depressed years for the stock market. Therefore, the data actually used covered the five-year period from 1969 through 1973. The study showed, "The mean discount for lack of marketability for the years 1969–1973 amounted to 35.43 percent."[11] Maher further eliminated the top and bottom 10 percent of purchases in an effort to remove especially high- and low-risk situations. The result was almost identical with the outliers removed, with a mean price discount of 34.73 percent.

Standard Research Consultants Study

In 1983, Standard Research Consultants analyzed recent private placements of common stock to test the current applicability of the SEC study.[12] Standard Research Consultants studied 28 private placements of restricted common stock from October 1978 through June 1982. Price discounts ranged from 7 percent to 91 percent, with a median of 45 percent.

Willamette Management Associates Study

Willamette Management Associates analyzed private placements of restricted stocks for the period January 1, 1981, through May 31, 1984. The early part of this study overlapped the last part of the SRC study, but few transactions took place during the period of overlap. Most of the transactions in the Willamette Management Associates study occurred in 1983.

Willamette Management Associates identified 33 transactions during that period (1) that could reasonably be classified as arm's length and (2) for which the price of the restricted shares could be compared directly with the price of trades in identical but unrestricted shares of the same company at the same time. The median price discount for the 33 restricted stock transactions compared with the prices of their freely tradable counterparts was 31.2 percent.

The slightly lower average percentage price discounts for private placements during this time may be attributable to the somewhat depressed pricing in the public stock market. This, in turn, reflected the recessionary economic conditions prevalent during most of the period of the study.

Silber Study

In a 1991 article in the *Financial Analysts Journal*, William L. Silber presented the results of his analysis of 69 private placements of common stock of publicly traded

---

[10] J. Michael Maher, "Discounts for Lack of Marketability for Closely-Held Business Interests," *Taxes*, September 1976, pp. 562–71.
[11] Ibid., p. 571.
[12] William F. Pittock and Charles H. Stryker, "Revenue Ruling 77-287 Revisited," *SRC Quarterly Reports*, Spring 1983, pp. 1–3.

companies between 1981 and 1988.[13] He found that the average price discount was 33.75 percent, which is very consistent with earlier studies.

Silber also found that the size of the price discount tended to be higher for private placements that were larger as a percentage of the shares outstanding. He found a small effect on the price discount on the basis of the size of the company as measured by revenues.

FMV Opinions, Inc., Study

An article in the January/February 1994 issue of *Estate Planning* referenced a study by FMV Opinions, Inc., that "examined over 100 restricted stock transactions from 1979 through April 1992."[14] The FMV study found a mean price discount of only 23 percent.

Management Planning, Inc., Study

A detailed study of restricted public securities was conducted by the valuation firm Management Planning, Inc. This study is titled "Analysis of Private Sales of Unregistered Common Stock, January 1, 1980–December 31, 1996." The results of this study are reported in *The Handbook of Advanced Business Valuation*.[15]

There was clear size effect in the Management Planning Study, with smaller companies tending to have larger discounts, as shown in Exhibit 17–4.

The purpose of the Management Planning restricted stock study was to compare (1) the per share prices paid in private placements of restricted stock with (2) the same company's freely traded, stock market price. The Management Planning study shows that in the vast majority of cases, restricted shares are privately placed at a lower price than the concurrent publicly traded price of the same stock. The difference in price, or discount, stems from the burden of the holding period, and resultant lack of liquidity, placed on the restricted stock. The restricted shares, it should be remembered, can be expected to have marketability after the initial two- to three-year holding period (a one- to two-year holding period for shares privately placed after April 29, 1997) and the various other Rule 144 requirements are met. In contrast, there is little likelihood that the typical privately held security will ever have the ready liquidity of a public stock or access to the infrastructure that supports our efficient public stock markets. Nonetheless, research and understanding of the discounts in private placements of restricted stock provide a good starting point for estimating the size of discounts for lack of marketability.

The private placement of restricted stock is a means by which corporations raise capital. This alternative is selected when, for reasons related to control issues, costs, or timing, it is not advantageous or practical to raise new equity capital in the already established market for a company's stock. Management Planning found three

---

[13] William L. Silber, "Discounts on Restricted Stock: The Impact of Illiquidity on Stock Prices," *Financial Analysts Journal,* July–August 1991, pp. 60–64.

[14] Lance S. Hall and Timothy C. Polacek, "Strategies for Obtaining the Largest Valuation Discounts," *Estate Planning*, January/February 1994, pp. 38–44.

[15] Robert Oliver and Roy Meyers, "Discounts Seen in Private Placements of Restricted Stock: The Management Planning, Inc., Long-Term Study (1980–1996)" (Chapter 5) in Robert F. Reilly and Robert P. Schweihs, eds. *The Handbook of Advanced Business Valuation*, (New York: McGraw-Hill, 2000).

Exhibit 17–4

Analysis of Restricted Stock Discounts by Revenue Size
Based upon Data from the Management Planning, Inc., Study

Revenues	Percent of Sample	Average Revenues ($ Millions)	Average Discounts	Standard Deviations	Range of Discounts	
					Low	High
Under $10 million	28.6%	6.6	32.9%	15.6%	2.8%	57.6%
$10-$30 million	22.4%	22.5	30.8%	11.2%	15.3%	49.8%
$30-$50 million	20.4%	35.5	25.2%	15.1%	5.2%	46.3%
$50-$100 million	16.3%	63.5	19.4%	7.3%	11.6%	29.3%
Over $100 million (adjusted) *	8.2%	224.9	14.9%	10.5%	0.0%	24.1%
Overall sample averages	95.9%	47.5	27.7%	14.1%	0.0%	57.6%
*Over $100 million (actual calculation)	4.1%	187.1	25.1%	17.9%	0.0%	46.5%

NOTE: Excludes Sudbury Holdings, Inc., whose private placement consisted of 125 percent of the pre-transaction shares outstanding. Excludes Starrett Housing Corp. which is one of the five most thinly traded companies in the sample.

publications to be excellent sources of private placement transactions. All are now published by Securities Data Publishing (SDP), located in New York. (They were formerly published by Dealer's Digest, Inc.) Up until 1989, Management Planning reviewed *Investment Dealers Digest*. When *Investment Dealers Digest* reduced its coverage of private placements in 1989, Management Planning first switched to *Private Placement Letter* and, later, to *Private Equity Week*. Using these three publications as a source, Management Planning reviewed all the private placements that were reported from January 1, 1980, to December 31, 1996. In selecting the transactions for further analysis, they established the following initial tests, or screening.

- The company selling stock in a private placement should make its financial statements available to the public.
- The company should have a publicly held and actively traded common stock "counterpart" equal in all other respects to the unregistered stock.
- Sufficient data on the private transaction should be readily available.
- The publicly traded common stock counterpart should be selling at a price of at least $2 per share.
- The company should be a domestic corporation.
- The company should not be characterized as being in the "developmental" stage at the time of the transaction.

In order to obtain the most meaningful group of private placement transactions that would have the most relevance to business valuation analysts, Management Planning established three additional tests that had to be met by each transaction.

- If the company issuing the restricted shares lost money in the year prior to the transaction, it was excluded.
- All start-up companies were excluded. Companies with less than $3 million in sales volume were also excluded.
- If the transaction involved restricted shares and the terms of the transaction conferred on the holder the right to register the shares for public trading, the transaction was excluded.

Management Planning reached the following conclusions about the final 53 transactions included in their study:

- The average lack of marketability discount was about 27 percent.
- The median lack of marketability discount was about 25 percent.
- These median and average lack of marketability discounts are slightly lower than the median (28 percent) and the average (29 percent) discounts of the entire prescreen group of 231 transactions.
- Only one of the 53 transactions occurred at a price equal to the market price.
- The remaining 52 transactions all occurred at lack of marketability discounts ranging from a low of 3 percent to a high of 58 percent.

Summary of Empirical Studies on Restricted Stock Transactions through 1996

The 10 empirical studies cover several hundred restricted stock transactions spanning the late 1960s through 1996.[16] Considering the number of independent researchers and the very long time span encompassing a wide variety of market conditions, the results are remarkably consistent, as summarized in Exhibit 17–5.

In many of the cases of restricted stock transactions tabulated in Exhibit 17–5, the purchaser of the stock had the right to register the stock for sale in the existing public market. Sometimes investors get a commitment from the issuer to register the securities at a certain future date. Sometimes investors have "demand" rights, where they can force the issuer to register the securities at a time of their choosing. Sometimes investors get "piggyback" rights where there is no obligation other than to include the securities on any future registration that the issuer undertakes. And, sometimes the purchaser has to rely on SEC Rule 144, where he or she can sell after one year if other parts of the rule are followed. In recent years, more transactions have occurred under SEC Rule 144(a), which relaxes some of the restrictions on such transactions, thus making the restricted securities more marketable. In any case, investors generally expect to be able to resell the stock in the public market in the foreseeable future.

The Internal Revenue Service specifically recognized the relevance of restricted stock transaction data as evidence for quantification of the discount for lack of marketability in Revenue Ruling 77-287. Revenue Ruling 77-287 is presented in Exhibit 17–6.

Studies of Private Transactions before Initial Public Offerings

Before the 1980s, virtually all the empirical research directed at quantifying the value impact of marketability (or the discount for lack of marketability) focused on comparisons between the prices (1) of freely tradable shares of stock and (2) of restricted but otherwise identical shares of stock. There is a general consensus among analysts that price discounts for lack of marketability for ownership interests of

[16] As we go to press, a new restricted stock study (analyzing restricted stock sales in 1997 and 1998) has just been completed that concludes a range of discounts from 0 to 30 percent with a mean of 13 percent and a median of 9 percent. This does not mean that lack of marketability discounts have declined, but rather that restricted stock studies are far less relevant for estimating such discounts for interests in closely held companies. For further details, see Kathryn Aschwald, "Restricted Stock Discounts Decline as a Result of 1-Year Holding Period," *Shannon Pratt's Business Valuation Update*, May 2000, pp. 1–3.

Exhibit 17–5

Summary of Restricted Stock Studies Through 1996

Empirical Study	Years Covered in Study	Average Price Discount (%)
SEC overall average [a]	1966–1969	25.8
SEC nonreporting OTC companies [a]	1966–1969	32.6
Gelman [b]	1968–1970	33.0
Trout [c]	1968–1972	33.5
Moroney [d]	[k]	35.6
Maher [e]	1969–1973	35.4
Standard Research Consultants [f]	1978–1982	45.0 [l]
Willamette Management Associates [g]	1981–1984	31.2 [l]
Silber [h]	1981–1988	33.8
FMV Opinions, Inc. [i]	1979–April 1992	23.0
Management Planning, Inc. [j]	1980–1996	27.1

a. "Discounts Involved in Purchases of Common Stock (1966–1969)," *Institutional Investor Study Report of the Securities and Exchange Commission*, H.R. Doc. No. 64, Part 5, 92nd Congress, 1st Session, 1971, pp. 2444–56.
b. Gelman, Milton, "An Economist-Financial Analyst's Approach to Valuing Stock in a Closely Held Company," *Journal of Taxation*, June 1972, p. 353.
c. Trout, Robert R., "Estimation of the Discount Associated with the Transfer of Restricted Securities," *Taxes*, June 1977, pp. 381–85.
d. Moroney, Robert E., "Most Courts Overvalue Closely Held Stocks," *Taxes*, March 1973, pp. 144–55.
e. Maher, J. Michael, "Discounts for Lack of Marketability for Closely Held Business Interests," *Taxes*, September 1976, pp. 562–71.
f. Pittock, William F., and Charles H. Stryker, "Revenue Ruling 77-276 Revisited," *SRC Quarterly Reports*, Spring 1983, pp. 1–3.
g. Willamette Management Associates study (unpublished).
h. Silber, William L., "Discounts on Restricted Stock: The Impact of Illiquidity on Stock Prices," *Financial Analysts Journal*, July–August 1991, pp. 60–64.
i. Hall, Lance S., and Timothy C. Polacek, "Strategies for Obtaining the Largest Valuation Discounts," *Estate Planning*, January/February 1994, pp. 38–44.
j. Oliver, Robert P., and Roy H. Meyers, "Discounts Seen in Private Placements of Restricted Stock: The Management Planning, Inc., Long-Term Study (1980–1996)" (Chapter 5) in Robert F. Reilly and Robert P. Schweihs, eds. *The Handbook of Advanced Business Valuation* (New York: McGraw-Hill, 2000).
k. Although the years covered in this study are likely to be 1969–1972, no specific years were given in the published account.
l. Median discounts.

closely held companies were greater than those for restricted shares of publicly held companies. This is because the closely held ownership interests had no established market in which they could eventually sell following the removal of certain trading restrictions. However, data for quantifying how much greater this price discount should be had not yet been collected and analyzed.

During the 1980s, an investment banking firm and a valuation consulting firm independently undertook the assemblage of data with which to address this question. The research proceeded along basically parallel lines, although each firm was unaware of the other's efforts until their respective research was far along and each had enough data to reach some conclusions.

Both firms used data from *registration statements*, forms that companies must file with the SEC when they sell securities to the public. Each of the series of studies reported in the following sections used data from these forms in order to analyze prices of the private transactions relative to the public offering prices and market prices following initial public offerings.

Exhibit 17–6

Revenue Ruling 77–287

SECTION 1. PURPOSE.

The purpose of this Revenue Ruling is to amplify Rev. Rul. 59-60, 1959-1 C.B. 237, as modified by Rev. Rul. 65-193, 1965-2 C.B. 370, and to provide information and guidance to taxpayers, Internal Revenue Service personnel, and others concerned with the valuation, for Federal tax purposes, of securities that cannot be immediately resold because they are restricted from resale pursuant to Federal securities laws. This guidance is applicable only in cases where it is not inconsistent with valuation requirements of the Internal Revenue Code of 1954 or the regulations thereunder. Further, this ruling does not establish the time at which property shall be valued.

SEC. 2 NATURE OF THE PROBLEM.

It frequently becomes necessary to establish the fair market value of stock that has not been registered for public trading when the issuing company has stock of the same class that is actively traded in one or more securities markets. The problem is to determine the difference in fair market value between the registered shares that are actively traded and the unregistered shares. This problem is often encountered in estate and gift tax cases. However, it is sometimes encountered when unregistered shares are issued in exchange for assets or the stock of an acquired company.

SEC. 3. BACKGROUND AND DEFINITIONS.

.01 The Service outlined and reviewed in general the approach, methods, and factors to be considered in valuing shares of closely held corporate stock for estate and gift tax purposes in Rev. Rul. 59-60, as modified by Rev. Rul. 65-193. The provisions of Rev. Rul. 59-60, as modified, were extended to the valuation of corporate securities for income and other tax purposes by Rev. Rul. 68-609, 1968-2 C.B. 327.

.02 There are several terms currently in use in the securities industry that denote restrictions imposed on the resale and transfer of certain securities. The term frequently used to describe these securities is "restricted securities," but they are sometimes referred to as "unregistered securities," "investment letter stock," "control stock," or "private placement stock." Frequently these terms are used interchangeably. They all indicate that these particular securities cannot lawfully be distributed to the general public until a registration statement relating to the corporation underlying the securities has been filed, and has also become effective under the rules promulgated and enforced by the United States Securities & Exchange Commission (SEC) pursuant to the Federal securities laws. The following represents a more refined definition of each of the following terms along with two other terms—"exempted securities" and "exempted transactions."

(a) The term "restricted securities" is defined in Rule 144 adopted by the SEC as "securities acquired directly or indirectly from the issuer thereof, or from an affiliate of such issuer, in a transaction or chain of transactions not involving any public offering."

(b) The term "unregistered securities," refers to those securities with respect to which a registration statement, providing full disclosure by the issuing corporation, has not been filed with the SEC pursuant to the Securities Act of 1933. The registration statement is a condition precedent to a public distribution of securities in interstate commerce and is aimed at providing the prospective investor with a factual basis for sound judgment in making investment decisions.

(c) The terms "investment letter stock" and "letter stock" denote shares of stock that have been issued by a corporation without the benefit of filing a registration statement with the SEC. Such stock is subject to resale and transfer restrictions set forth in a letter agreement requested by the issuer and signed by the buyer of the stock when the stock is delivered. Such stock may be found in the hands of either individual investors or institutional investors.

(d) The term "control stock" indicates that the shares of stock have been held or are being held by an officer, director, or other person close to the management of the corporation. These persons are subject to certain requirements pursuant to SEC rules upon resale of shares they own in such corporations.

(e) The term "private placement stock" indicates that the stock has been placed with an institution or other investor who will presumably hold it for a long period and ultimately arrange to have the stock registered if it is to be offered to the general public. Such stock may or may not be subject to a letter agree-ment. Private placements of stock are exempted from the registration and prospectus provisions of the Securities Act of 1933.

(f) The term "exempted securities" refers to those classes of securities that are expressly excluded from the registration provisions of the Securities Act of 1933 and the distribution provisions of the Securities Exchange Act of 1934.

(g) The term "exempted transactions" refers to certain sales or distributions of securities that do not involve a public offering and are excluded from the registration and prospectus provisions of the Securities Act of 1933 and distribution provisions of the Securities Exchange Act of 1934. The exempted status makes it unnecessary for issuers of securities to go through the registration process.

SEC. 4. SECURITIES INDUSTRY PRACTICE IN VALUING RESTRICTED SECURITIES.

.01 *Investment Company Valuation Practices.* The Investment Company Act of 1940 requires open-end investment companies to publish the valuation of their portfolio securities daily. Some of these companies have portfolios containing restricted securities, but also have unrestricted securities of the same class traded on a securities exchange. In recent years the number of restricted securities in such portfolios have increased. The following methods have been used by investment companies in the valuation of such restricted securities:

(a) Current market price of the unrestricted stock less a constant percentage discount based on purchase discount;

(b) Current market price of unrestricted stock less a constant percentage discount different from purchase discount;

(c) Current market price of the unrestricted stock less a discount amortized over a fixed period;

(d) Current market price of the unrestricted stock; and

(e) Cost of the restricted stock until it is registered.

The SEC ruled in its Investment Company Act Release No. 5847, dated October 21, 1969, that there can be no automatic formula by which an investment company can value the restricted securities in its portfolios. Rather, the SEC has determined that it is the responsibility of the board of directors of the particular investment company to determine the "fair value" of each issue of restricted securities in good faith.

.02 *Institutional Investors Study.* Pursuant to Congressional direction, the SEC undertook an analysis of the purchases, sales, and holding of securities by financial institutions, in order to determine the effect of institutional activity upon the securities market. The study report was published in eight volumes in March 1971. The fifth volume provides an analysis of restricted securities and deals with such items as the characteristics of the restricted securities purchasers and issuers, the size of transactions (dollars and shares), the marketability discounts on different trading markets, and the resale provisions. This research project provides some guidance for measuring the discount in that it contains information, based on the actual experience of the marketplace, showing that, during the period surveyed (January 1, 1966, through June 30, 1969), the amount of discount allowed for restricted securities from the trading price of the unrestricted securities was generally related to the following four factors.

(a) *Earnings.* Earnings and sales consistently have a significant influence on the size of restricted securities discounts according to the study. Earnings played the major part in establishing the ultimate discounts at which these stocks were sold from the current market price. Apparently earnings patterns, rather than sales patterns, determine the degree of risk of an investment.

(b) *Sales.* The dollar amount of sales of issuers' securities also has a major influence on the amount of discount at which restricted securities sell from the current market price. The results of the study generally indicate that the companies with the lowest dollar amount of sales during the test period accounted for most of the transactions involving the highest discount rates, while they accounted for only a small portion of all transactions involving the lowest discount rates.

(c) *Trading Market.* The market in which publicly held securities are traded also reflects variances in the amount of discount that is applied to restricted securities purchases. According to the study, discount rates were greatest on restricted stocks with unrestricted counterparts traded over-the-counter,

continued on next page

Exhibit 17–6

Revenue Ruling 77–287 (continued)

followed by those with unrestricted counterparts listed on the American Stock Exchange, while the discount rates for those stocks with unrestricted counterparts listed on the New York Stock Exchange were the smallest.

(d) *Resale Agreement Provisions.* Resale agreement provisions often affect the size of the discount. The discount from the market price provides the main incentive for a potential buyer to acquire restricted securities. In judging the opportunity cost of freezing funds, the purchaser is analyzing two separate factors. The first factor is the risk that underlying value of the stock will change in a way that, absent the restrictive provisions, would have prompted a decision to sell. The second factor is the risk that the contemplated means of legally disposing of the stock may not materialize. From the seller's point of view, a discount is justified where the seller is relieved of the expenses of registration and public distribution, as well as of the risk that the market will adversely change before the offering is completed. The ultimate agreement between buyer and seller is a reflection of these and other considerations. Relative bargaining strengths of the parties to the agreement are major considerations that influence the resale terms and consequently the size of discounts in restricted securities transactions. Certain provisions are often found in agreements between buyers and sellers that affect the size of discounts at which restricted stocks are sold. Several such provisions follow, all of which, other than number (3), would tend to reduce the size of the discount:

(1) A provision giving the buyer an option to "piggyback," that is, to register restricted stock with the next registration statement, if any, filed by the issuer with the SEC;

(2) A provision giving the buyer an option to require registration at the seller's expense;

(3) A provision giving the buyer an option to require registration, but only at the buyer's own expense;

(4) A provision giving the buyer a right to receive continuous disclosure of information about the issuer from the seller;

(5) A provision giving the buyer a right to select one or more directors of the issuer;

(6) A provision giving the buyer an option to purchase additional shares of the issuer's stock; and

(7) A provision giving the buyer the right to have a greater voice in operations of the issuer, if the issuer does not meet previously agreed upon operating standards.

Institutional buyers can and often do obtain many of these rights and options from the sellers of restricted securities, and naturally, the more rights the buyer can acquire, the lower the buyer's risk is going to be, thereby reducing the buyer's discount as well. Small buyers may not be able to negotiate the large discounts or the rights and options that volume buyers are able to negotiate.

.03 *Summary.* A variety of methods have been used by the securities industry to value restricted securities. The SEC rejects all automatic or mechanical solutions to the valuation of restricted securities, and prefers, in the case of the valuation of investment company portfolio stocks, to rely upon good faith valuations by the board of directors of each company. The study made by the SEC found that restricted securities generally are issued at a discount from the market value of freely tradable securities.

SEC. 5 FACTS AND CIRCUMSTANCES MATERIAL TO VALUATION OF RESTRICTED SECURITIES.

.01 Frequently, a company has a class of stock that cannot be traded publicly. The reason such stock cannot be traded may arise from the securities statutes, as in the case of an "investment letter" restriction; it may arise from a corporate charter restriction, or perhaps from a trust agreement restriction. In such cases, certain documents and facts should be obtained for analysis.

0.2 The following documents and facts, when used in conjunction with those discussed in Section 4 of Rev. Rul. 59-60, will be useful in the valuation of restricted securities:

(a) A copy of any declaration of trust, trust agreement, and any other agreements relating to the shares of restricted stock;

(b) A copy of any document showing any offers to buy or sell or indications of interest in buying or selling the restricted shares;

(c) The latest prospectus of the company;

(d) Annual reports of the company for 3 to 5 years preceding the valuation date;

(e) The trading prices and trading volume of the related class of traded securities 1 month preceding the valuation date, if they are traded on a stock exchange (if traded over-the-counter, prices may be obtained from the National Quotations Bureau, the National Association of Securities Dealers Automated Quotations (NASDAQ), or sometimes from broker-dealers making markets in the shares);

(f) The relationship of the parties to the agreements concerning the restricted stock, such as whether they are members of the immediate family or perhaps whether they are officers or directors of the company; and

(g) Whether the interest being valued represents a majority ownership.

SEC.6 WEIGHING FACTS AND CIRCUMSTANCES MATERIAL TO RESTRICTED STOCK VALUATION.

All relevant facts and circumstances that bear upon the worth of restricted stock, including those set forth above in the preceding Sections 4 and 5, and those set forth in Section 4 of Rev. Rul. 59-60, must be taken into account in arriving at the fair market value of such securities. Depending on the circumstances of each case, certain factors may carry more weight than others. To illustrate:

.01 Earnings, net assets, and net sales must be given primary consideration in arriving at an appropriate discount for restricted securities from the freely traded shares. These are the elements of value that are always used by investors in making investment decisions. In some cases, one element may be more important than in other cases. In the case of manufacturing, producing, or distributing companies, primary weight must be accorded earnings and net sales; but in the case of investment or holding companies, primary weight must be given to the net assets of the company underlying the stock. In the former type of companies, value is more closely linked to past, present, and future earnings while in the latter type of companies, value is more closely linked to the existing net assets of the company. See the discussion in Section 5 of Rev. Rul. 59-60.

.02 Resale provisions found in the restriction agreements must be scrutinized and weighted to determine the amount of discount to apply to the preliminary fair market value of the company. The two elements of time and expense bear upon this discount; the longer the buyer of the shares must wait to liquidate the shares, the greater the discount. Moreover, if the provisions make it necessary for the buyer to bear the expense of registration, the greater the discount. However, if the provisions of the restricted stock agreement make it possible for the buyer to "piggyback" shares at the next offering, the discount would be smaller.

.03 The relative negotiation strengths of the buyer and seller of restricted stock may have a profound effect on the amount of discount. For example, a tight money situation may cause the buyer to have the greater balance of negotiation strength in a transaction. However, in some cases the relative strengths may tend to cancel each other out.

.04 The market experience of freely tradable securities of the same class as the restricted securities is also significant in determining the amount of discount. Whether the shares are privately held or publicly traded affects the worth of the shares to the holder. Securities traded on a public market generally are worth more to investors than those that are not traded on a public market. Moreover, the type of public market in which the unrestricted securities are traded is to be given consideration.

SEC. 7. EFFECT ON OTHER DOCUMENTS.

Rev. Rul. 59-60, as modified by Rev. Rul. 65-193, is amplified.

SOURCE: Rev Rul. 77-287, 1977-2 C.B. 319.

Robert W. Baird & Company Studies

Eight studies were conducted under the direction of John D. Emory, first vice president of appraisal services at Robert W. Baird & Company, a regional investment banking firm headquartered in Milwaukee.[17] The studies covered various time periods from 1981 through 1997.

The basic methodology for the eight studies was identical. The population of companies in each study consisted of initial public offerings during the respective period in which Baird & Company either participated or received prospectuses. The prospectuses of these over 2,200 offerings were analyzed to determine the relationship between (1) the price at which the stock was initially offered to the public and (2) the price at which the latest private transaction occurred up to five months prior to the initial public offering.

Emory gives the following explanation regarding the studies:

> In order to provide a reasonable comparison of prices before and at the IPO, I felt it necessary both for the company to have been reasonably sound, and for the private transaction to have occurred within a period of five months prior to the offering date.
>
> The transactions primarily took one of two forms: (1) the granting of stock options with an exercise price equal to the stock's then fair market value; or (2) the sale of stock. . . . In most cases, the transactions were stated to have been, or could reasonably be expected to have been, at fair market value. All ultimately would have had to be able to withstand SEC, IRS or judicial review, particularly in light of the subsequent public offering.[18]

Following the above guidelines, and after eliminating development-stage companies (i.e., companies with a history of operating losses) and companies with no transactions within the five months before the initial public offering, 310 qualifying transactions remained in the eight studies.

The mean price discount for the 310 transactions was 44 percent, and the median price discount was 43 percent. The fact that these averages are a little more than 10 percentage points greater than those shown in restricted stock studies is about what one might reasonably expect. This is because the transactions occurred when there was not yet any established market for the stocks at all.

A summary of the results of each of the eight Emory studies is presented as Exhibit 17–7.

---

[17] John D. Emory, "The Value of Marketability as Illustrated in Initial Public Offerings of Common Stock—January 1980 through June 1981," *Business Valuation News*, September 1985, pp. 21–24, also in *ASA Valuation*, June 1986, pp. 62–66; "The Value of Marketability as Illustrated in Initial Public Offerings of Common Stock, January 1985 through June 1986," *Business Valuation Review*, December 1986, pp. 12–15; "The Value of Marketability as Illustrated in Initial Public Offerings of Common Stock (August 1987–January 1989)," *Business Valuation Review*, June 1989, pp. 55–57; "The Value of Marketability as Illustrated in Initial Public Offerings of Common Stock, February 1989–July 1990," *Business Valuation Review*, December 1990, pp. 114–16; "The Value of Marketability as Illustrated in Initial Public Offerings of Common Stock, August 1990 through January 1992," *Business Valuation Review*, December 1992, pp. 208–12; "The Value of Marketability as Illustrated in Initial Public Offerings of Common Stock, February 1992 through July 1993," *Business Valuation Review*, March 1994, pp. 3–5; "The Value of Marketability as Illustrated in Initial Public Offerings of Common Stock, January 1994 through June 1995," *Business Valuation Review*, December 1995, pp. 155–60; "The Value of Marketability as Illustrated in Initial Public Offerings of Common Stock, November 1995 through April 1997," *Business Valuation Review*, September 1997, pp. 123–31.

[18] John D. Emory, "The Value of Marketability as Illustrated in Initial Public Offerings of Common Stock, November 1995 through April 1997," *Business Valuation Review*, September 1997, p. 124.

Exhibit 17–7

The Value of Marketability as Illustrated in Initial Public Offerings of Common Stock

Study	Number of IPO Prospectuses Reviewed	Number of Qualifying Transactions	Discount	
			Mean	Median
1995-97	732	91	43	42
1994-95	318	46	45	45
1991-93	443	54	45	44
1990-92	266	35	42	40
1989-90	157	23	45	40
1987-89	98	27	45	45
1985-86	130	21	43	43
1980-81	97	13	60	66
All 8 studies	2,241	310	44%	43%

SOURCE: John D. Emory, "The Value of Marketability as Illustrated in Initial Public Offerings of Common Stock, November 1995 through April 1997," *Business Valuation Review*, September 1997, p. 125.

Willamette Management Associates Studies

Over many years, Willamette Management Associates has conducted a series of studies on the prices of private stock transactions relative to those of subsequent public offerings of stock of the same companies. The studies covered the years 1975 through 1995.

The Willamette Management Associates studies differed from the Emory studies in several respects. One important difference was that the source documents for the Willamette Management Associates studies were complete SEC registration statements primarily on Form S-1 and Form S-18. By contrast, the source documents for the Emory studies were prospectuses. Although the prospectus constitutes a portion of the registration statement, it is required to disclose only transactions with affiliated parties. Form S-1 and Form S-18 registration statements require disclosure of *all* private transactions in the stock within the three years before the public offering, in a section of the registration statement separate from the prospectus portion.

The Willamette Management Associates studies attempted to include only transactions that were on an arm's-length basis. The data analyzed included sales of stock in private placements and repurchases of treasury stock by the companies. All stock option transactions and sales of stock to corporate insiders were eliminated, unless there was reason to believe they were bona fide transactions for full value. Many registrant companies were contacted by telephone to validate the arm's-length nature of the transaction.

The Willamette Management Associates studies considered all public offerings in the files of the *IPO Reporter*. According to the *IPO Reporter*, they included all public offerings during the respective period except for offerings of closed-end fund companies. Eliminated from each of the studies were financial institutions, natural resource companies, offerings priced at $1 or less per share, and offerings that included units or warrants since such offerings might be thought to have unique characteristics. The private transactions analyzed took place from 1 to 36 months before the initial public offering. If a company had more than one transaction that met the study's criteria, all such transactions were included.

For each transaction for which meaningful earnings data were available in the registration statement as of both the private transaction and public offering dates, the price/earnings multiple of each private transaction was compared with the subsequent public offering price/earnings multiple. Companies that had no meaningful earnings as of the private transaction date and/or the public offering date were eliminated.

Because the private transactions occurred over a period of up to three years prior to the public offering, Willamette Management Associates made adjustments to reflect differences in market conditions for stocks of the respective industries between the time of each private transaction and the time of each subsequent public offering. Price/earnings multiples were adjusted for differences in the industry average price/earnings multiple between the time of the private transaction and that of the public offering.

The formula used to derive the discount for the private transaction price from the public offering price was as follows:

$$\frac{P/E_o - P/E_p\left(\frac{IP/E_o}{IP/E_p}\right)}{P/E_o}$$

where:

P/E_o = Price per share of the public offering
P/E_p = Price per share of the private transaction
IP/E_o = Industry price index at time of offering
IP/E_p = Industry price index at time of private transaction

The results of the Willamette Management Associates studies described above are summarized in Exhibit 17–8. As the exhibit indicates, the average discounts varied from period to period. However, in all cases, the concluded discounts were higher than the average discounts presented in the studies for restricted stocks of companies that already had an established public trading market—which is the result one would expect.

Criticisms of Willamette Management Associates Studies

Over the years that Willamette Management Associates has used pre-IPO studies in support of the estimation of the lack of marketability discount, the work has been the subject of certain criticisms. In the following discussion, we will attempt to respond to some of these criticisms.

1. *The results are impossible to verify because Willamette Management Associates will not provide the underlying data or calculation.* The analyses are performed in response to individual client situations at great expense and are proprietary. However, (1) they are based entirely on publicly available data, and (2) all the calculations can be replicated when needed, as the methodology is set forth in detail in several books and articles published by Willamette Management Associates professional staff.

2. *There is a self-selection bias in the determination of "qualifying transactions," resulting in an overestimation of the discount for lack of marketability by excluding "troubled" companies.* The Willamette Management Associates studies

Exhibit 17–8

**Summary of Discounts for Private Transaction P/E Multiples
Compared to Public Offering P/E Multiples
Adjusted for Changes in Industry P/E Multiples**

Time Period	Number of Companies Analyzed	Number of Transactions Analyzed	Standard Mean Discount	Trimmed Mean Discount*	Median Discount	Standard Deviation
1975–78	17	31	34.0%	43.4%	52.5%	58.6%
1979	9	17	55.6%	56.8%	62.7%	30.2%
1980–82	58	113	48.0%	51.9%	56.5%	29.8%
1983	85	214	50.1%	55.2%	60.7%	34.7%
1984	20	33	43.2%	52.9%	73.1%	63.9%
1985	18	25	41.3%	47.3%	42.6%	43.5%
1986	47	74	38.5%	44.7%	47.4%	44.2%
1987	25	40	36.9%	44.9%	43.8%	49.9%
1988	13	19	41.5%	42.5%	51.8%	29.5%
1989	9	19	47.3%	46.9%	50.3%	18.6%
1990	17	23	30.5%	33.0%	48.5%	42.7%
1991	27	34	24.2%	28.9%	31.8%	37.7%
1992	36	75	41.9%	47.0%	51.7%	42.6%
1993	51	110	46.9%	49.9%	53.3%	33.9%
1994	31	48	31.9%	38.4%	42.0%	49.6%
1995	42	66	32.2%	47.4%	58.7%	76.4%

* Excludes the highest and lowest deciles of indicated discounts.

SOURCE: Willamette Management Associates.

exclude, by definition, companies that fail, or fail to go public. This is obvious because only companies that go public create a benchmark of liquidity for minority ownership interest shares. Conversely, companies that do not go public are useless for the purpose of deriving a marketable stock price. In order to estimate the lack of marketability discount, one should have a benchmark for comparison (i.e., a marketable price to compare with the nonmarketable price).

If there was a bias based upon the fact that the Willamette Management Associates studies include only "successful" companies, it would understate the size of the lack of marketability discount. One would expect a "troubled" company to be less liquid than a "successful" company, with fewer options for liquidity resulting in a greater lack of marketability discount.

An argument has been made that the less successful company may trade at a price below the price realized in an earlier transaction (presumably resulting in a premium, or negative lack of marketability discount). This may be true at first glance. However, since we adjust the pricing for changes in the price/earnings multiple, the resulting lack of marketability discount is more reliable. In other words, the exclusion of "troubled" companies, while necessary and logical, does not necessarily lead to an overestimation of the lack of marketability discount.

3. *Many of the transactions are not arm's-length transactions.* A comprehensive effort is made to eliminate non-arm's-length transactions. Each of the transactions included in the database has also passed the scrutiny of the SEC. Although the level of effort that Willamette puts forth to verify the validity of the arm's-length nature of the pre-IPO transaction is subject to challenge, the small number of

non-arm's-length transactions that may have been inadvertently included would not skew the results.

Summary of Conclusions from Private Transaction Studies

The evidence from the Emory and Willamette Management Associate studies, taken together, is compelling. The studies covered hundreds of transactions over more than 20 years. Average differentials between private transaction prices and public market prices varied under different market conditions, ranging from about 40 percent to 63 percent, after eliminating the outliers.

This is very strong support for the hypothesis that the fair market values of non-controlling ownership interests in privately held businesses are greatly discounted from their publicly traded counterparts.

Other Analysis of Discounts for Lack of Marketability for Minority Ownership Interests

Ultimately, of course, the value of the nonmarketable, minority ownership interest is the present value of the benefits it will produce for its owner. This fact is recognized in the *Quantitative Marketability Discount Model* (QMDM).[19] The model simply estimates a time horizon at which the interest will be liquidated, a liquidating price based on annual percentage growth in value from the valuation date, and interim cash flows to the holder.

These estimated values are discounted back to a present value in the QMDM at a discount rate that is higher than the normal discount rate for cash flows for the subject company to reflect the illiquidity and extra uncertainty of being "locked up" for an indeterminate time. There are several factors to consider, and approximate percentage points for each factor add to the discount rate.

The model is sound, but the inputs require substantial subjective estimation. It is useful for identifying situations where the discount should be significantly above or below the averages shown by the restricted stock or pre-IPO studies.

QMDM also analyzes some of the studies discussed in this chapter in detail.

Discounts for Lack of Marketability for Controlling Ownership Interests

It is often necessary to agree on the cash equivalent value as of a valuation date for a controlling business ownership interest. This is true whether or not the business will actually be sold. Examples of situations where this cash equivalency analysis is necessary include *federal estate tax cases* (in the case of a death of the controlling business owner) and *marital property cases* (in the case of a marital dissolution).

---

[19] Z. Christopher Mercer, *Quantifying Marketability Discounts* (Memphis: Peabody Publishing, 1997).

Federal estate taxes, by law, require a cash equivalency value as of a date certain. The estate taxes themselves are paid in cash, not in kind by tendering shares of stock. Therefore, it seems reasonable to make an adjustment from the estimated (but uncertain) sale value of the subject controlling business interest at some undetermined time in the future to a cash equivalency value as of the valuation date, reflecting the time, costs, and risks attendant to achieving such a sale. And, of these three factors, the risk of actually being able to consummate the business sale is typically much more significant than the timing and the costs of the business sale.

This valuation adjustment, or discount, is the discount for illiquidity (i.e., the discount for lack of marketability of the controlling business ownership interest).

In many reported decisions, the U.S. Tax Court has recognized that discounts for lack of marketability for controlling ownership interests in closely held companies are appropriate. The courts have used language such as the following:

> Even controlling shares in a nonpublic corporation suffer from lack of marketability because of the absence of a ready private placement market and the fact that flotation costs would have to be incurred if the corporation were to publicly offer its stock.[20]

Similarly, in the marital dissolution situation, the spouse most actively involved in the closely held business usually gets the controlling ownership interest in the business. And the nonoperating spouse usually gets much more liquid assets, such as cash, marketable securities, and real estate.

A rational argument can be made that the same factors discussed above should be reflected in the value of the illiquid controlling business ownership interest for marital dissolution valuation purposes.

Illiquidity Factors Affecting Controlling Ownership Interests

Unlike the owner of publicly traded securities, the owner of a controlling ownership interest in a closely held business cannot (1) call up a securities broker, (2) sell that controlling ownership interest in seconds at a predetermined price and with a nominal transaction commission, and (3) realize the cash proceeds of the sale in three business days. Rather, selling a controlling business ownership interest is a lengthy, expensive, and uncertain undertaking. This assertion is equally true even if the subject investment is a 100 percent (i.e., absolute controlling) ownership interest in a closely held business enterprise.

The typical means of liquidating a controlling business ownership interest are as follows:

1. Consummate a public offering of the controlling block of stock.
2. In a private transaction:
   a. Sell the overall business enterprise (and equitably allocate the sale proceeds to all of the business owners).
   b. Sell the controlling ownership interest only (to the other minority ownership stockholders or to an independent third-party buyer).

Under various conditions in the public capital markets for stocks and the merger/acquisition markets for companies, one or more of the above transactional alter-

---

[20] *Estate of Woodbury G. Andrews*, 79 T.C. 938 (1982).

natives may be clearly more or less attractive—at any given point. The values realizable from these transactional alternatives usually have some relationship to each other. This is because potential acquirers of a closely held business may be public companies.

The controlling owner of a closely held business who wishes to liquidate his or her controlling ownership interest generally faces the following transactional considerations:

1. Uncertain time horizon to complete the offering or sale.
2. Cost to prepare for and execute the offering or sale.
3. Risk concerning eventual sale price.
4. Noncash and deferred transaction proceeds.
5. Inability to hypothecate.

Time Horizon. It may take many months, and in some cases years, to complete either an offering or a sale of a closely held business. To some extent, the time factor may be offset by cash flows available to the owner awaiting sale, if they are equal to or greater than the company's cost of capital on a stand-alone basis.

Costs. There will be many costs attendant to the sale:

1. Auditing and accounting fees, to provide potential buyers the financial information and assurances they demand.
2. Legal costs, at a minimum to draft all the necessary documents and often to clear away potential perceived contingent liabilities and/or to negotiate warranties.
3. Administrative costs on the part of business owners to deal with the accountants, lawyers, potential buyers, and/or their representatives.
4. Transaction and brokerage costs if a business broker, investment banker, or other transactional intermediary is involved.

Risk. There is a high degree of risk concerning the amount of the actual sale price that will be realized relative to the estimated sale price. This is (1) partly because business valuations are only estimates and (2) partly because internal and/or external factors may influence the business value during the sale negotiation period.

Furthermore, in many cases, there is substantial risk concerning whether the business can be sold at all. There is always considerable risk as to whether a transaction or an initial public offering can actually be completed at any given stock price. The capital markets are more or less receptive to stocks of companies in different industries at different points. And, some closely held companies will not be accepted by the public markets at all.

Form of the Proceeds. Even when a sale is complete, the business sale proceeds may not be all in cash. Often, the seller may receive part of the business sale proceeds in a note or contingent compensation, or in stock of the acquiring company (and usually restricted stock if the acquiring company is a publicly traded company).

From 1975 to 1980, almost half the reported business acquisitions were for all cash. In 1999, about 46 percent of the business acquisitions were all cash, 30 percent were all stock, and 24 percent were some combination of cash, debt, and stock.[21] In most of these cases, the stock received is restricted stock. Accordingly, the cash equivalency value of a closely held business sale transaction may be substantially lower than the announced deal price.

---

[21] *Mergerstat Review 2000* (Los Angeles: Applied Financial Information, LP, 2000), p. 15.

For closely held company sales through business brokers, seller financing through a note is involved in the vast majority of transactional cases. Usually, these seller paper notes are at interest rates below market rates for notes of comparable risk. Furthermore, many close corporation "deal prices" have a portion of the payments contingent on given levels of revenues or earnings, further reducing the cash equivalency value.

In the initial public offering transaction scenario, normally it is not possible to sell 100 percent of the company's stock at one time. Underwriters generally are not willing to sell an offering in which insiders are bailing out of all their stock. Thus, the closely held business seller usually is left with some unregistered (restricted) stock. This stock would still be subject to the discount for lack of marketability for restricted stocks as discussed in an earlier section.

Inability to Hypothecate. Ownership interests in closely held businesses, even controlling ownership interests, generally do not make satisfactory bank collateral. If, while awaiting a sale, an owner of a controlling ownership interest wants cash for an emergency or an opportunity or whatever, it will be time-consuming—and may be impossible—to borrow against the estimated value of the business interest.

Benchmark for the Illiquidity Discount for Controlling Ownership Interests

If the appropriate standard of value is fair market value, the price ultimately expected to be reached between "a willing buyer and a willing seller"—before the costs and risks listed above are considered—is a benchmark from which the illiquidity discount could be taken. Other possibilities concerning the appropriate base from which an illiquidity discount on a controlling business ownership interest basis should be taken are:

1. The price one might receive in an initial or secondary public stock offering (i.e., the publicly traded equivalent value).
2. The price achievable in the private sale of the entire closely held business enterprise.

In addition to the underwriting commissions and the direct expenses, underwriters frequently receive stock warrants, especially in connection with smaller initial public offerings. Although this is not an immediate cash expense, it is a very real cost of the transaction if the company is successful, possibly amounting to several percentage points of dilution.

There are also other indirect transaction costs, such as a large commitment of top management's time to negotiate and to carry out a successful stock offering. If the illiquidity discount is a critical issue in the subject business valuation, it may be appropriate to obtain the most current data with regard to the cost of a public flotation.

Many of the same or similar costs are involved in preparing a company for a private sale. In addition, the cost of an intermediary to effect the sale may need to be considered. Also, if the benchmark for the estimated sale price is valuation multiples observed in acquisitions of public companies, data indicate that valuation multiples for acquisitions of private companies tend to be lower. This pricing phenomenon is discussed in the following section.

Differences between Private and Public Company Acquisition Price/Earnings Multiples

Every year, *Mergerstat Review* publishes a table presenting the average price/earnings multiples for the acquisitions of private companies for which they have data—compared with the average price/earnings multiples for the acquisitions of companies that had been publicly traded. Almost every year, the average price/earnings multiple for the acquisitions of private companies is significantly lower than the average price/earnings multiple for the acquisitions of public companies.

The public versus private acquisition price/earnings multiple table from the *2000 Mergerstat Review* is presented in Exhibit 17–9.

Observers have hypothesized a number of reasons for this consistent and significant acquisition pricing differential. The most common reasons for this phenomenon are as follows:

1. Exposure to the market.
2. The quality of financial accounting and other information.
3. The size effect.

Exposure to the Market. The names and stock prices of publicly traded companies are published in hundreds of newspapers throughout the world every day. Publicly traded companies also issue many press releases every year with quarterly earnings and other information; these press releases are also published in hundreds of newspapers. Financial information on thousands of publicly traded companies is accessible on-line.

Publicly traded companies are required to file Forms 10-K, 10-Q, and 8-K, as well as other detailed financial information, with the SEC. Any company, or financial intermediary, interested in an acquisition in any industry has this list of publicly traded companies and the detailed financial information on them at its fingertips.

Exhibit 17–9

Median P/E Offered
Public versus Private
1989-1999

Year	Acquisitions of Public Companies		Acquisitions of Private Companies	
1990	17.1	(117)	13.2	(36)
1991	15.9	(93)	8.5	(23)
1992	18.1	(89)	17.6	(15)
1993	19.7	(113)	22.0	(14)
1994	19.8	(184)	22.0	(18)
1995	19.4	(239)	15.5	(16)
1996	21.7	(288)	17.7	(31)
1997	25.0	(389)	17.0	(83)
1998	24.0	(362)	16.0	(207)
1999	21.7	(434)	18.4	(174)

Note: ( ) denotes number of transactions reporting P/E.

SOURCE: *Mergerstat Review 2000* (Los Angeles: Applied Financial Information, LP, 2000), p. 20.

By contrast, there is no such comprehensive and reliable listing of closely held businesses. And privately owned businesses normally do not disclose financial data. Many privately owned businesses do not even disclose gross revenues. Therefore, acquisition seekers do not have privately owned businesses constantly exposed to them.

Business buyers have difficulty making a comprehensive list of available closely held businesses even if they attempt to do so. Generally, business buyers cannot get financial information regarding closely held businesses—short of a direct approach to the subject business, which they are often reluctant to take and which is often rebuffed. Often, private company sales are initiated by the seller, which may put downward pressure on the price paid for the private company.

Quality of Financial Accounting and Other Information. The SEC requirements for accounting information and other disclosures are far more stringent and extensive than what is required for an unqualified audit opinion under normal GAAP rules. Many analysts believe that this difference in the quantity and reliability of financial data has an impact on the differential in average price/earnings multiples paid for the acquisition of public companies versus the acquisition of private companies.

Size Effect. Empirical studies have proven that larger companies tend to be less risky than smaller companies. This phenomenon would generally result in a lower present value discount rate and a higher price for larger companies. On average, the privately owned companies reported in *Mergerstat Review* are smaller in size than the publicly traded companies reported in *Mergerstat Review*.

This appears to be a contributing factor to the price/earnings multiple differential between privately owned and publicly traded company acquisitions reported in the *Mergerstat Review*. However, it is highly questionable whether this difference in average acquisition size is significant enough to account for the large magnitude of difference between privately owned and publicly traded company acquisition price/earnings multiples.

It is not possible, with the data currently available, to completely explain the relative impact of the various influences that cause privately owned business acquisitions to trade at much lower price/earnings multiples than publicly traded company acquisitions. In any case, the data are clear that privately owned businesses realize lower acquisition price/earnings multiples, on average, when compared with publicly traded companies. Additional research on this point is clearly warranted. Nonetheless, the three factors listed above (i.e., exposure to market, quality of financial accounting, and size effect) generally explain this phenomenon.

If the analysis of the value of a controlling ownership interest in a privately owned business is based on market prices for the acquisitions of publicly traded companies, these data suggest that some amount of valuation adjustment is applicable. For convenience, we may refer to this valuation phenomenon as a part of the illiquidity discount of a controlling business ownership interest.

Empirical data clearly suggest that a valuation discount is appropriate for controlling ownership interests (and, for that matter, for 100 percent ownership interests) in closely held businesses. This illiquidity discount applies—although to varying degrees—regardless of whether the subject business is valued by reference to discounted or capitalized economic income analyses, to guideline publicly traded companies, to consummated guideline acquisitions, or to an asset-based valuation method.

Factors That Affect the Discounts for Illiquidity and Lack of Marketability

It is important to recognize that the discounts for illiquidity and lack of marketability are not a black-and-white issue. That is, an ownership interest is not necessarily simply "marketable," freely tradable in a public market, or "nonmarketable," not freely tradable. There are degrees of marketability. These *degrees* of marketability depend on the circumstances in each case.

The following are some of the factors that affect the degree of marketability. Although there is no empirically supported formula to assess the impact of each, consideration of these factors should guide the analyst's judgment about where the subject ownership interest should fall within the reasonable range of discounts for illiquidity and lack of marketability.

"Put" Rights

Generally, the most powerful factor that could reduce or eliminate a discount for lack of marketability would be the existence of a "put" right. A put is a contractual right that entitles the holder, at his or her option, to sell the ownership interest to a specified party at some time or under some specified circumstances, at the price (or mechanism for determining the price) specified in the contract. In other words, a put *guarantees* a market under specified circumstances. Put rights are most commonly found in connection with ESOP-owned stock.

Dividend Payments

Stocks with no or low dividends suffer more from lack of marketability than stocks with high dividends. Besides being empirically demonstratable, this makes common sense. If the stock pays no dividend, the holder is dependent *entirely* on some future ability to sell the stock to realize any return. The higher the dividend, the greater the return the holder realizes without regard for sale of the stock. For this reason, dividend-paying preferred stocks would typically be subject to a lower discount for lack of marketability than non-dividend-paying common stocks.

Potential Buyers

The existence of a reasonable number of potential buyers or even one strong potential buyer (often as demonstrated by past activity in the company's stock) could dampen the discounts for lack of marketability. For example, if an ESOP regularly purchases shares, the possibility of sometime selling shares to the ESOP may cause the discount for lack of marketability to be less than if the ESOP did not exist.

Size of Interest

Strictly from a marketability perspective, the empirical evidence cited in earlier sections suggests that larger blocks may tend to have larger discounts for lack of marketability than do smaller blocks. There may be fewer potential buyers for a large block, and a large block transaction may be more difficult to finance.

One may logically conclude that a larger ownership interest may have higher value because of possible elements of ownership control, such as a swing vote position or a seat on the board of directors. However, this is a discount factor different from lack of marketability, as discussed in the previous chapter.

Prospect of Public Offering or Sale of the Business

An imminent public offering or sale of the business could decrease the discount for lack of marketability. However, such prospects are almost never certain, and the degree of offset to the discount for lack of marketability is problematic since much of the empirical evidence that illustrates the discount is taken from companies that subsequently went public. In some cases, even if such an event were to occur, all noncontrolling shareholders may not necessarily have the right to participate.

Conversely, a business being absolutely committed to remaining private and in the hands of current control owners for the foreseeable future would tend to increase the discount for lack of marketability.

Information Access and Reliability

The degree to which information is made available to noncontrolling equity owners and the reliability of that information affects the discount for lack of marketability. For example, a recent article on partnership interest valuations states, "An important basis for illiquidity discounts is the difficulty faced by prospective purchasers in obtaining information."[22]

Restrictive Transfer Provisions

Many closely held stocks are subject to provisions that severely restrict the rights of the holder to transfer stock. Any provision that limits the right of the holder to transfer the stock would tend to increase the amount of the discount for lack of marketability.

In some cases, the restrictive provision may fix the value or put a ceiling on it. The impact of such restrictions is a matter of judgment that should be analyzed in light of the provisions in each case, in some cases with the advice of legal counsel regarding enforceability.

---

[22] Mark S. Thompson and Eric S. Spunt, "The Widespread Overvaluation of Fractional Ownership Positions," *Trusts & Estates*, June 1993, pp. 62–66. See also Michael J. Bolotsky, "Adjustments for Differences in Ownership Rights, Liquidity, Information Access, and Information Reliability: An Assessment of 'Prevailing Wisdom' versus the 'Nath Hypotheses,'" *Business Valuation Review*, September 1991, pp. 94–110. Bolotsky's position is that, conceptually, this is a factor separate from marketability, but he recognizes the reality that we have no good way to measure this factor separately.

Court Decisions on Discounts for Illiquidity and Lack of Marketability

There is a substantial body of judicial precedent with regard to the identification and quantification of the discounts for illiquidity and lack of marketability. Each of these judicial decisions depends on the facts and circumstances of the particular case in point. Therefore, it is inappropriate to rely on discount data from judicial precedent.

However, it may be useful for analysts to review published judicial precedent with regard to lack of marketability discounts. This review should *not* be used to extract a particular discount percentage. Rather, it may be used to better understand the various factors that the courts have considered in their estimates of the lack of marketability discounts.

There is a substantial amount of precedent related to lack of marketability discounts with respect to federal gift taxes, estate taxes, and income taxes. These cases are summarized in the *Federal Tax Valuation Digest*, published annually.[23] *Quantifying Marketability Discounts* also offers an overview of marketability discounts in the tax court and detailed analysis of four cases.[24]

The topics of illiquidity and lack of marketability arise in many other litigation contexts, including shareholder disputes, marital dissolution cases, and damages matters. One report, *Marketability Discounts in the Courts, 1991–1996*, covers (in addition to gift and estate tax cases) other federal and state cases where discounts were an issue in marital dissolutions, corporate disagreements, ESOPs, bankruptcy cases, income tax cases, dissenting stockholder cases, and other litigation.[25]

Mandelbaum v. Commissioner Reviews Lack of Marketability Factors

In *Bernard Mandelbaum, et al. v. Commissioner*.[26] The Tax Court listed numerous factors that it considers in its quantification of an appropriate lack of marketability discount.

> Valuers beware! The tax courts continue to emphasize the importance of detailed analysis of the closely held company being valued when using the many discount studies that practitioners often rely on to support their conclusions. In *Bernard Mandelbaum, et al. v. Commissioner* . . . the Court cites nine factors to be considered when selecting a discount for lack of marketability, one of the most controversial areas in business valuations. This valuation of minority blocks of Big M, Inc., a closely held chain of women's apparel retail stores, was for gift tax purposes.

---

[23] Idelle A. Howitt, ed., *Federal Tax Valuation Digest* (New York: Warren, Gorham & Lamont, 1999).

[24] Mercer, *Quantifying Marketability Discounts*.

[25] Janet Hamilton, "Marketability Discounts in the Courts, 1991–1996," *Shannon Pratt's Business Valuation Update*, March 1997.

[26] *Bernard Mandelbaum, et al. v. Commissioner*, T.C. Memo 1995-255 (June 12, 1995).

With these benchmarks established, the Court presented the following nine factors [among others] that should be considered in determining discounts for lack of marketability:

1. *Financial Statement Analysis.*
2. *Company's Dividend Policy.*
3. *The Nature of the Company, Its History, Its Position in the Industry, and its Economic Outlook.*
4. *Company's Management.*
5. *Amount of Control in Transferred Shares.*
6. *Restrictions on Transferability of Stock.*
7. *Holding Period for Stock.*
8. *Company's Redemption Policy.*
9. *Costs Associated with Making a Public Offering.*

The Court deserves praise for its willingness to address this important issue, as well as the depth of its analysis, even though some of its conclusions are arguable. The conclusions reached in this case continue a clear trend in the Tax Courts concerning discounts. They no longer seem satisfied by a blind application of discount studies. They want a much more detailed comparison of the particular characteristics of the ownership interest being valued with the characteristics of the companies that make up the studies, whether individually or in the aggregate.[27]

Estate of Barge v. Commissioner Considers Lack of Marketability Factors

In the *Estate of Barge v. Commissioner*,[28] the Tax Court also provided a very specific list of the factors that it considered in its estimation of the lack of marketability discount in this case.

> In a more recent case, *Barge*, the Court used a quantitative model quite similar to the "quantitative model" generally used by appraisers and analyzed by the Court in *Mandelbaum*. The basic difference in *Barge*, however, is that *all of the basic factors of a quantitative model were specified.*
>
> The discount for an undivided interest can be compared, by analogy, to the marketability discount applicable to minority interests in private businesses, since it deals specifically with the restrictions on sale and impediments to ultimate liquidity of the interest during a reasonably definable investment horizon. The factors considered by the Court included:

- *Base Value.*
- *Expected Holding Period.*
- *Expected Growth Rate of Value.*
- *Expected Dividends or Distributions.*
- *Required Holding Period Return.*

---

[27] James R. Hitchner, "Tax Court Reviews Nine Factors for Selecting Marketability Discounts," *CPA Expert,* Winter 1996, pp. 11–13.

[28] *Estate of Barge v. Commissioner*, TC Memo 1997-188, (April 23, 1997).

If, as we expect, the Tax Court continues to follow the line of reasoning found in *Mandelbaum* and furthered in *Barge*, there will be a growing expectation that business appraisers develop improved methodologies to quantify marketability discounts in the appraisal of non-marketable minority interests of private businesses *and* in estimating the appropriate discounts when valuing undivided interests in real property.[29]

Summary

This chapter presented a substantial amount of evidence to assist in estimating appropriate discounts (1) for lack of marketability related to noncontrolling business ownership interests and (2) for illiquidity related to controlling business ownership interests. In the final analysis, however, as with many other valuation issues, this estimation should be made in light of a studied examination of the facts and circumstances of each valuation assignment. The specific data that the analyst collects and relies on for each valuation should relate as closely as possible in time and other characteristics to the valuation subject.

Ownership interests in closely held businesses, most of which will never be freely tradable, suffer much more from lack of marketability than do restricted shares of publicly traded companies. In general, they also have fewer prospects of being marketable than do shares of companies that are considering (or are already in the process of attempting) an initial public offering.

Courts have tended to recognize higher discounts for illiquidity and for lack of marketability in recent years. The trend toward higher discounts for illiquidity and for lack of marketability has continued since publication of the third edition of this book. However, the levels of discounts allowed in most judicial decisions still seem to be below what the empirical evidence related to arm's-length transactions tends to suggest.

We hope that business owners, their legal and accounting advisers, and valuation analysts, will use the types of data presented in this chapter, along with continuing related research, to reduce the disparity between the (often low) discounts concluded in judicial decisions and the illiquidity and lack of marketability discounts empirically evidenced in actual market transactions.

Bibliography

Abrams, Jay B. "Discount for Lack of Marketability: A Theoretical Model." *Business Valuation Review*, September 1994, pp. 132–39.

Aschwald, Kathryn. "Restricted Stock Discounts Decline as a Result of 1-Year Holding Period." *Shannon Pratt's Business Valuation Update*, May 2000, pp.1–3.

Barron, Michael S. "When Will the Tax Court Allow a Discount for Lack of Marketability?" *Journal of Taxation*, January 1997, pp. 46–50.

Bogdanski, John A. "Dissecting the Discount for Lack of Marketability." *Estate Planning*, February 1996, pp. 91–95.

---

[29] Z. Christopher Mercer, "Are Qualifying Marketability Discounts New Or Not?," *Trusts & Estates*, February 1998, pp. 44–45

Budyak, James T. "Estate Freeze Rules Affect Partnership Valuation Discounts." *Taxation for Accountants*, December 1996, pp. 340–47.

Casey, Christopher. "Marketability Discounts for Controlling Interests Revisited." *Business Valuation Review*, March 2000, pp. 10–15.

Cavanaugh, James C. "Valuation Discounts Are Available in an Estate Plan." *Taxation for Accountants*, July 1995, pp. 31–37.

Chaffe, David B.H. III. "Option Pricing as a Proxy for Discount for Lack of Marketability in Private Company Valuations." *Business Valuation Review*, December 1993, pp. 182–88.

Curtiss, Rand M. "A Practical Methodology for Determining Premiums and Discounts." *Business Valuation Review*, December 1997, pp. 172–79.

Eckstein, David. "Black-Scholes and Marketability: Another View." *Valuation Strategies*, January/February 1999, p. 41.

Emory, John D. "The Value of Marketability as Illustrated in Initial Public Offerings of Common Stock—November 1995 through April 1997." *Business Valuation Review*, September 1997, pp. 3–7.

Fowler, Bradley A. "How Do You Handle It?" *Business Valuation Review*, September 1995, pp. 130–33.

Garber, Steven. "A Proposed Methodology for Estimating the Lack of Marketability Discount Related to ESOP Repurchase Liability." *Business Valuation Review*, December 1993, pp. 172–81.

Hall, Lance S., and Timothy C. Polacek. "Strategies for Obtaining the Largest Valuation Discounts." *Estate Planning*, January/February 1994, pp. 38–44.

Hamilton, Janet. "Marketability Discounts in the Courts, 1991–1996." (special report) *Shannon Pratt's Business Valuation Update*, March 1997.

Hayes, John W., and Scott D. Miller. "Marketability Issues in the Valuation of ESOPs." *CPA Expert*, Summer 1996, pp. 7–11.

Hertzel, Michael, and Richard L. Smith. "Market Discounts and Shareholder Gains for Placing Equity Privately." *Journal of Finance*, June 1993, pp. 459–85.

Hitchner, James R. "Tax Court Reviews Nine Factors for Selecting Marketability Discounts." *CPA Expert*, Winter 1996, pp. 11–13.

Hitchner, James R., and Gary Roland. "Marketability and Control Govern Value of Family Businesses." *Taxation for Accountants*, January 1994, pp. 24–28.

Hitchner, James R., and Kevin J. Rudd. "The Use of Discounts in Estate and Gift Tax Valuations." *Trusts & Estates*, August 1992, pp. 49–56, 60.

Howitt, Idelle A. "Estate of Joseph R. Cloutier." *Valuation Strategies*, November/December 1997, pp. 40–41.

Kubersky, Andrew S. "Marketability Discounting Issues for ESOP Acquisitions of Minority Shares." *Business Valuation Review*, September 1999, pp. 100–03.

———. "Marketability Discounts and ESOP Acquisitions of Minority Share Interests." *Journal of Employee Ownership Law & Finance*, Fall 1998, pp. 97–103.

Luft, Carl F., Lawrence M. Levine, and Jon Howe. "Illiquidity Considerations in Valuing Stock Options." *Valuation Strategies*, May/June 1998, pp. 14–21, 46, 48.

Maher, J. Michael. "Discounts for Lack of Marketability for Closely Held Business Interests." *Taxes*, September 1976, pp. 562–71.

Mercer, Z. Christopher. "Are Marketability Discounts Applicable to Controlling Interests in Private Companies?" *Valuation Strategies*, November/December 1997, pp. 31–36.

_____. "Are Qualifying Marketability Discounts New or Not?" *Trusts & Estates*, February 1998, pp. 39–46.

_____. *Quantifying Marketability Discounts*. Memphis: Peabody Publishing, 1997.

_____. "Revisiting the Quantitative Marketability Discount Model." *Valuation Strategies*, March/April 2000, pp. 12–21.

_____. "Should 'Marketability Discounts' Be Applied to Controlling Interests of Private Companies?" *Business Valuation Review*, June 1994, pp. 55–65.

Mercer, Z. Christopher, and Matthew R. Crow. "Black-Scholes Rather Than the Quantitative Marketability Discount Model?" *Valuation Strategies*, September/October 1998, pp. 5–13, 44.

Moroney, Robert E. "Why 25 Percent Discount for Nonmarketability in One Valuation, 100 Percent in Another?" *Taxes*, May 1977, pp. 316–20.

Paulsen, Jon. "More Evidence on IPO Marketability Discounts." *Business Valuation Review*, March 1998, pp. 10–12.

Peters, Jerry O. "Lack of Marketability Discounts for Controlling Interests: An Analysis of Public vs. Private Transactions." *Business Valuation Review*, June 1995, pp. 59–61.

Phillips, John R., and Neill W. Freeman. "What Is the Marketability Discount for Controlling Interests?" *Business Valuation Review*, March 1999, pp. 3–11.

Ressegieu, Matthew. "Valuation Discounts: What Is Required?" *Taxation for Lawyers*, March/April 1995, pp. 283–88.

Robinson, Debra A., and Edward J. Rappaport. "Impact of Valuation Discounts on Estate and Income Tax Basis." *Estate Planning*, June 1997, pp. 223–30.

Saliba, R. Gary, and Jason K. Chung. "When Linking Post-IPO Return Data with Pre-IPO Marketability Discount Data Should Initial Public Offering (IPO) Discounts Be Considered When Estimating Value at the Shareholder Level?" *Business Valuation Review*, December 1998, pp. 128–35.

Shenkman, Martin M., and Cal R. Feingold. "Minority, Marketability Discounts Affect Valuation of Partnership Interest." *Real Estate Finance Journal*, Summer 1993, pp. 18–25.

Shiffrin, Daniel. "Tax Court Disregards Stock Repurchase Agreement, Applies 40% Discount." *CPA Litigation Service Counselor*, December 1998, p. 3.

Silber, William L. "Discounts on Restricted Stock: The Impact of Illiquidity on Stock Prices." *Financial Analysts Journal*, July–August 1991, pp. 60–64.

Sliwoski, Leonard J. "Built-in Gains Tax, Discounts for Lack of Marketability, and Eisenberg v. Commissioner." *Business Valuation Review*, March 1998, pp. 3–6.

"Stock Marketability Restrictions That Apply to Decedent, but Not Estate, Will Affect Its Valuation." *The Tax Adviser*, September 1998, pp. 644, 646.

Wallgren, Don. "Jointly Owned Property May Not Be Subject to Valuation Discounts." *The Tax Adviser*, April 1999, pp. 218–20.

Chapter 18

Other Valuation Discounts

Introduction

In the two previous chapters, we have discussed two valuation discounts that are common to the valuation of many closely held businesses and business interests: (1) the discount for lack of control and (2) the discount for lack of marketability. In this chapter, we will consider several additional valuation discounts.

In practice, these miscellaneous valuation discounts are encountered less frequently than the discounts for lack of control and lack of marketability. The application of discounts for lack of control and lack of marketability are, in good measure, dictated by the valuation assignment. That is (depending on the valuation method used), the valuation of any noncontrolling ownership interest will require either an implicit or an explicit discount for lack of control. Also (depending on the valuation method used), the valuation of any closely held business will require either an implicit or an explicit discount for illiquidity or for lack of marketability.

Typically, the miscellaneous valuation discounts are not a function of the valuation assignment. Rather, they are a function of the valuation subject. These valuation discounts relate to the facts and circumstances of the subject business interest. Regardless of what level of value is determined by the valuation assignment, certain valuation discounts are appropriate if the appraisal subject has attributes or features that call for such an discount.

This chapter will explain the major categories of miscellaneous valuation discounts. Then, we will note examples of discounts that fall into each major category. Last, we will describe several methods for the practical quantification of valuation discounts within the major categories.

Major Categories of Valuation Discounts

Experienced analysts could list dozens of miscellaneous valuation discounts. However, upon reflection, each of these individual discounts can be grouped into the following two major categories:

1. Transferability restrictions category.
2. Nonsystematic risk attributes category.

The transferability restrictions category includes numerous discounts that relate to the transferability of the subject business interest. It is important to distinguish between the general illiquidity of a type of business interest and the specific illiquidity of the particular business or securities.

We have previously considered the difficulties the owner of an entire closely held business enterprise has converting his or her investment into cash. These difficulties include business sale "make ready" expenses and efforts, the time involved to find and negotiate with a business buyer, and the business brokerage costs and other transaction expenses that the business seller has to pay. We called this attribute of closely held business ownership *illiquidity*.

We also previously considered the additional difficulty that the owner of a noncontrolling block of stock in a closely held business has in the liquidation of that investment. It is much more time-consuming, expensive, difficult, and uncertain to find a buyer for a small block of securities than it is to find a buyer for the overall business. We called this attribute of noncontrolling securities ownership *lack of marketability*. And, we concluded that the typical lack of marketability discount was much greater than the typical illiquidity discount.

Transferability restrictions, however, relate to some internal feature of the securities subject to analysis. In addition to general liquidation difficulties, certain securities have additional liquidation constraints related to:

1. The size of the block of securities to be sold (compared with the sizes of other ownership interests in the business—or compared with some historical transactional activity).
2. Transfer restrictions that are conditions of ownership of the specific securities; these restrictions are often printed as legends directly onto the securities; these transfer restrictions often relate to either governmental securities laws or to conditions of executive or other employment.
3. Transfer restrictions that are imposed by a contract that is independent of the subject security—but that affects the ownership or transfer of the subject security; a fairly common example of a contractually imposed transfer restriction is a business ownership that is subject to a buy-sell agreement.

The nonsystematic risk attributes category includes numerous discounts that relate to individual features or unique attributes that directly affect the expected risk of an investment in the subject business or business interest. These risk factors are nonsystematic. That is, they relate to the subject business only. They do not consider systematic investment risks, such as inflation risk, interest rate risk, and so forth. Systematic risk attributes are normally encompassed in the application of general valuation methods.

In addition to the general risk of investing in the typical business in a certain industry, an investment in the subject business may involve unique risks. For example, the subject business may be relying upon outdated technology, may be producing only one or two principal products, may have very restricted distribution opportunities, may be selling most of its goods or services to just a very few customers, and may be relying on a very small handful of entrepreneurs to manage its operations.

Each of these attributes represents some sort of dependency. Each of these dependencies represents a nonsystematic risk. And, each of these nonsystematic risks may require the application of a specific valuation discount, if these risks haven't already been incorporated into the analysis via the specific-company risk premium in the present value discount rate (see Chapter 9).

Transferability Restrictions Discounts

While there are many different types of security-specific transfer restrictions, the most common transferability restrictions discounts are:

1. Blockage discount, related to size only or to size and SEC regulations.
2. Restricted stock discount, related to SEC regulations or to employment agreements.
3. Contractual transferability restriction discount, related to a shareholder or partner agreement or to a buy-sell agreement.

4. Family limited partnership (FLP) interest discount, which is a type of contractual transferability restriction related to the fact that only an assignee's interest—and not the actual limited partner's ownership interest—may be transferred according to the terms of most FLP agreements. This also may occur with interests in limited liability companies and limited liability partnerships.

We will briefly discuss these four common transferability restrictions discounts below.

Blockage and Federal Securities Laws

A recent article describes the interrelated effects of federal securities laws and blockage with regard to the ownership of certain securities in publicly traded companies:

Introduction. Sometimes a fortunate private business owner will hit the financial home run most entrepreneurs salivate over—a rich purchase price paid for his or her company in an acquisition by a public company. While the price may sometimes be paid all in cash, it is more common to receive part of the purchase price in cash and a portion in the shares of the acquiring public company. With public shares prices at an all-time high, public companies are eager to use their high priced share currency wherever possible to pay for some or all of the purchase. In such a transaction the company owner and his attorneys need to know the following:

- What is the actual value of the public company shares the seller receives, such as in computing the amount of the taxable gain?
- What is the value of the shares for estate tax purposes if the seller dies?

It seems simple. Just look up the trading price of the public company's shares in the paper. In reality, however, the public company shares might be worth significantly less than the actual trading value for the following reasons:

1. **Restrictions on Sale**—Shares received are often restricted from public sale for some period of time. . . .
2. **Not Registered for Public Sale**—Once restrictions on sale lapse, the shares cannot then be sold publicly unless they have undergone the expensive process of registration with the Securities and Exchange Commission. The smart business owner will typically require as a part of the transaction that the acquiring company agree to immediately undertake the efforts and costs to accomplish registration.
3. **Blockage**—The Seller may now own a large block of the public company's shares. If they were to be immediately sold this could cause a demand/supply imbalance in the public stock (i.e., more shares being offered for sale than the daily trading activity could normally absorb). To induce buyers to acquire such a large block, a substantial "blockage discount" from the traded daily price may be required.[1]

---

[1] George B. Hawkins, "Selling Out to a Public Company Buyer: Blockage, Restricted Shares, And Value—The Stated Price versus Reality," *Fair Value*, Spring/Summer 1997, pp. 1–2. Copyright 1997, Banister Financial, Inc., Charlotte, NC. A full reprint of this article is available at www.businessvalue.com.

Other analysts have considered this interrelationship of various security-specific transferability restrictions, as well. For example:

> The IRS and the courts have recognized two distinct and separate theories supporting a discount for valuation purposes in connection with Federal Estate Tax, Federal Gift Tax, and Federal Income Tax:
>
> 1. Federal securities law restrictions [Rev. Ruling 77-287 (1977)]
> 2. "Blockage" (when the block of stock in question is so large that it could not be sold within a reasonable time by a skilled broker without depressing the price of the stock) [See Adair v. Commissioner, T.C. Memo 1987-494 (1987); Revenue Ruling 77-287 (1977); Philip W. Moore, "Blockage Redux: The Challenge Posed By Blockage," Tr. & Est. Mag. Feb. 1992, at 35 et seq.; John V. Murray, "Securities Law Considerations in Valuing Stock for Tax Purposes," Tr. & Est. Mag., Dec. 1992; "Current Attitudes Towards Estate Tax Discounts for Restricted Securities and Underwriting Fees," Est. Plan. Mag., Sept. 1983.]
>
> It is clear that the application of the discount for Federal securities law restrictions applies for Federal Income Tax purposes as well as for Federal Estate Tax and Federal Gift Tax purposes. Thus, Rev. Ruling 77-287 states, in pertinent part, that:

>> The problem is to determine the difference in fair market value between the registered shares that are actively traded and the unregistered shares. This problem is often encountered in estate and gift tax cases. However, it is sometimes encountered when unregistered shares are issued in exchange for assets or the stock of an acquired company.

> It is also clear that the IRS and the courts apply the "blockage" concept in the context of Federal Income Tax as well as of the Federal Gift Tax and Federal Estate Tax.[2]

As the above article describes, the Securities Act of 1933 and other federal securities laws come into play when the security holder is an "affiliate" of the publicly traded corporation. According to SEC Rule 144(a), the term "affiliate" means any person or entity that is a control person of the publicly traded company. SEC Rule 405 defines a control person to include anyone who has the direct or indirect power to direct or cause the direction of management and management policies, whether through the ownership of voting securities, by contract, or otherwise.

The following is a description of the process of selling securities that are subject to SEC Rule 144 transferability restrictions:

> Under the 1933 Act, an affiliate can publicly sell stock in the corporation of which he or she is an affiliate only if (a) the shares are covered by a 1933 Act registration statement and prospectus, or (b) if the shares are sold pursuant to SEC Rule 144. Because in most cases, there is no registration statement and prospectus in effect covering the sale of the shares and the decedent's estate does not have any "registration rights" of either the "absolute" or "piggy-back" variety, the only avenue for public sale is Rule 144.

There are five conditions for a Rule 144 sale:

---

[2] Robert A. Barron, "Control and Restricted Securities," *Securities Regulation Law Journal*, Vol. 24: 82 1996, p. 83.

1. Current public information. If the issuer is a reporting company under the Securities Exchange Act of 1934 (1934 Act), it must be current in its 1934 Act reports. (Rule 144(c)(1)).

2. Volume limitation. In any three-month period, a Rule 144 seller can sell the greater of (a) 1 percent of the outstanding shares of the issuer on the one hand and (b) the average weekly volume in the prior four calendar weeks on the other hand. (Rule 144(e)).

3. Manner of sale requirement. There can be no solicitation of buy orders and no prearrangement of the transaction. (Rule 144(f) & 144 (g)).

4. Form 144 filing requirement. Form 144 must be filed with the SEC (in triplicate) on or before the trade date, and one copy must be filed with the national stock exchange, if any, on which the sale is to be executed.

5. In the case of "restricted securities," the securities must have been acquired and fully paid for at least two years [now one year] previously.[3]

The topic of the value effect of restricted stock (typically granted to executives of publicly traded corporations) was explored in detail in the last chapter. We reviewed all of the authoritative restricted stock studies that are used to quantify such a valuation discount. These empirical studies are referenced in the following excerpt from an article by two prominent tax accountants:

> The IRS issued Rev. Rul. 77-287 . . . to amplify Rev. Rul. 59-60 and to "provide information and guidance to taxpayers, Internal Revenue Service personnel, and others concerned with the valuation, for federal tax purposes, of securities that cannot be immediately resold because they are restricted from resale pursuant to federal securities laws." This Ruling recognizes that a discount should be associated with shares that are restricted from immediate access to an active public market.
>
> The Ruling cites four important factors to consider in determining the discount from a publicly traded price that should be applied in valuing restricted securities. These are:
>
> * The earnings and sales patterns of the company and the risk associated with those earnings.
> * The dollar amount of sales of the company's securities.
> * The trading market in which freely traded shares of the same class are traded.
> * The existence of resale agreement provisions or other provisions affecting the holders' rights.
>
> A number of empirical studies have been performed in an effort to quantify average levels of discounts for lack of marketability in the marketplace. These studies relate to one of two basic categories, depending on the type of market data on which the study was based. The categories are:
>
> * Restricted or letter stock studies.
> * Initial public offering studies.[4]

---

[3] Ibid., pp. 84–85.

[4] Charles H. Fisher, Jr. and Martin B. Solomon, "Valuation Discounts for Family Limited Partnerships—Why the Nature of the Underlying Assets Should Not Matter," *Valuation Strategies*, January/February 1999, pp. 31–32. Reprinted from *Valuation Strategies*. Copyright 1999, Warren, Gorhan & Lamont, 31 St. James Avenue, Boston, MA 02116, (800) 950-1216.

Contractual Transferability Restrictions

Similar to governmentally imposed restrictions on the transfer of publicly traded securities, there are often contractually imposed restrictions on the transfer of closely held securities.

These restrictions are typically imposed by the terms and conditions of:

1. Shareholder agreements.
2. Employment agreements.
3. Buy-sell agreements.
4. Limited partnership agreements.

These transferability restrictions are truly unique to each valuation subject—that is, each individual security and the transferability restrictions imposed on them by each individual contract or agreement. Analysts should consider the specific terms and conditions of the subject contract in their assessment of (1) the applicability and (2) the magnitude of any valuation discount. It is noteworthy, however, that these contract-specific transferability restriction discounts are often separate from—and incremental to—the general closely held security lack of marketability discount.

Nonsystematic Risk Discounts

Examples of the more common nonsystematic risk discounts include:

1. Discount for key person dependence.
2. Discount for key customer dependence.
3. Discount for key product dependence.
4. Discount for obsolescence of technology or facilities.
5. Discount for built-in capital gains.

This listing is not exhaustive with regard to nonsystematic risk factor valuation discounts. However, these discounts are the most common, and they are reasonably representative of the numerous other discounts.

Key person dependence indicates the subject company's unusually concentrated dependence on one executive or on a small group of executives. The key person could be "key" in any number of business operation functions: general management, finance, productions, new product development, sales and marketing, and so on. It is not uncommon for a business to have more than one key person.

The key person does not need to be the founder or the principal owner of the business. In fact, the key person may not own any equity in the subject business at all. A nonowner commissioned salesperson who brings in over half of all of the company orders could easily be a key person.

A company that has an unusually concentrated dependence on one or a small group of customers experiences the nonsystematic risk of key customer dependence. There is no one benchmark as to what level of customer concentration reflects key customer dependence. The Securities and Exchange Commission requires public companies to disclose to shareholders each instance when a customer is responsible for over 10 percent of annual company revenues. Accordingly, many analysts use this 10 percent of revenues SEC disclosure requirement as an indication of key customer dependence.

Similarly, the subject company may experience the nonsystematic risk of key product dependence. This occurs when a concentration of the company's sales come from one particular product or product model—particularly when the subject company competitors offer a broad array of products.

Another type of nonsystematic risk occurs when the subject company is dependent on either technologies or facilities (or both) that are outdated or that are being outdated. As with some other nonsystematic risks, it is important for the analyst to identify the benchmark (e.g., the subject industry, specifically identified competitors, etc.) that the subject company is being compared to in the assessment of a discount for obsolescence.

There have been numerous journal articles written recently with regard to the issue of a valuation discount for built-in capital gains. This has occurred after the publication of the following three tax-related court cases that specifically address this issue:

1. *Estate of Artemus D. Davis v. Commissioner.*[5]
2. *Estate of Helen Bolton Jameson v. Commissioner.*[6]
3. *Eisenberg v. Commissioner.*[7]

Each of these cases relates to the quantification of a valuation discount for built-in capital gains in the time period subsequent to the 1986 repeal of the General Utilities Doctrine. For further discussion of these cases, see Chapter 28.

Some analysts may consider built-in capital gains to be a transferability discount issue—and not a nonsystematic risk factor issue. However, built-in capital gains may be the most security-specific nonsystematic risk element of any valuation adjustment. This is because of the built-in capital gains associated with the individual securities themselves. That is, two identical blocks of stock in the very same company could have two very different levels of built-in capital gains. The analyst would need to know the current owner's income tax basis in each particular security in order to estimate the amount of the discount for built-in capital gains (if any).

Methods to Quantify Transferability Restriction Valuation Discounts

Two common types of restrictive holding periods are:

1. A mandatory holding period (e.g., one year), during which the security holder cannot sell the securities.
2. A period during which the security holder can sell small increments of stock (i.e., "trickle out" the stock) so as to:
    a. Be in compliance with SEC rules regarding the volume of securities that may be trickled out in comparison with the subject company trading volume.
    b. Not depress the subject company public security price.

---

[5] *Estate of Artemus D. Davis v. Commissioner*, 110 T.C. 530 (1998).

[6] *Estate of Helen Bolton Jameson v. Commissioner*, T.C. Memo 1999-43 (Feb. 9, 1999).

[7] *Eisenberg v. Commissioner*, No. 97-4331 U.S. App. (2d Cir. Aug. 18, 1998) *rev'g* T.C. Memo 1997-483 (Oct. 27, 1997).

Since the analyst has to consider both (1) federal securities laws requirements and (2) the effect of the trickle out on the supply and demand for the subject security, the analyst first estimates the appropriate trickle-out holding period.

Second, the analyst documents the public trading price of the subject company stock at the beginning of the trickle-out period.

Third, the analyst estimates the appropriate required rate of return to compensate the investor to hold the subject security during the trickle-out period.

Fourth, the analyst estimates the expected growth rate in the trading price of the subject securities during the trickle-out period.

The analyst then performs this calculation: Project the number of securities that can be sold during each period in the trickle-out period and then multiply by the current public trading price to yield the projected sales proceeds for each period. The analyst continues with this calculation: Estimate the present value of the projected sales proceeds using the required rate of return less the expected security price growth rate as the present value discount rate.

The result of this present value calculation is the indicated value of the restricted securities. The implicit valuation discount is the difference between (1) this present value conclusion and (2) the sales proceeds that could be realized if all of the subject securities could be sold at today's stock market price.

The empirical restricted stock studies were presented in detail in the previous chapter. The results of these empirical studies can be broadly applied when there are finite time periods associated with the transferability restrictions (governmental, contractual, etc.) on the subject securities.

Using the empirical block trade discount method, the analyst surveys business brokers and investment bankers who participate in the block trade market. Many of these financial intermediaries participate in the private placement of blocks of closely held securities. However, the only measurable empirical data relate to the private placement of substantial blocks of publicly traded securities. In this analysis, the analyst inquires of the financial intermediaries as to the typical pricing discount (compared with the stock market trading price) for the private placement of blocks of publicly traded securities.

Methods to Quantify Nonsystematic Risk Valuation Discounts

The three most common methods to quantify the valuation discount related to security-specific nonsystematic risk factors are:

1. The cost to cure method.
2. The scenario analysis method.
3. The effect on guideline companies method.

Each of these methods has strengths and weaknesses. And, the analyst should carefully consider when each method is appropriate in a particular situation.

The cost to cure method may be used when it is possible (1) to identify the nonsystematic risk deficiency and (2) to estimate an expense that could possibly be incurred by the subject business to remedy the deficiency.

This method is sometimes used to estimate a discount for key person dependence, for example. The analyst estimates the annual salary and other employment costs related to hiring a second key employee (e.g., someone from the industry who would be capable of taking over if the key executive departed). This additional compensation expense is the cost to cure the deficiency. This additional compensation expense is typically capitalized as an annuity in perpetuity. The result of this capitalization is the dollar amount of the key person dependence discount.

Many analysts also capitalize either (1) the insurance premiums associated with a hypothetical business interruption insurance policy or (2) the insurance premiums associated with a hypothetical key person life insurance policy in order to estimate the key person discount. The result of the capitalizations of hypothetical insurance premiums expense is another indication of the dollar amount of the key person dependence discount.

The scenario analysis method may be used when it is possible to estimate (1) the economic impact of this nonsystematic risk factor and (2) the probability occurrence of this nonsystematic risk factor. This method is sometimes used to estimate the discount for key customer dependence, for example.

Using this method, the analyst creates various scenarios related to the loss of a key customer, such as:

1. The customer withdraws all of its business.
2. The customer withdraws half of its business.
3. The subject company reduces its prices to retain the customer.

The analyst models the economic effect of each of the selected scenarios on the value of the subject business. The analyst next assigns a probability of occurrence to each of these scenarios. The sum of (1) each scenario economic impact (2) times its probability of occurrence is (3) the mathematical expectation of the effect of that nonsystematic risk factor. And, that nonsystematic risk factor is one indication of the valuation discount for that particular nonsystematic risk.

The effect on guideline companies method is less frequently used in practice. This method requires that the analyst identify pairs or groups of guideline publicly traded companies that are comparative to each other except for one attribute: the nonsystematic risk factor. For example, the analyst collects matched sets of guideline companies that are otherwise very similar except:

1. One group uses older technology and the other group uses new technology.
2. One group suffers from key person dependence and the other group does not.
3. One group suffers from key customer dependence and the other group does not.

The analyst compares the market-derived pricing multiples for the guideline company group with the nonsystematic risk to those for the guideline company group without the nonsystematic risk. The difference in the pricing multiples would indicate how the market perceives the occurrence of a nonsystematic risk factor. The analyst applies (1) the difference in the pricing multiples (2) to the financial fundamentals of the subject company. The product is an indication of the valuation discount for that particular nonsystematic risk factor.

This method is less commonly used because of the difficulty in finding matched sets of guideline publicly traded companies. However, it is noteworthy that the guideline companies should be comparative to each other—and not to the subject company. This method attempts to quantify the market perception of a factor like key customer dependence. Therefore, we do not need to analyze companies in the same industry and of the same size as the subject. Rather, we want to analyze two groups of otherwise comparative public companies with (1) one group experiencing key customer dependence and (2) the other group not experiencing key customer dependence.

Summary

This chapter introduced several miscellaneous valuation discounts. Since these discounts relate to the facts and circumstances of the particular valuation subject, they are not as common as the discount for lack of control or the discount for lack of marketability.

These various valuation discounts may be grouped into two categories:

1. Transferability restrictions discounts.
2. Nonsystematic risk factor discounts.

Transferability restrictions usually relate to federal securities laws, the size of the subject block of securities, employment agreement conditions, or buy-sell agreement restrictions. Nonsystematic risk factors usually relate to dependencies of the subject business that are not common throughout the industry. Examples include key person dependence, key customer dependence, and key product dependence.

This chapter introduced several categories of analytical methods that are commonly used to quantify the valuation discounts related to typical (1) transferability restrictions and (2) nonsystematic dependencies.

Bibliography

Barron, Michael S. "Is a Discount for Locked-In Capital Gains Tax Justified after General Utilities Repeal?" *Journal of Taxation*, April 1992, pp. 218–23.

Barron, Robert A. "Control and Restricted Securities." *Securities Regulation Law Journal*, Spring 1996, pp. 82–90.

_____. "Control and Restricted Securities, Part 2." *Securities Regulation Law Journal*, Summer 1996, pp. 199–207.

Becker, Brian, and Gary Gutzler. "Should a Blockage Discount Apply? Perspectives of Both a Hypothetical Willing Buyer and a Hypothetical Willing Seller." *Business Valuation Review*, March 2000, pp. 3–9.

Crow, Matthew R. "Discounts and Family Limited Partnerships Holding Only Marketable Securities." *CPA Litigation Service Counselor*, May 1999, pp. 9–12.

Finkel, Sidney R. "The Portfolio Discount for Closely Held Investment Holding Companies." *Valuation Strategies*, January/February 1999, pp. 20–25, 46, 48.

Fisher, Charles H. Jr., and Martin B. Solomon. "Valuation Discounts for Family Limited Partnerships." *Valuation Strategies*, January/February 1999, pp. 26–37.

Gasiorowski, John R. "Is a Discount for Built-In Capital Gain Tax Justified?" *Business Valuation Review*, June 1993, pp. 76–79.

Hawkins, George B. "Selling Out to a Public Company Buyer: Blockage, Restricted Shares, And Value—The Stated Price versus Reality." *Fair Value*, Spring/Summer 1997, pp. 1–2.

Hitchner, James R. "Large Discounts Allowed in Real Estate Partnership." *CPA Expert*, Spring 1997, pp. 10–11.

Larson, James A., and Jeffrey P. Wright. "Key Person Discount in Small Firms: An Update." *Business Valuation Review*, September 1998, pp. 85–94.

Lerch, Mary Ann. "Discount for Key Man Loss: A Quantitative Analysis." *Business Valuation Review*, December 1992, pp. 183–94.

Mulligan, Michael D., and Angela Fick Braly. "Family Limited Partnerships Can Create Discounts." *Estate Planning*, July/August 1994, pp. 195–204.

O'Shea, Kevin C., and Robert M. Siwicki. "Stock Price Premiums for Voting Rights Attributable to Minority Interests." *Business Valuation Review*, December 1991, pp. 165–71.

Osteryoung, Jerome S., and Derek Newman. "Key Person Valuation Issues for Private Businesses." *Business Valuation Review*, September 1994, pp. 115–19.

Shiffrin, Daniel. "Recent Developments in the Treatment of Built-in Gains: Davis, Jameson, and Eisenberg." *CPA Litigation Service Counselor*, May 1999, pp. 3–4.

_____. "Tax Court: No Discount for Built-in Gains Tax." *CPA Litigation Service Counselor*, March 1998, pp. 1–2.

_____. "Tax Court Reduces Blockage Discount: Estate of Foote." *CPA Litigation Service Counselor*, March 1999, p. 4.

_____. "Value Adjusted to Reflect Built-in Gains." *CPA Litigation Service Counselor*, August 1998, pp. 3–4.

Sliwoski, Leonard. "Built-in Gains Tax, Discounts for Lack of Marketability, and Eisenberg v. Commissioner." *Business Valuation Review*, March 1998, pp. 3–6.

Sonneman, Donald, "The Single Customer Business—Valuation of a Captive Business." *Business Valuation Review*, March 2000, pp. 44–48.

Chapter 19

Valuation Synthesis and Conclusion

When all the relevant valuation factors have been individually analyzed and assessed, they should be brought together to arrive at a final estimate that represents the valuation conclusion. Sometimes it may be obvious that the analyst should rely on the indications of a single valuation approach. This could be due to (1) the nature of the company or (2) the nature of the business interest subject to valuation. In other cases, two or more valuation approaches may produce such similar value indications that it is not mathematically significant how much weight each approach receives. However, in many cases, business valuation approaches and methods generate apparently inconsistent value indications. When the different valuation approaches result in materially different value indications, and the objective of the subject analysis is a point value estimate, the indications should be reconciled into a single value estimate.

This chapter describes this reconciliation process, a process that encompasses both quantitative and qualitative analyses and judgments.

The Reconciliation Process

During the reconciliation process, it is important for the analyst to review all of the procedures conducted during the valuation. Sometimes the reconciliation process is undertaken with a "cold" review by an independent analyst who challenges the most important valuation factors. The first step in this reconciliation process is for the analyst to review the valuation assignment itself. At this point, the analyst should address these three questions:

1. Did I value the right thing?
2. Did I value it the right way?
3. Did I conclude the right value?

The first question covers the issue of the valuation subject. Did the valuation assignment encompass the total assets of the business, the invested capital of the business, the shareholders' equity of the business, the common stock only, one class of common stock only, and so on? This question also considers the level of value—that is, controlling ownership interest versus noncontrolling ownership interest, marketable securities versus nonmarketable securities, and so on.

The second question addresses the issue of the appropriateness of the valuation methods that were used. Were equity methods used to value assets, or vice versa? Were methods applicable to the valuation of an overall business enterprise used to value a small block of securities, or vice versa?

The third question considers the reasonableness of the value indications. Are they mutually supportive or mutually contradictory? Do the value indications pass a basic "smell test" or reasonableness threshold for a business interest of the size and nature of the valuation subject?

A review of the valuation assignment should help the analyst answer the three questions listed above. This review should consider:

1. The purpose and objective of the valuation.
2. The business ownership interest to be valued.
3. The bundle of legal rights to be valued.
4. The ownership characteristics of the business interest to be valued.
5. The date of the valuation.

6. The standard (or definition) of value to be estimated.
7. The premise of value to be used (based upon the highest and best use of the subject business interest).

The valuation is performed to answer a specific question regarding the value of a business or business interest. Even within the same valuation approach, different methods will typically result in different value indications. For example, it is not uncommon for different indicated values to result from the application of two different income approach methods (e.g., from a direct capitalization method versus a discounted economic income method).

The process of reconciliation is the analysis of the alternative valuation indications in order to arrive at a final value estimate. Before reaching a final value estimate, the analyst should review the entire business valuation for appropriateness and accuracy. The review of the business valuation work product is the subject of Chapter 22. The definition of value estimated and its relationship to each procedure in the valuation process should be reviewed during the reconciliation process.

Criteria for the Selection of Valuation Approaches and Methods

Of the recommended valuation approaches discussed in this text, each approach will be more or less applicable based on the facts and circumstances of the particular analysis.

There is also no precise guideline or quantitative formula for selecting which approach or approaches are most applicable in a given situation. However, the following list presents the common factors to be considered by the analyst when selecting among alternative valuation approaches.

1. The quantity and quality of the available financial and operational data.
2. The degree of the analyst's access to the available financial and operational data.
3. The supply of industry private sale transactional data.
4. The supply of industry publicly traded company data.
5. The type of business, nature of business assets, and type of industry subject to valuation.
6. The nature of the business interest subject to valuation.
7. Statutory, judicial, and administrative considerations.
8. The informational needs of the valuation audience.
9. The purpose and objective of the valuation.
10. The professional judgment and expertise of the analyst.

Quantity and Quality of Available Data

Practically, this may be the most important of the valuation approach selection criteria. The analyst usually cannot perform a valuation approach (no matter how conceptually robust it is or how applicable it is based on industry observations) if the requisite financial, operational, or empirically market-derived data are not available.

Degree of Access to Available Data. In valuations performed, for example, for litigation support, dispute resolution, or other controversy purposes, the analyst may not have unrestricted access to company data, company management, company facilities, and so forth. In these cases, all the desired historical and prospective data may exist. However, the analyst may not be granted reasonable access to the existing data. Accordingly, in selecting among the valuation approaches, the analyst may have to consider not only what data exist, but also what data will be made available in analysis.

Supply of Industry Transactional Data and Public Company Data. Some industries have a large quantity of publicly available data regarding business purchase and sale transactions. When the supply of such reliable industry private sale transactional data is substantial, then the analyst will more likely select and rely on transaction-based, market approach methods. Also, some industries have a large quantity of publicly traded companies that provide useful valuation pricing guidance. Other industries have few or no pure play publicly traded companies. And, some industries have publicly traded companies that are infrequently traded or have other characteristics that made them inapplicable for providing meaningful valuation pricing guidance.

Type of Business, Nature of Business Assets, and Type of Industry Subject to Valuation

Certain industries have rules of thumb that industry participants may use as quick estimates regarding the value of businesses. While these industry rules of thumb, guidelines, or conventions should not be considered as rigorous as a business valuation analysis, they should not be ignored altogether. Depending on the nature of the subject business (e.g., whether it is capital asset–intensive or intangible asset–intensive), different valuation approaches may be more or less applicable.

Nature of the Business Interest Subject to Valuation

Obviously the valuation of a marketable, controlling ownership interest in a business enterprise is a different assignment from the valuation of a nonmarketable, noncontrolling ownership interest in the restricted, nonvoting common stock of the same business enterprise. In selecting the most appropriate valuation approach, the analyst should consider that some valuation approaches are more appropriate for overall business enterprise valuations, while other approaches are more appropriate for the analysis of ownership interests representing less than 100 percent of the business.

Statutory, Judicial, and Administrative Considerations

For those valuations performed for certain taxation, ESOP, and other regulatory purposes, the analyst should consider whether certain valuation approaches are required—and whether associated valuation approaches are prohibited—by the appropriate regulatory authority. For example, the IRS has published valuation procedures and guidelines for appraisals performed for federal gift and estate tax purposes, such as the specific Chapter 14 guidelines that apply to business valuations performed for estate freeze purposes. And some states (often as a matter of either statutory authority or judicial precedent) require some valuation approaches—and prohibit other valuation approaches—for valuations performed for appraisal rights pursuant to minority squeeze-out mergers, other shareholder appraisal rights cases, marital dissolution cases, and so forth. The analyst should be generally aware of specific statutory requirements, administrative guidance, or judicial precedent that may affect the subject valuation. Of course, most valuation analysts are not practicing attorneys and therefore should not practice law. In some cases, legal counsel should be consulted regarding the applicability of statutory, judicial, or administrative considerations.

Informational Needs of the Valuation Audience

The ultimate audience for the valuation may affect the selection of valuation approaches. These considerations include the level of sophistication of the audience and the degree of familiarity of the audience with the subject company. The ultimate purpose of the valuation—as either notational or transactional—may also affect which valuation approach (and how many valuation approaches) will be selected.

Purpose and Objective of the Analysis

Overall, the purpose and objective of the business valuation may influence the selection of the valuation approaches. The factors encompassed in the valuation objective include the description of the subject business ownership interest, the description of the ownership characteristics (e.g., the bundle of ownership legal rights) of the subject business interest, the definition (or standard) of value applied, the premise of value applied (including consideration of the highest and best use of the subject business interests), the level of value applied, and the valuation date. The factors encompassed in the valuation purpose include (1) the audience for the valuation and (2) the decision (or decisions) that will be made based on the value conclusion.

Professional Judgment and Expertise of the Analyst

Ultimately, the most important factors that affect the selection of the appropriate valuation approach or approaches are the professional judgment, technical expertise, and experienced common sense of the analyst.

Reconciling Divergent Indications among Valuation Methods

Ideally, the analyst will use two or more approaches in the subject valuation, and these approaches will yield virtually identical value indications. In practice, of course, this rarely happens.

Experienced analysts expect to derive a range of value indications when alternative valuation approaches are used. Frequently several valuation approaches all conclude a reasonably narrow dispersion of value indications. These alternative indications, then, imply the reasonable range of values for the subject business. They also provide mutually supportive evidence as to the final value estimate.

Occasionally, two or three valuation methods produce value indications within a reasonable range—and then one valuation method produces an obvious value estimate outlier.

An illustrative example of this value indication outlier phenomenon is presented in Exhibit 19–1:

Exhibit 19–1

Illustrative Business Enterprise, Inc.
Fair Market Value of Total Equity
Valuation Synthesis and Conclusion
Example of Outlier Phenomenon
As of December 31, 2000

Valuation Approach	Valuation Method	Value Indication
Market approach	Guideline publicly traded company method	$38,000,000
Income approach	Discounted economic income method	$40,000,000
Asset-based approach	Capitalized excess earnings method	$42,000,000
Asset-based approach	Asset accumulation method	$20,000,000
	Valuation synthesis and conclusion	$42,000,000

In this example, the value indication of the asset accumulation method is an obvious outlier compared with the three other indications. Accordingly, this valuation reconciliation would initiate further analysis and consideration before a final value estimate is concluded.

The question is: What is the analyst to do regarding such an outlier value indication? There are three alternatives.

First, the analyst could discard the valuation method that yields the outlier value indication. This action is based on the rationale that the outlier valuation method simply does not apply to the specific subject set of facts and circumstances.

Second, the analyst could include the outlier valuation method in the valuation reconciliation but assign a very low weight to the outlier value indication. This action is based on the rationale that if the method is fundamentally sound, even an unreasonable value indication should be given some weight in the final value estimate

Third, the analyst could thoroughly investigate why the particular valuation method is producing outlier value indications. The analyst could attempt to reconcile all the value indications. The analyst could search for an answer, or at least an explanation, to this apparent anomaly. As part of this reconciliation process, the analyst should recheck all the quantitative analyses and rethink all the qualitative conclusions. The analyst may find that an error was made in the analysis and application of the outlier method. For example, this reconciliation could reveal that one or more intangible assets were inadvertently not included in the asset accumulation method. Or, the reconciliation could reveal that the asset accumulation method was applied so as to conclude a noncontrolling level of value, while all of the other valuation methods were applied to conclude the enterprise valuation assignment—that is, a controlling level of value.

If an analytical or data error is discovered, it can be corrected. Then, the outlier method may produce a more reasonable, and more consistent, value indication.

Of course, this third alternative to handling the phenomenon of an outlier value indication (which involves additional analyses and reconciliation procedures) is the preferred procedure. Only with such analysis can a discrepancy be adequately explained and reconciled with the other value indications.

If, after careful review, one of the valuation methods that appears to have merit still produces an outlier, then it becomes a matter of the analyst's professional judgment as to the extent to which the factors reflected in the valuation method actually contribute to the estimate of value of the subject business or business interest. And, the analyst will weight that outlier method accordingly in the final value estimate.

Weighting of Valuation Method Results

As with the selection of which valuation methods to use, there are no scientific formulas or specific rules to use with regard to the weighting of the results of two or more valuation methods. In fact, the same factors or guidelines that affect the selection of the valuation methods will influence the analyst with regard to weighting the conclusions of these valuation methods.

This section is really only a brief summary of the relative applicability of different methods in different circumstances. The chapters on the various approaches and methods contain more extensive discussion of the circumstances under which each approach is more or less useful. The reader is encouraged to review those sections for guidance in the weighting of approaches and methods.

The different valuation approaches are not totally independent. Rather, they often have some degree of conceptual and practical overlap. For example, within the market approach, heavy emphasis may be appropriately placed on a pricing multiple of a certain economic income measure, such as a price/earnings multiple. Some analysts say this is a shortcut form of an income approach, thus lessening the need for a separate weight to be assigned to the income approach per se. Similarly, income approach methods are dependent on empirical data regarding market-derived conditions in order to estimate appropriate discount and capitalization rates. Thus, the better the job the income approach does of capturing and documenting market-derived discount and/or capitalization rate data, the less the need for a separate weight to be assigned to the market approach per se.

The analyst should ask, "What attributes of the ownership of the subject business or business interest create the economic value associated with its ownership?" If the income available for distribution to the business owner is the primary value driver, then it may be appropriate that one or more methods within the income approach dominate the value conclusion. Of course, a capitalization (1) of dividends (for a noncontrolling ownership interest) or (2) of dividend-paying capacity (for a controlling ownership interest) within the market approach could very well also capture this income-related value.

If the ability to sell the subject business or business interest is the primary value driver, then it may be appropriate that one or more methods within the market approach dominate the value conclusion.

If the economic value derives primarily from the ownership or use of the business assets, then one or more methods within the asset-based approach may dominate the value conclusion. A market approach using a pricing multiple of stock price to underlying net asset value may also be a satisfactory way to capture this asset-driven economic value. As a general rule, the asset-based approach tends to be more appropriate when valuing a controlling ownership interest than a noncontrolling ownership interest. This is because one of the important factors that the controlling owner controls—and a minority owner does not—is the commercialization (e.g., license, lease, sale, or use) of the subject business assets.

Through all of this, the analyst should keep in mind (1) the applicable standard of value, (2) the applicable premise of value, and (3) the applicable level of value.

For example, family law courts in some states adhere to a strict definition of *fair market value* on the premise of value in exchange. In such cases, the personal goodwill of the business owner that could not be easily transferred with the business sale may not be considered a marital asset. This may be the case even though that personal goodwill may give rise to considerable economic value to the business owner and it would be considered if *investment value* was the applicable standard of value.

The final value estimate should typically be a number within the range of value indications derived from the various methods used in the valuation analysis. The final value estimate may be a number indicated by one of the valuation methods. Or, it may be heavily weighted to the result of the valuation method relied on most. Or, it may be another number from within the indicated range of values.

Occasionally, an arithmetic average to arrive at a final value estimate is appropriate. Using the arithmetic average implies that all of the valuation methods have equal validity and equal weight. While this may occur in certain instances, this is usually not the case. When this is the case, it should be based on a conscious decision on the part of the analyst—and not on a naive averaging of all value indications.

The final value opinion regarding the subject business enterprise or business interest should be derived from the analyst's reasoning and judgment of all the factors considered and from the impartial weighting of all of the market-derived valuation evidence.

At What Point Are Valuation Discounts and Premiums Applied?

The appropriate point in the analysis at which to apply valuation discounts and premiums depends on the level of value indicated by each method used. As discussed in earlier chapters, the most important discounts or premiums are usually related to the degree of ownership control or lack of ownership control of the subject business interest and the degree of marketability or lack of marketability of the subject business interest. Therefore, it is necessary to examine, for each valuation method included in the reconciliation process, the extent to which that valuation method indicates: (1) a controlling or noncontrolling ownership interest and (2) a readily marketable or a less than readily marketable ownership.

If all the methods used indicate values at the same level of value (e.g., a marketable, noncontrolling ownership interest value), then any applicable premiums and/or discounts may be applied at the conclusion of the analysis, after the relative weightings are applied to the various methods. If, on the other hand, the various valuation methods used indicate values at different levels of value, then premiums and/or discounts normally would be applied separately to each individual method before the relative weightings of the methods.

For example, let's assume a guideline publicly traded company method and a discounted economic income (cash flow) method were used. Let's assume that no adjustments were made to the subject company economic income to reflect the influence of ownership control. Let's also assume that valuation pricing multiples and the present value discount rates were derived from public capital market minority share transactional data. In this case, both the methods used would indicate the marketable, noncontrolling ownership interest level of value. If the business interest being valued is a noncontrolling ownership interest in a closely held company, the results of the two methods could be synthesized. Then, a discount for lack of marketability could be applied to the combined value indication in order to estimate a nonmarketable, noncontrolling ownership interest level of value.

Let's assume now that, in addition to the two above-mentioned methods, a market approach using guideline merged and acquired company transaction data also was used. The valuation pricing multiples derived from merger and acquisition transactional data frequently reflect ownership control and/or acquisition price premiums. If that is true in the instant case, it would be appropriate to apply a minority ownership interest discount to the value indications of the guideline merged and acquired company method before weighting these indications in with the indication of the other two valuation methods.

A common error that inexperienced analysts make is to apply valuations of a single premium or discount to a value indication developed from two or more valuation methods that indicate different levels of value. This error can result in a serious distortion to the value estimate. Such a value conclusion that mixes two or more different levels of value is truly a meaningless valuation conclusion.

Accordingly, it is important for analysts to ensure in each situation that any discount or premium applied is appropriate to adjust from the level of value indicated in the valuation method to the level of value to be estimated in the valuation assignment.

Concluding the Value Estimate

Explicit Weighting

An intuitively appealing method of concluding the value estimate is for the analyst: (1) to use subjective but informed judgment and decide on a percentage weight to assign to the indications of each meaningful valuation approach or method and (2) to base the final value estimate on a weighted average of the indications of the various methods. Let's assume that the analyst is valuing a noncontrolling ownership interest in a closely held manufacturing company. The analyst ultimately relies on three value measures developed through the guideline publicly traded company method. The subject is an operating company. However, it has a substantial asset base, and the analyst concludes that the appropriate price-to-earnings pricing multiple should be accorded 60 percent of the total weight, the direct capitalization of dividends method a 10 percent weight, and the price-to-net-asset value pricing multiple a 30 percent weight. Let's assume, in this case, that the company has been unable to generate an adequate rate of return on its net asset base. Accordingly, the value estimate would be synthesized as presented in Exhibit 19–2.

In the case presented in Exhibit 19–2, let's assume that companies in the subject industry generally are selling at below net book value. However, the subject company is valued at a greater discount from net book value than the average company in the subject industry. This is because of the subject company's inadequate earnings. However, the net asset base is accorded some weight, and the company is valued at a lower discount from net book value than it would be if it were valued strictly on a price-to-earnings multiple basis. In this case, the effect of the direct capitalization of dividends on the final value estimate valuation method is neutral.

Regarding the above-described valuation synthesis procedure, it is noteworthy that no specific mathematical model is available for use in deriving the weights to assign to the indications of each valuation method. The relative weight to assign to

Exhibit 19–2

Illustrative Business Enterprise, Inc.
Fair Market Value of Total Equity
Valuation Synthesis and Conclusion
Example of Explicit Weighting
As of December 31, 2000

	Indicated Value per Share	Assigned Weight	Value Indication
Price to earnings multiple: $2.00 per share × 5.0	$10.00	0.6	$6.00
Direct capitalization of dividends multiple: $0.60 per share ÷ 0.05	$12.00	0.1	$1.20
Price to net asset value multiple: $20.00 book value × 0.8	$16.00	0.3	$4.80
			$12.00
Less: Discount for lack of marketability (at assumed 35%) 35% × 12.00			$4.20
Value conclusion per share			$7.80

each method depends on the analyst's judgment. However, one benefit of the explicit weighting valuation synthesis is that it forces the analyst to present his or her thinking in clearly quantified terms. The valuation synthesis narrative description, coupled with the explicit weighting, provides important information as to the analyst's thought process. The explicit weighting synthesis procedure also has the appeal of being relatively simple for the valuation audience to understand. If someone reviewing the valuation disagrees with some aspect of the analyst's judgment, the point of departure can be easily identified and quantified—by adjusting the valuation synthesis explicit weighting schema.

Numerous court cases in which business and security values have been estimated under dissenting stockholders' appraisal rights have relied on this explicit weighting procedure. However, Revenue Ruling 59-60 does not appear to enthusiastically embrace the explicit weighting synthesis procedure:

> Because the valuations cannot be made on the basis of a prescribed formula, there is no means whereby the various applicable factors in a particular case can be assigned mathematical weights in deriving the fair market value. For this reason, no useful purpose is served by taking an average of several factors (for example, book value, capitalized earnings, and capitalized dividends) and basing the valuation on the result. Such a process excludes active consideration of other pertinent factors, and the end result cannot be supported by a realistic application of the significant facts in the case except by mere chance.[1]

---

[1] Rev. Rul. 59-60 (1959-1 C.B. 237).

However, a balanced reading of this revenue ruling indicates that the IRS is not prohibiting the use of the explicit weighting procedure. Rather, it is discouraging a naive application of a weighted average procedure that is not based on reasoned judgment. Analysts can certainly comply with this guidance by thoughtfully considering each factor delineated in Revenue Ruling 59-60 in their selection of the specific weights to assign to each value indication.

Also, despite the above language from this revenue ruling, the explicit weighting procedure has been used successfully in many federal gift and estate tax cases, both in audit negotiations with the IRS and in cases decided in court. The wording of Revenue Ruling 59-60 indicates concern that the averaging or weighted average method allows for the omission of pertinent factors. Of course, it is possible to use the basic weighted average of factors procedure and still, at one stage or another, incorporate active consideration of all the pertinent factors mentioned in Revenue Ruling 59-60. Accordingly, it is important to demonstrate in each taxation-oriented valuation that all other pertinent factors were actively considered and reflected in the final value estimate.

Implicit Weighting

Some analysts use an implicit weighting scheme in the valuation reconciliation process. These analysts present the value indications for each method performed, and then they present the final value estimate without an explicit quantitative weighting. The implicit weighting procedure does not quantitatively justify the valuation synthesis process.

An example of this implicit weighting scheme is provided in Exhibit 19–3.

This valuation synthesis and conclusion presents the final value estimate. However, it does not explicitly or quantitatively explain the reconciliation process. However, this implicit weighting procedure is still informative to the valuation audience if the analyst adequately explains the reconciliation process in the narrative section of the valuation report. The narrative explanation can cover both (1) the conceptual preferability among the methods used and (2) the degree of the analyst's confidence in each method used—based on the relative quantity and quality of available data.

Final Value Estimate

Any of the following types of final value estimates may be appropriate, given the purpose and objective of the valuation:

1. A point estimate—usually the business valuation final value estimate is stated as a single figure or point estimate.
2. A range of value—in this conclusion, the business valuation value estimate is said to fall somewhere within a stated range of values. This may be reported solely, as the conclusion of value, or in conjunction with a single point estimate.
3. A relationship value—in this conclusion, the value estimate is expressed as a relationship to a stated value. For example, the value estimate is indicated to be "no less than $X million" or "no more than $Y million."

Exhibit 19–3

Illustrative Business Enterprise, Inc.
Fair Market Value of Total Equity
Valuation Synthesis and Conclusion
Example of Implicit Weighting
As of December 31, 2000

Valuation Approach	Valuation Method	Value Indication
Market approach	Guideline publicly traded company method	$38,000,000
Income approach	Discounted economic income method	$40,000,000
Asset-based approach	Asset accumulation method	$44,000,000
	Valuation synthesis and conclusion	$42,000,000

Summary

The final value estimate is ultimately based on an analysis and assessment of the accumulated market-derived pricing evidence by the reasoned professional judgment of the analyst. The valuation process should be presented in such a way as to lead the valuation audience to the same final value estimate concluded by the analyst. Accordingly, all of the relevant qualitative and quantitative data and analyses should be summarized in the valuation. And, the analyst's significant judgments and thought processes should be summarized in the valuation. In this way, the audience of the valuation should understand—and be able to re-create—how the analyst concluded the final value estimate.

Part V

Writing and Reviewing Business Valuation Reports

Chapter 20

Writing the Business Valuation Report

This chapter will discuss the following topics related to the preparation and issuance of business valuation reports:

1. An overview of the valuation reporting process.
2. USPAP business valuation reporting standards.
3. The form, format, and content of various common types of reports, as categorized by USPAP.
4. The valuation work paper documentation and retention requirements of USPAP.
5. The confidentiality requirements of USPAP.
6. Other valuation industry standards with regard to reports.

In addition, this chapter will present some general suggestions with regard to effective writing of business valuation reports.

Overview of the Business Valuation Report

According to the 2000 edition of the *Uniform Standards of Professional Appraisal Practice* (USPAP), the definition of an appraisal is: "the act or process of developing an opinion of value; an opinion of value . . ."[1] The USPAP definition of an appraisal report is: "any communication, written or oral, of an appraisal, appraisal review, or consulting service that is transmitted to the client upon completion of an assignment."[2] And, the USPAP definition of an assignment is: "an appraisal, appraisal review, or consulting service provided as a consequence of an agreement between an appraiser and a client."[3] See Chapter 1 for the background, history, and purpose of USPAP.

As we will discuss below, USPAP does provide standards with regard to "business appraisal reporting." However, USPAP does not define either a "business appraisal" or a "business appraisal report." And, while there are USPAP reporting standards with regard to the form and format of real estate appraisal reports, USPAP does not provide specific guidance with regard to the form or format of business valuation reports.

Accordingly, the length, type, and (to a certain extent) content of a business valuation report may be influenced by:

1. The valuation client.
2. Any applicable regulatory requirements.
3. Any applicable statutory authority.
4. The courts, through published judicial precedent.
5. The type of business ownership interest being valued.
6. The nature of the business valuation problem.

USPAP Reporting Standards

The *Uniform Standards of Professional Appraisal Practice* describe minimum standards to be applied in many types of appraisal reports. USPAP states that each written or oral "business appraisal report" must:

---

[1] *Uniform Standards of Professional Appraisal Practice*, 2000 edition, (Washington, DC: The Appraisal Foundation, 2000), p. 10.
[2] Ibid., p. 12.
[3] Ibid., p. 10.

1. Clearly and accurately set forth the appraisal in a manner that will not be misleading.
2. Contain sufficient information to enable those who receive or rely on the report to understand it properly.
3. Clearly and accurately disclose any extraordinary assumption or limiting condition that directly affects the appraisal, and indicate its impact on the concluded value.

The professional standards related to reporting the results of a business are presented in USPAP Standard 10. Since this standard provides clear and cogent professional guidance to analysts who prepare valuation opinion reports, whether or not those reports have to be prepared in accordance with USPAP standards, it is presented in its entirety in Exhibit 20–1.

Written Business Valuation Reporting Standards

As it relates to business valuation, USPAP provides the guideline that each written "business appraisal report" comply with the following disclosure requirements:

1. Identify and describe the business or the business ownership interest that is the subject of the valuation.
2. State the purpose of the valuation and the client's intended use of the valuation opinions and conclusions.
3. Define the standard of value to be estimated.
4. Indicate the effective or "as of" date of the valuation and the date of the valuation opinion report.
5. Describe the extent of the valuation process.
6. Set forth all assumptions and limiting conditions that affect the analyses, opinions, and conclusions.
7. Set forth the information considered, the analytical procedures followed, and the reasoning that support the valuation opinions and conclusions.
8. Explain the analyst's rationale for the valuation methods used and the valuation procedures considered.
9. Set forth any additional information that may be appropriate to demonstrate compliance with, or clearly identify and explain permitted departure from, the requirements of the USPAP "business appraisal development" standards.
10. Include a signed certification in compliance with USPAP Standards Rule 10-3 (which is included in Exhibit 20–1).

Oral Business Valuation Reporting Standards

USPAP Standards Rule 10-4 provides professional guidance with regard to oral business valuation reports. Oral reports are often presented within the context of expert witness testimony, either in deposition or in trial.

Effectively, USPAP does not distinguish between oral reports and written reports, at least with regard to professional standards. That is, USPAP Standards Rule 10–4 indicates that an oral report "must, at a minimum, address the substantive matters set forth in Standards Rule 10–2(a)" (i.e., the Standards Rule that describes the content of written business valuation reports).

Exhibit 20–1

USPAP Standard 10—Business Appraisal Reporting

In reporting the results of a business or intangible asset appraisal, an appraiser must communicate each analysis, opinion, and conclusion in a manner that is not misleading.

> Comment: STANDARD 10 addresses the content and level of information required in a report that communicates the results of a business or intangible asset appraisal developed under STANDARD 9.

> STANDARD 10 does not dictate the form, format, or style of business or intangible asset appraisal reports, which are functions of the needs of users and providers of appraisal services. The substantive content of a report determines its compliance.

Standards Rule 10-1 (**This Standards Rule contains binding requirements from which departure is not permitted.**)

Each written or oral business or intangible asset appraisal report must:
(a) clearly and accurately set forth the appraisal in a manner that will not be misleading.
(b) contain sufficient information to enable the intended user(s) to understand it. Any specific limiting conditions concerning information should be noted.
(c) clearly and accurately disclose any extraordinary assumption or hypothetical condition that directly affects the appraisal and indicate its impact on value.

> Comment: This requirement calls for a clear and accurate disclosure of any extraordinary assumptions or hypothetical conditions that directly affect any analysis, opinion, or conclusion. Examples might include items such as the execution of a pending agreement, atypical financing, infusion of additional working capital or making other capital additions, or compliance with regulatory authority rules. The report should indicate whether the extraordinary assumption or hypothetical condition has a positive, negative, or neutral impact on value.

Standards Rule 10-2 (**This Standards Rule contains specific requirements from which departure is not permitted.**)

Each written business or intangible asset appraisal report must be prepared in accordance with one of the following options and prominently state which option is used: Appraisal Report or Restricted Use Appraisal Report.

> Comment: When the intended users include parties other than the client, an Appraisal Report must be provided. When the only intended user is the client, a Restricted Use Appraisal Report may be provided.
> The essential difference between these options is the content and level of information provided.
> An appraiser may use any other label in addition to, but not in place of, the label set forth in this Standard for the type of report provided.
> The report content and level of information requirements set forth in this Standard are minimums for both types of report. An appraiser must ensure that any intended user of the appraisal is not misled and that the report complies with the applicable content requirements set forth in this Standards Rule.
> A party receiving a copy of an appraisal report does not become an intended user of the appraisal unless the client identifies such party as an intended user as part of the assignment.

(a)   The content of an Appraisal Report must be consistent with the intended use of the appraisal and, at a minimum:
    (i)   state the identity of the client and any intended users, by name or type;
        > Comment: An appraiser must use care when identifying the client to ensure a clear understanding and to avoid violations of the Confidentiality section of the ETHICS RULE. In those rare instances where the client wishes to remain anonymous, an appraiser must still document the identify of the client in the workfile, but may omit the client's identity in the report.
    (ii)   state intended use of the appraisal; [a]
    (iii)   summarize information sufficient to identify the business or intangible asset appraised;
        > Comment: The identification information must include property characteristics relevant to the assignment.
    (iv)   state as relevant to the assignment, the extent to which the business interest or the interest in the intangible asset appraised contains elements of ownership control, including the basis for that determination;
    (v)   state the purpose of the appraisal, including the standard of value (definition) and its source;
        > Comment: Stating the standard of value requires the definition itself and any comments needed to clearly indicate to the reader how the definition is being applied.
    (vi)   state the effective date of the appraisal and the date of the report;
        > Comment: The effective date of the appraisal establishes the context for the value opinion, while the date of the report indicates whether the perspective of the appraiser on the market or property use conditions as of the effective date of the appraisal was prospective, current, or retrospective.
    (vii)   summarize sufficient information to disclose to the client and any intended users of the appraisal the scope of work used to develop the appraisal;
        > Comment: This requirement is to ensure that the client and intended users whose expected reliance on an appraisal may be affected by the extent of the appraiser's investigation are properly informed and are not misled as to the scope of work. The appraiser has the burden of proof to support the scope of work decision and the level of information included in a report.
    (viii)   state all assumptions, hypothetical conditions, and limiting conditions that affected the analyses, opinions, and conclusions;
        > Comment: Typical or ordinary assumptions and limiting conditions may be grouped together in an identified section of the report. An extraordinary assumption or hypothetical condition must be disclosed in conjunction with statements of each opinion or conclusion that was affected.

continued on next page

Exhibit 20–1

USPAP Standard 10—Business Appraisal Reporting (continued)

    (ix)   **summarize the information analyzed, the appraisal procedures followed, the reasoning that supports the analyses, opinions, and conclusions;**

        Comment: The appraiser must attempt to determine that the information provided is sufficient for the client and intended users to adequately understand the rationale for the opinion and conclusions.

    (x)   **state and explain any permitted departures from specific requirements of STANDARD 9, and the reason for excluding any of the usual valuation approaches;**

        Comment: An Appraisal Report must include sufficient information to indicate that the appraiser complied with the requirements of STANDARD 9, including any permitted departures from the specific requirements. The amount of detail required will vary with the significance of the information to the appraisal.

        When the DEPARTURE RULE is invoked, the assignment is deemed to be a Limited Appraisal. Use of the term Limited Appraisal makes clear that the assignment involved something less than or different from the work that could have and would have been completed if departure had not be invoked. The report of a Limited Appraisal must contain a prominent section that clearly identifies the extent of the appraisal process performed and the departures taken.

    (xi)   **include a signed certification in accordance with Standards Rule 10-3.**

(b)   **The content of a Restricted Use Appraisal Report must be for client use only and consistent with the intended use of the appraisal and, at a minimum:**

    (i)   **state the identity of the client;**

        Comment: An appraiser must use care when identifying the client to ensure a clear understanding and to avoid violations of the Confidentiality section of the ETHICS RULE.

    (ii)   **state intended use of the appraisal;**

        Comment: The intended use of the appraisal must be client use only.

    (iii)   **summarize information sufficient to identify the business or intangible asset appraised;**

        Comment: The identification information must include property characteristics relevant to the assignment.

    (iv)   **state as relevant to the assignment, the extent to which the business interest or the interest in the intangible asset appraised contains elements of ownership control, including the basis for that determination;**

    (v)   **state the purpose of the appraisal, including the standard of value (definition) and its source;**

    (vi)   **state the effective date of the appraisal and the date of the report;**

        Comment: The effective date of the appraisal establishes the context for the value opinion, while the date of the report indicates whether the perspective of the appraiser on the market or property use conditions as of the effective date of the appraisal was prospective, current, or retrospective.

    (vii)   **state the extent of the process of collecting, confirming, and reporting data or refer to an assignment agreement in the appraiser's workfile, which describes the scope of work to be performed;**

    (viii)   **state all assumptions, hypothetical conditions, and limiting conditions that affected the analyses, opinions, and conclusions;**

        Comment: Typical or ordinary assumptions and limiting conditions may be grouped together in an identified section of the report. An extraordinary assumption or hypothetical condition must be disclosed in conjunction with statements of each opinion or conclusion that was affected.

    (ix)   **state the appraisal procedures followed, and the value opinion(s) and conclusion(s), and reference the workfile;**

        Comment: An appraiser must maintain a specific, coherent workfile in support of a Restricted Use Appraisal Report. The contents of the workfile must be sufficient for the appraiser to produce an Appraisal Report. The file must be available for inspection by the client (or the client's representatives, such as those engaged to complete an appraisal review), such third parties as may be authorized by due process of law, and a duly authorized professional peer review committee.

    (x)   **state and explain any permitted departures from applicable specific requirements of STANDARD 9; state the exclusion of any of the usual valuation approaches; and state a prominent use restriction that limits use of the report to the client and warns that the appraiser's opinions and conclusions set forth in the report cannot be understood properly without additional information in the appraiser's workfile;**

        Comment: When the DEPARTURE RULE is invoked, the assignment is deemed to be a Limited Appraisal. Use of the term Limited Appraisal makes clear that the assignment involved something less than or different from the work that could have and would have been completed if departure had not be invoked. The report of a Limited Appraisal must contain a prominent section that clearly identifies the extent of the appraisal process performed and the departures taken.

        The Restricted Use Appraisal Report is for client use only. Before entering into an agreement, the appraiser should establish with the client the situations where this type of report is to be used, and should ensure that the client understands the restricted utility of the Restricted Use Appraisal Report.

    (xi)   **include a signed certification in accordance with Standards Rule 10-3.**

Standards Rule 10-3 (This Standards Rule contains binding requirements from which departure is not permitted.)

Each written business or intangible asset appraisal report must contain a signed certification that is similar in content to the following:

    I certify that, to the best of my knowledge and belief:

    —   **the statements of fact contained in this report are true and correct.**

continued on next page

Exhibit 20–1

USPAP Standard 10—Business Appraisal Reporting (continued)

— the reported analyses, opinions, and conclusions are limited only by the reported assumptions and limiting conditions, and are my personal, impartial, unbiased professional analyses, opinions, and conclusions.

— I have no (or the specified) present or prospective interest in the property that is the subject of this report, and I have no (or the specified) personal interest with respect to the parties involved.

— I have no bias with respect to the property that is the subject of this report or to the parties involved with this assignment.

— my engagement in this assignment was not contingent upon developing or reporting predetermined results.

— my compensation for completing this assignment is not contingent upon the development or reporting of a predetermined value or direction in value that favors the cause of the client, the amount of the value opinion, the attainment of a stipulated result, or the occurrence of a subsequent event directly related to the intended use of this appraisal.

— my analyses, opinions, and conclusions were developed, and this report has been prepared, in conformity with the *Uniform Standards of Professional Appraisal Practice*.

— no one provided significant professional assistance to the person signing this report. (If there are exceptions, the name of each individual providing significant professional assistance must be stated.)

Standards Rule 10-4 (This Standards Rule contains binding requirements from which departure is permitted. See DEPARTURE RULE.)

An oral business or intangible asset appraisal report must, at a minimum, address the substantive matters set forth in Standards Rule 10-2(a).

Comment: See Record Keeping in the ETHICS RULE for corresponding requirements.

Standards Rule 10-5 (This Standards Rule contains binding requirements from which departure is not permitted.)

An appraiser who signs a business or intangible asset appraisal report prepared by another, even under the label "appraisal reviewer," must accept full responsibility for the contents of the report.

Comment: This requirement is directed to the employer or supervisor signing the report of an employee or subcontractor. The employer or supervisor signing the report is as responsible as the individual preparing the appraisal for the content and conclusions of the appraisal and the report. Using a conditional label next to the signature of the employer or supervisor or signing a form report on the line over the words appraisal reviewer does not exempt that individual from adherence to these Standards.

[a] See Statement on Appraisal Standards No. 9 (SMT-9) on page 93.

SOURCE: *Uniform Standards of Professional Appraisal Practice* (Washington, DC: The Appraisal Foundation, 2000), pp. 66–70. Reprinted with permission. The complete annual edition of USPAP is available for purchase from The Appraisal Foundation, 1029 Vermont Avenue, N.W., Suite 900, Washington, DC 20005.

USPAP Ethics Provisions

The USPAP Ethics Rule applies to all valuations (or other professional services) prepared in compliance with USPAP. Accordingly, these ethics provisions encompass business valuations, as well as other types of valuation.

Many analysts do not have an administrative or judicial requirement to comply with USPAP. However, the USPAP ethics provisions relate to basic professional conduct issues. Accordingly, all analysts may benefit from the useful professional guidance provided by the USPAP Ethics Rule.

The USPAP Ethics Rule is divided into four sections: (1) conduct, (2) management, (3) confidentiality, and (4) record keeping. The following sections will summarize the professional guidance provided by USPAP in the areas of record keeping/retention and client confidentiality.

Retention of Valuation Reports and Work Paper Files

The record keeping section of the USPAP ethics provision provides the following professional guidance:

> An appraiser must prepare a workfile for each assignment. The workfile must include the name of the client and the identity, by name or type, of any other intended users; true copies of any written reports, documented on any type of media; summaries of any oral reports or testimony, or a transcript of testimony, including the appraiser's signed and dated certification; all other data, information, and documentation necessary to support the appraiser's opinions and conclusions and to show compliance with this rule and all other applicable Standards, or references to the location(s) of such other documentation.
>
> An appraiser must retain the workfile for a period of at least five (5) years after preparation or at least two (2) years after final disposition of any judicial proceeding in which testimony was given, whichever period expires last, and have custody of his or her workfile, or make appropriate workfile retention, access, and retrieval arrangements with the party having custody of the workfile.[4]

Confidentiality Provision

The confidentiality section of the USPAP ethics provision addresses the confidential nature of the valuation analyst–valuation client relationship. The confidentiality provisions of USPAP provide the following professional guidance:

> An appraiser must protect the confidential nature of the appraiser-client relationship.
>
> An appraiser must not disclose confidential information or assignment results prepared for a client to anyone other than: 1) the client and persons specifically authorized by the client; 2) state enforcement agencies and such third parties as may be authorized by due process of law; and 3) a duly authorized professional peer review committee. It is unethical for a member of a duly authorized professional peer review committee to disclose confidential information presented to the committee.[5]

Valuation Industry Reporting Standards

Numerous valuation industry professional membership organizations also have addressed the issue of business valuation reporting standards. These trade association standards do not have the same legislative authority as USPAP. Nonetheless, these standards are usually binding on each organization's respective membership. And, these standards collectively do provide useful guidance to analysts as to what is the standard practice in the industry with regard to business valuation reports.

---

[4] Ibid., p. 4.

[5] Ibid., p. 3.

Valuation analyst and author Jay Fishman compared various professional organization valuation reporting standards in a recent article. This discussion summarizes that article.[6]

American Society of Appraisers

The Fishman article first summarizes the American Society of Appraisers business valuation standards with regard to report writing. In particular, the chapter focuses on the requirements of ASA BVS-VIII. All ASA business valuation standards, including BVS-VIII, are presented in Appendix B. We recommend that the reader review the actual language of BVS-VIII.

The Canadian Institute of Chartered Business Valuators

In its discussion of the CICBV business valuation reporting standards, the Fishman article mentions the following:

> The Canadian Institute of Chartered Business Valuators (CICBV) specifically addresses the format and content of appraisal reports in their Standard 110. The CICBV differentiates between Valuation Reports, Advisory Reports, and Expert Reports. A Valuation Report is defined as:
>
>> Any written communication on letterhead and/or where the author(s) is identified, containing a valuation conclusion of shares, assets, or an interest in a business, prepared by a valuator acting independently and is not clearly marked as being in draft form.
>
> Advisory Reports deal with reporting requirements when a valuator is not acting independently, and Expert Reports deal with the reporting requirements offering an independent opinion "containing a conclusion as to the damages or the quantum of financial gain or loss."
>
> At a minimum, a Valuation Report must contain the standard elements that are seen in most appraisal reports. These include valuation date, description of the shares, purpose of the valuation, and definition of the term value. Appendix A of this standard is a summary of the CICBV valuation reporting requirements for these types of reports. Appendix A indicates the following:
>
>> While it is not required that sufficient information be provided to enable the reader to perform his or her own independent valuation, a valuation report should contain sufficient narrative and schedules to support opinion and calculations for the purposes at hand. The source of any fact, which is material to the formal valuation, must be clearly stated, including sufficient details so that the significance of the fact can be reasonably assessed by the reader of the report. Adequate disclosure will usually include a comparison of valuation calculations and conclusions arrived at through different methods, a discussion of the rationale for accepting or rejecting each

---

[6] Jay E. Fishman, "Appraisal Reports: The Long and Short of It," *The Journal of Business Valuation* (Proceedings of the Fourth Joint Business Valuation Conference of The Canadian Institute of Chartered Business Valuators and the American Society of Appraisers) (Toronto: The Canadian Institute of Chartered Business Valuators, 1999).

methodology, and the relative importance or weighting of relevant methodologies in arriving at a final valuation conclusion.[7]

National Association of Certified Valuation Analysts

Mr. Fishman discusses the NACVA business valuation reporting standards as follows:

> The most recent version of National Association of Certified Valuation Analysts' (NACVA) Professional Standards is as of May 31, 1998. Reporting standards are covered in Section 4. In Section 4.2.2., NACVA indicates the following:
>
> > Any reporting of an opinion of value must be in writing and set forth the following information concerning the valuation engagement and its results:
> >
> > - identification of the subject being valued;
> > - description of the interest being valued;
> > - valuation date;
> > - report date;
> > - purpose of the valuation;
> > - identification of the standard of value;
> > - identification of the premise of value;
> > - identification of the assumptions, limiting conditions, and scope limitations;
> > - conclusion as to Opinion of Value;
> > - limitations on use of the report;
> > - responsible valuation analyst signature;
> > - a statement of independence;
> > - enterprise background and description;
> > - ownership size, nature, restrictions, and agreements;
> > - a description of the fundamental analysis;
> > - valuation approaches and methodologies;
> > - historical financial statement summaries, when applicable;
> > - adjustments to historical financial statements, when applicable;
> > - adjusted financial statement summaries, when applicable; and
> > - projected/forecasted financial statements including the underlying assumptions, when applicable.[8]

Institute of Business Appraisers

As part of the discussion of the IBA business valuation reporting standards, the Fishman article provides the following guidance:

> Perhaps more than any other appraisal society, the Institute of Business Appraisers (IBA) has more written concerning reporting requirements. According to the IBA, there are: oral reports, expert testimony, letter reports, formal reports and lastly, preliminary reports. Standard 1 of the IBA deals

---

[7] Ibid., pp. 192–93.
[8] Ibid., pp. 193–94.

with professional conduct and ethics. This standard refers to communicating appraisal results in a general way. It indicates that:

> It is essential that a business appraiser communicate the research and thought processes which lead to his [or her] opinions and conclusions in a manner that is clear, meaningful and not misleading. Said communication, whether oral or written, shall not be rendered in a careless or negligent manner.[9]

American Institute of Certified Public Accountants

As of this writing, the AICPA has no report writing or other standards specifically relating to business valuation. However, the AICPA has ethical standards relating to consulting (which includes business valuation). These standards cover many of the same issues as the USPAP ethical standards.

The above sections summarized relevant business valuation reporting standards as promulgated (1) by the *Uniform Standards of Professional Appraisal Practice* and (2) by recognized valuation industry professional membership organizations. The next sections do not report published professional standards. Rather, the following discussions will provide general suggestions to analysts for the preparation of clear, concise, and convincing business valuation reports.

Guidelines for Effective Report Writing

Obviously, it is important for the analyst to comply with applicable professional standards with regard to the conduct and the reporting of the business valuation. Nonetheless, compliance with applicable professional standards will not ensure an effective valuation report presentation. Unfortunately, many technically correct valuations fail to convince their intended audience to make the appropriate investment, transaction, regulatory, or judicial decision. This is because the valuation opinion report did not effectively communicate the analyses and conclusion to the report reader.

Previous chapters have focused on the quantitative and qualitative rigor of business valuation approaches and methods. The previous sections of this chapter have focused on technical compliance with professional standards related to valuation reporting (and work paper documentation and client confidentiality). This section will provide practical recommendations with regard to improving the content and style of valuation opinion reports.

What Causes Ineffective Report Writing

In recent years, many commentators have lamented the fact that valuation reports often ineffectively communicate the intended valuation conclusion. These commentators are usually representative of the audience for valuation opinions, such as investors, lawyers, and judges. Most of these criticisms of valuation reports are the

---

[9] Ibid., p. 195.

result of the analyst's failure to follow the fundamental "golden rule" of effective valuation report writing:

1. Say what you did, and
2. Do what you said.

While this "golden rule" may seem simplistic, compliance with it would satisfy many valuation report criticisms. Active consideration of this simple rule will assist the analyst in more effective communication of the valuation analyses and conclusion. Also, active consideration of this simple rule will assist the analyst in the general compliance of many valuation reporting professional standards.

Investment manager and valuation analyst Robert Willis wrote an article in which he effectively described many of the common mistakes that analysts make in ineffectively communicating their valuation opinions:

> Three broad criticisms explain why most appraisal reports and testimony are ineffective and unpersuasive. First, the court is dismissive of superficial reports lacking thoroughness and depth. Second, the court gives little weight to reports that fail to connect the particular facts and circumstances of the case to the proffered studies and the methodologies applied ("connectivity"). Third, the court is increasingly irritated with reports and testimony that fail to adequately consider the position of the hypothetical seller.[10]

In particular, Willis comments on what is arguably the most common criticism of valuation opinion reports: that they do not effectively support the stated valuation conclusion. In many cases, the valuation report presents the appropriate supporting data and analyses. However, the report fails to communicate how the analyst reached the value conclusion from the stated data and analyses.

> The second area of deficiency is the lack of *connectivity* in valuation reports. By this, I mean there is little connection made between the facts of the subject company and the empirical data proffered or the studies cited; and governing legal documents and state law are not connected to valuation issues (e.g., a connection is not shown between a family limited partnership (FLP) agreement and state statutes). There seems to be a general belief that all one has to do is cite the standard lack of marketability studies and, voila, a 35% discount appears! I have noted this tendency in many reports that cross my desk. The court increasingly is challenging such a rote approach of appraisers who do not make the effort to connect the facts and circumstances of the subject company to relevant legal documents, state law, empirical data, and discount studies.[11]

In the same article, Willis explains that the inability of the analyst to effectively organize and present the valuation report causes the reader to doubt the very credibility of the valuation analyses. In the following passage, Willis provides suggestions for enhancing the credibility of the valuation analyses by improving the quality of the valuation report.

> In this regard, the credibility of a valuation report is enhanced by commenting on the impact and outcome of using a range of assumptions (e.g., varying growth and discount rates). By exploring the valuation effect of

---

[10] Robert T. Willis Jr., "Preparing Valuation Reports to Withstand Judicial Challenge," *Estate Planning*, December 1998, p. 455.
[11] Ibid., p. 457.

several different assumptions (instead of just one set of assumptions), the appraiser illustrates a higher level of analysis and investigation, and the report takes on a higher level of credibility and objectivity by appearing less "results driven."[12]

Suggestions for Effective Report Writing

In addition to members of the valuation audience community, many analysts also have commented on the fact that valuation reports often fail to effectively communicate. Fortunately, some analysts also have offered practical suggestions to improve the effectiveness of valuation report communication. In a recent article, analyst Rand Curtiss offered the following constructive suggestions for improving the communicative effectiveness of valuation opinion reports:

1. Make sure the standard of value is consistent with the purpose of the appraisal.
2. Draw implications from economic, industry, company, and financial analysis.
3. In fair market value valuations, list the factors which must be considered according to Revenue Ruling 59-60, and describe how they apply or do not.
4. Support all subjective assumptions with independent facts, case information, logic, and most important, reasonability tests.
5. Make sure all valuation methods yield results at the same level of value.
6. Reconcile your results.
7. Avoid common technical errors.
8. Do not be overly precise: It is grossly misleading.[13]

In this article, Mr. Curtiss discusses procedures for the practical implementation of the above-listed suggestions. The Curtiss article is recommended to analysts who want to improve their report writing skills.

The following discussion presents guidelines for effective valuation opinion reports. These guidelines are not intended to correspond to promulgated professional standards. Rather, they are intended to be practical suggestions to make a valuation report more clear, convincing, and cogent.[14]

Guideline 1. Analysts should avoid the use of "mystery" valuation variables. These are valuation variables that mysteriously appear in the valuation opinion report text—or in the valuation report analytical exhibits. No empirical evidence or analytical procedures are presented to support these "mystery" variables.

Rather, the valuation report reader is left to wonder exactly where that particular valuation variable came from. We believe that the use of unsupported "mystery" variables often undermines the credibility of an otherwise sound valuation analysis. For example, instead of "companies in this industry tend to sell at six to nine times EBITDA," the analyst should provide specific evidence, such as "the six guideline companies, as shown in Exhibit X were priced at six to nine times EBITDA as of the valuation date."

---

[12] Ibid., p. 456.

[13] Rand M. Curtiss, "Improving Your Appraisal Reports: Some Constructive Suggestions," *Business Appraisal Practice*, Winter 1999, pp. 42–49.

[14] These guidelines are adapted from Robert F. Reilly, "10 Guidelines for Reporting Business and Property Appraisals for Tax Purposes," *Valuation Strategies*, May/June 1998, pp. 12–13.

Guideline 2. Analysts should avoid the use of "mystery" valuation data. These "mystery data" are data for which the valuation opinion report presents no citation or other empirical data source. Clearly, the source of significant data elements (e.g., inflation rates, risk-free rate of return, capital market performance indices) should be referenced and documented in the valuation opinion report.

Such references should be specific enough so that the valuation opinion report reader can verify the subject data. For example, the phrase "economists' consensus of the near-term inflation rate is 2.5 percent" would not qualify as an adequately supported data source reference within a valuation report. A better statement would be: "As of December 1999, the Livingston Survey, published by the Federal Reserve Bank of Philadelphia, estimated the long-term inflation rate at 2.5 percent."

Guideline 3. Analysts should avoid the use of vague or ambiguous statements. If the valuation opinion report reader has to ask, "What does the analyst mean by this statement?" then the report has failed to adequately communicate the analysis.

Often, a vague statement in a valuation opinion report can be more misleading than a factually incorrect statement. This is because the valuation opinion report reader can check and correct an incorrect fact. However, the valuation opinion report reader may never know if he or she has simply misinterpreted a vague or ambiguous statement.

Guideline 4. Analysts should avoid the use of superfluous narrative. This sometimes occurs (1) when the valuation opinion report includes generically prepared "boilerplate" descriptions of empirical data sources or analytical procedures or (2) when the analyst has attempted to "cut and paste" narrative sections of previous valuation opinion reports for insertion in the subject report.

All statements in the valuation report should have a purpose. It should also be fairly obvious (1) where and (2) how each statement or data element is used in the valuation analysis. If the valuation report reader has to wonder, "Where (or how) does the analyst use this statement (or data element) in the analysis?" then the valuation report will not be clear, convincing, and cogent.

Guideline 5. Analysts should include a valuation-related analysis of the historical results of financial performance related to the valuation subject. Such an analysis is clearly appropriate if the valuation subject is itself an income-producing business enterprise. This would be the case with any valuation subject that generates operating profits, rental income, license, royalty, or other income.

Such a historical financial performance analysis is also appropriate if the valuation subject is directly associated with an income stream, such as historical revenues, production volume, or cost savings.

It is informative for the valuation opinion report reader to understand the historical results of the valuation subject's financial performance, especially if one or more methods within the income approach is used in the particular valuation analysis. By a "valuation-related analysis," we mean that the analysis of historical performance results should be accompanied by comments on their impact on value.

Guideline 6. Analysts should include an explanation for any adjustments made (1) to the historical financial statements or (2) to the historical operational data subject to analysis. It may be entirely appropriate for the analyst to make these adjustments. The adjustments may relate to the effects of discontinued operations, excess or nonoperating tangible or intangible assets, or extraordinary items (including nonrecurring revenue, expense, or investment items).

Adjustments also may be appropriate to allocate revenues, expenses, and profits between or among various tangible and intangible assets.

It is usually appropriate for the analyst to list and explain any such adjustments in the valuation opinion report. When adjustments to historical financial detail are either aggregated or not adequately explained, the valuation report does not allow the reader to recreate all of the valuation analysis. For example, it is not adequate to say, "We adjusted Mr. Gotrocks' compensation for 1999 from $700,000 to $100,000." How did the analyst arrive at that number? The analyst should cite the compensation data source used and the job description that corresponds to Mr. Gotrocks' position.

This use of "mystery" adjustments represents a valuation opinion report deficiency, even if all of the "mystery" adjustments are appropriate and correctly made.

Guideline 7. Analysts should ensure that there are no inconsistent valuation variables (1) used in alternative analyses or (2) presented on different pages of the valuation opinion report. For example, without a very convincing explanation, it would be inappropriate to use (1) different present value discount rates or (2) different expected growth rates in alternative analyses of the same business valuation subject.

It is generally inappropriate to use related valuation variables that are internally inconsistent with each other. For example, without a very convincing explanation, it would be inappropriate (1) to derive a yield capitalization (i.e., present value discount) rate of 18 percent and an expected long-term growth rate of 5 percent and then (2) use a direct capitalization rate of 10 percent. Assuming they all apply to the same measure of economic income, a present value discount rate of 18 percent less an expected growth rate of 5 percent mathematically indicates a direct capitalization rate of 13 percent.

Such mathematical inconsistencies (especially if unexplained) cause the valuation opinion report audience to doubt the credibility of the subject business valuation analysis.

Guideline 8. Analysts should ensure that there are no inconsistent valuation variables presented between (1) the analysis and (2) the valuation opinion report. If a certain valuation variable is derived in the report narrative then it should be used in the quantitative analysis, and vice versa.

For example, if a 20 percent present value discount rate is derived in the valuation report narrative, then a 20 percent rate (and not a 15 percent or a 25 percent rate) should be used in the valuation analysis.

It is particularly confusing to the valuation opinion report reader if, for example, one figure for a valuation variable is derived on "page 18" of the business valuation report and a different figure of the same valuation variable is used in the analysis presented in "Exhibit III" of the same business valuation report.

Guideline 9. Analysts should avoid using undefined terms in the business valuation report. Also, analysts should avoid using different terms with the same meaning or definition. Moreover, analysts should avoid defining the same term in two different ways in different sections of the same business valuation report.

The jargon of business valuation is confusing enough for most valuation opinion report readers. The analyst should avoid making the valuation report more confusing with the use of inconsistent or imprecise language.

Analysts should also avoid creating their own glossaries. There is a fairly well accepted lexicon with regard to business valuation terminology. It is usually unnecessary (and generally confusing to the valuation report reader) for the analyst to create new terminology.

Guideline 10. The most common business valuation report-writing error is to present the analytical conclusions without any supporting logic.

Analysts should avoid the use of these "leap-of-faith" conclusions. Leap-of-faith conclusions are usually followed by the word "therefore": therefore, the royalty rate is . . . ; therefore, the remaining useful life is . . . ; therefore, the amount of the damage estimate is. . . .

Ideally, the analytical value conclusion should be presented with the logical rigor and inescapable certainty of a mathematical proof. Of course, this is not always the case.

There is a fair amount of professional judgment involved in many business valuation analyses. However, if the valuation opinion report reader cannot follow the valuation analysis from point A to point B to conclusion C, then the valuation synthesis and conclusion is not adequately supported.

Summary

This chapter presented the professional standards related to reporting the results of the business valuation. In particular, the standards rules related to USPAP Standard 10 were discussed. There are many instances when business valuations do not have to be prepared in accordance with the USPAP reporting standards. However, USPAP provides valuable professional guidance for analysts, even in the instances when the valuation report does not technically have to comply with USPAP. Accordingly, we recommend that analysts generally consider the guidance provided by USPAP with regard to most business valuation reports.

This chapter summarized the valuation reporting standards of several prominent valuation industry professional membership organizations. Of course, only members of each professional organization are bound to follow their individual reporting standards. Nonetheless, a summary of these professional standards provides the analyst with a good indication of what is the current standard of practice with respect to business valuation reports. Accordingly, we recommend that even analysts not associated with these organizations be generally familiar with their professional guidance with regard to business valuation reports.

Many competent analysts cannot effectively communicate their valuation analyses and conclusions. Effective valuation opinion reports are clear, convincing, and cogent. Therefore, this chapter also discussed both the content and organization of an effective business valuation report. Several basic communication principles related to effective report writing were presented.

These reporting principles do not rise to the level of professional standards. Rather, they are recommendations intended to assist the analyst to more effectively (and convincingly) present an otherwise competent valuation.

Well-researched and well-documented valuation opinion reports, presented in a complete, logical, and readable manner, can be instrumental (1) in expediting sound transactions and (2) in reducing the risks of litigation subsequent to the subject transactions. Conversely, poorly written valuation opinion reports may delay or prevent a transaction and may invite litigation—even if the transaction itself was basically sound.

This chapter is intended to assist analysts in the presentation of sound valuation opinion reports that will be readable by—and be acceptable to—the valuation audience, business buyers, business sellers, financier's beneficiaries, fiduciaries, governmental or other regulators, judges, juries, or other parties who will rely upon the subject business valuation.

Bibliography

Articles

Curtiss, Rand M. "Improving Your Appraisal Reports: Some Constructive Suggestions." *Business Appraisal Practice*, Winter 1999, pp. 42–49.

Fishman, Jay E. "Appraisal Reports: The Long and Short of It." *Journal of Business Valuation* (Proceedings of the 4th Joint Business Valuation Conference of The Canadian Institute of Chartered Business Valuators and the American Society of Appraisers). Toronto: The Canadian Institute of Chartered Business Valuators, 1999, pp. 189–214.

Fishman, Jay E., Shannon P. Pratt, et al. "Valuation Reports" (Chapter 9). In *Guide to Business Valuations*, 10th ed. Fort Worth, TX: Practitioner's Publishing Company, 2000.

Glass, Carla. "Keys to Successful Reporting Writing." Presentation to the International Appraisal Conference of the American Society of Appraisers, June 1996. Available from *Business Valuation Review*, P.O. Box 19237, Denver, CO 80219, (303) 975-8895.

Pratt, Shannon P. "Quality Report Writing Eludes Many Appraisers." *Shannon Pratt's Business Valuation Update*, August 1996, pp. 1,3.

Reilly, Robert F. "Ten Guidelines: Business and Property Appraisals." *Valuation Strategies*, May/June 1998, pp. 9–13.

Trugman, Gary R. "The Appraisal Report" and "Sample Appraisal Reports" (Chapters 12 and 13). In *Understanding Business Valuation*. Jersey City, NJ: American Institute of Certified Public Accountants, 1998.

Wietzke, Robert R. "Common Errors in Business Valuation Reports Revisited." *CPA Litigation Service Counselor*, June 1999, pp. 1–2, 11–12.

Willis, Robert T. Jr. "Preparing Valuation Reports to Withstand Judicial Challenge." *Estate Planning*, December 1998, pp. 455–62.

Yeanoplos, Kevin R. "The Creation of an Effective Valuation Report." Presentation to the AICPA National Business Valuation Conference, December 1999. Available on www.BVLibrary.com.

Technical Report Writing

Himstreet, William C. *Communicating the Appraisal: The Narrative Report*. Chicago: Appraisal Institute, 1991.

Houp, Kenneth W., Elizabeth Tebeaux, and Thomas E. Pearsall. *Reporting Technical Information*, 9th ed. New York: John Wiley & Sons, 1998.

English Style and Usage

The Chicago Manual of Style, 14th ed. Chicago: University of Chicago Press, 1993. *The Chicago Manual of Style* has long been the standard reference text for writers in many fields. Its precise rules leave little room for doubt about style matters.

Hodges, John C., Winifred Bryan Horner, et al. *Harbrace College Handbook*, rev. 13th ed. San Diego: Harcourt Brace Jovanovich, 1998. The staying power of the *Harbrace College Handbook* can be attributed to its straightforward instruction in grammar, mechanics, and punctuation. It provides a wide variety of excellent examples and leads the reader through the information in a logical and concise manner. It includes the Modern Language Association documentation guide.

Strunk, William Jr., and E. B. White. *Elements of Style*, 3rd ed. New York: Macmillan, 1979.
This is one of the standards in the composition field, and for a very good reason: In fewer than 100 pages, Strunk effectively communicates the most important aspects of good writing.

Chapter 21

Sample Report

Fair Market Value of a Noncontrolling Ownership Interest in the Common Stock of Warm Chicken Company as of December 31, 1998

Warm Chicken Company is a sample case contrived to illustrate the application of many of the principles and procedures presented in several chapters of this book.

This is a hypothetical company and is not intended to be patterned after any real-world company. The reader should not be concerned whether or not any of the assumptions bear resemblance to the reader's perception of reality in the poultry industry. The point of the case is to demonstrate an example of a valuation report and to illustrate, by example, the application of some of the procedures commonly used in valuation reports.

Introduction

Description of the Assignment

We were retained by Warm Chicken Company ("Warm Chicken" or "the Company") to provide our opinion of the fair market value of Warm Chicken's common stock on a nonmarketable, noncontrolling ownership interest basis, as of December 31, 1998 (the "valuation date"), to assist with a contemplated 5.45 percent ownership interest gift of common stock. A summary of our valuation is presented as Exhibit 21–1. All exhibits in this report are presented at the end of this chapter.

Standard and Definition of Value. The appropriate standard of value for federal gift tax purposes is fair market value. The Treasury Regulations define fair market value as follows:

> The price at which such property would change hands between a willing buyer and a willing seller, neither being under any compulsion to buy or to sell, and both having reasonable knowledge of relevant facts.[1]

Court decisions frequently state in addition that the hypothetical buyer and seller are assumed to be able, as well as willing, to trade and to be well informed about the property and the market for such property.

Our valuation analysis takes into consideration Revenue Ruling 59–60, which outlines and reviews the general factors to be considered in the valuation of the capital stock of closely held companies and thinly traded public corporations, as follows:

1. The nature of the business and the history of the enterprise from its inception.
2. The economic outlook in general and the conditions and outlook of the specific industry in particular.
3. The book value of the stock and the financial condition of the business.
4. The earning capacity of the company.
5. The dividend-paying capacity.
6. Whether or not the enterprise has goodwill or other intangible value.
7. Sales of the stock and the size of the block of stock to be valued.
8. The market prices of stocks of corporations engaged in the same or a similar line of business having their stocks actively traded in a free and open market, either on an exchange or over-the-counter.[2]

---

[1] Gift Tax Reg. §25.2512-1.
[2] Rev. Rul. 59-60, 1959-1 C.B. 237.

Summary Description of the Company

Warm Chicken was founded by Simon P. Warm in 1920 as a table egg poultry farm in Galena, Illinois. Today Warm Chicken is a fully integrated producer, processor, marketer, and distributor of fresh and further processed poultry products.

The Company's focus on providing a quality product is reflected by the fact that it averages two to three times more quality control checks than required by the U.S.D.A. and provides a money-back guarantee to consumers.

As of December 31, 1998, the Company was headquartered in Chicago, Illinois, and operated out of five production facilities throughout the Midwest. Sales of fresh poultry are currently concentrated throughout the Midwest. The Company's goal is to supply food services nationwide.

Capitalization and Ownership

Warm Chicken is a closely held company capitalized with one class of common stock that has a par value of $0.10.

The Company's common stock is owned 93.0 percent by the Warm family and 7.0 percent by various members of the Company management and directors. Exhibit 21–2 presents a detailed list of the Company's shareholders, along with their respective ownership percentages.

As of the valuation date, there were 5,000,000 shares of common stock authorized and 1,577,420 shares issued and outstanding.

Shareholders	Number of Common Shares Outstanding	% of Total Shares Outstanding
Simon P. Warm	733,500	46.5
Jake Warm	366,750	23.3
Sydney Warm	183,375	11.6
Gayle Warm	183,375	11.6
Paige Poulet	44,168	2.8
Alan Abacus	44,168	2.8
Fred Fryer	22,084	1.4
Total	1,577,420	100.0

Sources of Information

We used the following information and documents in the valuation analysis.

1. Company audited financial statements for the fiscal years ended March 31, 1994 through 1998.
2. Company unaudited financial statements for the nine-month periods ended December 31, 1997 and 1998.
3. Management's financial projections for the fiscal years ending March 31, 1999 through 2003.
4. Company's summary operating plan, overhead budget, and capital budget for fiscal year 1999.
5. Summary of product and divisional financial information for the 12 months ended December 31, 1998.

6. Schedule of ownership of common stock outstanding as of December 31, 1998.

7. In our analysis of the U.S. economy, we relied on information from *Forecast 1997-1998*, First Interstate Bancorp; *Business Week*; *The Wall Street Journal*; *Outlook and Trends & Projections*, Standard & Poor's Corporation; *U.S. Financial Data*, Federal Reserve Bank of St. Louis; *Economic Trends*, Federal Reserve Bank of Cleveland; *Barron's; Reuters; Nation's Business; United & Babson Investment Report*; and *The Outlook for Interest Rates and the Economy in 1997*, Sheshunoff Information Services Inc.

8. In our analysis of the poultry industry, we relied on information from *Watt Poultry Yearbook 1997*; *Industry Surveys*, Standard & Poor's; *Livestock, Poultry, and Dairy Situation and Outlook*, Economic Research Service of the U.S. Department of Agriculture; *Feedstuffs*; *Journal of Commerce & Commercial*; and Warm Chicken management.

9. For financial and descriptive information on publicly traded guideline companies, we relied upon information from Securities and Exchange Commission Forms 10-K and 10-Q, annual reports to shareholders, Standard & Poor's *Compustat* and *Dialog-on-Disc*, and Disclosure's *Compact D/SEC*.

In addition, we conducted discussions with Warm Chicken's management at the Company's headquarters in Chicago, Illinois.

Analysis of the U.S. Economy

In the valuation of any business interest, the general economic outlook as of the valuation date should be considered, since the national economic outlook influences how investors perceive alternative investment opportunities at any given time. In our analysis, we considered the general economic climate that prevailed at the end of 1998.

Overview

The U.S. economy expanded faster than expected in the last quarter of 1998. Gross domestic product (GDP) surged ahead at a 5.6 percent rate for the quarter, the fastest pace in two and one-half years, while inflation was near a 40-year low. GDP growth for all of 1998 matched 1997's advance. The United States, however, was an island of prosperity amid global chaos in Asia, Latin America, and Russia. U.S. consumers accounted for much of the economic growth in 1998, spurred by low inflation, low interest rates, and low unemployment. There were worker shortages in some industries. However, manufacturing activity weakened during most of the year.

On November 17, 1998, the Federal Reserve Board reduced interest rates for the third time in seven weeks to cushion the U.S. financial system against the spillover from financial turmoil in Russia. After each of the Federal Reserve Bank's interest rate cuts, major banks cut their prime rate.

The U.S. Labor Department reported that energy prices decreased in 1998. Food prices increased moderately, and prescription drug and education costs both jumped significantly. New car prices were unchanged and clothing costs were down slightly for the year. Computer prices fell substantially in 1998.

Nonfarm payroll employment increased moderately in December 1998. More service jobs were created than manufacturing jobs destroyed by the Asian crisis.

The year 1998 had the strongest peacetime job market in 41 years. Unemployment in December 1998 decreased slightly.

The employment cost index, which measures wages, salaries, and fringe benefits, increased modestly in 1998's fourth quarter. Wages and salaries increased moderately in 1998, as did employee benefit costs and personal income.

Consumer spending increased moderately in 1998's fourth quarter. However, spending on durable goods increased at a high rate. For the entire year, consumer spending was ahead moderately.

The Dow Jones Industrial Average closed out 1998 by gaining 16.0 percent for the entire year. The Standard & Poor's 500 index gained 26.7 percent, and the Nasdaq Composite index gained 39.6 percent. It was the fourth consecutive year with gains of more than 20.0 percent in the S&P 500 and the Nasdaq Composite.

During 1998, a global slump decreased foreign demand for many American-made goods, but domestic demand remained strong. For all of 1998, new orders for durable goods had the smallest gain since 1991. In December 1998, durable goods orders increased slightly.

After decreasing during the third quarter of 1998, capital goods spending by businesses increased in the last quarter of 1998. Companies faced a tighter labor market and scrambled to improve labor productivity and keep costs in control.

Outlook

Estimating economic growth for 1999 was more difficult than usual for economists because of a myriad of global uncertainties. The consensus estimate of the 54 economists polled by *The Wall Street Journal* at the end of 1998, however, called for continued growth in 1999, albeit at a slower pace than in 1998. One reason given for the slowdown in economic growth was that companies were experiencing a profit squeeze, which could produce a slowdown in capital spending. Many of the surveyed economists believed that inflation would increase slightly in 1999, and a majority thought there was a chance the stock market would enter a bear market during the year. More crises abroad could crimp growth in the U.S. economy in 1999. The Company is not overly worried about a negative impact on the poultry industry, since poultry consumption has not been shown to vary significantly with changes in U.S. prosperity.

Analysis of the Poultry Processing Industry

As an integrated poultry processing company, Warm Chicken's performance is directly related to the poultry processing industry. As part of our analysis, we researched the poultry processing industry in order to determine the current state of the industry as well as to identify any trends that may affect the industry in the future.

Overview

Beginning in the early 1930s, the poultry industry was dominated by many small growers and processors. The U.S. poultry business evolved into a vertically integrated industry in the mid-1930s, in which a few top companies accounted for most of the country's broiler and turkey production. Vertical integration combined the previously independent and fragmented operation of feedmills, hatcheries, farms, slaughterers, and processors into giant conglomerates that managed all stages of production.

Broilers, which are chickens raised specifically for table consumption, represented by far the largest segment of the industry, with the value of production exceeding $11.8 billion in 1995, compared with $3 billion for turkey. Other poultry, such as ducks and geese, accounted for only about $300 million in industry sales. Broiler production is mainly concentrated in 17 southeastern states on the eastern seaboard and along the Gulf of Mexico. This so-called "broiler belt" is the source of 90 percent of production.

Profitability in the poultry industry is related to consumer demand and feed grain prices. Feed grain accounts for approximately 50 percent of the cost of poultry production. An agricultural business such as Warm Chicken, which purchases and sells perishable commodities, is cyclical and very sensitive to market supply and demand pressures. Supply and demand are affected by such factors as weather conditions, pricing and supply of alternative products, changes in export markets, government policy, and current industry production capacity.

Demand for consumer food products is affected significantly by population growth. The U.S. population is expanding by less than 1 percent annually, and immigrants constitute about one-fourth of this increase. The population is continuing to age as the size of the average U.S. household shrinks. A shift in demographics is expected as the population age groups above 40 years of age constitute a larger total percentage of the population. The diet concerns of an aging population combined with the recent focus on health concerns has already affected U.S. food consumption. Consumers are eating more poultry and fish, and less red meat, as a result of health concerns.

The increased demand for poultry products has encouraged the introduction of several value-added products such as ground turkey, chicken nuggets, and other convenience-type poultry products. The favorable reception of rotisserie chicken in fast-food outlets has also increased demand. This could result in slightly higher margins on average.

The Current Market

The U.S. poultry industry is dominated by several large, vertically integrated companies, with approximately 65 percent of total production concentrated among the top 10 firms.

Exports

After experiencing a near decade of double-digit export growth, U.S. poultry exports faltered in 1998 as financial crisis in the Russian market halted trade to that market. Despite a last-minute rally by U.S. broiler exports in December 1998, poultry meat exports came in 2 percent below those of 1997—the first export decline since 1984.

The 1999 outlook for U.S. poultry meat shipments remains lackluster. Slowing international demand for poultry meat, aggravated by sluggish and uncertain demand from the Russian market in the aftermath of the ruble devaluation in August 1998, is expected to exert downward pressure on poultry exports, by an additional 5 percent in 1999.

Lower prices, and a slight recovery in consumer demand in Hong Kong/China, induced recovery in shipments to Hong Kong (up 13 percent), Mexico, and Japan (both up 11 percent). Price responsiveness was revealed in some of the smaller markets in Latin America, the Caribbean, and the Middle East also, with shipments to those regions increasing 42 percent in 1998.

Uncertainty characterizes the 1999 outlook for U.S. broiler meat with import demand hinging on the economic environment in Russia and China and the ability of the U.S. industry to adhere to Mexico's Avian Influenza (AI) regulations. In addition, the devaluation of the Brazilian real will test the United States' ability to compete effectively in the Japanese market.

Against these competing factors, U.S. poultry exports in 1999 are forecast to drop 5 percent to 2.4 million tons. As broiler meat shipments slide (forecast at 2 million tons), exports will account for 15 percent of domestic output, down from the peak of 17 percent in 1997.

Constrained export prospects for U.S. poultry meat in 1999 contrasts with the overall favorable outlook for the entire U.S. broiler industry. Despite low leg-quarter prices, domestic broiler meat prices have remained robust and, combined with low feed prices, are generating favorable net returns for the industry. Consequently U.S. production is predicted to increase by 5 percent to 15.8 million tons.

Sluggish demand for the overall U.S. poultry export market is occurring against a backdrop of increasing broiler meat output in 1999. U.S. broiler production in 1998, beset by hatchery supply flock problems and higher heat-induced bird mortality, experienced the slowest output growth since 1982.

Constrained production gains and strong domestic demand from the fast-food sector allowed the U.S. industry, despite record U.S. meat supplies and declining export prices, to maintain relatively high broiler prices in 1998. These robust prices, combined with the lowest feed costs since 1987, supported producer net returns in 1998 that were considerably higher than five-year averages.

Favorable producer returns are prompting a rise in anticipated U.S. broiler production of 5 percent to 6 percent in 1999. Indicators reveal that the industry's planned expansion includes (1) large increases in the broiler-type chick hatch, (2) a 3 percent to 5 percent increase in egg sets in incubators for broiler production, and (3) a steady increase in average unit weight gain as the industry moves to produce heavy broilers for cut-ups.

Identification of Guideline Companies

Overview

In order to gain market-derived pricing guidance from the guideline publicly traded company valuation method, one should identify a group of publicly traded companies that are similar to the subject company from an investment perspective. The first step in finding such guideline companies is to identify the most appropriate Standard Industrial Classification (SIC) code. Warm Chicken most closely resembles companies in the following SIC codes:

SIC 0251:   Broiler, Fryer & Roaster Chickens
SIC 0252:   Chicken Eggs

SIC 0259:   Poultry and Eggs, Not Elsewhere Classified
SIC 2015:   Poultry Slaughtering & Processing

We performed a search for publicly traded companies with SIC codes of 0251, 0252, 0259, and 2015. Standard & Poor's *Dialog-on-Disc* provides detailed information on more than 12,000 publicly traded companies. Detailed descriptions of the general operations, plant locations, subsidiaries, financial structure, and securities of these public companies are available. Disclosure's *Compact D/SEC* provides detailed information on more than 15,000 public companies. All information in these databases is updated monthly from various documents filed with the SEC.

From these databases, we obtained information on numerous potential guideline companies. Our next step was to identify companies that satisfied the following criteria:

- Industry and specific business lines that are comparable to Warm Chicken.
- Relative asset size and revenues that are comparable to Warm Chicken.
- Absolute and relative values of earnings and cash flow that are comparable to Warm Chicken.
- Information on each guideline company was available for the entire relevant time period.

Some of the most common reasons for rejection at this point were:

- Company serves unrelated business or geographic markets.
- Company is too diversified.
- Company is in poor financial condition.
- Company has a pending merger/acquisition.

After giving consideration to the above selection criteria, it was determined that five companies were most comparable to Warm Chicken. A description of each of the five comparable companies follows.

Descriptions of Selected Guideline Companies

Cagle's, Inc. Cagle's, Inc. ("Cagle's") operates an integrated poultry enterprise, including the breeding, hatching, raising and feeding of chickens, and the processing and marketing of fresh and frozen poultry products.

Cagle's products are sold to national and regional independent and chain supermarkets, food distributors, food processing companies, national fast-food chains, and institutional users, such as restaurants, schools, and distributors.

Pilgrim's Pride Corporation. Pilgrim's Pride Corporation ("Pilgrim") produces chicken products, and controls the breeding, hatching, and growing of chickens and the processing, preparation, and packaging of its product lines. Pilgrim also produces table eggs, animal feeds, and ingredients.

Pilgrim is one of the largest producers of prepared and fresh chicken products in North America and has one of the best known brand names in the chicken industry. Pilgrim is the fourth largest producer of chicken in the United States and one of the two largest in Mexico.

Products consist mainly of prepared foods, including portion-controlled breast fillets, tenderloins and strips, formed nuggets, patties, and bone-in chicken parts, which are sold frozen and may be either fully cooked or raw; fresh chicken, including refrigerated (nonfrozen) whole or cut-up chicken, sold to the food service industry either premarinated or nonmarinated, and prepackaged chicken, including various combinations of freshly refrigerated, whole chickens and chicken parts in trays, bags, or other consumer packs, labeled and priced ready for the retail grocer's fresh meat counter; and bulk packaged chicken, including parts and whole chicken, either refrigerated or frozen for U.S. export or domestic use.

Pilgrim also sells fresh eggs under the Pilgrim's Pride brand name as well as under private labels in various sizes of cartons and flats to domestic retail grocery and institutional food service customers located mainly in Texas. Pilgrim has a housing capacity for about 2.3 million commercial egg laying hens which can produce about 41 million dozen eggs annually.

Sanderson Farms, Inc. Sanderson Farms, Inc. ("Sanderson") produces, processes, markets, and distributes fresh and frozen chicken, and processes, markets, and distributes processed and prepared food items.

Sanderson produces, processes, markets, and distributes fresh and frozen chicken and other prepared food items. Sanderson sells its chicken products under the Sanderson Farms brand name to retailers, distributors, and fast-food operators in the southeastern, southwestern, and western United States. Through its foods division, Sanderson also sells over 200 processed and prepared frozen entrees and other specialty food products to distributors, food service establishments, and retailers.

In 1997, a new era in Sanderson development began with the opening of state-of-the-art poultry complexes in Brazos and Robertson Counties, Texas. Plans are underway to double-shift both lines of the Texas processing plant during fiscal 1998. Double-shifting will allow the plant to reach its full operating capacity of 1.2 million birds per week by the end of fiscal 1998. Once the processing plant is running at full two-shift capacity, the company's total employment in Texas will increase from 716 people to about 1,400.

Seaboard Corporation. Seaboard Corporation ("Seaboard"), a diversified international agribusiness and transportation company, processes poultry and pork; operates an ocean liner service for containerized cargo; operates bakeries in Puerto Rico; trades commodities; produces and processes fruits, vegetables, shrimp and pen-raised salmon; produces polypropylene bags; operates power generation facilities; and mills flour.

Seaboard produces and processes poultry in the U.S. and sells processed chicken and chicken parts, both directly and through commercial distributors, to retail, food service, and institutional markets, primarily in the eastern half of the United States. Seaboard also produces hogs and processes pork in the United States and sells fresh pork to domestic and foreign markets. Ocean liner service is operated between Florida and ports in Central and South America and the Caribbean Basin. Seaboard also operates bulk carriers primarily in the Atlantic Basin. In Puerto Rico, Seaboard mills flour and produces and distributes a full line of baked goods. These goods are distributed directly within Puerto Rico and neighboring islands to food-service and retail outlets. Commodities traded, primarily in the Eastern Mediterranean and the Atlantic Basin, include bulk grains and oil seeds.

WLR Foods, Inc. WLR Foods, Inc. ("WLR") produces, processes, and sells turkey and chicken products in the eastern United States, as well as in the upper Midwest, California, and 64 foreign countries. WLR also makes and distributes ice in the mid-Atlantic region.

WLR markets a full line of chicken and turkey products, including individually packaged fresh and frozen whole birds and bulk parts, and a large assortment of further processed products. WLR is currently expanding its offering of further processed products, including sliced luncheon meats, turkey burgers and sausages, and various fully cooked breast products.

WLR markets branded, as well as private-label, poultry products to retailers, fast-food operators, and food service customers. WLR's products are sold primarily under the Wampler Foods, Trim Free, and Rockingham brand names.

In addition, WLR operates a cold storage and ice manufacturing and distribution business. WLR is the largest ice retail manufacturer in the mid-Atlantic and its products are sold under the Cassco brand name.

Financial Statement Analysis

Overview

An important step in the valuation of any company is an analysis of its financial performance over time. Past sales and earnings growth can provide an indication of future growth and can put a company's earnings in a historical context. Other things being equal, a company with rapidly rising sales and earnings is worth more than one with little or no growth.

The following section examines significant trends in Warm Chicken's balance sheets, income statements, statements of cash flow, and pertinent financial ratios over the past five years. In addition, the Company's financial performance is compared to its peers in the poultry industry as a means of measuring the Company's relative historical performance.

Balance Sheets

Exhibit 21–3 presents Warm Chicken's balance sheets as of the March 31, 1994, through December 31, 1998.

Over this period, total assets increased $126.3 million, from $191.7 million at March 31, 1994, to $317.9 million as of December 31, 1998. As of December 31, 1998, net property, plant, and equipment, accounted for the largest percentage of total assets with 35.2 percent. Other assets increased from $4.3 million at March 31, 1994, to $48.2 million at March 31, 1995. Most of the increase in other assets may be attributed to an increase in intangible assets.

Total liabilities increased $88.9 million, from $81.5 million at March 31, 1994, to $170.4 million at December 31, 1998. Most of this increase may be attributed to an increase in interest-bearing debt. Over the past five years, interest-bearing debt increased from $14.5 million (representing 7.6 percent of total liabilities and stockholders' equity) to $67.2 million (representing 21.1 percent of total liabilities and stockholders' equity).

Stockholders' equity increased $37.4 million, from $110.2 million at March 31, 1994, to a five-year high of $147.6 million at December 31, 1998.

Income Statements

Exhibit 21–4 represents Warm Chicken's income statements for fiscal years ended March 31, 1994 through 1998, and the latest 12-month (LTM) period ended December 31, 1998.

The table below presents the Company's annual revenues over the past five fiscal years and the LTM period.

	LTM Ended	Fiscal Years Ended March 31,				
	12/98	1998	1997	1996	1995	1994
	$000	$000	$000	$0000	$000	$000
Net sales	754,600	743,999	725,015	635,970	501,378	450,311
Growth (%)	1.4	2.6	14.0	26.8	11.3	15.0

As presented, the Company reported increases in sales in each of the past five years. However, sales growth has declined from a five-year high of 26.8 percent in fiscal 1996 to a five-year low of 1.4 percent in the LTM period. Net sales increased $304.3 million, or 11.5 percent compounded annually, between fiscal 1994 and the LTM period. Compared to the guideline companies, Warm Chicken's 11.5 percent revenues growth over the past five years exceeds the guideline companies' median growth rate of 8.8 percent.

Cost of products sold increased $257.3 million, from $389.4 million in fiscal 1994 to $646.7 million in the LTM period. More importantly, cost of products sold as a percentage of revenues increased from 86.5 percent in fiscal 1994 to a five-year high of 90.4 percent in fiscal 1998. This increase was mainly the result of an increase in average grain prices.

The poultry industry is extremely dependent on the cost of key inputs. Consequently, the Company's profitability has been volatile. For instance, the Company's pretax profit margin increased from 3.4 percent in fiscal 1994 to a five-year average high of 5.4 percent in fiscal 1995. Since fiscal 1995, the Company's pretax profit margin has declined and remained below the fiscal 1995 pretax profit margin. Since fiscal 1996, the Company's profitability has improved. Pretax profit margin increased from a five-year low of negative 1.1 percent in fiscal 1996 to 4.7 percent in the LTM period.

Adjustments

In estimating an indication of value for a company, it is sometimes necessary to make adjustments to the company's historical balance sheets and income statements in order to eliminate items such as nonoperating assets and nonrecurring or unusual income or expense. Exhibit 21–8 presents the adjustments we made to Warm Chicken's earnings.

Financial and Operating Ratios

Exhibit 21–6 presents pertinent financial and operating ratios for Warm Chicken for the fiscal years ended March 31, 1994 through 1998, and for the latest 12-month period ended December 31, 1998 (the "LTM period"). Exhibit 21–7 presents comparative ratios for Warm Chicken and the five guideline publicly traded companies.

The current and quick ratios provide a rough indication of a company's liquidity (i.e., the degree to which current liabilities are covered by the most liquid assets). For Warm Chicken, these measures of liquidity decreased from 2.5 and 0.9, respectively, at March 31, 1994, to 1.8 and 0.7, respectively, at December 31, 1998.

Working capital, another measure of liquidity, reflects a company's ability to finance current operations. Warm Chicken's working capital increased from $60.4 million at March 31, 1994, to $69.9 million at December 31, 1998.

Activity ratios indicate how efficiently a company utilizes its assets. Warm Chicken's activity ratios indicate fairly consistent performance during the five-year period. Inventory turnover decreased from 6.9 at March 31, 1994, to 6.5 at December 31, 1998. The Company's operating cycle increased from 70 days at March 31, 1994, to 77 days at December 31, 1998.

Coverage ratios and debt ratios provide an indication of how heavily leveraged a company is. Highly leveraged companies are more vulnerable to business downturns than those with lower interest-bearing debt positions. Warm Chicken's interest expense ratios have increased since fiscal 1996, indicating the Company's turnaround from the fiscal 1996 pretax losses. The Company's debt/equity ratio has decreased since fiscal 1995 as a result of a decrease in interest-bearing debt.

In addition to indicating profits and returns over a period, profitability ratios assist in evaluating management performance. As previously mentioned, the cyclicality of the poultry industry has a strong influence on the Company's profitability. As shown by the margins in Exhibit 21–6, all of Warm Chicken's profitability ratios have increased since fiscal 1996. For example, return on investment increased from a negative 1.8 in fiscal 1996 to 10.2 in the LTM period. This financial strength leads us to believe that the Company is not significantly more risky in operating characteristics than the guideline publicly traded companies.

Valuation of Common Stock

Overview

In general, the factors outlined in Revenue Ruling 59–60 can be categorized into three general approaches for valuing the common stock of closely held companies. Valuation analysts use one or more of these three approaches to estimate the value of closely held company common stock. Of course, the objective of using more than one approach is to develop mutually supporting evidence as to the conclusion of value.

While the specific titles of these three approaches may vary, the generic names are as follows:

1. Market approach.
2. Income approach.
3. Asset-based approach.

After giving consideration to each of these approaches, we concluded that two approaches are the most relevant for our analysis of Warm Chicken's common stock: (1) the market approach, particularly the guideline publicly traded company method, and (2) the income approach, particularly the discounted cash flow method.

We considered the asset-based approach, but we did not rely upon this approach. This is because a noncontrolling equity owner in Warm Chicken does not have access to the value of the underlying assets.

The Guideline Publicly Traded Company Method

It has been stated that values are best determined and tested in the marketplace. One of the fundamental approaches to estimating the value of a closely held company is to look to the public market for evidence of the prices investors are willing to pay for similarly situated companies. Such a comparison to "guideline" publicly traded companies is the basis of the guideline publicly traded company method.

The following section outlines the theory, procedures, and conclusions of our analysis using the guideline publicly traded company method.

Valuation Theory and Procedures. There are four primary steps involved in the guideline publicly traded company method:

1. Identification of guideline publicly traded companies.
2. Calculation of market-derived pricing multiples based upon the guideline companies' trading prices and financial fundamentals.
3. Selection of appropriate market-derived pricing multiples to be applied to Warm Chicken's financial fundamentals.
4. Calculation of indicated values for Warm Chicken based upon the application of the selected market pricing multiples.

Qualitative Adjustment. In order to make an accurate comparison between Warm Chicken and the guideline publicly traded companies, we applied a qualitative adjustment to the market-derived pricing multiples selected in our analysis. This adjustment is necessary to reflect the modest additional risk factors inherent in an investment in Warm Chicken compared with an investment in the guideline companies. Such factors include:

1. **Geographical diversification.** Several of the guideline companies have significantly wider market areas than does Warm Chicken. Warm Chicken's operations are concentrated in the Midwest. As a result, the Company has greater exposure to regional economic fluctuations.
2. **Product-line diversification.** Several of the guideline companies have significantly broader product lines than Warm Chicken. Warm Chicken offers primarily chicken products while several of the guideline companies offer chicken, turkey, beef, pork, and even seafood products. As a result, Warm Chicken has greater exposure to fluctuating consumer tastes and demands.

Within the guideline publicly traded company method, we used an invested capital valuation method. The following section discusses the invested capital valuation method.

Invested Capital Valuation Method. An invested capital valuation method is commonly used in the valuation of closely held companies in order to minimize the differences between the subject company and the guideline companies, which may have significantly different capital structures. Certain adjustments are made to the financial fundamentals of both the subject and the guideline companies in order to minimize the effects of leverage on the companies' capital structures. These adjustments consist primarily of adding back interest expense to the relevant earnings measure.

Since the effects of leverage are minimized, the invested capital valuation method results in a value indication for a company's total capital (including both interest-bearing debt and equity). For purposes of our analysis, we refer to this indication of value as the *market value of invested capital* (MVIC), which we define as follows:

>   Market value of short-term interest-bearing debt
> + Market value of long-term interest-bearing debt, including capitalized leases
> + Market value of preferred stock outstanding
> + Market value of common stock outstanding
> = Market value of invested capital

Since MVIC consists of the market-derived pricing value of both debt and equity, the value of Warm Chicken's interest-bearing debt should be subtracted from its MVIC in order to arrive at a value indication for its total stockholders' equity.

We calculated the following market-derived pricing multiples in the invested capital valuation method of our guideline publicly traded method analysis:

1. MVIC/earnings before interest and taxes (EBIT)
2. MVIC/earnings before interest, taxes, depreciation, and amortization (EBITDA)
3. MVIC/debt-free net income (DFNI)
4. MVIC/debt-free cash flow (DFCF)
5. MVIC/revenues

We calculated these market-derived pricing multiples on both a LTM and five-year average basis.

The invested capital valuation method relies upon the five publicly traded companies described above in the section on identification of guideline companies. The calculations of invested capital market pricing multiples are presented in Exhibit 21–9.

MVIC/EBIT. Exhibit 21–9B presents the five guideline companies' EBIT performance in comparison to each other and Warm Chicken for the past five years. Warm Chicken's EBIT increased at a compound annual growth rate of 18.0 percent over the past five years, which is greater than the guideline companies median of 9.4 percent.

Last 12 Months. The MVIC/EBIT multiple for the last 12 months (LTM) for the guideline companies ranged from 4.3 to 18.0 with a mean of 9.8 and a median of 8.5.

In our opinion, Warm Chicken would command an MVIC/EBIT multiple slightly above the low end of the range of these guideline companies. Warm Chicken experienced a higher growth in the LTM period than that of the guideline companies. Warm Chicken's LTM EBIT profit margin of 4.8 percent is greater than the guideline companies' low of 2.6 percent but is smaller than the guideline company mean of 5.6 percent (see Exhibit 21–9G).

Applying the selected pricing multiple of 6.5 to the LTM EBIT of $36,355,000 for Warm Chicken results in a market value of invested capital of $236,308,000.

Five-Year Average. Five-year average EBIT multiples ranged from a low of 9.2 to a high of 20.7, with a mean of 15.5 and a median of 16.1.

Warm Chicken's five-year average EBIT profit margin of 2.9 percent is below the low end of the range of these guideline companies. However, Warm Chicken experienced faster growth than any of the guideline companies.

Applying the selected pricing multiple of 12.0 to Warm Chicken's five-year average EBIT of $19,735,000 results in a market value of invested capital of $236,820,000.

MVIC/EBITDA. Exhibit 21–9C presents the five guideline companies' EBITDA performance in comparison to each other and Warm Chicken for the past five years. Warm Chicken's EBITDA increased at a compound annual growth rate of 13.7 percent over the past five years, which is greater than the median of the guideline companies of 8.6 percent.

Depreciation and amortization are noncash items used by companies to manipulate their operating earnings to result in lower taxable income. Eliminating the effects of depreciation and amortization in a company provides a more realistic earnings level for that company. The more capital-intensive a company is, the greater the difference will be between EBIT and EBITDA. The poultry industry is extremely capital intensive. For example, four out of five guideline companies, as well as the subject company, have an EBITDA fundamental that is significantly greater than their respective EBIT fundamental.

	LTM Financial Fundamentals	
	EBIT $000	EBITDA $000
Cagles, Inc.	30,819	39,179
Pilgrim's Pride Corp.	89,006	122,198
Sanderson Farms, Inc.	32,077	55,318
Seaboard Corporation	62,156	121,052
WLR Foods, Inc.	24,097	50,649
Warm Chicken Company	36,355	56,719

Last 12 Months. The MVIC/EBITDA pricing multiple for the last 12 months (LTM) for the guideline companies ranged from 3.4 to 9.2 with a mean and median of 5.7.

In our opinion, Warm Chicken would command an MVIC/EBITDA multiple at the low end of the range indicated by the guideline companies. Warm Chicken's LTM EBITDA profit margin of 7.5 percent is greater than the guideline companies' low of 5.5 percent.

Applying the selected pricing multiple of 4.5 to the LTM EBITDA of $56,719,000 for Warm Chicken results in a market value of invested capital of $255,237,000.

Five-Year Average. Five-year average EBITDA multiples were also examined. These multiples ranged from a low of 6.3 to a high of 10.8, with a mean of 8.5 and a median of 8.4.

Warm Chicken's EBITDA profit margin of 6.0 percent is greater than the low end of the range of the guideline companies, but is smaller than the median of the range of the guideline companies.

Applying the selected pricing multiple of 6.3 to Warm Chicken's five-year average EBITDA of $40,143,000 results in a market value of invested capital of $252,900,900.

MVIC/DFNI. Exhibit 21–9D presents the five guideline companies' DFNI performance in comparison with each other and Warm Chicken for the past five years. EBIT and DFNI are identical except for income taxes. Consequently, both EBIT and DFNI financial fundamentals and pricing multiples follow similar trends.

Last 12 Months. The MVIC/DFNI pricing multiple for the LTM for the guideline companies ranged from 6.7 to 27.9, with a mean of 15.6 and a median of 13.9.

It is our opinion that Warm Chicken would command an MVIC/DFNI multiple greater than the low end of the range of these guideline companies, but less than the median of the range of these guideline companies. Warm Chicken experienced growth in the LTM period above that of the guideline companies. Warm Chicken's LTM DFNI profit margin of 2.9 percent is greater than the guideline companies' low of 1.6 percent but is less than the guideline company median of 3.9 percent.

Applying the selected pricing multiple of 11.0 to the LTM DFNI of $21,813,000 for Warm Chicken results in a market value of invested capital of $239,943,000.

Five-Year Average. Five-year average DFNI pricing multiples were also examined. These multiples ranged from a low of 14.0 to a high of 30.7, with a mean 24.4 and a median of 26.4.

Warm Chicken had greater growth than all of the guideline companies. However, Warm Chicken's five-year average DFNI profit margin of 1.8 percent is less than the low end of the range of the guideline companies.

Applying the selected pricing multiple of 20.0 to Warm Chicken's five-year average DFNI of $11,841,000 results in a market value of invested capital of $236,820,000.

MVIC/DFCF. Exhibit 21–9E presents the five guideline companies' DFCF performance in comparison to each other and Warm Chicken for the past five years. EBITDA and DFCF are identical except for taxes. Consequently, both EBITDA and DFCF financial fundamentals and pricing multiples follow similar trends.

Last 12 Months. The MVIC/DFCF multiple for the LTM for the guideline companies ranged from 4.7 to 11.3, with a mean of 7.4 and a median of 7.3.

Warm Chicken would command an MVIC/DFCF multiple greater than the low end of the range but less than the median of the range indicated by the guideline companies. Warm Chicken's LTM DFCF profit margin of 5.6 percent is greater than the guideline companies low of 4.5 percent, but is less than the guideline companies median of 6.5 percent.

Applying the selected pricing multiple of 5.5 to the LTM DFCF of $42,177,000 for Warm Chicken results in a market value of invested capital of $231,975,000.

Five-Year Average. Five-year average DFCF pricing multiples were also examined. These multiples ranged from a low of 7.6 to a high of 13.1, with a mean and median of 10.3.

Warm Chicken had greater growth than the median of the selected guideline companies, but less than the high of the selected guideline companies. Warm Chicken's DFCF profit margin was greater than the low end of the range of the guideline companies, but smaller than the median of the guideline companies.

Applying the selected pricing multiple of 7.6 to Warm Chicken's five-year average DFCF of $32,249,000 results in a market value of invested capital of $245,092,000.

MVIC/Revenues. Exhibit 21–9F presents the historical revenues reported by the guideline companies and Warm Chicken and presents various returns on revenues for both the LTM and five-year average.

A revenue-based valuation method can be considered a derivative of an earnings-based valuation method, since generally there is an implicit assumption that a certain level of revenues should be able to generate a certain level of earnings in a given type of business.

In selecting a multiple of revenues to apply to the revenues of Warm Chicken, we reviewed returns on revenues investors are willing to pay. The following table present the EBITDA returns and the MVIC/revenues pricing multiples for the guideline companies.

	LTM EBITDA/ Return on Revenues	MVIC/LTM Revenues
Cagles, Inc.	11.6	0.39
Pilgrim's Pride Corp.	9.2	0.56
Sanderson Farms, Inc.	10.6	0.61
Seaboard Corporation	6.6	0.61
WLR Foods, Inc.	5.5	0.22
Warm Chicken Company	7.5	NM

Applying the selected pricing multiple of 0.30 to Warm Chicken's LTM revenues of $754,600,000 results in a market value of invested capital of $226,380,000.

A similar pattern exists when looking at the five-year average for both the guideline companies and Warm Chicken. Since the five-year average is slightly lower than the Company's currently level, it is appropriate to use a slightly higher pricing multiple. Based on this information, the estimated MVIC/five-year average revenue pricing multiple for Warm Chicken is 0.35.

Applying a selected multiple of 0.35 to Warm Chicken's five-year average revenues of $672,192,000 results in a market value of invested capital of $235,267,000.

Summary of Indicated Values. The indicated values for the guideline publicly traded company method are summarized in Exhibit 21–10.

As presented in Exhibit 21–10, this method resulted in a range of indicated values—from a low of $226,380,000 to a high of $255,237,000. Since we are estimating an indication of value of the Company on a going-concern basis, we placed primary emphasis on the Company's earnings capacity. We also gave equal weighting to the LTM period and the five-year average. As a result, this method resulted in an indicated MVIC of approximately $239,700,000.

The Discounted Cash Flow Method

Overview. The second method that we relied on was the discounted cash flow method (DCF) of the income approach. This method is intuitively appealing, since it reflects the tradeoff between risk and expected return that is critical to the investment process. Generally, common stocks are purchased in light of anticipated stock price appreciation, which, in turn, is strongly influenced by expectations about a company's cash flow capacity.

The discounted cash flow method estimates value on the basis of future return flows over an investment horizon using empirical market data, macroeconomic and industry evidence, and the underlying fundamental trends for the subject company. The DCF method then applies a present value discount rate, known as the required rate of return on investment, to the projected future cash flows, which results in an estimation of the net present value of a series of cash flows.

We conducted the DCF method on an after-tax, invested capital basis, and we selected net cash flow as the measure of economic income. We used an invested capital method to eliminate the impact of the Company's leverage on the value of the Company common stock.

The DCF method estimates the value of a company by projecting the cash flows that the Company is expected to produce and discounting those cash flows back to the valuation date using a discount rate that reflects the related risk. This method requires an in-depth analysis of the Company's revenues, fixed and variable expenses, and capital structure.

The DCF method can result in an indication of value on either a controlling ownership interest or a noncontrolling ownership interest basis, depending on the nature of (1) the cash flows and (2) the discount rate that have been incorporated in the analysis. In this case, we did not incorporate any adjustments to the Company's results of operations or to its capital structure that would be considered of a controlling ownership interest nature. Therefore, our DCF analysis results in an indication of value on a noncontrolling ownership interest basis.

Valuation Calculations. The variables and calculations essential to our analysis using the DCF method are outlined below.

Present Value Discount Rate. In a rational investment environment, an investor faces various alternatives for investing current funds, all of which may earn future returns to compensate for: (1) the time the invested funds are committed, (2) the expected rate of inflation or loss of purchasing power experienced over the investment time horizon, and (3) the relative uncertainty of the future returns. The expected return on investment is therefore a function of the investment risk inherent in the future returns.

We estimated the appropriate present value discount rate for Warm Chicken's projected cash flows by analyzing the Company's weighted average cost of capital (WACC). The WACC incorporates the present cost of the Company's debt capital and equity capital as determined from market-derived empirical evidence. These capital costs, expressed as required rates of return, are then weighted according to the Company's capital structure (calculated on an estimated market value basis).

We estimated the cost of Warm Chicken's debt capital by analyzing the current rates on its various debt issues. Since corporate interest expense is tax deductible, we estimated the Company's after-tax cost of debt to be approximately 4.80 percent $(0.08 \times (1 - 0.40))$, using management's projected income tax rate of 40.0 percent.

We estimated the cost of Warm Chicken's equity capital using the capital asset pricing model (CAPM) which incorporates certain market rates of return and risk premiums, including: (1) a risk-free rate, (2) a long-term equity risk premium, (3) an industry beta, (4) a size premium, and (5) a company-specific risk premium. Each of these factors is discussed below.

Since our DCF analysis is based upon a long-term investment horizon, the appropriate risk-free rate is represented by a long-term government security. The most appropriate proxy for this rate is the yield to maturity of long-term (20-year) U.S. Treasury bonds. These bonds yielded approximately 5.4 percent as of the valuation date.

Equity risk premiums are quantified annually by Ibbotson Associates[3]. Ibbotson calculates the long-term equity risk premium as the total annual rates of return from common stocks less the long-term rates of return on 20-year U.S. Treasury bonds. According to the Ibbotson data, the arithmetic mean risk premium for the period 1926 to 1997 was approximately 7.8 percent.

Beta is a measure of the systematic risk inherent in a company's investment returns. We calculated betas for the five guideline publicly traded companies used in our guideline publicly traded company analysis. We unlevered and relevered the guideline companies' betas—as well as the selected beta for Warm Chicken—in order to eliminate any significant differences in capital structure. We used this beta to adjust the previously estimated long-term equity risk premium of 7.8 percent. This calculation resulted in a beta-adjusted, long-term equity risk premium of approximately 6.2 percent.

---

[3] *Stocks, Bonds, Bills, and Inflation, 1998 Yearbook* (Chicago: Ibbotson Associates, 1998).

Ibbotson also calculates the difference between the total returns of all public companies (7.8 percent as mentioned above) and returns exhibited by smaller, more thinly capitalized companies. According to the Ibbotson *1998 Yearbook*, stocks with a total capitalization in the neighborhood of Warm Chicken reflected an arithmetic mean annual return of approximately 2.56 percent above the overall equity risk premium exhibited by the S&P 500 common stock index. Therefore, we have applied a size premium of 2.56 percent.

A company-specific equity risk premium is often appropriate to reflect certain risks specific to an investment in a closely held company. In comparison with the universe of publicly traded companies from which the above equity risk premiums are calculated, a noncontrolling ownership interest investment in the common stock of Warm Chicken carries some unsystematic risk. Some of the factors that contributed to this unsystematic risk are listed below and are discussed under the guideline publicly traded company method above.

1. Geographical diversification.
2. Product-line diversification.

Based on these and other factors, we selected a company-specific equity risk premium of 0.5 percent.

The CAPM results in a total estimated cost of the Company's equity capital of approximately 14.7 percent. Based upon the Company's cost of debt capital and cost of equity capital, as calculated above, and its estimated capital structure of approximately 28 percent debt and 72 percent equity, we calculated a WACC of approximately 12.5 percent. The calculations to this effect are presented in Exhibit 21–12.

Projected Cash Flows. Using management's financial projections for fiscal 1999 through 2003 and our discussions with management in connection with this year's analysis, we prepared a projected income statement for the fiscal years 1999 through 2003. In our opinion, these projections present a reasonable estimate of the Company's future earnings capacity.

We selected net cash flow (NCF) as the appropriate measure of economic income to use in this valuation method. Net cash flow represents the maximum amount of cash that could be distributed to company stakeholders without affecting the Company's normal operational cash requirements. We calculated net cash flow on an invested capital basis by adding back projected interest expenses (on an after-tax basis). The following is our definition of net cash flow on an invested capital basis:

>   Net income (after taxes)
> \+   Depreciation and amortization
> \+   Interest expense, net of taxes
> –   Capital expenditures
> –   Incremental working capital requirements
> =   Net cash flow

Exhibit 21–13 illustrates the calculation of Warm Chicken's NCF for fiscal years 1999 through 2003. As presented in the exhibit, we calculated the present value of the Company's NCF for this discrete time period as approximately $55,591,000.

Of course, Warm Chicken will continue to generate cash flows beyond the discrete projection period. Therefore, our DCF analysis also projects a terminal value.

In estimating an appropriate terminal growth rate for the Company's net cash flows, we considered several factors, including: (1) the expected growth for the poultry processing industry, (2) the projected growth for the guideline companies, (3) the expected long-term rate of inflation, and (4) our discussion with Company management. Based upon this information, we selected a long-term growth rate of 4.0 percent as appropriate for the Company's net cash flow. By applying the terminal growth rate to the Company's projected fiscal 2003 normalized net cash flow, we arrived at an estimate of net cash flow for fiscal 2004.

In estimating the Company's terminal value, we considered a net cash flow pricing multiple based on the mathematical inverse of the direct capitalization rate. As presented in Exhibit 21–13, this process resulted in an overall terminal value indication of approximately $283,899,000 for Warm Chicken. The terminal value was then discounted to its present value by applying the fiscal 2003 present value discount factor. As a result, the present value of the terminal cash flows is approximately $181,284,000.

Valuation Indication. Combining the present value of the terminal cash flow value with the present value of the discrete cash flow projection results in an indicated MVIC of approximately $236,900,000.

Overall Valuation Conclusion

We used two valuation methods in estimating the value of Warm Chicken's common stock.

1. The guideline publicly traded company method resulted in an overall indication of MVIC of approximately $239,700,000.
2. The DCF method resulted in an overall indication of MVIC of approximately $236,900,000.

Based on our assessment of the relative merits of each of the two methods, we concluded an MVIC of approximately $238,300,000.

As previously discussed, this indicated MVIC includes the value of both debt and equity. Therefore, in order to estimate the value of the Company's total equity, we subtract the value of its interest-bearing debt. As of the valuation date, Warm Chicken had total interest-bearing debt of approximately $67,228,000. As a result, the Company's indicated value of total equity is approximately $171,072,000.

Discount for Lack of Marketability

A major difference between Warm Chicken's shares and those of its publicly traded counterparts is the lack of marketability of the Warm Chicken shares. All other things being equal, an investment is worth more if it is marketable than if it is not, since investors prefer liquidity over lack of liquidity. Interests in closely held businesses are illiquid relative to most other investments.

The market places a far greater value differential on the liquidity factor alone in its pricing of common stocks than in its pricing of any other class of investment assets, for sound reasons. For common stocks as a group, investors expect to realize the majority of their return in the form of capital gains at the time of the stock's sale and only a small part of their total return in the form of dividends while they hold the stock. This situation is taken to the extreme, of course, in the case of common stock that has not paid dividends in the past, such as that of Warm Chicken. Thus,

Discounts wont be major factor

the ability to sell the stock is crucial to the realization of the investor's expected return for buying and holding it.

A stock that pays no dividends, has no market, and cannot be legally offered to the general public but may possibly be salable under certain limited circumstances and at a totally undeterminable price must be discounted heavily from an otherwise comparative stock that is both legally salable to the general public and that has an established market.

Another reason that liquidity takes on a high degree of importance for common stocks is that prices of common stocks tend to be much more volatile than prices of real estate or other securities such as preferred stocks or bonds. Consequently, the investor's choice as to the timing of the sale of the stock is much more important in determining the amount of return to be earned on the investment than is the case with other security investments. Numerous studies of empirical evidence regarding the size of lack of marketability discounts have been published.[4]

Summary and Conclusion of Empirical Research

The restricted stock studies prior to 1996 are quite consistent in indicating an average discount for lack of marketability of at least 35 percent. In addition, the pre-IPO studies provide convincing support for a somewhat higher discount for lack of marketability of approximately 45 percent.

Such a result seems rational since the restricted securities included in the published studies will have access to an established public market upon the expiration of the restrictions. Also, the discounts based on private transactions before access to a public capital market (i.e., the pre-IPO studies) would be expected to more closely represent the actual discount for lack of marketability required by an actual investor in connection with the investment in the shares of a closely held security.

Selection of the Applicable Lack of Marketability Discount for a Warm Chicken Noncontrolling Ownership Interest

For a noncontrolling ownership interest in Warm Chicken, we considered the following factors that have an impact on the selection of the appropriate discount for lack of marketability:

- **Size of the block.** The 5.45 percent block is a noncontrolling ownership interest with very little ability to influence corporate policies.
- **Transaction activity.** There have been no transactions in the common stock of Warm Chicken over the last five years.
- **Dividends.** The Company has historically paid no cash dividends to shareholders and has indicated its intention not to pay any in the foreseeable future.

Based on the analysis set forth above regarding the factors that influence the lack of marketability of Warm Chicken shares, it is our opinion that the appropriate

---

[4] These studies normally would be presented in a valuation report. However, due to the limited amount of space available in presenting this sample case, we have not presented them here. See Chapter 17, Discounts for Illiquidity and Lack of Marketability, for a detailed discussion.

discount for lack of marketability falls within the range of 40 percent to 45 percent from the indicated publicly traded, noncontrolling ownership interest value based on the publicly traded guideline company method and the discounted cash flow method. Therefore, we selected a lack of marketability discount of 40 percent to apply to the subject securities.

Based upon our analysis as outlined herein, including a lack of marketability discount for the common stock, it is our opinion that the fair market value of Warm Chicken's common stock per share, on a nonmarketable, noncontrolling ownership interest basis, as of the valuation date, is:

<u>**$65.09**</u> (rounded)

Exhibit 21–1

Warm Chicken Company
Valuation Summary

	Indicated Value $000
Guideline publicly traded company method (rounded)	239,700
Discounted cash flow method (rounded)	236,900
Overall indicated market value of invested capital	238,300
Less interest-bearing debt	(67,228)
Indicated value of total equity	171,072
Less discount for lack of marketability @ 40%	(68,429)
Indicated value of total equity	102,643
Common shares outstanding (000s)	1,577
Indicated nonmarketable per share value of common equity (rounded)	$65.09

SOURCE: Exhibits 21–9, 21–10, and 21–13.

Exhibit 21–2

Warm Chicken Company
Summary of Shares Outstanding

	Common	
	Shares	%
WARM FAMILY:		
Simon P. Warm	733,500	46.5
Jake Warm	366,750	23.3
Sydney Warm	183,375	11.6
Gayle Warm	183,375	11.6
TOTAL WARM FAMILY	1,467,001	93.0
NONFAMILY SHARHOLDERS:		
Paige Poulet	44,168	2.80
Alan Abacus	44,168	2.80
Fred Fryer	22,084	1.40
TOTAL NONFAMILY MEMBERS	110,419	7.0
TOTAL SHARES OUTSTANDING	1,577,420	100.0

SOURCE: Statement of shareholders supplied by management.

Exhibit 21–3

Warm Chicken Company
Historical and Common-Size Balance Sheets

	As of 12/31/98 $000	As of March 31, 1998 $000	1997 $000	1996 $000	1995 $000	1994 $000	As of 12/31/98 %	As of March 31, 1998 %	1997 %	1996 %	1995 %	1994 %
ASSETS												
Current assets:												
Cash and cash equivalents	8,540	298	293	9,247	11,091	1,686	2.7	0.1	0.1	2.7	3.7	0.9
Short-term investments	9	14	294	266	263	7,418	0.0	0.0	0.1	0.1	0.1	3.9
Receivables	47,337	50,120	46,910	45,209	33,792	26,213	14.9	16.9	14.6	13.2	11.4	13.7
Inventory	93,119	92,805	111,437	105,083	80,699	61,504	29.3	31.4	34.7	30.7	27.2	32.1
Other current assets	5,968	6,455	7,986	7,313	4,596	5,280	1.9	2.2	2.5	2.1	1.5	2.8
Total current assets	154,972	149,692	166,919	167,118	130,441	102,100	48.7	50.6	52.0	48.9	44.0	53.3
Property, plant and equipment:												
Land and improvements	NA	16,379	16,100	15,862	12,546	10,366	NA	5.5	5.0	4.6	4.2	5.4
Buildings	NA	59,183	59,425	58,118	49,615	38,833	NA	20.0	18.5	17.0	16.7	20.3
Machinery and equipment	NA	190,520	188,813	183,542	165,338	130,931	NA	64.4	58.8	53.7	55.8	68.3
Construction in progress	NA	5,771	2,325	9,727	10,674	10,892	NA	2.0	0.7	2.8	3.6	5.7
Subtotal	NA	271,852	266,664	267,248	238,173	191,022	NA	91.9	83.0	78.2	80.3	99.7
Accumulated depreciation	NA	(171,869)	(157,648)	(139,278)	(120,259)	(105,752)	NA	(58.1)	(49.1)	(40.7)	(40.6)	(55.2)
Net property, plant, and equipment	111,976	99,984	109,016	127,971	117,914	85,270	35.2	33.8	33.9	37.4	39.8	44.5
Other assets	51,005	46,226	45,218	46,814	48,187	4,312	16.0	15.6	14.1	13.7	16.2	2.2
Total Assets	317,953	295,902	321,154	341,902	296,542	191,681	100.0	100.0	100.0	100.0	100.0	100.0
LIABILITIES AND STOCKHOLDERS' EQUITY												
Current liabilities:												
Accounts payable--trade	44,465	38,302	38,015	38,104	29,474	20,917	14.0	12.9	11.8	11.1	9.9	10.9
Accrued expenses and other	32,664	26,731	26,979	30,246	21,359	18,581	10.3	9.0	8.4	8.8	7.2	9.7
Short-term borrowings	4,197	13,780	25,651	21,628	11,952	-	1.3	4.7	8.0	6.3	4.0	-
Current portion of LTD	3,771	2,753	2,753	2,697	1,938	1,599	1.2	0.9	0.9	0.8	0.7	0.8
Deferred income taxes	-	-	-	-	518	572	-	-	-	-	0.2	0.3
Total current liabilities	85,097	81,565	93,398	92,675	65,240	41,668	26.8	27.6	29.1	27.1	22.0	21.7
Long-term liabilities:												
Long-term debt	59,260	61,231	75,797	99,250	74,113	12,886	18.6	20.7	23.6	29.0	25.0	6.7
Deferred income taxes	17,684	19,323	21,449	21,813	24,059	21,342	5.6	6.5	6.7	6.4	8.1	11.1
Other liabilities	8,320	6,839	6,219	5,005	5,107	5,602	2.6	2.3	1.9	1.5	1.7	2.9
Total long-term liabilities	85,265	87,392	103,464	126,068	103,280	39,830	26.8	29.5	32.2	36.9	34.8	20.8
Total liabilities	170,362	168,957	196,863	218,742	168,520	81,498	53.6	57.1	61.3	64.0	56.8	42.5
Stockholders' equity:												
Common stock, $0.10 par	157	157	157	157	158	158	0.0	0.1	0.0	0.0	0.1	0.1
Additional paid-in capital	11,712	10,693	10,406	10,328	10,610	10,448	3.7	3.6	3.2	3.0	3.6	5.5
Retained earnings	135,721	116,096	113,728	112,675	117,254	99,577	42.7	39.2	35.4	33.0	39.5	51.9
Total stockholders' equity	147,590	126,945	124,291	123,160	128,022	110,183	46.4	42.9	38.7	36.0	43.2	57.5
Total Liabilities and Stockholders' Equity	317,953	295,902	321,154	341,902	296,542	191,681	100.0	100.0	100.0	100.0	100.0	100.0

SOURCE: Company financial statements.

Exhibit 21–4

Warm Chicken Company
Historical and Common-Size Income Statements

	LTM Ended 12/98 $000	1998 $000	1997 $000	1996 $000	1995 $000	1994 $000	LTM Ended 12/98 %	1998 %	1997 %	1996 %	1995 %	1994 %
		Fiscal Years Ended March 31,						Fiscal Years Ended March 31,				
Net sales	754,600	743,999	725,015	635,970	501,378	450,311	100.0	100.0	100.0	100.0	100.0	100.0
Cost of products sold	646,691	672,290	655,300	573,928	422,010	389,387	85.7	90.4	90.4	90.2	84.2	86.5
Gross margin	107,909	71,710	69,716	62,042	79,367	60,923	14.3	9.6	9.6	9.8	15.8	13.5
Operating expenses:												
Selling, general, and administrative expense	47,644	41,375	36,475	41,247	34,666	30,081	6.3	5.6	5.0	6.5	6.9	6.7
Depreciation and amortization	20,364	20,949	22,590	21,536	16,600	14,240	2.7	2.8	3.1	3.4	3.3	3.2
Total operating expenses	68,009	62,324	59,065	62,783	51,266	44,321	9.0	8.4	8.1	9.9	10.2	9.8
Income (loss) from operations	39,900	9,385	10,650	(742)	28,102	16,602	5.3	1.3	1.5	(0.1)	5.6	3.7
Other income (expense):												
Other income	850	1,498	423	709	907	(240)	0.1	0.2	0.1	0.1	0.2	(0.1)
Interest expense	(5,440)	(6,079)	(7,967)	(6,665)	(2,167)	(1,263)	(0.7)	(0.8)	(1.1)	(1.0)	(0.4)	(0.3)
Total other income (expense)	(4,590)	(4,581)	(7,544)	(5,956)	(1,260)	(1,503)	(0.6)	(0.6)	(1.0)	(0.9)	(0.3)	(0.3)
Income before income taxes	35,310	4,804	3,106	(6,698)	26,841	15,100	4.7	0.6	0.4	(1.1)	5.4	3.4
Provision for income taxes	14,124	1,922	1,242	(2,679)	10,737	6,040	1.9	0.3	0.2	(0.4)	2.1	1.3
Net income before accounting change	21,186	2,883	1,864	(4,019)	16,105	9,060	2.8	0.4	0.3	(0.6)	3.2	2.0
Cumulative effect of accounting change	-	-	-	-	-	19,892	-	-	-	-	-	4.4
Net Income	21,186	2,883	1,864	(4,019)	16,105	28,952	2.8	0.4	0.3	(0.6)	3.2	6.4

SOURCE: Company financial statements.

Exhibit 21–5

Warm Chicken Company
Historical Cash Flow Statements

	For Fiscal Years Ending March 31,				
	1998 **$000**	**1997** **$000**	**1996** **$000**	**1995** **$000**	**1994** **$000**
Cash flows from operating activities:					
Net income	3,534	1,811	(3,575)	17,251	15,830
Adjustments provided by operating activities					
Depreciation and amortization	20,949	22,590	21,536	16,600	14,240
Net loss on disposal of property, plant, and equipment	605	428	2,282	33	155
Restructuring charge	6,854	(1,329)	4,184	-	-
(Increase) decrease in:					
Receivables	(2,831)	(1,701)	(11,390)	(2,145)	(6,489)
Inventories	18,814	(6,354)	(21,121)	(3,991)	(11,696)
Other current assets	1,547	(772)	(2,681)	1,410	(3,100)
Other assets	(7,875)	596	863	(429)	(375)
Increase (decrease) in :					
Accounts payable—trade	(241)	(88)	8,630	853	4,782
Accrued expenses and other payables	(664)	(705)	7,947	(2,746)	695
Current deferred income taxes	-	-	(518)	518	-
Deferred income taxes	(2,126)	(364)	(2,246)	54	(5,136)
Other liabilities	620	1,214	(103)	(1,830)	1,518
Net cash provided (used) from operating activities	39,186	15,326	3,810	25,577	10,424
Cash flows from investing activities:					
Business acquisitions, net of cash received	-	-	(15,035)	(65,622)	(3,825)
Net sales (purchases) of short-term investments	(598)	(529)	(980)	6,385	15,467
Proceeds on disposal of fixed assets	174	4,040	309	134	781
Additions to property, plant and equipment	(12,221)	(5,281)	(25,091)	(16,117)	(21,989)
Net cash provided (used) from investing activities	(12,645)	(1,770)	(40,797)	(75,219)	(9,566)
Cash flows from financing activities:					
Proceeds from issuance of common stock	22	194	116	116	683
Payment for purchases of common stock	(106)	(257)	(545)	(350)	(3,371)
Short-term borrowings	(11,886)	951	9,675	11,952	-
Repayments of long-term debt	(14,896)	(23,397)	(20,471)	(8,171)	(1,603)
Issuance of long-term debt	330	-	46,367	55,500	-
Net cash (used) in financing activities	(26,536)	(22,510)	35,143	59,047	(4,291)
Net (decrease) in cash and cash equivalents	5	(8,954)	(1,844)	9,405	(3,433)
Cash and cash equivalents, beginning of year	292	9,247	11,091	1,686	5,118
Cash and cash equivalents, end of year	298	292	9,247	11,091	1,686

SOURCE: Company financial statements.

Exhibit 21–6

Warm Chicken Company
Historical Ratio Analysis

	LTM Ending 12/98	Fiscal Years Ended March 31,				
		1998	1997	1996	1995	1994
LIQUIDITY						
Current ratio	1.82	1.84	1.79	1.80	2.00	2.45
Quick ratio	0.66	0.62	0.51	0.59	0.69	0.85
Working capital ($millions)	69.87	68.13	73.52	74.44	65.20	60.43
ACTIVITY						
Turnover:						
Working capital	10.80	10.92	9.86	8.54	7.69	7.45
Inventory	6.53	6.58	6.05	6.18	5.94	6.94
Receivables	16.31	15.34	15.74	16.10	16.71	19.61
Total asset	2.29	2.41	2.19	1.99	2.05	2.41
Average collection period (days)	22	23	23	22	22	18
Days to sell inventory	55	55	59	58	61	52
Operating cycle (days)	77	78	82	81	82	70
PERFORMANCE						
Sales/net property, plant and equipment	6.74	7.44	6.65	4.97	4.25	5.28
Sales/stockholder equity	5.11	5.86	5.83	5.16	3.92	4.09
PROFITABILITY (%)						
Operating margin before depreciation	7.99	4.08	4.58	3.27	8.92	6.85
Operating margin after depreciation	5.29	1.26	1.47	(0.12)	5.60	3.69
Pretax profit margin	4.68	0.65	0.43	(1.05)	5.35	3.35
Net profit margin	2.81	0.39	0.26	(0.63)	3.21	2.01
Return on:						
Assets	6.66	0.97	0.58	(1.18)	5.43	4.73
Equity	14.35	2.27	1.50	(3.26)	12.58	8.22
Investment	10.24	1.53	0.93	(1.81)	7.97	7.36
Average assets	6.42	0.93	0.56	(1.26)	6.60	4.84
Average equity	15.43	2.29	1.51	(3.20)	13.52	8.64
Average investment	9.87	1.48	0.88	(1.89)	9.90	7.64
LEVERAGE						
Interest coverage before tax	7.49	1.79	1.39	(0.00)	13.39	12.96
Interest coverage after tax	4.89	1.47	1.23	0.40	8.43	8.17
Long-term debt/shareholders' equity (%)	40.15	48.23	60.98	80.59	57.89	11.69
Total debt/invested capital (%)	31.30	37.99	45.60	50.08	40.74	11.62
Total debt/total assets (%)	21.14	26.28	32.45	36.14	29.68	7.56
Total assets/common equity	2.15	2.33	2.58	2.78	2.32	1.74

SOURCE: Exhibits 21-3, 21-4, and 21-5.

Exhibit 21–7

Warm Chicken Company
Comparative Ratios

	Cagles Mar-98	Pilgrim's Pride Sep-98	Sanderson Farms Oct-98	Seaboard Dec-98	WLR Foods Jun-98	Mean	Median	Warm Chicken Mar-98
LIQUIDITY								
Current ratio	2.19	2.32	3.34	1.65	2.40	2.38	2.32	1.84
Quick ratio	0.74	0.96	1.36	0.98	0.87	0.98	0.96	0.62
Working capital ($millions)	28.28	147.04	59.67	235.81	118.70	117.90	118.70	68.13
ACTIVITY								
Turnover:								
Working capital	8.10	11.27	11.90	14.53	12.23	11.61	11.90	10.92
Inventory	9.71	8.09	10.25	7.07	5.78	8.18	8.09	6.58
Receivables	18.00	16.67	16.28	9.97	12.57	14.70	16.28	15.34
Total asset	2.47	2.26	1.97	1.52	2.37	2.12	2.26	2.41
Average collection period (days)	20	22	22	36	29	26	22	23
Days to sell inventory	37	45	35	51	62	46	45	55
Operating cycle (days)	57	66	57	87	91	72	66	78
PERFORMANCE								
Sales/net property, plant & equipment	5.78	4.02	2.91	3.18	6.15	4.41	4.02	7.44
Sales/stockholder equity	6.25	5.77	4.03	3.96	9.11	5.82	5.77	5.86
PROFITABILITY (%)								
Operating margin before depreciation	2.10	8.17	10.56	7.13	0.78	5.75	7.13	4.08
Operating margin after depreciation	(0.18)	5.80	6.10	3.84	(2.22)	2.67	3.84	1.26
Pretax profit margin	1.19	4.24	4.67	4.79	(4.70)	2.04	4.24	0.65
Net profit margin	0.76	3.76	2.93	2.94	(2.98)	1.48	2.93	0.39
Return on:								
Assets	1.89	8.32	5.74	4.28	(7.39)	2.57	4.28	0.97
Equity	4.78	21.66	11.78	11.64	(27.16)	4.54	11.64	2.27
Investment	2.55	11.59	6.78	6.67	(9.62)	3.59	6.67	1.53
Average assets	1.89	8.47	5.75	4.46	(7.07)	2.70	4.46	0.93
Average equity	4.86	24.20	12.39	12.34	(24.48)	5.86	12.34	2.29
Average investment	2.55	11.91	6.62	7.02	(13.27)	2.97	6.62	1.48
LEVERAGE								
Interest coverage before tax	2.12	3.62	4.15	3.64	(0.97)	2.51	3.62	1.79
Interest coverage after tax	1.72	3.32	2.98	2.62	(0.25)	2.08	2.62	1.47
Long-term debt/shareholders' equity(%)	87.71	86.53	73.91	73.25	182.14	100.71	86.53	48.23
Total debt/invested capital(%)	49.43	47.66	44.29	64.60	69.12	55.02	49.43	37.99
Total debt/total assets (%)	36.70	34.20	37.54	41.46	53.07	40.59	37.54	26.28
Total assets/common equity	2.53	2.61	2.05	2.72	3.67	2.72	2.61	2.33

SOURCE: Standard & Poor's *Compustat* and Exhibit 21–6.

Exhibit 21–8

Warm Chicken Company
Pro Forma Adjustments and Representative Financial Fundamentals

	LTM 12/98 $000	Fiscal Years Ended March 31,					5-Year Average $000	LTM 12/98 %	Fiscal Years Ended March 31,				
		1998 $000	1997 $000	1996 $000	1995 $000	1994 $000			1998 %	1997 %	1996 %	1995 %	1994 %
Total revenues	754,600	743,999	725,015	635,970	501,378	450,311	672,192	100.0	100.0	100.0	100.0	100.0	100.0
Pretax income	35,310	4,804	3,106	(6,698)	26,841	15,100	12,673	4.7	0.6	0.4	(1.1)	5.4	3.4
After-tax income	21,186	2,883	1,864	(4,019)	16,105	9,060	7,604	2.8	0.4	0.3	(0.6)	3.2	2.0
Effective tax rate	40.0%	40.0%	40.0%	40.0%	40.0%	40.0%							
Adjustments to income:													
Net loss on disposal of plant, property and equipment	605	605	428	2,282	33	155	791	0.1	0.1	0.1	0.4	0.0	0.0
Restructuring charges	-	6,854	(1,329)	4,184	-	-	1,942	-	0.9	(0.2)	0.7	-	-
Hedging (gain)/loss	-	-	(1,200)	-	-	-	(240)	-	-	(0.2)	-	-	-
Litigation settlement	(5,000)	(468)	-	-	-	-	(1,094)	(0.7)	(0.1)	-	-	-	-
Total adjustments	(4,395)	6,991	(2,102)	6,466	33	155	1,399	(0.6)	0.9	(0.3)	1.0	0.0	0.0
Adjusted income:													
Pretax	30,915	11,795	1,004	(232)	26,875	15,255	14,071	4.1	1.6	0.1	(0.0)	5.4	3.4
After-tax	18,549	7,077	603	(139)	16,125	9,153	8,443	2.5	1.0	0.1	(0.0)	3.2	2.0
Depreciation and amortization	20,364	20,949	22,590	21,536	16,600	14,240	20,408	2.7	2.8	3.1	3.4	3.3	3.2
Interest expense	5,440	6,079	7,967	6,665	2,167	1,263	5,664	0.7	0.8	1.1	1.0	0.4	0.3
Adjusted fundamentals:													
EBIT	36,355	17,874	8,971	6,433	29,042	16,518	19,735	4.8	2.4	1.2	1.0	5.8	3.7
EBITDA	56,719	38,823	31,561	27,970	45,641	30,758	40,143	7.5	5.2	4.4	4.4	9.1	6.8
DFNI	21,813	10,724	5,383	3,860	17,425	9,911	11,841	2.9	1.4	0.7	0.6	3.5	2.2
DFCF	42,177	31,673	27,973	25,396	34,025	24,150	32,249	5.6	4.3	3.9	4.0	6.8	5.4

SOURCE: Exhibit 21-4 and discussions with Company management.

Exhibit 21–9A

Warm Chicken Company
Market Approach
Guideline Publicly Traded Company Method
Market Value of Invested Capital

Company	Market/ Symbol	FYE	Latest Quarter				As of or for Period Ending	Bid/Close Price Per Common Share 12/31/98 $	Common Shares Outstg. [b] 000s	Market Value of Common $000	MVIC $000
			TBV $000	BVIBD $000	TBVIC $000	MVIBD [a] $000					
Cagles, Inc.	ASE/CGL A	Mar-98	68,582	39,373	107,955	39,373	Dec-98	19.500	4,790	93,414	132,787
Pilgrim's Pride Corp.	NYSE/CHX	Sep-98	246,377	189,984	436,361	189,984	Dec-98	19.938	27,589	550,074	740,058
Sanderson Farms, Inc.	NDQ/SAFM	Oct-98	129,482	99,723	229,205	99,723	Oct-98	15.125	14,396	217,743	317,466
Seaboard Corporation	ASE/SEB	Dec-97	416,981	487,979	904,960	487,979	Sep-98	422.000	1,488	627,733	1,115,712
WLR Foods, Inc.	NDQ/WLRF	Jun-98	137,519	64,015	201,534	64,015	Dec-98	8.500	16,477	140,053	204,068
Warm Chicken Company	NM	Mar-98	107,431	67,228	174,659	67,228	Dec-98	NM	1,577	NM	NM

Definitions, sources, and footnotes are found on Exhibit 21-9I.

Exhibit 21–9B

Warm Chicken Company
Market Approach
Guideline Publicly Traded Company Method
Earnings before Interest and Taxes

Company	LTM		Earnings before Interest and Taxes (EBIT)					5-Year Average [c]	Average Annual Compound Growth [d]	MVIC	MVIC/EBIT	
	EBIT $000	Ending	1998/7 $000	1997/6 $000	1996/5 $000	1995/4 $000	1994/3 $000	EBIT $000	%	$000	LTM	5-Year Average
Cagles, Inc.	30,819	12/98	7,793	4,952	7,083	21,697	14,787	14,469	16.7	132,787	4.3	9.2
Pilgrim's Pride Corp.	89,006	12/98	78,122	65,898	21,375	24,916	60,756	50,213	9.4	740,058	8.3	14.7
Sanderson Farms, Inc.	32,077	10/98	32,077	7,610	1,173	21,320	28,488	18,134	3.0	317,466	9.9	17.5
Seaboard Corporation	62,156	9/98	74,434	26,201	49,880	56,912	32,747	53,917	14.4	1,115,712	18.0	20.7
WLR Foods, Inc.	24,097	12/98	(19,943)	(40,562)	2,253	33,831	34,575	(65)	(7.7)	204,068	8.5	DF
LOW	24,097								(7.7)		4.3	9.2
HIGH	89,006								16.7		18.0	20.7
MEAN	47,631								7.2		9.8	15.5
MEDIAN	32,077								9.4		8.5	16.1
Warm Chicken Company	36,355	12/98	17,874	8,971	6,433	29,042	16,518	19,735	18.0	NM	NM	NM

Definitions, sources, and footnotes are found on Exhibit 21-9I.

Exhibit 21–9C

Warm Chicken Company
Market Approach
Guideline Publicly Traded Company Method
Earnings before Interest, Taxes, Depreciation, and Amortization

Company	LTM EBITDA $000	Ending	1998/7 $000	1997/6 $000	1996/5 $000	1995/4 $000	1994/3 $000	5-Year Average [c] EBITDA $000	Average Annual Compound Growth [d] %	MVIC $000	MVIC/EBITDA LTM	MVIC/EBITDA 5-Year Average
Cagles, Inc.	39,179	12/98	15,633	12,713	12,372	26,192	19,686	21,218	15.5	132,787	3.4	6.3
Pilgrim's Pride Corp.	122,198	12/98	110,713	95,694	49,399	51,043	85,933	78,556	8.6	740,058	6.1	9.4
Sanderson Farms, Inc.	55,318	10/98	55,318	28,977	20,917	39,759	44,092	37,813	5.8	317,466	5.7	8.4
Seaboard Corporation	121,052	9/98	131,330	77,115	94,824	90,315	67,176	102,927	13.2	1,115,712	9.2	10.8
WLR Foods, Inc.	50,649	12/98	8,378	(12,474)	30,496	58,648	55,908	27,139	(2.2)	204,068	4.0	7.5
LOW	39,179								(2.2)		3.4	6.3
HIGH	122,198								15.5		9.2	10.8
MEAN	77,679								8.2		5.7	8.5
MEDIAN	55,318								8.6		5.7	8.4
Warm Chicken Company	56,719	12/98	38,823	31,561	27,970	45,641	30,758	40,143	13.7	NM	NM	NM

Definitions, sources, and footnotes are found on Exhibit 21-9I.

Exhibit 21–9D

Warm Chicken Company
Market Approach
Guideline Publicly Traded Company Method
Debt-Free Net Income

Company	LTM DFNI $000	Ending	1998/7 $000	1997/6 $000	1996/5 $000	1995/4 $000	1994/3 $000	5-Year Average [c] DFNI $000	Average Annual Compound Growth [d] %	MVIC $000	MVIC/DFNI LTM	MVIC/DFNI 5-Year Average
Cagles, Inc.	19,829	12/98	4,988	3,567	4,533	14,465	9,511	9,476	16.7	132,787	6.7	14.0
Pilgrim's Pride Corp.	53,404	12/98	46,873	39,539	12,825	14,950	36,454	30,128	9.4	740,058	13.9	24.6
Sanderson Farms, Inc.	20,092	10/98	20,092	4,433	704	13,191	17,757	11,235	3.1	317,466	15.8	28.3
Seaboard Corporation	39,979	9/98	51,046	17,837	33,957	38,745	22,294	36,313	13.1	1,115,712	27.9	30.7
WLR Foods, Inc.	14,966	12/98	(12,644)	(25,929)	1,453	21,043	21,606	(222)	(7.8)	204,068	13.6	DF
LOW	14,966								(7.8)		6.7	14.0
HIGH	53,404								16.7		27.9	30.7
MEAN	29,654								6.9		15.6	24.4
MEDIAN	20,092								9.4		13.9	26.4
Warm Chicken Company	21,813	12/98	10,724	5,383	3,860	17,425	9,911	11,841	18.0	NM	NM	NM

Definitions, sources, and footnotes are found on Exhibit 21-9I.

Exhibit 21–9E

Warm Chicken Company
Market Approach
Guideline Publicly Traded Company Method
Debt-Free Cash Flow

Company	LTM DFCF $000	Ending	1998/7 $000	1997/6 $000	1996/5 $000	1995/4 $000	1994/3 $000	5-Year Average [c] DFCF $000	Average Annual Compound Growth [d] %	MVIC $000	MVIC/DFCF LTM	5-Year Average
Cagles, Inc.	28,189	12/98	12,828	11,328	9,822	18,960	14,410	16,225	15.1	132,787	4.7	8.2
Pilgrim's Pride Corp.	86,596	12/98	79,464	69,335	40,849	41,077	61,631	58,471	8.3	740,058	8.5	12.7
Sanderson Farms, Inc.	43,333	10/98	43,333	25,800	20,448	31,630	33,361	30,914	6.8	317,466	7.3	10.3
Seaboard Corporation	98,875	9/98	107,942	68,751	78,901	72,148	56,723	85,324	12.4	1,115,712	11.3	13.1
WLR Foods, Inc.	41,518	12/98	15,677	2,159	29,696	45,860	42,939	26,982	(0.7)	204,068	4.9	7.6
LOW	28,189								(0.7)		4.7	7.6
HIGH	98,875								15.1		11.3	13.1
MEAN	59,702								8.4		7.4	10.3
MEDIAN	43,333								8.3		7.3	10.3
Warm Chicken Company	42,177	12/98	31,673	27,973	25,396	34,025	24,150	32,249	12.4	NM	NM	NM

Definitions, sources, and footnotes are found on Exhibit 21-9I.

Exhibit 21–9F

Warm Chicken Company
Market Approach
Guideline Publicly Traded Company Method
Revenues

Company	LTM Revenues $000	Ending	1998/7 $000	1997/6 $000	1996/5 $000	1995/4 $000	1994/3 $000	5-Year Average [c] Revenues $000	Average Annual Compound Growth [d] %	MVIC $000	MVIC/Revenues LTM	5-Year Average
Cagles, Inc.	338,042	12/98	344,886	353,567	308,749	349,770	312,696	339,003	1.6	132,787	0.39	0.39
Pilgrim's Pride Corp.	1,329,746	12/98	1,331,545	1,277,649	1,139,310	931,806	922,609	1,120,584	9.0	740,058	0.56	0.66
Sanderson Farms, Inc.	521,394	10/98	521,394	481,789	455,100	392,896	371,502	444,536	8.8	317,466	0.61	0.71
Seaboard Corporation	1,841,263	9/98	1,780,333	1,464,362	1,173,977	983,804	1,142,144	1,448,748	10.6	1,115,712	0.61	0.77
WLR Foods, Inc.	922,960	12/98	945,967	994,591	997,632	908,776	727,270	953,985	5.4	204,068	0.22	0.21
LOW									1.6		0.22	0.21
HIGH									10.6		0.61	0.77
MEAN									7.1		0.48	0.55
MEDIAN									8.8		0.56	0.66
Warm Chicken Company	754,600	12/98	743,999	725,015	635,970	501,378	450,311	672,192	11.4	NM	NM	NM

Definitions, sources, and footnotes are found on Exhibit 21-9I.

Exhibit 21–9G

Warm Chicken Company
Market Approach
Guideline Publicly Traded Company Method
Revenue Performance Ratios

Company	LTM Return on Revenues				5-Year Average Return on Revenues			
	EBIT %	EBITDA %	DFNI %	DFCF %	EBIT %	EBITDA %	DFNI %	DFCF %
Cagles, Inc.	9.1	11.6	5.9	8.3	4.3	6.3	2.8	4.8
Pilgrim's Pride Corp.	6.7	9.2	4.0	6.5	4.5	7.0	2.7	5.2
Sanderson Farms, Inc.	6.2	10.6	3.9	8.3	4.1	8.5	2.5	7.0
Seaboard Corporation	3.4	6.6	2.2	5.4	3.7	7.1	2.5	5.9
WLR Foods, Inc.	2.6	5.5	1.6	4.5	DF	2.8	DF	2.8
LOW	2.6	5.5	1.6	4.5	3.7	2.8	2.5	2.8
HIGH	9.1	11.6	5.9	8.3	4.5	8.5	2.8	7.0
MEAN	5.6	8.7	3.5	6.6	4.1	6.3	2.6	5.1
MEDIAN	6.2	9.2	3.9	6.5	4.2	7.0	2.6	5.2
Warm Chicken Company	4.8	7.5	2.9	5.6	2.9	6.0	1.8	4.8

Definitions, sources, and footnotes are found on Exhibit 21-9I.

Exhibit 21–9H

Warm Chicken Company
Market Approach
Guideline Publicly Traded Company Method
Book Value of Invested Capital and Performance Ratios

Company	MVIC $000s	MVIC/ Lat. Qtr. TBVIC	BV of IBD/ TBVIC %	MV of IBD/ MVIC %	LTM Return on TBVIC				5-Year Average Return on TBVIC			
					EBIT %	EBITDA %	DFNI %	DFCF %	EBIT %	EBITDA %	DFNI %	DFCF %
Cagles, Inc.	132,787	1.23	36.5	29.7	28.5	36.3	18.4	26.1	13.4	19.7	8.8	15.0
Pilgrim's Pride Corp.	740,058	1.70	43.5	25.7	20.4	28.0	12.2	19.8	11.5	18.0	6.9	13.4
Sanderson Farms, Inc.	317,466	1.39	43.5	31.4	14.0	24.1	8.8	18.9	7.9	16.5	4.9	13.5
Seaboard Corporation	1,115,712	1.23	53.9	43.7	6.9	13.4	4.4	10.9	6.0	11.4	4.0	9.4
WLR Foods, Inc.	204,068	1.01	31.8	31.4	12.0	25.1	7.4	20.6	DF	13.5	DF	13.4
LOW		1.01	31.8	25.7	6.9	13.4	4.4	10.9	6.0	11.4	4.0	9.4
HIGH		1.70	53.9	43.7	28.5	36.3	18.4	26.1	13.4	19.7	8.8	15.0
MEAN		1.31	41.8	32.4	16.4	25.4	10.2	19.3	9.7	15.8	6.1	12.9
MEDIAN		1.23	43.5	31.4	14.0	25.1	8.8	19.8	9.7	16.5	5.9	13.4
Warm Chicken Company	NM	NM	38.5	NM	20.8	32.5	12.5	24.1	11.3	23.0	6.8	18.5

Definitions, sources, and footnotes are found on Exhibit 21-9I.

Exhibit 21–9l

Warm Chicken Company
Market Approach
Guideline Publicly Traded Company Method
Definitions, Footnotes, and Sources to Exhibits

Definitions:
BV = Book value
DF = Deficit
FYE = Fiscal year-end
IBD = Interest-bearing debt
IC = Invested capital
LTM = Latest 12 months
MV = Market value
MVIC = LTD + ST interest-bearing debt + MV of preferred + MV of common equity
NA = Not available
NM = Not meaningful
T = Tangible
TBVIC = Stockholders' equity – goodwill + LTD + ST interest-bearing debt

Footnotes:
a. Book value if not publicly traded.
b. Per most recently available data prior to the valuation date.
c. Includes latest 12 months if at least six months beyond latest fiscal year-end.
d. From earliest year on the table to the latest 12-month period.

SOURCE: SEC Forms 10-K and 10-Q, Annual Reports to Shareholders, Standard & Poor's *Compustat* and *Dialog-on-Disc*, and Disclosure's *Compact D/SEC*.

Exhibit 21–10

Warm Chicken Company
Market Approach
Guideline Publicly Traded Company Method
Valuation Summary

Fundamental	Warm Chicken $000	Industry Multiples					Indicated Value $000
		Low	High	Mean	Median	Selected	
Latest Twelve Months							
EBIT	36,355	4.3	18.0	9.8	8.5	6.5	236,308
EBITDA	56,719	3.4	9.2	5.7	5.7	4.5	255,237
DFNI	21,813	6.7	27.9	15.6	13.9	11.0	239,943
DFCF	42,177	4.7	11.3	7.4	7.3	5.5	231,975
Revenues	754,600	0.22	0.61	0.48	0.56	0.30	226,380
						Indicated value	238,000
Five-Year Average							
EBIT	19,735	9.2	20.7	15.5	16.1	12.0	236,820
EBITDA	40,143	6.3	10.8	8.5	8.4	6.3	252,900
DFNI	11,841	14.0	30.7	24.4	26.4	20.0	236,820
DFCF	32,249	7.6	13.1	10.3	10.3	7.6	245,092
Revenues	672,192	0.21	0.77	0.55	0.66	0.35	235,267
						Indicated value	241,400
						Market value of invested capital	239,700

SOURCE: Exhibit 21-9.

Exhibit 21–11

Warm Chicken Company
Pro Forma Consolidated Income Statements

	Pro Forma Years Ending March 31,					Pro Forma Years Ending March 31,				
	1999 $000	**2000** $000	**2001** $000	**2002** $000	**2003** $000	**1999** %	**2000** %	**2001** %	**2002** %	**2003** %
Net sales	818,399	900,239	990,263	1,089,289	1,198,218	100.0	100.0	100.0	100.0	100.0
Growth	*10.0%*	*10.0%*	*10.0%*	*10.0%*	*10.0%*					
Operating expenses	781,613	857,559	943,313	,035,184	,136,483	95.5	95.3	95.3	95.0	94.8
Operating income	36,786	42,680	46,950	54,105	61,735	4.5	4.7	4.7	5.0	5.2
Other income/(expense):										
Interest expense	(4,458)	(4,842)	(5,598)	(5,487)	(4,791)	(0.5)	(0.5)	(0.6)	(0.5)	(0.4)
Other	(1,530)	(1,699)	(1,703)	(1,719)	(1,704)	(0.2)	(0.2)	(0.2)	(0.2)	(0.1)
Total other income/expense	(5,988)	(6,541)	(7,300)	(7,205)	(6,495)	(0.7)	(0.7)	(0.7)	(0.7)	(0.5)
Pretax income	30,799	36,139	39,649	46,900	55,240	3.8	4.0	4.0	4.3	4.6
Income taxes	12,319	14,456	15,860	18,760	22,096	1.5	1.6	1.6	1.7	1.8
Net Income	18,479	21,683	23,790	28,140	33,144	2.3	2.4	2.4	2.6	2.8

SOURCE: Management projections and management discussions.

Exhibit 21–12

Warm Chicken Company
Weighted Average Cost of Capital

Cost of Equity Capital:		**Source:**
Risk-free rate of return	5.40%	*The Wall Street Journal,* December 31, 1998
Long-term equity risk premium	7.80%	*Stocks, Bonds, Bills, and Inflation,* Ibbotson Associates, 1998
Industry beta	0.80	Standard &Poor's *Compustat* Database
Beta-adjusted equity risk premium	6.24%	
Size premium	2.56%	*Stocks, Bonds, Bills, and Inflation,* Ibbotson Associates, 1998
Unsystematic risk premium	1.50%	WMA estimate
Total equity rate	15.70%	
Cost of Debt Capital:		
Average cost of debt	8.00%	Company actual cost of debt
Tax rate	40.00%	Corporate tax rate
After-tax debt rate	4.80%	
Capital Structure:		
Equity/invested capital	72.00%	Company actual capital structure
Debt/invested capital	28.00%	Company actual capital structure
Total invested capital	100.00%	
WACC (Rounded)	**12.5%**	

SOURCE: As indicated in exhibit.

Exhibit 21–13

Warm Chicken Company
Discounted Cash Flow Method

	Fiscal Years Ending March 31,					Norm.
	1999	2000	2001	2002	2003	2003
Present Value of Discrete Net Cash Flows	$000 [a]	$000	$000	$000	$000	$000
Net income	4,620	21,683	23,790	28,140	33,144	33,144
Plus depreciation and amortization	4,199	14,477	14,020	16,422	14,261	-
Plus interest expense, net of taxes	669	2,905	3,359	3,292	2,874	2,874
Less capital expenditures	(4,000)	(16,000)	(16,000)	(16,000)	(16,000)	-
Less working capital requirements	(2,188)	(9,628)	(10,591)	(11,650)	(12,815)	(12,815)
Net cash flow	3,299	13,438	14,577	20,203	21,465	23,203
Present value factor @ 12.5% [b]	0.9854	0.9137	0.8108	0.7195	0.6385	
Present value of discrete cash flows	3,251	12,277	11,819	14,537	13,706	
Total present value of discrete cash flows	55,591					

Present Value of Terminal Net Cash Flow	
Fiscal 2004 net cash flow	24,131
Capitalization multiple [b], [c]	11.8
Terminal value	283,899
Present value factor @ 12.5%	0.6385
Present value of terminal cash flow	181,284

Valuation Summary	
Interim flows value	$55,591
Terminal value	181,284
Market value of invested capital (rounded)	$236,900

a. Represents three months of cash flow.
b. Calculated as if cash flows received at mid-year.
c. Incorporating a long-term nominal growth rate of 4.0%.

SOURCE: Exhibits 21-11 and 21-12.

Chapter 22

Reviewing a Business Valuation Report

Identification of the Subject Property
Relevant Dates
Definition of Value
    Standard of Value
    Reason for the Selected Standard of Value
Purpose of the Valuation
Actual or Assumed Ownership Characteristics
    Degree of Marketability
    Degree of Ownership Control
Basic Company Information
Economic and Industry Outlook
Sources of Information
    Site Visits
    Management Interviews
    Economic and Industry Data
    Company Financial Statements
    Income Approach Data
    Market Approach Data
    Asset-Based Approach Data
Financial Statement Analysis
    Financial Statement Adjustments
    Comparative Financial Statement Analysis
Valuation Methodology
    Income Approach
    Market Approach
    Asset-Based Approach—Asset Accumulation Method
    Asset-Based Approach—Capitalized Excess Earnings Method
Are the Data Used Appropriate for the Valuation Date?
    Cost of Capital Data
    Market Approach Data
    Asset-Based Approach Data
Valuation Synthesis and Conclusion
Analyst's Qualifications

Professional Accreditations
Education
Professional Association Memberships
Experience and Professional Involvement
Appraisal Certification
Statement of Contingent and Limiting Conditions
Overall Evaluation

This chapter is designed to serve as a convenient checklist for initial review of a written business, professional practice, or intangible asset valuation report. *Permission is granted to make copies of this chapter to use in connection with report reviews* (not for distribution or resale).

The checklist is presented more or less in the order that the material is typically found in valuation reports, although order of presentation varies among reports. Some of the items on this checklist are either required or highly recommended (1) by the *Uniform Standards of Professional Appraisal Practice* or (2) by the standards of the various business valuation professional associations. These "required" or "highly recommended" items are cross-referenced to the appropriate professional standards, as follows:

U   *Uniform Standards of Professional Appraisal Practice*
A   American Society of Appraisers Business Valuation Standards
I   Institute of Business Appraisers Standards
N   National Association of Certified Valuation Analysts Standards

Contact information for obtaining copies of these professional standards is provided in Chapter 1, Business Valuation Credentials and Standards.

Identification of the Subject Property

❑   Name of company.
❑   State of incorporation or registration.
❑   Form of ownership (e.g., C corporation, S corporation, limited partnership, general partnership).
❑   Ownership interest to be appraised (e.g., number of shares, percent general or limited partnership interest).

U 9-2 and 10-2; A VIII-IV and VIII-V; I 5.3; N 3.1 and 3.2

Relevant Dates

❑   Effective valuation date.
❑   Reason for the selected date (e.g., statute, agreement, transaction).

_____
_____

❑   Date report prepared. _____

U 10-2; A I-II and VIII-IV; I 5.3; N 3.1 and 4.2

Definition of Value

Standard of Value
❑ Fair market value.
❑ Fair value.
❑ Investment value.
❑ Other._____

Reason for the Selected Standard of Value
❑ Statute, buy-sell agreement, judicial precedent, transaction, and so forth.

_____
_____

U 9-2 and 10-2; A I-II and VIII-IV; I 5.3, N 3.1

Purpose of the Valuation

❑ Is the purpose of the valuation (use to which it is to be put) clearly stated (e.g., gift tax, estate tax, charitable contribution or redemption, marital dissolution, ESOP, buyout of owner(s), issuance of new stock, dissenting stockholder suit, minority dissolution suit)?
❑ Is the audience for the valuation clearly indicated?
❑ Is the standard (definition) of value stated appropriate to the stated use of the appraisal?

U 9-5; A VI-IV

Actual or Assumed Ownership Characteristics

Degree of Marketability
❑ Publicly traded.
❑ Closely held.
❑ Buy-sell agreement, put option, transferability restrictions, or other lack of marketability factors.

_____
_____

Degree of Ownership Control
❑ 100%.
❑ Less than 100%, but more then 50%.
❑ Less than 50%.
❑ Other control/lack of control ownership characteristics.

_____
_____

U 9-2 and 9-4; A I-III and VIII-V; N 3.2

Basic Company Information

- ❏ Brief history of the company.
- ❏ Description of major tangible and intangible assets.
- ❏ Products/services.
- ❏ Markets (industry and/or geographical).
- ❏ Competitive situation.
- ❏ Depth and quality of management.
- ❏ Capital structure (e.g., classes of common, convertible, and preferred stock). If more than one ownership class, the characteristic of each should be described.
- ❏ Distribution of ownership (and important relationships).
- ❏ Recent past transactions in the ownership of the company (or lack thereof).

U 9-4 and 10-2; A I-III, IV-III, and VIII-V; N 3.2

Economic and Industry Outlook

- ❏ Economic outlook as of the valuation date.
- ❏ Industry outlook as of the valuation date. The main thing to look for here is whether the factors stated are relevant to the value of this company (versus boilerplate). It is even better if the relevance is pointed out.

U 9-4; A I-III and VIII-V; N 3.2

Sources of Information

Site Visits
- ❏ Yes (should specify).   ❏ No.   ❏ Undisclosed.

Management Interviews
- ❏ Yes (should specify names and positions).   ❏ No.   ❏ Undisclosed.

Economic and Industry Data
- ❏ Economic data sources relied on.
- ❏ Industry data sources relied on.

Company Financial Statements
- ❏ Periods for which financial statements received.
- ❏ Assurance status of financial statements (e.g., audited, reviewed, compiled, internally prepared).

Income Approach Data
- ❏ Sources of economic income estimates or projections (who made them, when, and for what purpose?).
- ❏ Source(s) of cost of capital data (publications, on-line services, dates of publication, etc.).

❏ Are the discount or capitalization rates used adequately supported, and are they the appropriate rates for the measure of the economic income variable being discounted or capitalized?

A IV and V; N 3.6 and 3.7

Market Approach
❏ Are the criteria for selection of guideline publicly traded companies or guideline merged and acquired companies clearly delineated?
❏ Is the population from which the companies and/or transactions have been drawn clearly specified?
❏ Is it clear that all companies and/or transactions from the specified population that meet the criteria have been considered?
❏ Does the report clearly specify what market-derived pricing multiples are used and why they are appropriate?
❏ In selecting each pricing multiple to be applied to the subject company, out of the range of observed multiples for that company, does the report justify the level of the pricing multiple selected?
❏ Does the report provide an adequate explanation of the weight ultimately accorded to each of the indicated pricing multiples?

A III

Asset-Based Approach—Asset Accumulation Method
❏ Are all the asset and liability accounts adjusted that should be adjusted?
❏ Are all off–balance sheet assets and liabilities, actual or contingent, recognized and taken into consideration (or is there a statement that there are no off–balance sheet assets or liabilities)?
❏ Is the support for the amounts of the adjustments convincing?

A III

Asset-Based Approach—Capitalized Excess Earnings Method
❏ Are all categories of tangible assets correctly adjusted to current values?
❏ Is there a satisfactory explanation of how the market-derived required rate of return or the company's operating tangible assets was estimated?
❏ Is the level of economic income being capitalized clearly defined?
❏ Is the estimate of economic income being capitalized reasonably supported as being representative of ongoing earning power?
❏ Has an appropriate amount of reasonable owner's compensation been deducted as an expense in arriving at the amount of earning power to be capitalized?
❏ Is the direct capitalization rate applied to excess earnings adequately supported?
❏ Is there some type of "sanity check" (check for reasonableness) on the result (e.g., Is the overall capitalization rate reasonable, or is the number of years that would be required for the business or practice's earnings to pay the alleged value reasonable)?

A III-II

Market Approach Data

❑ Specification of population from which guideline publicly traded compan)
and/or guideline merged and acquired company transactions are drawn.

❑ Specification of criteria for selection of guideline companies and/or transactions

❑ Specification of sources for guideline company and/or guideline transaction data

Asset-Based Approach Data

❑ Sources of data for discrete tangible and intangible asset values relied on.

❑ Sources of data for discrete recorded and contingent liability values relied on

NOTE: *One of the criteria being sought is* **replicability**—*that is, can a competen
analyst independently check the accuracy and thoroughness of all the data pro
vided.*

I 1.8, 1.19, and 1.20; N 3.9 and 4.2

Financial Statement Analysis

Financial Statement Adjustments

❑ Is there adequate explanation of what adjustments were made to the compa
ny's historical financial statements, or an explanation of why none were nec
essary?

❑ Are the magnitudes of the adjustments adequately supported?

❑ If guideline company (usually public company) financial statements were use
in the market approach, is there an adequate explanation of what adjustment
were made to the guideline company statements, or an explanation of why non
were necessary?

Comparative Financial Statement Analysis

❑ Have the company's financial ratios been compared with individual guidelin
companies and/or industry averages?

❑ If so, have the accounting policies and definitions of the computed financia
ratios been put on a comparable basis between the subject company and th
guideline companies and/or industry averages used for comparison?

❑ Are the strengths and weaknesses resulting from the financial analysis pointe
out?

❑ Are the valuation parameters used (e.g., discount or capitalization rates in th
income approach, pricing multiples in the market approach) reasonable in ligh
of the financial statement analysis strengths and weaknesses?

A II-II, II-III, V-III, V-IV, and III-VI; N 3.5 and 4.2

Valuation Methodology

Income Approach

❑ Are the economic income variables used clearly defined (e.g., net cash flow to
equity, net cash flow to invested capital, net income, pretax income)?

❑ Are the estimates of prospective economic income to be discounted or capitalized adequately supported as being representative of future earning power?

Are the Data Used Appropriate for the Valuation Date?

Cost of Capital Data

If the build-up or CAPM procedure is used:
- ❏ Is the risk-free rate of return as of the effective valuation date?
- ❏ Are other components, such as equity risk premiums, current as of the date of valuation?

Market Approach Data

If the guideline publicly traded company method is used:
- ❏ Are the market prices for the guideline companies the prices as of the effective valuation date?
- ❏ Are the financial fundamental data for the guideline companies for the same time periods as the fundamental data for the subject company?

NOTE: Publicly traded companies report earnings quarterly and detailed income and balance sheet data annually. If the valuation date is at the end of a fiscal period, some analysts would not use that period's data because it would not have been published as of the valuation date. The more prevalent view, however, is that the data were susceptible to being known, or at least closely estimated, as of the valuation date, so it is preferable to use both subject and guideline company data as of the end of the fiscal period.

If the guideline merged and acquired company method is used:
- ❏ Are the transactions close enough to the valuation date to be relevant?
- ❏ If the transactions are somewhat removed from the valuation date, are adjustments for differences in industry and market conditions addressed?

Asset-Based Approach Data
- ❏ Are all tangible and intangible asset valuations relied on in reasonable proximity to the valuation date?
- ❏ If asset valuations are somewhat removed in time from the valuation date, are adjustments for differences in market conditions addressed?

A V-IV and VI; I 1.20; N 3

Valuation Synthesis and Conclusion

- ❏ Is the relative degree of weight accorded to each valuation approach satisfactorily explained?
- ❏ Considering the level of value produced by each method, are the proper discounts or premiums applied, if applicable?
- ❏ Are all indicated valuation discounts and/or premiums adequately identified and appropriately quantified?
- ❏ If there are nonoperating or excess assets, have they been treated appropriately in light of the definition of value sought and the subject ownership characteristics?
- ❏ Is the synthesis and conclusion appropriate in light of the legal context (e.g., statutory law, judicial precedent)?

A VI-III; I 1.1, 1.7, 1.25, and 1.26

Analyst's Qualifications

Professional Accreditations

American Society of Appraisers
❑ FASA.   ❑ ASA.   ❑ AM.

Institute of Business Appraisers
❑ MCBA.   ❑ FIBA.   ❑ CBA.   ❑ AIBA.   ❑ BVAL.

American Institute of Certified Public Accountants
❑ CPA/ABV.

National Association of Certified Valuation Analysts
❑ CVA.   ❑ GVA.   ❑ AVA.

The Canadian Institute of Chartered Business Valuators
❑ FCBV.   ❑ CBV.

Association for Investment Management & Research
❑ CFA.

See Chapter 1 for a description of the above accreditations.

Education
❑ Academic degree(s).
❑ Professional education (e.g., professional association courses, seminars).

_____

_____

Professional Association Memberships
❑ ASA.   ❑ IBA.   ❑ AICPA.
❑ NACVA.   ❑ CICBV.   ❑ AIMR.
❑ Other._____

Experience and Professional Involvement
❑ Length and type of experience.
❑ Professional involvement (e.g., teaching, speaking, writing, committee/officer, professional association involvement).

U 10-3; A VIII-II and VIII-III; I 1.25; N 2.3 and 4.2

Appraisal Certification

❑ Statement of disinterestedness (or disclosure of interest).
❑ Conformance (or lack of conformance) to any professional standards (e.g., USPAP, ASA BV Standards).
❑ Compensation is not contingent on value reported or on any predetermined value.
❑ No person(s) other than those identified had any significant professional input.
❑ To the best of the analyst's knowledge, all statements are true and correct.

U 10-2 and 10-3; A VIII-III; I 1.25; N 3.3., 4.1, and 4.2

Statement of Contingent and Limiting Conditions

❏ The opinion of value is valid only for the stated effective valuation date and only for the stated valuation purpose.

❏ No reliance on data supplied by others without independent verification.

NOTE: The typical valuation report will have a fairly lengthy list of assumptions and limiting conditions of which the reviewer should be aware.

U 10-1; A VIII-III; I 1.9; N 4.2

Overall Evaluation

❏ Is the report *understandable* to the reader?

❏ Did the analyst clearly appraise the property that was identified to be appraised?

❏ Is the valuation methodology appropriate for the purpose of the valuation, the relevant standard of value, the ownership characteristics (e.g., a noncontrolling, nonmarketable interest) and any judicial precedent?

❏ Is the report *internally consistent* (i.e., nothing in one place that seems to contradict something somewhere else)?

❏ Is the *methodology appropriate* for the stated definition of value and controlling statutes and judicial precedent?

❏ Is the report *comprehensive* (e.g., Does it do everything it promises to do; Are all the topics and information included that seem necessary to support the conclusion(s) reached)? (To some extent, this question addresses questions of omission rather than commission.)

❏ Does the report logically lead to convincing support for the conclusion(s) reached?

U 9-4 and 9-5; A I-II, I-IV, VI-III, and VIII-VIII; I 1.6, 1.9, 1.16, and 4.3; N 3.4 and 4.2

Part VI

Valuing Specific Securities and Interests

Chapter 23

Valuing Debt Securities

Lender: "At least you could pay me the interest on it."
*Debtor: "It is not my interest to pay the principal, nor my principle to pay
the interest."*

Although debt securities play an important role in the analysis and appraisal of closely held companies, their valuation can in no way be thoroughly discussed in a single chapter. Therefore, this chapter confines discussion to general areas of reference that the analyst may want to consider when valuing debt securities. References to more extensive discussions of the areas of interest to the reader, including complete books on fixed-income analysis and valuation, are included in the bibliography at the end of this chapter.[1]

Corporate securities can be classified many different ways. As long as investors find them attractive, traditional features of corporate securities will be replaced with newly created ones. The word "debt" sounds straightforward, but financial arrangements that look suspiciously like debt are often accounted for differently. For example, instead of borrowing money to buy equipment, many companies lease or rent the equipment on a long-term basis. Such arrangements are economically equivalent to secured long-term debt. Also, preferred stock typically offers a fixed dividend that resembles interest payments on debt and yet preferred stock is legally an equity security whose divided payment is not tax-deductible.

Extensive financial innovation has regularly introduced new varieties of debt securities: domestic and eurobonds; coupons and zeros; secured and unsecured; fixed-rate and floating-rate; senior and junior; callable, extendible, retractable; and so on. The use of derivatives has become a routine tool of corporate finance, allowing firms to protect themselves from adverse changes in external factors, such as interest rates, exchange rates, or commodity prices.

This chapter first discusses common situations that require the valuation of debt securities; it then moves to the general method of valuing them. The chapter also discusses the discount for lack of marketability, if any, and then examines the impact on value of special characteristics that many debt securities have.

Common Situations Requiring Valuation of Debt Securities

The most frequently encountered reasons for needing to value debt securities are the following:

1. Purchase or sale for cash.
2. Exchange of equity for debt, or vice versa.
3. Gift and estate taxes.
4. Allocating total enterprise value among classes of securities in a leveraged buyout, recapitalization (including tax-free reorganizations), or bankruptcy reorganization.
5. Adjusting a balance sheet for debt securities owned or owed.

Purchase or Sale for Cash

From time to time, a company may have occasion to purchase or sell debt securities for cash. If they are existing securities, it is necessary to estimate their cash

[1] See, for example, Frank J. Fabozzi, *Handbook of Fixed-Income Securities*, 5th ed. (New York: McGraw-Hill, 1997).

equivalent value. If they are to be newly issued securities, it is necessary to structure the provisions so that the value will be equal to the price paid or received.

Exchange of Equity for Debt

If debt securities are to be exchanged for some consideration other than cash, such as stock or other property, it usually is most expedient to estimate the cash-equivalent values of both the debt securities and the stock (or other consideration) to be exchanged.

Most typically, a company, or some or all of its stock, is to be sold and a debt security received as all or part of the consideration. The seller needs to know the cash-equivalent value of the consideration being received in return for the company or stock being given up. It is not uncommon for notes or other debt securities issued in connection with the acquisition of a company to have a cash-equivalent value of 20 percent or more below the securities' face value.[2]

Gift and Estate Taxes

Debt securities may be gifted or may reside in an asset in an estate. As in all gift and estate tax situations, the standard of value is fair market value. Quite often, debt securities transferred as a gift or included in an estate have a fair market value considerably below the face value. Depending on the fair market value of a decedent's debt securities, a variety of planning opportunities are available for the estate's personal representative to consider.[3]

Allocation of Total Enterprise Value among Classes of Securities

A leveraged buyout, by its nature, results in the creation of new classes of securities, almost always including at least one class of debt. Therefore, in dealing with the valuation for a leveraged buyout, it usually is necessary not only to value the entire enterprise but to allocate this total value among the various classes of participants.

Recapitalizations involving debt securities may be undertaken for a variety of reasons. One common reason is a leveraged recapitalization—issuing high-yield debt for the purpose of redeeming a substantial portion of outstanding equity to create a more optimal capital structure. Popular during the 1980s, high-yield debt is still used in transactions where several layers of capital are appropriate.

Bankruptcy recapitalizations, by their nature, involve debt securities, sometimes both before and after the recapitalization. Creative structuring of debt and other securities to meet the varying objectives of the parties at interest can be an essential tool in achieving a successful bankruptcy reorganization.

---

[2] While this may be true in a business of any size, it is particularly prevalent in the sale of small businesses. For an extended discussion of this, see Chapter 27, "Trade-Off between Cash and Terms," in Shannon P. Pratt, Robert F. Reilly, and Robert P. Schweihs, *Valuing Small Businesses and Professional Practices*, 3rd ed. (New York: McGraw-Hill, 1998).

[3] M. Read Moore and D. Alan Hungate, "Valuation Discounts for Private Debt in Estate Administration," *Estate Planning*, June 1998, pp. 195–203.

Adjusting a Balance Sheet for Debt Securities Owned or Owed

For various reasons, the balance sheet may be analyzed to adjust each line item to its fair market value. In many cases, debt may need to be adjusted to market on both the asset and liabilities sides of the balance sheet. An example would be the use of market value of invested capital valuation methods to value the common stock, as discussed in Chapter 11.

The extent of analysis undertaken for the valuation of debt securities will vary with the assignment and the accuracy required. For example, generally more analysis will be undertaken in the valuation of a debt security when that security is to be gifted (and thus subject to gift tax consequences) than when the assignment is to value the common stock of a closely held company by a market value of invested capital valuation method. Even if the analyst does not contemplate going through all the steps in the analysis of debt securities, it is important to understand them in order to have a general idea of the potential impact of an adjustment in the value of a debt security to market value.

Lease Financing

Lease financing is a substitute for secured debt financing. Just as with secured debt financing, the consequences for failure to make timely lease payments is the same as the failure to make debt payments: The lessor becomes a creditor and can force the lessee into bankruptcy. Therefore, for financial analysis purposes, the company's lease payment obligations are considered in the same category as the company's interest and principal repayment obligations. The disadvantages to the lessee of leasing as compared with conventional debt financing are that (1) The lessee gives up depreciation tax advantages of asset ownership and (2) the asset and the value of the asset are surrendered at the conclusion of the term of the lease.

The advantages of leasing are that (1) the financing terms of the lease usually take into consideration the lessor's ability to more efficiently use the tax advantages of asset ownership, (2) most leases are short-term operating leases, and that reduces the transaction costs (i.e., identifying qualified buyers and complications associated with equipment obsolescence) at the end of the anticipated period of use, and (3) there is less of a capital commitment so that equity and borrowing power are freed for other financing. The financial terms of a lease will typically also reflect the fact that special provisions of bankruptcy law give the lessor greater flexibility to seize the asset because the lessor owns the asset. For many smaller or less creditworthy companies, utilizing the asset under the terms of a lease is an attractive alternative to conventional debt financing.

The Internal Revenue Service has established guidelines to distinguish operating leases from capital leases, installment sales agreements, and secured loans. If the terms of the lease satisfy the guidelines, the taxpayer can deduct for tax purposes the full amount of each lease payment.

For financial analysis purposes, long-term debt is usually defined to include conventional long-term debt plus capitalized lease obligations.

Exhibit 23–1

Formulas for Key Ratios

1. EBIT interest coverage = $\dfrac{\text{Earnings from continuing operations* before interest and taxes}}{\text{Gross interest incurred before subtracting (1) capitalized interest and (2) interest income}}$

2. EBITDA interest coverage = $\dfrac{\text{Earnings from continuing operations* before interest, taxes, depreciation, and amortization}}{\text{Gross interest incurred before subtracting (1) capitalized interest and (2) interest income}}$

3. Funds from operations/total debt = $\dfrac{\text{Net income from continuing operations plus depreciation, amortization, deferred income taxes, and other noncash items}}{\text{Long-term debt** plus current maturities, commercial paper, and other short-term borrowings}}$

4. Free operating cash flow/total debt = $\dfrac{\text{Funds from operations minus capital expenditures, minus (plus) the increase (decrease) in working capital (excluding changes in cash, marketable securities, and short-term debt)}}{\text{Long-term debt** plus current maturities, commercial paper, and other short-term borrowings}}$

5. Return on capital = $\dfrac{\text{EBIT}}{\text{Average of beginning of year and end of year capital, including short-term debt, current maturities, long-term debt**, non-current deferred taxes, and equity}}$

6. Operating income/sales = $\dfrac{\text{Sales minus cost of goods manufactured (before depreciation and amortization), selling, general and administrative, and research and development costs}}{\text{Sales}}$

7. Long-term debt/capitalization = $\dfrac{\text{Long-term debt**}}{\text{Long-term debt + shareholders' equity (including preferred stock) plus minority interest}}$

8. Total debt/capitalization = $\dfrac{\text{Long-term debt** plus current maturities, commercial paper, and other short-term borrowings}}{\text{Long-term debt plus current maturities, commercial paper, and other short-term borrowings + shareholders' equity (including preferred stock) plus minority interest}}$

*Including interest income and equity earnings; excluding nonrecurring items.
**Including amount for operating lease debt equivalent.

SOURCE: *Standard & Poor's Corporate Ratings Criteria* (New York: Standard & Poor's Corporation, 2000), p. 55. Available on www.standardpoor.com/ratings/corporates/index.htm.

ratings for nearly all of the securities. As would be expected, the lower-rated indexes have higher yields to maturity than the higher-rated indexes at any point in time.

The list of prospective guideline publicly traded debt securities compiled from one of these two debt listings should then be narrowed to those with characteristics or provisions similar to the privately held debt security. Thus winnowing the selection will help eliminate securities whose yields to maturity differ because of varying contract provisions. If unable to eliminate any publicly traded debt securities whose provisions differ from those of the closely held debt security from the guideline list, the analyst should carefully consider the differences in the securities' provisions and the associated risk characteristics when determining the appropriate yield to maturity to apply to the closely held debt security.

Standard & Poor's attaches one of approximately 200 industry codes or sub-codes to nearly all the corporate bonds included in its listing. The analyst may want to consider including only publicly traded debt securities within the same general industry as that of the closely held debt security issuer, if enough publicly traded debt securities within that industry are available to provide meaningful insight into yields to maturity within that industry. Standard & Poor's description of the impact of industry analysis on its debt rating methodology is shown in Exhibit 23–2.

After gathering an appropriate set of publicly traded equivalent securities, the analyst should examine several quantitative and qualitative factors of the privately held debt security issuer and compare them with those of the publicly traded debt security issuers. This analysis is similar to that for valuing common stock in a closely held business.

The analyst should quantitatively analyze and compare the operating performance and financial position of the debt security issuer with those of the guideline publicly traded debt security issuers. This analysis is similar to that described above in comparing the operating performance and financial condition of the closely held debt security issuer with the broad population of its publicly traded counterparts. This comparison will offer the analyst insight into the appropriate yield to maturity for the closely held debt security relative to those of the guideline publicly traded debt securities.

If the valuation is to be done in considerable depth, the appraiser may wish to analyze relevant economic and industry data, as well as the company's fundamental position, in some detail, as discussed elsewhere in the book.

After completing the quantitative and qualitative analysis discussed above, the analyst must develop an opinion of the risk associated with the payments from the

Exhibit 23–2

Standard & Poor's Rating Methodology

Each rating analysis begins with an assessment of the company's environment. To determine the degree of operating risk facing a participant in a given business, Standard & Poor's analyzes the dynamics of that business. This analysis focuses on the strength of industry prospects, as well as the competitive factors affecting that industry.

The many factors assessed include industry prospects for growth, stability, or decline, and the pattern of business cycles. It is critical to determine vulnerability to technological change, labor unrest, or regulatory interference. Industries that have long lead times or that require fixed plant of a specialized nature face heightened risk. The implications of increasing competition are obviously crucial. Standard & Poor's knowledge of investment plans of the major players in any industry offers a unique vantage point from which to assess competitive prospects.

While any particular profile category can be the overriding rating consideration, the industry risk assessment goes a long way toward setting the upper limit on the rating to which any participant in the industry can aspire. Specifically, it would be hard to imagine assigning 'AA' and 'AAA' debt ratings or 'A-1+' commercial paper ratings to companies with extensive participation in industries of above-average risk, regardless of how conservative their financial posture. Examples of these industries are integrated steel makers, tire and rubber companies, homebuilders, and most of the mining sector.

Conversely, some industries are regarded favorably. They are distinguished by such traits as steady demand growth, ability to maintain margins without impairing future prospects, flexibility in the timing of capital outlays, and moderate capital intensity. Industries possessing one or more of these attributes include manufacturers of branded consumer products, drug firms, and publishing and broadcasting. Again, high marks in this category do not translate into high ratings for all industry participants, but the cushion of strong industry fundamentals provides helpful support.

The industry risk assessment also sets the stage for analyzing more specific company risk factors and establishing the priority of these factors in the overall evaluation. For example, if an industry is determined to be highly competitive, careful assessment of a firm's market position is stressed. If the industry has large capital requirements, examination of cash flow adequacy assumes major importance.

SOURCE: *Standard & Poor's Corporate Ratings Criteria* (New York: Standard & Poor's Corporation, 2000), pp. 17–18. Available at www.standardpoor.com/ratings/corporates/index.htm.

closely held debt security in relation to the risk associated with the payments of the publicly traded debt securities. Based on the closely held security's risk and the publicly traded debt securities' yields to maturity, the analyst estimates the appropriate yield to maturity to apply to the closely held debt security payments.

Valuation Conclusion. Having estimated the appropriate yield to maturity to apply to the future payments associated with a closely held debt security, the analyst may value the debt security simply by computing the present value of its payments, using the formula presented earlier in the chapter.

Marketability Aspects of Closely Held Debt Securities

Chapter 17, "Lack of Marketability Discounts," presents a great deal of evidence in support of a discount for lack of marketability for the common stock of closely held businesses. The volume of trading in corporate bonds is lower than the volume in common stocks. Bonds are less liquid than stocks and have higher trading costs. On the surface, it appears that such a discount for lack of marketability might also be appropriate for closely held debt securities. However, such a discount often is not required or, if required, would be much less than such a discount for a common stock.

Unlike investment returns on common stock, which are generated primarily by appreciation in the price of the common stock and contingent on the ability to sell the stock to realize the price appreciation, investment returns on most debt securities are generated predominantly by cash flows in the form of interest payments over the securities' lives. These payments are anticipated to be received by the debt security holder regardless of the security's marketability, and the repayment of principal is a contractual obligation for a given amount at a fixed point in time. Therefore, if the marketability of a debt security is to be considered at all, the discount associated with the security's lack of marketability should be much less than that associated with closely held common stock.

There are a few differences between publicly traded debt securities and privately placed debt securities. Private placements of debt are less standardized and usually have more strings attached. Privately issued debt can be as simple as an IOU, whereas publicly traded debt securities are more complicated contracts that include additional conditions such as procedures for the payment of interest and principal and who is to represent the holders in subsequent negotiations. Private placements of debt can be more simply arranged and can be more customized to match the concerns of the issuer and the holder. Private placements tend to have lower issuance costs but might have a higher rate of interest.

There may be a discount for lack of marketability for bonds, but it is hidden. Private bonds are tailored to the needs of both buyers and sellers and their yields reflect this. The marketability discount associated with a bond is a function of its risk class which is a function of the creditworthiness of the company and the size of the issue. Illiquid junk bonds sell at significantly higher yields than liquid junk bonds.

If the analyst thinks that marketability is a valid consideration in the valuation of a particular closely held debt security, the adjustment can be handled by either increasing the appropriate yield to maturity to apply to the debt security payments to compensate for the additional risk associated with lack of marketability or taking a discount from the value estimated by applying a yield to maturity unadjusted for marketability considerations.

Special Characteristics of Various Debt Securities

In estimating the value of a debt security, it is extremely important to analyze the security's various characteristics or provisions that may impact on its value. In addition, if guideline publicly traded debt securities are used in the valuation, any differences between the provisions of the security being valued and those of the guideline securities should be considered. The following discussion focuses on some of the most common provisions of various debt securities that should be analyzed in the valuation process.

Call Provisions

A feature associated with some debt securities, including most public debt, is a *call* provision. This allows the debtor to repay the debt prior to its maturity. Usually, the debt may not be called for some period early in its life, often the first five years. Furthermore, the debtor usually must pay a premium in addition to the amount of debt outstanding to the debtholder when the debt is called. A call provision benefits the debtor, since it allows the debtor to repay the debt early in a period of declining interest rates. A debt security with a call provision usually will require a higher yield to maturity than an identical security without such a provision. This is due to the fact that if the debt security is called, the investor usually will be unable to find a comparable alternative investment vehicle with a yield to maturity as high as that of the original debt issue that was called. If the stated interest rate on the debt is above market rates, making exercise of the call provision likely, the analyst usually will focus on the yield-to-call data rather than on the yield to maturity.

Whether a call provision requires a yield premium is a function of the likelihood of the call being exercised. There is no significant call premium associated with deep discount bonds.

Sinking Fund Provisions

A debt security also may have a *sinking fund* provision. This provision requires the debt issuer to call or retire a contractually determined portion of the entire debt issue periodically over time prior to the issue's maturity date. When a portion of a debt issue is retired under sinking fund provisions, the actual debt security to be retired is usually determined by lottery and the holder of the security typically is paid the security's face or par value. Although sinking fund provisions increase the uncertainty of the timing of future payments associated with a particular debt security, they also are thought to reduce the risk associated with the security. The sinking fund provisions ensure that a portion of the debt is retired periodically, thus reducing the amount of debt that will have to be paid off at maturity and lowering the risk of default on the debt.

Collateral Provisions

A debt security that has no pledge of specific property or assets as collateral for the debt is called a *debenture*. Although a debenture clearly will require a higher yield to maturity than an identical security secured by a specific asset, indenture provisions designed to protect the debtholder will reduce the relative risk associated with the debenture. Such indenture provisions might include restrictions on the amount of additional debentures the debtor can issue before paying off the original debentures; restrictions on the payment of cash dividends to equity owners of the debt issuer while the debentures are outstanding; and provisions that require the issuer to meet minimum liquidity (such as working capital) requirements while the debentures are outstanding. Despite the protection of such provisions, however, debentures generally are considered more risky than similar secured debt. Usually, the floor price for secured debt is the net liquidation value of the underlying collateral.

Income Tax Status

Interest earned on debt is subject to federal and state income taxation, with several exceptions. Interest earned on U.S. Treasury obligations and on many U.S. government agency obligations generally is exempt from income tax at the state level. Interest earned on most municipal obligations is exempt from federal income taxation and also may be exempt from state income taxation if the obligation originated in the state assessing the income tax. In addition, the purchaser must reside in the same state. As a result of this preferential tax status, debt securities not subject to some form of income taxation will require a lower yield to maturity than an identical security subject to income taxation. Conversely, a debt security subject to income taxation will require a higher yield to maturity than an identical security exempt from income taxation to compensate for the income tax liability associated with the interest on the debt security.

Zero Coupon Debt

An interesting form of debt security, known as a zero coupon debt security, allows the issuer to avoid paying cash to the debt holder for interest prior to the debt's maturity. The only cash payment from the debt issuer comes at maturity, when the debt's face value is repaid to the security holder. However, when the debt is originally issued, the debtor will receive proceeds substantially discounted from the debt's face amount. The difference between the amount of the proceeds the debtor receives at issue and the amount of debt the debtor repays at the maturity date is the investor's compensation in lieu of interest. The yield to maturity is simply the compound rate of return that equates the present value with the face value.

Because there are no annual interest payments and the holder is subject to tax on the amortization of the original issue discount, the taxable holder has negative cash flow. Therefore, zero coupon bonds sell at higher yields to maturity than bonds paying cash interest.

Convertible Debt

Corporations periodically issue bonds with conversion privileges, known as convertible bonds. These conversion privileges give the holder the right to convert the bond into a given number of shares of the issuing corporation's common stock at some future point. The bondholder has no obligation to convert the bond to stock if the conversion is not to the holder's advantage. The terms of the conversion privilege are usually set such that at the time the convertible debt is issued, there is no economic benefit in immediately converting the debt to stock. For example, if a $1,000-par-value convertible bond is issued for $1,000 and is convertible into 20 shares of the issuer's common stock that pays no dividend, there will be no economic benefit in converting the debt to stock as long as the common stock is selling for less than $50 per share.

A convertible bond is unique in that its value depends, to a certain extent, on the value of the common stock into which it can be converted. The convertible bond has a minimum value equal to its value as straight debt with no conversion privilege. However, as the value of the common stock into which the bond is convertible rises, the bond's value also will begin to depend on the common stock's value. Finally, as the common stock price continues to rise, there will be a point at which the incremental increase in the bond's value is nearly equal to the increase in the aggregate value of the number of common shares into which the bond can be converted. Once this relationship begins, the bond value has entered what is known as the *equity-equivalent region*. Continuing with the above example, if the bond value is indeed in the equity-equivalent region, as the value of a single share of common stock increases $1, the bond's value will increase $20 ($1 increase × 20 common shares per bond).

The valuation of closely held convertible debt securities presents a problem not associated with publicly traded convertible debt securities. Closely held debt securities are usually convertible into closely held stock with no readily determinable market price. Although it is theoretically correct to value closely held convertible debt by direct comparison with publicly traded convertible debt with comparable conversion privileges and other provisions, it is extremely difficult to find publicly traded convertible debt that meets these criteria. As a consequence, it is difficult to estimate the value of the closely held convertible debt by comparison with publicly traded convertible debt other than when determining the minimum value of the convertible debt as a straight, nonconvertible issue.

One reasonable alternative approach to this dilemma is to segregate the convertible debt security into two parts: a straight, nonconvertible debt security and a derivative security in the form of an option or warrant to purchase the common stock at a given price. The nonconvertible debt portion of the security would then be valued in the manner for valuing nonconvertible debt securities described above. The option portion of the security would be valued in a manner described in Chapter 25, "Valuing Stock Options." These two values would then be added together to estimate the value of the convertible debt security. This may result in a slight overvaluation of the convertible bond, however, because the warrant and the bond cannot be separated. There is no empirical basis to measure the difference and it is relatively minor.

Summary

Debt security valuations are required for a wide range of purposes. Some of the more common reasons include the possible purchase or sale of a debt security, an exchange of equity securities for debt securities, gift and estate taxes on debt securities, allocation of the enterprise value of a business entity among debt and other classes of securities, and the adjustment of the balance sheet for debt securities owned or owed.

The debt security valuation process includes an analysis of the debt security contract provisions to determine the amount and timing of payments associated with the security's ownership. Various contract provisions or characteristics that affect the amount, timing, and riskiness of payments include call provisions, sinking fund provisions, collateral provisions, income tax status, and whether the debt is a zero coupon issue or has conversion privileges.

The risk or uncertainty associated with the payments is further assessed through the use of guideline quantitative and qualitative analysis. This involves comparing the closely held debt security with a broad population of debt securities in order to estimate the general ratings classification into which the security would fall if it were publicly traded. Then the closely held debt security is compared with specific guideline publicly traded debt securities similar in debt rating and nature in order to estimate an appropriate yield to maturity to apply to the subject security. The present value of the debt security payments is estimated by discounting the future payments at the appropriate yield to maturity. The analyst should consider the marketability of the debt security and determine whether a discount for lack of marketability or an increase in the debt security's yield to maturity is appropriate. However, such discounts, if any, are minor compared with discounts for lack of marketability for common stocks.

Finally, if a convertible debt security is being valued, the valuation process is further complicated by the security's "optionlike" features.

Bibliography

Budgyk, Marko A. "Valuation of Fixed-Income Securities: Bonds and Preferred Stock" (Chapter 7). In *Financial Valuation: Businesses and Business Interests*, James H. Zukin, ed. New York: Warren, Gorham & Lamont, 1990.

Fabozzi, Frank J. *Advances in Fixed Income Valuation Modeling and Risk Management*. New Hope, PA: Frank J. Fabozzi Associates, 1997.

_____. *Bond Markets: Analysis and Strategies*, 4th ed. Paramus, NJ: Prentice Hall, 1999.

_____. *Fixed Income Mathematics: Analytical & Statistical Techniques*, 3rd ed. New York: McGraw-Hill, 1996.

_____. *Fixed Income Securities.* New Hope, PA: Frank J. Fabozzi Associates, 1997.

_____. *Handbook of Fixed-Income Securities*, 5th ed. New York: McGraw-Hill, 1997.

Julius, J. Michael. "The Skinny on Convertible Securities." *CPA Litigation Service Counselor*, October 1999, pp. 9–10.

Moore, M. Read, and D. Alan Hungate. "Valuation Discounts for Private Debt in Estate Administration." *Estate Planning*, June 1998, pp. 195–203.

Reilly, Frank K., and Keith C. Brown. "Part 4: Analysis and Management of Bonds" and "Part 6: Drivative Security Analysis." In *Investment Analysis and Portfolio Management*, 5th ed. Fort Worth, TX: The Dryden Press, 1997.

Wilson, Richard S., and Frank J. Fabozzi. *Corporate Bonds: Structures & Analysis.* New York: McGraw-Hill, 1996.

Chapter 24

Valuing Preferred Stock

There are two basic types of equity ownership of companies and both (common stock and preferred stock) are frequently used in closely held companies. The main characteristic of preferred stock is that the holder is contractionally promised a fixed dividend every period until its expiration. This dividend is typically required to be paid before any dividend can be paid to the common stockholders, hence the term *preferred*. The preferred distribution to a particular class of ownership also can exist in partnerships and limited liability companies.

In addition to the stated dividend, preferred stock can have many other characteristics that make it unique from the common stock. For example, preferred stock usually has a preference over common stock in the event that the corporation liquidates. Preferred stock need not have voting rights. Hence, preferred stock falls between debt and common stock in legal priority, privilege, and in the risk of ownership.

A good case can be made that preferred stock is really debt in disguise, a kind of equity bond. Unlike debt, however, preferred stock dividends cannot be deducted as interest expense when calculating the taxable income of the corporation. To the individual holder of preferred stock, the dividends received are taxable income. To the corporate owner, 70 percent of the dividends received are excluded from taxation.[1] It is no surprise to find that corporations hold most publicly traded preferred shares.

In this chapter, we consider the common situations that require the valuation of preferred stock, the special characteristics of closely held preferred stock, and the methods of valuing preferred stock.

Common Situations Requiring Valuation of Preferred Stock

There are many reasons for valuing preferred stock; these reasons are very similar to those for valuing debt securities, as discussed in Chapter 23. The most frequently encountered reasons are:

1. Purchase or sale of preferred stock for cash.
2. Exchange of common equity or debt for preferred stock, or vice versa.
3. Gift and estate taxes.
4. Allocating total enterprise value among classes of securities in a leveraged buyout, recapitalization, or bankruptcy reorganization.
5. Adjusting a balance sheet for preferred securities owned or outstanding.

Purchase or Sale for Cash

As is the case with debt securities, a company may have occasion to purchase or sell preferred stock for cash. If the preferred stock is existing stock, it is necessary to determine the cash-equivalent value. If it is to be newly issued, it will be necessary to structure the provisions so that the value will be equal to the price paid or received. Transactions that have reached a stalemate can often be successfully structured by taking advantage of the financial and legal flexibility available from preferred stock.

---

[1] According to Internal Revenue Code Section 243(a)(1). This 70 percent "dividends received deduction" applies as long as the corporation owns less than 20 percent of the distributing corporation. According to Section 243(c), the "dividends received deduction" is increased to 80 percent where the receiving corporation owns 20 percent or more of the distributing corporation. There is a 100% deduction if the company is in the same affiliated group.

Exchange of Common Equity or Debt for Preferred Stock

If preferred stock is to be exchanged for some consideration other than cash, such as common stock, debt securities, or other property, it usually is most expedient to determine the cash-equivalent values of both the preferred stock and the other consideration.

The most typical situation encountered is one in which a company, or some or all of its stock, is to be sold and a preferred stock received as all or part of the consideration. In this case, it is important that the seller know the cash-equivalent value of the consideration being received for the company or stock being sold.

Gift and Estate Taxes

Preferred stock may be gifted or may be an asset in an estate. In either situation, a determination of the preferred stock's fair market value is needed for tax purposes. It is not at all uncommon to find that the fair market value of a preferred stock is considerably less than its par value.

Allocating Total Enterprise Value among Classes of Securities

In many acquisitions, attracting capital requires creativity. For example, a leveraged buyout, by its very nature, results in the creation of new classes of securities, almost always including at least one class of debt. In addition, preferred stock may be issued in a transaction. Therefore, it is usually necessary not only to value the total enterprise but also to allocate the total value among the various classes of securities.

The issuance of preferred stocks as part of an acquisition is becoming increasingly popular, especially in situations involving ESOPs. Typically, the preferred stock is issued to the ESOP with other shareholders taking common stock. Issuing the preferred stock to the ESOP gives the ESOP a claim that is senior to the common shareholders' and at the same time allows a form of equity participation, thereby reducing the risk to the employees in a leveraged situation. One of the attractions of preferred stocks for ESOPs is the fact that, under the current tax law, dividends paid on preferred ESOP stock can be a tax-deductible expense to the corporation in most circumstances (see Chapter 32 on Employee Stock Ownership Plans).

Recapitalizations very often involve preferred stock, thereby requiring a valuation of the security. In recapitalizations involving preferred stock, a new class of preferred is issued, which the current owners of the business typically retain, while the common stock is passed along to other shareholders.

As noted in Chapter 23, bankruptcy reorganizations, by their nature, involve debt securities. Preferred stock often is issued along with the debt securities. As Chapter 23 notes, creative structuring of debt and preferred stock can be an essential tool in achieving a successful bankruptcy reorganization.

Adjusting a Balance Sheet for Preferred Stock Owned or Outstanding

The most common situation requiring a balance-sheet adjustment for preferred stock outstanding occurs when the analyst is using invested capital valuation methods to value common stock. In this situation, the market value of any preferred stock must be estimated as well as the market value of any debt outstanding. As discussed in Chapters 9 through 12, when the market value of debt and preferred stock is deducted from the value of the company's total invested capital, what remains is the value of the company's common equity.

Also, the company may own some preferred stock that may need valuing if the analyst is adjusting the various line items on the balance sheet to fair market value.

Special Characteristics of Closely Held Preferred Stocks

Preferred stock is often used to recognize that certain potential investors will have unique characteristics that call for special allocations of the proceeds of ownership. While the investor in preferred stock may be surrendering some of the "upside" potential that common shareholders have, the preferred stockholder will expect to be protected from some of the "downside" potential by demanding special characteristics and contingencies.

The special characteristics of the preferred stock that we typically[2] encounter include:

- Dividend rate.
- Liquidation preference.
- Cumulative versus noncumulative dividends.
- Redeemable (e.g., call options) versus nonredeemable rights (i.e., expected life).
- Put options.
- Voting versus nonvoting rights.
- Participating versus nonparticipating rights in any future earnings.
- Convertible versus nonconvertible rights into common equity.

The difficulties encountered in valuing closely held preferred stock result primarily from estimating the required yield rate given the stock's myriad characteristics. Because of the flexibility in characteristics, the ability to estimate the value of preferred stock of a closely held business depends on the analyst's experience and subjective judgment. The following discussion focuses on some of the most common special characteristics found in closely held preferred stock.

Dividend Rate

The dividend rate in and of itself is not special, but the type of dividend can be unique.

---

[2] In order to meet unique corporate governance situations, more complex preferred stock issues are often used, as in ESOP transactions. Beyond standard convertible preferred securities, complex ESOP securities include floor put convertible preferred stock, high yield convertible preferred stock, super common stock, tracking stock, and performance stock. See Chester A. Gougis, "Use of Alternative Equity Securities in the Capital Structure of ESOP Companes" (Chapter 12) in *The Handbook of Advanced Business Valuation*, Robert F. Reilly and Robert P. Schweihs, eds. (New York: McGraw-Hill, 2000).

Fixed Dividend Rate. The most common form of dividend is one that is fixed at an amount usually stated as a percentage of the preferred stock's par value. For example, a $100-par-value, 10 percent preferred stock would pay an annual dividend of $10 per share. The value attributable to the stated dividend rate of the preferred stock depends on the issuing company's current and expected ability to pay the stated dividend rate and the current market yields of preferred stocks with similar dividend payment risk.

Adjustable Dividend Rate. A somewhat less common form of dividend is an adjustable-rate dividend. This form of dividend typically is adjustable within a stated range and is pegged to the general level of interest rates. However, the adjustable rate can be pegged to just about anything. The dividend rate could be adjustable based on a given time period—for example, 10 percent from 1997 to 2000, 11 percent from 2000 to 2003, and so forth. There are situations in which the dividend rate is adjusted based on the corporation's profits (in effect, a specialized form of participating preferred stock). In this case, the dividend might have equaled some percentage of the average of the corporation's last three fiscal years' earnings or some other measure of profits.

In order to estimate the appropriate yield, or discount rate, to apply to the subject company's adjustable-rate preferred stock, publicly traded adjustable-rate preferred stocks may be used as a benchmark, although the number of these in the public market has dwindled in recent years. The analyst must be careful to note the differences between the basis for the adjustability of the subject company's preferred stock dividend and that of the publicly traded guideline company's preferred stock dividends. The adjustability differences in the subject preferred stock compared to its publicly traded adjustable counterparts will require either an increase or a decrease in the adjustable dividend yield evidenced in the market. Just as the case with a "straight" or fixed-dividend preferred stock, the subject company's ability to pay the adjustable dividend and its liquidation preference must also be analyzed, making appropriate adjustments to the publicly traded adjustable dividend yields as necessary.

In general, all other things being equal, adjustable-rate preferred stocks require a lower dividend yield, thereby increasing the preferred stock's value. As presented in Exhibit 24–1, in November 1999, market evidence indicated that adjustable-rate preferred stocks generally required yields in the range of 230 to 300 basis points[3] below the yields required on similar fixed-rate preferred stocks. However, at any given time, the reduction in required yield will depend on the level of interest rates prevailing in the market at the valuation date and the stated range of the adjustable dividend rate of the subject company's closely held preferred stock. For example, if market interest rates are at historically high levels at the valuation date, the likelihood of their going much higher is smaller. In this situation, the potential for a higher dividend rate in the future is diminished, thereby reducing the necessary adjustment to the yield. If the adjustable-rate range (or *collar*) on the closely held preferred stock is very small, there is less potential for an increase in the dividend, thereby reducing the required yield adjustment relative to an issue with a wider adjustable-dividend-rate range.

Liquidation Preference

Another important characteristic of a preferred stock is its liquidation preference and the subject company's ability to pay it in full at liquidation. In almost all cases, preferred

---

[3] 100 basis points = 1 percentage point.

Exhibit 24–1

Preferred Stock Yield Comparison

S&P Rating	Average Yield as of November 1999				
	Adjustable %	Number of Observations	Fixed rate %	Number of Observations	Yield Differential in Basis Points
BBB-	6.5	1	8.8	15	230
NR	7.1	4	10.1	31	297

SOURCE: *Standard & Poor's Corporation Records*, *Standard & Poor's Stock Guide*, and WMA calculations.

stock carries a contractual right to preference (advantage) in the distribution of the issuing corporation's assets upon liquidation. The preferred stock's liquidation preference usually is stated as a certain dollar amount per share, such as $100 per share.

Revenue Ruling 83-120 requires that the issuing corporation's ability to pay the full liquidation preference at liquidation be taken into account in estimating the preferred stock's fair market value. According to the ruling, this risk can be measured by the protection afforded by the corporation's net assets. The ruling sets out the method of measuring this protection as follows:

Formula 24–1

$$\text{Liquidation coverage} = \frac{\text{Market value of assets} - \text{Market value of liabilities}}{\text{Aggregate liquidation preference of preferred stock}}$$

This ratio should be high enough that any unforeseen business downturns would not jeopardize the issuing corporation's ability to pay the liquidation preference. This ratio should be compared with ratios of publicly traded preferred stocks. All other things being equal, if the subject company's preferred stock liquidation coverage ratio is higher than the publicly traded preferred stock ratios, a lower yield (or, conversely, a higher value) will be required on the subject company preferred stock due to the lower risk of nonpayment of the liquidation preference upon liquidation. However, it should be noted that since most investors look at investments in preferred stock on a going-concern basis, the liquidation coverage ratio generally is a less important factor in the valuation than the dividend coverage ratio.

It should be noted that it is extremely difficult, if not impossible, to obtain adequate data about the guideline publicly traded preferred stocks to compute the market value of assets called for in the above liquidation coverage ratio. Therefore, as a practical matter, analysts will often use the book value of the issuing corporation's assets and liabilities in calculating the liquidation coverage ratios.

Cumulative versus Noncumulative Dividends

The term *cumulative*, when applied to preferred stock dividends, means that if the dividends are not paid for one or more periods, the corporation has a contractual obligation to make up the lapsed payments before declaring and paying any dividends on the common stock or on other junior issues. Furthermore, many cumulative issues also give preferred stockholders voting rights and/or the right to elect one or more members to the board of directors following the nonpayment of one or more dividends.

Cumulative dividends imply that the risk of nonpayment of dividends becomes secondary, because the cumulative feature requires that the shareholder not suffer a loss in income in the long run unless the company is never able to pay. In addition, when dividends are cumulative, liquidation coverage tends to become more important than dividend coverage, because in the event of liquidation, cumulative dividends in arrears must be paid in addition to the stated liquidation preference before making any assets available for distribution to common shareholders.

However, cumulative dividends on convertible preferred stock may be illusory, as the cumulated dividends are normally lost when the preferred is converted. Many venture deals offer cumulative convertible preferred stock where investors know in advance that they will never get the dividends except as a preference in liquidation.

Noncumulative preferred stocks are rare in the public market, and those few that do exist typically have special characteristics, making them unlikely to be useful as comparative securities. In general, all other things being equal, the value of a noncumulative preferred stock would be significantly less than an otherwise comparable cumulative preferred stock, because dividends not paid on a noncumulative issue are lost permanently. Revenue Ruling 83-120 addresses the cumulative-versus-noncumulative feature as follows:

> The absence of a provision that preferred dividends are cumulative raises substantial questions concerning whether the stated dividend rate will, in fact, be paid. Accordingly, preferred stock with noncumulative dividend features will normally have a value substantially lower than a cumulative preferred stock with the same yield, liquidation preference and dividend coverage.[4]

According to Graham, Dodd, and Cottle:

> One of the chief objections to the noncumulative provision is that it permits the directors to withhold dividends even in good years, when they are amply earned, the money thus saved inuring to the benefit of the common stockholders. Experience shows that noncumulative dividends are seldom paid unless they are necessitated by the desire to declare dividends on the common; and if the common dividend is later discontinued, the preferred dividend is almost invariably suspended soon afterward.[5]

However, the analyst also must look at the subject company's history of dividend payments on noncumulative preferred stock and evidence of the company's intention to pay or not to pay preferred stock dividends. If the company has a solid history of paying dividends on its noncumulative preferred stock and a stated intention to do so in the future, and the company has the financial capability to pay dividends in the future, the diminution in value resulting from the noncumulative feature will be minimal. In addition, if the holder of a noncumulative preferred stock has full voting control of the corporation, the noncumulative feature becomes moot, since the shareholder controls the votes to pay or withhold dividends. With all these factors to consider, the impact of the noncumulative feature on value requires a considerable amount of experienced subjective judgment.

---

[4] Rev. Rul. 83-120, 1983-2 C.B. 170.

[5] Benjamin Graham, David L. Dodd, and Sidney Cottle, *Security Analysis—Principles and Technique* (New York: McGraw-Hill, 1962), p. 391.

Redeemable versus Nonredeemable

Most privately held preferred stock is nonredeemable—that is, the issue has an infinite life. However, in many instances, a preferred stock has a contractual redemption provision. The type of redemption provision can vary significantly. The most common forms of redemption provisions found in privately held companies are as follows:

1. The entire issue is redeemable at the option of the issuing corporation at a specified price (typically par value) over a designated time period. These types of issues are commonly referred to as *callable*.
2. The entire issue is redeemable at the option of the issuing corporation at a specified price contingent upon a certain event, such as the death of a major shareholder, a change in ownership control, or issuance of other securities.
3. Future redemption by the issuing company is mandatory and based on a specific redemption schedule. These types of issues have sinking fund provisions similar to the vehicle by which bonds are retired at intervals up to their maturity dates and are referred to as *sinking fund preferreds*.

The impact on value of the redemption privilege varies depending on the specific redemption provisions. Therefore, it is extremely important that the analyst be aware of all the contractual provisions and contingencies of the redemption.

In general, the most important factors of the redemption provisions that affect value are:

1. Call (or redemption) price.
2. Length of time the issuing company is *not* permitted to call the preferred.
3. Likelihood that the contingent event triggering redemption will occur.
4. Redemption schedule.
5. Whether or not a sinking fund or some other means of financing the redemption is established.
6. Issuing company's financial ability to cash out the preferred shares without some sort of redemption financing fund.

For a preferred issue that is redeemable at the issuing corporation's option at a specified price, the most important provisions affecting value are the call price and the length of time the issuing company is not permitted to call the preferred stock (the call protection period). All other things being equal, the shorter the call protection period, the lower the preferred stock's value. This is because redemption of the entire issue of preferred stock eliminates the shareholder's right to a future stream of income and forces the shareholder to accept a price (equal to the call price) for the stock that may be substantially lower than the fair market value the preferred stock might have in the absence of the redemption feature. A lower redemption, or call, price also reduces value to the shareholder, both by increasing probability that the preferred will be called (assuming that redemption is not contingent upon some future event) and by reducing the proceeds to shareholders upon redemption.

Fortunately, the public market for preferred stocks makes the task of estimating the appropriate yield rate to apply to a callable preferred stock, such as that described above, relatively straightforward. To value this type of issue, the analyst uses the same procedure discussed in the section "Method of Valuation" with one important distinction: The guideline publicly traded preferred stocks will be callable preferred stocks with similar call protection periods. As discussed in that section, the analyst chooses the appropriate yield based on a comparison of the dividend and liquidation payment risk of the subject preferred and the publicly traded callable preferred stock. An additional risk factor to consider in valuing callable preferred stock is the subject company's ability to fund redemptions.

When the preferred stock is redeemable contingent upon a future event, it is extremely difficult to ascertain the impact on value. This stems from the fact that the analyst is forced to make an educated guess as to the likelihood that the event triggering redemption will or will not occur. In addition, "contingent" redemption privileges are extremely rare, if not nonexistent, in the public market. Because the redemption of this type of issue is contingent upon some certain event, the importance of the likelihood of its occurring may outweigh the importance of the issuing corporation's financial ability to redeem the preferred shares should the contingent event occur when determining the appropriate yield to apply to the stock's future income stream.

One way to approach the valuation of a "contingently" redeemable preferred stock is to estimate the appropriate yield to apply to the future income stream absent the contingent redemption privilege and then adjust the yield based on an analysis of the likelihood of the contingent event occurring. Alternatively, the matter of the contingency can be handled as a separate adjustment. It should be noted that if the redemption is contingent upon the death of a major stockholder, the ability to use life insurance proceeds to redeem the preferred stock and the adequacy of those proceeds, or other evidence of the company's ability to pay, are important factors to consider in determining the appropriate yield adjustment.

Sinking fund preferred stocks differ from the types of redeemable preferred stocks discussed above in that it is known with certainty that the preferred stock will be redeemed at a specified price over a given time period. Both the redemption price and the redemption schedule are specified in the preferred stock contract. Sinking fund preferred stocks provide two advantages to their holders that are worth noting. First, the continuous reduction in the issue's size increases the likelihood that dividends will be paid. Second, the specified redemption guarantees a market, albeit limited, for the preferred stock.

The primary impact on the value of a sinking fund preferred stock results from the fact that redemption creates a finite stream of income to the investor plus a terminal value versus an infinite stream of income available to the nonsinking fund preferred stockholder. This can be illustrated with a simplified example. Assume that issue A is $100-par-value, nonredeemable, fixed-rate, voting, cumulative preferred stock that requires a market-derived yield of 10 percent. Issue A's fixed dividend rate is 7 percent, or $7 per share. The value of issue A before consideration of lack of marketability is calculated as follows:

Formula 24–2

$$\text{Value} = \frac{\text{Dividend}}{\text{Required yield}} = \frac{\$7.00}{0.10} = \$70 \text{ per share}$$

Now assume that issue B is identical to issue A in all respects except that it is a sinking fund preferred stock that is redeemable at par value beginning in Year 5, with 10 percent of the entire issue redeemable each year. There are 100 shares of issue B outstanding. In order to determine the appropriate required yield for issue B, the procedure outlined in the "Method of Valuation" section is followed using guideline publicly traded, redeemable, fixed-rate, voting, cumulative, sinking fund preferred stock *with similar redemption schedules*. It is important to note that the appropriate yield measure for sinking fund preferred stock is yield to maturity (YTM) as opposed to the stated yield implied by the dividend rate alone.

For simplicity, we will assume that the appropriate yield to maturity given an analysis of issue B's dividend and liquidation payment risk is 10 percent. The value of issue B before consideration of lack of marketability, if applicable, is calculated as shown in Exhibit 24–2. In these examples, the value of issue B (the sinking fund preferred) is greater than the value of issue A (nonsinking fund preferred) because issue B is redeemed at par value, which, because the required yield is higher than the stated yield, is higher than its value absent the sinking fund provision. Therefore, a portion of issue B's return is derived from capital gains from the time of purchase to the time of redemption. If the stated yield and required yield in both issue A and issue B were equal, their values would be equal to par in both instances.

Put Option

A common characteristic of closely held preferred stock is a *put* option on the preferred shareholder's behalf. This option allows the shareholder to require the issuing corporation to buy back the stock at some fixed price, usually par value. When a preferred stock can be put back to the company at par value, its value usually is, at a minimum, its par value assuming the company has the financial ability to honor the put. This is true because if the preferred stock's value is determined to be less than par value based on the stock's other characteristics, the holder always has the right to put the stock back to the company at par value.

Voting versus Nonvoting

In general, voting rights increase the value of preferred stock, for obvious reasons. Numerous studies of publicly traded preferred stocks have been conducted in an attempt to isolate the reduction in yield (and thus increase in value) investors accord to voting preferred stock. Unfortunately, these studies have yet to produce any meaningful results. Significant patterns of yield differentials due to voting versus nonvoting preferred stocks in the public market have not been developed on any consistent basis. Generally, this is because voting rights in publicly traded preferred stocks are incidental relative to the total outstanding voting power. Therefore, they have no significant impact on yield.

Lacking any concrete public market evidence, it is thus necessary for the analyst to subjectively adjust the required yield downward in valuing voting preferred stock. Industry practice dictates a discount in yield for voting stock ranging from 5 percent to 10 percent of the yield otherwise indicated.

In closely held companies, it is common for the preferred stock as a class to have voting control of the corporation. If the voting preferred stock being valued represents a controlling interest, the value increases considerably more (or the yield decreases even more). Perhaps the easiest way to approach the valuation of preferred stock in this situation is to value the stock absent the control feature and then add a premium for control.

Exhibit 24–2

Value of Sinking Fund Preferred

Year End	Income Stream			Present Value Factor @10.0% YTM	Value
	Dividends	Redemption	Total		
1	$700	$0	$700	0.909	$636.30
2	700	0	700	0.826	578.20
3	700	0	700	0.751	525.70
4	700	0	700	0.683	478.10
5	700	1,000	1,700	0.621	1,055.70
6	630	1,000	1,630	0.564	919.32
7	560	1,000	1,560	0.513	800.28
8	490	1,000	1,490	0.467	695.83
9	420	1,000	1,420	0.424	602.08
10	350	1,000	1,350	0.386	521.10
11	280	1,000	1,280	0.350	448.00
12	210	1,000	1,210	0.319	385.99
13	140	1,000	1,140	0.290	330.60
14	70	1,000	1,070	0.263	281.41
					8,258.61
				Shares outstanding	÷ 100
				Value per share	$82.59

YTM = Yield to maturity

Participating versus Nonparticipating

A participating preferred stock gives the preferred stockholder the right to share in additional earnings beyond the amount described in the preferred stock contract (beyond the stated dividend rate). On the other hand, a nonparticipating preferred stockholder can receive dividends only in the amount specified in the contract. A fully participating preferred stock allows the stockholder to share with the common stockholder in any earnings disbursements after the common stockholders have received a certain specified annual payment. The incremental amount to the preferred shareholders in such a case normally is equal to that paid to the common stockholders.

Another form of participating preferred stock, which is something less than fully participating, allows the preferred stockholder to share earnings disbursements with the common stockholder up to a certain dividend rate, and after this dividend has been paid in any one year, the right of the preferred stock to participate in the earnings ceases. The degree of participation allowed in any preferred stock can vary significantly from one issue to another, limited only by the creativity of financial advisers, legal counsel, and controlling stockholders' imaginations in designing the features of the issue. This is especially true of privately held participating preferred stock. Therefore, it is critical that the analyst review the preferred stock provisions to determine the level of participation.

The value of the participating feature in a preferred stock is derived from the stockholder's right to *potentially* higher dividends and depends on the likelihood that these potentially higher dividends will in fact be paid. Thus, the increment to value attributable to the participating feature is higher the greater the likelihood that dividends exceeding the stated dividend rate will be paid and the greater the participation (the higher the potential dividend).

When valuing a participating preferred stock, the analyst will need to analyze projected income statements, if available, and look at the common stock dividend payment history in order to estimate a level of future dividends to capitalize that can reasonably be expected given the preferred stock's contractual participation features.

A variation of a participating stock is a hybrid cumulative preferred stock. For example a company might issue a preferred stock that has a stated cumulative dividend and also participates in common stock dividends. Theoretically, one might logically approach a valuation of this type of preferred stock by valuing the fixed dividend and participating dividends separately and then adding these values together to get the preferred's total value. This approach requires that the required yield to be applied to the participating dividends be higher than the yield applied to the cumulative fixed dividends, because the risk of nonpayment of the participating dividends is much higher. Whether or not the preferred shareholder will receive additional dividends as a result of the participating feature depends upon whether or not dividends are declared on the common. The analyst must look at the subject company's history of paying dividends on common stock and assess the likelihood that its payment history will continue in order to assess the additional risk inherent in the preferred shareholder's receipt of participating dividends. In addition, the analyst should not view the appropriate required yield on the participating dividend portion of the preferred stock in isolation from the fact that the stock does, in fact, carry a stated cumulative dividend right. This fact, combined with the participation, reduces the overall risk of the participating portion of the issue compared with an issue that has only participating dividend rights. Thus, determining the appropriate required yield for the participating dividend requires a great deal of experienced subjective judgment.

Given these factors, perhaps a more appropriate approach to the valuation of such a hybrid preferred stock is to value both the cumulative stated dividends and the participating dividends together, adjusting the required yield to compensate for the added risk of nonpayment of the participating dividends. This process somewhat lessens the subjectivity required in estimating the appropriate required yield. Using this approach, the analyst can estimate the appropriate required yield to apply to the issue assuming that it lacked the participation feature by using public market evidence. Then the required yield is adjusted to reflect the added dividend payment risk attributable to the participating feature. If the valuation is approached by separating the cumulative stated dividend and the participating dividend, the analyst will be forced to determine the required yield on the participating dividend portion with no empirical market evidence base from which to start.

Convertible versus Nonconvertible

Convertible preferred stock is similar to a convertible bond in that it is a combination of a preferred stock issue and an option on a common equity issue. The conversion feature gives the preferred stock a speculative quality in addition to its investment value as a fixed-income security, which is derived through future dividend payments. Because of the speculative quality that the equity conversion feature imparts to the preferred stock, the stock's value depends not only on its conversion rights and expected future income stream, but on the value of the common stock as well.

Method of Valuation

Simply stated, the value of a preferred stock lacking any common equity kicker, such as convertibility or other special features, is equal to the present value of its future income stream discounted at its required rate of return, or yield. The higher the risk inherent in the investment, the higher the required yield.

Assessing Dividend and Liquidation Payment Risk

The single most important factor in the value of most preferred stock is the stock's dividend rate. Another factor would be redemption in the case of a preferred stock that has a prospect of being redeemed. In most instances, the primary source of value to the preferred stockholder is the right to future levels of income through the receipt of dividends. Therefore, in estimating the appropriate required yield for the subject company preferred, the risk that the dividends on the preferred stock will not be paid is critical.

The most prevalent measure for assessing the likelihood of receiving future preferred dividends is the company's fixed-charge coverage ratio, commonly defined as the sum of pretax income plus interest expense divided by the sum of interest expense plus preferred dividends adjusted for taxes. The higher this ratio, the greater the subject company's capacity to pay its preferred dividends (or, conversely, the lower the risk that the company will miss dividend payments) and, therefore, the lower the required yield. Rating agencies use the fixed-charge coverage ratio as part of the analysis conducted to determine the appropriate rating to assign a particular preferred stock issue. Moreover, Revenue Ruling 83-120 (to be discussed later) specifically requires analysis of the fixed-charge coverage ratio for preferred stock valuations involving federal gift, estate, or income taxes.

Other ratios than the fixed-charge coverage ratio are used to assess the subject company's dividend payment risk. One example is the return on total capital, defined as the sum of pretax income plus interest expense divided by the sum of long-term debt and shareholders' preferred and common equity. Several variations of this ratio also can be used, such as pretax cash flow, return on total capital, or pretax earnings before interest and depreciation charges return on total capital. A higher ratio indicates superior profitability and, thus, a greater ability to meet preferred dividend obligations.

Another often-calculated ratio is the liquidation coverage ratio, defined as the sum of the market value of total assets less the market value of total liabilities divided by the aggregate liquidation value of the preferred stock. This ratio helps the analyst identify the risk that the preferred shareholder will not receive the full liquidation payment in the event of the corporation's liquidation. Analysis of this ratio also is specifically required in Revenue Ruling 83-120. A higher ratio implies greater protection of the shareholder's investment in the event of liquidation of company assets.

The problem with the above ratios is that they address the subject company's dividend payment risk only as of a certain point in time. Because many companies exhibit cyclical earnings fluctuations, recent operating results may not accurately reflect a company's long-term dividend payment risk. A company subject to large swings in profits is more likely to suspend preferred dividends in down years, even though its average earnings may far exceed the annual preferred stock dividend requirements. Depending on the situation, the analyst may want to compute the above ratios using historical average financial statement figures.

The subject company's capitalization ratio is another measure of long-term dividend payment risk. The capitalization ratio is defined as the sum of long-term debt and the aggregate liquidation value of preferred stock divided by the sum of the long-term debt and total equity. This ratio measures the company's leverage and indicates how vulnerable the company will be in cyclical downturns. The higher the capitalization ratio, the greater the company's vulnerability to cyclical downturns; therefore, the risk of losing out on preferred dividend payments over the long term is higher.

The methods of calculating these ratios are shown in Exhibit 24–3. If the analyst is valuing a preferred stock that has not yet been issued, a situation that often occurs in recapitalizations, the subject company ratios must be calculated on a pro forma basis, assuming that the subject preferred issue is outstanding.

Comparison with Publicly Traded Preferred Stocks

None of the ratios discussed above indicate, in and of themselves, the appropriate required yield to apply to the subject preferred stock's income stream. In order to estimate the appropriate required yield, and thus the value of the preferred stock, the ratios determined for the subject company must be compared with similarly calculated ratios for a group of publicly traded preferred stocks having the *same rights and privileges as the subject company*. Once these ratios are calculated, the comparable publicly traded preferred stocks must be grouped by rating category.

Quantitative Comparison. Both Moody's and Standard & Poor's rate publicly traded preferred stock issues. Exhibit 24–4 shows Standard & Poor's ratings and its explanation of the nature of the risk of the preferred stocks contained in each category. Exhibit 24–5 shows the yields of nonconvertible publicly traded preferred stocks as they existed at the end of 1999. As can be seen from Exhibit 24–5, there were 134 nonconvertible fixed-dividend-rate preferred stocks issued by 120 different companies listed in the November 1999 *Standard & Poor's Stock Guide*.

It is extremely important that the guideline publicly traded preferred stocks used to estimate appropriate yields for the subject stock be as similar as possible to the subject stock in rights, privileges, and all relevant characteristics. Differences among these factors can have a significant impact on the required yield. In addition, the analyst will probably want to exclude preferred stocks issued by utilities, banks, insurance companies, and other financial institutions when selecting guideline publicly traded preferred stocks (unless the preferred stock to be valued is issued by a utility, bank, or insurance company). The criteria the rating agencies use differ somewhat for these types of issues due to their unique financial statement presentation and the fact that they are regulated. Because preferred stock ratings affect the investor's perception of risk, they also impact the required yield.

Once the ratios are calculated for both the subject company and the guideline publicly traded companies and the publicly traded issues are categorized by rating, the yields of each issue must be calculated and averaged for each rating category. The ratios for each issue also need to be averaged in each rating category.

Exhibit 24-3

Preferred Stock Dividend and Liquidation Payment Risk Ratios

$$\text{Fixed charge coverage} = \frac{EBIT}{1 + (\text{Preferred dividends}) \div (1-t)}$$

$$\text{Liquidation coverage} = \frac{(\text{Market value of assets} - \text{Market value of liabilities})^{a}}{\text{Aggregate liquidation value of preferred stock}}$$

$$\text{Capitalization ratio} = \frac{\text{Total debt} + \text{Liquidation value of all preferred stock}}{\text{Total debt} + \text{Total equity}}$$

$$\text{Pretax return on total capital} = \frac{\text{Pretax income} + \text{Interest expense}}{\text{Long - term debt} + \text{Total equity}}$$

a. From a practical standpoint, total book value of equity is often used.

NOTE: All net income and cash flow figures are before preferred stock dividends, discontinued operations, nonrecurring items, and extraordinary items.

EBIT = Earnings before interest expense and taxes
t = Effective tax rate

Exhibit 24-6 shows an example of the end result of this process. Generally, the more favorable the ratios, the higher the rating and the lower the yield. In addition, once financial institutions and utilities are excluded, the number of guideline preferred stocks drops significantly. In most circumstances, it is not necessary to compute dividend yields and ratios for each rating category. This is because once the dividend and liquidation payment risk ratios for the subject company have been calculated, it often becomes clear to the analyst into which rating category the subject preferred generally would fit.

Once all the necessary guideline data are available, the next step is to determine the rating category into which the subject preferred stock would fall given the subject company's dividend and liquidation payment risk. The appropriate yield is selected for the subject company based on the yields in the appropriate rating category.

Qualitative Factors. At this point, the analyst must consider any unique qualitative factors that might cause the required yield to be higher or lower than that based solely on the quantitative ratio analysis. These include many of the nonquantitative factors generally considered in valuing common stock that would increase or decrease the issuing company's risk. However, when assessing risk, the preferred shareholder will be most concerned with qualitative factors that may change the company's ability to meet its preferred stock obligations. These qualitative factors might include the following:

1. The competitive environment in the industry.
2. Depth and competence of management.
3. Proposed federal regulation of the business.

Exhibit 24–4

Standard & Poor's Preferred Stock Rating Definitions

"AAA" This is the highest rating that may be assigned by Standard & Poor's to a preferred stock issue and indicates an extremely strong capacity to pay the preferred stock obligations.

"AA" A preferred stock issue rated "AA" also qualifies as a high-quality, fixed income security. The capacity to pay preferred stock obligations is very strong, although not as overwhelming as for issues rated "AAA."

"A" An issue rated "A" is backed by a sound capacity to pay the preferred stock obligations, although it is somewhat more susceptible to the adverse effects of changes in circumstances and economic conditions.

"BBB" An issue rated "BBB" is regarded as backed by an adequate capacity to pay the preferred stock obligations. Whereas it normally exhibits adequate protection parameters, adverse economic conditions or changing circumstances are more likely to lead to a weakened capacity to make payments for a preferred stock in this category than for issues in the "A" category.

"BB", "B", "CCC" Preferred stock rated "BB", "B", and "CCC" are regarded, on balance, as predominantly speculative with respect to the issuer's capacity to pay preferred stock obligations. "BB" indicates the lowest degree of speculation and "CCC" the highest degree of speculation. While such issues will likely have some quality and protective characteristics, these are outweighed by large uncertainties or major risk exposures to adverse conditions.

"CC" The rating "CC" is reserved for a preferred stock issue in arrears on dividends or sinking fund payments but that is currently paying.

"C" A preferred stock rated "C" is a non-paying issue.

"D" A preferred stock rated "D" is a non-paying issue with the issuer in default on debt instruments.

"r" The "r" is attached to highlight derivative, hybrid, and certain other obligations that S&P believes may experience high volatility or high variability in expected returns due to non-credit risks. Examples of such obligations are: securities whose principal or interest return is indexed to equities, commodities, or currencies; certain swaps and options; and interest only and principal only mortgage securities.

The absence of an "r" symbol should not be taken as an indication that an obligation will exhibit no volatility or variability in total return.

NR This indicates that no rating has been requested, that there is insufficient information on which to base a rating, or that S&P does not rate a particular type of obligation as a matter of policy.

Plus (+) or Minus (–) To provide more detailed indications of preferred stock quality, the ratings from "AA" to "CCC" may be modified by the addition of a plus or minus sign to show relative standing within the major rating categories.

SOURCE: *Standard & Poor's Stock Guide*, October 1999 (New York: Standard & Poor's Corporation, 1999), p. 4.

Exhibit 24–5

Nonconvertible Preferred Stock Yields

S&P Rating	Number of Companies	Number of Issues	Dividend Yield Range		Dividend Yield	
			Low %	High %	Mean %	Median %
AA-	1	1	8.5	8.5	8.5	8.5
A+	2	2	7.9	8.4	8.2	8.2
A	8	11	6.2	9.5	8.3	8.3
A-	12	13	5.6	8.9	7.8	8.0
BBB+	17	19	6.6	9.5	8.4	8.4
BBB	9	9	8.1	11.2	9.1	8.6
BBB-	12	16	6.1	10.1	8.7	8.6
BB+	16	18	0.6	10.7	8.8	9.2
BB	6	6	8.6	9.5	9.2	9.4
B+	1	2	9.6	10.5	10.1	10.1
B	2	2	13.4	14.6	14.0	14.0
NR	34	35	0.8	18.7	9.7	9.4

SOURCE: *Standard & Poor's Corporation Records, Standard & Poor's Stock Guide,* and WMA calculations.

Exhibit 24–6

Nonconvertible, Nonsinking Fund, Fixed Rate Cumulative Preferred Stocks Excluding Financial Institutions and Utilities

S&P Rating	Number of Issues	Yield Range		Average			
		Low %	High %	Yield %	Interest Coverage	Total Debt/ Equity	Return on Equity
A	2	6.2	7.6	6.9	6.0	3.2	22.5
A-	2	5.8	7.1	6.5	12.4	1.0	29.0
BBB+	4	6.6	8.4	7.6	3.0	0.9	4.4
BBB	3	8.4	8.6	8.5	2.3	1.0	5.8
BBB-	2	9.5	9.8	9.7	-2.1	0.8	-2.6
BB+	8	7.9	9.9	9.1	1.9	0.9	4.2
BB	1	9.5	9.5	9.5	0.1	1.3	-7.6
B+	1	9.6	9.6	9.6	4.9	0.9	25.4
NR	1	7.1	7.1	7.1	NM	0.0	1.1

NM = Not meaningful

SOURCE: *Standard & Poor's Corporation Records*, *Standard & Poor's Stock Guide*, and WMA calculations.

4. Rights of lenders and other stockholders to influence dividend policy.
5. Trends in and diversification of supply sources.
6. Trends in and diversification of revenue sources.[6]

Standard & Poor's performs an extensive analysis of a company's qualitative factors in determining a security's appropriate rating. In addition, the outlook for the industry and economy also play an important role in assessing the subject company's preferred stock income stream risk.

Capitalizing the Income Stream

Once the appropriate required yield is estimated, the next step is to capitalize the preferred stock's future income stream by its required yield. Mechanically, this is a simple present value calculation. For a noncallable, nonsinking-fund preferred stock with no maturity and lacking a conversion feature, the formula for determining the value is as follows:

Formula 24–3

$$\text{Present value} = \frac{\text{Dividend}}{\text{Required yield}}$$

If the issue is nonconvertible and callable or subject to a sinking fund, its value is calculated as follows:

Formula 24–4

$$\text{Present value} = \sum_{i=1}^{n} \frac{E_i}{\left(1 + k_p\right)^i}$$

---

[6] Gerald R. Martin and E. Halsey Sandford, "Valuation of Preferred Stock," *Business Valuation Review*, March 1991, p. 35.

where:

E_i = Cash flow (including redemption price and dividends) in the ith period in the future

i = Period when cash flows are generated

k_p = Required yield at which preferred stock cash flows are to be discounted back to the present

n = Number of periods until redemption

It is important to note that even if a preferred stock is callable at the company's option, it usually is appropriate to value the issue as if it were noncallable if the stated dividend rate is below the rate currently required by the market for comparable issues. For example, if a $100-par-value preferred stock, callable at $100 per share and with a stated dividend of 6 percent, requires a yield of 10 percent under current market conditions, the call feature has little or no effect as a practical matter. If the required yield is above the stated yield, the company will not exercise its option to call the issue, which renders the call feature irrelevant for the preferred stockholder.

Marketability Aspects of Closely Held Preferred Stock

Chapter 17, Lack of Marketability Discounts, presented a great deal of evidence in support of a discount for lack of marketability on common stock of closely held businesses. On the surface, it appears that such a discount might also be appropriate for closely held preferred stocks. However, such a discount for preferred stocks, if required, would be different from such a discount for common stocks. Unlike investment returns on closely held common stock, which are predominantly generated by appreciation in the common stock's price and contingent upon the ability to sell the stock to realize the price appreciation, investment returns on most preferred stocks, as on debt securities, are predominantly generated by cash flows in the form of dividend payments over the life of the security. These cash flows are anticipated to be received by the holder of the preferred stock regardless of how marketable the preferred stock happens to be. Therefore, the discount associated with the lack of marketability of a preferred stock is different from that associated with closely held common stock.

If the analyst thinks that marketability is a valid consideration in the valuation of a particular closely held preferred stock, the adjustment can be handled by either increasing the appropriate yield to apply to the preferred stock's dividends or by taking a discount from the value determined by applying a yield unadjusted for marketability considerations.

Revenue Ruling 83-120

At this writing, the only regulatory guidelines established for the valuation of closely held preferred stock are those issued by the Internal Revenue Service in Revenue Ruling 83-120 (see Exhibit 24-7). Although applicable to any valuation of preferred stock in a closely held corporation, the ruling was specifically designed to prevent the relative overvaluation of preferred stock and concurrent undervaluation of common stock in "estate freezing recapitalizations" in closely held corporations.

Exhibit 24–7

Revenue Ruling 83–120

Rev. Rul. 83-120

SECTION 1. PURPOSE

The purpose of this Revenue Ruling is to amplify Rev. Rul. 59-60, 1959-1 C.B. 237, by specifying additional factors to be considered in valuing common and preferred stock of a closely held corporation for gift tax and other purposes in a recapitalization of closely held businesses. This type of valuation problem frequently arises with respect to estate planning transactions wherein an individual receives preferred stock with a stated par value equal to all or a large portion of the fair market value of the individual's former stock interest in a corporation. The individual also receives common stock which is then transferred, usually as a gift, to a relative.

SEC. 2. BACKGROUND

.01 One of the frequent objectives of the type of transaction mentioned above is the transfer of the potential appreciation of an individual's stock interest in a corporation to relatives at a nominal or small gift tax cost. Achievement of this objective requires preferred stock having a fair market value equal to a large part of the fair market value of the individual's former stock interest and common stock having a nominal or small fair market value. The approach and factors described in this Revenue Ruling are directed toward ascertaining the true fair market value of the common and preferred stock and will usually result in the determination of a substantial fair market value for the common stock and a fair market value for the preferred stock which is substantially less than its par value.

.02 The type of transaction referred to above can arise in many different contexts. Some examples are:

(a) A owns 100% of the common stock (the only outstanding stock) of Z Corporation which has a fair market value of 10,500x. In a recapitalization described in section 368(a)(1)(E), A receives preferred stock with a par value of 10,000x and new common stock, which A then transfers to A's son B.

(b) A owns some of the common stock of Z Corporation (or the stock of several corporations) the fair market value of which stock is 10,500x. A transfers this stock to a new corporation X in exchange for preferred stock of X corporation with a par value of 10,000x and common stock of corporation, which A then transfers to A's son B.

(c) A owns 80 shares and his son B owns 20 shares of the common stock (the only stock outstanding) of Z Corporation. In a recapitalization described in section 368(a)(1)(E), A exchanges his 80 shares of common stock for 80 shares of new preferred stock of Z Corporation with a par value of 10,000x. A's common stock had a fair market value of 10,000x.

SEC. 3. GENERAL APPROACH TO VALUATION

Under section 25.2512-2(f)(2) of the Gift Tax Regulations, the fair market value of stock in a closely held corporation depends upon numerous factors, including the corporation's net worth, its prospective earning power, and its capacity to pay dividends. In addition, other relevant factors must be taken into account. See Rev. Rul. 59-60. The weight to be accorded any evidentiary factor depends on the circumstances of each case. See section 25.2512-2(f) of the Gift Tax Regulations.

SEC. 4. APPROACH TO VALUATION—PREFERRED STOCK

.01 In general the most important factors to be considered in determining the value of preferred stock are its yield, dividend coverage and protection of its liquidation preference.

.02 Whether the yield of the preferred stock supports a valuation of the stock at par value depends in part on the adequacy of the dividend rate. The adequacy of the dividend rate should be determined by comparing its dividend rate with the dividend rate of high-grade publicly traded stock. A lower yield than that of high-grade preferred stock indicates a preferred stock value of less than par. If the rate of interest charged by independent creditors to the corporation on loans is higher than the rate such independent creditors charge their most credit worthy borrowers, then the yield on the preferred stock should be correspondingly higher than the yield on high quality preferred stock. A yield which is not correspondingly higher reduces the value of the preferred stock. In addition, whether the preferred stock has a fixed dividend rate and is nonparticipating influences the value of the preferred stock. A publicly traded preferred stock for a company having a similar business and similar assets with similar liquidation preferences, voting rights and other similar terms would be the ideal comparable for determining yield required in arms length transactions for closely held stock. Such ideal comparables will frequently not exist. In such circumstances, the most comparable publicly-traded issues should be selected for comparison and appropriate adjustments made for differing factors.

.03 The actual dividend rate on a preferred stock can be assumed to be its stated rate if the issuing corporation will be able to pay its stated dividends in a timely manner and will, in fact, pay such dividends. The risk that the corporation may be unable to timely pay the stated dividends on the preferred stock can be measured by the coverage of such stated dividends by the corporation's earnings. Coverage of the dividend is measured by the ratio of the sum of pre-tax and pre-interest earnings to the sum of the total interest to be paid and the pre-tax earnings needed to pay the after-tax dividends. *Standard & Poor's Ratings Guide, 58* (1979). Inadequate coverage exists where a decline in corporate profits would be likely to jeopardize the corporation's ability to pay dividends on the preferred stock. The ratio for the preferred stock in question should be compared with the ratios for high quality preferred stock to determine whether the preferred stock has adequate coverage. Prior earnings history is important in this determination. Inadequate coverage

indicates that the value of preferred stock is lower than its par value. Moreover, the absence of a provision that preferred dividends are cumulative raises substantial questions concerning whether the stated dividend rate will, in fact, be paid. Accordingly, preferred stock with noncumulative dividend features will normally have a value substantially lower than a cumulative preferred stock with the same yield, liquidation preference and dividend coverage.

.04 Whether the issuing corporation will be able to pay the full liquidation preference at liquidation must be taken into account in determining fair market value. This risk can be measured by the protection afforded by the corporation's net assets. Such protection can be measured by the ratio of the excess of the current market value of the corporation's assets over its liabilities to the aggregate liquidation preference. The protection ratio should be compared with the ratios for high quality preferred stock to determine adequacy of coverage. Inadequate asset protection exists where any unforeseen business reverses would be likely to jeopardize the corporation's ability to pay the full liquidation preference to the holders of the preferred stock.

.05 Another factor to be considered in valuing the preferred stock is whether it has voting rights and, if so, whether the preferred stock has voting control. See, however, Section 5.02 below.

.06 Peculiar covenants or provisions of the preferred stock of a type not ordinarily found in publicly traded preferred stock should be carefully evaluated to determine the effects of such covenants on the value of the preferred stock. In general, if covenants would inhibit the marketability of the stock or the power of the holder to enforce dividend or liquidation rights, such provisions will reduce the value of the preferred stock by comparison to the value of preferred stock not containing such covenants or provisions

.07 Whether the preferred stock contains a redemption privilege is another factor to be considered in determining the value of the preferred stock. The value of a redemption privilege triggered by death of the preferred shareholder will not exceed the present value of the redemption premium payable at the preferred shareholder's death (i.e., the present value of the excess of the redemption price over the fair market value of the preferred stock upon its issuance). The value of the redemption privilege should be reduced to reflect any risk that the corporation may not possess sufficient assets to redeem its preferred stock at the stated redemption price. See Section .03 above.

SEC. 5. APPROACH TO VALUATION—COMMON STOCK

.01 If the preferred stock has a fixed rate of dividend and is nonparticipating, the common stock has the exclusive right to the benefits of future appreciation of the value of the corporation. This right is valuable and usually warrants a determination that the common stock has substantial value. The actual value of this right

continued on next page

Exhibit 24–7

Revenue Ruling 83–120 (continued)

---

depends upon the corporation's past growth experience, the economic condition of the industry in which the corporation operates, and general economic conditions. The factor to be used in capitalizing the corporation's prospective earnings must be determined after an analysis of numerous factors concerning the corporation and the economy as a whole. *See* Rev. Rul. 59-60, at page 243. In addition, after-tax earnings of the corporation at the time the preferred stock is issued in excess of the stated dividends on the preferred stock will increase the value of the common stock. Furthermore, a

corporate policy of reinvesting earnings will also increase the value of the common stock.

.02 A factor to be considered in determining the value of the common stock is whether the preferred stock also has voting rights. Voting rights of the preferred stock, especially if the preferred stock has voting control, could under certain circumstances increase the value of the preferred stock and reduce the value of common stock. This factor may be reduced in significance where the rights of common stockholders as a class are protected under state law from actions by another class of shareholders,

see Singer v. Magnavox Co., 380 A.2d 969 (Del. 1977), particularly where the common shareholders, as a class, are given the power to disapprove a proposal to allow preferred stock to be converted into common stock. See ABA-ALI Model Bus. Corp. Act, Section 60 (1969).

Sec. 6. Effect on Other Revenue Rulings

Rev. Rul. 59-60, as modified by Rev. Rul. 65-193, 1965-2 C.B. 370 and as amplified by Rev. Rul. 77-287, 1977-2 C.B. 319, and Rev. Rul. 80-213, 1980-2 C.B. 101, is further amplified.

SOURCE: Rev. Rul. 83-120, 1983-2 C.B. 170.

In the section entitled "Approach to Valuation—Preferred Stock," Revenue Ruling 83-120 invokes the standard tools of security analysis for the valuation of the closely held preferred stock based on the issuing company's ability to pay its dividend yield and its liquidation preference. Revenue Ruling 83-120 specifically addresses the following factors affecting the value of preferred stock:

1. Stated dividend rate and the risk associated with payment of it.
2. Cumulative versus noncumulative dividends.
3. Ability to pay the preferred stock's liquidation preference at liquidation.
4. Voting rights.
5. Redemption privileges.

Specifically, the ruling calls on the valuation analyst to compute "coverage ratios" for the subject company's preferred stock dividend and liquidation value and to compare these ratios with those found for guideline publicly traded preferred stocks. The ruling indicates that if the ratios for the subject stock are substandard, the value of the subject preferred should be discounted from its par value on the basis of these criteria. Although the ruling is very specific with respect to these two factors, it leaves a wide area of uncertainty as to the value of features such as voting control and redemption rights, two extremely valuable features often found in closely held preferred stocks.

Summary

The combination of rights and privileges found in closely held preferred stock are limited only by the imaginations of the issuer, the financial adviser, and the legal counsel. It is the flexibility of the myriad of characteristics of closely held preferred stock that makes the estimation of value so difficult. Some guidance is found in Revenue Ruling 83-120, but the ruling fails to address the specific value implications of several of the most important features often found in closely held preferred stocks but not in publicly traded preferreds.

A judge's opinion in a 1981 estate tax case, in which the fair market value of closely held preferred stock was at issue, sums up the difficulties in valuing closely held preferred stock with many features not found in publicly traded preferred stocks:

> Since these consummate negotiators, who invariably achieve an agreeable bargain, are mythical persons endowed with characteristics prescribed in authoritative writings, the undertaking of determining what they would decide on given evidence not exactly like any recounted in precedents, might better be discharged with the benefit of interpretive insights and skills associated more often with the theater than with the court. Like the actor or actress who recreates the character from the guidelines the playwright has given, I must try first to understand the characters created in the authoritative statute regulations and precedents, and then, departing from the custom of the stage, occupy not one but two roles simultaneously—those of the willing buyer and the willing seller—coming finally to an agreement with myself—or more precisely between the two whom I am simultaneously impersonating—on the value of the stock at issue. A judge might be daunted by such an undertaking were it not for the reassuring thought that as surely as one who. . .

> . . . never saw a moor,
> [And] never saw the sea;
> Yet [may] know . . . how the heather looks,
> And what a wave must be.[7]

Bibliography

Barenbaum, Lester, and Walter Schubert. "Determining the Required Rate of Return for Preferred Stock of a Closely Held Firm." *Valuation*, June 1997, pp. 111–18.

Bloom, Gilbert D. "Certain Preferred Stock Gets the 'Boot'—But Does It Fit?" *Journal of Taxation*, February 1998, pp. 69–73.

Cortese, Christopher D. "The Subtraction Method of Valuing Preferred Stock: Chapter 14 Rules vs. Economic Reality." *Business Valuation Review*, June 1994, pp. 71–73.

Ferreira, Eurico J., Michael F. Spivey, and Charles E. Edwards. "Pricing New-Issue and Seasoned Preferred Stocks: A Comparison of Valuation Models." *Financial Management*, Summer 1992, pp. 52–62.

Houston, Arthur L., Jr., and Carol Olson Houston. "The Changing Use of Preferred Stock." *Management Accounting*, December 1991, pp. 47–49.

Julius, J. Michael. "The Skinny on Convertible Securities." *CPA Litigation Service Counselor*, October 1999, pp. 9–10.

Schneider, Willys H., and Sydney E. Unger. "TRA '97 Curtails Tax-Free Spinoffs and Use of Preferred Stock in Tax-Free Acquisitions." *Journal of Taxation*, December 1997, pp. 334–40.

Shayne, Mark. "Valuation Issues under Chapter 14." *Tax Management: Estates Gifts & Trusts Journal*, September 9, 1993, pp. 146–52.

---

[7] *Wallace v. United States*, 82-1 U.S.T.C. paragraph 13,442 (D. Mass. 1981). Verse from "Time and Eternity," in *Poems by Emily Dickinson*, vol. IV, George Monteiro, ed. (Delmar, NY: Scholars' Facsimiles & Reprints, 1967), p. XVII.

Sherman, Lawrence F. "Valuation of Preferred Capital Stock for Business Enterprises." *ASA Valuation*, March 1994, pp. 72–83.

Switzer, Ralph V. Jr., and Douglas E. Chestnut. "Evolution of the Estate Freeze." *National Public Accountant*, January 1994, pp. 20–25+.

Thompson, James. "Letter Ruling 9420001: A Taxable Gift on Conversion of Preferred Stock to Common Stock." *Tax Adviser*, October 1994, p. 611.

Chapter 25

Valuing Stock Options

Stock options are derivative securities. *Derivative securities* are securities whose values are contingent upon the value of other more basic underlying variables. In many situations, hedgers and speculators are better able to meet their financial objectives by trading newly created securities whose values are contingent upon the value of other more basic underlying variables.

There are publicly traded derivative securities that depend on stock indices, currencies, futures contracts, and interest rates. Derivatives can be contingent on almost any variable, from the price of beans to the amount of snow falling at a certain ski resort. There are even options on options, called compound options. Some stock options are created specifically by a corporate acquirer to meet the particular needs of the holder of the equity of a corporate seller. Others are made available to corporate clients by financial institutions or added to new issues of securities by underwriters. Derivative securities are being used more frequently by closely held businesses when their owners plan their estates, create an employee stock ownership plan, provide incentives to employees, and make corporate acquisitions and divestitures.

The derivative securities that this chapter addresses are options to purchase stock of either a publicly traded or a closely held company, but in either case there is no public trading market for the option itself.

This chapter explores the components of stock option values, including employee incentive stock options. It discusses the factors relevant to the value of stock options, and it explains and discusses the most widely recognized model in current use for the valuation of stock options. Finally, so called "real options" are introduced.

Some of the securities we discuss in this chapter are more correctly called *warrants* in the public markets rather than options. When warrants are exercised, the company issues treasury shares, thereby increasing its shares outstanding. The exercise period for warrants is usually years rather than months. Instruments called options in the public stock market differ from warrants in that options are issued by third parties (so that at exercise they are satisfied by already outstanding shares) rather than the company itself and are issued for periods of months rather than years. Nevertheless, we use the term *options* here, (1) because these instruments frequently arise in the familiar context of employee incentive stock options, (2) because contracts conveying such instruments in connection with private placements of capital usually use the term *option* rather than *warrant*, and (3) because the valuation methodology for options is usually easily adjusted in order to accommodate the valuation of warrants.

Common Situations Requiring Valuation of Options

The situations commonly requiring valuation of such securities are the following:

1. When they are designed, granted, exchanged, or terminated.
2. For company proxy statement disclosure.
3. When financial statement footnote disclosure requires that their value be recognized.
4. For determination of compensation of executives for SEC or for income tax purposes.
5. For transfer of ownership of the option to a third party.
6. In damage suits where the value of the option is at issue, such as a breach of contract suit between an existing or former executive and the issuing company.

7. For repurchase of an option by the issuing company.
8. For the divorce of an executive who holds an option.

Terminology

The financial analysis of derivative securities has become a specialty area in its own right complete with its own jargon. Here is an explanation of some of the more common terms.

- A *stock option* is a derivative security whose value is contingent on the price of a stock. An option gives the holder the right to do something—to buy or to sell the underlying stock. The holder does not have to exercise this right. This discretion distinguishes options from "forwards" and "futures" where the holder is obligated to buy or sell the underlying asset.
- A *call option* gives the holder the right to buy the underlying stock by a certain date for a certain price.
- A *put option* gives the holder the right to sell the underlying stock by a certain date at a certain price.
- A *stock warrant* is usually of a longer duration than a stock option and is issued by the company rather than by third parties. The pricing of a warrant must take into consideration the potential dilution effect on earnings.
- The *strike price* is the fixed price at which the option is exercisable, sometimes called the exercise price.
- The *expiration date* is the last date on which the holder may exercise his or her right. *American options* are exercisable any time up to the expiration date while *European options* can only be exercised on the expiration date itself.
- *Intrinsic value* is the difference between the current price for the underlying stock and its strike price, but is never less than zero. An American option is worth at least as much as the advantage in price it gives its holder to buy the underlying stock.

  If the value of the underlying stock exceeds the exercise price, the option is referred to as being *in the money*. If the value of the underlying stock and the exercise price are equal, the option is referred to as being *at the money*. If the value of the underlying stock is less than the exercise price, the option is referred to as being *out of the money*. For options that are at the money or out of the money, the intrinsic value is zero but the option may still have time value.
- The *time value* of a stock option is the present value of the expected difference between the value of the stock at the option's expiration date and the option's intrinsic value on a certain date. It may be optimal for the holder to wait rather than to immediately capture the intrinsic value (and begin to collect dividends and to vote the shares) in order to benefit from the time value of the option. The total value of an option is the sum of its intrinsic value and its time value.

Components of Stock Option Values

The components of stock option values are:

1. The current price of the underlying stock. As the stock price increases, call options become more valuable and put options become less valuable.
2. The strike price. As the strike price decreases, call options become more valuable and put options become less valuable.
3. The time to expiration. The owner of a longer-lived option has more exercise opportunities available than the owner of a shorter-lived option. Put and call options become more valuable as the time to expiration increases.
4. The volatility of the stock price. Volatility is the relative fluctuation of the underlying stock price. Put and call options become more valuable as the volatility increases.
5. The risk-free interest rate. While the investor's carrying cost increases with an increase in the risk-free interest rate, the expected growth rate in the underlying stock price tends to dominate this effect. As the risk-free interest rate increases, the price of call options increases and the price of put options decreases.
6. The dividends expected during the life of the option. The payment of dividends on the underlying stock detracts from an option's value because the option holder does not receive the dividends and the company pays out retained earnings that otherwise might be available for reinvestment and would contribute to the growth in value of the underlying stock. Call options are more valuable when expected dividends are zero or small. Put options are more valuable when dividends increase in size.

To value marketable stock options, most of the valuation models incorporate time to expiration date, the risk-free interest rate during the period, estimated dividends, stock price volatility, and a probability distribution of ending share prices. There are many option valuation models, including Shelton, Kassouf, Noreen-Wolfson, and the Cox, Ross, & Rubinstein binomial model. The most widely recognized stock option valuation formula is Black-Scholes.

Discussion of Option Valuation Models

Econometric versus Theoretical Models

The models currently in use for the valuation of stock options can be classified into two groups based on how they were developed: econometric models and theoretical models. This chapter briefly describes and discusses several models from these two groups.

In one sense, the models can be compared to approaches to valuation of businesses. The econometric models could be compared to the market approach, where one observes the market prices of similar assets. The theoretical models could be compared to the income approach, where a theoretical present value is estimated on the basis of all the factors that relate to future benefits to the holders.

Econometric Models. An *econometric model*, sometimes called an *empirical model*, is a statement of functional relationship that uses regression analysis of historical relationships among economic variables to estimate statistically the expected value of an economic variable. Econometric stock option valuation models were developed by studying historical relationships observed in the market between factors thought to have a bearing on the values of options and the options' actual market prices. The historical relationships thus observed are used to predict the current market price of an option contract given current values of the independent variables incorporated in the model and the assumption that the relationship between those variables and the option's value remains somewhat stable through time. The Shelton and Kassouf models are two econometric option valuation models.

Theoretical Models. *Theoretical models*, sometimes called *statistical* or *probability models*, can be distinguished from econometric models in several ways. The most important distinction is that econometric models deal with historical relationships and, therefore, do not produce a theoretical value, while theoretical models are forward-looking and attempt to determine what the option should sell for in the market given the option terms and the underlying stock's salient characteristics. Theoretical stock option valuation models are premised on a number of assumptions, generally similar to those implicit in capital asset pricing theory models, regarding the nature and behavior of the markets for both the underlying stock and the option. One essential assumption is that the price of the underlying stock behaves in such a way that possible future prices can be accurately modeled by some probability distribution. Other assumptions are listed in the context of the discussion of the Black-Scholes model. Given these assumptions and the data regarding the relevant independent variables, the models determine the theoretical value of the instrument—that is, the price at which the option should sell in the marketplace. The Black-Scholes and Noreen-Wolfson models are two theoretical models.

The Black-Scholes Option Pricing Model

In 1973, Fisher Black, Myron Scholes, and Robert Merton derived what remains as the most widely used and best known theoretical model for the valuation of marketable options. The 1997 Nobel Prize in economics recognized the model as one of the most useful works that economics has ever produced. The model is based on the assumption that it is possible to set up a perfectly hedged position consisting of owning the shares of stock and selling a call option on the stock. Any movement in the price of the underlying stock will be offset by an opposite movement in the option's value, resulting in no risk to the investor. This perfect hedge is riskless and, therefore, should yield the riskless rate of return. If it does not yield the riskless rate, the option is mispriced, the hedge is not perfect, and the option should be revalued until the hedge yields the riskless rate. The model inferred that when the option is correctly priced, the perfect hedge results.

The assumptions underlying the Black-Scholes model are not intuitively pleasing—nevertheless, it is important to be aware of them. These assumptions are as follows:

1. The short-term interest rate is known and is constant through time.
2. The stock price follows a random walk in continuous time with a rate of variance in proportion to the square of the stock price.
3. The distribution of possible stock prices at the end of any finite interval is lognormal.
4. The variance of the rate of return on the stock is constant.
5. The stock pays no dividends and makes no other shareholder distributions.
6. The option can be exercised only at maturity.
7. There are no commissions or other transaction costs in buying or selling the stock or option.

8. It is possible to borrow any fraction of the price of a security to buy it, or to hold it, at the short-term interest rate.

9. A seller who does not own a security (a short seller) will simply accept the price of the security from the buyer and agree to settle with the buyer on some future date by paying him an amount equal to the price of the security on that date. While this short sale is outstanding, the short seller will have the use of, or interest on, the proceeds of the sale.

10. The tax rate, if any, is identical for all transactions and all market participants.

The Black-Scholes model is expressed as follows:

$$\text{Call value} = S \times N(d_1) - Ee^{-rt} \times N(d_2)$$

where:

S	=	Stock price
E	=	Exercise (strike) price
$N(\ )$	=	Value of cumulative normal distribution at the point ( )
d_1	=	$\dfrac{\ln(S/E) + (r + 0.5\sigma^2)t}{\sigma\sqrt{t}}$
d_2	=	$d_1 - \sigma\sqrt{t}$
ln	=	Natural logarithm
r	=	Short-term riskless rate (continuously compounded)
t	=	Time to expiration, in years
e	=	Base of natural logarithms
σ	=	Annual standard deviation of return (usually referred to as *volatility*)

There are many assumptions and computations required to derive the option value using the Black-Scholes formula. For example, the model was developed to value "European" options, which can be exercised only at maturity, as opposed to "American" options, which can be exercised at any time. Dividends are ignored and when dividends are paid, they are paid at one point in time, not continuously. Also, fluctuations in the economy preclude rational acceptance of the assumption that investors can borrow or lend at a constant riskless interest rate. Over the years, much additional empirical research has been conducted, and adjustments have been made to the Black-Scholes model in order to correct for the original model's limitations. One with relatively good results is the Noreen-Wolfson model.

The Noreen-Wolfson variation of the Black-Scholes model has some of the same problems that its parent has. However, this model allows for dividends and incorporates the dilution that will occur on exercise. The problem of estimating the volatility factor continues to limit its usefulness for appraisers of closely held companies.

Empirical Tests of Option Valuation Models

In conjunction with the second edition of this book (1989), we conducted empirical tests of the Shelton, Kassouf, and Noreen-Wolfson models. We concluded that the Noreen-Wolfson adaptation of Black-Scholes does not provide as accurate an estimate of the market prices of warrants as either the Shelton or Kassouf model. The Kassouf model worked best, in both accurately estimating the values and maintaining low variability of the estimates relative to the actual market prices. The difficulty of using the Kassouf model—namely estimating the volatility of the stock price and re-estimating the coefficients of the regression relationship—points to the Shelton model as an easy and relatively accurate model for estimating warrant values. In a sense, this is comforting to valuation analysts, because most warrants or options they encounter are on closely held stocks with little or no historical pricing data. These data are necessary for calculating the volatility factor incorporated in both the Kassouf model and the Noreen-Wolfson adaptation.

Nevertheless, on the whole, the Black-Scholes model is the most widely recognized and accepted of the models. There are many proprietary variations used by professional traders and under specific circumstances. The original Black-Scholes model does not provide the best explanation for market prices.

Employee Incentive Stock Options

In creating employee stock options, the issuing company usually endeavors to set the strike price of the option at the fair market value of the underlying shares. When the strike price is set at fair market value, the intrinsic value is zero and the only value of the option is its time value. Under these circumstances, the Internal Revenue Service[1] has determined that the recipient has no income to report during the year of issuance. The typical assignment for the business valuation professional is to estimate the fair market value of the underlying common stock so that management can establish the strike price of the employee incentive stock options (ISOs) to eliminate (or at least minimize) the income tax expense of issuing the options.

Income that is eventually derived from the option is determined to be ordinary income to the recipient if the recipient exercises the option to buy the underlying securities and subsequently sells the securities within 12 months. To get a tax break, (1) the owner holds the shares for at least one year and (2) the ISO was granted at least two years before the stock is sold. Any gain from the time of the exercise to the time of the sale is taxed at capital gains rates, which are lower than ordinary income rates. Holding the shares for more than 12 months after exercise and before selling them puts the owner in the 20 percent capital gains tax bracket. A special, lower tax rate of 18 percent (8 percent for individuals in the 15 percent income tax bracket) applies to transactions after December 31, 2000, when the asset has been held for more than five years (Code Sec. 1.(h)(2)(A)). Planning around the Alternative Minimum Tax is important.

For nonqualified stock options (NSOs), it is usually tax advantageous to consider exercising the options early on, especially if the company's stock has great upside potential. Any appreciation above the option-grant price is taxed as ordinary income, payable at the time of exercise. When the stock is sold, any appreciation subsequent to exercise is taxed as capital gains as long as the shares are held for more than one year. Exercising an NSO early in order to minimize the ordinary income tax hit and to make the most of the income from a capital gain reduces taxes.

Of course, whether the owner comes out ahead by exercising early depends on how the underlying stock performs during the holding period, on dividends, on voting rights, and so on.

[1] See Internal Revenue Code Section 422.

Currently, to the issuing company, the issuance of employee incentive stock options is an event that is reported in its financial statement footnotes. This practice has come under intense scrutiny in recent years.

To date, the FASB, the SEC, and most compensation consultants have endorsed the Black-Scholes option-pricing model for the purpose of quantifying value, although they do not forbid the use of other models. Originally developed to value a fully transferable short-term call on a European-type option for non–dividend paying instruments, the model has been tweaked, squeezed, and reshaped numerous times to conform to nontransferable, long-term American warrants on dividend-paying instruments where exercise is contingent on employment and where the holder cannot be expected to behave like a highly liquid well-diversified investor.

Publicly traded call options need not be exercised in order to realize the profits from an increase in the price of the underlying security, because they can be sold to another investor, who receives the rights associated with the contract. Executive or employee stock options do not have this advantage, since the options are usually nonmarketable; however, the basic determinants of the value of traded options are also relevant to the value of any option-type contract. It is often possible to adopt a hedging strategy for protecting the value of options.

Employee stock options have special risks of forfeiture (e.g., termination of employment), required holding periods (e.g., to take advantage of capital gain treatment), nontransferability restrictions (sometimes the employee options at a publicly traded company are options on shares that are not registered for public trading or, in a privately held company are shares subject to a strict buy-sell agreement), and other contingencies that make employee stock options much different from publicly traded options.

Volatility is an important factor in many option valuation models. As volatility increases, the chance that a stock will do very well or very poorly increases. Since the employee owns a call option, he would be expected to benefit from price increases but to be protected from the downside risk since he has nothing to lose. But, for many reasons, volatility is not a critical factor in the valuation of employee incentive stock options because of their many restrictions. This is one of the disadvantages of using a theoretical model such as Black-Scholes, which is highly dependent on volatility for valuing private options.

To reiterate, employee stock options cannot be sold; they cannot be exercised until they vest; the underlying stock may be restricted from sale to third parties; and, once exercised, the employee faces a tax incentive to hold the stock for at least one year.

While volatility is an important factor in the valuation of publicly traded stock options, its impact on the value of employee stock options is not clear. The volatility factor is a function of the past variability in the returns on the stock as measured by changes in the stock price. When valuing the options of a privately held company, reliable historical prices are not available. Using the price series of a comparable public company to estimate the volatility factor may not be an acceptable proxy.

No universally accepted replacement for the Black-Scholes model has surfaced. This means that different analysts would arrive at different valuations for the options of two companies with identical characteristics. When the valuation methodology is not consistent across competitors, the results will not be widely embraced. While the Black-Scholes results for a particular company may seem reasonable, most managers and executives may perceive the models as block boxes that can be exchanged for new ones if the results do not square with intuition or earnings objectives.

Real Options

Real option valuation (ROV) theory applies option pricing theory more broadly than just for valuing options. It can be used as a strategic tool. ROV also incorporates "proactive" attributes of options—the holder can take action that increases the value of the investment. ROV has its roots in capital expenditure decision-making but is being applied in many other areas.

ROV seems to fit certain situations that are characterized by high levels of investment in research and development, and in manufacturing and marketing. An option buyer pays today's price for the investment and then may use his or her influence to improve the value of the investment.

Under ROV, the initial investment (similar to the price of the typical financial option) gives the investor the flexibility to invest more later, but only after some degree of uncertainty over the value is resolved. ROV captures the net present value of the investment plus its flexibility value.

Reactive flexibility—the ability to quickly buy or sell an option—is already part of the typical financial option's market value.

Proactive flexibility—where the value of an option can be increased after the option is owned by pulling the option pricing levers before exercising the option—is part of its real option value.

With financial options and with real options, the investor decides whether and when to initially invest. However, with real options, the investor faces other subsequent decisions. The investor in real options has the ability to influence the levers that affect the value of the option. In this way, real option holders use the investment value standard more than the typical fair market value standard.

This distinguishes real options from traditional financial options: Management uses its skills to improve the real option's value before exercising the option. Exhibit 25–1 depicts how, recognizing the components of options, management actions can influence an investment's value.

ROV challenges the validity of net present value methodology. According to ROV, net present value methodology does not adequately capture the expected future cash flow and the cost of capital of many investment opportunities.

The importance of ROV theory is that it introduces a mechanism to systematically think through the components of value. It provides a means to challenge the premise behind the net present value method of business valuation because the net present value method relies on the fixed, multi-year investment model at a fixed cost of capital. Under the fair market value standard, analysts use static investment plans to develop a one-time value indication. That method may provide one indication of value at a certain point in time but it does not necessarily reflect the full vision of management.

It is possible for management to view and price investment opportunities more dynamically. Management can, after consideration of subsequent information, change the course of an investment or even abandon a project after it has been launched. Managers who rely on a static long-term projection for many years ahead may find it more difficult to change course quickly.

ROV strategies incorporate the features of options into real-market investments. ROV discourages the use of static net present value measures for "go/no go" business

Exhibit 25–1

Influence of Management Actions on the Value of an Investment

Black-Scholes Variables	Management Actions
Time to expiration	Extend the option's duration. Maintain the regulatory barriers. Signal ability to exercise. Innovate to hold technology lead.
Risk-free interest rate	Monitor the impact of changes in the risk-free interest rate.
Exercise price	Reduce present value of fixed costs. Leverage economies of scale. Leverage economies of scope. Leverage economies of learning.
Stock price	Increase present value of expected cash flows. Develop marketing strategies. Develop alliances with low cost suppliers.
Uncertainty of stock price movements	Increase uncertainty of expected cash flows. Extend opportunity to related markets. Encourage complementary products, product. innovations, product bundling.
Dividends	Reduce value lost by waiting to exercise. Create implementation hurdles for competition. Lock up key resources.

decisions for long-term investments in intangible assets like research and development or even tangible assets like plant capacity.

For the valuation analyst, ROV theory includes elements of investment value because, to a great extent, it is based upon the opportunity that the holder of the option has to influence the value of the option after acquiring it. ROV theory may provide some insight into the traditional interpretation of levels of value and the definitions of investment value, fair market value, and fair value.

ROV theory has at least three implications for financial advisers:

1. Guideline transactions that are used to derive value indications may be the result of ROV theory and may include elements of investment value, not just fair market value.
2. When identifying acquisition or divestiture opportunities, consider simultaneous, multistage investments where the buyer can influence the value at some later point in time. This perspective might help the buyer compete at higher bid prices.
3. Pricing and structuring transactions may benefit from consideration of option variables by giving the participants proprietary rights, escalating financial obligations with expiration dates.

ROV includes a noteworthy departure from net present value theory. This is the power of real options: ROV encourages uncertainty and risk. ROV changes the way opportunities are valued by—and influenced by—management. It changes the way value is created.

Summary

Derivative securities permit their holders to alter return distributions to satisfy particular investment objectives. Derivative securities come in all sizes and types. The derivatives addressed in this article are those issued by the company on whose stock the option constitutes a call, usually as part of an employee incentive stock option or in conjunction with raising capital for the company.

The most famous stock option valuation formula is Black-Scholes. It incorporates all of the components of stock options: the current price of the underlying stock, the strike price, the time to expiration, the volatility of the stock price, the risk-free interest rate, and the dividends expected during the life of the option.

Real option valuation theory applies financial option pricing theory more broadly than just for valuing options. It is possible for management to view and price investment opportunities more dynamically. Management can, after consideration of subsequent information, change the course of an investment or even abandon a project after it has been launched. Managers take action on existing investments as if those investments were options. In this way, real option valuation theory relies on the investment value standard and uses financial option theory to make capital expenditure and other investment decisions.

Bibliography

Articles

Czaplinski, Nancy M. "How to Value and Treat Options." *American Journal of Family Law*, Spring 1998, pp. 15–21.

Dufendach, David C. "Real Options: Extending Project Finance Techniques to Valuations of High Growth Enterprises." *Valuation Strategies*, September/October, pp. 4–11.

Fowler, Bradley A., and Edward C. Fowler. "Pricing of Employee Options in Pre-IPO Venture Capital Backed Companies." *Business Valuation Review*, December 1997, pp. 180–82.

Franz, Diana R., Dean Crawford, and Linda Campbell. "How to Value Gifts of Employee Stock Options." *The Tax Adviser*, December 1998, pp. 848–55.

Gagliardi, Elaine Hightower. "Service Issues Rulings on Compensatory Stock Options." *Valuation Strategies*, November/December 1998, pp. 43–45.

Goodman, David H. "Valuation of Invested Stock Options." *The Valuation Examiner*, January/February 2000, pp. 18, 27–29.

Greene, Jeffrey R. "Is Estimated Value Analysis Stunting Your Growth?" *Valuation Strategies*, September/October 1997, pp. 26–28.

Johnson, George L., and David C. Dufendach. "Valuation of Options on Restricted Stock Using Simple Modifications of the Black-Scholes Model." *Business Valuation Review*, June 1998, pp. 35–41.

Madden, Robert E., and Lisa H.R. Hayes. "New Ruling Turns Golden Handcuffs of Stock Options into Estate Planning Ball and Chain." *Estate Planning*, August/September 1998, pp. 310–13.

Nadel, Alan, Benjamin Neuhausen, and Gregory Kopp. "Measuring Components of Value When Accounting for Stock Options." *Employee Ownership Report*, July/August 1998, p. 7.

"Repricing Stock Options." *Employee Ownership Report*, July/August 1998, pp. 8, 14.

"The Right Option." *The Economist*, October 18, 1997, pp. 75–78.

Schweihs, Robert P., and Richard N. Erickson. "Management Stock Options." Presentation to the Advanced Business Valuation Conference of the American Society of Appraisers, November 1997. Available on www.BVLibrary.com.

Shiffrin, Daniel. "Valuation of Stock Options for Gift Tax Purposes." *CPA Litigation Service Counselor*, July 1998, pp. 11–12.

Siwicki, Robert. "The Gifting of Stock Options as an Estate Planning Strategy." *Trusts & Estates*, November 1999, pp. 49–60.

Thompson, Susan, Alan Nadel, Benjamin Neuhausen, and Gregory Kopp. "Black-Scholes and the Value of Options." *Employee Ownership Report*, September/October 1997, p. 7.

Weinstein, Jeremy D. "Valuing Private Equity Warrants on Initial Issuance." *Valuation Strategies*, September/October 1999, pp. 12–19, 48.

Wing, Timothy R., and Hans Sprohge. "The Valuation of Employee Stock Options." *The Journal of Business Valuation* (Proceedings of the 4th Joint Business Valuation Conference of The Canadian Institute of Chartered Business Valuators and the American Society of Appraisers). Toronto: The Canadian Institute of Chartered Business Valuators, 1999, pp. 151–59.

Books

Amram, Martha, and Nalin Kulatilaka. *Real Options: Managing Strategic Investment in an Uncertain World.* Boston: Harvard Business School Press, 1999.

Brennan, Michael J., and Lenos Trigeorgis. *Project Flexibility, Agency, and Competition: New Developments in the Theory and Application of Real Options.* New York: Oxford University Press, 2000.

Damodoran, Aswath. *Corporate Finance: Theory and Practice.* New York: John Wiley & Sons, 1997.

Kolb, Robert W. *Futures, Options, and Swaps*, 3rd ed. Maiden, MA: Blackwell Publishers Ltd., 1999.

Trigeorgis, Lenos. *Real Options: Managerial Flexibility and Strategy in Resource Allocation.* Cambridge, MA: The MIT Press, 1996.

Chapter 26

Pass-Through Entities

Businesses are most commonly structured as corporations or as partnerships. Among other forms, we also see businesses that are formed as sole proprietorships, S corporations, and limited liability companies.

This chapter discusses these various forms of businesses and the impact that the form of the business may have on its value.

In most cases, the form of the business has an impact on its value, especially when the appraiser is analyzing the value of a minority interest in the business. Depending on the purpose of the appraisal assignment, the impact on the value of the business due to its form of ownership could be significant.

Characteristics of the Organizations

The analyst should understand the characteristics of the business's legal form. The legal form of the business defines its business-related characteristics and its tax-related characteristics.

Sole Proprietorships

The simplest form of a business is the sole proprietorship. Its simplicity is both its strength and its weakness. It is started without a lot of paperwork. Inexpensive, over-the-counter computer software allows for easy business recordkeeping. All earnings and losses of the business are taxed to the sole proprietor personally. All risks of the business are the sole proprietor's, and all of the sole proprietor's personal assets will be subject to those risks.

Corporations

Insulating personal assets from the liabilities of a business is frequently the reason that the corporate form is selected. A corporation is a separate entity for tax purposes, too. Shareholders own the corporation, and they elect a board of directors to govern the company. C corporations pay income taxes on taxable income, so the shareholder-owners might be subject to double taxation: once at the corporate level and again when corporate earnings are distributed as dividends. Instead of paying the extra layer of taxes, closely held corporation shareholder-owners often pay themselves additional, but reasonable, compensation—which reduces the level of taxable income of the corporation.

Partnerships

Two entities are required to form a partnership, and partnerships can be either general or limited. In a general partnership, all partners are jointly and severally liable for the obligations of the partnership and are permitted to participate in the management of the partnership. Individual general partners act primarily in their own interest subject only to their fiduciary duty owed to the other partners. In a limited partnership, the liability of the limited partners is limited to their agreed-upon capital contributions, but they are typically not permitted to participate in the management of the business (which right is reserved for the general partners). The net earnings of partnerships are taxed only at the partner level, thus avoiding double income taxation.

S Corporations

Generally, double taxation may also be avoided by electing S corporation status. Limited legal liability is also maintained. Generally, an S corporation's earnings are taxed only at the shareholder level. There are restrictions, however, on S corporation equity ownership, which will be discussed later in the chapter.

Limited Liability Companies

Limited liability companies (LLCs) are rapidly growing as a favored form of ownership. At least two "members" are required to form an LLC in most states. Members have limited legal liability and may participate in the management of the organization, but they are taxed on earnings only once—at the member level like a partnership. The LLC may have multiple classes of members, members other than individuals, and foreign members. One drawback to this form of business is that, because this ownership structure is relatively new, there is only limited uniform legislation among the states. This means that multistate businesses may face different rules regarding business operations than they had expected. States are moving, however, toward LLC legislation that gives them most all of the advantages of partnerships, plus the advantage of limited liability.

Pass-Through Entities

The businesses that pass through earnings to their owners, subject only to federal taxation at the owner's personal income tax rate, are referred to as "pass-through entities." Of the previously discussed legal organizations, the traditional corporation, sometimes called a "Type C Corporation," is the only one that is not a pass-through entity. While the tax-related advantages are real, the business-related implications of a particular business form are complex, and there are many disadvantages to be considered.

Effective January 1, 1997, Treasury Regulations Sections 301.7701-1 through 301.7701-3 were adopted giving guidance for determining what classification of entity a business should fall into. These regulations are now referred to as the "check-the-box" regulations. Readers are referred to the above regulation for definitions of types of entities.

Partnerships

The partnership agreement will describe the specific characteristics of the partnership and the rights, privileges, and risks of each partner's ownership position. Usually, general partners are jointly and severally responsible for the partnership's obligations, but general partners also have management responsibility.

The theory underlying the rule that there will be centralized management even though the limited partners own more than 80 percent of the partnership interests is that a general partner owning a relatively small interest is managing the business primarily for the other passive owners—which is the essence of centralized management—but a general partner that owns a significant interest is managing the business to a substantial degree for himself or herself.

S Corporations

S corporations were created in 1958 as part of a tax program to aid small businesses, although they are not limited to small businesses. The congressional intent was to lessen the influence of income tax considerations in the choice of business form by giving certain corporate entities and shareholders the option of being taxed as if they were partnerships. Hence, S corporations achieved the coveted corporate characteristics of limited liability combined with the income flow-through attributes of a partnership. Currently, to qualify for S corporation status, certain requirements must be met:

1. The corporation must have no more than 75 shareholders (all of whom must be U.S. citizens).
2. Shareholders must be individuals (except for estates, certain trusts, and other S corporations). No shareholder may be a nonresident alien.
3. All shareholders must participate equally in the allocation of profits, losses, and distributions.
4. Only common stock can be issued by an S corporation. The corporation may not have more than one class of stock, except that there can be voting and nonvoting shares as long as there are no unequal distribution rights.

Since 1998, the Internal Revenue Code allows ESOPs to own stock in an S corporation (and the ESOP counts as a single shareholder).

These limitations present qualification barriers and necessitate continued monitoring in order to prevent a subsequent inadvertent termination of S status.

The shareholders of the S corporation increase or decrease the basis of their ownership interest in the S corporation to the extent of the income or loss of the corporation recognized by each shareholder. The consequences of such basis adjustment is that income or loss is not taxable to the shareholder again upon distribution or, in the absence of distribution, upon the sale or exchange of the shareholder's interest in the corporation. This allows earnings to be distributed to shareholders free of federal income tax, avoiding the double taxation inherent in C corporations—where federal income taxes are levied on earnings at the corporate level and on dividends or distributions at the shareholder level.

It makes sense that the companies gaining this income tax benefit are unlikely to be high-growth companies, because high-growth companies typically plow profits back into the company to fund growth, leaving little or no earnings to pay out to shareholders.

Therefore, S corporations that have a handful of shareholders, where employee-shareholders of the corporation are in the minority, and/or where the corporation has significant cash flow to distribute, achieve the greatest advantage as measured by the income tax savings from their S election.

It is helpful for the analyst to be aware of the advantages and disadvantages of S corporation status, so that these attributes are reflected in the process of estimating the value of the subject company.

The major advantage of the S corporation status is avoiding the double income taxation on shareholder distributions. Income and loss items pass directly through to shareholders, where income is taxed at the personal tax rate of the shareholder—rather than at the corporate tax rate. This means that the S corporation can sell assets (at a purchase price that is often greater than a similar sale of stock) and distribute the proceeds without the corporate level tax (which would apply prior to a C corporation's dividend distribution).

S corporations are not subject to the accumulated earnings tax and there are no personal holding company taxes applicable to S corporations. Non–tax shelter S corporations are allowed to use the cash method of accounting. At the point of conversion to an S corporation, the C corporation's deferred income tax charges are adjusted to retained earnings, often improving the appearance of the balance sheet.

Other distinctions between S corporations and C corporations include:

1. S corporation shareholders are liable for taxes on income whether the income is distributed or not. Tax-free distributions are allowed only to the extent of the shareholder's basis in the stock. Shareholders typically demand enough cash distributions to pay their taxes, which may limit the amount of earnings available for reinvestment (see Exhibit 26–1).
2. S corporations must generally conform their tax years to their owner's tax years (usually calendar years).
3. Each shareholder's deductible share of the S corporation's loss in any year is limited to his adjusted basis in stock and direct shareholder loans, in general. Losses can be carried forward indefinitely at the shareholder level to future S corporation years in which the shareholder creates basis.
4. State and local tax compliance can be complicated with multistate S corporations.
5. Many fringe benefits for shareholders who own more than 2 percent of the S corporation's stock cannot be deducted by the S corporation.
6. The deductibility of pass-through losses for inactive owners is limited.

Limited Liability Companies (LLCs)

LLCs are not subject to the ownership restrictions applicable to S corporations and, thus, they can offer increased flexibility. An unlimited number of persons or entities (including partnerships, corporations, and nonresident aliens) may own interests in an LLC, and an LLC may be used in multi-tiered structures. LLCs may issue more than one class of equity, giving them the flexibility to use special allocations and to offer equity interests designed to meet the needs of different investors.

A large number of owners, however, may not be feasible from a practical standpoint, because the unanimous consent of all the remaining "members" may be required to prevent dissolution upon the withdrawal of a single member. Obtaining unanimous consent to continue an LLC's business upon the occurrence of an event of dissolution (e.g., death or bankruptcy of a member) may be extremely burdensome, especially for large organizations and fragile family arrangements.

Exhibit 26–1

Depending upon Distributions
The S Corporation Election May Be Unfavorable

	C Corporation	S Corporation	
100% Earnings Distributed			
Profit before tax	$100.00	$100.00	
Corporate tax at 35%	35.00	—	
Net profit	65.00	100.00	
Retain 0%	—	—	
Dividends	65.00	100.00	
Personal tax at 39.6%	25.74	39.60	
Net after tax	$39.26	$60.40	[a]
0% Earnings Distributed			
Profit before tax	$100.00	$100.00	
Corporate tax at 35%	35.00	—	
Net profit	65.00	100.00	
Retain 100%	65.00	65.00	[b]
Dividends	—	35.00	
Personal tax at 39.6%	—	39.60	[c]
Net after tax	$ —	$(4.60)	[d]

a. When 100 percent of earnings are distributed, the advantage is greater than 51 percent.
b. Assumes same dollar amount is retained; this implies same growth requirement.
c. Personal tax is due on the reported net profit.
d. When earnings are retained, the shareholder in the 39.6 percent bracket has negative cash flow.

Obviously, the structure and flow of the rights and privileges of the subject ownership position need to be understood by the analyst before its value can be determined.

Comparing the LLC with the S Corporation

An S corporation may continue in perpetuity and is not subject to the fixed termination date imposed upon LLCs in many states. The possibility of an inopportune termination may be of significance to a family-owned entity that may plan to continue operating through multiple generations.

S corporations have flexibility concerning restrictions on the transferability of their stock, and there is no risk of dissolution on the occurrence of the death, disability, bankruptcy, retirement, or resignation of a shareholder. Many LLCs must restrict the transferability of their interests and provide for dissolution upon the occurrence of certain events. The consent requirements to transfer interests and to continue the business upon the occurrence of an event of dissolution may not be feasible.

The taxation of S corporations may be simpler in many situations than the taxation of LLCs. Because an S corporation may have only one class of stock, its items of income, loss and gain, and deductions are shared pro rata. Thus, the complexities associated with special allocations, available to an LLC, are avoided with an S corporation.

Changing the Form of the Business from Taxable to Pass-Through

An existing C corporation that meets the requirements of an S corporation can make an S election tax-free (although undistributed earnings and profits may eliminate the benefit). Because an LLC is taxed as a partnership, the tax-free-reorganization provisions don't apply to the conversion of a C corporation to a partnership or to an LLC. The conversion involves a liquidation of the C corporation, followed by the formation of a partnership or an LLC. The C corporation will be subject to tax on any appreciation in its assets, and each shareholder will be taxed on the excess of the fair market value of his or her share of the distributed assets over his or her stock basis. This double taxation means that an S election is the only viable option for pass-through taxation to most C corporations.

The major disadvantage of the S corporation when converted from C corporation status is that any gain that the corporation recognizes within the 10 post-conversion years (i.e., the built-in gain) is taxed to the extent the asset giving rise to the gain or income was owned at the conversion date. Not only is the corporation subject to the "built-in gains tax" on these items, but the gain or income flows through to the shareholders net of corporate-level tax paid. This creates near double-level tax to the corporation and to its shareholders. Generally, C corporations converting to S status will want to know the fair market value of each of their assets and their stock as of the date of the conversion. That determines the property's unrealized built-in gain (UNBIG). Any gain in excess of the UNBIG is not taxed at the S corporation level, even if the sale occurs within the 10 post-conversion years.

Other tax disadvantages of the conversion to S corporation status are that carryover tax attributes are generally lost (but may be available for built-in gains purposes). There also may be a LIFO inventory method recapture tax.

The LLC is a unique entity that presents opportunities for innovative and flexible tax planning. Under present entity classification rules, LLCs can be structured to receive partnership tax treatment and may avoid many of the disadvantages associated with using other types of entities. There are, however, tax and state law uncertainties. It is uncertain how much flexibility can be built into the structure while still maintaining pass-through status. S corporations may continue to be the preferred form of doing business for many taxpayers because limited liability is certain, and the applicable tax rules are familiar, predictable, and, in many cases, simpler.

Valuation Issues

In the valuation of the ownership interest of the pass-through entity, the central valuation issues are two-fold. First, is there an incremental value attributable to the income tax advantages of the pass-through status? If so, how can this incremental value be accounted for in the valuation process? Second, if the value of the pass-through entity is derived at by comparison with the valuation characteristics of non–pass-through entities, what adjustments are necessary? The answers to these questions may vary from one business valuation situation to the next. The answers are very facts-and-circumstances specific. As we have said many times earlier in this book, the analyst should revisit the assignment's purpose and objective before selecting the business valuation approaches. In the simplest case, the analyst may want to rely on the advice of the Internal Revenue Service:

> S corporations lend themselves readily to valuation approaches comparable to those used in valuing closely held corporations (C corporations). You need only to adjust the earnings from the business to reflect estimated corporate income taxes that would have been payable had the Subchapter S election not been made.[1]

Business Enterprise Value

If the purpose of the valuation is to estimate the fair market value of a controlling interest in the pass-through entity for buying, selling, or merging the company, the company's tax attributes may have little or no impact on value. If the most likely buyer is a C corporation, then the C corporation would be unwilling to pay for the pass-through entity's income tax benefits which are not available to it by definition of its being a C corporation. If the most likely buyer were eligible to carry on with the S corporation status, why would the buyer pay a premium just for the election? Often, especially in appraisals for transaction purposes, valuation methodologies using pre-tax earnings fundamentals are used, because it is the buyer's tax status that is relevant—not the historical tax status of the selling company.

Valuation of Noncontrolling Interests

If the business interest being appraised is a minority ownership interest—that is, the appraisal of an ownership interest not having the prerogatives of control—then a direct comparison with values of other minority interests is the most appropriate approach to valuation. As discussed earlier in this book, the prices at which the daily transactions in noncontrolling interests of publicly traded companies take place offer guidance for the valuation of noncontrolling interests.

When the direct comparison approach (guideline publicly traded company method) is not applicable, the capitalization of owner's distribution method is usually used. However, direct comparison with other noncontrolling interests is not always an appropriate approach (for any of a variety of reasons, such as a lack of publicly traded guideline companies), so a discounted economic income approach should be considered.

Capitalization of Owner's Distribution Method

If the only appropriate guideline companies are C corporations, then the appraiser is faced with deciding how to apply empirical market data derived from C corporations to the pass-through entity's fundamentals. The analyst should keep in mind the specific tax-related and business-related characteristics of the pass-through entity that is the subject of the valuation assignment. Often, the business-related characteristics (such as limited life and limited transferability) are taken into consideration as a separate step in the valuation process. There are three alternatives to

---

[1] *IRS Valuation Training for Appeals Officers* (Chicago: CCH Incorporated, 1998), pp. 7–12. Also available at www.BVLibrary.com.

quantifying the tax-related characteristics of the pass-through entity when using C corporation market data:

1. Apply the statutory C corporation income tax rate to the pass-through entity's earnings and apply price/earnings (P/E) multiples derived from the C corporation guideline analysis.

   This procedure does not recognize the income tax advantages accruing to the owner of the pass-through entity interest—from the positive differential between the highest corporate marginal income tax rate and the maximum marginal income tax rate for individuals. Some appraisers use this procedure and add a premium to the indicated values to capture the economic advantage of pass-through entity status.

2. Capitalize the pass-through entity income (before taxes to owners) by applying guideline company P/E multiples.

   This procedure does not recognize the pass-through entity owners' exposure to taxes on the income that they don't receive in distributions from the company. It further suffers from a classic apples-to-oranges comparative flaw in its application of an after-tax-derived multiple being applied to a pretax earnings stream.

3. The third procedure is to apply the pass-through entity owner's highest personal income tax rate to the earnings and apply after-tax multiples derived from the guideline (C corporation) companies.

   This procedure captures the economic benefit that accrues to the pass-through entities from the lower personal income tax rates. However, such a capitalization of earnings fails to capture the pass-through entity's ability to distribute earnings on a tax-free basis.

In order to capture the incremental value attributable to the tax advantages of the pass-through entity, one must capitalize owners' paid-out distributions (as opposed to the K-1 distributive share of income, which may or may not be paid out). The capitalization of dividends or owners' distributions is given relatively minor weight in most minority interest valuations of C corporations. Ultimately, whether a C corporation or a pass-through entity, dividends are possible only as a result of earnings. In the valuation of a minority ownership interest, actual dividends—rather than dividend-paying capacity—are relevant, since the minority interest owner cannot force the payment of dividends, regardless of the dividend-paying capacity of the company. Since many closely held C corporations either don't pay dividends or pay only minimal dividends because of double taxation on dividends, the capitalization of dividends generally receives relatively less weight than other earnings-based approaches. It should be noted, however, that for investors owning a nonmarketable minority interest position in a closely held C corporation, dividends *do* represent the only return that the investor is able to realize.

However, the typical pass-through entity distributes a portion of earnings to its owners. In addition, it is the pass-through entity's ability to distribute proceeds on a tax-free basis (i.e., only taxed at one level—at the personal tax rate) that is at the crux of the entity's incremental value relative to the C corporation, as shown in Exhibit 26–1. Capitalizing the owners' distributions captures the incremental value reflected by both the difference in corporate and individual income tax rates and the elimination of double taxation. If a pass-through entity distributes all of its earnings, this advantage can result in a 51 percent higher after-tax cash flow at the owner's level (see Exhibit 26–1). Thus, when valuing a pass-through entity or an interest in it, the capitalization of owners' distributions method should receive a relatively greater proportion of the total weight given to earnings-based methods than is appropriate when valuing a C corporation or an interest in it.

Estimation of Appropriate Distribution Rate

If guideline companies are C corporations, dividend yields are inappropriate to apply to the pass-through entity's distributions.

If the subject pass-through entity is only distributing earnings sufficient to cover income taxes, then the capitalization of owners' distributions may not be a meaningful method of valuation. Arguably, if a pass-through entity distributes earnings in addition to those necessary to pay taxes, capitalizing those earnings only (total distribution less that portion of distributions necessary to pay taxes) may provide an indication of the value of the subject interest.

Discounted Economic Income Method

Often, a discounted economic income method is used in the appraisal of controlling interests. In such appraisals, the potential or hypothetical buyer will not pay for the pass-through entity's income tax advantages if they are not expected to continue in the future. However, if a discounted economic income method is being used in the appraisal of a minority ownership interest, or the pass-through entity's status of the company is expected to continue in the future, then one approach is to apply the highest applicable personal tax rate to the taxable income and calculate net cash flow. It is appropriate to select a discount rate as discussed in Chapter 9.

To capture the avoidance of double income taxation on net cash flow within this valuation framework, one must calculate the future income tax savings that would accrue to the pass-through entity because of its status. These income tax savings should then be reduced to their present value by applying a discount rate sufficient to reflect the risks that:

1. Future distributions may be insufficient to cover taxes.
2. The pass-through entity may lose its status
3. The impact of tax legislation relative to personal tax rates may change.

These risks would seem to imply an equity rate of return as the appropriate base to be used to develop a present value discount rate.

In estimating the appropriate present value discount rate applicable to the net free cash flow of a pass-through entity, the appraiser needs to take into consideration whether the pass-through entity status of the subject company increases its cost of capital. The reason that the company's cost of debt capital may be adversely impacted is that some banks are reluctant to lend to pass-through entities because of their distribution policies. A pass-through entity's cost of equity capital may be affected by its more circumscribed sources of capital—restricted by both number of investors (owners) and type. This increased cost of capital may offset any value increment from the present value of future income tax benefits.

Other Valuation Issues

The above methods of estimating value have attempted to explicitly deal with the incremental economic value of pass-through entities, which stems from the different income tax rates paid by a pass-through entity compared with a C corporation. However, the appraiser must take into consideration some of the other characteristics of pass-through entities and their implications on value. Earlier in this chapter, we listed a number of tax-related advantages and disadvantages of pass-through entities as well as business concerns for pass-through entities. These characteristics need to be examined in the valuation of each pass-through entity in order to determine whether there are risks specific to the subject company that are not reflected in the comparative valuation methods discussed above. Specific factors to analyze are the outlook for continuation of the pass-through entity status; the proportion of earnings paid out both currently and prospectively (examine the historical record, capital needs, and management intentions); owner agreements; and the categories of potential buyers (of the entire company or the interest). These specific risks need to be taken into account in valuing a pass-through entity. These additional risks can be taken into account either in specific discounts or in the valuation multiples or capitalization rates used.

As an example, what would be the impact (presumably negative) of a pass-through entity paying out distributions insufficient to meet the owners' income tax obligations? Typically, distributions are set to meet the income tax obligations of the owner with the highest tax rate. Pass-through entities typically have strong cash flows, making this scenario unlikely. If it was anything but a short-term aberration, there would be little advantage to pass-through entity status, and owners would presumably act to disqualify the election. A more likely scenario that the appraiser may encounter is that distributions are made and then loaned back to the corporation by the owners in order to meet, for example, a large, one-time capital expenditure requirement. This creates debt to the shareholder, which subsequently can be repaid without consequences.

Lack of Marketability

A lack of marketability discount is still applicable to a pass-through entity having no ready market for its securities. However, several additional factors need to be considered in estimating the appropriate level of such a discount. The valuation discount may be higher than an identical corporation organized as a C corporation because the pool of eligible buyers for an S corporation is limited. The valuation discount may be lower because dividends or distributions are more likely to be paid by a pass-through entity, providing the owner a significant cash yield. In fact, the typical pass-through entity may be distributing a large portion of its earnings. On the other hand, the marketability discount for stock of a pass-through entity that is not paying out sufficient distributions to cover the income tax obligations of its shareholders may be significantly increased. Furthermore, pass-through entities may be subject to greater limitations than C corporations with respect to their ability to continue to operate as a going concern (continuity of life) and to the transferability of the ownership interest (which may require approval of other owners).

Summary

Whether a premium or a discount should be applied to the business valuation simply because of the pass-through status of the legal organization structure should be examined on a case-by-case basis. Unfortunately, there isn't a simple answer that applies universally. Factors affecting the business valuation conclusion include:

- The purpose and objective of the assignment.
- The income tax rates of the company, the buyer, and the seller.
- Controlling versus noncontrolling ownership characteristics of the business interest subject to analysis.
- The magnitude of the distributions expected to be made to the owner of the interest.
- The expected holding period of investment.

The advantages and disadvantages of the pass-through form of business lead to the following important business concerns:

1. The articles of organization of the pass-through entity may significantly affect the rights, privileges, and risks of ownership and, hence, the value of ownership.
2. The pool of hypothetical willing buyers (i.e., the marketability of the subject business) may be limited because of the restrictions on ownership of partnership interests and S corporations, and the lack of legislative history regarding LLC owners' rights.
3. The value of ownership of a pass-through entity is not only affected by its tax attributes. Other attributes such as its ability to continue in operation and the restrictions on the transferability of ownership can impact its value.

Bibliography

Ackerman, David. "Technical Issues under the New S Corporation ESOP Laws." *Journal of Employee Ownership Law & Finance*, Winter 1999, pp. 3–20.

Aschwald, Kathryn F., and Donna J. Walker. "Valuing S Corporation ESOP Companies." *The Journal of Employee Ownership Law and Finance*, Summer 1999, pp. 27–34.

Banoff, Sheldon I. "New Ruling Adds Further Encouragement for Large Firms to Form LLCs." *Journal of Taxation*, July 1994, pp. 12–17.

Banoff, Sheldon I., Richard M. Lipton, and Burton W. Kanter. "LLC Members: More Like General or Limited Partners?" *Journal of Taxation*, June 1994, p. 380.

Barragato, Charles A. "The Final S Corporation Single-Class-of-Stock Regulations." *CPA Journal*, May 1993, pp. 46–49.

Berg, Mark E. "Pass-Through Entities." *Journal of S Corporation Taxation*, Summer 1993, pp. 84–91.

Brenman, Lawrence H. "Service Businesses Switch to LLC." *Journal of Partnership Taxation,* Summer 1994, pp. 167–74.

Buss, David B. "LLCs Still Beat S Corps Despite IRS's Reversal." *Practical Accountant*, January 1995, pp. 52–53.

Cassiere, George G. "The Value of S-Corp Election—The C-Corp Equivalency Model." *Business Valuation Review*, June 1994, pp. 84–91.

Clariday, Mary J. "The Limited Liability Company: An S Corporation Alternative or Replacement?" *Journal of S Corporation Taxation*, Winter 1993, pp. 202–25.

Clolery, Paul. "LLPs/LLCs: Bulletproofing Your Firm." *Practical Accountant*, September 1994, pp. 24–32.

Condren, Gary. "S Corporations and Corporate Taxes." *Business Valuation Review*, December 1993, pp. 168–71.

Crow, Matthew R. "The Basics on Fairness Opinions in Transactions Involving ESOPs." *CPA Litigation Service Counselor*, August 1999, pp. 9–10.

Dufendach, David C. "Valuation of Closely Held Corporations: 'C' v. 'S' Differentials." *Business Valuation Review*, December 1996, pp. 176–79.

Duffy, Robert E., and George L. Johnson. "Valuation of 'S' Corporations Revisited: The Impact of the Life of an 'S' Election under Varying Growth and Discount Rates." *Business Valuation Review*, December 1993, pp. 155–67.

Eastland, S. Stacy. "Family Limited Partnerships: Non-Transfer Tax Benefits." *Probate & Property*, March/April 1993, pp. 11–13.

Engel, Barry S., and Ronald L. Rudman. "Family Limited Partnerships: New Meaning for 'Limited.'" *Trusts & Estates*, July 1993, pp. 46–48.

Englebrecht, Ted D., Dana M. LeFever, and Steven C. Colburn. "Shareholder Guarantees of an S Corporation: Review and Analysis of the Basis Dilemma." *Taxes*, February 1993, pp. 114–25.

Graber, Adrian. "Business Valuations for S Corporation Elections." *Business Valuation Review*, December 1996, pp. 174–75.

Griswold, Terence L. "S Corporation Vauation: Is It Art or Science?" *Business Valuation Alert*, December 1999, pp. 1, 5–9.

Hodgman, David R. "Grantor Retained Annuity Trusts and S Corporation Stock." *Trusts & Estates*, December 1993, pp. 38–58.

Horwood, Richard M. "Limited Liability Companies Provide New Planning Options." *Estate Planning*, September/October 1994, pp. 266–74.

Horwood, Richard M., and Jeffrey A. Zaluda. "Asset Protection by Design." *Tax Management Estates, Gifts and Trusts Journal*, July 14, 1994, pp. 119–29.

Houren, Jay R. "Family Limited Partnerships." Presentation to the ABA Tax Section Midyear Meeting, 1999. Available on www.BVLibrary.com.

Ives, H. Bryan III. "Valuation Discounts for Partnership and LLC Member Interests." *Journal of Limited Liability Companies*, Winter 1994, pp. 110–17.

Julius, J. Michael. "Converting Distributions from S Corporations and Partnerships to a C Corporation Dividend Equivalent Basis." *Business Valuation Review*, June 1997, pp. 65–67.

Kato, Kelly. "Valuation of 'S' Corporations—Discounted Cash Flow Method." *Business Valuation Review*, December 1990, pp. 117–22.

Johnson, Linda M., and Rodger A. Bolling. "Bringing an S Corporation Back to Life." *Practical Accountant*, June 1993, pp. 20–31.

Karlinsky, Stewart S., and Hughlene Burton. "S Corporation Current Developments: S Corporation Eligibility and Elections, Operations, Reorganizations and Proposed Legislation." *Tax Adviser*, October 1994, pp. 629–36.

Kubersky, Andrew S. "Marketability Discounting Issues for ESOP Acquisitions of Minority Shares." *Business Valuation Review*, September 1999, pp. 100–03.

Lemons, Bruce N., and Richard D. Blau. "Significant Issues May Remain for S Corporation Partners Despite IRS's Newest Ruling." *Journal of Taxation*, September 1994, pp. 132–36.

Lemons, Bruce N., Richard D. Blau, and Thomas P. Rohman. "Final Basis and Distribution Regs. Provide Additional Guidance for S Corporations." *Journal of Taxation*, April 1994, pp. 226–30.

Looney, Stephen R. "Important Developments Affecting S Corporations Since the Tax Reform Act of 1986." *Journal of S Corporation Taxation*, Spring 1993, pp. 312–44.

Pluth, Robert R., Jr. "The Limited Liability Company: A New Alternative." *Trusts & Estates*, September 1994, pp. 14–17.

Price, Charles E. "Tax Aspects of Limited Liability Companies." *Journal of Accountancy*, September 1992, pp. 48–52.

Simpson, William E., and Peter D. Wrobel. "Income Tax Issues in Valuing S Corporations." *CPA Expert*, Spring 1996, pp. 1–7.

Sliwoski, Leonard. "Reflections on Valuing S Corporations." *Business Valuation Review*, December 1998, pp. 141–46.

Ware, Robert C. "The Limited Liability Company." *Life & Health Insurance Sales*, January 1994, pp. 85–92.

Part VII

Valuations for Specific Purposes

Chapter 27

Valuations for Estate and Gift Tax Purposes

Say not that you know another entirely until you have shared an inheritance with him.

Johann Kaspar Lavater
Swiss theologian, 1788

Introduction

The three most important objectives of estate planning for owners of closely held businesses are:

1. Provision for liquidity for themselves or their heirs, or both.
2. Minimization of federal gift and estate taxes and state inheritance taxes.
3. Provision for continuity of the business.

Liquidity during the owner's lifetime can be achieved by going public, selling the company, selling shares to an employee stock ownership plan (ESOP), or selling shares by other means. Liquidity at the owner's death can be provided by any of the same means or through a buy-sell agreement funded by life insurance. The need for liquidity relates to the business owner's desires not only to cash in on the company's successful growth, but also to have funds available to pay the associated income or estate taxes that the above transactions typically trigger. This chapter discusses the valuation issues that arise in connection with estate and gift planning based on these three key objectives.

Other chapters in Part VII carry this topic further. Chapter 29 focuses on buy-sell agreements. Additional estate planning–related information is contained in Chapter 33 on ESOPs. Elsewhere in the book, Chapter 24 discusses the valuation of preferred stocks, which often have been utilized in estate freezing recapitalizations.

The first section of this chapter sets forth the nature of estate and gift taxes and the current rates, exemptions, special provisions, and penalties under the current Internal Revenue Code and Regulations. The next section discusses the guidelines for valuation for estate and gift tax purposes (which also can be applied to income tax matters) and includes the complete texts of the most relevant IRS Revenue Rulings. The last section deals with valuation issues arising from specific estate and gift tax planning techniques, including the special valuation rules under Chapter 14. No doubt, over time, new estate planning techniques will be developed in response to the constantly changing economic and tax environment.

The material in this book generally is limited to discussion of valuation issues. Anyone involved in valuation services with tax planning or tax litigation implications should consult a competent attorney and CPA for guidance with regard to legal and tax issues.

Current Tax Rates and Penalties

Estate and gift taxes are a unified system of excise taxes levied on the transfer of wealth during life and at death. In other words, in calculating an individual's final estate taxes, the amount of all taxable gifts that were made during life are added to the estate's gross value and all gift taxes that were paid during life are subtracted from the estate tax payable. The current rates on taxable amounts are set forth in Exhibit 27–1.

The law provides for several basic exemptions and exclusions from the amount of net assets that otherwise would be taxable. These adjustments include:

- The first $650,000 of the fair market value of estate or previously gifted assets.[1]
- Any amounts given to one's spouse, either by gift or by will.[2]
- Up to $10,000 (indexed for inflation in $1,000 increments) gifted annually from any one donor to each of any number of donees.

Other special provisions affect:

- The value of farm or small-business, special-use real estate (Internal Revenue Code Section 2032A), and the value of "qualified family-owned business interests" (Section 2057).
- The time over which estate tax payments can be made and the interest rate charged on such payments on the portion of the estate consisting of interests in a privately owned company engaged in an active trade or business (Section 6166).
- The income tax treatment of redemptions of corporate stock owned by the estate whose proceeds are used to pay estate expenses and taxes (Section 303).
- The choice of the estate asset valuation date (either as of date of death or an alternative valuation date six months after death).

An additional tax can be levied on certain generation-skipping transfers of assets.

There are also penalties for the undervaluation of estate and gift assets (Section 6662). These penalties are presented in Exhibit 27–2. The Section 6662 penalties presented in Exhibit 27–2 are triggered by asset undervaluation and computed as a percentage of the tax underpayment. The IRS may decide not to apply these penalties if the reported value was made in good faith and had a reasonable basis. A qualified appraisal prepared by a competent valuation analyst may constitute part of the establishment of a "reasonable basis."

Valuation analysts are subject to a civil penalty of $1,000 for aiding and abetting an understatement of tax liability (Section 6701). Even more serious, the IRS may impose an administrative sanction barring the appraiser from submitting probative evidence in future IRS tax proceedings.

Guidelines for Federal Gift and Estate Tax Valuations

The basic guidelines for the valuation of closely held business equity are set forth in the Internal Revenue Code, the Treasury Regulations to the Code, and various Revenue Rulings. Technical Advice Memorandums and Private Letter Rulings can provide additional insights regarding the IRS positions on business valuation issues.

The Internal Revenue Code addresses the valuation of closely held securities in Section 2031(b). The standard of value applied to all gift, estate, and income tax matters concerning the IRS is fair market value. Fair market value is defined as the

---

[1] This amount applies to decedents dying and gifts made in 1999. The credit will increase annually to a maximum of $1,000,000 in 2006. The phase-in schedule is as follows: $675,000 in 2000 and 2001; $700,000 in 2002 and 2003; $850,000 in 2004; and $950,000 in 2005.

[2] The transfers to the spouse must be "qualified," that is, they must be in a form which would cause the property to be taxed in the spouse's estate if retained until death. These rules are different for spouses who are not U.S. citizens.

Exhibit 27–1

Current Unified Transfer Tax on Gifts and Estates

Column A Taxable Amount Over	Column B Taxable Amount Not Over	Column C Tax on Amount in Column A	Column D Rate of Tax on Excess over Amount in Column A
—	10,000	—	18%
10,000	20,000	1,800	20%
20,000	40,000	3,800	22%
40,000	60,000	8,200	24%
60,000	80,000	13,000	26%
80,000	100,000	18,200	28%
100,000	150,000	23,800	30%
150,000	250,000	38,800	32%
250,000	500,000	70,800	34%
500,000	750,000	155,800	37%
750,000	1,000,000	248,300	39%
1,000,000	1,250,000	345,800	41%
1,250,000	1,500,000	448,300	43%
1,500,000	2,000,000	555,800	45%
2,000,000	2,500,000	780,800	49%
2,500,000	3,000,000	1,025,800	53%
3,000,000	—	1,290,800	55%

SOURCE: *2000 U.S. Master Tax Guide* (Chicago: Commerce Clearing House, 2000), pp. 43-44. The rates change depending on the year of decease or of gift. The current tax regulations and tables should always be consulted.

Exhibit 27–2

Undervaluation Penalties

For Estate and Gift Taxes over $1,000:	
Value Claimed on the Tax Return as a Percentage of the Value Finally Determined	Additional Penalty
50% or more	0%
25%–49%	20%
below 25%	40%

price at which the property would change hands between a willing buyer and a willing seller when neither is under any compulsion to buy or to sell, both parties having reasonable knowledge of the facts.

The next most important source of guidance for valuation are the Treasury Regulations which set forth the IRS's interpretation of the laws set forth in the IRC. Each regulation is numbered in the same fashion as the code section to which it relates. Regulation Section 20.2031-2(f) covers corporate stock and Section 20.2031-3 covers unincorporated interests in businesses. Parallel regulations cover gift taxes in Sections 25.2512-2(f) and 25.2512-3.

Revenue Rulings are similar to regulations, except they are drafted to provide guidance for general types of situations not requiring a specific change in the regulations. The basic guidelines for the valuation of closely held common stocks are contained in Revenue Ruling 59-60, which is presented in its entirety in Exhibit 27–3.

Exhibit 27–3

Revenue Ruling 59–60

SECTION 2031.—DEFINITION OF GROSS ESTATE
26 CFR 20.2031-2: Valuation of stocks and bonds. Rev. Rul. 59-60
(Also Section 2512.)
(Also Part II, Sections 811(k), 1005, Regulations 105, Section 81.10)

In valuing the stock of closely held corporations, or the stock of corporations where market quotations are not available, all other available financial data, as well as all relevant factors affecting the fair market value must be considered for estate tax and gift tax purposes. No general formula may be given that is applicable to the many different valuation situations arising in the valuation of such stock. However, the general approach, methods, and factors which must be considered in valuing such securities are outlined. Revenue Ruling 54-77, C.B. 1954-1, 187, superseded.

SECTION 1. PURPOSE.

The purpose of this Revenue Ruling is to outline and review in general the approach, methods and factors to be considered in valuing shares of the capital stock of closely held corporations for estate tax and gift tax purposes. The methods discussed herein will apply likewise to the valuation of corporate stocks on which market quotations are either unavailable or are of such scarcity that they do not reflect the fair market value.

SEC. 2. BACKGROUND AND DEFINITIONS.

.01 All valuations must be made in accordance with the applicable provisions of the Internal Revenue Code of 1954 and the Federal Estate Tax and Gift Tax Regulations. Sections 2031(a), 2032 and 2512(a) of the 1954 Code (sections 811 and 1005 of the 1939 Code) require that the property to be included in the gross estate, or made the subject of a gift, shall be taxed on the basis of the value of the property at the time of death of the decedent, the alternate date if so elected, or the date of gift.

.02 Section 20.2031-1(b) of the Estate Tax Regulations (section 81.10 of the Estate Tax Regulations 105) and section 25.2512-1 of the Gift Tax Regulations (section 86.19 of Gift Tax Regulations 108) define fair market value, in effect, as the price at which the property would change hands between a willing buyer and a willing seller when the former is not under any compulsion to buy and the latter is not under any compulsion to sell, both parties having reasonable knowledge of relevant facts. Court decisions frequently state in addition that the hypothetical buyer and seller are assumed to be able, as well as willing, to trade and to be well informed about the property and concerning the market for such property.

.03 Closely held corporations are those corporations the shares of which are owned by a relatively limited number of stockholders. Often the entire stock issue is held by one family. The result of this situation is that little, if any, trading in the shares takes place. There is, therefore, no established market for the stock and such sales as occur at irregular intervals seldom reflect all of the elements of a representative transaction as defined by the term "fair market value."

SEC. 3. APPROACH TO VALUATION.

.01 A determination of fair market value, being a question of fact, will depend upon the circumstances in each case. No formula can be devised that will be generally applicable to the multitude of different valuation issues arising in estate and gift tax cases. Often, an appraiser will find wide differences of opinion as to the fair market value of a particular stock. In resolving such differences, he should maintain a reasonable attitude in recognition of the fact that valuation is not an exact science. A sound valuation will be based upon all the relevant facts, but the elements of common sense, informed judgment and reasonableness must enter into the process of weighing those facts and determining their aggregate significance.

.02 The fair market value of specific shares of stock will vary as general economic conditions change from "normal" to "boom" or "depression," that is, according to the degree of optimism or pessimism with which the investing public regards the future at the required date of appraisal. Uncertainty as to the stability or continuity of the future income from a property decreases its value by increasing the risk of loss of earnings and value in the future. The value of shares of stock of a company with very uncertain future prospects is highly speculative. The appraiser must exercise his judgment as to the degree of risk attaching to the business of the corporation which issued the stock, but that judgment must be related to all of the other factors affecting value.

.03 Valuation of securities is, in essence, a prophesy as to the future and must be based on facts available at the required date of appraisal. As a generalization, the prices of stocks which are traded in volume in a free and active market by informed persons best reflect the consensus of the investing public as to what the future holds for the corporations and industries represented. When a stock is closely held, is traded infrequently, or is traded in an erratic market, some other measure of value must be used. In many instances, the next best measure may be found in the prices at which the stocks of companies engaged in the same or a similar line of business are selling in a free and open market.

SEC 4. FACTORS TO CONSIDER.

.01 It is advisable to emphasize that in the valuation of the stock of closely held corporations or the stock of corporations where market quotations are either lacking or too scarce to be recognized, all available financial data, as well as all relevant factors affecting the fair market value, should be considered. The following factors, although not all-inclusive are fundamental and require careful analysis in each case:

(a) The nature of the business and the history of the enterprise from its inception.

(b) The economic outlook in general and the condition and outlook of the specific industry in particular.

(c) The book value of the stock and the financial condition of the business.

(d) The earnings capacity of the company.

(e) The dividend-paying capacity.

(f) Whether or not the enterprise has goodwill or other intangible value.

(g) Sales of the stock and the size of the block of stock to be valued.

(h) The market price of stocks of corporations engaged in the same or a similar line of business having their stocks actively traded in a free and open market, either on an exchange or over-the-counter.

.02 The following is a brief discussion of each of the foregoing factors:

(a) The history of a corporate enterprise will show its past stability or instability, its growth or lack of growth, the diversity or lack of diversity of its operations, and other facts needed to form an opinion of the degree of risk involved in the business. For an enterprise which changed its form of organization but carried on the same or closely similar operations of its predecessor, the history of the former enterprise should be considered. The detail to be considered should increase with approach to the required date of appraisal, since recent events are of greatest help in predicting the future; but a study of gross and net income, and of dividends covering a long prior period, is highly desirable. The history to be studied should include, but need not be limited to, the nature of the business, its products or services, its operating and investment assets, capital structure, plant facilities, sales records and management, all of which should be considered as of the date of the appraisal, with due regard for recent significant changes. Events of the past that are unlikely to recur in the future should be discounted, since value has a close relation to future expectancy.

(b) A sound appraisal of a closely held stock must consider current and prospective economic conditions as of the date of appraisal, both in the national economy and in the industry or industries with which the corporation is allied. It is important to know that the company is more or less

continued on next page

Exhibit 27–3

Revenue Ruling 59–60 (continued)

successful than its competitors in the same industry, or that it is maintaining a stable position with respect to competitors. Equal or even greater significance may attach to the ability of the industry with which the company is allied to compete with other industries. Prospective competition which has not been a factor in prior years should be given careful attention. For example, high profits due to the novelty of its product and the lack of competition often lead to increasing competition. The public's appraisal of the future prospects of competitive industries or of competitors within an industry may be indicated by price trends in the markets for commodities and for securities. The loss of the manager of a so-called "one-man" business may have a depressing effect upon the value of the stock of such business, particularly if there is a lack of trained personnel capable of succeeding to the management of the enterprise. In valuing the stock of this type of business, therefore, the effect of the loss of the manager on the future expectancy of the business, and the absence of management succession potentialities are pertinent factors to be taken into consideration. On the other hand, there may be factors which offset, in whole or in part, the loss of the manager's services. For instance, the nature of the business and of its assets may be such that they will not be impaired by the loss of the manager. Furthermore, the loss may be adequately covered by life insurance, or competent management might be employed on the basis of the consideration paid for the former manager's services. These, or other offsetting factors, if found to exist, should be carefully weighed against the loss of the manager's services in valuing the stock of the enterprise.

(c) Balance sheets should be obtained, preferably in the form of comparative annual statements for two or more years immediately preceding the date of appraisal, together with a balance sheet at the end of the month preceding that date, if corporate accounting will permit. Any balance sheet descriptions that are not self-explanatory, and balance sheet items comprehending diverse assets or liabilities, should be clarified in essential detail by supporting supplemental schedules. These statements usually will disclose to the appraiser (1) liquid position (ratio of current assets to current liabilities); (2) gross and net book value of principal classes of fixed assets; (3) working capital; (4) long-term indebtedness; (5) capital structure; and (6) net worth. Consideration also should be given to any assets not essential to the operation of the business, such as investments in securities, real estate, etc. In general, such nonoperating assets will command a lower rate of return than do the operating assets, although in exceptional cases the reverse may be true. In computing the book value per share of stock, assets of the investment type should be revalued on the basis of their market price and the book value adjusted accordingly. Comparison of the company's balance sheets over several years may reveal, among other facts, such developments as the acquisition of additional production facilities or subsidiary companies, improvement in financial position, and details as to recapitalizations and other changes in the capital structure of the corporation. If the corporation has more than one class of stock outstanding, the charter or certificate of incorporation should be examined to ascertain the explicit rights and privileges of the various stock issues including: (1) voting powers, (2) preference as to dividends; and (3) preference as to assets in the event of liquidation.

(d) Detailed profit-and-loss statements should be obtained and considered for a representative period immediately prior to the required date of appraisal, preferably five or more years. Such statements should show (1) gross income by principal items; (2) principal deductions from gross income including major prior items of operating expenses, interest and other expense on each item of long-term debt, depreciation and depletion if such deductions are made, officers' salaries, in total if they appear to be reasonable or in detail if they seem to be excessive, contributions (whether or not deductible for tax purposes) that the nature of its business and its community position require the corporation to make, and taxes by principal items, including income and excess profits taxes; (3) net income available for dividends; (4) rates and amount of dividends paid on each class

of stock; (5) remaining amount carried to surplus; and (6) adjustment to, and reconciliation with, surplus as stated on the balance sheet. With profit and loss statements of this character available, the appraiser should be able to separate recurrent from nonrecurrent items of income and expense, to distinguish between operating income and investment income, and to ascertain whether or not any line of business in which the company is engaged is operated consistently at a loss and might be abandoned with benefit to the company. The percentage of earnings retained for business expansion should be noted when dividend-paying capacity is considered. Potential future income is a major factor in many valuations of closely held stocks, and all information concerning past income which will be helpful in predicting the future should be secured. Prior earnings records usually are the most reliable guide as to the future expectancy, but resort to arbitrary five-or ten-year averages without regard to current trends or future prospects will not produce a realistic valuation. If, for instance, a record of progressively increasing or decreasing net income is found, then greater weight may be accorded the most recent years' profits in estimating earning power. It will be helpful, in judging risk and the extent to which a business is a marginal operator, to consider deductions from income and net income in terms of percentage of sales. Major categories of cost and expense to be so analyzed include the consumption of raw materials and supplies in the case of manufacturers, processors and fabricators; the cost of purchased merchandise in the case of merchants; utility services; insurance; taxes; depletion or depreciation; and interest.

(e) Primary consideration should be given to the dividend-paying capacity of the company rather than to dividends actually paid in the past. Recognition must be given to the necessity of retaining a reasonable portion of profits in a company to meet competition. Dividend-paying capacity is a factor that must be considered in an appraisal, but dividends actually paid in the past may not have any relation to dividend-paying capacity. Specifically, the dividends paid by a closely held family company may be measured by the income needs of the stockholders or by their desire to avoid taxes on dividend receipts, instead of by the ability of the company to pay dividends. Where an actual or effective controlling interest in a corporation is to be valued, the dividend factor is not a material element, since the payment of such dividends is discretionary with the controlling stockholders. The individual or group in control can substitute salaries and bonuses for dividends, thus reducing net income and understating the dividend-pay capacity of the company. It follows, therefore, that dividends are less reliable criteria of fair market value than other applicable factors.

(f) In the final analysis, goodwill is based upon earning capacity. The presence of goodwill and its value, therefore, rests upon the excess of net earnings over and above a fair return on the net tangible assets. While the element of goodwill may be based primarily on earnings, such factors as the prestige and renown of the business, the ownership of a trade or brand name, and a record of successful operation over a prolonged period in a particular locality, also may furnish support for the inclusion of intangible value. In some instances it may not be possible to make a separate appraisal of the tangible and intangible assets of the business. The enterprise has a value as an entity. Whatever intangible value there is, which is supportable by the facts, may be measured by the amount by which the appraised value of the tangible assets exceeds the net book value of such assets.

(g) Sales of stock of a closely held corporation should be carefully investigated to determine whether they represent transactions at arm's length. Forced or distress sales do not ordinarily reflect fair market value nor do isolated sales in small amounts necessarily control as the measure of value. This is especially true in the valuation of a controlling interest in a corporation. Since, in the case of closely held stocks, no prevailing market prices are available, there is no basis for making an adjustment for blockage. It follows, therefore, that such stocks should be valued upon a consideration of all the evidence affecting the fair market value. The size

continued on next page

Exhibit 27–3

Revenue Ruling 59–60 (continued)

of the block of stock itself is a relevant factor to be considered. Although it is true that a minority interest in an unlisted corporation's stock is more difficult to sell than a similar block of listed stock, it is equally true that control of a corporation, either actual or in effect, representing as it does an added element of value, may justify a higher value for a specific block of stock.

(h) Section 2031(b) of the Code states, in effect, that in valuing unlisted securities the value of stock or securities of corporations engaged in the same or a similar line of business which are listed on an exchange should be taken into consideration along with all other factors. An important consideration is that the corporations to be used for comparisons have capital stocks which are actively traded by the public. In accordance with section 2031(b) of the Code, stocks listed on an exchange are to be considered first. However, if sufficient comparable companies whose stocks are listed on an exchange cannot be found, other comparable companies which have stocks actively traded in on the over-the-counter market also may be used. The essential factor is that whether the stocks are sold on an exchange or over-the-counter there is evidence of an active, free public market for the stock as of the valuation date. In selecting corporations for comparative purposes, care should be taken to use only comparable companies. Although the only restrictive requirement as to comparable corporations specified in the statute is that their lines of business be the same or similar, yet it is obvious that consideration must be given to other relevant factors in order that the most valid comparison possible will be obtained. For illustration, a corporation having one or more issues of preferred stock, bonds or debentures in addition to its common stock should not be considered to be directly comparable to one having only common stock outstanding. In like manner, a company with a declining business and decreasing markets is not comparable to one with a record of current progress and market expansion.

Sec. 5. Weight to be Accorded Various Factors.

The valuation of closely held corporate stock entails the consideration of all relevant factors as stated in section 4. Depending upon the circumstances in each case, certain factors may carry more weight than others because of the nature of the company's business. To illustrate:

(a) Earnings may be the most important criterion of value in some cases whereas asset value will receive primary consideration in others. In general, the appraiser will accord primary consideration to earnings when valuing stocks of companies which sell products or services to the public; conversely, in the investment or holding type of company, the appraiser may accord the greatest weight to the assets underlying the security to be valued.

(b) The value of the stock of a closely held investment or real estate holding company, whether or not family owned, is closely related to the value of the assets underlying the stock. For companies of this type the appraiser should determine the fair market values of the assets of the company. Operating expenses of such a company and the cost of liquidating it, if any, merit consideration when appraising the relative values of the stock and the underlying assets. The market values of the underlying assets give due weight to potential earnings and dividends of the particular items of property underlying the stock, capitalized at rates deemed proper by the investing public at the date of appraisal. A current appraisal by the investing public should be superior to the retrospective opinion of an individual. For these reasons, adjusted net worth should be accorded greater weight in valuing the stock of a closely held investment or real estate holding company, whether or not family owned, than any of the other customary yardsticks of appraisal, such as earnings and dividend paying capacity.

Sec. 6. Capitalization Rates.

In the application of certain fundamental valuation factors, such as earnings and dividends, it is necessary to capitalize the average or current results at some appropriate rate. A determination of the proper capitalization rate presents one of the most difficult problems in valuation. That there is no ready or simple solution will become apparent by a cursory check of the rates of return and dividend yields in terms of the selling prices of corporate shares listed on the major exchanges of the country. Wide variations will be found even for companies in the same industry. Moreover, the ratio will fluctuate from year to year depending upon economic conditions. Thus, no standard tables of capitalization rates applicable to closely held corporations can be formulated. Among the more important factors to be taken into consideration in deciding upon a capitalization rate in a particular case are: (1) the nature of the business; (2) the risk involved; and (3) the stability or irregularity of earnings.

Sec. 7. Average of Factors.

Because valuations cannot be made on the basis of a prescribed formula, there is no means whereby the various applicable factors in a particular case can be assigned mathematical weights in deriving the fair market value. For this reason, no useful purpose is served by taking an average of several factors (for example, book value, capitalized earnings and capitalized dividends) and basing the valuation on the result. Such a process excludes active consideration of other pertinent factors, and the end result cannot be supported by a realistic application of the significant facts in the case except by mere chance.

Sec. 8. Restrictive Agreements.

Frequently, in the valuation of closely held stock for estate and gift tax purposes, it will be found that the stock is subject to an agreement restricting its sale or transfer. Where shares of stocks were acquired by a decedent subject to an option reserved by the issuing corporation to repurchase at a certain price, the option price is usually accepted as the fair market value for estate tax purposes. See Rev. Rul. 54-76, C.B. 1954-1, 194. However, in such case the option price is not determinative of fair market value for gift tax purposes. Where the option, or buy and sell agreement, is the result of voluntary action by the stockholders and is binding during the life as well as at the death of the stockholders, such agreement may or may not, depending upon the circumstances of each case, fix the value for estate tax purposes. However, such agreement is a factor to be considered, with other relevant factors, in determining fair market value. Where the stockholder is free to dispose of his shares during life and the option is to become effective only upon his death, the fair market value is not limited to the option price. It is always necessary to consider the relationship of the parties, the relative number of shares held by the decedent, and other material facts to determine whether the agreement represents a bona fide business arrangement or is a device to pass the decedent's shares to the natural objects of his bounty for less than an adequate and full consideration in money or money's worth. In this connection see Rev. Rul. 157 C.B. 1953-2, 255, and Rev. Rul. 189, C.B. 1953-2, 294.

Sec. 9. Effect on Other Documents.

Revenue Ruling 54-77, C.B. 1954-1, 187, is hereby superseded.

SOURCE: Rev. Rul. 59-60, 1959-1 C.B. 237.

Other forms of IRS opinions are issued in the form of Technical Advice Memorandums (TAMs) and Private Letter Rulings (PLRs), which refer to specific situations in which advice has been sought on a specific matter from the national office of the IRS. PLRs arise when taxpayers seek guidance on an issue for a specific case. TAMs arise when an inquiry on a specific issue in a case is initiated by a field office of the IRS. Although these TAMs and PLRs cannot be cited as precedent for anyone but the individual taxpayer, they do provide good evidence of the direction of the IRS thinking on a topic.

Of course the courts have final jurisdiction over tax matters. IRS regulations and positions taken in revenue rulings can be overturned by a single or series of adverse judicial rulings. The U.S. Tax Court, Federal District Court, and Court of Federal Claims systems all hear cases involving valuation issues for gift and estate taxes.

Revenue Ruling 59-60 also has been modified and amplified by other subsequent revenue rulings.

Revenue Ruling 77-287, presented as Exhibit 17–7 in Chapter 17, amplifies Revenue Ruling 59-60 by specifically recognizing criteria for determining an appropriate discount for lack of marketability. It also provides guidance for discounts to be applied to publicly traded securities restricted under federal securities laws (see Chapter 17). Revenue Ruling 83-120, discussed in Chapter 24, contains guidelines for valuing preferred stock. Revenue Ruling 93-12, presented in Exhibit 27–4, acknowledged that stock interest transfers among family members, who in the aggregate own a controlling interest in the company, would not be valued as controlling interests solely due to the family relationship among the shareholders. This acknowledgement that noncontrolling ownership interest transfers among relatives would normally be treated as noncontrolling interests for valuation purposes follows a long series of IRS losses in court on this issue.

If the analyst follows the valuation procedures presented in this book with reasonable thoroughness, the requirements of these rulings should be satisfied. Consequently, beyond including the relevant rulings as exhibits, this section will simply call attention to a few points in Revenue Ruling 59-60. The following chapter discusses a variety of key factors in the context of various positions taken and decisions reached in court cases.

Revenue Ruling 59-60, Section 3, "Approach to Valuation," makes the general point that the public marketplace best reflects the consensus of the investing public, and it concludes by suggesting as a measure of value "the prices at which the stocks of companies engaged in the same or similar line of business are selling in a free and open market." The section also recognizes that the value can change as a result of factors internal to the company and external economic factors. The section emphasizes the complexity of the factors affecting valuation and the degree of uncertainty involved.

Revenue Ruling 59-60, Section 4, "Factors to Consider," lists the eight key factors to consider with regard to the valuation of closely held corporations and elaborates on each. In any valuation involving gift and estate taxes, the analyst should review Section 4 to ensure that each of the eight points has been addressed in the valuation process.

Revenue Ruling 59-60, Section 4.01(c) notes, "In computing the book value per share of stock, assets *of the investment type* should be revalued on the basis of their market price and the book value adjusted accordingly [emphasis supplied]." It

Exhibit 27–4

Revenue Ruling 93–12

REVENUE RULING 93-12

ISSUE

If a donor transfers shares in a corporation to each of the donor's children, is the factor of corporate control in the family to be considered in valuing each transferred interest, for purposes of section 2512 of the Internal Revenue Code?

FACTS

P owned all of the single outstanding class of stock of X corporation. P transferred all of P's shares by making simultaneous gifts of 20 percent of the shares to each of P's five children, A, B, C, D, and E.

LAW AND ANALYSIS

Section 2512(a) of the Code provides that the value of the property at the date of the gift shall be considered the amount of the gift.

Section 25.2512-1 of the Gift Tax Regulations provides that, if a gift is made in property, its value at the date of the gift shall be considered the amount of the gift. The value of the property is the price at which the property would change hands between a willing buyer and a willing seller, neither being under any compulsion to buy or to sell, and both having reasonable knowledge of relevant facts.

Section 25.2512-2(a) of the regulations provides that the value of stocks and bonds is the fair market value per share or bond on the date of the gift. Section 25.2512-2(f) provides that the degree of control of the business represented by the block of stock to be valued is among the factors to be considered in valuing stock where there are no sales prices or bona fide bid or asked prices.

Rev. Rul. 81-253, 1981-1 C.B. 187, holds that, ordinarily, no minority shareholder discount is allowed with respect to transfers of shares of stock between family members if, based upon a composite of the family members' interest at the time of the transfer, control (either majority voting control or de facto control through family relationships) of the corporation exists in the family unit. The ruling also states that the Service will not follow the decision of the Fifth Circuit in Estate of Bright v. United States, 658 F.2d 999 (5th Cir. 1981).

In Bright, the decedent's undivided community property interest in shares of stock, together with the corresponding undivided community property interest of the decedent's surviving spouse, constituted a control block of 55 percent of the shares of a corporation. The court held that, because the community-held shares were subject to a right of partition,

the decedent's own interest was equivalent to 27.5 percent of the outstanding shares and, therefore, should be valued as a minority interest, even though the shares were to be held by the decedent's surviving spouse as trustee of a testamentary trust. See also, Propstra v. United States, 680 F.2d 1248 (9th Cir. 1982). In addition, Estate of Andrews v. Commissioner, 79 T.C. 938 (1982), and Estate of Lee v. Commissioner, 69 T.C. 860 (1978), nonacq., 1980-2 C.B. 2, held that the corporation shares owned by other family members cannot be attributed to an individual family member for determining whether the individual family member's share should be valued as the controlling interest of the corporation.

After further consideration of the position taken in Rev. Rul. 81-253, and in light of the cases noted above, the Service has concluded that, in the case of a corporation with a single class of stock, notwithstanding the family relationship of the donor, the donee, and other shareholders, the shares of other family members will not be aggregated with the transferred shares to determine whether the transferred shares should be valued as part of a controlling interest.

In the present case, the minority interests transferred to A, B, C, D, and E should be valued for gift tax purposes without regard to the family relationship of the parties.

HOLDING

If a donor transfers shares in a corporation to each of the donor's children, the factor of corporate control in the family is not considered in valuing each transferred interest for purposes of section 2512 of the Code. For estate and gift tax valuation purposes, the Service will follow Bright, Propstra, Andrews, and Lee in not assuming that all voting power held by family members may be aggregated for purposes of determining whether the transferred shares should be valued as part of a controlling interest. Consequently, a minority discount will not be disallowed solely because a transferred interest, when aggregated with interest held by family members, would be a part of a controlling interest. This would be the case whether the donor held 100 percent or some lesser percentage of the stock immediately before the gift.

EFFECT ON OTHER DOCUMENTS

Rev. Rul. 81-253 is revoked. Acquiescence in issue one of Lee, 1980-2 C.B. 2.

SOURCE: Rev. Rul. 93-12, 1993-1, C.B. 202.

is important to recognize that this requirement to adjust asset values specifically applies to assets "of the investment type," not operating assets.

Section 4.02(d) notes that the profit and loss statements to be considered should be for a "representative period." The section states that the analyst should separate recurrent from nonrecurrent items and operating income from investment income. It suggests putting more weight on recent years if there appears to be a trend in the earnings pattern.

Section 4.02(h) re-emphasizes that the prices of stocks of publicly traded companies in the same or similar lines of business should be considered and the greatest care possible taken in analyzing the companies in order to select the ones that are most comparative to the subject securities. Chapter 11 discusses the identification and selection of guideline publicly traded companies.

Weight to Be Accorded Various Factors

Section 5, "Weight to Be Accorded Various Factors," essentially makes the point that earnings should be accorded the most weight in valuing operating companies and asset values the most weight in valuing holding companies.

The section also notes that assets should be adjusted to market values if they are a factor in an operating company. For family-held investment companies, comparisons of per share value to underlying asset value can then be made on the basis of the ratios of market value to net asset value for closed-end investment companies, since such companies report the values of their assets at market on a regular basis. For closely held real estate holding companies, deriving a per share value by reference to publicly traded real estate holding companies is not quite as easy, since most real estate companies do not report their assets' market values. However, in the last few years quite a few real estate investment trusts (REITs) have started reporting market values. There now are enough reporting such market values that a table of REITs with the ratios of market prices to adjusted asset values can be constructed to provide guidance in valuing closely held real estate holding company shares.

Capitalization Rates

Section 6, "Capitalization Rates," makes further reference to publicly traded shares and notes that appropriate capitalization rates vary considerably both among companies and over time due to economic conditions.

Average of Factors

Section 7, "Average of Factors," is the section referred to in Chapter 19 that discourages use of a mathematical weighting of various factors. The reason is that "such a process excludes active consideration of other pertinent factors." However, as noted in Chapter 19 and in the examples presented in that chapter, mathematical weighting frequently is used in practice, even by government representatives, and relied on in court decisions despite the wording of this section.

Restrictive Agreements

Section 8, "Restrictive Agreements," makes the point that to be binding for estate tax valuation purposes, a price fixed under a buy-sell agreement must be binding during the life as well as at the death of the stockholder and not "a device to pass the decedent's shares to the natural objects of his bounty for less than adequate and full consideration in money or money's worth." See Chapter 29, "Buy-Sell Agreements," for additional discussion.

Summary of Guidelines

Although Revenue Ruling 59-60 was written over 40 years ago, it still offers considerable insight into the basic criteria and processes for valuing closely held common stocks. With minor modifications and amplification, it has stood the test of time.

Nevertheless, the nature of the process necessarily leaves much room for subjectivity and disagreement. Interpretations by IRS agents and by the courts have been somewhat less than consistent. It is not a subject that lends itself to such sharp definition of criteria that gray areas can be eliminated.

Chapter 14 Special Valuation Guidelines

Aside from the basic guidelines that have evolved over the years for valuing closely held securities for federal estate and gift taxes, in 1990 Congress passed a series of special valuation rules listed under a newly created Chapter 14 of the Internal Revenue Code to stem what the IRS convinced Congress to be certain abusive practices that involved valuation issues. Each of the four sections of Chapter 14, Sections 2701 through 2704, addresses a different series of issues and is discussed below. Because of the limitations on the size of this book, we can only address the major topics with which a valuation analyst is likely to deal under Chapter 14.

These special valuation rules potentially apply to all transactions (or modifications to prior existing arrangements) that occur after October 8, 1990, the effective date of the Chapter 14 statute.

It is very important to note that, if the Chapter 14 special valuation rules do not apply, the basic guidelines discussed in the previous section of this chapter, and other generally accepted techniques used to determine fair market value, will apply. The special valuation rules themselves are designed to override the generally accepted valuation guidelines for gift and estate tax valuation. Nonetheless, the structure of the special valuation rules clearly shows that Congress did not intend to eliminate consideration of discounts for lack of control for noncontrolling interest transfers or discounts for lack of marketability for estate and gift tax issues, even when family members as a group own control of an enterprise.

Valuing Recapitalizations and Senior Equity Interests under Section 2701

Section 2701 of Chapter 14 sets forth special valuation rules utilized for lifetime gifts when a junior equity interest (corporate, partnership or limited liability company) is transferred from one family member to another and the transferor (or an "applicable family member") retains a senior equity interest in the company. In other words, Section 2701 deals with the classic preferred estate "freeze."

Triggering the Special Valuation Rules. To fall under the rules of 2701, the following characteristics must be present in a transaction:

- The retained security must be of a class senior to the transferred junior security.
- The subject securities (both the retained senior preferred and transferred junior securities) must be non–publicly traded.
- The transaction must result in a transfer (directly or indirectly) between members of the family.[3]

---

[3] *Member of the family* is defined as the transferor's spouse, the transferor's (or spouse's) lineal descendants (and their spouses). In other words, any natural or adopted children or offspring of the children of the transferor and all associated spouses. Notice that such transfers do not apply to transfers from uncles and aunts to nieces and nephews.

- Immediately before the transfer, the transferor and applicable family members[4] in the aggregate have 50 percent or more (by vote or value) control of the corporate stock, or of the capital or profits interests in a partnership or limited liability company. Or, the transferor and the applicable family members must own any general partnership interest in a limited partnership.
- The transfer is not a proportionate transfer of all senior and junior equity interests and, as mentioned, the transferor must retain a senior equity interest.

If the transfer has these characteristics, then certain retained rights of the "applicable retained interest" (as the preferred senior security is called in Section 2701) must be ignored, and a special subtraction method of valuation must be followed, in determining fair market value for federal gift tax purposes.

Section 2701 basically requires that all rights and features of the preferred senior security that have any optional features in terms of payment amounts or timing that can potentially be manipulated by the controlling family be ignored or valued in a manner that results in the lowest possible value for the preferred senior interest.

As a result, all noncumulative distribution rights (such as dividends) are valued at zero regardless of family control. Similarly, any extraordinary payment right, such as a put, call, conversion, liquidation right, or option to acquire equity interests, is valued at zero—with certain exceptions described below.

The practical effect of these rules, from a valuation standpoint, is that only a few features will provide a basis for attributing value to the applicable retained senior securities. These include:

- *Cumulative dividends or distribution rights.* These can be either fixed in amount or variable if linked by a fixed ratio to a public market interest rate. These are called "qualified distribution rights." The taxpayer may make a permanent election to treat any noncumulative distribution right as a cumulative, qualified distribution right.[5] Therefore, the analyst should check with the client or the client's tax advisers to see if such an election has been made or will be made. If such qualified distributions are not actually made within four years of their scheduled payment date, then these unpaid distributions are treated as gifts and compounded forward for ultimate payment when the holder dies or transfers his interest.
- *Voting rights.* In valuing voting rights, any of the extraordinary payment rights discussed above are assumed either not to exist, or are exercised under the "lower of" rule, discussed below.
- *Mandatory redemption rights.* This category of redemption rights must require the retained preferred senior interest to receive a specific amount at a specific date. Optional extraordinary payment redemption rights that can be voluntarily exercised by either the holder or the company do not count.
- *Nonlapsing conversion rights.* Conversion rights that add value under Section 2701 must require that the senior interests be convertible into a stated number

---

[4] *Applicable family member* is defined differently than "member of the family." An applicable family member includes: (1) the transferor and spouse, (2) the transferor's (or spouse's) ancestors (or their ancestors' spouses). For purposes of measuring control, the transferor's brothers, sisters, or other lineal descendants of the parents of the transferor (or spouse) are also included as part of the measuring group of interest holders. Indirect applicable family member holdings through corporations, partnerships, and trusts are also included. Some background in genealogy is thus required as part of the due diligence for estate and gift tax valuation under Chapter 14.

[5] The taxpayer also can elect not to treat a cumulative dividend right as a qualified distribution right. This would be rather unusual, as the distribution right is then valued at zero for gift tax purposes. This may make sense when the subject company cannot be certain that distributions can be made consistently within the four-year grace period for payment under Section 2701(d).

of shares or percentage of the same class as the transferred interest. Obviously, this will tend to make the preferred interest increase in value with the underlying junior equity securities, and thus frustrate a freeze of the senior preferred interest. The timing of conversion can be optional.

There is also an additional "lower of" valuation rule which requires that the analyst determine if any of the extraordinary payment rights, if exercised in conjunction with any qualified distribution right, would lower the total value of the preferred security. If so, then the lower of the values must be used as the value of the applicable retained interest in the preferred securities.

As an example of this "lower of" rule, if a preferred stock had a high fixed, cumulative dividend yield that would cause it to be valued in excess of par value, but the preferred stock also had a put right or right to compel liquidation at par value, then the value utilized for the preferred interest would be par value—the lower of the two values.

Applying the Subtraction Method. Once it is established that the transaction falls under the special valuation rules of Section 2701, and that certain rights and features of the applicable retained interest in the senior preferred securities either do or do not add value under Section 2701, then the value of the transferred junior equity interest is determined under the Section 2701 subtraction method. The value is determined by following a four-step process:

Step 1. Estimate the fair market value of all of the capital securities of the subject company held by: the transferor (or spouse), any applicable family members, and any lineal descendants of the parents of the transferor (or spouse), utilizing standard business interest valuation procedures. Under Section 2701, the analyst should assume that all of these family-held interests are owned by one person, using a consistent set of assumptions. At this point it is also appropriate to determine what percentage of each class of the senior and junior equity interests the transferor and his applicable family members own in the aggregate, as this information will be used in Step 2. In many cases Step 1 may require the valuation of the entire company on a control basis as either a going concern or under a liquidation premise, when the family owns 100 percent of the securities.

Step 2. From this value subtract:
1. The fair market value of all family-held senior equity interests, other than those of the transferor and applicable family members. Also, as discussed immediately below in number 2, any percentage of the retained senior equity interests owned by the transferor and applicable family members in excess of the maximum percentage of junior equity interest classes held by the same transferor and the applicable family member group, is added back at this point in Step 2. These senior equity interests are valued utilizing standard business interest valuation procedures (see Revenue Ruling 83-120 and Chapter 24 on valuing preferred stock). In most family-owned businesses this calculation will not come into play, as all family member interest holders will be included in number 2 below.
2. The value determined under the Section 2701 special valuation rules of the transferor's and his applicable family members' retained senior equity interests. As noted above, this amount is further adjusted by reducing this amount so that it does not exceed the largest percentage

interest owned by the transferor and his applicable family members of any of the junior classes of equity interests.

As an example, if the transferor and applicable family members owned 100 percent of the preferred stock in a recapitalized company, but only owned 90 percent of the common class of stock (the rest being held by non–family member employees), then the number of preferred shares valued under the special valuation rules of Section 2701 would be 90 percent of the preferred share class. The remaining preferred shares would be valued utilizing standard business interest valuation procedures, as noted immediately above in number 1.

This procedure recognizes that any advantage in not exercising the nonqualified distribution and extraordinary payment rights of the senior securities may benefit all junior equity holders, not just the immediate members of the family.

Step 3. Allocate the remaining value to the family-held junior equity securities. If there are more than one class of junior equity securities, then the allocation must start with the class of junior equity securities with the greatest preference over the other junior equity classes. The allocation of the remaining value is made by continuing with the same set of assumptions utilized for valuing the entire family-held equity in Step 1 and the senior equity in Step 2 (i.e., using the "lower of" rule and zero value rules).

A final special "minimum value" rule under Section 2701 provides that the total allocated value to the junior equity interests can never be less than 10 percent of the sum of: (1) the total value of *all* of the enterprise's equity interests, plus (2) the total amount of any indebtedness owed to the transferor and any applicable family members.

Step 4. Determine the amount of the gift. The allocated values of the transferred junior equity interests are typically adjusted for discounts for (1) lack of ownership control and (2) lack of marketability. In the IRS Final Regulations,[6] the IRS provides some examples that do not include such discounts for some situations in which appraisers (and existing case law) would ordinarily allow discounts. We assume that since these final regulations pre-date Revenue Ruling 93-12, the examples would be altered to show such discounts if they were issued currently.

The final regulations also suggest that the total reduction to the allocated value, for lack of ownership control and lack of marketability discounts, should not cause the value of the transferred junior equity interests to be less than their fair market value utilizing standard business interest valuation procedures.

Also, any consideration paid to the transferor by the transferee would also require a reduction adjustment to the allocated value at this point in the process before determining the value of the gift under Section 2701. If this consideration is additional preferred stock, for example, swapped by the transferee to the transferor for common stock, the value of the preferred stock consideration is the value determined under the special valuation rules of Section 2701 (and not fair market value).

---

[6] Treasury Decision 8395 (RIN: 1545-AP44), effective January 28, 1992.

Lastly, any value determined under Section 2702 (regarding retained life, annuity, or unitrust interests in trust) is also subtracted during this step.

The remaining adjusted value allocated to the transferred junior equity shares is the deemed amount of the gift.

The discussion in the final regulations regarding the "minimum value" rule in Step 3 and the maximum reduction for discounts in Step 4 suggests that an additional iteration is also part of the subtraction process under Section 2701. Many practitioners believe that the analyst also needs to estimate the fair market value of the applicable retained senior equity interests and the junior transferred equity interests, without regard to the Section 2701 special valuation rules, in order to check these results against the results of the special valuation calculations.

Because value is assigned under Section 2701 only to payment of cumulative dividends on preferred stock, much of the current recapitalization activity is focused on partnerships and limited liability companies. Such entities do not have the income tax problem of having to pay taxes at the entity level before preferred interest payments are distributed.

However, the harsh and sometimes unpredictable application of the special valuation rules under Section 2701 has encouraged most estate planners to avoid transactions requiring its use. Consequently, the use of the traditional preferred stock estate freeze has greatly declined in popularity. However, there are still a number of private businesses with old pre–Chapter 14 preferred stock estate freezes outstanding that may require additional gifting of common stock after October 8, 1990. These new transactions will fall under the rules of Section 2701. It is recommended that all analysts who may become involved with a valuation under the special valuation rules of Section 2701 read the statute language, final regulations, technical corrections, subsequent clarifying revenue rulings and private letter rulings, and court cases on this subject carefully.

Valuation Issues under Section 2702

Because Section 2702 deals with retained life, annuity, and unitrust interests transferred via trusts for lifetime gift tax purposes, there are no special valuation rules included in this section that directly relate to closely held business interests.

Closely held business interests are often placed into various grantor retained annuity trusts (GRATs) and grantor retained unitrusts (GRUTs), or charitable remainder annuity trusts (CRATs), or charitable lead trusts (CRUTs). But the primary valuation issue in these cases is the application of the IRS annuity and life expectancy tables.

Buy-Sell Agreements or Sale of Options under Section 2703

Chapter 29 discusses buy-sell agreements in detail. For now, let us note that there are four factors that determine whether the buy-sell agreement is conclusively binding for estate tax purposes:

1. The agreement must restrict the transfer of the securities to the buy-sell price during the owner's life as well as at death.
2. There must be a valid business purpose for establishing the agreement.

3. The value established in the agreement must have been an adequate and fair price at the time the agreement was executed.
4. The value must reflect those typical of arm's-length transactions in the subject company's industry.

Thus, a properly drawn, "grandfathered" buy-sell agreement (i.e., one that predates Chapter 14) with a fixed transfer price may, over time, have provided a way to freeze the value of family members' shares at a value perhaps less than fair market value as of a subsequent date of death. Since October 9, 1990, this technique is unworkable from an estate tax standpoint for newly created or substantially modified buy-sell agreements due to the passage of Section 2703 of Chapter 14.

Valuation Rules for Lapsing Rights and Other Restrictions under Section 2704

This section of Chapter 14 addresses two basic areas of valuation issues. Subsection (a) of 2704 treats certain lapsed voting or liquidation rights in a family controlled corporation, partnership, or limited liability company as a deemed transfer subject to gift or estate tax. Subsection (b) requires the analyst to ignore certain restrictions on liquidation rights of business interests when valuing a transfer of an interest in a family controlled enterprise.

Lapse of Certain Rights. Section 2704(a) will come into play under the following set of circumstances:

- The holder of the lapsed voting or liquidation power and any applicable family members own, in the aggregate, a controlling interest in the subject company. The definitions of "applicable family member" and "control" are defined in the same manner as is Section 2701, discussed above.[7]
- Whenever a lapse of a voting right or liquidation right occurs.[8] If it occurs during life, it is treated as a gift; at death it is considered an estate tax issue. A lapse is defined as occurring at the time a presently exercisable right is restricted or eliminated. The sale or transfer of a voting or liquidation right is not included under this section, as these types of transactions are valued under the existing gift and income tax statutes.

Section 2704(a) does not apply if the transfer was already valued under the special valuation rules of Section 2701, in order to prevent double taxation. Also, if there is a change in a state law that causes the lapse, then Section 2704(a) does not apply. Of course, if the family does not have control over the unilateral capacity to liquidate, then Section 2704(a) does not apply. As an example, for a company requiring unanimous consent of all interest holders to liquidate, the presence of non–family member interest holders causes Section 2704(a) not to apply.

The practical effect of Section 2704(a) is to create the potential for additional gift or estate tax value only when the holder's interest has its highest fair market value under a premise of liquidation on a controlling ownership interest basis. This most often tends to affect companies in asset-intensive industries like heavy manufacturing, farming and ranching, and real estate development, in addition to holding companies.

---

[7] The IRS's use of a 50 percent ownership level as the threshold for control in this context is curious and not supported by financial valuation theory or legal rights theory, as a 50 percent voting interest cannot unilaterally vote to compel a liquidation.

[8] The Treasury is also given the right under this statute to determine if other lapsing rights should be added to this list.

Disregarding Applicable Restrictions. Under Subsection 2704(b), the analyst should disregard an applicable restriction on the ability to liquidate a company (in whole or in part) if the following conditions apply:

- If an interest is transferred to or for the benefit of a member of the transferor's family (either directly or indirectly).
- If the transferor and members of the transferor's family control the company immediately before the transfer. The definition of *control* is defined in the same manner as in Section 2701, discussed above. However, the definition of *member of the family* is slightly different from that contained in Section 2701, and echoes the more inclusive definition utilized in Section 2702 and for determining family control under Section 2701. Under Section 2704, a member of the family for any individual includes: (1) the individual's spouse, (2) any ancestor of the individual and spouse, (3) any lineal descendant of the individual and spouse, (4) any brother or sister (and their spouses) of the individual.
- The applicable restriction is more restrictive than the limitations that would apply under the state law generally applicable to the entity in the absence of the restriction.
- The restriction either lapses after such a transfer, or the transferor and member of the transferor's family have the right, either individually or as a group, to remove (in whole or in part) such a restriction.

Section 2704(b) does not apply in the case of a restriction on liquidation that is imposed under federal or state law. Thus, the basic default statutes of the state laws under which a company was formed can have a significant impact on the degree to which the analyst should consider the liquidation values of the company in valuing an individual interest.

In addition, Section 2704(b) does not apply if a restriction on liquidation arises as part of the company's financing and is a commercially reasonable restriction imposed by an unrelated arm's-length third party. A typical example of this is the restriction on distributing asset sale proceeds to shareholders, while a loan is outstanding, contained in standard bank loan covenants.

An option or other agreement that is subject to Section 2703 regarding buy-sell agreements is not regarded as an applicable restriction. This provision avoids double coverage of the same issue under Chapter 14.

Section 2704(b) concerns itself primarily with restrictions that are more onerous than the basic rights contained in state statutes—that could be conveniently applied and then removed by the controlling family at appropriate times. Like 2704(a), the practical effect of Section 2704(b) is to create the potential for additional gift or estate tax value only when the holder's interest has its highest fair market value under a premise of liquidation on a controlling interest basis. This most often tends to affect companies in asset-intensive industries like heavy manufacturing, farming and ranching, and real estate development, in addition to holding companies.

Locking in the Three-Year Gift Tax Statute of Limitations

The Taxpayer Relief Act of 1997 amended IRC Section 6501(c)(9) to provide that the three-year statute of limitations starts with the filing of a gift tax return, whether or not any tax is paid, *provided that the gift is adequately disclosed on the gift tax return.*

The IRS has issued its final regulations relating to the value of prior gifts for purposes of computing estate and gift tax.[9] The three-year statute of limitations on gift taxes will commence to run only if the gift is "adequately disclosed." The final regulations, issued December 3, 1999, state that the submission of a valuation will meet the adequate disclosure requirements with respect to the gift transfer value if the valuation meets the following two categories of disclosure requirements.

Category I—disclosures with respect to the person(s) who prepares the valuation report:

1. The person must be an individual who holds himself or herself out to the public as an appraiser, or performs appraisals on a regular basis.
2. The appraiser is qualified to make appraisals of the type of property being valued.
3. The appraiser is not the donor, donee, or any employee or either, or a member of the family of any of these parties.

Category II—the valuation report must contain the following information:

1. The date of the appraisal.
2. The date of the transfer.
3. The purpose of the appraisal.
4. A description of the property.
5. A description of the appraisal process employed, including the valuation method(s) utilized.
6. A description of the assumptions utilized.
7. A description of any hypothetical conditions considered.
8. Descriptions of any restrictions or other limiting conditions present.
9. The information considered in determining the value, including all financial information in sufficient detail to allow the reader to replicate the appraisal analysis and valuation.
10. The reasoning that supports the analysis, opinions, and conclusions.
11. Any specific comparative transactions utilized in the valuation analysis.
12. The fair market value of 100 percent of the entity determined without regard to any discounts in valuing the entity or the assets owned by the entity, unless this information is not relevant or material in determining the value of the interest.

Shifting the Burden of Proof from the Taxpayer to the IRS

The IRS Restructuring and Reform Act of 1998, signed by President Clinton on July 22, 1998, includes new IRC Section 7491, a provision shifting the burden of proof from the taxpayer to the IRS *if the taxpayer provides "credible evidence" supporting its position.*

---

[9] 1999 TNT 232-6 (Dec. 3, 1999).

In Tax Court, the taxpayer is the petitioner, or the "plaintiff." Thus, to the extent a valuation issue is a factual issue, if Section 7491 does not apply, the taxpayer has the burden of proof, and there is a rebuttable presumption of correctness of IRS-proposed tax deficiencies.

As of this writing, there is no case or regulation attempting to define "credible evidence of value." There is consensus, however, that it raises the standards for valuation evidence, reports, and litigation strategy. The taxpayer should cooperate with IRS requests for documents, meetings, interviews, information, and witnesses. It certainly means that taxpayers should obtain timely and complete valuations of any nonpublic equity interests involved in a gift or estate transfer of ownership.

Valuation Issues in Estate and Gift Tax Planning

Placing Family Assets in Corporate, Limited Liability Company, or Partnership Form

It may be worthwhile to consider incorporating various family assets into a family-controlled holding company before transferring interests to heirs. Aside from the business purposes of such transfers, such as centralization of supervision, reduction of potential personal exposure to creditors, assurance of smoother management succession, and prevention of the assets' waste by inexperienced heirs, there also may be estate planning advantages. The assets could be almost anything, such as marketable securities, real estate, art, coins, or any kind of collectibles. Since publicly traded securities of companies holding such assets (such as closed-end investment companies and REITs) tend to sell at a discount from underlying net asset value, so should shares of family-controlled corporations. Interests in this type of closely held company also are valued at a further discount for lack of marketability.

Of course, in making the decision to incorporate a family holding company to execute a portion of the family estate plan in this manner, one should realize that the justification for the discounted values is real, not contrived; that is, the heir who receives a gift of a minority interest of a family holding company or limited partnership representing an undivided interest in a portfolio of assets will not have control over those assets. Owning 15 percent of the assets and owning 15 percent of the stock of the company that owns them are two different things. The power to liquidate, transfer assets, declare dividends, and exercise all the other various elements of control will not go to the donee. There also may be income tax considerations, so such a move should not be undertaken without the aid of competent tax counsel. If the donor understands and is satisfied with the various implications, the creation of a family-owned holding company could be a tax saving feature of the total estate plan.

An extension of this technique has been placement of family assets in S corporations and limited partnerships, which allows pass-through of most types of income generated by the underlying assets without being subjected to income tax at the corporate level (see Chapter 26, Valuing Pass-Through Entities). This technique has become more important with the repeal of the *General Utilities* doctrine in the Tax Reform Act of 1986. Under the *General Utilities* doctrine, a corporation selling its assets to another corporation, as in an acquisition, generally was allowed to liquidate within one year of sale without having to recognize gain on the assets' sale at the corporate level.[10]

Family assets also have been placed in partnerships or limited liability companies to facilitate the estate planning techniques described in the next two sections on noncontrolling ownership interest transfers and recapitalizations.

Minimizing Taxes by a Series of Timely Noncontrolling Ownership Interest Transfers

In general, estate planning techniques for minimizing transfer taxes revolve around timing transfers when the value of the stock is relatively low and structuring them such that they have the least possible value.

The more rapidly a company is growing in value, the more important it is to effect stock transfers to heirs early rather than later, after the value has increased. However, if the business is cyclical in nature, it may be possible to time transfers at a cyclical trough in the company's value.

For structure, the best technique usually is to plan transfers as a series of small noncontrolling ownership interests. To begin, a married couple can give up to $20,000 ($10,000 per donor) in value to each of as many persons as they wish each year without paying federal gift tax. More important for transfers of substantial size, however, is that, at least under the law and court rulings at this writing, noncontrolling ownership interests are subject to substantial discounts in value per share compared with the per share value of a controlling ownership interest. Noncontrolling ownership interests are further discussed in Chapter 16.

Discounts for lack of marketability are discussed in Chapter 17. Noncontrolling shares in closely held companies can be valued for tax purposes by estimating their potential market value as publicly traded stock and then discounting them for lack of marketability. In general, the smaller the noncontrolling ownership interest, the greater the extent to which this approach can be applied. The net result may be that transfers of shares of closely held companies can be made at quite large discounts below the undiscounted control value of the entire company.

Although the IRS has conceded in Revenue Ruling 93-12 that family relationships will not be the sole reason to challenge noncontrolling ownership interest transfers when a family owns control of an enterprise, it remains sensitive to this issue. Analysts should review all the facts and circumstances of each gift in a series of gifts for companies in which a single family owns control, as, infrequently, some noncontrolling ownership interests deserve lesser discounts for relative lack of ownership control and lack of marketability. This could be due to some factor relating to the relative distribution of ownership (a so-called "swing vote" issue)[11] or the ability to unilaterally elect one or more directors to the board, and thereby influence the policies of the company.

---

[10] Mitchell M. Gans, "The Repeal of *General Utilities*: Estate Tax Implications," *Trusts & Estates*, July 1987, pp. 43–48.

[11] The IRS addressed the swing vote issue in a National Office Technical Advice Memorandum (Letter Ruling 9436005, May 26, 1994). We find swing vote issues a relative rarity as real-world willing buyers, even those already owning shares in a company, are rarely willing to bid much in excess of the amount a potential investor without existing ownership would pay for an interest. There is also an issue of whether a swing vote assumption is improperly based on the notion that the willing buyer possesses a special relationship with the seller that is not typical of the hypothetical willing seller/willing buyer standard of fair market value for estate and gift tax matters.

Loss of Key Person

Often the analyst faces the valuation of closely held stock in the estate of the president, founder, or other key executive of a business. In this circumstance, it is reasonable to investigate the possibility that the value of the company—and, thus, of its securities—has been impaired due to the loss of the services of a *key person* in the business's management. Several of the methods available to quantify the key person discount are discussed in Chapter 18.

Whether such decline in value actually has occurred depends on the facts of the individual case. The following are some of the elements to be investigated in establishing any discount or diminution from the loss of a key person.

First, the analyst determines the deceased executive's actual duties and areas of active involvement. A key person may contribute value to a company in both day-to-day management duties and from strategic judgment responsibilities based on long-standing contacts and reputation within an industry.

Second, the analyst assesses the ability of existing successor management to move up the organizational ladder and take over the duties of the vacated position. Ideally, a strong and stable corporate organization will provide this capability. This assumes that a succession plan actually exists. All too often, however, private business owners create "spider web" organization structures with themselves at the center—that is, all management decisions are made by the key executive-owner. The extent of organizational damage also may be related to the suddenness of the key manager's death.

Third, the analyst calculates the amount of compensation necessary for replacing the key executive or filling the positions vacated or created when successors move up.

Fourth, to this quantitative calculation the analyst adds the damages arising from risks to the company in bringing in replacement executives who may be unfamiliar with the company's operations. These risks can be compounded by the analyst's assessment of the complexity or precariousness of the company's competitive or financial position. This is especially true if the deceased was personal guarantor of the company's debts, as often is the case with closely held business loans. Sometimes these risks can be quantified as estimates of sales losses or profit margin declines over estimated future periods.

There are at least two offsets to these potential losses. One is the compensation, net of any continuing obligations, that the company ceases to pay to the deceased executive. The other is any insurance on the key person's life that is payable to the company and not earmarked for other purposes, such as repurchase of the deceased's stock in the company.

The estimates of key person losses can be directly incorporated into the valuation methods appropriate for the particular case. This may be accomplished by (1) adjusting normalized earnings or price to earnings multiples, or (2) as a reduction in estimated future cash flows to be discounted. Otherwise, the loss can be subtracted from the company's indicated value as a separate item, much like the discount for lack of marketability.

Evidence for the amount of the loss from the key person's death from securities' values in the public market shows that the magnitude of the decline varies with the particular circumstances. Generally, public companies have larger and more flexible professional management teams and thus can better absorb the shock of the loss of any one key person. An instructive example of a catastrophic loss of key executives, however, was the tragic death of most of the top management of Arrow Electronics in a hotel fire in December 1980. Arrow's New York Stock Exchange listed common stock fell approximately 20 percent after the announcement of the news.

Trapped-in Capital Gains Discounts

One of the most sudden and important changes in the Tax Court's position was the recognition, starting in 1998, of a discount for trapped-in capital gains taxes on appreciated property. The important cases establishing this precedent up to the time of this writing are discussed in the following chapter.

Other Estate Planning Situations Requiring Valuations

Strictly speaking, the two techniques reviewed below do not require consideration of any valuation factors different from those mandated under Revenue Ruling 59-60. But, the analyst should be aware of these techniques, as he or she may be called upon to prepare a valuation of a closely held business that will be used in this fashion.

Sale of Remainder Interest. In this technique, the owner of a closely held business security sells to an heir a remainder interest in the security and retains a life interest in the current enjoyment of income and the security's voting rights. The *remainder interest* is valued by taking the security's estimated fair market value and discounting it to a present value under the IRS actuarial tables based on the seller's projected remaining life. Assuming a present value interest factor of 10 percent, the present value of the remainder interest could be a small fraction of the security's current fair market value if the seller is relatively young. Upon the seller's death, the life interest terminates, leaving the security, including any appreciation after the sale, to pass, untaxed, to the heir outside the seller's gross estate.

Valuation is crucial to this technique, because if the sale transaction is not for full and adequate consideration, the asset's entire value will be brought back into the seller's estate at fair market value as of the date of death.

Sale for a Private Annuity or a Self-Canceling (or other Promissory) Note. In this technique, the business owner sells the entire business to an heir (or a trust for the benefit of an heir) in exchange for a *private annuity*—a fixed periodic payment made to the seller for the rest of his or her life.

A *self-canceling note* is similar to an annuity. The advantage of the self-canceling note is that, if it is structured correctly (with a proper principal and/or interest premium for the self-canceling feature, for example), there is no unpaid balance to be subject to the estate tax if the seller dies before the note is paid. One of the key issues in the structure of this technique is the correct valuation of the closely held business interest sold and the terms of the annuity or note received so as to avoid gift taxes on the initial sale and possible estate taxes at the seller's death.

Other Estate and Gift Valuation Issues

There are several additional issues regarding valuation for estate and gift taxes that analysts should be aware of.

In Revenue Ruling 85-75,[12] the IRS held that it will not necessarily be bound by values that it accepted for estate tax purposes as the correct cost basis for determining depreciation deductions or income taxes on capital gains from an asset's subsequent sale.

On the other hand, it may be possible to use one value for calculating the gross estate value of a block of closely held stock and a different value for calculating the value of a portion of the block of stock that will be exempted from estate taxes as a marital deduction (i.e., the portion of the estate transferred to a spouse).[13]

The final valuation issue is the lower value for closely held business stock that may result if real estate used in a family-owned trade or business is valued for estate tax purposes for actively involved family members under the provisions of Section 2032A, "Special-Use Valuation." A detailed discussion of this section is beyond the scope of this book. Here simply note that closely held company valuation methods based on net asset values may be lower if a valuation of the underlying operating real property follows the guidelines of this section. This issue is particularly relevant for family-owned farming or other agricultural business securities.

Summary

The entire area of estate and gift tax valuation can be a constantly shifting minefield of laws, regulations, and court decisions. Because of this, it is important that the analyst be able to function as a knowledgeable contributor to the client's team of estate planning professionals.

With the top federal transfer tax rate at 55 percent, the tax implications of estate planning and gift and estate tax valuations can be huge. Inclusion into an estate of additional values that were originally thought to be transferred away via estate planning transactions also can create tremendous problems. The tax implications are exacerbated by the penalties that may be imposed on taxpayers for undervaluation for gift and estate tax purposes and overvaluation for charitable contribution purposes. Valuation analysts are also subject to significant penalties.

It is essential that valuations involving federal tax implications be done in accordance with guidelines discussed in this chapter, as clarified and modified by ever-evolving case law.

Bibliography

Abraham, Mel H. "Kerr v. IRS—A Gift for Taxpayers and Family Limited Partnerships." *Valuation Strategies*, March/April 2000, pp. 28–34, 48.

Adams, Roy M., David A. Herpe, and Thomas W. Abendroth. "Highlights of the Chapter 14 Final Regulations." *Trusts & Estates*, April 1992, pp. 35–49.

Alerding, R. James Jr. "IRS Valuation Methods Lag behind Business Practice." *Taxation for Accountants*, July 1992, pp. 4–9.

---

[12] Rev. Rul. 85-75, 1985-1 C.B. 376.
[13] See *Estate of Chenoweth*, 88 T.C. No. 90 (1987).

Aucutt, Ronald D. "Fourteen Tips and Traps in Dealing with Chapter 14." *Estate Planning*, September/October 1993, pp. 259–66.

_____. "IRS Proposes New Rules for Reporting Gifts." *Judges & Lawyers Business Valuation Update*, February 1999, pp. 6–7.

August, Jerald D. "Artificial Valuation of Closely Held Interest: Sec. 2704." *Estate Planning*, November/December 1995, pp. 339–44.

Bishop, David M. "Trapped-in Capital Gains: Where Do We Go from Here?" *Business Valuation Review*, June 1999, pp. 64–68.

Bradley, Wray E. "Tax Court Valuation Standards Go Beyond 'Relevant and Reliable.'" *Valuation Strategies*, November/December 1999, pp. 34–39.

Brier, Kenneth P. and Joseph B. Darby III. "Family Limited Partnerships: Decanting Family Investment Assets into New Bottles." *The Tax Lawyer*, Fall 1995, pp. 127–64.

Brown, William J., Mark I. Wolk, and Leo N. Hitt. "Family Limited Partnerships: The Roles of the Players with a Focus on Valuation Discounts." *Business Entities*, May/June 1999, pp. 4–13.

Budyak, James T. "Estate Freeze Rules Affect Partnership Valuation Discounts." *Taxation for Lawyers*, January/February 1997, pp. 228–34.

Caudill, William H., and James T. Budyak. "New IRS Position on Valuation May Result in Reduced Marital and Charitable Deductions." *Journal of Taxation*, September 1993, pp. 176–79.

Chandler, William F., and Harold Dubroff. "Funding GRATs with S Stock, Partnership or LLC Interests." *Estate Planning*, November/December 1994, pp. 331–39.

Cooper Scott J. "A Guide through the Estate Freeze Maze." *Journal of Taxation of Estates and Trusts*, Winter 1992, pp. 5–10.

Eastland, S. Stacy. "The Art of Making Uncle Sam Your Assignee Instead of Your Senior Partner: The Use of Family Partnerships in Estate Planning." White paper available on www.BVLibrary.com.

_____. "Family Limited Partnership Interests Enjoy 40 to 85% Discounts from NAV." *Shannon Pratt's Business Valuation Update*, January 1997, pp. 1–3.

Eggers, Michael. "FLP Settlement Discount Study." Presentation to the IBA National Conference, January 2000. Available on www. BVLibrary.com.

Elliot, Charles E. "Family Limited Partnerships." Presentation to the AICPA National Business Valuation Conference, November 1998. Available on www. BVLibrary.com.

_____. "An Outline of Valuation Considerations Related to Limited Partnerships." Presentation to the AICPA National Business Valuation Conference, November 1998. Available on www. BVLibrary.com.

Englebrecht, Ted D., and James M. Turner. "Alternate Valuation Election Has Side Effects." *Estate Planning*, May/June 1994, pp. 154–61.

Fiore, Owen G. "Partnership between Appraiser and Tax Attorney." *Shannon Pratt's Business Valuation Update*, May 1997, pp. 1–3.

_____. A Tax Lawyer's Attitude Toward the Estate and Gift Tax Business Valuation Appraisal Process." White paper available on www.BVLibrary.com.

_____. "Valuation Adjustment Planning: Solid Reality or Fleeting Fantasy?" White paper available on www.BVLibrary.com.

_____. "Valuation Discount Planning—Especially FLPs & IRC 2703." Presentation to the Minnesota Chapter of the American Society of CLU and ChFC, April 1997. Available on www. BVLibrary.com.

Fowler, Bradley A. "How Do You Handle It? Family Partnership Valuations." *Business Valuation Review*, March 1997, pp. 41–44.

Gardner, John H. "Planning with Chapter 14 and GST Interaction." *Estate Planning*, May/June 1994, pp. 146–53.

Gibbs, Larry W. "What You Can Do if the Government Uses Rambo Tactics (Estate Valuation Audit)." Parts I and II. *Trusts & Estates*, June and July 1994, pp. 60–65 and 57–61.

Gingiss, Randall J. "The Gift of Opportunity." *DePaul Law Review*, Winter 1992, pp. 395–429.

Hall, Lance. "Corporate Structure Discount and Valuation of Asset-Holding C Corps." *Trusts & Estates*, September 1996, pp. 45–48.

Harris, Richard W., and Edith E. Silvestri. "Estate Tax Valuation of Contingent Claims." *Trusts & Estates*, December 1993, pp. 29–32+.

Hatcher, Milford B. Jr., and Gregory E. Kniesel. "Preferred Limited Partnerships: The FLPs of Choice?" *Valuation Strategies*, July/August 1999, pp. 12–33.

Herpe, David A. "Climate for Valuation Discounts Remains Good Despite IRS Obstinancy." *Trusts & Estate*, January 1995, pp. 66–76.

Hitchner, James R. "Valuation of Closely Held Businesses: Estate and Gift Tax Issues." *Tax Adviser,* July 1992, pp. 471–79.

Hitchner, James R., and Kevin J. Rudd. "The Use of Discounts in Estate and Gift Tax Valuations." *Trusts & Estates*, August 1992, pp. 49–56, 60.

Houren, Jay R. "Family Limited Partnerships." Presentation to the 1999 ABA Tax Section Midyear Meeting. Available on www.BVLibrary.com.

IRS Valuation Training for Appeals Officers. Chicago: Commerce Clearing House Inc., 1998.

Jeffries, Spencer, and Bruce A. Johnson. "Publicly Registered Limited Partnership Interests." *Business Valuation Review*, December 1996, pp. 155–56.

Kasner, Jerry A. "Valuation of Family Partnership Interests." *Tax Analysts —Special Reports*, 97 TNT 50-47, March 14, 1997.

Keligian, David L. "Appraisal Issues Now Require Greater Attention for Tax Planning to Be Effective." *Journal of Taxation*, February 1994, pp. 98–103.

Kimball, Curtis R. "Discount Settlements on Recent Family Limited Partnership Cases." Presentation to the ASA International Appraisal Conference, August 1999. Available on www.BVLibrary.com.

Laro, The Hon. David. "A View from the U.S. Tax Court." Presentation to the AICPA National Business Valuation Conference, November 1998. Available on www.BVLibrary.com.

Moore, M. Read "Honey, Who Shrunk My Deduction?" *Probate & Property*, January/February 1997, pp. 9–14.

Murray, John V. "Securities Law Considerations in Valuing Stock for Tax Purposes." *Trusts & Estates*, December 1992, pp. 40–45.

Nager, Ross W., Byrle M. Abbin, and David K. Carlson. "Significant Recent Development in Estate Planning." Parts I, II, and III. *Tax Adviser*, October, November, December 1994, pp. 587–605; 698–709; and 723–38.

Painter, Andrew D., and Jonathan G. Blattmachr. "How the Final Chapter 14 Anti-Freeze Regulations Affect Estate Planning Strategies." *Journal of Taxation of Estates and Trusts*, Spring 1992, pp. 5–14.

Rapkin, Stephanie. "The Basics of the S Corporation for the Estate Planner." *Trusts & Estates*, September 1996, pp. 38–44.

Robinson, Debra A., and Edward J. Rappaport. "Impact of Valuation Discounts on Estate and Income Tax Basis." *Estate Planning*, June 1997, pp. 223–30.

Schlenger, Jacques T., Robert E. Madden, and Lisa H.R. Hayes. "Blocks of Stock Are Aggregated when Determining Estate Tax Values." *Estate Planning*, May/June 1994, pp. 176–78.

Shore, H. Allen and Craig T. McClung. "Beyond the Basic Superfreeze—An Update and Additional Planning Opportunities." *Taxes*, January 1997, pp. 41–55.

Siwicki, Robert. "The Gifting of Stock Options as an Estate Planning Strategy." *Trusts & Estates*, November 1999, pp. 49–60.

Soled, Jay A. "Gifts of Partnership Interests: An Income Tax Perspective." *Business Entities*, May/June 1999, pp. 30–35.

Strauss, Benton C., and James K. Shaw. "Final Chapter 14 Regs. Clarify GRATs, Business Planning." *Estate Planning*, September/October 1992, pp. 259–66.

_____. "Final Chapter 14 Regulations Refine Estate Freeze Rules." *Estate Planning*, July/August 1992, pp. 195–202.

Switzer, Ralph V. Jr., and Douglas E. Chestnut. "Evolution of Estate Freeze." *National Public Accountant*, January 1994, pp. 20–25+.

Tiernan, Peter B. "How 50% Ownership Affects Estate Planning for Closely Held Stock." *Journal of Taxation*, October 1999, pp. 232–40.

Tucker, Gerald R., Gary A. Mall, and Scott E. Grimes. "IRS Finalizes Guidance on Adequate Disclosure." *Valuation Strategies*, March/April 2000, pp. 22–27, 46.

Vaughan, Patrick J., and Donna Esposito Fincher. "Saving Estate and Gift Taxes with Intrafamily Discounts." *Journal of Financial Planning*, January 1994, pp. 32–34.

Ward, Burke T., and Malcolm L. Cowen. "Should the Service Have Two Opportunities to Revalue Gifts?" *Trusts & Estates*, November 1994, pp. 40–43.

Warnken, Wayne L., and Pamela R. Champine. "Anti-Estate Freeze Rules Can Have Wide Scope." *Estate Planning*, July/August 1993, pp. 220–25.

Wise, Richard M. "Practice Standards, Tax Valuations and Valuation Methodologies—CICBV vs. ASA." *The Journal of Business Valuation* (Proceedings of the 12th Biennial Conference of the CICBV. Toronto: The Canadian Institute of Chartered Business Valuators, 1997, pp. 235–58.

Chapter 28

Estate and Gift Tax Court Cases

Always read the opinions on valuation that were written by the judge handling the case.[1]

This chapter summarizes federal courts' positions on many frequently encountered valuation issues. Out of the many hundreds of reported opinions, we have referenced a sampling that are generally representative of the federal courts' positions.

The published decisions cited are mostly from the period 1995–1999, although important earlier precedential cases are included as well. It is not possible to be comprehensive in a single chapter on federal courts' various positions on the myriad of valuation issues addressed. However, the full text of each decision cited usually includes reference to earlier precedent on point for the issues discussed.

The chapter is generally organized by type of primary valuation issue. In some cases, the federal court's position on issues other than the main issue are also mentioned. Other precedent may be referenced under more than one primary valuation issue section if the court's opinion was particularly important on more than a single issue.

Approaches to Value

The court's acceptance, rejection, or relative weight accorded to various valuation approaches and method generally revolves around three factors:

1. The type of company.
2. The quality of available evidence relevant to the respective methods.
3. The prospects for liquidation or continued operation.

As suggested in Revenue Ruling 59-60, the Tax Court tends to rely more on an asset-based approach in valuing holding companies and on an earnings-related method (either an income approach or a market approach emphasizing economic income variables) for operating companies. For hybrid companies, the Tax Court often accords partial weight to methods related to assets and partial weight to approaches related to earnings. Thus, the relative characterization of a company as a holding company or an operating company often is a major issue.

Sometimes the relative qualifying evidence available to support the respective approaches becomes the driving force as to which approach or approaches are accepted.

For example, in *Estate of Jung*, the Tax Court accepted the discounted cash flow (DCF) method over the guideline publicly traded company method.

> In the instant case, we believe the DCF approach to valuing Jung Corp. is more reliable than the market comparable approach. The market comparable approach does not work well in the instant case because the comparable corporations do not have the same product mix (health and elastic textile) as Jung Corp.[2]

> In *Rakow v. Commissioner*, the Tax Court accepted the IRS expert's DCF method over the taxpayer's market approach, and then applied a 31 percent discount for lack of control.[3]

---

[1] David Laro, "Judge Laro's Views on Discounts & Valuation Reports" (Part two), *Judges & Lawyers Business Valuation Update*, June 1999, p. 4.

[2] *Estate of Mildred Herschede Jung v. Commissioner*, 101 T.C. 412 (1993).

[3] *Rakow v. Commissioner*, T.C. Memo 1999-177 (May 27, 1999).

In *Dockery v. Commissioner*, the Tax Court accepted a valuation derived by the discounted dividend method. It also accepted the 40 percent combined lack of control and lack of marketability discount applied by the analyst to the undiscounted value derived by the discounted dividend method.[4]

Estate of Jameson involved a controlling ownership interest in a holding company with timber as its principal asset. The Tax Court decided that the asset-based approach is "most reasonable in a case like this one, where the corporation functions as a holding, rather than an operating, company and earnings are relatively low in comparison to the fair market value of the underlying assets."[5]

The matter of the prospects for liquidation versus continued operation are especially important for companies like family limited partnerships that may own very valuable underlying assets. The relevant state laws and the partnership agreements may have a major bearing on this determination. A classic case in point is *Estate of Watts*,[6] which involved a noncontrolling ownership interest in a partnership that owned extensive and very valuable timber and operated a sawmill and a plywood mill. The IRS used a liquidation basis and the taxpayer used a going-concern basis. Because of the binding partnership agreement, the Court concluded, "There was no reasonable prospect of liquidation. Therefore, we accept petitioner's going-concern valuation approach." The Court then accepted the taxpayer's expert's guideline publicly traded company valuation method and 35 percent discount for lack of marketability.

In *Estate of McFarland* on the other hand, the Tax Court denied a motion to value the partnership interest only on a going-concern basis. Distinguishing from *Watts*, the Tax Court noted that the trustee for the interest in the decedent's estate had the right, but not the obligation, to continue the partnership in the event of decedent's death.[7]

In *Furman v. Commissioner*, the Tax Court rejected "in toto" the valuation offered by the analyst retained by the IRS, and relied primarily on the taxpayer's expert's valuation, which used both (1) a capitalized economic income method using Ibbotson data and (2) an EBITDA pricing multiple method. The Court used the EBITDA pricing multiple method, modifying the expert's pricing multiple from 5.0 to 6.0. The expert had applied a 30 percent discount for lack of control and a 35 percent discount for lack of marketability. The Court allowed a combined 40 percent discount, plus a 10 percent key person discount proferred by the taxpayer's expert.[8]

Selection of Guideline Companies

The Tax Code, revenue rulings, IRS practice, and the Tax Court all appear to favor the market approach. However, dozens of analysts' market approach conclusions have been rejected because of the selection of the guideline companies used in their analysis.

In *Estate of Brookshire*, valuing a stock interest in a retail grocery chain, the taxpayer's expert used public retail grocery chains and adjusted pricing multiples to apply to Brookshire in order to account for increased competition from Wal-Mart and decreasing net income, which the Court accepted. The expert for the IRS used three

[4] *Dockery v. Commissioner*, T.C. Memo 1998-114 (Mar. 19, 1998).

[5] *Estate of Helen Bolton Jameson v. Commissioner*, T.C. Memo 1999-43 (Feb. 9, 1999).

[6] *Watts v. Commissioner*, 51 T.C.M. 60 (1985), *aff'd* No. 86-8504 U.S. App. (11th Cir. Aug. 4, 1987).

[7] *Estate of Vera M. McFarland v. Commissioner*, T.C. Memo 1996-424 (Sept. 19, 1996).

[8] *Furman v. Commissioner*, T.C. Memo 1998-157 (Apr. 30, 1998).

guideline companies that had significant sales other than retail grocery, which the Court determined were not comparable to Brookshire. The Court, therefore, rejected the IRS expert's market approach.[9]

In *Estate of Hendrickson*, the Tax Court accepted the guideline bank stocks selected by the taxpayer's expert and rejected those selected by the IRS expert. The IRS expert used geography as his primary selection criterion. In addition, all the selected companies were significantly larger than the subject, offered more services, and were multi-branch operations. The Tax Court characterized the taxpayer's expert's selection as "significantly more exacting" based on size and operating characteristics that more closely resembled the subject.[10]

Revenue Ruling 59-60 says that guideline companies should be in lines of business that are "the same or similar" relative to the subject company. In *Estate of Gallo*,[11] there were no sufficiently comparative guideline publicly traded wineries, so the experts on both sides used distilleries, breweries, soft drink companies, and even high brand recognition food companies. In *Estate of Hall*,[12] there was only one publicly traded greeting card company similar to Hallmark, so the Tax Court accepted a group of high market share consumer disposable products companies, such as Parker Pens.

Buy-Sell Agreements

The extent to which a buy-sell agreement may be determinative of value for gift or estate tax purposes—or a factor to consider—is a frequently disputed issue. If the buy-sell price is very low and not concluded to be determinative of value for estate tax purposes, even though legally binding on the estate, the estate may have to sell the stock or interest at a price that does not even cover the estate taxes.

Bommer Revocable Trust v. Commissioner is an illustrative case in point.[13] The Tax Court started its opinion by listing requirements for making a buy-sell agreement price controlling for federal estate tax:

- The price must be fixed or determinable.
- The agreement must be binding on the parties both during life and after death.
- The agreement must have been entered into for a bona fide business reason.
- It must not be a substitute for testamentary disposition.

The Tax Court quoted Regulations Section 20.2031-2(h):

> Such price will be disregarded in determining the value of the securities unless it is determined under the circumstances of the particular case that the agreement represents a bona fide business arrangement and not a device to pass the decedent's shares to the natural objects of his bounty for less than full and adequate consideration in money or money's worth.

With respect to the agreement's price, the Tax Court made the following observations:

[9] *Estate of Ann H. Brookshire v. Commissioner*, T.C. Memo 1998-365 (Oct. 8, 1998).
[10] *Estate of James Waldo Hendrickson v. Commissioner*, T.C. Memo 1999-278 (Aug. 23, 1999).
[11] *Estate of Mark S. Gallo v. Commissioner*, 50 T.C.M. 470 (1985).
[12] *Estate of Hall v. Commissioner*, 92 T.C. 312 (1989).
[13] *Cameron W. Bommer Revocable Trust v. Commissioner*, T.C. Memo 1997-380 (Aug. 20, 1997).

- The purchase price . . . was fixed . . . not subject to any reevaluation. . . . We find it unrealistic to assume that decedent . . . would have negotiated a fixed price . . . if he had been bargaining with unrelated parties. . . .
- The generous payment terms . . . are a further indication of their testamentary nature. . . .
- An inference of the testamentary device can be drawn from the manner in which the parties selected the $11,333.30 price. . . . Decedent was an experienced businessman, yet he failed to obtain a professional appraisal. . . .

Failure to have a professional valuation at the time of entering into a buy-sell agreement or a transaction is a red flag to both the IRS and the courts. Cases like this should help make attorneys more aware of the need for independent, professional valuations for buy-sell agreements and transactions, especially those involving insider control owners.

Covenants Not to Compete

A common controversy is the value of covenants not to compete. The controversy can arise in both estate tax cases and income tax cases.

The issue in *Thompson v. Commissioner* was whether the company, a distributor of beauty supply products, could amortize $2.5 million for noncompete covenants. The IRS disallowed the deduction in full, stating that the amount paid for the covenants was a disguised payment for the company's stock.[14]

To determine whether or not to allow the deductions, the Tax Court applied an 11-factor "economic reality" test.

When the Tax Court considered these "economic reality" factors, it decided that an overwhelmingly strong need and a corresponding high relative value existed for the noncompete agreements.

The taxpayer's expert, using a discounted cash flow method, valued the company with the covenants in place and then made assumptions concerning the probability of competition and the impact that competition from the key employees would have on the company in the first three years after the sale. In his final analysis, the taxpayer's expert valued the two noncompete agreements at approximately $2.5. million.

The Tax Court specifically stated, "We found [the IRS's] expert report to be of no assistance," and rendered its decision in favor of the taxpayer.

Reliance on Subsequent Sales

There have been several instances in which the Tax Court has relied primarily on sales of the business or an interest in it months or even years after the valuation date. The theory in support of this procedure is that the sale did not affect the value, but provided evidence of value that existed as of the valuation date. Many attorneys and

---

[14] *Thompson v. Commissioner*, T.C. Memo 1997-287 (June 24, 1997).

analysts believe that the Tax Court has taken this procedure to unwarranted extremes in some cases. However, if a subsequent sale has occurred, most analysts now agree that it would be prudent to reconcile the valuation date value concluded by other approaches with the subsequent event transaction price.

In *Estate of Scanlan*, the date of death was July 16, 1991, and the stock at issue was a noncontrolling ownership block. The Tax Court ultimately relied on an offer to buy the entire company in March of 1993, resulting in a sale consummated in January 1994. The Tax Court rejected the taxpayer's expert's valuation of $35.20 per share for various aspects of inadequacy of the valuation discussed elsewhere in this chapter. The IRS offered no expert testimony. However, the IRS claimed a value of $72.15 per share—the January 1994 sale price of $75.15 per share less 4 percent "to account for minority interest in the company, a minor increase in earnings . . . and the deflation of the dollar."[15]

The Tax Court said: "We find it incredible that the 4 percent discount . . . adequately accounts for both a marketability and minority discount, as well as the change in the setting from the . . . date of the Decedent's death." The Court then decided to discount the $75.15 sale price by 30 percent, to conclude a value of $50.51 per share on the date of death. It is likely that the estate tax value filed may well have held up in court had it been adequately supported.

In *Estate of Cidulka*, the Tax Court relied primarily on a sale of the company, structured as an asset sale, to the company's arch competitor, four years following the valuation date. Not only was the sale four years removed in time, but it obviously involved a high level of *investment value*, as opposed to *fair market value*. Furthermore, the price certainly could have been influenced by the structure of the transaction as an asset sale, while the estate owned stock.[16]

In *Estate of Jung*, while the Court emphasized that the valuation should be based on what was known or knowable at the valuation date, and that the subsequent sale of the company was not forseeable, the opinion nevertheless made a major point of being able to reconcile the analyst's date of death estimate of value with the subsequent sale price (about two years later).[17]

Discounts for Lack of Control and for Lack of Marketability

Discounts for lack of marketability have been creeping up slowly, influenced by the Willamette Management Associates studies and the John Emory pre-IPO studies (see Chapter 17). Nevertheless, at this writing, the highest discount purely for lack of marketability (i.e., not combined with any other factors) recognized by the Tax Court has been 40 percent.[18]

In *Estate of Mandelbaum*, the only issue before the Tax Court was the discount for lack of marketability. The Court stated that it used both the restricted stock studies and the pre-IPO studies as a starting place, and then considered several factors

---

[15] *Estate of Arthur G. Scanlan v. Commissioner*, T.C. Memo 1996-331 (July 25, 1996).

[16] *Estate of Joseph Cidulka v. Commissioner*, T.C. Memo 1996-149 (Mar. 26, 1996).

[17] *Estate of Jung*.

[18] A 50 percent discount for lack of marketability was upheld in an ESOP case, *Howard v. Shay* (see Chapter 33).

to adjust up or down from the average. Concluding that the balance of the adjustments was downward, the allowed lack of marketability discount was 30 percent.[19]

In *Estate of Davis*,[20] the taxpayer's experts testified to a 35 percent discount (exclusive of the capital gains issue), and the IRS expert opined to a 23 percent discount. The Tax Court ultimately concluded about a 32 percent discount. The significant point, noted in the published decision, in coming closer to the taxpayer's experts' opinion, was:

> . . . [the expert for the IRS] should have considered the . . . data reflected in those pre-IPO studies because they, together with the restricted stock studies, would have provided a more accurate base range and starting point for determining the appropriate lack of marketability discount. . . .

In *Estate of Simplot*, the Tax Court allowed a 35 percent lack of marketability discount for voting shares and a 40 percent lack of marketability discount for nonvoting shares.[21]

In *Estate of Brookshire*, the Tax Court concluded a 40 percent discount for lack of marketability. Importantly, the taxpayer's expert utilized the pre-IPO as well as the restricted stock studies in quantifying the lack of marketability discount.[22]

In *Estate of Mellinger*, the decedent held stock—both outright and through two trusts—in Frederick's of Hollywood, a publicly held company. Based on the very large size of the blocks relative to very limited trading volume, the Tax Court allowed a 25 percent blockage discount. (This is very high for a blockage discount, although the Tax Court also referred to it as a "marketability discount" at one point in the published decision.)[23]

Estate of Branson[24] demonstrates the fact that every case depends on its own unique facts and circumstances. The Tax Court rejected the testimony of *both* the expert for the taxpayer and the expert for the IRS as to the proffered discount for lack of marketability, which ranged from 20 percent to 55 percent, and allowed only a 10 percent discount for blockage. The Tax Court explained:

> The fact that Savings maintained a waiting list of willing buyers is evidence that the stock's history of low trading volume is due to the shareholder's preference to hold Savings shares for investment, rather than sale.

In *Estate of Fleming*,[25] valuing a 50 percent ownership interest, the Court said, "We conclude that, in addition to a minority discount, some amount of marketability discount should be applied. . . ." While the Court didn't specify the amounts of the respective discounts, the judicial conclusion was almost exactly a 27 percent discount from the value arrived at by the guideline merged and acquired company method. The wording suggests that this may imply a 19 percent lack of marketability discount applied in chain on top of a 10 percent lack of control discount opined to by one of the analysts.

---

[19] *Mandelbaum v. Commissioner*, T.C. Memo 1995-255 (June 12, 1995).

[20] *Estate of Artemus D. Davis v. Commissioner*, 110 T.C. 530 (1998).

[21] *Estate of Richard R. Simplot v. Commissioner*, 112 T.C. 13 (1999).

[22] *Estate of Brookshire*.

[23] *Estate of Harriett R. Mellinger v. Commissioner*, 112 T.C. 4 (1999).

[24] *Estate of Frank A. Branson v. Commissioner*, T.C. Memo 1999-231 (July 13, 1999).

[25] *Estate of Thomas A. Fleming v. Commissioner*, T.C. Memo 1997-484 (Oct. 27, 1997).

Discounts for Lack of Marketability—Controlling Ownership Interests

Discounts for lack of marketability for controlling interests (otherwise known as *illiquidity discounts*, as discussed in Chapter 17) have ranged all the way from zero to 30 percent.

In *Estate of Hendrickson*,[26] the IRS expert applied a 10 percent discount for lack of marketability to a controlling ownership interest, and the taxpayer's expert used a 30 percent discount. The Tax Court concluded that a 30 percent lack of marketability discount was reasonable, citing the following factors:

1. Peoples had few opportunities for growth.
2. Peoples earnings were subject to significant interest rate risk.
3. Peoples had no employee stock ownership plan or history of repurchasing shares.
4. There was no readily available public or private market for Peoples shares.

The Tax Court then went on to explain its decision as follows:

While we recognize that elements of control may enhance marketability, we do not think that the estate shares were rendered marketable by virtue of their affective [sic] control . . . A buyer of the estate shares would either have to sell the block privately, cause Peoples to make a public offering, or seek an acquiror. Any of these three options could take a number of months, and require significant transaction costs for the services of accountants, lawyers, and investment bankers.

Blockage Discounts

Blockage discounts may apply to publicly traded stock where the size of the block is large enough relative to normal trading volume that it could not be sold in a short time without depressing the market price. Blockage discounts concluded in most Tax Court cases are relatively modest—generally in the range of 3 percent to 10 percent—but have been as high as 25 percent. Also, there have been a number of cases in which the court has denied a blockage discount.

A typical case is a 3.3 percent blockage discount in *Estate of Foote*, where the block constituted 2.2 percent of the stock outstanding and was equal to 29 days of average trading volume.[27]

The *Estate of Wright* involved a large block of thinly traded stock, with a valuation date market price of $50 per share. The IRS expert said there should be no blockage discount, and the taxpayer's expert claimed a $12 discount for a net value

---

[26] *Estate of Hendrickson.* The 31-page opinion in this case explains the Court's position on many valuation issues and is particularly instructive reading for those interested in valuations for tax purposes.

[27] *Estate of Dorothy B. Foote v. Commissioner*, T.C. Memo 1999-37 (Feb. 5, 1999).

of $38, reflecting various factors including blockages. The Tax Court used the $38 as a starting point, but concluded a value of $45 per share due to the company's "excellent financial condition," thus resulting in a final discount of 10 percent from the $50 market price.[28]

One of the largest blockage discounts was found in *Estate of Mellinger*, which involved significant blocks of the thinly traded public stock of Frederick's of Hollywood. After thoroughly reviewing the testimony and qualifications of the experts, the Tax Court concluded that the appropriate blockage discount was 25 percent, as testified by the taxpayer's expert.[29]

Key Person Discount

The Tax Court often allows a discount for the loss or potential loss of a key person.

In *Estate of Paul Mitchell*, the Tax Court applied a $15 million discount (10 percent) to the $150 million enterprise value for the death of Paul Mitchell, the company's primary key person. The Tax Court then dealt with other discounts (lack of control, lack of marketability, lawsuit contingency) at the 40 percent noncontrolling ownership interest level.[30]

Contingent Liability Discounts

Discounts for contingent liabilities can cover a wide spectrum, such as environmental liabilities and pending lawsuits.

In *Estate of Paul Mitchell*, after taking a 10 percent key person discount at the enterprise level (as discussed above), the Tax Court then took a $1.5 million dollar discount for a pending compensation lawsuit *after* computing the estate's 40 percent pro rata interest in the enterprise value and *after* deduction of a 35 percent combined lack of control/lack of marketability discount.[31]

In *Estate of Desmond*, the primary issue was a discount for potential environmental liability for a controlling ownership interest in a closely held paint and coating manufacturing company. The expert for the IRS claimed 0 to 5 percent. The taxpayer's expert, using equally weighted asset-based, income, and market valuation approaches, claimed 25 percent. The Tax Court decided that the asset-based and income approaches should be discounted 25 percent. However, the Tax Court concluded that this discount should not be applied to the result of the unadjusted guideline publicly traded company valuation method. This was because the market prices of the guideline public companies had already taken the potential environmental liability into account.[32]

---

[28] *Estate of W. Clyde Wright v. Commissioner*, T.C. Memo 1997-53 (Jan. 29, 1997).
[29] *Estate of Mellinger*.
[30] *Estate of Paul Mitchell v. Commissioner*, T.C. Memo 1997-461 (Oct. 9, 1997).
[31] Id.
[32] *Estate of William J. Desmond v. Commissioner*, T.C. Memo 1999-76 (Mar. 10, 1999).

Trapped-In Capital Gains Taxes

One of the most dramatic shifts in Tax Court decisions, starting in 1998, was explicit recognition of liability for capital gains taxes on significantly appreciated property.

Until 1986, a corporation could liquidate, distribute all proceeds to stockholders within a year, and avoid paying any capital gains tax at the corporate level under the so-called *General Utilities Doctrine*. The Tax Reform Act of 1986 repealed the General Utilities Doctrine, leaving no practical means for C corporations to avoid paying capital gains tax on the sale of appreciated assets. Nevertheless, the IRS steadfastly held to the position that, when valuing a corporation with appreciated assets, a discount to reflect the liability for the capital gains tax was illegal as a matter of law.

In *Estate of Davis*,[33] a family holding company's primary asset was stock in Winn-Dixie Stores, with close to a zero cost basis. The Tax Court concluded:

> We reject respondent's position that, as a matter of law, no discount or adjustment attributable to ADDI&C's built-in capital gains tax is allowable in the instant case.
>
> We are convinced on the record in this case, and we find, that, even though no liquidation of ADDI&C or sale of its assets was planned or contemplated on the valuation date, a hypothetical willing seller and a hypothetical willing buyer would not have agreed on that date on a price for each of the blocks of stock in question that took no account of ADDI&C's built-in capital gains tax.

Shortly before the *Davis* case, the Tax Court had rejected a discount for trapped-in capital gains, and the case was on appeal at the time of the *Davis* case. Soon after the *Davis* decision, the Second Circuit Court of Appeals, citing favorably the *Estate of Davis*, reversed *Estate of Eisenberg*:

> In the past, the denial of a reduction for potential capital gains tax liability was based, in part, on the possibility that the taxes could be avoided by liquidating the corporation. . . . These tax-favorable options ended with the Tax Reform Act of 1986 (TRA). . . .
>
> Now that the TRA has effectively closed the option to avoid capital gains tax at the corporate level, reliance on these cases in the post-TRA environment should, in our view, no longer continue.[34]

In a March 1999 decision, *Estate of Simplot*,[35] the Tax Court allowed deduction of the full amount of the trapped-in gains tax liability on the appreciated value of a large block of stock in a publicly traded company in its valuation of the company holding the block of stock.

This result was applauded by much of the professional business valuation community. Typical is the comment of a well-known valuation analyst who reviewed the case:

---

[33] *Estate of Davis.*

[34] *Eisenberg v. Commissioner*, No. 97-4331 U.S. App. (2d Cir. Aug. 18, 1998), *rev'g* T.C. Memo 1997-483 (Oct. 27, 1997).

[35] *Estate of Richard R. Simplot v. Commissioner.*

The Court's finding is consistent with the position I have long advocated. This is an exciting result. Good economic evidence is the basis for sound decisions by the courts.[36]

One more 1999 case, *Estate of Jameson*,[37] also made clear the recognition of the trapped-in capital gains tax discount, in this case for a timber company. The Tax Court found:

> Where a timber company must recognize built-in capital gains under IRC §1231, because of its IRC §631(a) election, each time it cuts and sells timber, valuation of the company must take this built-in capital gains into account.

The IRS finally posted a notice on its Web site (www.irs.gov), acquiescing that there is no legal prohibition against a discount for trapped-in capital gains. Referring to the *Eisenberg* case, the notice stated:

> The Second Circuit reversed the Tax Court and held that, in valuing closely held stock, a discount for the built-in capital gains tax liabilities could apply depending on the facts presented. The court noted that the Tax Court itself had recently reached a similar conclusion in *Estate of Davis v. Commissioner.* . . .
>
> We acquiesce in this opinion to the extent that it holds that there is no legal prohibition against such a discount. The applicability of such a discount, as well as its amount, will hereafter be treated as factual matters to be determined by competent expert testimony based upon the circumstances of each case and generally applicable valuation principles.

Focus on Willing Seller as Well as on Willing Buyer

Recent judicial precedents have increasingly emphasized the point that the expert should consider the hypothetical willing seller as well as the hypothetical willing buyer.

In *Estate of Lehmann*, the Tax Court stated:

> [The taxpayer's expert] focuses exclusively on the hypothetical willing buyer. [He] failed to consider whether a hypothetical seller would sell his or her interest in the partnership for $399,000. . . . Ignoring the views of the willing seller is contrary to this well-established rule.[38]

In *Estate of Kaufman*, the Court observed:

> [The taxpayer's expert] seems to have focused too much on the willing buyer portion of the fair market value definition. He failed to consider whether a seller, under no compulsion to sell, would discount the pro rata value of his interest by 40 or 50 percent in order to consummate the sale.[39]

---

[36] Z. Christopher Mercer, "Tax Court Accords Superpremium to Small Voting Block: Allows Deduction of 100% of Trapped-in Capital Gains Tax," *Judges & Lawyers Business Valuation Update*, April 1999, pp. 1, 6–7.

[37] *Estate of Jameson v. Commissioner.*

[38] *Estate of George A. Lehmann v. Commissioner*, T.C. Memo 1997-392 (Aug. 26, 1997).

[39] *Estate of Alice Friedlander Kaufman v. Commissioner*, T.C. Memo 1999-119 (Apr. 6, 1999).

Inadequacy of the Valuation

The instances and factors contributing to inadequate valuations for tax purposes by both taxpayer and IRS experts, could easily fill an entire book of this size. Some of the most common inadequacies are the following:

- The valuation is out of date.
- Lack of site visits and/or management interviews.
- Inadequate selection and/or analysis/explanation of selected guideline company comparability.
- Inadequate empirical support for the valuation variables selected (e.g., pricing multiples, discount/capitalization rates, discounts/premiums).

The Court rejected the taxpayer's expert's report in *Estate of Scanlan*[40] for several reasons, including:

- He was unable to explain certain parts of the analysis contained in the reports.
- He arbitrarily applied a 35 percent lack of marketability discount.
- He made no mention of a hypothetical seller.
- Whereas the report prepared by the expert two years prior to the date of death states that he toured the facilities, there is nothing in his testimony or in his report as of the date of death to suggest that he did likewise before preparing the report for estate tax purposes.
- The report does not adequately account for the fact that the company's earnings in the year of the estate tax report increased dramatically over the years covered by the earlier report.
- The report does not adequately take into account that the company began paying dividends after the time covered by the earlier report.
- The report refers to the financial data of publicly traded companies, yet never explains how those companies were selected, or in what respects their lines of business were similar to the subject company.

Another case where the Tax Court rejected the taxpayer's expert's valuation was in *Estate of Kaufman*.[41] The opinion of the Tax Court discusses, among others, the following flaws:

- Did not sufficiently explain why the guideline publicly traded companies he selected for his analysis were comparative, and why other publicly traded companies that appeared more comparable were not used. "A proper valuation report must contain enough data on each similar corporation to allow the Court to make an informed, independent decision as to whether the corporations are sufficiently similar to the subject corporation to perform a proper valuation analysis."
- Did not analyze all three valuation approaches. "Valuation experts must thoroughly analyze all applicable methods of valuation, and they may not simply assert without sufficient explanation that they have concluded that a particular method is irrelevant." (The valuation approach that was not used in this case was the asset-based approach.)

---

[40] *Estate of Scanlan.*

[41] *Estate of Kaufman.* The expert in this case wrote a very interesting rebuttal to Judge Laro's criticisms. See *Judges & Lawyers Business Valuation Update*, January 1999, pp. 11–13.

- Relied upon faulty assumptions regarding the equivalent value of different share blocks (of different sizes).
- Assumed that there was no market for the estate's stock, when several factors cited by the Tax Court indicated that there was a market for the stock.
- Did not address the nature of the two classes of stock issued by the corporation, whether they had cumulative voting rights or what differences existed between the two classes of stock.

In *Estate of Freeman*, the Tax Court accorded the taxpayer's expert's value no weight. Among other faults the Tax Court noted:

> [The taxpayer's expert] analyzed financial statements for the four fiscal years ended March 31, 1986 through 1989, but no interim statements between March 31, 1989 and the valuation date.
>
> He capitalized 1989 earnings at a rate he considered "appropriate" after discussing the "price/earnings ratio of Dow Jones Industrial Average at October 20, 1989, and the range of that average for 5 years." He capitalized 1989 revenues, but did not explain the capitalization rate that he used. He used a price/book value ratio, again referring to the DJIA but not to any specific comparable companies.[42]

The Tax Court ultimately made "corrections" to the IRS expert's valuation to arrive at a conclusion. The Court has to work with the evidence available to it, but it is likely that more complete evidentiary testimony on behalf of the taxpayer would have led to a lower value conclusion.[43]

Must Use Empirical Data to Quantify Variables

While it is appropriate to use judicial precedent in support of valuation *positions*, the analyst should use relevant market data to quantify valuation variables. Such variables would include, for example, market-derived pricing multiples, discount and capitalization rates, and magnitudes of discounts or premiums.

In *Estate of Berg*,[44] the taxpayer's expert relied on judicial precedent to quantify discounts for lack of control and lack of marketability, while the IRS experts used market-derived data. The Tax Court rejected the taxpayer's expert's reliance on judicial precedent, and found in favor of the IRS expert's position. The case was appealed to the Eighth Circuit Court of Appeals[45] and the Tax Court's decision on the valuation was upheld.

In *Estate of Foote*, the taxpayer's expert reviewed 18 reported Tax Court cases that involved a blockage discount. Using the discounts awarded in those cases, he calculated a blockage discount of 22.5 percent. The IRS expert analyzed 16 factors relevant to the decedent's block and concluded a blockage discount of 3.3 percent, which the Court accepted because it "properly considered all the relevant factors."[46]

---

[42] *Estate of Ross H. Freeman v. Commissioner*, T.C. Memo 1996-372 (Aug. 13, 1996).

[43] See case summary and commentary in *Shannon Pratt's Business Valuation Update*, October 1996, pp. 14–15.

[44] *Estate of Edgar A. Berg v. Commissioner*, T.C. Memo 1991-279 (June 20, 1991).

[45] *Berg v. Commissioner*, No. 91-3198 U.S. App. (8th Cir. Oct. 5, 1992).

[46] *Estate of Foote.*

Summary

Perhaps what comes through loudest and clearest in this chapter is that the courts demand strong, relevant evidence in support of each valuation position taken and each valuation variable used. Clearly, in selecting and weighting valuation approaches, the quality of relevant evidence is an important consideration.

It is also clear that the Tax Court exercises considerable discretion regarding what valuation factors are relevant under what circumstances and what constitutes adequate evidence for the quantification of the myriad of variables affecting the valuation conclusion. Both valuation analysts and lawyers should heed Judge David Laro's advice to read the relevant judicial precedent, especially the opinions of the judge who will hear their cases.

The Tax Court is very receptive to discounts for factors that buyers and sellers in the real world would take into consideration. However, the reasoning for—and the quantification of—such discounts should be well-supported.

In summary, attorneys should not only retain competent valuation analysts for their clients but they also should critically evaluate the analyst's work product in light of the anticipated judicial reaction.

References

Electronic Sources

Business Valuation Update Online Library, www.BVLibrary.com. Includes full text of tax case opinions involving valuation from 1990 forward and frequently referenced cases from earlier years. Searchable by keyword, name of judge, and name of expert.

CCH Incorporated, www.tax.cch.com. CCH has various on-line and CD-ROM services that provide full-text of Tax Court decisions, revenue rulings, letter rulings, and other tax-related information.

Kleinrock's Tax Library (CD-ROM). A comprehensive tax library of tax cases (from Tax Court and other relevant courts) dating back to 1918, revenue rulings, letter rulings, technical advice memorandums, complete IRS Code and Regulations, IRS publications, and other relevant information. Fully searchable by keyword or citation. Available monthly or quarterly from Kleinrock Publishing, 11300 Rockville Pike, Rockville, Maryland 20852-3030, (800) 890-1503, www.kleinrock.com.

U.S. Tax Court, www.ustaxcourt.gov. Opinions section includes all applicable Tax Court opinions since January 3, 1999, posted the day they are released. Searchable by release date, petitioner's name, and judge's name.

Print Sources

CPA Expert. Quarterly newsletter that frequently contains commentary on significant court cases of all types by leading valuation practitioners, as well as articles on valuation and litigation issues. Published by the American Institute of Certified Public Accountants, Harborside Financial Center, 201 Plaza Three, Jersey City, New Jersey 07311-3881, (800) 862-4272, www.aicpa.org.

CPA Litigation Service Counselor. Monthly newsletter that frequently contains commentary on significant court cases of all types by leading valuation practitioners, as well as articles on valuation and litigation issues. Published by Harcourt Professional Publishing, 6277 Sea Harbor Drive, Orlando, Florida 32887-4600, (800) 831-7799.

Howitt, Idelle A., ed. *Federal Tax Valuation Digest.* Published annually, this cumulative digest contains summaries of all tax cases dealing with valuation issues from 1946 through the year prior to publication. Contains various indexes by keyword, judge, court, case name, and valuation issue. Published by Warren, Gorham & Lamont, 31 St. James Avenue, Boston, Massachusetts, (800) 431-9025, www.wgl.com.

Judges & Lawyers Business Valuation Update. Monthly newsletter that summarizes tax cases with valuation issues, with commentary by Shannon Pratt and leading estate attorneys. Published by Business Valuation Resources, 7412 S.W. Beaverton-Hillsdale Highway, Suite 106, Portland, Oregon 97215, (888) BUS-VALU, www.BVLibrary.com.

Shannon Pratt's Business Valuation Update. Monthly newsletter that summarizes tax cases with valuation issues, with commentary by Shannon Pratt and other leading business appraisers. Published by Business Valuation Resources (see above).

Valuation Case Digest. Quarterly newsletter summarizing court cases relating to valuation issues. The last page of each issue provides information on how to find the complete decision of each case (mostly from free, on-line sources). Published by Valuation Information, Inc., 33117 Hamilton Court, Suite 200, Farmington Hills, Michigan 48334-3355, (248) 324-1875.

Chapter 29

Buy-Sell Agreements

One of the most critical planning tasks facing a business owner is providing for the continuity of the enterprise. A buy-sell agreement can effectively prevent many potential problems regarding disposition of stock or a partnership interest of a departing or deceased stockholder or partner. The buy-sell agreement can accomplish the following objectives:

1. Smooth ownership transition while continuing the operation of the business.
2. Provide a mechanism with which an owner can liquidate the ownership interest in the event of death, disability, termination, or retirement.
3. Reduce uncertainty for noncontrolling shareholders.
4. Document a framework to quantify the efforts of management's stewardship and the success of business operations.
5. Prevent the ownership interest from being sold or otherwise transferred to any party not acceptable to the other owners.
6. Provide litigation support or dispute resolution procedures regarding equity valuation matters, such as shareholder marital dissolution issues or business interruption and insurance issues.
7. Provide a payment scheme that is affordable in the least disruptive manner to the subject company.
8. Provide a benchmark for valuation of the entire business or partial interest for sale, initial public offering, or collateralization purposes.

It is important to recognize that the makeup of the ownership of closely held businesses is quite varied. Some closely held businesses are owned by members of a family, all of whom work at the company. Some businesses (for instance, some medical practices) are owned by professionals who are in essence owner/managers. Some closely held businesses are primarily owned by one individual who exercises the prerogatives of control. And, some businesses are owned by passive owners (outsiders who do not work at the company). As a result of these various ownership situations, there are many types of buy-sell agreements.

Types of Buy-Sell Agreements

Buy-sell agreements used in closely held corporations or partnerships to provide for liquidation of the interest of a withdrawing or deceased shareholder or partner fall into one of three categories:

1. *Repurchase agreements* (also called *entity purchase agreements* or *redemption agreements*), in which the issuing corporation or partnership buys the interest from the withdrawing party or from the estate of the deceased party.
2. *Cross-purchase agreements*, in which one or more other individuals or entities buy the interest from the withdrawing party or from the estate of the deceased party.
3. *Hybrid agreements* (also called *wait-and-see agreements*) which usually allow the issuer first priority to buy the interest and other stockholders or partners the second-place option to buy. Such agreements can be drafted to allow both the company and the other shareholders the opportunity of waiting until after the date of death to determine which is in the better tax and liquidity condition to purchase the shares.

Each type of agreement may be either mandatory—that is, binding on both parties—or optional on the part of one of the parties, usually the purchaser. Sometimes agreements are written with one set of buy-out options during an owner's lifetime and with another set of options for a decedent's estate.

It is not necessary that the same agreement apply to all the owners of a particular entity. One or a few owners may be subject to an agreement while others are not, or different owners may be subject to different agreements. For example, it is common to find noncontrolling owners of an enterprise subject to a buy-sell agreement while the controlling owner is not. In limited partnerships, provisions applicable to limited partners normally differ from those applicable to general partners.

It is not necessary for the price to apply in all events. The valuation provisions of the buy-sell agreement may be affected by the event that triggered them. For example, some buy-sell agreements price the subject shares differently if the shareholder's employment is terminated voluntarily rather than involuntarily, or if the employee leaves to go to work for a competitor.

The provisions of any buy-sell agreement should, of course, be designed to best carry out the objectives of all the parties. From a seller's viewpoint, an important objective is to provide liquidity in the event of withdrawal from the business or death. From a purchaser's viewpoint, an important objective typically is to provide continuity of ownership and management without possible interference from outside parties. From the viewpoints of both seller and purchaser, an additional purpose is to establish the circumstances under which the agreement will become effective and a means of determining the price and terms of the transaction.

One consideration in the choice between the cross-purchase versus redemption form of buy-sell agreement is the number of shareholders or partners involved. The more there are, the more complicated the cross-purchase plan becomes relative to the redemption. In the cross-purchase arrangement, the number of party-to-party relationships, life insurance policies required, and so on rises exponentially with the number of parties involved. One solution to these problems is to create an insurance trust agreement, but this requires drafting another complicated agreement. In the redemption type of agreement, the corporation owns the life insurance policies, so there are not administrative or tax problems arising from the necessity to transfer policies at the death of one party (except for the possible alternative minimum tax, discussed later).

Naturally, the tax implications will be a major consideration in deciding which type of agreement to use. The tax implications, which are complicated and often subject to change, are beyond the scope of this book. Several references on tax implications appear in the bibliography at the end of this chapter.

Valuation Provisions of the Buy-Sell Agreement

The provision for valuation is a critical element of the buy-sell agreement. The parties have a great deal of flexibility in structuring this provision, but often it is neglected or done hastily and thus eventually turns out to be unfair to one or the other party.

Need for Clear Direction

The importance of having the valuation provisions of the buy-sell agreement thought through thoroughly by someone who understands valuation and understood by all parties before the agreement is signed cannot be overemphasized. Attitudes and relationships change, and one cannot assume that any ambiguity in the buy-sell agreement will be resolved amicably when the time comes to consummate a transaction pursuant to the agreement. Most disputes relating to buy-sell agreements arise because one or several of the details of the agreement either were inadequately defined or were misunderstood by one or more of the parties.

For example, in one arbitration case over the value of a business interest under a buy-sell agreement, the document was so ambiguous about the applicable valuation date that the valuation of the interest as of four different dates was required so that the arbitration panel could select the most applicable one. The value differences on the various dates were considerable, because the business was undergoing a series of significant and somewhat unpredictable changes during the relevant time period. The ambiguity as to the applicable valuation date substantially increased the time and cost involved for the analysis as well as the uncertainty of the outcome of the arbitration.

Even when the valuation criterion for the buy-sell agreement is simply book value, there can be disagreements over the definition of terms. Book value could be that determined for tax purposes or for business purposes, on a cash basis or on an accrual basis. It could be computed as of the date of death, as of the end of the month preceding death, as of the end of the last regular accounting period of the entity, as of the end of the fiscal year of the entity nearest the date of death, or as of some other date.

Chapters 3 and 16 discussed the fact that the fair market value of a minority ownership interest usually is less than a pro rata share of the value of the entire enterprise. Many parties to buy-sell agreements have been unpleasantly surprised to learn that the fair market value of their interest (the standard of value specified in the agreement that they hastily read and signed) was less than a proportionate share of the total enterprise value.

Buy-sell agreements may specify that the shares be valued strictly at their fair market value as noncontrolling ownership interests, at a proportionate share of the enterprise value with no discount for lack of control and/or no discount for lack of marketability, or at a specified percentage discount from a proportionate share of total enterprise value.

We suggest that the reader contemplating a buy-sell agreement read Chapter 2, Defining the Assignment, carefully and be sure that the agreement covers all the relevant points. In addition, the terms of payment should be specified. The payment terms may differ under various circumstances, and the agreement may allow the company some flexibility, making allowance for the company's ability to pay. *The key point to keep in mind is that the buy-sell agreement is a legal document that will have to stand on its own at the time a triggering event occurs.*

One unique aspect of the price-fixing mechanism in a buy-sell agreement, as opposed to other valuation problems, is the extreme uncertainty concerning when a future event that triggers a transaction under the agreement will occur. This is one of the key reasons why there is no single approach to the problem of establishing the price for a buy-sell agreement that one can recommend as completely satisfactory for all situations.

Most of the mechanisms for setting prices in buy-sell agreements generally fall into one or a combination of three categories:

1. Some type of formula based on the financial statements, such as book value, some type of adjusted book value, capitalization of earnings, or some combination of such variables.

2. Negotiation among the parties.

3. Independent outside appraisal.

Formula Approaches

Formula approaches for setting the price in a buy-sell agreement can easily turn out to be unfair to one party or the other when the transaction eventually occurs. As this book indicates, the valuation process should reflect a complex set of factors—usually too complex to be adequately embodied in a formula. A formula that might produce an appropriate value in one year might not do so in another year when circumstances in the company and the economy differ. For example, in the case of *St. Louis County Bank v. United States*, the court refused to honor for estate tax purposes an agreement that gave a corporation the right to purchase the decedent's stock under a formula that produced a zero value, even though the formula may have originally produced an acceptable value.[1] Having made this point, we will consider some of the most common formulas for fixing the price in a buy-sell agreement.

The most popular basis for a formula approach is to use book value or some type of adjusted book value. Earlier chapters made the point that book value only occasionally coincides with fair market value or any other standard of value of a business or business interest.

One of the obvious attractions of using book value is its simplicity. Even so, however, it must be well defined. Some buy-sell agreements call for book value with certain adjustments, such as adding back the LIFO inventory reserve or adjusting certain assets to current market value. Unless they are carefully defined, such adjustments can be subjects of dispute among the parties. Some agreements specify that an independent appraiser or an accountant be responsible for making the adjustments in order to avoid disputes among the parties.

Of course, if a business is on a cash basis, it is almost always necessary to make some adjustments to book value to reach a price that more nearly approximates an accrual basis book value, at least recognizing the receivables and payables.

If an asset accumulation method is used to establish the buy-sell agreement value in a repurchase agreement funded by life insurance, one must keep in mind whether the company's net asset value will be affected by the proceeds from the policy on the stockholder's death.

If a capitalization of earnings formula is used, it seems almost essential to base it on an average or weighted average of several years' earnings to avoid aberrations in the result that could occur from one or two exceptionally good or poor years. Perhaps formula valuations that rely heavily on the most recent earnings (or even projected earnings) would be preferred if such earnings better represent the expectation of the current earnings capacity of the company applicable to the interest being valued. This is often more appropriate in a growing company or one that is undergoing changes compared with recent historical results. Of course, as discussed elsewhere in this book, earnings should be adjusted to eliminate extraordinary items, although again such adjustments could be a source of disputes. The direct capitalization rate or multiplier is a critical variable, and a multiplier that is appropriate one year might not be so for another year because of changing economic conditions.

---

[1] *St. Louis County Bank v. United States*, 674 F.2d 1207 (8th Cir. 1982).

One common criticism of formula approaches that are based on the balance sheet or the income statement or both is that closely held companies have considerable latitude in reporting figures within the boundaries of generally accepted accounting principles, as well as control over such important variables as paying compensation to owner-employees versus retaining earnings. For this reason, controlling stockholders have the power to make decisions that could be detrimental to the noncontrolling stockholder whose value will be determined by a formula approach.

Negotiation among the Parties

Many practitioners believe that negotiation among the owners—usually annually—is the best approach to setting the buy-sell agreement price. The parties themselves usually have the most intimate knowledge of their own estate objectives as well as of their attitudes toward one another. They also may have a better idea than anyone else about the future operations of the business and its worth; in most cases, however, owners would benefit from professional outside guidance on that point.

The problems with this approach arise when the annual valuation is neglected or when the parties cannot agree. In our experience, the annual valuations seem to be neglected more often than not. The buy-sell agreement must provide for dealing with both of these eventualities.

The most common method of handling potential neglect of the annual valuation is to stipulate that if the price is not set annually on a timely basis, after some period (typically 12 to 24 months following the last price agreement), the price-fixing mechanism automatically reverts to either a formula approach or an independent appraisal. In the latter case, it is necessary to either name the appraisal firm or specify the method by which the appraiser will be selected. If a firm or person is named, provision must be made for an alternative selection procedure if the named appraiser is unable to serve.

O'Neal and Thompson offer the following guidance regarding provision for selecting appraisers in the buy-sell agreement. This guidance would apply whether appraisers are to be used in any case or to be used only in the event of inability to agree through negotiation:

> If the price of shares is to be fixed by appraisal, the names of the appraisers or a method of choosing them must be specified; and a statement should be made that the decision of a majority of the appraisers will be binding. . . . A typical appraisal provision states that the optionee or purchaser, as the case may be, shall select one appraiser, the offeror or vendor a second, and that the two appraisers shall choose a third. . . . Occasionally an independent third party, such as a corporate fiduciary, is given the power to appoint the third appraiser; or the third appraiser is designated by office . . . Sometimes the appraisers are selected in advance and designated by name. . . . If that is done, provision must be made for a method of appointing substitutes should the designated appraisers die, become incapacitated, or refuse to serve.[2]

Some buy-sell agreements provide for two or three appraisers to submit reports to an arbitration panel, which will make the final determination in case of a dispute, but this can get quite expensive.

One suggestion for avoiding the problem of neglecting the annual valuation is to ask one of the company's professional advisers, such as the attorney, accountant,

---

[2] F. Hodge O'Neal (deceased) and Robert B. Thompson, *O'Neal's Close Corporations*, 3rd ed. (St. Paul, MN: West Group, 1996, supplemented 1999), pp. 134–35. Reprinted with permission.

insurance agent, or appraiser, to put a memo in his or her "tickler" file to remind the company to make its annual valuation.

Reversion to formula or outside appraisal approaches is also the most common type of provision for dealing with circumstances in which the parties cannot agree on a value through negotiation.

Exhibit 29–1 is a sample valuation article for a buy-sell agreement, providing for negotiation and for the price to be determined by an arbitration panel if negotiation fails.

Buy-sell agreements with negotiation-based pricing for enterprises in which a family group holds 50 percent or greater controlling ownership interests are not likely to be regarded by the IRS as binding for estate and gift tax filings, because of the presumption that the family members have a donative intent toward each other that prevents impartial arm's-length transactions.

Independent Outside Appraisal

The advantages of having a formal, independent outside appraisal, kept current with periodic updates, are many. From a business planning perspective, the typical strong management/ownership relationship in a closely held business often requires a valuation study in order to support various ownership strategies, business directions, and investment alternatives. A formal, professionally prepared appraisal incorporates current economic conditions and is more likely to assure fair treatment to all concerned. When an independent valuation program is implemented in a consistent manner during cordial points in time, the parties have an opportunity to challenge and discuss the results with less bias and an acceptable valuation philosophy is developed. A common compliment given to professional appraisers is that their annual investigation provides not only an opinion as to the value of a closely held business, but also an analysis of that business from a management consultant's point of view.

The obvious disadvantage of the formal appraisal with regular updates is the cost. However, the appraisal does not necessarily have to result in quite as lengthy and detailed a report as an ESOP valuation, since there usually are fewer beneficiaries to be satisfied and the appraiser and the directors need not be concerned with meeting ERISA requirements.

Whether or not a full, written appraisal report is prepared when pricing the buy-sell agreement, some degree of guidance from an independent professional business appraiser usually is helpful in arriving at a value that will be equitable to all parties and will forestall subsequent disputes.

Understanding an Agreement's Pricing Philosophy

Since business valuations rarely can be made with undisputable precision, there usually will be some relevant range of reasonable prices that will be acceptable to all the parties. Some flexibility in setting the price is possible.

Appraisers of real estate, equipment, or other physical property informally assert that their appraisals are accurate to within plus or minus 10 percent. However, few business interests can be appraised within such tolerances. Just look at how widely the prices of many publicly traded stocks fluctuate over relatively short periods. For many closely held businesses, it is not unreasonable for the high end of a value range to be 50 percent above the low end. For highly dynamic or speculative businesses, the reasonable range may be much wider.

Exhibit 29–1

Sample Valuation Provision for Buy-Sell Agreement
(Corporation Stock Redemption Example)

As soon as practical after the end of each fiscal year, the stockholders shall agree on the value per share of the stock that is applicable to this agreement. Such value will be set forth in Schedule A, which shall be dated, signed by each stockholder, and attached hereto. Such value shall be binding on both the corporation and the estate of any deceased stockholder whose date of death is within one year of the last dated and signed Schedule A.

If more than a year has elapsed between the date when Schedule A was last signed and the date of death of a deceased stockholder, then the value per share shall be determined, as of the date of death of the stockholder, by mutual agreement between the surviving stockholders and the personal representative or administrator of the deceased stockholder's estate.

If the surviving stockholders and the personal representative of the deceased stockholder's estate are unable to agree upon such a value within 90 days after such personal representative or administrator has qualified to administer the estate of the deceased stockholder, then such value shall be determined by binding arbitration. Either party may give written notice of such binding arbitration pursuant to this agreement to the other party. Within 30 days of such notice of arbitration, each party shall appoint one arbitrator. Within 30 days of the appointment of the two arbitrators, the arbitrators so appointed will select a third arbitrator. The first two arbitrators will have sole discretion in the selection of the third arbitrator, except that he must be an individual or qualified representative of a firm that regularly engages, as a primary occupation, in the professional appraisal of businesses or business interests. In the event that the first two arbitrators are unable to agree on a third arbitrator within 30 days of their appointment, the Executive Director of the ABC Trade Association shall appoint the third arbitrator.

The standard of value to be used by the arbitrators shall be fair market value of the shares being valued as of the date of death, under the assumption that the stockholder is deceased and the corporation has collected the proceeds, if any, of insurance on the life of the deceased stockholder payable to the corporation.

Each arbitrator shall use his sole discretion in determining the amount of investigation he considers necessary in arriving at a determination of the value of the shares. The corporation shall make available on a timely basis all books and records requested by any arbitrator, and all material made available to any one arbitrator shall be made available to all arbitrators.

Concurrence by at least two of the three arbitrators shall constitute a binding determination of value. The value concluded by the arbitrators shall be reported to the corporation and to the personal representative or administrator of the estate of the deceased in writing, signed by the arbitrators concurring as to the concluded value, within 90 days of the appointment of the third arbitrator unless an extension of time has been agreed upon between the corporation and the personal representatives of the estate.

The corporation and the estate shall each be responsible for the fees and expenses of the arbitrators they appoint. The fees and expenses of the third arbitrator shall be divided equally between the corporation and the estate.

Considering this flexibility, if the buy-sell agreement price is to be determined by an independent outside appraiser for unrelated parties, the appraiser can present the parties with a relevant price range, and the parties can make a decision based on their wishes. Of course, it is not uncommon for the various parties to the agreement to have differing circumstances and objectives that motivate them toward opposite pricing philosophies. In general, in arm's-length bargaining one would expect parties who anticipate withdrawing earlier to opt for a higher value and parties who expect to survive in the business the longest to choose a lower value. If the decision is left to the outside appraiser, it is, of course, incumbent on the appraiser to balance these conflicting self-interests in the fairest possible manner. For estate and gift tax valuations, the fair market value standard requires the appraiser to consider only those motives typical of hypothetical, arm's-length willing buyers and willing sellers.

The consensus among the many articles that address this subject leans from the middle of the range to a somewhat conservative valuation when setting up a buy-sell agreement, whether the value standard is one of fair market value or some other standard. There are several valid arguments for inclining toward a conservative value. One is that recognizing that valuation is an imprecise matter, the parties tend to feel that they will enhance their favorable working relationship by leaning over backwards (a little) to be fair to one another. We have encountered some feeling that if some benefit is to be gained in the pricing by one party or another, it most properly should accrue to those who will remain with the business. This attitude is based on a recognition that none of the parties knows exactly when or for which owner a buy-sell agreement transaction may first be necessary, but that the surviving parties will bear the dual burden of carrying off the financing and payment of the transaction and of carrying on the management of the company during this process.

In a very close family situation, it is common to find the desire to minimize the price so as to lessen tax consequences. In these instances, it is especially important to have thoroughly documented justification of the price or basis selected, since the combination of a low price and a non-arm's-length family situation certainly will invite the scrutiny of the IRS and the state taxing authorities.

Terms and Funding

Two decisions that necessarily are integrally related in creating the buy-sell agreement are the provisions for payment terms and for funding.

Terms can run anywhere from immediate cash to payments spread out over several years, usually with interest. Funding can come from life insurance, from corporate funds in the case of a redemption, or from personal assets in the case of a cross-purchase. In some cases, borrowings may be used to fund either a redemption or a cross-purchase. In order for a buy-sell agreement to work, it is essential that funding adequate for carrying out its terms be available one way or another. Thus, provision for funding is an essential ingredient for a viable buy-sell agreement.

Term Payment Provisions

From the purchaser's viewpoint, the typical reason for preferring a term payment program to cash is to ease the funding burden. From the seller's viewpoint, the attraction of an installment payment program is the spreading out of the tax on the seller's gain over several of the seller's tax years. The seller, however, becomes a creditor subject to credit risk.

As this edition goes to press, a controversial "tax extender bill" is in effect, disallowing most installment tax payments for installment sales on or after December 17, 1999, for accrual method taxpayers. This provision was passed with little publicity, but since has stirred a firestorm of protest, and stands a high chance of being repealed or revised.

If a term payment plan is used, careful consideration must be given to establishing the interest rate, because this is really an integral part of the pricing decision. Attention also should be given to the matter of collateral or other protection to ensure that the seller will receive the contractual payments in the full amount and on a timely basis.

As discussed elsewhere in this book, if the interest rate on a term contract is below the market interest rate for similar instruments at the time of the event that triggers the transaction, the cash equivalent value the seller receives will be less than the contract's face value. Similarly, if the interest rate is above the relevant market rate, the cash equivalent value will be greater than the face value. The arithmetic for computing the present value of a contract bearing interest above or below a comparable market rate is shown in Chapter 9 (see Exhibit 9–1).

However, in setting the interest rate in the buy-sell agreement, we face the problem that market interest rates fluctuate considerably over time, and we have no way of knowing at what time in the future the buy-sell transaction will be triggered nor what the market level of interest rates will be at that time. There are several possible approaches to dealing with this dilemma.

One approach is simply to agree on an interest rate despite these uncertainties and hope that it does not prove grossly off the mark in the future. If the price under the buy-sell agreement is set by annual negotiation or appraisal, the interest rate could be reviewed and adjusted annually at the same time. Another alternative is to set the interest rate by tying it to some index of interest rates at the time of the transaction. The interest rate index used should represent intermediate- to long-term rates, since such rates fluctuate less than short-term rates and would be more appropriate for a term payment contract. The yield on *Barron's* intermediate grade bonds or *Moody's* BBB bonds could provide benchmarks for setting the interest rate. The agreement could specify that the index rate or some specified amount above or below it be used depending on the credit of the company involved, the degree of security provided, and the desires of the parties to the agreement.

It might be appropriate to use an interest rate index that represents securities whose maturities coincide with the payout terms of the buy-sell agreement. For example, an index representing five-year maturities can be used if the payout term is five years. The *Federal Reserve Bulletin* gives indexes of interest rates on U.S. Treasury bonds maturing in 1, 2, 3, 5, 7, 10, 20, and 30 years.

Income tax considerations could suggest the desirability of some trade-off between the price and the interest rate. The portion of the contract payments designated as interest will be a deductible expense to the buyer and income to the seller. The portion of the contract payments designated as principal will not be deductible to the buyer (unless there is an ESOP involved) and will be taxed as capital gains to the seller to the extent that they exceed the seller's basis. Thus, if the seller is in a low tax bracket and the buyer in a high one, it may be advantageous to structure the program to increase the interest rate and lower the price. Conversely, if the seller is in a high tax bracket and the buyer in a low one, it may be advantageous to lower the interest rate and increase the price. As noted earlier, these tax choices may not be available to companies using accrual accounting in conjunction with an installment sale.

Minimum interest rates based on U.S. Treasury rates are required for transactions among family members, and such applicable federal rates are published regularly.

The buy-sell agreement should also provide for adequate collateral or security for the seller in a term payment agreement. Security could take the form of a mortgage or lien on physical assets, such as real estate or equipment. It is also common to require that certain financial criteria, such as some minimum level of working capital, specified minimum current ratio, and specified maximum debt-to-equity ratio, be met. A typical sanction for enforcing such protective standards would be to provide that the entire amount become due and payable immediately if any of the standards are violated. These are the types of protections that a bank would require in making a loan, and many people feel that a seller of a business interest should be no less protected. The obvious problem is that such collateral may prevent the buyer from utilizing other financing. The seller could accommodate this by taking a second position, with some limits or safeguards.

Funding the Buy-Sell Agreement with Life Insurance

Life insurance can serve as an important source of funding for stock purchase agreements pertaining to deceased shareholders. The advantages of using life insurance for this purpose are several. First, deceased shareholders' estates get paid in cash, eliminating their need to rely on the corporation's continuing prosperity. Second, the corporation's investment in the cash value of an ordinary life policy is a business asset. Third, any excess insurance the corporation carries over and above the value of the stock purchase agreement can be retained as earned surplus.

In general, the use of life insurance can fulfill three basic needs:

1. Liquidation of the stock of a departed or disabled stockholder, either by the corporation or by other stockholders.
2. Payment of estate taxes.
3. Provision for continuity of the business after loss of a key person.

The owner should constantly monitor the value of the business in order to know how much life insurance is needed to fulfill these needs and update the coverage accordingly. The owner should seek out and periodically consult with a professional who knows how to apply life insurance to businesses, especially the tax implications of the many types of policies and the various configurations of ownership and beneficiaries.

For example, under current tax laws for C corporations, the receipt of life insurance proceeds from a policy owned by a corporation can give rise to additional corporate taxable income under the Alternative Minimum Tax calculations.

Liquidation of Departed or Disabled Owner's Stock. The beneficiary of life insurance purchased for the purpose of acquiring a deceased owner's stock is logically determined by the buy-sell agreement: The corporation is the beneficiary in connection with a repurchase agreement, and the various stockholders are the beneficiaries in connection with a cross-purchase agreement. The repurchase agreement, with the corporation as the beneficiary of the life insurance policies, usually is simpler administratively if there are three or more stockholders involved, but tax and other considerations may outweigh this advantage.

Funding of the purchase of a stockholder's interest if the stockholder is terminated but not deceased can be accomplished through an annuity or through life insurance with a cash value feature. The matter of insurance for covering needs in the event of the stockholder's permanent disability often is overlooked, but such needs are a common occurrence.

Payment of Estate Taxes. Estate taxes become a problem only to the extent that the estate's value exceeds the amounts exempted from estate taxes, under the unified credit, as discussed in Chapter 27. If the value exceeds the amount eligible for the unified credit exemption, the estate tax liability can be estimated from the estate and gift tax table in Chapter 27 (Exhibit 27–1). Provision for payment of the estimated amount of estate tax can be made with life insurance in that amount, as long as the insurance proceeds are structured so that they are not taxable as part of the estate.

Providing for Business Continuity. Life insurance payable to the corporation also can provide funding to ensure continuity of the business following the loss of a key person. It is common to find a key person contributing far more to the business's annual cash flow than he or she is taking out in salary and benefits. The company can be protected against the financial impact of the loss of such a valuable person by estimating the potential earnings or cash flow shortfall to be compensated for until the key person can be replaced and the replacement brought up to speed. The company can then cover the estimated amount of that risk with life insurance on the key person.

Review of Prior Life Insurance Funding. If funding of the foregoing requirements has been provided for through life insurance taken out in prior years, that
insurance should be reviewed as to both amount and type.

The necessary amounts of insurance can change for several reasons. One, of
course, is general inflation. Another likely reason is the increased value of the business due to its success. Still another could be changes in the makeup of the business's
ownership. Finally, the value of a particular person in the role of a key person can
change over time due to a variety of circumstances.

There is a wide variety of life insurance products available and important changes
continue to occur at this writing. A review of the life insurance funding may very well
reveal new products that are better suited to the owner's objectives and/or are more
cost efficient.

Restrictions on Transfer

Most buy-sell agreements contain restrictions on the transfer of the ownership
interest.

This is of particular importance for corporations who have elected to be taxed
as an S corporation. These agreements should prohibit shareholders from transferring stock to anyone in such a way as would terminate the S election.

Generally, restrictions on transfer require that before transferring shares to any
outside party they first be offered to the corporation and/or to other stockholders. The
price at which the shares must be offered to the company and/or other stockholders
may be the price offered by the outside party. More often, however, the price is the
one that would be determined by the buy-sell agreement price-fixing mechanism. Such
restrictions often are determinative of, or at least useful evidence of, value for other
purposes since they limit both the shares' marketability and the potential amount
received for them.

In a case where there is more than one class of stock, the buy-sell agreement may
provide that the shares automatically be converted from one class to another if transferred, such as from voting to nonvoting.

If the parties to a buy-sell agreement desire to have restrictive transfer provisions
apply to involuntary transfers, such as in the cases of divorces or foreclosures when
the securities have been hypothecated and a loan defaulted, such extensions of the
restrictions should be spelled out in the agreement. Otherwise, courts may rule that
the restrictions do not apply to such involuntary transfers.

Buy-Sell Agreement Values for Estate and Gift Tax Valuation
under Chapter 14

Generally speaking, the price as determined by a buy-sell agreement will be binding on the Internal Revenue Service for estate tax purposes if the value falls within
the range of what would be determined under Revenue Ruling 59-60 at the time of
death. Of course, that value would be binding even in the absence of a buy-sell
agreement, but it usually is easier to substantiate—or at least usually more readily

acceptable to the IRS—in the presence of a buy-sell agreement, especially to the extent that the agreement value was established by arm's-length negotiation.

A review of the law, the literature, and the court cases indicates that the most important criterion is the extent to which the price was established on an arm's-length basis. Following is the complete text of Section 8 of Revenue Ruling 59-60, which addresses the effect of stockholder agreements on gift and estate tax values:

> Frequently in the valuation of closely held stock for estate and gift tax purposes, it will be found that the stock is subject to an agreement restricting its sale or transfer. Where shares of stock were acquired by a decedent subject to an option reserved by the issuing corporation to repurchase at a certain price, the option price is usually accepted as the fair market value for estate tax purposes. See Rev. Rul. 54-76, C.B. 1954-1, 194. However, in such case the option price is not determinative of fair market value for gift tax purposes. Where the option, or buy and sell agreement, is the result of voluntary action by the stockholders and is binding during the life as well as at the death of the stockholders, such agreement may or may not, depending upon the circumstances of each case, fix the value for estate tax purposes. However, such agreement is a factor to be considered, with other relevant factors, in determining fair market value. Where the stockholder is free to dispose of his shares during life and the option is to become effective only upon his death, the fair market value is not limited to the option price. It is always necessary to consider the relationship of the parties, the relative number of shares held by the decedent, and other material facts, to determine whether the agreement represents a bona fide business arrangement or is a device to pass the decedent's shares to the natural objects of his bounty for less than an adequate and full consideration in money or money's worth. In this connection, see Rev. Rul. 157 C.B. 1953-2, 255, and Rev. Rul. 189, C.B. 1953-2, 29.[3]

It also should be pointed out that a value fixed by a buy-sell agreement may be legally binding on the estate for transaction purposes even if it is not binding on the IRS for estate tax purposes. This could result in a situation where the estate ends up paying taxes on a value substantially higher than the price the estate actually receives.

Valuation Requirements under Section 2703

The Chapter 14 special valuation rules are applied to all applicable transfers after October 8, 1990. Section 2703 of Chapter 14 deals with buy-sell agreements, options, and other similar influences on value for estate or gift tax transfers.

Section 2703 applies to any family-owned business in which the family members (defined in the regulations) control 50 percent or more of the vote or value of the company.[4] Any buy-sell agreement, restriction, or other similar factor relating to the right to use or sell the property will be ignored for estate, gift, and generation-skipping tax purposes unless the agreement meets all three of the following tests:

---

[3] Rev. Rul. 59-60, 1959-1 C.B. 237, Section 8.

[4] We find the use of 50 percent as a threshold for control an odd choice. A 50 percent interest in a company is not per se a controlling interest, but merely a right to deadlock the company's decision-making process.

1. It is a bona fide business arrangement.
2. It must not be a device to transfer the property to the natural objects of the transferor's bounty (such as family members) for less than adequate and full consideration in money or money's worth.
3. Its terms must be comparable to similar arrangements entered into by persons in an arm's-length transaction.

Because of the effective date of the statute, many old buy-sell agreements will be "grandfathered" under the law, and transactions under these agreements need only follow the requirements in Revenue Ruling 59-60 and any court decisions involving similar fact patterns. The regulations for Section 2703 make it plain that any grandfathered agreement that is substantially modified after October 8, 1990, will thereafter be required to follow the rules under Section 2703. The IRS defines "substantial modification" as any change in the buy-sell agreement or other restriction that would alter (beyond a *de minimis* amount) the quality, timing, or amount of the rights of the parties to the agreement. Also, if any parties of a generation younger than those originally participating in the agreement as of October 8, 1990, are added by voluntary modification of the agreement (i.e., added as parties to the agreement by some discretionary method other than by a mandatory action such as inheritance), this will be considered a substantial modification.

Changes that are necessary to update the value of an agreement or restriction to make the value or terms of the agreement more nearly approximate fair market value are not to be considered material changes. An example of this would be a formula-based change in the earnings multiple utilized to calculate a value under the agreement. Failure to update an agreement requiring, say, an annual determination of value, constitutes a substantial modification.

What kind of formula-based value will work with buy-sell agreements under Section 2703? Under the pre–Chapter 14 rules, all that was basically necessary to make a buy-sell agreement (or other restriction) binding for estate and gift taxes was:

1. The agreement be binding during life as well as at death.
2. The agreement create a determinable value as of a specifically determinable date.
3. The agreement have at least some bona fide business purpose (this could include the promotion of orderly family ownership and management succession, so this was a pretty easy test to meet).
4. The agreement resulted in a fair market value for the subject business interest when it was originally executed. Often, the buy-sell agreement value would generate future date of death or gift date values substantially below what the fair market value otherwise would have been for the subject interest—even though the value was reasonable when the agreement was made.

In the regulations on this fourth test, it was noted that this standard is not met by showing a few isolated comparables, but rather the general business practice in the industry. If several different valuation formulas are in general use, it is permissible to utilize only one of these.[5]

If more than one right or restriction is set forth in the buy-sell agreement, each is tested separately under the rules of Section 2703.

---
[5] Regulations, Section 25.2702-1(b)(4).

Summary

Buy-sell agreements can be very useful tools for controlling ownership and liquidating the interests of deceased or departed shareholders or partners. They may take the form of cross-purchase agreements (among owners), repurchase agreements (between owner and company), or some combination of the two. Agreements may be funded in any of several ways, most commonly with some type of life insurance and/or annuity product. Under some circumstances, the buy-sell agreement value may determine estate taxes.

A key provision in any buy-sell agreement, and one that often receives inadequate attention in its drafting, is the provision for valuation. Aspects of the valuation provision that are not addressed, addressed in an unclear manner, and/or not understood in the same way by all the parties can lead to irreconcilable divisiveness and protracted litigation. It is extremely important that the implications of every aspect of the valuation provision be understood and considered in detail by all the parties. If independent appraisal is being contemplated, the procedure for selecting the appraiser(s) should be precise and complete. The agreement should give clear direction to the appraisers on all aspects of the appraisal assignment, including the valuation date and a clear definition of the applicable standard of value.

Care also should be taken in the planning stage to avoid the potentially disastrous estate tax consequences of transfers among family members or with others at less than full and adequate consideration.

Bibliography

Abatemarco, Michael J., and Alfred Cavallaro. "The Importance of Buy-Sell Agreements for Closely Held Corporations." *CPA Journal*, February 1992, pp. 57–59.

Adams, Roy M., David A. Herpe, and James R. Carey. "Buy-Sell Agreements after Chapter 14." *Trusts & Estates*, May 1993, pp. 22–32.

Bell, Lawrence L. "Valuation of Buy-Sell Agreements under Chapter 14 of the Internal Revenue Code." *Journal of the American Society of CLU & ChFC*, September 1992, pp. 48–53.

Birnbaum, Bruce L. "Practitioners Have Several Ways of Using Buy-Sell Agreements." *Taxation for Accountants*, April 1994, pp. 220–26.

Bogdanski, John A. "Hard Times for Buy-Sell Agreements." *Estate Planning*, June 1998, pp. 235–39.

"Buy-Sell Agreement Ignored in Valuing Decedent's Stock." *Estate Planning*, January 1998, pp. 32–35.

Drake, Dwight J., Kent Whiteley, and Timothy J. McDevitt. "The Ten Most Common Mistakes of Buy-Sell Agreements." *Journal of Financial Planning*, July 1992, pp. 104–12.

Ellentuck, Albert B. "Establishing the Estate Value of Stock by Using a Buy-Sell Agreement." *The Tax Adviser*, September 1998, pp. 637–38.

_____. "Reviewing a Buy/Sell Agreement." *The Tax Adviser*, November 1999, pp. 809–12.

Etkind, Steven M. "How a Professional Practice Can Be Sold Effectively." *Estate Planning*, May/June 1994, pp. 162–68.

Gamble, E. James. "How Do We Handle Buy-Sell Agreements under Chapter 14?" *Trusts & Estates*, March 1991, pp. 38–46.

_____. "Tax Law Notes: Buy-Sell Agreements, Section 2703, and the Final Regulations." *Michigan Bar Journal*, July 1992, pp. 664–66.

Gross, Mark P. "Buy-Sell Agreements and Divorce." *CPA Litigation Services Counselor*, February 2000, pp. 11–12.

Hales, Robert E. "To Buy-Sell or Not to Buy-Sell." *Practical Tax Lawyer*, Fall 1994, pp. 31–38.

Howitt, Idelle A. "Estate of Cameron W. Bommer." *Valuation Strategies*, September/October 1998, pp. 38–39, 42.

Johnson, Linda M., and Brian R. Greenstein. "Using Buy-Sell Agreements to Establish the Value of a Closely Held Business." *Journal of Taxation*, December 1994, pp. 362–68.

Kasner, Jerry A. "The IRS Loses One in the Buy-Sell Valuation Battle." *Tax Notes*, April 12, 1993, pp. 231–32.

Kelly, James P. III. "Waiving Rights under Buy-Sell Agreement Affects Stock Value." *Estate Planning*, September/October 1991, pp. 284–91.

Marcus, Fred J., and Douglas K. Freeman. "Valuation of Closely-Held Stock." *Journal of the American Society of CLU & ChFC*, September 1993, pp. 24–25.

Mezzullo, Louis A. "Buy-Sell Agreements after Chapter 14." *Trusts & Estates*, June 1994, pp. 49–59.

O'Connell, John J. "Net Gifts at Death and New Buy-Sell Agreement Problems." *Journal of the American Society of CLU and ChFC*, January 1994, pp. 72–76.

Peterson, James. "Ducking the Cross Fire: Avoiding Disputes in Buy-Sell Agreements." *Journal of Accountancy*, January 1991, pp. 65–69, 71.

Robbins, Valerie C. "Buy-Sell Agreement with a Twist." *Tax Adviser*, August 1992, pp. 524–25.

Stoneman, Christopher. "Buy-Sell Agreements: Accomplishing Planning Objectives with Optimal Tax Consequences." *Tax Management Estates, Gifts & Trusts Journal*, December 15, 1992, pp. 423–36.

Strouse, Jonathan E. "Redemption and Cross-Purchase Buy-Sell Agreements: A Comparison." *Practical Accountant*, October 1991, pp. 44–53+.

Switzer, Ralph V., and Edward D. Jones. "Orchestrating a Continuation Provision." *National Public Accountant*, December 1992, pp. 30–37.

Willens, Robert. "Buy-Sell Agreements: Constructive Dividend Dangers Lurk." *Journal of Accountancy*, February 1992, pp. 49–52.

Wise, Richard M. "Buy-Sell Valuation." *Canadian Tax Highlights*, June 22, 1993, pp. 44–45.

Chapter 30

Valuation for Income Tax Purposes

Introduction

First, this chapter will discuss many of the reasons to value business entities and business interests for federal income tax purposes. These income taxation–related valuation purposes may be grouped into two general categories: (1) tax planning opportunities and (2) compliance opportunities. Tax planning opportunities include valuations that may cause the deferral of income tax liability or that may reduce a current or future income tax liability. Tax compliance opportunities typically involve transactions that trigger an immediate taxable event that must be quantified or otherwise measured in terms of value.

As part of this discussion, we will list several income taxation transactions where a valuation is relevant. We will describe the taxation-related reason for the valuation requirement—often in terms of a reference to the appropriate statutory authority, administrative rulings, or judicial precedent. And, we will discuss any unusual or particular valuation considerations that relate directly to that particular taxation-related valuation requirement.

Second, we will briefly discuss several of the valuation-related federal income tax penalties. Valuation practitioners, tax practitioners, and taxpayers should all be mindful of these penalties when accounting for a taxable transaction where valuation is relevant.

Third, we will briefly discuss a common state income taxation–related reason to conduct a valuation analysis. This common reason relates to the state income tax consequences of an intercompany (and interstate) transfer of corporate intellectual properties—and the resulting intercompany (and interstate) royalty payments related to the intellectual property transfer.

This chapter will exclude consideration of federal gift and estate tax–related valuation issues, which were addressed in Chapter 27. This chapter also will exclude a discussion of state and local ad valorem property tax valuation issues. These issues will be addressed in Chapter 34.

As with all chapters in this book, this chapter is written from a valuation and economic analysis perspective. It is not intended to offer legal, accounting, or taxation advice. Appropriate professional advisers should be consulted for such advice.

Federal Income Tax Reasons to Conduct an Appraisal

Exhibit 30–1 lists several federal income tax transactions where valuation is relevant. This list is not intended to be exhaustive. This list is intended to illustrate many of the more common income taxation–related reasons to conduct a valuation. Several of the most common income taxation–related reasons to conduct a valuation will be described in greater detail in the following sections.

While Exhibit 30–1 does indicate that numerous taxable transactions may require a valuation, most of these transactions may be grouped into a fewer number of more general categories of taxable "events." For example, the first general category of taxable events that may require a valuation is when a taxpayer (whether individual, partnership, or corporation) claims a deduction for property that the taxpayer abandons or donates. Such a deduction occurs in the case of abandonment losses, casualty losses, charitable contributions, and so forth.

The second general category of taxable events involves a valuation that is needed when a business owner and/or employee receives noncash distributions from a business (whether the business is a proprietorship, corporation, or partnership). This type of transaction occurs in the case of property distributed to employees as compensation, property distributed to shareholders as dividends, property distributed to shareholders as part of a partial or complete liquidation, employee stock options or other stock rights distributed to employees, and so on. In these instances, the valuation may affect the amount of the tax deduction available (if any) to the business. And, the valuation may affect the amount of income (as compensation or otherwise) recognized by the employee or shareholder.

A third general category of taxable events relates to the amount of recognition of income (if any) associated with economic benefits received by a business. Examples of this category of taxable events include: (1) the valuation of property received, such as rents and (2) the valuation (or the solvency/insolvency test) related to the recognition (or nonrecognition) of cancellation of indebtedness income by a business involved in a debt restructuring.

Exhibit 30–1

Taxable Transactions Requiring Valuations

Abandonment losses	Foreclosure of mortgaged property
Bargain purchases	Incorporation of a business
Basis of property (for depreciation and amortization)	Insolvent corporation recapitalization
"Boot" in tax-free transfer	Intercompany transfer of goods or services
Cancellation of indebtedness income	Liquidation, when property is received by a shareholder
Casualty losses	Lump sum acquisition of various assets or properties
Charitable contributions of property	(purchase price allocation)
Compensation received in the form of property	"Reasonableness" of compensation (determination of)
Conversion of C corporation to S corporation	Rents received in the form of property
Dividends received in the form of property	Recapitalization
Employee stock options	Residence converted to a rental property
Excess accumulated earnings (quantification of)	Stock rights
Exchange of properties	Tax shelters

A fourth general category of taxable events involves the conversion of one property (or form of property) to another. Examples of this category of taxable events, which may require valuations, are the conversion of C corporations to S corporations (and the estimation of the associated built-in gains associated with the assets subject to the conversion of corporate form) and the general taxable or tax-free exchange of properties.

A fifth category of taxation-related events that may involve valuations are tests of reasonableness. These tests of reasonableness include, for example, the reasonableness of the amount of compensation paid to the owner of a business, the reasonableness of the amount of undistributed "excess" accumulated earnings retained in a corporation, or the reasonableness of the transfer price (or royalty payment) related to the intercompany transfer of goods, services, or properties between controlled or otherwise related taxpayers.

A sixth (and very common) category of taxable events that typically requires a valuation involves establishing the value-related tax basis for assets transferred into, purchased by, or transferred out of a business (whether a proprietorship, partnership, or corporation). Examples of this category of valuation opportunities include the incorporation of a business (i.e., when assets other than cash are transferred into the corporation in exchange for securities) and the allocation of a lump-sum purchase price paid for an assemblage of assets, properties, or business interests (i.e., for purposes of establishing a basis in each asset purchased).

The following sections will describe several of these income taxation–related valuation opportunities in greater detail.

Valuation of Property Received in a Transaction

When any type of property (other than cash) is received on a sale, exchange, or other disposition, the amount recognized upon receipt of that property is its fair market value. This basic rule of income taxation valuation in property transactions is presented in Internal Revenue Code Section 1001(b). The definition of fair market value used for property transaction and property basis purposes is the familiar: the most probable price that, at a particular time, will induce a willing buyer to buy and a willing seller to sell, neither being under undue pressure to buy or to sell.[1]

This familiar definition of value has been slightly expanded with regard to the income taxation valuation of transactional property so as to include consideration of: (1) the availability of a buyer at the particular time and place and (2) the assumption that the buyer is not only willing but also able to pay for the particular quantity involved.[2]

Determining Basis in a Property

When there is a sale or exchange of property, the taxpayer must determine the amount of the property transaction gain or loss, and whether it is taxable or deductible. For income tax purposes, the following factors are considered in calculating the amount of the property transaction gain or loss:

---

[1] See *H.H. Marshman*, 279 F.2d 27 (6th Cir. 1960), *cert. denied*, 364 U.S. 918 (1960).
[2] See *Helvering v. Walbridge*, 70 F.2d 683 (2d Cir. 1934), *cert. denied*, 293 U.S. 594 (1934).

$$Basis + Additions - Reductions = Adjusted\ basis$$
$$Amount\ realized - Adjusted\ basis = Gain$$
$$Adjusted\ basis - Amount\ realized = Loss$$

Basis is the measurement of the taxpayer's investment in the property for income tax purposes. A taxpayer must know the property's basis in order to determine such taxation-related elements as depreciation, casualty losses, and gain or loss on the property's sale or exchange. Basis is ordinarily the property's original cost or purchase price (including transaction costs such as sales taxes and delivery costs, for instance). Basis normally includes cash, debt assumed, and the fair market value of any other property given up. However, if a taxpayer receives property by some other form, such as by gift or inheritance, the taxpayer must normally use the property's basis rather than its cost.

Various transactional and taxation events may occur that change the taxpayer's original basis in the property. These events increase or decrease the original basis. The result is called the adjusted basis.

In certain situations, the fair market value of property on a particular date is the key factor in determining its basis. When using value to determine basis, actual sales prices of similar property on the open market are typically reliable evidence of value. For example, for this purpose, various courts have concluded that stock exchange quotations represent good evidence of a stock's fair market value.

A taxable exchange involves an exchange of property in which the gain is taxable or the loss is deductible. If a taxpayer acquires one property in return for another property in a taxable exchange, then the basis of the property received is generally its fair market value at the time of the exchange.

There are two allowable methods for determining the basis of property received in exchange for other property:

1. The basis is the fair market value of the property when it is received.
2. The basis is the fair market value of the property exchanged for it, increased by any payments made or decreased by any payments received, when the two properties are of unequal value.

Occasionally, it may be impracticable to estimate the fair market value of the property given up (in order to measure the cost of the property received). In these situations, taxpayers may presume the values of the exchanged properties are equal, if the exchange took place at arm's length.

If a taxpayer receives property for services, then the original basis of the property to that taxpayer is its fair market value. According to Treasury Regulation Section 1.61-2(d), the taxpayer will include this amount in his or her taxable income. The basis of any restricted property received as payment for services is the sum of any amount paid for the property, plus any amount the taxpayer includes in gross income when the property is no longer subject to a substantial risk of forfeiture. The results related to restricted property received as payment for services are presented in Regulation Section 1.83-4.

Joint Ownership of Property

The death of a joint tenant or a tenant by the entirety may create a problem in determining a property's basis for the survivor. The portion of the property included in the decedent's estate is considered to be acquired from the decedent by the survivor.

The survivor's basis in this inherited portion of the property is its fair market value on the date of death (or on the alternate valuation date). The basis of that part of the joint property not included in the decedent's estate is its cost or other basis, per Internal Revenue Code Section 2040. These rules apply to *all* joint interests in property *except* for those involving a husband and wife, as discussed below.

Only half of the joint ownership interest's fair market value is included in the gross estate regardless of who paid for the property. For married decedents, qualified joint interests include *any* interest in property held by the decedent and by the spouse as tenants by the entirety, or as joint tenants with right of survivorship (but only if decedent and spouse are the only joint tenants).

Property Acquired from a Decedent

Generally, if a taxpayer inherits property from a decedent, then the property's basis will be its fair market value when the decedent died. This property valuation rule is according to Internal Revenue Code Section 1015. However, if the executor of the estate elects the alternate valuation date for estate tax purposes, then the property's basis will be its fair market value on that alternate valuation date.

Valuation Requirements for Charitable Contribution Deductions

Individuals may deduct contributions they make to—or for the use of—qualified charitable organizations. A qualified charitable organization may be a public, private, or a governmental unit.

A list of qualified charitable organizations, to which contributions are tax-deductible, is contained in U.S. Treasury Department Publication 78.

Individual taxpayers are subject to a percentage limitation as to the amount of charitable contributions allowed for any one tax year; this annual deduction limitation is based on their "contribution base." According to Internal Revenue Code Section 170(b)(1), this percentage limitation is based on two factors:

1. The type of the organization to which the charitable contribution is made.
2. The type of the property donated.

An individual taxpayer's "contribution base" is his or her adjusted gross income, computed without regard to any net operating loss carryback.[3]

The 1993 Omnibus Budget Reconciliation Act added considerable documentation and substantiation requirements with regard to the charitable contribution of property. This section will summarize these appraisal-related documentation and substantiation requirements.

Documentation Requirements—Contributions of Property

A corporate or individual taxpayer making a charitable contribution of property—other than money—must have a receipt from the donee charitable organization and

---

[3] According to Code Section 170(b)(1)(F).

a reliable written record of specified information with respect to the donated property, per Regulation Section 1.170A-13(b)(2).

The receipt must include the name of the donee, the date and location of the contribution, and a description of the property in detail reasonable under the circumstances, including the value of the property.

A reliable written record should include the following information:

1. Name and address of the donee organization.
2. Date and location of the contribution.
3. A description of the property in reasonable detail, including the value of the property (including, in the case of securities, the name of the issuer, the type of security, and whether such security is regularly traded on a stock exchange or over-the-counter).
4. In the case of ordinary income property (including capital gain property held for less than 12 months), the cost or basis of the property.
5. If less than a 100 percent interest in the property is contributed, the total amount claimed as a deduction for the tax year and for prior years and the name of any person other than the donee organization that has actual possession of the property.
6. The terms of any agreement entered into by the taxpayer relating to the use, sale, or other disposition of the contributed property.
7. If an election is made to treat contributions and carryovers of 30 percent capital gain property as ordinary income property, the years for which the election is made and the contributions to which the election is made.

Noncash Property Contributions

No deduction is allowed for any charitable contribution of $250 or more unless the taxpayer substantiates the contribution by a contemporaneous written acknowledgement from the donee organization of the contribution.

However, substantiation is not required if the donee organization files a return with the Internal Revenue Service reporting the information that is required to be included in the written acknowledgement to substantiate the amount of the deductible contribution.

An acknowledgement must include the following information:

1. The amount of cash and a description, but not the value, of any property other than cash contributed.
2. Whether the donee organization provided any goods or services in consideration, in whole or in part for any property contributed.
3. A description and good-faith estimate of the value of any goods or services provided to the donor, or, if the goods and services consist solely of intangible religious benefits, a statement to that effect.

Appraisals for Noncash Contributions

Most donors, including individuals, partnerships, S corporations, closely held corporations, and personal service corporations, must attach Form 8283, Noncash Charitable Contributions, to their federal income tax return when claiming charitable contributions deductions that include noncash gifts of more than $500.

However, C corporations, other than personal service corporations and closely held corporations, need to attach Form 8283 to their income tax returns only when the amount of the noncash contribution deduction is more than $5,000.

Form 8283 must be completed by all donors if the aggregate claimed or reported value of such property—and all similar items of property for which charitable deductions are claimed or reported by the same donor for the same tax year (whether or not donated to the same donee)—is more than $5,000. The phrase *similar types of property* means property of the same generic category or type, such as stamps, books, land, buildings, or non-publicly-traded stock.

In cases where the noncash charitable contributions deduction includes items with a value in excess of $5,000, Form 8283 must include an acknowledgment of receipt signed by the donee charity and a signed appraiser's certification of appraisal, per Regulation Section 1.170A-13(c)(3).

Publicly Traded Stock. Neither a qualified appraisal nor an appraisal summary is required for securities that are publicly listed and regularly traded on a national, regional, or over-the-counter established securities market or for mutual funds for which quotations are published daily in general circulation newspapers.

Closely Held Stock. Qualified appraisals are not required for deductions of $10,000 or less of nonpublicly traded stock. However, a partially completed appraisal summary signed by the donee must be attached to his or her tax return for charitable contributions of closely held stock valued between $5,000 and $10,000.

Qualified Appraisals. Pursuant to Regulation Section 1.170A-13(c)(3), a qualified appraisal is an appraisal document that:

1. Relates to an appraisal that is made not earlier than 60 days before the date of contribution of the appraised property and that must be updated if made earlier.
2. Is prepared, signed, and dated by a qualified appraiser.
3. Does not involve a prohibited type of appraisal fee, such as that in which a part or all of the fee arrangement is based on a percentage (or set of percentages) of the appraised value of the property.
4. Includes the following information:
    a. A description of the donated property.
    b. In the case of tangible property, the physical condition of the property.
    c. The date of contribution.
    d. The terms of any agreement entered into by the donor which relates to the use, sale, or other disposition of the contributed property.
    e. The name, address, and taxpayer identification number of the qualified appraiser and the appraiser's employer or partnership.
    f. The qualifications of the qualified appraiser.
    g. A statement that the appraisal was prepared for income tax purposes.
    h. The date on which the property was valued.
    i. The appraised fair market value of the property on the date of contribution.
    j. The method of valuation used.
    k. The specific basis for valuation, if any, such as any specific comparable sales transactions.
    l. A description of the fee arrangement between the donor and the appraiser.

The appraisal summary, which is made on Form 8283, must be signed and dated by both the donee and the qualified appraiser, and it must be attached to the donor's return on which a deduction of the appraised property is first claimed or reported.

The person who signs the appraisal summary for the donee must be an official authorized either to sign the tax or information returns of the donee or to sign appraisal summaries. The signature of the donee does not indicate concurrence with the appraised value of the contributed property.

No part of the fee paid for a charitable contribution appraisal can be based on a percentage of the appraised value of the property—that is, the appraiser's fee cannot be a contingent fee (or other similar arrangement).

Also, the appraisal fees may not be deducted as part of the charitable contribution.

Qualified Appraisers. According to Regulation Section 1.170A-13(c)(5), a qualified appraiser is an individual who:

1. Holds himself out to the public as an appraiser or who regularly performs appraisals.
2. Is qualified to appraise property because of his qualifications.
3. Is aware of the appraiser penalties associated with the overvaluation of charitable contributions.

Certain individuals, however, may not act as qualified appraisers, including:

1. The property's donor (or the taxpayer who claims the deduction).
2. The property's donee.
3. A party to the property transfer transaction (with certain very specific exceptions).
4. Any person employed by, married to, or related to any of the above persons.
5. An appraiser who regularly appraises for the donor, donee, or party to the transaction and does not perform a majority of his or her appraisals for other persons.

Year-End Charitable Gifting Considerations

Year-end personal tax planning is an important process for high income and high net worth individuals—especially owners of closely held businesses. The use of charitable contributions (e.g., the contribution of appreciated stock to a charitable organization) is one year-end personal tax planning technique that may be used to (1) reduce current year taxable income and (2) reduce the individual taxpayer's gross estate.

This tax planning technique is particularly relevant to high income or high net worth individuals who would otherwise not be inclined to financially support religious, academic, or other charitable organizations. This section will present some of the common taxpayer planning strategies—and some of the federal taxation considerations—with regard to year-end charitable contributions.

The following paragraphs summarize year-end charitable gifting techniques that are intended to reduce current year taxable income.

1. **Prepay Contribution Pledges.** The taxpayer may prepay any outstanding charitable contribution pledges. Accelerating tax deductions allows taxpayers to reduce income taxes now—as opposed to in the future. Another alternative is to make a larger charitable contribution this year, above the amount otherwise due on the pledge. It is noteworthy that charitable pledge payments (and other cash gifts) are deductible in the year in which they are paid to the charity and not in the year in which the pledge is made.
2. **Contribute Appreciated Assets.** The taxpayer may contribute appreciated assets. Writing a contribution check to a charitable organization is a simple procedure. However, when the taxpayer contributes appreciated property (i.e., property held for more than a year), the taxpayer can claim a deduction for the property's full fair market value. Thus, the taxpayer avoids tax on the appreciation of the contributed assets.

Generally, the fair market value of marketable securities is the mean between their high and low trading prices on the date of delivery of the securities to the charity. For mutual fund shares (e.g., open-end investment companies), their fair market value is the redemption price of these shares on the date of their delivery to the charity.

Exhibit 30–2 illustrates the added federal income tax benefit that a donor can realize by a gift of appreciated securities to a charity. Let's assume that the appreciated stock is now worth $40,000 and that the stock originally cost only $10,000. Therefore, this stock has a built-in gain of $30,000.

It is noteworthy that the indicated income tax savings are even greater for a taxpayer in a higher income tax bracket. State income taxes can also increase the tax savings associated with this illustrative charitable gift.

3. **Select Appropriate Delivery Date.** The taxpayer should be careful about the date of delivery of the gift to the charity. This date determines the year in which the income tax deduction is available. If you mail a check to the charity, the date of mailing is the delivery date. For securities, the date of delivery determines both (1) the date of valuation and (2) the year of the charitable contribution deduction.

   A stock certificate properly endorsed or a separate stock power also should be provided to the charity. If the securities are handed to the charity or to the charity's agent, that determines the delivery date. If securities are mailed to the charity, then the date of mailing is the date of delivery. If the taxpayer arranges for stock certificates to be reissued in the charity's name, then delivery is effective on the date when the security is transferred to the charity on the corporation's books—that is, the date on the new stock certificate.

4. **Take a Capital Loss.** The taxpayer may take a capital loss on the sale of depreciated securities. If the taxpayer owns securities worth less now than when they were bought, the taxpayer (1) may sell them and (2) may then contribute the proceeds to the charity.

   The result is that the taxpayer can take a capital loss on his or her federal income tax return. It is noteworthy that a taxpayer cannot take a capital loss if the taxpayer donates the depreciated securities directly to the charity.

5. **Contribute Nonmarketable Assets.** The taxpayer may contribute real estate or other closely held property to a charity. Such assets are not actively traded on a public stock exchange (such as the over-the-counter market). Therefore, the fair market value of the contributed property is the price at which such property would change hands between a willing buyer and a willing seller. The fair market value of the contributed property should be substantiated by an independent professional appraiser.

   For such a contribution, the date of delivery is the date that the contributed property is received by the charity. For real estate, the date of the charitable contribution deduction is the date that the charity receives a properly executed deed (or its recording date in some states).

Limitations on Charitable Contribution Deductions

The Internal Revenue Code limits an individual taxpayer's charitable deduction each year to a percentage of adjusted gross income, depending on the type of gift. However, for each type of charitable gift described below, the individual taxpayer

Exhibit 30–2

**Comparison of the "Cost" of a Charitable Gift of Appreciated Stock
versus a Charitable Gift of Cash**

	Charitable Gift of Cash	Charitable Gift of Appreciated Stock
Fair market value of gift	$40,000	$40,000
Income tax savings in the 28% bracket	11,200	11,200
Capital gains tax avoided (20%× $30,000)		6,000
Net (of taxes) cost of $40,000 charitable gift	**$28,800**	**$22,800**

is allowed a five-year "carryover" of any amount that falls outside the deduction limit in the current year. These carryover amounts can be used as tax deductions in succeeding years.

Subsequent to the 1993 Omnibus Budget Reconciliation Act, the substantiation and documentation requirements have increased with regard to the appraisal of non-cash property claimed for charitable contribution deductions.

Taxpayers, and their valuation advisers, should be familiar with these appraisal substantiation and documentation requirements when planning a noncash charitable contribution.

Valuation of Worthless and Abandoned Property

When misfortune strikes, leaving a taxpayer with worthless property, the taxpayer normally has a deductible loss equal to the adjusted basis of the worthless property. It is noteworthy, however, that the loss in these situations does not technically arise from a sale or exchange. The following discussion will summarize how the taxpayer is to justify and to quantify this deductible loss.

Worthless Securities

In the event that a qualifying security[4] becomes worthless at any time during the taxable year, the resulting loss is treated as having arisen from the sale or exchange of a capital asset on the last day of the taxable year. Losses from worthless securities are then treated as either short-term or long-term capital losses, depending on the taxpayer's holding period with regard to the subject securities.

Whether a security actually becomes worthless during a given year is a question of fact. And, the burden of proof is on the taxpayer to show that the security became worthless during the tax year in question.

---

[4] For purposes of the worthlessness deduction, a *security* is defined (in Code Section 165(g)(2)) as (1) bonds, debentures, notes, or certificates, or other evidence of indebtedness issued by a corporation (including those issued by a government or its political subdivision), with interest coupons or in registered form; (2) a share of stock in a corporation; or (3) a right to subscribe for, or to receive, a share of stock in a corporation.

Worthless Securities in Affiliated Corporations. The basic rule for worthless securities is modified for a corporate taxpayer's investment in the securities of an affiliated corporation. If securities of an affiliated corporation become worthless, then the loss is treated as an ordinary loss and the limitations that normally apply if the loss were a capital loss are avoided.[5]

A corporation is considered affiliated to a parent corporation if the parent owns at least 80 percent of the voting power of all classes of stock and at least 80 percent of each class of nonvoting stock of the affiliated corporation. In addition, to be treated as an affiliated corporation for purposes of the worthless security provisions, the defunct corporation must have been truly an operating company. This test is met if the corporation has less than 10 percent of the aggregate of its gross receipts from passive sources such as rents, royalties, dividends, annuities, and gains from sales or exchanges of stock and securities. This condition prohibits ordinary loss treatment for what are really investments.

Abandoned Property. While the tax law creates a fictional sale or exchange for worthless securities, it takes a different approach for abandoned property. When worthless property (other than stocks and securities) is abandoned, the abandonment is not considered a sale or exchange. Consequently, any loss arising from an abandonment is treated as an ordinary loss rather than a capital loss—a much more favorable taxation result. It is noteworthy, however, that the loss is deductible only if the taxpayer can demonstrate that the property has been truly abandoned and not simply taken out of service temporarily.

Valuation Aspects of Section 165

Businesses that own worthless assets or worthless security interests should consider the possibility of taking an abandoned asset or worthless security loss deduction under Internal Revenue Code Section 165. Particularly as businesses generate taxable income, this deduction would give rise to either current or future income tax benefits.

The federal income tax rules for taking the loss deduction vary greatly, depending on the type of nondepreciable business asset or security interest involved and the taxpayer's actions.

The taxpayer "shall be allowed as a deduction any loss sustained during the taxable year and not compensated for by insurance or otherwise."[6] The amount of the loss equals the adjusted basis of the property calculated under Code Section 1011, as if the asset had been sold or exchanged at a loss.

However, the amount of the loss must be adjusted for any salvage value or for compensation received. If the loss arises from a capital asset, Code Sections 1211 and 1212 (relating to the capital loss limitation and carryover) restrict the deductibility of the loss.

A deduction is not permitted if the loss results from an actual sale or exchange of the worthless or abandoned property. In addition, if the abandonment or worthless net loss was incurred by an individual, it must have been incurred in a trade or business, in a transaction entered into for profit, or from an event classified as a casualty or theft.

The worthlessness or abandonment loss is deductible in the year sustained. However, it cannot be deducted if there is a reasonable prospect of recovery. The possibility of recovery is a question of fact that must be determined by the particular circumstances involved.

Abandonment Loss for Nondepreciable Business Assets

The loss is deductible when "evidenced by closed and completed transactions and as fixed by identifiable events occurring in such taxable year."[7]

The deduction of a loss is permitted for "the sudden termination of the usefulness in such business or transaction of any nondepreciable property, in a case where such business or transaction is discontinued or when such property is permanently discarded from use therein. . . ."[8]

Accordingly, an abandonment loss on nondepreciable business assets (other than securities) is deductible, even though the assets may not be totally worthless.

The criteria for establishing an abandonment loss for nondepreciable business assets—in cases other than worthlessness—are:

1. The occurrence of a closed and completed transaction coupled with the termination of the asset's usefulness.
2. The discontinuance of the use of the asset.
3. The discontinuation of the business.

An event that meets either of the latter two conditions qualifies as the abandonment of the asset. For a taxpayer to claim an abandonment loss for a business asset, there must be both the intent to abandon plus an actual act designed to accomplish that intent. The actual proof of an asset abandonment will be determined based on the facts and circumstances of the event.

The deductibility of an abandonment is effective when the taxpayer discontinues the use of the asset or the business in which the asset is used.[9]

Worthless Stock Deduction

In addition to allowing a deduction for the abandonment of nondepreciable business assets, Internal Revenue Code Section 165(g) allows a deduction for the loss sustained by a taxpayer resulting from the worthlessness of a security.

For there to be a deduction without a sale, the security must be totally worthless and, therefore, unsalable. The loss deduction must be taken only for the year in which the security becomes completely worthless. A partial worthlessness of a security caused simply by a drop in value in the market price is not deductible until the taxpayer has sold the security. If the security is a capital asset, the loss is a capital loss. To determine if the capital loss is treated as long-term or short-term, the taxpayer is considered to have held the worthless stock or security until the last day of the year in which it became worthless.

The loss from a worthless security is treated as resulting from a sale or exchange on the last day of the tax year in which the security becomes worthless. In most cases, this worthlessness event will result in a long-term capital loss for the taxpayer.

As mentioned above, the worthless security loss will be treated as an ordinary deduction if it involves the security of an affiliated corporation (e.g., the stock of a

---

[7] Regulation Section 1.165-1(b) and (d).
[8] Regulation Section 1.165-2(a).
[9] Ibid.

subsidiary). To qualify as an affiliated corporation, the taxpayer must own stock possessing at least 80 percent of the voting power and at least 80 percent of each class of nonvoting stock. In addition, the "worthless" subsidiary must obtain over 90 percent of its gross receipts from active sources.

The determination of worthlessness is a question of fact. In a case in which the Internal Revenue Service had urged a finding that stock did not become worthless in the year chosen by the taxpayer, for want of an "identifiable event," such as appointment of a receiver, cessation of normal business operation, bankruptcy, or liquidation, the Tax Court held that exceptional circumstances—that is, the lack of liquidating value and potential operating value—justified the taxpayer's choice.[10]

A taxpayer's deduction for a loss sustained on a worthless security is based on his or her adjusted basis in the security. A cash-method taxpayer may deduct, for worthless stock purchased on the installment basis and not entirely paid for, only the amount paid up to the close of the tax year.

Summary of Worthless and Abandoned Property Valuation

From time to time, many business taxpayers suffer economic losses. In addition to operating losses, many businesses abandon nondepreciable business assets or experience the worthlessness of owned securities (in particular, the stock of corporate subsidiaries). This section has briefly summarized the rules relating to substantiating a deduction for the abandonment of nondepreciable business assets or the worthlessness of owned securities.

Valuation Aspects of Cancellation of Indebtedness Income

When creditors cancel all or part of a business's debt, its tax consequences are determined by whether the business is in bankruptcy proceedings or is insolvent.[11] When debt is canceled under bankruptcy proceedings, there is no taxable income currently. The taxpayer has a choice as to how the reduction is recorded. First, the recognition of any income associated with the cancellation of debt may be offset by seven tax attributes.

1. Net operating losses (NOLs) and NOL carryovers
2. The general business credit.
3. The minimum tax credit.
4. Capital loss carryovers.
5. The basis of the taxpayer's property.
6. Passive activity loss and credit carryovers.
7. Foreign tax credit carryovers.

Although not involved in a bankruptcy proceeding, a business may still be financially insolvent—that is, the value of its liabilities exceed the value of its assets. And the question of business insolvency (and the relative values of assets and liabilities) is answered by a business valuation.

---

[10] See *Steadman v. Commissioner*, 424 F.2d 1 (6th Cir. 1970), *cert. denied*, 400 U.S. 869 (1970).
[11] Code Section 198(1).

If a business remains insolvent after debt cancellation, the decrease in debt is offset by the seven tax attributes listed above. If, however, the business is insolvent before, but solvent after, the debt cancellation, then the debt cancellation—to the extent of solvency—is subject to the rules governing solvent businesses. In contrast, when the debt of a solvent business not in bankruptcy is canceled, then the taxpayer must report the debt reduction as taxable income.

Unfavorable Tax Consequences of Debt Restructuring

In almost every debt restructuring, some amount of debt is forgiven by the lender. As introduced above, there are usually unfavorable income tax consequences associated with such debt restructurings. Without adequate tax planning, and without a thorough and rigorous valuation analysis, these unfavorable tax consequences may surprise the unwary taxpayer.

These negative tax consequences typically occur when the taxpayer can least afford them. Income recognition may occur without the taxpayer enjoying any cash receipts. When this happens, a tax liability becomes due even though the taxpayer may not have any cash to pay the tax liability. And, this tax liability is triggered when the borrower is trying to restructure debt. Presumably, the debt restructuring is due to the severe economic condition of the borrower and attempts to avoid the stigma and costs associated with bankruptcy. In any event, the tax liability is created when the borrower is least able to pay it.

The two most common negative tax consequences of debt restructuring are (1) the recognition of gain or loss on the direct transfer of property to a creditor in exchange for debt discharge and (2) the recognition of discharge of indebtedness income when debt is partially or totally forgiven. Both of these common negative income tax consequences are directly affected by the valuation of the borrower's property.

Insolvency Provisions of Code Section 108

Internal Revenue Code Section 61(a)(12) includes as gross income the "discharge of indebtedness" associated with the reduction or forgiveness of debt. Code Section 108 provides for an exclusion of "discharge of indebtedness" income from gross income if the debt discharge occurs when the taxpayer is insolvent. The Code Section 108 income exclusion is limited to the amount by which the taxpayer is insolvent at the time of the discharge.

A taxpayer will not recognize income from the discharge of indebtedness if the discharge occurs when the taxpayer is insolvent, even if the taxpayer is not in Title 11 bankruptcy proceedings.[12] An insolvent taxpayer is permitted to exclude from gross income any amount of indebtedness forgiven by a creditor—subject only to the limitation that the amount excluded cannot exceed the amount of insolvency.

Code Section 108(d)(3) defines *insolvency* as the amount by which a taxpayer's liabilities exceed the fair market value of the taxpayer's assets immediately before the discharge of indebtedness. Accordingly, the determination of insolvency is entirely a valuation matter. This determination requires the fair market value appraisal of all the assets owned by the borrower just before the debt forgiveness.

---

[12] Ibid.

The statutory authority and judicial precedent related to Code Section 108 make it clear that all of the taxpayer's assets are subject to appraisal in the determination of insolvency. These assets include: tangible personal property (e.g., machinery and equipment), tangible real estate (e.g., land and buildings), intangible real property (e.g., leasehold interests and easements), and intangible personal property (e.g., trademarks and goodwill). And the statutory and judicial guidance is clear that traditional valuation approaches (i.e., cost approach, market approach, and income approach) are appropriate for the appraisal of the fair market value of the taxpayer's assets.

Unquestionably, a rigorously prepared and thoroughly documented independent appraisal is required to support a claim of insolvency under Code Section 108.

The Internal Revenue Code does not provide a definition of *liabilities* in the determination of insolvency. Accordingly, the determination of what liabilities are included in the solvency test has become a matter of judicial and administrative interpretation. The rationale for Code Section 108 has been to provide the economically distressed taxpayer with a fresh start, not hampered by the imposition of an income tax liability that the taxpayer is not able to pay.

Insolvency Test Illustrative Example

The following simple example illustrates the application of the Code Section 108 insolvency test.

Real Estate Development Corporation is in financial distress. It has successfully negotiated with its bank for a partial reduction of the loan associated with its current office building construction project. The analysis of insolvency for Real Estate Development Corporation is presented in Exhibit 30–3.

Real Estate Development Corporation is "insolvent" in the amount of $1,600,000 (i.e., the $9,100,000 of total liabilities less the fair market value of $7,500,000 in total assets).

Accordingly, Real Estate Development Corporation could exclude up to $1,600,000 of discharge of indebtedness income from its gross income. In other words, its bank could discharge, or forgive, up to $1,600,000 in debt without the recognition of discharge of indebtedness income to Real Estate Development Corporation.

The "Costs" of Code Section 108

Of course, this Code Section 108 exclusion from discharge of indebtedness income is not without any negative income tax consequences. Taxpayers will not recognize income from the discharge of indebtedness if they are in bankruptcy, to the extent they are insolvent (as illustrated above). However, in exchange for this income exclusion, taxpayers are required to reduce certain favorable tax attributes. These tax attributes are reduced by the amount of the discharge of indebtedness income that is excluded from gross income by the taxpayer. General business credits and foreign tax credits are reduced at the rate of 33.3 cents for every dollar of excluded discharge of indebtedness income.

Unless the taxpayer elects to reduce the basis in his or her depreciable assets (e.g., real estate) before reducing other tax attributes, the taxpayer must reduce tax attributes in the following sequence:

Exhibit 30–3

Real Estate Development Corporation
Analysis of Assets and Liabilities
As of Date of Debt Discharge

	Tax Basis	Fair Market Value Basis
Assets		
Cash and other assets	$ 100,000	$ 100,000
Office building	10,000,000	7,000,000
Goodwill and other intangibles	0	400,000
Total Assets	$10,100,000	$7,500,000
Liabilities		
Current liabilities	$ 100,000	$ 100,000
Construction project debt	9,000,000	9,000,000
Total Liabilities	$ 9,100,000	$9,100,000

1. Net operating losses or carryovers.
2. Carryovers of the general business tax credit.
3. Capital losses and carryovers.
4. Basis in depreciable and nondepreciable assets.
5. Foreign tax credit carryovers.

As an alternative to the reduction of tax benefits, the borrower may elect to reduce the basis of any depreciable assets, but not below his or her basis in the assets.

In summary, the Code Section 108 insolvency discharge of indebtedness income exclusion is designed to provide a borrower with greater flexibility in arranging his or her financial affairs. It is not intended to allow taxpayers to avoid future taxes. Therefore, depending on the beneficial tax attributes otherwise available to the borrower, the Code Section 108 discharge of indebtedness income exclusion may provide some taxpayers with a permanent income exclusion and some taxpayers with only a temporary income exclusion.

Summary of Cancellation of Indebtedness Income Valuation

In the current economic climate, particularly as magnified in many real estate markets, debt restructurings are a normal part of the business environment. These debt restructurings take many forms and include direct forgiveness of (partial or total) debt and direct transfers of assets to creditors in exchange for (partial or total) debt cancellation. Without proper planning and structured valuation analysis, these debt restructuring techniques could have unexpected—and undesirable—income tax consequences.

In this section, we considered the unfavorable taxation consequences of debt restructuring and the discharge of indebtedness income exclusion provisions of Code Section 108. All these unfavorable taxation consequences of debt restructuring are affected by the valuation of the taxpayer's assets.

Valuation-Related Income Tax Penalties

There are several taxation-related penalties that may be assessed as a result of adjustments made to valuation issues. These valuation issues may affect income tax returns (e.g., charitable contributions) as well as gift and estate tax returns. Most of these penalties are assessed against the taxpayer. However, certain penalties also may be assessed against the tax return preparer.

In this section, we will discuss not only those penalties that deal exclusively with valuation issues, but also those general accuracy-related penalties that may be applicable to valuation issues. We will discuss the current penalties related to valuation issues—that is, on those changes to the tax law that occurred since the passage of the Omnibus Budget Reconciliation Act of 1989 (OBRA).

Analysts who prepare valuations for taxation-related purposes should be familiar with these penalties. In addition, analysts who prepare tax returns that include valuation issues (even if the valuations were prepared by other consultants) should be familiar with these penalties.

The Section 6662 Accuracy-Related Penalties

OBRA consolidated into one Internal Revenue Code section (Section 6662) several different accuracy-related taxation penalties:

1. The negligence penalty.
2. The substantial understatement of income tax penalty.
3. The substantial valuation overstatement penalty.
4. The substantial estate or gift tax valuation understatement penalty.
5. The substantial overstatement of pension liabilities penalty.

The accuracy-related penalty is applied to the portion of any underpayment of tax that is attributable to one or more of the above five issues.

The penalties under Section 6662 have a penalty rate of 20 percent of the tax underpayment. This is true except with respect to underpayment attributable to one or more "gross valuation misstatements."[13] The penalty rate increases to 40 percent of the tax underpayment when there is a "gross valuation misstatement."

Only the substantial valuation overstatement penalty[14] and the substantial estate or gift tax valuation understatement penalty[15] are limited exclusively to valuation issues. However, the other accuracy-related penalties may be applicable to valuation issues, as well. For example, there is nothing to prevent a negligence penalty[16] from being applied to a valuation issue, assuming the facts of the position support the assertion of taxpayer negligence. This is noteworthy because the negligence penalty does not have a minimum threshold of a $5,000 tax understatement, as do the penalties related exclusively to valuation.

---

[13] Defined under Section 6662(h)(2).
[14] Section 6662(e).
[15] Section 6662(g).
[16] Section 6662(b)(12).

The accuracy-related penalties are assessed on an issue by issue basis. And, each of the accuracy-related penalties is applied only to that part of the tax underpayment that is caused by the allegedly proscribed conduct.

Negligence Penalty

The negligence penalty is applied only to the portion of the tax underpayment attributable to negligence. This represents a change from prior tax law, when the negligence penalty was applied to the entire amount of the tax underpayment. The definition of negligence remains the same as under the prior law.

The negligence-related penalty will be imposed (1) for negligence in the case of any careless, reckless, or intentional disregard of rules or regulations, and (2) for any failure to make a reasonable attempt to comply with the provisions of the tax law. No penalty is imposed if it can be shown (1) that there was reasonable cause of the tax underpayment and (2) that the taxpayer acted in good faith with respect to the tax underpayment.

Substantial Valuation Overstatement Penalty

The substantial valuation overstatement penalty:

1. Can apply to all taxpayers.
2. May exist if the value or adjusted basis of any property claimed on a return is 200 percent (up from the previous 150 percent) or more of the correct value or adjusted basis.
3. Applies only if the amount of the tax underpayment attributable to a valuation overstatement exceeds $5,000 ($10,000 for a corporation other than an S corporation or personal holding company). This is a major increase in the threshold, as the previous penalty required an understatement of only $1,000 (under old Section 6659(d)).
4. Is 20 percent of the tax underpayment if the value or adjusted basis is 200 percent or more—but less than 400 percent—of the correct value or adjusted basis. The penalty is doubled to 40 percent if the value or adjusted basis is 400 percent or more of the correct value or adjusted basis.[18]

Substantial Overstatement of Pension Liabilities Penalty

The substantial overvaluation of pension liabilities was changed so as to be assessable only if the valuation difference is 200 percent or more. The minimum tax underpayment for the pension overvaluation penalty to apply remains at $1,000. The rate of the tax penalty is doubled to 40 percent, if pension liabilities are overstated by 400 percent.[19]

---

[17] Sections 6662(b) and (c).
[18] This penalty is codified in Sections 6662(b)(3), 6662(f), and 6662(h).
[19] This penalty is codified in Sections 6662(b)(4), 6662(f), and 6662(h).

Definitions and Special Rules under Section 6664

The penalties under Sections 6662 and 6663 apply only if a tax return is actually filed. For this purpose, a tax return does not include a return filed under Section 6020(b), where the Service filed the return based on information available. The fraudulent failure to file a tax return is covered by Section 6651(f).

No accuracy-related penalties will be imposed (1) if there was reasonable cause of the tax underpayment and (2) if the taxpayer acted in good faith.[20] The valuation overstatement penalty will not apply to charitable contribution property if:

1. The claimed value was based on a "qualified appraisal" by a "qualified appraiser" as defined in the regulations under Section 170(a)(1), and
2. In addition to the appraisal, the taxpayer made a good faith investigation of the value of the property.[21]

Tax Return Preparer Penalties

Tax return preparers are subject to a different set of tax penalties than are taxpayers. First, preparers may be assessed a $250 penalty[22] for any tax return that understates a taxpayer's tax liability due to an undisclosed position for which there was not a realistic possibility of being sustained on the merits. Second, preparers may be subject to a $1,000 penalty[23] for any willful, reckless, or intentional understatement of tax liability. This penalty could relate to a valuation-related tax understatement.

Summary of Valuation-Related Income Tax Penalties

The accuracy-related penalty encompasses the entire spectrum of income tax, gift tax, and estate tax–related valuation matters (including, for example, the valuation aspects of transfer pricing under Section 482). The negligence penalty may be assessed on valuation-related tax disputes if the taxpayer acted in a careless or reckless manner.

In addition, the person who prepared the tax return could be assessed a penalty[24] related to a willful understatement of tax liability associated with an insupportable valuation position.

Valuation Aspects of Intercompany Transfer Pricing

As part of an intercompany transfer, an explicit or implicit price is used to value the goods, services, or resources exchanged in the transaction. Since this transfer price is agreed upon by two related parties, the influence of market forces may be less prevalent than what unrelated parties would experience. Therefore, the actual

---

[20] Section 6664(c).
[21] Section 6664(c)(2).
[22] Section 6694(a).
[23] Section 6694(b).
[24] Ibid.

intercompany transfer price may differ from that which would be established by two independent parties engaged in an arm's-length exchange.

As a result of the intercompany transaction, the revenue or expenses and, therefore, the taxable income of each related party is affected by the magnitude of the transfer price. To the extent that the related parties have some discretion in establishing their "internal" transfer price, this price may be set so as to minimize the combined companies' global tax liability, by shifting taxable income between companies according to differences in national tax rates.

Internal Revenue Code Section 482 authorizes the Secretary of the Treasury to allocate income, deductions, and other tax items among related taxpayers to prevent the evasion of taxes or to clearly reflect income. The Tax Reform Act of 1986 amended Section 482 by providing that the income from a transfer or license of intangible property must be "commensurate with the income" attributable to the intangible.

In July 1994, the Internal Revenue Service issued the final regulations on the intercompany pricing of both tangible and intangible property under Section 482. This section briefly outlines the key features of the final Section 482 regulations, discusses the purposes and roles of the intercompany transfer pricing consultants and experts, presents the prescribed methods for analyzing transfer prices involving both tangible and intangible assets, and finally outlines the current penalty and safe harbor provisions with regard to valuation misstatements.

Key Features of the Final Section 482 Regulations

The final 1994 transfer pricing regulations elaborate on the issue that may arise when a company transacts with an affiliate on terms that are not at "arm's length." The issue is whether the company is required to report the "true taxable income" rather than the results of the actual transactions.

The 1994 regulations provide that, "if necessary to reflect an arm's-length result, a controlled taxpayer may report . . . the results of its controlled transactions based upon prices different from those actually charged."[25]

Taxpayers wishing to use Section 482 must affirmatively report the results on a timely filed tax return and may not do so on an amended return.

The construction of "true taxable income" remains the fundamental remedy of Section 482. According to the final regulations, true taxable income is a condition that exists when a controlled taxpayer reports financial results that are consistent with the results that an uncontrolled taxpayer would have attained under comparable circumstances.

This formulation contains two core components: "consistency" with uncontrolled results and "comparable circumstances." Consistency tests a controlled taxpayer's financial results against the "arm's-length results" of a comparable uncontrolled taxpayer. The arm's-length results are established by using methods determined under the "best method rule." Rather than being the most accurate measure, the best method under the final regulations provides the most reliable measure of an arm's-length result.

The series of factors to be considered in searching for the most reliable result under the arm's-length standard of transfer pricing are: (1) the particular facts and circumstances of the transaction, (2) the completeness and accuracy of available data, and (3) the degree of comparability between controlled and uncontrolled transactions.

---

[25] Reg. Section 1.482-1(a)(3).

Consistency with an arm's-length result is determined by creating an arm's-length range based on comparable information. The arm's-length range is established by a group of comparables in the case where all the information of both the controlled transaction and the uncontrolled comparables is sufficiently complete, and any material differences that have an ascertainable effect on the prices or profits of the comparables can be adequately reconciled by adjustments. If the data on the comparables are not sufficiently complete, then all comparables with a similar level of comparability and reliability are considered with their reliability enhanced using appropriate statistical techniques.

The most useful portions of the regulations are the factors to determine comparability. All factors that could affect a financial result are to be taken into account.

The factors to be considered in determining comparability include:

1. *Functional Analysis*—An analysis of the economically significant activities of the controlled and uncontrolled taxpayers including research and development, manufacturing, marketing, distribution, and managerial functions. In order for the two transactions (i.e., the controlled and the uncontrolled) to be comparable, the entities should perform similar economic functions with respect to those transactions.
2. *Contractual Terms*—To be considered comparable, an uncontrolled transaction must have similar significant contractual terms that could affect the prices that would be earned.
3. *Risk Analysis*—The risks borne by each party in the controlled and uncontrolled transactions must be analyzed, including market risks, research and development, financial risks, product liability risks, and general business risks. The economic substance of transactions will be reviewed by the IRS to determine risks borne. Taxpayers must be certain not to mismatch the allocation of risks and potential rewards for bearing those risks.
4. *Economic Conditions*—The economic conditions surrounding the transactions must be similar and must consider factors such as: (1) alternatives realistically available to the buyer and seller (e.g., make versus buy); (2) the similarity of the geographic markets; (3) the relative size of each market and the extent of economic development; and (4) the level of the market, market share for items transferred, location specific costs, and competition in the market.

Special Circumstances

There are three special circumstances that may affect comparability: (1) market share strategies, (2) differences in geographic markets, and (3) extraordinary or tax-motivated transactions.

Multiple Year Data

The results of a controlled transaction ordinarily will be compared with the results of uncontrolled comparables occurring in the taxable year under review. It is appropriate to consider earlier or later year data to examine circumstances—such as the assumption of risk and market share strategies—that are perceived as involving longer time periods.

Multiple year averages are acceptable to establish a range. If the taxpayer's results for a particular year fall outside of the multiple year range, however, a new provision states that the requisite adjustment should ordinarily be based on the range of the uncontrolled comparable results for the single year and not the multiple year average. This requirement appears to be unfavorable to taxpayers and undermines the more economically relevant use of the multiple year averages.

Purposes and Roles of Valuation and Economic Analysis Experts

The critical element in evaluating, developing, and presenting transfer pricing issues from the standpoint of the taxpayer or tax administrator is the development and interpretation of the facts relevant to the matter at hand. The importance of the development of pricing positions has been highlighted by the Section 482 penalty provisions under Section 6662 and the reasonable cause exception thereto in Section 6662(e).

There are typically three steps that need to be followed in developing and presenting transfer pricing positions: (1) identify the pertinent facts and circumstances, (2) evaluate the facts and circumstances to determine the appropriate pricing methodology and result, and (3) present the position.

These steps are critical regardless of the purpose of the evaluation: development of a tax return position, identification of positions by the IRS in an examination, response to an examination by the IRS, formulation of a transfer pricing mechanism in an Advance Pricing Agreement context, or presentation of the position in a court of law.

The potential range of purposes that may necessitate an intercompany transfer pricing study is quite broad and may include the following:

1. An evaluation of existing or new intercompany pricing policies.
2. Required documentation.
3. Assessment of exposure in the event of an IRS—or a foreign taxing authority— examination.
4. IRS examination positions.
5. An Advance Pricing Agreement submission.
6. Due diligence for a "reasonable documentation" opinion for Section 6662(e) purposes.
7. State tax planning matters.
8. Other purposes unique to particular situations.

Types of Experts

The development and presentation of an intercompany transfer pricing position often requires the use of experts for the purpose of developing certain data, evaluating proper pricing methods, and determining the result of specific issues.

A frequent issue in transfer pricing cases is the appropriate financial accounting treatment of the respective elements of a multinational taxpayer's business. This is often critical to an appropriate determination of the situation, especially when the selected pricing method involves the use of financial margin analyses, such as the comparable profits method. In order to apply this method properly, the financial data of the entities or the product lines in question must be accurately determined. In these cases, it may prove useful to engage the services of a financial expert to prepare and present this type of product line segmentation.

A financial expert can assist the taxpayer in making a redetermination of the pertinent financial information on a profit center basis. This redetermination may include the partitioning of the taxpayer's sales revenue into major product categories. Net profits for each category can then be estimated by tracing all of the direct costs to each type of product revenue and by allocating the common costs (such as the fixed costs of production or research, engineering, selling, advertising, and general and administrative expenses) to each profit center using an appropriate allocation method.

Financial expertise can thereby be effectively used to present ambiguous or unreliable data in a manner appropriate for the pricing issues that develop in taxation disputes or with respect to intercompany transactions occurring in later periods. The need for financial expertise also can arise in a variety of circumstances, including the comparability of guideline transactions, the application of foreign accounting principles, and various other related matters.

Taxpayers also can draw upon the expertise of valuation consultants and experts to assess their exposure to potential IRS transfer pricing adjustments before the fact and to develop a defense of existing pricing practices once the IRS has begun a transfer pricing examination. Valuation consultants and experts also can develop planning strategies that minimize tax burdens and audit-associated risks. Among their virtues, both defense and planning have the salutary effect of reducing the likelihood of double taxation. Equally important, a well-conceived and economically defensible transfer pricing policy significantly reduces the likelihood of valuation misstatement penalties.

Summary of Transfer Pricing Valuation Issues

The principles and mechanics of the final Section 482 regulations set the stage for elaborate routines of investigation, analysis, comparison, and documentation. The final regulations also require careful analysis of the facts and circumstances surrounding each intercompany transaction—including comparable transactions—and impose a substantial factual burden of proof on the taxpayer—including detailed documentation of his or her intercompany transfer pricing policy and analysis in support of his or her prices at arm's-length.

As a result, multinational taxpayers will have to devote significant resources in order to comply with these regulations. Taxpayers need to rely increasingly on their advisers to assist in choosing and documenting the method(s) that best determines the most appropriate intercompany price—given the economic business circumstances of a controlled transaction.

Valuation of Intellectual Properties for State Income Taxation Purposes

In recent years, many national corporations have formed intellectual property holding companies and then transferred legal title to various intellectual properties to them. In the most common structure for this program, the entity transfers intellectual properties such as trademarks and trade names to the newly organized intellectual property holding company. As part of its normal business operations, the holding company licenses the use of the trademarks and trade names to the related business interests in other states. The business pays a license fee or royalty payment to the holding company for the use of the trademarks and trade names now owned by the holding company.

There is no tax liability in many states on the income derived from the licensing or leasing of intellectual properties, such as royalties received for the use of trademarks. The intercompany payments from outside the holding company state—the royalty payments for the use of the trademarks—represent deductible expenses for determining taxable income in other states in which the entity generates business income. The net result, therefore, can be a reduction in the total state income tax obligation of the consolidated entity. The taxpayer's consolidated federal income tax expense, however, is obviously not affected by this intercompany intellectual property transfer program.

This section presents the valuation, economic, and corporate management aspects related to the design and implementation of an intellectual property transfer program. Some of the issues include identification of specific intellectual properties to transfer, creation of the holding company, methods of quantifying arm's-length transfer prices for the intangible assets, and the most significant economic pros and cons of implementing an intellectual property transfer program.

Trademarks and Trade Names

Corporate trademarks and trade names are the most common intangible assets found in intellectual property transfer programs. Because of the critical importance of corporate trademarks and trade names combined with the need to protect, manage, and control their use, corporations in the retail industry frequently avail themselves of this intellectual property transfer strategy. Corporations in wholesale distribution, manufacturing, service, and other industries also may have the same needs, making the use of an interstate intellectual property transfer program a viable strategic option for many industries.

Transfer of Intellectual Properties

In determining which intellectual properties to include in an interstate transfer program, a taxpayer should consider which corporate intellectual properties:

- Have legal existence.
- Have economic substance.
- Can be legally transferred to a holding company.
- Have a practical business reason for being transferred to the holding company.
- Are actually used, or used up, in normal business operations in other states.
- Can be associated with a determinable royalty rate or other transfer price, in order to effectively quantify the intellectual property transfer program.
- Have a reasonably long-term and determinable, remaining useful life.
- Will not have to be sold, abandoned, or otherwise transferred back out of the holding company in the foreseeable future.

In the case of trademarks and trade names, a number of additional issues should be considered including:

- Should all trademarks and trade names be transferred?
- Should only the overall corporation trademark be transferred?
- Should all individual brand, product, and service marks be transferred?
- Should future trademarks and trade names be transferred as they are developed?
- Should the trademarks be transferred in perpetuity or for a specific limited term?

These questions cannot be answered in a vacuum. They can be answered only after careful consideration of the above selection criteria and after thorough consideration of the business purpose and objectives of the intellectual property transfer program.

Creation of the Intellectual Property Holding Company

Besides advising in the creation of an intellectual property holding company, qualified legal counsel is also necessary before the taxpayer implements any intellectual property transfer program. Title to the trademarks, trade names, and/or other intellectual properties should be effectively transferred to the newly created holding company, using legal counsel familiar with intellectual property law.

The newly created holding company should have both form and substance. There should be a legitimate business purpose other than the exclusive goal of minimizing consolidated state tax liability. One traditional corporate purpose for the intellectual property transfer program is to allow the business entity to better control its intellectual properties. This means internal, as well as external, control, and this would include accounting, legal, administrative, and operational controls.

Another common corporate purpose for the intellectual property transfer program is to allow the corporation to explore the possibility of licensing its trademarks, trade names, technology, copyrights, and other intellectual properties. The holding company would be the vehicle to license various intellectual properties to independent, third-party licensees in arm's-length transactions. As with all stated corporate goals and objectives, these purposes do not ultimately have to be achieved.

To accomplish its business purpose, and to achieve substance as well as form, it is not unusual for the corporate parent to transfer assets, other than intangibles, to the newly created holding company. Often, the parent will transfer cash balances and certain banking relationships to the state of the holding company incorporation. Also, employees are frequently placed on the payroll of the holding company. These employees may be responsible for the management and control of the company's intellectual properties. They also may be accountable for developing and implementing the company's intellectual property licensing program.

As with any functioning business enterprise, the newly created holding company should prepare financial statements on a periodic basis. These statements should report the results of operations and the financial position of the corporation. The results of operations will include any licensing and investment income less the payroll, rent, utilities, and administrative costs of the business operations. Administrative, accounting, or other services provided to the holding company business operations should be charged through intercompany accounts to the holding company. The holding company's balance sheet will include among its assets the transferred intellectual properties.

Valuation of the Transferred Intellectual Properties

Intellectual properties included in an intercompany intellectual property transfer program are valued using the traditional cost approach, market approach, and income approach valuation methods.[26]

Other Considerations

As with any asset management or other corporate strategy program, there are costs as well as benefits. These costs should be understood and budgeted before management chooses to implement an intellectual property transfer program.

The intellectual property transfer program could include significant setup costs such as qualified legal and valuation advice, a new holding company entity, as well as the costs associated with transferring assets, personnel, and operations. Also, consideration should be given to the indirect costs associated with possible disruption to the business enterprise during the creation and implementation of the intellectual property program.

In addition to the start-up costs, there will probably be continuing administrative costs associated with maintaining the intellectual property transfer program. These costs, as noted earlier, include ongoing periodic legal and valuation advice. In addition, various states may challenge the appropriateness of the intellectual property transfer price. These challenges may come as part of an audit of the impact of the intercompany transfer pricing on the parent corporation's total state income tax liability.

The greatest risk facing a prospective user in an intellectual property transfer program is an unexpected change in the value of the transferred intangible asset—and the corresponding change in the transfer price. After the program is implemented and the intangible assets are transferred, the fair arm's-length transfer price may change due to unanticipated asset obsolescence or economic changes in the industry or in the subject business entity. This is one reason many corporations re-evaluate the fair transfer price formula periodically. Such events could materially affect the cost/benefit considerations concerning an asset transfer program. There is no effective way to ensure against the occurrence of such events.

A valuation analyst experienced with intercompany transfer pricing analysis should be able to reasonably estimate a fair transfer price formula and an expected remaining life of the transfer agreement on a preliminary basis. These preliminary estimates should be adequate for planning, evaluation, and decision-making purposes. A more rigorous and thorough valuation and analysis of the remaining economic life of the intellectual property would be required in the actual pricing and structuring phase of implementing the intellectual property transfer program.

Summary of Intellectual Property Valuation for State Income Taxation

As with any strategic planning technique, there are pros and cons to implementing an intellectual property transfer program.

---

[26] For more information regarding the valuation and analysis of intangible assets and intellectual properties, see Robert F. Reilly and Robert P. Schweihs, *Valuing Intangible Assets* (New York: McGraw-Hill, 1999).

In terms of the pros, the business entity may enjoy increased internal and external control over its intellectual properties. It may implement a legal and an organizational structure to investigate licensing, or otherwise maximize the value of its intellectual properties. And there may be substantial state income tax management opportunities associated with an intellectual property transfer program.

As to the cons, the business entity may experience significant transfer program implementation costs, including the expenses of a cost/benefit analysis study, legal fees, valuation consulting fees, and all the temporary organizational disturbances associated with implementing the program. There may be recurring legal and valuation consulting fees, particularly if certain states decide to challenge the transfer pricing formula. Last, there is the risk that the value—and the associated transfer price—of the transferred assets may change over time. And, this risk is not always within the control of corporate management.

Summary

This chapter discussed some of the many reasons to value business entities and business interests for federal (and state) income tax purposes. In this chapter, we also explored several specific reasons to conduct federal income taxation–related valuations, including setting basis after a property transfer transaction, substantiating charitable contribution deductions, substantiating property abandonment and worthless security deductions, assessing corporate insolvency with regard to the nonrecognition of cancellation of indebtedness income, and intercompany transfer pricing. In addition, we presented the accuracy-related federal income tax penalties associated with the undervaluation or overvaluation of assets, properties, or business interests. Lastly, we discussed the valuation aspects of the interstate transfer of intellectual properties for state income taxation–related purposes.

Each of these topics was presented from a valuation and economic analysis perspective. This chapter was not intended to provide legal, accounting, or taxation advice. Appropriate professional advisers should be consulted for such advice.

Bibliography

Casinelli, Elio J., Kevin M. Hennessey, and Richard F. Yates. "Final Intercompany Transaction Regs. Focus on Broad Concepts Rather Than Mechanics." *The Journal of Taxation*, December 1995, pp. 325–32.

Eason, Pat, Raymond A. Zimmerman, and Tim Krumwiede. "A Changing Environment in the Substantiation and Valuation of Charitable Contributions." *Taxes*, April 1996, pp. 251–59.

"Failure to Obtain Qualified Appraisals of Nonpublicly Traded Stock Limits Charitable Deductions to Basis, Not FMV." *The Tax Adviser*, January 1998, pp. 64–68.

Levey, Marc M., and Casey J. Schoen. "Better Comparable Analysis Persuades Tax Court in Westreco." *The Journal of International Taxation*, January 1993, pp. 39–42.

Lowell, Cym H. "Relationship of Section 482 to International Corporate Tax Planning." *The Journal of Corporate Taxation*, Spring 1996, 36–56.

_____. "Strategies for Transfer Pricing Disputes." *Valuation Strategies*, May/June 1999, pp. 10–19, 46.

Millon, Thomas J., and Robert F. Reilly. "Valuation of Tangible and Intangible Assets as Part of a Transfer Pricing Analysis." *ASA Valuation*, June 1997, pp. 46–54.

Reilly, Robert F. "Tax Penalties Related to Valuation Issues." *CPA Expert*, Spring/Summer 1998, pp. 9–11.

_____. "Valuation Requirements for Charitable Contribution Deductions." *CPA Expert*, Winter 1997, pp. 7–10.

Rich, Jeffrey A. "Valuation of Intangible Property Transactions under the Final Transfer Pricing Regulations." *Valuation Strategies*, November/December 1999, pp. 26–33.

Robinson, Debra A., and Edward J. Rappaport. "Impact of Valuation Discounts on Estate and Income Tax Basis." *Estate Planning*, June 1997, pp. 223–30.

Schlesinger, Sanford J. "IRS Adopts Final Regulations Providing Exceptions to Use of Valuation Tables." *Estate Planning*, May 1996, pp. 182–85.

Simpson, William E., and Peter D. Wrobel. "Income Tax Issues in Valuing S Corporations." *CPA Expert*, Spring 1996, pp. 1–7.

Smith, Gordon V., and Russell L. Parr. "Valuation Issues in Transfer Pricing." (Chapter 2A). In *Valuation of Intellectual Property and Intangible Assets*, 2nd ed.,1996 Cumulative Supplement. New York: John Wiley & Sons, 1996.

Soled, Jay A. "Gifts of Partnership Interests: An Income Tax Perspective." *Business Entities*, May/June 1999, pp. 30–35.

Springsteel, Ian. "Transfer Pricing: Separate but Unequal." *CFO Magazine*, August 1999, pp. 89–91.

Wrappe, Steven C., Ken Milani, and Julie Joy. "The Transfer Price Is Right." *Strategic Finance*, July 1999, pp. 39–43.

Chapter 31

Income Tax Court Cases

Introduction

This chapter presents summaries of numerous federal income taxation–related court cases. The case summaries presented represent only a small fraction of the federal income tax valuation cases decided in the last several years. The cases selected are not necessarily the "best" judicial decisions—from either a judicial or a valuation perspective. However, they are intended to be a representative sample of federal judges' current thinking with regard to: valuation principles and standards, valuation methodology, selection of the appropriate market, and minimum qualifications for valuation analysts and valuation expert reports.

The income tax case summaries are presented in the following categories:

1. General valuation methodology issues.
2. Charitable contribution issues.
3. Reasonable compensation issues.
4. Intangible asset valuation issues.

Obviously, these four categories do not encompass all valuation and economic analysis aspects of federal income taxation. Again, these categories are intended to represent the areas of federal income taxation that are affected by valuation and related economic analyses.

General Valuation Methodology Issues

Pabst Brewing Company v. Commissioner

In *Pabst Brewing Company v. Commissioner,*[1] the tax issue was the fair market value of certain assets. After stipulating to values of several assets, the remaining disputed values were of two breweries and brands of beer. The IRS claimed that these assets were transferred at less than their fair market values.

This case is particularly instructive to valuation analysts because the Tax Court articulates a number of principles regarding the estimation of fair market value. In addition, the Tax Court decision specifically comments on (1) the specific weaknesses of the respective experts' credentials for estimating fair market value and (2) the specific weaknesses in their methodology.

The Tax Court's Valuation Principles. The following are several quotes from the Tax Court's decision in this case. These quotes are illustrative of fundamental valuation principles:

1. "The willing buyer and the willing seller are hypothetical persons, rather than specific individuals or entities, and the characteristics of these hypothetical persons are not necessarily the same as the personal characteristics of the actual seller or a particular buyer."
2. "Fair market value is determined as of the valuation date, and no knowledge of unforeseeable future events which may have affected the value is given to the hypothetical persons."

---

[1] *Pabst Brewing Company v. Commissioner*, T.C. Memo 1996-506 (Nov. 12, 1996).

3. "Fair market value equals the highest and best use to which the property could be put on the valuation date, and fair market value takes into account special uses that are realistically available due to the property's adaptability to a particular business. Fair market value is not affected by whether the owner has actually put the property to its highest and best use. The reasonable, realistic, and objective possible uses for the property in the near future control the valuation thereof. Elements affecting value that depend upon events or a combination of occurrences which, while within the realm of possibility, are not reasonably probable, are excluded from this consideration."

4. "As typically occurs in a case of valuation, the parties rely primarily on their experts' testimony and reports. . . . Expert testimony sometimes aids the Court in determining valuation. Other times, it does not. For example, expert testimony is not useful to the Court when the expert is merely an advocate for the position argued by the party."

In this case, the Tax Court concluded: "We do not accept the conclusion of any of the experts in toto, but we find parts of each of their opinions to be helpful in understanding the operation of the beer industry."

Tax Court Review of Expert Credentials. The expert for the IRS was with a consulting firm that assists management in developing corporate strategy. With respect to his credentials and expertise, the Tax Court said, "That fact that [he] is knowledgeable about this industry does not compel us to credit the testimony on the Transferred Assets' fair market value. . . . We do not find that he has expertise in valuing assets for federal income tax purposes. The thrust of [his] expertise centers on marketing, economics, and the like, rather than on the ascertainment of fair market value."

The Tax Court also specifically commented that he was also "disturbed by [the expert's] lack of regard for comparable sales."

The experts for Pabst were (1) an investment banker with many years of valuation experience and (2) an individual with 40 years' experience as a brewing industry executive.

Tax Court Review of Valuation Methodology. With respect to the first taxpayer expert, the Court was complimentary about his valuation credentials. However, the Court rejected his methodology with limited discussion of the details.

With respect to the second Pabst expert, the Court concluded: "We find his testimony on the valuation issue to be unpersuasive." In the decision, the Court listed the following specific factors:

1. The dates of many of the purported comparable sales were too far removed from the valuation date.
2. The report did not set forth enough data on the comparable breweries to allow the Court to make a meaningful comparison. A proferred comparable sale without enough identifying data in order to explain the components of the sale was unhelpful to the Court.
3. The Court was troubled by the fact that his methodology focused on the views of the buyer, to the exclusion of the seller. Ignoring the views of the willing seller is contrary to the well-established criteria of a hypothetical willing buyer and hypothetical willing seller.

The Court's Decision. Ultimately, the Tax Court concluded the following:

Although the values ascribed in the Allocation Agreement are not necessarily determinative of the actual fair market values of the underlying assets, these values are very persuasive as to the assets' true fair market value, given the fact that the parties to the agreement were dealing at arm's length and the agreement had independent economic significance. . . . We hold that the value of the Transferred Assets equals the $190,287,375 of consideration . . . remitted to petitioner in connection with the transfer.

Summary and Conclusion. This case is informative to valuation analysts because the Tax Court comments specifically with regard to (1) expert professional credentials and (2) valuation principles and methodologies.

Nathan and Geraldine Morton v. Commissioner

Introduction. In *Nathan and Geraldine Morton v. Commissioner*,[2] the Tax Court provides a critical review of the discounted cash flow valuation method.

The tax issue in this case was the fair market value of Soft Warehouse, Inc. (SWI) stock purchased by a key employee. Nathan Morton left Home Depot to join SWI (later CompUSA), which had three large computer stores at the time. Mr. Morton agreed to purchase 500 shares of SWI, at $60.98 per share pursuant to a recently adopted stock plan.

The share purchase was on a five-year vesting schedule. Income tax on any gains between purchase price and fair market value normally would be spread over the transaction consummation period. However, Section 83(b) allows an exception to realize gross income from any gain at the time of the agreement to purchase. Mr. Morton made the Section 83(b) election. And, he reported the fair market value of the stock to be $60.98 per share, resulting in no gross income.

The Facts of the Case. The stock plan did not require the stock to be sold at fair market value. No valuation of the SWI stock was made at the time the stock plan was adopted nor at the time of the purchase agreement.

The IRS concluded that the fair market value of the SWI stock was $1,739.82 per share, resulting in taxable income to Mr. Morton of $839,420.

In addition, the IRS asserted that taxpayer was liable for the penalty prescribed under Section 6662—for negligence in underreporting the value.

The Issues at Trial. A legal issue common to many Tax Court cases was the admissibility of documents prepared after the valuation date. In this case, the following post-transaction data documents proved controversial at the trial.

1. A valuation of a noncontrolling equity interest in SWI one year later prepared by a major accounting firm.
2. A confidential private placement memorandum 14 months after the purchase, prepared by two well-known investment banking firms.
3. A prospectus for CompUSA (the successor company to SWI) almost two and a half years after the purchase, prepared by two other well-known investment banking firms.

Regarding these document admissibility issues, the Tax Court stated the following:

This court has drawn a distinction between subsequent events which affect the value of the property and those which merely provide evidence of such value on the valuation date.

---

[2] *Morton v. Commissioner*, T.C. Memo 1997-166 (Apr. 1, 1997).

Subsequent events or conditions which affect the value of the property can be taken into account only if they are reasonably foreseeable on the valuation date.

Conversely, subsequent events which merely provide evidence of the value of the property on the valuation date can be taken into account regardless of whether they are foreseeable on the valuation date.

The valuation prepared by [the accounting firm] and the confidential private placement memorandum . . . both contain information regarding the value of SWI stock within a reasonable time after that date, and neither describes subsequent evens which affected the value of SWI stock. Both documents also represent valuations of SWI stock by third parties who were not influenced by the biases of litigation. The fact that they were prepared after the valuation date is a factor that we must consider in determining the probative value of the evidence, but does not automatically make the documents irrelevant.

The CompUSA prospectus, on the other hand, is not relevant to our determination of the value of the stock at issue. This document describes a public offering of SWI stock almost 2½ years after the valuation date. Based upon the record of this case, we cannot find that the public offering was sufficiently foreseeable by the parties on the valuation date. Accordingly, we will sustain petitioners' objection insofar as the CompUSA prospectus is concerned.

In valuation reports prepared for trial, the taxpayer's expert valued the SWI stock at $55 per share. The expert hired by the IRS valued the SWI stock at $1,798 per share.

The IRS's Position. The Tax Court noted that taxpayer had the burden of proof. And the Tax Court's written opinion offered no discussion whatsoever of the government expert's valuation methodology. The government expert used a guideline publicly traded company valuation method. He selected Home Depot, Toys R Us, and Staples as his guideline companies, based on the theory that SWI, in becoming CompUSA, was a "category killer retailer," in spite of the fact that SWI only had three stores at the time of the valuation date.

The Taxpayer's Position. The taxpayer's expert relied solely on the income approach to valuation—and particularly the discounted cash flow method. He justified this decision (1) because in his opinion, there were no sufficiently comparable companies in existence as of the valuation date, and (2) because the cost approach, in his opinion, tended to minimize the value of assets and failed to consider intangible assets such as goodwill. He used a standard discounted net cash flow model.

The taxpayer's expert assumed that increments to working capital would equal 7 percent of the increase in sales over the previous year. He used a present value discount rate of 35 percent, which he described as necessary to justify the high degree of risk involved. He described SWI as a venture capital situation. And, he wanted to account for that risk in his discount rate. Finally, the taxpayer's expert reduced his value estimate with a combined lack of control and lack of marketability discount of 50 percent.

The Tax Court's Opinion. The Tax Court noted wild fluctuations of the income approach value estimates when minor valuation assumptions were changed. One reason for this was that the company was extremely highly leveraged at the valuation date.

The Tax Court pointed out that just a 1 percentage point change in incremental working capital, from 7 percent to 6 percent of incremental sales, caused the income approach value per share to increase substantially. The Tax Court found this "troubling in light of the fact that [the taxpayer's expert] agreed on cross-examination that six percent was a reasonable figure for incremental working capital."

The Tax Court also found the 35 percent present value discount rate "bothersome." The Court noted that the expert did not provide any objective support, either at trial or in his expert valuation report, for selecting a discount rate in this range.

The Court calculated that changing the present discount rate to 33 percent produced a value of $1,161 per share and changing the discount rate to 30 percent produced a value of $3,551 per share.

Summary and Conclusion. In this case, the Tax Court was critical of the taxpayer expert's use of the discounted cash flow valuation method. In particular, the Court was critical of the fact that the taxpayer's analyst had never fully explained nor fully documented key and sensitive valuation variables in his valuation opinion report. This criticism should be noteworthy to valuation practitioners.

Charitable Contribution Issues

John T. and Linda L. Hewitt v. Commissioner

Introduction. In the case of *John T. and Linda L. Hewitt v. Commissioner,*[3] the U.S. Tax Court held that the taxpayers did not substantially comply with Section 1.170A-13 of the Income Tax Regulations and, therefore, were not entitled to charitable contribution deductions in excess of that allowed by the Internal Revenue Service.

The Facts of the Case. The petitioners, John and Linda Hewitt, were part of an investor group that acquired Mel Jackson's Tax Service. At the time of the acquisition, Mel Jackson's Tax Service, Inc., which was headquartered in Tidewater, Virginia, operated multiple offices and generated over $1 million in revenue. Later, the name of the company was changed to Jackson Hewitt Tax Services, Inc. ("the Company" or "Jackson Hewitt").

During the taxable year of 1990, the petitioners made gifts of the Company stock to the Hewitt Foundation and to the Foundry United Methodist Church. At the time of the gifts, there were approximately 700,000 shares of Jackson Hewitt stock outstanding and in the hands of around 400 individuals and organizations. These stockholders included employees, franchisees, and others related to the company. Also, at the time the gifts were made, the Company stock was not traded on an organized exchange or market.

Rather, the market for the Company stock operated primarily through individuals or organizations contacting the Company. These contacts took the form of offers to buy or sell shares in the stock of the Company at a given price. In making these offers, the potential market participants only had access to information regarding trades and offers to sell made by other shareholders.

In addition to transactions funneled through the Company, a separate market operated through Wheat First Securities, Inc., in which hundreds to thousands of shares of Jackson Hewitt common stock were traded between 1990 and 1992. During the period between May 1, 1990, and December 31, 1991, the Company recorded 317 stock transfers involving approximately 100,000 shares. The petitioners filed timely joint federal tax returns for the 1990 and 1991 taxable years.

---

[3] *Hewitt v. Commissioner,* 109 T.C. 258 (1997), *aff'd* No. 98-1386 U.S. App. (4th Cir. Nov. 19, 1998).

In their 1990 federal tax return, the petitioners included Form 8283 (noncash contributions), on which they reported the donation of two blocks of Jackson Hewitt stock valued at $26,000 and $7,000. As part of petitioners' 1991 tax return, they reported two contributions of stock valued at $48,000 (with a basis of $2,832) and $40,000 (with basis of $3,057).

Petitioners did not obtain a qualified appraisal to support the values of the Jackson Hewitt common stock they donated in 1990 and 1991. The fair market values claimed by the petitioners were based upon the average per share price of Company stock traded in arm's-length transactions at approximately the same time as the petitioners' donations of stock.

In their notice of deficiency, the IRS only allowed the petitioners' deductions for their gifts in the stock of the Company in the amounts of their original tax bases.

The Issues of the Case. The provisions relevant to this case state that the Secretary of the Treasury shall prescribe regulations which require any individual, closely held corporation, or personal service corporation claiming a charitable contribution deduction to:

1. Obtain a qualified appraisal for the contributed property.
2. Attach an appraisal summary to the tax return.
3. Include on the tax return such additional information (including the cost basis and acquisition date of the contributed party).[4]

Contributions to which these requirements apply include those of property (other than publicly traded securities) with a value greater than $5,000.

The IRS did not dispute that the Hewitts made charitable contributions to qualified organizations within the respective tax years or that the claimed values represented the fair market values of these contributions. The IRS disallowed the charitable contribution deductions claimed by the Hewitts for the stock in Jackson Hewitt in excess of the basis due to the lack of qualified appraisals.

It is quite clear that the Hewitts did not obtain any qualified appraisals to support their claimed deductions. However, they maintained that they should be allowed the value of the claimed deductions because their use of the average per share price of Jackson Hewitt stock traded in bona fide arm's-length transactions constituted substantial compliance with the requirements of Regulation Section 1.170A-13.

The Hewitts' tax returns, which did not even include an appraisal summary, only reflected the gifts of stock without identifying the gifts as Jackson Hewitt stock, without any indication of the number of shares. These returns only set forth the cost basis and the claimed values.

To sustain their position that a qualified appraisal is not a requirement under their circumstances, the Hewitts cited *Bond v. Commissioner*,[5] which held that the taxpayer had substantially complied with the requirements of the statute and regulations even though a separate appraisal had not been obtained and the qualifications of the appraiser were omitted from the appraisal summary attached to the tax return.

The Court's Decision. In the *Hewitt v. Commissioner* matter, the Court found nothing in *Bond v. Commissioner* that relieves the Hewitts of the requirements of obtaining a qualified appraisal. No deduction is allowed for a contribution of property for which an appraisal is required unless the appraisal requirements are satisfied. The donor must obtain and retain a qualified written appraisal by a qualified

---

[4] Section 170(a)(1).
[5] *Bond v. Commissioner*, 100 T.C. 32 (1993).

appraiser for the property contributed and must attach a signed appraisal summary to the return on which the deduction is first claimed.

The Court ruled that the Hewitts furnished practically none of the information required. The IRS must be provided with enough information to alert taxpayers to potential overvaluations. The Hewitts were found not to fall within the permissible boundaries of *Bond v. Commissioner*. In *Bond* an appraisal summary was completed by a qualified appraiser, and it contained most of the required information. The summary could therefore be treated as a written appraisal and be attached to the return.

The taxpayers also tried to support their position claiming that there was a market which provided support for their use of the average per share price of the Jackson Hewitt stock. This position was found to be without merit. Given the amounts of the gifts in this case, the exemption from the qualified appraisal requirements is statutorily limited to publicly traded securities.

The principal objective of the appraisal report requirement is to enable the IRS to deal more effectively with the prevalent use of overvaluations. Such need exists even though in a particular case, such as this, it turns out that the taxpayers' deduction was in fact based on the fair market value of the property. This happenstance is insufficient to constitute substantial compliance with a statutory condition to obtain the claimed deduction. In the Court's opinion, what the petitioners were seeking was not the application of the substantial compliance principle but an exemption from the clear requirement of the statute and regulations in a situation where there is no overvaluation of the charitable contribution.

The Court held that the taxpayers were not entitled to deduct amounts in excess of those allowed by the IRS for the contributions of Jackson Hewitt stock.

Appeals Court Decision. The taxpayers appealed the decision to the U.S. Court of Appeals for the fourth circuit. The Appeals Court affirmed the decision of the Tax Court, noting that the legislative history indicates that Congress intended the qualified appraisal requirement to be mandatory. The Appeals Court concluded deductions are a matter of "legislative grace," and a taxpayer seeking the benefits of a deduction must show that every condition Congress imposes has been "fully satisfied."

Summary and Conclusion. This case offers important lessons to taxpayers claiming charitable contribution deductions for gifts of shares of closely held, nonpublicly traded common stock. Even though the fair market value of closely held stock involved in a gift or transfer is known with almost absolute certainty, the taxpayer is still required to provide the IRS with supporting evidence, in the form of an appraisal summary.

Gerald D. and Catherine Leibowitz v. Commissioner

Introduction. In *Leibowitz v. Commissioner*,[6] the U.S. Tax Court provided guidance with regard to the appropriate market from which to extract valuation pricing data for movie memorabilia.

The tax issues in this case were (1) the fair market value of the movie memorabilia ("the collection") donated by taxpayer Gerald Leibowitz to the American Museum of the Moving Image (AMMI) for purposes of determining the charitable contribution deductions to which petitioners were entitled for the year of the gift, and for the later years by way of carryovers and (2) whether the taxpayers were liable for a valuation overstatement.

---

[6] *Leibowitz v. Commissioner*, T.C. Memo 1997-243 (May 29, 1997).

The Tax Court found the value of the collection to be less than the taxpayers claimed, but more than the IRS allowed. The Tax Court held that the taxpayers were not liable for a valuation overstatement.

The Collection. The collection donated to AMMI consisted of 7,378 items, including 546 duplicates, of movie memorabilia from 659 different films. The exact number of items in each category was based on an inventory conducted by AMMI. Most of the titles in the collection were of films from the 1950s through the 1970s. The overall physical condition of the collection was mint, with many items having never been handled.

The duplicate items were physically separated from the rest of the collection and held for subsequent sale or trade. However, none of the duplicates had been disposed of at the time of trial.

The Taxpayer's Valuation. Leibowitz obtained two appraisals of the collection. The second appraisal, for $188,085, was used as the basis for a charitable contribution reported in the taxpayer's tax return. A copy of the report of that appraisal was attached to the return.

The Taxpayer's Trial Expert. The appraisers had performed approximately 1,500 appraisals of "reproduction masters" of works of art in connection with questionnable tax shelters.[7] Both appraisers, by reason of the inflated values in those appraisals, were also named as defendants in numerous lawsuits by investors in those tax shelters.

The Tax Court rejected both the appraisals, which exceed by more than 20 percent the values asserted by the taxpayer's expert at the trial. "The record fails to support either of these appraisals," the Tax Court concluded.

Leibowitz retained a different appraiser to appraise the collection and to prepare an expert valuation report for trial. At the time of trial, this appraiser had been a collector and dealer of movie memorabilia.

The taxpayer's trial expert based his valuation of the collection on prices in the retail store and catalog sales market as of the valuation date. In preparation for assigning values to the collection, the appraiser consulted dealers whom he knew or had dealings with who had owned or operated retail stores as of the valuation date. He also consulted various trade publications.

Taxpayer's expert included all 7,378 items in the inventory in his valuation, including the 546 duplicates. He assigned one or more premium units to the more desirable of the 659 titles, valued as a multiple of the "average value" assigned to items in that category. For example, each three-sheet poster was assigned an "average value" of $30. If the appraiser assigned three premium units to a title, the three-sheet would be valued at $90, or three times the "average value."

He took into account the overall mint condition of the collection and the development of the market. He believed that the market was developing slowly throughout the relevant time period. He took into account in his valuation report events that occurred both prior to and shortly after the donation when he valued the collection.

The IRS's Experts. The IRS retained an appraiser to estimate the fair market value of the collection and prepare an expert valuation report for trial. This expert was the author of a price guide, an editor of magazines devoted to movie memorabilia, a member of the International Appraiser's Society, and a senior price editor for a major comic book pricing guide.

---

[7] See *Rose v. Commissioner* 88 T.C. 386, 398-399 (1987), *aff'd* 868 F.2d 851 (6th Cir. 1989).

The IRS expert began collecting memorabilia prior to the valuation date and became a dealer in movie memorabilia after the valuation date. Eventually, the IRS expert became a major dealer in movie memorabilia. At the time of trial, he maintained a database of prices of over 100,000 items of movie memorabilia.

He assumed that the relevant market was the movie memorabilia convention. He asserted that the single key element in pricing movie memorabilia is demand by collectors who conduct an appropriate amount of research prior to entering the convention market.

The IRS appraiser heavily discounted the value of foreign posters because he maintained that there was little or no demand for them as of the valuation date. In his view, collectors viewed foreign posters of American films as inauthentic novelties, and that only when domestic posters began to rise dramatically in price after the valuation date did collectors begin to show interest in foreign posters of American films.

The IRS expert considered the collection as a whole to have little intrinsic value because it consisted of "minor or unknown films." He evaluated the collection as little more than a hoard, virtually unsalable within a short period of time, even at distress sale prices in the convention market.

Based upon these foregoing considerations, the IRS expert assigned values as low as 25 cents to individual items. He appraised the collection at the time of its donation to AMMI in 1985 at $5,733.49.

Tax Court's Conclusion of the Relevant Market. The Tax Court noted that: "Selection of the proper market for valuation purposes is a question of fact." In determining the appropriate market to use in valuing most types of property, a sale "to the public" normally refers to a sale to the retail customer who is the ultimate consumer. A sale to an ultimate consumer is any sale to those persons who do not hold the item for subsequent resale. However, when used in this context, the term "retail" does not mean that the most expensive source is the only source for determining fair market value. Fair market value is determined in the market most commonly used by the ultimate consumer, which may or may not be the most expensive, since ultimate consumers may simultaneously participate in multiple markets with different price structures.

Stores specializing in movie memorabilia were located in such major metropolitan areas as New York, Los Angeles, and San Francisco. These stores also competed in nationwide markets through catalog sales along with dealers who specialized in catalog sales. Despite the lack of specific comparative sales data in the record concerning the different markets, the Tax Court concluded that it is more likely than not, based upon the testimony of both experts, that retail stores were the most common form of sale to "ultimate consumers" of movie memorabilia at the time.

The mint condition of the collection particularly suited it to sale on consignment in the retail store setting or in the catalog sales market. The absence of "high-end" titles would have precluded sale of most of the collection on an item-by-item basis in the auction market. These factors supported the Tax Court's finding that retail stores were the relevant market for the Leibowitz collection. In the written decision, the Tax Court reported: "We therefore reject [the IRS expert's] overall valuation of the collection."

The taxpayer's expert chose the correct market in which to value the collection. However, for other reasons, the Tax Court also rejected his valuation. The IRS expert conceded in testimony that the taxpayer's expert's valuation was accurate for the New York retail store market because retail store prices were markedly higher than those found at conventions. However, the Court's analysis of the record indicated that the taxpayer's valuation was too high.

The appraiser's use of flawed methodology in determining base prices inflated the entire valuation. In determining a base price for each category of item, the taxpayer's expert used an "average price" for that category. As the IRS correctly pointed out on brief, this meant that the taxpayer's appraiser assumed that each item in the collection was worth at least the average value in the marketplace of all such items for sale. Even when taking into account the mint condition of the collection, this approach improperly inflates the valuation.

The Tax Court rejected the expert for the taxpayer's valuation, even though he chose the correct market and his overall methodology of assigning premium values to more desirable titles relative to all the items in a category would have been a reasonable approach if he had used a valid base price.

The Tax Court's Valuation of the Collection. The parties' experts differed on the amount of time that it would take to sell the collection. The IRS expert postulated a period of no less than one to two years because of the difficulties attendant in gaining access to the market. However, this expert did not consider how long it would take a skilled dealer in movie memorabilia already present in the retail store market to sell the collection. The taxpayer's expert estimated that the collection could be sold on consignment in a retail store within a year without affecting the prices obtained for each individual item. The collection was relatively small in relation to the inventory carried by a movie memorabilia store or chain of stores.

A year to liquidate the collection at full retail store prices would not be unreasonable under the circumstances. The minimal physical storage requirements and comparatively stable prices in the movie memorabilia markets over the course of a year support such a finding.

Based upon the foregoing considerations, the Tax Court did not apply a blockage discount to the fair market value of petitioner's collection.

The Tax Court considered a number of factors in arriving at a fair market value of the collection. The agreed mint condition of the collection played a major role, both in determining the relevant market, as discussed above, and in valuing each item for sale on an individual basis. The taxpayer's testimony that the collection's mint condition would tend to increase the prices commanded in a retail store was strongly supported by commentary in all of the movie memorabilia pricing guides in evidence.

The level of collector demand for the titles in the collection was also very important. The taxpayer's appraiser characterized the collection as "middle-of-the-road." The pricing guides, the IRS expert's concession that at least some of the titles were marketable, and the evidence in the record that the collection as a whole could be sold support this characterization.

For several categories, the Tax Court found that the petitioners failed to carry their burden of proof in establishing a fair market value. Therefore, the IRS's valuation was used for those categories.

Summary and Conclusion. Ultimately, the Tax Court concluded that the total fair market value of the collection was $50,412. This case is instructive to both taxpayers and valuation practitioners. It illustrates how the Tax Court can select the relevant market and pick and choose the various components of each expert's valuation analysis and report. It also illustrates how the Tax Court can conclude its own value for property when it is not satisfied with either party's valuation experts.

Reasonable Compensation Issues

Labelgraphics, Inc. v. Commissioner

Introduction. In *Labelgraphics, Inc. v. Commissioner*,[8] the Tax Court provides practitioners with a five factor test for assessing the reasonableness of the executive compensation income tax deduction related to employee/owners of closely held corporations.

The main issue in this case was the amount that Labelgraphics, Inc., was entitled to deduct as reasonable compensation to its president, Lon Martin. Mr. Martin was the president and sole shareholder of this corporation during the year in question.

The IRS claimed Mr. Martin's compensation of $878,913 was overstated by $633,313. This amount, therefore, represented taxable income to the company.

The Tax Court's Five Factor Test. The Tax Court's Five Factor Test comprises the following factors.

Factor Number One. The first factor that the Tax Court considered was the employee's role in the company. The Tax Court determined that Mr. Martin was the primary reason for the company's success over the years from its inception. The Tax Court made note of the substantial contributions that he provided to the company over his years of service. However, the Tax Court questioned why his bonus was almost three times the amount of any other bonus that Mr. Martin had ever received. The taxpayer's first expert argued that the unusually high compensation was justified because Mr. Martin had been undercompensated in prior years. This expert offered no analysis or explanation in support of his claim. Because of this, however, the Tax Court gave his opinion little weight. The Tax Court found no other evidence to support the abnormal jump in Mr. Martin's bonus for the year in question.

Factor Number Two. The second factor that the Tax Court considered was a comparison of the compensation paid to similarly situated employees in similar companies. Both taxpayer experts believed that the bonus was reasonable based on their comparisons with other executives in high-tech companies.

Both taxpayer experts failed to offer any details concerning which companies they used to base their opinions on. Both experts failed to provide specifics on the particular executives involved, pertinent information on their particular qualifications and skills, and the exact compensation that was received.

Accordingly, the Tax Court was unable to determine: (1) how similar these other unidentified companies and their businesses were to the petitioner and (2) how similar the services their executives rendered were to the services that Mr. Martin performed.

The taxpayer's second expert argued that Mr. Martin was entitled to even more compensation because he was performing the tasks of four different executives. However, the Tax Court gave little weight to this argument, just as it has in prior cases. This is due to the Court's opinion that it simply is not possible for one person to perform work equal to four full-time executives.

The taxpayer's second expert also contended that Mr. Martin should be receiving royalties for a new process that he developed, just as chief technical officers of high-tech companies receive royalties for products that they help develop. The Tax Court found that the expert did not elaborate enough to give this argument weight.

---

8 *Labelgraphics, Inc. v. Commissioner*, T.C. Memo 1998-343 (Sept. 28, 1998).

The IRS expert (1) used three comparable publicly traded companies in the printing industry and (2) considered two surveys of executive compensation in the printing industry to determine that reasonable compensation for Mr. Martin should have totaled $230,000. The Tax Court rejected the IRS expert's opinion for several reasons. First, two of the comparable companies that he used were exceedingly large and the third company was not nearly as profitable as Labelgraphics. Second, the surveys that he used were, admittedly, of limited use in determining what may be reasonable compensation. Third, he failed to take into consideration the substantial stock options that the executives of these companies received.

Factor Number Three. The third factor considered by the Tax Court was the character and condition of the company. The company had, over the years, been run well and profitably. The management had been able to build an excellent reputation in the label and printing industry.

Factor Number Four. The fourth factor examined whether a relationship existed between the company and employee that may permit the company to disguise nondeductible corporate distributions as deductible compensation. Labelgraphics suffered a loss of $98,639 that resulted in a –6.19 percent return on equity for the year in question.

The Tax Court did not agree that an independent investor would be satisfied with these results in light of the high salary payout.

Factor Number Five. The fifth factor focused on whether the compensation was paid pursuant to a (1) structured, (2) formal, and (3) consistently applied program. Mr. Martin's bonuses in prior years had been tied to the performance of the company.

The Tax Court concluded that there were no substantial changes in performance that would provide a reasonable explanation for paying Mr. Martin such an unusually high bonus.

Summary and Conclusion. The Tax Court determined that Mr. Martin deserved a larger than normal bonus for his development of a new process. However, the Court concluded that the bonus that he received was abnormally high.

The Tax Court determined that a total compensation of $406,000 was reasonable compensation, as it provided for a 10.20 percent return on stockholders' equity.

O.S.C. & Associates, Inc. v. Commissioner

Introduction. In *O.S.C. & Associates, Inc. v. Commissioner*,[9] the U.S. Court of Appeals for the Ninth Circuit presented a hidden danger in a strategy used by some owners of closely held corporations—that is, those who pay themselves excessive deductible compensation to avoid paying nondeductible dividends.

In this case, the usual taxpayer fallback position in reasonableness of compensation cases—in which the stockholder-employees expected to be able to at least deduct the reasonable compensation portion, if challenged—backfired. This occurred when, as a result of the disguised dividend taint, the Appeals Court denied a sizable portion of what the IRS had already admitted was reasonable compensation.

The Facts of the Case. As a result of their hard work and unique skills, the two stockholder-employees owned a successful silk-screening business. The taxpayer business, originally purchased for $180, grew from a kitchen table to a 65,000

---

[9] *O.S.C. & Associates, Inc. v. Commissioner*, No. 97-71199 U.S. App. (9th Cir. Aug. 16, 1999), *aff'g* T.C. Memo 1997-300 (June 30, 1997).

square-foot plant, with over 200 employees. The taxpayer corporation grossed over $13 million a year.

During this increasingly successful 20-year journey, the owners incorporated, with (1) one becoming president and chief executive officer with 90 percent of the company's stock and (2) the other becoming vice president with the remaining 10 percent of the company's stock.

The taxpayer corporation formally adopted an incentive compensation plan. This compensation plan had the purpose of recognizing the two shareholders for their contributions to the business. The employee/shareholders were the plan's only participants. Payments were made "according to stock ownership." As a practical matter, this stock ownership–based allocation resulted in the corporation distributing nearly all of its net income as incentive payouts to the two owners in the years in question.

The Court's Two-Part Test. The Appeals Court, citing an earlier case[10] applied, a two-prong test to determine the deductibility of payments to the stockholder-employees. The two-part test included: (1) reasonableness of amount and (2) compensatory intent.

In the earlier case, the Ninth Circuit Court of Appeals acknowledged that most courts concentrate on the first prong—that is, reasonable amount—using that result to infer compensatory purpose. The Appeals Court, however, held that, "In the rare case where there is evidence that an otherwise reasonable compensation payment contains a disguised dividend, the inquiry may expand into compensatory intent apart from reasonableness."

In this case, however, the Appeals Court observed that this was just such a case where reasonableness alone was not sufficient to satisfy the compensatory intent prong.

Was the Compensation Disguised Dividends? As evidence that the corporations' compensation plan allocations were not intended as compensation but, rather, as disguised dividends, the Appeals Court noted that the percentages of the corporation's net income paid to its two stockholder-employees ranged from 81 percent to 94 percent. The Court concluded that this was a strong indication that profits were being siphoned out of the taxpayer corporation disguised as compensation.

In addition, the Appeals Court noted that the taxpayer corporation had never paid or declared a dividend. This was relevant in light of the taxpayer corporation's history of high profitability. Also, the 90 percent employee/owner had rejected professional advice to pay dividends.

Furthermore, the taxpayer corporation's accountant manipulated the actual implementation of the compensation plan in order to increase the allocations above what the plan would have authorized.

Finally, the Appeals Court determined that the design of the compensation plan was inconsistent with compensatory intent because: (1) the plan applied only to the corporation's shareholders and no other employees; (2) the payments were calculated with reference to their proportionate stock ownership; and (3) the method of calculation was not based on the value of services rendered to the corporation, but was structured to distribute every dollar of net profit.

Summary and Conclusion. This case provides a very effective road map as to what a closely held business owner should not do in order to protect the "reasonable" component of an excessive compensation deduction.

---

[10] *Elliots, Inc. v. Commissioner*, No. 81-7173 U.S. App. (9th Cir. Sept. 26, 1983).

Law Offices—Richard Ashare, P.C. v. Commissioner

Introduction. In *Law Offices—Richard Ashare*,[11] the U.S. Tax Court provides guidance to professional corporations involved in conflicts with the IRS regarding whether substantial amounts of compensation paid to their professional employees (e.g., doctors, lawyers, consultants, etc.) can be deducted by the corporation as reasonable compensation expense.

In this case, the Tax Court gave significant latitude to the professional corporation in allowing it to prove that a $1.75 million payment made to an attorney in a single year was intended solely as compensation. And, as reasonable compensation, the entire $1.75 million payment was totally deductible by the corporation.

The Tax Court's reasonable compensation finding is particularly noteworthy to professional firm owners. This is because the taxpayer corporation reported a taxable loss in the amount of $1,857,933 for the year of the $1.75 million compensation payment.

The Facts of the Case. Richard Ashare was the taxpayer corporation's sole shareholder attorney. He was also the taxpayer corporation's only professional employee. His compensation related exclusively to one class-action case.

The taxpayer corporation achieved a $70 million settlement after 15 years of litigation. The settlement included $12,567,000 in legal fees paid to the corporation over four years.

The taxpayer corporation paid the shareholder attorney $12,242,000 in salary over five years. This included the $1.75 million salary that was the subject of the IRS challenge.

The Court's Decision. In a surprising taxpayer victory, the Tax Court found that the $1.75 million payment to the attorney/employee met the first test for deductibility (i.e., reasonableness of amount). This was because the amount was reasonable for compensation paid by a personal service corporation, such as the law firm in the present case, to its key employee for his services. The employee's qualifications for his position with the employer firm justified high compensation.

In addition, the Tax Court noted the fact that the attorney was vital and indispensable in the operation of the employer's business. The nature of the employer's business was complex and highly specialized, requiring this employee's expertise.

The Tax Court warned however, that the fact that the $1.75 million was reasonable did not necessarily mean that it was fully deductible to the employer. Under the second test for deductibility, a deduction for compensation is only allowed to the extent that the compensation is paid for services actually rendered by the employee—in or before the year of payment.

The Tax Court concluded that the $1.75 million met this second test for deductibility. This was because it was paid to the attorney to compensate him for his work on the class litigation for which the employer received over $12 million in court-ordered legal fees.

The Tax Court also noted that the employer's board of directors determined that the employee was entitled to receive the $1.75 million in compensation for his past and present services on one case. That one case constituted the firm's work during the years of the employee's tenure. The taxpayer corporation's board, through the exercise of sound business judgment, resolved that the employee was entitled to the $1.75 million in spite of the IRS's conclusions to the contrary.

---

[11] *Law Offices—Richard Ashare, P.C. v. Commissioner*, T.C. Memo 1999-282 (Aug. 24, 1999).

The Tax Court was aware of the fact that the corporation's board of directors was made up of the practitioner himself, his wife, and his longtime tax adviser. Nonetheless, the Court refused to second-guess the taxpayer corporation board's determination.

Summary and Conclusion. In its decision, the Tax Court noted that careful scrutiny of the facts is appropriate in a case such as this one—that is, where the employer payer is controlled by the payee/employee. Nevertheless, the Court's published opinion did not include any of the usual analysis of whether the $1.75 million paid to the corporation's sole shareholder employee should have been characterized as a nondeductible dividend rather than as deductible compensation.

Alpha Medical, Inc. v. Commissioner

Introduction. In *Alpha Medical, Inc. v. Commissioner,*[12] the Sixth Circuit U.S. Court of Appeals reversed the judgment of the Tax Court.

The Tax Court held that $2.3 million (of the $4.4 million actual compensation) paid to the president and sole shareholder of a company could be claimed as a business expense deduction.

Reasonableness of Owner/Employee Compensation. Although the Appeals Court essentially agreed with the Tax Court's conclusions with respect to the individual factors examined to determine the reasonableness of the compensation, the Appeals Court concluded that the compensation was reasonable because it did not exceed the amount needed to remedy undercompensation in prior years.

The Facts of the Case. Mr. William Rogers incorporated Alpha Medical Management, Inc., in Tennessee with an initial capital contribution of $1,000. The company provided management services to home health care agencies and hospitals with home health care departments.

Mr. Rogers was the president, sole director, and sole shareholder of the company through the year in question. Mr. Rogers, who earned a doctorate degree in pharmacology, founded a durable medical equipment business and a drugstore chain, which he had previously sold.

After selling the medical equipment business, Mr. Rogers turned down a management position in California with an annual salary of over $1 million so that he could stay in Tennessee and concentrate on developing Alpha Medical Management, Inc., as a successful business concern.

The shareholders' equity of Alpha Medical increased to $3.4 million for the year in question, from $97,000 four years earlier.

The salary of Mr. Rogers increased to $4,439,180 as deductible compensation and $1,500 as nondeductible dividends for the year in question, from $67,000 four years earlier.

The compensation of Mr. Rogers was equal to 64.6 percent of the taxpayers' net taxable income before the deduction of Mr. Rogers's compensation ($6,871,433) and 44.9 percent of gross receipts ($9,880,760).

The Internal Revenue Service allowed only $400,000 as a deduction for reasonable compensation of Mr. Rogers.

The Tax Court's Decision. The Tax Court examined nine relevant factors in order to determine the reasonableness of Mr. Rogers' compensation and concluded

---

[12] *Alpha Medical, Inc. v. Commissioner*, No. 98-1406 U.S. App. (6th Cir. Apr. 19, 1999), *rev'g* T.C. Memo 1997-464 (Oct. 14, 1997).

for each factor whether it favored the taxpayer, favored the Commissioner, or was neutral.

The factors considered by the Tax Court are listed below.

1. Employee's qualifications—favored taxpayer.
2. The nature, extent, and scope of the employee's work—favored taxpayer.
3. The size and complexities of business—favored taxpayer.
4. A comparison of salaries paid with gross income and net income—favored Commissioner.
5. The prevailing general economic conditions—favored Commissioner.
6. Comparison of salaries with distributions to stockholders—favored taxpayer.
7. The prevailing rates of compensation for comparable positions in comparable concerns—neutral.
8. The salary policy of the taxpayer as to all employees—favored Commissioner.
9. The amount of compensation paid to the employee in previous years—favored taxpayer.

The Tax Court concluded that the compensation paid to Mr. Rogers was in part unreasonable, agreeing with neither the taxpayer nor with the Commissioner. The Tax Court held that $2.3 million constituted reasonable compensation for Mr. Rogers for services rendered the year in question and prior years.

The Appeals Court Decision. The Appeals Court decision noted that the Tax Court did not explain how it reached the $2.3 million figure and that it appeared to split the difference between the Internal Revenue Service's original position and the taxpayer's position.

The Appeals Court reviewed the nine factors considered by the Tax Court and agreed with the conclusions with respect to all but one. Regarding the salary policy of the taxpayer as to all employees, the Tax Court stated that this factor pointed to the conclusion that Mr. Rogers' compensation was in part unreasonable.

This conclusion was based on the great disparity between the compensation of the sole shareholder, Mr. Rogers, and the nonshareholders and the fact that his compensation plan was not the result of a longstanding arm's-length agreement.

The Appeals Court disagreed "in light of the fact that Rogers was grossly underpaid for several consecutive years." Furthermore, the Appeals Court noted that, in five years, Mr. Rogers had taken the company from nothing to a net profit of nearly $7 million, stating: "In this situation, the factual record and some notion of parity with other highly successful executives requires a different result from that reached by the Tax Court."

The Appeals Court reversed the judgment of the Tax Court, acknowledging Mr. Rogers' qualifications, responsibility for the success of the company, long hours, risks assumed in founding and developing the company, and opportunity cost in turning down the $1 million-plus position in California.

The Appeals Court concluded that Mr. Rogers' "compensation . . . did not exceed the amount needed to remedy prior years of undercompensation, and was therefore reasonable."

Summary and Conclusion. *Alpha Medical, Inc. v. Commissioner* demonstrates that a level of compensation to a sole shareholder that may seem unreasonable at first glance may, in fact, be reasonable when all factors are considered, most notably undercompensation in prior years.

Exacto Spring Corporation v. Commissioner

Introduction. The CEO was the cofounder, chief executive officer, and principal owner of the Exacto Spring Corporation. For the two years in question, Exacto paid the CEO $1.3 million and $1 million in salary. Upon audit, the Internal Revenue Service concluded that these amounts were excessive. The IRS assessed a deficiency based on the disallowance of the excess compensation.

The Tax Court's Decision. In *Exacto Spring Corporation*,[13] the Tax Court concluded the amount of deductible reasonable compensation for the CEO. Based on a traditional seven-factor test, the Tax Court concluded that the amount of reasonable compensation for the CEO was approximately midway between his actual compensation and the IRS determination.

In *Exacto Spring Corporation*,[14] the Court of Appeals reversed the Tax Court's decision. The seven-factor test applied by the Tax Court was "unclear and incomplete," according to the Appeals Court.

The Seven Factor Reasonable Compensation Case. The Tax Court applied a reasonableness of compensation test that involves the consideration of the following seven factors. However, none of these seven factors is entitled to any specified weight relative to another:

1. Type and extent of the services rendered.
2. Scarcity of qualified employees.
3. Qualifications and prior earning capacity of the employee.
4. Contributions of the employee to the business venture.
5. Net earnings of the employer.
6. Prevailing compensation paid to employees with comparable jobs.
7. Peculiar characteristics of the employer's business.

The Appeals Court Reaction to the Seven Factor Test. The Appeals Court concluded that this seven factor test leaves much to be desired. To begin with, the test is nondirective. No indication is given of how the seven factors are to be weighted in the likely event they do not all line up on one side. And, many of the seven factors (such as the type and extent of services rendered, the scarcity of qualified employees, and the peculiar characteristics of the employer's business) are vague, the Appeals Court concluded.

Second, the seven factors do not bear a clear relationship either (1) to each other or (2) to the primary purpose of Section 162(a)(1). The purpose of Section 162(a)(1) is to prevent dividends (or in some cases gifts) that are not deductible from corporate income from being disguised as salary, which is deductible.

Suppose that an employee like the CEO, the founder and the chief executive officer and principal owner of Exacto, rendered no services to the company at all—but received a huge salary. It would be absurd to allow the whole (or, for that matter, any part) of his salary to be deducted as an ordinary and necessary business expense, even if he were well qualified to be the company's chief executive officer, the company had substantial net earnings, chief executive officers of similar companies were paid a lot, and it was a business in which high salaries were common.

The Appeals Court noted that the seven factor test would not prevent the Tax Court from allowing a deduction in such a case, even though Exacto obviously was

[13] *Exacto Spring Corporation v. Commissioner* (aka *Heitz v. Commissioner*), T.C. Memo 1998-220 (June 24, 1998).
[14] *Exacto Spring Corporation*, 196 F. 3d 833 (7th Circ. Nov. 16, 1999).

seeking to reduce its taxable income by disguising earnings as salary. In that case, the Tax Court would not allow the deduction. But, this disallowance would have nothing to do with the seven factor test.

Third, the Appeals Court concluded that the seven factor test sets up the Tax Court as the ultimate personnel department for closely held corporations. The Appeals Court concluded that this is a role unsuitable for courts.

The test invites the Tax Court to decide what seven factors should be considered when deciding the amount that the Exacto employees should be paid on the basis of the judges' own ideas of what jobs are comparable, what relation an employee's salary should bear to the corporation's net earnings, what types of business should pay abnormally high (or low) salaries, and so forth. The Appeals Court noted that the judges of the Tax Court are not equipped by training or experience to determine the salaries of corporate officers.

Fourth, since the seven factor test cannot itself determine the outcome of a dispute because of its nondirective character, it invites the making of arbitrary decisions based on discretion or unprincipled rules of thumb. The Tax Court in this case essentially added the IRS's conclusion of the maximum that the CEO should have been paid to what he was actually paid, and divided the sum by two.

Fifth, the Appeals Court noted that the reaction of the Tax Court to a challenge to the deduction of executive compensation is unpredictable under the seven factor test. Accordingly, corporations run unavoidable legal risks in determining a level of compensation that may be indispensable to the success of their business.

The Facts of the Case. The drawbacks of the seven factor test are well illustrated in this case. The Tax Court found that the CEO was indispensable to the Exacto business and essential to its success. The CEO was not only its chief executive officer. He was also the company's chief salesman and marketing man, plus the head of its research and development (R&D) efforts and its principal inventor. The company's entire success appears to have been due (1) on the one hand to the R&D conducted by him and (2) on the other hand, to his marketing of these innovations. (The CEO did receive some additional compensation for his marketing efforts from a subsidiary of Exacto Spring Corporation.)

Likewise, the design of precision springs (which is the Exacto Spring Corporation specialty) is an extremely specialized branch of mechanical engineering. The Tax Court recognized that there are very few engineers who have made careers specializing in this area, let alone engineers like the CEO who have the ability (1) to identify and attract clients and (2) to develop springs to perform a specific function for that client.

The Tax Court noted that the CEO was highly qualified to run Exacto as a result of his education, training, experience, and motivation. He had over 30 years of highly successful experience in the field of spring design. And, the Tax Court concluded that his efforts were of great value to Exacto.

With regard to Exacto net earnings, the Tax Court was noncommittal. Exacto had reported a loss in the first year in question and very little taxable income in the second year. But it conceded having taken some improper deductions in those years unrelated to the CEO's salary. After adjusting the Exacto Spring Corporation income to remove these deductions, the Tax Court concluded that Exacto had earned more than $1 million in each of the years at issue, net of CEO's supposedly inflated salary.

The Tax Court was noncommittal with regard to earnings of comparable employees as well. Expert witnesses had presented evidence, and the Tax Court was critical of both.

Exacto Spring Corporation's witness had arrived at his estimate of the CEOs maximum reasonable compensation in part by aggregating the salaries that Exacto would have had to pay to hire four people. The more roles or functions an employee performs, the more valuable his or her services are likely to be. However, the Tax Court concluded that an employee who performs four jobs, each on a part-time basis, is not necessarily worth as much to a company as four employees each working full time at one of those jobs. The Tax Court ruled that it is arbitrary to multiply the normal full-time salary for one of the jobs by four to compute the reasonable compensation of the employee who fills all four of them.

The expert witness for the IRS considered whether the CEO's compensation was consistent with Exacto investors' earning a reasonable return (adjusted for the risk of its business), which he calculated to be 13 percent. However, he neglected to consider the concessions of improper deductions, which led to adjustments to taxable income. The Tax Court determined that, with those adjustments, the investor's annual return was more than 20 percent, despite the CEO's large salary.

Finally, the Tax Court dismissed the IRS's argument that the Exacto low level of dividends (zero in the two years at issue, but never very high) was evidence that the corporation was paying the CEO dividends in the form of salary.

The Tax Court pointed out that shareholders might not want dividends. The Exacto shareholders may prefer the corporation to retain its earnings. That would cause the value of the corporation to rise and, therefore, allow the shareholders to obtain corporate earnings in the form of capital gains taxed at a lower rate than ordinary income.

The Tax Court also noted that, while the CEO, as the owner of 55 percent of Exacto common stock, obviously was in a position to influence his salary, the corporation's two other major shareholders (each with 20 percent of the stock) had approved it. These other shareholders had not themselves been paid a salary or other compensation and are not relatives of the CEO. Also, they had no financial or other incentive to allow the CEO to siphon off dividends in the form of salary.

Summary and Conclusion. It is noteworthy that the Appeals Court did not hold that a chief executive officer's salary is always reasonable. It did note that there could be situations in which a high rate of return was not due to the chief executive officer's exertions. In such situations, the presumption of reasonableness would be rebutted.

In addition, the IRS could still have prevailed if it could show that, while the CEO's salary was reasonable, Exacto did not in fact intend to pay him that amount as salary, and that this amount really did include a concealed dividend (even though it need not have). In such a case, because any deductible business expense must be bona fide (as well as reasonable), the deduction could be disallowed.

Intangible Asset Valuation Issues

Nestle Holdings, Inc. v. Commissioner

Introduction. In *Nestle Holdings, Inc. v. Commissioner*,[15] the corporate taxpayer appealed a decision of the Tax Court.[16]

[15] *Nestle Holdings, Inc. v. Commissioner*, Nos. 96-4158, 96-4192 U.S. App. (2d Cir. July 31, 1998).
[16] *Nestle Holdings, Inc. v. Commissioner*, T.C. Memo 1995-441 (Sept. 14, 1995).

In its decision, the Appeals Court reached two important conclusions. First, the Appeals Court ruled that the taxpayer realized a capital gain when it sold intangible assets to its parent company. Second, the Appeals Court ruled that the Tax Court erred in solely relying upon the relief-from-royalty method in its valuation of the taxpayer's trademarks.

Of these two conclusions, the second is much more important (1) to corporate owners of marketing-related intangibles such as trademarks and trade names and (2) to intangible asset and intellectual property valuation analysts.

This Appeals Court decision discusses the conceptual pros and cons of the use of (and of the sole reliance upon) the relief-from-royalty valuation method.

Fact Set Summary. Nestle Holdings, Inc. ("Nestle") is a first-tier subsidiary of Nestle S.A. ("NSA").

The IRS concluded income tax deficiencies regarding the Nestle sale to NSA of various intangible assets, including patents, trademarks and trade names, and proprietary technology. Nestle claimed that it had realized a capital loss on the sale. The IRS concluded that Nestle had overstated the fair market value of (and, in turn, its tax basis in) the transferred intangible assets. Accordingly, the IRS concluded that Nestle had realized a capital gain on the sale of the subject intangible assets.

Nestle went to the Tax Court regarding the matter. The Tax Court, in good measure, adopted the IRS's intangible asset valuations. And, the Tax Court concluded that Nestle had realized a capital gain.

The Appeals Court agreed with the Tax Court that Nestle realized a capital gain on the intangible asset sale transaction. However, the Appeals Court rejected the Tax Court's exclusive reliance on the relief-from-royalty method of estimating the fair market value of the Nestle trademarks.

The Facts of the Case. Nestle purchased the stock of Carnation Company ("Carnation"). Nestle intended to finance the acquisition with a capital contribution of $525 million from NSA and a $2.5 billion loan from third-party financing sources. Ultimately, this acquisition financing plan was revised.

Actually, the Carnation acquisition was financed by commercial loans of $1.6 billion and related-party loans of $1.325 billion. NSA provided some of the related-party loans, but it made no capital contributions to Nestle.

After the acquisition, Nestle made the required principal and interest payments to the related parties, and Nestle deducted the interest expense for federal income tax purposes.

As a result of the acquisition, Nestle became the owner of the Carnation intangible assets. It was an NSA policy to own all of the trademarks and trade names used by Nestle companies. Accordingly, Nestle sold the acquired Carnation intangibles to NSA. These intangible assets included trademarks and trade names, patents, and proprietary technology. Nestle and NSA agreed (1) that NSA would pay fair market value for the intangibles, and (2) that NSA would cancel a portion of the Nestle debt in exchange for the subject intangibles.

To estimate the fair market value of the Carnation intangible assets, Nestle commissioned an appraisal. The appraiser valued the Carnation trademarks and trade names at $315,000,000, the proprietary technology at $106,018,700, and the patents at $4,612,000—for an aggregate fair market value of $425,630,700. Accordingly, NSA cancelled $425,630,700 of the Nestle debt in exchange for the Carnation intangible assets.

Nestle accounted for the purchase of the Carnation stock as a purchase of the Carnation assets. Accordingly, Nestle adjusted the basis of the acquired assets to their fair market values.

Nestle also allocated to these intangible assets a small portion of the total price paid to acquire Carnation over and above the fair market value of the tangible and intangible assets Nestle had received.

As a result, the basis of the Nestle intangible assets was "stepped up" to $435,837,000, an amount that was in excess of the assets' fair market value. Consequently, Nestle claimed a capital loss on the subsequent sale of the acquired Carnation intangible assets to NSA.

The IRS challenged the claimed capital loss. In particular, the IRS challenged the Nestle valuation of the acquired intangible assets. The IRS ultimately valued the Carnation trademarks and trade names at $150,300,000 and its proprietary technology at $21,204,000.

The IRS agreed to the valuation of the Carnation patents at $4,612,000. It assigned the Nestle acquired intangible assets an aggregate basis of $163,556,000.

The IRS then alleged that since Nestle had received $425,630,700 from its parent for intangible assets that had a basis of $163,556,000, Nestle had realized a short-term capital gain of $262,074,700 on the sale of these intangibles. Since Nestle failed to report this "gain," the IRS determined a tax deficiency.

The Tax Court's Decision. Nestle argued that when a related party pays more or less than fair market value for an asset, the excess or shortfall should be attributable to the parties' relationship and should be reclassified accordingly. In this case, the relationship between the parties was that of a shareholder to a corporation. Therefore, the excess over the assets' fair market value that NSA paid to Nestle was a capital contribution.

The Tax Court rejected this argument. The Tax Court concluded that allowing the excess purchase price to be treated as a capital contribution would impermissibly "allow petitioner retroactively to convert debt into equity, without any adverse tax consequences."

Nestle argued that even if there were a capital gain, the IRS had overestimated the tax deficiency by underestimating the fair market value of the trademarks and trade names that Nestle sold to NSA.

Nestle provided expert testimony that the fair market value of the Carnation trademarks and trade names was $346,000,000. The IRS provided expert testimony that the fair market value of the Carnation trademarks and trade names was only $146,100,000.

The Tax Court concluded that Nestle was not entitled to claim a "second-tier step-up" in the basis of the acquired assets. Accordingly, Nestle could only adjust the basis of the intangible assets to their fair market value.

The Tax Court also disagreed with the Nestle valuation expert and his estimate of the fair market value of the Carnation intangibles. The Tax Court concluded that the only trademark valuation method used by the IRS's expert—the relief-from-royalty method—was reasonable. And, the Tax Court concluded that Nestle had not "demonstrated that the Carnation trademarks and trade names are worth more than the value determined by [the IRS expert]."

Accordingly, the Tax Court concluded that the trademarks and trade names Nestle sold to NSA had a value of $146,100,000. The Tax Court concluded that the aggregate basis in all of the Carnation intangibles—including patents and proprietary technology—was $219,482,000. Therefore, the Tax Court concluded that Nestle realized a capital gain of $206,148,700 on the sale on the Carnation intangible assets to NSA.

Nestle appealed two aspects of the Tax Court's opinion.

The Appeals Court Decision—Tax Treatment of Sale. Nestle claimed that the excess of price over fair market value paid by NSA for the Carnation intangibles should be treated as a capital contribution. The Appeals Court concluded that such treatment would constitute a retroactive change in the form of the transaction with NSA.

Nestle already had selected the form of the transaction between Nestle and NSA, the Appeals Court concluded. Therefore, because the NSA transaction was structured as a sale of assets, any gain realized by Nestle must be treated as a capital gain.

The Appeals Court Decision—Valuation of Carnation Intangibles. The Tax Court had ruled that the evidence that Nestle presented regarding the fair market value of its trademarks was flawed. The Tax Court adopted the valuation provided by the IRS's expert.

That expert estimated the fair market value of the Nestle acquired trademarks using the relief-from-royalty method as his only valuation method. Underlying this valuation method is the premise that the only value that a purchaser of a trademark receives is the "relief" from paying a royalty for its use.

Using this method, the fair market value of a trademark is estimated by quantifying the present value of the stream of market-derived royalty payments that the owner of a trademark is "relieved" of paying. This royalty stream is estimated by the following steps:

1. Conclude whether the trademarks are profitable or capable of being commercialized.
2. Select a market-derived royalty rate for each trademark.
3. Multiply this market-derived royalty rate by the estimated revenue stream of the product associated with the trademark.

The IRS expert concluded that most of the Carnation trademarks were profitable and that the range of royalty rates in the food industry was from 0 to 5 percent. He then assigned royalty rates to the subject trademarks and quantified the present value of the estimated royalty payments. The Tax Court found this valuation method to be reasonable and adopted the conclusion of the IRS expert.

On the other hand, the Appeals Court disagreed with the sole reliance upon the relief-from-royalty method. The Appeals Court concluded that the relief-from-royalty method necessarily undervalues trademarks.

The Appeals Court concluded that the sole use of a relief-from-royalty method in the case of a sale is not appropriate. This is because it is the fair market value of a trademark, and not the cost of its use, that is at issue. The Appeals Court concluded that the relief-from-royalty method fails to capture the value of all of the rights of intangible asset ownership, such as: (1) the power to determine when and where the trademark may be used and (2) the ability to move the trademark into or out of product lines.

The Appeals Court concluded that the Tax Court's exclusive reliance on this valuation method fundamentally misunderstands the nature in trademarks and the reasons why the law provides for exclusive rights of ownership in a trademark.

Summary and Conclusion. This case illustrates how creative tax planning depends upon credible, independent valuation opinions. Given the inherent shortcomings of the relief-from-royalty valuation methodology, the Appeals Court concluded that the Tax Court erred when it adopted the Service's trademark valuations. The Appeals Court instructed the Tax Court to examine alternate methods for estimating the fair market value of the transferred Carnation trademark.

This case provides useful guidance with regard to the valuation of trademarks and trade names for federal income taxation purposes. In particular, the Appeals Court decision describes: (1) the analytical limitations of the relief-from-royalty valuation method, and (2) the potential problems associated with the exclusive reliance on the relief-from-royalty method to value trademarks and trade names.

Thompson v. Commissioner

Introduction. In *Thompson v. Commissioner*,[17] the Tax Court concluded the valuation of a noncompete agreement intangible asset, using an 11 factor "economic reality test."

The tax issue in this case was whether State Supply, a distributor of beauty supply products organized as an S corporation, could amortize $2.5 million for noncompete covenants.

The Facts of the Case. Group One Capital, Inc., an investment company, executed a cash merger for State Supply for $6 million. State Supply's previous year's pretax earnings were approximately $1.5 million.

The due diligence uncovered the fact that State Supply had two employees who could potentially put them out of business if they were to quit working for State Supply and become competitors. These two employees were: (1) Holliday, who had been with State Supply for 26 years, and (2) Beaurline, who had been in the beauty supply business for 36 years. Therefore, as a condition of acquiring a loan to fund the acquisition, the bank required that Holliday and Beaurline execute noncompete agreements with State Supply.

The principals of Group One Capital, Inc., and their attorney met with Beaurline, Holliday, and State Supply's attorney and negotiated one-year employment agreements and a three-year noncompete agreement with the following terms: "Beaurline and Holliday would each be paid $17,540 per month the first 24 months and $23,040 per month for the last 36 months for a total of $1,250,000 each for the noncompete agreements."

Taxpayer State Supply claimed amortization deductions for the noncompete agreements. The IRS disallowed the deductions in full. It claimed that the amount paid for the covenants was a disguised payment for State Supply's stock.

The Tax Court's Decision. To determine whether or not to allow the deductions, the Tax Court applied the 11 factors of the "economic reality" test which include:

1. The grantor's (i.e., covenantor's) having the business expertise to compete.
2. The grantor's intent to compete.
3. The grantor's economic resources.
4. The potential damage to the buyer posed by the grantor's competition.
5. The grantor's contacts and relationships with customers, suppliers, and other business contacts.
6. The duration and geographic scope of the covenant.
7. Enforceability of the covenant not to compete under state law.
8. The age and health of the grantor.

---

[17] *Thompson v. Commissioner*, T.C. Memo 1997-287 (June 24, 1997).

9. Whether payments for the covenant not to compete are pro rata to the grantor's stock ownership in the company being sold.
10. Whether the payments under the covenant not to compete cease upon breach of the covenant or upon the death of the grantor.
11. The existence of active negotiation over the terms and value of the covenant not to compete.

When the Tax Court considered these 11 "economic reality" factors, it decided that an overwhelmingly strong need and a corresponding high relative value existed for the noncompete agreements.

The Service argued that the one year employment agreement effectively prevented the possibility of competition for the first year they were in effect. And, after the possibility of competition has been eliminated for one year, even the taxpayer's calculations support the value of the noncompete agreements to be only $400,000.

In deciding the issue of the employment agreement, the Tax Court decided that since (1) the possibility existed that the employment relationship could be terminated by either side, in which case, absent a noncompete agreement, Beaurline and Holliday could engage in competition, and (2) the noncompete agreements were, as required by the bank, part and parcel of the stock-sale transaction, the one year employment agreement did not preclude the necessity of the noncompete agreement in the first year.

The Tax Court considered the testimony of a valuation engineer for the IRS and an independent appraiser who testified for State Supply. Both experts agreed that State Supply was worth approximately $8.5 million with the covenants in place. Their valuations differed, however, in the amount to be placed on the noncompete agreements.

The IRS expert simply concluded that the present value of the future earnings stream plus the excess cash was $8.6 million. And, since the total purchase price was $8.6 million, that "leaves, at best, a nominal value for allocation to the covenants."

The taxpayer's expert, on the other hand, using a discounted cash flow model, valued State Supply with the covenants in place. He then analyzed the probability of competition and the impact that competition from Holliday and Beaurline would have on State Supply in the first three years after the sale. In his final analysis, the taxpayer's expert valued the two noncompete agreements at approximately $2.5 million.

Summary and Conclusion. This case provides an 11 factor "economic reality" test for noncompete covenants and encourages careful analysis. The Tax Court specifically stated, "We found [the IRS] expert report to be of no assistance," and the Tax Court rendered its decision in favor of the taxpayer.

DHL Corporation and Subsidiaries v. Commissioner

Introduction. In *DHL Corporation and Subsidiaries v. Commissioner*,[18] the Tax Court quantified the fair market value of the DHL Corporation trademark. This case is instructive to analysts who perform valuations, demographic analyses, or transfer price analyses with regard to intellectual properties.

The Facts of the Case. DHL and its subsidiaries provide services related to the pickup and delivery of time sensitive documents (and other materials) to domestic and

---

[18] *DHL Corporation and Subsidiaries v. Commissioner*, T.C. Memo. 1998-461 (Dec. 30, 1998).

international markets. During the 1970s and 1980s, DHL expanded rapidly and became the third largest courier service, operating in 195 countries.

The DHL subsidiaries served the international market while DHL operated domestically. DHL and its subsidiaries had common ownership. Its subsidiaries did quite well, while the domestic operations lost money in an unsuccessful attempt to compete with the domestic leaders such as Federal Express. The international operations accounted for two-thirds of the DHL business.

Domestic DHL and its subsidiaries all used the same trademark. Under a license agreement with its subsidiaries, domestic DHL owned the trademark. However, the trademark title was besmirched because in some countries, the DHL subsidiaries had registered the trademark in their own name.

In the late 1980s, three foreign airline companies became interested in integrating their airlines with the DHL delivery network. The airlines offered to purchase (1) a 57.5 percent interest in the foreign subsidiaries for $450 million and (2) the DHL trademark for $50 million. After the transaction was negotiated, the total purchase price remained unchanged, but the amount of the purchase price allocated to the trademark was reduced to $20 million. Later, an appraisal confirmed that value.

The IRS's Position. The Internal Revenue Service concluded that the value of the DHL trademark was $300 million. The IRS presented two expert witnesses, who testified as to the value of the trademark. Both experts assumed that the entire DHL revenue stream was attributable to the trademark and not to any other existing intangible asset(s).

The first government expert valued the trademark using the relief-from-royalty method. After surveying a variety of businesses regarding royalty rates, he concluded that a 1 percent royalty rate was appropriate. In estimating the value under this method, he used a discounted cash flow analysis. In this analysis, he assumed that the income tax rate would be 30 percent and the expected long-term growth rate would be 6 percent. Using a present value discount rate of 12.5 percent, he estimated the trademark's fair market value to be $287 million.

The government's second expert valued the trademark using the relief-from-royalty method (and the discounted cash flow technique) coupled with the "other anticipated value" method. The secondary method "quantifies economic benefits accruing to an asset that may not be reflected in other income approaches, including marketing cost savings, operating synergies, lower costs of funds, etc. This benefit is supposedly measured in the form of incremental cash-flows that the expert believes are 'not necessarily the result of excess earnings or avoided royalties.'" Using slightly different valuation variables including a 3.6 percent expected long-term growth rate and a 1.15 percent royalty rate, he estimated that the value of the trademark was $327.5 million.

The Taxpayer's Position. At trial, the taxpayer also presented expert testimony regarding the value of the trademark. DHL initially argued that the $20 million allocated to the trademark was the fair market value of that asset. It claimed that the amount was arrived at through arm's-length negotiations. DHL attributed considerable value to other off–balance sheet assets, especially the DHL network which "enjoyed an intangible benefit from its existing infrastructure and operating know-how that created a 'barrier to entry' of others into the same marketplace."

The taxpayer's expert calculated the value of the trademark at $55.2 million, based on a 0.31 percent royalty rate and a 7.6 percent expected long-term growth rate. The taxpayer's analyst discounted that amount by a 14.1 percent present value discount rate to arrive at fair market value.

The Tax Court's Decision. The Tax Court concluded that the amount allocated to the trademark in the purchase agreement was not arrived at through arm's-length negotiations. It found that the initial $50 million offer was an attempt to bolster the DHL financial condition in the wake of its attempted expansion. However, the Court concluded that the purchase price was negotiated down because the buyers refused to negotiate the overall transaction price of $500 million.

The Tax Court also disregarded the taxpayer's expert valuation. It stated:

> We find it peculiar that petitioners' expert could expect to derive an independent fair market value by accepting the parties' values and rates, because his objective was to reach a fair market value. However, petitioner's expert accepted rates used in the transaction under consideration and then reduced their effect by discounting them to a present value. That approach does not serve to assist the Court in measuring . . . whether the value they used was a "fair market value."

The Tax Court also declined to accept the Internal Revenue Service claimed position. The Court reasoned that the entire value is not attributed solely to the DHL name recognition. The Court concluded that the DHL existing network had significant intangible value.

The Court concluded its own valuation by accepting the IRS $300 million figure as the value of all of the DHL intangible assets. The Court then reduced that amount by one-half. The Tax Court reasoned that the DHL in-place operating infrastructure had significant value at least equal to the DHL name recognition.

After concluding that the trademark had a $150 million value worldwide, the Tax Court separated the amount of value attributable to the DHL international business and then applied a lack of marketability discount to that amount. "A marketability discount is generally thought to be necessary where the buyer may incur out-of-pocket expenses or other costs due to some aspect or defect in the asset being purchased."

In this case, the Tax Court concluded that a 50 percent discount was appropriate because "The potential for delay, expense, inconvenience, etc. could be immense and would present a huge potential for out-of-pocket expenses or other costs [in securing the DHL's trademark rights in the foreign countries] to a potential willing buyer."

Based on this analysis, the Tax Court concluded that the fair market value of the DHL trademark and trade name was $100 million.

Summary and Conclusion. In *DHL Corporation and Subsidiaries v. Commissioner*, the Tax Court had to conclude the fair market value of a service company's trademark with the contexts of (1) a purchase price allocation and (2) Section 482. In this case, the Tax Court rejected the analyses and conclusions of both the IRS experts and the taxpayer's experts.

In a classic compromise, the Tax Court concluded its own value for the DHL trademark.

Summary

This chapter presented summary reviews of the valuation aspects of numerous federal income tax court cases. The cases that were reviewed were not selected based on their judicial precedent or noteworthy legal merits. Rather, they were selected because they were informative to taxpayers, their legal counsel, and to valuation practitioners with regard to issues of valuation principles and practices.

However, analysts should not naively rely upon the judicial decisions in these cases in their valuation practices for several reasons. First, all of the cases reviewed are very specific with regard to facts and circumstances. It is very unlikely that the facts and circumstances of another assignment would be sufficiently similar to the cases reviewed to allow for the naive application of a judicial guideline. Second, federal judges apply a specific set of legal and (sometimes) valuation principles in their decisions. These same valuation principles may not apply in valuations performed for purposes other than federal income taxation. Third, federal judges are not trained valuation analysts. A judicial decision that makes good legal sense may not be based on sound valuation principles or economic theory. And, fourth, decisions of federal judges (particularly in the U.S. Tax Court) seem to have a tendency to pick a point between the two valuation positions. Court decisions (particularly decisions that compromise between the taxpayer's and the IRS's position) may be judicially fair. But, they may not always be technically correct from a more academic valuation and economic analysis perspective.

Chapter 32

Valuations for Employee Stock Ownership Plans

An employee stock ownership plan (ESOP) is a qualified retirement plan under the Internal Revenue Code of 1986, as amended (the Code). The plan is designed to invest primarily in employer stock. The Code and the Employee Retirement Income Security Act of 1974, as amended (ERISA) impose a number of requirements for the ESOP to gain qualified status. The ESOP must comply with most of the requirements of other qualified retirement plans. There are additional requirements specific to ESOPs. Additionally, ESOPs are "exempt" from other qualified plan requirements due to prohibited transaction exemptions. For example, the ESOP may use borrowed funds from the sponsoring company to purchase employer stock.

As of this writing, there are approximately 12,000 to 14,000 ESOPs in the United States. In addition, the ESOP concept is currently expanding globally. During 1997, legislation was passed that allows S corporations to sponsor ESOPs.

ESOP transactions are complex because they encompass the incorporation of knowledge from various disciplines. The following is a summary of these disciplines:

- Valuation.
- Legal and regulatory.
- Qualified plan administration.
- Finance.
- Fiduciary concerns.

There is also a great deal of crossover among disciplines on some issues. This chapter will generally cover the major aspects of each of these disciplines and how each affects the ESOP transaction. To reduce one of the complexities and for ease in understanding, the S Corporation ESOP issues will be addressed in a separate section. Thus, all the other sections of this chapter assume the company sponsoring the ESOP is a C corporation.

General ESOP Framework

The starting point for understanding the complexities involved in ESOPs is the general ESOP framework. ESOPs have served the dual purpose of meeting corporate finance and compensation objectives. The following is a summary of various purposes for use of an ESOP:

- Liquidity for shareholders.
- Estate planning.
- Management succession planning.
- Capital for expansion.
- Acquisitions.
- LBO by management.
- Divestiture.
- Recapitalization.
- Takeover defense.
- Motivating employees.
- Employee benefit.
- Privatization.
- Charitable giving.
- Going private.

Types of ESOPs

Nonleveraged ESOPs

The nonleveraged ESOP does not use debt to purchase employer securities. The nonleveraged ESOP acquires employer securities through tax deductible stock contributions or tax deductible cash contributions that are used to purchase employer securities. Stock is purchased gradually each year based on the company's annual contribution amount. The ESOP percentage ownership increases with each contribution. Thus, debt financing is not necessary.

Leveraged ESOPs

The typical leveraged ESOP transaction is accomplished through a series of steps that are best illustrated by the diagram presented in Exhibit 32–1.

ABC Company borrows money from the bank (the "Bank Loan"). The Company then loans the proceeds from the Bank Loan to a newly created ESOP, evidenced by the "ESOP Loan." The ESOP purchases stock from existing shareholders in return for the cash from the proceeds of the ESOP Loan.

Exhibit 32–2 illustrates the effects of the leveraged ESOP transaction on an annual basis. Annually, ABC Company makes tax-deductible employer contributions to the ESOP (or pays dividends on the ESOP stock). The ESOP uses its cash from these employer contributions to make payments on the ESOP Loan. ABC

Exhibit 32–1

Leveraged ESOP Transaction

Exhibit 32–2

Annual ESOP Cash Flows

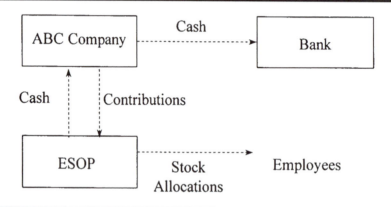

Company now actually has the cash it used for employer contributions and the ESOP has merely been a conduit for the cash. Therefore, ABC Company can now use the cash to make payments on the Bank Loan. As the ESOP Loan is paid back, employer securities are allocated to ESOP participant accounts.

All Parties to a Leveraged ESOP Transaction Benefit

The tax and economic advantages of a leveraged ESOP transaction benefit all parties to the transaction, including the company, the shareholders, the employees, and the lenders.

The Company. The most significant benefit for the company is the ability to effectively deduct the principal payments on the ESOP acquisition loan. This is a substantial tax savings for the company and increases after-tax cash flow as compared to conventional financing. These tax benefits also increase the company's debt-carrying capacity and thus enhance the ability to obtain financing.

The company also may experience productivity gains due to employee ownership. In addition, the ESOP should be helpful in attracting and retaining employees.

The Shareholders. The most significant benefit for the selling shareholder is the availability of the 1042 election. Under Code Section 1042, the selling shareholder can defer the capital gains tax on the sale to the ESOP. The specific requirements of Section 1042 are discussed in detail later in this chapter. Therefore, the shareholder would realize greater net after-tax proceeds when selling to an ESOP.

The ESOP transaction is also a liquidity event for the selling shareholder. Many owners of privately held business have a significant portion of their net worth invested in the business. The sale to an ESOP can provide needed liquidity—and yet the selling shareholder can maintain ownership control. These events also can be beneficial to the individual shareholder's estate plan.

Additional equity incentives for management are still available in the ESOP company. In fact, equity-based incentive plans are common in ESOP companies because the ESOP is considered a passive financial investor—that is, the ESOP does not participate in daily management decisions.

The Employees. The major benefit for employees is the ability to share in the equity growth of the company. Since the value of the company is dependent on its performance, employees may be more motivated to act in ways that maximize shareholder value.

Generally, ESOP contributions are larger than typical profit sharing contributions. ESOP contributions can even exceed 25 percent of annual compensation in some transactions.

And, just as in other qualified retirement plans, the employee does not recognize taxable income in the year the shares are allocated to the accounts. Rather, taxable income is recognized when the participant receives a distribution from the ESOP. During the period the stock is held by the ESOP, the appreciation in value is also not currently taxed.

The Lenders. The major benefit for the lenders in ESOP transactions is the reduced credit risk associated with the effective ability to deduct principal. The tax savings increase after-tax flow and provide a greater chance that the company can meet its debt obligations.

Most lenders prefer to be sure that the company can handle the debt obligations based on current cash flow. But the lender also looks to the balance sheet for collateral protection. The ESOP transaction also can enhance credit through a pledge of the qualified replacement property (QRP) purchased by the selling shareholder in a Section 1042 rollover transaction as collateral for the Bank Loan.

Valuation of a Company for ESOP Purposes

The first step in assessing the feasibility of an ESOP is estimating the value of the business. In estimating the value of a business for ESOP purposes, most of the valuation concepts discussed in prior chapters are applicable. However, ESOPs bring added complexities to the valuation process. This chapter assumes the reader has a basic knowledge of general valuation theories and expands upon the specific valuation issues related to ESOPs.

Adequate Consideration

ERISA requires that ESOPs pay no more than "adequate consideration" when investing in employer securities. Adequate consideration generally follows the specific guidelines for the definition of fair market value under Revenue Ruling 59-60. On May 17, 1988, the Department of Labor (DOL) issued the "Proposed Regulation Relating to the Definition of Adequate Consideration" for ESOP transactions. The full contents of the adequate consideration regulations are available on the Department of Labor's web site at www.dol.gov. As of this writing, the DOL may issue new regulations in the near future.

For purposes of ERISA and the adequate consideration regulations, fair market value is defined as:

> The price at which an asset would change hands between a willing buyer and a willing seller when the former is not under any compulsion to buy and the latter is not under any compulsion to sell, and both parties are able, as well as willing, to trade and are well informed about the asset and the market for such asset.[1]

An ESOP appraisal is required to be performed, (1) when the ESOP makes an acquisition of employer securities, (2) at least annually thereafter (although some companies routinely have their stock appraisals updated semiannually or quarterly), (3) whenever there is a transaction between the plan and a party in interest, and (4) if the ESOP sells out of its stock position.

The DOL adequate consideration regulations provide that the written document include an assessment of all "relevant factors" including:

(A) The nature of the business and the history of the enterprise from its inception;

(B) The economic outlook in general, and the condition and outlook of the specific industry in particular;

(C) The book value of the securities and the financial condition of the business;

(D) The earning capacity of the company;

(E) The dividend-paying capacity of the company;

(F) Whether or not the enterprise has goodwill or other intangible value;

(G) The market price of securities of corporations engaged in the same or a similar line of business, which are actively traded in a free and open market, either on an exchange or over-the-counter;

(H) The marketability, or lack thereof, of the securities. Where the plan is the purchaser of securities that are subject to "put" rights and such rights are taken into account in reducing the discount for lack of marketability, such assessment shall include consideration of the extent to which such rights are enforceable, as well as the company's ability to meet its obligations with respect to the "put rights" (taking into account the company's financial strength and liquidity);

(I) Whether or not the seller would be able to obtain a control premium from an unrelated third party with regard to the block of securities

---

[1] Proposed Regulation Relating to the Definition of Adequate Consideration, 53 Fed. Reg. 17,632 (1988), p. 17,634.

being valued, provided that in cases where a control premium is taken into account:

(1) Actual control (both in form and substance) passes to the purchaser with the sale, or will pass to the purchaser within a reasonable time pursuant to a binding agreement in effect at the time of the sale, and

(2) It is reasonable to assume that the purchaser's control will not be dissipated within a short period of time subsequent to acquisition.[2]

The requirement to assess factors (A) through (G) as well as all "relevant factors" is consistent with Revenue Ruling 59-60. Factors (H) and (I) are additional factors specific to ESOP valuations.

Independence of the Appraiser and the Appraiser's Role

The DOL adequate consideration regulations require that someone that is independent of all parties to the ESOP transaction conduct ESOP appraisals. The DOL notes that under Code Section 401(a)(28)(C), ESOP fiduciaries must employ an independent appraiser meeting requirements similar to Regulation 1.170A-13(c)(5) of the Code which relates to independent appraisals of donations to charitable organizations.

A qualified independent appraiser under these regulations is a person who, among other qualifications:

1. Is not a party to the transaction, is not related to any party to the transaction, is not married to any person with relationship to the transaction, and is not regularly used by any of the parties to the transaction and does not perform a majority of appraisals for these persons.
2. Holds himself or herself out to the public as an appraiser or performs appraisals on a regular basis.
3. Is qualified to make appraisals of the type of property being valued including, by background, experience, education, and memberships, if any, in professional associations.
4. Understands that an intentionally false or fraudulent overstatement of value may subject the valuation practitioner to a civil penalty.
5. Receives an appraisal fee that is not based on a percentage of the appraised value of the property.

The role of the independent appraiser is to provide the fiduciary with the financial data and the documents that are required by law in order for the fiduciary to make its decisions on behalf of the ESOP participants. The fiduciary is actually the party responsible for the value and fairness decision—not the appraiser.

Providing investment advice to the plan on such matters as investment policies or strategies, overall portfolio composition, or diversification of plan investments could imply that the appraiser is a fiduciary. The law indicates that the fiduciary is determined not by label but by function. The appraiser does not make the decision to close the transaction. The fiduciary does.

---

[2] Ibid., pp. 17,637–38.

Reporting Requirements

The DOL proposed adequate consideration regulations also address the ESOP valuation reporting requirements. In order to comply with the regulations the ESOP valuation report must contain the following information:

(A) A summary of the qualifications to evaluate assets of the type being valued of the person making the valuation;
(B) A statement of the asset's value, a statement of the methods used in estimating that value, and the reasons for the valuation in light of those methods;
(C) A full description of the asset being valued;
(D) The factors taken into account in making the valuation, including any restrictions, understandings, agreements, or obligations limiting the use or disposition of the property;
(E) The purpose for which that valuation was made;
(F) The relevance or significance accorded to the valuation methods taken into account;
(G) The effective date of the valuation; and
(H) In cases where a valuation report has been prepared, the signature of the person or firm making the valuation and the date the report was signed.[3]

Valuation Approaches and Methods

The three generally accepted approaches to valuation are the income approach (Chapters 9 and 10), the market approach (Chapters 11 and 12), and the asset-based approach (Chapters 13 and 14). In addition, the ESOP appraisal also includes a detailed qualitative and quantitative analysis of the subject ESOP company. While all of the three approaches may be used to value shares of company stock held by an ESOP, the asset-based approach is used less often than the other two approaches (and mainly for holding or investment companies).

ESOP-Specific Adjustments

ESOP Contributions

It has been accepted practice to add back the employer corporation ESOP contributions in estimating the normalized earnings of the business, if the contributions are in excess of normal retirement plan benefits. However, if ESOP contributions represent compensation in lieu of wages or benefits, or are expected to remain in place over an indefinite period of time, contribution expenses should not be added back in arriving at normalized earnings. If the ESOP is replacing another plan but

---

[3] Ibid.

at a higher level, the analyst also should make the adjustment for normalized employee benefit costs discussed below.

Normalized Employee Benefit Costs

If the company did not have an ESOP, the sponsoring company would probably consider another employee benefit plan. Or, the ESOP may be replacing another employee benefit plan for a period of time. Thus, the appraiser needs to assess the normalized level of employee benefit costs and subtract this as an expense from normalized earnings. Historical practices in the subject ESOP company are good indications of the market level of benefits expected by the employees.

This adjustment in combination with the ESOP contribution adjustment discussed previously basically adjusts the ESOP company's normalized earnings as the willing buyer would if they did not intend to continue the ESOP. Since ESOPs are specific buyers, the willing buyer test would require that the analyst make this assumption.

Compensation Adjustments

Analysts sometimes consider an adjustment for excess compensation if some members of management are earning amounts in excess of the market level of compensation. In an ESOP valuation, these adjustments are only appropriate if the compensation policies will be changed to reflect the reduced level of compensation. Even if excess compensation is being paid, if the higher level of compensation is expected to continue, the ESOP valuation should reflect the ongoing compensation practices.

ESOP Compensation Adjustment

Under SOP 93-6, defined and discussed in the section of this chapter on ESOP Accounting Standards, the audited income statement contains a recording of compensation expense associated with the ESOP at fair market value. This compensation expense is not cash compensation and should not be reflected as such. The true economics of the cash transactions indicate that the appreciation in the value of the shares held by the ESOP trust is actually earnings of the plan. Thus, when valuing ESOP stock, most analysts adjust for the fair market value component of the ESOP compensation expense in determining the normalized earnings of the company.

Control Premiums

Valuation practitioners generally agree that the basis for the ESOP valuation will differ depending on whether or not the block of stock subject to the valuation carries elements of control. Generally, a buyer of a controlling ownership interest will pay more for the stock, as discussed in Chapter 15.

In some control ESOP transactions, no changes are expected to enhance cash flows. Although technically a control premium may be applied to these transactions, the application of a control premium may not be prudent. Even though interim cash flows may not reflect enhanced cash flows, the ESOP, as a control shareholder, could sell the company and receive a control price. Most analysts take the position that the ESOP should be able to pay whatever a hypothetical third-party buyer would pay for the block of stock being purchased, including control.

The following are some factors, among others, to consider when estimating the appropriate control premium, if any, to apply in ESOP valuations:

1. The elements of control inherent in the particular block of stock.
2. The degree of control—effective, operating, and absolute.
3. The aggregate interest purchased or held by the ESOP regardless of whether the sellers constituted minority or controlling interests.
4. The potential for control, such as binding agreements with other shareholders that result in the passing of control to the ESOP.
5. The effects related to the distribution of stock ownership.
6. Any empirical evidence of control premiums actually paid in similar transactions.
7. Any value enhancements that may result from the passing of control (e.g., effective use of leverage, elimination of excess compensation paid to selling shareholders, sale of undervalued assets).
8. Any value enhancement due to a put right.
9. The rights and obligations under the employer corporation's articles of incorporation and state law.
10. Whether the company's articles of incorporation or state law provides for cumulative voting.
11. Contractual restrictions under the company's debt agreements or employment contracts.
12. Effects of regulations, including state statutes (i.e., what constitutes majority for voting purposes).
13. The current financial condition and policies of the company.

If the ESOP purchases control over a period of time instead of in one transaction, the issue of whether a control premium applies becomes more complex. Evidence in the public marketplace generally suggests that control premiums are paid along the entire spectrum of creeping control, although at different levels. Consistency among ESOP valuations from year to year is essential for the fair treatment and nondiscrimination of employee participants. Thus, if a control premium has been applied in past ESOP valuations, there is a tendency among analysts to continue this practice.

Discount for Lack of Marketability

There is still continuing controversy surrounding the extent to which a lack of marketability discount should be applied in ESOP valuations. Marketability is the ability of the stock to be sold and turned into cash quickly. On the one end of the marketability spectrum, there are relatively few potential buyers for shares in most closely held companies (especially of noncontrolling ownership interests). On the other end of the spectrum, shares in publicly traded corporations have almost instant marketability on an organized exchange and high liquidity, since the seller can receive cash within three business days.

Put Option and Repurchase Liability

The economic factor that generally distinguishes ESOP shares in closely held corporations is that a "put option" is required to be attached to the ESOP shares. Without this put option, employees could be forced to hold employer securities for extended periods of time. The put option requires the employer to provide the needed liquidity by repurchasing the distributed employer securities. This employer obligation to purchase shares is referred to generally as the repurchase obligation. Under Code Section 409(h)(1)(B), employer securities that are acquired by an ESOP after December 31, 1979, must be subject to a put option if the securities are not readily tradable on an organized market at the time of the distributions to employee participants.

Employer corporation securities acquired with the proceeds of an ESOP loan after September 30, 1976, must also be subject to a put option, if the shares are not readily tradable on distribution. For employer securities not subject to these mandatory put option requirements, the company may provide a voluntary put option.

The DOL proposed regulations guide the analyst to consider (1) the extent to which the put rights are enforceable and (2) the company's ability to meet its obligation. Most ESOP valuation practitioners "interpret the ESOP put right as substantially mitigating, if not eliminating, any marketability discount that would otherwise apply."[4]

The principal economic factors that influence the discount for lack of marketability with regard to ESOP employer securities are as follows:

1. The provisions of the ESOP plan documents, including the put rights.
2. The financial strength and solvency of the employer corporation.
3. The size of the share block owned by the ESOP.
4. The degree of liquidity in the ESOP trust and the company.
5. The extra borrowing capacity of the employer corporation.
6. The repurchase liability and the expected funding requirements.
7. The extent to which the company has planned and managed the repurchase liability.
8. Past practices in repurchases by the company.
9. The form and timing of payments to selling shareholders and ESOP lenders.
10. The overall priority of acknowledged and contingent claims that may conflict with achieving liquidity for plan participants over time.

The ESOP company can best plan for the repurchase liability by setting corporation policies regarding how repurchases will be handled. These policies will aid the analyst in assessing the lack of marketability discount. The repurchase liability is discussed in greater detail later in this chapter.

Current Controversies

The *Eyler* case (discussed in Chapter 33) and others have created a resurgence of the lack of marketability discount issue in ESOPs. The general trend is an attempt by the IRS to significantly increase the lack of marketability discount applied in ESOP trans-

---

[4] J. Michael Julius, "ESOP Appraisals and Non-ESOP Shareholders," *CPA Litigation Service Counselor*, July 1998, p. 9.

actions to reduce deductions from taxable income available to the ESOP company. The bases for these opinions are not entirely justified. First of all, *Eyler* was a fact pattern that included violations of ESOP valuation and fiduciary guidelines. The marketability issue was a minor issue that was not even technically debated. The judge merely commented on marketability as an issue in the opinion.

In addition, in order to justify such a position, the analyst has to assume that the DOL misunderstood the definition of fair market value when drafting the language relating to lack of marketability discounts in the adequate consideration regulations. The other erroneous assumption needed is that the true economics of the put option should not be considered because it is not a right that is attached to the security. The put right is, however, a statutory right under the Code. The ESOP does not sell this right but most noncontrolling investors negotiate some buyout provision when the investment decision is made.

Despite all the debate over substantial lack of marketability discounts for ESOP transactions, the typical practice remains that these discounts should be under 10 percent. However, due to the recent controversies, many ESOP fiduciaries are taking the position that some discount should be applied to protect from protracted litigation.

Post-Transaction Value in Leveraged ESOPs

After the ESOP purchases employer securities, the company has a significant demand on cash flow for debt repayments. Unless the sponsoring company receives substantial future cost or tax savings, the fair market value of the ESOP shares immediately after the transaction is reduced. This reduction in value is directly attributable to the reduction in cash flow available to the common equity as a result of the company's obligation to amortize the ESOP debt.

The tax shield created by the ESOP debt mitigates the reduction in value. This ESOP tax shield can be quantified by computing the present value of the tax savings over the period of the ESOP Loan. The present value of the ESOP tax shield would then be added back to equity value. It is important to note that, if the ESOP Loan and Bank Loan payments are not congruous, the present value of the tax shield is coincident with payments made on the ESOP Loan—not the Bank Loan. Payments on the ESOP Loan trigger the deductibility of principal payments.

If the value of the company does not change over the period the ESOP Loan is amortized, this reduction in value is recovered. However, it is important to note that the valuation impact is tied to the Bank Loan—not the ESOP Loan. It is the company's obligation to outside lenders that triggers the effect on common equity value.

Legislative and Regulatory Issues in ESOPs

The valuation practitioner conducting ESOP valuations needs to have a general understanding of the legislative and regulatory issues that impact ESOPs. The following is a general discussion of some of the legislated rules regarding ESOPs. These legal aspects of ESOPs are complex and further discussions with qualified ERISA counsel are necessary before implementing an ESOP.

Section 1042 Rollover

Code Section 1042 generally provides that, if certain requirements are met, no gain will be recognized by the selling shareholder upon the sale to an ESOP. The requirements of this tax deferral include:

- Immediately after the sale to the ESOP, the ESOP must own at least 30 percent of the voting stock of the business or 30 percent of the value of the business.
- Qualified replacement property (QRP) must be purchased with the proceeds within a 15-month period beginning three months prior to the sale to the ESOP. QRP is generally defined as stocks and bonds of domestic operating corporations.
- The selling shareholder must have owned the securities sold to the ESOP for at least three years prior to the sale.

The gain is deferred until the sale of the QRP. And, if the selling shareholder holds the QRP in his estate, the gain is never taxed, due to the step up in basis allowed upon death.

409(l) Employer Securities

The ESOP must purchase an employer security that meets the requirements of Code Section 409(l). This Code section generally provides that the security purchased by the ESOP be (1) the highest voting common stock, or (2) convertible into the highest voting common stock.

Principal Deductibility and Code Section 415

The company may deduct dividends paid on employer securities held by a leveraged ESOP, provided that the dividends paid are reasonable and are either (1) paid in cash directly to the participants after receipt by the ESOP trust, or (2) used to make payments on the ESOP Loan. At times, the ESOP valuation analyst may be asked to opine on the reasonableness of the ESOP dividend.

Dividends used to make payments on the ESOP Loan are not included in ESOP participants' annual additions for purposes of the Code Section 415 contribution limitations. This provision allows an ESOP design that provides for a dividend-paying security to enhance the debt payment abilities under the ESOP Loan without the constraints of the 25 percent of compensation limitations under Code Section 415.

Code Section 133 Interest Exclusion

There are still some Code Section 133 loans in existence, so this provision does bear mentioning—although briefly. Code Section 133 provided for an exclusion from taxable income of 50 percent of the interest earned on the ESOP debt by the ESOP lender. Certain conditions had to be met. Code Section 133 was repealed in August of 1996.

The IRS Audit Guidelines

The IRS has audited ESOPs from time to time. IRS Announcement 95-33 contains finalized examination guidelines for (among other things) audits of ESOPs. Familiarity with these guidelines will assist the valuation practitioner when analyzing the ESOP transaction structure and valuation issues so as to protect the transaction and valuations from attack by the IRS. These guidelines address the issues of (1) how much is "primarily invested," (2) the ESOP exempt loan, (3) the Code Section 1042 rollover, (4) the Code Section 415 limitations, (5) dividends paid on ESOP stock, (6) the ESOP put option, (7) voting rights, (8) the date of the appraisal, (9) adequate consideration, (10) the independence of the appraiser, (11) appraisal conclusions, (12) subsequent events, and (13) proceeds from the sale of unallocated shares.

ESOP Specific Plan Administration Issues

The ESOP Association has published an Administration Handbook that was designed to assist its members on ESOP administration, record keeping, compliance, and technical issues. The following is a general discussion of some of the plan administration issues in ESOPs. These plan administration aspects of ESOPs are complex, and further discussions with a qualified, experienced ESOP plan administrator is necessary before implementing an ESOP.

An ESOP is a qualified plan and must therefore meet the minimum coverage, distribution, vesting, and participation requirements under ERISA. This section will focus on the issues specific to ESOP plan administration. Knowledge of the general requirements of qualified plans is assumed.

A general understanding of ESOP plan administration issues is an important concept for the ESOP valuation practitioner because it impacts the size and timing of the company's repurchase obligation.

Allocations to Participant Accounts

The ESOP plan document governs the operation of the ESOP. Therefore, the starting point in determining the allocations to participant accounts is the plan documents. The company then completes an employee census that consists of gathering certain demographic data on employees. The plan administrator then determines who among the employees is eligible to participate in the ESOP allocations.

The number of shares that are released from the plan is determined based on a choice between two methods. The first method is an allocation based on the ratio of principal paid in the current year over the total principal obligation. The second method is similar except that principal and interest are considered. Since interest payments are greater in the first years of an ESOP, participant allocations will be faster under the principal and interest method.

This ratio is then applied to the number of shares in the suspense account. Immediately after the leveraged ESOP transactions, all the shares are in suspense or "encumbered by debt." As the debt is paid, the shares are no longer encumbered and are thus released from suspense and allocated to eligible participant accounts.

Exhibit 32–3 is a graphical depiction of the allocation of ESOP shares over a seven-year ESOP loan. The participant account is further subject to vesting provisions on allocated shares.

Dividends are allocated in a different manner. Dividends on allocated shares that are not used to make payments on the ESOP debt are allocated to respective accounts of the participants to whom the shares are allocated. When dividend payments on allocated shares are used to repay an ESOP loan, shares will be released from the suspense account due to such payments.

Distribution Policy

Distribution of benefits from an ESOP must commence no later than one year after the close of the plan year (1) in which the participant terminates employment due to reaching normal retirement age, disability, or death; or (2) which is the fifth plan year following the plan year in which the participant separates from service with the employer.

Distributions of securities acquired with the proceeds of an ESOP loan may be delayed until the loan is repaid. Benefits to ESOP participants may be distributed in installments over five years (up to 10 years where the benefits exceed $710,000). The ESOP participant has the right to demand a distribution of employer securities unless the articles of incorporation or bylaws restrict ownership of employer securities to employees.

Diversification

Qualified ESOP participants may elect to diversify their accounts. A qualified participant includes one who has attained age 55 and has at least 10 years participation in the ESOP. The election period is a six-year period that begins with or in the plan year during which the participant becomes qualified. The first five elections

Exhibit 32–3

Illustrative Example of the Allocation of ESOP Shares

are limited to 25 percent of the participant's account balance. The final year, the qualified participant may diversify up to 50 percent of the account balance attributable to such participant.

Since the company also must provide the liquidity necessary for these diversification requirements, the company must consider these obligations in estimating the cash flow requirements of the ESOP.

Finance Issues in Leveraged ESOPs

Other qualified retirement plans are prohibited from borrowing funds under the prohibited transaction rules. ERISA Section 408(b)(3) and Code Section 4975(d)(3) contain the provisions that exempt the ESOP from this prohibited transaction rule. The following is a *general discussion* of some of the finance issues in ESOPs. These finance aspects of ESOPs are complex, and further discussion with an experienced ESOP lender is necessary before implementing an ESOP.

At times the ESOP valuation practitioner also may render a fairness opinion that includes a statement that the leveraged ESOP transaction is fair from a financial point of view. This fairness opinion requires an understanding of the typical terms and conditions offered by lenders in this type of transaction.

The leveraged ESOP transaction is significantly different from conventional financing. The inexperienced ESOP lender typically is concerned with the accounting provisions that can result in negative equity on the ESOP company's balance sheet. The ESOP lender also must consider the enhanced cash flow associated with the deductibility of principal payments in order to be competitive. Generally, the debt service coverage analysis is performed on a pretax basis. In addition, the pledge of Code Section 1042 securities is a typical structure in the ESOP financing that can make up for collateral shortfalls.

ESOP lenders also need to have an understanding of the leveraged ESOP to complete these transactions. For example, the ESOP lender may be concerned if the ESOP valuation is extremely aggressive. Benefit allocation issues can affect cash flows and thus the ability of the ESOP lender to be repaid. The repayment terms of an ESOP loan may be tied to Code Section 415/404 limitations. Certainly these constraints are important in the financing structure of the leveraged ESOP transaction. Other issues considered by the ESOP lender include environmental issues, product liability or other contingent liability issues, change of control issues, management continuity issues, and trustee issues.

If the ESOP valuation practitioner is issuing a fairness opinion, a review of the credit agreement is necessary to understand all the terms of the financing. A clear understanding of the constraints and benefits of the ESOP transaction is essential to the review of this document and the fairness of a transaction.

Repurchase Liability

Does repurchase liability affect the fair market value of ESOP stock? This has been a long debated and still unanswered question. However, today there is a better understanding of the repurchase liability and its impact on the economics of the ESOP company.

The repurchase liability is created by the employer's obligation to purchase shares from the ESOP trust at the time the participant receives a distribution. There are two methods that can be used by the company to satisfy the obligation. The general effect of each of these transactions on fair market value is discussed below.

Repurchase or Recycling

The first method is called a repurchase or recycling transaction. In a "repurchase," the ESOP trust purchases the shares of withdrawing participants and recycles them to other ESOP participants in the plan. The trust's cash for the purchase comes from the company in the form of a deductible employer contribution. If the amount of this employer contribution is in excess of a market level of employee benefits, the recycling transaction can be dilutive. The recycling transaction is a transfer of ownership between former and current ESOP participants. Exhibit 32–4 illustrates this repurchase transaction.

Redemption

The second method is called a redemption transaction. In a "redemption," the shares are purchased directly by the company and then canceled. Redemptions by design are nondilutive. Exhibit 32–5 illustrates this method.

Although redemptions do not use tax-deductible contributions, since the shares are no longer considered outstanding, the net effect on fair market value should be negligible if the transaction occurs at fair market value. The transfer of ownership in the redemption transaction is between former participants and all remaining shareholders. Since the shares are canceled in the redemption, the percentage ownership of all the remaining shareholders, including ESOP participants, increases. However, the amount of the ESOP trust's ownership percentage declines.

Exhibit 32–4

Repurchase of Shares from Participants

Exhibit 32–5

Redemption of ESOP Shares by the Company

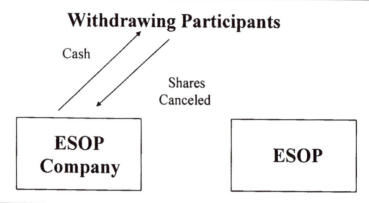

Managing the Repurchase Liability

When the ESOP company decides to recycle shares, a compensation event occurs. The redemption more closely resembles a capital transaction. The complexities of the ESOP contain the concept that the same dollar compensates employees as well as creates an equity obligation.

In order to manage the repurchase liability, management must decide on a compensation policy separate from the decision on who should be the shareholders of the company over the long term. Then, the decisions regarding repurchases of shares are clear. The following three choices indicate what actions would be necessary to comply with both objectives.

1. If the contributions (net of tax and dividends) necessary to fund the repurchase liability are within the amount agreed upon in the compensation policy, then recycling makes sense.
2. If the contributions (net of tax and dividends) necessary to fund the repurchase liability are below the amount agreed upon in the compensation policy, then an additional cash contribution may be necessary.
3. If the contributions (net of tax and dividends) necessary to fund the repurchase liability are greater than the agreed upon compensatory amount, then the company should redeem the shares above the set limit and recycle for the compensatory amount.

The employer can use any combination of redemption and recycling transactions. And, just as the ESOP solves an ownership transition problem, it creates one. However, the ESOP operates like a perpetual redemption program for ESOP participants if recycling is always chosen. And, the timing of the obligation is determined through the operation of the plan provisions. Planning for and managing this obligation should be completed annually both on a short-term and on a long-term basis. Repurchase liability studies that consider actuarial assumptions are helpful tools in this process.

Methods of Funding

There are a number of alternative strategies for funding the repurchase obligation. The following listing contains some options.

- Current cash flow.
- Additional cash contributions.
- Company debt.
- Company sinking fund.
- Life insurance.
- Sale to a third party.
- Initial public offering.
- Employee purchases.
- Use of 401(k) balances.
- Liquidation.

Management must consider the effect of these decisions have on both compensation and share ownership.

Fiduciary Issues in ESOPs

The following is a *general discussion* of some of the fiduciary issues in ESOPs. These fiduciary aspects of ESOPs are complex, and further discussion with an independent fiduciary or ERISA counsel are necessary before implementing an ESOP. Valuation practitioners are not fiduciaries and should be sure that their actions would not make them a fiduciary.

The independent valuation adviser is hired directly by the ESOP fiduciary or trustee even though the valuation fees are paid by the company. Thus, the ESOP's independent financial adviser needs an understanding of the role of the ESOP trustee and how the valuation assignment interfaces with that role. Valuation analysts should pay particular attention to voting rights as they affect the fairness of the leveraged ESOP transaction.

General fiduciary duties that apply to ESOP fiduciaries are outlined in ERISA (the Overriding ERISA Fiduciary Standards). These duties apply to all trustee actions. ERISA requires the fiduciary to manage and administer the ESOP trust (1) solely in the interests of plan participants and beneficiaries; (2) for the exclusive purpose of providing benefits to plan participants and their beneficiaries and defraying reasonable expenses of administering the ESOP trust; (3) with the care, skill, prudence, and diligence that, under the circumstances then prevailing, a prudent man or woman acting in like capacity and familiar with such matters would use in the conduct of an enterprise of a like character and with like aims; (4) in accordance with the plan and trust agreement in most circumstances; and (5) in accordance with applicable requirements of the law.

Voting Issues

When the ESOP holds unregistered securities (privately held stock not traded on an exchange), the participants in the plan must be given the right to vote allocated shares with respect to any corporate matter that involves the voting of such shares with respect to any corporate merger or consolidation, recapitalization, reclassification, liquidation, dissolution, or sale of substantially all assets of a trade or business, or such similar transaction as may be prescribed by regulation (Code Section 409(e)(3)).

Trustee's Voting Rights

The ESOP trustee votes the unallocated shares. However, voting of both allocated and unallocated shares is subject to the Overriding ERISA Fiduciary Standards discussed in the previous section. The ESOP plan's provisions for voting unallocated shares can include any of the following three options:

1. The fiduciary can vote the stock as directed by an ESOP committee.
2. The fiduciary can vote the unallocated stock in the same proportions as the employees vote allocated stock.
3. The fiduciary can always vote the stock in its discretion.

Although one of the Overriding ERISA Fiduciary Standards is to follow the provisions of the plan document, the fiduciary has the final responsibility and fiduciary duty with respect to voting of the stock. This is true regardless of the provisions in the plan document. In his or her discretion, a fiduciary can override the participant's direction if the fiduciary believes the directions are not in the best interests of the plan.

Circularity of Control

The Board of Directors of a company selects the ESOP trustee. The shareholders of the company vote on the members of the Board of Directors. If the ESOP trustee owns a controlling interest in the company, then the ESOP selects the Board of Directors. For obvious reasons this is sometimes referred to as the circularity of control.

Independent, Directed, or Internal Trustee

It is not required that companies retain an independent trustee. In practical terms, the trustee of the ESOP can be an officer or group of employees from the sponsoring company or members of the administration committee. However, due to the extent of fiduciary liability, it is prudent for the ESOP company to hire an independent bank or trust company. The ESOP plan document clearly defines the duties and responsibilities of the trustee and other fiduciaries. A directed trustee is typically an independent bank or trust company that is directed by the ESOP committee selected by the Board of Directors.

Each type of trustee is still required to meet the Overriding ERISA Fiduciary Standards previously discussed. Thus, it is important for ESOP trustees to have a complete understanding of their fiduciary duties and the resulting fiduciary liability. A complete discussion of these items is beyond the scope of this chapter.

Various actions can be taken against a fiduciary for breach of the fiduciary duties. Generally, any person who is a fiduciary with respect to a plan who breaches any of the responsibilities or duties imposed upon fiduciaries by ERISA, shall be *personally* liable to make good to such plan any losses to the plan resulting from each such breach. Therefore, this liability extends beyond the liability protection provided by incorporating a business. There are also civil penalties. It is entirely possible that an uneducated ESOP trustee could unknowingly breach a fiduciary duty.

Accounting for ESOPs

Most of the accounting rules that govern the accounting for ESOP related transactions are contained in the American Institute of Certified Public Accountants Statement of Position 93-6 (SOP 93-6). The following is a summary of its provisions excerpted from The ESOP Association's booklet on ESOP accounting standards.

Liabilities—All ESOP debt will be recorded on balance sheet of plan sponsor, no exceptions. Issue of push down of obligation to subsidiary is still present, but not discussed in SOP 93-6

Equity—Contra equity account will still be the offsetting entry. Contra account will change as compensation is recognized. Mezzanine capital issue is still present, but not discussed in SOP 93-6. Equity recorded may be adjusted for immediate post-transaction valuation changes.

Income—Compensation cost will be based upon the *fair market value* of the shares released or deemed to be released for the period.

Dividends—Any compensation cost obligation will not be reduced to the extent satisfied with dividends on allocated shares. Dividends on allocated shares retain character of true dividends.

Earnings per share—Unreleased shares will *not* be considered to be outstanding. All convertible preferred shares will be considered to be common stock equivalents.

Disclosures—Repurchase liability as reflected by the current value of allocated shares must be disclosed, the use of an actuarial estimate of this future obligation is not authorized.

Effective Date—The SOP 93-6 is effective for ESOP stock acquisitions after December 31, 1992. Sponsors of ESOPs that were formed prior to the effective date can elect the SOP 93-6. The reporting in the standard is required for financial periods beginning after December 15, 1992.[5]

Since the ESOP company's auditor needs the fair market value of the ESOP shares to complete the income statement, there is a timing issue. The ESOP valuation practitioner needs the audit in order to complete the valuation. The typical procedure is for the ESOP valuation analyst to work with a preliminary audit that is only preliminary due to the ESOP compensation adjustment. The valuation is then conducted and the conclusion is communicated to the auditor. Then the audited financial statements can be finalized. The valuation is actually further finalized to reflect the fair market value entry made by the auditors. However, since the compensation expense entry is adjusted in the determination of normalized earnings, there is no valuation impact after the final audit report is issued.

---

[5] *ESOP Accounting Standards* (Washington, DC: The ESOP Association, 1999), p. 3.

There are no regulations that specifically say that the auditor cannot also be the ESOP valuation adviser. However, since the valuation is an input to the audit, it seems difficult to say that the auditor is independent with respect to the valuation. Leading ESOP attorneys strongly advise against an ESOP using the company's auditor as its valuation adviser. As of this writing, the Independence Standards Board is considering this issue.

Nuances of S Corporation ESOPs

The Small Business Job Protection Act of 1996 (the 1996 Act) amended the Code to allow ESOPs to hold shares of an S corporation, effective for tax years beginning after December 31, 1997; and the Taxpayer Relief Act of 1997 (the 1997 Act) added an exemption for S corporation ESOPs to the unrelated business income tax (UBIT Exemption). The following is a general summary of the specific aspects of S corporation ESOPs as they differ from C corporation ESOPs.

The new laws have only been in place for two years. Although some of the issues have been settled, there is still significant uncertainty regarding some important technical issues. In addition, legislative changes are still expected. Two proposals to limit the benefits of S corporation ESOPs have already been considered by Congress.

The combination of S corporation tax law, ERISA, qualified plan requirements, and ESOPs adds even more complexities to the leveraged ESOP transaction.

Limitations on S Corporation Tax Benefits

Code Section 1042. The Section 1042 election is not available to shareholders in S corporations. However, in many cases, shareholders of S corporations have built up significant tax bases in the shares of their S corporations. S corporation shareholders realize an increase in tax basis equivalent to their pro rata share of the corporation's earnings annually. Shareholder basis in S corporations is reduced by distributions. The benefits of Section 1042 become less important the higher the shareholder's basis in the stock.

Dividend Deductibility. Dividend deductibility provisions of Code Section 404(k) do not apply in the S corporation context. In situations in which the annual ESOP loan payments exceed the maximum amount that can be contributed to an ESOP under Code Section 415, it is possible in C corporations to cover this shortfall with tax deductible dividends. The S corporation does not have this structuring option.

Limitations on Contributions to the Plan. The increased limit for tax deductions for contributions to a leveraged ESOP, when used to pay principal and interest, is not available to the S corporation. These limitations are 25 percent of compensation for C corporations and 15 percent of compensation for S corporations. However, an S corporation can increase the limits by implementing a combined ESOP/Money Purchase Pension Plan.

In addition, interest expense may be excluded from the Code Section 415 limitations if certain tests are met with respect to highly compensated employees. This exclusion is not available to S corporation ESOPs.

Voting Issues

Since the S corporation ESOP is not publicly traded, the voting issues reflect that circumstance. Thus, the voting rights of the participants in an S corporation ESOP may be limited to certain matters as previously discussed in the previous section on voting rights.

Form of Distribution

Not all possible shareholders are eligible S corporation shareholders (i.e., nonresident aliens, IRAs, certain trusts, etc.). In addition, if individual shareholder participants are allowed to maintain share ownership upon a distribution, the S corporation could reach a point in which it violated the 75 shareholder limit. The ESOP trust is considered one shareholder for purposes of this S corporation rule, but departing participants would not be included. Thus, inadvertent terminations of S corporation status could occur. The S corporation ESOP company may, therefore, require employees to take their benefits in the form of cash.

S Corporation Distributions

Distributions on Allocated Shares. As of this writing, the IRS has taken the position that distributions by S corporations on stock that is not pledged as collateral to secure the ESOP loan cannot be used to make payments on that loan, even though this is not so in the C corporation context, although the technical arguments for this position are not coincident with legislative history and the intent of the S corporation ESOP laws.

Distributions Paid in Cash to Participants. In the C corporation context, dividends paid on ESOP shares that are distributed directly to participants are not subject to the excise tax on premature distributions. The ability to have participants receive company dividends without incurring an excise tax does not extend to S corporations.

Steps to Implementing an ESOP

The following is a summary of the steps to implementing a leveraged ESOP. These steps are intended to follow a logical sequence.

1. Retain qualified advisers with areas of expertise described in this chapter.
2. Conduct a feasibility study that addresses all of the constraints in ESOP transactions to see if an ESOP makes sense from a financial point of view.
3. Design and structure a transaction that addresses those constraints.
4. Estimate the value of the company.
5. Consider the design of the plan and trust provisions.
6. Obtain financing for the transaction.
7. Estimate the repurchase liability.

8. Begin the process of plan administration.
9. Use an effective communication program to inform employees.

Summary

The reader should now be equipped with an understanding of the ESOP valuation issues as they differ from typical valuation techniques. The other professional disciplines involved in the ESOP transaction interface with the valuation professional. Therefore, it is important that the valuation professional also have a general knowledge of the other areas of expertise.

In a typical leveraged ESOP transaction, the valuation adviser may rely on other professionals in their areas of expertise to assist in resolving the issues that surface. The sections of this chapter addressing the expertise of other professionals involved in the ESOP transaction are intended to assist the appraiser in "surfacing issues" and addressing "fairness" concerns.

Bibliography

Articles

Abello, Kim S., and Robert S. Socol. "The Leveraged ESOP Transaction" (Chapter 8A). In *Financial Valuation: Business and Business Interests, 1997 Update*, Robert F. Reilly and Robert P. Schweihs, eds. New York: Warren Gorham & Lamont, 1997.

Ackerman, David. "Technical Issues under the New S Corporation ESOP Laws." *Journal of Employee Ownership Law and Finance*, Winter 1999, pp. 3–19.

Berka, Jack W. "An ESOP Update Review of Current Issues." Presentation to the International Conference of the American Society of Appraisers, June 1997. Available on www.BVLibrary.com.

Bonn, Karen. "Feasibility Studies Help Avoid ESOP Foibles." *The Tax Adviser*, February 1999, pp. 82–83.

Brown, Karen W. "Payment of Control Premiums by ESOPs." *ESOP Report*, November/December 1993, pp. 6–8.

Hall, C. Wells III. "The S Corporation ESOP: Incentivised Employee Stock Ownership or Tax Gimmickry?" *Business Entities*, January/February 1999, pp. 14–19, 62.

Kober, John A. "A Tool for Shareholder Liquidity, Estate Planning and Management Succession Planning." White paper (1999) available on www.BVLibrary.com.

Kubersky, Andrew S. "Marketability Discounts and ESOP Acquisitions of Minority Share Interests." *Journal of Employee Ownership Law and Finance*, Fall 1998, pp. 97–103.

Julius, J. Michael. "ESOP Appraisals and Non-ESOP Shareholders." *CPA Litigation Service Counselor*, July 1998, pp. 9–10.

Long, Dennis J. "Creating an ESOP Distribution Policy." *The Journal of Employee Ownership Law and Finance*, Summer 1997, pp. 85–92.

Long, Dennis J., Peter J. Prodoehl, and John P. Prodoehl. "Tracking ESOP Shares." *The Journal of Employee Ownership Law and Finance*, Summer 1995.

Mueller, Susan L. and Judith C. Gehr. "Valuation Issues in Multi-Investor ESOP LBOs" (Chapter 2). In *ESOP Valuation*, Scott S. Rodrick, ed. Oakland, CA: The National Center for Employee Ownership, 1999.

Reilly, Robert F. "Current Issues in the Valuations of ESOP-Owned Securities." *Journal of Pension Planning & Compliance*, Winter 1996, pp. 47–60.

Regnitz, Timothy J. "Understanding the ESOP Repurchase Obligation." *The Journal of Employee Ownership Law and Finance*, Winter 1999, pp. 21–34.

"Repurchase Liability: What ESOP Companies Should Know About It." *The ESOP Newsletter of McBride Baker and Coles*, Winter 2000.

Sandquist, Andrew, and John J. Cresto. "Anticipating and Avoiding ESOP Financing Obstacles," *The Journal of Employee Ownership Law and Finance*, Summer 1999, pp. 63–72.

Suhre, Karen K. "Should the ESOP-Owned Company Elect to Become an S Corporation?" *Benefits Law Journal*, Spring 1998.

Books

Ash, Merri E., Virginia J. Bartlett, et al. *The ESOP Association Administration Handbook*. Washington, DC: The ESOP Association, 1996.

An Employer's Guide to Employee Stock Ownership Plans. St. Paul, MN: Minnesota Small Business Assistance Office, Minnesota Department of Trade and Economic Development, 1994.

ESOP Accounting Standards. Washington, DC: The ESOP Association, 1999.

Fisch, Robert A. *The ESOP Handbook: Practical Strategies for Achieving Corporate Financing Goals*. New York: John Wiley & Sons, 1994, supplemented 1998.

How the ESOP Really Works. Washington, DC: The ESOP Association, 1997.

An Introduction to ESOP Valuations. Washington, DC: The ESOP Association, 1997.

Kaplan, Jared, John E. Curtis Jr., and Gregory K. Brown. *ESOPs* (Tax Management Portfolio). Washington, DC: Tax Management Inc., 1991.

Report on Valuation Considerations for Leveraged ESOPs. Washington, DC: The ESOP Association, 1998.

Rodrick, Scott S., ed. *Leveraged ESOPs and Employee Buyouts*. Oakland, CA: The National Center for Employee Ownership, 1998.

_____. *ESOP Valuation*. Oakland, CA: The National Center for Employee Ownership, 1999.

Rosen, Cory. *Understanding ESOP Valuation*. Oakland, CA: The National Center for Employee Ownership, 2000.

Smiley, Robert W. Jr., and Ronald J. Gilbert, eds. *Employee Stock Ownership Plans: Business Planning, Implementation, and Law and Taxation*. New York: Warren, Gorham & Lamont, 1991, supplemented annually.

Structuring Leveraged ESOP Transactions. Washington, D.C: The ESOP Association, 1999.

ESOP Association Briefs

"The Benefits of Employee Stock Ownership" (1995).

"Employee Ownership & Corporate Performance" (1997).

"ESOP Accounting" (1995).

"The ESOP as an Employee Benefit" (1995).

"ESOP Distributions" (1997).

"ESOP Diversification" (1996).

"ESOP Dividends" (1996).

"ESOP Facts & Figures" (1996).
"ESOP Fiduciary Issues" (1996).
"ESOP Financing" (1996).
"ESOP/401(k) Plans" (1995).
"ESOP Repurchase Obligation" (1996).
"The ESOP Tax-Free Rollover" (1997).
"ESOPs and Subchapter S Corporations" (1997).
"Federal Legislative History" (1997).
"How to Establish an ESOP" (1997).
"The Policy of Broadened Ownership" (1995).
"Tax Advantages for Business Planning" (1996).
"Using Convertible Preferred Stock in ESOPs" (1996).
"The Valuation of ESOP Stock" (1997).
"Voting Rights of ESOP Stock" (1996).
"What is an ESOP?" (1995).

Associations
The ESOP Association
1726 M Street N.W., Suite 501
Washington, DC 20036
(202) 293-2971
www.esopassociation.org

The National Center for Employee Ownership
1736 Franklin Street, 8th floor
Oakland, CA 94612
(510) 272-9461
www.nceo.org

Chapter 33

ESOP Court Cases

Introduction
Sommers Drug Stores
    Introduction
    The Facts of the District Court Case
    The Facts of the Appeal
    The Plaintiff's Position
    The Defendants' Position
    Commentary and Conclusion
Hines v. Schlimgen
    Introduction
    Commentary and Conclusion
U.S. News & World Report
    Introduction
    The Facts of the Case
    The Valuation Issues
    The District Court's Decision
    The Appeals Court's Decision
    Commentary and Conclusion
Andrade v. Parsons
    Introduction
    The Facts of the Case
    The Facts of the Complaint
    The District Court's Decision
    The Appeals Court's Decision
    Commentary and Conclusion
Reich v. Valley National Bank of Arizona
    Introduction
    The District Court's Findings
    Commentary and Conclusion
Howard v. Shay
    Introduction
    The Facts of the Case
    The District Court's Decision
    The District Court's Decision—Commentary and Conclusion
    The Appeals Court's Decision

Introduction

The judicial decisions selected for review in this chapter should be of particular interest to ESOP valuation practitioners and ESOP financial advisers. Many of these decisions indicate what the courts are looking for with regard to (1) the content of valuation analyses and (2) the quality of valuation reports.

In addition, many of these decisions should be of interest to ESOP trustees, ESOP attorneys, and other ESOP practitioners. In addition to employer corporation stock valuation issues, many of these cases involve the fiduciary responsibilities of ESOP trustees—particularly with regard to reliance upon independent financial advisers during an ESOP stock purchase or sale transaction.

Because of the mix of fiduciary and valuation issues, unlike the other court case chapters, we have organized this chapter by case, rather than by valuation issue. As is true with the other court case chapters in this book, the full texts of cases are available to on-line library subscribers at www.BVLibrary.com.

Sommers Drug Stores

Introduction

In *Sommers Drug Stores Co. v. Corrigan Enterprises, Inc.,*[1] the U.S. Court of Appeals provided useful guidance with regard to what factors a valuation analyst

---

[1] *Sommers Drug Stores Co. v. Corrigan Enterprises, Inc.,* 793 F.2d 1456 (5th Cir. 1986).

should consider with regard to the valuation of close corporation stock for ERISA compliance purposes. Valuation practitioners should note the guidance provided by the Appeals Court in this case.

The Facts of the District Court Case

In December 1997, the trustee of the Sommers Drug Stores Company ("Sommers") employee profit sharing trust accepted an offer to sell the trust's holdings of stock in the company back to the company for $10,000 per share. Before the time of the stock sale, the company had sold its drug store operations. At the time of the sale from the profit sharing trust, Sommers was primarily a holding company owning cash and real estate. At that time, the trust owned approximately 20 percent of the Sommers outstanding stock.

In December 1980, the trust sued the company and its principal stockholder for breach of fiduciary duty under ERISA and under common law in connection with the stock sale. At the trial court level, the trust's expert witness testified that the stock was worth $27,171 per share. The defendants' expert testified at the trial level that the stock was worth only $8,500 per share.

At the trial, the jury found that both the principal stockholder and the company had breached their fiduciary duty under ERISA. It found that the stock was worth $27,171 per share. After granting the defendants' motion for a remittitur (i.e., a petition to reduce the damages that the jury had assessed), the District Court entered a judgment in favor of the trust for $552,612 in actual damages and $1,250,000 for punitive damages. The punitive damages were assessed $500,000 against the principal stockholder and $750,000 against the company.

The Facts of the Appeal

The principal stockholder and the company appealed. The U.S. Court of Appeals for the Fifth Circuit remanded the case for further proceedings. The Appeals Court held that "there is insufficient evidence in the record to support the jury's finding of fair market value, upon which the district court's judgment of actual damages was based." The Appeals Court also held that the trust could not recover punitive damages under the applicable section of ERISA.

The Plaintiff's Position

The method of the plaintiff's expert for estimating fair market value per share was (1) to sum all the Sommers net assets—including the discounted present value of a 10-year employment contract received by the principal stockholder in connection with the sale of the drug store operations—and (2) to then divide by the number of shares outstanding.

The Defendants' Position

The defendants' principal contention was that the testimony of the plaintiff's expert lacked probative value. This is because his valuation conclusion was based on an asset liquidation value rather than on fair market value of the business.

The Appeals Court agreed with the defendants' position, stating:

> On cross-examination [the witness] acknowledged that market value and asset value were different measures, but he asserted that in this case they were the same. We conclude that [the witness's] testimony was so conclusory and lacking in analysis that no jury could reasonably have relied on it in determining the fair market value of the Trust's stock.

A particularly informative part of this decision from the perspective of the valuation practitioner is what the Appeals Court said the expert *should have* considered in estimating the fair market value of the trust's shares of stock for purposes of ERISA. The Court's comments are presented in the following excerpts from the published opinion:

> Although ERISA does not define the term "fair market value," it is defined in other contexts as the price that a willing buyer would pay a willing seller, both having reasonable knowledge of the pertinent facts. . . . We conclude that this definition is appropriate for purposes of ERISA.
>
> Determining fair market value for the stock of a closely held company can be difficult; typically no readily available market exists in which to determine what willing buyers are prepared to pay. This problem has arisen most frequently in the estate tax context, and it is to that area of law that we turn for guidance. The Internal Revenue Service's estate tax regulations provide that closely held stock for which there is no available market price should be valued according to "the company's net worth, prospective earning power and dividend-paying capacity, and other relevant factors."

The Appeals Court noted that the "other relevant factors" that should have been considered by the expert include the following:

> The goodwill of the business; the economic outlook in the particular industry; the company's position in the industry and its management; the degree of control of the business represented by the block of stock to be valued; and the values of securities of corporations engaged in the same or similar lines of business which are listed on a stock exchange.

Particularly noteworthy to ESOP valuation practitioners is the Court's critique of the analysis of the plaintiff's appraiser:

> [The witness's] valuation ignored most of these factors. Of particular significance, he failed to consider that the Trust's stock represented a minority position in [the company]. He also neglected to consider the prices at which shares of comparable companies were traded on the national exchanges. He did not take account of the prices at which Sommers stock had changed hands in a series of tender offers between 1970 and 1977, one of the factors mentioned in Rev. Rul. 59-60. See Rev. Rul. 59-60 & 4.02(g), 1959-1 C.G. 237, 241-42; see also *Fitts' Estate v. Commissioner*, 237 F.2d 729, 731 (8th Cir. 1956). ("In determining the value of unlisted stocks, actual sales made in reasonable amount at arm's length, in the normal course of business, within a reasonable time before or after the basic date, are the best criterion of market value."); (*Duncan Industries, Inc. v. Commissioner*, 73 T.C. 266 91979) (same). Nor did [the witness] consider whether a discount for lack of marketability should be applied to the Trust's stock. See *Estate of Andrews v. Commissioner*, 79 T.C. 938, 953, 957 (1982).

We do not suggest that consideration of these factors would necessarily have changed [the witness's] valuation of the Trust's shares. Indeed in support of his apparent approach, we note that under Rev. Rul. 59-60, "[t]he value of the stock of a closely held investment or real estate holding company [which (the company) arguably was] . . . is closely related to the value of the assets underlying the stock." Rev. Rul. 59-60, & 5(b), 1959 1 C.B. 237, 243. But [the witness's] utter failure to consider other relevant factors, or to explain his reasons for disregarding them, renders his testimony unworthy of credit.

Commentary and Conclusion

The Appeals Court was blunt in its disapproval of the valuation analysis performed by the plaintiff's appraiser. In this case, the analyst applied the wrong standard of value (i.e., asset liquidation value versus fair market value), and the analyst effectively disregarded each and every one of the valuation factors delineated in Revenue Ruling 59-60. This classic (i.e., almost 15 years old at the time of this writing) decision still provides useful guidance to ESOP valuation analysts as to what factors should be considered in the ESOP valuation.

Hines v. Schlimgen

Introduction

In *Martin Hines et al. v. Frederick P. Schlimgen, Mark C. Rowley, and Rowley & Schlimgen, Inc.*,[2] the District Court both (1) concluded the value of the close corporation stock purchased by the ESOP and (2) faulted the conduct of the ESOP trustees for allowing the stock purchase to take place based on an obviously flawed stock valuation.

In the *Martin Hines* case, brought by a beneficiary, both the trustees and the company were held liable for the ESOP stock overvaluation.

On August 15, 1980, the Rowley & Schlimgen, Inc., employee stock ownership plan purchased 740 newly issued shares of common stock from the company for $125 per share. This ESOP stock purchase was made on the basis of a valuation of the company stock by an individual who subsequently became the controller of Rowley & Schlimgen, Inc. The District Court ultimately found the value of the Rowley & Schlimgen, Inc., stock to be $56 per share.

The District Court's decision determined that there had been a breach of fiduciary duty on the part of the ESOP trustees. The Court found (1) that the trustees had allowed the ESOP to purchase stock from the company at a price determined by an individual who was not independent and (2) that the stock valuation "was flawed in several respects." The Court held that both the trustees and the company were liable for the difference in the amount, plus costs and attorneys' fees.

In determining a $56 per share value for the ESOP stock, the court made frequent reference to Revenue Ruling 59-60. The following are some of many factors that the Court considered in its conclusion that the stock valuation was flawed:

---

[2] *Martin Hines et al. v. Frederick P. Schlimgen, Mark C. Rowley, and Rowley & Schlimgen, Inc.*, No. 85-C-1037-S U.S. Dist. Ct. (W.D. Wisc., Oct. 10, 1986).

1. A loss year was ignored without explanation in calculating the company's normalized earnings base.
2. Many company-specific facts were not considered, including management voids and weaknesses, lack of diversification, lack of computerization, and undercapitalization.
3. An inappropriate earnings pricing multiple was used.
4. There was no recognition of the fact that the ESOP stock was a noncontrolling ownership interest.

The District Court concluded that the appropriate discount for lack of control was 20 percent. The Court noted that "such discounts are often in the range of 20 to 30 percent and may go as high as 50 percent."

The Court finally concluded that the trustees' business judgment "was not in any way directed to the best and sole interests of the participants, which the law requires."

Commentary and Conclusion

This is another classic case of an ESOP appraisal that was prepared with total disregard of Revenue Ruling 59-60. To make matters worse, the analyst who performed the stock valuation was clearly not independent of the management of the employer corporation.

Perhaps most noteworthy to ESOP practitioners is the District Court's assessment of the due diligence (or lack thereof) performed by the ESOP trustees. This was one of the first in a line of judicial precedents in which the courts have concluded that ESOP trustees cannot naively rely upon the results of ESOP valuation reports.

U.S. News & World Report

Introduction

This case actually involves two related decisions: (1) *Charles S. Foltz, et al., v. U.S. News & World Report, Inc., et al.*, and (2) *David B. Richardson, et al., v. U.S. News & World Report, Inc., et al.*.[3] The Foltz case, a class-action case, dealt with the years 1973 through 1980; the Richardson case, not a class action case, covered 1981.

Although *U.S. News & World Report* cases concerned a profit-sharing plan and a stock bonus plan, the issues were similar to those that would have been involved in an ESOP. The case was, therefore, followed with great interest by ESOP valuation practitioners.

The Facts of the Case

Suits were brought by retirees who claimed that they were underpaid at retirement because the closely held stock of U.S. News & World Report, Inc. (U.S. News), was

---

[3] *Charles S. Foltz, et al., v. U.S. News & World Report, Inc., et al.*, No. 84-0447, U.S. Dist. Ct. (D.C. June 22, 1987) and *David B. Richardson, et al., v. U.S. News & World Report, Inc.*, et al., No. 85-2195, U.S. Dist. Ct. (D.C. June 22, 1987).

undervalued by independent appraisers in the years 1973 through 1981. The defendants included: (1) U.S. News, (2) certain U.S. News directors, (3) the U.S. News Profit-Sharing Plan (the plan), and (4) the independent appraisal company.

During their employment, the plaintiffs had participated in the profit sharing plan. The retired employees were also beneficial owners of stock in the company under its stock bonus plan. Upon retirement or separation, U.S. News employees liquidated their plan accounts and redeemed their stock interests.

The plaintiffs sought recovery of benefits they claimed were owed to them by virtue of an alleged undervaluation of the company's stock during the class period.

In 1962, the U.S. News stock was sold to various parties associated with the company, including the profit sharing plan, for a total consideration of $15 million. That transaction price was based on an independent appraisal.

In 1975, the U.S. News stock was appraised at $69 per share. By 1980, the appraised stock price had risen to $152 per share. And, in 1981, the U.S. News stock was appraised at $470 per share.

From 1962 until the company was sold in 1984, at $2,842 a share, the same independent appraisal firm appraised the company stock each year.

The amount of profit-sharing plan benefits distributed to retirees was based on the annual appraisal. In addition, the company exercised its option to purchase stock from certain stockholders who left the firm, at a price based on the annual appraisal.

Early in the 1970s, the profit-sharing plan ownership interest increased to the point of constituting a majority of the outstanding stock. The profit-sharing plan stock, as well as most of the nonplan stock, was voted by a voting trust.

After 1977, the voting trust could have been dissolved by a vote of the stock held by the profit sharing plan. However, there was never any movement to do so.

The company owned real estate at its headquarters located in Washington, D.C. During the 1970s, real estate values in the area increased significantly. There were discussions about developing the real estate for alternative uses, but no definite plans were implemented until 1981. At that time, an agreement was reached with Boston Properties for development of the property.

The Valuation Issues

In a 106-page memorandum opinion, the U.S. District Court judge stated that "the central issue requiring resolution in this litigation has always been the propriety of the methodology employed in appraising the U.S. News stock." The primary valuation issues in the case were as follows:

1. **Controlling versus Noncontrolling Ownership Interest Level of Value.** The annual appraisals valued the stock on a noncontrolling ownership interest basis. The plaintiffs contended that the stock should have been valued on a controlling ownership interest level of value.
2. **Discount for Lack of Marketability.** Most of the annual appraisals applied a 10 percent discount for lack of marketability. The plaintiffs contended that no discount for lack of marketability should have been taken. It is noteworthy that the stock had no put option. The company had a call option at the appraised price. The company exercised its call option consistently to retire stock from the stock bonus plan when employees left. Most such calls were for cash. However, on certain occasions, the company exercised its option to purchase the stock on

extended terms and at a low interest rate. This payment scheme was allowed under the call option.

3. **Importance of Real Estate and Other Assets.** The annual appraisals placed various weights on the real estate values in different years, depending on the circumstances at the time. In all years, however, the primary emphasis of the valuation was on the company's earning power. The plaintiffs argued that considerably more weight should have been accorded to the analysis and values of the real estate and certain other assets.

4. **Subsequent Events.** The annual appraisals valued the stock on a going-concern basis, taking into consideration only facts and circumstances as they were known or knowable as of the valuation date. The plaintiffs argued that prospects for future changes, such as those that would be instituted by a strategic buyer of the company (and thus impounded into the price that a buyer would be willing to pay for the company), should have been considered and reflected in the annual appraisals. As noted above, U.S. News was sold in 1984 at a price of $2,842 per share.

5. **Other Issues.** There were a variety of other allegations as to adjustments that the valuation analysts should have or should not have made to the company's income statements and balance sheets during the course of the annual appraisals.

The District Court's Decision

The Court's decision is particularly noteworthy for ESOP valuation practitioners. This abstract will highlight the most salient points. The Court concluded:

> After consideration of the expert testimony presented, the Court is not persuaded that the per share price arrived at each year by [the appraisal company] did not fall within a reasonable range of acceptable values.

Controlling versus Noncontrolling Ownership Interest Issue. Regarding the stock held by the plan, the District Court stated:

> [S]ince the terms of the U.S. News plan did not contemplate anything other than a series of minority-interest transactions… the valuation of its stock on a minority basis does not offend ERISA. . . .
>
> [V]arious individuals concurrently held undivided, minority interests in a control block of stock. . . . The mere fact that Plan members' interest, if added together, amounted to a majority of the outstanding shares in the company does not, standing alone, entitle them to pro rata control value.

The following language from the published decision addresses the control-versus-noncontrol ownership issue. In addition, this narrative strongly supports the acceptance of the analyst's judgment when reasonable valuation alternatives exist:

> Clearly, in the absence of any statutory, administrative or judicial authority for the proposition that a control value might have been indicated, defendants cannot be faulted for employing a minority valuation. . . . ERISA does not require plan fiduciaries to maximize the benefits of departing employees . . . ; it only requires them to make a reasonable choice from among possible alternatives.

The District Court also noted that the noncontrolling ownership interest level of value was consistent with the level of value used when the plan purchased the U.S. News stock in 1962 and in 1966.

Discount for Lack of Marketability Issue. The District Court concluded that:

[T]he company was under no obligation to repurchase the stock. It has, rather, an option to call the stock. . . . Moreover, . . . the company could—and from time to time did—exercise its option . . . to pay for the stock on terms that would not have been accepted gladly by an outside investor. . . . [T]he modest 10 percent marketability discount that [the appraisal company] applied generally to the U.S. News stock in the aggregate was perfectly appropriate.

Real Estate and Other Assets Issue. With regard to the valuation implications of the various U.S. News nonoperating assets, the Court concluded:

In a minority valuation . . . assets may or may not play an important part in arriving at a per share figure, because a minority shareholder cannot reach those assets. . . . Generally speaking, if the valuation being undertaken is of a business, such as U.S. News, that produces goods or services, primary consideration will be given to the earnings of the company and the resultant return on a shareholders' investment.

Subsequent Events Issue. With regard to the consideration of subsequent events in the stock valuation, the Court noted:

[T]he approach to be used is not retrospective, but prospective. One must look at the situation as of the time that each employee separated from the company. Therefore, the appropriate inquiry is whether the company was properly valued during the class period, not whether former employees become eligible for a greater share of benefits upon the contingency of a subsequent sale.

With respect to the possible future development of the real estate holdings, the Court cited testimony that:

Any realizable value should be attributed to the real estate only if it was evident that the controlling interest had a firm and clear intent to dispose of the real estate within a very short or reasonable period of time [, that is,] absolute evidence . . . not mere development plans.

The Appeals Court's Decision

On January 13, 1989, the U.S. Court of Appeals for the District of Columbia Circuit issued an opinion affirming on all counts the decision of the U.S. District Court involving the value of stock of U.S. News & World Report.[4]

Of considerable interest to ESOP valuation practitioners are several of the Appeals Court's statements rejecting plaintiffs' contention that the plan fiduciaries had a duty to maximize pecuniary benefits to individual plan participants:

---

[4] *Charles S. Foltz, et al., v. U.S. News & World Report, et al.,* No. 87-7151 U.S. App. (D.C. Jan. 13, 1989); *Charles S. Foltz, et al., John Kirby, appellant v. U.S. News & World Report, et al.,* No. 87-7152, U.S. App. (D.C. Jan. 13, 1989); and *David B. Richardson, et al., v. U.S. News & World Report, Inc., et al.,* No. 87-7153, U.S. App. (D.C. Jan. 13, 1989).

Where the controlling instruments contemplate employee ownership, all participants are on notice that maximization of the firm's pecuniary value is not to serve as an exclusive goal. . . .

Also of interest to ESOP valuation practitioners, are statements of the Appeals Court supporting the proposition that, when valuing noncontrolling ownership interests, little weight should be accorded to potential liquidation value of assets. That is particularly true with regard to nonoperating assets (1) that are currently producing little or no income and (2) to which no firm decision has been made regarding development of those assets' income-producing capability in the near term.

Regarding the nonoperating assets, the Appeals Court concluded:

After reviewing the testimony of the expert witnesses, the District Court found that [the] decision to give some, but very limited, weight to the value of the real estate "adequately took account of the Company's underlying assets." 663 F.Supp. at 1531. We find no error here.

Commentary and Conclusion

The Appeals Court decision concluded with the note that the filings in the U.S. News case (the trial of which lasted four months) are reported to be the largest in any civil case in the history of the District Court for the District of Columbia, and that "the district court threaded its way through the maze with patience and skill."

While not specifically an ESOP case, the various U.S. News decisions provide valuable professional guidance to ESOP valuation practitioners. The Court's detailed opinion in this case is very instructive regarding a multitude of valuation issues.

Andrade v. Parsons

Introduction

The Ralph M. Parsons Company employee stock ownership plan participated in a leveraged buyout (LBO) of the Parsons Corporation (Parsons) in September of 1984. After the LBO, the ESOP became the 100 percent owner of Parsons stock. This case is informative to all ESOP practitioners as to what constitutes prudent behavior on the part of the ESOP fiduciary.

The Facts of the Case

The case was brought as a class action by participants in the ESOP alleging that the LBO transaction violated ERISA.[5]

Counts I, II, and IV of the complaint were dismissed by the District Court prior to trial. The remaining counts III, V, and VI were tried by the Court and dismissed

---

[5] *Andrade v. Parsons Corp.*, No. CV 85-3344-RJK, U.S. Dist. Ct., 12 Employee Benefits Cas. (BNA) 1954 (C.D. Cal. June 21, 1990), *aff'd* 972 F. 2d 1336 (9th Cir. July 31, 1992).

following the presentation of the plaintiffs' case. Count III alleged (1) that the members of the Parsons board of directors, certain senior executives of Parsons, and the members of the retirement committee were fiduciaries of the ESOP under ERISA and (2) that they breached their fiduciary duties in carrying out the LBO. Counts V and VI related exclusively to the "crossover election." This election allowed the ESOP participants who had been participants in predecessor plans to the ESOP the opportunity to invest up to 100 percent of their account balances in Parsons stock.

The District Court's Decision

The Court ruled that although the members of the Parsons board of directors were fiduciaries of the ESOP by virtue of their exclusive authority to appoint the members of the retirement committee, the members' fiduciary responsibility could not extend beyond the appointment of the retirement committee.

The Court determined that the three members of the retirement committee were "competent and trustworthy individuals." Therefore, the Parsons board had not breached its duty in appointing those members.

The Court then considered whether certain senior executives of Parsons should be deemed fiduciaries of the ESOP. The Court concluded that the plaintiffs failed to carry what it characterized as the "extraordinary light burden" of showing that the senior executives exercised any control or authority over the retirement committee or plan assets.

The plaintiffs' claim was based on the fact that the Parsons chief financial officer (1) resigned as chairman of the retirement committee immediately prior to the LBO, (2) helped select the financial adviser and legal adviser ultimately hired by the retirement committee, and (3) met separately with the members of the special committee to negotiate the tender offer price without the presence of any member of the retirement committee.

The Court ruled that based solely on the testimony of the members of the retirement committee, they understood their fiduciary obligations and acted independently and exclusively for the benefit of the ESOP participants. Accordingly, the Court determined that the senior executives were not fiduciaries under ERISA and could not be held liable for a breach of fiduciary duty.

Finally, the Court ruled that the members of the retirement committee had complied with their obligations to act exclusively in the interests of the plan participants and prudently in the performance of their duties. With respect to the first standard, the Court relied on each member's testimony (1) that he was aware of and understood his obligations under ERISA and (2) that he made an independent determination that the LBO was in the best interest of the participants.

The Court stated that in order to prove a breach of the prudent standard, the plaintiffs had an obligation to show that the retirement committee did not conduct a careful and impartial investigation prior to entering into the LBO. The Court concluded that the retirement committee (1) properly retained independent and competent legal and financial advisers, (2) considered the potential disadvantages of the LBO and implemented mechanisms such as the "prop price" to counteract any negative impact of the transaction, and (3) determined that the ESOP participants would receive substantial long-term benefits from the transaction. All of these factors demonstrated that the retirement committee acted prudently under ERISA.

The Appeals Court's Decision

On July 31, 1992, the U.S. Court of Appeals for the Ninth Circuit issued a memorandum opinion affirming the decision of the District Court in *Andrade v. Parsons Corporation* in favor of the defendants.

Commentary and Conclusion

The case involved the conduct of the individual ESOP fiduciaries in approving the 1984 leveraged buyout of Parsons Corporation by its ESOP. The District Court's 1990 opinion provides valuable guidance to individual fiduciaries for demonstrating that they have complied with ERISA by acting independently and with advice of independent legal and financial advisers in arranging and approving ESOP transactions.

This case is also noteworthy to all ESOP practitioners with regard to the District Court's assessment of what constitutes prudent behavior for an ESOP fiduciary.

Reich v. Valley National Bank of Arizona

Introduction

Reich v. Valley National Bank of Arizona,[6] is also commonly referred to as the "Kroy" case. In this case, the U.S. District Court for the Southern District of New York provided an important precedent (1) for financial advisers and (2) for fiduciaries to ESOP-owned companies with regard to assessing the fairness of mergers and acquisitions transactions.

The Kroy case involves an action brought by the Department of Labor (DOL) against Valley National Bank of Arizona (Valley National) in its capacity as trustee of the Kroy, Inc., Employee Stock Ownership Plan (Kroy ESOP).

ESOP practitioners had anticipated that the resolution of this case would establish long-awaited guidelines for the equity allocation within multi-investor ESOP leveraged buyouts. Unfortunately, the District Court's decision only tangentially addresses the issue of multiple investor equity allocation.

The District Court's Findings

The District Court held that Valley National breached its fiduciary duty by causing the Kroy ESOP to purchase Kroy stock without obtaining "adequate consideration." Specifically, Valley National failed to conduct a good faith investigation in connection with the management-led leveraged buyout in which Kroy, Inc., was taken private (the "Transaction").

The District Court concluded Valley National failed to perform the proper due diligence in order to determine the following:

1. Whether the price to be paid by the ESOP for the Kroy stock was in excess of the fair market value of the underlying stock.

---

[6] *Reich v. Valley National Bank of Arizona*, 89 Civ. 8361 (CBM) (S.D.N.Y. 1993).

2. Whether the Transaction was fair to the ESOP from a financial point of view.

This resulted in the Court concluding that Valley National caused the ESOP to engage in various nonexempt prohibited transactions under ERISA.

The facts of this case and the Court's decision provide numerous insights for ESOP fiduciaries and for ESOP financial advisers. Among the more significant fiduciary issues are those pertaining to the fact that a fiduciary must:

1. Be an active participant in negotiating the price and terms of the transaction.
2. Retain its own financial advisers.
3. Conduct a thorough and diligent investigation of the company and of the security that it is purchasing.

Commentary and Conclusion

The District Court defined fair market value as the price at which an asset would exchange hands between a willing buyer and a willing seller when the former is not under any compulsion to buy and the latter is not under any compulsion to sell, and both parties are able, as well as willing, to trade and are well informed about the asset and the market for that asset. The published decision provides valuable insights to ESOP practitioners with regard to the responsibilities (1) of ESOP fiduciaries and (2) ESOP financial advisers with regard to their assessment of an ESOP stock sale or purchase transaction.

Howard v. Shay

Introduction

Howard v. Shay,[7] is also commonly called the "PAE" case. In this case, the U.S. District Court for the Central District of California found that the ESOP committee did not breach its fiduciary duties in selling ESOP stock to an entity created by the majority shareholder of the ESOP sponsor.

In *Howard v. Shay*, the District Court held that the administrative committee (the "Committee") of the ESOP of Pacific Architects and Engineers, Inc. (the "PAE ESOP") did not breach its fiduciary duties under ERISA by selling all of the Pacific Architects and Engineers, Inc. (PAE) stock held by the PAE ESOP to the E. & A. Shay Irrevocable Trust (the "Shay Trust"). The Shay Trust was an entity created by the majority shareholder of PAE.

The Facts of the Case

The plaintiffs were participants in an ESOP created for the benefit of employees of Pacific Architects and Engineers, Inc. (PAE), a California corporation. PAE was

---

[7] *Newman Howard, et al., v. Edward A. Shay, et al.*, No. CV-91-146 DT, U.S. Dist. Ct., LEXIS 20153 (C.D. Cal. Sept. 15, 1993), *rev'd and rem'd* 100 F.3d 1484 (9th Cir. 1996), *retried* No. CV 91-146 DT (GHKX), U.S. Dist. Ct. 1998 WL 526500 (C.D. Cal. May 29, 1998).

primarily a real estate holding company, but it also had engineering and architecture operations. The real estate owned by PAE was both foreign and domestic. The company also held a 50 percent ownership interest in K.K. Halifax, a Japanese real estate corporation.

The PAE ESOP was originally created in 1972 as an employee benefit plan. In 1974, the ESOP purchased approximately 40 percent of the PAE stock from Edward Shay, the president and chairman of PAE (and an ESOP fiduciary) for $10.67 per share. There was no put option in connection with the ESOP stock, and no put option was ever created. Prior to the sale, Edward Shay owned 100 percent of the outstanding stock of PAE.

In 1987, Richard Smith, a PAE senior executive and co-fiduciary, consulted with a financial adviser regarding the possibility of terminating the ESOP. The financial adviser informed Richard Smith about potential problems associated with the valuation methodology used by the appraisal firm that had conducted the valuation of the PAE stock for ESOP annual update purposes.

On November 9, 1988, the Committee voted to sell all of the shares of PAE stock (38.05 percent of PAE) held by the PAE ESOP to the Shay Trust for $14.40 per share, for a total sum of $5,479,241.21. This stock sale was in connection with the termination of the PAE ESOP.

The stock sale occurred and was based on an independent stock valuation performed by an accounting firm. The independent valuation estimated a fair market value of $14.40 per share, the highest value ever assigned to the PAE stock held by the PAE ESOP. The stock valuation was accompanied and supported by a fairness opinion.

The accounting firm separated the PAE value into three components: (1) the PAE 50 percent interest in K.K. Halifax, which held Japanese real estate, (2) the PAE interests in other real estate, and (3) the PAE engineering and architecture operations.

The valuation was based on the standard of fair market value on a going-concern basis, based in part on PAE's attorney's assertion that California Corporations Code Section 1800 did not give the ESOP the right to trigger an involuntary dissolution of PAE.

The values for (1) and (2) above were based on independent appraisals of the domestic and Japanese real estate, provided by the defendants. The Japanese real estate held by K.K. Halifax was valued at $120.2 million, or approximately $60 million for PAE's 50 percent interest, before consideration of any discounts or built-in capital gains taxes. The PAE interest in other real estate had been appraised at $18.2 million. The accounting firm valued the PAE engineering and architecture operations at $5.3 million, based on the market approach.

The accounting firm next considered the amount of valuation discounts to apply to the above values. First, a 60 percent discount was applied to the PAE ownership interest in K.K. Halifax. The valuation report justified this valuation discount in part by explaining that (1) the Japanese real estate market was overvalued and volatile, (2) PAE did not have a controlling ownership interest in K.K. Halifax, (3) the other 50 percent owner was more powerful than PAE, and (4) there would be very substantial taxes on any sale.

Second, a 40 percent to 50 percent discount for lack of control was applied on all real estate–related interests, including K.K. Halifax, to reflect the fact that the ESOP only owned approximately 40 percent of the PAE stock.

Third, a 50 percent discount for lack of marketability was applied, resulting in a fair market value of the ESOP stock of $14.40 per share. The discount for lack of marketability reflected the facts that (1) the PAE stock was not publicly traded and (2) the ESOP plan participants did not have the right to "put" the stock to the company.

The complaint was filed in the District Court on January 10, 1991. The complaint sought equitable and monetary relief from the Committee and PAE. The complaint alleged that the Committee breached its fiduciary duties under ERISA (1) by engaging in prohibited self-dealing and (2) by improperly selling the PAE stock to the Shay Trust for less than its fair market value.

The District Court's Decision

In reviewing the independent valuation and fairness opinion, the District Court found nothing wrong either (1) with the Committee's selection of the accounting firm or (2) with the valuation procedures performed by that firm. The Court also found that (1) the lack of control discount and (2) the lack of marketability discount were neither improper nor excessive under the circumstances. Details of transactions involving 25 percent to 49.9 percent of a company's stock (from the Willamette Management Associates proprietary database), presented through expert testimony, were instrumental in supporting the 50 percent lack of marketability discount.

The District Court's Decision—Commentary and Conclusion

The District Court's comment regarding whether independent or neutral fiduciaries should have been retained for purposes of the PAE ESOP's sale of the PAE stock to the Shay Trust is noteworthy to ESOP practitioners. The District Court concluded that it was not "fatal" that an independent or neutral fiduciary was not involved.

In this case, the possible appointment of an independent or neutral fiduciary was considered and rejected because an international public accounting firm had been retained to render (1) an independent valuation of the PAE stock and (2) a fairness opinion with respect to the transaction.

The Appeals Court's Decision

The Ninth Circuit Court of Appeals reversed the District Court's decision, finding for the plaintiffs on breach of fiduciary duties of care and loyalty to the ESOP plan participants in engaging in a self-dealing transaction.

The Ninth Circuit Court decision focused in particular on the lack of thoroughness of the investigation by the fiduciaries. The Court stated:

> To justifiably rely on an independent appraisal, a conflicted fiduciary need not become an expert in the valuation of closely held corporations. But the fiduciary is required to make an honest, objective effort to read the valuation, understand it, and question the methods and assumptions that do not make sense. If after a careful review of the valuation and discussion with the expert there are still uncertainties, the fiduciary should have a second firm review the valuation. Adopting the alternative rule—that an independent appraisal is a complete defense to a charge of imprudence—should be foolish, especially

in cases in which there is a strong possibility of self-dealing.... A fiduciary determined to self-deal has ample opportunity to sway the final valuation that will set the transaction.... This case illustrates the danger. Not only did Smith discuss liquidity and minority interest discounts with prospective valuators, but also, at least one firm . . . balked at his conditions of retention. Conflicted fiduciaries do not fulfill ERISA's investigative requirements by merely hiring an expert. Shay, Smith, and Lehrer did nothing else. A day after they got [the] valuation, they completed the transaction. They did not meaningfully review, discuss, or question the valuation.

The District Court Retrial

On remand in 1998, the U.S. District Court reaffirmed its 1993 decision that the "price of $14.40 per share is found by the Court to be fair and adequate consideration for the self-dealing transaction."

However, based on the Ninth Circuit 1996 decision for the plaintiff regarding the breach of fiduciary duty, the District Court granted the PAE ESOP and/or any of its participants the election to buy back their PAE shares owned previously by tendering $14.40 per share to the trustee of the E. & A. Shay Irrevocable Trust. Additionally, the plaintiffs were allowed to recover their attorney's fees and costs.

The District Court Retrial—Commentary and Conclusion

This case offers important lessons both (1) to ESOP financial advisers and (2) to ESOP fiduciaries. For ESOP financial advisers, the case illustrates in particular the importance of providing ample case-specific support when selecting the discounts for lack of control and for lack of marketability used in the valuation report.

With regard to the fiduciary issues, the District Court provided an overview of requirements for fiduciaries in ESOP transactions. In particular, the District Court stated that a conflicted fiduciary "is required to make an honest, objective effort to read the valuation, understand it, and question the methods and assumptions that do not make sense."

Eyler v. Commissioner

Introduction

In *Gary L. Eyler v. Commissioner*, the petitioner appealed the earlier decision of the U.S. Tax Court. [8]

The Issues of the Case

Gary Eyler, the former CEO and majority shareholder of Continental Training Services, Inc. (CTS), disputed the Internal Revenue Service Commissioner's determination

---

[8] *Gary L. Eyler v. Commissioner*, No. 95-2482, 1996 U.S. App. LEXIS 15831 (7th Cir. July 2, 1996), *aff'g* T.C. Memo 1995-123 (Mar. 23, 1995).

that he had engaged in a prohibited transaction with CTS's ESOP when he sold $10 million worth of CTS stock to the ESOP in December 1986. Eyler appealed the Commissioner's determination to the Tax Court.

In 1995, the Tax Court concluded that Eyler was not exempt from liability for the excise taxes imposed in connection with his sale of CTS stock to the ESOP because he failed to establish: (1) that the fair market value per share of CTS stock on the transaction date was at least $14.50 per share or (2) that any fiduciary named in the ESOP made a good-faith determination that the fair market value per share of CTS stock on the transaction date was at least $14.50.

Internal Revenue Code Sections 4975(a) and (b) impose a two-tier excise tax on prohibited transactions between an ESOP and disqualified persons. A prohibited transaction includes any sale of stock between a plan and a disqualified person, and a disqualified person is an owner of 50 percent or more of the stock of a corporation whose employees are covered by the plan.

Internal Revenue Code Section 4975(a) imposes a yearly 5 percent tax on the amount involved. Internal Revenue Code Section 4975(b) imposes a second tier of tax equal to 100 percent of the amount involved if the prohibited transaction is not corrected (i.e., reversed) within the taxable period. Eyler was assessed on both tiers.

The Facts of the Case

From 1973 (when he started CTS), until 1986 (when he sold CTS), Eyler was its sole or majority shareholder as well as its chairman of the board and chief executive officer. CTS operated a series of vocational schools to train truck drivers and heavy equipment operators.

Government deregulation of the industry resulted in enormous growth for CTS. Enrollment at CTS schools increased from about 2,000 students in 1980 to more than 37,000 students in 1986. By 1986, it was the largest proprietary vocational training system in the United States.

In 1985, Eyler began exploring either selling CTS or taking it public. CTS had received inquiries and solicitations from a number of investment banking firms.

In early 1986, Eyler and CTS decided to take the company public through an initial public offering (IPO). During 1986, the underwriters conducted a due diligence investigation, which consisted of reviewing the financial records and history of CTS, visiting the company's facilities, interviewing the management, and evaluating financial and economic forecasts.

As a result of the due diligence, an estimated IPO price range of $13 to $16 per share was established.

The underwriters attempted to determine whether there was interest in purchasing CTS stock in the price range of $13 to $16 per share. Marketing the proposed IPO during October and the first week of November 1986, the underwriters determined that the "circled interest" for CTS stock at $13 to $16 was only around $1 million. ("Circled interest" is an investment banking term of art meaning specifically identified likely syndicate participation in an offering.)

In November 1986, Eyler decided to look into establishing an ESOP for CTS and thereafter selling a substantial portion of his shares to the ESOP. On November 24, 1986, CTS approached a bank to negotiate a $10 million loan to be secured by the shares to be sold by Eyler to the ESOP.

At a meeting on December 12, 1986, the CTS board considered the proposed ESOP. Under the terms of the ESOP, CTS was designated plan administrator and named fiduciary. CTS's duties under the plan included appointing and overseeing the plan committee. The board approved the establishment of the plan under the terms proposed by the CTS chief financial officer during the meeting.

As a related aside, sometime in late 1986 or early 1987, seven of the CTS board members each purchased 1,882 shares of CTS stock from a minority shareholder of CTS, at $14.50 per share, for a total purchase price of just over $27,000. One of the directors paid cash for his stock. The remaining six directors received funds for the purchase from Eyler by way of informal, unsecured "bridge loans," the terms of which were not reduced to writing. Eventually, the stock certificates evidencing the directors' purchases were prepared in March 1987, when loans from the bank for the purchase were formally approved.

In addition, in September 1986, two investigations of CTS were pending. The first investigation, by the attorney general of California, concerned allegations that CTS engaged in certain fraudulent practices and used untrue or misleading advertising with respect to its courses. The second, by the U.S. Department of Education, focused on the same areas. In 1988, the United States, on behalf of the Department of Education, filed a $366 million lawsuit against CTS.

The federal government also withdrew CTS's eligibility to participate in various government student loan programs. This withdrawal was later judicially determined to be a violation of CTS's constitutional right to due process, but by the time this news arrived, CTS was financially ruined.

The Issues before the Court

In 1991, the Internal Revenue Service began investigating the ESOP transaction. In April 1992, the Commissioner of the IRS determined that Eyler was a disqualified person who engaged in a nonexempt prohibited transaction within the meaning of Internal Revenue Code Section 4975. Eyler was said to be liable for the excise tax penalty, and a notice of deficiency was issued to him for assessments covering the years 1986 to 1990.

Eyler filed a petition in Tax Court seeking a redetermination of the deficiency. Eyler argued first that the $14.50 price paid by the ESOP for his stock was fair market value. Eyler's alternative argument was that even if $14.50 was not fair market value, the CTS board of directors acted in good faith in determining that it was, and thus "adequate consideration" was still received by the ESOP.

The Tax Court rejected both arguments.

First, it held that Eyler failed to meet his burden of establishing $14.50 as the fair market value on the date of the prohibited transaction. The underwriters' range of $13 to $16 per share did not, in the Tax Court's view, represent a final price determination, and it was also based on a number of assumptions that had not come to pass.

Second, the Tax Court found that because the board members knew that many of the assumptions underlying the underwriters' price range had changed and yet they did nothing further to investigate the suggested price, their actions did not rise to the level of prudence imposed on ERISA fiduciaries. Since "adequate consideration" was not received by the ESOP when it purchased Eyler's stock, the Tax Court sustained the deficiencies determined by the Commissioner.

The Petitioner's Position

Eyler argued that the fair market value of CTS stock was at least $14.50 based on the valuation set by the underwriters. Eyler also argued that the Tax Court erred when it adopted the Commissioner's argument regarding a lack of marketability discount. He also argued that the purchases of CTS stock by several directors for $14.50 per share shortly after the ESOP transaction was for a basis establishing fair market value.

Eyler argued that the ESOP still received adequate consideration when it purchased his stock because the CTS fiduciaries acted in good faith in determining that the fair market value of CTS stock was $14.50 per share.

The Appeals Court Decision—The Valuation Issues

The Appeals Court agreed with the Tax Court that there are several reasons why the underwriters' estimated price range of $13 to $16 per share did not establish the fair market value to be at least $14.50 on the date of the sale.

First, that price range was established after the underwriters conducted a due diligence investigation and as a part of CTS's anticipated IPO. That price range did not purport to determine the fair market value of CTS stock at any specific point in time; nor did it in any way purport to be a final determination. The purpose of selecting that price was to see how investors might respond.

Second, that price range was not binding and did not represent a firm commitment by the underwriters.

The Appeals Court concluded that the lack of public interest in CTS stock also weighed against Eyler's reliance on the underwriters' valuation. When the stock was offered nationally to individual and institutional investors, the "circled interest" was small, no more than $1 million. Clearly, the public showed little interest in buying CTS stock within the underwriters' price range.

The Appeals Court noted that many significant factors changed from the time the prospectus was filed by the underwriters in September to the date of completion of the ESOP sale on December 22, 1986. The $13 to $16 estimated price range was based on certain assumptions that did not come to fruition at the time of the ESOP transaction.

First, the underwriters assumed that as a result of the IPO, CTS would be a publicly traded corporation.

A second important assumption was that the IPO would result in a positive cash flow for CTS. When the IPO was shelved and the ESOP established, the CTS cash flow actually worsened because CTS committed itself to making contributions to the ESOP in amounts large enough for the plan to repay the $10 million loan.

In particular, the Appeals Court noted a significant factor not assumed, let alone considered, by the underwriters in preparing the preliminary prospectus was the establishment of the ESOP itself. Upon formation of the ESOP, CTS undertook two obligations that affected its balance sheet and future-operating income

First, CTS guaranteed the $10 million loan to the ESOP, which was required to be classified as debt on CTS's balance sheet and a charge to shareholders' equity.

Second, CTS obligated itself to make contributions to the ESOP in an amount sufficient to cover the loan payments, or at least $2 million per year, resulting in a significant cash drain on the company.

The Appeals Court firmly stated that significant changes in these underlying assumptions, together with the limited nature of the underwriters' estimated price range and minimal circled interest, demonstrated that the valuation did not provide a basis for establishing fair market value.

With regard to the marketability discount, the Appeals Court concluded that Eyler's argument failed for the fundamental reason that, as of the date of the ESOP transaction, CTS had no history of paying ESOP distributions in cash. Whatever effect the CTS history of payouts might have had on the fair market value of CTS stock at the time of the ESOP transaction was pure speculation.

Similarly, the Appeals Court rejected Eyler's assertion that the marketability discount was inappropriate because the ESOP put option had no fixed price and could be paid out over five years under the terms of the ESOP.

The Appeals Court stated: "Nothing in the record convinces us that the Tax Court clearly erred when it concluded that the marketability discount should apply to the [underwriters'] valuation."

Regarding the allegedly arm's-length pre-ESOP sales at $14.50 per share, the Appeals Court stated that it was not unreasonable for the Tax Court to conclude that the sale of stock from the minority shareholder to the directors was not at arm's length. The purchases involved directors of CTS and a noncontrolling shareholder, not the corporation. Eyler, who benefited from the sale in his effort to establish the $14.50 value, provided unsecured bridge loans to six of the seven directors who purchased stock from the noncontrolling shareholder.

Concluding the valuation issue, the Appeals Court stated:

> For all of these reasons, we are unable to say that the Tax Court committed clear error when it found that Eyler failed to meet his burden of establishing that the fair market value of CTS stock on December 22, 1986, was at least $14.50.

The Appeals Court Decision—The Fiduciary Issues

The trustee and plan administrator of the ESOP was the vice president of human resources at CTS. Under the terms of the ESOP, the trustee was not responsible for day-to-day operations of the plan, but rather served in an administrative capacity, carrying out the discretionary decisions of the plan committee.

The Appeals Court concluded that the trustee played no role in pricing the CTS stock for the ESOP, made no good-faith determination of its fair market value, and, therefore, his actions failed to support Eyler's argument.

The Appeals Court also concluded that the actions of the members of the plan committee, who were appointed at the December 12, 1986, board meeting, were not helpful. There was no evidence that the committee even met in the 10 days between the board meeting and the ESOP purchase. There was also no evidence that any of the committee members conducted any investigation to determine the fair market value of the stock.

The Appeals Court stated: "Thus, as the Tax Court properly found, Eyler is not relieved of excise tax liability on the basis of the committee's alleged good-faith determination of fair market value of the stock."

Eyler argued that CTS, acting through its board of directors, qualified as a fiduciary of the ESOP. Eyler argued that in light of the opinion letter prepared by CTS's attorneys, and the board's knowledge of earlier takeover valuation opinions, the board acted in good faith in determining the price of the stock.

The Tax Court had rejected Eyler's contention, finding that the board's actions did not rise to the exacting level of prudence imposed on ERISA fiduciaries. The Appeals Court affirmed the Tax Court's conclusion.

With regard to the fiduciary issues, the Appeals Court concluded:

> In sum, the law requires a fiduciary of an ESOP to act with the care, skill, and diligence that a prudent person would undertake in acting on behalf of ESOP beneficiaries. The degree to which a fiduciary makes an independent inquiry is critical. We find no merit to Eyler's contention that the board of directors was well-informed and, therefore, made a good-faith determination of the fair market value of the stock. The record does not show that even one director, let alone a majority, sought independent information on the fair market value of the stock. Rather, on the same day the project was presented, the board voted to guarantee a $10 million loan, the proceeds of which would be used to buy the majority shareholder's stock. A prudent person would not have relied upon the dated [underwriters'] estimated price range for the ESOP stock purchase in light of the failed IPO and changing financial conditions at the corporation. Moreover, there is not evidence that the board was knowledgeable about the effects of these changing conditions on the fair market value of CTS stock. Thus, it was not clear error for the Tax Court to conclude that Eyler did not meet his burden of showing that the directors acted in good faith in determining fair market value.

Commentary and Conclusion

This case, particularly due to the strong affirmation of the Tax Court decision by the Appeals Court, is instructive both (1) to ESOP financial advisers and other ESOP practitioners and (2) to any individuals who assume the responsibility of an ESOP fiduciary.

This case provides useful guidance with respect to (1) ESOP share purchase valuation issues (i.e., how much analysis is required to determine fair market value) and to (2) ESOP fiduciary issues (i.e., how much due diligence is required to assess adequate consideration).

The virtual unanimity of the Tax Court and the Appeals Court on these issues makes this judicial precedent particularly important and informative.

Davis v. Torvick

Introduction

In the case of *Davis v. Torvick, Inc.*,[9] the U.S. District Court decided a case involving both (1) ESOP valuation issues and (2) ESOP fiduciary duty issues. Accordingly, this case has relevance to both ESOP valuation analysts and ESOP trustees.

---

[9] *William R. Davis, et al.v. Torvick, Inc., et al.*, C-93-1343 CW, 1996 WL 266217 (N.D.Cal. May 2, 1996).

The Facts of the Case

The plaintiffs were employees of Torvick, Inc., a Mercedes-Benz dealership in Santa Rosa, California. One defendant was Torvick, Inc., the Mercedes-Benz dealership, and a California corporation. Torvick, Inc., was the employer of the plaintiffs and the corporate custodian of the Amended Profit Sharing Plan and Trust Agreement of Torvick, Inc. ("Profit Sharing Plan"). Another defendant was Robert C. Torvick, a member of the board of directors of Torvick, Inc., and a trustee for the Profit Sharing Plan and the Torvick, Inc., Employee Stock Ownership Plan (ESOP).

Defendants Roy F. Bracket and Blain R. Torvick were members of the board of directors for Torvick, Inc., and trustees of the Profit Sharing Plan.

The lawsuit also named the company's accounting firm and law firm as defendants. The accounting firm settled with the plaintiffs for an undisclosed amount. Accordingly, the charges against them were dismissed by the time of the trial.

The Profit Sharing Plan was a trust fund to which the plaintiffs contributed a percentage of their salary. Torvick, Inc., was to make matching contributions in an amount depending on its profitability. The plaintiffs received periodic statements detailing the amount that they were supposed to have in their respective accounts.

The ESOP was a trust fund created after the Profit Sharing Plan. The only asset of the ESOP was Torvick, Inc., stock. The plaintiffs exchanged their assets in the Profit Sharing Plan in return for Torvick, Inc., stock. The amount of stock allotted to each plaintiff was proportional to each plaintiff's account balance in the Profit Sharing Plan.

The Issues of the Case

The plaintiffs alleged that Robert Torvick utilized the Employees' Profit Sharing Plan funds for his own use, the use of Torvick, Inc., or the use of other entities controlled by Robert Torvick. The total amount of money that should have been in the Profit Sharing Plan on March 31, 1990, was $870,152.75.

By Robert Torvick's own estimate, the maximum amount that was actually funded was $30,000 to $40,000. Over $800,000 was either never placed into the plan or was borrowed from the plan by Robert Torvick or by entities controlled by Torvick.

By Robert Torvick's own estimate, he—or entities controlled by him—owed over $200,000 to the Profit Sharing Plan in notes. The rest of the missing money was never contributed.

The plaintiffs alleged that Robert Torvick and Torvick, Inc., caused periodic statements to be distributed to the plaintiffs that misrepresented that the Profit Sharing Plan assets were safely invested.

The plaintiffs alleged that Torvick, Inc., employees, at the direction of Robert Torvick, negligently prepared inflation projections that were used by Torvick, Inc.'s CPA firm, in the valuation of Torvick, Inc. (the "Valuation Report"). The Torvick, Inc., employees prepared the projections within the span of a few days, and they based them only on past performance extrapolated into the future. The projections did not take into account any other factors, such as the outlook of the specific business. Robert Torvick ordered at least one of the projections to be made more "optimistic."

In addition to including the negligent projections, the Valuation Report did not include any clear reference to the large debt owed the Profit Sharing Plan.

Robert Torvick, in or about late 1989 and early 1990, met with the plaintiffs and presented the Valuation Report. The purpose of the meeting was to promote the

ESOP and assure the plaintiffs that it was a good investment to transfer funds from the Profit Sharing Plan into the ESOP.

Allegedly, the defendants intentionally misled the employees by concealing the state of the Profit Sharing Plan. The employees relied on the representations to their detriment when they voted to transfer their Profit Sharing Plan assets to the ESOP in or about late 1989 or early 1990.

Torvick, Inc., subsequently went bankrupt. The value of the employees' shares in the corporation went to zero. The gross amount of the employees' loss was approximately $450,000 as of March 31, 1990.

The Plaintiffs' Position

Robert Torvick and Torvick, Inc., were acting as fiduciaries when they had the Valuation Report prepared by their accounting firm. They also were acting as fiduciaries when they met with the plaintiffs to encourage the employees to switch to the ESOP plan.

Valuations and representations concerning the future of a business are normally standard business practices, and are not connected with plan administration. When the valuation is created and used to make representations about the future of an alternative plan, and to convince participants to leave the current plan, however, it is an act of plan administration.

The Defendants' Position

Robert Torvick proposed two related defense arguments. The first argument is that the plaintiffs would have opted for the transfer even had they known of his misconduct. The second argument is that the plaintiffs had not been damaged because they received full value for their unfunded Profit Sharing Plan in the form of Torvick, Inc., stock when the ESOP plan was formed.

Robert Torvick argued that the Valuation Report was accurate and that Torvick, Inc., simply failed in the marketplace, a risk that all stockholders take.

The Valuation Report represented that Torvick, Inc. was worth approximately 1 million dollars at the time of the employees' transfer to the ESOP. Robert Torvick argued that the employees were not damaged because if Torvick, Inc., had done well, as all parties hoped, the plaintiffs would have assets in the amount owed them in the form of Torvick, Inc., stock.

The fact that Torvick, Inc., went bankrupt does not change the value of what the employees received in 1990. According to this argument, the employees took the risk of failure in the marketplace.

The District Court's Decision

The District Court concluded that Robert Torvick violated ERISA and damaged the fund. The loans that Robert Torvick caused to be made from the Profit Sharing Plan to himself, and to entities controlled by him, were transactions between the plan and a party in interest, and were a violation of ERISA. The loans that Robert Torvick caused to be made from the Profit Sharing Plan to himself were transactions between the plan and a fiduciary and were a violation of ERISA.

The periodic statements provided to the plaintiffs clearly stated the amounts that were supposed to be in the Profit Sharing Plan. The plaintiffs were entitled to rely on these representations unless they were given timely notice that the information was incorrect.

By causing the Profit Sharing Plan to remain unfunded, and then lying about the state of the plan in these periodic statements, Robert Torvick engaged in a serious breach of duty to discharge his responsibilities as a trustee solely in the interest of the participants.

The District Court concluded that, as a result of these ERISA violations, Robert Torvick committed at least one more violation. In convincing the employees to switch to the ESOP by concealing his past ERISA violations, representing to the employees that all of the Profit Sharing Plan assets were being held in cash and that Torvick, Inc., would receive those assets, and causing the Valuation Report to be based, at least in part, on negligent projections, Robert Torvick did not operate in the interest of anyone other than himself.

Materially misleading the employees to erase his own debt and conceal his violations of ERISA is entirely inconsistent with Robert Torvick's fiduciary duties, the District Court concluded.

Commentary and Conclusion

This case offers important lessons both to ESOP valuation analysts and to ESOP fiduciaries. With regard to the valuation issues, the District Court specifically noted: "The Court has grave doubts about the accuracy of the Valuation Report based not only on the negligent projections used to formulate it, but also on the lack of any concrete reference to the large debt owed the Profit Sharing Plan."

With regard to the fiduciary issues, the District Court concluded: "A fiduciary that breaches any of the responsibilities imposed by ERISA is personally liable to make good to such plan any losses to the plan from such a breach, and shall be subject to such other equitable or remedial relief as the court may deem appropriate."

Summary

This chapter has reviewed numerous court cases that are noteworthy to ESOP valuation practitioners. The cases subject to review have been informative with regard to (1) the acceptable (and unacceptable) employer corporation stock methodology and (2) the preferred content of ESOP valuation opinion reports.

In addition to ESOP valuation analysts, many of these cases are instructive to ESOP trustees and other ESOP practitioners. These cases discuss the responsibilities of ESOP fiduciaries—particularly with regard to employer corporation stock purchase or sale transactions. ESOP practitioners should be familiar with the professional guidance provided by these court cases.

Chapter 34

Valuations for Ad Valorem Taxation

Introduction

Business valuation techniques are used in many situations. When analysts are familiar with the techniques described in this book, they will become comfortable with their many applications.

This chapter will present many business valuation analyses that are conducted for purposes of ad valorem property taxation. These purposes include: (1) compliance (i.e., the annual administrative filing of property tax renditions), (2) assessment appeal, and (3) valuation and equalization litigation (including expert witness testimony).

First, we will define certain terminology that is specific to the ad valorem taxation assessment and appeal process. Second, we will introduce the basic principles of the property tax valuation process. Third, we will introduce the basic principles of the property tax equalization process. Fourth, we will introduce the basic principles of the property tax appeal process. Fifth, we will discuss the general functions that appraisers perform in the ad valorem taxation planning and compliance process. Sixth, we will present several special topics related to specific analyses that valuation analysts typically perform to assist taxpayers in the property taxation assessment, appeal, and litigation process. These special topics include the identification and quantification of functional obsolescence, the identification and quantification of external (or economic) obsolescence, the identification and valuation of intangible assets for taxpayers assessed under the unitary method of valuation, and the identification and application of appropriate income approach methods for ad valorem unitary valuation.

Definitions of Ad Valorem Taxation Terminology

The following brief definitions will acquaint the reader with some general terms that are used regularly in the ad valorem taxation planning and compliance process.

These definitions are consistent with, but not necessarily identical to, those presented in *Property Taxation*, published by the Institute of Professionals in Taxation, a prominent organization of professionals involved in the ad valorem taxation process.[1]

- **Assess**—to make an appraisal of the property in connection with a listing of the property liable to ad valorem taxation. It implies the exercise of discretion on the part of the public officials charged with the duty of property assessment, including the listing—or inventory—of the property involved and the conclusion of an appropriate, defined value on that property. The word assess is sometimes used interchangeably with the word *levy*.
- **Assessor**—a public official elected or appointed to discover, list, and appraise privately owned property for ad valorem property tax purposes.
- **Assessed valuation**—the value placed on each taxable unit by the assessor, which provides the basis to which the applicable property tax rate is applied to determine the amount to be paid by the property owner as property taxes.

[1] *Property Taxation*, 2nd ed. (Washington, DC: Institute of Professionals in Taxation, 1993).

- **Assessment roll**—a list, or roll, of all privately owned taxable property within a taxing authority jurisdiction completed, verified, and deposited by the local assessor.
- **Tax rate**—typically developed by dividing the total cost of the local government's annual budget by the total assessed value on the tax roll (i.e., all privately owned property within the local taxing jurisdiction). An example of the way taxing authorities set the property tax rate in their jurisdiction follows:

$$\frac{\text{Annual muncipal budget}}{\substack{\text{Total assessed value of} \\ \text{private property per the tax role}}} = \frac{\$2,000,000}{\$100,000,000} = \substack{\text{a tax rate of 20 mills} \\ (\$2 \text{ per } \$100 \text{ or } \$20 \\ \text{per } \$1,000 \text{ of assessed} \\ \text{property valuation})}$$

- **Equal and uniform taxation**—ad valorem taxes are considered to be equal and uniform when no taxpayer or class of taxpayers in the taxing district—whether it be a state, county, city, town, or village—is taxed at a rate different from other taxpayers in the same taxing district upon the same value or the same type of property. The concept of equal and uniform taxation is a basic statutory and judicial goal of ad valorem property taxation. The departure of this standard by a taxing authority is one of the principal justifications for a taxpayer's assessment appeal.
- **Equalization ratio**—the percentage of market value at which a property is assessed. The equalization ratio is often simply called the ratio.
- **Ratio study**—generally the comprehensive comparison of actual property sales or of appraised values of selected parcels to the taxing jurisdiction's assessments in order to determine the effective equalization rate or ratio.
- **Ad valorem**—literally, this phrase means "according to value." The term ad valorem tax means a tax or duty on the value of the property subject to taxation. Such property could include tangible personal property, a parcel of tangible real estate, or a mass collection of income-producing assets (as in the case of a business subject to the unitary property assessment method).
- **Certiorari**—the name of a writ of review or inquiry. In ad valorem property tax practice, it brings the taxpayer's assessment appeal into a superior court, based on the record of the administrative tribunal (e.g., a board of tax review) or of an inferior judicial tribunal.

Market Value as the General Basis of Property Assessment

The most common basis for assessing real estate and personal property in the United States is market value. This market-derived property assessment basis is often referred to in state statutes, in judicial opinions, and in the property tax literature by such terms as fair cash value, fair value, cash value, true value, true cost value, economic value, and other similar terminology.

Notwithstanding these local statutory phrases, all these definitions have generally come to mean the most likely price at which a property will sell from a willing seller to a willing buyer, both cognizant of all pertinent facts and neither being under duress.

However, this classic "willing buyer–willing seller" definition should sometimes be tempered when there are no comparable sales transactions in the appropriate competitive market. This is often the situation in the case of special purpose properties such as mining operations, certain chemical processing operations, timber or other special agricultural businesses, or any other properties that are special purpose or unique properties. In these instances, a form of the cost approach to property valuation is often the most appropriate valuation approach when recent market data regarding property sale transactions are not available.

Nonetheless, when either a cost approach or an income approach is used to value special purpose assessable property—because a lack of recent transactional data regarding such special purpose properties does not allow the effective use of the market approach—the objective of the analysis is still to estimate the market value of the subject property.

The Property Tax Valuation Process

As with the valuation of tangible and intangible properties for any purpose, there are three basic approaches to the valuation of property for ad valorem taxation purposes: the cost approach, the income approach, and the sales comparison (or market) approach.

In the cost approach to property valuation, four basic steps are involved:

1. The subject land (if any) is valued as if vacant and unimproved.
2. The reproduction or replacement cost of the building, site improvements, or personal property is estimated at current prices.
3. Allowances for physical depreciation, functional obsolescence, technological obsolescence, and external (including location and economic) obsolescence are subtracted.
4. The land value (if any) is added to this estimate of the depreciated replacement cost of the improvements and the personal property.

In the income approach to property valuation, the value of the property is based on its ability to produce either a net operating income or a net rental income. A capitalization rate is then divided into this economic income stream to convert it into an estimate of the taxable property's current value.

In the sales comparison or market approach, actual sales of similar properties are analyzed and a value is estimated for the subject property by a process of comparison.

Each of these three valuation approaches is described in greater detail in Chapter 14, which discusses the asset-based approach to business valuation.

The Property Tax Equalization Process

In determining the equalized valuations required by state statutes, local property tax assessment authorities often make and issue comprehensive assessment ratio studies. These assessment ratio studies analyze the average level of assessment, the degrees of assessment, uniformity, and the overall compliance with the assessment and classification requirements for each major class of property in each jurisdiction. These assessment ratio studies are performed to indicate (1) the degree of compliance with the law and rules and regulations of the assessment jurisdiction and (2) the proper classification of property in each assessment jurisdiction.

To ensure the equalization of the assessment process, assessment authorities typically collect and tabulate information relative to the sales of properties within their jurisdiction. They also cause valuations to be made of properties of various classes in their jurisdiction (selected on a basis of random sampling or otherwise) to (1) confirm the assessment ratio derived from property sale prices, (2) assist in determining the appropriate assessment ratio when the number of actual property sales is insufficient to represent a specific class of properties in the jurisdiction, (3) provide a substitute for the actual sale prices of properties of a unique character or that are sold at infrequent intervals, and (4) establish an assessment ratio for the tangible personal property (as opposed to the real estate) assessed in their jurisdiction.

Assessment Ratio Studies

Assessment ratio studies, designed to compare the assessed value with the market value of property, are performed principally for evaluating the accuracy of the assessment process and for ensuring valuation equalization in the assessment process. Property tax assessment authorities often use assessment ratio studies: (1) to establish the necessity for general revaluations, (2) to identify any problems with their appraisal procedures, (3) to "trend" property valuations between general reappraisal dates, (4) to adjust actual property sale prices for time, and (5) to develop property depreciation factors. Tax equalization officials also use assessment ratio studies to estimate the total market value of taxable property in their jurisdiction. This estimation is made, in part, to bring centrally assessed properties in line with locally assessed properties, from an assessment fairness perspective.

Use of Assessment Ratio Studies in Administrative Appeals and Litigation

An assessment ratio study is a means of testing the fairness of the property assessment procedure in a given jurisdiction. Property tax assessment authorities are generally required by law to assess all property in an assessing district uniformly. Only through an assessment ratio study can one determine whether the assessor meets this statutory requirement.

After reviewing some basic tax equalization concepts, the following section will discuss how to determine whether an assessment ratio study is justified, how to conduct one, and how to use it in property tax assessment negotiations. To understand how to use an assessment ratio study, taxpayers and their valuation advisers should understand the following basic concepts in ad valorem taxation: uniformity, changing values and their impact on uniformity, market values, and the assessment ratio.

Uniformity. The concept of uniformity in property tax assessment equalization is related to the most basic principle of ad valorem taxes. As mentioned above, ad valorem means "according to value." In very practical terms, this means that each dollar of property value is to be assessed so it will contribute the same amount of tax revenue to operate the local government. A $1 million personal residence should be assessed so the owner's tax burden will equal exactly the owner's tax burden that will result from a $1 million assessment on a retail commercial property, or a $1 million multifamily apartment house, or a $1 million parcel of vacant land, or a $1 million industrial building, or any other type of property in the assessment jurisdiction having a $1 million value on the same date.

A logical extension of this concept is that, as of a given date, the value of each separate property on an assessment roll in the taxing jurisdiction will be established for assessment purposes. This value will presumably relate to market value. The assessor then assesses each property in proportion to its market value. The assessment may be at 100 percent of market value (i.e., full value assessment), or, if the statute permits, the assessment may be at some fraction of market value (i.e., uniform assessment). So long as each property is treated equally, the assessment process has been equalized, and the ad valorem tax burden has been equalized.

Changing Values. Changing property values may create the need for an assessment ratio study. Even if the assessment roll was properly assembled and represented an equalized distribution of assessments at a given date, over time, the values of the various properties will typically change at different rates. Some types of property (for example, retail commercial property) may increase in value at a greater rate than other types of property.

Within a comparatively short time period, therefore, the assessment roll (which may have been uniform when it was assembled) is no longer equalized. The longer this situation continues without correction, the more inequitable the assessment roll becomes. If the assessments on these properties are not adjusted—that is, equalized—to reflect the varying rates of change in property value that occur over time, then the assessments no longer represent either (1) a full value assessment or (2) a uniform assessment.

Market Value. The definition of market value in the assessment process is no different from the definition of market value generally. In estimating market value, the valuation analyst considers all the usual marketplace factors involved in and affecting the value of property. Among other criteria, appraisers consider income potential, typical financing patterns, zoning, development capacity, street frontage, land area and/or plottage, neighborhood characteristics and influences, availability and sufficiency of municipal utilities and services, functional utility of the structural and site improvements, convenience of and proximity to transportation facilities, marketability, and all other factors usual and necessary to the formulation of an opinion of value.

The Assessment Ratio. The assessor begins with market value in assessing property for ad valorem tax purposes. Market value is generally the basis on which any assessment equalization is made. When an assessment roll is no longer uniform or equalized, one of the two items necessary to prove an inequitable or discriminatory property tax assessment is the market value of the subject property. The other item is the assessment ratio—that is, the ratio of the property's assessment to the property's market value—and whether the assessment ratio for the individual property exceeds the assessment ratio applicable to all other property on the same assessment roll as of the same date.

The Property Tax Unitary Valuation Process

Estimating the fair market value of an individual property such as an office building or an apartment complex is relatively straightforward. The taxable location of the property is readily ascertainable, and its value can be directly obtained by analyzing comparable sales, market-derived rental rates, and replacement or reproduction cost.

Many properties, however, are components of interrelated and interdependent operating business systems that span numerous taxing jurisdictions. Examples of such operating business systems include: traditional utilities, such as electric power generating companies; partially regulated but highly competitive businesses, such as long-distance telecommunications companies, railroads and airlines; and businesses in transition, such as telephone companies.

The reason for the unitary valuation concept is the recognition that it is not possible to accurately value, for property tax purposes, the property of (for example) a railroad in one taxing jurisdiction simply by analyzing that property in isolation. Rather, it is more practical to value the entire operating system and then apportion some of that value to each taxing jurisdiction. This is the basic concept of unit value, sometimes referred to as *unitary value* or as *system value*.

This approach to valuing an integrated bundle of operating assets has been extended to value business enterprise types other than railroads. This extension logically covers other interstate, capital-intensive businesses that employ operating systems of interdependent interrelated assets in multiple taxing jurisdictions. Historically (although much less so today), these companies were almost always publicly regulated utilities.

One issue that is implicitly present in the unit valuation process is that the going-concern value of the entire operating business is being estimated rather than the market value of the taxpayer's tangible property only. In other words, a fundamental question of the unitary valuation process is: Does this process value the overall business enterprise or does it value only the assessable assets of a taxpayer (albeit on a collective basis)?

The Property Tax Appeal Process

When assessment and millage rate formulas are consistently applied, the ad valorem assessment and taxation process is inherently fair and equitable. Disputes regarding valuation and/or equalization are inevitable, however.

Such disagreements usually arise when property owners believe that the market value placed on their property is excessive or overstated (either in absolute terms or in comparison with other properties in the same taxing jurisdiction).

For this reason, ad valorem assessments of property values are often vigorously contested and appealed. Such disputes are often resolved (at varying points in the administrative or judicial appeal process) through soundly reasoned, rigorously prepared, and comprehensively documented independent appraisals.

The ad valorem property tax assessment appeal process encompasses systematic procedures employed to answer specific questions regarding the value of real estate and tangible personal property. This process starts with the identification of the valuation problem and ends with a reporting on the valuation results.

For each ad valorem assessment appeal valuation, the analytical and quantitative procedures depend on the nature of the assignment, the type of properties appraised, the purpose and objective of the valuation, and the quantity and quality of available data.

Steps in the Ad Valorem Taxation Valuation Process

All ad valorem assessment appeal valuations generally follow the process below:

1. Definition of the scope, objective, and purpose of the valuation.
2. Identification, inspection, and inventory of the assets subject to valuation.
3. Market research and analysis of all available valuation data.
4. Contemplation of the three generally accepted approaches to property valuation.
5. Selection of the quantitative and qualitative valuation methods and procedures to be used in the subject valuation.
6. Performance of the selected valuation approaches, methods, and procedures.
7. Integration and synthesis of the results of the various valuation approaches, methods, and procedures.
8. Reporting of the final conclusion of property value.

The Assessing Authority's Objective

The objective of the property tax assessing authorities in setting ad valorem taxes is to estimate the value of all taxable properties within a given jurisdiction fairly and equitably—yet also efficiently and economically. Assessing authorities are supposed to treat owners of similar properties fairly and equally.

The Property Owner's Objective

The objective of a property owner is to ascertain the correct market value of his or her property and to file a property tax return reflecting that value. If an initial assessment is overstated or if the assessing authority does not accept a property owner's value for the property, extensive administrative and judicial appeal processes are available.

The Independent Valuation Analyst's Objective

The objective of the independent valuation analyst is to prepare the most soundly reasoned and thoroughly documented valuation possible. The analyst should also remain independent and objective during the ad valorem assessment appeal process. While valuation analysts can perform certain advisory and consultative services—and act as intermediaries on behalf of their taxpayer clients—independent valuation analysts cannot become advocates or perform advocacy functions with regard to valuation or equalization appeals.

Special Topics

Many ad valorem taxation valuation issues are best addressed in textbooks related to real estate appraisal or personal property appraisal. However, financial valuation analysts often become involved in the economic analysis aspects of property taxation valuation. These "special topics" are appropriately covered in this book.

In the next few sections of this chapter, we will explore several "special topics" in which financial valuation analysts may be particularly helpful to property owners in the ad valorem tax property valuation and equalization process—and in the ad valorem tax assessment appeal process.

Identification and Quantification of Functional Obsolescence

While functional obsolescence is most closely associated with the cost approach to property valuation, it is a consideration in the sales comparison and the income approaches to property valuation as well. In the sales comparison approach, the analyst attempts to select and analyze comparable properties with similar levels of functional obsolescence. In the income approach, the analyst attempts to ensure that the subject property's economic income stream is properly adjusted for the economic detriments associated with the subject property's functional obsolescence.

Definition of Functional Obsolescence. Functional obsolescence is an impairment of the functional utility of a property according to current market tastes and standards. To apply the concept properly—and it applies to all types of property—one needs to be aware that functional obsolescence can be curable or incurable. In addition, functional obsolescence represents more than practical usefulness—that is, it can take the form of superadequacies, as well as inadequacies.

A superadequacy is an excess in the capacity or quality of a property as compared with market standards. One example of a superadequacy is a warehouse with a ceiling height far greater than that required by the existing operations of the tenant or of the marketplace at large. An inadequacy is a characteristic of the subject property that is of a lower standard as compared with the marketplace. A three-bedroom apartment with only one bathroom is an example of an inadequacy.

Sample Situations. It is possible to construct an endless list of examples of functional obsolescence. The following examples are intended only to be illustrative in nature:

- Commercial office buildings may have public spaces such as corridors that are abnormally wide or oversized.
- Some commercial amenities are considered standard in office complexes (e.g., express elevators, telecommunication hookups, inside parking, and retail space); the lack of these amenities may indicate the existence of functional obsolescence.
- Shopping centers that are nonenclosed or have an inappropriate floor plan (e.g., one with an unsuccessful skating rink in the center).
- Instances of inadequate lighting, heating, or air conditioning typically represent functional obsolescence. These instances occur mostly in older buildings. They also may occur in cases in which facilities are currently being used for a purpose other than that for which they were constructed. Instances of excessive (and therefore partially unused) lighting, heating, or air conditioning also can represent functional obsolescence.
- A manufacturing or processing plant that is too large to accommodate the current or planned levels of business operations. In other words, there is significant excess capacity. Or a manufacturing or processing plant may be too small to accommodate the current level of business operations, so there are operating inefficiencies and a paucity of capacity.

- For the particular type of production or processing operation in the facility, the plant ceilings may be too low—or too high. Likewise, for the particular type of production or processing operating in the facility, the plant floors may be too thin—or too thick.
- There may be excess construction costs in an older plant because the walls are too thick (as compared with modern construction techniques and materials). Likewise, in older plants, the walls may be too thin to allow for the current production or processing operations to occur on higher floors. In addition, in many older plants, concrete or other types of load-bearing columns consume excessive plant floor area or disrupt an otherwise efficient materials or production flow.
- Other than the load-bearing columns mentioned previously, there may be numerous examples of structural or physical impediments to material-processing flow or product-manufacturing flow. Inefficient layout or design, related both to real estate and to tangible personal property, are among the most common examples of functional obsolescence.

Identification of Functional Obsolescence. Many property owners realize that their existing properties are experiencing functional obsolescence only after they have purchased or constructed new properties. When the input, output, or operations of the older properties are compared with those of the newer properties, instances of functional obsolescence become clearly evident.

In some cases, the property owner may identify functional obsolescence not by comparison of the subject properties with new properties, but rather by comparison of the subject properties with competitors' properties. When competitors have purchased new assets or constructed new facilities, these new properties provide a basis for comparison with the subject properties. Such a comparison can indicate instances of functional obsolescence.

Proper Applications. Functional obsolescence enters the property valuation process in each of the three traditional approaches to property value.

Income Approach. Property tax assessors often estimate a fair market value indication using the income approach by projecting a prospective economic income stream and then capitalizing it. This simple approach may ignore the future costs to be incurred to make necessary corrections of design deficiencies (e.g., the costs involved in eliminating excess office space in an office/warehouse). Because of this design deficiency, the prospective economic income may not be stable. Furthermore, the comparable properties used to estimate the appropriate capitalization rate may not be suffering from the same amount of functional obsolescence as the subject property is subject to.

Sales Comparison Approach. Any sales comparison approach to analysis depends on the degree of comparability of the "comparable" property sales considered. Adjustments to comparable properties are made to account for, among other things, the functional deficiencies of the subject property—as compared with the functional deficiencies experienced by the comparable properties.

Cost Approach. Property tax assessors often use some version of the cost approach, particularly with regard to the valuation of special purpose properties. Original costs are often increased based on indexing factors that adjust for property inflation factors and are then adjusted downward in an attempt to adjust for all forms of depreciation and obsolescence, including functional obsolescence. When used properly, the cost approach considers the various functional obsolescence factors impacting the subject property. To be curable, the cost of correcting the functional obsolescence must be the same or less than the anticipated increase in the subject property value. Functional obsolescence is curable if correcting it on the date of the appraisal is economically feasible—otherwise, it is incurable. Curable functional obsolescence is typically measured by the cost to correct the deficiency.

Quantification of Functional Obsolescence. Clearly, after identifying and documenting significant instances of functional obsolescence, the next step in the property tax valuation process is the quantification of functional obsolescence. Although many individual methods and procedures are available to quantify specific instances of functional obsolescence, all these procedures and techniques are often categorized into one or two methods.

The first method of quantifying functional obsolescence involves calculating the difference between the reproduction cost new and the replacement cost new of the subject property. The second method of quantifying functional obsolescence involves the capitalization of excess operating expenses (i.e., the costs of materials, labor and overhead) associated with the operation of the subject property.

Reproduction versus Replacement Cost New. This method is particularly useful when estimating incurable functional obsolescence associated with special purpose real estate and tangible personal property. In fact, the principal difference between the reproduction cost and the replacement cost of the subject property is the amount of incurable functional obsolescence. Those elements of functional obsolescence that are incurable should be eliminated before the estimation of replacement cost new (i.e., the cost to purchase or construct a new, state-of-the-art productive asset or property).

Although it is a complex engineering and appraisal process to estimate both the reproduction cost new and the replacement cost new for the subject property, it is relatively easy to estimate the associated functional obsolescence. Once both the reproduction cost and the replacement cost have been estimated, the amount of incurable functional obsolescence is typically the mathematical difference between the two cost estimations.

Capitalization of Excess Operating Expenses. This method typically quantifies the amount of curable functional obsolescence associated with the subject property. The approach quantifies the economic penalty associated with operating the subject property (given all its elements of functional obsolescence) instead of curing the subject property (and thereby eliminating the excess operating costs).

As mentioned previously, excess operating expenses include the material, labor, and overhead expenses associated with operating the subject property. In the appraisal of tangible personal property, for example, excess material expenses should include the expense of carrying excess raw material and work-in-process inventory, as well as the excess expense of waste and scrappage due to a functionally obsolete machine or process. Excess labor expenses should include the costs of employee fringe benefits and employment taxes, as well as the direct expenses of excess machine operators, material handlers, and so on. Excess overhead expenses should include the costs of excess electricity, gas, water, property and casualty insurance, rent, security, and property tax expense associated with operating the functionally obsolete property.

It is somewhat more difficult to quantify the amount of curable functional obsolescence associated with the capitalized excess operating expense method than with the replacement cost versus reproduction cost method. First, the excess expenses have to be identified and documented. This requires an estimation of what a normal level of operating expenses would be. Normal operating expenses may mean industry norms, expense data from specific competitors, expense data from other facilities operated by the same property owner, or historical operating expense data related to the subject property. Next, these excess operating expenses must be projected over the remaining useful life of the subject property. For the purposes of this projection, the remaining useful life typically means the lowest of the subject property's physical life or economic life.

The projection of excess operating expenses should be quantified as a present value, using an appropriate present value discount rate. This discount rate should reflect the property owner's cost of capital, the time value of money, and the risk associated with property ownership. Accordingly, the quantification of functional obsolescence using the capitalized excess operating expense method requires the appraiser to perform several detailed analyses.

Summary of Functional Obsolescence Issues. Functional obsolescence is an impairment (inadequate or superadequate) of the functional utility of a property according to current market tastes and standards. It can be curable or incurable. The cost to correct incurable functional obsolescence exceeds the resulting increase in value.

Using the income approach to property valuation, functional obsolescence is quantified indirectly. That is because a property with functional obsolescence will generate less economic income to be capitalized in the income approach analysis. In the sales comparison approach to property valuation, functional obsolescence also will be quantified indirectly. That is because the analyst will be required to make a number of adjustments to allow for the noncomparability of less functionally obsolete properties in the market data comparison base. In the cost approach to property valuation, functional obsolescence is specifically identified and quantified. This direct approach to the quantification of functional obsolescence requires the application of appraisal procedures to the financial and operational results caused by the elements of functional obsolescence.

In many ad valorem property assessments, functional obsolescence is not adequately identified or quantified by either the property owner or the assessing authority. However, a competent and comprehensive ad valorem property tax valuation will both identify and quantify all elements of functional obsolescence—and thus properly estimate the fair market value of the subject property.

Identification and Quantification of the Economic Component of External Obsolescence

There are two components to external obsolescence: (1) locational obsolescence and (2) economic obsolescence. Both of these components can directly impact the valuation of properties for ad valorem assessment purposes.

Locational obsolescence is a decrement in the value of a property due to changes in the physical environment in which the property operates. An example of locational obsolescence would be the construction of a nuclear power plant next to a luxury hotel—presumably the value of the hotel would decrease. Another example would be the construction of a high-rise office building between the subject office building and the lakefront—without its current lakefront views, the rental rates of the subject office building will decline and the value of the subject office property will decrease.

Economic obsolescence is the decrement in the value of a property due to changes in the economic condition of the industry in which that property operates. For example, as the trucking industry proves to be a cost-effective substitute to the railroad industry (and railroad industry profit margins decline due to the effect of the competition), then the value of special purpose properties used in the railroad industry will decrease.

Locational obsolescence is a topic that may more fully be explored in a text related to real estate appraisal. In this section, we will further discuss economic obsolescence and its effect on the value of properties for ad valorem assessment purposes.

Definition of Economic Obsolescence. Economic obsolescence is a reduction in the value of real estate and of tangible personal property due to the impact of events or conditions that are external to and not controlled by the physical nature or the structural or mechanical operation of the property.

Due to the dual characteristics of being (1) beyond the control of the property owners and (2) physically separate from the property, economic obsolescence is considered to be a form of external obsolescence. Although economic obsolescence manifests itself externally to the subject property, its valuation impact is as real and quantifiable as any other form of obsolescence.

Identification of Economic Obsolescence. Of all the forms of obsolescence, economic obsolescence is, arguably, the most difficult to identify and quantify. In fact, economic obsolescence is often best evidenced by a reduction in the value of property that cannot be explained by any of the other forms of obsolescence.

With respect to special purpose properties, the following conditions may indicate the existence of economic obsolescence:

- Changes in zoning or zoning requirements.
- A significant increase in the number of comparable properties on the market.
- Changes in pedestrian or other traffic flow patterns around the subject property.
- The plan for or the erection of unsightly or incongruous-use properties near the subject property.
- A sudden or gradual decrease in the maintenance of properties in the subject locale (e.g., the deterioration of an older residential neighborhood).
- Otherwise unexplained decreases in occupancy or rental rates and increases in tenant turnover.
- Increases in local or regional unemployment, local or regional interest rates, or local or regional utility rates.
- Changes in local or regional government policies regarding economic development and local or regional industry mix.

Forms of Economic Obsolescence. There are two significant categories or forms of economic obsolescence. The first category deals with curability; the second deals with universality. Curability relates to whether the economic obsolescence is curable or incurable. Universality relates to whether the economic obsolescence is local, regional, or national.

Curable economic obsolescence means the events or conditions that caused the obsolescence can be cured (i.e., fixed, repaired, or terminated) as the result of some expenditure of time, effort, or money. Incurable economic obsolescence means the events or conditions that caused the obsolescence cannot be changed, at least not by the owner of the property, regardless of the amount of expenditure of time, effort, or money.

Because economic obsolescence is caused by factors external to the physical structure of the property, most economic obsolescence is considered to be incurable. That is, the owner of the property cannot change the events or conditions that are causing the decrease in the value of the subject property. However, as there are not absolutes in valuation science, it is erroneous to assume all economic obsolescence is incurable.

For example, a real estate developer may construct a luxury hotel. Shortly after the hotel's construction, the neighborhood zoning is changed to allow a garbage dump to be operated next to the new hotel. Clearly, as occupancy rates dwindle, the otherwise luxurious hotel will experience substantial economic obsolescence. However, such economic obsolescence may be curable. It is conceivable, and perhaps economically astute, for the real estate developer to purchase the garbage dump site and turn it into an appealing, verdant park. In this example, the curative expenditure was not made on the subject property, yet the substantial economic obsolescence was cured.

However, it is true that most economic obsolescence is incurable. For example, suppose the same real estate developer constructed his luxury hotel at what was to be a major exit of a planned limited-access interstate highway. After the hotel is built, federal funds are canceled and the highway is never constructed. Clearly, this luxury hotel will experience prodigious economic obsolescence. Without the powers of eminent domain, it would be impossible, if not otherwise impractical and uneconomical, for the real estate developer to complete the highway. Thus, this hypothetical situation illustrates incurable economic obsolescence.

Universality. The universality of economic obsolescence relates to its geographic impact. The degree of the impact of universality on the value of a property is a function of two factors. First, the special purpose versus general purpose nature of the property determines the impact of universality. Second, the breadth and scope of the secondary market for that property type determine the level of influence on universality.

Local economic obsolescence affects the value of properties located only within a locally defined geographic vicinity. For example, changes in zoning affect only those properties within a certain business district. Regional economic obsolescence affects the value of properties on a regional, statewide, or multistate basis. For example, when the semiconductor industry becomes depressed, real estate up and down the Silicon Valley will experience some economic obsolescence. Of course, national economic obsolescence affects all properties used in a certain industry, or in some other global category, on a nationwide basis. For example, when spot oil prices drop below $10 per barrel, the secondary market values for oil well drilling equipment decrease materially, due to economic obsolescence, on a nationwide basis.

Typically, properties that are very general purpose in nature are affected more by local economic obsolescence. Properties that are very special purpose in nature are affected more by national economic obsolescence. For example, the value of a general purpose commercial office building would be affected by local zoning requirements, local economic conditions, local interest rates, and local supply and demand for leased office space. A special purpose sulfuric acid processing plant would be affected by national economic trends, national and international trends in the sulfuric acid industry, and the supply and demand from both plant inputs and outputs on a global basis.

Properties that sell in specialized local secondary markets are affected more by local economic obsolescence. Properties that sell in broad general secondary markets are affected more by national economic obsolescence.

Quantification of Economic Obsolescence. On a local level, economic obsolescence affects real estate to a greater extent than tangible personal property. Each of the three real estate valuation approaches encompasses procedures to quantify economic obsolescence.

Multiple regression analyses—or other quantitative procedures—are often used in the sales comparison approach. These procedures allow for the identification and quantification of the impact of several independent variables on the value of the dependent variable (i.e., the value of the subject property). The actual independent variable elements that are used in the analysis will vary, based on the quality and quantity of available data, the kind of property valued, and the judgment and experience of the analyst. However, independent variables such as interest rates, time adjustments (i.e., elapsed time while the property was listed on the market before sale), and rental rates, or changes in rental rates, are not uncommon. Such independent variables encompass measures of local economic obsolescence.

The income approach to property valuation requires both current analyses of—and prospective projections of—rental income, vacancy and collection losses, tenant renewal rates, operating expenses, and capitalization rates. Clearly, projections that encompass lower rental rates, higher vacancy and collection losses, lower renewal rates, higher operating expenses, and higher capitalization rates have included implicitly, if not explicitly, a quantification of local economic obsolescence.

The specific identification and quantification of economic obsolescence are most closely associated with the cost approach to property valuation. The cost approach requires an estimate of either the replacement cost or the reproduction cost of the subject real property. From this estimate, allowances are subtracted for all forms of accrued depreciation and obsolescence—including economic obsolescence.

Using the cost approach, there are several commonly used methods for quantifying local economic obsolescence. One method involves estimating the reduction in annual net operating income associated with the specific economic obsolescence factors. This reduction in annual net operating income is capitalized to estimate the total amount of local economic obsolescence.

As with local economic obsolescence, there are several methods for quantifying national or industrywide economic obsolescence. For the most part, these methods all involve factors that are relatively macroeconomic and affect an industry on a global basis. Also, these methods typically involve an analysis of the relative change in these factors—for example, a specific macroeconomic factor today compared with the five-year average value for that factor.

One element frequently associated with industrywide economic obsolescence is the change in product selling prices. Typically, if average product selling prices across the industry decline materially, and with some anticipated level of permanence, then economic obsolescence occurs with respect to the special purpose real property and tangible personal property used in that industry. For example, a general and prolonged reduction in the price of a barrel of crude oil will cause economic obsolescence to occur in the assets used in the oil and gas exploration industry.

A general and prolonged reduction in the number of units produced, on an industrywide basis, is also indicative of industrywide obsolescence. This is true if there is relatively low price elasticity of demand for the products produced in the subject industry. A reduction of the total number of units produced in an industry could be the result of changes in consumer demand and preference or changes in competition, production quotas, or import or export quotas. For example, an industry that has historically produced 1 million units per year and now produces only 700,000 units per year, where there is little or no product price elasticity, will experience economic obsolescence associated with the properties used in that industry.

A current and sustained reduction in the level of investor returns, compared with historical industry averages, also indicates economic obsolescence on an industry-wide basis. Appropriate measures of investor returns would include return on net assets, return on total assets, return on investment, return on equity, and return on tangible assets.

When rates of investor return are reduced industrywide, property owners cannot afford to replace worn-out productive properties with either new or used properties. If the property owners are earning an inadequate rate of return on their investments in the productive properties, they will not expect to earn an adequate rate of return on investment in new or replacement properties. Since the "return" portion of the formula is controlled by macroeconomic events, the "investment" portion of the formula will be affected by the property owners. That is, the property owners will continue to bid down or reduce the value of the subject properties until their level of investment in the subject properties is low enough to allow them to earn a fair return on investment. For example, as across-the-board rates of investor return declined in the steel industry a few years ago, the value of properties employed in the steel industry correspondingly declined, due to industrywide economic obsolescence.

Associated with rates of investor return, current and sustained reductions in the levels of profit margins also may be indicative of industrywide economic obsolescence. For example, in an industry that has historically earned a 10 percent net profit margin (e.g., return on sales) and now earns only 6 percent, industrywide economic obsolescence associated with the special purpose real estate and tangible personal property will become evident.

A general and sustained increase in present value discount rates or income capitalization rates for an industry, when compared with historical industry norms, also may be indicative of economic obsolescence. Such discount rates or capitalization rates are derived from the cost of capital components—both debt and equity—available to property owners in the industry. As with increases in the costs of labor and materials, increases in the costs of capital components have a deleterious effect on the value of the properties employed in the business. Accordingly, increases in the discount rates or capitalization rates that property owners require may cause a decrease in the value of the properties employed in the subject industry, due to economic obsolescence.

One method that may be used to quantify both company-specific (nonsystematic) economic obsolescence and industrywide (systematic) economic obsolescence involves the estimation of a company's business enterprise value. The business enterprise valuation encompasses the going-concern value of all the company's assets, including financial assets, real estate, tangible personal property, and intangible personal property. To determine the existence of economic obsolescence, the business enterprise value is compared with the depreciated replacement cost of the company's productive assets. If the business enterprise value is less than the depreciated replacement cost of the company's assets, then economic obsolescence typically exists.

Issues in Unit Valuation for Ad Valorem Purposes

Under the summation concept, each real property and personal property asset of the taxpayer is appraised individually. The respective values for all of the individual real property and personal property assets are summed (hence, the name "summation concept"). The sum of the individual asset values represents the collective valuation of all of the industrial or commercial taxpayer assets subject to property taxation.

Under the unitary concept, first, the entire business enterprise of the industrial or commercial taxpayer is valued as a "unit"—or as a single mass assemblage of operating assets. Second, the value of any individual asset or property type not assessable as part of the taxable unit is removed from the overall unit valuation. The residual, or remainder, is the taxable unit—that is, the value of the industrial or commercial taxpayer's assets subject to assessment. Third, for businesses that operate in several different taxing jurisdictions, an allocation of the taxpayer's total unit value to a particular jurisdiction is made. Last, the value of any assets exempt from unitary assessment in the local jurisdiction (e.g., locally assessed assets or over-the-road vehicles) is removed from the allocated taxable unit.

The summation valuation concept is a topic for exploration in a discussion related to real estate or tangible personal property valuation. It is appropriate to explore the unit valuation concept in a financial valuation context. In all material respects, the first—and the principal—analyses in the unit valuation process are business enterprise valuation analyses.

As we will explore in our discussion of "what is the unit subject to ad valorem taxation?" the objective of the taxpayer's unit valuation is not always the same as the objective of the taxpayer's business enterprise valuation. Nonetheless, the approaches, methods, and procedures generally used in both valuations are essentially the same.

In this section, we will summarize the generally accepted unit valuation approaches. We will compare and contrast these unit valuation approaches with the generally accepted business enterprise valuation approaches. Next, we will consider the related questions of:

1. What is the "unit" subject to ad valorem taxation?
2. Do the generally accepted unit valuation approaches actually value that appraisal subject?

Then, we will explore some of the current controversial issues related to the application of the individual unit valuation approaches. Lastly, we will consider some of the valuation differences between an assemblage of operating assets and a capitalization structure of negotiable securities—from an investment risk and expected return perspective.

Unit Valuation. First, we will describe the types of industrial and commercial companies that are typically subject to unit valuation for ad valorem taxation purposes. Second, we will introduce the standard unit valuation approaches. And, third, we will compare the standard unit valuation approaches with the standard business valuation approaches.

The Background of Unit Valuation. Traditionally, the unit valuation concept was applied to transportation, communication, and utility companies. These categories of industries include railroads and airlines; local exchange, long-distance, and cellular telephone companies; gas, water, and electric utilities; and oil and gas pipeline companies. The rationale for applying the unit valuation concepts to these types of taxpayers includes the following arguments:

1. The taxpayer assets are located in numerous taxing jurisdictions; in fact, they often cross numerous state lines.
2. The taxpayer assets are fully integrated from a physical, functional, and an economic perspective; it does not make sense to analyze any one set of assets separately from the overall operating unit.

3.   The individual taxpayer assets are physically, functionally, technologically, and economically part of one system; most of the systematic and nonsystematic risk factors that affect the system also affect the individual assets.

4.   The value of any of the taxpayer assets is a function of the assets being part of an income-producing mass assemblage of assets; the independent values of the individual assets are not reflective of the contributory value of the assets to the overall unit.

5.   For some of these taxpayers (e.g., railroads and airlines), the taxpayer assets physically move; it may be difficult—and unfair—to independently value the individual assets based upon their physical location on any one particular assessment (i.e., valuation) date.

Many of these arguments for the use of the unit valuation concept are factual and logical. However, there is an additional factor that distinguishes companies in most (if not all) of the above-mentioned industries: Historically, they were all regulated. And, many of these industries were rate regulated—that is, subject to the mechanism of an allowed maximum rate of return on investment times an allowed "rate base" (i.e., the level of investment of assets placed in service).

The unit valuation concept essentially equates the value of the taxpayer's debt and equity instruments (sometimes called the market value of invested capital) to the value of the taxpayer's assessable assets in place as of a particular valuation date. For many reasons that are not relevant to this discussion, the concept of unit valuation may have been much more appropriate when these taxpayers were regulated (and, particularly, when they were subject to a "rate base" related regulatory environment).

However, most of the taxpayers that are currently subject to unit valuation are no longer regulated companies. In fact, most transportation, communications, and (to some extent) utilities now operate in an unregulated, competitive economic structure. In a free market, competitive economic structure, prices, rates of return, and profits are much less predictable. Therefore, the basic premise of unit valuation (i.e., that the value of negotiable securities equals the value of assessable assets) may not be as applicable as it once was.

Some local assessment taxing jurisdictions have expanded the category of companies that are subject to unit valuation to include physically local (i.e., located within one taxing jurisdiction) but still functionally integrated business operations. Examples of such companies include: cable television operators; mining operations; racetracks and sporting facilities; hotels and resort properties; and complex, process-type manufacturing facilities.

Some taxing jurisdictions assert that such businesses can be described as integrated and independent systems of operating assets. However, most of these businesses have always operated in an unregulated, competitive economic environment. And, these businesses typically compete against other taxpayers that are assessed under the summation valuation concept. For these reasons, such corporate taxpayers often question the applicability of unit valuation in their ad valorem property tax assessment.

Unit Valuation Approaches. The three standard and generally accepted unit valuation approaches are the cost approach, the income approach, and the market approach. Assuming that the taxpayer is subject to the unit valuation concept, these three approaches are used to provide independent indications of value for the taxpayer's overall operating unit. The value indications of the three approaches are synthesized and correlated into a final value reconciliation.

Unit Valuation and Business Valuation. Clearly, there are direct comparisons between the standard unit valuation approaches and the standard business valuation approaches. While the names of the unit valuation approaches, methods, and procedures are somewhat different, the differences are more semantic than substantive. The conceptual underpinnings and theoretical principles are basically the same. The practical application of the analytical procedures is basically the same.

The cost approach shares the same conceptual development as the asset-based business valuation approach. In both approaches, the total tangible assets of the overall business enterprise are adjusted to a current market value. In both approaches, the total intangible value of the overall business enterprise is estimated on an aggregate basis.

In both approaches, the enterprise's intangible value is measured by some version of a capitalized excess earnings procedure. In the unit valuation, this intangible value is called *entrepreneurial profit* if positive or *economic obsolescence* if negative. In the business valuation, this intangible value is called *goodwill* if positive or *negative goodwill* (and a reduction of tangible asset value) if negative.

The income approach shares the same conceptual development as the income-based business valuation approach. In both approaches, the value of the total enterprise is estimated by capitalizing a measure of prospective economic income. In both approaches, the overall capitalization rate represents a risk-adjusted rate of return to the total investors in the enterprise.

In both approaches, the alternative valuation methods involve (1) the present value of a future stream of income with the consideration of a future enterprise value—at the conclusion of the discrete projection period or (2) the present value of an annuity in perpetuity where the annuity income is a stabilized estimate of next period income.

The market approach shares the same conceptual development as the market-based business valuation approach. In the stock and debt method, the values of the unit's total debt and equity securities are estimated by reference to capital market–derived security pricing data. In the guideline publicly traded company business valuation method, the values of the enterprise's total debt and equity securities are estimated by reference to the same capital market–derived security pricing data.

The results of all three approaches—whether called unit valuation or business valuation approaches—are an estimate of the value of (1) the total asset structure and (2) the total capital structure of the subject overall business enterprise. As a basic economic premise—and as a basic accounting premise—the value of a business's total asset structure must equal the value of the business's total capital structure. This is true in a unit valuation performed for property tax purposes. And, this is true in a business valuation performed for any other purpose.

Asset Structure of the Going-Concern Business. Let's examine the content of the total asset structure of a going-concern business enterprise. The components of the asset structure are as follows:

1. Current assets.
2. Tangible assets:
   a. Tangible real estate.
   b. Tangible personal property.
3. Intangible assets:
   a. Identified intangible assets.
   b. Unidentified intangible assets.

The current assets include cash, receivables, and inventory. The tangible real estate includes land and buildings. The tangible personal property includes machinery and equipment.

The identified intangible assets include (1) intangible real property—for example, leasehold and possessory interests, easements, air and water rights, and subsurface exploitation rights; and (2) intangible personal property—for example, contracts, licenses, trademarks, patents, copyrights, software, employees, suppliers, customers, and the going-concern value of the business.

Going-concern value is often defined as the incremental value associated with the assemblage of all of the enterprise's identified tangible assets (e.g., plant and equipment) and all of the enterprise's identified intangible assets (e.g., employees, products, customers, suppliers).

The unidentified intangible asset category is principally the goodwill of the enterprise. Goodwill is often defined as the present value of future income not associated with any of the other tangible or intangible assets—that is, the tangible or intangible assets currently in place as of the valuation date.

So, goodwill could relate to the sale of future products that have not yet been developed as of the valuation date. It could relate to sales to future customers that are not yet known as of the valuation date. And, it could relate to future income generated from physical plant and facilities not yet constructed on the valuation date. It could even relate to the future income to be earned from investors' expectations of business mergers and acquisitions that are not yet consummated on the valuation date.

Accordingly, unidentified intangible value (e.g., goodwill) relates to assets (tangible or intangible) that are not yet in existence as of the valuation date.

The sum of all of these categories of tangible and intangible assets represents the total asset structure of a going-concern business enterprise. The value of the total asset structure is estimated by the application of any of the unit valuation and the business valuation approaches described above.

Capital Structure of the Going-Concern Business. Let's examine the content of the total capital structure of a going-concern business enterprise. The components of the capital structure are as follows:

1. Current liabilities.
2. Long-term debt.
3. Preferred stock.
4. Common stock.

The current liabilities include salaries, accounts, notes, and taxes payable. The long-term debt includes bonds, notes, mortgages, and debentures. The preferred stock includes all classes of the company's preferred stock outstanding. And, the common stock includes all classes of the company's common stock outstanding.

Also, implicit in the common stock value is the value effect on the company's contingent liabilities. Contingent liabilities are the unrecorded liabilities associated with the company's environmental, litigation (including employee, product, and general commercial), taxation, and potential bankruptcy issues. These contingent liabilities have the effect of reducing the value of the company's common stock. That is, investors implicitly consider the likelihood, amount, and timing of these contingent liabilities, in their pricing of the company's common stock.

The sum of all of these components of debt and equity capital represent the total capital structure (sometimes called total invested capital) of a going-concern business enterprise. The value of the total capital structure is estimated by the application of any of the unit valuation or the business valuation approaches described above.

Appraisal of the Going-Concern Business. The concluded asset structure and capital structure values achieve the desired appraisal objective of the business valuation of a going-concern business enterprise. However, do the concluded asset structure and capital structure values achieve the appraisal objective of a unit valuation for ad valorem property tax purposes? We will consider that question next.

The Unit Subject to Valuation. The definition of the unit subject to valuation is a matter of statutory authority, administrative rulings, and judicial precedent. It is a question that must be asked—and answered—on a state-by-state basis. In some states, the definition of the unit subject to ad valorem property taxation is clear and unambiguous. In many states, however, the statutes, rulings, and precedents are not clear and unambiguous.

Jurisdictional Differences. In some jurisdictions, there is uncertainty on the parts of—and controversy between—taxpayers and assessing authorities as to what exactly is included in (or excluded from) the taxable unit. The following paragraphs will outline some of the issues with regard to assets that may be either included in—or excluded from—the taxable unit.

In some jurisdictions, current assets are excluded from the taxable unit. These current assets (e.g., cash, receivables, inventory, etc.) may be excluded from property taxation altogether. Or, they may be subject to a different level of property taxation than that applied to the overall unit.

In some jurisdictions, over-the-road vehicles are excluded from the taxable unit. This is because the vehicles are subject to a different type of taxation—through the vehicle licensing procedures.

In some jurisdictions, construction work-in-process is excluded from the unit subject to taxation. This is because those assets are not yet fully functional as of the assessment date.

In most jurisdictions, locally assessed properties (e.g., buildings, plants, etc.) are excluded from the taxable unit. This exclusion is to avoid double taxation of the same property. That is, if a facility is locally assessed as real property (for example, at the county level), it should not also be included in the overall unit subject to centrally assessed property taxation.

In many jurisdictions, identified intangible assets are excluded from the unit subject to ad valorem taxation. Depending upon the jurisdiction, all identified intangible assets may be excluded from property taxation—or only certain statutorily specified intangible assets (e.g., software, trademarks, patents, copyrights) may be excluded from property taxation.

In virtually all jurisdictions, only assets in place as of the assessment date are subject to taxation. However, this concept has not been fully developed—either in practice, in the literature, or in judicial deliberations. This point relates to the fact that the asset structure appraised in the unit valuation includes the goodwill of the taxpayer business enterprise. And, the goodwill of the taxpayer business enterprise includes the economic value of both tangible and intangible assets not yet in existence as of the valuation date.

Value Excluded from the Taxable Unit. Accordingly, it is important for both taxpayers and assessing authorities to understand the total composition of the asset structure that is the result of the unit valuation (and the business valuation) process. Those assets that are statutorily excluded from the taxable unit should be removed from the overall unit value conclusion—prior to the property tax assessment procedure.

Some of the assets to be excluded are easy to identify. Obvious examples include cash account balances, over-the-road vehicles, and construction work-in-progress. Some of the other assets to be excluded are not as easy to identify. Less obvious examples include identifiable intangible assets (e.g., customer relationships, a trained and assembled workforce, proprietary technology, etc.). And, perhaps the least obvious example—but arguably the most universal example—would be unidentifiable intangible value in the nature of goodwill. This unidentifiable intangible goodwill (or the present value of the future income from tangible and intangible assets not in existence on the assessment date) may be an important element in the reconciliation of:

1. The taxpayer's overall business enterprise value (as estimated by the standard unit valuation methods).
2. The value of the portion of the taxpayer's unit subject to ad valorem property taxation.

Identification and Valuation of Intangible Assets in the Unit Method of Assessment

Using the unit method of property tax assessment, the indicated values derived from the income approach (using either the direct capitalization method or the yield capitalization method) and from the market approach (using the stock and debt method) represent the total value of the assets of the subject taxpayer business enterprise, including all tangible and all intangible assets. However, in many taxing jurisdictions, intangible personal property assets are not subject to ad valorem taxation. Therefore, in jurisdictions in which they are not subject to property taxation, the value of the intangible personal property assets should be identified and deducted from the indicated total asset value of the unit (derived from either the income approach or the market approach) to arrive at the residual value of the taxpayer's assessable tangible assets.

Numerous examples of intangible personal property assets are commonly found in the business enterprise unit. Intangible personal property assets are identifiable, separable, and capable of systematic valuation and may include, for example, the following: trademarks and trade names, a trained and assembled workforce, computer software and systems, customer relationships, patents, supplier contracts, and royalty agreements.

Identification and Application of Appropriate Income Approach Methods for Ad Valorem Unitary Valuation

The capital asset pricing model (CAPM)[2] was developed by William F. Sharpe in the 1960s, in the course of his study of the valuation of securities and the mechanics of portfolio theory. Along with his other work in investment analysis and portfolio management, the development of CAPM won Sharpe the Nobel Prize in economics in 1990.

---

[2] See Chapter 9 of this book, pp. 162–68.

While CAPM is, arguably, the most important univariate model to describe rational investment decision making that has come along, this section will focus on the practical limitations and conceptual weaknesses of using CAPM for ad valorem property tax valuation purposes.

In particular, we will consider the use of CAPM to quantify the required rate of return on property subject to ad valorem property taxation. We will also consider the use of CAPM to estimate a required capitalization or discount rate for either direct (income) capitalization or yield (income) capitalization valuation methodologies.

For purposes of this section, we will assume that property subject to ad valorem tax is a centrally assessed *unit*—that is, a property that is assessed as an income-producing collection of tangible real property and tangible personal property.

Weaknesses of Using CAPM

One of the major conceptual and practical weaknesses of using CAPM to estimate a capitalization rate for property tax purposes is whether, fundamentally, a theory developed for understanding the value of investment securities within a diversified portfolio is applicable to the understanding of the value of illiquid assets operating within an individual going-concern company.

CAPM was designed to estimate the fair rate of return on investment securities—not the capitalization rate on the controlling interest in illiquid asset components of individual corporations. Since different investment assets are subject to different degrees of risk, it is clear that they have different expected rates of investment return. For example, cash or cash equivalents—such as marketable securities—change hands regularly in well-established money markets, which are generally recognized as being highly efficient. Thus, these types of investment assets have rates of return that are closely followed by investors.

Tangible production assets, such as income-producing real estate and operating tangible personal property, are fundamentally different from marketable securities. For one thing, the market for exchanging ownership of operating real estate or operating tangible personal property is not nearly as efficient as either the established money markets or the capital markets for exchanging investment securities. The next section discusses several of the differences in the market for securities exchange transactions and the market for operating real estate/tangible personal property exchange transactions. These differences in marketplace mechanics—and in particular, differences in marketplace efficiency—partly explain why CAPM is more effective for estimating an investor's required rate of return on security investments than it is for estimating that same rate of return for real estate/personal property investments.

Exhibit 34–1 presents some of the more salient differences between the typically efficient and organized markets in which investment securities are transacted and the typically inefficient unorganized markets in which real estate/personal property operating assets transact. Thus, although the CAPM model works well for estimating non-diversified risk and required rate of return in the securities market, it may not work well for estimating those same variables in the real estate/personal property markets.

Exhibit 34–2 summarizes some of the intrinsic differences between securities (whether debt or equity instruments) and operating real estate/personal property (either individual assets or going-concern assemblages of assets) as investment alternatives.

Exhibit 34–1

Differences between Securities Exchange Markets and Real Estate/Personal Property Exchange Markets

Securities Transactions Market	**Operating Real Estate/Personal Property Transactions Market**
1. Generally homogeneous properties competing for investment funds.	1. Substantially heterogeneous properties competing for investment funds.
2. Large number of buyers and sellers.	2. Few buyers and sellers in any one price range at any one location (particularly for special purpose assets).
3. Relatively uniform, stable, and low transaction prices.	3. Relatively high and fluctuating transaction prices.
4. Low cost of individual transactions (including brokerage, information, and title-transfer fees).	4. High cost of individual transactions (including brokerage, information, and title-transfer fees).
5. Relatively few government restrictions on secondary market transactions.	5. Secondary market transactions subject to regulations, registration, and legislation at all levels.
6. Supply and demand of properties never far out of balance	6. Volatile demand for and sluggish supply of properties.
7. Reasonably knowledgeable and generally informed buyers and sellers.	7. Potentially uninformed buyers and sellers who interact infrequently.
8. Public disclosure of substantial financial and operational information regarding properties.	8. Restricted disclosure of limited information (if any disclosure at all) regarding properties.
9. Organized market mechanism, allowing for rapid consummation and confirmation of transaction.	9. Small, fragmented, overlapping market segments causing delayed consummation of transaction.
10. Readily "consumed," quickly supplied, and easily transported properties.	10. Durable, relatively immobile, and illiquid properties.

Exhibit 34–2

Intrinsic Differences between Securities and Operating Real Estate/Personal Property

Securities (Debt or Equity Instrument)	**Real Estate/Personal Property (Individual or as a Mass Assemblage)**
1. Liquid, marketable investments.	1. Illiquid investments.
2. Noncontrolling interest income production and distribution.	2. Controlling interest in income production and distribution.
3. Small absolute dollar investment required.	3. Large absolute dollar investment required.
4. Small percentage of overall wealth committed to investment.	4. Large percentage of overall wealth committed to investment.
5. Diversified portfolio of investments.	5. Nondiversified portfolio of investments.
6. Short-term investment time horizon.	6. Long-term investment time horizon.
7. Does not require investment to maintain investment base.	7. Requires replenishment investment to maintain investment base.
8. Investments expected to appreciate over time.	8. Investments expected to depreciate over time.
9. Income typically subject to only individual tax (from investor's perspective).	9. Income typically subject to both corporate and individual tax (from investor's perspective).
10. Portfolios can be created in limitless combinations of risky securities and risk-free securities.	10. Portfolio limited to the particular combination of real estate and personal property that operates the business.

As Exhibit 34–2 indicates, there are fundamental investment risk and return differences between marketable minority interests in debt and equity securities and nonmarketable controlling interests in operating real estate and tangible personal property. Because of these differences, it is unlikely that a model that effectively correlates nondiversified risk and expected return for securities will be able to serve the same function for such real estate or personal property.

Another weakness in using the CAPM for ad valorem tax property valuation is the measurement of the various components of the CAPM equation. (This weakness also applies when using CAPM for its original purpose of understanding the value of securities in a portfolio.)[3] That is, there is no single accepted source of data or method for measuring the beta coefficient component of the model.

Another problem with using CAPM to estimate the cost of equity capital for ad valorem valuation analysis is that the associated valuation model and resulting valuation conclusion generally include the value of assets not yet in place as of the property tax lien date. Since CAPM implicitly incorporates investors' expectation of security appreciation, it will impart a value to the returns from expected future investments in both tangible assets and intangible assets—assets not in existence on the assessment date.

Since the empirical data used in a CAPM analysis are market derived, they indicate a consensus of investors' expectations regarding the prospective performance of the subject investment and/or the guideline investments. If the subject business is successful, these expectations will include the present value of future returns for two types of business assets that may not be subject to ad valorem taxation: (1) goodwill and (2) expected future capital expenditures in tangible real and personal property.

Goodwill is sometimes defined as the present value of future income from future customers. According to this definition, these are unidentified customers the subject business may serve at some point in the future—as opposed to expected, recurring income for the current, identified, repeat customers of the subject business. While investors' expectations of future income from new customers is an important component of a going-concern business, the associated goodwill represents the intangible value of business relationships that do not exist (and are not subject to specific identification) as of the property tax lien date.

In their security pricing decisions, investors also will assign a value to the positive net present value of future capital expenditures of the subject business. (A positive net present value occurs when the business expects to earn a rate of return on its investment greater than its cost of capital.) Investors' expectations of future capital expenditures may, themselves, have two components: (1) future merger and acquisition activity at the subject firm and (2) future investments in plant, property, and equipment at the subject firm. It is reasonable for investors to expect that competent management of the subject business will continue to make new net investments (that is, expenditures greater than what is required to simply replace worn-out assets) in order to expand the business in new locations, new product lines, new services, and so forth. While these investor expectations are perfectly reasonable, valuation analyses that incorporate these expectations (through CAPM or otherwise) will include the present value of capital expenditures for tangible assets (and/or mergers and acquisitions) that do not physically exist as of the property tax lien date.

Additional Difficulties

CAPM is difficult to adjust when estimating the required rate of return commensurate with measures of economic income other than net cash flow available to investors. For example, it is difficult to adjust CAPM to accommodate pretax net income, operating income, operating cash flow, or economic income streams other than net cash flow.

---

[3] See Exhibit 9–12.

There are also numerous and difficult adjustments that have to be made when applying betas estimated for guideline companies to the valuation of the company subject to ad valorem taxation, including:

1. Different degrees of leverage between the guideline companies (or the industry average) and the subject company.
2. Different degrees of diversification—that is, the differences between the subject subsidiary or division (perhaps a business operating in one product line or in one location) and guideline diversified holding companies.
3. Differences between the closely held subject company and the publicly traded guidelines (particularly significant, of course, if the subject company is closely held or is the "closely held" division or subsidiary of a public corporation).
4. Difficulties that arise when the subject company is in only one line of business and the "best" available guidelines are not pure play companies.
5. Difficulties that arise when the "best" (or any) guideline companies are more diversified than the subject company (that is, when the guideline companies are more in the nature of "portfolio" companies).

Alternatives to CAPM

There are several alternatives to CAPM for estimating the cost of equity capital in either a direct capitalization or a yield capitalization valuation analysis. For purposes of identifying these alternatives only, the following methods can be used for estimating the cost of equity capital:

1. The cost of debt of the subject company plus an equity risk premium.
2. The sum of the dividend yield plus the capital gain yield for selected guideline companies.
3. The arbitrage pricing theory.

All of these alternative methods have strengths and weaknesses. However, none of these methods corrects for all of the problems encountered when using CAPM.

The conceptual and practical problems with CAPM are even greater in the valuation of operating properties subject to ad valorem taxation when using a standard yield capitalization method on a net cash flow basis. However, problems are not as severe when using the model in the valuation of operating properties subject to ad valorem taxation, if the following valuation methods are utilized:

1. An asset accumulation method, including the aggregate appraisal of all real and tangible personal property (typically using a cost approach), and including going-concern and goodwill value (but based on the capitalization of historical and not prospective economic income).
2. A yield capitalization method that assumes no future growth in economic earnings. The implicit assumption in the use of this method is either:
   a. Capital expenditures equal annual depreciation expense (so that there is only direct asset replacement in the valuation model), or
   b. Incremental (new) capital expenditures yield exactly the subject firm's weighted average cost of capital (so that there is no increase in unit value due to these incremental capital expenditures).
3. A direct capitalization method that assumes no growth in economic earnings. The implicit assumption in the use of this method is that annual depreciation

expense exactly equals prospective capital expenditures, so that there is a stable asset base in the valuation model. In addition, the following factors should be taken into account in using this method:

a. The naive use of earnings to price (E/P) multiples is generally inappropriate when estimating a capitalization rate for property taxation direct capitalization analyses, since E/P multiples consider both income yield and expected capital appreciation. Thus, the use of E/P multiples will typically subject the valuation to the inclusion of assets not in existence on the lien date.

b. Security investors demand a return of and a return on their investments. They sell their investments after a defined holding period and enjoy appreciation in the value of their investments. This appreciation typically does not occur for operating properties subject to ad valorem taxation.

c. Investors' yields on operating property must be adjusted when compared with yields earned by security investors. Operating businesses do not sell their portfolio of operating properties after a defined holding period, and they do not generally enjoy appreciation in these properties.

There are two fundamental valuation objectives that analysts should keep in mind when attempting to use CAPM for property tax valuation purposes: (1) Operating properties (either collectively or individually) are *not* the same as marketable debt or equity security instruments, and (2) operating properties in place on the lien date do not have the same value as the prospective income to be generated by future properties.

Clearly, analysts need to carefully consider all of the implications of using CAPM for the valuation of operating properties, either individually or on a unitary basis, for ad valorem property tax purposes.

Problems with the Use of Stock Market Data in Property Tax Valuations

Introduction

In this section, we will summarize the conceptual and the practical problems with the use of stock market data sources in the property tax valuation of any unit of real estate. This will include the use of stock market data to extract direct capitalization rates, present value (yield capitalization) discount rates, and pricing multiples. As part of this discussion, we will focus on the valuation differences between an investment in operating real estate (i.e., the property tax valuation subject) and an investment in negotiable securities (i.e., often the property tax valuation data source). We will consider these differences from an investment risk and expected return perspective.

There are general comparability problems regarding the use of capital market data (i.e., pricing multiples, capitalization rates, and security prices) in all unit valuation methods—including both income and market approach methods. These general comparability problems include: (1) the potential lack of comparability of the selected guideline companies and the taxpayer unit of operating property and (2) the lack of comparability of the selected guideline securities (i.e., marketable, non-controlling securities traded on efficient stock exchanges) and the taxpayer unit (i.e., nonmarketable, controlling ownership interests in operating property for which there is no ready secondary market).

In addition to these general comparability problems, there may be several other analytical problems associated with the use of capital market–derived data in unit valuation methods:

1. Security prices are substantially variable (and sometimes erratic) in the short term.
2. Security prices are often affected by macroeconomic events not related to the subject company.
3. Security prices can be quickly and substantially distorted based upon short-term industry-specific or company-specific phenomena.
4. Security prices are always forward looking—accordingly they reflect investors' expectations of income that has not yet been (and may never be) earned.
5. Capital market pricing multiples tend to artificially inflate the value indications of the more successful companies in an industry—particularly if the multiples include consideration of companies that have poor financial performances.

Security prices change quickly and substantially. Daily changes of 10 percent, 20 percent, or more in the stock prices of public companies are not uncommon. Daily changes of 100 points, 200 points, or more in broad market indices such as the Dow Jones Industrial Average are also not uncommon. While these rapid and significant price changes clearly reflect investors' perceptions of security values, they do not necessarily reflect investors' perceptions of underlying operating property values. If the price of a guideline company security was to change (increase or decrease) 20 percent in one day, no rational investor—or informed analyst—would expect that the market value of that guideline company's operating property also would change 20 percent in one day. Nonetheless, the use of capital market data in unit valuation methods can lead to that conclusion.

Security prices can change substantially when there has been no fundamental change whatsoever in the guideline company or in the guideline industry. Rather, security prices often change substantially in response to macroeconomic or political conditions. For example, announced or perceived changes in Federal Reserve monetary policy, changes in Congressional fiscal policy, changes in economists' consensus of inflation forecasts, and so on, all may cause substantial changes in stock prices. Similarly, the election or appointments of political candidates in the United States—or as far away as Russia, China, or Israel—can cause substantial changes in stock prices. Clearly, after any of these macroeconomic or political announcements, there is not a corresponding change in the market value of the operating property of the guideline companies or of the subject taxpayer. Nonetheless, the use of capital market data in unit valuation methods can lead to that conclusion.

Security prices can change materially based upon short-term phenomena. For example, when a guideline company—or the subject taxpayer—either attains or fails to obtain quarterly earnings expectations, then stock prices often change materially. This is true even though the operating results that triggered the price change are very short-term and may not be reflective of longer-term trends. Likewise, a single event can materially change the stock price levels in an entire industry. For example, after the 1996 crash of the Value Jet flight in the Florida Everglades, the stock price of Value Jet and many other discount airlines decreased materially. At the same time, the stock price of many major airlines increased materially. These price changes would have direct effects on the corresponding multiples. Clearly, the short-term operational results or the one-time events that occurred to one industry participant should not have an impact on the market value of the operating property of all guideline companies or of the subject taxpayer. Nonetheless, the use of capital market data in unit valuation methods can lead to that conclusion.

Both portfolio management theory and empirical data indicate that security prices are forward looking—or ex ante. That is, they depend on investor's expectations of the future results of operations of the guideline companies and of the subject taxpayer. First, when there is a difference between expected operating results and historical operating results, there are practical problems associated with the application of the market-derived ex ante multiples to the ex post financial data of the subject taxpayer. Second, and perhaps more importantly, security prices are based upon what investors think may happen in the future. Of course, these expected results of operations may never actually materialize. And, actual future results of operations may turn out to be considerably below the expected future results of operations. Therefore, if these ex ante security prices are used in the unit valuation, then the taxpayer will be assessed based upon the results of business operations that have not yet occurred as of the valuation date—and that may never occur. Accordingly, the use of capital market data in unit valuation methods can lead to this conclusion.

Often, when the results of operations deteriorate, security prices do not decline in the same proportion. For example, when guideline companies in an industry have a "bad year" financially, their stock prices will decline. However, typically they will not decline to the same extent as their decrease in operating results. Therefore, capital market multiples actually tend to increase when an industry—or when particular guideline companies—have declining financial results. (One explanation for this phenomenon is that security prices are forward looking—and that investors are expecting a future rebound in the subject industry.) When the subject taxpayer has a financially successful year, the indicated value of the taxpayer property is artificially inflated. This is because the inflated multiples (of the less profitable than average guideline companies) are applied to the (more profitable than average) subject taxpayer results. The result is that the indicated value of the taxpayer is overstated due to the inflated multiples of the less profitable companies in the subject industry. Clearly, the value of the currently successful taxpayer should not be estimated by reference to investors' expectations for the rebound of less successful guideline companies. Nonetheless, the use of capital market data in unit valuation methods can lead to that conclusion.

Income Approach Valuation Issues

This section will explore several of the current issues with regard to the application of the income approach to property valuation. This discussion will address the relative weighting of the yield capitalization method versus the direct capitalization method.

Many analysts assign a greater weighting to the yield capitalization method than to the direct capitalization method in the valuation synthesis and conclusion. This section describes some of the reasons for this relative weighting.

In the application of the yield capitalization method, both the measurement of economic income and the yield capitalization rate are intended to be specific to the subject property. The discrete income projection is the best estimate of the prospective income generation of the subject property. And, the yield capitalization rate (or present value discount rate) is typically estimated based on a risk analysis of the subject property compared with all other classes of investment opportunities.

The yield capitalization method is specific to the subject property. It can accommodate projected cyclical changes in economic income. It can accommodate uneven expected rates of changes in prospective economic income. And, it can accommodate expected fundamental changes in the economic income—or in the investment risk—of the subject property.

In the direct capitalization method, the economic income subject to capitalization is intended to relate directly to the subject property. However, the guideline publicly traded companies from which direct capitalization rates are often estimated are, at best, indirectly related to the subject property. For several reasons, as will be discussed below, these guidelines companies often do not provide useful valuation guidance with regard to direct capitalization rates.

First, with regard to the income subject to capitalization, the direct capitalization method requires the estimation of a single period stabilized income projection. Since this estimation is for a single period, it cannot vary over time. In other words, the direct capitalization method does not allow for (1) any expected cyclical changes in income or (2) any changes in income not represented by a constant growth rate.

Second, while the estimation of the single period stabilized income is very important to direct capitalization, it is difficult to project this stabilized income. Careful analysis is required in order to determine if the stabilized income should be based on (1) last year's actual income, (2) an average of the last three years, (3) an average of the last five years, or (4) some other base period. The projection of stabilized income is intended to be an estimate of the most likely level of income, on average, in the future. However, many analysts simply inflate a prior period's actual income in order to estimate the prospective stabilized income.

Third, with regard to the typical direct capitalization rate estimation process, there are two serious comparability problems:

1. The guideline companies selected for analysis are often not comparable enough to the taxpayer business to provide meaningful valuation guidance.
2. The guideline company data subject to analysis relate to marketable, noncontrolling securities that trade in efficient capital markets; the taxpayer property unit relates to nonmarketable, controlling ownership interests in operating properties that have no organized secondary market.

Accordingly, there may be a fundamental lack of comparability between the capital market data used to estimate the direct capitalization rate and the operating property included in the taxpayer unit.

Fourth, there are well defined comparability criteria for the application of the direct capitalization method to the valuation of real estate. There are also well defined criteria of the identification and quantification of adjustments (to increase the comparability of the comparable properties with the subject property) in the application of the direct capitalization method to the valuation of real estate. However, many analysts do not follow these same well defined criteria for comparability and adjustments in the application of the direct capitalization method for unit valuation purposes. If these well defined criteria are not followed, then the results of the direct capitalization analysis may be unreliable.

Many analysts prefer to weight the yield capitalization method more heavily than the direct capitalization method in the overall valuation synthesis and conclusion. This section has summarized some of the reasons for this preference of the yield capitalization valuation method as compared with the direct capitalization valuation method. The yield capitalization method uses income and yield capitalization rate (i.e., risk and expected return) factors that are more directly associated with the subject taxpayer. The direct capitalization method often uses capital market data that are indirectly associated with the subject taxpayer.

Within the unit valuation context, the direct capitalization method may lead to unreasonable valuation conclusions for several reasons. The analyst may attempt to identify and quantify adjustments to the capital market–derived data in order to mitigate the problems with the direct capitalization method. However, if the quantity and magnitude of these adjustments are significant, then it is logical to assign a weighting preference to the yield capitalization method in the value reconciliation and correlation procedure.

Market Approach Valuation Issues

This section will explore several of the current issues with regard to the application of the market approach—and particularly the stock and debt method—to unit valuation. The following discussion will address these issues:

1. The appropriate weighting of the stock and debt method in the overall valuation conclusion.
2. The proper categorization of direct capitalization as either an income approach method or a market approach method.

The Appropriate Weighting of the Stock and Debt Valuation Method. Many analysts believe that little weight should be applied to the stock and debt method value indication in the reconciliation and correlation phase of the valuation. This section will summarize some of the issues with regard to this question.

Within the context of the unit valuation of operating property for ad valorem taxation purposes, there are several significant weaknesses associated with the stock and debt valuation method. These weaknesses are both conceptual and practical in nature. These stock and debt method weaknesses can generally be grouped into three categories:

1. Comparability weaknesses.
2. Applicability weaknesses.
3. Application weaknesses.

Each of these three categories of weaknesses will be summarized below.

When the subject taxpayer securities are publicly traded, capital market data with regard to the subject taxpayer are typically used directly in the stock and debt method. This procedure assumes that the subject taxpayer is a good comparable for itself. On the surface, this assumption may seem self-evident. Upon closer inspection, however, this assumption may not be valid at all.

Unless the subject taxpayer is (and is expected to continue to be) a single product line "pure play" company, then the taxpayer's security capital market data reflect investors' perceptions of—and expectations regarding—the entire portfolio of businesses owned by the subject publicly traded taxpayer. Often, however, the unit subject to valuation represents only one of many business lines of the subject publicly traded taxpayer. Often, in addition, the unit subject to valuation is owned by one subsidiary of a multiple business unit "holding company" or "portfolio" publicly traded taxpayer. So, in addition to the subject unit representing only one of many lines of business, it is actually owned by a nonmarketable closely held corporation—as opposed to a marketable publicly traded taxpayer.

These phenomena have long been recognized with regard to the application of the stock and debt method. In the application of this method, adjustments are made for the "influence" of the subject single business, closely held unit on the value of the "portfolio," publicly traded parent taxpayer. These adjustments are often made by quantifying the "asset influence," the "revenue influence," or the "income influence" of the subject unit—compared with the publicly traded taxpayer.

The objectives of making these influence adjustments are appropriate. However, the application of these influence adjustments is generally ineffective and inefficient. This is because the relative value influence of a single business unit on a portfolio parent is not a function of unit assets as a percent of total taxpayer assets or of unit income as a percent of total taxpayer income. Rather, the relative value influence is a function of the risk and expected return investment characteristics of the subject unit compared with the risk and expected return of the portfolio parent taxpayer corporation.

However, these relative risk and expected return investment characteristics are very difficult to identify and to quantify. Therefore, the considerably more simple asset and income influence adjustment conventions are often used by many analysts. One fundamental weakness of the stock and debt method is that these influence conventions are often not adequate to appropriately quantify the amount of the parent taxpayer publicly traded security prices that may be allocated to the subject single business, closely held unit.

In addition to the comparability issues summarized above, there is an overall weakness regarding the application of the stock and debt method to the valuation of a unit of operating property. The stock and debt method uses data related to marketable, noncontrolling ownership interests in publicly traded stock and debt securities. These securities are traded on efficient capital markets. The taxpayer unit subject to assessment typically involves a nonmarketable, controlling ownership interest in operating property. There is typically no efficient secondary market on which to trade these operating properties.

There are numerous risk and expected return investment differences between the ownership of negotiable securities and the ownership of operating property. These investment differences have already been documented in the valuation literature. Basically, these many risk and expected return differences may be grouped into the following categories of investment characteristics:

1. Marketability.
2. Ownership control.
3. Investment time horizon.
4. Investment diversification.
5. Investment wealth concentration.
6. Limitation on the amount of financial liability.
7. Expected appreciation versus depreciation.
8. Effects of regulation.

Many of these risk and expected return investment differences will be discussed below. Due to the number—and magnitude—of these investment differences between marketable securities and operating property, the use of capital market data in the stock and debt method may call into question the applicability of that valuation method in a unit valuation analysis.

General comparability and applicability weaknesses regarding the use of capital market data (i.e., pricing multiples, capitalization rates, and security prices) in the stock and debt method were mentioned above. These general comparability and applicability weaknesses include: (1) the potential lack of comparability of the subject taxpayer "portfolio" parent corporation to the subject taxpayer single business, closely held unit of operating property and (2) the inevitable lack of comparability of the taxpayer marketable, noncontrolling securities (traded on efficient stock exchanges) to the taxpayer unit properties (i.e., nonmarketable, controlling ownership interests in operating property for which there is no ready secondary market).

These weaknesses are sometimes summarized by the assertion that "the stock and debt method values the wrong thing." In addition, it is sometimes said that "the stock and debt method values the wrong thing in the wrong way."

The Proper Categorization of the Direct Capitalization Method. This discussion will explore the question: Is direct capitalization valuation a market approach method or an income approach method? Quantitatively, the answer to this question may affect how we estimate the economic income subject to capitalization, how we estimate the appropriate capitalization rate, how we make adjustments to the comparable property data that we use in our analysis, and so on.

Qualitatively, the answer to this question may help us understand the application limitations of direct capitalization, help us define what is the unit subject to valuation, help us focus on the data sources for our valuations—and if, in fact, those data are really relevant to our analysis—and help us question the ultimate applicability of direct capitalization to the unit valuation process.

If we review the authoritative literature with respect to direct capitalization, we may quickly arrive at the conclusion that direct capitalization is an income approach valuation method. The authoritative real estate appraisal texts introduce direct capitalization as an income approach method. The authoritative tangible personal property appraisal texts cover direct capitalization within their income approach chapters. And, the authoritative business valuation and security analysis treatises include direct capitalization within their income approach valuation sections (as we do in this book).

Nonetheless, there are fairly distinct and salient differences between how these literature sources describe the application of the direct capitalization process to the types of properties they are considering and how the direct capitalization process is typically applied in the unit valuation context. Let's explore these differences as we decide whether direct capitalization is an income approach method or a market approach method—for unit valuation purposes.

In the literature regarding income approach valuation methods, we can find ample discussion of the direct capitalization method. This is true in the appraisal of real estate, of tangible personal property, of intangible assets, of business enterprises, and of debt and equity securities.

However, in all of these discussions, direct capitalization is presented as an analysis that is internal to the property. In other words, the estimate of the income subject to capitalization is derived from an analysis of the income earning capacity of the property itself. The estimate of the capitalization rate comes, of course, from market-derived data. And, there are several recognized methods for estimating overall direct capitalization rates. Nonetheless, all of these methods involve an analysis (in some form) of either the subject property itself and/or of empirical transactional data regarding directly comparable properties.

While the income data may have to be extracted from the appraisal subject, they do not generally need to be adjusted using quantitative, qualitative, or comparative techniques. Also, while the capitalization rate data may have to be extracted from the marketplace, they do not generally need to be adjusted for fundamental differences (or comparability concerns) between the transactional properties and the subject property.

The following is the formula for the direct capitalization valuation method:

$$PV = \frac{E}{c}$$

where:

PV = the present value of the property subject to appraisal

E = the economic income associated with the ownership of the subject property

c = the appropriate overall capitalization rate associated with the subject income estimate

For example, in an illustration of the direct capitalization method to the valuation of a hotel property, we would expect to see the following types of data used—all of which are internal to or integral to the subject property:

E = the net operating income from the rental of the hotel land and building from the property owner to the hotel operator

c = a blending of the current cost of mortgage debt to the hotel owner and the cost of equity of hotel property ownership, weighted at the typical debt to value ratio observed from contemporaneous mortgages on hotel properties

PV = would then be the value estimate of a fee simple ownership interest in the hotel land and building, based upon an analysis that is fairly specific to the subject property

In the literature regarding the application of market approach valuation methods, we do not find much discussion of the direct capitalization method. However, we do find voluminous discussions of a topic that may be particularly relevant: the identification and quantification of adjustments. These adjustments are analyzed and applied in the market approach when the analyst obtains data from properties that are somehow different from the subject—and then attempts to make that data applicable to the subject.

In real estate appraisal, for example, the more common market approach adjustments include: property rights conveyed, financing terms, conditions of sale, market conditions, location, physical characteristics, economic characteristics, use, and nonrealty components. And, as we may recall from basic real estate appraisal principles, we adjust the comparables to the subject property—not the subject property to the comparables. That is, when the comparable properties are somehow different from the subject, we identify these differences and adjust the comparable property transactional data to what it would have been if the comparables were identical to the subject.

In all appraisal disciplines—that is, real estate, personal property, intangible assets, debt and equity securities, and so on—the measurement and sequencing of these adjustments are fundamental to the market approach. And, all of these adjustments are generally quantified by reference to data that are external to the subject property—and which must be extracted from the appropriate secondary marketplace.

In the typical property appraisal assignment, the direct capitalization analysis would likely be considered an income approach method. However, let's now consider the following hypothetical valuation. Let's appraise the same hotel property that we described above. In this appraisal, we will conduct a unit property valuation. For purposes of this illustration, let's define our valuation variables as follows:

E = the net operating income of all of the business operations conducted within the hotel property, including room rental, restaurant operations, cocktail lounge, gift shop, conference and convention business, and banquet operations

c = a rate of return derived from negotiable equity securities traded on the New York Stock Exchange; these equity securities relate to international hospitality companies that derive most of their income from franchising as opposed to operating hotels—and that derive virtually none of their income from owning hotel properties and leasing these properties to hotel operators

PV = one is not certain what this value estimate indicates, as it combines a measurement of broadly defined hospitality business income (that is subject to seasonal, cyclical, and other factors) with a rate derived from marketable, noncontrolling ownership interests in negotiable equity securities

Perhaps, no experienced taxpayer or taxing authority would ever create the appraisal situation in the above hypothetical. However, if we accept the situation for purposes of illustration, it is clear that the identification and measurement of adjustments would be essential elements to the appraisal. These adjustments—to both income and capitalization rate data—could be based upon quantitative, qualitative, or comparative analysis techniques. Nonetheless, it also would be clear that these adjustments would be made from data that are external to the subject property—and that should be extracted from the marketplace.

In conclusion, the direct capitalization analysis appears to be an income approach method when it is applied to a summation valuation of individual assets. However, the direct capitalization analysis appears to be a market approach method when it is applied—as it customarily is—to the unit valuation of an assemblage of operating property. This conclusion is reached when one considers the type of and sources of data used in the unit valuation direct capitalization analysis. And, this conclusion is reached when one considers the number of and magnitude of adjustments required to make the direct capitalization analysis applicable to the unit valuation.

Differences in the Risk and Expected Return Investment Characteristics between Operating Property and Negotiable Securities

This section explores the use of capital market–derived data (e.g., price/earnings multiples, earnings/price capitalization rates, and security prices) in the income approach and the market approach to unit valuation. This discussion focuses on the differences between the risk and expected return investment characteristics of capital market–derived data (i.e., data derived from negotiable securities) and the appraisal subject (i.e., the unit of taxpayer operating property).

Typically, there are 12 differences in the risk and expected return investment characteristics identified between operating property and negotiable securities. These differences are listed below:

1. Lack of marketability.
2. Lack of absolute control.
3. Investment time horizon.
4. Regulatory risk.

5. Litigation risk (a form of unlimited liability risk).
6. Bankruptcy risk (a form of unlimited liability risk).
7. Environmental risk (a form of unlimited liability risk).
8. Lack of diversification (with regard to the subject investment).
9. Concentration of wealth (with regard to the subject investor).
10. Transaction cost.
11. Market inefficiency.
12. Investment depreciation.

Each of these 12 investment characteristics is summarized below.

Lack of Marketability. Negotiable securities are eminently liquid. They trade easily and quickly on organized stock market exchanges (e.g., the New York Stock Exchange). Investors know that their securities trade will occur on the day of their market order, and that they will receive the proceeds from their transaction (in the case of a sale) within three trading days.

Operating property, on the other hand, is eminently illiquid. It is difficult and expensive to sell special purpose operating property—such as most industrial and commercial real estate. Operating property owners have no organized exchange market to go to; they are not sure what price their transaction will result in; they do not know when the transaction will occur; and, they do not know when they will receive the proceeds from a sale transaction.

Lack of Absolute Control. Controlling owners of many types of businesses can unilaterally decide most important business management decisions. For example, they can decide which customers to service—and which not to serve; they can decide which product lines to offer—and which not to offer; they can decide which assets to buy and which assets to sell; and, they can decide which services and territories to discontinue—in order to quickly change strategic direction and to maximize their profits.

Controlling owners in regulated (or partially regulated) industries need to obtain regulatory approval in order to implement certain critical management decisions—such as a merger, acquisition, liquidation, or divestiture. Therefore, control is not as substantial a value increment in regulated industries as it is in nonregulated industries, because management does not enjoy "absolute control."

Investment Time Horizon. Typically, investors in capital market negotiable securities, on average, turn over their investments every two to three years. In other words, they only expect to hold the investment for a two- to three-year horizon. They can then remain liquid—or they can invest in other negotiable securities.

Capital-intensive businesses (such as most industrial and commercial companies), on average, turn over their investments in operating assets every 20 to 30 years. In other words, they expect to hold their investments in operating assets for long periods of time.

The longer the expected investment time horizon, the greater the risk to the investor (due to missed alternative investment opportunities, inflation risk, and other factors). This concept is the theoretical basis for the well-known upward sloping curve of the "term structure of interest rates" for both corporate and government bonds.

Regulatory Risk. Transactions involving negotiable securities are, for the most part, unregulated. And, once the securities are owned by the investor, the securities themselves are almost totally unregulated.

Transactions involving operating property in a regulated industry are, for the most part, highly regulated. And, once the operating property is owned by the business, the operating property itself is subject to considerable regulation.

The greater the restrictions placed on any property type—whether negotiable securities or operating property—the lower the value of the property.

Litigation Risk. Securities owners are not subject to any risk greater than the cost of their original investment. If the business they invest in loses a substantial lawsuit (of any type), the most the investor can lose is his or her original investment in the subject stocks or bonds.

Operating property owners are subject to the direct risk of litigation claims. There is no limit to the amount of their liability. If a taxpayer corporation has a $100 million net worth investment in operating property, and the taxpayer loses a $500 million lawsuit, then the taxpayer is responsible to pay the judgment (out of other resources or out of future profits, if necessary). The taxpayer owner can lose much more than the original cost investment in the operating property.

Bankruptcy Risk. Securities owners are not subject to any risk greater than the cost of their original investment. If the business they invest in becomes bankrupt, the most the investor can lose is his or her original investment in the subject stocks or bonds.

Operating property owners are subject to the direct risk of bankruptcy. There is no limit to the amount of their liability. If a taxpayer corporation suffers a bankruptcy action, the operating property owner is responsible to pay creditors (out of other resources or out of future profits, if necessary). The taxpayer is at risk for much more than the original cost of investment in the operating property.

Environmental Risk. Securities owners are not subject to any risk greater than the cost of their original investment. If the business they invest in has an environmental problem, the most the investor can lose is his or her original investment in the subject stocks or bonds.

Operating property owners are subject to direct environmental risk—including the cost of environmental cleanup. If a taxpayer corporation must clean up an environmental problem, the operating property owner is responsible to pay the costs (out of other resources or out of future profits, if necessary). The taxpayer is at risk for much more than the original cost of investment in the operating property.

Lack of Diversification. Portfolio management theory tells us that capital market investors should—and do—diversify their investment portfolio. This portfolio diversification is performed in order to reduce—and, in theory, to eliminate nonsystematic risk.

Capital-intensive industrial and commercial businesses cannot as easily diversify their investments. For example, transportation, communications, and utility companies will invest primarily in industry-specific property. Therefore, operating property owners cannot easily reduce the nonsystematic risk that securities investors can easily eliminate.

It is true that the corporate parents of taxable units can—and do—diversify their holding company corporations. However, for this discussion, we are only interested in the operating property in the taxable operating unit.

Concentration of Wealth. Investment analysis theory tells us that investors should—and do—practice asset allocation. That is, they invest (or allocate) a portion of their wealth in (1) stocks and bonds; (2) real estate; (3) cash; (4) money market instruments; (5) personal assets, such as automobiles, jewelry, and art work; (6) precious metals; and (7) other assets. This asset allocation—and the periodic asset allocation "rebalancing"—reduces risk to the securities investor.

Capital intensive industrial and commercial businesses cannot—and do not—practice asset allocation. For example, an industrial or commercial company may invest 100 percent of its wealth in industry-specific operating property. And, this allocation (or lack thereof) cannot be periodically rebalanced. Accordingly, capital intensive operating property owners experience much greater investment risk than securities investors do.

Transaction Costs. Transaction costs to capital market securities investors are low—and predictable. This predictability (and competitiveness) of securities brokerage fees is one of the hallmarks of trading on organized securities exchanges.

Transaction costs to capital intensive industrial and commercial operating property owners are high—and unpredictable. For example, if an industrial or commercial company decides to sell some excess operating property, brokerage fees (as a percent of the final sale price) are relatively high and relatively noncompetitive.

Market Inefficiency. The organized stock exchange markets (e.g., the New York Stock Exchange) are the very paradigm of an efficient trading market. Market participants (i.e., investors) essentially know when, where, and how their trade will take place. They are confident that a buyer will be found (if they are a seller) and that a seller will be found (if they are a buyer). They know that there is a system of brokers, dealers, and market specialists that will make the transaction quick, inexpensive, and painless.

The secondary market in which capital-intensive industrial and commercial operating property trades is the antonym of market efficiency. There are few market participants. There are few brokers and dealers. There are not market specialists (at least as they exist in the stock exchanges). Operating property buyers and sellers are uncertain as to when—or if—their transaction will take place and at what price the transaction will take place.

Investment Depreciation. Capital market investors expect their investments to appreciate. And, over time, negotiable security investments generally do appreciate. Therefore, capital market investors do not need to replenish their investment portfolio (i.e., continue to invest in their portfolio) just to maintain their investment base. Rather, even without replenishment, capital market investment portfolios tend to appreciate over time.

Operating property investors expect their investments to depreciate. And, over time, capital intensive industrial and commercial operating property generally does depreciate. Therefore, capital intensive businesses need to constantly replenish their operating property portfolios (i.e., continue to make investments in replacement operating property) just to maintain their investment base. Accordingly, without constant replenishment, operating property investment portfolios tend to depreciate over time.

Capitalization of Leased Equipment Rental Expense

Introduction

Some taxing authorities add back the rental expense associated with operating leased equipment to the level of the taxpayer's economic income subject to capitalization. This add-back is made by some taxing authorities in the application of both income approach and market approach valuation methods, including the direct capitalization method, the yield capitalization method, and the stock and debt method.

These taxing authorities perform this add-back procedure because they believe that the value of the operating leased equipment (1) would otherwise not be included in the unit value of the taxpayer and, therefore, (2) would otherwise escape property taxation during the term of the lease. This conclusion is based upon the premises that (1) the lessee is responsible for paying the property tax on the leased equipment during the lease term, and (2) the lessor is responsible for paying the property tax on the leased equipment after the conclusion of the lease term. These property tax payment responsibilities are typically assigned in the actual equipment operating lease contract.

These taxing authorities justify this add-back adjustment with the following arguments: (1) All the income derived from the use of the operating leased equipment is not being included in the taxpayer's unit valuation (because the rental expense of the equipment is subtracted before arriving at the level of economic income subject to capitalization), and (2) because the taxpayer uses the leased equipment in its business operations, the leased equipment should be valued as if it were an owned asset, but this is not occurring because the rental expense is greater than the corresponding ownership expense (i.e., depreciation expense).

Reasons Not to Capitalize Operating Lease Rental Expense

Corporate taxpayers typically assert that there are several reasons not to capitalize operating lease rental expense in the application of either income approach or market approach methods of unit valuation. These reasons are both conceptual and practical in nature. Several of these reasons are discussed here.

Consistency. As a basic methodological axiom, any adjustment that is made to the operating results of the subject taxpayer also should be made to the operating results of the selected guideline companies. For purposes of this argument, guideline companies are the publicly traded securities from which direct capitalization rates, capital market multiples, or stock and debt security pricing data are derived.

If the rental expense add-back is made to subject taxpayer data, it should also be made to the guideline companies' data. Such a consistency adjustment is often difficult to make, because the analyst typically does not have adequate rental expense data for all the guideline companies.

It is noteworthy that this argument does not address whether the rental expense adjustment is methodologically correct. Rather, this argument indicates that unless this adjustment (or any other adjustment) is not made consistently both to the subject taxpayer and to the guideline companies, it is procedurally incorrect, and it will result in distorted valuation conclusions.

Ownership Interest Subject to Appraisal. Some taxing authorities assert that taxpayers should be taxed on the fee simple ownership interest in operating leased property. Whether it correctly does so or not, add-back of the associated rental expense is intended to tax the fee simple interest in the leased property. However, many taxpayers assert that this basic position is fundamentally flawed. Taxpayers do not own a fee simple interest in operating leased equipment. Therefore, this add-back attempts to value a bundle of legal rights that the taxpayer does not own.

Regarding operating leased equipment, the taxpayer owns the lessee's rights to the property only, and the lessor continues to own the lessor's rights on the property. For example, the taxpayer lessee typically cannot sell or otherwise transfer, borrow against, hypothecate or otherwise pledge, enjoy, and value appreciation in, and so on, the operating leased equipment. At most, the taxpayer owns a term interest in the equipment. The lessor retains the reversionary interest in the equipment.

If the taxpayer is taxed on the fee simple interest in the leased equipment (by effectively capitalizing the add-back as annuity in perpetuity), then (1) the taxpayer is taxed on a bundle of legal rights that it does not enjoy, and (2) the fee simple interest in the property will be subject to double taxation, once to the taxpayer (during the lease term) and once to the lessor (at the conclusion of the lease term).

Leased Equipment Economic Income Already Included in Taxpayer Unit. If the unit valuation methods are applied appropriately, the appropriate level of economic income related to leased equipment is already encompassed in the valuation conclusion. This argument does not imply that the same level of economic income is analyzed for owned versus leased equipment. Rather, a reconcilable level of economic income for owned versus leased equipment is appropriate, because there are several subtle economic differences between owned and leased equipment.

The revenue generated by the taxpayer from the use of owned equipment is identical to that generated by the use of leased equipment. Accordingly, the only difference between owned and leased equipment in the level of economic income generated relates to the expense of operating the equipment.

The expense of owning equipment includes depreciation expense and interest expense. The expense of leasing equipment includes the rental expense. The rental rate is set by the lessor (1) to cover the lessor's depreciation expense and interest expense and (2) to provide a profit to the lessor as compensation for the risks of the leasing business.

In a capitalization analysis based on net operating income, the only relevant equipment ownership expense is depreciation. Typically, the taxpayer's rental expense on leased equipment is greater than the taxpayer's depreciation expense on identical owned equipment. However, these two expense levels can be reconciled.

First, the taxpayer depreciates owned equipment over the life of the equipment. However, the lease term (i.e., the period of equipment use to the taxpayer) is usually shorter than the life of the equipment. If the cost of owned equipment were depreciated over the (shorter) lease term, the adjusted depreciation expense would more closely approximate the rent expense. It is argued that such an adjustment is appropriate because the taxpayer will not enjoy the use of the leased equipment for as long a period as the taxpayer will enjoy the use of owned equipment.

Second, it is appropriate for the rent expense to include a profit increment for the lessor. Effectively, the taxpayer has transferred many of the risks of asset ownership to the lessor. Since the taxpayer does not actually own the leased equipment (with all of the attendant risks), it is reasonable for the expense of a leased asset to be slightly greater than the expense of an identical owned asset.

In summary, after an adjustment is made to depreciation expense to recognize the shorter use period for leased equipment, the only material difference in the expense of owned versus leased assets is explained by the fact that the taxpayer has transferred certain risks of asset ownership to the lessor.

Not a Standard Business Valuation Procedure. Going-concern businesses are appraised for many reasons in addition to ad valorem taxation. There is a well-established body of literature on the valuation of going-concern businesses. There are promulgated professional standards with respect to the valuation of going-concern businesses. In addition, a voluminous body of published judicial precedent addresses the valuation of going-concern businesses for purposes other than ad valorem taxation.

Other than the positions postulated by certain taxing authorities, there is no literature, professional standard, or judicial support for the lease expense add-back.

Accordingly, the lease expense add-back is not a standard or generally accepted procedure in the valuation of operating business units.

Summary

This chapter presented many of the reasons to conduct a valuation analysis for ad valorem property tax assessment purposes. These purposes include: initial assessments for newly constructed properties, re-assessments for properties that have transferred ownership, periodic property tax compliance (i.e., filing) purposes, and ad valorem property tax assessment appeal purposes. The basis of such an appeal could be either on grounds of property valuation (i.e., an overassessment) or on grounds of assessment equalization (i.e., an unfair assessment). In either case, a valuation analysis is required.

In addition to general topics related to ad valorem property tax terminology and procedural methodology, we discussed several special topics of particular interest to financial valuation analysts, including: the identification and quantification of functional obsolescence, the identification and quantification of economic obsolescence, the identification and valuation of intangible assets under the unit assessment method, and the identification and application of appropriate income approach methods for ad valorem unit valuation purposes. Issues such as the use of the capital asset pricing model in property tax valuation, the use of stock market data in property tax valuation, and capitalization of leased equipment rental expense were also discussed.

Bibliography

Ancel, Mark G. "Should Intangibles Be Used as a Basis for Determining Market Value?" *Journal of Multistate Taxation*, September/October 1993, pp. 166–73.

Cook, Cline G. "The Appraiser's Role in the Tax Appeal Process." *Real Estate Appraiser,* August 1991, pp. 17–20.

Davis, Joseph M., and John R. Cesta. "The Valuation of Operating Leased Property in the Unitary Method." *ASA Valuation*, August 1994, pp. 42–56.

Donias, Claire H. "Valuation for Ad Valorem Taxation" (Chapter 13). In Robert F. Reilly and Robert P. Schweihs, eds. *The Handbook of Advanced Business Valuation*. New York: McGraw-Hill, 2000.

Fletcher, Gregory G. "Significant Court Cases Concerning Ad Valorem Taxation of Public Utility and Railroad Property." *Assessment Journal*, January/February 1994, pp. 43–55.

Fowler, Bruce A. "Unit Valuation: Oklahoma's Illegal Tax on Intangible Property." *Tulsa Law Journal*, Winter 1995, pp. 367–93.

Hanke, Steve H., and Stephen J.K. Walters. "Tax Appraisal in Evolving Industries: An Econometric Approach." *Journal of Legal Economics*, Fall 1995, pp. 43–54.

Hellerstein, Walter. "State and Local Taxation of Intangibles Generates Increasing Controversy." *Journal of Taxation*, May 1994, pp. 296–302.

Hess, Alan C. "Do Regulated Utilities Have Growth Opportunities?" *Assessment Journal*, July/August 1995, pp. 45–53.

Matonis, Stephen J., and Daniel R. DeRango. "The Determination of Hotel Value Components for Ad Valorem Tax Assessment." *Appraisal Journal*, July 1993, pp. 342–47.

Mo, Douglas. "Ad Valorem Taxation of Cable Television Intangibles: The Search for the Holy Grail." *Assessment Journal*, May/June 1996, pp. 33–36.

Rabe, James G., and Robert F. Reilly. "Valuation of Intangible Assets for Property Tax Purposes." *National Public Accountant*, April 1994, pp. 26–28+.

_____. "Valuing Intangible Assets as Part of a Unitary Assessment." *Journal of Property Tax Management*, Winter 1994, pp. 12–20.

Reilly, Robert F. "Assessing Your Assessment: Valuation Techniques for Finding out What Your Property's Really Worth." *Commercial Investment Real Estate Journal*, Summer 1995, pp. 30–33.

_____. "Valuation of Trademarks for Property Tax Purposes." *Journal of Property Tax Management*, Fall 1999, pp. 36–50.

Rife, Knute. "Appealing Property Tax Assessments." *Practical Real Estate Lawyer*, January 1991, pp. 69–88.

Shank, David W. "How Regulation Affects the Valuation of Public Utility Property." *Valuation*, July 1993, pp. 46–52.

Walters, Lawrence C., et al. "Measuring Obsolescence in Regulated Firms: Enhancements to the Cost Approach." *Assessment Journal*, May/June 1994, pp. 47–58.

Wiley, Richard N. "The Unit Valuation Method: Not a License to Commit Unit Taxation." *Journal of Property Tax Management*, Spring 1996, pp. 49–61.

Chapter 35

Dissenting Stockholder and Minority Oppression Actions

The incidence of adjudicated actions brought by minority stockholders increased dramatically during the last half of the 1990s. All indications are that this trend will continue.

These actions brought by minority shareholders generally fall into one of two categories:

1. Dissenting stockholder actions.
2. Minority oppression actions.

Either may be accompanied by claims of breach of fiduciary duty.

Dissenting Stockholder Actions

All states and the District of Columbia have dissenting stockholder statutes. These statutes essentially provide that if a company effects an extraordinary corporate action—typically identified in the statutes—stockholders may dissent from the action and be paid the *fair value* of their shares.

The "triggering events" allowing a dissent action vary somewhat from state to state. They apply in all states if a stockholder is forced to give up his or her stock, such as a cash-out merger (sometimes called a "squeeze-out") or a merger where the stockholders would get stock in the acquiring corporation. In many states, dissenters' rights are triggered by the sale of major corporate assets, as defined in the respective states' statutes.

Most states require that if a minority stockholder wishes to dissent from a corporate action, the decision must be registered in writing at or within a few days following the stockholder meeting at which the action is approved by the majority of stockholders. This process often is referred to as *perfecting dissenters' appraisal rights*. The courts are virtually unanimous in prohibiting dissenters' appraisal rights unless they have been perfected within the time specified in the statute and pursuant to the procedures specified therein. In addition, there typically are other procedural "hoops" that a stockholder must jump through.

In virtually all states, the statutory standard of value is *fair value*. The Revised Model Business Corporation Act, which many of the states have adopted, defines fair value as:

> The value of the shares immediately before the effectuation of the corporate action to which the dissenter objects, excluding any appreciation or depreciation in anticipation of the corporate action unless exclusion would be inequitable.[1]

None of the state statutes give any further definition to the standard of fair value. According to the official comment of the Model Business Corporation Act, the definition of fair value leaves to the parties (and, ultimately, to the courts) the details by which fair value is to be determined within the broad outlines of the definition. Thus, case law precedent provides guidance as to how each state interprets the standard of fair value. The interpretations vary greatly, as discussed in the next chapter, but virtually no state specifically equates *fair value* with *fair market value*. In some

---

[1] Model Business Corporation Act, Section 13.01(3) (1998).

cases, the ultimate value standard that is applied is fair market value but this is a consequence of following the fair value guidance rather than the other way around. Many states have no precedential case law on fair value, in which case they look at decisions from other states for guidance.

Interpretation of the Fair Value Standard in Dissent Cases

"That Which Has Been Taken"

A typical interpretation of the philosophy of fair value in a dissenting stockholder situation is the following:

> Fair value, in an appraisal context measures "that which has been taken from [the shareholder], viz., his proportionate interest in a going concern." *Tri-Continental Corp. v. Battze*, Del. Supr. 74 A.2d 71, 72 (1950).[2]

The Delaware Block Method

Prior to 1983, dissenting stockholder cases primarily utilized the "Delaware block method." This method develops values in each of three categories:

1. Investment value.
2. Market value.
3. Asset value.

Mathematical weightings are then assigned to the indications of value from each of the three categories (although the weight to one, or even two in extreme cases, could be zero), and the resulting weighted average is the concluded value.

The definitions of *investment value* and *market value* in the context of the Delaware block method are different from those discussed in the three basic approaches to value (Part III of this book).

Investment value in the context of the Delaware block method means value based on expected earnings and/or dividends. It is akin to the value based on the income approach in the three basic approaches to value. It may be arrived at by discounted cash flow (DCF), capitalization of earnings, or capitalization of dividends. In this sense, it mixes the traditional income approach and market approach in that it may derive capitalization rates either by traditional income approach methods (see Chapters 9 and 10) or by traditional market approach methods (see Chapters 11 and 12).

Market value, on the other hand, has historically been based on prior transactions in the subject company's securities. This contrasts with the traditional appraisal concept of *market value*, as discussed in Chapters 11 and 12, where market value uses multiples of both income statement and balance sheet parameters based on comparable transactions.

A summary of a valuation conclusion under the Delaware block method would typically appear in the form presented in Exhibit 35–1.

---

[2] *In Matter of Shell Oil Co.*, 607 A.2d 12B (Del. Supr. 1992).

Exhibit 35–1

Delaware Block Method
Sample Valuation Conclusion

	Indicated Value per Share	Weight	Weighted Value
Investment value			
Capitalization of earnings	$10.00	0.40	$4.00
Capitalization of dividends	6.00	0.10	0.60
Market value	12.00	0.25	3.00
Asset value	15.00	0.25	3.75
Weighted value per share			$11.35

Should Consider All Relevant Factors

A landmark case in 1983 said that the traditional factors considered under the Delaware Block Rule alone were not necessarily sufficient; instead, "all relevant factors" should be considered. In that particular case, the court specifically made the point that projections of future earnings were available and should be considered. The court also made the point that a determination of *fair value* "must include proof of value by any techniques or methods which are generally considered acceptable in the financial community."[3]

The interpretation of fair value is a subject of continued debate and is difficult to generalize. Most states, however, have embraced the notion that "all relevant factors should be considered." Note that the Delaware block method factors are not abandoned by *Weinberger*; the case just states that all relevant factors must be considered. Both historically and currently, courts have treated *investment value* (defined in this context as value based on earning capacity) as the most important of the three categories of value.

Requirement for Entire Fairness

There are many subtleties to the application of fair value for corporate law purposes. For example, some states consider concepts of "entire fairness." There are two major aspects of entire fairness:

1. Fair consideration.
2. Procedural fairness.

Fair Consideration

The notion of fair consideration within the context of entire fairness also encompasses two criteria:

1. Absolute fairness.
2. Relative fairness.

---

[3] *Weinberger v. UOP, Inc.*, 457 A.2d 701 (Del. 1983).

Absolute fairness generally addresses whether the consideration received was adequate relative to the value of the interest that was given up.

Relative fairness means whether the consideration received was fair in comparison with what other stockholders received. For example, are the controlling stockholders receiving some consideration that actually should be shared with all stockholders (e.g., an "employment agreement" for which no services are required and which contributes nothing to the buying company)?

Procedural Fairness

Within the concept of procedural fairness, there generally are two broad criteria:

1. Independence.
2. Competence and thoroughness.

Independence refers both to parties affiliated with the company and also to outside legal and financial advisers.

If there are potentially conflicted board members, some companies appoint a committee of outside directors with authority to retain independent legal counsel and independent financial advisers, and to negotiate on an arm's-length basis. They have the fiduciary responsibility to protect the interests of all the stockholders, especially those not a part of the control group.

Independence with respect to outside advisers means retaining legal counsel and financial advisers who are independent of the control parties. Generally speaking, this means professional advisers who do not have a direct or indirect financial interest in the company or the parties to the dispute.

Competence and thoroughness similarly applies to parties affiliated with the company and also to their outside advisers.

It is not expected that board members themselves be expert in either legal matters or in financial valuation or deal structuring. It is, however, expected that they use prudent diligence and care in evaluating the qualifications of the expert that they choose to retain. It is also expected that they exert the time and effort necessary to understand and evaluate the recommendations of the outside experts in exercising their fiduciary responsibility to make recommendations in reliance on those experts. The experts merely provide advice. It is the directors who have the fiduciary responsibility to recommend action based on that advice.

It obviously is beyond the scope of this book to address the issue of competence or thoroughness of legal counsel. With respect to competence of financial advisers, considerable guidance is provided in Chapter 1 on business valuation credentials. With respect to thoroughness of the financial adviser, the responsible fiduciary can find guidance in evaluating the financial adviser's work in Chapter 22, Reviewing a Business Valuation Report.

Consequences of Lack of Entire Fairness

Lack of entire fairness implies that the directors violated some duty owed to the shareholders. If the plaintiffs establish such liability, then the measure of damages may go beyond simply fair value as contemplated in the dissenters' rights statutes.

As explained by Vice Chancellor Jack Jacobs of the Delaware Court of Chancery:

> The statutory appraisal case limits damages, on the upside, in that the value is fixed at one point in time, and is not supposed to include any synergies. There is no issue of burden of proof. If the court does not accept the valuation presented by one side or the other, it must perform independently its own valuation.
>
> In a breach of fiduciary duty case, the traditional burden of proof rules apply, whereby if the evidence on both sides is even (we say "in equipoise") then the party that has the burden of proof loses.
>
> Another bright line difference is that in a fiduciary duty action, other measures of damages may be available, including damages calculated as of a date after the transaction. "Rescissory" damages would be an example. Damages measured by that method would be available in a breach of fiduciary duty action, but not in a statutory appraisal case.[4]

Minority Interest Dissolution Actions

An increasing number of states have been enacting "judicial dissolution statutes." These generally allow minority shareholders to sue for dissolution of the corporation or partnership if they can demonstrate minority oppression or a deadlock on decision making. As can be seen in Exhibit 35–2, a majority of states now have such statutes.

The triggering events vary from state to state. In some states, the minority bringing suit must constitute some minimum percentage of the ownership, while other states have no minimum percentage requirement.

In California, the leading state in minority dissolution actions, if stockholders owning 33⅓ percent or more of a company's stock can demonstrate minority oppression, their remedy is a dissolution of the corporation. The majority stockholders can prevent such a dissolution by paying, in cash, the fair value pursuant to California Corporations Code Section 2000. The following is the process involved:

1. Minority stockholders sue for dissolution.
2. The court determines whether conditions warranting the dissolution have occurred.
3. If so, and parties cannot agree on a price to buy out the minority stockholders, majority stockholders move to stay the dissolution pending valuation to determine how much the minority stockholders would receive if liquidation proceeded.
4. Court appoints three appraisers. Parties can agree upon, and seek court confirmation in an appointee process, or can allow the court to select the appraisers. Unless otherwise agreed by the parties, the conclusion of the appraisers is advisory to the court rather than binding.
5. The court adopts a value.
6. The court enters a decree "which shall provide in the alternative for winding up and dissolution of the corporation unless payment is made for the shares within the time specified by the decree."

---

[4] Shannon P. Pratt, "Fair Value: A View from the Delaware Court of Chancery" (interview with Jack B. Jacobs), *Shannon Pratt's Business Valuation Update*, September 1999, p. 2.

Exhibit 35–2

Dissolution Statutes

Has Judicial Dissolution Statute

Alabama, Alaska, Arizona, Arkansas, California, Colorado, Connecticut, District of Columbia, Florida, Georgia, Idaho, Illinois, Indiana, Iowa, Kentucky, Louisiana, Maine, Maryland, Massachusetts, Michigan, Minnesota, Missouri, Montana, Nebraska, New Hampshire, New Jersey, New Mexico, New York, North Carolina, North Dakota, Ohio, Oregon, Pennsylvania, Rhode Island, South Carolina, South Dakota, Tennessee, Texas, Utah, Vermont, Virginia, Washington, West Virginia, Wisconsin, Wyoming

No Judicial Dissolution Statute

Delaware, Hawaii, Kansas, Nevada, Oklahoma, Guam, Northern Mariana Islands, Puerto Rico, Virgin Islands

SOURCE: John E. Hempstead, "Conduct of the Parties Now a Factor in New Jersey Fair Value Determinations," *Judges & Lawyers Business Valuation Update*, September 1999, p. 3.

7. The majority stockholders may elect to pay the amount in cash prior to the deadline.
8. If the majority stockholders decline to pay, the company is liquidated and all shareholders receive a proportionate share of the resulting cash proceeds.[5]

Interpretation of the Fair Value Standard in Dissolution Cases

Courts in different states vary from one to another (and sometimes from one case to the next in the same state) in their interpretation of fair value for dissolution cases, and may not interpret this standard in the same manner as for dissenting stockholder cases.

California has what might seem at first reading an internally contradictory definition of fair value in the context of its dissolution statutes:

The fair value shall be determined on the basis of the liquidation value as of the valuation date but taking into account the possibility, if any, of sale of the entire business as a going concern in a liquidation.

While the above may seem abstruse at first blush, the evolution of case law makes it clear. The value may be based on a liquidation of assets and/or selling all or parts of the operations as a going concern if that would produce higher net proceeds.

In any case, as with fair value in the context of dissent cases, the definition of fair value in dissolution cases is missing some of the elements of the traditional definition of fair market value. As California corporate attorney Art Shartsis points out, many of the assumptions underlying fair market value are not present:

- There is no willing seller. In the dissolution the seller is involuntarily disposing of the assets.
- The seller is under compulsion to sell.

---

[5] Arthur J. Shartsis, "Dissolution Actions Yield Less Than Fair Market Enterprise Value," *Judges & Lawyers Business Valuation Update*, January 1999, p. 5.

- The involuntary seller under compulsion does not have the luxury of waiting for a top offer; the sale must be completed under the adverse conditions of a corporate dissolution conducted in accordance with California law.
- Implicitly, the buyer is aware of the seller's weakened position.[6]

Summary

Stockholder disputes that are resolved under the statutory standard of fair value typically fall clearly into one of two distinct categories:

1. Dissenting stockholder actions.
2. Minority owner dissolution actions.

Actions under both types of statutes have been on the increase in recent years.

All states have dissenting stockholder statutes. The standard of value is usually fair value.

A majority of states now have "judicial dissolution statutes" which allow minority shareholders demonstrating oppression to sue for dissolution of the entity. To prevent dissolution, the controlling owners can pay the oppressed minority owners the fair value of their shares.

For both types of actions, the respective states' court case precedents interpret the standard of fair value. Some states do not have precedential case law on fair value, in which instance they tend to look at case precedents from other states. In almost any case, the strict definition of fair value differs from the traditional definition of fair market value, although, in some cases, the outcome is the same.

The next chapter provides a sampling of cases showing the states' varying interpretations of the standard of fair value in various contexts.

Bibliography

Calio, Joseph Evan. "New Appraisals of Old Problems: Reflections on the Delaware Appraisal Proceeding." *American Business Law Journal*, May 1994.

Emory, John D. Jr. "The Role of Discounts in Determining 'Fair Value' under Wisconsin's Dissenters' Rights Statutes: The Case for Discounts." *Wisconsin Law Review*, March 1996, pp. 1155–75.

Fishman, Jay E., Shannon P. Pratt, et al. "Fair Value under Shareholder Dissent and Minority Oppression Actions" (Chapter 15). In *Guide to Business Valuations*, 10th ed. Fort Worth, TX: Practitioners Publishing Company, 2000.

Fishman, Jay E., and Anne C. Singer. "Fair Value for Oppressed and Dissenting Shareholders" (Chapter 15). In Robert F. Reilly and Robert P. Schweihs. *The Handbook of Advanced Business Valuation*. New York: McGraw-Hill, 2000.

Hempstead, John E. "Conduct of the Parties Now a Factor in New Jersey Fair Value Determinations." *Business Valuation Review*, September 1999, pp. 131–33.

---

[6] Ibid., pp. 5–6.

Lee, M. Mark, and Gilbert E. Matthews. "Fairness Opinions" (Chapter 16). In Robert F. Reilly and Robert P. Schweihs. *The Handbook of Advanced Business Valuation*. New York: McGraw-Hill, 2000.

O'Neal, F. Hodge, and Robert B. Thompson. *O'Neal's Oppression of Minority Shareholders*, 2nd ed. St. Paul, MN: West Group, 1999.

Pratt, Shannon P. "Shareholder Suit Valuation Criteria Vary from State to State." *Valuation Strategies*, January/February 1999, pp. 12–15.

Shartsis, Arthur J. "Dissolution Actions Yield Less Than Fair Market Enterprise Value." *Judges & Lawyers Business Valuation Update*, January 1999, pp. 5–6.

Van Vleet, Daniel R., and Frederick W. Axley. "Fair Value in Dissenting Stockholder Disputes" (Chapter 9A). In Robert F. Reilly, Robert P. Schweihs et al., eds. *Financial Valuation: Businesses and Business Interests*, 1997 Update. New York: Warren, Gorham & Lamont, 1997, pp. U9A-1–26.

Chapter 36

Dissenting Stockholder and Minority Oppression Court Cases

Delaware has by far the most judicial precedent in the realm of dissenting stockholder actions. Many states have none at all or none that may have addressed certain specific issues. When states lack their own precedent, they often look to other states' precedents. Delaware tends to be the leader, but states also look particularly at decisions in other states that have statutes worded the same or similarly to their own.[1]

In the realm of stockholder oppression cases for judicial dissolution, California has by far the most precedential case law. As noted in the previous chapter, Delaware is one of the states that does not have a judicial dissolution statute.

Readers Must Interpret Cases Carefully

A study of the relevant case law is an essential prerequisite to estimation of fair value for either a dissenting stockholder action or a suit for dissolution in any jurisdiction. After having done one's best, however, rarely will the reader have clear-cut guidance as to the court's likely posture on every possible valuation issue.

The facts and circumstances of cases vary significantly from one to another. Thus, while prior cases should be studied for guidance, one must be very careful in interpreting them as a bright line of final authority.

Vice Chancellor Jack Jacobs of the Delaware Court of Chancery clearly sounds this warning:

> Both my Court and the Delaware Supreme Court recognize that valuation cases are *extremely* fact-driven. Very few conclusions on valuation issues have universal applicability, though statements found in some opinions may have the appearance, and might be interpreted by some, as having sweeping generality.[2]

A case in point is a decision by the Supreme Court of Kansas on a dissenting stockholder suit arising out of a reverse stock split forcing a cash-out of minority stockholders. The Westlaw head-notes make the sweeping statement, without qualification, that "minority and marketability discounts are not appropriate when the purchaser of the stock is either the majority shareholder or the corporation itself." It would seem misleading to accept this broad interpretation, since the question put to the Kansas Supreme Court was limited to a forced cash-out, not to all events that could trigger a dissenting stockholder action.

The question put to the Kansas Supreme Court was:

> Is it proper for a corporation to determine the "fair value" of a fractional share pursuant to K.S.A. § 17-6405 by applying minority and marketability discounts when the fractional share resulted from a reverse stock split intended to eliminate the minority shareholder's interest in the corporation?[3]

The court concluded as follows:

---

[1] Because statutes of several states undergo revision every year, it is impractical to publish even summaries of all of them in a book such as this. Many state government web pages provide their state statutes on-line or they are available at law libraries.

[2] Shannon P. Pratt, "Fair Value: A View from the Delaware Court of Chancery" (interview with Jack B. Jacobs), *Shannon Pratt's Business Valuation Update*, September 1999, p. 2.

[3] *Katherine B. Arnaud, et al. v. Stockgrowers State Bank of Ashland, Kansas, et al.*, No. 82,909, 1999 WL 1000415 (Kan. Nov. 5, 1999).

In answering the certified question before us, we hold that minority and marketability discounts should not be applied when the fractional share resulted from a reverse stock split intended to eliminate a minority shareholder's interest in the corporation.[4]

The sweeping generality of the Westlaw head-notes combined with the actual very specific applicability prompted the following comment:

I think that it is important to recognize that this decision's applicability is limited to the narrow circumstances of the question put to the court. . . . There are many other actions where dissenters' rights are triggered even though the stockholders are not forced to be pushed out, a fact set which would seem to be very distinguishable from this case.[5]

Fair Value Is Not Fair Market Value

In most states, the standard of value for dissenting stockholder suits and for minority oppression suits is fair value. Several state statutes indicate that either "fair cash value" or simply "value" is the appropriate standard. While the various states interpret fair value quite differently from one another, and sometimes differently under differing facts and circumstances, they do *not* strictly equate fair value with fair market value.

This point is illustrated well by a New York court's rejection of an expert's valuation report based on fair market value in a dissenting stockholder case. The court stated:

Because the petitioner's expert . . . in its valuation report (on title page) and on 15 occasions refers to its valuation to be based on Fair Market Value, and the Business Corporation Law only uses the term Fair Value . . . the Court considers it a threshold question as to whether Fair Value and Fair Market Value are synonymous.

The Standard upon which [the company's expert's] valuation was based was Market Value. . . . the statutory standard is much broader. . . . The Court may give *no weight* [emphasis supplied] to market value if the facts of the case so require.[6]

The court ultimately did reject the report based on the standard of fair market value (concluding $52 per share) and awarded the dissenters $99 per share.

In *LeBeau v. M.G. Bancorporation, Inc.*, the investment banker had issued a fairness opinion on a squeeze-out merger based on fair market value rather than on fair value. The Delaware Court of Chancery stated that this was "legally flawed" as evidence regarding fair value.[7]

---

[4] Ibid.

[5] Shannon P. Pratt, "Kansas Supreme Court Disallows Discounts in Reverse Split Forced Cashout," *Judges & Lawyers Business Valuation Update*, December 1999, p. 6.

[6] *Matter of Slant/Fin. Corp. v. The Chicago Corp.*, (N.Y. Sup. Ct. Oct. 5, 1995), *aff'd* 236 A.D.2d 547, 654 N.Y.S.2d 627 (N.Y. App. Div. Feb. 18, 1997).

[7] *LeBeau v. M.G. Bancorporation, Inc.*, No. Civ. A. 13414, 1998 WL 44993 (Del. Ch. Jan. 29, 1998).

Breach of Fiduciary Duty Expands Plaintiffs' Potential Damages

As noted in the previous chapter, the concept of "entire fairness" includes both procedural fairness and fair consideration paid. If the test of entire fairness is not met, then plaintiffs' damage may go well beyond the simple dissenting stockholder appraisal rights remedy.

An example of lack of entire fairness is discussed in the Delaware case of *M.G. Bancorporation v. LeBeau*:

> In assessing the validity of the substantive unfairness claims, at least two factors are pivotal. The first is the defendants' failure to establish an independent committee of directors to represent the minority stockholders' interests. . . . [I]n the [short-form merger] context the absence of a negotiating committee of independent directors, without more, does not constitute unfair dealing as a matter of law. Nonetheless, that circumstance is evidence of unfair dealing that, when combined with other pleaded facts, may state a cognizable unfair dealing claim that the fiduciaries will ultimately have the duty to negate.
>
> The second critical factor, of which the Court takes judicial notice, is that the fair value of the plaintiffs' shares has now been adjudicated at $85 per share [in the judicial appraisal action]. The significant gap between the $41 merger price and the $85 appraisal value, combined with the other substantive unfairness allegations (including the improper manner in which the $41 merger price was arrived at), create an inference that the Merger was the product of unfair dealing.[8]

We noted in the previous chapter that the issue of independence went not only to the appointment of a committee of independent directors, but also to the requirement that the committee retain legal counsel and financial advisers that are independent of the control parties. Failure on the latter requirement is illustrated by a case in which the trial court was willing to accept that the procedure was fair based on appointment of an independent committee of the board. The decision, however, was reversed at the appellate level because neither the legal counsel nor the financial advisers retained were deemed independent of the control parties.

In *Kahn v. Tremont Corporation*,[9] the Delaware Court of Chancery found that Tremont's appointment of a special committee of disinterested directors adequately shifted the burden of proof to the plaintiffs on the issue of fairness. Plaintiffs appealed and the Supreme Court of Delaware noted that the committee chose as its financial adviser a bank that had lucrative past dealings with related companies controlled by the same stockholder as the subject company. Furthermore, the committee's legal adviser was previously retained by two of the controlling stockholders' related companies in connection with past transactions. The court concluded that the special committee did not act in an independent and informed manner. The case was reversed and remanded for a new fairness determination with the burden of proof remaining with the defendants.

[8] *M.G. Bancorporation v. LeBeau*, No. 153, 1998 (Del. Apr. 30, 1999). See also, for example, *Boyer v. Wilmington Materials, Inc.*, No. 12549, 1999 WL 393549 (Del. Ch. Jan. 20, 1999).
[9] *Kahn v. Tremont Corporation*, No. 170, 1996, 1997 WL 332976 (Del. June 10, 1997).

A classic case in which the directors' breach of fiduciary duty resulted in damages not being limited to fair value is *Ryan v. Tad's Enterprises, Inc.*.[10] Certain salient facts of the transactions were as follows:

1. The Townsend brothers owned 72.6 percent of the stock.
2. Prior to the merger, Tad's sold its chain of six restaurants. In conjunction with the restaurant sale, the two Townsend brothers received $1 million each for noncompete and consulting agreements.
3. An attorney acted in the capacity of a board member, represented the corporation in the transactions, and represented the Townsend brothers personally in negotiating the consulting and noncompete agreements.
4. Tad's board did not retain any unaffiliated law firm, financial adviser, or other independent representative to represent or negotiate the merger on behalf of Tad's minority shareholders.
5. Tad's board did hire an investment banking firm to furnish an opinion that the $13.25 merger price was fair to the minority stockholders. However:
   a. It was not asked to, nor did it, opine on the fairness of the Townsends' noncompete and consulting agreements.
   b. At the board meeting when the merger was approved, the firm did not discuss its valuation analysis or provide any written materials.
   c. The investment banking firm's subsequent written opinion listed information considered, but no projections or forecasts were provided by the board.

The court noted that it normally would defer to a board's judgment, on the presumption of due care and good faith.

However, that presumption vanishes in cases where the minority shareholders are compelled to forfeit their shares in return for a value that is "determined as a result of a bargaining process in which the controlling shareholder is in a position to influence both bargaining parties." In such cases, the Court will carefully scrutinize the board's actions to ascertain:

- whether the board instituted measures to ensure a fair process, and
- whether the board achieved a fair price for the disinterested stockholder minority. . . .

The business judgment review standard will not apply where the decision under challenge is made by a board, a majority of whom have a material conflict of interest in the transaction.

The court concluded:

Defendants are liable to the plaintiffs for breaching their fiduciary duty of loyalty. The question then becomes, what is the extent of that liability. . . . *the measure of damages for breach of fiduciary duty is not limited to the corporation's fair value as determined in an appraisal.* [emphasis supplied]

Ultimately, the court ordered the noncompete proceeds to be distributed to all shareholders, and dissenters were awarded a total of $23.86 per share, compared with $13.26 originally offered.

---

[10] *Ryan v. Tad's Enterprises, Inc.*, Nos. 10229, 11977, 1996 WL 204502 (Del. Ch. Apr. 24, 1996).

Approaches to Value

Most courts embrace all three broad approaches to value (income, market, and asset-based approaches) in dissenting stockholder and judicial dissolution cases. The Chancery Court of Delaware has repeatedly expressed a preference for the discounted cash flow method (citations will be provided in sections to follow on the income approach). However, reliance on the DCF method is dependent on reasonable projections, which are not always available.

Should Consider Market Value, Asset Value, and Investment Value

In Utah's dissenters' case of first impression, *Oakridge Energy v. Clifton*,[11] the Supreme Court of Utah reviewed and cited case law from other states that had similar statutes, including Iowa, Maryland, Maine, Delaware, and Massachusetts. The company (which was public before the triggering event) paid dissenting stockholders $2.75 per share, based on a $2.50 market price plus a $0.25 dividend. Plaintiffs claimed $3.57 per share based on a pro forma balance sheet after taking the effect of the proceeds of the asset sale that triggered dissenters' rights.

The court noted that the consensus of the cases cited is that the component elements to be relied on in estimating fair value are market value, net asset value, and investment value, and "the courts have traditionally favored investment value,[12] rather than asset value, as the most important of the three elements." The court stated:

> We conclude that the trial court erred in using the stock market price . . . as the sole criterion for determining the fair value. . . . We agree with the courts cited above that a dissenting shareholder disclaims both the burden and the benefit of the disfavored corporate action . . . under the plain language of the statute, any effect of the Cometra sale must be excluded. . . . No informed expert even ventured to suggest the Oakridge assets could be valued at $21.5 million prior to Cometra's offer. . . . "fair value" is not measured by any unique benefits that will accrue to the acquiring corporation. . . . the sale price here was not reinforced by several buyers bidding against each other.

The defendants had introduced testimony that net asset value before the events was $2.13 per share. Neither side had introduced evidence of investment value. Therefore, the Supreme Court concluded:

> The stock market price and a reasonable approximation of the asset value were before the trial court, each supported by substantial evidence of investment value. . . . Absent evidence of investment value, the trial court should at least have considered the asset value as well as the market price of the stock.
>
> However, since the per share value based on asset value ($2.13) is less than the stock market price ($2.50), no choice of weighting would have resulted in a per share value greater than $2.50 for the Oakridge stock. Thus

---

[11] *Oakridge Energy, Inc. v. Clifton*, No. 960049, 1997 WL 191487 (Utah Apr. 18, 1997).

[12] Investment value, as used here, is as defined in the previous chapter (a value based on earnings), as opposed to the definition of investment value in contexts other than fair value determinations—that is, the value to a particular buyer or seller.

the trial court's error is harmless, indeed beneficial to the dissenters since Oakridge has not sought an adjustment of the $2.75 already paid.

We affirm the judgment of the trial court.

Unfortunately, courts' interpretations of market value, investment value, and asset value vary. For example, asset value usually means the net assets adjusted to some premise of current value. However, one decision used the market price to the book value pricing multiple of a group of guideline companies as a proxy for asset value, resulting in asset value being measured as 1.29 times book value.[13]

Consideration of all these major elements, that is, market value, investment value, and asset value, does not necessarily mean that all three will be utilized in the final analysis. In some cases weight will be accorded to all three, in some cases, only two, and some cases will be decided entirely on the basis of one of the three major elements. Investment value typically is accorded the greatest weight, followed by market value, with asset value usually accorded the least weight. Some Delaware cases, for example, have ultimately been decided entirely on the basis of investment value measured by the discounted cash flow method and others based entirely on guideline companies.

Market Approach Accepted

As is true with tax cases, the acceptance of evidence and conclusions using the market approach is very sensitive to the comparability of the guideline companies chosen.

In *Borruso v. Communications Telesystems International*,[14] both experts used only the guideline publicly traded company method, both relying primarily on multiples of revenue, because the financial history was insufficient to provide a basis for a DCF analysis or even multiples of economic income variables such as EBITDA. Each expert used eight guideline companies. The court used the five that were in common between the two experts, plus one from the dissenters' expert's group. The court opinion provided a discussion worth reading about its reasons for acceptance and rejection of various guideline companies offered by the experts.

The dissenters' expert started with the median of the pricing multiples of his guideline companies, and adjusted from there for differences in general between the guideline group and the subject company. The company's expert applied adjustments to the multiples of each individual company to reflect differences between each of them and the subject. The court adopted the latter procedure. The court rejected the upward adjustment made by the dissenters' expert to reflect superior growth in the most recent fiscal year, because there was no evidence in the record that this growth was sustainable.

The court's position on discounts and/or premiums applicable to the result of the guideline company analysis is discussed in the subsequent section on discounts and premiums.

Another case that accepted the market approach involved shares of a bank stock in a dissenting stockholder case. The court ultimately relied on a pricing multiple of total capital and a price/earnings multiple.[15]

---

[13] *Berens v. Ludwig, Comptroller of the Currency,* No. A-94-984 U.S. Dist. Ct., 1997 WL 64073 (N.D. Ill. Feb. 13, 1997).

[14] *Carl Borruso and William Lee v. Communications Telesystems International*, C.A. No. 16316-NC, 1999 LEXIS 197 (Del. Ch. Sept. 24, 1999).

[15] *Mark H. Berens v. Eugene A. Ludwig*, No. 97-3545 U.S. App., 1998 WL 797169 (7th Cir. Nov. 17, 1998), *aff'g Berens v. Ludwig, Comptroller of the Currency*, No. A-94-984 U.S. Dist. Ct., 1997 WL 64073 (N.D. Ill. Feb. 13, 1997).

An opinion in a dissenting stockholder case concluded that a multiple of EBIT-DA procedure was better than the DCF method in that particular case. It based its concluded multiple on that paid by the subject company in two prior acquisitions that it had made.[16]

Guideline Merged and Acquired Company Method

In contrast to most Delaware appraisal cases, the court in a bank holding company case, *LeBeau v. M.G. Bancorporation*[17] rejected both the discounted cash flow and the guideline publicly traded company analysis, both of which were presented by experts on both sides, because of perceived errors. Instead of adjusting the experts' valuations for the alleged errors, the court relied on an analysis of guideline merged and acquired companies, which it normally rejects as unpermissably including a control premium. The Court justified the methodology in this case by reference to *Rapid American* (see section on control premiums):

> In *Harris v. Rapid American*, the Supreme Court ruled that a holding company's ownership of a controlling interest in its subsidiaries is an independent element of value that must be taken into account in determining a fair value for the parent company.
>
> Although the respondents argued that this decision should apply only to subsidiaries operating in different businesses, the Vice Chancellor disagreed.[18]

In reviewing the case, Gil Matthews criticized the decision:

> This reasoning leads to the absurd conclusion that a business conducted through a subsidiary is entitled to a control premium, but an identical business conducted through a division is not! The application of a control premium at a subsidiary level, when such premium is not permitted at the parent level, is an anomaly that is difficult to justify.[19]

Discounted Cash Flow Method

In *Grimes v. Vitalink*,[20] the Delaware Court of Chancery characterized the DCF method as "increasingly the model of choice for valuations in this Court." In the *Grimes* case, both experts used the DCF method. Differences occurred in:

- Forecast assumptions.
- Selection of comparable companies used to estimate multiples for the terminal value.[21]

---

[16] *Connector Service Corporation v. Jeffrey Briggs*, No. 97 C 7088 U.S. Dist. Ct., 1998 LEXIS 18864 (N.D. Ill. Oct. 30, 1998).

[17] *LeBeau v. M.G. Bancorporation, Inc.*

[18] Gilbert E. Matthews, "Delaware Court Relies on Comparable Acquisition Method," *Shannon Pratt's Business Valuation Update*, March 1998, p. 11.

[19] Ibid.

[20] *Charles L. Grimes v. Vitalink Communications Corporation*, No. C.A. 12334, 1997 WL 538676 (Del. Ch. Aug. 28, 1997), *aff'd* No. 425, 1997 (Del. Apr. 1, 1998).

[21] Note that, as discussed in Chapter 9, despite many investment bankers' preference to use market multiples for terminal values, we favor using the Gordon growth model for estimating the terminal values to avoid mixing up a market approach with an income approach.

Based on the credibility of the experts, their methods, and the data relied on, the court relied on the company's expert and concluded the value put forward by the company's expert.

In *Gilbert v. M.P.M. Enterprises*,[22] both sides presented both a guideline publicly traded company method and a DCF method. The court decided to base its conclusion on the DCF method. The dissenters presented what they called a "buy side DCF" and a "sell side DCF." The court said that the sell side model was the only appropriate one to consider because the law requires valuation as a going concern without "any element of value arising from the accomplishment or expectation of a merger." After an argument over whether to use the build-up or CAPM procedure to develop a discount rate, the court decided in favor of CAPM.

In *Hintmann v. Fred Weber*, the Delaware Court of Chancery was presented with both the build-up method and the CAPM method for estimating the appropriate present value discount rate. The court rejected the build-up method, noting that, "This method differed from the CAPM in only one respect: It did not employ beta. The CAPM would seem to be more useful than the 'build-up' method because it offers more complete information. Specifically, the CAPM includes a measure of the stock's systematic risk."[23]

Excess Earnings Method

Although it is not common in fair value cases, the excess earnings method has been accepted. The method was accepted over defendants' objections, and was upheld on appeal, in a New Jersey case, *Balsamides v. Protameen Chemicals, Inc.*[24] The Supreme Court explained:

> The court noted that although not preferred, "excess earnings" is an acceptable method, and [plaintiff's expert] chose it, in part, because defendants would not provide the information needed to employ any other method.

> This suggests to us that resisting providing information for valuation probably does not serve the company's best interests.

Weighting of Methods

Sometimes courts assign specific mathematical weights to the results of the analysis by each of two or more valuation methods. An example of this is found in a Nevada case, *Steiner v. Benninghoff*.[25] In that case, the court weighted methods as presented in Exhibit 36–1.

While the above breakdown is unique to the particular case, there have been many cases that have reached conclusions by some form of mathematical weighting of results of two or more appraisal methods.

---

[22] *Gilbert v. M.P.M. Enterprises, Inc.*, No. CA 14416-NC, 1998 LEXIS 60 (Del. Ch. Apr. 24, 1998), *aff'd M.P.M. Enterprises, Inc. v. Jeffrey D. Gilbert*, 731 A.2d 790 (Del. June 25, 1999).

[23] *Hintmann v. Fred Weber, Inc.* No. 12839 Del. Ch., 1998 WL 853052 (Feb. 17, 1998).

[24] *Emanuel Balsamides, et al. v. Protameen Chemicals, Inc., et al.*, 1999 WL 492630 (N.J. July 14, 1999).

[25] *Steiner v. Benninghoff*, No. CV-N-94-0840-ECR U.S. Dist. Ct., 1998 WL 276136 (D. Nev. May 26, 1998).

Exhibit 36–1

Example of Mathematical Weighting

Enterprise Value:

	Per Share	Weight		Weight	Final Value
Discounted cash flow	$1,273.64	70%	$1,479.22	75%	
Mergers and acquisitions	1,958.95	30%			$1,407.22
Market Value:					
Guideline public companies			1,191.98*	25%	

*After a 25% discount for lack of marketability

SOURCE: *Steiner v. Benninghoff,* No. CV-N-94-0840-ECR U.S. Dist. Ct., 1998 WL 276136 (D. Nev. May 26, 1998).

A South Carolina appellate court upheld a minority oppression case decision where one appraiser used only an asset approach, one used only an income approach, and the trial court's decision was an average of the two.[26]

Discounts and Premiums

A major issue in many fair value cases is whether or not discounts and/or premiums are applicable. If so, there is always the issue of the magnitudes of such discounts and/or premiums.

The primary issues are lack of control (i.e., minority ownership interest) discounts, ownership control premiums, and discounts for lack of marketability. The published opinions that have addressed these issues vary considerably from state to state:

1. Some do not allow either lack of control or lack of marketability discounts.
2. Some allow both lack of control and lack of marketability discounts.
3. Some allow discounts for lack of control but not for lack of marketability.
4. Some allow discounts for lack of marketability but not for lack of control.
5. Several states have taken the position that discounts for lack of control and lack of marketability must be decided in each case on the basis of the facts and circumstances of that case.
6. Some states have applied ownership control premiums under certain specific circumstances.

Lack of Control Discounts Rejected

In its case of first impression on the issue of a lack of control discount in a dissenting stockholder suit, the Wisconsin Court of Appeals rejected the 30 percent minority

---

[26] *McDuffie v. O'Neal,* No. 2553, 1996 WL 452905 (S.C. App. Aug. 12, 1996).

interest (i.e., lack of control) discount that had been applied by the trial court. The court reviewed cases from several states (including Delaware, New York, and Oklahoma) and concluded that lack of control discounts should not be applied. The court agreed with the rationale that was stated in *Cavalier Oil Corp. v. Harnett*:

> Discounting individual shareholdings injects into the appraisal process speculation on the various factors which may dictate the marketability of minority shareholdings. More important, to fail to accord to a minority shareholder the full proportionate value of his shares imposes a penalty for lack of control, and unfairly enriches the majority shareholders who may reap a windfall from the appraisal process by cashing out a dissenting shareholder, a clearly undesirable result.[27]

Because of this "clearly undesirable result," the Wisconsin Court of Appeals held that lack of control discounts are inappropriate in dissenters' rights cases as a matter of law, and it remanded to the lower court to award SSM the pro rata share of HMO-W's net assets without a lack of control discount.[28]

A 1999 Montana Supreme Court decision demonstrates the need to always research the latest decisions. The Montana Supreme Court reversed itself! In a 1999 dissenting stockholder case,[29] the Supreme Court disallowed a lack of control discount, overruling its own decision to allow a lack of control discount in a 1996 shareholder oppression suit.[30]

Ownership Control Premium Accepted

The Delaware Court of Chancery has accepted the application of an ownership control premium under two specific circumstances:

1. When the base valued is a publicly traded equivalent value derived by the guideline publicly traded company method.
2. When valuing a controlling ownership position in a subsidiary company.

In *Borruso v. Communications Telesystems International*,[31] the court relied on the guideline publicly traded company method. Both experts agreed that an ownership control premium should be applied, but disagreed as to the stage of the analysis at which it should be applied. The dissenters' expert applied a premium to the MVIC to revenue pricing multiples to reflect the control issue. The company's expert applied the control premium to the guideline publicly traded company analysis result. The court accepted the latter procedure, noting that the dissenters' expert's procedure had the effect of altering the methodology itself.

Two cases in which the Delaware Court of Chancery placed an ownership control premium on the indicated values of wholly owned subsidiaries are *Rapid American Corporation v. Harris*[32] and *Hintmann v. Fred Weber, Inc.*[33] In *Rapid American*, the court valued the subsidiaries by the guideline publicly traded company method. The Delaware Supreme Court concluded that an ownership control

---

[27] *Cavalier Oil Corp. v. Harnett*, 564 A.2d 1137 (Del. 1989).

[28] *HMO-W v. SSM Health Care System*, No. 98-2834, 1999 WL 395650 (Wis. App. June 17, 1999).

[29] *Hansen v. 75 Ranch Company*, No. 97-249, 1998 WL 180831 (Mont. Apr. 9, 1998).

[30] *McCann Ranch, Inc. v. Sharon Quigley-McCann*, 276 Mont. 205, 208, 915 P.2d 239, 241 (1996).

[31] *Carl Borruso and William Lee v. Communications Telesystems International.*

[32] *Rapid American Corporation v. Harris*, 603 A.2d 796 (Del. 1992).

[33] *Hintmann v. Fred Weber, Inc.*

premium was appropriate, explaining, "The exclusion of a control premium artificially and unrealistically treated Rapid as a minority shareholder."

In *Hintmann v. Fred Weber*, the court valued the subsidiaries on the basis of a simple average of the guideline publicly traded company method and the DCF method. Saying that the case was analogous to *Rapid American*, the court then added a 20 percent ownership control premium to the resulting indicated values of the subsidiaries. However, a commentator on the decision, investment banker Gil Matthews, criticized the decision as distinguishable from *Rapid American* in that the subsidiary values were based partly on the DCF method:

> DCF value should represent the full value of the future cash flows of the business. Excluding synergies, a company cannot be worth a premium over the value of its future cash flows. Thus, it is improper and illogical to add a control premium to a DCF valuation.[34]

In another case, the Delaware Court of Chancery implicitly allowed an ownership control premium by accepting the guideline merged and acquired company method (see *LeBeau v. M.G. Bancorporation* referenced earlier).

Lack of Marketability Discounts Rejected

The Delaware Court of Chancery is one venue that has regularly rejected discounts for lack of marketability. For example, in *Borruso v. Telesystems International*,[35] the court rejected the company's expert's "discount for lack of liquidity," citing *Cavalier Oil*[36] and saying that it was essentially a discount for lack of marketability which is inappropriate in a fair value determination.

Iowa courts have not issued a definitive opinion on discounts for lack of marketability. In *Sieg v. Kelly*,[37] the trial court disallowed the lack of marketability discount and the case was appealed. The Supreme Court of Iowa noted: "Iowa was clear at the time Sieg made its valuation that a . . . discount is not permitted." It noted, however, that some jurisdictions allow lack of marketability discounts and other do not. In the final analysis, it found no error in rejecting the lack of marketability discount, but did not issue a generalized pronouncement on the issue.

In the New Jersey dissenting stockholder case of *Wheaton v. Smith*,[38] the Supreme Court overturned the trial court's acceptance of a discount for lack of marketability, which had been affirmed by the New Jersey Appellate Division. Relying on 2 ALI, *Principles of Corporate Governance: Analysis and Recommendations*, ¶7.22(a), the trial court concluded that the application of a lack of marketability discount was appropriate because of "extraordinary circumstances" that were present. The New Jersey Supreme Court explained as follows:

> Such circumstances require more than the absence of a trading market in shares; rather, the court should apply this exception only when it finds that the dissenting shareholder has held out in order to exploit the transaction

---

[34] Gilbert E. Matthews, "Delaware Court Adds Control Premiums to Subsidiary Value," *Shannon Pratt's Business Valuation Update*, May 1998, p. 10.

[35] *Carl Borruso and William Lee v. Communications Telesystems International.*

[36] *Cavalier Oil Corp. v. Harnett.*

[37] *Sieg Company v. Kelly*, No. 96-61, 1997 WL 575996 (Iowa Sept. 17, 1997).

[38] *Lawson Mardon Wheaton, Inc. v. Smith, et al.*, 1999 WL 492634 (N.J. July 14, 1999).

giving rise to appraisal so as to divert value to itself that could not be made available proportionately to other shareholders.

On the same day, the New Jersey Supreme Court accepted a lack of marketability discount in the minority oppression case of *Balsamides v. Protameen Chemicals*, discussed in the next section.

Lack of Marketability Discounts Accepted

In a New Jersey minority oppression case, *Balsamides v. Protameen Chemicals, Inc.*,[39] the trial court accepted a 35 percent discount for lack of marketability. The New Jersey Superior Court, Appellate Division, reversed, and, on appeal, the New Jersey Supreme Court upheld the lack of marketability discount. The New Jersey Supreme Court explained as follows:

> The position of the Appellate Division ignores the reality that Balsamides is buying a company that will remain illiquid because it is not publicly traded and public information about it is not widely disseminated. Protameen will continue to have a small base of available purchasers. If it is resold in the future, Balsamides will receive a lower purchase price because of the company's closely-held nature.
>
> If Perle and Balsamides sold Protameen together, the price they received would reflect Protameen's illiquidity. They would split the price and also share that determent. Similarly, if Balsamides pays Perle a discounted price, Perle suffers half of the lack-of-marketability markdown now; and Balsamides suffers the other half when he eventually sells his closely-held business. Conversely, if Perle is not required to sell his shares at a price that reflects Protameen's lack of marketability, Balsamides will suffer the full effect of Protameen's lack of marketability at the time he sells. Accordingly, we find that Balsamides should not bear the brunt of Protameen's illiquidity merely because he is the designated buyer.

On the same day, the New Jersey Supreme Court rejected a lack of marketability discount in the dissenting stockholder case of *Wheaton v. Smith*, discussed in the previous section.

It is not unheard of to apply some particular discount to the results of one or more valuation methods but not to the results of one or more other methods. For example, as seen in an earlier case reference, the court applied a 25 percent discount for lack of marketability to the results of the guideline publicly traded company method, but no discount to the results of the DCF method or the guideline merged and acquired company method.

Discounts Left to Court's Discretion

Opinions in several states have rejected the notion that there should be a sweeping policy that lack of control discounts, ownership control premiums, and/or lack of marketability discounts should be either accepted or rejected in all fair value cases.

---

[39] *Emanuel Balsamides, et al. v. Protameen Chemicals, Inc., et al.*

Instead they have taken the position that the issue of lack of control and lack of marketability discounts should be decided on a case-by-case basis depending on the facts and circumstances of the particular case.

The essence of this position is articulated in a 1999 Missouri decision:

> The most important guidance of this case, relied on heavily by Defendant, is its holding that the application of both marketability and minority discounts "in determining fair value pursuant to § 351.455, when a shareholder of a corporation objects to a merger or consolidation, rests within the sound discretion of the trier of facts after every relevant fact and circumstance is considered." 765 S.W.2d at 305, 306. Although both parties in their thorough briefs argue at various junctures that this case or that policy mandates that the Court apply or decline to apply discounts, the principle which emerges most strongly and clearly from *King* is that such a decision is discretionary. The Court's discussion of Missouri case law, as well as that of other states, must, therefore, proceed with the understanding that no law or policy requiring or forbidding the application of discounts may hold sway with the Court, which is required by its interpretation of Missouri law to rest its decision on its own discretion, after considering every relevant fact and circumstance.[40]

Colorado is another state where the matter of discounts is to be made on a case-by-case basis. In *WCM Industries, Inc. v. Wilson*, the company claimed that, as a matter of law, a discount for lack of marketability must be applied to closely held shares. The appeals court disagreed:

> A marketability discount may, in appropriate circumstances, be applied, but . . . such a determination is a factual one that must be made on an ad hoc, case-by-case basis . . . [and] our review of the out-of-state cases cited by WCM reveals a majority rule that a marketability discount is not required as a matter of law but, rather, may be employed by a fact finder, depending upon the particular facts and circumstances.[41]

The court emphasized that the valuation analyst and the trial court may consider any relevant factors relative to the worth of the stock that are reasonable under the circumstances and justified by the evidence presented.

Illinois is also in the camp of leaving lack of control and lack of marketability discounts to the courts' discretion. In *Weigel Broadcasting v. Smith*,[42] a reverse split squeeze-out, the company's independent expert concluded $115 per share, reflecting a combination discount for lack of control and lack of marketability of 50 percent. The Dissenter's expert was at $578.14 per share. The Appellate Court of Illinois concluded $126 per share. The appellate court cited case law supporting discounts for lack of control and lack of marketability and concluded, "Applying such discounts is left to the trial court's discretion."

---

[40] *Swope, et al. v. Siegel-Robert, Inc.*, No. 97-CV-2016 U.S. Dist. Ct. (E.D. Mo. June 23, 1999). The reference to *King* is *King v. F.I.J., Inc.*, 765 S.W.2d 301 (Mo. App. 1989). The case provides an extensive discussion of dissenting stockholder case law, citing cases from several states.

[41] *WCM Industries, Inc. v. Wilson*, 948 P.2d 36 (Colo. App., Div. I, Dec. 15, 1997).

[42] *Weigel Broadcasting Company v. Smith, et al.*, 682 N.E.2d 745 (Ill. App. July 24, 1997).

"Dr. Pangloss and Mr. Scrooge"

Vice Chancellor Steele expressed a degree of cynicism toward the desired objectivity of experts in *Gilbert v. MPM Enterprises*.

> One might expect the experts' desire to convince the Court of the reasonableness and validity of their assumptions and financial models would produce a somewhat narrow range of values, clearly and concisely supported, despite the individual parties' obvious conflicting incentives. Unfortunately, as this case and other cases most decidedly illustrate, one should not put much faith in that expectation, at least when faced with appraisal experts in this Court. . . .
>
> Reading petitioner's submissions, one might easily conclude that MPM was poised to become the Microsoft of the SMT industry. By contrast, respondent's submissions give the impression that a more likely comparison, given MPM's myriad management, technical and legal problems, is Apple. In sum, one report is submitted by Dr. Pangloss, and the other by Mr. Scrooge."[43]

The courts seek a high degree of objectivity with regard to valuation expert witnesses. The courts place great weight on the credibility of the valuation analyst in deciding what evidence and testimony to accept or not accept. Typically, the courts will find an apparently neutral valuation expert to be much more credible than an apparently biased or goal-oriented valuation expert.

Summary

By selected examples, this chapter has demonstrated the great diversity of positions taken by courts in interpreting the standard of fair value in dissenting stockholder and minority oppression cases. One conclusion that is obvious is that virtually no court specifically equates "fair value" with "fair market value."

It also seems apparent that both the valuation analyst and/or the attorney need to read relevant judicial precedent with great care. In particular, analysts should be careful about attributing broad applicability to seemingly sweeping statements. Facts and circumstances vary greatly from one case to another, and courts will consider these variations in deciding whether a principle articulated in one case is applicable to the instant case at bar.

Another important point in estimating fair value is whether or not there was procedural fairness in the entire transaction. If controlling owners acted unfairly toward noncontrolling stockholders (or vice versa), there may, in some jurisdictions, be considerable elements of damages incurred beyond just the basic appraisal under dissenters' stockholder rights.

Generally speaking, the elements of market value, investment value, and asset value should all be considered, although the final conclusion may be based on only one or two of these elements. The most important element in most cases is *investment value,* followed by market value and asset value. Investment value in this context

---

[43] *Gilbert v. MPM Enterprises, Inc.*, No. 14416, 1997 WL 633298 (Del. Ch. Oct. 9, 1997).

means value based on production of income, as opposed to value to a particular owner or investor, as the standard of investment value is defined in other appraisal contexts.

Accepted valuation methods vary greatly, depending on the type of company, the facts and circumstances of each case, the relative quality of evidence available for different valuation methods, and the preferences of the court. Courts sometimes weight two or more methods and other times ultimately depend on the results of a single method.

The courts' postures toward discounts and premiums is highly variable, both from jurisdiction to jurisdiction and, in many jurisdictions, depending on the distinguishable facts and circumstances from one case to another within a jurisdiction.

Many states have no precedential case law in the area of dissenting stockholder suits and/or minority oppression suits. Others have some case law, but most have not addressed all the various issues that may arise. In the face of lack of their own precedential case law, courts usually look to precedential case law from other states. Thus, although dissent and oppression valuation cases are nominally state-specific, it is important for valuation analysts and attorneys working in this area to have a broad familiarity with the various precedents of many states. This chapter has not attempted to provide a comprehensive treatise, but has provided examples to illustrate variations of courts' positions on issues commonly encountered.

Chapter 37

Valuations for Marital Dissolution Purposes

Although marital dissolutions may be a small proportion of the typical business valuation practice, they account for a high proportion of the times that business valuation experts appear in court as expert witnesses. Often the business or business interest is the largest asset in the marital estate. And, the resolution of the value of the subject business property often cannot be settled by logical negotiation between disputing spouses.

To make matters worse, guidelines for business valuations prepared for marital dissolution purposes are less well settled in most states than for business valuations prepared for virtually any other purpose. For example, no state marital dissolution statute specifies a definition of value. Even in states with an abundance of marital dissolution judicial precedent, family law trial courts have wide latitude in exercising their discretion. Published judicial precedent is often confusing and (sometimes) contradictory.

The Marital Estate

The marital estate comes into being upon filing for divorce. It represents the assets that must be divided according to the property laws of the state. Currently, each state adheres to either (1) the *community property* standard or (2) the *equitable distribution* standard with regard to the division of assets included within the marital estate.

The question as to what property is or is not included in the marital estate is often a major issue. The analyst sometimes must value property before the court has determined the extent to which it is or is not included in the marital estate.

Community Property

In states adhering to the community property standard, distributable property is referred to as community property. The community property standard is based on the premise of joint and equal ownership of the marital estate. In a community property standard state, all assets acquired during a marriage are assumed (1) to be acquired by the marital community and (2) to be owned jointly by the community. These states generally follow the practice of an equal division of the marital estate upon divorce.

Equitable Distribution

Most states follow the standard of equitable distribution. Under this concept, equitable distribution of the marital estate may mean equal distribution, or it may not. The court may make adjustments and decisions related to the allocation process based on the specific facts and circumstances.

Active or Passive Appreciation During Marriage

Many states take the position that appreciation in the value of property that was separate at the time of marriage is part of the marital estate. This would be the case if the appreciation was due to the active efforts of one spouse, but not if the appreciation was "passive"—that is, due to external factors such as the market. This distinction may require the analyst to value the property both as of the date of marriage and also at the marital dissolution valuation date. In some cases, the valuation analyst is asked to opine as to whether the appreciation was due to the spouse's efforts or not.

Active or Passive Post–Valuation Date Appreciation

Some states (e.g., North Carolina) have enacted legislation to include passive appreciation in the marital estate *after* the basic valuation date. For example, if the valuation date is the date of separation, but the trial to determine the property division is two years later, a portion of the passive appreciation after the date of separation in the property awarded to one spouse may have to be shared with the other spouse. This distinction creates yet another element of valuation. This increase in value is accounted for at the time of the actual property distribution, and it is called *divisable property*.

Standard of Value

Since state statutes are silent with respect to the standard of value for marital property valuation, it is necessary to look at each state's judicial precedent for guidance. In general, the standards of value adopted by the family law courts are *investment value*, *fair market value*, and *intrinsic value*.

Investment Value

Investment value, as defined in Chapter 2, is the value of a business (or business interest) to a specific owner. Unlike the fair market value standard, this standard considers (1) the specific owner's expectation of risks, (2) the potential synergy associated with ownership of the subject business, (3) the specific earnings expectations resulting from the subject ownership, and, in some cases, (4) the relationship of the spouse/owner to the other owners of the business.

Those practitioners espousing the investment value standard say that the marital property value should be "current value to the marital community in the hands of the present owner."[1]

Fair Market Value

Many state courts have adopted fair market value as the relevant standard of value. Fair market value is based on the price that would be negotiated between an informed hypothetical buyer and an informed hypothetical seller, as discussed in Chapter 2. The fair market value concept is more thoroughly defined in Revenue Ruling 59-60.

Those practitioners espousing the fair market value standard say that it is unfair to value the property that one spouse will receive at more than that spouse could realize on a sale. Proponents of the fair market value standard explain, for example:

---

[1] Alan S. Zipp, "Business Valuation Standard for Divorce is Different from Fair Market Value," *American Journal of Family Law*, Fall 1997, pp. 167–72.

The relevant point to the court should be the amount the business assets could bring in cash or cash equivalent at the appropriate date. The point of whether or not the business or any other asset will actually be sold is beside the point. In fact, there is a sale of sorts which occurs within the dissolution. The net effect of the separation of marital assets is that each spouse purchases a (let's assume) 50% interest in certain assets from their spouse and pays for the purchase by selling back their 50% interest in other assets. The transfers occur and the marital assets are separated. The end result is not substantially different than when both spouses agree jointly to each sell a marital asset and divide the funds received. The primary difference is they are the buyers and sellers, there are no outside parties involved, and the mode of payment is the exchange of interests in the marital assets.[2]

Bishop and Schroeder make the point that lack of marketability discounts should be recognized, just as they are in Tax Court, because one spouse usually gets liquid assets while the other spouse lacks the flexibility and safety of being able to "cash out" readily at the owner's option. They also make the point that "underlying principles are much more consistent and broadly accepted" under the fair market value standard than they are in marital dissolutions not using the fair market value standard.

Intrinsic Value

Intrinsic value, also discussed in Chapter 2, is a concept of value based on the fundamental or real value of the asset. Intrinsic value assumes a higher level of insight and knowledge about the asset than a typical investor may possess. For example, for a publicly traded company, the intrinsic value would represent someone's estimate of the "true" value of the stock of the company versus the published stock price.

Internal Contradictions in the Case Law

Most state courts claim to espouse the philosophy that the value of assets in the marital estate should *not* include any value attributable to either spouse's post marital efforts nor any value resulting from restrictions on post marital efforts. Having said that, the courts often go on to decide on values of companies or professional practices where post-marital efforts or restrictions thereon are clearly reflected in the valuation methods accepted. Some specific situations illustrating this are discussed in the next chapter.

For example, the "capitalized excess earnings method," often used in family law courts, includes a value that can only be realized if the operating spouse continues to work. Otherwise, the "excess earnings" that are capitalized will never be realized (unless it can be shown that they are tied completely to the entity, rather than to the individual).

When the courts use *market value*, they often rely on comparable business sales that include a covenant not to compete that restricts the activities of the sellers. Yet, the values of the covenants not to compete are not subtracted out of the total consideration received by the sellers in the allegedly comparable sale transactions.

---

[2] David M. Bishop and Steven F. Schroeder, "Business Valuation Standard of Value for Divorce Should Be Fair Market Value," *American Journal of Family Law*, Spring 1999, pp. 48–52.

And, it is not at all uncommon for courts to use the term *market value* or *fair market value* and then to conclude a value that incorporates elements of investment value or some other standard.

The analyst should carefully study the case law in the relevant family law jurisdiction and discuss the interpretations with the client's attorney. In many situations this will still leave room for a high level of confusion. It is incumbent upon the attorney to educate the analyst as to the valuation methods that are acceptable in the subject jurisdiction.

Valuation Date

Selecting the appropriate valuation date is an important step in the valuation process. In a marital dissolution valuation, relevant state-specific statutory authority and judicial precedent sometimes specifies the appropriate valuation date or dates. In many instances, however, the appropriate valuation date is unclear based on the state-specific judicial precedent. Accordingly, the appropriate valuation date for the ownership interest included in the marital estate is a question most appropriately answered by legal counsel, and not by the valuation analyst.

Based on judicial precedent in numerous states and jurisdictions throughout the country, and based on the specific circumstances of the particular marital dissolution, the valuation date is generally one or more of the following dates:

1. The date of marriage.
2. The date of separation.
3. The date of filing.
4. The date of the trial.

Since the selection of the appropriate valuation date can affect the value of the subject business, it is important that the attorney instruct the analyst regarding the applicable valuation date (or dates) early in the valuation process. However, the analyst may have to go to court prepared to testify as to the value on several different dates if the court does not address that issue beforehand.[3]

Discovery

There are often obstacles in the discovery process for the analyst in a marital dissolution proceeding. In the case where the analyst is working for a nonowner spouse, information regarding the subject business or professional practice may be difficult to obtain. Also, the owner spouse may not readily share strategic and financial information with the analyst.

In these cases, it is advisable for the analyst to prepare a comprehensive data and document request to give to the client or to the client's attorney. Often, it is difficult to add to or amend an initial document request. Therefore, the analyst is advised to

[3] The date of valuation is a frequent issue. See, for example, *Else v. Else*, No. A-95-488, 1997 WL 22615 (Neb. App. Jan. 14, 1997), where the appellate court decided that the trial court erred by using the date of trial rather than the date of separation. See also *Quillen v. Quillen*, No. 29502-9608-CV-531, Sup. Ct. Ind. (Aug. 6, 1996), where the court decided the date should be before the husband lost financing capacity for his construction company because of sex offenses against his daughter since he brought it on himself.

prepare as comprehensive a document request list as possible for submission. Exhibit 4–1 (in Chapter 4) presents a sample document request list. Some of these documents may be accessible from the subject company's accountants, attorneys, or bankers.

Most valuation experts consider it preferable to conduct discovery in the most informal (from a legal point of view) and most direct manner possible, with the greatest possible interaction. In this sense, most analysts prefer direct management interviews over depositions and depositions over interrogatories. The answers to each question may raise other questions. The management interview provides opportunity for dialogue. If forced to do discovery through depositions rather than interviews, the attorney rather than the analyst usually has to ask the questions. It is highly desirable to have the analyst present at any depositions in order to provide the attorney with follow-up questions.

Interrogatories are the most cumbersome and generally least satisfactory form of discovery, lacking virtually all interaction. If they are absolutely necessary, the attorney should try to leave the door open for follow-up sets of interrogatories to fill in unanswered questions, including those that may arise throughout the course of the valuation process.

The independent valuation analyst should be objective and not an advocate for the client's position. If this can be communicated to the operating spouse, that spouse may be more open to direct contact with the analyst. It is the operating spouse's opportunity to fully expose the analyst to his or her side of the story. A competent and objective analyst will take all factors presented into consideration. In many cases, the analyst can get a more complete understanding directly from the operating party than through other means of discovery. This may narrow the differences between the analysts, and may sometimes facilitate a settlement.

Goodwill

In many divorce cases, the inclusion and/or measurement of goodwill as a marital asset is by far the largest issue in the valuation of the marital estate's business or professional practice.

The classic definition of goodwill is "the propensity of customers to return for repeat business." The criterion as to whether goodwill exists usually is the ability to earn a rate of return in excess of a normal rate of return on the net assets of the business, after reasonable compensation to operating personnel. The measurement of goodwill often is performed by capitalizing amounts of economic return in excess of a normal rate of return on the net other assets of the business (see Chapter 13 on the Capitalized Excess Earnings Method).

In marital dissolution cases, goodwill may require allocation between two types: (1) institutional (or practice) goodwill and (2) professional (or personal) goodwill. Professional or personal goodwill may be described as the intangible value attributable solely to the efforts of or reputation of an owner spouse of the subject business. Institutional or practice goodwill may be described as the intangible value that would continue to inure to the business without the presence of that specific owner spouse.

As with many matters related to marital dissolution valuations, the consideration of goodwill varies among states. In general, the various judicial precedents follow one of three positions regarding the consideration of goodwill:

1. Goodwill is never a distributable marital asset.
2. Business or practice goodwill *only* is a distributable marital asset.
3. All intangible value in the nature of goodwill (both personal and practice goodwill) related to the business or practice is distributable.

States that adhere strictly to the fair market value standard in marital property dissolution follow option number two above. That is, they recognize the fact that the value of personal goodwill can only be realized as a result of the continuing involvement of that person (post-marital efforts), and, therefore, only the business goodwill is a marital asset. (An exception could be genuine celebrity goodwill, where a person may receive a royalty from endorsing a product or service, with no actual future effort expended by that person.)[4]

The analyst should consult the attorney regarding the appropriate treatment of goodwill early in the assignment. This consultation procedure should be performed in order to determine what information should be requested and what valuation methods should be used. The analyst also should carefully study the relevant judicial precedent. There are literally hundreds of cases dealing with goodwill as a marital asset. A representative sampling of these is discussed in the next chapter.

Valuation Methods

Family law courts generally recognize each of the three basic approaches to value:

1. Income approach (both direct capitalization and, increasingly, discounted cash flow).
2. Market approach.
3. Asset-based approach (including the capitalized excess earnings method).

Having said this, however, it should be noted that the courts often take considerable latitude in their applications of these valuation approaches. This situation makes it even more important for the analyst to consider any applicable state statutes and relevant judicial precedent when concluding which valuation approaches and methods are most appropriate.

Income Approach

The commonly used income approach valuation methods (especially for valuing operating companies) are (1) the discounted future economic income (often cash flow) method and (2) the direct capitalization of economic income (often earnings) method. The trend in many family law courts is to emphasize income approach methods more than asset-based approach and market approach methods of valuation.

---

[4] See especially Michael C. Wierwille and Neil J. Beaton, "Valuing of Celebrity or Professional Goodwill—A New Paradigm," *The Journal of Business Valuation* (Proceedings of the Fourth Joint Business Valuation Conference of The Canadian Institute of Chartered Business Valuators and the American Society of Appraisers, 1998), pp. 269–78. Also available at www.BVLibrary.com.

The capitalized economic income method (discussed in Chapter 10) is one of the more frequently used methods in marital dissolution valuations.[5] However, recent family law court cases have indicated that the courts are turning more frequently to other valuation methods. This is because these other methods (such as the discounted cash flow method) have achieved wide acceptance in the valuation community at large.

In the direct capitalization of economic income method, the value of the company is estimated by dividing the expected economic income of a company by an appropriate direct capitalization rate. If the economic income measure is net cash flow, this direct capitalization rate is generally equal to the present value discount rate less the expected long-term growth rate for the cash flow stream.

In the discounted cash flow method (one version of the discounted economic income method, discussed in Chapter 9), the value of a company is based on the present value of the future economic income (measured as cash flow), discounted at a yield capitalization rate (present value discount rate) appropriate to the level of risk associated with an investment in the subject company. This valuation method is gaining more widespread acceptance by the family law courts.[6]

Market Approach

The market approach valuation methods rely on prices paid for (1) guideline publicly traded companies (discussed in Chapter 11) or (2) for guideline merged and acquired companies (discussed in Chapter 12) as the basis for estimating the value of a business. As discussed in these chapters, the market approach has become increasingly feasible in recent years because of the development and accessibility of both publicly traded guideline company data and also data on the sales of privately held companies.

Asset-Based Approach

Asset-based approach methods (discussed in Chapters 13 and 14) are often recognized by courts in marital dissolution valuations. These methods rely on the adjusted balance sheet of the subject company in order to estimate the value of the subject ownership interest in the subject company. This method, although widely used, is often incorrectly performed.

Often—and inappropriately—the net book value of the business assets less the book value of the liabilities is used to value the subject ownership interest. Rather, an asset accumulation method should be used to value the subject ownership interest by valuing all of the assets and all of the liabilities of the subject business. This valuation should include adjustments for off–balance sheet items as well. Such items may include unrecorded liabilities, unrecorded intangible assets, and unrecorded (or nonoperating) assets. The net difference in the value of all of the assets and all of the liabilities will indicate the value of the subject business equity. Adjustments to that business value in order to value the subject ownership interest will depend on the individual facts and circumstances.

---

[5] See, for example, *DeLucia v. DeLucia*, No. FA 950249319S, 1997 WL 16832, Conn. Super. Ct. (Jan. 10, 1997), and *Giuliani v. Giuliani*, No. CA 930526886S, 1996 WL 409324, Conn. Super. Ct. (June 19, 1996).

[6] See, for example, *Guiffre v. Baker*, No. 95-G-1904, 1996 WL 535254, Ohio Ct. App. 11th Dist. (Aug. 30, 1996), and *Sergi v. Sergi*, No. 17476, 1996 WL 425914, Ohio Ct. App. 9th Dist. (July 31, 1996). In both these cases, the courts rejected the excess earnings method and accepted the discounted cash flow method.

The Capitalized Excess Earnings Method

An asset-based approach method that is used extensively in marital dissolution valuations is the *capitalized excess earnings method* (see Chapter 13). Although this method is sometimes disparaged in valuation texts, it remains a common valuation method in analyses performed for marital dissolution purposes.

Under this method, the value of the subject business is the sum of the value of the tangible assets and the intangible assets less the value of the outstanding liabilities. The method takes its name from the fact that the intangible asset value is estimated based on the direct capitalization of the economic income earned by the business in excess of a fair return on its tangible assets.

Usually Employ More Than One Method

Other valuation methods have been used in marital dissolution cases. However, the above paragraphs describe the most common valuation methods. The selection of the appropriate valuation method(s) will depend on the facts and circumstances of the particular case. However, the latitude afforded judges in the marital dissolution process should persuade the analyst to adopt more than one valuation method—in order to provide mutually supportive evidence as to the valuation conclusion.

In general, once the valuation method(s) has been selected, implementing it in the divorce context is similar to implementing it outside of the divorce context. However, certain issues are dealt with differently or assume unique significance in a divorce proceeding. Some of these nuances are addressed in the following chapter on Marital Dissolution Court Cases.

Compensation

Another area in which the analyst may perform procedures of particular significance to the marital dissolution assignment is in the area of adequate compensation. In certain cases, the court may want to establish whether or not the amount paid to an owner spouse in salary and benefits has adequately compensated the marital estate for the owner spouse's efforts. This issue usually arises in the case of a spouse who is the owner of a business that is arguably a nonmarital asset.

Using "marital income" that is not paid in the form of compensation may be considered an investment in the nonmarital asset. An attorney may want to discern whether the value of a nonmarital business has been enhanced because the owner spouse has not withdrawn adequate compensation from the company. This issue could trigger some argument as to the extent of the exclusion of the enterprise from the marital estate.[7] Thus, the analyst in a valuation for divorce purposes should be familiar with compensation issues and with sources of information regarding reasonable compensation (see Chapter 6 on Gathering Economic and Industry Data for useful sources of compensation information).

[7] The issue of adequate compensation may be a factor in the court deciding whether (or the extent to which) appreciation in the value of a company was active or passive. To the extent that the operating spouse was adequately compensated, the appreciation may be attributed to other factors. To the extent that the spouse was undercompensated, the appreciation may be attributed to the spouse's efforts for which the marital estate was not adequately compensated during the marriage.

Noncompete Covenants

Noncompete covenants and employment agreements require special attention in a marital dissolution proceeding. If the sale of the marital asset business occurs, a noncompete covenant and/or an employment agreement may be required of the owner spouse. This issue may trigger argument over whether the value of the proceeds attributable to the noncompete covenant and/or employment agreement are part of the marital estate.

In addition, in the case of a jointly owned business, one spouse may be required to buy out the other—and some form of a noncompete and/or employment agreement could be required. The value assigned to these agreements may have special significance in the divorce valuation.

Generally speaking, the value of the noncompete covenant would *not* be a marital asset because it restricts the postmarital activity of the spouse and the employment agreement would not be a marital asset because it involves future efforts of the spouse. However, these agreements may need to be valued to ascertain whether the amount allocated to them is the fair market value of these agreements.[8]

As noted earlier, family law courts often (perhaps even usually) ignore the implications of these elements of value in the market approach when using pricing multiples derived from private sales of guideline companies.

Buy-Sell Agreements

One of the very common controversies is whether a buy-sell agreement value should be controlling for marital dissolution purposes, or whether it should be accorded any weight at all. Family law court decisions on this issue vary greatly.

As a broad generality, in states where professional (personal) goodwill is considered a marital asset, the buy-sell agreement price (the amount that would be realized if the spouse withdrew from the enterprise) usually is not found to be controlling. In other states a buy-sell agreement may be controlling or the issues may be decided on the basis of individual facts and circumstances.

In some cases, the buy-sell agreement value may be given some weight even though it is not controlling. Examples of the treatment of buy-sell agreements for divorce valuations are presented in the next chapter.

Treatment of Trapped-In Capital Gains Taxes

Another issue that is often important in the marital dissolution analysis is the inclusion of the capital gains tax effect with regard to the value conclusion. This influence is often considered in the valuation of business ownership interests using asset-based methods. This influence is intended to reflect the contingent tax liability for the unrealized capital gains on appreciated business assets. In concluding whether

---

[8] See, for example, *In re Marriage of Monaghan*, 899 P2d 841 (Wash. App. Aug. 9, 1995) and *Sweere v. Gilbert-Sweere*, 534 NW2d 294 (Minn. App. July 18, 1995), discussed in the next chapter.

this adjustment is appropriate, it is noteworthy that the repeal of the so-called General Utilities doctrine (by the Tax Reform Act of 1986) makes it virtually impossible for a corporation to sell or distribute appreciated assets without incurring a taxable gain.

In marital dissolution proceedings, however, courts have generally found that consideration of tax consequences is appropriate only (1) when the tax liability is imminent or (2) when the tax will arise directly from the court's property disposition. In situations where there is some speculation as to when (or if) the assets will be sold and the magnitude of the associated tax liability, family law courts have generally found that it is inappropriate to consider the tax consequences related to the sale.[9] However, it often falls to the analyst to determine—and to defend—an independent opinion regarding the appropriate consideration of capital gains taxes.

In 1998, the U.S. Tax Court and the Second Circuit Court of Appeals finally recognized that trapped-in capital gains were appropriate to recognize as a valuation factor and the IRS has acquiesced to this position (see Chapter 27 and 28 on gift and estate valuations and related court cases). Family law courts often quote IRS authority and Tax Court cases in support of positions taken. And, this movement on the part of the Tax Court and the IRS could be a catalyst in family law courts for increased recognition of trapped-in capital gains liability. Many practitioners believe that it is unfair to distribute free and clear liquid assets to one spouse and give the other spouse what would be an equal value except for assuming the liability for capital gains taxes when and if the spouse decides to sell.

Nevertheless, in some jurisdictions, the recognition of the trapped-in capital gains tax liability may result in the court using an equitable distribution technique—rather than an equal division of the marital property.

Valuation Discounts and Premiums

The applicability of valuation discounts and premiums offers further challenges in a marital dissolution valuation. The size of valuation discounts and premiums is often a matter of informed professional judgment on the part of the analyst. The situations in which discounts and premiums are applicable—and the reasonable range of these valuation adjustments—are fairly well addressed within most legal contexts, such as federal income, gift, and estate tax and ESOP transactions. In a valuation for divorce, however, the state-specific nature of the statutes and judicial precedent encourages the analyst to become familiar with both (1) the types of valuation adjustments and (2) the circumstances under which each has been accepted within each state. The analyst should form an independent opinion regarding the appropriate application of discounts and premiums. This includes valuation adjustments that are fairly common, such as the discount for lack of marketability, the discount for lack of ownership control or the ownership control premium, and the discount for key person dependence.

One argument often made against discounts is that there should be none because there is no change of ownership. Many consider this argument to be fatally flawed because, as noted earlier in the chapter, one spouse is, in effect, buying out the other spouse's interest.

---

[9] See, for example, *In re the Marriage of Hay*, No. 14368-6-111, 1995 WL 757772, Wash. Ct. App. (Dec. 26, 1995).

As seen in Chapters 15 through 18, differences of opinion about the discount and premium adjustments are often a much larger dollar issue than differences about the value of the company itself. Some examples of court opinions on discount and premium issues are given in the next chapter.

The Role of the Analyst

The valuation of businesses and business interests for marital dissolution purposes is a complex and challenging task due to the diverse jurisdictions and unique issues in these cases. In addition, the analyst in a marital dissolution engagement may often assume an expanded role. In addition to performing a valuation, the analyst may often assume a more forensic accounting or forensic economics role, by assisting attorneys in identifying distributable assets and tracing their origins. The valuation process may require the analysis of the flow of financial resources into and out of the subject business enterprise. However, in some instances, the analyst will defer such investigative analysis to a forensic accountant.

Since many divorce valuations are performed within a litigation environment, the analyst should function effectively and should offer several services to legal counsel. These services should begin with assisting counsel in the discovery process. In addition, the analyst may be asked to analyze and evaluate settlement offers that occur frequently during the marital dissolution process. In this capacity, the analyst would be called upon to evaluate the reasonableness of a settlement offer in light of the value or estimated value of the assets in the marital estate.

A consideration sometimes present in family law engagements that is not found in engagements for other purposes is a tradeoff between the value determined for property distribution and awards of ongoing spousal support or alimony. Frequently, the value of the business exceeds all other marital assets combined, so that it is not possible to achieve an equitable distribution if the operating spouse is awarded the business and the nonoperating spouse all the other assets. One way to handle this problem is to give the nonoperating spouse a note for a portion of the difference. Some courts, however, prefer to set a very conservative value on the business and offset that with more generous support or alimony payments. The analyst should be aware of these considerations if consulting with the attorney on settlement options.

As with most litigation support assignments, the analyst may be called upon to assist legal counsel in the deposition and subsequent trial examination of opposing valuation experts. This may involve assessing the strengths and weaknesses of the opposing expert's position in terms of both factual interpretation and valuation methodology.

Throughout all of the processes, the analyst should remain objective. More often in family law than in any other area of valuation, the courts justifiably accuse experts of bias and advocacy in favor of their clients. This does not help the client, the analyst, or the profession. The client is best served by having the court accept a reasonable value rather than having the court reject the expert's evidence as not credible.

Adequacy of Evidence

Our study of appellate opinions in the 1990s reveals that there is a larger incidence of remand for lack of adequate supporting evidence for business value conclusions in family law cases than in taxation, shareholder dispute, bankruptcy, or any other category of business valuation.

On the one hand, trial courts have wide discretion in deciding factual matters, such as value, especially in family law courts. On the other hand, appellate courts do, quite consistently, require that the trial court must have an adequate evidentiary basis for reaching its conclusion of fact. Appellate courts have remanded many cases for new evidence and hearings on the value of the business because the evidence presented by the "experts" at the trial court was insufficient to support the court's conclusion of value. This usually results in money that has been spent on "experts" and the related attorney fees being wasted. Attorneys should be able to avoid such remands by hiring competent experts, critically reviewing their work product (see Chapter 22 on Reviewing a Business Valuation Report), and being sure to make a complete record at trial.

It is important for the analyst to present his or her opinions credibly and persuasively in deposition and in court testimony. The analyst should be able to effectively explain complicated financial issues to a judge or attorney whose expertise is not accounting or finance. The analyst should be experienced in the application of valuation procedures within a contrarian environment.

Summary

Many aspects of valuations for marital dissolution differ totally or in some respects from valuation assignments for other purposes.

For example, the analyst may become involved in an issue as to whether or not certain property should or should not be included in the marital estate. The most common debate that may involve the appraiser is whether or not appreciation in the value of a business during marriage is classified as active or passive.

The applicable standard of value is generally less clear in the context of marital dissolution than for practically any other valuation purpose. The expert needs to study the relevant case law and interpret it from a valuation point of view. Often, family law courts lean toward *investment value* (value to the particular spouse), even though they may use the phrase *fair market value*.

The date of valuation is important, and the analyst may have to prepare valuations for more than one effective date. However, sometimes the court will bifurcate the matter and rule on the valuation date ahead of the trial addressing the property settlement.

Discovery is often more of an issue in marital dissolution cases than in other types of valuation engagements, because the operating spouse may resist permitting access to records, premises, and/or management, or may even conceal relevant information. This problem may lead to engaging a forensic accountant.

The issue of goodwill tends to loom larger in family law valuations than in other areas of valuation. The problem is not just the measurement of the value of goodwill, but the issue as to who owns it—the individual or the marital estate. Sometimes an allocation must be made between personal and business (or professional) goodwill.

Valuation methodology varies greatly, with much discretion on the part of the court. Family law courts gradually are moving toward acceptance of the valuation methods typically used in the financial community, such as the discounted cash flow valuation method.

Owners' compensation adjustments are often a bigger issue in marital dissolutions than in other types of cases. Sometimes the question of whether an owner was adequately compensated during marriage bears on the issue of whether appreciation in the value of the business or business interest is or is not a marital asset.

The value of noncompete covenants and employment agreements is another major issue being accorded growing recognition (and deservedly so). The value of such agreements is usually (but not always) regarded as personal rather than marital property. Yet most courts so far have not adjusted comparable company sale prices for the inclusion of such agreements in the market approach to valuation, probably because valuation experts have presented little evidence on this important matter.

Deduction of liability for trapped-in capital gains on appreciated assets is often an issue. Courts have generally disallowed such a deduction unless a sale is imminent, but recent IRS and Tax Court acquiescences to such a deduction may lead family law courts to be more prone to consider it.

Few state family law courts treat valuation discounts and premiums the same way that they would be treated in a conventional fair market value context. The analyst should study the relevant case law when it comes to discount or premium issues.

The analyst should be objective and must avoid any inclination or pressure toward bias in favor of the client. Although this applies to all types of cases, a reading of the opinions suggests that lack of objectivity may be a more prevalent problem in family law than in other types of cases.

The role of the valuation analyst is critical. It is important to bring in a competent, experienced analyst at the outset and to have the analyst involved at every step. It is important for the analyst and the attorney working together to build an adequate evidentiary record at trial. On appeal, courts look to the question of whether or not the lower court had adequate evidence on which to base its decision. If so, the decision normally is upheld. If not, the decision often is remanded for further proceedings.

Bibliography

Articles

Berning, Richard C., and Michele G. Miles. "Surviving a Divorce Engagement." *Shannon Pratt's Business Valuation Update*, October 1999, pp. 1–4.

Bishop, David M. and Steven F. Schroeder. "Business Valuation Standard of Value for Divorce Should Be Fair Market Value," *American Journal of Family Law*, Spring 1999, pp. 48–52.

Brandes, Joel R., and Carole L. Weidman. "Valuation of a Professional License." *New York Law Journal*, December 24, 1996, pp. 3–5.

Cenker, William J., and Carl J. Monastra. "The Basics of Business Valuation in Divorce Settlements." *Practical Accountant*, January 1991, pp. 18–26.

Cohen, Robert S., and Arthur H. Rosenbloom. "The Whole May Be Worth Less Than the Sum of Its Parts." *New York Law Journal*, December 18, 1995, pp. 1–4.

Connell, John R., and William H. Vincent. "Valuing Pension Benefits in Divorce: Look before You Leap." *Journal of Accountancy*, January 1994, pp. 98–100.

Cowhey, Gregory J., Lester Barenbaum, and Sandra R. Klevan. "Putting a Price Tag on the Company." *Family Advocate*, Spring 1995, pp. 44–52.

Darrah, William C. "The Antolik Case and the Determination of Professional Goodwill." Presentation to the International Appraisal Conference of the American Society of Appraisers, June 1998. Available on www.BVLibrary.com.

Dennis, Stephen G. "Selecting and Using a Financial Expert in Dissolution Practice." *Family Law Quarterly*, Spring 1992, pp. 17–25.

Felder, Myrna. "A Blueprint for a 'McSparron' Evaluation." *New York Law Journal*, October 29, 1996, pp. 3–5.

Feder, Robert D. "Direct Examination of a Business Appraiser in a Divorce Action." *American Journal of Family Law*, Spring 1993, pp. 1–11.

Fishman, Jay E., Shannon P. Pratt, et al. "Premiums and Discounts in Business Valuation." *Fair$hare: The Matrimonial Law Monthly*, June 1992, pp. 14–16.

Gitlin, Gunnar J. "Business Valuation in Divorce—What Is Double-Dipping and How Is it Quantified?" *American Journal of Family Law*, Summer 1997, pp. 109–18.

Goodman, Beverly. "Appraisers Find Band of Gold in Dissolving Ties That Bind." *Accounting Today*, August 7, 1995, pp. 3–4.

Goodman, Stanley L. "The Three Big Issues in Business and Professional Practice Valuation." *Fair$hare: The Matrimonial Law Monthly*, April 1996, pp. 2–3.

Gross, Mark P. "Buy-Sell Agreements and Divorce." *CPA Litigation Service Counselor*, February 2000, pp.11–12.

Hitchner, James R. "Valuation Date Is Critical in Divorce Case." *CPA Expert*, Fall 1998, pp. 7–10.

Jimmerson, James J. "Celebrity Goodwill: Is it Real or Is it a Mirage?" *American Journal of Family Law*, Summer 1997, pp. 145–51.

Kendig, Robert E. "Discovery Issues in Valuation Cases." *American Journal of Family Law*, Spring 1992, pp. 55–74.

Kinser, Katherine A. "Practical Approaches to the Presentation of Business Values in Divorce." *Fair$hare: The Matrimonial Law Monthly*, August 1992, pp. 3–5.

Lieber, Frederick E. "Adjusting the Income Statement in Business Valuations." *Fair$hare: The Matrimonial Law Monthly*, November 1992, pp. 3–5.

Mason, Miriam E., and Michael S. Cohen. "From a Matrimonial Lawyer's Perspective—The Ten (and a Few More) Most Frequent Errors Made by Business Appraisers." Presentation to the AICPA National Business Valuation Conference, 1999. Available on www.BVLibrary.com.

Mastracchio, James N., and Nicholas J. Mastracchio. "Professional License Value in a Divorce." *CPA Journal*, December 1996, pp. 34–39+.

Miod, Donald John. "The Double Dip in Valuing Goodwill in Divorce" (Parts I and II) *CPA Litigation Service Counselor*, April 1998, pp. 1–4, and May 1998, pp. 5–7.

Person, Stanley. "Reasonable Compensation." *Journal of Accountancy*, October 1995, pp. 37, 127.

Pia, Kenneth J. "Who Is Qualified to Value a Business?" *Family Advocate*, Spring 1995, pp. 22–24.

Pratt, Shannon P. "Coping with Business Valuation in Family Law." *American Journal of Family Law*, Winter 1998, pp. 212–17.

_____. "Lack of Clear Definition of Value Confounds Both Attorneys and Appraisers." *Valuation Strategies*, January/February 2000, pp. 35–37.

_____. "Separating Entity from Personal Intangible Assets." *Valuation Strategies*, May/June 1999, pp. 4–9.

_____. "What Is Value?" *Family Advocate*, Spring 1995, pp. 28–33.

Raymond, Richard. "A Biased Valuation: The Treatment of a Professional Degree in Divorce Actions." *American Journal of Economics and Sociology*, July 1995, pp. 268–87.

Reilly, Robert F. "The Differences in Valuing Big and Small Businesses for Divorce." *Fair$hare: The Matrimonial Law Monthly*, September 1995, pp. 3–8.

_____. "The Identification and Qualifications of Business Valuation Discounts and Premia." *Fair$hare: The Matrimonial Law Monthly*, July 1996, pp. 2–5.

Reilly, Robert F., and Robert P. Schweihs. "Valuation Testimony Guidelines in the Post *Daubert* Era." *Fair$hare: The Matrimonial Law Monthly*, March 2000, pp. 7–9.

Riesebell, H.F. "Divorce of a Closely Held Business Owner." *Fair$hare: The Matrimonial Law Monthly*, May 1992, pp. 3–8.

Shayne, Mark. "The Role of the Business Valuator in Marital and Family Business Litigation," *American Journal of Family Law*, Fall 1991, pp. 239–49.

Shenkman, Martin M. "When Should Professional Goodwill Be Valued?" *The Matrimonial Strategist*, March 1997, pp. 1–3.

Skoloff, Gary N., and Cary B. Cheifetz. "Direct Examination of Marital Property Valuation Experts." *The Practical Litigator*, May 1992, p. 25.

Trugman, Gary R. "An Appraiser's Approach to Business Valuation." (Parts I and II) *Fair$hare: The Matrimonial Law Monthly*, July 1991, pp. 3–8, and August 1991, pp. 8–13.

Weinstein, Jeffrey P. "The Use and Abuse of Economic Experts in Divorce Litigation." *Fair$hare: The Matrimonial Law Monthly*, February 1995, pp. 3–6.

Wierwille, Michael C. and Neil J. Beaton, "Valuing of Celebrity or Professional Goodwill—A New Paradigm," *The Journal of Business Valuation* (proceedings of the Fourth Joint Business Valuation Conference of The Canadian Institute of Chartered Business Valuators and the American Society of Appraisers, 1998), pp. 269–78.

Wise, Richard M. "Valuing Private Shares in Divorce Litigation: The Whole Seldom Equals the Sum of the Parts." *Canadian Family Law Quarterly*, August 1990, pp. 295–319.

Zipp, Alan S. "Business Valuation Standard for Divorce is Different from Fair Market Value," *American Journal of Family Law*, Fall 1997, pp. 167–72.

Books

Barson, Kalman A. *Investigative Accounting in Divorce*. New York: John Wiley & Sons, 1996 (cumulative supplement 1999).

Bateman, Tracy A. Annotation. *Divorce and Separation Consideration of Tax Consequences in Distribution of Marital Property*, 9 A.L.R. 5th (1993).

Brown, Ronald L., ed. *Valuing Professional Practices and Licenses: A Guide for the Matrimonial Practitioner*, 3rd ed. New York: Aspen Law and Business, 1999.

Feder, Robert D. *Valuation Strategies in Divorce*, 4th ed. New York: Aspen Law & Business, 1997 (cumulative supplement 1999).

Fishman, Jay E., Shannon P. Pratt, J. Clifford Griffith, and D. Keith Wilson. *Guide to Business Valuations*, 10th ed. Fort Worth, TX: Practitioners Publishing Company, 2000.

Goldberg, Barth H. *Valuation of Divorce Assets*. St. Paul: West Publishing Company, 1984.

Goldberg, Barth H. and Joseph N. DuCanto. *Valuation of Divorce Assets*, 1994 Supplement. St. Paul: West Publishing Company, 1994.

Kleeman, Robert E. Jr., ed. *Valuation Strategies in Divorce*, 2nd ed. New York: John Wiley & Sons, 1992.

Kleeman, Robert E. Jr., R. James Alerding, and Benjamin D. Miller. *The Handbook for Divorce Valuations*. New York: John Wiley & Sons, 1999.

Meltzer, Stanton L., David A. Rooney, et al. *Guide to Divorce Engagements*, 7th ed. Fort Worth: Practitioners Publishing Company, 1998.

Moriarty, Robert B., and David J. Zaumeyer. *The Valuation Expert in Divorce Litigation: A Handbook for Attorneys and Accountants*. New York: American Bar Association, 1992.

Oldfather, Ann, Janice E. Kosel, et al. *Valuation and Distribution of Marital Property*. New York: Matthew Bender & Co., January 1996.

Oldham, J. Thomas. *Divorce, Separation and the Distribution of Property*. New York: Law Journal Seminars Press, 1996 (updated annually).

Orenstein, Theodore P., and Gary N. Skoloff. *When a Professional Divorces: Strategies for Valuing Practices, Licenses, and Degrees*, 2nd ed. Chicago: American Bar Association, 1994.

Pierson, Eric. *1999 Wiley Family Law Update*. New York: Aspen Law & Business, 1999.

Periodicals

American Journal of Family Law, quarterly. Aspen Law & Business, 1320 Edgewood Drive, Altoona, WI 54720, (715) 835-3338, www.aspenpublishers.com.

CPA Litigation Services Counselor, monthly. Harcourt Brace Professional Publishing, 6277 Sea Harbor Drive, Orlando, FL 32887, (800) 831-7799, www.hbpp.com.

Fair$hare: The Matrimonial Law Monthly, monthly. Aspen Law & Business, 7201 McKinney Circle, Frederick, MD 21704, (800) 638-8437, www.aspenpublishers.com.

Family Advocate, quarterly. American Bar Association, P.O. Box 10892, Chicago, IL 60610-0892, (312) 988-5522, www.abanet.org/family/advocate/home.html.

Judges and Lawyers Business Valuation Update, monthly. Business Valuation Resources, 7412 S.W. Beaverton-Hillsdale Highway, Suite 106, Portland, OR 97225, (888) 287-8258, www.BVLibrary.com.

The Matrimonial Strategist, monthly. Leader Publications, 345 Park Avenue South, New York, NY 10010, (800) 888-8300, www.lawcatalog.com.

Shannon Pratt's Business Valuation Update, monthly. Business Valuation Resources, 7412 S.W. Beaverton-Hillsdale Highway, Suite 106, Portland, OR 97225, (888) 287-8258, www.BVLibrary.com.

Chapter 38

Marital Dissolution Court Cases

Treatment of various factors in business and professional practice valuation are more diverse from one jurisdiction to another in marital disolution cases than in any other context of business valuation. Furthermore, the statutes provide very limited guidance. Therefore, the analyst needs to be knowledgeable about the case law as relates to divorce for each jurisdiction in which the analyst practices.

The purpose of this chapter is to provide a small but representative sampling of the often diverse positions that various state appellate courts have taken on some of the most important business valuation issues frequently encountered in the context of marital dissolution. When state courts address a particular issue for the first time, they often look to precedents in other states for guidance. Therefore, it is helpful to have a general knowledge of various states' positions on issues and to have the ability to research case precedent on controversial issues.[1]

Standards of Value

Most decisions give no explicit definition of the acceptable standard of value. It usually is necessary to infer the court's acceptable standard(s) of value from the language of decisions and valuation methods and procedures accepted. Thus, this section gives only a few examples of clearly articulated standards of value.

Fair Market Value

Several states adhere quite consistently to the standard of fair market value. These include, for example, Wisconsin,[2] Illinois,[3] Pennsylvania,[4] Florida,[5] and South Carolina.[6] These states do not include any personal goodwill in the value of the business on the grounds that personal goodwill is the property of the individual and not marital property.

Investment Value

Without specifically saying so, many family law courts utilize *investment value*— that is, value to a *particular* buyer or seller. They tend to zero in on value to the operating spouse.

A good example is a Colorado case that said that the accepted valuation of business goodwill is based on the value of the business to the operating spouse.[7]

In Virginia, business interests normally are valued at fair market value. For closely held companies, the goal is to arrive at a fair market value for a stock for which there is no market. However, in Virginia, interests in law practices cannot be bought or sold.

---

[1] Full texts of virtually all precedential marital dissolution case opinions involving business or professional practice valuations are available at www.BVLibrary.com.

[2] See *Siker v. Siker*, 1999 WL 74599 (Wis. Ct. App. Feb. 18, 1999); *Huebner v. Huebner*, No. 96-2397-F, 1997 WL 106572 (Wis. Ct. App. Mar. 12, 1997); and *Sommerfield v. Sommerfield*, 454 N.W.2d 55, 58 (Wis. Ct. App. 1990).

[3] See *Grunsten v. Grunsten*, 1999 WL 64479 (Ill. App. Ct. Feb. 11, 1999).

[4] See *Campbell v. Campbell*, 483 A.2d 363, 367 (Pa. Super. Ct. 1986).

[5] See *Christians v. Christians*, 732 So.2d 47 (Fla. Dist. Ct. App. 1999) and *Makowski v. Makowski*, 613 So.2d 924 (Fla. Dist. Ct. App. 1999).

[6] See *Hickum v. Hickum*, 463 S.E.2d 321, 325 (S.C. Ct. App. 1995); *RGM v. DEM*, 410 S.E.2d 564, 568 (S.C. 1991); and *Reid v. Reid*, 312 S.E.2d 724, 727 (S.C. Ct. App. 1984).

[7] *In re Marriage of Nichols*, 606 P.2d 1314 (Colo. Ct. App. 1979).

So the court has adopted what it termed "intrinsic value," which comports to what we have called "investment value" in this book—that is, value to a *particular* owner, in this case, the operating spouse. The Court stated, "the highest and best use for defendant's share is to remain with Hunton & Williams." The Court thus accepted a valuation that included a goodwill component, even though the buy-sell agreement did not.[8]

The Court in the case above quoted from another case:

> Goodwill is an asset of a professional practice subject to valuation as marital property . . . to hold otherwise would result in a windfall to the professional spouse. This would derive from the failure to consider part of the value of an asset already classified as marital property.[9]

California is one of the few states in which courts have clearly taken the position that the standard of value should be investment value rather than market value:

> We hold section 4800, subdivision (a) of the Family Law Act (Civ. Code, SS 4800, subd. (a)) is satisfied when the investment value of closely held shares is determined rather than their market value.[10]

The *Hewitson* case notes three approaches that have been accepted to determine investment value:

> The three basic approaches, or their variations, which have been recognized in determining the investment value of closely held shares are commonly termed (1) capitalization of earnings approach #3 (see Worthen v. United States (D.Mass. 1961) 192 F.Supp. 727; Cohan, Valuation of Interests in Closely Held Businesses (1966) 44 Taxes 504, 508), (2) dividend paying capacity #4 (see Estate of Goar v. Comm'r. (1950) 9 T.C.M. 854; Righter v. United States, supra, 439 F.2d 1204, 1210), and (3) book value #5 or net asset value #6 (see Estate of Rowell (1955) 132 Cal.App.2d 421, 428). The application of these approaches, or their variations, will determine the investment value of the closely held shares, not their market value.[11]

Active versus Passive Appreciation

States are divided on the issue of whether appreciation in a pre-marriage separate asset is a marital asset, or the conditions to determine that issue.

"Active" Appreciation a Marital Asset

Many states consider the amount of appreciation in an asset that was separate property before marriage to be a marital asset. For example, an Arizona case said that classification of increase in community property depends on whether the increase resulted from natural growth of the business (separate property) or from an individual's management skills (community property).[12]

---

[8] *Howell v. Howell*, No. HH-1013-3 Va. Cir. Ct., 1998 WL 972312 (Sept. 4, 1998)

[9] *Russell v. Russell*, 11 Va. App. 411 (1990).

[10] *In re Marriage of Hewitson*, 142 Cal.App.3d 874, 191 Cal. Rptr. 392 (Part 1) (1983).

[11] Ibid.

[12] *Baum v. Baum*, 584 P.2d 604, 609 (Ariz. Ct. App. 1978)..

In Tennessee, if the separate property of one spouse appreciates in value during the marriage as a result of the efforts of either spouse, the appreciation becomes a marital asset.[13]

"Active" Appreciation Must Be Proven

As of this writing, only New York has considered the value of a license to practice to be a marital asset. However, the wife in a North Carolina case tried to have the *appreciation* in her husband's medical license during the marriage classified as a marital asset. The Court said that:

> Active appreciation of separate property is marital property, but appreciation must be proven . . . to demonstrate active appreciation of separate property, there must be a showing of:
>
> • Value of the asset at time of acquisition.
> • Value of the asset at time of separation.
> • Difference between the two values.[14]

In this case, the court found that the evidence presented tended to show that marital efforts led to the acquisition of the medical license rather than to an active appreciation in its value.

Valuation Date

It is difficult to generalize about courts' positions regarding valuation dates. Even states that have generally fixed policies on this issue often allow trial courts considerable discretion to make exceptions.

Many courts use date of trial (or as close to it as practical) as the valuation date.[15] In a similar vein, some accept a date as near as possible to the final divorce decree.[16]

The effective date in some cases is the date the complaint was filed.[17] Some use date of separation.[18] Trial courts may exercise discretion in determining valuation

---

[13] *Brown v. Brown*, 913 S.W.2d 163, 167 (Tenn. Ct. App. 1994).

[14] *Conway v. Conway*, 1998 WL 865157 (N.C. Ct. App. 1998).

[15] See, for example, *Hargrave v. Hargrave*, 209 Cal. Rptr. 764, 769 (Cal. Ct. App. 1985); *Aufmuth v. Aufmuth*, 152 Cal Rptr. 668, 670 (Cal. Ct. App. 1979); *Moffitt v. Moffitt*, 813 P.2d 674, 678 (Alaska 1991), *Ogard v. Ogard*, 808 P.2d 815, 818–19 (Alaska 1991); *Taylor v. Taylor*, 736 S.W.2d 388, 391 (Mo. 1987); *Butler v. Butler*, No. 82077, 1998 WL 933354, at *2 (N.Y. App. Div. Dec. 30, 1998).

[16] For example, *In re Marriage of Olinger*, 707 P.2d 64, 68 (Or. Ct. App. 1985); *Koch v. Koch*, 874 S.W.2d 571, 576 (Tenn. Ct. App. 1993); *Wilson v. Wilson*, 741 S.W.2d 640, 643 (Ark. 1987); *In re Marriage of Talty*, 623 N.E.2d 1041, 1046 (Ill. App. Ct. 1993); *In re Marriage of Thomas*, 608 N.E.2d 585, 587 (Ill. App. Ct. 1993); *In re Marriage of Lopez*, 841 P.2d 1122, 1125 (Mont. 1992); *In re Marriage of Swanson*, 716 P.2d 219, 222 (Mont. 1986); *Vivian v. Vivian*, 583 P.2d 1072, 1074 (Mont. 1978); *In re Marriage of Wagner*, 679 P.2d 753, 758 (Mont. 1984); *Dunn v. Dunn*, 802 P.2d 1314, 1320 (Utah Ct. App. 1990); *Sommerfield* 454 N.W.2d at 60.

[17] *Mallett v. Mallett*, 473 S.E.2d 804, 810 (S.C. Ct. App. 1996); *Hickum v. Hickum*, 463 S.E.2d 321, 323 (S.C. Ct. App. 1995); *Hillebrand v. Hillebrand*, 546 A.2d 1047, 1049 (N.H. 1988); *Rosenberg v. Rosenberg*, 510 N.Y.S.2d 659, 662 (App. Div. 1987), *Muller v. Muller*, 456 N.Y.S.2d 918, 922 (Sup. Ct. 1982); *Siegel v. Siegel*, 523 N.Y.S.2d 517, 520 (App. Div. 1987) (because possibility of dissipation of corporate assets existed).

[18] *Kilbourne v. Kilbourne*, 284 Cal. Rptr. 201, 204 (Ct. App. 1991); *Moffitt*, 813 P.2d at 678; *Ogard*, 808 P.2d at 818–19; *Richmond v. Richmond*, 779 P.2d 1211, 1214 (Alaska 1989); *Carlson v. Carlson*, 487 S.E.2d 784, 786 (N.C. Ct. App. 1997).

dates.[19] And, unlike estate tax valuations, the date does not always have to be the same for all assets.[20]

An interesting case involving a dispute as to the appropriate valuation date erupted because the husband was arrested and incarcerated for child molestation the day before the wife's expert's going-concern valuation date, jeopardizing the construction company's ability to obtain financing. The husband ultimately was convicted. The trial court accepted the wife's expert's valuation, which included goodwill. The Court of Appeals reversed, opining that, as long as husband was incarcerated or under threat of incarceration, financing was not available. Thus, the goodwill (defined as "the expectation of public patronage") was eliminated. However, the Indiana Supreme Court concluded:

> The selection of the valuation date for any particular marital asset has the effect of allocating the risk of change in the value of that asset between the date of valuation and the date of the hearing. We entrust this allocation to the discretion of the trial court.[21]

The Supreme Court thus upheld the $328,000 valuation of the trial court, which included the value of the goodwill.

Goodwill

The "Market Value of Goodwill" Paradox

The paradox of many family law courts' conclusions as to the value of goodwill is well illustrated in the California case of *Fortier*.[22] The case states that goodwill value is separate and must be established without dependence upon the potential or continuing net income of the selling doctor. It then goes on to say that the community goodwill value is the market value at which the goodwill could be sold, assuming the expectancy of continuity of the practice.

But "continuity of the practice" would seem to somehow involve the future actions of the spouse. It is rare that a practice is sold without a noncompete agreement, which would limit the spouse's activities. Furthermore, practice sales usually involve transition services of the selling party for several months, sometimes a year or even longer. Yet the cases don't mention that the "market value" usually includes a noncompete covenant and an agreement for services, which would seem to be assets personal to the spouse.

Similarly, in a subsequent case, the Court stated:

> Value must be established without dependence on the potential or continuing net income of the professional spouse. (In re Marriage of Fourtier, supra, 34 Cal.App.3d 384, 388, 109 Cal. Rptr. 915.)

---

[19] *Scalero v. Scalero*, No. 71738, 1998 WL 23845, at *3 (Ohio Ct. App. Jan. 22, 1998); *Wallace v. Wallace*, 733 S.W.2d 102, 106 (Tenn. Ct. App. 1987); *Reese v. Reese*, 671 N.E.2d 187, 191 (Ind. Ct. App. 1996); *Favell v. Favell*, 957 P.2d 556, 462 (Okla. Ct. App. 1997).

[20] *Green v. Green*, No. 97CA2333, 1998 WL 363840, at *3 (Ohio Ct. App. June 30, 1998).

[21] *Quillen v. Quillen*, 671 N.E.2d 98 (Indiana 1996).

[22] *In re Marriage of Fortier*, 34 Cal.App.3d 384, 109 Cal. Rptr. 915 (1973).

In sum, we conclude the applicable rule in evaluating community goodwill to be that such goodwill may not be valued by any method that takes into account the post-marital efforts of either spouse. . . .[23]

Having said this, the Court of Appeals accepted a goodwill value of $27,000, based on expert witness testimony described, in part, as follows:

He explained that if appellant continued in his practice, his business had a value of $27,000 in excess of tangible items, but that it depended on how long appellant let the practice "sit," whether he abandoned it, or whether he passed away. He said he had no opinion as to whether appellant could obtain $27,000 for goodwill from a buyer, but stated he would receive an amount for goodwill if he sold the practice. Heller reiterated that the $27,000 valuation for goodwill did not mean that appellant could obtain that sum by selling the medical practice and that he had no opinion as to the amount of money that could be obtained for goodwill upon a sale.[24]

So, post marital efforts do not count, but the goodwill value of $27,000 "if the appellant continued in his practice" is a marital asset. Is this a paradox or what?

North Carolina cases regularly reflect the same paradox. The case most often cited states:

Any legitimate method of valuation that measures the present value of goodwill by taking into account past results *and not the postmarital efforts of the professional spouse*, is a proper method of valuing goodwill (emphasis supplied).[25]

The case then goes on to list methods to value the goodwill of a professional practice that have been accepted in various jurisdictions:

- The price a willing buyer would pay.
- Capitalization of excess earnings.
- One year's average gross income
- Evidence of sales of comparable practices.

All of these valuation methods reflect, to some extent, implied continuing participation and/or a noncompete covenant.

The opinion notes "the execution of a covenant not to compete, in connection with the sale of a business, is essentially a sale of the goodwill of the business."[26] Many would consider this a very confused statement, because they would regard the covenant not to compete as a contract giving up the practitioner's *personal* goodwill rather than the goodwill of the business or practice.

In the same vein, a Maine case determined that goodwill of an insurance company is marital property, even though the Court assumed that the goodwill of the agency and its customer pool would be protected by a noncompetition agreement.[27]

---

[23] *In re Marriage of Foster*, 42 Cal.App.3d 577, 117 Cal. Rptr. 49 (1974).

[24] *Id.*

[25] *Poore v. Poore*, 75 N.C.App. 414, 331 S.E.2d 266 (July 2, 1985).

[26] *Jewel Box Stores v. Morrow*, 272 N.C. 659, 158 S.E. 2d 840 (1968).

[27] *Lord v. Lord*, 454 A.2d 830, 833 (Me. 1983).

Personal Goodwill Not a Marital Asset in Many States

Typical of those states that reject the inclusion of personal goodwill as a marital asset is Nebraska. A 1999 case, citing *Taylor*[28] explained:

> If goodwill depends on the continued presence of a particular individual, such goodwill, by definition, is not a marketable asset distinct from the individual. Any value which attaches to the entity solely as a result of the personal goodwill represents nothing more than probable future earning capacity, which, although relevant in determining alimony, is not a proper consideration in dividing marital property in a dissolution proceeding . . . "There is a disturbing inequity in compelling a professional practitioner to pay a spouse a share of intangible assets at a judicially determined value that could not be realized by a sale or another method of liquidating value."[29]

Virginia defines goodwill and distinguishes business goodwill from personal goodwill with the following explanation:

> Goodwill has been defined as "the increased value of the business, over and above the value of its assets, that results from the expectation of continued public patronage." The reputation of an individual, as well as his or her future earning capacity, are not considered to be components of goodwill. Russell v. Russell, 11 Va. App. 411, 415–16 (1990).[30]

Professional Goodwill Is a Marital Asset in Many States

Washington is one of the states that recognizes professional goodwill as an intangible asset subject to division in a divorce. Its value is determined by considering the *Fleege*[31] factors which include, but are not limited to the practitioner's:

- Age.
- Health.
- Past earning power.
- Reputation in the community for judgment, skill, and knowledge.
- Comparative professional success.[32]

In Montana, the Court accepted a wife's expert's analysis of the medical doctor husband's earnings compared with similar medical doctors to value goodwill as a marital asset.[33]

---

[28] *Taylor v. Taylor*, 222 Neb. 721, 386 N.W. 2d 851 (1986).

[29] *Kriscfeld v. Kriscfeld*, No. A-97-720 Neb. App., 1999 WL 8819 (Jan. 5, 1999). See also *Utter v. Utter*, No. A-94-984 Neb. App. Ct., 1996 WL 169911 (Apr. 9, 1996).

[30] *Howell v. Howell*, No. HH-1013-3 Va. Cir. Ct., 1998 WL 972312 (Sept. 4, 1998).

[31] *In re Marriage of Fleege*, 91 Wash. 2d 324, 588 P.2d 1136 (1979).

[32] *Crosetto v. Crosetto*, No. 17911-3-11 Wash. App. Div. 2, 1996 WL 389337 (July 12, 1996), also citing *In re Marriage of Luckey*, 73 Wash. App. 201, 206, 868 P.2d 189 (1994).

[33] *In re Marriage of Hull*, 712 P.2d 1317, 1321 (Mont. 1985).

Valuation Methods in the Family Law Courts

A study of the valuation methods accepted in family law cases of the 50 states and other jurisdictions reveals a picture so convoluted it is hard to imagine and impossible to describe. Probably the most incisive summary statement is that "there is no uniform rule for fixing the value of a going business for equitable distribution."[34]

Similarly, one opinion explained that the choice of method used to value a company depends on the "unique status of each corporation."[35]

The worst that can be said is that courts have accepted many "methods" which have no definition in the literature of business valuation and are not described in the opinions that accepted them. The best that can be said is that the more enlightened courts seem to be moving toward trying to adopt methods that are actually favored in the financial community.

Typical of the latter is a gradual movement toward recognition of the discounted cash flow method. An example is an Ohio case that accepted a value of $14 million based on the DCF method as opposed to a value of $24.6 million based on the capitalized excess earnings method.[36] An abstract of the case makes the following comment:

> The trial judge stated from the bench that the DCF method had never been used before within her family law jurisdiction. She was willing to consider it based on testimony that members of the professional financial community would be likely to use the method in valuing a company of this type. It goes to show that "we haven't used the method here before" isn't adequate cause for rejection, as long as it is a method generally accepted in the financial community.
>
> Also, this case again demonstrates the importance of making a thorough record of evidence at trial, adequate to be persuasive to an appellate court that the trial court's decision was based on competent, credible, and sufficient evidence.[37]

Unlike practice in the U.S. Tax Court and most state courts dealing with shareholder disputes, valuation decisions in family law courts are not usually neatly classified into variations of the income, market, and asset-based approaches. In fact, the courts often mix standards of value with valuation methods. For example, one opinion recognized "fair acceptable methods" for valuing goodwill:

1. The price a willing buyer would pay.
2. Capitalization of excess earnings method.
3. One year's average gross income of the practice.
4. Evidence of sale of comparable practice.[38]

To most valuation analysts, the price a willing buyer would pay would be regarded as a standard of value (specifically fair market value), not a method of valuation. To most valuation analysts, something to be called a "method" would have to deal

[34] See *Amodio v. Amodio*, 509 N.E.2d 936 (N.Y. 1987).

[35] *Cheatham v. Cheatham*, No. 01A01-9508-CH-00380 Tenn. Ct. App., 1997 WL 731784 (Nov. 25, 1997).

[36] *Sergi v. Sergi*, No. 17476 Ohio Ct. App., 9th Dist., 1996 WL 425914 (July 31, 1996).

[37] *Shannon Pratt's Business Valuation Update*, September 1996, p. 9. Other cases that have accepted the DCF method include, for example, *Giuffre v. Baker*, No. 95-G-1904 Ohio Ct. App., 1996 WL 535254 at *4 (Aug. 30, 1996), and *Oatey v. Oatey*, No. 67809, 67973 Ohio Ct. App., 1996 WL 200273 at *7 (Apr. 25, 1996).

[38] *Conway v. Conway*, No. COA97-1439 N.C. Ct. App., 1998 WL 865157 (Dec. 15, 1998).

with the question of how one estimates what the willing buyer would pay, which might include numbers 2 and 4. But, number 3, "one year's average gross income," is a specific pricing multiple, but the "method" should imply an exercise in arriving at what the pricing multiple should be.

The capitalization of excess earnings method is encountered far more in family law cases than in any other type of cases. Unfortunately, as discussed in Chapter 13, the details of its implementation are extremely varied.

With little truly definitive case law on proper methodology, it is incumbent on the analyst, through the written report and/or testimony, to educate the court on the details of the methodology used and why it is the proper methodology for the specific case at bar.

An area of contention in some cases is whether or not the guideline publicly traded company method should be used to value closely held companies or interests in them. The most frequently cited case rejecting the method is a California case, *In re Marriage of Lotz*, in which the appellate court reversed the trial court's value of $469,000 that was based on guideline publicly traded companies' price/earnings multiples. The Appellate Court explained as follows:

> We agree that the price earnings ratios of publicly traded corporations have little relevance in valuing a closely held corporation. There are enormous differences between the two types of corporations. The sales volume of publicly traded corporations is much higher than the volume of closely held corporations. The stock in a publicly traded corporation has liquidity value because its owners can sell stock and get money in a matter of days, whereas the stock in "Your Own Things" has no liquidity value. There is less risk in owning stock in public corporations because they can "miss on two or three lines" without being hurt too much. Finally, the cost "to go public" is between $150,000 and $200,000 for legal and accounting fees. Therefore, there is no substantial support for the use of the above formula in evaluating a closely held corporation, even considering the attempts to adjust the formula.[39]

A subsequent oft-cited California case, *Hewitson*, relied on *Lotz* and also rejected a valuation based on publicly traded company market-derived pricing multiples. The *Hewitson* case added another dimension in that multiples seen in *acquisitions* of publicly traded companies were also used, and were also rejected by the Court, even though the business interest being valued was 100 percent of the stock.

In justifying its rejection of acquisition prices paid for public companies, the Court explained:

> Cash is rarely paid for the acquired company. The company is usually acquired in exchange for stock in the acquiring company. The shares used to acquire the comparable company are normally issued without any substantial effect on the stock exchange price of the acquiring company. Hence, the acquiring company will pay a premium to acquire the company because (1) it is paying cheaper than cash consideration, and (2) such a controlling interest in the acquired company will insure the safety of its investment.[40]

The second point would seem to have no merit at all, since it would apply equally to acquisitions of public or private companies, and would affect the investment value as well as the market value. The first point should be able to be handled by

---

[39] *In re Marriage of Lotz*, 120 Cal. App. 3d 379, 174 Cal.Rptr. 618 (1981).

[40] *In re Marriage of Hewitson*.

adjusting to an estimate of cash equivalent value in those cases where there may be a disparity between face value and cash equivalent value.

The wife in *Hewitson* argued that the case should be distinguished from *Lotz* because the company was much bigger. The Court found that argument "without merit" because the "primary difference" between public and closely held corporations is the "lack of marketability, i.e., liquidity of close corporation stock."

It should be noted that, even if one accepts the courts' findings in light of conditions at the time (1981 and 1983), conditions have changed to the extent that the guideline publicly traded company method and the acquisition transaction method (acquisitions of *either* public or private companies) would not suffer, at least to the same extent, from the same criticisms today.

The Size Argument

As of this writing, partly due to congressional encouragement and partly due to market reaction, there are thousands of public companies with equity values under $10 million, so the generalization about public companies always being much larger than private companies is no longer valid.

The Liquidity Argument

For controlling ownership interests, two significant factors have changed. First, as noted in the previous paragraph, it is much easier today than 15 or 20 years ago for smaller companies to gain liquidity through an initial public offering (IPO). Second, the business of business intermediaries (business brokers and small to mid-market company merger and acquisition specialists) has burgeoned in the late 1990s, making it much easier for private companies to find acquirers.

For noncontrolling ownership interests, the matter of lack of marketability is no less of a negative factor, but the issue of making an appropriate valuation adjustment has been greatly facilitated by development of noncontrolling ownership interest lack of marketability discount databases over the last 15 years, as discussed in detail in Chapter 17. The restricted stock studies were in their infancy at the time of the *Lotz* and *Hewitson* cases, and the pre-IPO studies didn't even exist. Today there are substantial empirical data to help quantify an adjustment from an "as if publicly traded" level of value to a nonmarketable, noncontrolling level of value.

The Risk Argument

The notion that there is less risk in publicly traded companies because they can "miss on two or three lines" without being hurt too much certainly is not valid for many of today's smaller public companies that have only one or a few lines.

The Cost of Flotation Argument

While there certainly is a size below which it is not economical to go public, the lower limit is much lower today than in the early 1980s. This is largely because Congress passed legislation, implemented by SEC regulations, that allows smaller companies to go public with far lower accounting and legal requirements than are necessary for larger company registrations. These smaller company IPOs have been further facilitated by a substantial network of investment banking companies that specialize in such smaller offerings.

Noncompete Covenants

Most, but not all, states that have addressed the issue conclude that a noncompete covenant is separate property, *not* a marital asset, since it restricts the future activities of the spouse. For example, in its first case to address the issue, the Nebraska Court of Appeals looked to other jurisdictions and concluded that the covenant not to compete is *not* a marital asset.[41]

In a Washington case, a dentist sold his practice, including a noncompete covenant. Of the total proceeds of $180,000, $109,000 was allocated to the noncompete covenant, which the trial court found was separate property, not part of the marital estate. The Appellate Court agreed that the covenant not to compete was separate property. However, it found nothing in the record to substantiate the fairness of the portion of the total proceeds allocated to the covenant. Therefore, the Appellate Court stated, "On remand, the trial court is to segregate the value of the practice from the value of the covenant not to compete based on all of the evidence rather than one party's bold assertions."[42]

In South Carolina's case of first impression on the noncompete issue, the Court of Appeals found that the husband's contract receivable for a noncompete covenant was *not* a marital asset. Seeking precedent from other states, the Court concluded:

> Although we find no definitive majority view, we are persuaded by the reasoning of cases which find that a covenant not to compete is not marital property and, therefore, is not subject to equitable distribution. . . We remand this issue for the family court to distribute the husband's share of the purchase price of the Insurance Centre assets as marital property. However, the court should exclude from the marital estate the value of the husband's share of the covenant not to compete.[43]

The Supreme Court of New Mexico concluded that the $10,000 per year proceeds of a covenant not to compete resulting from the sale of a funeral home company should be separate property.

> Appellee successfully argued at the trial level that the payments to be received under the covenant constituted additional compensation for the sale of stock and as such, was community property within the meaning of Section 40- 3-8(B), N.M.S.A. 1978. The trial court reached its decision by finding that the terms of the covenant were too extreme and invalidated

[41] *Kriscfeld v. Kriscfeld.*

[42] *In re the Marriage of Delores A. Monaghan and Robert D. Monaghan,* 78 Wash. App. 918, 899 P.2d 841 (Aug. 9, 1995). Other cases cited regarding fairness of allocation to covenant included *Lucas v. Lucas*, 95 N.M. 283, 285, 621 P.2d 500, 502 (1980); *Carr v. Carr*, 108 Idaho 684, 701 P.2d 304 (1985); and *In re Marriage of Quay*, 18 Cal. App. 4th 961, Cal. Rptr. 2d 537, 541–42 (1993).

[43] *Ellerbe v. Ellerbe*, 323 S.C. 283, 473 S.E.2d 881 (S.C. Ct. App. 1996). Citations referenced were *Cutsinger v. Cutsinger*, 917 S.W.2d 238 (Tenn. Ct. App. 1995) (court excluded monetary amounts for covenant not to compete from purchase price of chiropractic practice); *Hoeft v. Hoeft*, 74 Ohio App. 3d 809, 600 N.E.2d 746 (Ohio Ct. App. 1991) (court determined that while proceeds received for the sale of the husband's dental practice were marital property, monies received from a covenant not to compete were nonmarital); *Johnston v. Johnston*, 778 S.W.2d 674 (Mo. Ct. App. 1989) (covenant not to compete properly excluded in the valuation of dental practice); *Donahue v. Donahue*, 299 S.C. 353, 384 S.E.2d 741 (1989) (goodwill of a professional practice is not subject to equitable distribution).

the covenant thereby adding $100,000 to the sale price of the stock. Neither view is correct in light of the record.

Although the covenant was contemporaneously negotiated with the sale of the stock, a review of the record fails to indicate that the $100,000 due under the covenant was to be considered as part of the stock's purchase price. To the contrary, the record is replete with evidence that the price paid for the stock was both fair and reasonable. The price paid exceeded the total assets of the corporation after allowing for depreciation. Other evidence indicated that covenants not to compete are common in the mortuary business and there is nothing in the record which suggests that the terms of appellant's covenant were so extreme as to make it invalid.

Upon the lawful dissolution of marriage, the right to compete becomes a personal right and as such, the separate property of the owner, who may then relinquish or exercise that right to his or her own benefit.[44]

As with many issues, the positions do vary from state to state. The Court of Appeals of Indiana concluded that the proceeds of a covenant not to compete *is* a marital asset.

Theodore next contends that the trial court's determination that the proceeds he received from the covenant not to compete were marital property and subject to distribution was error. Theodore's argument fails. Theodore characterizes the proceeds of the covenant not to compete as future income. Future earnings of one spouse are not marital property subject to division in a dissolution proceeding. *Bressler v. Bressler*, 601 N.E.2d 392, 397 (Ind. Ct. App. 1992). However, a restrictive covenant not to compete which is signed in conjunction with the sale of a business represents the goodwill of that business absent evidence to the contrary. *Berger v. Berger*, 648 N.E.2d 378, 383 (Ind. Ct. App. 1995). The value of the goodwill of a business is included in the marital estate. *Cleary v. Cleary*, 582 N.E.2d 851, 853 (Ind. Ct. App. 1991).

Here, Theodore signed the covenant not to compete in conjunction with the sale of his interest in Petro-Chem. The total proceeds were $11,450,000. There is evidence in the record that the value of his interest in the business was approximately $11 million. There is also evidence that Theodore's goal was to sell the business for between $10 million and $12 million. This evidence all supports the determination that the noncompete agreement was to protect the goodwill of the business. Absent evidence to the contrary, the noncompete agreement represents the goodwill of the company, which is includable in the marital estate.[45]

California distinguishes between a covenant actually executed and one that probably would have to be executed to sell the business. A California decision says:

Consideration paid for a noncompetition agreement, or the value of that agreement, is the separate property of the covenanting spouse if such a covenant actually has been negotiated as part of the sale of the property. (Carr v. Carr (Idaho App. 1985) 701 P.2d 304; Dillion v. Anderson (Tex. App. 1962) 358 S.W.2d 694; Lucas v. Lucas (N.M. 1980) 621 P.2d 500.)

---

[44] *Lucas v. Lucas.*

[45] *Reese v. Reese.*

However, it is inappropriate when awarding the property to one spouse to reduce the value of the business by the speculative value of a hypothetical noncompetition agreement. (Mitchell v. Mitchell (N.M. App. 1986) 719 P.2d 432; McGehee v. McGehee (La. App. 1 Cir. 1989) 543 So.2d 1126.)[46]

The Appellate Court thus reversed the trial court's decision to deduct from the estimated proceeds if a sale were to take place the portion of those proceeds estimated to be attributable to a covenant not to compete.

Consistent with the above decision, a subsequent California appellate opinion concluded that the entire $1,320,000 proceeds from a covenant not to compete executed in conjunction with the sale of a business was separate property.[47]

Buy-Sell Agreements

It is uncommon but not unheard of for the valuation provisions of a buy-sell agreement to be controlling in a valuation for marital dissolution distribution purposes.

Cases Rejecting Buy-Sell Agreements

Virginia, for example, has rejected buy-sell agreement valuation provisions as being controlling for interests in professional practices.[48]

Other examples of rejecting buy-sell or restrictive agreements for valuation purposes include *Ullom v. Ullom*;[49] *Argyle v. Argyle*, in which the buy-sell agreement did not contemplate evaluation for such purposes;[50] *In re Marriage of Brooks*, where the buy-sell agreement was made in close proximity to the divorce;[51] *Berenberg v. Berenberg*;[52] and *In re Marriage of Bowen*.[53]

Cases Finding Buy-Sell Price Controlling

A buy-sell agreement price was found determinate when the court concluded that if the husband were to sell his shares in an insurance company, he would do so according to the stipulations of the buy-sell agreement.[54]

A buy-sell agreement was found controlling for a block of unregistered stock of a public company, according other shareholders a right of first refusal. The Court said, "Any appraisal of the value of the stock based on a potential sale outside the terms of the agreement would have been purely speculative."[55]

---

[46] *In re Marriage of Czapar*, 232 Cal. App. 3d 1308, 284 Cal. Rptr. 41 (1991).

[47] *In re Marriage of Quay.*

[48] *Howell v. Howell*, discussed further in the section on investment value earlier in this chapter.

[49] *Ullom v. Ullom*, 559 A.2d 555, 558 (Pa. Super. Ct. 1989).

[50] *Argyle v. Argyle*, 688 P.2d 468, 471 (Utah 1984).

[51] *In re Marriage of Brooks*, 756 P.2d 161, 163 (Wash. Ct. App. 1988).

[52] *Berenberg v. Berenberg*, 474 N.W.2d 843, 847 (Minn. Ct. App. 1991).

[53] *In re Marriage of Bowen*, 473 A.2d 73, 78 (N.J. 1984).

[54] *In re Marriage of Gillespie*, No. 19978-5-11 Wash. Ct. App., 1997 WL 795692 (Dec. 31, 1997).

[55] *Rosenberg v. Rosenberg*, 510 N.Y.S.2d 659, 662 (N.Y. App. Div. 1987).

A Supreme Court of New Mexico case found a law firm's buy-sell agreement to be controlling, partly because over 150 transactions had taken place, all in accordance with the agreement.[56]

Another case also affirmed a buy-sell agreement price because it was what had been paid in arm's-length transactions and was all the owner could receive under the buyout agreement.[57]

Buy-Sell Agreement May Be Considered

It is quite common for a buy-sell or similar agreement to be considered as one factor affecting the valuation, although it isn't necessarily determinative in valuing the stock.[58]

Discounts for Lack of Control and Lack of Marketability

Discount for Lack of Control

Many jurisdictions have recognized that a lack of control discount is frequently appropriate if the spouse does not own a controlling interest in the subject company. For example, an Alaska case, referencing other jurisdictions, rejected as a matter of law testimony to the effect that no discount for lack of control was appropriate.[59]

In a North Dakota case, the Court rejected the testimony of one expert who said that "there should be no minority discount in a family-owned business in divorce cases, where, as here, Lillian's family owns the corporation and the minority shares are not being sold to unrelated, unknown buyers." However, the Court concluded a discount for lack of control of only 11.3 percent rather than the 25 percent to 40 percent sought by the party being awarded the business interest in question.[60]

There have been many other cases in which discounts for lack of control have been accepted.[61] On the other hand, there have been many cases where experts' testimony in favor of a discount for lack of control has been rejected.[62]

---

[56] *Hertz v. Hertz*, 657 P.2d 1169, 1174–75 (N.M. 1983).

[57] *Johnson v. Johnson*, 771 P.2d 696, 698 (Utah Ct. App. 1989).

[58] See, for example, *Bosserman v. Bosserman*, 384 S.E.2d 104, 107–08 (Va. Ct. App. 1989) (spouse did not consent to buy-sell agreement or is not bound by its terms); *Naddeo v. Naddeo*, 626 A.2d 608, 610–11 (Pa. Super. Ct. 1993) (partner did not have the ability to sell interest); *Stearns v. Stearns*, 494 A.2d 595, 598 (Conn. App. Ct. 1985) (closely held, family-run business); *Mitchell v. Mitchell*, 732 P.2d 208, 212 (Ariz. 1987); *Lyon v. Lyon*, 439 N.W.2d 18, 20 (Minn. 1989); *Buckl v. Buckl*, 542 A.2d 65, 69 (Pa. Super. Ct. 1988); *Rogers v. Rogers* 296 N.W.2d 849, 852 (Minn. 1980); *Schecter v. Schecter*, No. FA 9703276678 Conn. Super. Ct., 1999 WL 34857 (Jan. 12, 1999); *Drake v. Drake*, 809 S.W.2d 710, 713 (Ky. Ct. App. 1991) (closely held corporation); *In re Marriage of Dieger*, No. 97-1493 Iowa Ct. App., 1998 WL 690075 (June 24, 1998).

[59] *Hayes v. Hayes*, 756 P.2d 298 (Alaska 1988).

[60] *Kaiser v. Kaiser*, No. 960013 N.D. Sup. Ct., 1996 WL 663189 (Nov. 18, 1996).

[61] *Priebe v. Priebe*, 556 N.W.2d 78, 81 (S.D. 1996) (40 percent); *DeCosse v. DeCosse*, No. 96-118 Mont., 1997 WL 19374 (Apr. 15, 1997) (20 percent); and *Arneson v. Arneson*, 355 N.W. 2d 16 (Wis. Ct. App. 1984) (25 percent).

[62] For example, *Howell v. Howell*; *Oatey v. Oatey*, No. 67809, 67973 Ohio Ct. App., 1996 WL 200273 at *22 (Apr. 25, 1996); *Nardini v. Nardini*, 414 N.W. 2d 184, 189 (Minn. 1987); and *Cross v. Cross*, 586 P.2d 547, 549 (Wyo. 1978).

Discount for Lack of Marketability

States vary in their treatment of discounts for lack of marketability. In one case, for example, one expert testified in favor of a discount and the other opined that marketability is not a factor in cases where a business is not being sold to a third party. The Court concluded:

> Where a sale of the business is not contemplated, the value of the stock should be determined without discounting for lack of marketability. Under these circumstances, the fact that H & H stock is not publicly traded does not warrant application of the discount to reduce the value of Linda's interest. See and compare Mexic v. Mexic, 577 So.2d 1046, 1050 (La. App. 4th Cir. 1991).[63]

Many other cases have rejected discounts for lack of marketability.[64] On the other hand, there are many cases in which discounts for lack of marketability have been accepted.[65]

Adequacy of Evidence

As noted in the previous chapter, while trial courts have broad discretion regarding findings of fact, the record must indicate that there was adequate evidence to support those findings. The incidence of remand for lack of adequate evidence supporting business values is higher in family law case appeals than in any other business valuation litigation context.

Typical of court opinions to this effect is the following:

> In allocating property between the parties to a divorce and in making an award of sustenance alimony, the trial court must indicate the basis for its award in sufficient detail to enable a reviewing court to determine that the award is fair, equitable and in accordance with the law.[66]

Citing the above case, a subsequent appellate decision remanded a case on similar grounds:

> The trial court failed to indicate the basis of its award and valuation of Get Out of Town on a Rail, Inc. with sufficient detail to enable this court to conduct a meaningful review of the award.[67]

Another typical example is a Louisiana case:

> The evidence presented by both parties as to the valuation of the corporation is patently unsound. . . . We are unable to make a determination of the valuation of the husband's medical corporation based upon the record before

---

[63] *Head v. Head*, No. 30,585-CA La. App., 1998 WL 257217 (2d Cir. May 22, 1998).

[64] See, for example, *Howell v. Howell* (no amount specified) and *Neuman v. Neuman*, 842 P.2d 575, 579 (Wyo. 1992) (35 percent).

[65] For example, *In re Marriage of Tofte*, 895 P.2d 1387, 1392 (Or. Ct. App. 1995) (35 percent); *Ellis v. Ellis*, No. 77407 N.Y. App. Div., 1997 WL 35218 at *2 (Jan. 30, 1997) (25 percent); and *Michael v. Michael*, 469 S.E.2d 14, 17 (W. Va. 1996) (25 percent).

[66] *Kaechele v. Kaechele*, 35 Ohio St.3d 93, 97 (1988).

[67] *Giuffre v. Baker*.

us. . . . The matter should be remanded to the trial court for an evidentiary hearing.[68]

Similarly, in a North Carolina case:

The trial court . . . should clearly indicate the evidence on which its valuations are based, preferably noting the valuation method or methods on which it relied. . . . We vacate that portion of the equitable distribution order which determines the value of defendant's goodwill in his medical practice, and remand this case to the district court for a proper determination of such value. . . .[69]

In one case, a certified public accountant employed the income approach to place a value on the corporation, although he avowed that he had insufficient information to give an opinion on the value at the time of the marriage in 1989.

The trial court, using the figures the CPA considered insufficient, purported to find the corporation's value on that date. The Court of Appeals determined that if the information available to the CPA was insufficient for that purpose, it was inadequate to support a finding of value by the court. The Court of Appeals declared that the judgment decreeing a division of the community estate was to be reversed and remanded to the trial court.[70]

The Virginia Court of Appeals upheld the striking of the wife's expert's testimony (using the discounted cash flow method for a start-up business) on the basis that it was speculative. The trial court concluded, "I don't think it's the law that you can get somebody to get on the stand and project earnings of a company that has done no business, has no record of income. That's pure speculation. Couldn't be more pure." The Court of Appeals concluded, "Based on the evidence presented to the court at trial, we find no error in this ruling."[71]

A Washington case emphasizes to both the expert and the attorney the necessity of making a good record at trial. Professional goodwill, defined as "the expectation of continued public patronage," is recognized as intangible property subject to division in a divorce. The Court must first determine whether goodwill exists, and, if so, determine its value considering several factors (discussed in the earlier section on goodwill). One expert testified that there was no goodwill, and the value of the business was $2,040 (assets minus liabilities). The other expert testified that the business was worth $125,582 (1.5 times the last four years' average gross income less operating expenses). The trial court determined that the value of the business was $50,000. The Court of Appeals explained:

The trial court must state on record which factors . . . were used . . .; failure to do so will deem the valuation to be unsupported by sufficient evidence, necessitating reversal and remand. . . .

We cannot determine from the record before us whether the trial court actually found "goodwill." Once the trial court finds goodwill, it must set forth on the record the factors and method used in reaching a finding of goodwill and its value. . . . Because the trial court here did not state how it reached the valuation figure, we remand and direct the trial court to set forth the factors and methods used in valuation if it indeed finds goodwill exists.[72]

[68] *Fox v. Fox*, No. 97-1914 La. App. 1 Cir., 1998 WL 781651 (Nov. 6, 1998).

[69] *Conway v. Conway*.

[70] *In re Marriage of Cassel*, No. 07-96-0268-CV Tex. App., 1997 WL 260099 (May 19, 1997).

[71] *Shoolts v. Shoolts*, Nos. 2205-96-4 Vir. Ct. App., 1998 WL 201536 (Apr. 28, 1998).

[72] *Crosetto v. Crosetto*, No. 17911-3-11 Wash. App. Div. 2, 1996 WL 389337 (July 12, 1996), also citing *Hall*, 103 Wash.2d at 247, 692 P.2d 175, and *Marriage of Monaghan*, 78 Wash. App. 918, 927–28, 899 P.2d 841 (1995).

An Appellate Court reversed and remanded a trial court's conclusion of value for a hair transplant practice: "Because no evidence supports the valuation, we reverse and remand for new trial."[73]

In another case, the husband offered no expert testimony, and the Appellate Court found inadequate the wife's expert's testimony, which the trial court had accepted. The Appellate Court reversed and remanded.[74]

In another case example, the wife presented no expert testimony, and the trial court found the testimony and analysis of the husband's expert not to be credible. The Appellate Court stated:

> The burden of presenting . . . sufficient evidence . . . does not fall on the petitioning spouse alone, but . . . is an obligation existing with both parties . . . [and] neither party met this burden with respect to the valuation of the three corporations. . . .
>
> On review of a case such as this, where the record does not support any valuation of a very substantial marital asset, we conclude that the only reasonable course is for us to order further proceedings at which sufficient evidence on the question of valuation can be presented. . . . Accordingly, we reverse and remand the case so that the trial court can take additional evidence on the valuation. . . .[75]

What a waste! Another case with no credible evidence on either side, resulting in extended delay and costs on both sides to resolve the matter!

The incidence of lack of credible evidence on one side or both in family law cases involving business valuation is amazing. There is a great need to educate the legal community that there is a professional community with thousands of qualified valuation analysts, and that clients are best served by engaging these qualified professionals at the onset of any actual or potential dispute regarding the value of a business or professional practice.

Treatment of Tax Liabilities

As noted in the previous chapter, family law courts rarely allow the deduction of a tax liability assumed in connection with a business or other property unless the payment of the liability is imminent.

For example, "theoretical tax liabilities should not have been deducted in valuing Sun Well Service, Inc., and Marvin's retirement accounts."[76]

Similarly typical is the statement in a California case:

> It is improper to take into consideration the tax consequences of an order dividing a community asset unless the tax liability is immediate and specific and will arise in connection with the division of the community property. (See *In re Marriage of Fonstein* (1976) 17 Cal.3d 738, 749, fn. 5; *In re Marriage of Davies* (1983) 143 Cal.App.3d 851, 857; *In re Marriage of*

---

[73] *Kelsey v. Kelsey*, 918 P.2d 1067 (Ariz. App. Div. 1 Jan. 1, 1996).

[74] *Simmons v. Simmons*, No. 95 T 5237 Ohio Ct. App., 1996 WL 297003 (May 10, 1996).

[75] *Blackstone v. Blackstone*, No. 1-94-2780 Ill. App. (1st Dist. May 30, 1997).

[76] *Kaiser v. Kaiser.*

Sharp (1983) 143 Cal.App.3d 714, 718; *In re Marriage of Slater* (1979) 100 Cal.App.3d 241, 249.[77]

In one case, an Appellate Court reversed a decision that valued stock options after a deduction of capital gains taxes. The Court of Appeals stated:

> A trial court must consider tax consequences related to the disposition of marital property. However, "the statute requires the trial court to consider only the direct or inherent and necessarily incurred tax consequences of the property disposition." Future tax consequences incident to the disposition of stock awarded one party is not a proper consideration before the trial court. Reversed.[78]

In Washington, the wife successfully appealed the trial court's decision that reduced the value of a real estate partnership by the capital gains tax that would have to be paid if the property were sold. Since it was the first Washington case addressing this issue, the Court looked to other states for precedent, citing cases in seven other states. In denying the deduction for the impounded capital gains tax liability, the Court explained:

> Courts have generally found that consideration of tax consequences is either required or at least appropriate where the consequences are immediate and specific and/or arise directly from the court's decree, but find they are not an appropriate consideration where speculation as to a party's future dealings with property awarded to him or her would be required. . . .[79]
>
> We agree with the rule adopted by most jurisdictions. . . . Mr. Hay testified at trial that he had no plans to sell his partnership interest. . . . We remand to enable the trial court to consider the property division without regard to the capital gains tax consequences of a hypothetical sale of H & L Investments.[80]

This and similar cases lead us to raise a question as to the appropriate valuation approach or approaches. If the sale of the assets is so remote a possibility as to eliminate consideration of the capital gains tax liability, that calls into question using asset value as the only primary valuation approach. Perhaps an income approach would be more appropriate or maybe an income approach should be blended with an asset-based approach.[81]

Summary

This chapter has discussed various states' appellate decisions on a variety of business valuation issues in the context of a marital dissolution. About the only issue on which there is general agreement is that the trial court must have adequate, credible evidence on which to base its findings.

---

[77] *In re Marriage of Czapar.*

[78] *Knotts v. Knotts*, No. 32405-9710-CV-430 Ind. Ct. App., 1998 WL 159207 (Apr. 7, 1998).

[79] Tracy A. Bateman, *Annotation Divorce and Separation: Consideration of Tax Consequences in Distribution of Marital Property*, 9 A.L.R. 5th 568, 592, 52[a] (1993).

[80] *Hay v. Hay*, No. 14368-6-III Wash. Ct. App. (Div. 3 Dec. 26, 1995).

[81] See Shannon P. Pratt, "Trapped-in Capital Gains Affects Real-World Value," *Shannon Pratt's Business Valuation Update*, February 1996, pp. 1, 3.

Decisions varied considerably on most other issues:

- Standard of value.
- Active versus passive appreciation.
- Effective date of valuation.
- When goodwill is or isn't marital property and how to value it.
- Valuation methods.
- The marital or nonmarital status of the value of actual or potential noncompete covenants and/or employment agreements.
- The weight accorded buy-sell agreements.
- Discounts for lack of control and/or lack of marketability.
- Treatment of trapped-in capital gains tax liabilities.

It is a frequently encountered paradox that courts say that they will not accept valuations that are dependent on future efforts of a spouse, and then in the same case accept valuation methods that inherently impound future efforts of the spouse (or restrictions on the spouse's future activities). An important part of the analyst's job is to educate the courts as to what credible evidence is available and why certain valuation methods are and are not appropriate in the particular situation. There is no business valuation litigation context in which this need is greater than in the family law courts.

In any case, within the marital dissolution context, it is incumbent on the attorney to provide the valuation analyst with a thorough review of the relevant judicial precedent.

Part VIII

Litigation and Dispute Resolution

Chapter 39

Litigation Support Services

Valuation-Related Controversy Matters
Types of Litigation
    Contract Disputes
    Commercial Torts
    Business Interruption Claims
    Antitrust Claims
    Securities Litigation
    Marital Dissolution
    Personal Injury or Wrongful Termination Cases
    Estate, Gift, and Income Taxes
    State and Local Property Taxes
    Bankruptcy/Insolvency/Reorganization Situations
    Intellectual Property Rights Infringement
Engaging the Appraiser
    Qualifications
    Conflicts of Interest
    Engagement Agreement
Assessing the Case
Critique of the Opposition
Expert Testimony
Rebuttal
Assistance in Preparing Briefs
Discovery
Business Appraisal Discovery
    Permanent Files
    Accountant's Files
    Bank Files
    Invoices
    Interrogatories
    Depositions
    Research
Calculating the Amount of Damages
    The Before-and-After Method
    The Yardstick (Comparable) Method
    Sales Projections ("But For") Method

Frequently, commercial, taxation, or family law litigation involves a controversy over the value of assets, properties, or business interests. Appraisals that are performed within a litigation environment require that the analyst understand the legal context within which the appraisal is being made. The analyst should tailor his or her valuation work to address the facts and circumstances of the case, while taking into consideration all relevant statutory authority, judicial precedent, and administrative rulings. Prevailing statutory, judicial, or administrative law often varies considerably from one valuation purpose to another and even from one jurisdiction to another for valuations for the same purpose (e.g., dissenting stockholder actions or marital property distribution). This means that the very same business interest could have a different value depending on the legal context in which it applies.

This chapter precedes the chapter on expert witness testimony, deliberately separating the subject of general litigation support from the subject of expert testimony. In this chapter, we discuss several valuation consulting, economic analysis, and financial advisory services within the context of litigation support and controversy resolution.

Valuation-Related Controversy Matters

Many valuation-related disputes can be resolved before a trial is necessary. The odds of a favorable resolution are substantially increased when clients work closely from the very beginning with an appraiser who is experienced in litigation and dispute resolution matters. An experienced appraiser can be very helpful in assessing the merits of the case, both in estimating a reasonable range of values and in weighing the risks involved in going to court. If the case cannot be resolved outside the courtroom, then, at least, the decision to go to court will be based on a sound assessment of the situation from a valuation viewpoint. And, the preparation for the litigation may be more orderly, thorough, and cost-efficient.

When clients or their counsel assess valuation-related litigation issues without the assistance of an experienced appraiser, then the interests of the client are not best served. These situations usually arise when principals or their counsel attempt to minimize the expert's fees, when they do not know how to locate an appraiser experienced in controversy matters, or when they do not fully understand the best way to utilize the appraiser's experience and expertise. In any event, when contacted late, the appraiser's ability to provide the best advice may be constrained.

It is also important to integrate expert witness testimony with other litigation support services. In order to support or refute a plaintiff's claim of damages, expertise in several areas is often required in order to assess the significant factors affecting the plaintiff's likely activities (absent the alleged wrongful action) and in order to ascertain whether the defendant's actions were indeed the principal cause for the harm to the plaintiff. Damage cases in which significant dollar amounts are at stake may require that numerous experts—including industry, accounting, finance, and economics experts—be retained by both the plaintiff and by the defendant, in order to adequately address the specific questions relating to their areas of expertise.

An appraiser can sometimes help select and supervise other experts. Specialized experts may be needed to address certain elements that impact the value of an asset, property, or business interest, such as industry experts or experts in specific types of property. Appraisers often maintain relationships with such advisers because they need to call on them from time to time for informational or other purposes. For various reasons, the attorney may call in more than one appraisal expert: (1) in order to get more than one expert's opinion before the trier of fact; (2) in order to have an expert concentrate on certain especially controversial or critical aspects of the case, such as the appropriateness of a certain method or the quantification of some premium or discount; or (3) in order to have one expert for rebuttal and another for the case in chief.

One valuable litigation support service of an experienced appraiser is to review and critique materials and expert reports prepared by other experts on the same side of the case. In some situations, for a variety of reasons, such a review can be part of the input an attorney needs in order to decide whether to call in a particular expert to testify. In other cases, the review may help focus and buttress the testimony to be presented by a particular expert.

An independent appraiser is an advocate for his or her position only, and not an advocate for the client. The independent appraiser may assist both the client and the lawyer in preparing the best possible case. However, when it comes to the independent expert's opinion, the expert must present an unbiased, impartial position on all substantive issues on which he or she has been asked for an opinion. The independent expert must remain free from both actual bias and the appearance of bias. If the attorney believes that any litigation support functions that the independent expert otherwise might logically perform would create the perception of a bias, then the attorney might wish to have these services performed by other professionals.

The vast majority of valuation-related controversy matters never reaches the stage of requiring expert testimony before a trier of fact (judge, jury, or other tribunal). Accordingly, thoroughly documented appraisals can contribute significantly to successful settlements of valuation-related controversies. The same level of analytical rigor and appraisal documentation that leads to successful settlements also can provide the underpinnings for proper trial preparation. It is often said that the best way to facilitate a successful settlement is to begin preparing from the outset as if the case were going to court.

Types of Litigation

Commercial litigation claims typically involve the determination of the occurrence of an action, the cause of the action, and the amount of damages that are related to the action. Appraisers and economists are frequently called upon to assist attorneys in evaluating these claims—and especially in estimating the existence of, and the amount of, commercial damages. In many instances, the appraisers and economists also are asked to provide expert testimony as to the damage issues.

The following paragraphs summarize some of the more common reasons why parties become involved in litigation involving the valuation of assets, properties, and business interests.

Contract Disputes

Breach of contract or warranty involves all types of products or services. The Uniform Commercial Code generally describes the laws of damages regarding breaches of contract. Different remedies are prescribed, depending on the breaching party. For instance, only commercial buyers may claim consequential damages (i.e., losses resulting from an act or a breach that are not direct or immediate) under certain circumstances.

Commercial Torts

These involve claims of negligence or intentional torts that include interference with business, unfair competition, fraud, or interference with a contract. Damages are often measured by lost earnings; and in some cases, damages are measured by the lost profits resulting from negligence and lost profits resulting from intentional torts.

Business Interruption Claims

Businesses organized for the purpose of carrying on a business for profit can suffer contract or tort claims that may be measured in terms of lost profits. Some business interruptions also are caused by casualty. Business interruption insurance can cover either the loss of earnings caused by the casualty or the loss of income sustained and any expenses incurred in order to resume normal business operations. This category of business interruption insurance may sometimes cover events related to eminent domain, condemnation, and expropriation issues.

Antitrust Claims

Examples of these claims are predatory pricing, price fixing, and other anticompetitive actions. Damages are frequently measured by estimating the difference between the "inflated" anticompetitive price and the "normal" competitive price—or by estimating the amount of lost profits that resulted from the anticompetitive practices of another company or companies.

Securities Litigation

These legal actions result from disputes involving the value of corporate or other securities including, for instance, corporate and partnership dissolutions, buy-sell agreements, minority shareholder rights, and going public or going private transactions. Also included in this category of types of litigation are damages that occur in cases involving securities fraud. In such cases, damages are often measured as the difference between the "true" or "intrinsic" value of the securities involved and the actual price at which shares were exchanged.

Marital Dissolution

The valuation of a closely held business is often a contested issue in the division of property (i.e., the marital estate) between spouses involved in a marital dissolution. The value of the family-owned business on several valuation dates (e.g., date of the marriage, date of the filing of the dissolution action, etc.) is often a matter of controversy between the spouses. This topic is covered in detail in Chapters 37 and 38.

Personal Injury or Wrongful Termination Cases

A party injured or wrongfully terminated often requires the estimation of lost employment earnings that were suffered as a result of the wrongful action. In the case of a self-employed individual involved in a personal injury matter, for example, the lost profits of the owner's business are sometimes used as a measure of the individual's earnings.

Estate, Gift, and Income Taxes

In these cases, the federal government, usually the Internal Revenue Service, opposes the taxpayer. These cases may include, for example, the allocation of the purchase price paid for a bundle of assets, gift and estate tax claims, employee compensation issues such as employee incentive stock options grants, debt forgiveness in restructurings, corporate reorganizations of entities, recapitalizations, charitable contributions, abandonment losses, property contribution issues, intercompany transfer pricing issues (of tangible and intangible assets), use of NOL carryforwards, and S corporation built-in gains tax. See Chapters 27 and 28 for further discussion of gift and estate tax issues and Chapter 30 and 31 for further discussion of income tax–related valuation matters.

The reason that a valuation dispute may arise in conjunction with an NOL is that Code Section 382(b) limits the annual NOL deduction to the value of the old loss corporation immediately before the ownership change multiplied by the federal long-term tax exempt rate (with some modifications). For a short tax year, the amount is prorated.

State and Local Property Taxes

Special-purpose properties and income-producing properties subject to state and local property taxes are often the subject of valuation controversies. Such properties include, for example, cable and broadcast television properties, mining operations, timberland and forestry operations, chemical processing plants, gas and electric utilities and power generation plants, data processing and telecommunications facilities, high-technology properties, railroads and regulated industries, farm land and agricultural properties, hotels and motels, strip and enclosed shopping malls, and mixed-use properties. In such valuation controversies, it is often important to separately identify and appraise nontaxable intangible personal property (or other nonassessable) assets. See Chapter 34 for further discussion on the topic of ad valorem taxation–related valuation matters.

Bankruptcy/Insolvency/Reorganization Situations

The appraiser may be called upon to independently create or assess a reorganization plan, to analyze debt and equity capital restructuring proposals, to review financial forecasts and projections, to value various classes of collateral, to test the going-concern versus liquidation presumptions of plans of reorganization or liquidation, to identify spinoff opportunities, to prepare fraudulent conveyance analyses, or to express a solvency or insolvency opinion—to name a few typical financial advisory services.

Intellectual Property Rights Infringement

In what has become a common occurrence in the information age, claims of intellectual property rights infringement involve trademarks, trade names, copyrights, patents, proprietary technology, computer software, and many other intangible assets and intellectual properties.[1]

Engaging the Appraiser

An appraiser providing expertise in a litigated valuation case serves as a "forensic economist" in that the appraiser is using expertise in the microeconomic analysis of property valuation. It is important to retain appraisers who can not only use their education and experience to develop and support a sound position but who also can communicate that position in terms that a judge and/or jury can understand. It is important to evaluate appraisers' abilities through the examination of their credentials and experience, their reputations, their references, and/or personal interviews. There have been three U.S. Supreme Court cases upholding the lower courts' exclusions of expert testimony. These cases are discussed futher in the following chapter on expert testimony.

Qualifications

Although previous litigation experience is helpful, it is also important for the appraiser to have the benefit of "real-world" transactional experience along with the experience of doing battle in a courtroom.

Valuation issues are affected by a wide variety of legal mandates and precedents. Such mandates and precedents differ significantly in their application to various valuation purposes. Even for valuations for similar purposes, both statutory authority and judicial precedent are subject to considerable variation from one jurisdiction to another. Many statutes and court decisions contain vague or ambiguous wording, so that an understanding of different interpretations from one jurisdiction to another may require study of several cases. Ignorance of these variations can result in misdirection in litigation-related valuation work. Of course, the attorney must finally decide any legal matter; nevertheless, such decisions can be greatly enhanced by appraisers who have a good working knowledge of the valuation-related aspects of the law.

---

[1] For further information on this subject, see Robert F. Reilly and Robert P. Schweihs, *Valuing Intangible Assets* (New York: McGraw-Hill, 1999).

The research and other professional resources of the appraiser's firm are often an essential component of the appraiser's ability to successfully perform litigation support and dispute resolution services. Accordingly, the appraiser should have a collegial staff with appropriate qualifications, with the ability to meet the required deadlines, and of a size necessary to carry out the research and analytical requirements of the case. Library and other research resources are time-consuming and expensive to develop. Even in this age of on-line services, a crucial task in the controversy process is to index and organize documents, articles, statistical data, published court cases, and miscellaneous economic, industry, and corporate reports. Having the relevant research material is critical to the appraiser involved in a controversy matter, but so is having that material well-organized, indexed, and easily accessible.

Active involvement in professional organizations and activities may increase an appraiser's ability to provide effective litigation support. These activities include attending seminars sponsored by leading professional appraisal organizations and by specific industry trade associations, speaking at such programs, and writing for well-recognized professional publications. These activities help to keep the appraiser current on the thinking and the developments in the mainstream of the profession and to expose the appraiser's own thinking to peer scrutiny.

To establish whether there is a concurrence of valuation philosophy, the attorney may wish to approach the prospective witness with a hypothetical scenario. In this way, the attorney can get some idea of the methods and parameters the witness would use in reaching the value conclusion without revealing the client's name or identifying the actual asset, property, or business interest to be valued. One of the nuances of this exercise is that the credibility of the potential witness is maintained if it can be established that he or she was hired to ascertain a value independently, and not to testify to some value predetermined by the interested party.

This comparison of valuation philosophies is as important to the appraiser as it is to the client, since no reputable appraiser wants to be under pressure to testify to a conclusion that cannot be professionally supported. Usually, a brief dialogue between an experienced attorney and an experienced appraiser is all that is necessary to determine whether the appraiser can be useful as a witness on the specific case.

Conflicts of Interest

The appraiser should be independent of the parties on both sides of the case. Very early in the proceedings, the attorney must disclose the names of all of the parties in the case to the prospective witness in order to ascertain that there is no conflict of interest. Apart from having already been retained by the opposing party, the most common conflict of interest would be having a financial or investment interest that would introduce the appearance of a conflict of interest. Potential conflicts should be promptly disclosed to the client and/or the client's attorney, because the appearance of a conflict can discredit a witness (whether the witness considers it a conflict or not).

In general, it is not a disqualifying conflict for the appraiser to have performed services for the opposing party. It is never a disqualifying conflict that the appraiser has been retained on unrelated assignments by the opposing party's law firm. On the contrary, that may be viewed as a sign of professional integrity and independence. For example, our firm has performed quite a number of taxation-related valuation and economic analysis assignments both for the Internal Revenue Service and for corporate and individual taxpayers.

One common problem is the appraiser who is interviewed by one side and not retained, and then is contacted by the other side. A potential problem can be avoided if the appraiser makes it clear to the attorney in initial interviews that no confidential information or analysis should be shared until after the appraiser has been formally retained.

Engagement Agreement

In many cases, engagement agreements for litigation support services give very little detail, often because the attorneys have not yet determined exactly what services they will need from the appraiser. It is not uncommon for the appraiser to assist the attorney at various points in the case with regard to focusing the issues, gathering the data, and developing the scope of the assignment. While it is important to include as many of the elements of the assignment as possible, the engagement agreement may become discoverable by the other side, along with drafts and modifications to the agreement. Since the legal strategy of the case may change after the engagement has commenced—and since attorneys don't want their legal strategies to be discovered—standardized, nondescriptive engagement letters are often used for litigation support projects.

If the appraiser knows enough about the property to be analyzed to estimate the time required, the assignment itself may be performed for a fixed fee or within a narrow estimated fee range. Otherwise, a fee based upon hourly billing rates is usually adopted.

Often, litigation cases can be structured in advance around specific tasks and a specific work product. For example, the first phase, at a predetermined budgeted amount, could include an assessment of the case, some preliminary consultation with the attorney regarding the apparent merits of the case, and a brief critique of the opponent's work product. Subsequent phases might include a detailed valuation work plan, a review of material provided in response to a document request, a preliminary range of value conclusions, an analysis of the benefits and costs of pursuing litigation, a full narrative valuation opinion report, and so forth.

The amount of time to be spent in depositions, preparation with attorneys for court, observation and testifying in court, and other aspects of litigation support are normally beyond the appraiser's control. For that reason, the compensation for these services usually is made on an hourly basis, at a specific hourly rate. The attorney and the appraiser often cooperate in order to structure the compensation to be flexible enough to accommodate the many uncertainties involved in litigation but rigid enough that the expert will not become a party at interest to the outcome of the case.

> Make sure you receive the check for your airfare, estimated hotel expenses and three days of your time before you leave home for a trial. . . . If it comes out in court that you have not been paid lately, the jury may think the outcome of the case is very important to you. Your objectivity may be suspect. . . .
>
> **Q:** *Does your client owe you any money?*
>
> **A:** *No. My bills have been paid to date and my expenses for this trip were paid in advance. My being paid does not depend on the outcome of this case.*[2]

---

[2] Daniel F. Poynter, *Expert Witness Handbook* (Santa Barbara, CA: Para Publishing, 1987).

Assessing the Case

Matters such as the applicable standard of value and the relevant valuation date or dates are not always as obvious as they might appear on the surface. In many controversy cases, there is no statutorily defined standard of value or applicable valuation date. Sometimes the relative rights of various parties at interest are very complex and careful definition of the property and its relevant rights and restrictions is a crucial prerequisite to the assignment itself. Ultimately, the attorney must decide the question or questions to ask the appraiser to address. Often the appraiser's knowledge and experience can be very helpful in focusing the relevant questions, in defining the case to the client's advantage, and to achieving a successful outcome.

Once the basic work plan is framed, the appraiser may be asked to do some preliminary work to suggest a reasonable range of value within which the final conclusion might be expected to fall. Often, it is possible to provide such information on a preliminary basis. The preliminary range of values can help the attorney decide on the litigation posture. Sometimes the most valuable service that an appraiser can perform for clients is to tell them what they don't want to hear—that the value is not what they suspected and, at least from a monetary standpoint, the case is not what it appeared to be. Heading off financially unproductive litigation can save the client tens of thousands of dollars. When each side is provided with an opinion as to a reasonable range of value from a genuinely competent appraiser, the groundwork for a settlement is often laid. On the other hand, if a settlement cannot be reached, the preliminary range of value the appraiser provides lends some confidence to a decision to proceed with litigation.

Often the appraiser can facilitate the identification and quantification of areas of financial uncertainty so that the attorney can better assess the risks of litigation. Sometimes reasonable people will reach different conclusions because of different assessments of the economic or other exogenous factors affecting the subject asset, property, or business interest. Sometimes there may be contingent assets or liabilities that may have a substantial impact on the appraiser's estimation of value. It often helps to try to quantify the risk that arises from various uncertainties. For example, if the preliminary range of value is between $8 million and $12 million, the litigation posture could be significantly different than if the preliminary range of value is between $0 and $20 million.

After the valuation issues have been framed and a preliminary range of values has been estimated, the attorney is in a better position to assess the relationship between the litigation's potential benefits and costs. In making this analysis, the attorney may ask the appraiser to estimate some range of likely or possible costs to complete the case, including preparation for testimony, depositions, direct- and cross-examination at trial, and the preparation of post-trial briefs. Possibly the most important of all of these fees are those related to pre-trial preparation between the appraiser and the attorney handling the case. Also, in the heat of litigation, costs tend to run over expectations more often than under. Appraisers, attorneys, and clients should fully consider the difficulty of controlling deposition and court time and, especially, the costs of responding to possible unknown material that the opposition may present.

Critique of the Opposition

In many litigated valuations, the process of critiquing the opposition's position is as important to reaching a satisfactory resolution as preparing the valuation case in chief—or even more so. After all, if the opposition's position is found to be unsound and indefensible, there probably would be no case.

The critique of an opposing expert's report or presentation may take place at any time from the outset of possible litigation throughout the trial itself. If an expert's report is available at the beginning stage of assessing the case, it is important to review it at that time. It may be an entirely sound piece of work, and an early review may result in a recommendation to accept it or possibly to negotiate some minor modifications, thus forestalling thousands of dollars of futile litigation costs.

If the opposition's expert is off base, it is good to know why as soon as possible. The more sophisticated the expert on the other side, the more likely it is that a settlement can be reached through narrowing and compromising on the valuation issues that are genuinely arguable. If the other side has used an inexperienced expert, then it is usually much more difficult to engage in a constructive exchange leading to a resolution short of the courtroom. In any case, the appraiser must provide the attorney with an understanding of the strengths and weaknesses of the opposing expert's position.

Expert Testimony

Obviously, one of the most important litigation support services available from appraisers and economists is expert witness testimony. Deposition and court testimony are the subjects of the next chapter.

Rebuttal

The type of rebuttal needed largely depends, of course, on what is wrong with the other expert's work. If the expert has made a mathematical error, that should be brought to the court's attention, along with its impact on the conclusion. If the expert has taken a position unsupported by the preponderance of authority on an issue, evidence as to the preponderance of authority must be researched and developed. For example, if the opposition takes the position that there should be no discount from enterprise value when estimating the fair market value of a noncontrolling stock interest, then the rebuttal should cite authoritative regulations, texts, articles, and other sources that make it clear that such a discount should be taken. If the expert's approaches are basically sound, but the expert has reached a poor conclusion because of inadequate and/or erroneous data, then the best rebuttal approach may be to recalculate the results with his or her own methodology, but using complete and accurate data.

Assistance in Preparing Briefs

Appraisers who have testified and either listened to or read the testimony of an opposing expert tend to have a sharp sense of the difference between their own and their opponents' positions on the important valuation issues. Briefs in a case are enriched by a good expert's insights; the appraiser can help bring these differences into sharp focus, particularly as they apply to issues that have the greatest monetary impact, and can express clear, concise reasons why his or her position is superior. The attorney may want to take advantage of the appraiser's insights by discussing the briefs before preparing them or by having the appraiser review the briefs in draft form.

Similarly, the appraiser often can provide a special understanding of the opponent's briefs. One thing to look for is any mischaracterization of the appraiser's own evidence or testimony, another is any unjustifiable conclusions or implications made on the basis of the opposing expert's testimony. Sometimes the appraiser reviewing the opposing briefs will notice a clearly erroneous factual statement on some valuation matter that the attorney reading the brief might not realize is an error. A review by the appraiser is a good safety check for ensuring that any unwarranted contentions do not go unnoticed but are treated with a firm and convincing reply.

Discovery

Within the area of litigation, one of the most important tasks that can be performed by the appraiser or economist is assisting the attorney with discovery. Unfortunately, many appraisers concentrate on selecting the correct valuation procedures, which are then applied to either meaningless or unreliable financial information. It is extremely important that the appraiser be brought into the early stages of a case in order to assure that the necessary information is gathered before the actual valuation is started.

In most cases, the more cooperative and less formalized the discovery process, the better both parties are served. If all parties are willing to cooperate, it is often easiest for experts to gather sufficient information for a thorough understanding by directly contacting the information sources rather than by working through the attorneys. It is not unusual for an unconstrained discovery process to uncover previously misinterpreted facts, leading to a settlement of the case.

When the parties are unwilling to cooperate, the experts must, of course, rely on the attorneys to enforce discovery of the necessary information. If the information is delayed or documents do not arrive on a timely basis, then the attorneys must follow up immediately and vigorously. Further, it is up to the experts to keep the attorneys informed about whether the requested information is arriving in a timely manner. Keeping the attorneys apprised in this way will facilitate their follow-up and make it possible for them to accurately report to the court about the receipt of information.

In virtually all valuation cases, there is a standard set of documents that are needed for the business valuation. For private companies, these documents will usually include historical and (if available) prospective operating statements, income tax returns, ownership lists, prior transaction information, important contracts, and documentation of the ownership of the subject assets, properties, and business interests (for an example of a document request list, see Exhibit 4–1). Public companies also may have additional documents such as management or outside advisers' presentations to the board of directors.

The appraiser should compose a list tailored as specifically as possible to the particular situation, given what is known about it at the time, and provide for one or more follow-up requests. This is because it is usually impossible to know what every relevant document will be until the appraiser has reviewed the initial batch of data and knows more about the appraisal subject.

If the appraiser can expect to receive the parties' cooperation, then the initial documents request need cover only the known essentials, and the expert can inspect additional documents during a field visit and/or include them in a supplementary request as necessary. If the parties refuse to cooperate, then the initial documents list must be as complete as possible. Even so, lists that demand voluminous material of little or no direct relevance serve no useful purpose and often delay discovery on the grounds that the demand is unreasonably burdensome. The appraiser's experience and judgment can help generate a reasonable and manageable documents list for the specific circumstances.

Business Appraisal Discovery

A business valuation is heavily influenced by the company's financial condition and its operations, so it is important for the appraiser to have the necessary and meaningful financial data regarding the subject company. Many times this data comes from outside the company and from atypical places.

Discovery can be very time-intensive. Engagements often require a high-level professional to be on site (someone who can think on his or her feet as information is discovered). In some cases, it may not be possible to delegate the assignment at all. Scheduling also becomes quite important in terms of properly managing the engagement.

Permanent Files

A set of documents that may provide meaningful information is the company's permanent files, such as the stock register, articles of incorporation, bylaws, shareholder and/or board of director meeting minutes, and other legal documents. The originals of these documents are sometimes maintained by the company's corporate counsel. Many times, these documents will contain financial projections, buy-sell agreements, evidence of prior sales of interests in the company, and so on.

Accountant's Files

The company's independent accounting firm is often a source of information. These files contain working copies of the historical financial statements and tax returns, but also will contain supporting documents, legal documents, accountants' notes, correspondence with the company, and other data which are not necessarily part of the company's records. When reviewing these records, the appraiser should understand the accountant's materiality standard. The materiality standard adopted by the accountant for financial statement reporting purposes may not be consistent with the materiality standard required for the subject litigation. For example, the company's capital expenditure practices and fixed asset recordkeeping practices may be summarized by the accountant for financial statement reporting purposes but may contain details that would be extremely relevant to the litigation. Another example is when employee stock option grants are not required to be reported on financial statements but would be critical to accurately report the per share valuation conclusion. An offer to buy or sell the company may be in the accountant's files, too.

Many times, the accountant's working papers will resolve questions that the appraiser may have, thus saving the time and expense of the appraiser replicating the already completed work. As an example, the accountant's papers may explain why certain expense categories increased or decreased from normal levels during a single accounting period, or may disclose unusual or nonrecurring income or expenses of the business. The analyst should always realize, of course, that generally accepted accounting principles allow substantial flexibility, and accounting practices for many closely held businesses may be influenced by tax issues.

Bank Files

If the company has an operating line of credit, or has used bank financing to finance the purchase of business assets, then the bank that provides the financing will maintain a loan file on the company. This bank loan file may contain many documents that are relevant to the subject valuation, including the following:

1. The loan application and financial worth statement of the company and/or the company's owner.
2. Prior financial statements of the company.
3. Memorandums from the loan officer that disclose additional information on the company or the financial statements which may not be apparent from a review of those statements.
4. Articles and other data on the company and on the industry in which the company participates.

The analyst must always consider, of course, the extent to which information submitted to the bank may paint an especially optimistic picture to support the credit accommodation. It also should be noted that accountants' files legally belong to the accountant, and bank files are the property of the bank. Therefore, in some cases, these files may not be accessible, even by subpoena, in a litigation.

Invoices

Many times a review of selected company invoices may be necessary. As an example, if the company is being valued for purposes of a marital dissolution and if the appraiser notices that the legal and accounting expenses for the business have increased substantially in the most recent financial statements, a review of the paid invoices may be in order. A review may disclose that the fees were not for business purposes but were primarily related to the owner's own personal legal and accounting problems. Also, payments near year-end may be prepayments of future expenses even though they were classified as payments for goods or services already rendered.

Interrogatories

Interrogatories are far more cumbersome than interactive questions and answers. For one thing, the next logical question often depends upon the answer to the prior question. Moreover, in an interactive situation, the respondent has the opportunity to clarify and perhaps narrow the scope of a broad inquiry, which may save considerable time and expense in complying with the inquiry. As with the documents request list, the burden of the initial interrogatories can be eased for both parties if they provide for follow-up interrogatories. In developing suggested questions, the appraiser must keep in mind both the scope of the inquiry and the clarity of wording in order to elicit what is intended and relevant. Also, as with the document request list, the appraiser's experience and judgment can be invaluable in developing relevant and incisive interrogatories.

Depositions

Information can be gathered from depositions of fact witnesses and from other expert witnesses. The appraiser can help the attorney prepare for both categories of deposition. The appraiser can suggest areas of questioning that will enhance the information on which to base his or her expert opinion. The purpose of deposing the fact witness is to get information and to ensure that the witness is as committed as far as possible to whatever the factual testimony will be.

The purpose of deposing opposing experts usually is to understand what they have done, what they have concluded, and the basis for their conclusions. In some cases, where settlement is the object, the deposition can be a powerful tool of persuasion by exposing the weaknesses in the expert's analysis. Attorneys can widen their perspective by calling on their own experts for some guidance in deposing opposing experts.

The attorney may have his or her own expert, or a member of the expert's staff, on hand when deposing the opponent's experts. The appraiser can thus point out lines of questioning that might elude the attorney but are perfectly logical to one with specific knowledge of information sources, various valuation techniques, and all the calculations and jargon current in the valuation profession. A meaningful deposition prevents experts from going into court still wondering exactly what the opposing experts did in developing their opinions. In many cases, information and insights gained through an incisive deposition can lead the parties to a settlement.

Research

Appraisers and their staffs can support litigation by providing research on such topics as economic and industry data, guideline company data, comparative transaction data, authority for positions on valuation issues, and many others. Specific research assignments may be tailored to the needs of a particular case.

The results of this research may eventually be incorporated into expert testimony or brought into evidence in other ways. Attorneys in cross-examination, arguments, and briefs also may use such information.

Calculating the Amount of Damages

Although the burden of proof regarding damages rests with the plaintiff, and at times may appear to represent a near monumental task, defendants assume significant risk when they rely upon a plaintiff's inability to calculate exact damages. This is because the court may merely require that the plaintiff's presentation be reasonable. It is essential that defendants provide expert evidence as to the actual amount of damages (or lack of damages). Otherwise, a defendant may end up facing a significant liability at the conclusion of the trial, regardless of how weak the plaintiff's presentation may have been, because that presentation was the only proof provided.

Economic damages often require or may benefit from the use of business valuation methods. Both disciplines rely heavily on the income approach method. Damages experts need not consider more than one approach or method and need not limit their examination to data that were available prior to the valuation date. Any business valuation analyst who is asked to express an opinion regarding economic damages should be careful to recognize the many differences between these two disciplines.[3]

Though the circumstances surrounding different damage claims will determine the specific type of claim filed (e.g., breach of contract, antitrust, lost business opportunity), the methods used to calculate claims are fairly standard. With the exception of breach of contract, which is often covered by liquidated damages and other provisions within the contract itself, most damage claims can be calculated by administering one or more of the following methods:

1. Before and after.
2. Yardstick (comparable).
3. Sales projection ("but for").

The Before-and-After Method

Using the before-and-after method, economic income is estimated during the damage period based upon results (1) attained prior to the alleged damaging acts, and/or (2) after the effects of the alleged acts have subsided, and either or both of these is compared with results during the period of the effect of the alleged acts. The success of this method depends, of course, on the ability of the expert to establish and support a proven historical financial record for the subject property so that operations preceding and succeeding the event are able to serve as "damage bookends," clearly illustrating the effects of the interruption or the violation period. Ideally, operations before and after the damage period will show similar trends, thereby enabling the expert to estimate the subject property's performance during the damage period using either pre- or post-damage operations as a performance standard with comparable damage amounts resulting. In many cases, only the "before" period or the "after" period is available to use to predict the "but for" performance during the damage period.

---

[3] For more information on the differences between economic damages estimates and business valuation, see John R. Phillips and Michael Joseph Wagner, "Economic Damages: Use and Abuse of Business Valuation Concepts" (Chapter 14) in *The Handbook of Advanced Business Valuation,* Robert F. Reilly and Robert P. Schweihs, eds. (New York, McGraw-Hill, 2000).

The Yardstick (Comparable) Method

The yardstick, or comparable, method requires the expert to identify companies or industries that are comparable to the plaintiff's company and plot the performance of the plaintiff's company along the lines of the comparable companies' or industry's performances. This method, of course, requires that the expert not only satisfy the often difficult task of identifying similar companies or industries, but also that the companies or industries selected by the expert be, themselves, unaffected by the alleged damaging acts of the defendant. Applying as a proxy the performance of another company or a particular industry to project the performance of the subject company, absent the alleged damaging actions of the defendant, is a straightforward, understandable method in estimating losses. Once again, the key lies in carefully identifying the most appropriate guideline companies or industry. In some instances, a comparable but unaffected branch or division of the subject company may provide the needed yardstick.

Sales Projections ("But For") Method

The sales projections, or "but for," method entails the creation of a performance model for the subject company, complete with growth and return estimates. Using the model, operations for the subject company are projected during the damage period absent (i.e., "but for") the alleged effects of the defendant's actions. The returns suggested by the model are then compared with the actual results realized by the company during the period.

Of these three methods, probably the most often applied method is some variation of the sales projection method. Typically, most business operators are in a position to provide sales projections for their businesses, and fit within one of a countless number of industries subject to annual, semiannual, or even quarterly projections by a variety of both public and private data sources. Such circumstances lend themselves quite nicely to the development of simulation models designed specifically for the subject business. However, a key factor to keep in mind when developing a sales projection and the resulting profits is that courts tend to prefer projections based on historical track records, even in light of numerous concurring industry forecasts and other published financial data regarding "normal" growth and returns for participants within the relevant industry.

Regardless of the method undertaken, the extent to which projected results exceed actual results represents the plaintiff's loss. This loss often not only represents profits lost during the damage period, but also can, and often does, represent a decrease in overall business value separate from lost profits. Whatever is represented by the total damage claim, all concerned parties should bear in mind that the sum total of combined lost profits and any decrease in overall business value is limited to the present value of total future profits anticipated by the business prior to the alleged damaging acts. The reason is that the value of any business is the present (discounted) value of all expected future profits. Intuitively, this should serve as a recurring reasonableness check throughout the calculation process.

Mitigation

The principle of mitigation suggests that even victims of contract breaches have a duty to mitigate damages—that is, to keep them as low as possible—and that damages are not recoverable for losses that the injured party could have avoided without undue risk, burden, or humiliation. Even in fraud situations, courts have long held that once a plaintiff learns of the fraud, alleged damages that accrue thereafter are not caused by the fraud, but rather by the plaintiff's decision to continue its relationship with the defendant irrespective of the plaintiff's knowledge of the fraud.

With regard to buyers and sellers of goods or services, the buyer is required by the principle of mitigation to "cover" by making reasonable efforts to find replacement goods or services to purchase, while a breached seller is obligated to make reasonable efforts to find an alternative purchaser for the breached goods or services. Excess costs incurred by the buyer in acquiring replacement goods, differences between the contract price and the resale price incurred by the seller, and incidental damages such as expenses incurred in stopping the manufacture of goods, and inspecting, transporting, receiving, or storing goods that resulted from the breach are normally recoverable.

Summary of Damages

In general, damage cases require a creative, but realistic, approach to calculating "hypothetical" values absent the alleged effects of the damaging party's actions. A thorough understanding of the damaged party's industry is important in any damage calculation, and, if available, a historical record of the damaged party's operations should be beneficial. Knowledge of case law will provide the expert with important guidance regarding approaches and methods that the courts will or will not accept in the calculation of damages in the specific legal context in question.

Work Product

Reports that the expert may provide can range from an oral expression of the analysis and conclusions, a single letter addressing a single fact or conclusion, to a detailed narrative report.

Affidavits

The purpose of an affidavit is to put a sworn statement before the court without the author's physical presence. Affidavits are most commonly used in connection with pretrial matters, but sometimes they are introduced as evidence in a trial. The subject matter of an affidavit can be anything from scheduling information, such as the days on which an expert is and is not available for testimony, to a statement of an expert's opinion with a summary of the supporting reasons. Care must be given as to the information provided because it can be damaging to the credibility of the affiant if later his or her opinion changes during the course of the trial.

Written Reports

For valuation cases in some jurisdictions, it is mandatory for the opposing parties to exchange written reports no later than 30 days prior to the call of the trial docket. In U.S. Tax Court, for example, the expert report typically serves as the appraiser's direct testimony. In other jurisdictions, the manner in which expert opinion is expressed is a critical component of the litigation strategy and is left to the attorney's discretion. In such jurisdictions, some attorneys insist on a written report, others decide whether to have a written report on a case-by-case basis. Some attorneys believe that a written report or even knowledge that a written report is available detracts from the court's attention to the expert's testimony during the trial. If a written report is to be prepared for litigation purposes, then it normally will follow the guidelines discussed in Chapter 20, Writing an Appraisal Report.

Summary

This chapter has presented a brief discussion of many of the important litigation support services that an appraiser or economist can provide in addition to expert testimony. It is beneficial to engage the expert's assistance at an early point in the litigation proceedings so that such services, particularly as they relate to the discovery process, can be fully integrated with the anticipated expert testimony. Very often, the expert's services may facilitate a settlement rather than culminate in expert testimony in court.

Although the appraiser may be of great assistance in many ways in preparing and administrating the case, it is essential that the attorney and the client fully respect the appraiser's independence in arriving at any opinion. The appraiser should not only avoid bias in fact, the appraiser should also avoid the appearance of bias. For this reason, it may be preferable to have certain litigation support services performed by another appraiser. In any case, the effective use of the appraiser's expertise in providing litigation support services can facilitate an expeditious and satisfactory outcome in many controversy cases.

Chapter 40

Expert Testimony

"Give your evidence," said the King; "and don't be nervous, or I'll have you executed on the spot."[1]

Court testimony challenges an expert witness because it is part of an adversarial proceeding. If the opposite side were willing to accept the witness's valuation, there probably would be a settlement instead of a trial. Indeed, most valuation cases settle before they reach the courtroom, especially if the witness has prepared the case thoroughly and the attorney has drawn on the expert's research in negotiating with the opposition. Thus, if the case goes to court, it's because of sharp disagreement. Competent, thorough preparation must culminate in a clear and convincing presentation.

It is essential that an analyst be objective and unbiased when legal testimony is involved. One school of thought holds that since courts in some situations tend to split the difference between opposing positions, an analyst must take an extreme position, because that is the only strategy that will lead to a fair court result. To be effective, the expert witness should arrive at a figure that he or she expects to present and defend without compromise on cross-examination. Usually, a rigorously prepared, convincingly presented, objective case will prevail over an extreme position, which a competent judge will tend to discredit. The only reasonable expectation is that courts will adopt the well-supported position of one side of a case without compromise.[2] Before preparing the presentation of the analysis, consider the typical areas of impeachment:

- Unsatisfactory credentials.
- Advocacy or bias.
- Contrary prior opinions.
- Report inconsistencies.
- Faulty facts or foundation.
- Incompetent authority.
- Insufficient or inaccurate data.

This chapter follows the typical sequence of a business valuation expert witness engagement. As it relates to damage cases, this chapter focuses on the damages calculations and not on the "liability" or "causation" portions of such cases.

Background Preparation

When legal controversy is involved, there is no substitute for thorough homework and preparation. The expert witness virtually must prepare not only his or her own case, but the other side's as well. The expert valuation witness must attempt to anticipate any apparent weaknesses that the opposing attorney may seize upon in cross-examination and be prepared to defend against attacks on them. Also, the expert witness should be prepared to critique the case the opposing side presents.

Basic Preparation and Documentation

The basic research itself should follow the principles and procedures previously outlined in this book. In legal testimony, one must rely as much as possible on facts,

---

[1] Lewis Carroll, *Alice's Adventures in Wonderland* (Middlesex, England: Puffin Books, Penguin Books, Ltd., 1946).

[2] See, for example, *Estate of Saul R. Gilford v. Commissioner*, 88 T.C. 38 (1987); *Estate of Albert L. Dougherty v. Commissioner*, 59 T.C.M. 772 (1990); and *Estate of Eric Stroben v. Commissioner*, T.C. Memo 1992-350 (June 22, 1992).

not on conjecture. Documentation is the foundation of every step. It makes no difference how thoroughly the witness is personally convinced of the validity of the facts and conclusions if he or she is unable to convince the court. While complete documentation undoubtedly helps the opposition, omitting or obscuring helpful information deprives the judge and the jury of useful assistance.

If the witness were presenting the company in question to a prospective buyer, it might be valid to presume that the buyer knows something about the business or industry involved. However, an appraiser cannot presume that the court can have the prospective buyer's sophistication about every business brought before it. Every fact on which the witness intends to rely in reaching his or her conclusion must be presented, along with whatever supporting documentation is necessary for convincing the court that it should indeed rely upon that fact.

Moreover, unlike the situation of presenting the company to a prospective buyer, in which the analyst would have an opportunity, at the buyer's request, to research and provide supplementary information, the expert has no such chance in court. The analyst cannot take a couple of weeks to do additional homework and come back for another audience. The court, however concerned it may be with reaching an equitable decision, will make its determination based on the initial presentation, however inadequate. Thus, the research had better be thorough the first time around.

Federal Rules of Civil Procedure

Rule 26 of the *Federal Rules of Civil Procedure* took effect December 1, 1993. Particularly relevant for expert witnesses are the requirements for disclosure of expert testimony:

(2) *Disclosure of Expert Testimony.*

   (A) In addition to the disclosures required by paragraph (1), a party shall disclose to other parties the identity of any person who may be used at trial to present evidence under rules 702, 703, or 705 of the federal rules of evidence.

   (B) Except as otherwise stipulated or directed by the court. This disclosure shall, with respect to a witness, who is retained or specially employed to provide expert testimony in the case or whose duties as an employee of the party regularly involve giving expert testimony, be accompanied by a written report prepared and signed by the witness. The report shall contain a complete statement of all opinions to be expressed and the basis and reasons therefore; the data or other information considered by the witness in forming the opinions; any exhibits to be used as a summary of or support for the opinions; the qualifications of the witness, including a list of all publications authored by the witness within the preceding 10 years; the compensation to be paid for the study and testimony; and a listing of any other cases in which the witness has testified as an expert at trial or by deposition within the preceding four years.

   (C) These disclosures shall be made at the times and in the sequence directed by the court. In the absence of other directions from the court or stipulation by the parties, the disclosures shall be made at least 90 days before the trial date or the date the case is to be ready for trial or, if the evidence is intended solely to contradict or rebut evidence on the same subject matter identified by another party under paragraph (2)(b), within 30 days after the disclosure made by the other party. The parties shall supplement these disclosures when required under subdivision (e)(1).[3]

State Rules Often Less Stringent

Many states have less rigid requirements than the federal rules. In some states, no report is required. Sometimes the attorney obtains the opposing expert's views only at deposition. Sometimes the opposing expert's views are presented only in brief summary form in the opposing attorney's answers to interrogatories. In the extreme, there are times when the opposing expert's positions and evidence are only learned for the first time at trial. The expert should discuss with the attorney what the local requirements are.

Discovery

If the managers of the business being valued are unwilling to cooperate with the witness, they can make it difficult to get the information necessary for doing the job. The analyst must keep legal counsel apprised of what documents need to be reviewed, what facilities should be visited, and who needs to be interviewed. The expert witness must provide this information as early as possible so that if the opposition parties procrastinate, the analyst will not be responsible for failing to complete a thorough valuation study. As noted in the previous chapter, the expert witness also should keep the attorney informed of the timeliness and adequacy of the information received. That way, the attorney can follow up on missing data and report accurately to the court on how promptly and completely the information was supplied.

Reading Prior Cases and Articles

Part of the homework for testifying on a valuation issue is to become familiar, if possible, with relevant prior court cases. The full texts of the cases, rather than only the digests various services provide, often provide insight to the expert witness that would otherwise be overlooked. Although the digests help keep one abreast of day-to-day developments in the field, they are a weak substitute for the detail of the full text when addressing a specific case. It also can help to read articles by other experts analyzing particular cases or categories of cases.

Significant court cases on valuations for various purposes are cited throughout the book.[4] These are not to be considered substitutes for fresh research. The expert should ask counsel for any relevant cases he or she is aware of. The attorney should also provide the expert with any relevant cases he or she knows of. The expert also may do independent research for cases dealing with relevant issues.

Federal Rules of Evidence Regarding Expert Testimony

Federal Rules of Evidence 702 through 705 govern testimony by expert witnesses. As this edition goes to press, the U.S. Supreme Court has approved and forwarded

---

[3] FED. R. CIV. P. 26.

[4] See, especially, Chapters 28, 31, 33, 36, and 38. The full texts of cases cited in this book are available to subscribers of the business valuation on-line library at www.BVLibrary.com.

to Congress amendments to Rules 702 and 703. Unless Congress takes specific action, these changes become effective December 1, 2000. We consider it unlikely that Congress will change the Supreme Court recommendations. Therefore, Exhibit 40–1 presents Rules 702 through 705 as amended. The italicized portions of Rules 702 and 703 represent the language added by the amendments.

The most important parts of the amendments are the extension of Rule 702 to encompass the concepts of the *Daubert* and *Kumho Tire* cases (discussed later) to make them applicable to *all* expert testimony, not just scientific testimony.[5]

Use of Hearsay Evidence

The opposing attorney probably will object to any testimony the expert witness offers that might be classified as hearsay. The term *hearsay* refers broadly to any information obtained from third parties without personal verification. The expert witness should not, however, avoid collecting information and opinions from other people if they are relevant. The judge has a great deal of latitude in deciding what evidence to consider and usually wants to hear anything that might help reach an equitable decision. Most judges are reluctant to disallow any potentially relevant testimony on technical grounds, especially if there is no jury. Once the witness has been qualified to testify as an expert before the court, judges tend to want to hear what he or she has to say. They want to know how the witness reached his or her opinion, even if portions of the testimony would be disallowed as hearsay in certain other legal proceedings. The judge can then determine what weight, if any, to accord any statements in the testimony. Rule 703 of the Federal Rules of Evidence states:

> The facts or data in the particular case upon which an expert bases an opinion or inference may be those perceived by or made known to him at or before the hearing. If of a type reasonably relied upon by experts in the particular field in forming opinions or inferences upon the subject, the facts or data need not be admissible in evidence.[6]

Correctly analyzed, it is the opinion of the expert that is the evidence, not the hearsay information that supports it. The key phrase in the above quotation from the Federal Rules is "*reasonably relied upon by experts in the particular field in forming opinions.*" Particularly in business valuation, the expert often derives important portions of information from conversations with other people. The expert may conduct some interviews personally, and members of his or her project team may conduct others. If the use of such information may provoke controversy, the attorney should ask the expert a question, or a series of questions, on the stand to ensure that the court understands that analysts typically rely on such information in the course of valuing businesses.

Nevertheless, the witness runs the risk that anything that could be considered hearsay may be disallowed or accorded little or no weight in the court's deliberations. Therefore, the expert should take all feasible steps to make any research that might be considered hearsay both admissible and convincing. If the expert is surveying customers, suppliers, or competitors to obtain information on industry practices, the larger the sample, the better. Using specific names and companies to

---

[5] There are extensive and very relevant Advisory Committee notes too lengthy to reproduce here. They are available in full to subscribers at www.BVLibrary.com.

[6] FED. R. EVID. 703.

Exhibit 40–1

Federal Rules of Evidence Rules 702–705

Rule 702. Testimony by Experts
If scientific, technical, or other specialized knowledge will assist the trier of fact to understand the evidence or to determine a fact in issue, a witness qualified as an expert by knowledge, skill, experience, training, or education, may testify thereto in the form of an opinion or otherwise, *if (1) the testimony is based upon sufficient facts or data, (2) the testimony is the product of reliable principles and methods, and (3) the witness has applied the principles and methods reliably to the facts of the case.*

Rule 703. Bases of Opinion Testimony by Experts
The facts or data in the particular case upon which an expert bases an opinion or inference may be those perceived by or made known to the expert at or before the hearing. If of a type reasonably relied upon by experts in the particular field in forming opinions or inferences upon the subject, the facts or data need not be admissible in evidence *in order for the opinion or inference to be admitted. Facts or data that are otherwise inadmissible shall not be disclosed to the jury by the proponent of the opinion or inference unless the court determines that their probative value in assisting the jury to evaluate the expert's opinion substantially outweighs their prejudicial effect.*

Rule 704. Opinion on Ultimate Issue
    (a) Except as provided in subdivision (b), testimony in the form of an opinion or inference otherwise admissible is not objectionable because it embraces an ultimate issue to be decided by the trier of fact.
    (b) No expert witness testifying with respect to the mental state or condition of a defendant in a criminal case may state an opinion or inference as to whether the defendant did or did not have the mental state or condition constituting an element of the crime charged or of a defense thereto. Such ultimate issues are matters for the trier of fact alone.

Rule 705. Disclosure of Facts or Data Underlying Expert Opinion
The expert may testify in terms of opinion or inference and give reasons therefor without first testifying to the underlying facts or data, unless the court requires otherwise. The expert may in any event be required to disclose the underlying facts or data on cross-examination.

SOURCE: Excerpted from FED R. EVID. (Rules 702–705).

identify who said what will tend to make the testimony more acceptable than using confidential sources.

    To be on the safe side, though, the expert should structure the research and conclusion so that anything that could be considered hearsay is not essential to the conclusion. That way, rather than being dependent upon questionable evidence, the conclusion is supported by it.

Challenges to Testimony per *Daubert/Kumho*

In recent years, there have been three U.S. Supreme Court cases in which lower courts' decisions to exclude expert testimony have been upheld. It is no longer unusual for expert witness testimony to be disallowed because it does not comport with prevailing standards.

Daubert

In the *Daubert*[7] case, a doctor testified before the trial court and presented a radical medical opinion. That opinion was unsupported by either the relevant professional literature, the medical research scientific standards, the recognized professional

---

[7] *Daubert v. Merrell Dow Pharmaceuticals, Inc.*, 509 U.S. 579 (1993).

organizations, or any concurring medical research colleagues. With regard to the admission of this testimony, the questions that the trial court faced were (1) Was the doctor truly a scientific expert or merely a "hired gun?" and (2) Was the expert testimony based on medical expertise or on "junk science?" With regard to the admissibility of expert testimony, the *Daubert* court applied four factors to determine the reliability of a particular expert's scientific theory or technique:

1. Testing—can the theory or technique be tested, or has it been tested?
2. Peer reviews—has the theory been subjected to peer review or publication, which aids in determining flaws in the method?
3. Error rates—are there established standards to control the use of the technique?
4. Acceptability—is the technique generally accepted in the relevant technical community?

In its decision, the Supreme Court noted that the *Daubert* factors should be applied flexibly,[8] that the four factors were merely illustrative, and that other factors could argue in favor of testimony admissibility.

General Electric v. Joiner

In *General Electric Co. v. Joiner*,[9] the Supreme Court held that whether the specific *Daubert* factors are appropriate measures of reliability in a particular case is a matter the law grants the trial judge broad latitude to determine—the same broad latitude that the trial judge enjoys with respect to his or her ultimate reliability determination.

Kumho Tire Company

In *Kumho Tire Company v. Carmichael*,[10] the U.S. Supreme Court clearly ruled that the *Daubert* factors do not apply only to "scientific" experts, but to all "technical" or "other specialized" experts, as well. The defendants moved to exclude expert testimony at trial on the grounds that his methodology failed to satisfy Rule 702 of the Federal Rules of Evidence. The Appeals Court held that the District Court had erred as a matter of law in its application of the four *Daubert* factors. The Appeals Court ruled that (1) *Daubert* was limited only to a scientific context and (2) the *Daubert* factors could not be applied to testimony that was characterized as "skill-or-experience-based." The defendants appealed.

The Supreme Court made the following unambiguous statement:

> Rule 702 does not distinguish between "scientific" knowledge and "technical" and "other specialized" knowledge, but makes it clear that any such knowledge might be the subject of expert testimony.

Accordingly, the Court excluded the expert's testimony based on the *Daubert* factors.

---

[8] The court's gatekeeper function regarding admissibility of experts is not limited to scientific experts. See *Kumho Tire Company, Ltd., et al. v. Patrick Carmichael, et al.*, 119 S.Ct. 1167 (Mar. 23, 1999).

[9] *General Electric Co. v. Joiner*, 522 U.S. 136 (1997).

[10] *Kumho Tire Company v. Carmichael*, 199 S.Ct. 1167 (Mar. 23, 1999).

Other Cases Rely on *Daubert* Factors

Several trial courts (and appeals courts) have applied the *Daubert* factors to exclude valuation-related expert testimony. The damages issue in one case[11] involved the fair market value of the plaintiffs' shares of a closely held corporation. The plaintiffs' expert used only one valuation method (a discounted cash flow method) that relied upon speculative financial projections. Applying the four *Daubert* factors to test the admission of the expert testimony under Rule 702, the District Court judge concluded that undue prejudice would be caused if the court allowed the "highly speculative testimony."

In another case,[12] the opinion regarding fair market value of plaintiff's partnership interests in a real estate development company was not allowed. Again, the plaintiff's expert used only one valuation method (again, a discounted cash flow method) to value the subject partnership interests. Explaining its exclusion of the valuation-related expert testimony, the U.S. Court of Appeals specifically noted that the valuation expert "conceded that he did not employ the methodology that experts in valuation find essential."

Depositions

The term *depose* means to *state under oath but not in open court*. It is common practice for the opposing attorney to take an expert witness's deposition some time before the trial, for several reasons. One is to help the attorney assess the relative strengths of the opponent's case for guidance on whether to offer or accept a settlement and, if so, on what basis. Another reason is to try to learn enough about the witness and his or her testimony in advance to prepare a cross-examination that will damage the testimony's credibility. Still another reason is that an attorney can sometimes embarrass or discredit a witness by bringing out inconsistencies between deposition testimony and trial testimony.

The time and place of the deposition is determined by the attorneys subject to the expert's availability. Some attorneys like to take depositions of experts well in advance of trial, but also expect the experts to complete trial preparation prior to the deposition. Obviously, a witness cannot disclose the results of research not yet completed. Therefore, there is an inherent conflict between the desire for an early deposition and the desire for the work to be as complete as possible.

What to Take to the Deposition

The expert should ask the attorney what to take to the deposition, unless a subpoena with clear instructions has been served. The necessary materials will vary greatly from one situation to another. Instructions for depositions have varied all the way from taking absolutely nothing to taking every document and working paper in the file.

---

[11] *Andrew J. Whelan, et al. v. Tyler Abell, et al.*, Nos. 87-442 and 87-1763 U.S. Dist. Ct. (D.C.), Memorandum Opinion on the Disqualification of Plaintiffs' Proposed Expert Witness issued July 25, 1997 (prior to the case in chief).

[12] *Frymire-Brinati v. KPMG Peat Marwick*, 3 F.3d 183 (7th Cir., 1993).

Keep in mind that everything taken to a deposition must be made available to opposing counsel if demanded. The Federal Rules of Evidence[13] and many state rules also entitle the adverse party to demand production of any document used by a witness before a deposition or trial to refresh his or her memory for purposes of his or her testimony.

If there is any question, the expert's attorney should advise the expert as to which items opposing counsel are entitled to see and which they are not. Obviously, before the deposition, the attorney and the analyst should review all work papers, correspondence, memos, and any other material in the case file. By doing so, the attorney will gain a thorough knowledge of the information used and also get a chance to review the material for items, if any, that are not subject to discovery by the opposing attorney because of attorney-client privilege. The attorney should have this opportunity even when the deposition is pursuant to a subpoena that specifies what is to be brought.

Deposition Testimony

The witness will be sworn in, and the deposing attorney will introduce himself or herself and state a few basic ground rules, which include the witness's right to have any question repeated or clarified.

The opposing attorney will ask most, if not all, of the questions. The scope of allowable questions varies considerably from one situation to another, but often it is quite broad. It usually starts with the expert's background. Attorneys often ask about the expert's past valuation work, other testimony, and work on past cases of a similar nature in the hope of finding something that will appear to contradict the witness's positions in the current case.

The question of work done for other clients is sensitive, because much of the information may be confidential. According to the Ethics Provision of the *Uniform Standards of Professional Appraisal Practice*, "An appraiser must protect the confidential nature of the appraiser-client relationship." The expert must advise the attorney that he or she cannot divulge confidential information without the client's permission. If uncertain about how to handle this or any other matter, the witness may request a recess in order to consult with his or her attorney.

For the most part, the general rules applicable to courtroom testimony, discussed later in this chapter, also apply in deposition testimony. The expert is not required to provide any more information than the question specifically calls for—and normally should not. The two worst faults of some expert witnesses are unresponsiveness and over-responsiveness, that is, giving answers beyond the scope of the question. A good way for the witness to make sure that he or she understands the question is to repeat it in his or her mind. This process allows a few seconds to stay composed (and not say anything that might later be regretted) and permits the witness to think about the words used in the question. If any of the words or phrases are not clear, the witness should ask a question to clarify the meaning before answering.

Once certain that he or she understands the question, the expert should answer forthrightly, to the point, and as briefly as possible. It is not the witness's responsibility to assist examining counsel by rephrasing questions the way they should have been asked or to volunteer information, no matter how pertinent, that the question did not address.

---

[13] Fed. R. Evid. 612.

The attorney often tries to fence in the witness with a question such as, "Is that everything you considered in forming your opinion?" The witness usually should insist on leaving the gate open with something like, "That's everything I can recall at this time."

Also, the witness should not accept as true, assumptions made by the questioner. A document may not state exactly what an attorney says it states. "Isn't it true . . . ?" does not mean that it is true. Witnesses should beware of hypotheticals because they could be traps. The analyst should make sure the questioner clearly states all assumptions in the hypothetical, and write them down if necessary. Then he or she should consider repeating all of the assumptions in the answer including, if appropriate, a statement that these assumptions do not correspond with the facts of the case at hand.

The expert should remember that although the deposition results in a written transcript, pauses generally do not appear in the text. Before starting to talk, the witness should take time to frame a concise answer that will read well in the transcript.

After the Deposition

The witness has the right to receive, read, and make any corrections to the transcript of the deposition, or he or she may waive that right. Although court reporters generally are incredibly fast and accurate, they do make mistakes—and occasionally the mistakes can make a good point pointless or, at worst, totally change the meaning, such as by leaving out a "not." Also, reading over the transcript of the deposition is a constructive exercise for the witness, because it helps call attention to any weakness or disorganization, which the witness can correct before the trial.

Further, the witness has the right to check and recheck data as thoroughly as desired. Any errors found at any time between the deposition date and the court date should be corrected. If the opposing attorney tries to embarrass the witness with the inconsistency in court, the witness should state frankly that the material was preliminary at the time of the deposition and that the process of checking the material disclosed an error that subsequently was corrected.

Outlining Courtroom Testimony

In preparing for courtroom testimony, it is important to know what the format of the trial will be. Legal counsel will be pursuing his or her "theme" for the case, and the format of the expert witness testimony should complement the case's legal strategy (in presentation format, not in opinion). Whether a judge or a jury will be making the decision can affect how detailed the testimony must be, the nature and size of exhibits, and much of the style of testimony. Most business valuation cases are tried before a judge without a jury. Even if the parties have a right to a jury trial, attorneys on both sides usually opt to waive that right in business valuation cases, partly because of the extra time and cost of dealing with a jury. Moreover, it is very difficult to educate lay people about the complexities of business valuation within the tight time frame and structured format of a jury trial. Consequently, regardless of how conscientious and well intentioned the jury may be, most attorneys consider them too unpredictable for business valuation cases.

Regardless of the format, the expert witness and the attorney must spend time together preparing the presentation. The witness should know what areas of questions to expect in order to prepare direct and complete answers. The attorney needs to know what evidence the expert witness has prepared to be sure of getting all of it presented. Some attorneys like to put the expert witness on the stand and ask one broad question, such as, "Will you please describe your investigation and findings as to the value of XYZ Company?" Most attorneys prefer to develop the case logically and point by point in a format of questions and short answers between the attorney and the witness.

In some instances, the judge issues a pretrial order requiring each side of the case to prepare and exchange formal, written reports and then find areas of agreement and disagreement among themselves, limiting the verbal testimony to the unresolved issues.

It is legal counsel's decision as to who should prepare the first draft of the question list. Whether the attorney or the witness, the direct testimony usually proceeds in more or less the following sequence:

1. Identification and qualifications of the witness.
2. Description of the assignment.
3. Conclusion.
4. Steps taken in carrying out the assignment.
5. Findings.
6. Restatement of the conclusion.

Qualifying the Witness

Qualifying the witness as an expert is an essential first step in establishing the witness's credibility in the court's eyes. This step usually establishes not only the witness's expertise on the subject of business valuation, but his or her position and affiliations, making it clear that the witness is independent of the company being valued and the parties to the suit.

Frequently, opposing counsel gratuitously offers to stipulate that the witness qualifies as an expert. This offer should usually be rejected. The attorney calling the expert wants to acquaint the judge and/or jury firsthand with the expert and his or her qualifications relevant to the forthcoming testimony. This is his or her opportunity to sell the witness as a person with strong credentials to support the valuation opinion. The extent of the qualifying process varies considerably from one case to another, but it usually proceeds approximately along the following sequence and format.

Education. The qualifications usually start with academic degrees and relevant nondegree programs.

Professional Credentials. Professional credentials are the expert's professional designations and affiliations. Since appraisal and financial analysis designations (such as ASA and CFA) are less known to most courts than accounting designations such as CPA, it often is appropriate to explain to the court the nature of these designations and the qualifications required for attaining them. Professional involvements such as holding office and/or serving on committees also may be covered at this point, as well as special honors or recognition.

Publications and Teaching. Books and/or articles written, appraisal courses taught, and a summary of relevant professional appraisal lectures given usually logically follow professional credentials.

Employment History. The focus should be on the portion of the witness's employment history that bears on his or her qualifications as an appraiser. It may focus on the scope of the appraisal work of the firm that employs the analyst and on the analyst's involvement in that work.

Experience Particularly Relevant to the Case at Bench. The expert's relevant experience may be past appraisal work on companies in the same industry and/or may focus on past experience with appraisals involving similar issues.

Description of the Assignment

The description of the assignment usually includes such information as when and who retained the witness and what the assignment was, including the standard of value to be used. This information is similar to that included in the description of the assignment section of a written report as discussed in Chapter 2, Defining the Assignment.

The matter of the witness's compensation may be raised, either by the attorney on direct examination or by the opposing attorney on cross-examination. Whether the compensation is a flat fee or on an hourly basis, it is a good idea for the witness to come to court prepared to answer the question of how many hours have been spent in preparation. If the witness has carried out all the steps in the valuation process suggested in this book, he or she will have spent many hours, and testimony to that effect will lend further support to the thoroughness of the preparation.

Summary of Conclusion

Once the witness has been qualified and the assignment defined, most attorneys ask the witness to state his or her valuation conclusion, before describing the research undertaken to reach it, very much as the introduction to a written appraisal report summarizes the ultimate conclusion. Some attorneys prefer to wait until the entire research project has been described before having the witness present the conclusion. In this, as in all other procedural matters in testimony, the attorney's judgment should prevail. In some states, evidentiary rules require that the research testimony precede the opinion.

Description of Steps Taken

The description of the steps taken in reaching the valuation conclusion should include the sources of information, such as those that appear in the written report, plus brief statements of what was obtained from the various sources. For example, in listing persons interviewed, the witness might relate at this point in the testimony which subjects were discussed. In listing written information sources, the witness also might discuss which pieces of information were obtained from each source. On the other hand, the style of the testimony, as determined by legal counsel, may call for the expert witness to merely explain that information was gathered as was necessary to reach a reasonable conclusion.

Findings

According to the *Uniform Standards of Professional Appraisal Practice*:

Each written or oral business or intangible asset appraisal report must:

(a) clearly and accurately set forth the appraisal in a manner that will not be misleading.

(b) contain sufficient information to enable the intended user(s) to understand it. Any specific limiting conditions concerning information should be noted.

(c) clearly and accurately disclose any extraordinary assumption or hypothetical condition that directly affects the appraisal and indicate its impact on value.[14]

Even oral testimony about the research findings should cover the remainder of the information discussed in Chapter 20, Writing an Appraisal Report. Findings include pertinent aspects of the economic outlook, the industry in which the company operates and the company's position in that industry, a description of the company, and the analysis leading to the valuation conclusion.

Final Conclusion

Even though in valuing the company at issue the appraiser probably has used several valuation approaches and has come up with a reasonable range of possible values, the concluding statement usually should be a single figure and a restatement of the standard of value. The attorney probably will ask the witness to state the conclusion in a manner similar to this: "It is my opinion that the fair market value of ABC Grocery Company, as of the valuation date, is $163 per share." The attorney usually will also ask whether all the procedures followed in the valuation have been in accordance with generally accepted business valuation principles and procedures, or, more commonly recently, in conformance with USPAP.

Exhibits

Naturally, an important part of preparing for court testimony is creating exhibits that will help communicate the thoroughness and credibility of the valuation. In addition to the written valuation opinion report, such exhibits usually include any charts, pictures, or other supporting material that may assist the court in understanding the business and how it should be valued.

In courtroom testimony, the old adage, "A picture is worth a thousand words," is particularly true. It may be wise to avoid spreadsheets, and to use clearly understandable graphs and charts instead. The witness probably has seen and toured the company's facilities; the judge very likely has not. Since the court usually can't go to the facilities, the next best thing is to bring the facilities to the court. Through photographs, the witness can give a "walking tour" of the business, giving the court a better understanding of what is being valued and, one would hope, making the financial analysis more meaningful. The pictures used in the courtroom usually can be prints that the judge can see and that can be entered as official exhibits. If the proceeding is a jury trial, the attorney and witness may wish to present the pictures as slides so that all parties in the courtroom can see the same thing while the witness

---

[14] Standards Rule 10-1, *Uniform Standards of Professional Appraisal Practice*, 2000 edition (Washington, DC: The Appraisal Foundation, 2000), p. 66.

is describing the company's operations. If a slide or computer presentation is used, copies should be prepared for possible submission as exhibits.

For exhibits of a size and format that can be readily copied, such as 8½-by-11-inch pages, such as would be included in a written report, it is convenient to prepare an extra set for the judge in addition to the set to be labeled by the clerk and entered as the official exhibit in the court record. Doing so will make it convenient for the judge to look at the tables and other exhibits while the witness is discussing them in direct testimony, as well as during cross-examination. It is also a courtesy, and in some cases a requirement, to provide a set of copies for the opposing attorney.

The exhibits the witness proposes to use should be reviewed with the attorney who will conduct the examination to ensure that all are appropriate and are legally admissible.

Preparation with the Attorney

Once the testimony outline and exhibits have been drafted, the attorney should review them thoroughly with the expert. The attorney should understand the significance of the major points in the expert's work in order to be able to phrase questions most meaningfully, spend the most time on the most salient points, and know what topics, if any, to revisit on redirect examination. The expert should be sure to understand any legal issues that bear on the testimony and how his or her testimony fits into the overall case. Even though the trial attorney is preoccupied and under pressure, both he or she and the appraiser must understand how important it is to work together to prepare a well-focused and persuasive presentation of the expert's work. All too often the attorney fails to gain the full impact of the expert's knowledge and research because of inadequate preparation.

In the Courtroom

The expert should appear in court as rested, alert, and neatly groomed as possible. In general, the witness should take what he or she expects to have to refer to, a calculator, perhaps a note pad, and no more. If asked questions about any document, the witness is entitled to request a copy of it and examine it. Documents should be sufficiently organized so that the witness will have little trouble finding references.

The witness should not plan to read testimony except quotations from documents when it is important to have the record reflect the document's exact wording. An outline of testimony points might help ensure that the witness overlooks no important point. The expert should keep in mind, however, that opposing counsel may examine and copy all materials brought to or referred to while on the witness stand.

General Guidelines for Testimony

Perhaps the most critical thing for the witness to keep in mind in the courtroom is the need to be objective and unbiased—not an advocate. An advocate is defined as "one who pleads the cause of another" or "one who supports something as a cause." Pleading and supporting the client's cause is the attorney's role. The expert witness's role is to present the facts as they are and to use his or her professional expertise to interpret those facts to reach an objective conclusion.

Another key responsibility on the witness stand is to respond to the questions asked. The witness first must pay attention to the question and be sure of understanding it, and should pause long enough before answering to (1) allow any objections to be made by the attorneys, and (2) be *sure* that the answer will satisfy the question. If unsure whether the question is understood, the witness should ask for clarification.

Although answers should be concise but complete, how far to go is a matter of judgment. However, the witness definitely should avoid introducing material or ideas irrelevant to the question. Nevertheless, there is a fine line of judgment. A question may be worded such that a direct answer without clarification could leave a misleading impression. Naturally, in such cases the witness should volunteer the necessary clarification. (Of course, such questions are more likely to come from the opposing attorney during cross-examination, because he or she either doesn't understand the material or wishes to lead the witness into creating a false impression.)

The witness should speak distinctly and slowly enough for the judge and attorneys to understand the ideas and for the court reporter to type the words into the record. If it is necessary to use proper names or esoteric terminology, the appraiser should spell them so that the court reporter can enter them into the record correctly.

The witness should make enough eye contact with the judge and/or jury to ensure that they are following the testimony and understanding the ideas. If not sure whether the judge and/or jury understands, the witness should pause and rephrase the point more clearly. The key point is that the witness is trying to communicate to the trier of fact—either judge or jury—*not* to the client's counsel or opposing counsel.

In general, the expert witness should avoid technical language and jargon. Usually there is no reason to believe that the judge and/or jurors are trained in the very technical discipline of business valuation or in the specifics of the industry in which the subject business operates. If a technical term is necessary for making a point, it should be defined or explained in terms intelligible to a lay person.

In referring to an exhibit, the witness should say something like, "I direct your attention to Exhibit 10" and give the judge time to find Exhibit 10 before proceeding.

The witness should avoid distracting mannerisms and utterances such as "well," "ummm," and uhhh." Unconscious habits, such as clicking a ballpoint pen or tapping a pencil, should be eliminated.

Otherwise, the witness should be his or her natural self, exuding competence and confidence but never arrogance.

Direct Examination

The expert witness must be careful not to omit any material facts, even (or especially) if their implications do not support the client's case. One should always assume that the opposing attorney and expert witness are properly prepared (even if one suspects they are not) and will not allow any facts that help their position to be overlooked. If the expert witness omits material facts, whether because of incompetence or advocacy, his or her credibility with the court will be in question. It is also essential that the expert witness not distort any facts or their interpretations. "Straightforward" is a good key word to go by.

Whether the expert enters all exhibits in one batch at the beginning of the testimony or one by one as they become relevant is a matter of preference. Many attorneys think the latter approach helps keep the court's attention focused on the subject at hand. After the oral qualification of the expert witness, his or her written credentials may be entered as an exhibit. From that point forward, each exhibit can be introduced immediately before the witness discusses it so that the judge can view it as the witness describes and interprets it.

Exhibits are numbered by the court as they are entered, and usually other exhibits have been entered earlier in the case; therefore, the witness's Table II may be the court's Exhibit 15, for example. As the exhibits are entered, the witness should write the court's exhibit number at the top of his or her own copy, since that usually is how the exhibit will be identified when the witness is called to discuss it on cross-examination.

The witness should not be surprised if the opposing attorney raises frequent objections. He or she may object to the form or substance of a question, an answer given by a witness, or the introduction of an exhibit. When an objection is raised, the witness must pause while the attorneys argue it out, then proceed when so instructed by the judge or by the attorney conducting the examination.

Cross-Examination

It is the opposing attorney's job to expose to the court any weaknesses in the expert witness's testimony. The witness should not take it personally. The attorney may attempt to discredit the witness in various ways, such as asking questions designed to attack the witness's competence to present expert testimony on the valuation issue at hand or to bring out possible conflicts of interest that would impugn the witness's independence. If the witness has testified in previous cases, he or she should assume that the opposing attorney has read the transcripts of such cases and will ask questions to bring out any apparent inconsistencies between previous and present testimony. The witness also should assume that the attorney has reviewed all the books and articles that he or she has written.

As discussed earlier, in preparing for direct testimony the witness also must prepare for cross-examination. If the witness did not use a particular approach that may seem reasonable on the surface, he or she should be prepared to explain why. If the witness did not use a company as a comparative, he or she should be prepared to explain why the company was disqualified. (This particular problem will be taken care of almost automatically if the procedures outlined in Chapter 11, Market Approach: Guideline Publicly Traded Company Method, are followed and documented.)

Some attorneys use a cross-examination technique of asking questions in a manner designed to leave the court with an impression that they might like to convey but that may be misleading. A favorite ploy is to carefully frame a complicated question so as to leave a certain impression and then demand a yes or no answer. The witness should realize that he or she cannot be compelled to limit the answer to yes or no if it would not be completely appropriate. The witness has the right to clarify the answer and should demand to be allowed to do so if failure to clarify would leave a misimpression. The witness should first answer yes or no if it is possible to do so and then give the clarification. If it is a compound question and the answer is yes to one or more parts and no to others, the witness should make clear to which part or parts each response refers. If the question simply cannot be answered yes or no, the witness should explain why. The witness also may request the attorney to rephrase a question, either for clarification or to "unbundle" a compound question.

Another cross-examination ploy is to ask a question that contains a misleading presumption. In such a case, the witness must correct the false presumption in the answer; otherwise, he or she will risk leaving the impression of accepting the false premise.

It also is common for cross-examining attorneys to mischaracterize a witness's prior testimony, reading into it some impression that was never intended. In replying to such a misrepresentation, the witness may need to preface the answer with wording such as, "To put the answer to your question in proper context, I need to correct the misunderstanding of my prior testimony that was implied in your paraphrasing of it."

The hardest questions to deal with are those that are so abstruse that they are unintelligible. Usually the expert should not heroically attempt to interpret such questions but admit not understanding them and request clarification.

Through all of this, the witness should try to remain courteous. Nevertheless, he or she must also be firm and not feel intimidated by an overbearing attorney.

A witness must avoid attempting to bluff if he or she does not know an answer. Any suspicion of bluffing could cast doubt on the credibility of the witness's entire testimony. If the witness does not know the answer, he or she must say so. Also, if there is some error in the data, the witness should admit it and correct it, making whatever adjustment to the conclusion the correction would indicate.

If the expert witness has done his or her homework thoroughly, the cross-examination actually can help the case. With each answer explaining why a particular approach was rejected, for example, the opposing position may be discredited.

Redirect Examination

Even when the cross-examination has been completed, it is not time for the witness to breathe a sigh of relief. The attorney who conducted the original examination usually will want to keep the witness on the stand to ask redirect examination questions. The limited purpose of redirect is to expand any points brought out in the cross-examination that the attorney thinks need elaboration. It is the attorney's opportunity to counter possible misimpressions that might have been left with the court during the cross-examination and to reinforce any positions about which the cross-examination may have raised doubts.

If there is a recess between cross- and redirect examinations and the witness feels the need to clarify any points further, he or she should inform legal counsel so that counsel can ask the appropriate questions (provided, of course, that the court hasn't prohibited discussion of the case). If the witness feels strongly that something should be brought out on redirect examination and there is no scheduled recess, he or she usually can request a conference with the attorney. The redirect and recross-examinations can go back and forth indefinitely, limited only by the material presented in the immediately preceding testimony, the attorneys' restraint, and the judge's patience.

The judge may break in at any time during the direct examination, cross-examination, or any part of the proceedings to ask questions. Some judges are more apt to do so than others. Questions from the judge usually are a good sign—at least the judge is paying attention, and judges often ask penetrating and perceptive questions. Also, the witness should prefer that the judge ask for clarification of something the witness has left unclear or omitted rather than just leaving the issue alone.

Rebuttal Testimony

Attorneys often ask experts to present testimony for the purpose of rebutting testimony presented by the opposition's expert. Such testimony can take a wide variety of forms. Rebuttal testimony is most often presented to correct factual errors or errors in appraisal procedure committed by the opposing expert. Of course, if factual errors are to be corrected, it is important to present complete documentation for the correction. If procedural errors are to be corrected, the appraiser must present as strong authority as is possible for the correct procedures.

In many cases, rebuttal testimony is at least as important as the basic testimony and it should be presented as constructively as possible. Often, when the errors are corrected, the different approaches of the opposing experts ultimately lead to similar conclusions.

Exclusion of Witnesses

From time to time, the opposing attorney may move to have the expert witness excluded from the courtroom when testimony of the opposing expert is presented. As a generality, the purpose of the exclusion rule is to keep fact witnesses from being influenced in their testimony by the testimony of other fact witnesses. It is often *very* important to have the expert in the courtroom to hear opposing expert testimony, sometimes to give the attorney technical advice about the testimony, especially for cross-examination, and sometimes so the expert can rebut testimony of an opposing expert. A witness cannot be excluded when that person's presence is essential to the presentation of the party's cause[15]. Rarely, if ever, will a judge exclude an expert when this is called to the court's attention.

Courts' Expectations Regarding Expert Testimony

There are several common expectations that triers of fact have as to a valuation practitioner's expert testimony. This listing of expectations is not necessarily presented in order of relative significance.

1. Courts are increasingly expecting valuation analysts to comply with USPAP as the valuation industry professional standard, even in cases where compliance with USPAP is not required by statutory authority or by judicial precedent.
2. Judges expect expert valuation reports to be more comprehensive, more thorough, more rigorous—and more readable—than was the industry standard even a few years ago. The expectation is that the valuation report will stand on its own, and that it will tell the entire valuation "story."
3. Courts look for the presentation of market-derived, empirical data as the justification for a valuation analysis (e.g., transactional pricing multiples, direct and yield capitalization rates, valuation discounts and premiums). Courts are less persuaded by the analytical justification of "in my opinion . . ." and more persuaded by the analytical justification, "based on the market-derived, empirical evidence presented in my appraisal report. . . ."

[15] FED. R. EVID. 615.

4. Quantitative analysis and qualitative explanation for the selection of valuation variables (e.g., pricing multiples, capitalization rates, comparable sale pricing data, valuation adjustments—such as discount/premium percentages) are what judges want. Courts have come to realize that it is unusual that the naive selection of averages (means or medians) is appropriate with regard to the application of valuation variables to the subject property valuation analysis. The use of averages implies that everything about the facts and circumstances of the subject property in the instant case is average; in practice, this situation is very rarely the case.

5. Courts prefer expert witnesses to avoid the use of vague phrases such as "in my opinion . . .," "based on my judgment . . .," or "based on my experience. . . ." When possible, triers of fact seem to prefer that valuation experts use positive phrases such as "my analysis indicates . . .," "the data supports . . .," or "the market tells us. . . ." These positive phrases provide the triers of fact with explanations and justifications of their ultimate opinions.

6. In recent years, courts seem to be more willing to consider *Daubert*[16] motions. Based on the U.S. Supreme Court *Daubert* decision, these *Daubert* motions (usually made by motions in limine or after the voir dire phase of the examination) ask the judge to exclude the testimony of an expert witness that is based on "junk science"—or, in the case of a business valuation, on "junk economics."

7. In recent years, triers of fact more commonly seem to prefer that valuation experts avoid statements such as, "It is the State's position that . . ." or "It is my firm's position that. . . ." Analysts should be mindful of the fact that they are the experts—not their corporate or governmental employers. All valuation opinions should be an analyst's professional opinion, based on his or her personal professional training, experience, expertise, and reasoned judgment—and not based on the employer's or organization's dogma.

8. Courts seem to prefer for valuation experts to rely upon authoritative treatises, credentialling society courses, and promulgated professional standards—as opposed to the positions (published or otherwise) of single individuals (however well credentialled). What this implies is that valuation witnesses should generally endorse valuation industry practices. As a corollary, valuation witnesses should generally avoid relying upon a single individual's unproven position, such as "Dr. Jones says . . ." or "Professor Smith says. . . ."

9. The professional valuation practitioner should not let his or her expert testimony deteriorate into personal attacks on the opposing valuation experts. Courts don't seem to like "he said" versus "she said" expert valuation testimony. Courts appear to prefer to rely upon empirical and market-derived pricing evidence, authoritative literature, and informed professional judgment—and not upon juvenile comments between temperamental experts.

10. Courts appear to desire that the valuation experts bring all aspects of the valuation analysis back to the specific facts and circumstances of the instant case. Abstract formulas and conceptual theories are great—but triers of fact seem to want to understand how they apply to the specific set of facts and circumstances in front of them in the instant litigation.

---

[16] *Daubert v. Merrell Dow Pharmaceuticals, Inc.*

Summary

Providing expert testimony in an adversarial proceeding is considered by most professional business analysts to be the most challenging aspect of the profession. By the time an adversarial proceeding reaches the courtroom, settlement efforts have been exhausted and the disagreements are razor-sharp.

Many aspects of the courtroom drama are very much like theater in style, posturing, and pace. However, when legal controversy is involved, the expert witness has no substitute for thorough homework and preparation. The expert witness virtually prepares not only for his or her own case, but for the other side's as well.

Bibliography

Bingham, Dennis. "Making Persuasive Presentations in Court." *Business Appraisal Practice*, Fall 1999, pp. 13–23.

Bradley, Wray E. "Tax Court Valuation Standards Go Beyond 'Relevant and Reliable.'" *Valuation Strategies*, November/December 1999, pp. 34–39.

Brinig, Brian. "Business Valuation Litigation." Presentation to the Advanced Business Valuation Conference of the American Society of Appraisers, October 1996. Available on www.BVLibrary.com.

Crain, Michael A., Dan L. Goldwasser, and Everett P. Harry. "Expert Witnesses—In Jeopardy?" *Journal of Accountancy*, December 1994, pp. 42–48.

Dennis, Stephen G. "Selecting and Using a Financial Expert in Dissolution Practice." *Family Law Quarterly*, Spring 1992, pp. 17–25.

Feder, Robert D. "Direct Examination of a Business Appraiser in a Divorce Action." *American Journal of Family Law*, Spring 1993, pp. 1–11.

Ford, David J. "Plan to Succeed: Prepare, Prepare, Prepare." *CPA Litigation Service Counselor*, August 1999, pp. 7–8.

Jackson, Daniel L. "The Next Hurdle: The Second Prong of the Daubert Test." *CPA Litigation Service Counselor*, November 1999, pp. 1–2, 4–5.

Kendig, Robert E. "Discovery Issues in Valuation Cases." *American Journal of Family Law*, Spring 1992, pp. 55–74.

Lewis, Elaine. "Effective Valuation Expert Testimony: Preparation and Practice Are the Keys." *Judges & Lawyers Business Valuation Update*, October 1999, pp. 1, 3–4.

_____. "Preparing for Trial: Packaging the Presentation." *Shannon Pratt's Business Valuation Update*, October 1998, pp. 1–3.

Locke, R. Christopher. "Expert Testimony in the Post-Daubert Era." *CPA Expert*, Spring 1996, pp. 3–7.

Markel, John R. "Experts Should Be Alert to New Trends in Deposition Questioning Tactics." *CPA Litigation Service Counselor*, June 1999, pp. 5–8.

McFarland, Matt. "Beyond Daubert: The Rules Have Changed." *CPA Litigation Service Counselor*, August 1999, pp. 1–5.

Pratt, Shannon P. "Questions to Ask Expert Business Valuation Witnesses." *Fair$hare*, June 1999, pp. 9–11.

_____. "Recent Court Decisions Raise the Standards for Valuation Experts." *Valuation Strategies*, September/October 1999, pp. 35–39.

Reilly, Robert F. "Expert Witness Procedures for Accountants: Dos and Don'ts for Success in the Courtroom." *The CPA Journal*, March 1999, pp. 25–28.

_____. "Guidelines for Guarding against Daubert Challenges to Expert Testimony." *CPA Expert*, Summer 1999, pp. 15–19.

Reilly, Robert F., and Robert P. Schweihs. "Expert Testimony: Lessons Learned from Sons of Daubert." *Valuation Strategies*, January/February 2000, pp. 26–31, 42.

Russell, Deirdre, and Steven F. Schroeder. "Kumho Tire—A View of Your Future as an Expert Witness." *Business Appraisal Practice*, Fall 1999, pp. 5–12.

Weinstein, Jeffrey P. "The Use and Abuse of Economic Experts in Divorce Litigation." *Fair$hare: The Matrimonial Law Monthly*, February 1995, pp. 3–6.

Wise, Richard M. *Financial Litigation: Quantifying Business Damages and Values.* Toronto: The Canadian Institute of Chartered Accountants, 1990.

_____. "The Use and Abuse of Experts" (Chapter 40). In *Handbook of Business Valuation*, 2nd ed. Thomas L. West and Jeffrey D. Jones, eds. New York: John Wiley & Sons, 1999.

Chapter 41

Arbitration and Mediation

Clogged courts and escalating litigation costs have made arbitration as a solution for civil disputes and claims of conflict more necessary than ever before. Arbitration is a process by which a dispute is settled by an impartial, disinterested person or group who is authorized to render a decision that is legal, final, and binding. Arbitration is used as an alternative to litigation because it provides for an expeditious and inexpensive resolution of disputes by arbitrators having expert knowledge within a particular field, who act in an informal process that maintains the privacy of business transactions.[1]

The process of "arbitration" usually results in a binding conclusion, as opposed to "mediation," the product of which is advisory rather than binding. Mediators do not decide disputes; their only role is to encourage the parties to reach an equitable settlement of their differences.

Depending on the directive giving rise to the arbitration, the arbitrator(s)' conclusion may be contractually binding by itself, or it may be subject to limited review and confirmation by a court. Whether or not the product is binding, these services are categorized as "alternative dispute resolution" (ADR).

Business valuation disputes lend themselves exceedingly well to the arbitration process, partly because there normally is a single, unambiguous conclusion—that is, a value. The authors have had extensive experience serving as arbitrators, expert witnesses before arbitrators, and consultants to attorneys contemplating or conducting an arbitration process. Whenever the arbitrators themselves are experts in the field, as suggested in the above quote, our experiences have been very positive with respect to the fairness of the conclusion, and, in most cases, the expeditiousness of the process.

Advantages of ADR over Court Trial

The primary advantages of ADR over a court trial are the following:

1. The hearings are private rather than public, and in many cases are not recorded by a court reporter, a compelling advantage in many circumstances. This often allows the parties a chance to maintain an ongoing business relationship.
2. There is less likelihood of an outlandish result in favor of one side over the other, provided the arbitrators are qualified, professional business appraisers. In cases where the issue is a dispute over the value of a business or a business interest, an appraiser, if properly chosen, is usually in a better position as a result of experience and knowledge to assess the testimony regarding the value of a business or business interest than either a judge or jury.
3. ADR usually takes less elapsed time from start to finish.
4. Scheduling normally can be made more convenient for all parties involved.
5. Arbitration usually costs less. Attorneys' time and experts' fees frequently are considerably reduced. The appraisal process itself may not be less expensive than a court trial, but the amount of time required for preparing for cross-examination and rebuttal to an opposing expert in court can be substantially less.
6. Arbitration usually is less acrimonious, less formal, and less taxing on all participants, especially the principals in the disputed issue.

---

[1] Jerome N. Block, "The Process of Arbitration," *The Appraisal Journal*, April 1993, pp. 234–38.

7. The award of the arbitrators in most situations is final and binding and can be confirmed in court on motion.

8. The parties can handpick the trained professional who will conduct the ADR process.

Situations Suitable for Arbitration

Almost any dispute over the value of a business or a partial interest in a business can lend itself to resolution by arbitration instead of trial. If the parties in divorce and corporate or partnership dissolutions decide ahead of time to resolve any valuation issues by arbitration, they may never reach the point of dispute.

In mediation, the counselor can sometimes uncover unrealistic expectations and identify hidden concerns or objectives. This process can overcome personality conflicts and prevent the parties from some of the more humbling or embarrassing aspects of litigation in open court. This process usually narrows the issues, at least, if it does not reach a satisfactory conclusion between the parties.

The following have been the major categories, in our experience, where arbitration has proven most effective:

- Corporate and partnership dissolutions and buyouts of minority interests.
- Dissenting stockholder actions.
- Damage cases.
- Divorces.

Corporate and Partnership Dissolutions and Buyouts of Minority Interests

Like marriages, many business ownership relationships that appeared to be made in heaven end up with an agreement to disagree. Often the best solution is to sever the ownership relationship, usually sooner rather than later.

Arbitrating the valuation issue usually is a far lesser distraction of management's focus on running the business than is going to court. Arbitration in this very common situation also has all the other advantages listed above. Often especially relevant is the issue of fairness of the outcome, avoiding the tendency of judges and juries to become biased by the "good guy, bad buy" epithets that often characterize such court proceedings. Besides the issue of fairness, the arbitration process generally results in a far less rancorous parting of the ways than a court trial.

Arbitration also works well in those few states where a corporate or partnership dissolution occurs pursuant to a state dissolution statute, such as California[2] and Rhode Island.[3] Such dissolutions are discussed further in Chapter 35.

Dissenting Stockholder Actions

As discussed in Chapter 35, a merger, sale, or other major corporate action can give rise to dissenting stockholders' appraisal rights. The expediency and lower cost make

---

[2] Cal. Corp. Code §§1300 and 2000.
[3] R.I. Bus. Corp. Code §7-1.1-90.1.

the arbitration process an attractive alternative to a trial for determination of the value under appraisal rights in such cases, especially smaller ones for which prolonged and expensive court proceedings can result in a no-win situation for everyone.

Damage Cases

Damage cases, in which the valuation of a business or practice often is the central issue in determining the amount of relief, include the following:

1. Breach of contract.
2. Condemnation.
3. Antitrust.
4. Lost profits.
5. Lost business opportunity.
6. Amount of casualty insurance proceeds or allocation of proceeds among parties at interest.
7. Infringement of intellectual property.
8. Business torts.
9. Violation of securities laws.

We have observed that the risk of the court reaching an outlandish determination of value is greater in damage cases—especially those involving breach of contract and antitrust—than in any other major category of disputed valuation cases. One of the reasons for such extreme decisions is that some juries or courts allow their view that there should be liability for damages to affect their objectivity about the valuation issue; similarly, they may be swayed by some sentiment toward the parties involved. This risk can be significantly reduced through the use of an arbitration process using qualified appraisers as arbitrators.

Plaintiffs may resist arbitration by qualified valuers in favor of "rolling the dice" for a high award based on a jury's indignation over the defendants' egregious actions. However, witnesses testifying to extreme amounts may lack credibility (especially if faced with a strong rebuttal witness), and judges often have authority to vacate or substantially reduce jury awards. Furthermore, the costs of court trials often exceed the depths of plaintiffs' pockets when faced with the unlimited resources of some defendants.

Divorces

Of all situations involving disputed valuations of businesses or professional practices, those arising from divorces often are the most difficult for the parties to resolve by amicable negotiation. Although divorces are only a small part of our firm's valuation practice, they account for a large proportion of the occasions on which we prepare for, and appear on, the witness stand in court to present expert testimony.

Disputed valuation issues can become a major element in the already intense emotional strain accompanying divorce proceedings. Frequently, the valuation for the property settlement is the major, if not the only, disputed issue. Besides the time and cost advantages, arbitration spares the parties the tension and added antagonism of fighting it out in court.

We believe that the trend toward settling business valuation issues by arbitrating in marital property divisions will accelerate as more family law attorneys become familiar and comfortable with the arbitration process in this context.

The Arbitration Agreement

The arbitration agreement is critical, because it is a document governing the arbitration that is binding on both the parties and the arbitrators. The arbitration agreement usually originates in one of the following ways:

1. An arbitration clause is included as part of a corporate document or contract among the parties, such as a buy-sell agreement. When such an agreement is triggered, it generally is desirable for the attorneys to draw up—and for the parties to execute—a supplemental agreement addressing details discussed below that may not have been covered in the general arbitration clause.
2. An arbitration agreement is created specifically for the situation at hand, sometimes with direction or assistance from a court.

In any case, we highly recommend that a valuation consultant experienced in arbitration be engaged to assist the lawyer in drafting or reviewing the arbitration clause or agreement, so that the valuation clause will actually result in accomplishing the objective of the parties.

The arbitration document must be clear, complete, and unambiguous. We have seen incredible amounts of unnecessary frustration and wasted time and energy expended as a result of parties' and arbitrators' disagreements as to the interpretation of the arbitration agreement.

We also highly recommend that all parties to the arbitration agreement read and understand it before they agree to become bound by it. For example, many buy-sell agreements specify the standard of value as "the fair market value of the shares." Noncontrolling stockholders often are shocked when they learn that they have been forced to sell out under this clause at a price considerably lower than a pro rata portion of the enterprise as a whole.

Factors Specified in the Arbitration Agreement

Factors that should be mandated by the agreement include the following:

1. Procedure for selection of arbitrators.
2. Definition of the property to be appraised.
3. Date as of which the property is to be valued.
4. Standard of value to be used (as discussed in Chapter 2 and elsewhere in the book).
5. What constitutes a conclusion by the arbitrators, such as:
   a. Agreement by at least two out of three.
   b. Average of the two closest to each other.
   c. Conclusion of the third (neutral) arbitrator, such as in a "special master" situation.
6. Format and procedure for the arbitrators' rendering of their conclusion.
7. Terms of payment of the amount determined by the arbitrators, including interest, if any.
8. Time schedule for the various steps in the arbitration process, at least the selection of arbitrators and some outside time limit for the total process.

Failure to specify any of the above factors may leave the door open for costly and extensive legal battles.

The agreement may specify a reporting deadline, or a schedule may be worked out in conjunction with the process of engaging the arbitrators. In our experience, reporting deadlines written into arbitration agreements often are too optimistic to allow for the time necessary to work out legal details, collection and transmission of all the information necessary for the arbitrators, and accommodation of the schedules of the arbitrators, attorneys, parties, and witnesses.

Factors Left to the Arbitrators' Discretion

Factors that can, and in most cases should, be left to the discretion of the arbitrators include the following:

1. Whether or not each arbitrator is expected or required to make a complete, independent appraisal, or the extent to which each arbitrator considers it necessary to do independent work, as opposed to relying on certain data or analyses furnished by other arbitrators and/or appraisers.
2. The obligation of the arbitrators to communicate with each other (writing, telephone calls, personal meetings), and the rules for sharing information.
3. Scheduling of the arbitrators' work and meetings, within the constraint of the agreed upon reporting schedule.
4. The valuation approaches and criteria to be taken into consideration, within the constraints of any legally mandated criteria.
5. The facts, documents, and other data on which to rely (although the principals may agree to stipulate certain facts or assumptions, which could make the arbitrators' job easier with respect to some matters of possible factual uncertainty).

Other Factors to Address

As a generality, the arbitration agreement may specify rules on various matters, or, in the absence of specific rules, should contain some broad language giving the arbitrators authority to make rules on points not addressed in the agreement. An example would be rules regarding contacts between parties and the arbitrators. Often participants in arbitrations are given no rules as to whether ex parte contact is permitted, and arbitration statutes provide little or no guidance.

Another topic often not addressed is rules specifying whether the arbitrators are free to obtain property-specific information independent of that provided by the parties, or should rely solely on information presented to them by the parties and their witnesses and made part of the arbitration record.

Selection of Arbitrators

Two factors need to be delineated regarding the selection of arbitrators: (1) the criteria for selection and (2) the procedure for selection.

Criteria for Selection

The arbitration process produces the most equitable results for all parties if all the arbitrators (or the arbitrator) are experienced, qualified, professional appraisers of businesses, professional practices, intangible property, or whatever the subject property may be. If there are three arbitrators, it is most desirable that all three should be full-time professional appraisers, but two out of three are far better than only one or none at all.

In some cases, if the business or profession is highly specialized, it may be desirable to seek as arbitrators one or more appraisers who have experience in appraising the specific line of business or professional practice. It is generally not desirable to gain the desired industry expertise by utilizing as an arbitrator someone who is an active or retired participant in the industry or profession involved, or who has done ancillary functions such as accounting or economic analysis work in the industry or profession, but who is not experienced in matters related directly to valuation. Many of these people lack the requisite training to deal professionally with the specific issue of valuation, and there is also the risk that such people's biases toward the industry or profession could prevent objective valuation. The expertise of industry experts can be gained through informal discussion with the arbitrator(s) or by formal testimony presented to the arbitrator(s). This is preferable to having them act as arbitrators themselves.

We have observed sound valuation conclusions reached by arbitration panels composed of industry people knowledgeable in finance, along with attorneys knowledgeable in both the industry and valuation matters. However, in these instances, costs were incurred not only for the three arbitrators, but also for expert testimony to be presented to the arbitration panel by at least two appraisers (one or more retained by each party) in each case. We also have seen nonprofessional panels reach conclusions that we do not believe a consensus of responsible professional appraisers would consider supportable within a reasonable range of value.

Obviously, one criterion for selection is the availability of the desired arbitrator(s) so that the arbitration can taken place reasonably promptly.

Procedure for Selection

The most typical procedure is that each party selects one arbitrator and the two arbitrators select the third. It is preferable for the two arbitrators appointed by the parties to have complete authority to select the third, rather than having the selection of the third arbitrator subject to the approval of the principals. This avoids delays and dealing with pressures arising from the principals' biases, which are almost sure to be injected.

It is important that there be an alternative procedure for the selection of a third arbitrator in case of a deadlock. This contingency procedure should be planned in advance or in conjunction with entering into the arbitration agreement. There should be a deadline, at which time the alternate selection process takes effect if the first two arbitrators have failed to reach agreement on a third arbitrator. In case of a deadlock, the procedure should call for the appointment of the third arbitrator, who is a qualified appraiser, by some predetermined entity, such as the American Society of Appraisers, the American Arbitration Association, a court, or some designated official in the industry or profession. This procedure will almost assure that at least two of the three arbitrators will be professional appraisers, if one side has already chosen one. If one side insists that the third arbitrator be a qualified professional appraiser, and presents a list of appraisers who are independent of the principals involved, it is not likely that anyone charged with making such an appointment would select someone not so qualified over someone who is qualified.[4]

Another possibility is to establish the procedure so that the two arbitrators attempt to reach agreement, bringing in the third arbitrator only if they are unable to do so. In that case, we recommend, based on our experiences, that the prospective third arbitrator be agreed upon between the first two at the outset, before they get involved in other aspects of interaction with each other in the arbitration process.

American Arbitration Association Procedure

The American Arbitration Association (AAA) procedure for appointing arbitrators is different from that described in the foregoing section. When parties agree to submit a disputed matter to arbitration through the AAA, the association sends the parties a list of suggested arbitrators from the association's panel of arbitrators. Each party may veto nominees and indicate its preferences, but the final decision is made by the AAA.

In many AAA arbitrations, each party will retain its own expert appraiser who will present testimony before the arbitration panel, rather than having the expert actually participate as an arbitrator. In this sense, the preparation and presentation of expert testimony is similar to a court trial, although it is slightly less formal.

The next few sections of this chapter discuss the type of situation where the appraiser is acting as a member of the arbitration panel rather than as a presenter of expert testimony.

Engagement and Compensation of Arbitrators

Once the arbitrators have been appointed, the engagement should be committed to writing. The description of the engagement may take the form of a standard professional services agreement initiated by an appraiser serving as arbitrator, an engagement letter drafted by one of the attorneys or parties, or both. All aspects of the engagement should be adequately covered. Sometimes, addenda to the initial engagement document(s) may be necessary, since decisions on some items, such as schedules and some expenses, may be made or changed as the engagement progresses.

The engagement document(s) should include by reference the statute and/or document(s) giving rise to the arbitration (e.g., a buy-sell agreement) and should cover compensation of the arbitrator and all necessary instructions not addressed or not made clear in the arbitration document(s).

All documents relating to the engagement of an arbitrator should be signed by the arbitrator and whoever is responsible for compensating the arbitrator for his or her services. The most common compensation arrangement is that each party assumes

---

[4] Accredited senior appraisers of the American Society of Appraisers who are certified in business valuation may be found on the web site of the American Society of Appraisers, www.appraisers.org or by calling (800) ASA-VALU.

responsibility for the compensation and expenses of the arbitrator it has nominated or appointed, with the parties equally sharing the compensation and expenses of the third arbitrator. Such arrangements vary, however, from case to case.

The amount of compensation is usually based on each arbitrator's normal professional hourly or daily billing rate (or some mutually agreed upon rate) plus out-of-pocket expenses. It is much less common for an arbitrator's compensation to be based on a fixed fee, because it is very difficult to determine in advance just how much time the total appraisal and arbitration process will require. However, it is reasonable to expect to discuss some estimate of probable fees and the daily rate or other basis for the fees. Under the procedures of the American Arbitration Association, these arrangements are carried out by a representative of that organization. If the association is to be directed to appoint qualified business appraisers, it also should be directed to expect to pay the fees normally charged by such qualified appraisers.

The Arbitration Process

One of the major variables in the arbitration process is the extent to which each arbitrator is expected or required to carry out independent appraisal work. Some arbitration documents specify that each expert on the arbitration panel do a complete, independent appraisal. At the other extreme, some arbitration documents specify that the arbitrator(s) rely entirely on evidence presented by the parties or their witnesses. More commonly, however (and we think preferably in most cases), the extent of independent appraisal work to be done is left to the judgment of each individual arbitrator, or to the arbitration panel as a group. This subject should be discussed with the parties or their representatives before the arbitration commences. It would be useful to have this addressed in the arbitrators' engagement letter, preferably allowing them considerable discretion.

Review of Arbitration Document

Each arbitrator should begin with a careful review of the statute and/or document(s) giving rise to the arbitration. If there is any confusion or disagreement about any details of the assignment, such as the exact definition of the property, the effective date of the valuation, or the applicable standard of value, the arbitrators should seek clarification immediately. This should be done in writing to avoid any possible disputes later.

Initial Communication among Arbitrators

We recommend that the arbitrators establish communication among themselves at the earliest possible time after their appointment. A face-to-face meeting is ideal if geographic proximity to each other makes that feasible, but a conference call or a series of conference calls is usually sufficient, perhaps supplemented by correspondence. While each case is unique, the following is a generalized list of points to try to establish early:

1. Status of work already accomplished, if any (who has done what work up to that point).
2. An agreement as to sharing of information. (Our preference is to agree that all information gathered or developed by one arbitrator will be shared with the other arbitrators as quickly as possible.)
3. An agreement, if possible, as to the relevant valuation approaches to consider. (Where this becomes an issue, it seems fair to allow the parties' representatives to be heard as to their preferences. However, in our experience, this often results in highly biased supplications by parties' representatives who have no technical knowledge of relevant valuation approaches.)
4. A list of documents and data needed, and assignment of responsibility for obtaining each and seeing that the necessary distribution to other arbitrators is made. (It should be agreed up front that any such documents in the possession of the parties will be provided as evidence to the arbitrators promptly and completely.)
5. Any other possible division of the research effort, such as searches for comparable transactions, development of economic and/or industry data, and routine financial statement analysis (spreadsheets, ratio analysis, comparison with industry averages, and so on). Division of research effort, of course, must depend on each arbitrator's willingness to accept certain efforts of another, which must be based on a judgment of professional ability and unbiased presentation of data and analysis.
6. Scheduling.

Field Visit

In most cases, arbitrators will want to visit the operating premises and interview relevant principals and/or management. It works out best if the arbitrators can conduct this field trip together, if possible, rather than separately. Together, the arbitrators will see the same things at the same time, and all can benefit from hearing each other's questions and answers first-hand. A joint field trip also gives the arbitrators an opportunity to address any items not fully covered in their previous communications. Also, this gives arbitrators who did not know each other previously an opportunity to get to know each other and form a basis for working together.

Hearings

The arbitrators should offer each party the opportunity to present oral and written information and opinions if they so desire. It is frequently convenient to hold a meeting to accommodate such input in conjunction with the field trip.

The Valuation Meeting

Usually, the arbitrators will meet in person to reach the valuation conclusion. In some instances, this meeting may be replaced by a conference call. In either case, all should be as prepared as possible, having exchanged and assimilated as much information as possible prior to the meeting.

In the meeting, it is usually most productive to come to agreements issue by issue, identifying and keeping track of each point of agreement and disagreement.

Good notes should be kept so that it is clear exactly what points have been agreed upon, and what the respective positions are on points that have been addressed but on which agreement has not been reached. Each arbitrator should be receptive to the others' information and viewpoints and attempt to reach compromises on points where reasonable judgments may differ.

It is most desirable to come to a conclusion that can be endorsed as fair by all members of the arbitration panel. This agreement can usually be achieved if all of the arbitrators are qualified professional business appraisers. If unanimous agreement cannot be reached, the arbitrator in the minority position may render a dissenting opinion for the record if he or she so desires.

Reporting the Results of the Arbitration

The formal report of the valuation conclusion reached by the arbitrators is usually contained in a very brief letter that does no more than reference the arbitration agreement, state that the arbitrators have completed their assignment in accordance with the agreement, and state the conclusion reached. The arbitrators concurring in the conclusion sign the letter. In the parlance of arbitration, this is called an *award*. In some cases, the letter must be notarized as well as signed.

In a significant proportion of cases, the principals on both sides would like to have a brief report explaining how the valuation conclusion was reached. In arbitration parlance, this is called an *opinion*. In such situations, we suggest that such an advisory report be the sole responsibility of the third appraiser. To make such a report a joint task of two or more arbitrators, each of who probably judged various factors a little bit differently—though they were able to agree on a conclusion—would usually be an unnecessarily complicated and costly exercise.

If the valuation conclusion is reached unilaterally by a special master, normally he or she would be the only one to sign the report. An explanation of the procedures and criteria used is usually included.

Mediation

While an arbitrator's role is to reach a conclusion that is binding on the parties, the mediator's role is to reach closure by convincing the parties to come to a settlement.

> The ultimate goal of mediation is to assist the parties in designing a solution that specifically addresses their needs and interests. Mediation is much more flexible than either arbitration or litigation in that it allows the parties themselves to design a very particularized solution to their particular dispute that is as detailed or general as the parties desire. Additionally, at least in family mediation, attorneys are usually not present at most of the mediation sessions and therefore legal fees are reduced.[5]

---

[5] Deborah Iwanyshyn, "Mediation as a Form of Dispute Resolution," *Shannon Pratt's Business Valuation Update*, October 1998, p. 5.

How Mediation Differs from Arbitration and Litigation

Mediation is a voluntary process that involves the use of an impartial person or persons, by the parties to a dispute, to facilitate informed decision-making so as to assist parties to work together to design a customized solution to their dispute. The parties can customize their solution to suit their needs in a far more detailed fashion than will generally occur if a decision is made for them by either a judge or an arbitrator.

No party is ever forced to continue to mediate if she or he decides that mediation is not working. No party ever gives away rights during a mediation session. All decisions are subject to review no matter how far along in the process the parties may be.

Arbitration involves the use of a third person, sometimes selected by the parties and sometimes appointed for them, to listen to their arguments and to examine their evidence and to make a decision for them. Private arbitration, if agreed to by both parties, can be customized to eliminate a lot of the formalities and requirements of litigation. However, the arbitrator still makes the final decision and it generally is not as detailed as an agreement that the parties design themselves.[6]

Self-Determination Is the Fundamental Principle

The Standards of Conduct for Mediators published as joint standards for the American Bar Association (ABA) and The Society of Professionals in Dispute Resolution (SPIDR) states that, "Self-determination is the fundamental principle of mediation. It requires that the mediation process rely upon the ability of the parties to reach a voluntary, uncoerced agreement."

Role of the Business Valuation Expert in Mediation

Experts can act as co-mediators as well as neutral experts, although the roles are significantly different. If acting as a co-mediator the expert must comply with the ethical constraints of impartiality and neutrality and the goal of self-determination by the parties. The expert co-mediator can't give an opinion as to value but can provide information to assist the parties in making informative decisions and in formulating their own settlement.

When consulted as a neutral expert, the appraiser's role requires him or her to utilize his or her expertise to give an opinion that the parties can choose to either use or ignore. The recommendation by a mediator to employ the services of a neutral expert is far more common than the use by the mediator of an expert to co-mediate. Peter Adler, former president of SPIDR, noted that he has utilized the services of appraisers as both experts and co-mediators. In larger cases, where the parties themselves have independently employed two experts, it is also acceptable to ask the experts to select a third expert if the parties do not feel that they can rely upon either of the experts selected by the other.[7]

---

[6] Ibid.

[7] Ibid., p. 6.

Mediation in Family Law

One of the fastest growing applications of mediation in recent years has been in the area of divorce. A group called the Academy of Family Mediators has published a document titled *Standards of Practice for Family and Divorce Mediation.* It explains: "The role of the mediator includes reducing the obstacles to communication, maximizing the exploration of alternatives, and addressing the needs of those it is agreed are involved or affected."

Mediation in Federal Tax Disputes

The Internal Revenue Service authorized mediations to resolve gift and estate tax matters starting late in 1995, and several successful tax mediations have been concluded since then.

Summary

The two most critical elements for an expeditious and successful arbitration are:

1. *A definitive arbitration agreement that provides the arbitrators with unambiguous instructions on the key matters listed above and that all parties understand.*
2. *The appointment of competent and independent arbitrators with a high degree of relevant valuation expertise who will be fair in reaching a conclusion about the value of the subject property.*

If these two elements are properly addressed, the arbitration process can be a very efficient and fair way of resolving business or professional practice valuation matters.

Mediation is rapidly growing in popularity as a form of alternative dispute resolution. In order for mediation to succeed:

1. *The parties must desire to resolve the conflict.*
2. *There needs to be a well-qualified mediator.*
3. *If a business valuation is involved, the mediator, co-mediator, or neutral adviser to the mediator should be a well-qualified business valuation analyst.*

As of this writing, there are only a few valuation analysts qualified as mediators. Therefore, the valuation analyst's role usually would be as a co-mediator or neutral advisor to the mediator. In addition, valuation practitioners have an obvious role in providing expert testimony in mediation proceedings.

Bibliography

Berman, Peter J. "Resolving Business Disputes Through Mediation and Arbitration." *CPA Journal*, November 1994, pp. 74–77.

Block, Jerome N. "The Process of Arbitration." *The Appraisal Journal*, April 1993, pp. 234–38.

Brief, Matthew, and Vincent Love. "Alternative Dispute Resolution: The Pros and Cons." *CPA Expert*, Summer 1996, pp. 3–7.

Brinig, Brian P., et al. "Alternative Dispute Resolution" (Chapter 12). In *Guide to Litigation Support Services,* 5th ed. Fort Worth, TX: Practitioners Publishing Company, 1999.

Carper, Donald L. "Remedies in Business Arbitration." *Arbitration Journal*, September 1991, pp. 49–58.

Demery, Paul. "Is Mediation in Your Future?" *Practical Accountant*, January 1996, pp. 48–55.

Diana, James C. "The New Mediation Procedure in Appeals: The Latest Development in the IRS' ADR Initiative." *Tax Management Memorandum*, November 13, 1995, pp. 331–39.

Fiore, Nicholas. "Pros and Cons of the New IRS Mediation Program." *Journal of Accountancy*, May 1996, p. 36.

Ford, David J. "CPAs and ADR: A Civilized Alternative to Litigation." *CPA Litigation Service Counselor*, February 2000, pp. 1–5.

Goldsheider, Robert. "Measuring the Damages: ADR and Intellectual Property Disputes." *Dispute Resolution Journal*, October–December 1995, pp. 55–63.

Iwanyshyn, Deborah. "Mediation as a Form of Dispute Resolution." *Shannon Pratt's Business Valuation Update*, October 1998, pp. 5–6.

Kaufman, Steve. "See You Out of Court: Mediation Used in Resolving Business Disputes." *Nation's Business*, June 1992, pp. 58–60.

Klinefelter, Stanard T., and Sandra P. Gohn. "Alternative Dispute Resolution: Its Value to Estate Planners." *Estate Planning*, May/June 1995, pp. 147–54.

Koritzinsky, Allan R., Robert M. Welch Jr., and Stephen W. Schlissel. "The Benefits of Arbitration." *Family Advocate*, Spring 1992, pp. 45–52.

Kratchman, D. Michael, and William P. Walsh. "Mediation Instead of Litigation for Resolution of Valuation Disputes." *Michigan Business Law Journal*, Winter 1995, pp. 15–17.

Miller, Seymour W. "Mediation—An Alternate Dispute Resolution Methodology Whose Time Has Come." *CPA Journal*, July 1994, pp. 54–55.

Pearson, Claude M. "Using Streamlined Arbitration to Resolve Valuation Disputes for an Accounting Partnership." *Practical Accountant*, September 1987, pp. 116–17.

Saltzman, Michael I. "Tax Court Mediation: A Case Study." *Tax Executive*, November/December 1996, pp. 449–53.

Wilburn, Kay O., Lowell S. Broom. "Alternative Strategies for Litigation Battles." *Journal of Accountancy*, March 1994, pp. 77–80.

Wilburn, Kay O., and Frank M. Messina. "IRS Has Now Begun to Open the Door of Opportunity for Resolving Disputes in a More Effective Way." *CPA Journal*, July 1996, pp. 52–54.

Zimmerman, Philip. "A Practical Guide to Mediation for CPAs." *CPA Journal*, June 1995, pp. 42–46.

Professional Arbitration and Mediation Organizations

The Academy of Family Mediators
5 Militia Drive
Lexington, MA 02173
(781) 674-2663
www.mediators.org

American Arbitration Association
335 Madison Avenue, 10th floor
New York, NY 10017
(212) 484-4000
www.adr.org

American Bar Association Dispute Resolution Section
750 North Lake Shore Drive
Chicago, IL 60611
(312) 988-5522
www.abanet.org/dispute/home.html

Association for Family and Conciliation Courts
329 West Wilson Street
Madison, WI 53703
(608) 251-4001
www.afccnet.org

Center for Problem Resolution
320 Ft. Duquesne Boulevard
Pittsburgh, PA 15222
(412) 338-1477

Center for Public Resources Institute for Dispute Resolution
366 Madison Avenue
New York, NY 10017
(212) 949-6490
www.cpradr.org

Mediation and Conflict Management Services
8000 Bonhomme, Suite 201
St. Louis, MO 63105
(314) 721-4333
www.mediate.com

National Alliance of Mediators
145 West 67th Street
New York, NY 10023
(800) 787-1904

National Institute for Dispute Resolution
1726 M Street N.W., Suite 500
Washington, D.C. 20036
(202) 466-4764

The Society of Professionals in Dispute Resolution (SPIDR)
1621 Connecticut Ave. N.W., Suite 400
Washington, D.C. 20009
(202) 265-1927
www.spidr.org

Appendix A

International Glossary of Business Valuation Terms

To enhance and sustain the quality of business valuations for the benefit of the business valuation profession and the users of the services of its practitioners, the below identified societies and organizations whose members provide business valuation services have adopted the definitions for the terms included in this glossary.

The performance of business valuation services requires a high degree of skill, and imposes upon the valuation professional a duty to communicate the valuation process and conclusion, as appropriate to the scope of the engagement, in a manner that is clear and not misleading. This duty is advanced through the use of terms whose meanings are clearly established and consistently applied throughout the profession.

If, in the opinion of the business valuation professional, one or more of these terms needs to be used in a manner which materially departs from the enclosed definitions, it is recommended that the term be defined as used within that valuation engagement.

This glossary has been developed to provide guidance to the business valuation practitioners who are members of the listed societies, organizations, and others performing valuations of business interests or securities by further memorializing the body of knowledge which constitutes the competent and careful determination of value and, more particularly, the communication of how that value was determined.

Departure from this glossary is not intended to provide a basis for civil liability and should not be presumed to create evidence that any duty has been breached.

American Institute of Certified Public Accountants
American Society of Appraisers
The Canadian Institute of Chartered Business Valuators
National Association of Certified Valuation Analysts
The Institute of Business Appraisers

Adjusted Book Value — the value that results after one or more asset or liability amounts are added, deleted, or changed from their respective financial statement amounts.

Appraisal — see Valuation.

Appraisal Approach — see Valuation Approach.

Appraisal Date — see Valuation Date.

Appraisal Method — see Valuation Method.

Appraisal Procedure — see Valuation Procedure.

Asset (Asset-Based) Approach — a general way of determining a value indication of a business, business ownership interest, or security by using one or more methods based on the value of the assets of that business net of liabilities.

Benefit Stream — any level of income, cash flow, or earnings generated by an asset, group of assets, or business enterprise. When the term is used, it should be supplemented by a definition of exactly what it means in the given valuation context.

Beta — a measure of systematic risk of a security; the tendency of a security's returns to correlate with swings in the broad market.

Blockage Discount — an amount or percentage deducted from the current market price of a publicly traded security to reflect the decrease in the per share value of a block of those securities that is of a size that could not be sold in a reasonable period of time given normal trading volume.

Business — see Business Enterprise.

Business Enterprise — a commercial, industrial, service, or investment entity, or a combination thereof, pursuing an economic activity.

Business Valuation — the act or process of determining the value of a business enterprise or ownership interest therein.

Capital Asset Pricing Model (CAPM) — a model in which the cost of capital for any security or portfolio of securities equals a risk-free rate plus a risk premium that is proportionate to the systematic risk of the security or portfolio.

Capitalization — a conversion of a single period stream of benefits into value.

Capitalization Factor — any multiple or divisor used to convert anticipated benefits into value.

Capitalization Rate — any divisor (usually expressed as a percentage) used to convert anticipated benefits into value.

Capital Structure — the composition of the invested capital of a business enterprise; the mix of debt and equity financing.

Cash Flow — cash that is generated over a period of time by an asset, group of assets, or business enterprise. It may be used in a general sense to encompass various levels of specifically defined cash flows. When the term is used, it should be supplemented by a qualifier (for example, "discretionary" or "operating") and a definition of exactly what it means in the given valuation context.

Control — the power to direct the management and policies of a business enterprise.

Control Premium — an amount (expressed in either dollar or percentage form) by which the pro rata value of a controlling interest exceeds the pro rata value of a non-controlling interest in a business enterprise, that reflects the power of control.

Cost Approach — a general way of estimating a value indication of an individual asset by quantifying the amount of money that would be required to replace the future service capability of that asset.

Cost of Capital — the expected rate of return (discount rate) that the market requires in order to attract funds to a particular investment.

Discount — a reduction in value or the act of reducing value.

Discount for Lack of Control — an amount or percentage deducted from the pro rata share of value of one hundred percent (100%) of an equity interest in a business to reflect the absence of some or all of the powers of control.

Discount for Lack of Marketability — an amount or percentage deducted from the value of an ownership interest to reflect the relative absence of marketability.

Discount Rate — a rate of return (cost of capital) used to convert a monetary sum, payable or receivable in the future, into present value.

Economic Life — the period of time over which property may generate economic benefits.

Effective Date — see Valuation Date.

Enterprise — see Business Enterprise.

Equity Net Cash Flows — those cash flows available to pay out to equity holders (in the form of dividends) after funding operations of the business enterprise, making necessary capital investments, and reflecting increases or decreases in debt financing.

Equity Risk Premium — a rate of return in addition to a risk-free rate to compensate for investing in equity instruments because they have a higher degree of probable risk than risk-free instruments (a component of the cost of equity capital or equity discount rate).

Excess Earnings — that amount of anticipated benefits that exceeds a fair rate of return on the value of a selected asset base (often net tangible assets) used to generate those anticipated benefits.

Excess Earnings Method — a specific way of determining a value indication of a business, business ownership interest, or security determined as the sum of (a) the value of the assets obtained by capitalizing excess earnings and (b) the value of the selected asset base. Also frequently used to value intangible assets. See Excess Earnings.

Fair Market Value — the price, expressed in terms of cash equivalents, at which property would change hands between a hypothetical willing and able buyer and a hypothetical willing and able seller, acting at arm's length in an open and unrestricted market, when neither is under compulsion to buy or sell and when both have reasonable knowledge of the relevant facts. {NOTE: in Canada, the term "price" should be replaced with the term "highest price."}

Forced Liquidation Value — liquidation value at which the asset or assets are sold as quickly as possible, such as at an auction.

Going Concern — an ongoing operating business enterprise.

Going Concern Value — the value of a business enterprise that is expected to continue to operate into the future. The intangible elements of Going Concern Value result from factors such as having a trained workforce, an operational plant, and the necessary licenses, systems, and procedures in place.

Goodwill — that intangible asset arising as a result of name, reputation, customer loyalty, location, products, and similar factors not separately identified.

Goodwill Value — the value attributable to goodwill.

Income (Income-Based) Approach — a general way of determining a value indication of a business, business ownership interest, security, or intangible asset using one or more methods that convert anticipated benefits into a present single amount.

Intangible Assets — non-physical assets (such as franchises, trademarks, patents, copyrights, goodwill, equities, mineral rights, securities and contracts as distinguished from physical assets) that grant rights, privileges, and have economic benefits for the owner.

Invested Capital — the sum of equity and debt in a business enterprise. Debt is typically (a) long-term liabilities or (b) the sum of short-term interest-bearing debt and long-term liabilities. When the term is used, it should be supplemented by a definition of exactly what it means in the given valuation context.

Invested Capital Net Cash Flows — those cash flows available to pay out to equity holders (in the form of dividends) and debt investors (in the form of principal and interest) after funding operations of the business enterprise and making necessary capital investments.

Investment Risk — the degree of uncertainty as to the realization of expected returns.

Investment Value — the value to a particular investor based on individual investment requirements and expectations. {NOTE: in Canada, the term used is "Value to the Owner."}

Key Person Discount — an amount or percentage deducted from the value of an ownership interest to reflect the reduction in value resulting from the actual or potential loss of a key person in a business enterprise.

Levered Beta — the beta reflecting a capital structure that includes debt.

Liquidity — the ability to quickly convert property to cash or pay a liability.

Liquidation Value — the net amount that can be realized if the business is terminated and the assets are sold piecemeal. Liquidation can be either "orderly" or "forced."

Majority Control — the degree of control provided by a majority position.

Majority Interest — an ownership interest greater than fifty percent (50%) of the voting interest in a business enterprise.

Market (Market-Based) Approach — a general way of determining a value indication of a business, business ownership interest, security, or intangible asset by using one or more methods that compare the subject to similar businesses, business ownership interests, securities, or intangible assets that have been sold.

Marketability — the ability to quickly convert property to cash at minimal cost.

Marketability Discount — see Discount for Lack of Marketability.

Minority Discount — a discount for lack of control applicable to a minority interest.

Minority Interest — an ownership interest less than fifty percent (50%) of the voting interest in a business enterprise.

Net Book Value — with respect to a business enterprise, the difference between total assets (net of accumulated depreciation, depletion, and amortization) and total liabilities of a business enterprise as they appear on the balance sheet (synonymous with Shareholder's Equity); with respect to an intangible asset, the capitalized cost of an intangible asset less accumulated amortization as it appears on the books of account of the business enterprise.

Net Cash Flow — a form of cash flow. When the term is used, it should be supplemented by a qualifier (for example, "Equity" or "Invested Capital") and a definition of exactly what it means in the given valuation context.

Net Tangible Asset Value — the value of the business enterprise's tangible assets (excluding excess assets and non-operating assets) minus the value of its liabilities. {NOTE: in Canada, tangible assets also include identifiable intangible assets.}

Non-Operating Assets — assets not necessary to ongoing operations of the business enterprise. {NOTE: in Canada, the term used is "Redundant Assets."}

Orderly Liquidation Value — liquidation value at which the asset or assets are sold over a reasonable period of time to maximize proceeds received.

Premise of Value — an assumption regarding the most likely set of transactional circumstances that may be applicable to the subject valuation; e.g., going concern, liquidation.

Portfolio Discount — an amount or percentage that may be deducted from the value of a business enterprise to reflect the fact that it owns dissimilar operations or assets that may not fit well together.

Rate of Return — an amount of income (loss) and/or change in value realized or anticipated on an investment, expressed as a percentage of that investment.

Redundant Assets — see Non-Operating Assets.

Report Date — the date conclusions are transmitted to the client.

Replacement Cost New — the current cost of a similar new property having the nearest equivalent utility to the property being valued.

Reproduction Cost New — the current cost of an identical new property.

Residual Value — the prospective value as of the end of the discrete projection period in a discounted benefit streams model.

Risk-Free Rate — the rate of return available in the market on an investment free of default risk.

Risk Premium — a rate of return in addition to a risk-free rate to compensate the investor for accepting risk.

Rule of Thumb — a mathematical relationship between or among variables based on experience, observation,

hearsay, or a combination of these, usually applicable to a specific industry.

Special Interest Purchasers — acquirers who believe they can enjoy post-acquisition economies of scale, synergies, or strategic advantages by combining the acquired business interest with their own.

Standard of Value — the identification of the type of value being utilized in a specific engagement; e.g., fair market value, fair value, investment value.

Sustaining Capital Reinvestment — the periodic capital outlay required to maintain operations at existing levels, net of the tax shield available from such outlays.

Systematic Risk — the risk that is common to all risky securities and cannot be eliminated through diversification. When using the capital asset pricing model, systematic risk is measured by beta.

Terminal Value — see Residual Value.

Unlevered Beta — the beta reflecting a capital structure without debt.

Unsystematic Risk — the portion of total risk specific to an individual security that can be avoided through diversification.

Valuation — the act or process of determining the value of a business, business ownership interest, security, or intangible asset.

Valuation Approach — a general way of determining a value indication of a business, business ownership interest, security, or intangible asset using one or more valuation methods.

Valuation Date — the specific point in time as of which the valuator's opinion of value applies (also referred to as "Effective Date" or "Appraisal Date").

Valuation Method — within approaches, a specific way to determine value.

Valuation Procedure — the act, manner, and technique of performing the steps of an appraisal method.

Valuation Ratio — a fraction in which a value or price serves as the numerator and financial, operating, or physical data serve as the denominator.

Value to the Owner — see Investment Value.

Weighted Average Cost of Capital (WACC) — the cost of capital (discount rate) determined by the weighted average, at market value, of the cost of all financing sources in the business enterprise's capital structure.

Index